VOID IF DETACHED FROM BOOK OR ALTERED

AMERICAN HISTORIC I N N S
INCORPORATED

Certificate

&ᴓ *redeemable for* ᴓ&

One Free Night at a Bed & Breakfast or Country Inn

Advance reservations required.
See "How to Make a Reservation."

&ᴓ &ᴓ &ᴓ &ᴓ ᴓ& ᴓ& ᴓ& ᴓ&

Compliments of American Historic Inns, Inc. and participating Bed & Breakfasts and Country Inns.

This certificate entitles the bearer to one free night at any one of the more than 1,600 Bed & Breakfasts and Country Inns included in this book when the bearer buys the first night at the regular rate.
See back for requirements.

VOID IF DETACHED FROM BOOK OR ALTERED

VOID IF DETACHED FROM BOOK OR ALTERED

AMERICAN
HISTORIC
I N N S
INCORPORATED

This section should be completed by the innkeeper when the certificate is redeemed.
MAIL COMPLETED CERTIFICATE TO:
AMERICAN HISTORIC INNS, INC.
PO BOX 669, DANA POINT, CA 92629-0669

_____
Name of Guest

_____
Guest Home Address

_____
Guest City/State/Zip

_____
Guest Home Phone

_____
Guest Email Address

_____
Name of Bed & Breakfast/Inn

_____
Signature of Innkeeper

ဢ   ဢ   ဢ   ဢ   ൏   ൏   ൏   ൏

Certificate Expires December 31, 2005

IF BOOK IS PURCHASED AT THE INN, CERTIFICATE IS VALID ONLY FOR FUTURE VISIT

Media Comments

"...lighthouses, schoolhouses, stage coach stops, llama ranches ... There's lots to choose from and it should keep B&B fans happy for years." – Cathy Stapells, Toronto Sun

"Pay for one night at a nearby country inn and get the second night free...Among them is the very fine L'Auberge Provencale...The goal of the program, sponsored by the Association of American Historic Inns, is to introduce first-timers to inn stays but frequent inn guests also are eligible for the bargain."
– James Yenckel, Washington Post

"Anytime you can get superb accommodations AND a free night, well that's got to be great, and it is ... I've used this book before, and I must tell you, it's super ... The news, information and facts in this book are all fascinating." – On the Road With John Clayton, KKGO, Los Angeles radio

"...helps you find the very best hideaways (many of the book's listings appear in the National Register of Historic Places.)" – Country Living

"I love your book!" – Lydia Moss, Travel Editor, McCall's

"Delightful, succinct, detailed and well-organized. Easy to follow style..."
– Don Wudke, Los Angeles Times

"Deborah Sakach's Bed & Breakfasts and Country Inns continues to be the premier Bed & Breakfast guide for travelers and tourists throughout the United States." – Midwest Book Review

"One of the better promotions we've seen." – Baton Rouge Advocate

"...thoughtfully organized and look-ups are hassle-free...well-researched and accurate...put together by people who know the field. There is no other publication available that covers this particular segment of the bed & breakfast industry – a segment that has been gaining popularity among travelers by leaps and bounds. The information included is valuable and well thought out." – Morgan Directory Reviews

"Readers will find this book easy to use and handy to have. An excellent, well-organized and comprehensive reference for inngoers and innkeepers alike."
– Inn Review, Kankakee, Ill.

"This guide has become the favorite choice of travelers and specializes only in professionally operated inns and B&Bs rather than homestays (lodging in spare bedrooms)." – Laguna Magazine

"This is the best bed and breakfast book out. It outshines them all!"
– Maggie Balitas, Rodale Book Clubs

"Most of us military families have lived all over the world, so it takes an unusual book, service or trip to excite us! As I began to look through the book, my heart beat faster as I envisioned what a good time our readers could have visiting some of these very special historic bed and breakfast properties." – Ann Crawford, Military Living

"Absolutely beautiful!" – KQIL talk show radio

"This is a great book. It makes you want to card everything." – KBRT Los Angeles radio talk show

"All our lines were tied up! We received calls from every one of our 40 stations (while discussing your book.)" – Business Radio Network

"For a delightful change of scenery, visit one of these historical inns. (Excerpts from Bed & Breakfasts and Country Inns follow.) A certificate for one free consecutive night (minimum two nights stay) can be found in the book." – Shirley Howard, Good Housekeeping

"iLoveInns.com boasts independently written reviews, elegant design, and direct links to inns' URLs." – Yahoo! Internet Magazine referring to iLoveInns.com, winner of their 2002 Best B&B Site.

Comments From Innkeepers

"The guests we receive from the Buy-One-Night-Get-One-Night-Free program are some of the most wonderful people. Most are first time inngoers and after their first taste of the inn experience they vow that this is the only way to travel." – Innkeeper, Mass.

"Guests that were staying here last night swear by your guide. They use it all the time. Please send us information about being in your guide." – Innkeeper, Port Angeles, Wash.

"The people are so nice! Please keep up the great program!"
– K. C, The Avon Manor B&B Inn, Avon-By-the-Sea, N.J.

"We would like to express our appreciation for the Free Night programs. We had an excellent response to the certificates. It has helped us fill our vacancies during the weekdays and in the slower time of the season. Keep up the good work!" – Hacienda Vargas, Sante Fe, N.M.

"I have redeemed several certificates which have led to new loyal customers who, in turn, referred our inn to new guests!" - Manchester Inn Bed & Breakfast, Ocean Grove, N.J.

"We've just received the new edition. Congratulations on this magnificent book. You've done it again!" – Gilbert House B&B of Middleway, Charles Town, W.Va.

"We get many good leads from you throughout the year. Anything that we can do to support, we'll be glad to. Thanks for a great publication."
– A Grand Inn-Sunset Hill House, Sugar Hill, N.H.

"We want to tell you how much we love your book. We have it out for guests to use. They love it! Each featured inn stands out so well. Thank you for the privilege of being in your book."
– Fairhaven Inn, Bath, Maine

"We've had guests return two or three times after discovering us through your book. They have turned into wonderful guests and friends." – Port Townsend, Wash.

"I wanted to let you know that I have been getting quite a few bookings from your guide with the certificates."
– Quill Haven Country Inn, Somerset, Pa.

"The response to your book has been terrific and the guests equally terrific! Many are already returning. Thanks for all your hard work." – Rockport, Mass.

"We love your book and we also use it. Just went to New Orleans and had a great trip."
– Gettysburg, Pa.

"I love your directories and your special offers and very much appreciate being a part of American Historic Inns."
– The Hostetler House B&B, St. Glendive, Mt.

"Outstanding! We were offering a variety of inn guide books, but yours was the only one guests bought."
– White Oak Inn, Danville, Ohio

"This has been one of the best B&B programs we have done and the guests have been delightful. Thanks!" – Eastern Shore, Md.

"We have been thrilled with our relationship with American Historic Inns for many years. Many of the travelers you've led to us had never visited our area before. Many of them, likewise, have returned."
– The Thorpe House Country Inn, Metamora, Ind.

"We are grateful that so many of our old friends and new guests have found us through your book. We always recommend your publications to guests who wish to explore other fine country inns of New England."
– Innkeeper, Vt.

Comments About
Bed & Breakfasts and Country Inns

"I purchased 8 of these books in January and have already used them up. I am ordering 8 more. I've had great experiences. This year I've been to California, Philadelphia and San Antonio and by ordering so many books enjoyed getting two free nights at each place. The inns were fabulous."
– D. Valentine, Houston, Texas

"Our office went crazy over this book. The quality of the inns and the quality of the book is phenomenal! Send us 52 books." – M.B., Westport, Conn.

"My husband and I have really enjoyed our Bed & Breakfast free night for the past two summers. Such a good offer. Thanks!" – B.C., Houston, Texas

"The 300 women who attended my 'Better Cents' seminar went wild for the free-night book. I brought my copy and showed them the value of the free-night program. They all wanted to get involved. Thank you so much for offering such a great value."
– R.R., Making Cents Seminars, Texas

"Thank you for offering this special! It allowed us to get away even on a tight budget."
– D.L., Pittsburgh, Pa.

"I'm ordering three new books. We've never stayed in one we didn't like that was in your book!"
– M.R., Canton, Ohio

"My husband and I enjoyed the ambiance and delicious breakfasts! This is a lovely inn and a great offer. Thanks for making it possible for us to enjoy."
– J.D., Woodbury, N.J.

"This made our vacation a lot more reasonable. We got the best room in a beautiful top-drawer inn for half the price." – L.A., Irvine, Calif.

"I used your book and free night offer and took my 17-year-old daughter. It was our first B&B visit ever and we loved it. (We acted like friends instead of parent vs. teenager for the first time in a long time.) It was wonderful!" – B.F., Clinton, N.J.

"Thanks! Do we love your B&B offer! You betcha! The luxury of getting a two-day vacation for the cost of one is Christmas in July for sure. Keep up the good work."
– R.R., Grapevine, Texas.

"What a great idea for gifts. I'm ordering five to use as birthday, housewarming and thank-you gifts." – J.R., Laguna Niguel, Calif.

"The best thing since ice cream – and I love ice cream!" – M.C., Cape May, N.J.

"I keep giving your books away as gifts and then don't have any for myself. Please send me three more copies." – D.T., Ridgewood, N.J.

"The 50% savings on a memorable three-day getaway makes this deal one we cannot pass up!"
– P.T., Lafayette, Calif.

"Out of 25 products we presented to our fund raising committee your book was No. 1 and it generated the most excitement." – H.U., Detroit, Mich.

To Ethan's little sister

American Historic Inns™

Bed & Breakfasts
and
Country Inns

by Deborah Edwards Sakach

Published by

AMERICAN HISTORIC INNS
INCORPORATED

PO Box 669
Dana Point
California
92629-0669
www.iLoveInns.com

Bed & Breakfasts and Country Inns

COVER DESIGN:
David Sakach

PRODUCTION MANAGER:
Andy Prizer

SENIOR EDITOR:
Shirley Swagerty

ASSISTANT EDITORS:
Pamela Barrus, Tiffany Crosswy, Erika Jester,
Jan Lynn, Patricia Purvis, Stephen Sakach

DATABASE ASSISTANTS:
Matt Chronister, Jamee Danihels, Chaya Prizer

PROGRAMMING AND CARTOGRAPHY:
Chris Morton

SCANNING:
Jamee Danihels

PROOFREADING:
Eric Stewart, Suzanne Sakach

Publisher's Cataloging in Publication Data
Sakach, Deborah Edwards
American Historic Inns, Inc.
Bed & Breakfasts and Country Inns

1. Bed & Breakfast Accommodations - United States, Directories, Guide Books.
2. Travel - Bed & Breakfast Inns, Directories, Guide Books.
3. Bed & Breakfast Accommodations - Historic Inns, Directories, Guide Books.
4. Hotel Accommodations - Bed & Breakfast Inns, Directories, Guide Books.
5. Hotel Accommodations - United States, Directories, Guide Books.
I. Title. II Author. III Bed & Breakfast, Bed & Breakfasts and Country Inns.

American Historic Inns is a trademark of American Historic Inns, Inc.
ISBN: **1-888050-16-0**
Softcover
Printed in the United States of America.
10 9 8 7 6 5 4 3 2 1

Table Of Contents

How To Make A Reservation

1 Call

The FREE Night offer **requires advance reservations** and is subject to availability.*

To use the Free Night Certificate call the inn of your choice in advance of your stay and identify yourself as holding a Certificate from American Historic Inns, Inc.

Find out what meals, if any, are included in the rates and whether you will have to pay for meals. Some properties participating in this program do not offer a free breakfast.

2 Confirm

Verify your rate and the inn's acceptance of the Free Night Certificate for the dates you are staying. Make a written note of the name of the reservationist and confirmation code, if any.

Confirm availability of the dates you wish to stay. This offer is subject to availability. All holidays are excluded as well as certain local event dates. A consecutive two-night minimum is required.

Ask about cancellation policies as some inns may require at least a two-week notice in order to refund your deposit. (Also, please note some locales require bed tax be collected, even on free nights.)

3 Check-in

Don't forget to take this book with the Free Night Certificate along with you.

The FREE Night is given to you as a gift directly from the innkeeper in the hope that you or your friends will return and share your discovery with others. The inns are not reimbursed by American Historic Inns, Inc.

IMPORTANT NOTE

*"Subject to availability" and "anytime based on availability": each innkeeper interprets availability for their own property. Just as airlines may set aside a number of seats for discounted fares, so small inns in our program may use different formulas to manage the number of rooms and the times available for the Buy-One-Night-Get-One-Night-Free program. You must call the innkeeper to see if any of their vacant rooms are available for the free night. While innkeepers have proven to be extremely generous with the program, each reservation must be made by first stating that you wish to use the Free Night Certificate toward your two-night stay. When innkeepers foresee a full house during peak times, they might not be able to accept this certificate. Our innkeepers welcome your reservation and are looking forward to your visit.

How To Use This Book

You hold in your hands a delightful selection of America's best bed & breakfasts and country inns. The innkeeper of each property has generously agreed to participate in our FREE night program. **They are not reimbursed for the second night, but make it available to you in the hope that you will return to their inn or tell others about your stay. This is their gift to you.**

Most knowledgeable innkeepers enjoy sharing regional attractions, local folklore, history, and pointing out favorite restaurants and other special features of their areas. They have invested much of themselves in creating an experience for you to long remember. Many have personally renovated historic buildings. Others have infused their inns with a unique style and personality to enliven your experience with a warm and elegant environment. Your innkeepers are a tremendous resource. Treat them kindly and you will be well rewarded.

Accommodations

You'll find bed & breakfasts and country inns in converted schoolhouses, churches, lighthouses, 18th-century farmhouses, Queen Anne Victorians, adobe lodges, plantations and more.

Many are listed in the National Register of Historic Places and have preserved the stories and memorabilia from their participation in historical events such as the Revolutionary or Civil wars.

The majority of inns included in this book were built in the 18th, 19th and early 20th centuries. We have stated the date each building was constructed at the beginning of each description.

Each inn featured in this guidebook has agreed to honor the certificate for the free night when the first night is purchased at the regular rate. We hope you enjoy the choices we made, and we encourage you to suggest new inns that you discover.

A Variety of Inns

A **Country Inn** generally serves both breakfast and dinner and may have a restaurant associated with it. Many have been in operation for years; some, since the 18th century as you will note in our "Inns of Interest" section. Although primarily found on the East Coast, a few country inns are in other regions of the nation. Always check as to what meals are provided.

A **Bed & Breakfast** facility's primary focus is lodging. It can have from three to 20 rooms or more. The innkeepers usually live on the premises. Breakfast is the only meal served and can be a full-course, gourmet breakfast or a simple buffet. Many B&B owners pride themselves on their culinary skills.

As with country inns, many B&Bs specialize in providing historic, romantic or gracious atmospheres with amenities such as canopied beds, fireplaces, hot tubs, whirlpools, afternoon tea in the library and scenic views.

Some give great attention to recapturing a specific historic period, such as the Victorian or Colonial eras. Many display antiques and other furnishings from family collections.

A **Homestay** is a room available in a private home. It may be an elegant stone mansion in the best part of town or a charming country farm. Homestays have one to three guest rooms. Because homestays are often operated as a hobby-type business and open and close frequently, only a very few unique properties are included in this publication.

Area Codes

Although we have made every effort to update area codes throughout the book, new ones pop up from time to time. The phone companies provide recordings for several months after a change, but beyond that point, it can be difficult to reach an inn or B&B.

Although they are listed by state or province, the new codes were added only in certain sections of the state or province. For example, the new 747 area code in California applies only to certain areas in southern California.

The following list includes the most recent area code changes that were available at press time.

State/Province	Old Code	New Code	Effective Date of Change
California	310	424	TBD
California	818	747	TBD
California	909	951	7/17/04
New York	716	585	8/17/02
Utah	801	385	3/30/05
Virginia	540	276	TBD

Baths

Most bed & breakfasts and country inns provide a private bath for each guest room. We have included the number of rooms and the number of private baths in each facility.

Beds

K, Q, D, T, indicates King, Queen, Double or Twin beds available at the inn.

Meals

Continental breakfast: Coffee, juice, toast or pastry.

Continental-plus breakfast: A continental breakfast plus a variety of breads, cheeses and fruit.

Country breakfast: Includes all the traditional fixings of home-cooked country fare.

Full breakfast: Coffee, juice, breads, fruit and an entree.

Full gourmet breakfast: May be an elegant four-course candlelight offering or especially creative cuisine.

Teas: Usually served in the late afternoon with cookies, crackers or other in-between-meal offerings.

Vegetarian breakfast: Vegetarian fare.

Meal Plans

AP: American Plan. All three meals may be included in the price of the room. Check to see if the rate quoted is for two people or per person.

MAP: Modified American Plan. Breakfast and dinner may be included in the price of the room.

EP: European Plan. No meals are included. We have listed only a few historic hotels that operate on an EP plan.

Always find out what meals, if any, are included in the rates. Not every establishment participating in this program provides breakfast, although most do. Inns offering the second night free may or may not include a complimentary lunch or dinner with the second night. Occasionally an innkeeper has indicated MAP and AP when she or he actually means that both programs are available and you must specify which program you are interested in.

Please do not assume meals are included in the rates featured in the book.

Rates

Rates are usually listed in ranges, i.e., $65-175. The LOWEST rate is almost always available during off-peak periods and may apply only to the least expensive room. Rates are subject to change and are not guaranteed. Always confirm the rates when making the reservations. Rates for Canadian listings usually are listed in Canadian dollars. Rates are quoted for double occupancy for two people. Rates for this program are

calculated from regular rates and not from seasonal promotional offers.

Breakfast and other meals MAY or MAY NOT be included in the rates and may not be included in the discount.

Smoking

The majority of country inns and B&Bs in historic buildings prohibit smoking; therefore, if you are a smoker we advise you to call and specifically check with each inn to see if and how they accommodate smokers.

Rooms

Under some listings, you will note that suites are available. We typically assume that suites include a private bath and a separate living room. If the inn contains suites that have more than one bedroom, it will indicate as such.

Additionally, under some listings, you will note a reference to cottages. A cottage may be a rustic cabin tucked in the woods, a seaside cottage or a private apartment-style accommodation.

Fireplaces

When fireplaces are mentioned in the listing they may be in guest rooms or in common areas. The fireplace could be either a gas or wood-burning fireplace. If it mentions that the inn contains a fireplace in room, please keep in mind that not every room may have a fireplace. A few inns have fireplaces that are non-working because of city lodging requirements. Please verify this if you are looking forward to an intimate, fireside chat in your room.

State maps

The state maps have been designed to help travelers find an inn's location quickly and easily. Each city shown on the maps contains one or more inns.

As you browse through the guide, you will notice coordinates next to each city name, i.e. C3. The coordinates designate the location of inns on the state map.

Media coverage

Some inns have provided us with copies of magazine or newspaper articles written by travel writers about their establishments, and we have indicated that in the listing. Articles written about the inns may be available either from the source as a reprint, through libraries or from the inn itself. Some inns have also been featured by local radio and TV stations.

Comments from guests

Over the years, we have collected reams of guest comments about thousands of inns. Our files are filled with these documented comments. At the end of some descriptions, we have included a guest comment received about that inn.

Inspections

Each year we travel across the country visiting inns. Since 1981, we have had a happy, informal team of Inn travelers and prospective innkeepers who report to us about new Bed & Breakfast discoveries and repeat visits to favorite inns.

Although our staff usually sees many inns each year, inspecting inns is not the major focus of our travels. We visit as many as possible, photograph them and meet the innkeepers. Some inns are grand mansions filled with classic, museum-quality antiques. Others are rustic, such as reassembled log cabins or renovated barns or stables. We have enjoyed them all and cherish our memories of each establishment, pristine or rustic.

Only rarely have we come across a truly disappointing inn poorly kept or poorly managed. This type of business usually does not survive because an inn's success depends upon repeat guests and enthusiastic word-of-mouth referrals from satisfied guests. We do not promote these types of establishments.

Traveler or tourist

Travel is an adventure into the unknown, full of surprises and rewards. A seasoned "traveler" learns that even after elaborate preparations and careful planning, travel provides the new and unexpected. The traveler learns to live with uncertainty and considers it part of the adventure.

To the "tourist," whether "accidental" or otherwise, new experiences are disconcerting. Tourists want no surprises. They expect things to be exactly as they had envisioned them. To tourists we recommend staying in a hotel or motel chain where the same formula is followed from one locale to another.

We have found that inngoers are travelers at heart. They relish the differences found at these unique bed & breakfasts and country inns. This is the magic that makes traveling from inn to inn the delightful experience it is.

Minimum stays

Many inns require a two-night minimum stay on weekends. A three-night stay often is required during holiday periods.

Cancellations

Cancellation policies are individual for each bed & breakfast. It is not unusual to see 7- to 14-day cancella-

tion periods or more. Please verify the inn's policy when making your reservation.

What if the inn is full?

Ask the innkeeper for recommendations. They may know of an inn that has opened recently or one nearby but off the beaten path. Call the local Chamber of Commerce in the town you hope to visit. They also may know of inns that have opened recently. Please let us know of any new discoveries you make.

We want to hear from you!

We've always enjoyed hearing from our readers and have carefully cataloged all letters and recommendations. If you wish to participate in evaluating your inn experiences, use the **Inn Evaluation Form** in the back of this book. You might want to make copies of this form prior to departing on your journey.

We hope you will enjoy this book so much that you will want to keep an extra copy or two on hand to offer to friends. Many readers have called to purchase our Free Night Certificate book for hostess gifts, birthday presents, or for seasonal celebrations. It's a great way to introduce your friends to America's enchanting country inns and bed & breakfasts.

Visit us online at iLoveInns.com!

Would you like more information about the inns listed in this book? For color photos, links to the inns' web sites and more, search our web site at **iLoveInns.com**. You'll find thousands of inns from the United States and Canada. We think you'll agree with Yahoo! Internet Magazine who named iLoveInns.com "Best B&B Site."

How to Read an Inn Listing

Anytown ❶ *G6*

An American Historic Inn

❷ 123 S Main St
Anytown, MA 98765-4321
(123)555-1212 (800)555-1212 Fax:(123)555-1234
Internet: www.iLoveInns.com
E-mail: comments@iLoveInns.com

❸ **Circa 1897.** Every inch of this breathtaking inn offers something special. The interior is decorated to the hilt with lovely furnishings, plants, beautiful rugs and warm, inviting tones. Rooms include four-poster and canopy beds combined with the modern amenities such as fireplaces, wet bars and stocked refrigerators. Enjoy a complimentary full breakfast at the inn's gourmet restaurant. The chef offers everything from a light breakfast of fresh fruit, cereal and a bagel to heartier treats such as pecan peach pancakes and Belgium waffles served with fresh fruit and crisp bacon.

❹

❺ Innkeeper(s): Michael & Marissa Chaco. $125-195. 13 rooms with PB, 4 with FP, 1 suite and 1 conference room. ❽ Breakfast and afternoon tea included in rates. ❾ Types of meals: Full bkfst, country bkfst, veg bkfst, early coffee/tea, picnic lunch, gourmet lunch and room service. ❿ Beds: KQDT. ⓫ Phone, air conditioning, turndown service, ceiling fan, TV and VCR in room. Fax, copier and bicycles on premises. Handicap access. Antiques, fishing, parks, shopping, theater and watersports nearby.

⓬ Location: One-half mile from Route 1A.

⓭ Publicity: *Beaufort, Southern Living, Country Inns, Carolina Style, US Air, Town & Country.*

⓮ *"A dream come true!"*

⓯ **Certificate may be used:** December, January and February, Sunday through Wednesday night only. Good only for four rooms which have a rate of $175.

---

① Map coordinates
Easily locate an inn on the state map using these coordinates.

② Inn address
Mailing or street address and all phone numbers for the inn. May also include the inn's web site and email address.

③ Description of inn
Descriptions of inns are written by experienced travel writers based on visits to inns, interviews and information collected from inns.

④ Drawing of inn
Many listings include artistic renderings.

⑤ Innkeepers
The name of the innkeeper(s).

⑥ Rates
Rates are quoted for double occupancy. The rate range includes off-season rates and is subject to change.

⑦ Rooms
Number and types of rooms available.
PB=Private Bath   FP=Fireplace
HT=Hot Tub   WP=Whirlpool

⑧ Included Meals
Types of meals included in the rates.

⑨ Available meals
This section lists the types of meals that the inn offers. These meals may or may not be included in the rates.

⑩ Beds
King, Queen, Double, Twin

⑪ Amenities and activities
Information included here describes amenities or services available at the inn. If handicap access is available, it will be noted here. Nearby activities also are included.

⑫ Location
Type of area where inn is located.

⑬ Publicity
Newspapers, magazines and other publications which have featured articles about the inn.

⑭ Guest comments
Comments about the inn from guests.

⑮ Certificate dates
Indicates when inn has agreed to honor the Buy-One-Night-Get-One-Night-Free Certificate™. Always verify availability of discount with innkeeper.

Alabama

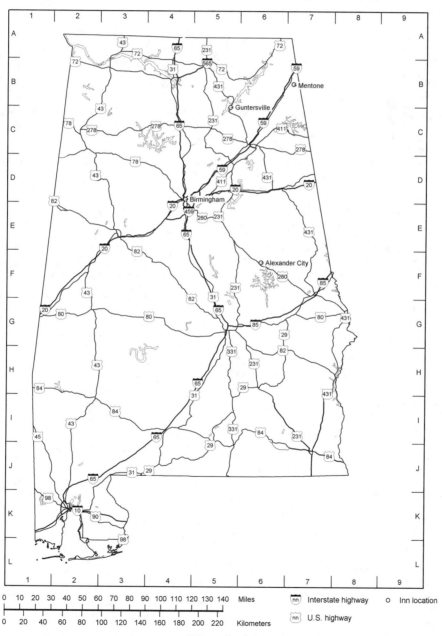

	Miles	Interstate highway	○ Inn location
0 10 20 30 40 50 60 70 80 90 100 110 120 130 140		
0 20 40 60 80 100 120 140 160 180 200 220	Kilometers	(nn) U.S. highway

Alexander City   **F6**

Mistletoe Bough
497 Hillabee St
Alexander City, AL 35010
(256)329-3717 (877)330-3707
Internet: www.bbonline.com/al/mistletoe
E-mail: mistletoe@webshoppe.net

Circa 1890. When Jean and Carlice Payne purchased this three-story Queen Anne Victorian, it had been in the Reuben Herzfeld family for 103 years. Surrounded by two acres of

lawns, tall oak and pecan trees as well as a tulip tree, Victorian Pearl bushes, camellias and brilliant azaleas, the home has a three-story turret and cupola, balconies, stained-glass windows and a wraparound porch. The porch ceiling is painted sky blue. A gracious foyer features tongue-and-groove wainscoting and opens to a ladies' parlor on one side and a gentlemen's parlor on the other. Fresh flowers, antiques and lace curtains are mixed with traditional and antique Victorian and European furnishings. Upon arrival, guests are pampered with refreshments and homemade cookies (frequently with ingredients from Mistletoe's fruit trees and Carlice's herb garden). Other goodies are always on hand. A four-course breakfast is served in the formal dining room with fine china, crystal and silver. The home is in the National Register.
Innkeeper(s): Jean & Carlice Payne. $85-120. 5 rooms with PB. Breakfast and snacks/refreshments included in rates. Types of meals: Full bkfst. Beds: KQD. Cable TV, ceiling fan, telephone and turn-down service in room. Air conditioning. Parlor games, fireplace, badminton and croquet on premises. Antiquing, golf, shopping and water sports nearby.
Location: City.
Certificate may be used: Jan. 10 through Dec. 10, Sunday through Thursday. Based on availability. Void during holidays and special events.

Birmingham   **D4**

The Tutwiler - A Wyndham Historic Hotel
2021 Park Place North
Birmingham, AL 35203
(205)322-2100 (800)678-8946 Fax:(205)325-1198
Internet: www.thetutwiler.com
E-mail: cmcelheney@wyndham.com

Circa 1914. Featuring a classic blend of traditional surroundings and present-day amenities, this hotel boasts a gracious service appreciated by the corporate or leisure traveler. The hotel is located in the center of the financial, business, historic and cultural districts. Charles Lindbergh held a press conference here, and Tallulah Bankhead made a post-wedding celebration. Well-appointed guest bedrooms feature generous conveniences including high-speed Internet access, shower massage, Golden Door Spa toiletries, luxurious linens, plush towels and the daily newspaper. A lounge on the private executive level offers breakfast, hors d'oeuvres and drinks. Laundry and valet service are available. Enjoy using the state-of-the-art health club, or visit the adjacent Linn Park and Museum of the Arts.

Innkeeper(s): General Manager, Patrick Hatton. Call for rates. Call inn for details.
Certificate may be used: January-December, Thursday, Friday, Saturday and Sunday only, subject to availability.

Guntersville   **C5**

Lake Guntersville B&B
2204 Scott St
Guntersville, AL 35976-1120
(256)505-0133 Fax:(256)505-0133
Internet: www.bbonline.com/al/lakeguntersville/
E-mail: lakeguntersvillebandb@konnekted.com

Circa 1910. The state's largest lake is just a short walk from this turn-of-the-century home that is furnished with many antiques. Boasting more than 900 miles of shoreline, the lake is

perfect for fishing and boating. Each of the well-appointed guest bedrooms have private outside access; several offer lake views. Weather permitting, breakfast is served on the veranda, surrounded by gorgeous scenery and serenaded by songbirds. The veranda also is appealing for relaxing on wicker chairs, a swing or hammock.
Innkeeper(s): Carol Dravis. $69-115. 7 rooms with PB. Breakfast included in rates. Types of meals: Full gourmet bkfst and early coffee/tea. Beds: KQDT. Cable TV, reading lamp, refrigerator, ceiling fan, clock radio and telephone in room. Air conditioning. Fax, parlor games, fireplace, e-mail and conference areas on premises. Handicap access. Antiquing, fishing, golf, live theater, parks, shopping, sporting events, tennis, water sports and walking trails nearby.
Location: Mountains. Peninsula.
Publicity: *Huntsville Times, Sun Herald, Mobile Press, Advertiser Gleam, Birmingham News, Off the Beaten Path, Alabama Public TV Special, WLRH and Huntsville Public Radio.*
Certificate may be used: Sunday-Thursday, year-round, no holiday weekends.

Mentone   **B7**

Mentone Inn
Hwy 117, PO Box 290
Mentone, AL 35984
(256)634-4836 (800)455-7470
Internet: mentoneinn.com

Circa 1927. Located at the top of Lookout Mountain amidst forests and meadows of wild flowers Mentone Inn offers a refreshing stop for those in search of the cool breezes and natural air conditioning of the mountains. This lodge has been welcoming travelers since 1927. Here antique treasures mingle with modern-day conveniences and favorite places are the fireplace in the main lounge and the gracious porch. Sequoyah Caverns, Little River Canyon and DeSoto Falls are moments away.
Innkeeper(s): Glenda Hollis. $85-115. 12 rooms with PB. Types of meals: Full bkfst and early coffee/tea. Beds: QT. TV, reading lamp, ceiling fan, desk and central heat in room. Central air. VCR, parlor games, telephone, fireplace and porch on premises. Antiquing, canoeing/kayaking, downhill skiing, golf, hiking, horseback riding, parks and water sports nearby.
Location: Lookout mountains.
Publicity: *Birmingham News, Weekend Getaways Magazine, Montgomery Advertiser and Nashville Traveler.*
Certificate may be used: Year-round, subject to availability.

Alaska

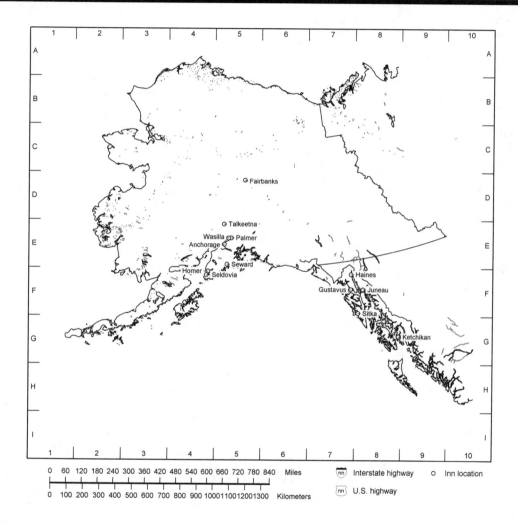

| | 0 | 60 | 120 | 180 | 240 | 300 | 360 | 420 | 480 | 540 | 600 | 660 | 720 | 780 | 840 | Miles |
| 0 | 100 | 200 | 300 | 400 | 500 | 600 | 700 | 800 | 900 | 1000 | 1100 | 1200 | 1300 | | Kilometers |

| nn Interstate highway | O Inn location |
| nn U.S. highway | |

Anchorage E5

Alaska's North Country Castle B&B

PO Box 111876, 14600 Joanne Cir
Anchorage, AK 99511
(907)345-7296 Fax:(907)345-7296
Internet: www.customcpu.com/commercial/nccbnb
E-mail: nccbnb@customcpu.com

Circa 1986. Surrounded by woods, this modern, multi-level Victorian cottage-style home offers gorgeous views of the Chugach Mountains and Cook Inlet. The B&B is not actually a castle, though guests are treated like royalty. Sit by the fire, play the piano or choose a book from the Alaskana library in the living room. Each guest bedroom boasts warm floors, vaulted ceilings, bay windows, robes, phone and modem. Two rooms can be combined with a deck and balconied sitting area. The Turnagain View Suite features a fireplace, double Jacuzzi, shower for two and private deck. Innkeepers Wray and Cindy serve a hearty, traditional breakfast in a gazebo-style nook with Alaska blueberry pancakes or baked French toast or specialty egg dishes and fresh fruit, reindeer sausage and juice. Use of a refrigerator, washer, dryer and barbecue grill are available.
Innkeeper(s): Cindy & Wray Kinard. $79-189. 3 rooms with PB, 1 with FP, 2 suites. Breakfast included in rates. Types of meals: Full gourmet bkfst. Beds: QT. Reading lamp, clock radio, turn-down service, desk and hot tub/spa in room. Fax, copier, library, telephone and fireplace on premises. Cross-country skiing, downhill skiing, fishing, live theater, parks, shopping, sporting events, bird sanctuary and wilderness mountain trails nearby.
Location: Mountains. Foothills.
Publicity: *Country.*
Certificate may be used: Sept. 15-Oct. 14, April 15-May 15.

Anchorage Mahogany Manor Historic Downtown Inn

204 East 15th Ave.
Anchorage, AK 99501
(907)278-1111 (888)777-0346 Fax:(907)258-7877
Internet: www.mahoganymanor.com
E-mail: mahoganymanor@compuserve.com

Circa 1947. This elegant inn in the heart of Anchorage stands on a half-acre on the crest of a hill with views of the countryside and mountains. From the rare woods used in construction, to the Alaskan artwork, to the unique floor-to-ceiling indoor waterfall, the beauty of this inn competes with the natural beauty surrounding it. The library is full of books on Alaska for explorers planning their next journey or for guests relaxing at the end of the day. The four guest bedrooms, including a three-room family suite, come with robes and slippers. A hearty continental breakfast is available to guests whenever they want it in the full-service guest kitchen that is stocked with delights like juice, fruit, rolls, breads, pastries, yogurt and hot and cold cereals. Hot drinks are always available, and hors d'oeuvres or dessert are offered each evening, as well. The inn is a perfect place for releasing creative energies at corporate meetings, and it's excellent for creating lifetime memories at family events. It has a swimming pool and outdoor whirlpool.
Innkeeper(s): Mary Ernst, CTC & Russ Campbell. $129-309. 4 rooms, 2 with PB, 1 with FP, 2 suites and 1 conference room. Breakfast, afternoon tea and snacks/refreshments included in rates. Types of meals: Cont plus, veg bkfst, early coffee/tea and room service. Beds: KQDT. Modem hook-up, data port, cable TV, VCR, reading lamp, stereo, clock radio, telephone, coffeemaker, turn-down service, desk, voice mail, fireplace, hair dryers, iron, ironing board, robes and slippers in room. Fax, copier, spa, library, parlor games, fireplace, laundry facility and gift shop on premises. Limited handicap access. Antiquing, art galleries, bicycling, canoeing/kayaking, cross-country skiing, downhill skiing, fishing, golf, hiking, horseback riding, museums, parks, shopping, sporting events, tennis, water sports, Performing Arts Center, Egan Convention Center and federal buildings and hospitals nearby.
Location: City.
Publicity: *Anchorage Daily News, Alaska Business Monthly* and MSNBC documentary.
Certificate may be used: Sunday-Thursday, Oct. 1-April 30, except holidays and special events.

Elderberry B&B

8340 Elderberry St
Anchorage, AK 99502-4245
(907)243-6968 Fax:(907)243-6968
Internet: www.elderberrybb.com
E-mail: elderberry-b-b@gci.net

Circa 1974. This homestay bed & breakfast is located in a quiet Anchorage residential neighborhood and offers three homey rooms with comfortable furnishings. It's not unusual to see moose walking around the neighborhood. The home is close to the airport, as well as shops and restaurants.
Innkeeper(s): Norm & Linda Seitz. $65-95. 3 rooms with PB. Breakfast included in rates. Types of meals: Full bkfst and early coffee/tea. Beds: QDT. TV, VCR, reading lamp, clock radio, telephone and desk in room. Fax, copier, fireplace and 45" surround sound TV system on premises. Cross-country skiing, downhill skiing, fishing, live theater, parks, shopping and water sports nearby.
Location: Airport.

"A friendly face, a lovely breakfast and a good bed made our stay in your wonderful state more enjoyable."
Certificate may be used: Sept. 15-May 15, Sunday-Thursday.

Glacier Bear B&B

4814 Malibu Rd
Anchorage, AK 99517-3274
(907)243-8818 Fax:(907)248-4532
Internet: www.touristguide.com/b&b/alaska/glacierbear
E-mail: gbear@alaska.net

Circa 1986. This cedar-sided contemporary home is located just three blocks from the world's largest float plane lake. The B&B is decorated with Victorian pieces. One bedroom includes a pencil canopy bed, while another offers an antique king bed and a fireplace. The landscaped grounds include an eight-person spa surrounded by ferns, trees and wild berry bushes. The innkeepers offer both a hearty full breakfast or continental fare. Freshly ground coffee, tea, soft drinks and snacks are available throughout the day.
Innkeeper(s): Cleveland & Belinda Zackery. $75-125. 5 rooms, 3 with PB, 1 with FP. Breakfast included in rates. Types of meals: Full bkfst, early coffee/tea and snacks/refreshments. Beds: KQT. Reading lamp, clock radio, telephone and desk in room. VCR, fax, spa, bicycles and parlor games on premises. Cross-country skiing, downhill skiing, fishing, parks, shopping, sporting events, water sports, float plane lake and nature walks nearby.
Location: City.
Certificate may be used: Oct. 1-April 1.

Jewel Lake B&B

8125 Jewel Lake Road
Anchorage, AK 99502
(907)245-7321 Fax:907-245-2313
Internet: www.jewellakebandb.com
E-mail: info@jewellakebandb.com

Circa 1979. Jewel Lake, a modern home built of cedar wood, is located just a few minutes from downtown Anchorage and the Anchorage International Airport. The five guest rooms are comfortably furnished and accented with the flavor of the Alaskan outdoors. The innkeepers offer a variety of helpful amenities, including use of the kitchen, freezer storage for fish their guests have caught, use of laundry facilities and business aids such as fax service and Internet access. Fishing, hiking and bicycling are just some of the outdoor activities, and Anchorage offers a variety of shops, galleries and restaurants.

Innkeeper(s): Troy Roberts. $40-225. 5 rooms, 4 with PB, 1 two-bedroom suite. Breakfast and snacks/refreshments included in rates. Types of meals: Cont plus, early coffee/tea and room service. Beds: KQDT. Modem hook-up, data port, cable TV, VCR, reading lamp, ceiling fan, clock radio, turn-down service and full kitchen in room. Fax, copier, telephone, fireplace and laundry facility on premises. Antiquing, art galleries, bicycling, cross-country skiing, downhill skiing, fishing, hiking, live theater, museums, parks, shopping and water sports nearby.
Location: City.
Publicity: *Arrington's Inn Traveler 2003 and 2004 book of list winner for Best in Alaska.*

Certificate may be used: Sept. 1 to May 15, any day of the week.

The Oscar Gill House

1344 W 10th Ave
Anchorage, AK 99501-3245
(907)279-1344 Fax:(907)279-1344
Internet: www.oscargill.com
E-mail: oscargill@gci.net

Circa 1913. This clapboard, Craftsman-style home was built in Knik, Alaska, but later disassembled and moved to Anchorage in 1916. The home is the city's oldest, and the innkeepers have kept the decor simple and comfortable, with antiques here and there, as well as vintage furnishings from the '30s and '40s. Down comforters and bathrooms stocked with toiletries are a few of the special touches guests will find. Breakfasts are served up in the cheery dining room, which features panoramic photos of Anchorage and the home in its original location. Innkeeper Susan Lutz prepares a variety of entrees for the morning meal, including items such as sourdough French toast or Mexican egg casseroles accompanied by freshly ground coffee, a selection of teas and homemade hot chocolate.

Innkeeper(s): Mark & Susan Lutz. $65-110. 3 rooms, 1 with PB and 1 conference room. Breakfast included in rates. Types of meals: Full bkfst and veg bkfst. Beds: QDT. Cable TV, reading lamp, clock radio, telephone, hair dryers, robes and body shop products in room. Fax, bicycles, library, fireplace and picnic table on premises. Antiquing, art galleries, bicycling, canoeing/kayaking, cross-country skiing, downhill skiing, fishing, hiking, live theater, museums, parks, shopping, sporting events, tennis, water sports, brew pubs, restaurants, courthouse and Delaney Parkstrip nearby.
Location: City, mountains, waterfront. Downtown park-Rose Garden.
Publicity: *Frommers, Fodors, Berkeley Guides "On the Loose" and NPR.*

Certificate may be used: Jan. 2-April 1, Oct. 1 through Nov. 22, Nov. 28 through Dec. 22.

Fairbanks D5

7 Gables Inn & Suites

PO Box 80488
Fairbanks, AK 99708
(907)479-0751 Fax:(907)479-2229
Internet: www.7gablesinn.com
E-mail: gables7@alaska.net

Circa 1982. There are actually 14 gables on this modern Tudor-style inn, which is located a short walk from the University of Alaska and the Chena River. Inside the foyer, a seven-foot waterfall is an amazing welcome. A two-story, flower-filled solarium and a meeting room are wonderful gathering places. Seasonally enjoy the magnificent aurora borealis or a white world of snowflakes and dog mushing, and then relax in a steaming in-room Jacuzzi tub. In summertime the midnight sun allows canoe trips down the river for a progressive dinner from restaurant to deck to dock. The innkeepers received the city's Golden Heart Award for exceptional hospitality.

Innkeeper(s): Paul & Leicha Welton. $50-150. 20 rooms, 9 with PB, 11 suites. Breakfast and snacks/refreshments included in rates. Types of meals: Full gourmet bkfst. Beds: KQT. Cable TV, VCR, reading lamp, clock radio, telephone, desk, hot tub/spa, wireless Internet, DVD, most with Jacuzzi tubs, some suites with fireplaces and all suites have full private kitchens in room. Fax, bicycles, library and laundry facility on premises. Antiquing, bicycling, cross-country skiing, downhill skiing, fishing, golf, hiking, museums, parks and shopping nearby.
Location: City.

Certificate may be used: Oct. 1-April 30.

Chena River B&B

1001 Dolly Varden Dr
Fairbanks, AK 99709-3229
(907)479-2532

Located on 10 acres along the Chena River, this inn offers spectacular views of the Northern Lights. Two of the rooms feature views of the river, woodlands and flower garden. (In the winter, moose are frequent visitors to the garden where they nibble its remnants.) The inn features hardwood floors, Oriental rugs and an enormous collection of books, many about Alaska. The innkeeper is a native Alaskan and has extensive knowledge about his home state. Breakfast features sourdough pancakes, bacon, sausage, eggs and fresh fruit salad. Guests are welcome to use the kitchen for snacks. Fairbanks is four miles. University museum, Riverboat Discovery and historic Chena Pump House are nearby.
Innkeeper(s): Steve Mease. $40-120. 5 rooms, 1 with PB. Breakfast included in rates. Types of meals: Full bkfst. Beds: QDT. TV in room.
Publicity: *Washington Post and Northwest Living.*

"Felt just like home, but the food was better."
Certificate may be used: September-May, based on availability.

Frog Pond B&B

131 Frog Pond Cir
Fairbanks, AK 99712
(907)457-4006 (888)457-4006 Fax:(907)457-4020
Internet: frogpondbb.com
E-mail: frogpondbb@usa.net

Circa 1983. Sitting among the birch trees, this spacious country home has a peaceful two-acre yard. Downtown is just minutes away providing easy access to popular attractions. Guest bedrooms offer comfortable Queen beds. A two-bedroom apartment can sleep up to six people. Kitchen and laundry facilities are included as well as a large living area to relax in.

An assortment of Alaskan videos are available to watch. A hearty country-style breakfast is prepared daily by the hosts, known for their excellent culinary skills and tasty food.

Innkeeper(s): Dave & Kerinda Johnson. $70-195. 4 rooms, 1 suite. Breakfast included in rates. Types of meals: Full bkfst. Beds: QT. Reading lamp and clock radio in room. VCR, fax, copier and telephone on premises. Downhill skiing, shopping and sporting events nearby.

Location: City.

Certificate may be used: Oct. 1-April 30.

Gustavus   F7

Glacier Bay's Bear Track Inn

PO Box 255
Gustavus, AK 99826
(907)697-3017 (888)697-2284 Fax:(907)697-2284
Internet: www.beartrackinn.com
E-mail: beartrac@aol.com

Circa 1997. This handsomely designed log inn offers a huge lobby with inspiring views of the water, mountains, forests and meadows. There are suede couches, a walk-around fireplace and moose antler chandeliers. Attractively furnished guest rooms are in keeping with the log decor and offer views and great comfort. Among the inn's specialities are Dungeness Crab, Alaskan spotted prawns, salmon and halibut. Favorite activities include a wide variety of chartered fishing excursions, whale watching, hiking, glacier tours, kayaking, "flight-seeing," golf and mountain biking. In addition, helicopter tours, mini-cruise ship excursions and bear viewing can be arranged by the innkeepers. The inn is family owned and operated.

Innkeeper(s): Mike Olney & Alice Park. $293. 14 rooms with PB and 1 conference room. Breakfast, afternoon tea, snacks/refreshments and dinner included in rates. Types of meals: Full bkfst, early coffee/tea, lunch and room service. Restaurant on premises. Beds: Q. Reading lamp, turn-down service and hair dryer in room. VCR, fax, copier, library, child care, parlor games, telephone, fireplace, croquet, horseshoes, volleyball and badminton on premises. Handicap access. Fishing, golf, parks, shopping, water sports and Glacier Bay National Park nearby.

Location: Mountains, waterfront. Country.

Certificate may be used: May 13 to July 1, Sunday-Saturday.

Haines   F7

The Summer Inn B&B

Box 1198
Haines, AK 99827
(907)766-2970 Fax:(906)766-2970
Internet: www.summerinnbnb.com
E-mail: summerinnb&b@wytbear.com

Circa 1912. This historic farmhouse has an infamous beginning, it was built by a member of a gang of claimjumpers who operated during the Gold Rush. The home affords stunning mountain and water views. The home is comfortably furnished, and one guest bathroom includes a clawfoot tub original to the home. Breakfasts include fresh fruit and entrees such as sourdough pancakes with ham. The area offers many activities, including museums and a historic walking tour, skiing, snowshoeing, ice fishing, hiking, fishing and much more.

$80-110. 5 rooms. Breakfast and afternoon tea included in rates. Types of meals: Full bkfst, early coffee/tea and snacks/refreshments. Beds: DT. Reading lamp and alarm clocks in room. Fax, library, telephone and BBQ on premises. Art galleries, beach, bicycling, canoeing/kayaking, cross-country

skiing, fishing, golf, hiking, live theater, museums, parks, shopping, tennis, water sports and birding nearby.

Location: Coastal town.

Publicity: *American History (April 2000) and Historic Sears Mail Order Houses Roebucks.*

Certificate may be used: Dec. 1-March 31, subject to availability.

Homer   F5

Beary Patch B&B Inn

PO Box 1544
Homer, AK 99603
(907)235-2483 (888)977-BEAR Fax:(907)235-2327
Internet: www.alaska-beary-patch.com
E-mail: bearybb@ptialaska.net

Circa 1985. Enjoy views of snow-capped peaks and forested wilderness at this bed & breakfast located in a cozy contemporary home within walking distance of downtown Homer. One guest room features a lace canopy bed piled high with pillows and decorated with a trail of ivy. Another fanciful room features a "beary" theme with twin beds covered with bear quilts. A large stuffed bear completes the look. The Beary American room features twin beds covered with red, white and blue quilts. Another patriotic quilt hangs from the wall. Guests can relax in the den or in the Victorian-appointed living room. Breakfasts include three courses. Guests start off with gourmet coffee and yogurt topped with a berry puree. From there, freshly baked muffins are served. The daily entrée might include blueberry pancakes topped with bananas, blueberries, blueberry syrup and whipped cream, accompanied by Alaskan reindeer sausage. Shops, restaurants and a museum are just a few minutes away.

Innkeeper(s): Raymond & Coletta Walker. $69-119. 4 rooms, 2 with PB. Breakfast and snacks/refreshments included in rates. Types of meals: Full gourmet bkfst. Beds: KQT. Reading lamp, ceiling fan, clock radio, telephone and turn-down service in room. TV, VCR, fax, copier, library, parlor games and fireplace on premises. Art galleries, beach, canoeing/kayaking, cross-country skiing, fishing, golf, hiking, horseback riding, live theater, museums, parks and shopping nearby.

Location: City.

Publicity: *Alaska Travel.*

Certificate may be used: October-March, excluding Christmas; September, Monday through Thursday.

Juneau   F8

Pearson's Pond Luxury Inn & Adventure Spa

4541 Sawa Cir
Juneau, AK 99801-8723
(907)789-3772 (888)658-6328 Fax:(907)789-6722
Internet: www.pearsonspond.com
E-mail: book@pearsonspond.com

Circa 1985. View glaciers, visit museums or take a chance at gold-panning streams while staying at this award-winning B&B resort. Landscaped gardens and blueberry bushes border the guests' decks. A full, self-serve breakfast and trail snacks are found in each private kitchenette or in the Breakfast Lounge. The Mendenhall Glacier is within an easy walk and nearby trails offer excellent hiking or mountain biking. River rafting, glacier trekking, or angling for world-class halibut, salmon or freshwater trout may interest the more adventuresome. Soak in a hot tub spa surrounded by a lush forest near a picturesque duck pond. Vacation condos are also available.

$119-349. 7 rooms with PB, 7 with FP, 2 suites. Breakfast, afternoon tea and snacks/refreshments included in rates. Types of meals: Cont plus and early coffee/tea. Beds: Q. Cable TV, VCR, reading lamp, stereo, refrigerator, clock radio, telephone, desk and 3 with spa in room. TV, fax, copier, spa, bicycles, library, parlor games, fireplace, boats and two hot tubs on premises. Antiquing, cross-country skiing, downhill skiing, fishing, live theater, parks, shopping, water sports and downhill and cross-country skiing nearby.
Location: Mountains. Glacier Lake.
Publicity: *Good Housekeeping, Cross Country Skier, Alaska Journal of Commerce, Senior Voice, Sunset, Atlantic Monthly, Pacific Northwest, Style, Cooking Light, News Herald, Travel Agent Magazine, CNN and MSN.*

"A definite 10!"
Certificate may be used: October through April, Sunday through Thursday.

Silverbow Inn & Bakery

120 2nd St
Juneau, AK 99801-1215
(907)586-4146 (800)586-4146 Fax:(907)586-4242
Internet: www.silverbowinn.com
E-mail: info@silverbowinn.com

Circa 1914. For more than 100 years, Alaska's oldest operating bakery has been located here. The innkeepers, an architect and urban planner, have brought the building to life with a luxurious lobby and romantic restaurant. The inn offers B&B and European-style pension rooms. Freshly made bagels, breads and pastries are served at breakfast. Within two blocks are the state capitol, convention center, waterfront and shopping district.
Innkeeper(s): Jill Ramiel/Ken Alper. $68-148. 6 rooms with PB and 2 conference rooms. Breakfast, afternoon tea and snacks/refreshments included in rates. Types of meals: Cont and early coffee/tea. Restaurant on premises. Beds: QT. Cable TV, VCR, reading lamp, refrigerator, snack bar, clock radio, telephone, desk and voice mail in room. Fax, copier, library, parlor games, social hour with wine and cheese and bakery on premises. Antiquing, cross-country skiing, downhill skiing, fishing, live theater, parks and shopping nearby.
Location: Urban, historic district.
Publicity: *Travel & Leisure, Destinos and Frommers Choice 2000.*
Certificate may be used: Oct. 1-April 1.

Ketchikan   G8

Almost Home B&B

412 D-1 Loop Rd N
Ketchikan, AK 99901-9202
(907)225-3273 (800)987-5337 Fax:(907)247-5337
Internet: www.ketchikan-lodging.com/bb15.html
E-mail: wanda@ketchikan-lodging.com

Circa 1981. These rural B&B accommodations, located a few minutes' drive north of Ketchikan, provide guests with a completely outfitted apartment. Guests can choose from two- or three-bedroom units. Each offers linens, phone, cable TV, washer and dryer and a gas barbecue grill. A special welcome is extended to fishing parties. Ketchikan is known for its excellent salmon and halibut fishing and offers several fishing derbies each summer.
Innkeeper(s): Darrell & Wanda Vandergriff. $150. 4 cottages. Breakfast included in rates. Types of meals: Cont plus. Beds: KDT. Cable TV, reading lamp, refrigerator, clock radio, telephone, gas BBQ, full outfitted kitchen and laundry facility in room. Fishing, live theater, parks, shopping, water sports, totem poles and native culture nearby.
Location: Wooded secluded lot.
Certificate may be used: Oct. 1-June 1.

Palmer   E5

Colony Inn

325 E Elmwood
Palmer, AK 99645-6622
(907)745-3330 Fax:(907)746-3330

Circa 1935. Historic buildings are few and far between in Alaska, and this inn is one of them. The structure was built to house teachers and nurses in the days when President Roosevelt was sending settlers to Alaska to establish farms. When innkeeper Janet Kincaid purchased it, the inn had been empty for some time. She  restored the place, including the wood walls, which now create a cozy ambiance in the common areas. The 12 guest rooms are nicely appointed, and 10 include a whirlpool tub. Meals are not included, but the inn's restaurant offers breakfast and lunch. The inn is listed in the National Register.
Innkeeper(s): Janet Kincaid. $90. 12 rooms with PB. Types of meals: Full bkfst & lunch. Restaurant on premises. Beds: QDT. Cable TV, reading lamp, clock radio and telephone in room. Parlor games and fireplace on premises. Antiquing, cross-country skiing, downhill skiing, fishing, golf, parks, shopping & tennis nearby.
Location: City.

"Love the antiques and history."
Certificate may be used: Oct. 1-May 1.

Rose Ridge B&B

PO Box 1943
Palmer, AK 99645
(907)745-8604 (877)827-ROSE Fax:(907)745-8608
Internet: www.roseridgebnb.com
E-mail: stay@roseridgebnb.com

Circa 1997. Fifteen secluded acres surround this quiet, modern home in the Matanuska Valley. Watch videos or play games in the family room. A reading area is perfect for curling up with a good book. Guest bedrooms, accented with hand-stitched quilts, also feature VCRs and private entrances. Enjoy a continental breakfast, or a full breakfast from a varied menu, served in the dining room. Walk in the woods or relax on the deck. Pan for gold at nearby Hatcher Pass when visiting Independence Mine and Historical Park.
Innkeeper(s): David & Diane Rose. $85-95. 2 rooms with PB. Breakfast included in rates. Types of meals: Country bkfst, veg bkfst and early coffee/tea. Beds: Q. Modern hook-up, TV, VCR, reading lamp, clock radio and desk in room. Fax, library, parlor games, telephone and laundry facility on premises. Limited handicap access. Art galleries, bicycling, canoeing/kayaking, cross-country skiing, fishing, golf, hiking, horseback riding, museums, parks, shopping, tennis, water sports and glacier hikes nearby.
Location: Country, mountains.
Certificate may be used: Anytime, subject to availability.

Seldovia   F4

Swan House South B&B

6840 Crooked Tree Dr
Anchorage, AK 99516-6805
(907)346-3033 (800)921-1900 Fax:(907)346-3535
Internet: www.alaskaswanhouse.com
E-mail: swan1@alaska.net

Circa 1999. In a peaceful setting on Seldovia Bay, this modern bed and breakfast offers relaxation and scenic splendor. The spacious guest suites have private decks to enjoy the waterfront sea otters, bald eagles and gorgeous views of Mt. Iliamna. See salmon swimming in the clear water below the private Boat House Guest Cottage (a favorite honeymoon spot). Expect a delicious gourmet breakfast that may include Belgian waffles with reindeer sausage and homemade berry syrups. A large greenhouse nurtures blueberries and raspberries; potatoes and fruit trees are cultivated as well.

Innkeeper(s): Judy & Jerry Swanson. $149-269. 5 rooms with PB, 4 suites. Breakfast and afternoon tea included in rates. Types of meals: Full gourmet bkfst and early coffee/tea. Beds: KQT. Modem hook-up, TV, VCR, reading lamp, CD player, clock radio, telephone, coffeemaker and desk in room. Fax, copier, spa, bicycles, parlor games and fireplace on premises. Art galleries, beach, bicycling, canoeing/kayaking, fishing, hiking, museums, parks and shopping nearby.
Location: Mountains, ocean community, waterfront. Remote island.
Publicity: *Travel & Leisure Magazine.*
Certificate may be used: May 1-15, Sept. 15-30, Sunday-Thursday.

Seward   E5

The Farm B&B Inn

PO Box 305
Seward, AK 99664-0305
(907)224-5691 Fax:(907)224-5698
Internet: www.alaskan.com/thefarm/
E-mail: thefarm@ptialaska.net

Circa 1906. The main house of this bed & breakfast is located on 20 acres of farm-like setting with plenty of fields to enjoy. Rooms are spacious and comfortable, one includes a king-size, canopied bed. The innkeepers also offer sleeping cottages. A three-room, economy bungalow and kitchenette suites are available, as well. Guests may use the laundry facilities. The home is three miles outside of Seward.

$65-105. 15 rooms, 11 with PB, 2 suites. Breakfast included in rates. Types of meals: Cont plus. Beds: KQT. Cable TV, reading lamp, clock radio, telephone and desk in room. VCR and fax on premises. Handicap access. Cross-country skiing, fishing, parks, shopping and water sports nearby.
Certificate may be used: September-May.

Sitka   F8

Alaska Ocean View Bed & Breakfast Inn

1101 Edgecumbe Dr
Sitka, AK 99835-7122
(907)747-8310 (888)811-6870 Fax:(907)747-3440
Internet: www.sitka-alaska-lodging.com
E-mail: info@sitka-alaska-lodging.com

Circa 1986. This Alaska-style red-cedar executive home is located in a quiet neighborhood one block from the seashore and the Tongass National Forest. Witness spectacular Alaska sunsets over stunning Sitka Sound and on clear days view majestic Mt. Edgecumbe, an extinct volcano located offshore on Kruzoff Island. Binoculars are kept handy for guests who take a special interest in looking for whales and eagles.

Innkeeper(s): Carole & Bill Denkinger. $109-169. 3 rooms with PB, 2 with FP, 1 suite and 1 conference room. Breakfast, afternoon tea and snacks/refreshments included in rates. Types of meals: Full gourmet bkfst, veg bkfst and early coffee/tea. Beds: KQT. Data port, TV, VCR, reading lamp, stereo, refrigerator, ceiling fan, snack bar, telephone, coffeemaker, turn-down service, desk, microwave, clock, radio, HEPA air purifier, iron, ironing board and some with whirlpool tubs and fireplace in room. Fax, copier, spa, library, parlor games, fireplace, free snack bar, gift shop and concierge service on premises. Antiquing, fishing, hiking, live theater, parks, shopping, water sports, whale watching, historical attractions, wildlife viewing, fly fishing, ocean fishing and kayaking nearby.
Location: Island community, mountains, ocean.
Certificate may be used: Sunday-Wednesday, October-March, Sunday-Wednesday, April-May 15. Space subject to availability.

Talkeetna   E5

Denali View Raft Adventures and B&B

Hc 89 Box 8360
Talkeetna, AK 99676-9703
(907)733-2778 Fax:(907)733-2778
Internet: www.denaliview.com
E-mail: info@denaliview.com

Circa 1987. This rich wood home is a newer building, but displays many Victorian elements, including a two-story turret. The inn boasts a view of Denali, otherwise known as Mt. McKinley, as well the surrounding wilderness. The interior features wood paneling and a hint of Victorian decor. The den is an especially fun room for hunters, the walls are decorated with bearskins and other hunting trophies, such as deer, mountain goat and pheasant. Guest rooms are warm and cozy with flowery touches and a few antiques. Breakfasts feature items such as a cheese souffle or perhaps eight-grain French toast. After the morning meal, guests can take advantage of the multitude of outdoor activities, from hunting to hiking to skiing.

Innkeeper(s): LesLee & Norm Solberg. $100-125. 3 rooms with PB and 1 conference room. Breakfast included in rates. Types of meals: Full gourmet bkfst and early coffee/tea. Beds: QT. Cable TV, VCR, reading lamp, clock radio and telephone in room. Fax, copier and bicycles on premises. Cross-country skiing, fishing, live theater, parks, shopping, rafting, flightseeing and jet boating nearby.
Location: Mountains, waterfront. Valley.
Publicity: *San Francisco Chronicle, International Travel, Eva Infomercial and Pat Robinson's Church TV.*

"Thank you for sharing your bit of heaven—you are most gracious hosts."

Certificate may be used: Feb. 1-April 30, no breakfast during these dates.

Wasilla   E5

Wasilla Lake B&B

961 N Shore Dr
Wasilla, AK 99654-6546
(907)376-5985 Fax:(907)376-5985
Internet: www.wasillalake.com
E-mail: waslake@gci.net

Circa 1974. Located on the north shore, this premier bed & breakfast features spectacular lake and mountain views and equally impressive flower gardens. This spacious country home offers guest bedrooms with private or shared baths in the main part of the house. Stay in a 900-square-foot apartment with fireplace, situated on the lower level. An all-glass front overlooks the large deck, dock and water. Ask about making arrangements to fish for a pontoon boat ride. A visit to Anchorage is only 45 miles away.

Innkeeper(s): Laverne & Arlene Gronewald. $85-150. 7 rooms, 2 with PB, 1 with FP, 1 suite. Breakfast included in rates. Types of meals: Full bkfst and early coffee/tea. Beds: KQDT. Cable TV, VCR, reading lamp, stereo, refrigerator, clock radio, telephone and desk in room. Fax, copier, swimming, bicycles and fireplace on premises. Antiquing, cross-country skiing, downhill skiing, fishing, golf, live theater, parks, shopping, water sports and national and state parks nearby.
Location: Mountains, ocean community, waterfront.
Certificate may be used: November to May.

Arizona

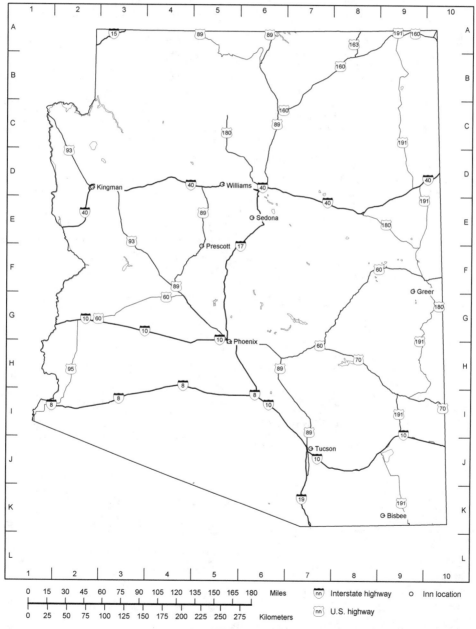

Miles

Kilometers

nn Interstate highway   o Inn location

nn U.S. highway

Bisbee   K9

Audrey's Inn

20 Brewery Ave
Bisbee, AZ 85603
(520)227-6120 (888)437-4263 Fax:(520)432-9022
Internet: www.bisbeerentals.us
E-mail: bisbeerentals@aol.com

Circa 1904. Situated in the historic Brewery Gulch in a small town just one and a half hours southeast of Tucson, this 100-year-old brick, three-story building has been renovated to offer one-story guest bedrooms and townhouse suites. The inn is pet friendly and each room is decorated in a different theme. Stay in the Wild Animal Room, Psychic Room, Chinese Unit, Six-Gun Wedding Honeymoon Suite or Patio Unit. Suites include cable TV with VCR, full kitchen, living room, dining area and phones with answering machines. On-site laundry facilities are provided. The rooftop patio with great views is popular for weddings. Schedule a psychic reading with Audrey. Browse through the Made in Bisbee art gallery located below the inn.

Innkeeper(s): Audrey Campbell. $85. 6 suites. Types of meals: Early coffee/tea. Beds: K. Modem hook-up, cable TV, VCR, reading lamp, refrigerator, ceiling fan, clock radio, telephone, coffeemaker and desk in room. Air conditioning. Handicap access. Antiquing, art galleries, bicycling, golf, hiking, live theater, museums, parks, shopping, tennis and wineries nearby.

Location: City.

Certificate may be used: Anytime, Sunday-Thursday except holidays with no other discounts.

Bisbee Grand Hotel, A B&B Inn

61 Main Street, Box 825
Bisbee, AZ 85603
(520)432-5900 (800)421-1909
Internet: www.bisbeegrandhotel.com
E-mail: bisbegrandhotel@msn.com

Circa 1906. This National Register treasure is a stunning example of an elegant turn-of-the-century hotel. The hotel originally served as a stop for mining executives, and it was restored back to its Old West glory in the 1980s. Each of the rooms is decorated with Victorian furnishings and wall coverings. The suites offer special items such as clawfoot tubs, an antique Chinese wedding bed, a fountain or four-poster bed. Try the Old Western Suite with an authentic covered wagon modified to fit a queen-size bed. The Grand Western Salon boasts the back bar fixture from the Pony Saloon in Tombstone. After a full breakfast, enjoy a day touring the Bisbee area, which includes mine tours, museums, shops, antiquing and a host of outdoor activities.

Innkeeper(s): Bill Thomas. $50-150. 8 rooms, 7 suites. Breakfast included in rates. Types of meals: Full bkfst.

Certificate may be used: Excluding Jan. 15-May 15, excluding weekends and holidays. Offer does not apply to suites.

Greer   F9

White Mountain Lodge

PO Box 143
Greer, AZ 85927-0143
(928)735-7568 (888)493-7568 Fax:(928)735-7498
E-mail: wmlodge@wmonline.com

Circa 1892. This 19th-century lodge affords views of Greer meadow and the Little Colorado River. The guest rooms are individually decorated in a Southwestern or country style. The common rooms are decorated with period antiques, Southwestern art and Mission-style furnishings. The Lodge's living room is an ideal place to relax with its stone fireplace. While dining on the hearty breakfasts, guests not only are treated to entrees that range from traditional country fare to the more gourmet, they also enjoy a view from the picture window. The cookie jar is always filled with homemade goodies and hot drinks are available throughout the day. The inn is near excellent hiking trails.

Innkeeper(s): Charles & Mary Bast. $85-155. 12 rooms, 6 with PB, 4 with FP and 6 cabins. Breakfast and snacks/refreshments included in rates. Types of meals: Full gourmet bkfst, veg bkfst and early coffee/tea. Beds: KQT. TV, VCR, reading lamp, refrigerator, ceiling fan, clock radio, coffeemaker, desk, hot tub/spa and two with whirlpool tubs in room. Fax, copier, spa, telephone and fireplace on premises. Antiquing, art galleries, cross-country skiing, downhill skiing, fishing, golf, hiking, museums and shopping nearby.

Location: Country, mountains.

Publicity: *Independent & Arizona Republic, Arizona Foothills, Vista Magazine, KOY Radio, Channel 3 and Phoenix Magazine.*

Certificate may be used: Sunday-Thursday (no holidays).

Kingman   D2

Hotel Brunswick

315 E Andy Devine Ave
Kingman, AZ 86401
(928)718-1800 Fax:(928)718-1801
Internet: www.hotel-brunswick.com
E-mail: rsvp@hotel-brunswick.com

Circa 1909. Built at the turn of the 20th century, the Hotel Brunswick was, for awhile, the tallest building in three counties. The hotel was built to accommodate the many railroad passengers who traveled through Kingman. Later in the century, the hotel fell into disrepair until the current owners purchased the property, restoring the historic charm. Each of the guest rooms has been appointed individually. Rooms range from the spacious honeymoon suite to the cozy, economical Cowboy and Cowgirl rooms. In addition to the accommodations, the hotel includes a European-style café, Mulligan's Bar, and a full-service business center. Your hosts can arrange a massage service or create a honeymoon package with flowers and champagne. Kingman, a stop along the famed Route 66, maintains many historic buildings and sites.

Innkeeper(s): Mr. Gerard Guedon. $25-110. 24 rooms, 7 with PB, 8 suites. Breakfast included in rates. Types of meals: Cont plus, early coffee/tea and gourmet dinner. Restaurant on premises. Beds: QDT. Modem hook-up, cable TV, VCR, reading lamp, refrigerator and telephone in room. Air conditioning. Fax, copier and laundry facility on premises. Handicap access. Antiquing, canoeing/kayaking, fishing, golf, hiking, horseback riding, museums, parks, shopping, water sports and ghost towns nearby.

Location: Arid plains.

Publicity: *Kingman Daily Miner, Standard News, Arizona Holidays and TV 77.*

Certificate may be used: June, July, August, subject to availability, holidays excluded. No other discounts apply.

Phoenix   F5

Maricopa Manor

15 West Pasadena Ave.
Phoenix, AZ 85013-2001
(602)274-6302 (800)292-6403 Fax:(602)266-3904
Internet: www.maricopamanor.com
E-mail: res@maricopamanor.com

Circa 1928. Secluded amid palm trees on an acre of land, this
Spanish-style house features four graceful columns in the entry
hall, an elegant living room with a marble mantel and a music
room. Completely refurbished suites are very spacious and distinctively furnished with style and good taste. Relax on the private patio or around the pool while enjoying the soothing
sound of falling water from the many fountains.

Innkeeper(s): Jeff Vadheim. $99-249. 7 rooms, 4 with FP, 7 suites. Breakfast
included in rates. Types of meals: Cont plus. Beds: KQ. Cable TV, VCR, reading lamp, stereo, refrigerator, ceiling fan, clock radio, telephone and desk in
room. Air conditioning. TV, fax, copier, spa, swimming, library, parlor games
and off-street parking on premises. Handicap access. Amusement parks,
antiquing, golf, live theater, parks, shopping, sporting events, tennis, water
sports and restaurants nearby.

Location: City.

Publicity: *Arizona Business Journal, Country Inns, AAA Westways, San
Francisco Chronicle, Focus and Sombrero.*

*"I've stayed 200+ nights at B&Bs around the world, yet have
never before experienced the warmth and sincere friendliness of
Maricopa Manor."*

Certificate may be used: April 1-Dec. 19.

Prescott   F5

Dolls & Roses Victorian Bed & Breakfast

109 N Pleasant St
Prescott, AZ 86301
(928)776-9291 (800)924-0883 Fax:(928)778-2642
Internet: www.dollsandroses-bb.com
E-mail: dollsandroses@yahoo.com

Circa 1883. Each of the guest rooms at this historic 19th-cen-
tury Victorian is decorated with a rose theme. The English Rose
is a spacious room with a sitting area decorated with a love seat
and antique rocker. The Rose Garden has an antique clawfoot
tub. The historic home is decorated in Victorian style with
antiques and a collection of porcelain dolls. A full breakfast is
served each morning featuring specialty egg dishes. Historic
downtown is within walking distance.

Innkeeper(s): Donna Perkins. $99-149. 4 rooms with PB. Breakfast includ-
ed in rates. Types of meals: Full bkfst, early coffee/tea and snacks/refresh-
ments. Beds: KQ. Reading lamp and ceiling fan in room. Air conditioning.
TV, VCR, fax, copier, parlor games, telephone, fireplace, lovely garden and
sitting area on premises. Limited handicap access. Antiquing, art galleries,
bicycling, canoeing/kayaking, fishing, golf, hiking, horseback riding, live theater, museums, parks, shopping, tennis, water sports and seasonal town
square events nearby.

Location: City, mountains.

Certificate may be used: Monday-Thursday, October through April, holidays
and special events excluded.

Juniper Well Ranch

PO Box 11083
Prescott, AZ 86304-1083
(928)442-3415
Internet: www.juniperwellranch.com
E-mail: juniperwell@earthlink.net

Circa 1991. A working horse ranch sits on the front 15 acres
of this 50-acre, wooded property, which is surrounded by the
Prescott National Forest. Guests are welcome to feed the horses, and children have been known to take a ride on a tractor
with innkeeper David Bonham. Two log cabins and the ranch
house sit farther back on the land where families can enjoy
nature, "unlimited" hiking and seclusion. A summer house is
available for ranch guests. It has no walls, a sloping roof with
skylights and a fire pit. Guest pets, including horses, are welcome on an individual basis.

Innkeeper(s): David Bonham & Gail Ball. $100. 6 rooms, 3 with PB, 3 with
FP and 3 cabins. Beds: QDT. Reading lamp, refrigerator, ceiling fan, clock
radio, desk and full kitchen in room. Stable, library, pet boarding, child care,
telephone, working horse ranch, unlimited hiking, horse feeding and summer
house on premises. Handicap access. Antiquing, cross-country skiing, fishing,
golf, live theater, parks and shopping nearby.

Location: City, mountains. Ranch.

Certificate may be used: Sunday through Thursday, all year. Holidays excluded.

Pleasant Street Inn

142 S Pleasant St
Prescott, AZ 86303-3811
(928)445-4774 (877)226-7128 Fax:(928)445-4774
Internet: www.pleasantstreetinn-bb.com
E-mail: jeannew@cableone.net

Circa 1906. Pleasant Street Inn was moved to its present site,
in the heart of historic Prescott, in 1991. Rooms at this quaint,
Victorian inn are stylishly decorated with comfort in mind. The
PineView Suite boasts a sitting room and fireplace. Another
suite includes a sitting room and private, covered deck. Prescott,
which served twice as the state territorial capital, offers a variety
of museums and art galleries to explore, as well as the historic
Court House Square. Nearby Prescott National Forest is a perfect place to enjoy hiking, climbing and other outdoor activities.

Innkeeper(s): Jeanne Watkins. $100-150. 4 rooms with PB, 2 suites.
Breakfast included in rates. Types of meals: Full bkfst. Beds: KQD. Modem
hook-up, data port, reading lamp, refrigerator, ceiling fan, fireplace and private deck in room. Central air. TV, VCR, fax, parlor games and telephone on
premises. Limited handicap access.

Location: Mountains.

Certificate may be used: Anytime, Jan. 1-March 31, subject to availability. Monday through Thursday, April 1-Dec. 31, excluding holidays and
special events.

Sedona   E6

A Territorial House - An Old West B&B

65 Piki Dr
Sedona, AZ 86336
(928)204-2737 (800)801-2737 Fax:(928)204-2230
Internet: www.territorialhousebb.com
E-mail: info@territorialhousebb.com

Circa 1977. Old West hospitality and elegance combine to create
an ambiance of yesterday while meeting today's modern expectations. This bed and breakfast is situated in a peacefully scenic
area on almost an acre sheltered by juniper and cottonwood

trees. Each guest bedroom reflects the overall theme, named after characters from classics like Miss Kitty from Gunsmoke, Cisco's Room and Indian Garden or a two-room suite called Ponderosa and the Bunkhouse. Choose one with a large jetted or whirlpool tub, oversize shower, refrigerator, leather recliner, fireplace and a private balcony. Just outside, walk a paved one-mile loop with incredible views. Horseback or airplane rides and balloon or jeep tours are some of the great activities that are only five minutes away. Relax in the hot tub after a rejuvenating day.

Innkeeper(s): Larry & Suzie Galisky. $125-215. 4 rooms with PB, 1 suite. Breakfast, afternoon tea and snacks/refreshments included in rates. Types of meals: Full gourmet bkfst. Beds: KQT. Cable TV, VCR, reading lamp, CD player, refrigerator, ceiling fan, clock radio, telephone, hot tub/spa and fireplace in room. Central air. Fax, copier, spa and fireplace on premises. Antiquing, art galleries, bicycling, cross-country skiing, downhill skiing, fishing, golf, hiking, horseback riding, parks, shopping and tennis nearby.

Location: City.

Certificate may be used: July-August, December-January, Sunday-Thursday. No holidays.

Casa Sedona Bed & Breakfast Inn

55 Hozoni Drive
Sedona, AZ 86336-3765
(928)282-2938 (800)525-3756 Fax:(928)282-2259
Internet: www.casasedona.com
E-mail: casa@sedona.net

Circa 1992. Red Rock views and a garden setting combine to create a romantic ambiance at Casa Sedona. The inn is located in Sedona and secluded on an acre of grounds. Each guest room has been decorated individually with romance in mind. Each room includes a fireplace and oversize Jacuzzi tub. There is also an outdoor hot tub where guests can relax and gaze at a starry sky. Guests are pampered with Southwestern-style fare for breakfast, which often is served outdoors under the shade of juniper trees. After a day exploring the area, return to the bed & breakfast and enjoy afternoon refreshments. The innkeepers provide hiking and driving maps, as well as a custom map for a day trip to the Grand Canyon.

Innkeeper(s): Bob & Donna Marriott. $170-275. 16 rooms with PB, 16 with FP and 1 conference room. Breakfast, snacks/refreshments and hors d'oeuvres included in rates. Types of meals: Full gourmet bkfst, veg bkfst and early coffee/tea. Beds: KQT. Data port, cable TV, VCR, reading lamp, CD player, refrigerator, ceiling fan, clock radio, telephone, turn-down service, hot tub/spa, fireplace, iron, robes, hair dryers, Jacuzzi and make-up mirror in room. Central air. Fax, spa, library, parlor games, gift shop and wedding gazebo on premises. Handicap access. Antiquing, art galleries, bicycling, fishing, golf, hiking, horseback riding, live theater, museums, parks, shopping, tennis and wineries nearby.

Location: City, mountains.

Publicity: *Country Inns, Cosmopolitan (Japan), Innside Scoop, Physicians, Money Magazine and Travel Channel.*

"Cozy with a warm inviting feeling."

Certificate may be used: January, June, July, August, Sunday-Thursday, holidays excluded, subject to availability.

Lodge at Sedona-A Luxury Bed and Breakfast Inn

125 Kallof Place
Sedona, AZ 86336-5566
(928)204-1942 (800)619-4467 Fax:(928)204-2128
Internet: www.lodgeatsedona.com
E-mail: info@lodgeatsedona.com

Circa 1959. Elegantly casual, this newly renovated mission-style B&B sits on three secluded acres with expansive red rock views, mature juniper and pinions, sculpture gardens, foun-

tains and a private labyrinth. Enjoy sunset snacks in the Fireplace Lounge, Celebration Porch or outdoor terrace. Artfully decorated guest rooms feature romantic fireplaces, double spa tubs, sitting areas, private decks and entrances. Linger over a five-course gourmet breakfast. Massage therapy is available. Exclusive receptions, weddings and executive meetings are accommodated. The lodge offers health club privileges, including access to two swimming pools. The Grand Canyon is a two-hour day trip, and the area includes hiking trails, jeep tours and hot air balloons.

Innkeeper(s): Shelley L Wachal. $160-325. 14 rooms with PB, 12 with FP, 1 with HT, 8 suites and 2 conference rooms. Breakfast, afternoon tea, snacks/refreshments and hors d'oeuvres included in rates. Types of meals: Full gourmet bkfst, veg bkfst and early coffee/tea. Beds: KQT. Cable TV, VCR, reading lamp, stereo, ceiling fan, snack bar, clock radio, desk, hot tub/spa, fireplace, stereo and large private deck in room. Central air. Fax, copier, spa, swimming, library, parlor games, telephone, laundry facility, gift shop, Celebration Terrace, DVD, one ADA suite and gift shop on premises. Handicap access. Antiquing, art galleries, bicycling, canoeing/kayaking, cross-country skiing, fishing, golf, hiking, horseback riding, live theater, museums, parks, shopping, tennis, wineries, Jeep tours, cycling, hot air balloon, biplane, casino, camping and adventure tours nearby.

Location: Country, mountains. Sedona Red Rock country.

Publicity: *Real Simple Magazine, Arizona Republic, Sedona, Red Rock News, San Francisco Examiner, Country Register, New York Post, Sedona, Bon Appetit, Mountain Living, Sunset Magazine and KPNX Channel 10 Phoenix.*

"What a wonderful hideaway you have! Everything about your inn was and is fantastic! The friendly service made me feel as if I was home. More importantly, the food made me wish that was my home!"

Certificate may be used: June 13-Aug. 28, Jan. 3-March 15, Sunday-Thursday.

Tucson   J7

Agave Grove B&B Inn

800 West Panorama Rd
Tucson, AZ 85704-3912
(520)797-3400 (888)822-4283 Fax:(520)797-0980
E-mail: agavebb@earthlink.net

Circa 1976. This private home is built in a hacienda style with courtyard, waterfall-fed swimming pool in view of the mountains, putting green and gazebo-like ramada on its two acres. There is a flagstone fireplace in the family room and guests enjoy playing billiards and board games. One of the guest rooms offers a Jacuzzi. Breakfast specialties may include caramelized French toast, fruit and sausage. Drive to the University of Arizona's observatory and museums as well as many other area attractions.

Innkeeper(s): John & Denise Kiber. $70-175. 5 rooms, 1 with PB, 3 suites. Breakfast and snacks/refreshments included in rates. Types of meals: Full gourmet bkfst, early coffee/tea and picnic lunch. Beds: KQ. Cable TV, reading lamp, refrigerator, ceiling fan, snack bar, clock radio, telephone, desk, hot tub/spa suites have microwave in room. Air conditioning. VCR, fax, copier, spa, swimming, library, child care, parlor games, fireplace and billiard table on premises. Handicap access. Amusement parks, antiquing, downhill skiing, golf, live theater, parks, shopping, sporting events, tennis, botanical gardens and day trips nearby.

Location: Mountains. Suburban desert estate.

Publicity: *Arizona Daily Star.*

Certificate may be used: June 1-Nov. 30.

Alta Vista Bed & Breakfast

11300 East Broadway Blvd.
Tucson, AZ 85748
(520)647-3037
Internet: www.altavistabedandbreakfast.com
E-mail: altavistabandb@aol.com

Circa 1978. Extraordinary panoramic views of the Santa Catalina and Rincon Mountains as well as the lush Tanque Verde Valley instill a sense of serenity at this desert oasis covering more than three acres. Built high on a hill with territorial-style architecture, the guest bedrooms offer a variety of decor. The spacious White Wicker Room blends traditional with cottage romance. The cheery Santa Fe Room boasts a lodge-pole bed and the cozy New England Room features a four-poster bed. A hearty breakfast includes fresh fruit, homemade baked goods, prickly pear cactus jams and an entree that may be a Spanish omelette, Grand Marnier French toast, or multigrain pancakes with real maple syrup. Special dietary needs and desires are gladly catered to. Relax on the front porch or sit by the fire in the living room. Walk the gardens, or explore nearby Saguaro National Park East.

Innkeeper(s): Peter & Gaila Smith. $65-125. 3 rooms with PB. Breakfast, afternoon tea and snacks/refreshments included in rates. Types of meals: Country bkfst, veg bkfst and early coffee/tea. Beds: KQ. TV, VCR, reading lamp, ceiling fan, clock radio, turn-down service, desk, satellite TV, two with refrigerator and microwave in room. Central air. Fax, copier, parlor games, telephone and fireplace on premises. Art galleries, bicycling, golf, hiking, horseback riding and Saguaro East National Park nearby.
Location: City. On the edge of Tucson in the East.
Certificate may be used: June 1-Sept. 30.

Casa Alegre B&B

316 E Speedway Blvd
Tucson, AZ 85705-7429
(520)628-1800 (800)628-5654 Fax:(520)792-1880
Internet: www.casaalegreinn.com
E-mail: alegre123@aol.com

Circa 1915. Innkeeper Phyllis Florek decorated the interior of this Craftsman-style home with artifacts reflecting the history of Tucson, including Native American pieces and antique mining tools. Wake to the aroma of fresh coffee and join other guests as you enjoy fresh muffins, fruit and other breakfast treats,  such as succulent cottage cheese pancakes with raspberry preserves. The Arizona sitting room opens onto serene gardens, a pool and a Jacuzzi. An abundance of shopping and sightseeing is found nearby.

Innkeeper(s): Phyllis Florek. $90-135. 4 rooms with PB, 1 with FP. Breakfast included in rates. Types of meals: Full gourmet bkfst. Beds: Q. Cable TV, reading lamp, ceiling fan and clock radio in room. VCR, fax, spa, swimming, parlor games, telephone and fireplace on premises. Antiquing, live theater, parks, shopping, sporting events and restaurants nearby.
Location: City.
Publicity: *Arizona Daily Star, Travel Holiday and Arizona Times.*

"An oasis of comfort in Central Tucson."
Certificate may be used: June 1 through Aug. 30.

Casa Tierra Adobe B&B Inn

11155 W Calle Pima
Tucson, AZ 85743-9462
(520)578-3058 (866)254-0006 Fax:(520)578-8445
Internet: www.casatierratucson.com
E-mail: info@casatierratucson.com

Circa 1988. The Sonoran Desert surrounds this secluded, adobe retreat. The mountain views and brilliant sunsets are spectacular. The interior arched courtyard, vaulted brick ceilings and Mexican furnishings create a wonderful Southwestern atmosphere. Each guest room has a private entrance and patios that overlook the desert landscape. The rooms open up to the courtyard. Freshly ground coffee and specialty teas accompany the full vegetarian breakfast. Old Tucson, the Desert Museum and a Saguaro National Park are nearby. The inn also provides a relaxing hot tub and telescope.

Innkeeper(s): Barb & Dave Malmquist. $135-325. 4 rooms, 3 with PB, 1 suite. Breakfast and snacks/refreshments included in rates. Types of meals: Full gourmet bkfst, veg bkfst and early coffee/tea. Beds: Q. Data port, reading lamp, refrigerator, ceiling fan, snack bar, clock radio and telephone in room. Air conditioning. TV, VCR, fax, spa and telescope on premises. Bicycling, golf, hiking and horseback riding nearby.
Location: Country.
Publicity: *Arizona Daily Star, Smart Money Magazine, Washington Post, Phoenix Magazine and Scottsdale Tribune.*
Certificate may be used: May 1-June 15, Aug. 15-Nov. 15.

Jeremiah Inn B&B, Ltd.

10921 E Snyder Rd
Tucson, AZ 85749-9066
(520)749-3072 (888)750-3072
Internet: www.jeremiahinn.com
E-mail: info@jeremiahinn.com

Circa 1995. The Catalina Mountains serve as a backdrop for this modern Santa Fe-style home. There are five guest rooms, four offer a sitting area, and all are decorated in Southwestern style. Guest rooms have a private entrance, and there is a refrigerator for guest use. Breakfast at the inn is an event. The menu might include a lavish selection of fresh fruit, a Southwestern-style potato saute and homemade cinnamon toast. Guests enjoy use of a pool and a spa. Guests can spend the day hiking, golfing, shopping or exploring the scenic area on horseback.

Innkeeper(s): Bob & Beth Miner. $90-120. 5 rooms with PB. Breakfast and snacks/refreshments included in rates. Types of meals: Full bkfst and early coffee/tea. Beds: QT. TV, reading lamp, ceiling fan, clock radio, telephone, DVD and VCR in room. Air conditioning. VCR, spa, swimming, parlor games, fireplace, laundry facility, gift shop and private outside entry to guest wing on premises. Limited handicap access. Amusement parks, antiquing, art galleries, bicycling, golf, hiking, horseback riding, live theater, museums, parks, shopping, sporting events and tennis nearby.
Location: Suburban ranch.

"We felt like honored guests at your inn-truly an oasis in the desert."
Certificate may be used: May 1 to Jan. 1, holidays excluded.

The Suncatcher

105 N Avenida Javalina
Tucson, AZ 85748-8928
(520)885-0883 (877)775-8355 Fax:(520)885-0883
Internet: www.thesuncatcher.com
E-mail: info@thesuncatcher.com

Circa 1991. From the picture window in your opulent guest room, you'll enjoy views of mountains and desert scenery. The bedchambers include beautiful furnishings, such as a bed draped in a luxurious canopy. A fireplace or double Jacuzzi tub are options. Guests enjoy the use of a heated pool and hot tub in the backyard patio, as well as use of four acres. All of Tucson's sites and shops are nearby.

Innkeeper(s): Janos & Nicola Siess. $80-145. 4 rooms with PB, 1 with FP. Breakfast included in rates. Types of meals: Full bkfst. Beds: Q. Cable TV, VCR, reading lamp, clock radio, telephone, turn-down service and desk in room. Air conditioning. Fax, copier, spa, swimming, fireplace and bar on premises. Handicap access. Golf, hiking, parks, shopping and birding nearby.

Location: Mountains.

Certificate may be used: July 1-Sept. 1.

Williams   D5

Mountain Country Lodge B&B

437 West Route 66
Williams, AZ 86046
(928)635-4341 (800)973-6210 Fax:(928)635-4341
E-mail: mclodge@grandcayon2.com

Circa 1909. Originally built as a mansion, this nostalgic lodge is centrally located in Grand Canyon country. The veranda overlooks historic Route 66. Each guest bedroom is distinctively decorated. Amenities include cable TV, an extensive video library and refrigerators. Breakfast is enjoyed in the intimate on-site restaurant called Special D's. There is much to experience nearby, from pine forests to the scenic red rocks of Sedona.

Innkeeper(s): Greg Lee. $69-125. 9 rooms, 8 with PB, 1 with FP and 1 conference room. Breakfast included in rates. Types of meals: Cont plus and gourmet dinner. Restaurant on premises. Beds: KQD. Cable TV, VCR, refrigerator, ceiling fan, clock radio and fireplace in room. Air conditioning. Antiquing, art galleries, bicycling, cross-country skiing, downhill skiing, fishing, golf, hiking, horseback riding and shopping nearby.

Location: City, mountains.

Publicity: *Channel 11.*

Certificate may be used: November-March, Sunday-Thursday, subject to availability.

The Sheridan House Inn

460 E Sheridan Ave
Williams, AZ 86046
(928)635-9441 (888)635-9345 Fax:(928)635-1005
Internet: www.grandcanyonbedandbreakfast.com
E-mail: sheridanhouseinn@msn.com

Circa 1988. This two-story house offers porches and decks from which to enjoy its two acres of ponderosa forest. For a queen-size bed and views of pine trees ask for the Willow Room or for sunset views the Cedar Room is the best choice. It also features a bay widow. CD stereo systems and cable TV are in all the rooms. Full breakfasts are served, often on the upstairs deck and a casual buffet dinner is available as well. A fitness room and den with pool table and piano are open to guests, and there is a seasonally available hot tub, as well. The Grand Canyon is 45 minutes away and the Grand Canyon Railroad is within a half mile.

Innkeeper(s): K.C. & Mary Seidner. $150-220. 8 rooms with PB, 2 suites and 1 conference room. Breakfast included in rates. Beds: KQDT. Cable TV, VCR, reading lamp, stereo, ceiling fan, clock radio and telephone in room. Fax, copier, spa, library, parlor games, fireplace and hiking trail on premises. Antiquing, cross-country skiing, downhill skiing, fishing, golf, horseback riding, parks, shopping, tennis and Grand Canyon Railroad nearby.

Location: Mountains.

Publicity: *Williams Grand Canyon News and KPAZ Flagstaff.*

Certificate may be used: Jan. 5-March 31, Sunday-Thursday, excluding holidays.

Arkansas

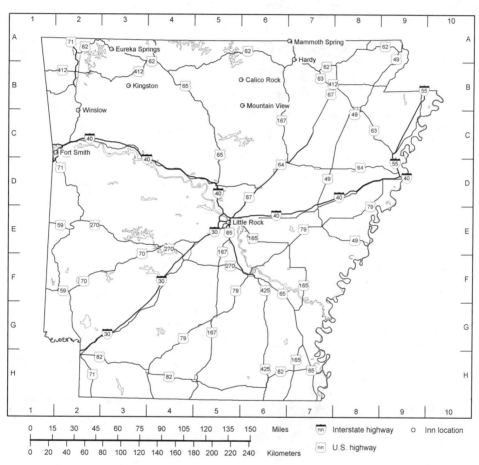

| | Interstate highway | ○ Inn location |
| nn | U.S. highway | |

0 15 30 45 60 75 90 105 120 135 150 Miles

0 20 40 60 80 100 120 140 160 180 200 220 240 Kilometers

Calico Rock   B5

Happy Lonesome Log Cabins

1444 Forest Home Lane
Calico Rock, AR 72519-9102
(870)297-8764
Internet: www.bbonline.com/ar/hlcabins
E-mail: hlcabins@centurytel.net

Circa 1988. The two rustic log cabins are located on a wooded, 194-acre property on the bluff above White River. The interiors are simple and comfortable and include a sleeping loft, small kitchen and wood stove. Continental fare is placed in the kitchenette so guests may enjoy a light breakfast at their leisure. The favorite activity is relaxing on the porch and enjoying the views of river and woodland. Calico Rock is an interesting historic town nearby, and there are plenty of old buildings and shops to browse. Explore the Ozark National Forest, Blanchard Springs Caverns, or try one of the area's popular river activities, such as float trips, canoeing or fishing.

Innkeeper(s): Carolyn & Christian J. Eck. $75-95. 4 rooms, 2 with PB. Breakfast included in rates. Types of meals: Cont plus. Beds: QD. Refrigerator, ceiling fan, clock radio and kitchenette in room. Air conditioning. Parlor games and telephone on premises. Amusement parks, antiquing, fishing, golf, live theater, parks, shopping, tennis and water sports nearby. Location: Mountains. Forest.
Certificate may be used: March through December.

Arkansas

Eureka Springs   A3

1884 Bridgeford House B&B

263 Spring St
Eureka Springs, AR 72632-3154
(479)253-7853 (888)567-2422 Fax:(479)253-5497
Internet: www.bridgefordhouse.com
E-mail: innkeeper@bridgefordhouse.com

Circa 1884. Victorian charm abounds at this Queen Anne-
Eastlake home, located in the heart of the historic district.
Experience generous Southern hospitality upon arrival, when
offered homemade treats. Several guest bedrooms
feature a double Jacuzzi, fireplace
and deck. Savor a gourmet breakfast served on fine china and flatware. The bed & breakfast is just
a few blocks from gift boutiques,
antique shops, spas, restaurants and
much more.

Innkeeper(s): Jeff & Nadara (Sam) Feldman. $99-165. 5
rooms with PB. Breakfast included in rates. Types of meals: Full bkfst,
early coffee/tea, snacks/refreshments and room service. Beds: KQ. Cable
TV, VCR, reading lamp, refrigerator, clock radio and fans in room. Air conditioning. Telephone on premises. Antiquing, fishing, golf, live theater, shopping and water sports nearby.
Location: City, mountains. Less than one hour from Branson, Mo.
Publicity: Times Echo Flashlight, Arkansas National Tour Guide and
Country Almanac.

"You have created an enchanting respite for weary people."
Certificate may be used: Anytime, subject to availability.

5 Ojo Inn B&B

5 Ojo St
Eureka Springs, AR 72632-3220
(479)253-6734 (800)656-6734 Fax:(479)363-9492
Internet: www.5ojo.com
E-mail: bnbinns@5ojo.com

Circa 1900. Guests at 5 Ojo choose between four restored
buildings ranging in vintage from an 1891 Victorian to a 1940s
cottage. Rooms are decorated with antiques but include modern amenities such as refrigerators and coffeemakers. Most
rooms include whirlpool tubs
and fireplaces. The Carriage
House Cottage and the
Anniversary Suite are ideal places
for honeymooners or those celebrating a special occasion.
Among its romantic amenities,
the Anniversary Suite includes a private porch with a swing.
Gourmet breakfasts are served in the Sweet House's dining
room, but private dining can be arranged. Eureka Springs with
its 63-65 springs, has been a sought after spa town for more
than a century.
Innkeeper(s): Richard & Jan Grinnell. $79-149. 10 rooms with PB, 7 with
FP, 2 suites and 1 cottage. Breakfast included in rates. Types of meals: Full
gourmet bkfst. Beds: QT. Cable TV, reading lamp, refrigerator, ceiling fan,
clock radio, coffeemaker, desk and nine with Jacuzzi tubs for two in room. Air
conditioning. TV, VCR, fax, spa, library, parlor games and telephone on
premises. Antiquing, art galleries, fishing, golf, live theater, parks, shopping,
sporting events, water sports, massage therapy and Victorian village nearby.
Location: City, mountains. Historic District.
Publicity: Arkansas Democrat Gazette, Southern Living and Country Inns.
Certificate may be used: Jan. 2-Dec. 30, Monday-Thursday, except October,
holidays and festivals.

Arsenic & Old Lace B&B Inn

60 Hillside Ave
Eureka Springs, AR 72632-3133
(479)253-5454 (800)243-5223 Fax:(479)253-2246
Internet: www.arsenicOldlace.com
E-mail: ArsenicOldLaceBB@aol.com

Circa 1992. This bed & breakfast is a meticulous reproduction of
Queen Anne Victorian style, and it offers five guest rooms decorated with antique Victorian furnishings. Popular with honeymooners, the guest rooms offer whirlpool tubs, balconies and fireplaces.
The inn's gardens complement the
attractive exterior, which includes a
wraparound veranda and stone wall.
Its location in the historic district
makes it an excellent starting point
for a sightseeing stroll or shopping.

Innkeeper(s): Debbie & Jens Hansen. $130-
195. 5 rooms with PB, 5 with FP. Breakfast
and snacks/refreshments included in rates. Types of meals: Full gourmet bkfst.
Beds: KQ. Cable TV, VCR, reading lamp, ceiling fan, hot tub/spa,
private patios and robes in room. Air conditioning. Parlor games, telephone and
video library on premises. Antiquing, fishing, golf, live theater, parks, shopping,
tennis, water sports, music festivals, car festivals and Passion Play nearby.
Location: City.
Publicity: Gail Greco's Romance of Country Inns, Houston Chronicle,
Oklahoma Living and KLSM-TV.

"It was well worth the 1,000 miles we traveled to share your home for
a short while...thanks for a four-star vacation."
Certificate may be used: January-September, Sunday through Thursday only.
November-December, Sunday through Thursday only. Tree Top suite and holidays excluded.

Candlestick Cottage Inn

6 Douglas St
Eureka Springs, AR 72632-3416
(479)253-6813 (800)835-5184 Fax:(479)253-2849
Internet: www.candlestickcottageinn.com
E-mail: candleci@mynewroads.com

Circa 1882. Woods and foliage surround this scenic country
home, nestled just a few blocks from Eureka Springs historic district. Guests are sure to discover a variety of wildlife strolling by
the home, including an occasional deer. Breakfasts are served on
the tree-top porch, which overlooks a waterfall and fish pond.
The morning meal begins with freshly baked muffins and fresh
fruit, followed by an entree. Innkeepers Bill and Patsy Brooks will
prepare a basket of sparkling grape juice and wine glasses for
those celebrating a special occasion. Guest rooms are decorated
in Victorian style, and some include two-person Jacuzzis.
Innkeeper(s): Bill & Patsy Brooks. $75-135. 6 rooms with PB and 1 cottage.
Breakfast included in rates. Types of meals: Full bkfst. Beds: KQT. Cable TV,
reading lamp, refrigerator, ceiling fan, clock radio, coffeemaker, hot tub/spa and
Jacuzzi in room. Air conditioning. VCR, fax, copier, parlor games, telephone and
laundry facility on premises. Antiquing, art galleries, canoeing/kayaking, fishing,
golf, hiking, horseback riding, museums, parks and shopping nearby.
Location: City.
Certificate may be used: Jan. 1-March 31, Sunday-Thursday.

Cliff Cottage Inn - Luxury B&B Suites & Historic Cottages

42 Armstrong
Eureka Springs, AR 72632
(479)253-7409 (800)799-7409
Internet: www.cliffcottage.com
E-mail: cliffctg@aol.com

Circa 1880. The only bed & breakfast in the heart of historic
downtown, it is comprised of three splendid houses in a row,

just 17 steps down to the shops
and restaurants of Main Street.
Cliff Cottage, an 1880 Eastlake
Victorian, is Sears' first kit home
and is a State and National
Historic Landmark. It features
suites with private front porches
overlooking downtown and
decks tucked into the three-story high rock bluff behind. The
Place Next Door is a Victorian replica boasting two upstairs
suites with balconies. The Artist's Cottage is a renovated 1910
Craftsman. Two elegant suites include pure-air whirlpool tubs,
20 shower settings, wetbars, a porch and a deck. A complimentary bottle of champagne or white wine is chilled in the refrigerator; a coffeemaker with imported tea, coffee, hot chocolate and
chai are provided. A full gourmet breakfast is delivered each
morning. The innkeeper will gladly arrange massages, horseback
riding, carriage rides, canoe trips and discounted golf.
Innkeeper(s): Sandra CH Smith. $185-230. 8 rooms with PB, 4 with FP, 2
with HT, 6 suites and 2 cottages. Breakfast, snacks/refreshments and wine
included in rates. Types of meals: Full gourmet bkfst, veg bkfst and early cof-
fee/tea. Beds: KQ. Modem hook-up, data port, cable TV, VCR, reading lamp,
CD player, refrigerator, ceiling fan, snack bar, clock radio, coffeemaker, desk,
hot tub/spa, fireplace, suites have two-person Jacuzzi and cottages have private hot tubs in room. Central air. Spa, library, parlor games and telephone
on premises. Amusement parks, antiquing, art galleries, beach,
canoeing/kayaking, fishing, golf, hiking, horseback riding, live theater, museums, parks, shopping, tennis, water sports and Great Passion Play nearby.
Location: Mountains. Six-minute drive to Passion Play.
Publicity: *Arkansas Democrat Gazette, Country Inns, Modern Bride,
Southern Living, Southern Bride, One of the Top Four Most Romantic Inns of
the South by Romantic Destinations Magazine, Winter 2003 published by
Southern Bride, 3 Star AAA and received the American Bed & Breakfast
Association highest rating as well as an Award for Excellence.*
Certificate may be used: Monday-Thursday, except May, October or special
events and holidays. Not valid with any other promotions. Colette's suite only
but upgrade possible. Must pay sales tax due on free night.

Gaslight Inn

19 Judah St
Eureka Springs, AR 72632
(479)253-8887 (888)253-8887 Fax:(479)253-2278
Internet: www.gaslightsquare.com
E-mail: info@gaslightsquare.com

Circa 1895. Exquisitely furnished with museum-quality
antiques and vintage treasures from the 1890s, this upscale
Victorian inn sits on a secluded hill in the historic district of
the village. Elegant surroundings and a comfortable ambiance
are the hallmarks of this award-winning inn. Chat over champagne, fruit and cheese in the splendid parlor. Romantic suites
feature Jacuzzis with separate showers, fireplaces, cable TV and
private entrances. Indulge in the pampered delight of a
gourmet breakfast. Relax on the veranda or stroll the impressive
gardens with a fountain, covered pavilion and fish pond. Walk
into town to explore the galleries, museums and shops.
Wedding, honeymoon and deluxe packages are available.
Innkeeper(s): Cynthia & Thomas Morin. $110-175. 5 rooms with PB, 4 with
FP, 2 suites. Breakfast, snacks/refreshments and wine included in rates.
Types of meals: Full gourmet bkfst and early coffee/tea. Beds: Q. Cable TV,
reading lamp, ceiling fan, clock radio, hot tub/spa, fireplace, antique bed and
armoire and two-person Jacuzzi in room. Central air. Spa, telephone, wedding
pavilion, fish pond, garden paths and romantic swings on premises. Limited
handicap access. Antiquing, art galleries, canoeing/kayaking, fishing, golf,
hiking, horseback riding, live theater, museums, parks, shopping, Great
Passion Play, tram tour of historic downtown Eureka Springs, romantic carriage rides and ghost tours at Crescent Hotel nearby.
Location: Mountains. In the Historic District of the village of Eureka Springs.
Certificate may be used: Anytime January-March; Sunday-Thursday April-
December except holidays, subject to availability.

Heart of The Hills Inn

5 Summit St
Eureka Springs, AR 72632
(479)253-7468 (800)253-7468
Internet: www.heartofthehillsinn.com
E-mail: mgreene@mynewroads.com

Circa 1883. Two suites and a Victorian cottage comprise this
antique-furnished homestead located just four blocks from
downtown. Suites have been restored and decorating in an
1880s style. The cottage is locat-
ed beside the inn and is
decorated in Victorian-
country style. The cottage
also offers a private deck
that overlooks the garden.
The village trolley stops at the inn, but the inn is within walking
distance of town. Trolley tickets available for purchase at the Inn.
Innkeeper(s): Joe Green. $80-139. 3 rooms with PB, 2 suites and 1 cottage.
Breakfast and snacks/refreshments included in rates. Types of meals: Full
bkfst and early coffee/tea. Beds: KD. Cable TV, VCR, refrigerator and coffeemaker in room. Air conditioning. TV, parlor games, telephone, private
decks, double Jacuzzi and quiet garden area on premises. Antiquing, art galleries, fishing, golf, live theater, shopping and water sports nearby.
Location: Mountains. Historic Loop.
Publicity: *Carroll County Tribune's Peddler and KHOG (ABC)
Fayetteville/Fort Smith.*

*"The decor and atmosphere of your inn was breathtaking; we were
able to relax and not want for a thing."*
Certificate may be used: Anytime, Sunday-Thursday.

The Heartstone Inn & Cottages

35 King's Hwy
Eureka Springs, AR 72632-3534
(479)253-8916 (800)494-4921 Fax:(479)253-5361
Internet: www.heartstoneinn.com
E-mail: info@heartstoneinn.com

Circa 1903. A white picket fence leads to this spacious
Victorian inn and its pink and cobalt blue wraparound porch
filled with potted geraniums and Boston ferns. Located on the
Eureka Springs historic loop the inn offers English country
antiques, private entrances and pretty linens. Private Jacuzzis,
refrigerators and VCRs are available. Pamper yourself in the
inn's massage therapy studio. Walk to shops, restaurants and
galleries or hop on the trolley to
enjoy all the pleasures of the
town. Golf privileges at a private club are extended to
guests. The New York Times
praised the inn's cuisine as the
"Best Breakfast in the Ozarks."
Innkeeper(s): Rick & Cheri Rojek. $89-
150. 11 rooms with PB, 4 with FP, 6 suites, 2 cottages and 1 conference
room. Breakfast and snacks/refreshments included in rates. Types of meals:
Full gourmet bkfst. Beds: KQ. Cable TV, VCR, reading lamp, refrigerator, ceiling fan, clock radio, coffeemaker, fireplace and whirlpool tub in room. Air conditioning. Fax, copier, spa, parlor games, telephone, gift shop, massage therapy and gift shop on premises. Limited handicap access. Amusement parks,
antiquing, art galleries, bicycling, canoeing/kayaking, fishing, golf, hiking,
horseback riding, live theater, parks, shopping, restaurants and opera nearby.
Location: City, mountains.
Publicity: *Innsider, Arkansas Times, New York Times, Arkansas Gazette,
Southern Living, Country Home, Country Inns and USA Today.*

"Extraordinary! Best breakfasts anywhere!"
Certificate may be used: Sunday through Wednesday arrivals during
November through April. Other times, last minute only, call for availability.

Sleepy Hollow Inn

4064 CR 152
Eureka Springs, AR 72632-9094
(479)253-5561 (800)805-6261
Internet: www.estc.net/sleepyhollow
E-mail: sleepyhollowbnb@aol.com

Circa 1881. Ideal for honeymooners or those in search of privacy, this three-story Victorian cottage with gingerbread trim provides a romantic retreat. Fine attention to detail has been given to the inn's elegant decor. Guest bedrooms and a luxurious main suite encompass all of the second floor, and a third-story guest bedroom boasts a view of impressive
limestone cliffs. For the ulti-
mate in intimacy and seclusion,
the entire cottage is available to
one or two couples at a time,
offering the freedom to relax
and make this a vacation home

away from home. Soak in the antique clawfoot tub or snuggle up on the porch swing. Fresh-baked pastries and other treats await in the spacious kitchen. Red bud trees give shade to the peaceful garden setting across the street from a historical museum. Chilled champagne and wedding packages are available.
Innkeeper(s): Janet Fyhrie. $129. 4 rooms, 2 with PB, 3 suites and 2 cottages. Breakfast and snacks/refreshments included in rates. Types of meals: Cont plus and early coffee/tea. Beds: QD. Cable TV, reading lamp, stereo, refrigerator, ceiling fan, snack bar, clock radio, telephone, coffeemaker, hot tub/spa and fireplace in room. Central air. Spa, fireplace and private parking on premises. Amusement parks, antiquing, art galleries, beach, canoeing/kayaking, fishing, golf, hiking, horseback riding, live theater, museums, parks, shopping, tennis, water sports and vintage train rides nearby.
Location: City. In historic downtown Eureka Springs.
Publicity: *Bestfares.com Magazine.*

"Truly a delightful experience. The love and care going into this journey back in time is impressive."
Certificate may be used: Anytime, Sunday-Thursday, subject to availability.

Taylor-Page Inn

33 Benton St
Eureka Springs, AR 72632-3501
(479)253-7315

Within easy walking distance of downtown restaurants, shopping and trolley, this turn-of-the-century Square salt-box inn features Victorian and country decor in its three suites and rooms. Guests often enjoy relaxing in the inn's two sitting rooms. The suites offer ceiling fans, full kitchens and sun decks. The inn offers convenient access to antiquing, fishing, museums and parks.
Innkeeper(s): Jeanne Taylor. $85. 3 rooms, 2 suites. Breakfast included in rates. Types of meals: Cont. Cable TV, reading lamp, refrigerator, ceiling fan, clock radio & telephone in room. Air conditioning. Antiquing & shopping nearby.
Location: City.
Certificate may be used: Anytime, January, February, March, April through December, Sunday through Thursday.

Fort Smith   C2

Thomas Quinn Suites

815 N B St
Fort Smith, AR 72901-2129
(501)782-0499
E-mail: thomasQuinnSuites@hotmail.com

Circa 1863. Nine suites with kitchenettes are available at this inn, which in 1916 added a second story and stately columns to its original structure. Located on the perimeter of Fort

Smith's historic district, it is close to the art center, historic sites, museums and restaurants. Several state parks are within easy driving distance. Early morning coffee and tea are served.
Innkeeper(s): Jan Bennett. $65-100. 9 suites. Types of meals: Early coffee/tea. Cable TV, VCR, refrigerator, clock radio, telephone and desk in room. Air conditioning. Hot tub on premises. Amusement parks, antiquing, fishing, parks, shopping and water sports nearby.
Location: City.
Certificate may be used: Anytime, subject to availability.

Hardy   A7

The Olde Stonehouse B&B Inn

511 Main St
Hardy, AR 72542-9034
(870)856-2983 (800)514-2983 Fax:(870)856-2193
Internet: www.oldestonehouse.com
E-mail: info@oldestonehouse.com

Circa 1928. The stone fireplace gracing the comfortable living room of this former banker's home is set with fossils and unusual stones, including an Arkansas diamond. Lace table-cloths, china and silver make
breakfast a special occasion.
Each room is decorated to keep
the authentic feel of the Roaring
'20s. The bedrooms have
antiques and ceiling fans. Aunt
Jenny's room boasts a clawfoot
tub and a white iron bed, while

Aunt Bette's room is filled with Victorian-era furniture. Spring River is only one block away and offers canoeing, boating and fishing. Old Hardy Town caters to antique and craft lovers. The innkeepers offer "Secret Suites," located in a nearby historic home. These romantic suites offer plenty of amenities, including a Jacuzzi for two. Breakfasts in a basket are delivered to the door each morning. The home is listed in the National Register. Murder-mystery weekends, romance packages, golf, canoeing and fly-fishing are available.
Innkeeper(s): Charles & JaNoel Bess. $85-149. 6 rooms with PB, 2 suites. Breakfast and snacks/refreshments included in rates. Types of meals: Full bkfst, early coffee/tea and picnic lunch. Beds: QD. Reading lamp, stereo, refrigerator, ceiling fan, clock radio and desk in room. Air conditioning. TV, VCR, fax, copier, library, parlor games, telephone, fireplace, guest refrigerator, coffee service and phones on premises. Antiquing, fishing, live theater, parks, shopping, water sports, museums, fly fishing with guide available and murder mystery weekends nearby.
Location: Small town.
Publicity: *Memphis Commercial Appeal, Jonesboro Sun, Vacations, Southern Living, Arkansas at Home, Democrat Gazette and Midwest Living.*

"For many years we had heard about 'Southern Hospitality' but never thought it could be this good. It was the best!"
Certificate may be used: November-April, anytime except special events. May-October, Sunday-Thursday.

Kingston   E4

Fool's Cove Ranch B&B

PO Box 10
Kingston, AR 72742-0010
(479)665-2986 (866)665-2986 Fax:(479)665-2986
E-mail: MJS@foolscoveranch.com

Circa 1979. Situated in the Ozarks' Boston Mountain range, this 6,000-square-foot farmhouse, part of a family farm, offers 130 acres of field, meadow and forest. Guests who have had their horses test negative on a Coggins test may bring them along and utilize the farm's corrals. Guests may angle for bass or catfish in the pond. Favorite gathering spots are the roomy parlor and the outdoor hot tub. Guests can check out the stars at the ranch's observatory. Area attractions include the Buffalo National River, and several fine fishing spots.

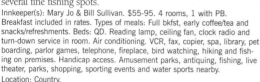

Innkeeper(s): Mary Jo & Bill Sullivan. $55-95. 4 rooms, 1 with PB. Breakfast included in rates. Types of meals: Full bkfst, early coffee/tea and snacks/refreshments. Beds: QD. Reading lamp, ceiling fan, clock radio and turn-down service in room. Air conditioning. VCR, fax, copier, spa, library, pet boarding, parlor games, telephone, fireplace, bird watching, hiking and fishing on premises. Handicap access. Amusement parks, antiquing, fishing, live theater, parks, shopping, sporting events and water sports nearby.
Location: Country.
Certificate may be used: May 15 to Dec. 15.

Little Rock E5

The Empress of Little Rock Small Luxury Hotel and B&B

2120 Louisiana St
Little Rock, AR 72206-1522
(501)374-7966 (877)374-7966 Fax:(501)375-4537
Internet: www.theEmpress.com
E-mail: hostess@theEmpress.com

Circa 1888. Day lilies, peonies and iris accent the old-fashioned gardens of this elaborate, three-story Queen Anne Victorian. A grand center hall opens to a double staircase, lit by a stained-glass skylight. The 7,500 square feet include a secret card room at the top of the tower. The Hornibrook Room features a magnificent Renaissance Revival bedroom set with a high canopy. The Tower Room mini-suite has a king-size Austrian bed. The two-course gourmet breakfast is served in the dining room "before the Queen" by candlelight.

Innkeeper(s): Sharon Welch-Blair & Robert Blair. $125-195. 5 rooms with PB, 3 with FP, 3 suites and 1 conference room. Breakfast and snacks/refreshments included in rates. Types of meals: Full gourmet bkfst, veg bkfst, early coffee/tea and picnic lunch. Beds: KQT. Data port, cable TV, reading lamp, refrigerator, ceiling fan, snack bar, clock radio, telephone, coffeemaker, turn-down service, desk, luxury robes, complimentary liquors, antique fireplace with gas logs, feather beds and high-speed Internet access in room. Central air. VCR, fax, copier, library, parlor games, fireplace, secret garden with Gothic summer house, spa and award winning gardens on premises. Antiquing, art galleries, bicycling, fishing, golf, hiking, horseback riding, live theater, museums, parks, shopping, sporting events, tennis, water sports, tours, high tea, bridal brunches and portraits nearby.
Location: City. Historic district.
Publicity: *National Geographic Traveler, Nation's Business, Victorian Home, Victorian Decorator & Life Styles, Southern Living and Home and Garden Television.*

"Staying at the Empress of Little Rock was a 'dream come true!' We've read about and admired it for years. It was definitely a trip to a more gracious time—one that we should all try to implement more in our daily lives."

Certificate may be used: Nov. 30-March 31 and June 1-Sept. 15, selected rooms only, any night, no holidays.

Mammoth Spring A7

Roseland Inn B&B

570 Bethel, PO Box 4
Mammoth Spring, AR 72554-0004
(870)625-3378
E-mail: roselond@ozarks.com

Tucked away in a picturesque country town, this Colonial Revival home is just a stone's throw from one of the world's largest natural springs. Innkeeper Jean Pace, a former Mammoth Spring mayor, has decorated her National Register inn with antiques, collectibles and bright flower arrangements. With its reception hall, large front porch and gazebo, the home has served as a site for parties and weddings. Spring River and Mammoth Spring State Park are nearby, and Jean will refrigerate your daily catch.
Innkeeper(s): Jean Pace. $52. 4 rooms. Breakfast included in rates. Types of meals: Full bkfst.
Certificate may be used: Monday through Thursday, year-round (one room, one night per visit only).

Mountain View B6

Ozark Country Inn

PO Box 1201
Mountain View, AR 72560-1201
(870)269-8699 (800)379-8699

Circa 1906. This historic two-story Federal-style inn is located within a block of Courthouse Square and downtown eateries and shops. A full breakfast is served at 8 a.m. before guests head out to explore the many attractions offered in the surrounding area, including Blanchard Springs Caverns and the Ozark Folk Center.
Innkeeper(s): Sissie & Don Jones. $65-70. 6 rooms with PB. Breakfast included in rates. Types of meals: Full bkfst. Beds: QDT. Cable TV, reading lamp and clock radio in room. Air conditioning. VCR, telephone and fireplace on premises. Antiquing, fishing, shopping, water sports and Ozark Folk Center and Blanchard Springs Caverns nearby.
Location: Mountains.
Certificate may be used: March 1 to Dec. 1, Sunday through Thursday.

Winslow C2

Sky-Vue Lodge B&B

22822 North Hwy 71
Winslow, AR 72959
(479)634-2003 (800)782-2003
Internet: www.bbinternet.com/sky-vue
E-mail: skyvue@valuelinx.net

Circa 1931. Since the 1930s, guests have enjoyed spectacular views of the Boston Mountains at this Ozark lodge. There are seven cabins and guest houses located on 83 scenic acres with fishing ponds and a playhouse for children. The cabins have a covered porch with a porch swing. Breakfasts are served in the lodge's dining room, which offers a view of the mountains. Horseback riding is available at a nearby stable, and several state parks are nearby offering fishing, swimming and hiking.
Innkeeper(s): Glenn & Janice Jorgenson. $45-70. 9 rooms with PB, 5 with FP, 1 suite, 4 cottages, 3 cabins and 1 conference room. Breakfast included in rates. Types of meals: Country bkfst and early coffee/tea. Beds: KQDT. Cable TV, refrigerator and coffeemaker in room. Air conditioning. VCR, fax, copier, parlor games, telephone and ADA compliant (American with Disabilities Act) handicapped and/or wheelchair accessible room available on premises. Limited handicap access. Antiquing, fishing, horseback riding, parks, tennis and Civil War battlefields nearby.
Location: Mountains.
Certificate may be used: Dec. 1-March 10, Sunday through Wednesday, closed for Christmas.

California

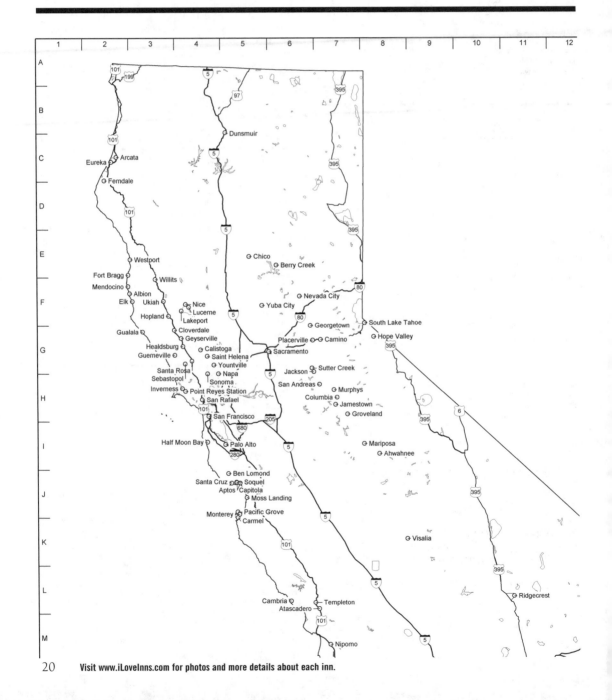

Visit www.iLoveInns.com for photos and more details about each inn.

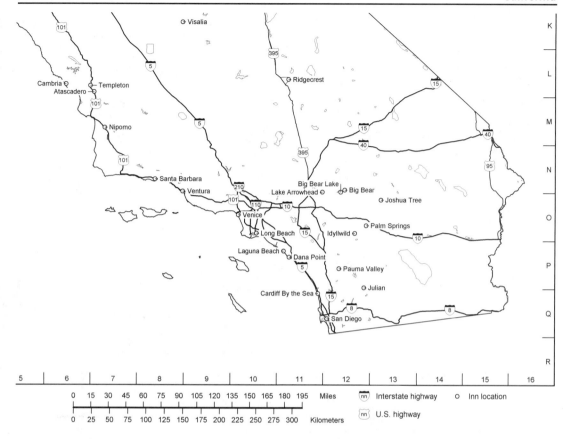

Map legend:
- nn Interstate highway
- nn U.S. highway
- ○ Inn location

Miles: 0 15 30 45 60 75 90 105 120 135 150 165 180 195
Kilometers: 0 25 50 75 100 125 150 175 200 225 250 275 300

Ahwahnee I8

Apple Blossom Inn B&B
44606 Silver Spur Tr
Ahwahnee, CA 93601
(559)642-2001 (888)687-4281
Internet: www.sierratel.com/appleblossominn
E-mail: appleblossominn@sierratel.com

Circa 1991. Surrounded by an organic apple farm, this peaceful bed & breakfast is just a stone's throw from Yosemite National Park and offers the ideal location for a stay in Gold Country. Relax by the woodburning stove in the sitting room or on the sundeck. Tastefully furnished guest bedrooms reflect a western decor with natural earth tones or traditional Victorian style. A video library is provided for in-room use. After a hearty breakfast visit the historic Sugar Pine Railroad or ski at nearby Badger Pass Resort. Swim in the inn's pool or soak in the spa overlooking the woods.

Innkeeper(s): Rick Mousaw. $96-135. 3 rooms with PB. Breakfast, afternoon tea and snacks/refreshments included in rates. Types of meals: Full bkfst and early coffee/tea. Beds: QD. TV, VCR, reading lamp, ceiling fan, clock radio, turn-down service and desk in room. Air conditioning. Spa, parlor games and telephone on premises. Antiquing, cross-country skiing, downhill skiing, fishing, live theater, parks, shopping and water sports nearby.
Location: Mountains.
Certificate may be used: Nov. 1-March 30, Sunday-Thursday. Holidays excluded.

Albion F2

Fensalden Inn
PO Box 99
Albion, CA 95410-0099
(707)937-4042 (800)959-3850 Fax:(707)937-2416
Internet: www.fensalden.com
E-mail: inn@fensalden.com

Circa 1860. Originally a stagecoach station, Fensalden looks out over the Pacific Ocean as it has for more than 100 years. The Tavern Room has witnessed many a rowdy scene, and if you look closely you can see bullet holes in the original redwood ceiling. The inn provides 20 acres for walks, whale-watching, viewing deer and bicycling. Relax with wine and hors d'oeuvres in the evening.

Innkeeper(s): Lyn Hamby. $119-239. 8 rooms with PB, 8 with FP, 3 suites, 1 cottage and 2 conference rooms. Breakfast, hors d'oeuvres and wine included in rates. Types of meals: Full bkfst. Beds: KQ. Reading lamp, CD player, refrigerator, ceiling fan, coffeemaker, fireplace and bungalow has Jacuzzi bathtub in room. Fax, copier, parlor games and telephone on premises. Handicap access. Antiquing, art galleries, beach, bicycling, canoeing/kayaking, fishing, golf, hiking, horseback riding, live theater, parks, shopping, tennis and wineries nearby.
Location: Country.
Publicity: *Sunset, Focus, Peninsula, Country Inns, Steppin' Out, LA Times,*

Vine Times and 1950s B movie *The Haunting of Hill House.*

"Closest feeling to heaven on Earth."

Certificate may be used: Anytime, November-April, subject to availability in selected rooms, excluding holidays and special events.

Aptos   J5

Bayview Hotel

8041 Soquel Dr
Aptos, CA 95003-3928
(831)688-8656 (800)422-9843 Fax:(831)688-5128
Internet: www.bayviewhotel.com
E-mail: lodging@bayviewhotel.com

Circa 1878. This Victorian hotel is the oldest operating inn on the Monterey Coast. Each of the rooms is decorated with antiques, sitting areas, and some have fireplaces. The inn is just half a mile from beautiful beaches, and a redwood forest is nearby. This inn is an ideal spot for those seeking relaxation or those on a coastal trip. Monterey and San Jose are less than an hour from the hotel, and San Francisco is 90 miles north. Breakfast is served in the inn's dining room. The hotel is close to an abundance of outdoor activities, as well as Nisene Marks State Park.

Innkeeper(s): Christina Locke & Peggie Lorenzo. $109-269. 12 rooms, 10 with PB, 2 with FP. Breakfast included in rates. Types of meals: Cont plus, early coffee/tea and afternoon tea. Beds: KQD. Cable TV, clock radio and fireplace in room. TV, fax, telephone, fireplace and gift shop on premises. Amusement parks, antiquing, parks, shopping and water sports nearby.
Location: Ocean community.
Publicity: *Mid-County Post and Santa Cruz Sentinel.*

"Thank you so much for all of your tender loving care and great hospitality."

Certificate may be used: Oct. 1-April 1, Sunday-Thursday, subject to availability.

Arcata   C2

Hotel Arcata

708 9th St
Arcata, CA 95521-6206
(707)826-0217 (800)344-1221 Fax:(707)826-1737
Internet: www.hotelarcata.com
E-mail: info@hotelarcata.com

Circa 1915. This historic landmark hotel is a fine example of Beaux Arts-style architecture. Several rooms overlook Arcata's downtown plaza, which is just outside the front door. A variety of rooms are available, each decorated in turn-of-the-century style. All rooms include pedestal sinks and clawfoot tubs. The hotel offers a full-service, renown Japanese restaurant, offering excellent cuisine, and there are many other fine restaurants within walking distance. Guests also enjoy free use of a nearby full-scale health club. The starting point of Arcata's architectural homes tour is within walking distance of the hotel.

Innkeeper(s): Virgil Moorehead. $120-200. 32 rooms with PB, 7 suites and 1 conference room. Breakfast included in rates. Types of meals: Cont, lunch, dinner and room service. Restaurant on premises. Beds: KQT. Cable TV, reading lamp, telephone and desk in room. Fax, copier and free health club privileges on premises. Handicap access. Parks, shopping, state parks, beaches, redwoods, rivers and theater nearby.
Location: City.
Certificate may be used: Anytime, subject to availability.

Atascadero   L7

Oak Hill Manor

12345 Hampton Court
Atascadero, CA 93422
(805)462-9317 (866)625-6267 Fax:(805)462-0331
Internet: www.oakhillmanorbandb.com
E-mail: macare@oakhillmanorbandb.com

Circa 1984. Situated on a hill surrounded by oaks, this English Tudor-style house overlooks the Santa Lucia Mountains. Decorated and furnished in unpretentious elegance, this enjoyable setting offers a relaxing getaway. Play pool, darts, games or watch the large screen TV in the pub. The parlor is perfect for reading by the fire. Quiet guest bedrooms and suites feature fireplaces and Jacuzzis. Savor breakfast in the formal dining room or on a private deck with a view. A business buffet is offered in the Sun Room for early birds. Appetizers and local wine are served in the afternoon. Cookies and beverages always are available. A steam bath is an added pleasure after the day's excursions.

Innkeeper(s): Maurice & Rise Macare. $155-235. 8 rooms, 6 with FP, 8 suites. Breakfast and snacks/refreshments included in rates. Types of meals: Full gourmet bkfst, veg bkfst, early coffee/tea, picnic lunch, afternoon tea, gourmet dinner and room service. Beds: KQ. Cable TV, reading lamp, ceiling fan, clock radio, turn-down service, desk, hot tub/spa, voice mail, 6 with fireplace and 5 with hot tub in room. Central air. VCR, fax, copier, sauna, parlor games, telephone, fireplace, laundry facility and gift shop on premises. Handicap access. Antiquing, art galleries, beach, bicycling, canoeing/kayaking, fishing, golf, hiking, horseback riding, live theater, museums, parks, shopping, sporting events, tennis, water sports and wineries nearby.
Location: Country, mountains.
Certificate may be used: Anytime, subject to availability.

Ben Lomond   J5

Fairview Manor

245 Fairview Ave
Ben Lomond, CA 95005-9347
(831)336-3355 (800)553-8840
Internet: www.fairviewmanor.com
E-mail: fairviewbandb@aol.com

Circa 1924. The Santa Cruz Mountains serve as a backdrop at this private and restful getaway. The inn is surrounded by nearly three acres of park-like wooded gardens. The Redwood County inn offers comfort and relaxation. The deck off the Great Room overlooks the San Lorenzo River. Built in the early 1920s, the décor reflects that era. Each of the cozy guest bedrooms boasts a private bath and delightful garden view. Enjoy a full country breakfast and afternoon snacks. The inn is an excellent place for family get-togethers as well as small meetings and outdoor weddings. Beaches, thousands of acres of state parks and many wineries are nearby.

Innkeeper(s): Nancy Glasson. $139-149. 5 rooms with PB and 1 conference room. Breakfast and snacks/refreshments included in rates. Types of meals: Full bkfst. Beds: KQ. Reading lamp, desk and sitting area in room. Parlor games, fireplace, refrigerator and complimentary drinks on premises. Antiquing, fishing, parks, shopping, water sports and wineries nearby.
Location: Mountains.
Certificate may be used: Sunday through Thursday.

Berry Creek · E6

Lake Oroville Bed and Breakfast
240 Sunday Dr
Berry Creek, CA 95916-9640
(530)589-0700 (800)455-5253 Fax:(530)589-3800
Internet: www.lakeorovillebedandbreakfast.com
E-mail: bnb@rontimco.com

Circa 1970. Situated in the quiet foothills above Lake Oroville, this country inn features panoramic views from the private

porches that extend from each guest room. Two favorite rooms are the Rose Petal Room and the Victorian Room, both with lake views and whirlpool tubs. The inn's 40 acres are studded with oak and pine trees. Deer and songbirds abound.

Innkeeper(s): Cheryl & Ron Damberger. $75-165. 6 rooms with PB and 1 conference room. Breakfast included in rates. Types of meals: Full bkfst and early coffee/tea. Beds: KQ. Cable TV, VCR, reading lamp, stereo, refrigerator, ceiling fan, snack bar, clock radio, telephone, turn-down service, desk, hot tub/spa, whirlpool tubs and tape player in room. Air conditioning. TV, fax, copier, spa, library, pet boarding, child care, parlor games and fireplace on premises. Handicap access. Antiquing, fishing, golf, live theater, parks, shopping, tennis and water sports nearby.
Location: Mountains. Lake and valley views.
Publicity: Oroville Mercury-Register, Chronicle, San Jose Mercury and Most Romantic Weekends.
Certificate may be used: Sunday-Thursday (except holidays). All year.

Big Bear · N12

Gold Mountain Manor Historic B&B
1117 Anita, PO Box 2027
Big Bear, CA 92314
(909)585-6997 (800)509-2604 Fax:(909)585-0327
Internet: www.goldmountainmanor.com
E-mail: info@goldmountainmanor.com

Circa 1928. This spectacular log mansion was once a hideaway for the rich and famous. Eight fireplaces provide a roaring fire in each room in fall and winter. The Lucky Baldwin Room offers a hearth made from stones gathered in the famous Lucky Baldwin mine nearby. In the Clark Gable room is the fireplace Gable and Carole Lombard enjoyed on their honeymoon. Gourmet country breakfasts and afternoon hors d'oeuvres are served. In addition to the

guest rooms, there are home rentals.
Innkeeper(s): Trish & Jim Gordon. $125-225. 7 rooms with PB, 7 with FP, 2 suites and 1 conference room. Afternoon tea and snacks/refreshments included in rates. Types of meals: Full gourmet bkfst and early coffee/tea. Beds: Q. Reading lamp, ceiling fan, desk, hot tub/spa and suites have Jacuzzi in room. VCR, fax, spa, bicycles, library, parlor games, telephone, fireplace and pool table on premises. Cross-country skiing, downhill skiing, fishing, parks, sporting events, water sports and hiking/forest nearby.
Location: Mountains. Forest at end of street.
Publicity: Best Places to Kiss, Fifty Most Romantic Places and Kenny G holiday album cover.

"A majestic experience! In this magnificent house, history comes alive!"
Certificate may be used: Jan. 2-Dec. 15, Sunday-Thursday.

Big Bear Lake · N12

Eagle's Nest B&B
41675 Big Bear Blvd, Box 1003
Big Bear Lake, CA 92315
(909)866-6465 (888)866-6465 Fax:(909)866-6025
Internet: www.eaglesnestlodgebigbear.com
E-mail: eaglesnestlodge@earthlink.net

Circa 1983. Named for the more than 50 American bald eagles that nest in and around Big Bear, this lodgepole pine inn features a river rock fireplace in the great room. Antiques, leather furniture and lodge decor provide a warm mountain setting. Surrounded by tall pine trees, the property also includes several cottage suites.
Innkeeper(s): Mark & Vicki Tebo. $85-125. 5 rooms with PB, 3 with FP. Breakfast and snacks/refreshments included in rates. Types of meals: Country bkfst. Beds: Q. Cable TV, reading lamp, ceiling fan, clock radio and fireplace in room. VCR, fax, parlor games, telephone, fireplace and gift shop on premises. Antiquing, bicycling, canoeing/kayaking, cross-country skiing, downhill skiing, fishing, golf, hiking, horseback riding, live theater, parks, shopping, water sports, mountain biking, rock climbing and movie theatres nearby.
Location: Mountains.

"Each breakfast was delicious and beautiful. A lot of thought and care is obvious in everything you do."
Certificate may be used: Anytime except holidays and weekends from Dec. 15-April 15, subject to availability.

Knickerbocker Mansion Country Inn
PO Box 1907
Big Bear Lake, CA 92315
(909)878-9190 (877)423-1180 Fax:(909)878-4248
Internet: www.knickerbockermansion.com
E-mail: knickmail@knickerbockermansion.com

Circa 1920. The inn is one of the few vertically designed log structures in the United States. The inn was built of local lumber by Bill Knickerbocker, the first dam keeper of Big Bear. The inn includes two historic buildings set on two-and-a-half wooded acres, backing to a national forest. Although, the inn offers a secluded setting, the village of Big Bear Lake is within walking distance. The village offers shopping, restaurants, fishing, hiking, mountain biking and excellent downhill skiing.
Innkeeper(s): Stanley Miller & Thomas Bicanic. $110-280. 11 rooms with PB, 2 with FP, 2 total suites, including 1 two-bedroom suite and 1 conference room. Breakfast included in rates. Types of meals: Full gourmet bkfst, early coffee/tea, picnic lunch, snacks/refreshments and gourmet dinner. Restaurant on premises. Beds: KQ. Modem hook-up, data port, cable TV, VCR, reading lamp, stereo, refrigerator, ceiling fan, clock radio, telephone, coffeemaker, desk, hot tub/spa, voice mail and fireplace in room. Fax, copier, library, parlor games and gift shop on premises. Handicap access. Antiquing, art galleries, bicycling, canoeing/kayaking, cross-country skiing, downhill skiing, fishing, golf, hiking, horseback riding, live theater, museums, parks, shopping, tennis and water sports nearby.
Location: Mountains.
Publicity: Los Angeles Magazine, Yellow Brick Road, San Bernardino Sun and Daily Press.

"Best breakfast I ever had in a setting of rustic elegance, a quiet atmosphere and personal attention from the innkeepers. The moment you arrive you will realize the Knickerbocker is a very special place."
Certificate may be used: Sunday-Thursday, non-holiday, subject to availability and prior booking.

Calistoga   G4

Chelsea Garden Inn

1443 2nd St
Calistoga, CA 94515-1419
(707)942-0948 (800)942-1515 Fax:(707)942-5102
Internet: www.chelseagardeninn.com
E-mail: innkeeper@chelseagardeninn.com

Circa 1940. Located in the heart of Napa Valley, this delightfully different California-style inn features two-room suites with fireplaces and private entrances. The romantic ground-level Rose Suite has a large sitting room with fireplace, day bed and library. The adjoining Burgandy Suite is perfect for couples traveling together. Named for its view of the mountains, the second-floor Palisades Suite boasts a four-poster bed and a small balcony overlooking the pool. A full gourmet breakfast is served in the dining room or garden with fresh-brewed coffee from a local roastery. Enjoy evening wine and cheese. Explore the extensive gardens with grapevines, flowers, fruit and nut trees. Swim in the pool or relax by the fire in the social room. Visit local shops, wineries, museums, spas, art galleries and restaurants just two blocks away.
Innkeeper(s): Diane Byrne, Dave and Susan DeVries. $160-225. 4 suites. Breakfast included in rates. Types of meals: Full bkfst. Beds: KQT. Cable TV, clock radio, coffeemaker, fireplace, central heating, refrigerator, iron, hair dryer and dressing gown in room. Central air. Fax, copier, swimming, library, telephone, Internet connection, social room with vaulted ceiling, gardens, complimentary wine and fruit and cheese each evening on premises. Antiquing, art galleries, bicycling, fishing, golf, hiking, horseback riding, museums, parks, shopping, tennis, wineries, mud baths, massage, ballooning, glider rides and natural wonders and historical sites nearby.
Location: Small town in the Wine Country.
Publicity: *Sunset Magazine, Access Press and The Best Places to Kiss in Northern California.*
Certificate may be used: Monday, Tuesday, Wednesday, Nov. 1 through April 30, subject to availability.

Fannys

1206 Spring St
Calistoga, CA 94515-1637
(707)942-9491 Fax:(707)942-4810
Internet: www.fannysnapavalley.com
E-mail: info@fannysnapavalley.com

Circa 1915. In a shingled Craftsman-cottage style, painted forest green and red, this inn offers an inviting shaded porch with swing, rockers and spots for dining. Inside, comfortable interiors include over-stuffed chairs, a fireplace, library and upstairs guest rooms with plank floors and window seats. The innkeeper, a former restaurateur, provides a full breakfast and knowledgeable touring suggestions.
Innkeeper(s): Deanna Higgins. $120-180. 2 rooms with PB. Breakfast included in rates. Types of meals: Country bkfst. Beds: Q. Reading lamp, ceiling fan and clock in room. Air conditioning. Fax, library, parlor games, telephone and fireplace on premises. Antiquing, golf, parks, shopping and winery tours & tasting nearby.
Location: Napa Valley.
Certificate may be used: Sunday-Thursday, subject to availability.

Cambria   L6

The J. Patrick House

2990 Burton Dr
Cambria, CA 93428-4002
(805)927-3812 (800)341-5258 Fax:(805)927-6759
Internet: www.jpatrickhouse.com
E-mail: jph@jpatrickhouse.com

Circa 1980. This charming log home and carriage house bed & breakfast is nestled in the woods above Cambria's east village. The picturesque grounds include a garden area that separates the main log home from the carriage house, where all but one of the guest rooms are located. Rooms are decorated in a romantic style with country/traditional decor, wood-burning fireplace or stove and private bath. Wine and hors d'oeuvres are served each evening in the main house's fireplaced living room. Fresh fruits, homemade granola and freshly baked breads and muffins are part of the full morning meal. "Killer" chocolate chip cookies and cold milk are served before bedtime.
Innkeeper(s): Ann O'Connor & John Arnott. $165-205. 8 rooms with PB, 7 with FP. Breakfast and wine included in rates. Types of meals: Full bkfst, veg bkfst and early coffee/tea. Beds: KQ. CD player, clock radio, turn-down service, fireplace, massage, champagne, one with wood burning stove, hair dryer and iron/ironing board in room. Fax, library, parlor games, telephone, gift shop, gift shop, wine and hors d'oeuvres, guest refrigerator and sitting room on premises. Antiquing, art galleries, beach, bicycling, canoeing/kayaking, fishing, golf, hiking, horseback riding, parks, shopping, tennis, wineries, Hearst Castle and Paso Robles wine region tasting nearby.
Location: Mountains. Woods.
Publicity: *Karen Brown's, Elmer Dills, KABC, Channel 7 and Select Registry.*
Certificate may be used: October through March, Monday-Thursday, excluding holiday periods. Based on availability.

The Squibb House

4063 Burton Dr
Cambria, CA 93428-3001
(805)927-9600 Fax:(805)927-9606
Internet: www.squibbhouse.net
E-mail: innkeeper@squibbhouse.net

Circa 1877. A picket fence and large garden surround this Victorian inn with its Italianate and Gothic Revival architecture. Guests may relax in the main parlor, stroll the gardens or sit and rock on the porch. The home was built by a Civil War veteran and young school teacher. The downstairs once was used as a classroom while an addition was being made in the town's school. Each guest room has a fire stove.
Innkeeper(s): Laurie. $105-185. 5 rooms with PB, 5 with FP. Breakfast included in rates. Types of meals: Cont plus. Beds: Q. Reading lamp in room. Parlor games, telephone, fireplace and retail shop in historic 1885 carpentry shop on premises. Antiquing, fishing, golf, parks, shopping, Hearst Castle, wine tasting and galleries nearby.
Location: Pine covered hills.
Publicity: *Cambrian.*
Certificate may be used: Sunday-Thursday only, November-March, not valid during holiday weeks.

Camino   G7

The Camino Hotel-Seven Mile House

4103 Carson Rd, PO Box 1197
Camino, CA 95709-1197
(530)644-7740 Fax:(530)647-1416
Internet: www.caminohotel.com
E-mail: inquire@caminohotel.com

Circa 1888. Once a barracks for the area's loggers, this inn now caters to visitors in the state's famed gold country. Just

east of Placerville, historic Camino is on the Old Carson Wagon Trail in Apple Hill. Nine guest rooms are available, including the E.J. Barrett Room, a favorite with honeymooners. Other rooms feature names such as Pony Express, Stage Stop and Wagon Train. The family-oriented inn welcomes children, and a local park offers a handy site for
their recreational needs. Popular area activities include apple picking, antiquing, hot air ballooning, white-water rafting, hiking and wine tasting. The inn also offers a Self-Indulgence Package, on-site wine tasting and an in-house masseuse.

Innkeeper(s): Paula Nobert. $68-98. 9 rooms, 3 with PB and 1 conference room. Breakfast and snacks/refreshments included in rates. Types of meals: Full bkfst, early coffee/tea and picnic lunch. Beds: QDT. Reading lamp, clock radio, turn-down service and coolers in room. Parlor games, telephone, fireplace, homemade chocolate chip cookies, wine tasting room and two massage therapists on premises. Antiquing, cross-country skiing, downhill skiing, fishing, golf, live theater, parks, shopping, water sports, wine tasting, white-water rafting and hot air ballooning nearby.
Location: Small agricultural town. Wine country.
Publicity: *Better Homes & Gardens, Sunset and Sierra Heritage.*
Certificate may be used: Year-round except weekends (Friday & Saturday) in September, October, November and December.

Capitola   Q11

Inn at Depot Hill
250 Monterey Ave
Capitola, CA 95010-3358
(831)462-3376 (800)572-2632 Fax:(831)462-3697
Internet: www.innatdepothill.com
E-mail: reserve@innsbythesea.com

Circa 1901. Once a railroad depot, this inn offers rooms with themes to represent different parts of the world: a chic auberge in St. Tropez, a romantic French hideaway in Paris, an Italian coastal villa, a summer home on the coast of Holland and a traditional English garden room, to name a few. Most rooms have garden patios with hot tubs. The rooms have many amenities, including a fireplace, white marble bathrooms and feather beds. Guests are greeted with fresh flowers in their room. Gourmet breakfast, tea, wine, hors d' oeuvres and dessert are offered daily.

Innkeeper(s): Tom Cole. $200-385. 12 rooms, 12 with FP, 4 suites and 1 conference room. Breakfast and snacks/refreshments included in rates. Beds: KQT. Cable TV, VCR, reading lamp, stereo, clock radio, telephone, turn-down service, desk and hot tub/spa in room. TV, fax, spa and fireplace on premises. Handicap access. Amusement parks, antiquing, fishing, golf, live theater, parks, shopping and water sports nearby.
Location: Ocean community.
Publicity: *Country Inn, Santa Cruz Sentinel, McCalls, Choices & Vacation, San Jose Mercury News, Fresno & Sacramento Bee, San Francisco Focus, American Airline Flight, SF Examiner and Sunset Magazine.*

"The highlight of our honeymoon. Five stars in our book!"
Certificate may be used: Monday-Thursday, November through April, based on availability, excludes holidays and special events.

Cardiff-By-The-Sea   Q11

Cardiff-By-The-Sea Lodge
142 Chesterfield Dr
Cardiff-By-The-Sea, CA 92007-1922
(760)944-6474 Fax:(760)944-6841
Internet: www.cardifflodge.com
E-mail: innkeeper@cardifflodge.com

Circa 1990. Each of the guest rooms at this romantic seaside retreat features an individual theme. For instance, the Santa Fe room is decorated with a whitewashed, four-poster log bed, a hand-crafted fireplace and a large Roman tub. This ocean view room also includes a wet bar. The Sweetheart room, with its hand-carved bed, heart-shaped whirlpool tub, fireplace and ocean view is a perfect place for romantics. Other rooms feature themes such as "Garden View," "Victorian," "Summer" and "Paradise." This inn, which offers convenient access to San Diego, is listed in "The Best Places to Kiss in Southern California."

Innkeeper(s): James & Jeanette Statser. $140-385. 17 rooms with PB, 5 with FP. Breakfast included in rates. Types of meals: Cont plus. Beds: QD. Cable TV, reading lamp, refrigerator, clock radio, telephone, desk, hot tub/spa and ocean views in room. Air conditioning. VCR, fax, copier, spa and fireplace on premises. Amusement parks, antiquing, fishing, golf, live theater, parks, shopping, tennis and water sports nearby.
Location: Ocean community.
Publicity: *Sunset, LA Times, Jeopardy, Wheel of Fortune, Channel 8 and Cable.*

"Simply fantastic! Everyone has raved about this place and with good reason."
Certificate may be used: January to June, October to December, excludes holidays and weekends. Excludes Feb. 14 week, Easter week. Monday-Thursday only.

Carmel   J5

Cobblestone Inn
PO Box 3073
Monterey, CA 93942-3073
(831)625-5222 (800)833-8836 Fax:(831)625-0478
Internet: www.cobblestoneinncarmel.com
E-mail: cobblestoneinn@foursisters.com

Circa 1950. An exterior of wood and cobblestone gathered from the Carmel River provide a friendly facade for visitors to this bed & breakfast located two blocks from the heart of Carmel. Each guest room has its own cobblestone fireplace. The inn's English country decor is enhanced with quilts, a colorful antique carousel horse and other early American antiques. In addition to breakfast and afternoon tea, evening wine and hors d'oeuvres are served. Guests can borrow one of the inn's bicycles to explore the area. The beach and shopping are nearby. There is a $20 fee for an additional guest in room, except for children less than 5 years old. Cobblestone is one of the Four Sisters Inns.

Innkeeper(s): Sharon Carey. $125-250. 24 rooms with PB, 24 with FP, 3 suites. Breakfast, afternoon tea, snacks/refreshments and wine included in rates. Types of meals: Full gourmet bkfst and early coffee/tea. Beds: KQ. Cable TV, VCR, reading lamp, stereo, refrigerator, snack bar, clock radio, telephone and turn-down service in room. Central air. Fax, bicycles, parlor games, fireplace and afternoon wine and hors d'oeuvres on premises. Handicap access. Antiquing, art galleries, beach, bicycling, canoeing/kayaking, fishing, golf, hiking, horseback riding, live theater,

museums, parks, shopping, tennis and wineries nearby.
Location: Ocean community.
Publicity: *Country Inns and Honeymoons.*
Certificate may be used: Sunday-Thursday, November-March, excluding holidays and special events and may exclude certain room types based on availability.

The Stonehouse Inn

PO Box 2939
Carmel, CA 93921
(831)624-4569 (800)748-6618
Internet: www.carmelstonehouse.com
E-mail: stonehouseinn@aol.com

Circa 1906. This quaint Carmel country house boasts a stone exterior, made from beach rocks collected and hand shaped by local Indians at the turn of the century. The original owner,

"Nana" Foster, was hostess to notable artists and writers from the San Francisco area, including Sinclair Lewis, Jack London and Lotta Crabtree. The romantic Jack London room features a dramatic gabled ceiling, a brass bed and a stunning view of the ocean. Conveniently located, the inn is a short walk from Carmel Beach and two blocks from the village.
Innkeeper(s): Terri Navailles. $139-199. 7 rooms. Breakfast included in rates. Types of meals: Full bkfst. Beds: KQDT. Reading lamp in room. Telephone on premises. Fishing, live theater, parks, shopping and water sports nearby.
Location: Ocean community.
Publicity: *Travel & Leisure and Country Living.*
"First time stay at a B&B — GREAT!"
Certificate may be used: Nov. 1 through May 31, Sunday through Thursday, except special events such as Thanksgiving, Christmas, New Year, AT&T Golf Tournament.

Chico   E5

L'Abri B&B

14350 Hwy 99
Chico, CA 95973
(530)893-0824 (800)489-3319
Internet: www.now2000.com/labri
E-mail: l.janak@att.net

Circa 1972. This ranch-style house is located on more than two acres, with a scenic seasonal creek. All three guest rooms offer a private, outside entrance and each is uniquely decorated. Full breakfasts are offered, often followed by special baked goods and an occasional peach or berry cobbler when in season. Cycle the country roads, go horseback riding or go into town and enjoy light opera and open-air summer concerts.
Innkeeper(s): Lauree & Stephen Janak. $75-125. 3 rooms with PB. Breakfast and snacks/refreshments included in rates. Types of meals: Country bkfst, veg bkfst, early coffee/tea and room service. Beds: Q. Modem hook-up, reading lamp, stereo, ceiling fan, clock radio and telephone in room. Air conditioning. Copier, library, parlor games and fireplace on premises. Antiquing, art galleries, bicycling, canoeing/kayaking, cross-country skiing, downhill skiing, fishing, golf, hiking, horseback riding, live theater, museums, parks, shopping, sporting events, tennis and water sports nearby.
Location: Country.
Certificate may be used: Jan. 2-Dec. 1, Sunday-Thursday, except holidays and special events.

Music Express Inn

1145 El Monte Ave
Chico, CA 95928-9153
(530)345-8376 Fax:(530)893-8521
Internet: www.now2000.com/musicexpress
E-mail: icobeen@chico.com

Circa 1977. Music lovers will delight in this inn's warmth and charm. Nine guest rooms, all with private bath and cable TV, provide country-style comfort to those visiting the college town of Chico. Jacuzzi tubs, private phone lines, refrigerators and microwaves are among the amenities. Visitors are welcome to tickle the ivories of the inn's Steinway grand piano. The innkeeper, a music teacher, is adept at many instruments and plays mandolin in a local band. The inn's library also lures many guests, and those who explore the surrounding area will find plenty of opportunities for antiquing and fishing.

Innkeeper(s): Barney & Irene Cobeen. $61-125. 9 rooms with PB, 1 suite, 1 cottage and 2 conference rooms. Breakfast included in rates. Types of meals: Full bkfst. Beds: KQDT. Cable TV, VCR, reading lamp, refrigerator, ceiling fan, telephone, desk, microwave, Jacuzzi tubs and refrigerators in room. Air conditioning. Fax, copier, library, parlor games and fireplace on premises. Handicap access. Antiquing, fishing, live theater, parks, shopping, sporting events and water sports nearby.
Certificate may be used: All year, Sunday-Thursday.

Cloverdale   G3

Old Crocker Inn

1126 Old Crocker Inn Road
Cloverdale, CA 95425
(707)894-4000 (800)716-2007 Fax:(707)324-8400
Internet: www.oldcrockerinn.com
E-mail: michel@oldcrockerinn.com

Circa 1890. Stay in historic luxury at this wine country getaway on five scenic acres in the hills overlooking Alexander Valley's award-winning vineyards. Originally the inn was a summer hunting ranch in 1890 for the founder of the Central Pacific Railroad and his empire builder cronies, known as California's Big Four. Renovations have created peaceful and inviting accommodations. Sit by the fire in the lobby or wander the gardens with comfy chairs and lounges. Lavish guest bedrooms and suites feature private entrances and gas fireplaces. Savor a generous breakfast in the impressive dining room or on the spacious deck that surrounds the main lodge. Lunch baskets and prix fixe dinners are available with advance notice. Work out in the spa and exercise room then swim in the refreshing pool.
Innkeeper(s): Michel & Susan Degive. $145-205. 10 rooms with PB, 10 with FP, 2 suites, 1 cottage, 3 cabins and 1 conference room. Breakfast, afternoon tea and snacks/refreshments included in rates. Types of meals: Full gourmet bkfst, early coffee/tea, picnic lunch and gourmet dinner. Restaurant on premises. Beds: KQT. Data port, cable TV, VCR, reading lamp, CD player, ceiling fan, clock radio, turn-down service, hot tub/spa, fireplace and free high-speed Internet in room. Fax, copier, spa, swimming, pet boarding, parlor games, telephone and gift shop on premises. Limited handicap access. Antiquing, beach, bicycling, canoeing/kayaking, fishing, golf, hiking, horseback riding, museums, parks and wineries nearby.
Location: Country.
Certificate may be used: Nov. 1-April 30, Sunday-Thursday, subject to availability.

Columbia   *H7*

Columbia City Hotel & Restaurant

PO Box 1870
Columbia, CA 95310
(209)532-1479 (800)532-1479 Fax:(209)532-7027
Internet: www.cityhotel.com
E-mail: info@cityhotel.com

Circa 1856. Built in 1856 during the height of the Gold Rush
Era, this two-story Victorian was known as the "What Cheer
House." Now a state historical site, it has been authentically
restored by the State of California, and the state owns the
hotel's antique furniture and fixtures. The hotel was listed in
Sunset Magazine's February 2000 issue as one of the 24 best
bed & breakfasts. No televisions or telephones intrude on the
historic ambiance of the hotel's 10 guest rooms. Indoor plumbing is the only historical compromise. Each room has a half-
bath, and showers are down the hall. The beautifully restored
restaurant offers fine selections of French cuisine, The hotel
hosts family reunions, meetings, and weddings. Inquire about
the Getaway Lodging, Dinner and Theatre Package for two.
Innkeeper(s): Tom Bender. $105-125. 10 rooms and 1 conference room.
Breakfast included in rates. Types of meals: Cont plus, early coffee/tea, lunch
and gourmet dinner. Restaurant on premises. Beds: QDT. Central air. Parlor
games on premises. Antiquing, art galleries, cross-country skiing, downhill
skiing, fishing, golf, hiking, horseback riding, live theater, museums, parks,
shopping, tennis and wineries nearby.
Location: Mountains.
Certificate may be used: Monday-Thursday, Sept. 9-May 1.

Dana Point   *P11*

Blue Lantern Inn

PO Box 3073
Monterey, CA 93942-3073
(949)661-1304 (800)950-1236 Fax:(949)496-1483
Internet: www.foursisters.com/inns/bluelanterninn.html
E-mail: info@foursisters.com

Circa 1990. The four-diamond inn is situated high on a
blufftop overlooking a stunning coastline and the blue waters of
Dana Point harbor with its pleasure craft, fishing boats and the
tall ship, Pilgrim. Each guest room fea-
tures both a fireplace and a whirlpool
tub and many offer private sun decks.
Afternoon tea, evening turndown service and bicycles are just a few of the
amenities available. In the evening,
wine and hors d'oeuvres are served.
Shops, restaurants and beaches are
nearby, and popular Laguna Beach is
just a few miles to the north. There is a

$20 fee for an additional guest in room, except for children less
than 5 years old. Blue Lantern is one of the Four Sisters Inns.
Innkeeper(s): Lin McMahon. $155-500. 29 rooms with PB, 29 with FP and
2 conference rooms. Breakfast, afternoon tea, snacks/refreshments and wine
included in rates. Types of meals: Full bkfst. Beds: KQ. Data port, cable TV,
VCR, reading lamp, stereo, refrigerator, ceiling fan, snack bar, clock radio,
telephone, coffeemaker, turn-down service, hot tub/spa, newspaper and
bathrobes in room. Air conditioning. Spa, bicycles, library, parlor games, fireplace and gym on premises. Handicap access. Amusement parks, antiquing,
art galleries, beach, bicycling, canoeing/kayaking, fishing, golf, hiking, horseback riding, live theater, museums, parks, shopping, water sports, beach and
Dana Point Harbor nearby.
Location: Ocean community, waterfront.

Publicity: *Los Angeles Magazine, Glamour, Oregonian and Orange County
Register.*
Certificate may be used: November-February, Sunday-Thursday, holidays and
special event periods, Point rooms and Tower suites excluded, based on promotional discount availability.

Dunsmuir   *B5*

Dunsmuir Inn

5423 Dunsmuir Ave
Dunsmuir, CA 96025-2011
(530)235-4543 (888)386-7684 Fax:(530)235-4154
Internet: www.dunsmuirinn.net
E-mail: jerryrig@joimail.net

Circa 1925. Comfortably situated in the Sacramento River
canyon, this country inn is a perfect home base for the assortment of outdoor activities available. Old-fashioned flower gardens and the family orchard surround picnic tables and barbecue facilities. Stay in a guest bedroom or suite with a clawfoot
tub. A hearty breakfast starts the day right. Sit on the front
porch swing before taking a stroll along the Historic District. A
short scenic walk to the river offers white water rafting, kayaking, world class trout fishing and popular swimming holes.
Gold panning is still a favorite pastime to try. Go skiing and
sledding nearby, or ice fish at Castle Lake. Visit breathtaking
Mount Shasta and Mossbrae Falls. Ask the innkeepers about
driving tours and sightseeing suggestions.
Innkeeper(s): Jerry & Julie Iskra. $75-85. 5 rooms with PB, 1 suite. Breakfast
included in rates. Types of meals: Country bkfst, veg bkfst, early coffee/tea,
picnic lunch and snacks/refreshments. Beds: KD. TV, VCR, reading lamp, ceiling fan and turn-down service in room. Air conditioning. Fax and telephone on
premises. Antiquing, bicycling, canoeing/kayaking, cross-country skiing, downhill skiing, fishing, golf, hiking, parks and world class trout fishing nearby.
Location: Country.
Certificate may be used: October-April, except holidays.

Elk   *F3*

Elk Cove Inn

PO Box 367
Elk, CA 95432-0367
(707)877-3321 (800)275-2967 Fax:(707)877-1808
Internet: www.elkcoveinn.com
E-mail: elkcove@mcn.org

Circa 1883. This mansard-style Victorian home was built as a
guest house for lumber baron L. E. White. Operated as a full-
service country inn for more than 35 years, Elk Cove Inn commands a majestic view from atop a scenic bluff. There are four
cabins and four new ocean-front luxury suites with large windows, fireplaces, spa tubs and balconies. There is also a new hot
tub with a view of the ocean. Most rooms have a fireplace and
an ocean view. Antiques, hand-embroidered linens and down
comforters add to the amenities. Below the inn is an expansive
driftwood-strewn beach. Gourmet breakfasts are served in the
ocean-view dining room. Guests can enjoy cocktails, beer or
wine in the ocean-front bar. Coffee makers with fresh ground
coffee, teas, cider and hot chocolate are available in the rooms.
$100-350. 15 rooms with PB, 14 with FP, 4 suites and 4 cottages.
Breakfast and snacks/refreshments included in rates. Types of meals: Full
gourmet bkfst. Beds: KQ. Reading lamp, CD player, refrigerator, clock radio,
coffeemaker, hot tub/spa, fireplace, luxurious bathrobes, imported French and
Swiss bath amenities, a decanter of port and chocolates for bedtime, welcome baskets with a split of wine, our signature cookies and fresh fruit in
room. Cottages include microwaves and refrigerators, and our spa suites
include all of the above plus espresso makers, CD/tape players and Jacuzzi

tubs in room. Fax, copier, spa, library, parlor games, telephone, fireplace, gift shop and daily afternoon hors d'oeuvres on premises. Antiquing, art galleries, beach, bicycling, canoeing/kayaking, fishing, golf, hiking, horseback riding, live theater, parks, shopping and wineries nearby.

Location: Ocean community, waterfront. Oceanfront.

"Quiet, peaceful, romantic, spiritual. This room, the inn, and the food are all what the doctor ordered."

Certificate may be used: Midweek, Sunday through Thursday, December and January, non-holiday weeks. Cannot be combined with other specials.

Eureka   C2

The Carter House Victorians

301 L St
Eureka, CA 95501
(707)444-8062 (800)404-1390 Fax:(707)444-8067
Internet: www.carterhouse.com
E-mail: reserve@carterhouse.com

Circa 1884. Superior hospitality is offered in these Victorian inns that grace the historic district. Perched alongside Humboldt Bay, the inn promises appealing views. Proud of their AAA four-diamond rating, luxurious guest bedrooms and suites feature fireplaces, antique furnishings and spas. Begin each morning with a highly acclaimed breakfast. Renowned for regional, seasonal cuisine, for many ingredients are grown in the garden or bought from local purveyors. Restaurant 301 boasts a coveted international Wine Spectator Grand Award, maintaining in its cellars an extensive collection of the world's finest vintages.

Innkeeper(s): Mark & Christi Carter. $155-497. 32 rooms with PB, 15 with FP, 15 suites, 2 cottages and 1 conference room. Breakfast and afternoon tea included in rates. Types of meals: Full gourmet bkfst, early coffee/tea, snacks/refreshments, hors d'oeuvres, wine, gourmet dinner and room service. Restaurant on premises. Beds: KQDT. Cable TV, VCR, reading lamp, stereo, refrigerator, snack bar, clock radio, telephone, turn-down service, desk and hot tub/spa in room. Fax, copier, spa, fireplace, bedtime tea & cookies and wine & hors d'oeuvres before dinner available on premises. Handicap access. Antiquing, fishing, live theater, parks, shopping, sporting events, water sports and beaches nearby.

Location: Ocean community, waterfront.

Publicity: *Sunset, U.S. News & World Report, Country Home, Country Living, Bon Appetit, San Francisco Focus, Northwest Palate, Gourmet, Art Culinare, San Francisco Chronicle, Wine Spectator, New York Times Magazine and Organic Gardening.*

Certificate may be used: Jan. 30-May 15, Friday-Monday.

Cornelius Daly Inn

1125 H Street
Eureka, CA 95501-1844
(707)445-3638 (800)321-9656 Fax:(707)444-3636
Internet: www.dalyinn.com
E-mail: innkeeper@dalyinn.com

Circa 1905. This 6,000-square-foot Colonial Revival mansion is located in the historic section of Eureka. The inn's gracious atmosphere includes four wood-burning fireplace and a third floor ballroom. Enjoy the romantic French bedroom suite with dressing table, armoire and bedstead in Annie Murphey's

Room. It offers a fireplace and a view over the Victorian garden. Miss Martha's Room features antique twin beds with inlaid pearl. Breakfast is served fireside in the inn's formal dining room or garden patio. In the evenings, refreshments are served.

Innkeeper(s): Donna & Bob Gafford. $90-170. 5 rooms, 3 with PB, 1 with FP, 2 suites. Breakfast and wine included in rates. Types of meals: Full

gourmet bkfst, early coffee/tea, afternoon tea, snacks/refreshments and hors d'oeuvres. Beds: QT. Reading lamp, refrigerator, clock radio, fireplace, Antique furnishings, plush robes and beautiful carpets in room. TV, VCR, fax, copier, library, parlor games, telephone, game room and billiard table on premises. Antiquing, art galleries, beach, bicycling, canoeing/kayaking, fishing, golf, hiking, live theater, museums, parks, shopping, State Redwood Park, National Redwood Park, Pacific Ocean and boating nearby.

Location: Ocean community. Redwoods.

"A genuine delight."

Certificate may be used: Nov. 1-May 1. Holidays & special event weekends excluded.

Old Town Bed & Breakfast Inn

1521 3rd St
Eureka, CA 95501-0710
(707)443-5235 (888)508-5235 Fax:(707)442-4390
Internet: www.oldtownbnb.com
E-mail: info@oldtownbnb.com

Circa 1871. This early Victorian was built in the Greek Revival style as the original family home of lumber baron William Carson. It was constructed of virgin redwood and Douglas fir and moved three blocks to its current location in 1905. Called a "Humboldt County jewel" by the local visitors and convention bureau, the inn is the original bed & breakfast of the area and was opened in 1983. Spacious guest rooms offer heirloom quilts, antiques, and TV/VCRs. (There's a large movie collection to peruse.) In the morning, a variety of gourmet breakfasts are served under the light of oil lamps and beside a flickering fireplace.

Innkeeper(s): Steve & Karen Albright. $110-140. 4 rooms with PB, 1 with FP. Breakfast included in rates. Types of meals: Country bkfst, veg bkfst and early coffee/tea. Beds: KQ. Cable TV, VCR and clock radio in room. Fax, library, telephone, fireplace, large movie collection and library with computer/DSL/fax on premises. Antiquing, art galleries, beach, bicycling, canoeing/kayaking, fishing, golf, hiking, horseback riding, live theater, museums, parks, shopping, tennis, water sports, eco-tours, Redwood State National and zoo nearby.

Location: City, ocean community.

Publicity: *Times-Standard, Country, San Francisco Chronicle, Sunset, San Francisco Examiner and L.A.Times.*

"From the moment we opened the door, we knew we had chosen a special place to stay."

Certificate may be used: November-March, anytime, subject to availability, holidays excluded.

Fawnskin   N12

Inn At Fawnskin

PO Box 378
Fawnskin, CA 92333
(909)866-3200 (888)329-6754 Fax:(909)878-2249
Internet: www.fawnskininn.com
E-mail: innatfawnskin@charter.net

Circa 1976. Listen to the quiet at this contemporary log home on an acre with scores of pine trees. The inn is located across the street from the North Shore of Big Bear Lake. It has four guest bedrooms and is decorated in elegant country style with antiques and reproductions. The large master suite has a rock fireplace, a sitting area and a private balcony that overlooks the lake. Guests are free to use the living room (with its large rock fireplace), TV/VCR/DVD and dining room. A country breakfast is served on china in the dining room. The meal includes such delicacies as fresh peaches, a brie and ham omelette with maple-smoked bacon, fresh-squeezed orange juice and freshly-ground coffee. The inn is minutes from boating, fishing, biking trails, ski areas, shops and restaurants. Guests enjoy moonlight walks by the lake and skies filled with stars. Guests who listen carefully may be rewarded by hearing innkeeper Nancy, who once sang at the White House, singing as she creates a perfect atmosphere for guests to relax and unwind.

Innkeeper(s): Nancy & Bill Hazewinkel. $115-285. 4 rooms with PB, 3 with FP, 3 suites and 6 cabins. Breakfast, hors d'oeuvres and wine included in rates. Types of meals: Full gourmet bkfst, veg bkfst, early coffee/tea and snacks/refreshments. Beds: KQ. Cable TV, VCR, reading lamp, CD player, refrigerator, ceiling fan, clock radio, desk, hot tub/spa and fireplace in room. Fax, copier, spa, parlor games and gift shop on premises. Limited handicap access. Antiquing, art galleries, bicycling, canoeing/kayaking, cross-country skiing, downhill skiing, fishing, golf, hiking, horseback riding, live theater, museums, parks, shopping and water sports nearby.

Location: Mountains.

Publicity: *LA Times, Inland Empire magazine and Valley Messenger.*

Certificate may be used: Anytime, subject to availability.

Ferndale   C2

Collingwood Inn Bed & Breakfast

PO Box 1134
Ferndale, CA
(707)786-9219 (800)469-1632 Fax:(707)786-9219
Internet: www.collingwoodinn.com
E-mail: innkeeper@collingwoodinn.com

Circa 1885. Considered a Showboat House, the architecture of this enchanting B&B built in 1885 is non-symmetrical Italianate with Queen Anne flair. Relax in the parlor amid casual elegance and Victorian splendor and enjoy the generous hospitality. Savor afternoon tea, bedtime port and chocolates. Choose a well-appointed guest bedroom or suite that features a private entrance with a deck or balcony, fireplace, feather bed, clawfoot tub, sitting area, garden or village view, robes, fruit basket, fresh flowers, inn-made soap and bubble bath. Designated pet-friendly rooms include treats and necessities. An incredible breakfast buffet is available when desired and made with local, organically grown ingredients. Browse Peter's art gallery and studio. On-site spa services can be arranged.

Innkeeper(s): Chris Hanks & Peter Consello. $99-203. 5 rooms with PB, 2 with FP, 1 two-bedroom suite. Breakfast, afternoon tea and wine included in rates. Types of meals: Full gourmet bkfst, veg bkfst, early coffee/tea, lunch, picnic lunch, snacks/refreshments, hors d'oeuvres, gourmet dinner and room service. Beds: QT. Reading lamp, turn-down service, desk, fireplace, terrycloth robes, complimentary fruit basket, bottled water and bedtime chocolates in room. TV, fax, copier, bicycles, library, pet boarding, parlor games, telephone, laundry facility and gift shop on premises. Limited handicap access. Antiquing, art galleries, beach, bicycling, canoeing/kayaking, fishing, hiking, horseback riding, live theater, museums, parks, shopping, water sports, Humboldt County Fair, Redwood National Forest and Avenue of the Giants nearby.

Location: Country, mountains. Victorian Village.

Publicity: *San Francisco Chronicle (2003), Fido-friendly Magazine (2003), Times-Standard, KQED San Francisco (2004), KPLU Seattle (2004), KVIE Sacramento (2004), KPBS San Diego (2004), Travel Channel (2004), HR Radio, Germany/Europe (2004), Outbreak, The Majestic and Blue Skies.*

Certificate may be used: Anytime, November-March, subject to availability.

Gingerbread Mansion Inn

PO Box 40, 400 Berding St
Ferndale, CA 95536-1380
(707)786-4000 (800)952-4136 Fax:(707)786-4381
Internet: gingerbread-mansion.com
E-mail: innkeeper@gingerbread-mansion.com

Circa 1899. Built for Dr. H.J. Ring, the Gingerbread Mansion is now the most photographed of Northern California's inns. Near Eureka, it is in the fairy-tale Victorian village of Ferndale (a National Historical Landmark). Gingerbread Mansion is a unique combination of Queen Anne and Eastlake styles with elaborate

gingerbread trim. Inside are spacious and elegant rooms including two suites with "his" and "her" clawfoot bathtubs. The Empire Suite is said to be the most opulent accommodation in Northern California. Another memorable choice would be "The Veneto", an imaginative experience where guests stay within a piece of artwork. Extensive formal English gardens beautifully surround the mansion and it is a stroll away to Victorian shops, galleries and restaurants. A Wilderness park and bird sanctuary are a half mile away.

Innkeeper(s): Robert & Juli McInroy and Vincent & Susan Arriaga. $150-400. 11 rooms with PB, 5 with FP, 5 suites. Breakfast and afternoon tea included in rates. Types of meals: Full bkfst and early coffee/tea. Beds: KQT. Reading lamp, clock radio, turn-down service and desk in room. Library, parlor games, telephone, fireplace and gardens on premises. Antiquing, fishing, hiking, live theater, parks and shopping nearby.

Location: Victorian village.

Publicity: *San Francisco Focus, Sunset, Travel Holiday, Country Inns, Los Angeles Times, Sunset, PBS (Inn Country USA), HGTV-Restore America and Outbreak (Warner Bros.).*

"Absolutely the most charming, friendly and delightful place we have ever stayed."

Certificate may be used: Nov. 1-March 15, Sunday-Friday, excluding holidays.

Fort Bragg   E2

Avalon House

561 Stewart St
Fort Bragg, CA 95437-3226
(707)964-5555 (800)964-5556 Fax:(707)964-5555
Internet: www.theavalonhouse.com
E-mail: anne@theavalonhouse.com

Circa 1905. This redwood California Craftsman house was extensively remodeled in 1988 and furnished with a mixture of antiques and willow furniture. Some rooms feature fireplaces, whirlpool tubs and ocean views and decks. The inn is in a quiet residential area, three blocks from the Pacific Ocean, one block west of Hwy. 1, and two blocks from the Skunk Train depot.

Innkeeper(s): Anne Sorrells. $85-155. 6 rooms with PB, 4 with FP. Breakfast included in rates. Types of meals: Full bkfst and early coffee/tea. Beds: QD. Reading lamp, clock radio and spa in room. Telephone and fireplace on premises. Antiquing, fishing, live theater, parks, shopping, water sports, whale watching and Skunk Train nearby.

Location: Ocean community.

Publicity: *Advocate News.*

"Elegant, private and extremely comfortable. We will never stay in a motel again."

Certificate may be used: Nov. 1 to April 30, Monday-Thursday, excluding holidays.

Country Inn

632 N Main St
Fort Bragg, CA 95437-3220
(707)964-3737 (800)831-5327 Fax:(707)964-0289
Internet: www.beourguests.com
E-mail: cntryinn@mcn.org

Circa 1893. The Union Lumber Company once owned this two-story townhouse built of native redwood. It features rooms with slanted and peaked ceilings, and several rooms have fireplaces. Camellia trees, flower boxes, and a picket fence accent the landscaping, while two blocks away a railroad carries visitors on excursions through the redwoods.

Innkeeper(s): Cynthia & Bruce Knauss. $75-145. 8 rooms with PB, 2 with FP. Breakfast and wine included in rates. Types of meals: Full gourmet bkfst and early coffee/tea. Beds: KQ. Clock radio, telephone, hot tub/spa and fireplace in room. Spa and parlor games on premises. Handicap access. Antiquing, art galleries, beach, bicycling, canoeing/kayaking, fishing, golf, hiking, horseback riding, live theater, museums, parks, shopping, tennis, water sports and wineries nearby.

Location: Country, ocean community.

Certificate may be used: Anytime, Sunday-Thursday.

Glass Beach B&B

726 N Main St
Fort Bragg, CA 95437-3017
(707)964-6774
Internet: www.glassbeachinn.com
E-mail: glassbeachinn@hotmail.com

Circa 1920. Each of the guest rooms at this Craftsman-style home is decorated in a different theme and named to reflect the decor. The Malaysian and Oriental Jade rooms reflect Asian artistry, while the Forget-Me-Not and Victorian Rose rooms are bright, feminine rooms with walls decked in floral prints. Antiques are found throughout the home and the back cottage, which includes three of the inn's nine guest rooms. The inn also offers a hot tub for guest use. Breakfasts are served in the inn's dining room, but guests are free to take a tray and enjoy the meal in the privacy of their own room.

Innkeeper(s): Nancy Cardenas/RichardFowler. $60-195. 9 rooms with PB, 4 with FP, 1 suite and 1 cottage. Breakfast and snacks/refreshments included in rates. Types of meals: Country bkfst, afternoon tea and room service. Beds: Q. Cable TV, VCR, reading lamp, refrigerator, clock radio, hot tub/spa and fireplace in room. Spa, parlor games and telephone on premises. Handicap access. Antiquing, art galleries, beach, bicycling, canoeing/kayaking, fishing, golf, hiking, horseback riding, live theater, museums, parks, shopping, water sports, wineries and scuba diving nearby.

Location: City, ocean community.

Certificate may be used: Jan. 5-June 4, Oct. 1-Dec. 31, Sunday-Thursday. Most holidays excluded.

Old Stewart House Inn

511 Stewart St
Fort Bragg, CA 95437-3226
(707)961-0775 (800)287-8392
Internet: www.oldstewarthouseinn.com
E-mail: pat@oldstewarthouseinn.com

Circa 1876. This is the oldest house in Fort Bragg and was built for the founding partner of the town mill. The Victorian theme is enhanced by rooms that may feature amenities such as a fireplace, as well as period furnishings. Within a three-block area of the inn are the Skunk Train Depot, restaurants, shops and beaches. Also nearby are ocean cliffs, stands of redwood, waterfalls and botanical gardens.

Innkeeper(s): Jim and Pat McKeever. $100-145. 5 rooms with PB, 2 with FP and 2 cabins. Breakfast and snacks/refreshments included in rates. Types of meals: Full bkfst. Beds: Q. TV and hair dryer in room. Library, parlor games, telephone and fireplace on premises. Handicap access. Antiquing, fishing, golf, live theater, parks, shopping, tennis and water sports nearby.

Location: Ocean community.

Certificate may be used: Jan. 30-May 10, excluding holidays, Sunday through Thursday only.

Georgetown   G6

American River Inn

PO Box 43, Gold Country
Georgetown, CA 95634-0043
(530)333-4499 (800)245-6566 Fax:(530)333-9253
Internet: www.americanriverinn.com
E-mail: ariinnkeeper@aol.com

Circa 1853. Just a few miles from where gold was discovered in Coloma stands this completely restored miners' boarding house. Mining cars dating back to the original Woodside Mine Camp are on-site. The lode still runs under the inn. There is a Jacuzzi, croquet field, chipping green and complimentary mountain bikes. In the evenings, guests are treated to complimentary wines and hors d'oeuvres. Georgetown was a designated site for the California gold discovery celebration.

Innkeeper(s): Maria, Will & Betty. $85-115. 12 rooms, 7 with PB, 1 with FP and 1 conference room. Types of meals: Full gourmet bkfst. Beds: KQ. Fax, copier and spa on premises. Handicap access. Fishing and hiking nearby.

Publicity: *Los Angeles Times, Sunset, Gourmet, Westways and 50 Romantic Getaways.*

"Our home away from home. We fell in love here in all its beauty and will be back for our fourth visit in April, another honeymoon for six days."

Certificate may be used: Sunday through Thursday, June 1-Oct. 1; anytime, Oct. 1 through May 30.

Geyserville   G4

Hope-Merrill House & Hope Bosworth House

PO Box 42
Geyserville, CA 95441-9637
(707)857-3356 (800)825-4233 Fax:(707)857-4673
Internet: www.hope-inns.com
E-mail: moreinfo@hope-inns.com

Circa 1870. The Hope-Merrill House is a classic example of the Eastlake Stick style that was so popular during Victorian times. Built entirely from redwood, the house features original wainscoting and silk-screened wallcoverings. A swimming pool, vineyard and gazebo are favorite spots for guests to relax. The Hope-Bosworth House, on the same street, was built in 1904 in the Queen Anne style by an early Geyserville pioneer who lived in the home until the 1960s. The front picket fence is covered with roses. Period details include oak woodwork, sliding doors, polished fir floors and antique light fixtures.

Innkeeper(s): Cosette & Ron Scheiber. $124-250. 12 rooms with PB, 5 with FP, 1 suite. Breakfast included in rates. Types of meals: Full gourmet bkfst, early coffee/tea and picnic lunch. Beds: Q. Reading lamp, ceiling fan and desk in room. Fax, copier, telephone, fireplace, coffee, tea and hot chocolate available 24 hours a day on premises. Antiquing, parks, shopping, water sports, wineries and redwoods nearby.

Location: Wine country.

Publicity: *New York Times, San Francisco Chronicle, San Diego Union, Country Homes, Sunset, Sacramento Union, Los Angeles Times and Bay Area Back Roads.*

Certificate may be used: From Dec. 1-March 31 anyday, Sunday-Thursday April 1-Nov. 30.

Groveland   H7

The Groveland Hotel at Yosemite National Park

18767 Main St, PO Box 481
Groveland, CA 95321-0481
(209)962-4000 (800)273-3314 Fax:(209)962-6674
Internet: www.groveland.com
E-mail: peggy@groveland.com

Circa 1849. Located 23 miles from Yosemite National Park, the 1992 restoration features both an 1849 adobe building with 18-inch-thick walls constructed during the Gold Rush and a 1914 building erected to house workers for the Hetch Hetchy Dam. Both feature two-story balconies. There is a Victorian

parlor, a gourmet restaurant and a Western saloon. Guest rooms feature European antiques, down comforters, some feather beds, in-room coffee, phones with data ports, and hair dryers. The feeling is one of casual elegance.
Innkeeper(s): Peggy A. & Grover C. Mosley. $145-285. 17 rooms with PB, 3 with FP, 3 suites and 1 conference room. Breakfast included in rates. Types of meals: Full bkfst, early coffee/tea, picnic lunch and room service. Restaurant on premises. Beds: KQT. Data port, reading lamp, ceiling fan, telephone, desk, voice mail, hair dryers, robes and irons in room. Air conditioning. VCR, fax, copier, library, parlor games and fireplace on premises. Handicap access. Antiquing, cross-country skiing, downhill skiing, fishing, golf, parks, shopping, tennis and water sports nearby.
Location: Mountains. 1/2 hour to Yosemite.
Publicity: Sonora Union Democrat, Los Angeles Times, Peninsula, Sunset (February 2001-West's Best Inns), Stockton Record, Country Inns Magazine (Top 10 Inns in U.S.), Men's Journal Magazine, 25 Best Hideaways, Associated Press and Wine Spectator Award of Excellence for our wine list.
Certificate may be used: Oct. 15-April 15, Sunday through Thursday, excluding holidays.

Gualala   G3

North Coast Country Inn

34591 South Hwy One
Gualala, CA 95445
(707)884-4537 (800)959-4537 Fax:(707)884-1833
Internet: www.northcoastcountryinn.com
E-mail: innkeeper@northcoastcountryinn.com

Circa 1944. Overlooking the Pacific Ocean, the six guest rooms that comprise North Coast Country Inn are tucked into a pine and redwood forested hillside. Each is furnished with

antiques, and include a fireplace, some wet-bar kitchenettes and private deck. There is a very private and secluded hot tub on the hillside or you may relax in the gazebo. Breakfast is served in the breakfast room. Barking sea lions are often heard in the distance.
Innkeeper(s): Maureen Topping & Bill Shupe. $146-215. 6 rooms with PB, 6 with FP and 1 conference room. Breakfast and snacks/refreshments included in rates. Types of meals: Full gourmet bkfst, veg bkfst, early coffee/tea and picnic lunch. Beds: KQ. Reading lamp, refrigerator, ceiling fan, clock radio, coffeemaker, turn-down service, hot tub/spa and fireplace in room. TV, VCR, fax, spa, parlor games, telephone, fireplace and gift shop on premises. Antiquing,

art galleries, beach, bicycling, canoeing/kayaking, fishing, golf, hiking, horseback riding, live theater, parks, shopping, tennis and wineries nearby.
Location: Ocean community.
Publicity: San Francisco Examiner, Wine Spectators, Wine Trader, Motortrend, Los Angeles Times and San Francisco Chronicle.

"Thank you so much for a very gracious stay in your cozy inn. We have appreciated all the special touches."
Certificate may be used: November-May 31, subject to availability and June-October 31, Sunday-Thursday.

Guerneville   G3

Fern Grove Cottages

16650 Highway 116
Guerneville, CA 95446-9678
(707)869-8105 Fax:(707)869-1615
Internet: www.ferngrove.com
E-mail: innkeepers@ferngrove.com

Circa 1926. Clustered in a village-like atmosphere and surrounded by redwoods, these craftsman cottages have romantic fireplaces, private entrances, and are individually decorated. The cottages were built in the 1920s and served as little vacation houses for San Francisco families visiting the Russian River. Some units have a kitchen or wet bar, some have double whirlpool tubs and other cottages are suitable for families. Guests enjoy use of the swimming pool. The cottages are just a few blocks from shops and restaurants, as well as a swimming beach on the river. Visit a nearby redwood state reserve or the Russian River Valley wineries for wine tasting and tours.
Innkeeper(s): Mike & Margaret Kennett. $79-219. 21 rooms with PB, 14 with FP, 20 cottages and 1 conference room. Breakfast included in rates. Types of meals: Cont plus. Beds: KQ. Cable TV, reading lamp, refrigerator and clock radio in room. Swimming, bicycles, fireplace and guest barbecue area on premises. Antiquing, beach, canoeing/kayaking, fishing, golf, parks, shopping, tennis, water sports, wineries, Armstrong Redwood State Park and ocean nearby.
Location: River and vineyards.
Certificate may be used: Anytime, November-April, subject to availability.

Ridenhour Ranch

12850 River Rd
Guerneville, CA 95446-9276
(707)887-1033 (888)877-4466 Fax:(707)869-2967
Internet: www.ridenhourranchhouseinn.com
E-mail: ridenhourinn@earthlink.net

Circa 1906. Located on a hill overlooking the Russian River, this ranch house is shaded by redwoods, oaks and laurels. There are eight guest rooms, including two cottages overlooking the informal gardens. Guests can relax in the hot tub below the majestic oak trees. The Korbel Champagne cellars are next door, and it's a five-minute walk to the river. The ranch offers easy access to wineries in Napa and Sonoma, old-growth redwoods, the Russian River and the dramatic Sonoma coast.
Innkeeper(s): Chris Bell & Meilani Naranjo. $105-185. 8 rooms with PB, 1 with FP, 1 suite. Breakfast and snacks/refreshments included in rates. Types of meals: Full gourmet bkfst and early coffee/tea. Beds: KQ. Cable TV and ceiling fan in room. Parlor games and fireplace on premises. Limited handicap access. Antiquing, bicycling, fishing, golf, hiking, live theater, parks, shopping and water sports nearby.
Location: Country, ocean community. Vineyards, river, ocean, redwoods.
Publicity: Los Angeles Times, Orange County Register and Los Altos Town Crier.

"Your hospitality and food will ensure our return!"
Certificate may be used: December-April, Sunday-Thursday.

Half Moon Bay   I4

Landis Shores Oceanfront Inn

211 Mirada Rd
Half Moon Bay, CA 94019
(650)726-6642 Fax:(650)726-6644
Internet: www.landisshores.com
E-mail: luxury@landisshores.com

Circa 1999. Luxuriate in pampered pleasure at this
Contemporary Mediterranean bed & breakfast inn overlooking
Miramar Beach. Guest bedrooms boast impressive extras that
include binoculars, private balconies, fireplaces, robes, radiant
heated floors, a generous assortment of personal grooming
amenities and mini-refrigerators with bottled water. Marble or
granite bathrooms feature whirlpools and separate showers
except for the ADA San Francisco Bay room, with a large limestone shower. Enjoy in-room entertainment centers and business services. Choose a movie selection from the library. Savor
a gourmet breakfast in the dining room at a table for two or on
a tray delivered to the door. The restaurant has a sommelier
and an award-winning wine list. Exercise in the fully equipped
fitness center or jog along the coastline trail. Guest services can
arrange horseback riding or bike rentals.
Innkeeper(s): Ken & Ellen Landis. $195-345. 8 rooms with PB, 8 with FP
and 1 conference room. Breakfast, hors d'oeuvres and wine included in rates.
Types of meals: Full gourmet bkfst and early coffee/tea. Beds: KQ. Modem
hook-up, data port, cable TV, VCR, reading lamp, CD player, refrigerator,
clock radio, telephone, coffeemaker, turn-down service, desk, hot tub/spa,
voice mail, fireplace, private balconies, wireless Internet access and radiant
heated floors in room. Fax, copier, library, parlor games, fitness center, movie
library and award-winning wine list on premises. Handicap access. Antiquing,
art galleries, beach, bicycling, canoeing/kayaking, fishing, golf, hiking, horseback riding, live theater, parks, shopping, tennis, water sports, wineries, tide
pools, redwoods and birdwatching nearby.
Location: Ocean community, waterfront. Beach access.
Publicity: *Half Moon Bay Review, Arrington's Bed & Breakfast Journal, Inn
Traveler and KGO Radio (Dining Around with Gene Burns).*
Certificate may be used: Monday-Thursday.

Old Thyme Inn

779 Main St
Half Moon Bay, CA 94019-1924
(650)726-1616 (800)720-4277 Fax:(650)726-6394
Internet: www.oldthymeinn.com
E-mail: innkeeper@oldthymeinn.com

Circa 1898. Spend enchanted nights in this "Princess Anne"
Victorian inn located on the historic Main Street of Old Town,
Half Moon Bay. Its lush, aromatic English flower and herb gar-

den with a bubbling fountain
provides a perfect backdrop for
casual conversations or romantic
tete-a-tetes. Just 28 miles from
San Francisco and less than one
hour from San Jose and the
Silicon Valley, the inn is within
walking distance of a crescent-
shaped beach, art galleries, shops and fine dining. Furnished in
antiques and adorned with the innkeeper's art collection, it
offers seven freshly decorated guest rooms, each with a queen
bed and hypoallergenic featherbed and down comforter. Two
rooms have both Jacuzzis and fireplaces. Savor the inn's tanta-
lizing full breakfast before a day of relaxing or sightseeing.
Innkeeper(s): Rick & Kathy Ellis. $140-325. 7 rooms with PB, 3 with FP.

Breakfast included in rates. Types of meals: Full bkfst. Beds: Q. TV, VCR, read-
ing lamp, stereo, refrigerator, clock radio, desk, hot tub/spa, some with Jacuzzi
tubs and fireplaces in room. Fax, telephone and fireplace on premises.
Antiquing, fishing, golf, live theater, parks, shopping and water sports nearby.
Location: Seashore.
Publicity: *California Weekends, Los Angeles, San Mateo Times, San Jose
Mercury News, Herb Companion and San Francisco Examiner.*
Certificate may be used: Nov. 1 to April 30, Sunday-Thursday (except for
Thanksgiving, year-end holidays and Valentine's/President's Day weekends),
valid for the Garden or Thyme room only, subject to availability.

Healdsburg   G4

Camellia Inn

211 North St
Healdsburg, CA 95448-4251
(707)433-8182 (800)727-8182 Fax:(707)433-8130
Internet: www.camelliainn.com
E-mail: info@camelliainn.com

Circa 1869. Just two blocks from the tree-shaded town plaza,
this Italianate Victorian townhouse elegantly graces a half-acre
of award-winning grounds. Architectural details include ceiling
medallions, ornate mahogany and Palladian windows. Gather in
the double parlor with twin marble fireplaces and antiques.
Spacious guest bedrooms feature inlaid hardwood floors with
Oriental rugs and chandeliers. Many feature whirlpool tubs for
two, gas-log fireplaces, canopy beds, sitting areas and private
entrances. The Memento can be used as a family suite with an
adjoining room. Savor a hearty breakfast buffet fireside in the
main dining room. Relax in the swimming pool, and enjoy the
more than 50 varieties of camellias.
Innkeeper(s): Ray, Del and Lucy Lewand. $129-229. 9 rooms with PB, 4 with
FP, 1 two-bedroom suite and 2 conference rooms. Breakfast and wine included
in rates. Types of meals: Full bkfst. Beds: QD. Modem hook-up, reading lamp,
hot tub/spa and fireplace in room. Air conditioning. TV, fax, swimming, telephone and gift shop on premises. Limited handicap access. Antiquing, art gal-
leries, beach, bicycling, canoeing/kayaking, fishing, golf, hiking, horseback rid-
ing, live theater, museums, parks, shopping, water sports and wineries nearby.
Location: Town surrounded by vineyards.
Publicity: *Sunset, Travel & Leisure, New York Times, San Fernando Valley
Daily News, San Diego Union, Sacramento Bee, Healdsburg Tribune,
Washington Post, Cooking Light and Food & Travel.*
"A bit of paradise for city folks."
Certificate may be used: Anytime, December-April, Sunday-Thursday, subject
to availability, excludes holidays & events.

The Honor Mansion

14891 Grove St
Healdsburg, CA 95448-4821
(707)433-4277 (800)554-4667 Fax:(707)431-7173
Internet: www.honormansion.com
E-mail: innkeeper@honormansion.com

Circa 1883. This Italianate manor, a short distance from
Healdsburg Plaza, is located on an acre of grounds with century-
old trees, including a graceful magnolia tree, flowers and a large
koi pond with a bridge and waterfall. The attractively decorated
historic home offers antiques and Victorian appointments.
Accommodations include five rooms in the main house and
four suites. The Tower Suite in the old water tower next to the
pool boasts an appealing queen bed, second-floor living room,
view of the vineyard and a private outdoor garden whirlpool
tub. Every possible wish seems to have been anticipated in all
the rooms, with items such as pool slippers, two sets of robes,
refrigerators, wet bars and make-up mirrors among the plethora
of amenities. An award-winning breakfast (Sunset Magazine)

includes such treats as its signature Honor Mansion Eggs Benedict. An extensive repertoire contains both a winter menu and a summer menu. Dishes include homemade chicken apricot sausage, Espresso Pears with vanilla ice cream, Grand Mariner French Toast, and Chardonnay Peach Bisque. Before dinner, an array of colorful hors d'oeuvres are presented, and after dinner, tempting treats such as Cathi's chocolate-dipped macaroons appear. The innkeepers are expert itinerary planners and will be able to help you find the best wineries, scenic trails and picnic spots, restaurants, canoe trips down the Russian River, organic farms, llama ranches and butterfly gardens.

Innkeeper(s): Cathi & Steve Fowler. $170-350. 13 rooms with PB, 5 with FP, 4 suites. Breakfast, afternoon tea and snacks/refreshments included in rates. Types of meals: Full gourmet bkfst and early coffee/tea. Beds: KQ. Cable TV, VCR, reading lamp, stereo, ceiling fan, clock radio, telephone, turn-down service, desk and hot tub/spa in room. Central air. TV, spa, swimming, parlor games and fireplace on premises. Limited handicap access. Antiquing, art galleries, bicycling, canoeing/kayaking, fishing, golf, hiking, horseback riding, live theater, museums, parks, shopping, tennis, water sports, wineries, guided fishing, Jeep tours, day spas, hot air ballooning, fitness club, dancing and live entertainment nearby.

Location: City. In the heart of Sonoma County wine country where Alexander Valley, Dry Creek Valley and the Russian River Valley converge.

Publicity: *Sunset Magazine ("West's Best Inns").*

"Far better than 'First class', it's more like 'World Class!'"

Certificate may be used: Jan. 1 through March 31, Sunday through Thursday.

Madrona Manor, Wine Country Inn & Restaurant

PO Box 818
Healdsburg, CA 95448-0818
(707)433-4231 (800)258-4003 Fax:(707)433-0703
Internet: www.madronamanor.com
E-mail: info@madronamanor.com

Circa 1881. This handsome estate consists of five historic structures including the Mansion, Schoolhouse and a Gothic-style Carriage House. Embellished with turrets, bay windows, porches and a mansard roof, the stately inn is surrounded by eight acres of manicured lawns, terraced flower and vegetable gardens and wooded areas. Elegant antique furnishings abound. The inn's noteworthy five-star restaurant offers California cuisine featuring fresh local ingredients served in romantic dining rooms.

Innkeeper(s): Joe & Maria Hadley. $185-445. 17 rooms with PB, 5 suites and 2 conference rooms. Breakfast included in rates. Types of meals: Full gourmet bkfst and dinner. Restaurant on premises. Beds: KQ. Telephone in room. Air conditioning. Fax, fireplace and data port on premises. Handicap access. Antiquing, bicycling, fishing, parks, shopping, sporting events, water sports and wineries nearby.

Location: Country.

Publicity: *Travel & Leisure, Conde Naste, Gourmet, Woman's Day Home Decorating Ideas, US News, Diversions, Money, Good Housekeeping, Wine Spectator, Wine and Spirits and Great Country Inns of America.*

"Our fourth visit and better every time."

Certificate may be used: All year, Sunday through Thursday, excluding holidays.

Hope Valley   G8

Sorensen's Resort

14255 Hwy 88
Hope Valley, CA 96120
(530)694-2203 (800)423-9949
Internet: www.sorensensresort.com
E-mail: sorensensresort@yahoo.com

Circa 1876. Where Danish sheepherders settled in this 7,000-foot-high mountain valley, the Sorensen family built a cluster of fishing cabins. Thus began a century-old tradition of valley hos-

pitality. The focal point of Sorensen's is a "stave" cabin — a reproduction of a 13th-century Nordic house. Now developed as a Nordic ski resort, a portion of the Mormon-Emigrant Trail and Pony Express Route pass near the inn's 165 acres. In the summer, river rafting, fishing, pony express re-rides and llama treks are popular Sierra pastimes. Lake Tahoe lies 20 miles to the north. Breakfast is included in the rates for bed & breakfast units only. All other cabins are equipped with kitchens.

Innkeeper(s): John & Patty Brissenden. $95-350. 33 rooms, 31 with PB, 23 with FP, 28 cottages and 2 conference rooms. Types of meals: Full bkfst, early coffee/tea, lunch, picnic lunch, snacks/refreshments and gourmet dinner. Restaurant on premises. Beds: QD. Reading lamp and refrigerator in room. Copier, sauna, library, parlor games, telephone, fireplace, e-mail hook-up, complimentary wine, tea and cocoa on premises. Handicap access. Antiquing, cross-country skiing, downhill skiing, fishing, parks and water sports nearby.

Location: Mountains.

Publicity: *Sunset, San Francisco Chronicle, Los Angeles Times, Motorland, Outside, New York Times and Travel & Leisure.*

"In one night's stay, I felt more comfortable, relaxed, and welcome than any vacation my 47 years have allowed. Thank you for the happiness you have given my children."

Certificate may be used: Monday through Thursday, non-holiday, excluding February, July, August and October.

Hopland   F3

The Hopland Inn

P.O. Box 660
Hopland, CA 95449
(707)744-1890 (800)266-1891 Fax:(707)744-1219
Internet: www.hoplandinn.com
E-mail: info@hoplandinn.com

Circa 1890. Enter the elegance and charm of this 1890 Victorian-era historic hotel. The Fireside Library with its rich wood bookshelves, marble fireplace and high back chairs is an inviting place to read a good book, and there are more than 4,000 volumes to choose from. Enjoy a full selection of Mendocino wines, fine liquors and ales at the mahogany bar with polished brass and marble accents. Guest bedrooms are appointed with floral period-style wallcoverings and antiques. The large and airy dining room with high ceilings opens onto a courtyard surrounded by lush flora. The more intimate Pomo Room is also available for special functions, holiday parties and rehearsal dinners diligently prepared by executive chef Sean Forsha. The innkeepers will help plan visits to local wineries as well as other interesting local attractions.

Innkeeper(s): Scott Heinonen & Sean Leland. $135-185. 21 rooms, 20 with PB, 1 suite. Breakfast included in rates. Types of meals: Cont plus and dinner. Restaurant on premises. Beds: KQT. Reading lamp, ceiling fan, clock radio, telephone and voice mail in room. Air conditioning. Library, parlor games, fireplace, swimming pool, communal wraparound deck, landscaped courtyard, cozy fireside library and on-site bistro and bar open nightly (closed Tuesday) on premises. Limited handicap access. Antiquing, art galleries, bicycling, canoeing/kayaking, fishing, hiking, museums, parks, shopping, water sports, wineries and casino nearby.

Location: Country. Wine country.

Publicity: *Johansen, Best Places of Northern California Guidebook and inspected/rated by California Association of Beds & Breakfasts.*

"We appreciate your attention to details and efforts which made our visit so pleasant."

Certificate may be used: Sunday through Thursday, all year, except holidays.

Idyllwild   O12

Cedar Street Inn

25870 Cedar Street PO Box 627
Idyllwild, CA 92549
(909)659-4789 Fax:(909)659-3540
Internet: www.cedarstreetinn.com
E-mail: cedarst@easyfeed.com

Circa 1988. Old-world sophistication blends with personal comfort at this Victorian country inn that is hidden in a quaint forest village. Developed from two 1930s homes, vintage decor and quality antique furnishings impart a casual elegance. Gather for socializing in the Guest Parlor or Great Room. Choose from themed guest bedrooms and suites with fireplaces, cable TV and private entrances or stay in separate cabins in a sylvan garden setting. A two-bedroom cottage boasts a fireplace, kitchen and large, secluded outdoor deck with a whirlpool tub. The Hobbit House includes a dry sauna. Thoughtful amenities make each visit a delight. Hike nearby trails and Strawberry Creek. Ask about monthly specials.
Innkeeper(s): Patty & Gary Tompkins. $75-175. 11 rooms. Types of meals: Early coffee/tea. Beds: KQT. Cable TV, reading lamp, refrigerator, ceiling fan, desk and coffeemakers in room. Fax, copier, library, parlor games and fireplace on premises. Amusement parks, antiquing, cross-country skiing, fishing, golf, live theater and shopping nearby.
Location: Mountains.
Certificate may be used: All year, Sunday-Thursday, except holidays.

The Pine Cove Inn

PO Box 2181
Idyllwild, CA 92549
(909)659-5033 (888)659-5033 Fax:(909)659-5034
E-mail: pinecoveinn@aol.com

Circa 1935. These rustic, A-frame cottages offer a variety of amenities in a natural, mountain setting. Refrigerators and microwaves have been placed in each unit, several of which include a wood-burning fireplace. One unit has a full kitchen. A full breakfast is served in a separate lodge which dates back to 1935. The village of Idyllwild is three miles down the road, and the surrounding country offers a variety of activities.
Innkeeper(s): Joel Hellinger. $80-110. 10 rooms with PB, 4 with FP, 4 suites and 1 conference room. Breakfast included in rates. Types of meals: Country bkfst. Beds: QT. Reading lamp, refrigerator, clock radio, microwave and some with fireplace in room. TV, VCR, fax, telephone and fireplace on premises. Antiquing, art galleries, bicycling, fishing, hiking, horseback riding, shopping, hiking and mountain hiking nearby.
Location: Mountains.
Certificate may be used: Sunday through Thursday only, any dates except Dec. 20 through Jan. 4.

Inverness   H4

Rosemary Cottage

PO Box 273
Inverness, CA 94937-0273
(415)663-9338 (800)808-9338
Internet: www.rosemarybb.com
E-mail: innkeeper@rosemarybb.com

Circa 1986. From the windows in this secluded cottage, guests can enjoy views of a wooded canyon and hillside in the Point Reyes National Seashore park. The cottage is a cozy, self-contained unit with a well-equipped kitchen, bedroom, and a living room with a wood-burning stove. The decor is French

country, highlighting the wood beams, red oak floors and terra cotta tiles. There is a hot tub in the garden.
Innkeeper(s): Suzanne Storch. $156-265. 6 rooms, 3 with PB, 3 with FP and 3 cottages. Breakfast included in rates. Types of meals: Full bkfst. Beds: QT. Reading lamp, refrigerator, clock radio and telephone in room. Spa, parlor games and fireplace on premises. Antiquing, fishing, parks, shopping and water sports nearby.
Location: Ocean community. Pt. Reyes National Seashore.
Certificate may be used: Nov. 1 through March 31, Sunday through Thursday, excluding holiday weeks.

Ten Inverness Way

10 Inverness Way, PO Box 63
Inverness, CA 94937-0063
(415)669-1648 Fax:(415)669-7403
Internet: www.teninvernessway.com
E-mail: inn@teninvernessway.com

Circa 1904. Shingled in redwood, this handsome bed & breakfast features a stone fireplace, a sunny library with many good books, and close access to a wonderful hiking area. After an afternoon of hiking, guests can enjoy a soak in the garden hot tub. Inverness is located on Tomales Bay, offering close access to nearby beaches at Point Reyes National Seashore. The Golden Gate Bridge is 45 minutes from the inn.

Innkeeper(s): Teri Mowery. $125-200. 5 rooms, 4 with PB, 2 suites. Breakfast and afternoon tea included in rates. Types of meals: Full gourmet bkfst, veg bkfst, early coffee/tea, picnic lunch and snacks/refreshments. Beds: Q. Reading lamp, ceiling fan and clock radio in room. Fax, copier, spa, library, parlor games, telephone, fireplace and gift shop on premises. Antiquing, art galleries, beach, bicycling, canoeing/kayaking, fishing, golf, hiking, horseback riding, live theater, museums, parks, shopping, water sports and wineries nearby.
Location: Mountains, ocean community.
Publicity: *Los Angeles Times* ("as snug as a Christmas stocking, as cheery as a roaring fire"), *New York Times, Travel & Leisure, Sunset, Gourmet* and *San Francisco Chronicle.*

"Everything we could have wanted for our comfort was anticipated by our hosts. Great hot tub. Lovely rooms and common areas."
Certificate may be used: Sunday through Thursday, Nov. 1 through April 30, holiday periods excluded.

Jackson   G6

Gate House Inn

1330 Jackson Gate Rd
Jackson, CA 95642-9539
(209)223-3500 (800)841-1072 Fax:(209)223-1299
Internet: www.gatehouseinn.com
E-mail: info@gatehouseinn.com

Circa 1902. This striking Victorian inn is listed in the National Register of Historic Places. Set on a hillside amid lovely gardens, the inn is within walking distance of a state historic park and several notable eateries. The inn's country setting, comfortable porches and swimming pool offer many opportunities for relaxation. Accommodations include three rooms, a suite and a romantic cottage with a gas log fireplace and whirlpool tub. All of the guest rooms feature queen beds and elegant furnishings. Nearby are several lakes, wineries and golf courses.

Innkeeper(s): Mark & Donna Macola. $130-205. 6 rooms with PB, 3 with FP, 1 suite and 2 cottages. Breakfast included in rates. Types of meals: Full bkfst, early coffee/tea and afternoon tea. Beds: Q. Reading lamp, ceiling fan, clock radio and desk in room. Air conditioning. Fax, copier, swimming, parlor games, telephone and fireplace on premises. Antiquing, cross-country skiing, downhill skiing, fishing, live theater, parks, shopping, water sports and casino nearby.
Location: Mountains.

"Most gracious, warm hospitality."
Certificate may be used: Sunday-Thursday, holidays excluded.

Wedgewood Inn

11941 Narcissus Rd
Jackson, CA 95642-9600
(209)296-4300 (800)933-4393 Fax:(209)296-4301
Internet: www.wedgewoodinn.com
E-mail: vic@wedgewoodinn.com

Circa 1987. Located in the heart of Sierra gold country on a secluded, five acres, this Victorian replica is crammed full of sentimental family heirlooms and antiques. Each room has been designed with careful attention to detail. A baby grand piano rests in the parlor. The carriage house is a separate cottage with its own private entrance. It boasts four generations of family heirlooms, a carved canopy bed, a wood-burning stove and a two-person Jacuzzi tub. The innkeepers'

1921 Model-T, "Henry," is located in its own special showroom. Gourmet breakfasts are served on bone china and include specialties such as cheese-filled blintzes, fruit and baked goods. Breakfast is available in selected guest rooms by request. There is a gift shop on the premises.
Innkeeper(s): Vic & Jeannine Beltz. $155-205. 5 rooms with PB, 1 suite. Breakfast included in rates. Types of meals: Full gourmet bkfst, early coffee/tea and snacks/refreshments. Beds: Q. Refrigerator, ceiling fan, clock radio, turn-down service, desk and Jacuzzi in room. Air conditioning. Fax, copier, parlor games, telephone, croquet, hammocks and horseshoes on premises. Antiquing, cross-country skiing, downhill skiing, fishing, golf, live theater and shopping nearby.
Location: Mountains. Gold Country Foothills.
Publicity: *San Francisco Chronicle, Contra Costa Times, Stockton Record, Country Magazine and Victorian Magazine.*
Certificate may be used: Sunday through Thursday inclusive, no holiday weekends.

Jamestown   H7

1859 Historic National Hotel, A Country Inn

18183 Main St, PO Box 502
Jamestown, CA 95327
(209)984-3446 (800)894-3446 Fax:(209)984-5620
Internet: www.national-hotel.com
E-mail: info@national-hotel.com

Circa 1859. Located between Yosemite National Park and Lake Tahoe, in Gold Country, this is one of the 10 oldest continuously operating hotels in the state. The inn maintains its original redwood bar where thousands of dollars in gold dust were once spent. Original furnishings, Gold Rush period antiques, brass beds, lace curtains and regal comforters grace the guest bedrooms. A soaking room is an additional amenity, though all rooms include private baths. Enjoy a daily bountiful buffet breakfast. Arrange for romantic dining at the on-site gourmet

restaurant, considered to be one of the finest in the Mother Lode. Order a favorite liquor or espresso from the saloon, or try the area's wine tasting. Favorite diversions include gold panning, live theatre and antiquing, golf and shopping.
Innkeeper(s): Stephen Willey. $90-140. 9 rooms with PB and 1 conference room. Breakfast included in rates. Types of meals: Cont plus, early coffee/tea, gourmet lunch, picnic lunch, snacks/refreshments and gourmet dinner. Restaurant on premises. Beds: QT. Cable TV, reading lamp and desk in room. Air conditioning. TV, VCR, fax, parlor games and telephone on premises. Antiquing, cross-country skiing, downhill skiing, fishing, live theater, parks and water sports nearby.
Location: Mountains.
Publicity: *Bon Appetit, California Magazine, Focus, San Francisco Magazine, Gourmet and Sunset.*
Certificate may be used: Anytime, Sunday-Thursday.

Joshua Tree   O13

Joshua Tree Inn

61259 29 Palms Hwy, P.O. Box 1966
Joshua Tree, CA 92252-0340
(760)366-1188 Fax:(760)366-3805
Internet: Joshuatreeinn.com
E-mail: frontdesk@JTinn.com

Circa 1940. Escape to the peaceful grandeur of the Mojave Desert at this secluded hacienda-style inn on four acres, only five miles from the national park. Feel enveloped by the awesome mountains while relaxing on the vine-covered veranda. The square horseshoe design allows for privacy with each ground-level guest bedroom and suite facing the large pool and courtyard. Stay in the leg-

endary Gram Parsons Room, named after the songwriter/musician who was one of the many celebrity guests. Hike, climb or simply stargaze from a lounge chair.
Innkeeper(s): Dan Verhoef. $75-145. 10 rooms with PB, 2 suites and 1 conference room. Types of meals: Cont, early coffee/tea and afternoon tea. Beds: KQDT. Cable TV, reading lamp, ceiling fan, clock radio and water cooler in room. VCR, fax, copier, swimming, parlor games, telephone and fireplace on premises. Antiquing, golf, live theater, parks, shopping, tennis and Joshua Tree National Park nearby.
Location: Mountains. Joshua Tree National Park (5 min).
Publicity: *Los Angeles Times and Press Enterprise.*

"Quiet, clean and charming."
Certificate may be used: Anytime, subject to availability.

Spin and Margies Desert Hide-A-Way

PO Box 1092
Joshua Tree, CA 92252
(760)366-9124 Fax:(760)366-2954
Internet: www.spinandmargiesdeserthideaway.com
E-mail: mindela@earthlink.net

Circa 1950. Escape to this Hacienda-style inn situated on three acres of desert landscape featuring palms, pines, native trees and succulents and a small pond. Three well-designed suites are arranged around an interior courtyard with cactus, yuccas and a soothing fountain. Blending an eclectic mix of Southwest, Mexican and modern furnishings and decor, the private suites include sitting rooms, kitchens and patios in some. Each offers everything needed to make coffee, tea, cereal, waffles or pancakes for breakfast and even margaritas to enjoy while watching the sunsets.
Innkeeper(s): Drew Reese/Mindy Kaufman. $75-145. 4 suites. Breakfast and

snacks/refreshments included in rates. Types of meals: Cont plus and early coffee/tea. Beds: Q. Cable TV, VCR, reading lamp, stereo, refrigerator, ceiling fan, snack bar, clock radio, telephone, coffeemaker, desk, fireplace, tape system and full kitchen with breakfast items available in room. Air conditioning. Library, parlor games and fireplace on premises. Antiquing, art galleries, bicycling, cross-country skiing, golf, hiking, horseback riding, live theater, museums, parks, shopping, wineries, gift Spin & Marty trading post and casino nearby.
Location: Country, mountains. Desert & National Park area.
Publicity: *Malibu Times.*
Certificate may be used: Anytime, Sunday-Thursday.

Julian P12

Butterfield B&B
PO Box 1115
Julian, CA 92036-1115
(760)765-2179 (800)379-4262 Fax:(760)765-1229
Internet: butterfieldbandb.com
E-mail: butterfield@abac.com

Circa 1935. On an ivy-covered hillside surrounded by oaks and pines, the Butterfield is a peaceful haven of hospitality and country comfort. Overlooking the countryside, several of the charming guest bedrooms feature fireplaces and fluffy featherbeds. A delicious gourmet breakfast is served in the gazebo during summer or by a warm fire in cooler months. The parlor is a delightful place to enjoy hot beverages and afternoon treats. Whether it is scheduling an in-room massage, or arranging a horse-drawn carriage, the innkeepers are always happy to oblige.
Innkeeper(s): Ed & Dawn Glass. $130-175. 5 rooms with PB, 2 with FP and 1 cottage. Breakfast and snacks/refreshments included in rates. Types of meals: Full gourmet bkfst and early coffee/tea. Beds: QD. Cable TV, VCR and ceiling fan in room. Air conditioning. Library on premises. Antiquing, fishing, golf, live theater, parks and shopping nearby.
Location: Mountains.
Publicity: *South Coast and Travel Agent.*
Certificate may be used: Jan. 7-Aug. 31, Sunday-Thursday.

Orchard Hill Country Inn
2502 Washington St, PO Box 2410
Julian, CA 92036-0425
(760)765-1700 (800)716-7242
Internet: www.orchardhill.com
E-mail: information@orchardhill.com

Circa 1992. This Craftsman-style inn is a perfect country getaway for those seeking solace from the city lights. There are four, 1920s-style cottages, and a new lodge built as a companion. Expansive, individually appointed cottage rooms offer amenities such as fireplaces, whirlpool tubs, hand-knitted afghans and

down comforters all surrounded by warm, country decor. Gourmet coffee, tea and cocoa also are provided in each cottage room, as are refrigerators. Guests can enjoy a breakfast of fruit, fresh baked breads and a special egg dish in the dining room. Wine and hors d'oeuvres are provided each afternoon. Dinner is served on selected evenings. The expansive grounds boast a variety of gardens highlighting native plants and flowers.
Innkeeper(s): Straube Family. $185-285. 22 rooms with PB, 11 with FP and 1 conference room. Breakfast and snacks/refreshments included in rates. Types of meals: Full bkfst, early coffee/tea, picnic lunch and gourmet dinner. Beds: KQ. Cable TV, VCR, reading lamp, stereo, refrigerator, ceiling fan, clock radio, desk, hot tub/spa, whirlpool tub and wet bar in room. Air conditioning. Fax, copier, parlor games, telephone, fireplace and modem access on premises. Handicap access. Antiquing, fishing, hiking, live theater, parks, shopping,

music/art festivals, horse trails and bird watching nearby.
Location: Mountains. Northeast San Diego County.
Publicity: *San Diego Union Tribune, Los Angeles Times, Orange County Register, Orange Coast, San Francisco Chronicle, San Bernardino Sun and Oceanside Blade-Citizen.*
"The quality of the rooms, service and food were beyond our expectations."
Certificate may be used: Monday-Thursday, other restrictions may apply.

Rockin' A Ranch B&B
1531 Orchard Ln
Julian, CA 92036-9607
(760)765-2820
Internet: www.julianbnb.com/rockina

Circa 1981. This contemporary wood-sided ranch inn found in the countryside outside Julian offers a relaxing getaway for city folk. The inn boasts a private bass fishing facility and guests also visit the farm animals found on the grounds. The three guest rooms have private baths, and amenities include ceiling fans, a fireplace, spa and turndown service. The inn is a very popular anniversary and honeymoon destination. Visitors enjoy a full breakfast and evening snack and will find Julian a fun place to explore in their spare time.
Innkeeper(s): Gil & Dottie Archambeau. $145. 2 rooms with PB, 2 with FP. Breakfast and snacks/refreshments included in rates. Types of meals: Full bkfst. Beds: QD. Reading lamp, ceiling fan, clock radio, turn-down service, hot tub/spa and wood-burning fireplace in room. VCR, spa, swimming, parlor games, telephone, fireplace, swimming pool (in season) and Jacuzzi on premises. Antiquing, cross-country skiing, fishing, live theater, parks and shopping nearby.
Location: Country, mountains.
Certificate may be used: Jan. 2-Dec. 30, Sunday through Thursday excluding holidays.

Laguna Beach P11

Casa Laguna B&B Inn
2510 S Coast Hwy
Laguna Beach, CA 92651-3932
(949)494-2996 (800)233-0449 Fax:(949)494-5009
Internet: www.casalaguna.com
E-mail: innkeeper@casalaguna.com

Circa 1924. A romantic combination of California Mission and Spanish Revival architecture, the Mission House and cottages were built in the early '30s. The casitas were added in the '40s. The hillside setting of secluded gardens, winding paths and flower-splashed patios invites guests to linger and enjoy ocean views. Be sure to arrive in time to watch the sunset from the Bell Tower high above the inn. Ask for a quiet room at the back of the property.
Innkeeper(s): Francois Leclair & Paul Blank. $130-450. 20 rooms with PB, 10 with FP, 5 with WP, 5 suites, 1 cottage and 1 conference room. Breakfast, afternoon tea, snacks/refreshments, hors d'oeuvres and wine included in rates. Types of meals: Cont plus, early coffee/tea and picnic lunch. Beds: KQT. Modem hook-up, data port, cable TV, reading lamp, CD player, refrigerator, ceiling fan, snack bar, clock radio, telephone, coffeemaker, desk, hot tub/spa, voice mail, microwave, pillowtop feather beds, down pillows, down comforters, Gilcrhist & Soames bath products, robes, special coffees and hot chocolate in room. Air conditioning. Fax, swimming, library, parlor games, fireplace, business center and DVD/CD library on premises. Amusement parks, antiquing, art galleries, beach, bicycling, fishing, golf, hiking, live theater, museums, parks, shopping, tennis, water sports, wineries and Pageant of the Masters nearby.
Location: Ocean community.
Publicity: *Sunset Magazine, Orange County Register, Real Orange, Home and Garden TV, Los Angeles Magazine and Houston Post.*
"What a fantastic place. Who needs a casa in Spain?"
Certificate may be used: Sept. 15-June 15, Sunday-Thursday, no holidays.

Eiler's Inn

741 S Coast Hwy
Laguna Beach, CA 92651-2722
(949)494-3004 Fax:(949)497-2215
Internet: www.eilersinn.com
E-mail: theeilersinn@aol.com

Circa 1940. This New Orleans-style inn surrounds a lush courtyard and fountain. The rooms are decorated with antiques and wallpapers. Wine and cheese is served during the evening in front of the fireplace. Named after Eiler Larsen, famous town greeter of Laguna, the inn is just a stone's throw from the beach on the ocean side of Pacific Coast Highway.

Innkeeper(s): Maria Mestas. $110-275. 12 rooms with PB, 1 with FP, 1 suite. Breakfast included in rates. Types of meals: Cont plus and afternoon tea. Beds: KQD. TV and telephone in room. Fireplace on premises. Amusement parks, antiquing, fishing, live theater and shopping nearby.
Location: City.
Publicity: *California Bride, Los Angeles Magazine, Westways, The Tribune and Daily News.*

"Who could find a paradise more relaxing than an old-fashioned bed and breakfast with Mozart and Vivaldi, a charming fountain, wonderful fresh-baked bread, ocean air."

Certificate may be used: October-May, Sunday-Thursday.

Lake Arrowhead   N11

Bracken Fern Manor

815 Arrowhead Villas Rd, PO Box 1006
Lake Arrowhead, CA 92352-1006
(909)337-8557 Fax:(909)337-3323
Internet: www.brackenfernmanor.com
E-mail: brakenfernmanor@earthlink.com

Circa 1929. Opened during the height of the '20s as Lake Arrowhead's first membership resort, this country inn provided refuge to Silver Screen heroines, the wealthy and the prominent. Old letters from the Gibson Girls found in the attic bespoke of elegant parties, dapper gentlemen, the Depression, Prohibition and homesick hearts. Each room is furnished with antiques collected from a lifetime of international travel. There is also a game parlor, wine tasting cellar, library, art gallery and garden Jacuzzi and sauna. Wine is offered in the afternoon. The Crestline Historical Society has its own museum and curator and a map of historical sites you can visit.

Innkeeper(s): Cheryl Weaver. $80-225. 10 rooms, 9 with PB, 3 suites. Breakfast included in rates. Types of meals: Full bkfst and early coffee/tea. Beds: KQDT. Reading lamp, refrigerator and hot tub/spa in room. VCR, telephone, fireplace, Jacuzzi, art gallery and garden & wine cellar on premises. Antiquing, cross-country skiing, downhill skiing, fishing, live theater, shopping and water sports nearby.
Location: Mountains.
Publicity: *Mountain Shopper & Historic B&B, The Press Enterprise, Sun and Lava.*

"My husband brought me here for my 25th birthday and it was everything I hoped it would be - peaceful, romantic and so relaxing .... Thank you for the wonderful memories I will hold close to my heart always."

Certificate may be used: March, April, May, January. No holidays.

Lakeport   F4

Thompson House

3315 Lakeshore Blvd
Lakeport, CA 95453
(707)263-4905 Fax:(707)263-6276
Internet: www.thompsonhouse.net
E-mail: thompsonhouse@thompsonhouse.net

Circa 1895. This Spanish stucco home's interior is decorated in an English Tudor style. Located on two acres, the home's grounds include lawns, a gazebo and space for 300-400 people for garden weddings and parties. Owners of Anthony's Restaurant nearby, the innkeepers offer kitchen dinners for 40 once a month at the inn and a 10% discount at Anthony's is also offered on Thursday. A 1,400-square-foot suite is the only accommodation offered. It's comprised of a bedroom with a romantically draped four-poster bed, a private bath and a living room with ceiling fan, fireplace and a wall of bookcases. Porcelain dolls, crafted by the innkeeper, are displayed. A popular breakfast item is puff pastry filled with home-canned fruits, home-baked muffins and fruit compote. The grounds feature a horseshoe pit. Berries are grown on the property and there's a grape arbor, roses, azaleas, rhododendrons and fruit and nut trees.

Innkeeper(s): Jan & Bill Thompson. $125. 1 room, 1 with FP, 1 suite. Breakfast included in rates. Types of meals: Cont plus. Beds: Q. Cable TV, VCR, reading lamp, CD player, refrigerator, ceiling fan, clock radio, coffeemaker and coffee/tea available in room. Air conditioning. Fax, copier, library, parlor games, telephone, laundry facility and fireplace on premises. Limited handicap access. Antiquing, art galleries, beach, bicycling, canoeing/kayaking, fishing, golf, hiking, horseback riding, live theater, museums, parks, shopping, tennis, water sports, wineries and water slides nearby.
Location: Country, mountains. Across from lake.
Publicity: *Lake County Record Bee.*

Certificate may be used: Anytime, subject to availability.

Long Beach   O10

Lord Mayor's B&B Inn

435 Cedar Ave
Long Beach, CA 90802-2245
(562)436-0324 (800)691-5166 Fax:(562)436-0324
Internet: www.lordmayors.com
E-mail: innkeepers@lordmayors.com

Circa 1904. This collection of carefully restored homes includes the Main House where the city's first mayor lived. Granite pillars flank the veranda of this historical landmark with a golden oak wood interior. The Eastlake Room boasts a family heirloom fainting couch. Hand-carved Austrian twin beds accent Margarita's Room. The Hawaiian Room has a small clawfoot tub. A four-poster bed and Dutch wardrobe adorn Beppe's Room. The Apple and Cinnamon Houses are suitable for families or large groups. The Garden House, a studio that was originally part of the horse barn, provides tranquil privacy. Breakfast is a tasty assortment of home-baked treats and a hot entree. Enjoy the city garden, or walk to the nearby convention center, restaurants and beach.

Innkeeper(s): Laura & Reuben Brasser. $85-140. 12 rooms, 10 with PB, 1 cottage and 1 conference room. Breakfast and snacks/refreshments included in rates. Types of meals: Full bkfst and early coffee/tea. Beds: QDT. Reading lamp and clock radio in room. TV, VCR, fax, library and telephone on premises. Antiquing, art galleries, beach, bicycling, golf, live theater, museums,

parks, Aquarium of Pacific, Gateway to Catalina and Island and Carnival Cruise Line terminal nearby.
Location: City, ocean community.
Publicity: *KCET Magazine, Daily News Los Angeles, Press Telegram and Yellow Brick Road.*

"Your hospitality and beautiful room were respites for the spirit and body after our long trip."
Certificate may be used: Anytime, subject to availability, excluding April 4-15.

Lucerne   F4

Kristalberg B&B
PO Box 1629
Lucerne, CA 95458-1629
(707)274-8009
Internet: www.kristalbergbb.com
E-mail: merv@kristalbergbb.com

Circa 1987. This country B&B affords a breathtaking panoramic view of Clear Lake. Each of the guest rooms is furnished and decorated in a different style. The master suite offers a whirlpool tub and early

American decor, other rooms feature French and Spanish decor. The parlor features Victorian and Italian influences. The expansive breakfast is served in the home's formal dining room. The cuisine features fresh fruit, vegetables and herbs from the garden and home-baked house specialties.
Innkeeper(s): Merv Myers. $85-175. 3 rooms. Breakfast included in rates. Types of meals: Full bkfst. Beds: QD. TV, reading lamp, ceiling fan, clock radio, two rooms with private balconies overlooking the lake and master suite has whirlpool tub in room. Central air. Swimming, library and parlor games on premises. Antiquing, canoeing/kayaking, fishing, golf, hiking, museums, parks, shopping, water sports, wineries, boating, bird watching and rock hounding nearby.
Location: Country. Within view of Clear Lake.

"First rate in food, hospitality, and comfort."
Certificate may be used: Anytime, Sunday-Thursday, subject to availability.

Mariposa   I8

Rockwood Gardens
5155 Tip Top Rd
Mariposa, CA 95338-9003
(209)742-6817 (800)859-8862 Fax:(209)742-7400
E-mail: ewigfal@sierratel.com

Circa 1989. Nestled among the pines in the Sierra foothills, this five-acre contemporary Prairie-style inn was designed and built to complement the natural beauty found nearby. A creek, oaks, pond and wildflower meadow all are part of the inn's setting. Guests often use the inn as headquarters when exploring the many breathtaking sights of Yosemite National Park. Visitors select from the Rose, Duck and Manzanita rooms. Stroll the grounds and relish the view of evening stars. The inn's suite can accommodate up to four people and is equipped with a dining area, microwave, small refrigerator and satellite TV.
Innkeeper(s): Gerald & Mary Ann Fuller. $70-110. 3 rooms, 1 suite and 1 conference room. Breakfast included in rates. Types of meals: Cont plus and picnic lunch. Beds: KQ. VCR, reading lamp, telephone, satellite TV and suite with kitchen in room. Air conditioning. Fax, copier, parlor games and fireplace on premises. Antiquing, cross-country skiing, downhill skiing, fishing, parks, shopping, water sports and Yosemite National Park nearby.
Location: Mountains. Yosemite National Park.
Certificate may be used: Jan. 2 to April 15 and Oct. 1 to Dec. 2, every day.

Mendocino   F2

Alegria Oceanfront Inn & Cottages
44781 Main St
Mendocino, CA 95460
(707)937-5150 (800)780-7905 Fax:(707)937-5151
Internet: www.oceanfrontmagic.com
E-mail: inn@oceanfrontmagic.com

Circa 1861. Sitting in the historic village on a bluff overlooking an ocean cove, this inn lightens the sprits just as the name Alegria means when translated. The main house was built in 1861 as a saltbox and recently renovated. Stay in one of the guest bedrooms or a private cottage. They all feature generous amenities and some include wood-burning stoves. The second-floor Pacific Suite boasts a microwave and wet bar sink. The ocean view dining room is the perfect spot for an incredible breakfast that is made with organically grown produce when possible. The ever-changing perennial garden includes antique roses and a relaxing hot tub. Take the trail 200 footsteps from the garden's edge down to Big River Beach.
Innkeeper(s): Elaine & Eric Wing Hillsland. $99-269. 6 rooms with PB, 1 suite and 4 cottages. Breakfast included in rates. Types of meals: Full gourmet bkfst, veg bkfst, early coffee/tea and picnic lunch. Beds: KQ. Cable TV, VCR, reading lamp, refrigerator, ceiling fan, clock radio, coffeemaker, fireplace, private decks, panoramic ocean views, some with wood burning stoves, microwave and wet bar sink in room. Fax, copier, spa, telephone and gift shop on premises. Art galleries, beach, bicycling, canoeing/kayaking, fishing, golf, hiking, horseback riding, live theater, museums, parks, shopping, tennis, wineries, used book store, Big River Beach, Big River Estuary, Headlands State Park, Montgomery Woods, Jackson State Demonstration Forest, Van Damme State Park & Beach, Russian Gulch State Park & Beach, Caspar State Beach, Mendocino Coast Botanical Gardens, Glass Beach and MacKerricher State Park & Beach nearby.
Location: Ocean community, waterfront. Wine country.
Publicity: *Country Inns Magazine and Horticulture Magazine.*
Certificate may be used: November-February, Sunday-Thursday, excluding holidays, subject to availability.

Brewery Gulch Inn
9401 Coast Hwy One N
Mendocino, CA 95460-9767
(707)937-4752 (800)578-4454 Fax:(707)937-1279
Internet: www.brewerygulchinn.com
E-mail: info@brewerygulchinn.com

Circa 1864. Ten acres of bliss are found at this distinctive Craftsman-style inn, built with eco-salvaged, old virgin redwood timbers from Big River. Sitting next to the original historic farmhouse on a scenic hillside, Arts and Crafts furnishings and ocean views create an eye-pleasing decor. The romantic guest bedrooms boast fireplaces, private decks, and pampering touches including terry robes and CD players. Mouth-watering breakfast al fresco on the common deck or fireside is prepared with organic ingredients by a French-trained chef. Relax in the fireplaced Great Room with afternoon wine and hors d'oeuvres.
Innkeeper(s): Glenn Lutge. $150-325. 10 rooms with PB, 10 with FP. Breakfast and snacks/refreshments included in rates. Types of meals: Full gourmet bkfst, early coffee/tea, picnic lunch, hors d'oeuvres and wine. Beds: KQT. Modem hook-up, data port, cable TV, VCR, reading lamp, stereo, clock radio, telephone, turn-down service, desk and fireplace in room. Fax, copier, library, parlor games, fireplace and gift shop on premises. Handicap access. Antiquing, art galleries, beach, bicycling, canoeing/kayaking, fishing, golf, hiking, horseback riding, live theater, museums, parks, shopping, tennis, water sports, wineries and Skunk steam engine train nearby.
Location: Ocean community.
Publicity: *Coastal Living, Food & Wine, Sunset Magazine, San Francisco Chronicle, Appellation, Steppin' Out, KGO Radio, was Travel & Leisure Magazine's Inn of the Month in November of 2001 and was chosen as one*

of 12 Great Gateways by Diablo Magazine.
Certificate may be used: Anytime, November-April, subject to availability, except during holidays or local special events.

C.O. Packard House B&B

PO Box 1065
Mendocino, CA 95460-1065
(707)937-2677 (888)453-2677 Fax:(707)937-1323
Internet: www.packardhouse.com
E-mail: info@packardhouse.com

Circa 1878. One of four landmark homes on Executive Row, this Carpenter's Gothic Victorian sits in the heart of the historic village. It features an elegant blend of antiques, custom-designed furnishings, decorative wall glazes and international art. Luxurious guest bedrooms and suites boast gorgeous views, a jetted tub for two, robes, slippers and VCRs. Savor a breakfast in the French Country kitchen that may include pear in puff pastry, Eggs Benedict, and banana bread or perhaps poached pear, frittata and muffins. Relax over afternoon wine, crudites and cheese. Stroll through the gardens, or walk to the Headlands State Park feeling refreshed by the ocean breeze.
Innkeeper(s): Maria & Dan Levin. $125-255. 6 rooms with PB, 6 with FP, 1 suite and 2 cottages. Breakfast and snacks/refreshments included in rates. Types of meals: Full gourmet bkfst, veg bkfst and picnic lunch. Beds: KQT. Cable TV, VCR, reading lamp, CD player, refrigerator, ceiling fan, clock radio, telephone, coffeemaker, hot tub/spa and fireplace in room. Central air. Parlor games, fireplace, gift shop, gardens and video library on premises. Art galleries, beach, bicycling, canoeing/kayaking, fishing, golf, hiking, horseback riding, live theater, parks, shopping, tennis, water sports, wineries, diving, whale watching and bird watching nearby.
Location: Ocean community. Village.
Publicity: *Marin IS, Via, Sunset Magazine and Pontiac Moon.*
Certificate may be used: Jan. 10-Feb. 30, Sunday-Thursday, subject to availability.

The Headlands Inn

PO Box 132
Mendocino, CA 95460-0132
(707)937-4431 (800)354-4431 Fax:(707)937-0421
Internet: www.headlandsinn.com
E-mail: innkeeper@headlandsinn.com

Circa 1868. A historic village setting by the sea complements this New England Victorian Salt Box. The quaintness of the past combines with amenities of the present. Meet new friends sharing afternoon tea and cookies in the parlor. Almost all of the romantic guest bedrooms feature fireplaces, comfortable feather beds with down comforters, fresh flowers and bedside chocolates. A cottage provides more spacious privacy. Indulge in a full breakfast delivered to the room with homemade treats and creative entrees. The front porch is an ideal spot for ocean views. Lawn seating gives ample opportunity to enjoy the year-round English garden.
Innkeeper(s): Denise & Mitch. $115-210. 7 rooms with PB, 6 with FP, 1 suite and 1 cottage. Breakfast, afternoon tea and snacks/refreshments included in rates. Types of meals: Full gourmet bkfst and veg bkfst. Beds: KQ. Reading lamp, clock radio, desk, fireplace, feather beds, hair dryers, robes, cottage has cable TV/VCR and refrigerator in room. Fax, copier, parlor games and telephone on premises. Limited handicap access. Antiquing, art galleries, beach, bicycling, canoeing/kayaking, fishing, golf, hiking, horseback riding, live theater, museums, parks, shopping, tennis and wineries nearby.
Location: Ocean community.
Publicity: *"Best Places to Kiss" Romantic Travel Guide and "Best Places to Stay" Travel Guide.*

"If a Nobel Prize were given for breakfasts, you would win hands down. A singularly joyous experience!!"
Certificate may be used: November-April, Monday-Thursday, rooms Strauss, Cottage, or Barry only.

The Inn at Schoolhouse Creek

PO Box 1637
Mendocino, CA 95460
(707)937-5525 (800)731-5525 Fax:(707)937-2012
Internet: www.schoolhousecreek.com
E-mail: innkeeper@schoolhousecreek.com

Circa 1860. The Inn at School House Creek offers private cottages and rooms on its eight acres of rose gardens, forests and meadows. (The inn's gardens have been featured in several magazines.) Many cottages include views of the ocean and all offer a fireplace. Located three miles from Mendocino, the inn was a motor court in the '30s. Private beach access to Buckhorn Cove allows guests to enjoy whale watching, sea lions and the crashing waves of the Pacific. Organize your day to include a picnic lunch (available by advance notice) to enjoy at a secluded waterfall in the redwoods. Then take a sunset soak in the inn's ocean view hot tub. The next morning's breakfast may include Fruit Basket Breakfast Pudding with whipped cream, eggs, fruit and a variety of freshly baked muffins and breads, jams and juices.
Innkeeper(s): Steven Musser & Maureen Gilbert. $85-275. 15 rooms with PB, 15 with FP, 1 with HT, 2 suites and 9 cottages. Breakfast, hors d'oeuvres and wine included in rates. Types of meals: Full bkfst, early coffee/tea, picnic lunch and afternoon tea. Beds: KQD. Modem hook-up, cable TV, VCR, reading lamp, CD player, refrigerator, clock radio, telephone, coffeemaker, desk, hot tub/spa, voice mail and fireplace in room. Fax, spa, library, pet boarding, child care, parlor games, gift shop and evening hors d'oeuvres on premises. Handicap access. Antiquing, art galleries, beach, bicycling, canoeing/kayaking, fishing, golf, hiking, horseback riding, live theater, parks, shopping, tennis, water sports and wineries nearby.
Location: Ocean community.
Certificate may be used: Nov. 1-Feb. 28, Sunday-Thursday, holidays and local festivals excluded.

Sea Rock B&B Inn

PO Box 906
Mendocino, CA 95460-0906
(707)937-0926 (800)906-0926
Internet: www.searock.com
E-mail: searock@mcn.org

Circa 1930. Enjoy sea breezes and ocean vistas at this inn, which rests on a bluff looking out to the Pacific. Most of the accommodations include a wood-burning Franklin fireplace and feather bed. Four guest rooms are available in the Stratton House, and each affords a spectacular ocean view. There are six cottages on the grounds, most offering a sea view. The innkeepers also offer deluxe accommodations in four special suites. Each has an ocean view, wood-burning fireplace, private entrance and a deck, whirlpool or ocean view tub. The grounds, which now feature gardens, were the site of an 1870s brewery. The inn is less than half a mile from Mendocino.
Innkeeper(s): Susie & Andy Plocher. $169-335. 14 rooms with PB, 14 with FP, 8 suites and 6 cottages. Breakfast included in rates. Types of meals: Cont plus. Beds: KQ. Cable TV, VCR, reading lamp, clock radio, telephone and desk in room. Fireplace on premises. Antiquing, fishing, golf, live theater, parks, shopping, tennis and water sports nearby.
Location: Ocean community.
Publicity: *California Visitors Review and Sunset Magazine.*
Certificate may be used: Jan. 3-March 1, Monday-Thursday, excluding holiday periods.

Whitegate Inn Bed and Breakfast

PO Box 150
Mendocino, CA 95460-0150
(707)937-4892 (800)531-7282 Fax:(707)937-1131
Internet: www.whitegateinn.com
E-mail: staff@whitegateinn.com

Circa 1883. When it was first built, the local newspaper called Whitegate Inn "one of the most elegant and best appointed residences in town." Its bay windows, steep gabled roof, redwood siding and fish-scale shingles are stunning examples of Victorian architecture. The house's original wallpaper and candelabras adorn the double parlors. There, an antique 1827 piano, at one time part of Alexander Graham Bell's collection, and inlaid pocket doors take you back to a more gracious time. French and Victorian antique furnishings and fresh flowers add to the inn's elegant hospitality and old world charm. The gourmet breakfasts are artfully presented in the inn's sunlit dining room. The inn is just a block from the ocean, galleries, restaurants and the center of town.

Innkeeper(s): Richard & Susan Strom. $169-289. 6 rooms with PB. Breakfast included in rates. Types of meals: Full gourmet bkfst and snacks/refreshments. Beds: KQ. Cable TV, VCR, reading lamp, refrigerator, snack bar, clock radio, telephone and desk in room. Fax, copier, fireplace, welcome basket, evening sherry, wine and cheese on premises. Antiquing, art galleries, beach, bicycling, fishing, golf, wineries and whale watching nearby.
Location: Ocean community.
Publicity: *Innsider, Country Inns, Country Home, Glamour, Santa Rosa Press Democrat, San Francisco Chronicle, Bon Appetit, Victoria Magazine, Sunset, San Francisco Examiner, Victorian Decorating and Country Gardener.*

"We have stayed at over 60 Inns and Whitegate is the best inn we have ever had the pleasure to be a guest at, the service and hospitality are the best."
Certificate may be used: Nov. 1 through April 30, Sunday-Thursday, no holiday periods, selected rooms.

Monterey   J5

The Jabberwock

598 Laine St
Monterey, CA 93940-1312
(831)372-4777 (888)428-7253 Fax:(831)655-2946
Internet: www.jabberwockinn.com
E-mail: innkeeper@jabberwockinn.com

Circa 1911. Set in a half-acre of gardens, this Craftsman-style inn provides a fabulous view of Monterey Bay with its famous barking seals. When you're ready to settle in for the evening,

you'll find huge Victorian beds complete with lace-edged sheets and goose-down comforters. Three rooms include Jacuzzi tubs. In the late afternoon, hors d'oeuvres and aperitifs are served on an enclosed sun porch. After dinner, guests are tucked into bed with homemade chocolate chip cookies and milk. To help guests avoid long lines, the innkeepers have tickets available for the popular and nearby Monterey Bay Aquarium.

Innkeeper(s): Joan & John Kiliany. $145-265. 7 rooms with PB, 4 with FP. Breakfast, afternoon tea, snacks/refreshments, hors d'oeuvres and wine included in rates. Types of meals: Full gourmet bkfst, veg bkfst, early

coffee/tea and picnic lunch. Beds: KQ. Reading lamp, clock radio and three with Jacuzzi in room. Fax, copier, spa, parlor games, telephone and fireplace on premises. Antiquing, art galleries, beach, bicycling, canoeing/kayaking, fishing, golf, hiking, horseback riding, live theater, museums, parks, shopping, tennis, water sports, wineries, restaurants, Cannery Row, Carmel shopping and Monterey Bay Aquarium nearby.
Location: City, ocean community, waterfront.
Publicity: *Sunset, Travel & Leisure, Sacramento Bee, San Francisco Examiner, Los Angeles Times, Country Inns, San Francisco Chronicle, Diablo and Elmer Dill's KABC-Los Angeles TV.*

"Words are not enough to describe the ease and tranquility of the atmosphere of the home, rooms, owners and staff at the Jabberwock."
Certificate may be used: Nov. 1-April 30, Sunday-Thursday.

Moss Landing   J5

Captain's Inn

PO Box 570
Moss Landing, CA 95039
(831)633-5550
Internet: www.captainsinn.com
E-mail: capt@captainsinn.com

Circa 1906. A meticulously restored historic Pacific Coast Steamship Company building and a newly built boathouse comprise this coastal getaway only an hour from San Jose. Relax in front of the parlor fireplace or peruse the reading library and browse through area guidebooks. The inn's nautical décor includes a touch of whimsy in the guest bedrooms that are furnished with antiques and thoughtful amenities like robes, plush-top mattresses and feather pillows. Stay in a room with a fireplace and soaking or clawfoot tub for two. Continental fare is available to early risers. Later in the dining room, a home-cooked breakfast full of traditional classics and recipes from German grandmothers are served. Walk to ocean beaches, shops and art studios.

Innkeeper(s): Captain Yohn & Melanie Gideon. $110-265. 10 rooms with PB. Breakfast and snacks/refreshments included in rates. Types of meals: Full bkfst, veg bkfst and early coffee/tea. Beds: KQ. Modem hook-up, cable TV, reading lamp, clock radio, telephone, turn-down service, desk, voice mail, fireplace, soaking tubs, oversized showers with two heads, comforters, quilts, feather pillows, cozy robes, bird lists, guidebooks to local area and antiques in room. Fax, copier, bicycles, library, parlor games, gift shop, local menus, voice mail, telephones, decks and outdoor tables and chairs on premises. Handicap access. Antiquing, art galleries, beach, bicycling, canoeing/kayaking, fishing, golf, hiking, horseback riding, museums, parks, shopping, water sports, wineries, Elkhorn Slough, Pacific Ocean, sea otter trips, whale watching, auto races, agriculture tours and live music nearby.
Location: Ocean community, waterfront. Monterey Bay.
Publicity: *AAA's Via magazine (2004), Huell Howser's California's Golden Coast, PBS, KCET-LA, June on the Road with Bette, KVIE-PBS, Sacramento, Travels with Romney Dunbar, Cable TV and KRML (jazz and blues station).*
Certificate may be used: December through February, excluding Dec. 25-Jan. 1 and Valentine's holiday. Boathouse rooms only.

Murphys   H7

Trade Carriage House

230 Big Trees Rd
Murphys, CA 95247
(209)728-3404 (800)800-3408 Fax:(209)728-2527
Internet: www.realtyworld-murphys.com
E-mail: sales@realtyworld-murphys.com

Circa 1930. A white picket fence surrounds the Trade Carriage House, originally built in Stockton and later moved to Murphys. There are two bedrooms, both furnished with antiques and wicker pieces. A sunroom overlooks a private deck. Three doors down is a second vacation home, Tree Top House, that boasts a

deck overlooking the treetops. This home has two bedrooms and two baths, a pine vaulted ceiling and, like the Trade Carriage House, is within two blocks of historical Main Street, with shops, restaurants and local wineries. Nearby are the gold rush towns of Columbia and Sonora. The Loft on Main is a third vacation house located on Main Street in the heart of downtown Murphys. Murphys is located between Lake Tahoe and Yosemite. Innkeeper(s): Cynthia Trade. $130-150. 3 cottages. Beds: QD. Cable TV, reading lamp, refrigerator and telephone in room. Air conditioning. One apartment on premises. Antiquing, cross-country skiing, downhill skiing, fishing, golf, live theater, parks, shopping, tennis, water sports and major area for wineries nearby.
Location: Mountains. Gold Country Foothills.
Certificate may be used: Oct. 1-April 30, Sunday-Thursday, except holidays.

Napa   H4

Arbor Guest House

1436 G St
Napa, CA 94559-1145
(707)252-8144 (866)627-2262 Fax:(707)252-7385
Internet: www.arborguesthouse.com
E-mail: Susan@arborguesthouse.com

Circa 1906. Innkeepers Jack and Susan Clare have decorated the exterior of their gracious bed & breakfast, which is surrounded by old trees, with lush gardens and five patios. Romantic guest quarters boast beautiful period furnishings. Two of the rooms include spa tubs and three offer fireplaces. Freshly made breakfasts feature homemade breads, scones, fruits and egg dishes and are served in the dining room or at a table in the sunny garden. The many wineries and shops of Napa Valley are nearby.
Innkeeper(s): Jack and Susan Clare. $120-210. 5 rooms with PB, 3 with FP, 2 with WP. Breakfast and snacks/refreshments included in rates. Types of meals: Full gourmet bkfst, veg bkfst and early coffee/tea. Beds: QD. Reading lamp, ceiling fan, clock radio, coffeemaker, desk, hot tub/spa, fireplace, iron and ironing board in room. Central air. Telephone and high-speed wireless access on premises. Limited handicap access. Amusement parks, antiquing, art galleries, bicycling, canoeing/kayaking, fishing, golf, hiking, horseback riding, live theater, museums, parks, shopping and wineries nearby.
Location: Wine country.
Certificate may be used: January-July, Monday-Thursday, excluding holidays.

Blackbird Inn

1755 First St
Napa, CA 94559
(707)226-2450 (888)567-9811
Internet: www.blackbirdinnnapa.com
E-mail: blackbirdinn@foursisters.com

Circa 2001. This meticulously restored hideaway, built with Greene and Greene-type architecture, is within an easy walk to town. The stone pillared porch, leaded glass and blackbird vines are a welcome setting for the wonderful atmosphere found inside. True to the Craftsman-style furnishings and decor, the period lighting accents the subdued colors and warm ambiance. Double-paned windows offer quiet views of the garden fountain. Many of the guest bedrooms feature private decks, spa tubs and fireplaces. Wine and hors d'oeuvres are served in the afternoon. There is a $20 fee for an additional guest in room, except for children less than 5 years old.
Innkeeper(s): Michael Harris. $135-275. 8 rooms with PB, 6 with FP. Breakfast, afternoon tea, snacks/refreshments, hors d'oeuvres and wine included in rates. Types of meals: Full bkfst and early coffee/tea. Beds: KQ. Data port, cable TV, VCR, reading lamp, stereo, clock radio, telephone, turndown service, hot tub/spa, jetted spa tub and/or private deck and some with

fireplace in room. Air conditioning. Fax, parlor games, fireplace, full signature breakfast, afternoon wine and hors d'oeuvres, morning newspaper delivery, evening turndown service, complimentary sodas and home-baked cookies on premises. Handicap access. Antiquing, art galleries, bicycling, golf, hiking, live theater, museums, parks, shopping, wineries and wine tasting nearby.
Location: City. Downtown Historic Napa.
Certificate may be used: Nov. 2-April 29, Sunday-Thursday, excluding holidays, special event periods and based on promotional discount availability.

Candlelight Inn

1045 Easum Drive
Napa, CA 94558-5524
(707)257-3717 (800)624-0395 Fax:(707)257-3762
Internet: www.candlelightinn.com
E-mail: mail@candlelightinn.com

Circa 1929. Located on a park-like acre with gardens, this elegant English Tudor-style house is situated beneath redwood groves and towering trees that shade the banks of Napa Creek. Seven rooms feature a marble fireplace and two-person marble Jacuzzi inside the room. The Candlelight Suite offers cathedral ceilings, stained-glass windows and a private sauna. The inn's breakfast room has French doors and windows overlooking the garden. Breakfast is served by candlelight.
Innkeeper(s): Mark & Wendy Tamiso. $139-350. 10 rooms with PB, 7 with FP. Breakfast and snacks/refreshments included in rates. Types of meals: Full gourmet bkfst and early coffee/tea. Beds: KQT. Cable TV, reading lamp, clock radio, telephone, hot tub/spa, voice mail and fireplace in room. Air conditioning. Fax, swimming and parlor games on premises. Limited handicap access. Amusement parks, antiquing, art galleries, bicycling, canoeing/kayaking, golf, hiking, horseback riding, live theater, museums, parks, shopping, wineries, hot air ballooning and spas nearby.
Location: Wine country.

"We still haven't stopped talking about the great food, wonderful accommodations and gracious hospitality."

Certificate may be used: December-February, Sunday-Thursday, holiday periods excluded, subject to availability.

La Belle Époque

1386 Calistoga Ave
Napa, CA 94559-2552
(707)257-2161 (800)238-8070 Fax:(707)226-6314
Internet: www.napabelle.com
E-mail: lynnette@napabelle.com

Circa 1893. This luxurious Victorian inn has won awards for "best in the wine country" and "best breakfast in the nation." Enjoy the experience in the wine cellar and tasting room where guests can casually sip Napa Valley wines. The inn, which is one of the most unique architectural structures found in the wine country, is located in the heart of Napa's Calistoga Historic District. Beautiful  original stained-glass windows include a window from an old church. Six guest rooms offer a whirlpool tub. A selection of fine restaurants and shops are within easy walking distance, as well as the riverfront, art museums and the Wine Train Depot.
Innkeeper(s): Lynnette & Steve Sands. $205-350. 9 rooms with PB, 6 with FP, 3 suites and 1 conference room. Breakfast, afternoon tea, snacks/refreshments, hors d'oeuvres and wine included in rates. Types of meals: Full gourmet bkfst and early coffee/tea. Beds: KQ. Cable TV, VCR, reading lamp, ceiling fan, clock radio, telephone, desk and whirlpools in room. Air conditioning. Fax, copier, parlor games, fireplace, gift shop and fireplaces on premises. Amusement parks, antiquing, golf, hiking, horseback riding, live theater, museums, parks, shopping, sporting events, tennis and wineries nearby.
Location: Wine country.

"At first I was a bit leery, how can a B&B get consistent rave reviews? After staying here two nights, I am now a believer!"
Certificate may be used: Dec. 1-23, Jan. 2-March 15, Monday-Thursday, holidays excluded.

Old World Inn

1301 Jefferson St
Napa, CA 94559-2412
(707)257-0112 (800)966-6624 Fax:(707)257-0118
Internet: www.oldworldinn.com
E-mail: theoldworldinn@aol.com

Circa 1906. The decor in this exquisite bed & breakfast is second to none. In 1981, Macy's sought out the inn to showcase a new line of fabrics inspired by Scandinavian artist Carl Larrson. Each romantic room is adorned in bright, welcoming

colors and includes special features such as canopy beds and clawfoot tubs. The Garden Room boasts three skylights, and the Anne Room is a must for honeymoons and romantic retreats. The walls and ceilings are painted in a warm peach and blue, bows are stenciled around the perimeter of the room. A decorated canopy starts at the ceiling in the center of the bed and falls downward producing a curtain-like effect. A buffet breakfast is served each morning and a delicious afternoon tea and wine and cheese social will curb your appetite until dinner. After sampling one of Napa's gourmet eateries, return to the inn where a selection of desserts await you.
Innkeeper(s): Sharon Fry & Russ Herschelmann. $165-280. 10 rooms with PB, 6 with FP, 1 suite and 1 cottage. Breakfast, afternoon tea and snacks/refreshments included in rates. Types of meals: Full gourmet bkfst and early coffee/tea. Beds: KQT. Cable TV, VCR, reading lamp, refrigerator, ceiling fan, clock radio, telephone and hot tub/spa in room. Air conditioning. Fax, spa, parlor games and fireplace on premises. Antiquing, fishing, golf, live theater, parks, shopping, sporting events and tennis nearby.
Location: City. Wine country.
Publicity: *Napa Valley Traveller.*

"Excellent is an understatement. We'll return."
Certificate may be used: Dec. 1 through March 1, Sunday-Thursday, except holidays.

Stahlecker House B&B Country Inn & Garden

1042 Easum Dr
Napa, CA 94558-5525
(707)257-1588 (800)799-1588 Fax:(707)224-7429
Internet: www.stahleckerhouse.com
E-mail: stahlbnb@aol.com

Circa 1949. This country inn is situated on the banks of tree-lined Napa Creek. The acre and a half of grounds feature rose and orchard gardens, fountains and manicured lawns. Guests often relax on the sun deck. There is an antique refrigerator stocked with soft drinks and lemonade. Full, gourmet break-

fasts are served by candlelight in the glass-wrapped dining room that overlooks the gardens. In the evenings, coffee, tea and freshly made chocolate chip cookies are served. The Napa Wine Train station is five minutes away. Wineries, restaurants,

antique shops, bike paths and hiking all are nearby.
Innkeeper(s): Ron & Ethel Stahlecker. $148-268. 4 rooms with PB, 4 with FP, 1 suite. Breakfast and snacks/refreshments included in rates. Types of meals: Full gourmet bkfst and afternoon tea. Beds: QT. TV, reading lamp, clock radio, telephone, turn-down service, desk, hot tub/spa and couple spa/couple shower in room. Air conditioning. Library, parlor games, fireplace and croquet on premises. Antiquing, fishing, golf, hiking, live theater, parks, shopping, tennis, wineries and hot air balloons nearby.
Location: City. Wine country.
Publicity: *Brides Magazine and Napa Valley Traveler.*

"Friendly hosts and beautiful gardens."
Certificate may be used: Monday-Thursday only, Nov. 1 to April 30 (not valid in summer, no holidays).

Nevada City   F6

Emma Nevada House

528 E Broad St
Nevada City, CA 95959-2213
(530)265-4415 (800)916-3662 Fax:(530)265-4416
Internet: www.emmanevadahouse.com
E-mail: mail@emmanevadahouse.com

Circa 1856. The childhood home of 19th-century opera star Emma Nevada now serves as an attractive Queen Anne Victorian inn. English roses line the white picket fence in front, and the forest-like back garden has a small stream with benches. The Empress' Chamber is the most romantic room with ivory Italian linens atop a French antique bed, a bay window and a massive French armoire. Some rooms have whirlpool baths and TV. Guests enjoy relaxing in the hexagonal sunroom and on the inn's wrap-around porches. Empire Mine State Historic Park is nearby.
Innkeeper(s): Colleen Carroll. $130-200. 6 rooms with PB, 2 with FP. Breakfast and afternoon tea included in rates. Types of meals: Full bkfst and early coffee/tea. Beds: Q. Reading lamp, desk, clawfoot and Jacuzzi tubs in room. Air conditioning. Fax, library, parlor games, telephone and fireplace on premises. Antiquing, downhill skiing, fishing, live theater, parks, shopping and water sports nearby.
Location: City, country, mountains, ocean community, waterfront. Town in foothills.
Publicity: *Country Inns, Gold Rush Scene, Sacramento Focus, The Union, Los Angeles Times, San Jose Mercury News, Sacramento Bee and Karen Browns.*

"A delightful experience: such airiness and hospitality in the midst of so much history. We were fascinated by the detail and the faithfulness of the restoration. This house is a quiet solace for city-weary travelers. There's a grace here."
Certificate may be used: Jan. 2 to April 30, Monday-Thursday, no holidays.

The Red Castle Inn Historic Lodgings

109 Prospect St
Nevada City, CA 95959-2831
(530)265-5135 (800)761-4766
Internet: www.historic-lodgings.com

Circa 1860. The Smithsonian has lauded the restoration of this four-story brick Gothic Revival known as "The Castle" by townsfolk. Its roof is laced with wooden icicles and the balconies are adorned with gingerbread. Within, there are intricate moldings, antiques, Victorian wallpapers, canopy beds and decorative wood stoves. Verandas provide views of the historic city through cedar, chestnut and walnut trees, and of terraced gardens with a fountain pond. A French chef prepares the inn's creative breakfasts.

Innkeeper(s): Conley & Mary Louise Weaver. $110-165. 7 rooms with PB, 3 suites. Breakfast and afternoon tea included in rates. Types of meals: Full gourmet bkfst and early coffee/tea. Beds: QD. Reading lamp, clock radio, turn-down service and desk in room. Air conditioning. Library, parlor games, telephone, phone upon request and private parking on premises. Antiquing, cross-country skiing, downhill skiing, fishing, live theater, parks, shopping and water sports nearby.
Location: City, mountains.
Publicity: *Sunset, Gourmet, Northern California Home & Garden, Sacramento Bee, Los Angeles Times, Travel Holiday, Victorian Homes, Innsider, U.S. News & World Report, USAir, McCalls, New York Times, Brides, San Francisco Focus and Motorland.*

"The Red Castle Inn would top my list of places to stay. Nothing else quite compares with it."—Gourmet
Certificate may be used: Sunday through Thursday, April 1-Aug. 31 except Easter week, Memorial Day and town special events; anyday Jan. 1-March 31 except holidays and town events. Saturdays may only be booked 3 days in advance.

Nice   F4

Featherbed Railroad Company B&B
2870 Lakeshore Blvd, PO Box 4016
Nice, CA 95464
(707)274-4434 (800)966-6322
Internet: featherbedrailroad.com
E-mail: rooms@featherbedrailroad.com

Circa 1940. Located on five acres on Clear Lake, this unusual inn features guest rooms in nine luxuriously renovated, painted and papered cabooses. Each has its own feather bed and private bath, most have Jacuzzi tubs for two. The Southern Pacific cabooses have a bay window alcove, while those from the Santa Fe feature small cupolas.
Innkeeper(s): Lorraine Bassignani. $102-180. 9 rooms with PB. Breakfast included in rates. Types of meals: Full bkfst. Beds: QDT. Cable TV and VCR in room. TV and spa on premises.
Publicity: *Santa Rosa Press Democrat, Fairfield Daily Republic, London Times, Travel & Leisure and Bay Area Back Roads.*
Certificate may be used: Sunday-Thursday, Oct. 15-April 15.

Nipomo   M7

The Kaleidoscope Inn & Gardens
130 E Dana St
Nipomo, CA 93444
(805)929-5444 (866)504-5444 Fax:(805)929-5440
Internet: www.kaleidoscopeinn.com
E-mail: info@kaleidoscopeinn.com

Circa 1887. Romantic and historic, this splendidly restored Victorian home is ocean close on the Central Coast. Built entirely from redwood in 1887, the original gingerbread, moon and sun detailing reflect its architectural heritage. Spacious guest bedrooms with stained-glass windows and 14-foot ceilings feature many luxuries. CD players, robes, hair dryers, down comforters, quilts, and private baths are delightful pleasures. Wake up to a fabulous gourmet breakfast. Roam the acre of lush gardens before touring nearby Hearst Castle. Special packages are available. Local golf courses offer reduced playing fees. Outdoor weddings, receptions and special events are popular around the Heart Gazebo under

the lawn's shade trees. Dancing is enjoyed on the brick patio.
Innkeeper(s): Carolayne, Holley & Kevin Beauchamp. $125. 4 rooms with PB. Breakfast included in rates. Types of meals: Full bkfst. Beds: KQ. Reading lamp in room. TV, VCR, library, parlor games, telephone and fireplace on premises. Antiquing, fishing, golf, live theater, parks, shopping, water sports, Hearst Castle, wineries, missions, beaches, hiking, biking and spas nearby.
Location: Small town.
"Beautiful room, chocolates, fresh flowers, peaceful night's rest, great breakfast."
Certificate may be used: Monday through Thursday, year-round. Holidays excluded.

Pacific Grove   J5

Centrella B&B Inn
612 Central Ave
Pacific Grove, CA 93950-2611
(831)372-3372 (800)433-4732 Fax:(831)372-2036
Internet: www.centrellainn.com
E-mail: concierge@innsbythesea.com

Circa 1889. Pacific Grove was founded as a Methodist resort in 1875, and this home, built just after the town's incorporation, was billed by a local newspaper as, "the largest, most commodious and pleasantly located boarding house in the Grove." Many a guest is still sure to agree. The rooms are well-appointed in a comfortable, Victorian style. Six guest rooms include fireplaces. The Garden Room has a private entrance, fireplace, wet bar, Jacuzzi tub and a canopy bed topped with designer

linens. Freshly baked croissants or pastries and made-to-order waffles are common fare at the inn's continental buffet breakfast. The inn is within walking distance of the Monterey Bay Aquarium, the beach and many Pacific Grove shops.
Innkeeper(s): Stephen Koski. $119-279. 26 rooms with PB, 6 with FP, 2 suites and 5 cottages. Breakfast and snacks/refreshments included in rates. Types of meals: Cont plus. Beds: KQT. Reading lamp and telephone in room. VCR, fax, copier, fireplace and TVs upon request on premises. Antiquing, golf, parks and water sports nearby.
Location: City.
Publicity: *Country Inns, New York Times and San Francisco Examiner.*
"I was ecstatic at the charm that the Centrella has been offering travelers for years and hopefully hundreds of years to come. The bed—perfect! I am forever enthralled by the old beauty and will remember this forever!"
Certificate may be used: Sunday-Thursday excluding July, August, holiday and special events.

Gatehouse Inn
225 Central Ave
Pacific Grove, CA 93950-3017
(831)649-8436 (800)753-1881 Fax:(831)648-8044
Internet: www.gatehouse-inn.com
E-mail: info@gatehouse-inn.com

Circa 1884. This Italianate Victorian seaside inn is just a block from the Monterey Bay. The inn is decorated with Victorian and 20th-century antiques and touches of Art Deco. Guest rooms feature fireplaces, clawfoot tubs and down comforters. Some rooms have ocean views. The dining room boasts opulent Bradbury & Bradbury Victorian wallpapers as do some of the guest rooms.

Afternoon hors d'oeuvres, wine and tea are served. The refrigerator is stocked for snacking.

$135-220. 9 rooms with PB, 6 with FP. Breakfast, afternoon tea and snacks/refreshments included in rates. Beds: KQT. Reading lamp, clock radio, telephone and turn-down service in room. Fax, copier, parlor games and fireplace on premises. Antiquing, fishing, live theater, parks, shopping and water sports nearby.

Location: Ocean community.

Publicity: *San Francisco Chronicle, Monterey Herald, Time, Newsweek, Inland Empire and Bon Appetit.*

"Thank you for spoiling us."

Certificate may be used: Anytime, November-April, subject to availability.

Gosby House Inn

PO Box 3073
Monterey, CA 93942-3073
(831)375-1287 (800)527-8828 Fax:(831)655-9621
Internet: www.foursisters.com/inns/gosbyhouseinn.html
E-mail: info@foursisters.com

Circa 1887. Built as an upscale Victorian inn for those visiting the old Methodist retreat, this sunny yellow mansion features an abundance of gables, turrets and bays. During renovation the innkeeper slept in all the rooms to determine just what antiques were needed and how the beds should be situated. Eleven of the romantic rooms include fireplaces and many offer canopy beds. The Carriage House rooms include fireplaces, decks and spa tubs. Gosby House, which has been open to guests for more than a century, is in the National Register. There is a $20 fee for an additional guest in room, except for children less than 5 years old. Gosby House is one of the Four Sisters Inns. The Monterey Bay Aquarium is nearby.

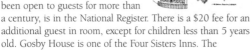

Innkeeper(s): Kalena Mittelman. $95-185. 22 rooms with PB, 11 with FP. Breakfast, afternoon tea, hors d'oeuvres and wine included in rates. Types of meals: Full bkfst and early coffee/tea. Telephone, turn-down service, hot tub/spa, bath robes, newspaper and eight with TV in room. TV, fax, copier, bicycles and fireplace on premises. Handicap access. Antiquing, shopping and Monterey Bay Aquarium nearby.

Publicity: *San Francisco Chronicle, Oregonian, Los Angeles Times and Travel & Leisure.*

Certificate may be used: November-March, Sunday-Thursday, certain rooms excluded. Based on promotional discount availability and excludes holidays & special event periods.

Green Gables Inn

PO Box 3073
Monterey, CA 93942-3073
(831)375-2095 (800)722-1774 Fax:(831)375-5437
Internet: www.foursisters.com/inns/greengablesinn.html
E-mail: info@foursisters.com

Circa 1888. This half-timbered Queen Anne Victorian appears as a fantasy of gables overlooking spectacular Monterey Bay. The parlor has stained-glass panels framing the fireplace and bay windows looking out to the sea. A favorite focal point is an antique carousel horse. Most of the guest rooms have panoramic views of the ocean, fireplaces, gleaming woodwork, soft quilts and teddy bears, and four rooms have spa tubs. Across the street is the Monterey Bay

paved oceanfront cycling path. (Mountain bikes may be borrowed from the inn.) There is a $20 fee for an additional guest in room, except for children less than 5 years old. Green Gables is one of the Four Sisters Inns.

Innkeeper(s): Lucia Root. $155-260. 11 rooms, 7 with PB, 6 with FP, 5 suites. Breakfast, afternoon tea, snacks/refreshments, hors d'oeuvres and wine included in rates. Types of meals: Full bkfst and early coffee/tea. Beds: KQD. Cable TV, VCR, reading lamp, stereo, ceiling fan, snack bar, clock radio, telephone, turn-down service, hot tub/spa, terry robes and newspaper in room. Fax, copier, bicycles, library, parlor games, fireplace and afternoon wine and hors d'oeuvres on premises. Handicap access. Antiquing, art galleries, beach, bicycling, canoeing/kayaking, fishing, golf, hiking, horseback riding, live theater, museums, parks, shopping, tennis, water sports, wineries and aquarium nearby.

Location: Ocean community, waterfront.

Publicity: *Travel & Leisure and Country Living.*

Certificate may be used: December and January, Sunday-Thursday excluding certain rooms, holidays, special event periods and is based on promotional discount availability.

Inn at 213 Seventeen Mile Dr

213 Seventeen Mile Dr
Pacific Grove, CA 93950-2400
(831)642-9514 (800)526-5666 Fax:(831)642-9546
Internet: www.innat17.com
E-mail: innkeeper@innat17.com

Circa 1925. The only challenging part of a visit to this 1920s craftsman-style house is figuring out where the deep blue sea ends and clear skies begin. Located in the heart of the Monterey Peninsula, this two-story, three-building inn offers sea or garden views from the main house, while you will find rustic ambiance, surrounded by oak and redwood trees, in the cottage and redwood chalet rooms. Relax in the spa beneath the tall trees in the gardens, which are often visited by deer and monarch butterflies, or enjoy a glass of champagne while observing Koi in the fountain ponds. Or, spend time in the wood-paneled dining, sitting and reading rooms while enjoying complimentary hors d'oeuvres and planning a day full of activities.

Innkeeper(s): Ozzy and Eva. $145-240. 14 rooms with PB and 1 cottage. Breakfast and snacks/refreshments included in rates. Types of meals: Full gourmet bkfst and veg bkfst. Beds: KQ. Data port, cable TV, refrigerator, clock radio and telephone in room. VCR, fax, copier, spa, library, parlor games and fireplace on premises. Handicap access. Antiquing, art galleries, beach, bicycling, canoeing/kayaking, fishing, golf, hiking, live theater, museums, parks, shopping, sporting events, tennis, water sports, wineries, Monterey Bay Aquarium and The Monarch Butterfly Sanctuary nearby.

Location: Ocean community.

Certificate may be used: Nov. 1 to June 1, Sunday-Thursday, except holidays, special events.

Martine Inn

PO Box 330
Pacific Grove, CA 93950-0232
(831)373-3388 (800)852-5588 Fax:(831)373-3896
Internet: www.martineinn.com
E-mail: don@martineinn.com

Circa 1899. This turn-of-the-century oceanfront manor sits atop a jagged cliff overlooking the coastline of Monterey Bay. Bedrooms are furnished with antiques, and each room contains a fresh rose and a silver Victorian bridal basket filled with fresh fruit. Thirteen rooms also boast fireplaces. Some of the museum-quality antiques were exhibited in the 1893 Chicago World's Fair. Other bedroom sets include furniture that belonged to Edith Head, and there is an 1860 Chippendale

Revival four-poster bed with a canopy and side curtains. Innkeeper Don Martine has a collection of old MGs, five on display for guests. Twilight wine and hors d'oeuvres are served, and chocolates accompany evening turndown service. The inn is a beautiful spot for romantic getaways and weddings.

Innkeeper(s): Don Martine. $139-359. 24 rooms with PB, 12 with FP and 6 conference rooms. Breakfast, snacks/refreshments, hors d'oeuvres and wine included in rates. Types of meals: Full gourmet bkfst, early coffee/tea, afternoon tea and dinner. Beds: KQD. Reading lamp, refrigerator, clock radio, telephone, turn-down service, desk and with 48-hour notice dinner is available in room. TV, fax, copier, spa, library, parlor games, fireplace, evening wine and DSL Internet on premises. Handicap access. Antiquing, art galleries, beach, bicycling, canoeing/kayaking, fishing, golf, hiking, horseback riding, live theater, museums, parks, shopping, sporting events, tennis, water sports, wineries, Monterey Bay Aquarium and Cannery Row nearby.

Location: Ocean community, waterfront.

Publicity: *Sunday Oregonian, Bon Appetit, Vacations APAC and Fresno Bee.*

"Wonderful, can't wait to return."

Certificate may be used: Anytime, November-April, subject to availability. No on Valentines and between Christmas and New Years.

Old St. Angela Inn

321 Central Ave
Pacific Grove, CA 93950-2934
(831)372-3246 (800)748-6306 Fax:(831)372-8560
Internet: www.sueandlewinns.com
E-mail: lew@redshift.com

Circa 1910. This Cape-style inn once served as a rectory then a convent. Guest rooms are decorated with period antiques. Three rooms include a fireplace, and two offer a cast-iron stove. Six rooms have a whirlpool tub. Breakfasts are served in a glass solarium. The ocean is a block away and it's just a short walk to the aquarium or fisherman's wharf.

Innkeeper(s): Lewis Shaefer & Susan Kuslis. $110-225. 9 rooms with PB. Breakfast, afternoon tea and snacks/refreshments included in rates. Types of meals: Full gourmet bkfst and early coffee/tea. Beds: KQT. Reading lamp, refrigerator, telephone and hot tub/spa in room. Fax, spa, parlor games and fireplace on premises. Antiquing, fishing, live theater, parks, shopping and water sports nearby.

Location: City, ocean community.

Publicity: *Best Places to Kiss.*

"Outstanding inn and outstanding hospitality."

Certificate may be used: Anytime, November-April, subject to availability.

Palm Springs   O12

Casa Cody Country Inn

175 S Cahuilla Rd
Palm Springs, CA 92262-6331
(760)320-9346 (800)231-2639 Fax:(760)325-8610
Internet: www.casacody.com
E-mail: casacody@aol.com

Circa 1910. Casa Cody, built by a relative of Wild Bill Cody and situated in the heart of Palm Springs, is the town's oldest continuously operating inn. The San Jacinto Mountains provide a scenic background for the tree-shaded spa, the pink and purple bougainvillea and the blue waters of the inn's two swimming pools. Each suite has a small kitchen and features terra cotta and turquoise  Southwestern decor. Several have wood-burning fireplaces. There are Mexican pavers, French doors and private patios. The area offers many activities, including museums, a heritage cen-

ter, boutiques, a botanical garden, horseback riding and golf.

Innkeeper(s): Elissa Goforth. $59-229. 23 rooms, 24 with PB, 10 with FP, 8 suites and 2 cottages. Breakfast included in rates. Types of meals: Cont plus. Beds: KQT. Cable TV, reading lamp, refrigerator, ceiling fan, telephone, desk, hot tub/spa and kitchen in room. Air conditioning. TV, fax, copier, spa and swimming on premises. Antiquing, bicycling, live theater, hiking, horseback riding, tennis, golf, ballooning and polo nearby.

Location: Heart of village.

Publicity: *New York Times, Washington Post, Los Angeles Times, San Diego Union Tribune, Seattle Times, Portland Oregonian, Los Angeles, San Diego Magazine, Pacific Northwest Magazine, Sunset, Westways, Alaska Airlines Magazine and Huel Howser California Gold.*

"Outstanding ambiance, friendly relaxed atmosphere."

Certificate may be used: May 1 to Dec. 21, Sunday through Thursday for any large studio or one-bedroom suite, except holidays.

Sakura, Japanese B&B Inn

1677 N Via Miraleste at Vista Chino
Palm Springs, CA 92262
(760)327-0705 (800)200-0705 Fax:(760)327-6847
Internet: www.travelbase.com/destination/palm-spring/sakura
E-mail: sakurajbb@aol.com

Circa 1945. An authentic Japanese experience awaits guests of this private home, distinctively decorated with Japanese artwork and antique kimonos. Guests are encouraged to leave their shoes at the door, grab kimonos and slippers and discover what real relaxation is all about. Futon beds, and in-room refrigerators and microwaves are provided. Guests may choose either American or Japanese breakfasts, and Japanese or vegetarian dinners also are available. The Palm Springs area is home to more than 100 golf courses and hosts annual world-class golf and tennis charity events. A favorite place for celebrity watching, the area also is the Western polo capital and offers the famous 9,000-foot aerial tram ride that climbs through several temperature zones. There are cycling trails, theater, horseback riding in the canyons and fine dining, skiing and antiquing. During the summer months, the innkeepers conduct tours in Japan.

Innkeeper(s): George & Fumiko Cebra. $45-90. 3 rooms, 2 with PB, 1 suite. Breakfast included in rates. Types of meals: Full bkfst, early coffee/tea, picnic lunch, afternoon tea and dinner. Beds: Q. Amusement parks, antiquing, cross-country skiing, fishing, live theater, parks and shopping nearby.

Location: City, mountains. California desert.

Certificate may be used: Anytime, Sunday-Thursday.

Palo Alto   I4

Adella Villa B&B

122 Atherton Ave.
Palo Alto, CA 94027-4021
(650)321-5195 Fax:(650)325-5121
Internet: www.adellavilla.com
E-mail: tricia@best.com

Circa 1923. This Italian villa is located in an area of one-acre estates five minutes from Stanford University. One guest room features a whirlpool tub; four guest rooms have showers. The music room boasts a 1920 mahogany Steinway grand piano. There is a seasonal swimming pool set amid manicured gardens.

Innkeeper(s): Tricia Young. $115-165. 5 rooms with PB. Breakfast, afternoon tea and snacks/refreshments included in rates. Types of meals: Full gourmet bkfst and early coffee/tea. Beds: KQ. Modem hookup, cable TV, VCR, reading lamp, stereo, clock radio, telephone, desk and DSL in room. Fax, copier, swimming, library, fireplace, laundry facility and DVD on premises.

Amusement parks, antiquing, art galleries, beach, bicycling, golf, live theater, museums, parks, shopping, sporting events, tennis and wineries nearby.
Location: City. Suburb of San Francisco.
Publicity: *L.A. Times- Reader's Choice.*

"This place is as wonderful, gracious and beautiful as the people who own it!"
Certificate may be used: Thursday, Friday, Saturday and Sunday nights only, excluding graduation weekend & holiday weekends.

Pauma Valley   P12

Cupid's Castle B&B

PO Box 580
Pauma Valley, CA 92061
(760)742-3306 Fax:(760)742-0279
Internet: www.cupidscastlebandb.com
E-mail: cupidscastle@earthlink.net

Circa 1995. Five acres of gardens with fountains, waterfalls and a fragrant lemon orchard surround this four-story castle. A fairy grotto garden with willow love seat and gazebos is a popular spot for weddings and anniversaries. Inside the B&B, cupids from the innkeeper's collection can be spotted. Romantic guest bedrooms feature two-person Jacuzzi tubs, canopy beds, VCRs and private balconies. A full breakfast is served daily. Arrangements can be made for a special dinner prepared with grilled salmon, New York steak and homemade cheesecake. Palomar Mountain and observatory, wineries and five casinos are nearby. Try hot-air ballooning, cycling or golf.
Innkeeper(s): Ted & Connie Vlasis. $200-275. 4 suites. Breakfast and snacks/refreshments included in rates. Types of meals: Full gourmet bkfst, early coffee/tea and dinner. Beds: K. Modem hook-up, cable TV, VCR, reading lamp, stereo, refrigerator, ceiling fan, clock radio, coffeemaker, desk, hot tub/spa and fireplace in room. Central air. Fax, copier, spa, library, parlor games, fireplace, gift shop and happy hour on premises. Handicap access. Amusement parks, antiquing, art galleries, beach, bicycling, fishing, golf, hiking, horseback riding, live theater, museums, parks, shopping, wineries and casinos nearby.
Location: Country, mountains. Farm.
Publicity: *Featured on San Diego T.V. News, San Diego Hideaways and Voted Most Romantic by Arlington's Bed and Breakfast Journal.*
Certificate may be used: Monday through Friday, Jan. 30 to Dec. 14.

Placerville   G7

Shafsky House B&B Inn

2942 Coloma St
Placerville, CA 95667
(530)642-2776 Fax:(503)642-2109
Internet: www.shafsky.com
E-mail: stay@shafsky.com

Circa 1902. Gold Country hospitality is offered at this Queen Anne Victorian bed and breakfast located just a stroll to the historic district and the shops of Old Hangtown. Enjoy a welcome snack and refreshments in the elegant living room. Pleasantly decorated guest bedrooms are furnished with antiques and offer individually controlled heat and air conditioning as well as feather beds and goosedown comforters during winter. The two-room Lighthouse Suite also boasts a sitting room for a private breakfast. Arrangements can be made for special occasions, or a personalized bouquet of flowers.
Innkeeper(s): Rita Timewell and Stephanie Carlson. $115-145. 3 rooms with PB. Breakfast, snacks/refreshments and wine included in rates. Types of meals: Full bkfst, veg bkfst, early coffee/tea and hors d'oeuvres. Beds: KQ. Reading lamp, ceiling fan, clock radio, turn-down service, desk and wireless Internet in room. Air conditioning. VCR, fax, copier, library, parlor games, telephone, fireplace, gift shop, satellite TV, video library, games and guest refrigerator on premises. Limited handicap access. Antiquing, art galleries,

canoeing/kayaking, cross-country skiing, downhill skiing, fishing, golf, hiking, horseback riding, live theater, museums, parks, shopping, tennis, water sports, wineries, Apple Hill, Sutter's Mill, Gold Bug Mine, Gold Discovery Park and whitewater rafting nearby.
Location: City, country, mountains. Located a short stroll from historic Placerville, aka Old Hangtown.
Publicity: *Mountain Democrat, San Francisco Chronicle, KCRA, KNCI and KAHI.*
Certificate may be used: Anytime, subject to availability.

Point Reyes Station   H4

Carriage House

325 Mesa Rd, PO Box 1239
Point Reyes Station, CA 94956-1239
(415)663-8627 (800)613-8351
Internet: www.carriagehousebb.com
E-mail: felicity@carriagehousebb.com

Circa 1960. This remodeled inn boasts a view of Inverness Ridge. One guest room and two suites are furnished in antiques and folk art with a private parlor, television, VCR and a fireplace. Children are welcome and cribs and daybeds are available. Point Reyes National Seashore has 100 miles of trails for cycling, hiking or horseback riding. Breakfast items such as freshly squeezed juice, muffins and breads are stocked in the room, so guests may enjoy it at leisure.
Innkeeper(s): Felicity Kirsch. $145-180. 3 rooms with PB, 2 with FP, 2 suites. Breakfast included in rates. Types of meals: Cont plus. Beds: QT. Cable TV, VCR, reading lamp and refrigerator in room. TV, telephone and fireplace on premises. Antiquing, fishing, parks and shopping nearby.
Location: Rural.
"What a rejuvenating getaway. We loved it. The smells, sounds and scenery were wonderful."
Certificate may be used: Jan. 3-June 15, Monday-Thursday. No holiday weeks, October-December, Monday-Thursday.

The Tree House

PO Box 1075
Point Reyes Station, CA 94956-1075
(415)663-8720 (800)977-8720
Internet: www.treehousebnb.com
E-mail: treehousebnb@juno.com

Circa 1970. This homestay offers an outstanding view of Point Reyes Station from the deck and some of the guest rooms. The King's Room features a king-size waterbed while Queen Quarter boasts its own fireplace. A hot tub is tucked away in a cozy spot of the garden.
Innkeeper(s): Lisa Patsel. $125-165. 3 rooms with PB, 2 with FP, 1 suite. Breakfast included in rates. Types of meals: Cont plus. VCR, reading lamp, ceiling fan, clock radio and telephone in room. TV, spa, pet boarding and fireplace on premises. Antiquing, parks and shopping nearby.
Location: Mountains. Hiking.
Certificate may be used: Sunday through Thursday, January to Dec. 31 (no holidays or weekends).

Ridgecrest   L11

BevLen Haus Bed & Breakfast

809 N Sanders St
Ridgecrest, CA 93555-3529
(760)375-1988 (800)375-1989 Fax:(760)375-6871
E-mail: BLH_B&B@iwvisp.com

Circa 1950. Country charm abounds at this bed & breakfast. Two antique cookstoves warm the home, one in the kitchen and another in the sitting room. The garden room includes a Franklin stove. Each of the three guest rooms features country decor with

quilt-topped beds. The home is near museums and outdoor attractions. Death Valley National Park is a popular day trip.
Innkeeper(s): Beverly & Leonard de Geus. $55-75. 3 rooms with PB. Breakfast included in rates. Types of meals: Full bkfst. Beds: QDT. Reading lamp, ceiling fan and desk in room. Central air. TV, fax, copier, spa, telephone and fireplace on premises. Antiquing, bicycling, fishing, golf, hiking, museums, parks, shopping and tennis nearby.
Location: Northern Mojave Desert.
Certificate may be used: Anytime, subject to availability.

Sacramento   G6

Amber House

1315 22nd St
Sacramento, CA 95816-5717
(916)444-8085 (800)755-6526 Fax:(916)552-6529
Internet: www.amberhouse.com
E-mail: info@amberhouse.com

Circa 1905. These three historic homes on the city's Historic Preservation Register are in a neighborhood of fine historic homes eight blocks from the capitol. Each room is named for a famous poet, artist or composer and features stained glass,

English antiques, and amenities such as bath robes and fresh flowers. Ask about the Van Gogh Room where you can soak in the heart-shaped Jacuzzi tub-for-two or

enjoy one of the rooms with marble baths and Jacuzzi tubs in either the adjacent 1913 Mediterranean mansion or the 1895 Colonial Revival. A gourmet breakfast can be served in your room or in the dining room at a time you request.
$149-299. 14 rooms with PB, 3 with FP and 1 conference room. Breakfast included in rates. Types of meals: Full gourmet bkfst and early coffee/tea. Beds: KQ. Cable TV, VCR, reading lamp, CD player, refrigerator, clock radio, telephone, turn-down service, desk, hot tub/spa, voice mail, hair dryer, iron/ironing board and breakfast in room. Air conditioning. TV, fax, bicycles, library, parlor games and fireplace on premises. Antiquing, cross-country skiing, downhill skiing, fishing, live theater, parks, shopping and water sports nearby.
Location: City.
Publicity: *Travel & Leisure and Village Crier.*

"Your cordial hospitality, the relaxing atmosphere and delicious breakfast made our brief business/pleasure trip so much more enjoyable."
Certificate may be used: Anytime, subject to availability.

Saint Helena   G4

Spanish Villa

474 Glass Mountain Rd
Saint Helena, CA 94574-9669
(707)963-7483
E-mail: valleyinnkeeper@sbcglobal.net

Circa 1981. This contemporary Mission-style Spanish villa is nestled in a wooded valley in the Napa wine country, three miles from town. Rooms feature king-size beds and private baths with hand-painted sinks. A stay in a suite adds plantation shutters and a private balcony. A large sitting room and fireplace are favorite gathering spots. The quiet, country roads found in the area are popular for biking, jogging or walking. Don't miss the chance to visit nearby Calistoga, with its hang gliding and famous mud baths.
Innkeeper(s): Roy & Barbie Bissember. $155-275. 3 rooms with PB. Breakfast included in rates. Types of meals: Early coffee/tea. Beds: K. Reading

lamp in room. VCR, telephone and fireplace on premises. Amusement parks, antiquing, fishing, live theater, parks, shopping and water sports nearby.
Location: Country.
Certificate may be used: December, January, February, March, Sunday-Thursday. Please inquire about other months.

San Andreas   H7

The Robin's Nest

PO Box 1408
San Andreas, CA 95249-1408
(209)754-1076 (888)214-9202 Fax:(209)754-3975
Internet: www.robinest.com
E-mail: info@robinest.com

Circa 1895. Expect to be pampered from the moment you walk through the door at this three-story Queen Anne Victorian. Guests are made to feel at home, and treated to an elegant, gourmet breakfast. The late 19th-century gem includes many fine architectural features, including eight-foot round windows, 12-foot ceilings on the first floor and gabled ceilings with roof windows on the second floor. Antiques decorate the guest rooms, with pieces such as a four-poster, step-up bed. One bathroom includes an original seven-foot bathtub. The grounds boast century-old fruit trees, grapevines, a brick well, windmill and the more modern addition of a hot spa.
Innkeeper(s): Karen & Bill Konietzny. $85-150. 9 rooms, 7 with PB, 1 suite. Breakfast, afternoon tea and snacks/refreshments included in rates. Types of meals: Full gourmet bkfst, veg bkfst and early coffee/tea. Beds: KQDT. Modem hook-up, cable TV, reading lamp, refrigerator, ceiling fan, clock radio, telephone, coffeemaker and desk in room. Central air. VCR, fax, copier, spa, library, parlor games, fireplace, laundry facility, outdoor kitchen, redwood deck and personal barbecues on premises. Limited handicap access. Antiquing, canoeing/kayaking, cross-country skiing, downhill skiing, fishing, golf, hiking, live theater, museums, parks, shopping, tennis, water sports, wineries, 3 caverns featuring walking, rappelling, spelunking and rafting nearby.
Location: Mountains. Gold-country foothills at 1,000 ft. elevations.
Publicity: *San Francisco Chronicle (featured twice in 1999).*

"An excellent job of making guests feel at home."
Certificate may be used: Jan. 1 to Dec. 31, Sunday through Thursday.

San Diego   Q12

A Victorian Heritage Park Inn

2470 Heritage Park Row
San Diego, CA 92110-2803
(619)299-6832 (800)995-2470 Fax:(619)299-9465
Internet: www.heritageparkinn.com
E-mail: innkeeper@heritageparkinn.com

Circa 1889. Situated on a seven-acre Victorian park in the heart of Old Town, this inn is two of seven preserved classic structures. The main house offers a variety of beautifully appointed guest rooms, decked in traditional Victorian furnishings and decor. The opulent Manor Suite includes two bedrooms, a Jacuzzi tub and sitting room. Several rooms offer ocean views, and guest also can see the nightly fireworks show at nearby Sea World. A collection of classic movies is available, and a different movie is

shown each night in the inn's parlor. Guests are treated to a light afternoon tea, and breakfast is served on fine china on candlelit tables. The home is within walking distance to the many sites, shops and restaurants in the historic Old Town.

Innkeeper(s): Nancy & Charles Helsper. $125-250. 12 rooms with PB, 1 suite and 1 conference room. Breakfast and afternoon tea included in rates. Types of meals: Full gourmet bkfst and early coffee/tea. Beds: KQT. Reading lamp, clock radio, telephone, turn-down service and desk in room. Air conditioning. VCR, fax, copier, parlor games and fireplace on premises. Antiquing, fishing, live theater, parks, shopping, sporting events, water sports, San Diego Zoo and Tijuana nearby.

Location: City.

Publicity: *Los Angeles Herald Examiner, Innsider, Los Angeles Times, Orange County Register, San Diego Union, In-Flight, Glamour and Country Inns.*

"A beautiful step back in time. Peaceful and gracious."

Certificate may be used: Call innkeeper for dates. Based on availability.

San Francisco   H4

Archbishop's Mansion

1000 Fulton St (at Steiner)
San Francisco, CA 94117-1608
(415)563-7872 (800)543-5820 Fax:(415)885-3193
Internet: www.sftrips.com
E-mail: abm@jdvhospitality.com

Circa 1904. This French Empire-style manor was built for the Archbishop of San Francisco. It is designated as a San Francisco historic landmark. The grand stairway features redwood paneling, Corinthian columns and a stained-glass dome. The parlor has a hand-painted ceiling. Each of the guest rooms is named for an opera. Rooms have antiques, Victorian window treatments and embroidered linens. Continental breakfast is served in the dining room, and guests also are treated to a complimentary wine and cheese reception each night.

Innkeeper(s): Greg Horner. $165-425. 15 rooms with PB, 11 with FP, 5 suites. Breakfast included in rates. Types of meals: Cont. Beds: KQ. Cable TV, VCR, reading lamp, clock radio, telephone, turn-down service, desk and hot tub/spa in room. Fax, copier and fireplace on premises. Parks nearby.

Location: City.

Publicity: *Travel-Holiday, Travel & Leisure and Country Inns.*

"The ultimate, romantic honeymoon spot."

Certificate may be used: Anytime, Sunday-Thursday, holidays excluded.

The Inn San Francisco

943 South Van Ness Ave
San Francisco, CA 94110-2613
(415)641-0188 (800)359-0913 Fax:(415)641-1701
Internet: www.innsf.com
E-mail: innkeeper@innsf.com

Circa 1872. Built on one of San Francisco's earliest "Mansion Rows," this 21-room Italianate Victorian is located near the civic and convention centers, close to Mission Dolores. Antiques, marble fireplaces and Oriental rugs decorate the opulent grand double parlors. Most rooms have featherbeds, Victorian wallcoverings and desks, while deluxe rooms offer private spas, fireplaces or bay windows. There is a rooftop deck with a 360-degree view of San Francisco. Complimentary beverages are always available. The inn is close to the opera, symphony, theaters, Mission Dolores, gift and jewelry centers and antique shopping.

Innkeeper(s): Marty Neely & Connie Wu. $95-265.

21 rooms, 19 with PB, 3 with FP, 3 suites and 1 cottage. Breakfast included in rates. Types of meals: Full bkfst and afternoon tea. Beds: QD. TV, reading lamp, refrigerator, clock radio, telephone, desk, hot tub/spa, one suite with redwood hot tub, flowers and truffles in room. Fax, fireplace, garden, rooftop view sundeck and parlor on premises.

Location: City.

Publicity: *Innsider, Sunset Magazine, San Francisco Chronicle and American Airlines Magazine.*

"Breakfast; marvelous. The best B&B we've visited. We were made to feel like family."

Certificate may be used: Monday-Thursday, subject to availability, holidays excluded. Check with innkeeper for weekend night availability.

Marina Inn

PO Box 3073
Monterey, CA 93942
(415)928-1000 (800)274-1420 Fax:(415)928-5909
Internet: www.marinainn.com

Circa 1924. Near Fisherman's Wharf in the Marina District, this historic Victorian Painted Lady provides easy access to all the city sights and activities. Upon entering the elegant marble lobby of this classic four-story hotel, stress and cares are left outside. Warm and inviting guest bedrooms feature pine poster beds, floral wall coverings and plush comforters. Chocolates accompany the evening turndown service. Enjoy a continental breakfast each morning in the cozy sitting room. After a day of adventures and exploration, relax over a glass of sherry.

Innkeeper(s): Kelly Wuthrich. $65-135. 40 rooms with PB. Snacks/refreshments included in rates. Types of meals: Cont and early coffee/tea. Beds: KQT. Cable TV, reading lamp, stereo, clock radio and telephone in room. Antiquing, art galleries, beach, bicycling, golf, hiking, live theater, museums, parks, shopping, sporting events and tennis nearby.

Location: City.

Certificate may be used: Sunday-Thursday, November-April, excluding holidays, special events periods and based on availability.

Petite Auberge

863 Bush St
San Francisco, CA 94108-3312
(415)928-6000 (800)365-3004 Fax:(415)775-5717
Internet: www.petiteaubergesf.com
E-mail: petiteauberge@jdvhospitality.com

Circa 1917. An ornate baroque design with curved bay windows highlight this five-story hotel that has now been transformed into a French country inn. This Joie de Vivre property boasts antiques, fresh flowers and country accessories. Most guest bedrooms feature working fireplaces. Take a short walk to the Powell Street cable car. In the evenings, wine and cheese, sherry, tea, coffee and cake are served. There is an extra fee for an additional guest in room, except for children less than five years old.

Innkeeper(s): Karlene Holloman. $99-219. 26 rooms with PB, 17 with FP, 1 suite. Breakfast and afternoon tea included in rates. Types of meals: Full gourmet bkfst, early coffee/tea and wine. Beds: KQ. Cable TV, reading lamp, refrigerator, clock radio, telephone, turn-down service, fireplace and terry robes in room. Fax, copier and valet parking on premises. Handicap access. Antiquing, art galleries, beach, canoeing/kayaking, fishing, golf, hiking, live theater, parks, shopping, sporting events, tennis, wineries, historic sites, museums and cable nearby.

Location: City. Nob Hill, Union Square.

Publicity: *Travel & Leisure, Oregonian, Los Angeles Times and Brides.*

"Breakfast was great, and even better in bed!"

Certificate may be used: November-February, Sunday-Thursday, excluding holidays and special events.

White Swan Inn

845 Bush St
San Francisco, CA 94108-3300
(415)775-1755 (800)999-9570 Fax:(415)775-5717
Internet: www.whiteswaninnsf.com
E-mail: whiteswan@jdvhospitality.com

Circa 1915. This four-story inn is near Union Square and the Powell Street cable car. Beveled-glass doors open to a reception area with granite floors, an antique carousel horse and English artwork. Bay windows and a rear deck contribute to the feeling of an English garden inn. The guest rooms are decorated with bold English wallpapers and prints. All rooms have fireplaces. Turndown service and complimentary newspapers are included, and in the evenings wine, sherry, tea, coffee, cake and hors d'oeuvres are served. There is a $20 fee for an additional guest in room, except for children less than 5 years old.

Innkeeper(s): Karlene Holloman. $139-309. 26 rooms with PB, 26 with FP, 3 suites and 1 conference room. Breakfast and afternoon tea included in rates. Types of meals: Full gourmet bkfst, early coffee/tea, snacks/refreshments and wine. Beds: KQT. Data port, cable TV, reading lamp, refrigerator, clock radio, telephone, coffeemaker, turn-down service, desk, fireplace, terry robes, newspaper and complimentary beverages in room. Fax, copier, library, parlor games and wireless Internet on premises. Antiquing, art galleries, beach, canoeing/kayaking, fishing, golf, hiking, live theater, museums, parks, shopping, sporting events, tennis and wineries nearby.
Location: City.
Publicity: *Travel & Leisure, Victoria* and *Wine Spectator.*

"Wonderfully accommodating. Absolutely perfect."
Certificate may be used: December and January, Sunday-Thursday, excluding holidays and special events.

San Rafael   H4

Casa Soldavini

531 C St
San Rafael, CA 94901-3809
(415)454-3140 Fax:(415)454-3140
E-mail: dnloasis@msn.com

Circa 1932. The first Italian settlers in San Rafael built this home. Their grandchildren now own it and proudly hang pictures of their family. Grandfather Joseph, a wine maker, planned and planted what are now the lush gardens surrounding the home. The many Italian antiques throughout the house complement the Italian-style decor. A homemade breakfast is included, and snacks and beverages are served throughout the day.
Innkeeper(s): Linda Soldavini Cassidy. $95-135. 3 rooms, 1 with PB. Breakfast included in rates. Types of meals: Cont plus, afternoon tea and snacks/refreshments. Beds: Q. Cable TV, VCR, CD player, ceiling fan, snack bar, clock radio, telephone, coffeemaker, turn-down service and voice mail in room. Fax, copier, bicycles, pet boarding, parlor games and fireplace on premises. Amusement parks, antiquing, art galleries, beach, bicycling, canoeing/kayaking, fishing, golf, hiking, horseback riding, live theater, museums, parks, shopping, sporting events, tennis, water sports and wineries nearby.
Location: City.
Certificate may be used: Anytime, upon availability.

Santa Barbara   N8

Cheshire Cat Inn & Spa

36 W Valerio St
Santa Barbara, CA 93101-2524
(805)569-1610 Fax:(805)682-1876
Internet: www.cheshirecat.com
E-mail: cheshire@cheshirecat.com

Circa 1894. This elegant inn features three Queen Anne Victorians, a Coach House and three cottages surrounded by fountains, gazebos and lush flower gardens. The guest bedrooms and suites are furnished with English antiques, Laura Ashley fabrics and wallpapers or oak floors, pine furniture and down comforters. Some boast fireplaces, Jacuzzi tubs, private balconies, VCRs and refrigerators. Wedgewood china set in the formal dining room or brick patio enhances a delicious breakfast. Local wine and hors d'oeuvres are served in the evening. Spa facilities offer massage and body treatments.
Innkeeper(s): Amy Taylor. $169-400. 21 rooms with PB, 3 with FP, 3 with HT, 4 suites, 3 cottages and 1 conference room. Breakfast, hors d'oeuvres and wine included in rates. Types of meals: Full bkfst, early coffee/tea and room service. Beds: KQT. Modem hook-up, cable TV, VCR, reading lamp, refrigerator, ceiling fan, clock radio, telephone, hot tub/spa and fireplace in room. Air conditioning. Spa and spa facilities on premises. Antiquing, art galleries, beach, bicycling, canoeing/kayaking, fishing, golf, hiking, horseback riding, live theater, museums, parks, shopping, sporting events, tennis, water sports and wineries nearby.
Location: City.
Publicity: *Two on the Town, KABC, Los Angeles Times, Santa Barbara, American In Flight* and *Elmer Dills Recommends.*

"Romantic and quaint."
Certificate may be used: Anytime, subject to availability.

Glenborough Inn

1327 Bath St
Santa Barbara, CA 93101-3630
(805)966-0589 (800)962-0589 Fax:(805)564-8610
Internet: www.glenboroughinn.com
E-mail: santabarbara@glenboroughinn.com

Circa 1885. The Victorian and California Craftsman-style homes that comprise the Glenborough are located in the theatre and arts district. Antiques, rich wood trim and elegant fireplace suites with canopy beds are offered. Some rooms also have mini refrigerators or whirlpools tubs. There's always plenty of hospitality and an invitation to try the secluded garden hot tub. Homemade breakfasts, served in the privacy of your room, have been written up in Bon Appetit and Chocolatier. Bedtime cookies and beverages are served, as well. It's a three-block walk to restaurants, shops and the shuttle to the beach.
Innkeeper(s): Marlies Marburg. $110-325. 18 rooms with PB, 12 with FP and 6 cottages. Breakfast included in rates. Types of meals: Full bkfst. Beds: KQD. TV, reading lamp, ceiling fan, clock radio, telephone, desk, hot tub/spa, coffeemaker, robes and some with A/C and mini-fridge in room. Fax, spa, parlor games and fireplace on premises. Antiquing, fishing, live theater, parks, shopping, sporting events and water sports nearby.
Location: City.
Publicity: *Houston Post, Los Angeles Times* and *Pasadena Choice.*

"Only gracious service is offered at the Glenborough Inn."
Certificate may be used: October through May, Sunday-Thursday, except holidays.

The Old Yacht Club Inn

431 Corona Del Mar
Santa Barbara, CA 93103-3601
(805)962-1277 (800)676-1676 Fax:(805)962-3989
Internet: www.oldyachtclubinn.com
E-mail: info@oldyachtclubinn.com

Circa 1912. One block from famous East Beach, this California Craftsman house was the home of the Santa Barbara Yacht Club during the Roaring '20s. It was opened as Santa Barbara's first B&B and has become renowned for its gourmet food and superb hospitality.
Innkeeper(s): Eilene Bruce. $110-239. 12 rooms with PB and 1 conference room. Breakfast included in rates. Types of meals: Full gourmet bkfst, early coffee/tea and gourmet dinner. Beds: KQ. TV, reading lamp, telephone and hot tub/spa in room. Fax, copier, bicycles, fireplace, wine social, beach chairs and beach towels on premises. Antiquing, fishing, live theater, shopping, sporting events and water sports nearby.
Publicity: *Los Angeles, Valley, Bon Appetit and Gourmet.*

"One of Santa Barbara's better-kept culinary secrets."
Certificate may be used: November, December, January, February, Monday-Thursday evenings only. Weekend and holiday periods excluded. Reservations taken within two weeks of date requested.

The Orchid Inn

420 W Montecito St
Santa Barbara, CA 93101-3879
(805)965-2333 (877)722-3657 Fax:(805)962-4907
Internet: www.orchidinnatsb.com
E-mail: info@orchidinnatsb.com

Circa 1920. It's a short walk to the beach and harbor from this Victorian inn, which offers accommodations in the main house and adjacent carriage house. Guest rooms are decorat-

ed in period style with antiques. Brass beds, tapestry pillows, and fluffy comforters add a romantic touch. Several rooms include fireplaces, Jacuzzi tubs or private balconies.
Innkeeper(s): Pete Chiarenza, Edward Skolak. $125-250. 8 rooms with PB, 5 with FP, 2 suites and 1 conference room. Breakfast and wine included in rates. Types of meals: Full gourmet bkfst and veg bkfst. Beds: KQT. Cable TV, VCR, clock radio, telephone, desk, hot tub/spa, voice mail and fireplace in room. Air conditioning. Fax, copier, library and parlor games on premises. Antiquing, art galleries, beach, bicycling, canoeing/kayaking, golf, hiking, horseback riding, live theater, museums, parks, shopping, water sports, wineries and roller skating nearby.
Location: City, ocean community.
Publicity: *Los Angeles Times.*
Certificate may be used: Year-round, Sunday through Thursday, excluding holidays.

Prufrock's Garden Inn By The Beach

600 Linden Ave
Carpinteria, CA 93013-2040
(805)566-9696 (877)837-6257 Fax:(805)566-9404
Internet: www.prufrocks.com
E-mail: innkeepers@prufrocks.com

Circa 1904. Tucked between a mountain wilderness, flower fields and an ocean, this inn is located one block from State Beach Park and 10 minutes from the City Center. Santa Barbara Independent named it a "Most Romantic Getaway," and the L.A. Times voted it a "Readers' Favorite." Other recognitions include being pictured in Land's End catalog and a "Community Beautiful" award. Explore Salt Marsh Park and

waterfront bluffs, or visit specialty shops and cafes. The inn is close to an Amtrak station. A quote from The Love Song of J. Alfred Prufrock, by TS Eliot is lived out at this inn: "Time for you and time for me, before the taking of a toast and tea."
Innkeeper(s): Judy & Jim Halvorsen. $179-299. 7 rooms, 5 with PB. Breakfast, afternoon tea and snacks/refreshments included in rates. Types of meals: Full bkfst and early coffee/tea. Beds: Q. Data port, cable TV, VCR, reading lamp, ceiling fan, clock radio, desk, hot tub/spa, fireplace, sitting area, daybeds and high-speed Internet in room. Fax, copier, spa, library, parlor games, telephone and gardens on premises. Handicap access. Antiquing, beach, bicycling, fishing, hiking, live theater, parks, shopping, sporting events, wineries and tide pools nearby.
Location: Ocean community. Charming seaside town.
Publicity: *Santa Barbara Independent's "Most Romantic Getaway," Carpinteria's "Community Beautification" award, pictured in Land's End catalog, L.A. Times ("Reader's favorite") and Sunset magazine.*
Certificate may be used: Oct. 1-June 30, Sunday-Thursday.

Secret Garden Inn and Cottages

1908 Bath St
Santa Barbara, CA 93101-2813
(805)687-2300 (800)676-1622 Fax:(805)687-4576
Internet: www.secretgarden.com
E-mail: garden@secretgarden.com

Circa 1908. The main house and adjacent cottages surround the gardens and are decorated in American and English-Country style. The Hummingbird is a large cottage guest room with a queen-size white iron bed and a private deck with a hot tub for your exclusive use. The two suites have private outdoor hot tubs. Wine and light hors d'oeuvres are served in the late afternoon, and hot apple cider is served every evening.
Innkeeper(s): Dominique Hannaux. $121-231. 11 rooms with PB, 1 with FP, 5 with HT, 3 suites and 9 cottages. Breakfast and snacks/refreshments included in rates. Types of meals: Full gourmet bkfst and early coffee/tea. Beds: KQ. TV, reading lamp, refrigerator, clock radio and hot tub/spa in room. Fax, copier, spa, parlor games, telephone and wine and cheese on premises. Antiquing, art galleries, beach, bicycling, canoeing/kayaking, fishing, golf, hiking, live theater, museums, parks, shopping, water sports and wineries nearby.
Location: City.
Publicity: *Los Angeles Times, Santa Barbara and Independant.*

"A romantic little getaway retreat that neither of us will be able to forget. It was far from what we expected to find."
Certificate may be used: Jan. 1 to June 1 and Sept. 1-Dec. 17, Sunday-Thursday, excluding holidays.

The Upham Hotel & Country House

1404 De La Vina St
Santa Barbara, CA 93101-3027
(805)962-0058 (800)727-0876 Fax:(805)963-2825
Internet: www.uphamhotel.com
E-mail: upham.hotel@verizon.net

Circa 1871. Antiques and period furnishings decorate each of the inn's guest rooms and suites. The inn is the oldest continuously operating hostelry in Southern California. Situated on an acre of gardens in the center of downtown, it's within easy walk-

ing distance of restaurants, shops, art galleries and museums. The staff is happy to assist guests in discovering Santa Barbara's varied attractions. Garden cottage units feature porches or secluded patios and several have gas fireplaces.
Innkeeper(s): Jan Martin Winn. $175-410. 50 rooms with PB, 8 with FP, 4 suites, 3 cottages and 3 conference rooms. Breakfast included in rates. Types of meals: Cont plus, early coffee/tea and snacks/refreshments. Beds: KQ. Cable TV, reading lamp, ceiling fan, clock radio, telephone, desk and master

suite has hot tub/spa in room. Fax, copier and fireplace on premises. Antiquing, golf, live theater, parks, shopping and water sports nearby.
Location: City.
Publicity: *Los Angeles Times, Santa Barbara, Westways, Santa Barbara News-Press and Avenues.*

"Your hotel is truly a charm. Between the cozy gardens and the exquisitely comfortable appointments, The Upham is charm itself."
Certificate may be used: Sunday-Thursday, Jan. 2-Dec. 30.

Santa Cruz   J4

Pleasure Point Inn
PO Box 1825
Lewiston, ME 04241-1825
(831)469-6161 (877)557-2567
Internet: www.pleasurepointinn.com
E-mail: inquiries@pleasurepointinn.com

Circa 2001. Located in front of the popular Pleasure Point Surfing Beach, this oceanfront estate was completely remodeled recently. The modern Mediterranean-style architecture and design has an upscale appearance. Guest bedrooms all feature gas fireplaces, custom furniture, private patios and entrances. Some offer heated floor tiles and Jacuzzi tubs. Enjoy the sights and sounds of the sea from the large roof top deck overlooking Monterey Bay. Chaise lounges encourage soaking up the sun by day. A heater gas lamp placed near the outdoor dining tables provides warmth for cool evenings. Gaze at the stars while relaxing in the big hot tub. Capitola Village, only two miles away, offers shopping, dining, a sandy beach and nightly entertainment. Cruises can be arranged at the local yacht harbor.
Call for rates. 4 rooms with PB. Breakfast and snacks/refreshments included in rates. Types of meals: Cont plus. Beds: KQ. TV, reading lamp, refrigerator, clock radio, telephone, coffeemaker, fireplace and some with Jacuzzi tubs in room. Fireplace on premises. Amusement parks, antiquing, shopping and sporting events nearby.
Certificate may be used: Sunday-Wednesday from Jan. 10-March 31.

The Darling House-A B&B Inn By The Sea
314 W Cliff Dr
Santa Cruz, CA 95060-6145
(831)458-1958
Internet: www.darlinghouse.com
E-mail: ddarling@darlinghouse.com

Circa 1910. It's difficult to pick a room at this oceanside mansion. The Pacific Ocean Room features a fireplace and a wonderful ocean view. The Chinese Room might suit you with its silk-draped, hand-carved rosewood canopy wedding bed. Elegant oak, ebony, and walnut woodwork is enhanced by the antique decor of Tiffanys and Chippendales. Roses, beveled glass and libraries add to the atmosphere. Beyond the ocean-view veranda are landscaped gardens. Guests often walk to the wharf for dinner.
Innkeeper(s): Karen & Darrell Darling. $95-260. 8 rooms, 1 with PB, 2 with FP, 1 suite, 1 cottage and 1 conference room. Breakfast included in rates. Types of meals: Cont plus. Beds: KQDT. Modem hook-up, VCR, turn-down service, desk, innkeepers provide wake-up service, message service, clothes press, reservation service and TV on request in room. Fax, copier, library, parlor games, telephone and fireplace on premises. Limited handicap access. Amusement parks, antiquing, art galleries, beach, bicycling, canoeing/kayaking, fishing, golf, hiking, live theater, museums, parks, shopping, sporting events, tennis, water sports, wineries, Narrow Gauge Railway, Aquarium, Ocean Research, Shakespeare Festival in July, Begonia Festival, Cabrillo Music Festival, Jazz Festival, PGA Tournaments and International Ocean Sport Contests nearby.

Location: City, ocean community.
Publicity: *Modern Maturity, Pacific, New York Times, LA Times, Sacramento Bee Fresno, San Francisco Chronicle, Oakland Tribune, Santa Cruz Sentinel, Bay Guardian, San Jose Mercury News and Thrill (an ABC made-for-TV movie).*

"So pretty, so sorry to leave."
Certificate may be used: November-April, Sunday-Thursday, holidays excluded.

Santa Rosa   G4

Hotel La Rose
308 Wilson St
Santa Rosa, CA 95401
(707)579-3200 (800)LAROSE8 Fax:(707)579-3247
Internet: www.hotellarose.com
E-mail: reservations@hotellarose.com

Circa 1907. Built by prominent Italian stonemasons almost a century ago, this family-operated boutique hotel in the heart of Railroad Square features the ambiance of a bed and breakfast. A rooftop garden includes a relaxing hot tub. Stay in the renovated, historic Main Building or in the newer Carriage House. Guest bedrooms feature many upscale amenities and offer modern technology. Some of the marble and brass bathrooms have whirlpool tubs. Twenty rooms with a private patio or balcony surround the rose garden courtyard. Enjoy a European breakfast each morning. Located in the lobby, Josef's Restaurant & Bar offers traditional French Continental cuisine for lunch or dinner. Stroll to the downtown business district, the Santa Rosa Plaza shopping center and many antique and specialty stores.
Innkeeper(s): Brian Larsen GM. Call for rates. 49 rooms. Beds: QT. Data port, telephone, desk, voice mail, high-speed wireless Internet, large screen cable TV, marble and brass bathrooms and some with whirlpool tubs in room. Air conditioning. Roof garden has hot tub on premises. Antiquing, art galleries, golf, hiking, live theater, museums, parks, shopping and wineries nearby.
Certificate may be used: Anytime, Sunday-Thursday, based on availability.

Sebastopol   G4

Vine Hill Inn
3949 Vine Hill Rd
Sebastopol, CA 95472
(707)823-8832 Fax:(707)824-1045
Internet: www.vine-hill-inn.com
E-mail: innkeeper@vine-hill-inn.com

Circa 1897. Situated between picturesque apple orchards and vineyards, this Victorian farmhouse is an eclectic country-style bed & breakfast. An intimate ambiance is imparted, with gathering places to play games or converse. Spacious guest bedrooms boast antiques, Egyptian towels and bathrobes. Choose between a clawfoot tub or Jacuzzi. Relax on private decks or porches with gorgeous views. Savor a satisfying breakfast that may include fresh fruit, chicken sausage, frittata and beverages. A swimming pool provides added enjoyment.
Innkeeper(s): Kathy Deichmann. $135-150. 4 rooms with PB. Breakfast included in rates. Types of meals: Full gourmet bkfst. Beds: Q. Reading lamp in room. Central air. Fax, copier, swimming, library, parlor games, telephone and fireplace on premises. Antiquing, art galleries, beach, bicycling, canoeing/kayaking, fishing, golf, hiking, horseback riding, live theater, parks, shopping and wineries nearby.
Location: Country.
Certificate may be used: Anytime, Sunday-Thursday, subject to availability.

Sequoia National Park   K9

Plantation B&B

33038 Sierra Hwy 198
Sequoia National Park, CA 93244-1700
(559)597-2555 (800)240-1466 Fax:(559)597-2551
Internet: www.plantationbnb.com
E-mail: relax@plantationbnb.com

Circa 1908. The history of orange production is deeply
entwined in the roots of California, and this home is located on
what once was an orange plantation. The original 1908 house
burned in the 1960s, but the current home was built on its
foundation. In keeping with the home's
plantation past, the innkeepers decorated the bed and breakfast with a
"Gone With the Wind" theme. The
comfortable, country guest rooms
sport names such as the Scarlett
O'Hara, the Belle Watling, and of
course, the Rhett Butler. A hot tub is
located in the orchard, and there also
is a heated swimming pool.

Innkeeper(s): Scott & Marie Munger. $129-219. 7 rooms with PB, 2 with FP, 2
suites. Breakfast and snacks/refreshments included in rates. Types of meals: Full
gourmet bkfst and early coffee/tea. Beds: KQDT. Cable TV, VCR, reading lamp,
ceiling fan and hot tub/spa in room. Air conditioning. Fax, spa, swimming, parlor
games, telephone and fireplace on premises. Antiquing, cross-country skiing,
fishing, golf, parks, shopping, sporting events and water sports nearby.
Location: Mountains.
Publicity: *Exeter Sun, Kaweah Commonwealth, Los Angeles Times, Fresno
Bee, Visalia Delta Times, Westways Magazine and Sunset Magazine.*

"Scarlett O'Hara would be proud to live on this lovely plantation."
Certificate may be used: Sept. 7-May 15.

Sonoma   H4

Brick House Bungalows

313 First St E
Sonoma, CA 95476
(707)996-8091 Fax:(707)996-7301
Internet: www.brickhousebungalows.com
E-mail: info@brickhousebungalows.com

Circa 1907. Just one hour north of San Francisco, in the heart of
Sonoma Wine Country, this 1907 brick house was built to reflect
an Italian stone farmhouse. The four bungalows were gradually
added in later years. Kitchenettes, fireplaces, fine linens, vibrant
patterned fabrics, distressed leather couches, antique Kilim carpets and private patios enhance a luxurious stay. In-suite massage
and spa services are available. Lush gardens and a secluded central courtyard impart a tranquil atmosphere for a perfect getaway.
Relax on the hammock or sip complimentary wine by the fire.
Enjoy many cultural events, museums, restaurants and shopping
one-half block away in Historic Sonoma Plaza.
Innkeeper(s): Denise and Anthony Salvo. $150-275. 5 cottages, 4 with FP, 2
suites. Breakfast included in rates. Types of meals: Cont plus. Beds: KQ. Cable
TV, VCR, reading lamp, stereo, refrigerator, ceiling fan, clock radio, telephone,
coffeemaker, desk and fireplace in room. Fax, child care, parlor games, fireplace and laundry facility on premises. Amusement parks, antiquing, art galleries, bicycling, golf, hiking, horseback riding, live theater, museums, parks,
shopping, tennis, wineries, hot air balloons and historical wineries nearby.
Location: Country. Wine country.
Publicity: *Tuscan Magazine and voted among "The Top 10 B&Bs in America"
by Arrington's B&B Journal.*
Certificate may be used: Anytime, November-April, subject to availability,
no holidays.

Inn at Sonoma

630 Broadway
Sonoma, CA 95476
(707)939-1340 (888)568-9818 Fax:(707)939-8834
Internet: www.innatsonoma.com
E-mail: innatsonoma@foursisters.com

Circa 2002. Located within walking distance to the historic
Sonoma Plaza, this delightful new inn is sure to please.
Reflecting a casual California decor, the well-furnished guest
bedrooms feature fireplaces and some offer private balconies.
Start the day with a sumptuous breakfast, then grab a bicycle
to explore the local area. Hors d'oeuvres and afternoon wine
are a welcome respite, and the rooftop Jacuzzi is a soothing
relaxer. There is a $20 fee for an additional guest in room,
except for children less than 5 years old.
Innkeeper(s): Chapman Retterer. $125-240. 19 rooms with PB, 19 with FP.
Breakfast, afternoon tea, snacks/refreshments and wine included in rates.
Types of meals: Full bkfst, veg bkfst and early coffee/tea. Beds: KQ. Data
port, cable TV, reading lamp, stereo, clock radio, telephone, coffeemaker,
turn-down service, DVD player, fireplace, private decks and terry robes in
room. Air conditioning. Fax, spa, bicycles, library, parlor games, fireplace and
afternoon wine and hors d'oeuvres on premises. Handicap access. Antiquing,
art galleries, bicycling, canoeing/kayaking, golf, hiking, live theater, museums,
parks, shopping and wineries nearby.
Location: Wine country.
Certificate may be used: November-March, Sunday-Thursday, based on promotional discount availability, excludes holidays and special event periods,
may exclude certain rooms.

Sonoma Creek Inn

239 Boyes Blvd
Sonoma, CA 95476
(707)939-9463 (888)712-1289 Fax:(707)938-3042
Internet: www.sonomacreekinn.com
E-mail: info@sonomacreekinn.com

Circa 2001. Offering a reasonable lodging alternative in
Sonoma Valley, this lively inn is located within easy access to
the region's wineries and many activities. Cheerful guest bedrooms offer amenities that include a refrigerator, coffee maker,
iron and hair dryer for added comfort. Some rooms feature private patios with fountains. Enjoy the Creekside Cafe, the locals'
favorite place for breakfast. It is conveniently situated on the
grounds and inn guests receive a a 10 percent discount.
Innkeeper(s): Chapman Rettner. $69-159. 15 rooms with PB. Restaurant on
premises. Beds: Q. Cable TV, reading lamp, refrigerator, ceiling fan, clock
radio, telephone, coffeemaker, desk, voice mail and private patios/decks in
room. Central air. Fax on premises. Handicap access. Antiquing, art galleries,
bicycling, golf, hiking, horseback riding, live theater, museums, parks, shopping, tennis, water sports and wineries nearby.
Location: Country.
Certificate may be used: November-April, Sunday-Thursday. Excludes holidays and special event periods, based on availability.

Victorian Garden Inn

316 E Napa St
Sonoma, CA 95476-6723
(707)996-5339 (800)543-5339 Fax:(707)996-1689
Internet: www.victoriangardeninn.com
E-mail: Vgardeninn@aol.com

Circa 1870. Authentic Victorian gardens cover more than an
acre of grounds surrounding this Greek Revival farmhouse.
Pathways wind around to secret gardens, and guests can walk to
world-famous wineries and historical sites. All rooms are decorated with the romantic flair of the innkeeper, an interior designer.
Ask to stay in the renovated water tower or in the Woodcutter's

Cottage which offers a private deck. Enjoy a therapeutic spa in the gardens.

Innkeeper(s): Donna Lewis. $139-259. 4 rooms, 3 with PB, 2 with FP, 1 suite. Breakfast included in rates. Types of meals: Cont plus, veg bkfst, early coffee/tea, snacks/refreshments and room service. Beds: QDT. Refrigerator, ceiling fan, clock radio, telephone, coffeemaker, hot tub/spa and some with fireplaces in room. Air conditioning. Spa, swimming, sauna, library, parlor games, fireplace, laundry facility, beautiful gardens, pool and massage on premises. Antiquing, live theater, wineries, therapeutic spa, beautiful gardens and restaurants nearby.

Location: Country.

Publicity: *Denver Post and Los Angeles Times.*

"I'll be back! So romantic, this place is for lovers! What a perfect spot for a honeymoon! Great! Wonderful! Fabulous! We could not have asked for anything more."

Certificate may be used: November-March, Sunday-Thursday, Tower rooms only.

Soquel   J5

Blue Spruce Inn

2815 S Main St
Soquel, CA 95073-2412
(831)464-1137 (800)559-1137 Fax:(831)475-0608
E-mail: info@bluespruce.com

Circa 1875. The Blue Spruce is located four miles south of Santa Cruz and one mile from Capitola Beach and the Monterey Bay Marine Sanctuary. Spa tubs, fireplaces and colorful gardens add to the pleasure of this renovated farmhouse. The Seascape is a favorite room with a private entrance and a bow-shaped Jacuzzi tub for two. The Carriage House offers skylights above the bed, a king-size featherbed and an in-room Jacuzzi. Plush robes and private baths are features and in the morning, hearty gourmet breakfasts, the inn's specialty, are served. Afterwards enjoy a ride along the beach or a hike through the redwoods.

Innkeeper(s): Nancy, Wayne & Carissa Lussier. $110-240. 6 rooms with PB, 6 with FP. Breakfast included in rates. Types of meals: Full bkfst and early coffee/tea. Beds: KQ. Cable TV, reading lamp, clock radio, telephone, desk, four with Jacuzzi tubs, five with deck or patio and private entrance in room. TV, parlor games and fireplace on premises. Antiquing, beach, golf, parks, shopping and wineries nearby.

Location: Resort area.

Publicity: *L.A. Weekly, Aptos Post, San Francisco Examiner and Village View.*

"You offer such graciousness to your guests and a true sense of welcome."

Certificate may be used: Monday-Thursday, winter only, subject to availability.

South Lake Tahoe   F8

Inn at Heavenly B&B

1261 Ski Run Blvd
South Lake Tahoe, CA 96150-8604
(530)544-4244 (800)692-2246 Fax:(530)544-5213
Internet: www.innatheavenly.com
E-mail: info@innatheavenly.com

Circa 1950. This inn is just half a mile from the Heavenly Ski Resort and one mile from Casinos. Guests will find this log cabin exterior with theme decorated rooms and rock fireplaces

cozy and inviting. We offer plenty of amenities, including in-room coffee makers, refrigerators, microwaves and cable TVs. All rooms offer VCRs, and there is a complimentary selection of videos. Guests can reserve to have private use of the hot tub. A free shuttle goes to casinos and the ski area.

Innkeeper(s): Nancy Kam & Paul Gardner. $125-195. 15 rooms with PB, 15 with FP, 3 cabins and 1 conference room. Breakfast, afternoon tea and snacks/refreshments included in rates. Types of meals: Cont plus and early coffee/tea. Beds: KQD. Cable TV, VCR, reading lamp, stereo, refrigerator, ceiling fan, clock radio and hot tub/spa in room. Fax, copier, spa, sauna, bicycles, library, parlor games, telephone, fireplace, park, swings and BBQs on premises. Amusement parks, cross-country skiing, downhill skiing, fishing, live theater, parks, shopping and water sports nearby.

Location: City, mountains.

"I've never felt so at home in any lodging. I give 5 stars for hospitality."

Certificate may be used: Anytime, Sunday-Thursday, holidays excluded.

Sutter Creek   G6

Grey Gables B&B Inn

161 Hanford St
Sutter Creek, CA 95685-1687
(209)267-1039 (800)473-9422 Fax:(209)267-0998
Internet: www.greygables.com
E-mail: reservations@greygables.com

Circa 1897. The innkeepers of this Victorian home offer poetic accommodations both in the delightful decor and by the names of their guest rooms. The Keats, Bronte and Tennyson rooms afford garden views, while the Byron and Browning rooms include clawfoot tubs. The Victorian Suite, which encompasses the top floor, affords views of the garden, as well as a historic churchyard. All of the guest rooms boast fireplaces. Stroll down brick pathways through the terraced garden or relax in the parlor. A proper English tea is served with cakes and scones. Hors d'oeuvres and libations are served in the evenings.

Innkeeper(s): Roger & Susan Garlick. $130-224. 8 rooms with PB, 8 with FP. Breakfast and afternoon tea included in rates. Types of meals: Full gourmet bkfst and early coffee/tea. Beds: KQT. Reading lamp, ceiling fan and clock radio in room. Air conditioning. Fax, copier, parlor games, telephone and fireplace on premises. Handicap access. Antiquing, cross-country skiing, downhill skiing, fishing, live theater, parks, shopping, water sports and wineries nearby.

Location: City, mountains. Mountains-Gold Country.

Certificate may be used: Anytime, Sunday-Thursday.

The Hanford House B&B Inn

PO Box 1450, 61 Hanford St, Hwy 49
Sutter Creek, CA 95685
(209)267-0747 (800)871-5839 Fax:(209)267-1825
Internet: www.hanfordhouse.com
E-mail: bobkat@hanfordhouse.com

Circa 1929. Hanford House is located on the quiet main street of Sutter Creek, a Gold Rush town. The ivy-covered brick inn features spacious, romantic guest rooms; eight have a fireplace. The Gold Country Escape includes a Jacuzzi tub, canopy bed, sitting area and a private deck. Guests can enjoy breakfast in their room or in the inn's cheerful breakfast room. Guests can relax in the front of a fire in the Hanford Room, which doubles as facilities for conferences, retreats, weddings and social

events. Wineries, antique shops and historic sites are nearby.
Innkeeper(s): Bob & Karen Tierno. $110-249. 9 rooms with PB, 8 with FP, 3 suites and 1 conference room. Breakfast, afternoon tea and snacks/refreshments included in rates. Types of meals: Full gourmet bkfst and early coffee/tea. Beds: KQ. Cable TV, reading lamp, ceiling fan and telephone in room. Air conditioning. VCR, fax and complimentary wireless Internet access on premises. Handicap access. Antiquing, fishing, golf, live theater, water sports, skiing, Gold Rush historic sites and 25 wineries nearby.
Publicity: *Best Places to Kiss and 50 Best Inns in Wine Country.*
Certificate may be used: Jan. 1-Dec. 31; Sunday-Thursday, excluding holidays, first night at peak rates. Second-floor suites are excluded from the program.

Templeton   L6

Carriage Vineyards Bed and Breakfast
4337 S. El Pomar Road
Templeton, CA 93465
(805)227-6807 (800)617-7911 Fax:(805)226-9969
Internet: www.carriagevineyards.com
E-mail: LarryDSmyth@cs.com

Circa 1995. Named after the owners' horse-drawn carriage collection, this 100-acre ranch is tucked away in the country of the Central Coast. Enjoy vineyards, orchards, pastures, gardens and a creek. Hike the hillsides or grab a mountain bike to be immersed in the peaceful scenery of the area. Tastefully decorated guest bedrooms are furnished with well-placed antiques. The Victoria Room is a second-story master suite featuring an oversize shower and Jacuzzi tub for two. Savor a hot gourmet breakfast served daily, and on Sunday enjoy upscale continental fare. Overnight horse facilities are available.
Innkeeper(s): Joanna Caldwell. $95-180. 3 rooms, 1 with PB. Breakfast included in rates. Types of meals: Full gourmet bkfst. Beds: KQDT. Clock radio, coffeemaker, desk and hot tub/spa in room. Central air. Fax, spa, telephone, fireplace, laundry facility and horse overnight stables on premises. Antiquing, art galleries, beach, live theater, museums, parks, sporting events, water sports and wineries nearby.
Location: Country.
Certificate may be used: Anytime, Sunday-Thursday except July through August on weekends.

Country House Inn
91 S Main St
Templeton, CA 93465-8701
(805)434-1598 (800)362-6032
Internet: www.wineriesofpasorobles.com
E-mail: countryhouse@tcsn.net

Circa 1886. Built by the founder of Templeton in 1886, this Victorian home and Carriage House is now a designated historic site. Fully restored and furnished in a quaint yet comfortable style, gather in one of the fireside common rooms to relax or chat with new friends. Guest bedrooms and suites boast an assortment of pleasures that includes terry cloth robes. Several rooms have clawfoot tubs, private entrances and a porch with wicker furniture. Enjoy a gourmet breakfast in the dining room. Elegant landscaping and gardens accent the grounds. Croquet is a popular activity on the front lawn. Tour the local vineyards of this rural wine country.
Innkeeper(s): Dianne Garth. $115-130. 5 rooms with PB, 1 with FP, 1 suite. Breakfast included in rates. Types of meals: Full gourmet bkfst, early coffee/tea and afternoon tea. Beds: KQ. Reading lamp, ceiling fan, desk and fireplace in room. Parlor games and telephone on premises. Antiquing, art galleries, beach, canoeing/kayaking, fishing, golf, hiking, horseback riding, live theater, museums, parks, shopping, tennis, water sports, wineries and wine tours nearby.
Location: Wine country.
Publicity: *Los Angeles Times and PM Magazine.*

"A feast for all the senses, an esthetic delight."
Certificate may be used: April-September, Sunday-Thursday; October-March, Sunday-Saturday.

Ukiah   F3

Vichy Hot Springs Resort & Inn
2605 Vichy Springs Rd
Ukiah, CA 95482-3507
(707)462-9515 Fax:(707)462-9516
Internet: www.vichysprings.com
E-mail: vichy@vichysprings.com

Circa 1854. This famous spa, now a California State Historical Landmark (#980), once attracted guests Jack London, Mark Twain, Robert Louis Stevenson, Ulysses Grant and Teddy Roosevelt. Nineteen rooms and eight cottages comprise the property. Some of the cottages are historic and some are new. The 1860s naturally warm and carbonated mineral baths remain unchanged. A hot soaking pool and historic Olympic-size pool await your arrival. A magical waterfall is a 30-minute walk along a year-round stream.
Innkeeper(s): Gilbert & Marjorie Ashoff. $115-265. 26 rooms with PB, 8 with FP, 1 suite, 8 cottages and 1 conference room. Breakfast and Sunday brunch included in rates. Types of meals: Full bkfst. Beds: QT. Modem hookup, data port, reading lamp, refrigerator, clock radio, telephone, coffeemaker, desk and fireplace in room. Central air. Fax, copier, spa, swimming, mineral baths, massages, facials and 700 acres of private park to explore on premises. Handicap access. Antiquing, beach, bicycling, canoeing/kayaking, fishing, golf, hiking, live theater, museums, parks, shopping, tennis, water sports, wineries, redwood parks, tallest trees in the world, lakes and rivers, Sun House Museum California Historic Landmark and Montgomery Woods nearby.
Location: Country, mountains. 700 acres on property.
Publicity: *Sunset, Sacramento Bee, San Jose Mercury News, Gulliver (Japan), Oregonian, Contra Costa Times, New York Times, San Francisco Chronicle, San Francisco Examiner, Adventure West, Gulliver (Italy), Bay Area Back Roads, Huell Hauser California Gold, PBS and Farm Bureau.*
Certificate may be used: Anytime, November-April, subject to availability.

Venice   O10

Venice Beach House
15 Thirtieth Avenue
Venice, CA 90291
(310)823-1966 Fax:(310)823-1842
Internet: www.venicebeachhouse.com
E-mail: info@venicebeachhouse.com

Circa 1911. Built by Warren and Carla Wilson in 1911 in the Craftsman style of architecture, this faithfully restored home is listed in the National Register. The Wilsons' friends and family included the founder of Venice, Abbot Kinney and a close-knit group of Hollywood stars and local personalities. An ever-growing circle of friends and family are invited to share its casual elegance. Romantic guest bedrooms and spacious suites are tastefully decorated and well-furnished. James Peasgood's Room boasts a double Jacuzzi, cathedral wood ceiling and private balcony. Enjoy the ocean vista in the Pier Suite with a fireplace and sitting room. Tramp's Quarters with a pine beam ceiling and the Olympia Suite with oversized dual shower offer delightful garden views. After breakfast explore the scenic area by bicycle or walk to the beach to rollerblade, surf and people-watch.
Innkeeper(s): Brian Gannon. $130-195. 9 rooms, 3 with PB, 1 with FP, 2 suites. Breakfast included in rates. Types of meals: Cont plus. Beds: KQDT. Modem hook-up, data port, cable TV, reading lamp, clock radio, telephone, desk and DSL high-speed Internet access in room. Fax, bicycles, library, fireplace and Venice Beach on premises. Amusement parks, beach, bicycling, canoeing/kayaking, hiking, shopping, water sports, rollerblading and surfing nearby.

Location: 1911 historical inn, California craftsman.
Publicity: *Washington Post - "In one of the most popular beach towns in the world, by far the most charming accommodation is the Venice Beach House" and MTV.*

"In one of the most popular beach towns in the world, by far the most charming accommodation is the Venice Beach House." — *Washington Post*
Certificate may be used: Nov. 30-April 1, subject to availability.

Ventura   N8

The Victorian Rose B&B
896 E Main Street
Ventura, CA 93001
(805)641-1888 Fax:(805)643-1335
Internet: www.victorian-rose.com
E-mail: victrose@pacbell.net

Circa 1888. Expect the unexpected at this 110-year-old church with Victorian Gothic, Eastlake, Mission and Norwegian architecture that is now a one-of-a-kind bed & breakfast filled with timeless treasures. Distinctive original details feature a 96-foot wooden steeple, stained-glass windows and 26-foot-high carved beam ceilings. The main room with cherubs, antiques and an indoor fountain includes separate sitting areas to read or play cards and enjoy the wine and cheese hour. A vintage barber shop chair and related décor influence one corner. The 12-foot spiral staircase leads to the balcony of the Emperor's Bedroom, which was once the choir loft and now boasts Oriental furnishings and ambiance. A gas fireplace and patio access is appreciated in the Victorian Rose, Wisteria Gardens and Fleur de Lis guest bedrooms. Grand settings of china and crystal accent gourmet breakfasts.
$99-175. 5 rooms with PB, 5 with FP, 2 with WP. Breakfast, afternoon tea, snacks/refreshments, hors d'oeuvres and wine included in rates. Types of meals: Cont plus, veg bkfst and early coffee/tea. Beds: KQ. Cable TV, refrigerator, turn-down service and fireplace in room. Air conditioning. Fax on premises. Antiquing, art galleries, beach, bicycling, canoeing/kayaking, fishing, golf, hiking, live theater, museums, parks, shopping, tennis, water sports, wineries and Channel Island nearby.
Location: City. Historical downtown.
Certificate may be used: January-April, Monday-Thursday, except Wisteria Bedroom.

Visalia   K8

Ben Maddox House B&B
601 N Encina St
Visalia, CA 93291-3603
(559)739-0721 (800)401-9800 Fax:(559)625-0420
Internet: www.benmaddoxhouse.com
E-mail: innkeeper@benmaddoxhouse.com

Circa 1876. Sequoia National Park is just 40 minutes away from this late 19th-century home constructed completely of redwood. The parlor, dining room and front guest bedrooms remain in their original pristine state and are tastefully furnished in period antiques. Other guest bedrooms boast a Jacuzzi bathtub or separate sitting area. Enjoy a leisurely breakfast served at private tables in the historic dining room or on the deck. The grounds feature a swimming pool, finch aviary, gardens and 100-year-old trees. Ask about small group special events such as weddings, showers, rehearsal dinners, family reunions, corporate retreats and meetings.
Innkeeper(s): Brenda & Michael Handy. $85-135. 6 rooms with PB. Breakfast included in rates. Types of meals: Full bkfst. Beds: KQ. Cable TV,

reading lamp, refrigerator, clock radio, telephone and data port in room. Air conditioning. Swimming, complimentary soft beverages and pool on premises. Antiquing, cross-country skiing, fishing, live theater, parks, shopping, sporting events, water sports, Sequoia National park, historic downtown area and restaurants nearby.
Location: City. Historic District.
Publicity: *Southland, Fresno Bee and has 3-diamond rating for AAA and CABBI.*
Certificate may be used: Anytime, subject to availability.

Westport   E3

Howard Creek Ranch
PO Box 121
Westport, CA 95488
(707)964-6725 Fax:(707)964-1603
Internet: www.howardcreekranch.com
E-mail: howardcreekranch@mcn.org

Circa 1871. First settled as a land grant of thousands of acres, Howard Creek Ranch is now a 60-acre farm with sweeping views of the Pacific Ocean, sandy beaches and rolling mountains. A 75-foot bridge spans a creek that flows past barns and outbuildings to the beach 200 yards away. The farmhouse is surrounded by green lawns, an award-winning flower garden, and grazing cows, horses and  llama. This rustic rural location offers antiques, a hot tub, sauna and heated pool. A traditional ranch breakfast is served each morning.
Innkeeper(s): Charles & Sally Grigg. $75-160. 14 rooms, 13 with PB, 5 with FP, 3 suites and 3 cabins. Breakfast included in rates. Types of meals: Full gourmet bkfst. Beds: KQD. Reading lamp, refrigerator, ceiling fan, desk and hot tub/spa in room. VCR, fax, copier, spa, swimming, sauna, library, parlor games, telephone and fireplace on premises. Antiquing, art galleries, beach, bicycling, canoeing/kayaking, fishing, golf, hiking, horseback riding, live theater, museums, parks, shopping, water sports, wineries, farm animals, hiking trails and birdwatching nearby.
Location: Mountains, ocean community.
Publicity: *California, Country, Vacations, Forbes, Sunset, Diablo and American Heartland.*

"This is one of the most romantic places on the planet."
Certificate may be used: Oct. 15-May 15, Sunday-Thursday, excluding holiday periods.

Willits   F3

Beside Still Waters Farm Luxury Bed & Breakfast Cottages
30901 Sherwood Rd
Willits, CA 95490
(707)984-6130 (877)230-2171
Internet: www.besidestillwatersfarm.com
E-mail: innkeeper@besidestillwatersfarm.com

Circa 2004. Luxury bed & breakfast cottages offer privacy and pampering in a peaceful setting amidst 22 picturesque acres. Indulge in daydreams and rekindle romance while staying at these newly built accommodations in Mendocino County. Each guest suite is a separate cottage situated near the Victorian-style farmhouse for easy access to borrow a game, puzzle or browse for a CD and video. Stroll through the garden flowers. Modern amenities include aromatherapy steam showers, foot spas, heated towel bars, whirlpools for two and cast iron stove fireplaces. Meadowood Guesthouse, ideal for families, groups and extended stays, boasts a full kitchen and laundry facilities. Breakfast is delivered to each cottage and may feature an egg entrée with fresh-picked herbs, or French toast with lavender maple syrup and homemade sausage.

Innkeeper(s): Earl & Christy Collins. $225-325. 3 cottages, 3 with FP. Breakfast and snacks/refreshments included in rates. Types of meals: Full gourmet bkfst, veg bkfst and afternoon tea. Beds: KQT. Modem hook-up, data port, cable TV, VCR, reading lamp, stereo, refrigerator, ceiling fan, snack bar, clock radio, telephone, coffeemaker, turn-down service, desk, hot tub/spa, voice mail, fireplace, aromatherapy steam-showers and foot spas in room. Air conditioning. Fax, copier, spa, library, parlor games, laundry facility, gift shop and picnic areas on premises. Antiquing, art galleries, beach, bicycling, canoeing/kayaking, fishing, golf, hiking, horseback riding, live theater, museums, parks, shopping, wineries and whale watching nearby.

Location: Country, mountains.

Certificate may be used: Sunday-Thursday, November-April, subject to availability.

Yountville   G4

Lavender

PO Box 3073
Monterey, CA 93942-3073
(707)944-1388 (800)522-4140 Fax:(707)944-1579
Internet: www.lavendernapa.com
E-mail: lavender@foursisters.com

Circa 1999. Stroll through lavender and flower gardens or relax on the veranda of this French farmhouse located in California's Napa Valley wine country. Privacy and elegant country comfort are the order of the day in the inn's eight guest rooms decorated in bold natural colors. The main house has one guest room upstairs and one downstairs. The six cottages, each with its own private entrance and private patio, have King-size beds, spacious bathrooms with two-person bathtubs. The farm breakfast is an all-you-can-eat buffet with a variety of courses sure to please the most discriminating palate. Typical menus include such items as egg entrees, breakfast potatoes, pancakes, muffins, fresh fruit, different breads, oatmeal and cereal. Each afternoon during the complimentary teatime, guests relax with wine, cheese, crackers and baked goods like cookies, pound cake and angel food cake. Guests can walk through the entire small town of Yountville with its Vintage 1870 shopping center, cafes and historic residential homes. Or guests may prefer to check out one of the inn's bicycles and soak up the relaxed atmosphere as they pedal through town. Naturally, many guests spend the day wine tasting and some take the three-hour tour on the Wine Train as it winds its way up the valley at a leisurely five miles per hour. Nearby Calistoga has its own geyser as well as day spas known for a variety of rejuvenating baths. There is a $20 fee for an additional guest in room, except for children less than 5 years old.

Innkeeper(s): Rachel Retterer. $150-250. 8 rooms with PB, 8 with FP. Breakfast, afternoon tea and wine included in rates. Types of meals: Full gourmet bkfst. Beds: K. Modem hook-up, data port, cable TV, reading lamp, telephone, turn-down service, desk, hot tub/spa and voice mail in room. Air conditioning. Fax, copier and bicycles on premises. Antiquing, art galleries, bicycling, fishing, golf, hiking, horseback riding, museums, parks, shopping, sporting events, tennis, water sports and wineries nearby.

Location: Wine country.

Certificate may be used: December-April, Sunday-Thursday excluding special event periods and holidays, based on promotional discount availability.

Maison Fleurie

PO Box 3073
Monterey, CA 93942-3073
(707)944-2056 (800)788-0369 Fax:(707)944-9342
Internet: www.maisonfleurienapa.com
E-mail: maisonfleurie@foursisters.com

Circa 1894. Vines cover the two-foot thick brick walls of the Bakery, the Carriage House and the Main House of this French country inn. One of the Four Sisters Inns, it is reminiscent of a bucolic setting in Provence. Rooms are decorated in a warm, romantic style, some with vineyard and garden views. Rooms in the Old Bakery have fireplaces. A pool and outdoor hot tub are available and you may borrow bicycles for wandering the countryside. In the evenings, wine and hors d'oeuvres are served. Yountville, just north of Napa, offers close access to the multitude of wineries and vineyards in the valley. There is a $20 fee for an additional guest in room, except for children less than 5 years old.

Innkeeper(s): Rachel Retterer. $130-225. 13 rooms with PB, 7 with FP. Breakfast, afternoon tea and wine included in rates. Types of meals: Full gourmet bkfst. Beds: KQD. Telephone, turn-down service, hot tub/spa, terry robes and newspaper in room. Fax, bicycles, fireplace, outdoor pool and hot tub on premises. Handicap access. Antiquing and wineries nearby.

Location: Napa Valley.

"Peaceful surroundings, friendly staff."

Certificate may be used: December-February, Sunday-Thursday, excluding certain room, holidays and special event periods, based on availability.

Yuba City   F5

Harkey House B&B

212 C St
Yuba City, CA 95991-5014
(530)674-1942 Fax:(530)674-1840
Internet: www.harkeyhouse.com
E-mail: lee@harkeyhouse.com

Circa 1875. An essence of romance fills this Victorian Gothic house set in a historic neighborhood. Every inch of the home has been given a special touch, from the knickknacks and photos in the sitting room to the quilts and furnishings in the guest quarters. Camilla's Cottage features a queen bed with a down comforter and extras such as an adjoining kitchen and a gas stove. Full breakfasts of muffins, fresh fruit, juice, waffles and freshly ground coffee are served in a glass-paned dining room or on the poolside patio.

Innkeeper(s): Bob & Lee Jones. $90-195. 4 rooms with PB, 2 with FP, 1 cottage and 1 conference room. Breakfast included in rates. Types of meals: Full bkfst and early coffee/tea. Beds: Q. Cable TV, reading lamp, stereo, ceiling fan, clock radio, telephone, turn-down service, desk and hot tub/spa in room. Air conditioning. TV, VCR, spa, library, parlor games, fireplace and pool on premises. Antiquing, fishing, golf, live theater, parks, shopping, water sports, birding and Sutter Buttes nearby.

Location: Mountains. Rivers.

Publicity: *Country Magazine.*

"This place is simply marvelous...the most comfortable bed in travel."

Certificate may be used: January to December, Sunday-Thursday.

Colorado

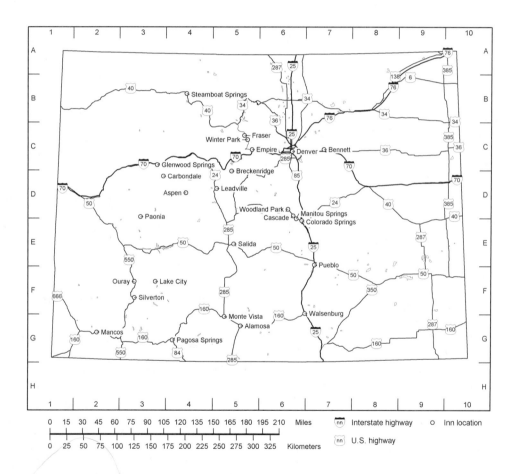

| | Miles | | Interstate highway | | Inn location |

0 15 30 45 60 75 90 105 120 135 150 165 180 195 210   Miles

0 25 50 75 100 125 150 175 200 225 250 275 300 325   Kilometers

nn Interstate highway   ○ Inn location

nn U.S. highway

Alamosa   G5

Cottonwood Inn & Gallery: A B&B Inn

123 San Juan Ave
Alamosa, CO 81101-2547
(719)589-3882 (800)955-2623 Fax:(719)589-6437
Internet: www.cottonwoodinn.com.
E-mail: relax@cottonwoodinn.com

Circa 1912. This refurbished Colorado Arts-and-Crafts inn is filled with antiques and paintings by local artists. Blueberry pancakes and banana crepes with Mexican chocolate are the inn's specialties. A favorite day trip is riding the Cumbres-Toltec Scenic Railroad over the La Manga Pass, site of an Indiana Jones movie. The inn offers five rooms, four suites and a carriage house.

Innkeeper(s): Deborah Donaldson. $56-125. 10 rooms, 6 with PB, 4 suites. Breakfast and afternoon tea included in rates. Types of meals: Full gourmet bkfst, veg bkfst and gourmet dinner. Beds: KQD. Cable TV, reading lamp, refrigerator, clock radio, telephone, coffeemaker and desk in room. Fax, library, child care, parlor games and courtyard hot tub on premises. Antiquing, art galleries, bicycling, cross-country skiing, fishing, golf, hiking, horseback riding, live theater, museums, parks, shopping, sporting events, tennis, historical train, sand dunes and hot springs nearby.

Location: Small town.

Publicity: *Colorado Expressions, Rocky Mountain News, Country Inns, Denver Post, Milwaukee Journal, Channel 4 Denver* and *Colorado Get Away.*

"Your place is so inviting, and with the front porch and birds singing, our visit was so peaceful and relaxing."

Certificate may be used: Anytime, excluding special engagements.

Aspen   D4

Little Red Ski Haus

PO Box 8288
Aspen, CO 81612-8288
(970)925-3333 (866)630-6119 Fax:(970)925-7123
Internet: www.littleredskihaus.net
E-mail: info@littleredskihaus.net

Circa 1888. People from all over the world stay at this historic Victorian bed & breakfast that is known to be the area's first. Little Red is in the historic registry and boasts a recent $1 million renovation. An elegant fireplace with an antique mantel graces the parlor and an upright piano is in the music room. Antiques furnish the elegant guest rooms. Enjoy a full gourmet breakfast in the Prospector's Cellar. In the afternoon and evening, guests gather in this charming room that boasts a fireplace and full service bar. Guests can also find time to meet friends and enjoy the hot tub deck. Located close to town, shuttle busses go to the nearby slopes. The gondola is walking distance away.

Innkeeper(s): Beverly Fiore. $137-389. 13 rooms with PB, 2 suites and 1 conference room. Breakfast included in rates. Types of meals: Full gourmet bkfst, picnic lunch and afternoon tea. Beds: KQT. Modem hook-up, data port, cable TV, VCR, reading lamp, ceiling fan, clock radio, telephone, turn-down service, desk, hot tub/spa, voice mail, some with whirlpool tubs and others have instant steam showers in room. Spa, library, parlor games, fireplace, laundry facility, ski lockers and boot room on premises. Handicap access. Antiquing, art galleries, bicycling, canoeing/kayaking, cross-country skiing, downhill skiing, fishing, golf, hiking, horseback riding, live theater, museums, parks, shopping, tennis, water sports, snowmobiling, hot air ballooning,

rodeos, white-water rafting, snowshoeing, ice skating, rock climbing, paragliding, Jeep trips and motorcross trips nearby.

Location: Mountains.

Publicity: *Aspen Magazine, Boulder Daily Camera, Ski Magazine* - voted November 2003 "Inn of the Month," *Aspen Times, Aspen Daily News, Du Page County Dairy Herald, Denver Post,* ABC Chicago Affiliate, *Janet Davies Show* and *In Gear Cable TV Show.*

Certificate may be used: April-May, October-November, Dec. 1-15.

Bennett   C7

Willow Tree Country Inn

PO Box 160
Bennett, CO
(303)644-5551 (800)257-1241 Fax:(303)644-3801
Internet: www.willowtreebb.com
E-mail: willowtreeinn@tds.net

Circa 1920. A peaceful setting permeates this English Tudor inn that sits on 60 acres with magnificent views of the Rocky Mountains. The country décor and antique furnishings are tastefully blended in an uncluttered and inviting way. Enjoy a light supper upon arrival. Watch a glorious sunset from the large covered porch. Read in the sunroom or watch a video by the fire in the parlor. Delightful guest bedrooms boast snow-capped mountain vistas, robes, slippers, a snack basket and a stocked refrigerator. Feel pampered with a complimentary hydrotherapy foot bath and herbal foot massage. Breakfast in the dining room may start with just-baked cinnamon rolls, a fruit plate and green chili strata. Soak in the hot tub after playing croquet, badminton or horseshoes.

Innkeeper(s): Deborah & Gerald Toczek. $69-139. 3 rooms with PB. Breakfast, afternoon tea, snacks/refreshments and dinner included in rates. Types of meals: Full gourmet bkfst, veg bkfst, early coffee/tea and room service. Beds: KD. Refrigerator, ceiling fan, snack bar, clock radio, turn-down service and desk in room. Air conditioning. TV, VCR, spa, parlor games and fireplace on premises. Golf, croquet, horseshoes, badminton and puzzles nearby.

Location: Country.

Certificate may be used: Anytime, subject to availability.

Breckenridge   D5

Abbett Placer Inn B&B

205 S French
Breckenridge, CO 80424
(970)453-6489 (888)794-7750 Fax:(970)453-1842

Circa 1897. Recently renovated to offer modern comforts, this Victorian inn reflects its heritage and is located in the heart of the Historic District. The custom decor is comfortable and stylish. Relaxation is easy, whether reading by the fire, playing a game or watching a video. Outdoor decks and a hot tub feature spectacular mountain views. Most of the guest bedrooms boast a fireplace, whirlpool tub and private balcony. Wake up to a satisfying breakfast before hiking, skiing or experiencing the many local activities.

Innkeeper(s): Lynn Cavalluzzi. $85-156. 5 rooms with PB, 4 with FP. Breakfast and snacks/refreshments included in rates. Types of meals: Full gourmet bkfst, veg bkfst, early coffee/tea and picnic lunch. Beds: KQT. Cable TV, VCR, reading lamp, refrigerator, clock radio, telephone, desk, hot tub/spa and fireplace in room. Fax, spa, parlor games and fireplace on premises. Antiquing, art galleries, bicycling, canoeing/kayaking, cross-country skiing, downhill skiing, fishing, golf, hiking, horseback riding, live theater, museums, parks, shopping, tennis and water sports nearby.

Location: Mountains.

Certificate may be used: May 1-Nov. 10, Sunday-Thursday.

Hunt Placer Inn

PO Box 4898
Breckenridge, CO 80424-4898
(970)453-7573 (800)472-1430 Fax:(970)453-2335
Internet: www.huntplacerinn.com
E-mail: info@huntplacerinn.com

Circa 1994. Set among woods in a historic, gold-mining town, this delightful mountain chalet is located on what was an actual mining claim. Guest rooms are decorated in a variety of
styles, from Southwestern to Victorian, each with an elegant flair. The room and suite names reflect the decor, such as the Bavaria Suite or the Gold Rush Room. The morning menu changes daily, offer-
ing items such as Swiss muesli, fresh fruit, French toast souffle with caramel sauce, creme brulee and quiche. A free shuttle takes guests to the nearby ski slopes and alpine slide.

Innkeeper(s): Trip & Kelly Butler. $149-199. 8 rooms with PB, 3 with FP. Breakfast, afternoon tea and snacks/refreshments included in rates. Types of meals: Full gourmet bkfst, veg bkfst and early coffee/tea. Beds: KQT. Modem hook-up, data port, reading lamp, clock radio, telephone, voice mail, fireplace and private balconies in room. TV, VCR, fax, pet boarding, parlor games, elevator to second floor and luxurious outdoor hot tub on premises. Handicap access. Antiquing, art galleries, bicycling, canoeing/kayaking, cross-country skiing, downhill skiing, fishing, golf, hiking, horseback riding, live theater, museums, parks, shopping and symphony nearby.

Location: Mountains. Breckenridge Ski Resort.

Publicity: *Denver Post, New York Newsday, Colorado Expressions, Travel Channel and Romantic Inns of America.*

Certificate may be used: April 7-Dec. 20, Sunday-Thursday.

Carbondale   D3

Ambiance Inn

66 N 2nd St
Carbondale, CO 81623-2102
(970)963-3597 (800)350-1515 Fax:(970)963-3130
Internet: www.ambianceinn.com
E-mail: ambiancein@aol.com

Circa 1976. This contemporary chalet-style home is located in the beautiful Crystal Valley between Aspen and Glenwood Springs. Each room is individually appointed with amenities such as four-poster bed or a two-person Jacuzzi. The Aspen Suite features knotty pine paneling and snowshoes hang on the walls, creating a ski lodge atmosphere. Other rooms feature motifs such as Southwestern or Hawaiian style.

Innkeeper(s): Norma & Robert Morris. $70-100. 4 rooms with PB, 1 suite. Breakfast included in rates. Types of meals: Full gourmet bkfst and early coffee/tea. Beds: Q. Cable TV, reading lamp, stereo, ceiling fan, clock radio, desk and hot tub/spa in room. TV, VCR, telephone and fireplace on premises. Antiquing, cross-country skiing, downhill skiing, fishing, parks, shopping and sporting events nearby.

Location: Mountains.

Certificate may be used: Excludes holidays, Christmas week and peak summer weekends.

Cascade   D6

Rocky Mountain Lodge & Cabins

4680 Hagerman Ave
Cascade, CO 80809-1818
(719)684-2521 (888)298-0348 Fax:(719)684-8348
Internet: www.rockymountainlodge.com
E-mail: info@rockymountainlodge.com

Circa 1936. Surrounded by mountains, this rustic log lodge is snuggled within the Ute Pass about five miles from Manitou Springs. There are five rooms in the lodge, as well as a cottage and cabin. Rooms are decorated in an upscale country style; poster and sleigh beds are topped with quilts and fluffy comforters. The great room includes a huge rock fireplace and plenty of places to relax. Three-course breakfasts are served to all guests staying in the lodge rooms. The cottage and cabin are within walking distance from the main lodge. The cabin dates to 1909 and includes two bedrooms, a living room with a fireplace and a kitchen. The two-story cottage, built during the 1930s, includes a bedroom and sitting area upstairs and a kitchenette and dining room downstairs.

Innkeeper(s): Brian and Debbie Reynolds. $80-199. 6 rooms with PB, 1 with FP, 1 with HT, 1 suite, 1 cottage, 1 guest house and 1 cabin. Breakfast, afternoon tea and snacks/refreshments included in rates. Types of meals: Full gourmet bkfst, veg bkfst, early coffee/tea, gourmet lunch and picnic lunch. Beds: QDT. Modem hook-up, cable TV, VCR, reading lamp, Luxury Suite has ceiling fan, clock radio, coffeemaker, DVD player, fireplace, refrigerator, telephone, two-person body spray shower, whirlpool air massage tub for two and private sitting room in room. Fax, spa, library, parlor games, telephone, fireplace, gift shop, refrigerator, microwave, coffeemaker and evening dessert on premises. Limited handicap access. Amusement parks, antiquing, art galleries, bicycling, fishing, golf, hiking, horseback riding, live theater, museums, parks, shopping, sporting events, tennis, white water rafting and train trips nearby.

Location: Mountains.

Certificate may be used: November-April, Sunday-Thursday, subject to availability, holidays excluded.

Chipita Park   D6

Chipita Lodge B&B

9090 Chipita Park Rd
Chipita Park, CO 80809
(719)684-8454 (877)CHI-PITA Fax:(719)684-8234
Internet: www.chipitalodge.com
E-mail: chipitainn@aol.com

Circa 1927. Overlooking Chipita Lake and at the base of Pikes Peak, this native stone and log lodge features a hot tub and gazebo with views of mountains on its two-acre knoll-top location. Formerly the local post office and general store, the lodge boasts rooms with fresh Western decor as well as rooms with Native American influences. A three-course breakfast is served with country-style entrees. Evening and afternoon refreshments are offered before the large stone fireplace in the handsome gathering room or on the deck overlooking the lake. The Garden of the Gods, Manitou Springs and Cripple Creek are nearby.

Innkeeper(s): Kevin & Martha Henry. $88-126. 3 rooms with PB and 1 conference room. Breakfast and snacks/refreshments included in rates. Types of meals: Full gourmet bkfst. Beds: Q. Modem hook-up, reading lamp, CD player, ceiling fan, clock radio and turn-down service in room. Fax, copier, spa, parlor games, telephone and fireplace on premises. Amusement parks, antiquing, art galleries, cross-country skiing, fishing, golf, hiking, horseback riding, live theater, museums, parks, shopping, sporting events and wineries nearby.

Location: Mountains.

Publicity: *Denver Post.*

Certificate may be used: Nov. 1-March 31, Sunday-Thursday, excluding Thanksgiving, Christmas, New Year's, Valentine's, Easter.

Colorado Springs E6

Black Forest B&B

11170 Black Forest Rd
Colorado Springs, CO 80908-3986
(719)495-4208 (800)809-9901 Fax:(719)495-0688
Internet: www.blackforestbb.com
E-mail: blackforestbb@msn.com

Circa 1984. Ponderosa pines, golden aspens and fragrant meadows surround this massive log home built on the highest point east of the Rocky Mountains. This rustic mountain setting is complete with 20 acres of beautiful country to explore. If you want to fully experience mountain living, the innkeepers will be more than happy to share their chores with you, which range from cutting firewood to planting Christmas trees on their tree farm. A greenhouse holds an indoor lap pool, sauna, fitness center and honeymoon suite.

Innkeeper(s): Rex and Susan Redden. $75-250. 8 rooms with PB, 5 with FP, 7 total suites, including 2 two-bedroom suites, 1 three-bedroom suite and 1 four-bedroom suite, 2 cottages, 3 guest houses, 2 cabins and 1 conference room. Breakfast and snacks/refreshments included in rates. Types of meals: Cont plus and early coffee/tea. Beds: KQDT. Modem hook-up, data port, cable TV, VCR, reading lamp, CD player, refrigerator, ceiling fan, snack bar, clock radio, telephone, coffeemaker, desk and fireplace in room. Fax, copier, swimming, sauna, library, child care, parlor games, laundry facility and gift shop on premises. Limited handicap access. Antiquing, art galleries, bicycling, canoeing/kayaking, cross-country skiing, fishing, golf, hiking, horseback riding, live theater, museums, parks, shopping, sporting events, tennis, water sports and focus on the family nearby.
Location: Mountains.
Certificate may be used: November through April, except Christmas and Thanksgiving holidays.

Cheyenne Canon Inn

2030 W Cheyenne Blvd
Colorado Springs, CO 80906
(719)633-0625 (800)633-0625 Fax:(800)633-8826
Internet: cheyennecanoninn.com
E-mail: info@cheyennecanoninn.com

Circa 1921. This massive, 10,000-square foot mansion features Arts and Crafts-style architecture. The manor was built as an upscale casino and bordello. During its heyday, the famous guests included the Marx Brothers and Lon Chaney. The casino room now serves as the location for the inn's nightly wine and cheese hour. The room has more than 100 panes of glass affording views of Cheyenne Canon and Cheyenne Mountain. The guest rooms and adjacent honeymoon cottage are decorated with treasures and antiques from around the world. There is a greenhouse spa on the second floor and complimentary beverages and fruit always are available. Modem outlets, TVs and in-room phones are among the amenities for business travelers. Downtown Colorado Springs is minutes away, and hiking trails and waterfalls are across the street.

Innkeeper(s): Keith Hampton. $95-200. 10 rooms with PB, 4 with FP, 3

suites, 1 cottage and 2 conference rooms. Types of meals: Full bkfst, early coffee/tea, snacks/refreshments and gourmet dinner. Beds: KQ. Cable TV, ceiling fan, telephone, turn-down service and hair dryers in room. Air conditioning. Fax, library and day spa on premises. Antiquing, fishing, golf, hiking, live theater, parks, shopping, sporting events and gambling nearby.
Location: City, mountains.
Publicity: *Denver Post, Colorado Source, Beacon, National Geographic Traveler and Country Inns.*

"It truly was 'home away from home.' You have made it so welcoming and warm. Needless to say our breakfasts at home will never come close to the Cheyenne Canon Inn!!"
Certificate may be used: October through April, Sunday-Thursday.

Lennox House Bed & Breakfast

1339 N Nevada Ave
Colorado Springs, CO 80903-2431
(719)471-9265 (800)471-9282 Fax:(719)471-0971
Internet: www.lennoxhouse.com
E-mail: info@lennoxhouse.com

Circa 1890. Whether traveling for pleasure or business, visitors to this recently renovated Queen Anne Victorian will find an abundance of comforts and generous amenities. Surrounded by historical homes on tree-lined streets, the inn is centrally located to enjoy all that downtown has to offer, as well as nearby Pikes Peak National Forest. Original woodwork highlights the custom-designed interior. Guest bedrooms feature fireplaces, tub-for-two, canopy beds and modern conveniences that enhance a delightful stay. A satisfying breakfast is served every morning at a flexible time. Snacks, beverages and use of a refrigerator and microwave are available around the clock. Enjoy an extensive video collection and small gift shop. Ask about special packages offered.

Innkeeper(s): Mark & Lisa Kolb. $99-129. 4 rooms with PB, 1 suite. Breakfast and snacks/refreshments included in rates. Beds: KQ. Cable TV, VCR, reading lamp, telephone and voice mail in room. Air conditioning. Fax, laundry facility and video collections on premises. Hiking and shopping nearby.
Certificate may be used: Nov. 1-April 30, Sunday-Thursday, excluding holidays.

Room at the Inn A Victorian Bed & Breakfast

618 N Nevada Ave
Colorado Springs, CO 80903-1006
(719)442-1896 (888)442-1896 Fax:(719)442-6802
Internet: www.roomattheinn.com
E-mail: roomatinn@pcisys.net

Circa 1896. A Colorado pioneer built this Queen Anne Victorian, a delightful mix of turret, gables and gingerbread trim. While restoring their century-old Victorian, the innkeepers discovered several hand-painted murals had once decorated the interior. Original fireplace mantels and a collection of antiques add to the nostalgic ambiance. Fresh flowers, turndown service and a bountiful breakfast are just a few of the amenities. Several rooms include a fireplace or double whirlpool tub.

Innkeeper(s): Dorian & Linda Ciolek. $109-160. 8 rooms with PB, 4 with FP, 2 suites. Breakfast, afternoon tea and snacks/refreshments included in rates. Types of meals: Full bkfst and early coffee/tea. Beds: Q. Reading lamp, telephone, turn-down service, desk, clocks and whirlpool tubs in room. Air conditioning. VCR, fax, copier, parlor games, fireplace and spa on premises. Handicap access. Antiquing, fishing, live theater, parks, shopping, sporting events, museums and fine arts center nearby.

Location: City.

Publicity: *Denver Post and Colorado Springs Gazette-Telegraph.*

Certificate may be used: Anytime, subject to availability.

Denver   C6

Capitol Hill Mansion Bed & Breakfast

1207 Pennsylvania St
Denver, CO 80203-2504
(303)839-5221 (800)839-9329 Fax:(303)839-9046
Internet: www.capitolhillmansion.com
E-mail: info@capitolhillmansion.com

Circa 1891. Although only open since 1994, owners James R. Hadley and Carl S. Schmidt II have mastered the art of innkeeping at this beautiful 1891 ruby sandstone mansion. Choose from eight antique-appointed guest rooms, all with private baths, some with a whirlpool tub for two, a fireplace or balcony. Each of the guest rooms is uniquely decorated. The Gold Banner Suite features a brass bed, fireplace and cozy sitting area. The Pasqueflower Room on the third floor boasts a six-foot, round whirlpool tub located in the turret of the mansion. Enjoy a full breakfast each morning and Colorado wine in the evening. Experience the Victorian luxury of yesterday in present-day Denver.

Innkeeper(s): Jay Hadley & Carl Schmidt II. $85-175. 8 rooms with PB, 2 with FP, 3 suites. Breakfast included in rates. Types of meals: Full bkfst. Beds: KQT. Cable TV, reading lamp, stereo, refrigerator, clock radio, telephone, whirlpool tubs, fireplaces and parlor games in room. Air conditioning. Fax, copier, parlor games and CD player on premises. Handicap access. Amusement parks, antiquing, cross-country skiing, downhill skiing, fishing, golf, live theater, parks, shopping, sporting events, tennis and water sports nearby.

Publicity: *Yellow Brick Road, Life on Capitol Hill, Journal Constitution, Denver Post, Rocky Mountain News, Westword and Citysearch.com.*

Certificate may be used: Dec. 1-March 31, Sunday through Thursday.

Empire   C5

Mad Creek B&B

PO Box 404
Empire, CO 80438-0404
(303)569-2003 (888)266-1498
Internet: www.madcreekbnb.com
E-mail: madmadam@aol.com

Circa 1881. There is just the right combination of Victorian décor with lace, flowers, antiques and gingerbread trim on the façade of this mountain town cottage. The home-away-from-home atmosphere is inviting and the Eastlake furnishings are comfortable. Relax in front of the rock fireplace while watching a movie, peruse the library filled with local lore or plan an adventure with local maps and guide books. Empire was once a mining town, conveniently located within 20 to 60 minutes of at least six major ski areas.

Innkeeper(s): Myrna & Tonya Payne. $75-105. 3 rooms with PB. Breakfast, afternoon tea and snacks/refreshments included in rates. Types of meals: Full bkfst and early coffee/tea. Beds: KQD. Reading lamp, ceiling fan, toiletries and down comforters in room. TV, VCR and outdoor hot tub and gazebo where breakfast is served when weather permits among the beautiful wildflower gardens on premises. Antiquing, cross-country skiing, downhill skiing, fishing, horseback riding, parks, shopping, water sports and gambling nearby.

Location: Mountains. Rivers.

Certificate may be used: Oct. 15-Nov. 20, Sunday-Thursday; April 16-May 20, Sunday-Thursday.

Fraser   C5

Wild Horse Inn Bed and Breakfast

PO Box 609
Fraser, CO 80442
(970)726-0456 Fax:(970)726-9678
Internet: www.wildhorseinn.com
E-mail: info@wildhorseinn.com

Circa 1994. Surrounded by majestic mountains, this inn was built from handhewn 400-year-old Engleman pine logs, moss-covered rock and huge picture windows. Sitting among acres of meadows and trees on a ridge above Fraser Valley, the casual lodge atmosphere exudes a rustic flair with superb hospitality and gracious service. Plan the next day's activities by the massive stone fireplace. Read a book from the library. Munch on a treat from the bottomless cookie jar. Each spacious guest bedroom features a private balcony, cozy robes and a whirlpool bath. Tastebuds are teased and tempted with locally roasted coffee, blackberry scones, orange muffins or brioche. Ham crisps with baked eggs and mushrooms, Mexican Frittata or Lemon Souffle Crepes are additional breakfast favorites served in the dining room. Schedule a massage, soak in the hot tub or lounge on a sun deck.

Innkeeper(s): John Cribari and Christine French. $160-215. 7 rooms with PB. Breakfast, afternoon tea and snacks/refreshments included in rates. Types of meals: Full gourmet bkfst, veg bkfst, early coffee/tea, picnic lunch and room service. Beds: KQT. Modem hook-up, data port, TV, VCR, reading lamp, clock radio, telephone, robes and slippers, private balconies and jetted tubs in room. Fax, spa, sauna, library, parlor games, fireplace, gift shop, massage services, fitness equipment, movie library and winter-season soups on premises. Antiquing, art galleries, bicycling, canoeing/kayaking, cross-country skiing, downhill skiing, fishing, golf, hiking, horseback riding, museums, parks, shopping, water sports, Rocky Mountain National Park, rafting, mountain biking, hot air ballooning, snowmobiling, dog sled rides and ice skating nearby.

Location: Mountains.

Publicity: *Quick Escapes and Travel & Leisure.*

Certificate may be used: April, May, October-Nov. 15.

Glenwood Springs   C3

Glenwood Springs Victorian B & B

1020 Colorado Ave
Glenwood Springs, CO 81601-3320
(970)945-0517
Internet: www.glenwood-colorado-inn.com
E-mail: reneevictorianbb@yahoo.com

Circa 1909. Decorative shingles in shades of purple and white with gingerbread trim accent the historic wood frame of this Victorian Stick house. Restored to reflect its original era, oak moldings and wainscoting mingle with wallpapers and lace as well as French, American and English antique furnishings. The parlor boasts an oak and marble fireplace mantle and chandelier. Lavish guest bedrooms include robes, comforters, quilts and fine linens. Ask about in-room mini spa treatments. An elegant and hearty breakfast is served in the dining room with crystal, silver and china. Enjoy afternoon tea with treats.

Innkeeper(s): Renee Pogrow. $125-150. 3 rooms, 1 with PB. Breakfast, afternoon tea and snacks/refreshments included in rates. Types of meals: Full gourmet bkfst, veg bkfst and early coffee/tea. Beds: Q. Reading lamp, clock radio, robes, fans and various sundries in room. TV, VCR, library, parlor games, telephone, fireplace, gift shop, front porch, gifts and mini spa treatments on premises. Amusement parks, antiquing, art galleries, bicycling, canoeing/kayaking, cross-country skiing, downhill skiing, fishing, golf, hiking, horseback riding, live theater, museums, parks, shopping, tennis, water sports, wineries, hot springs, vapor caves, caverns, spas, trails and rafting nearby.

Location: City, mountains.

Publicity: *Post Independent and Denver Post.*

Certificate may be used: November-April except holidays (Thanksgiving, Christmas, New Years, Valentines Day, Easter, etc) Sunday-Thursday.

Sunlight Mountain Inn B&B

10252 County Rd 117
Glenwood Springs, CO 81601
(970)945-5225 (800)733-4757 Fax:(970)947-1900
Internet: sunlightinn.com
E-mail: gddubois@aol.com

Circa 1968. Located at the foot of Sunlight Mountain Resort Ski Area, this lodge provides cozy guest rooms decorated in a casual Western style. One room has a fireplace and whirlpool tub. Four Mile Creek runs through the property, which is locat-

ed at 8,000 feet. The inn originally was known as the Apple Inn and was built by a prominent local citizen, instrumental in the development of the nearby Sunlight Ski Area. A full breakfast, including such items as blueberry pancakes,

haystack eggs or perhaps an apple dish is served in the inn's dining room, which overlooks the ski area. During the winter season, dinner is served. The inn's cuisine is American country — Western style. The inn has an outdoor hot tub. Snowmobiling and horseback riding excursions are available nearby. The inn is 12 miles from a renown hot springs.

Innkeeper(s): Pierre & Gretchenn DuBois. $65-164. 20 rooms with PB, 1 with FP. Breakfast included in rates. Types of meals: Full gourmet bkfst. Beds: KQDT. Clock radio, telephone and coffeemaker in room. TV, VCR, spa, fireplace and full bar on premises. Art galleries, bicycling, canoeing/kayaking, cross-country skiing, downhill skiing, fishing, golf, hiking, horseback riding, parks, shopping and water sports nearby.

Location: Mountains.

Certificate may be used: Anytime, subject to availability.

Lake City   F3

Old Carson Inn

8401 County Rd 30, PO Box 144
Lake City, CO 81235-0144
(970)944-2511 (800)294-0608
Internet: www.oldcarsoninn.com
E-mail: oldcarsoninn@aol.com

Circa 1990. Located at an elevation of 9,400 feet, this massive log house provides a secluded mountain setting in a forest of aspens and spruce. The Bonanza King Mine Room features a

cathedral ceiling and soaring windows overlooking an aspen grove. Native American artifacts and antiques are sprinkled throughout the inn.

Innkeeper(s): Clay & Bettina Wormington. $55-105. 7 rooms with PB. Breakfast included in rates. Types of meals: Full bkfst and picnic lunch. Beds: KQ. Reading lamp and ceiling fan in room. VCR, spa, parlor games, telephone, fireplace and satellite TV on premises. Antiquing, cross-country skiing, fishing, shopping, snowmobiling and Jeeping nearby.

Location: Mountains.

"Words are inadequate to express how very much we delighted in our stay at your beautiful home."

Certificate may be used: Between Memorial weekend and Sept. 30, excluding holidays, weekend and special events as available.

Leadville   D5

The Ice Palace Inn Bed & Breakfast

813 Spruce St
Leadville, CO 80461-3555
(719)486-8272 (800)754-2840 Fax:(719)486-0345
Internet: icepalaceinn.com
E-mail: stay@icepalaceinn.com

Circa 1899. Innkeeper Kami Kolakowski was born in this historic Colorado town, and it was her dream to one day return and run a bed & breakfast. Now with husband Giles, she has created a restful retreat out of this turn-of-the-century home built with lumber from the famed Leadville Ice Palace. Giles and Kami have filled the home with antiques and pieces of history from the Ice Palace and the town. Guests are treated to a mouth-watering gourmet breakfast with treats such as stuffed French toast or German apple pancakes. After a day enjoying Leadville, come back and enjoy a soak in the hot tub.

Innkeeper(s): Giles & Kami Kolakowski. $89-169. 5 rooms with PB, 5 with FP, 2 with HT. Breakfast, afternoon tea and snacks/refreshments included in rates. Types of meals: Full gourmet bkfst, veg bkfst, early coffee/tea and room service. Beds: KQDT. Cable TV, VCR, reading lamp, stereo, refrigerator, ceiling fan, clock radio, telephone, coffeemaker, turn-down service, desk, hot tub/spa and fireplace in room. Fax, copier, spa, library, parlor games, gift shop and hot tub on premises. Antiquing, art galleries, bicycling, canoeing/kayaking, cross-country skiing, downhill skiing, fishing, golf, hiking, horseback riding, live theater, museums, parks, shopping, tennis and water sports nearby.

Location: Mountains.

Publicity: *Herald Democrat, The Denver Post, The Great Divide, Good Morning America, CNN, The Fox Report and National Public Radio.*

Certificate may be used: Anytime, April, May, October, November, excluding holidays for November and May, subject to availability.

The Leadville Country Inn

127 E 8th St
Leadville, CO 80461-3507
(719)486-2354 (800)748-2354 Fax:(719)486-0300
E-mail: info@leadvillebednbreakfast.com

Circa 1892. Colorado's spectacular scenery follows along the route of the Silver Kings into Leadville at a height of 10,200 feet. Staying in this restored Victorian adds more magic to your experience. Built by a mining executive, this Queen Anne offers a romantic turret and many original features. There is a hot tub in the garden. The inn is often selected for anniversaries and is a popular romantic getaway for couples.

Innkeeper(s): Maureen & Gretchen Scanlon. $70-160. 9 rooms with PB. Breakfast included in rates. Types of meals: Full gourmet bkfst, early coffee/tea and snacks/refreshments. Ceiling fan and some with TV in room. VCR and spa on premises. Antiquing, cross-country skiing, downhill skiing, fishing, hiking and shopping nearby.

Location: City, mountains. Highest city in North America— 10,200 ft.

Publicity: *Rocky Mountain News, Herald Democrat, Country Travels, Sunset Magazine and Denver Post.*

"This Inn has more charm than a love story written for entertainment."

Certificate may be used: Sunday-Thursday, April and May, subject to availability. Not valid during Memorial Day weekend or Memorial Day.

Peri & Ed's Mountain Hide Away

201 W 8th St
Leadville, CO 80461-3529
(719)486-0716 (800)933-3715 Fax:(719)486-2181
Internet: www.mountainhideaway.com
E-mail: solder@mountainhideaway.com

Circa 1879. This former boarding house was built during the boom days of Leadville. Families can picnic on the large lawn sprinkled with wildflowers under soaring pines. Shoppers and history buffs can enjoy exploring historic Main Street, one block away. The surrounding mountains are a natural playground offering a wide variety of activities, and the innkeepers will be happy to let you know their favorite spots and help with directions. The sunny Augusta Tabor room features a sprawling king-size bed with a warm view of the rugged peaks.

Innkeeper(s): Eva Vigil. $49-129. 10 rooms with PB, 2 with FP and 2 cottages. Breakfast included in rates. Types of meals: Full bkfst. Beds: KQDT. Ceiling fan and clock radio in room. VCR, spa, library, parlor games and telephone on premises. Antiquing, cross-country skiing, downhill skiing, fishing, live theater, parks and shopping nearby.

Location: Mountains.

Certificate may be used: October-Dec. 15, April 15-June 30, Monday-Wednesday.

Mancos   G2

Bauer House

PO Box 1049
Mancos, CO 81328
(970)533-9707 (800)733-9707
Internet: www.bauer-house.com
E-mail: bauerhse@fone.net

Circa 1890. Built by town founder George Bauer, this three-story brick and stone Victorian home displays several of the prominent family's possessions as well as old newspapers, pictures and bank ledgers. Guest bedrooms and a suite feature a classic decor with antique furnishings and splendid mountain views. The third-floor Southwest-style penthouse includes a kitchen with a bar. Bobbi makes a changing creative menu for each day's breakfast. Enjoy popular favorites like her signature eggs Benedict, stuffed pancakes, homemade waffles or stratas accompanied by fresh fruit, muffins and breads. Relax on porches and patios, visit the inn's antique shop or take a ride to historic sites on the Bauer House Buggy (a horseless carriage). Practice on the putting green, play croquet or bocce ball. The entrance to Mesa Verde National Park is seven miles away.

Innkeeper(s): Bobbi Black. $95-125. 5 rooms with PB. Breakfast, afternoon tea, snacks/refreshments and hors d'oeuvres included in rates. Types of meals: Full gourmet bkfst, early coffee/tea and picnic lunch. Beds: QT. TV, reading lamp, CD player, ceiling fan, telephone, turn-down service, desk and penthouse has kitchenette in room. VCR, fax, copier, parlor games, fireplace and computer e-mail on premises. Limited handicap access. Antiquing, art galleries, fishing, golf, hiking, horseback riding, live theater, parks, shopping, sporting events, tennis and water sports nearby.

Location: Mountains. Historic town.

Publicity: *Colorado Life Styles, Durango Herald, Denver Post, Arrington's Book of Lists for Inns:* rated #5 for Best Customer Service in North America - 2003 & 2004, *Colorado History Now, Inside/Outside, Country Magazine* and CBS.

"Bobbi went out of her way to make our visit to Mancos more enjoyable. She is an excellent ambassador for the Mancos Valley and quite

an interesting person to know. The Bauer House should be recommended as the place to stay, to anyone visiting the area!"

Certificate may be used: April 1-July 1.

Manitou Springs   E6

1892 Victoria's Keep Bed & Breakfast Inn

202 Ruxton Ave
Manitou Springs, CO 80829
(719)685-5354 (800)905-5337 Fax:(719)685-5913
Internet: www.victoriaskeep.com
E-mail: info@victoriaskeep.com

Circa 1892. A stream passes by the wraparound front porch of this Queen Anne Victorian. Stained glass windows and a turret complete the picture. The home is furnished in period antiques, and there are coordinated wallpapers. Every room has a fireplace of its own as well as Queen beds. Most have whirlpool tubs for two and feather beds. Afternoon dessert is offered, and in the morning a gourmet breakfast is served.

Innkeeper(s): Jay Rohrer and Karen Cullen. $80-185. 6 rooms with PB, 5 with FP, 4 suites. Breakfast, afternoon tea and snacks/refreshments included in rates. Types of meals: Full gourmet bkfst, veg bkfst and early coffee/tea. Beds: Q. Reading lamp, CD player, refrigerator, clock radio, fireplace and Jacuzzi tub in room. Air conditioning. TV, VCR, library, parlor games and telephone on premises. Antiquing, art galleries, bicycling, canoeing/kayaking, fishing, golf, hiking, horseback riding, live theater, museums, parks, shopping, sporting events and United States Olympic Training Center nearby.

Location: Mountains. Base of Pikes Peak.

Certificate may be used: November-April, Sunday-Thursday, except special events and holidays.

Gray's Avenue Hotel

711 Manitou Ave
Manitou Springs, CO 80829-1809
(719)685-1277 (800)294-1277
Internet: www.graysbandb.com
E-mail: info@graysbandb.com

Circa 1886. This 1886 Queen Anne shingled Victorian inn is in the Manitou Springs Historic Preservation District, which is listed in the National Register of Historic Places. It was one of Manitou Spring's original hotels. The four guest rooms and three suites are comfortably appointed — from the cozy Bird Room with its bay window to the Orange Suite, which has three rooms, each with a double bed. Start off your day with a  hearty breakfast, including courses like waffles with fresh strawberries and whipped cream, bacon, fresh fruit, coffee and tea. Then relax on the large front porch, stroll through the town with its shops and restaurants or put on your hiking boots to explore the incredible natural wonderland. Within walking or driving distance is the Cog Railroad, Pikes Peak, the Cave of the Winds, Cliff Dwellings, the Air Force Academy, the Commonwheel Artist Co-op and a number of museums and art galleries. Hikers will enjoy Mueller State Park, Waldo Canyon, Intemann and Barr Trails, Garden of the Gods and more. Airport pickup and return can usually be arranged.

Innkeeper(s): Kevin Abney. $75-110. 7 rooms with PB, 3 with FP, 3 total suites, including 2 two-bedroom suites and 1 cottage. Breakfast and snacks/refreshments included in rates. Types of meals: Full bkfst, veg bkfst and early coffee/tea. Beds: KQDT. Cable TV, reading lamp, ceiling fan and clock radio in room. VCR, fax, copier, spa, library, parlor games, telephone, fireplace and massages on premises. Antiquing, art galleries, bicycling, fishing, golf, hiking, horseback riding, live theater, museums, parks, shopping, sporting events and tennis nearby.

Location: Mountains.

Certificate may be used: Anytime, Sunday-Thursday.

Red Crags B&B Inn

302 El Paso Blvd
Manitou Springs, CO 80829-2308
(719)685-1920 (800)721-2248 Fax:(719)685-1073
Internet: www.redcrags.com
E-mail: info@redcrags.com

Circa 1880. Well-known in this part of Colorado, this unique, four-story Victorian mansion sits on a bluff with a combination of views that includes Pikes Peak, Manitou Valley, Garden of the Gods and the city of Colorado Springs. There are antiques throughout the house. The formal dining room features a rare cherrywood Eastlake fireplace. Two of the suites include double whirlpool tubs.  Outside, guests can walk through beautifully landscaped gardens or enjoy a private picnic area with a barbecue pit and a spectacular view. Wine is served in the evenings.

Innkeeper(s): Howard & Lynda Lerner. $85-185. 8 rooms with PB, 8 with FP, 5 total suites, including 1 two-bedroom suite. Breakfast, afternoon tea, snacks/refreshments and wine included in rates. Types of meals: Full gourmet bkfst, veg bkfst and early coffee/tea. Beds: K. Data port, reading lamp, snack bar, clock radio, telephone, desk, hot tub/spa, fireplace, feather beds, TV available upon request, some with two-person jetted tubs and 3 with air conditioning in room. Fax, copier, spa, parlor games and gift shop on premises. Antiquing, art galleries, bicycling, cross-country skiing, fishing, golf, hiking, horseback riding, live theater, museums, parks, shopping, sporting events, tennis, Pikes Peak, Olympic Training Center, Focus on the Family, Glen Eyrie Castle and Cave of the Winds nearby.

Location: City, mountains.

Publicity: *Rocky Mountain News, Bridal Guide, Denver Post, Los Angeles Times, Springs Woman, Colorado Springs Gazette and Front Range Living.*

"What a beautiful, historical and well-preserved home - exceptional hospitality and comfort. What wonderful people! Highly recommended!"

Certificate may be used: Oct. 15 to April 30, Sunday-Thursday; excluding holidays, subject to availability.

Monte Vista   G5

The Windmill B&B

4340 W Hwy 160
Monte Vista, CO 81144
(719)852-0438 (800)467-3441

Circa 1959. This Southwestern-style inn affords panoramic views of the surrounding Sangre De Cristo and San Juan mountain ranges. The 22-acre grounds still include the namesake windmill that once was used to irrigate water in the yard and garden. Now it stands guard over the hot tub. Each of the guest rooms is decorated in a different theme, with a few antiques placed here and there. The plentiful country breakfast is served in a dining room with mountain views.

Innkeeper(s): Sharon & Dennis Kay. $65-99. 4 rooms with PB. Breakfast and snacks/refreshments included in rates. Types of meals: Full gourmet bkfst and early coffee/tea. Beds: KQT. Reading lamp, turn-down service and hot tub/spa in room. Telephone and fireplace on premises. Antiquing, cross-country skiing, downhill skiing, fishing, live theater, parks and shopping nearby.

Location: Mountains.

Certificate may be used: Sunday-Thursday.

Ouray   F3

Christmas House B&B Inn

PO Box 786
Ouray, CO 81427
(970)325-4992 (888)325-9627 Fax:(970)325-4992
Internet: www.christmashousebandb.com
E-mail: email@christmashousebandb.com

Circa 1889. Peace and goodwill abound at this delightful romantic Victorian lodge surrounded by the San Juan Range of the Rocky Mountains. The tiny town, population 700, is nine blocks long and six blocks wide. It sits at the northern end of the portion of Highway 550 known as "The Million Dollar Highway" because of its spectacular views. The inn has five deluxe suites, each with a double whirlpool tub and awesome views. Four have fireplaces and private entrances. Guests can enjoy the Dickensesque English Ivy suite with its antique Victorian bed and breathtaking mountain view. Or they may choose the Mistletoe (perfect for honeymooners and other lovers) with its fireplace and pink half canopy bed. Breakfast is a celebration of menus with names like "Joy To the World," "Up on the Housetop" and "Feliz Navidad." Happy, hungry guests will enjoy entrees like maple/rosemary grilled ham, crepes, waffles, omelets and juices.

Innkeeper(s): George Allyson Crosby. $95-170. 5 rooms, 4 with FP, 5 suites. Breakfast and snacks/refreshments included in rates. Types of meals: Full gourmet bkfst, veg bkfst, early coffee/tea and gourmet dinner. Beds: QT. Modem hook-up, data port, cable TV, VCR, reading lamp, stereo, refrigerator, ceiling fan, clock radio, telephone, coffeemaker, turn-down service, desk, hot tub/spa, fireplace, private Jacuzzis for two, private entrances, private & shared saunas for two, robes and dryers in room. Air conditioning. TV, fax, copier, sauna, library, parlor games, fireplace, gift shop, video/CD library, telescope, local menus, ice and iron/board on premises. Antiquing, art galleries, bicycling, canoeing/kayaking, cross-country skiing, downhill skiing, fishing, golf, hiking, horseback riding, live theater, museums, parks, shopping, tennis, water sports, wineries, Jeep tours and rentals, mine tours, ballooning, mountain biking, ice climbing, sledding, snowmobiling, snowshoeing and ice skating nearby.

Location: Mountains.

Publicity: *Westwind, West Life and KJYE.*

Certificate may be used: Jan. 4-May 24, Sunday-Thursday (does not include Feb. 14 or Ice Festival), not available with any other discounts or promotions.

Wiesbaden Hot Springs Spa & Lodgings

PO Box 349
Ouray, CO 81427-0349
(970)325-4347 Fax:(970)325-4358
Internet: www.wiesbadenhotsprings.com
E-mail: lodge@wiesbadenhotsprings.com

Circa 1879. Built directly above natural mineral hot springs, this historic lodging establishment has a European flair. Below the main lodge and into the mountain is the natural Vaporcave, where the hot springs flow from thousands of feet below the earth's surface into a 108 degree soaking pool. The remains of an adobe where Chief Ouray resided while using the sacred water for its medicinal and healing qualities can be seen on the property. The Vaporcave, outdoor swimming pool and Lorelei, a privately rented outdoor soaking spa are all continually flowing hot springs. Therapeutic massage, Raindrop, LaStone and Dry Brushings are also offered as well as Aveda Concept Spa facials, wraps and polishes. The Wiesbaden is considered a place of unequaled ambiance.

Innkeeper(s): Linda Wright-Minter. $85-335. 20 rooms with PB, 2 with FP, 2 total suites, including 1 two-bedroom suite, 2 cottages and 2 guest houses. Types of meals: Early coffee/tea. Beds: KQDT. Cable TV, reading lamp, refrigerator, ceiling fan and telephone in room. Fax, spa, swimming and fireplace on premises. Antiquing, art galleries, bicycling, cross-country skiing, downhill skiing, golf, hiking, horseback riding, museums, parks, shopping, tennis and water sports nearby.

Location: Mountains.

Publicity: *Travel & Leisure, National Geographics Traveler, Spa, Sunset, Money, Lifestyles, New York Times and many other publications.*

Certificate may be used: Nov. 15-May 15, Sunday through Thursday excluding all holidays. All natural hot springs pools on premises.

Pagosa Springs   G4

Canyon Crest Lodge

201A Yeoman Dr
Pagosa Springs, CO 81147
(970)731-3773 (877)731-1377 Fax:(970)731-5502
Internet: www.canyoncrestlodge.com
E-mail: canyoncrest@pagosa.net

Circa 1998. Sitting on 40 acres of tall pine trees and mountainous rocky terrain with magnificent views of Pagosa Peak, Valley and the Great Divide, this English Country House is a traditional rock structure with 18-inch thick walls. Gather by the large fireplace in the lounge and enjoy the relaxing ambiance. Guest suites are named after famous castles, and can be accessed from the private upper deck. Each suite includes a comfortable sitting area with a TV, and a walk-in closet with robes and slippers. Breakfast is served in the dining room and can be taken to the dining deck or back to the room. Other meals can be arranged in advance. Soak in the hot tub overlooking the gorgeous scenery.

Innkeeper(s): Valerie Green. $100-200. 6 rooms, 1 with FP, 6 suites and 1 conference room. Types of meals: Country bkfst, veg bkfst, early coffee/tea, picnic lunch, afternoon tea, gourmet dinner and room service. Beds: KQ. Modem hook-up, data port, TV, VCR, reading lamp, stereo, refrigerator, snack bar, clock radio, telephone, turn-down service, hot tub/spa and voice mail in room. Fax, copier, spa, sauna, bicycles, library, parlor games, fireplace and laundry facility on premises. Handicap access. Antiquing, art galleries, bicycling, canoeing/kayaking, cross-country skiing, downhill skiing, fishing, golf, hiking, horseback riding, live theater, museums, parks, shopping, sporting events, tennis, water sports and wineries nearby.

Location: Mountains.

Certificate may be used: Anytime, subject to availability, Sunday-Thursday.

Paonia   D3

The Bross Hotel B&B

PO Box 85
Paonia, CO 81428
(970)527-6776 Fax:(970)527-7737
Internet: www.paonia-inn.com
E-mail: brosshotel@paonia.com

Circa 1906. A group of artisans, carpenters and craftspeople restored this turn-of-the-century western hotel to its original splendor with front porch and balcony. Wood floors and trim, dormer windows and exposed brick walls all add to the Victorian decor. For pleasure, relax in the sitting area or library/TV/game room. A conference room and communications center is perfect for business. Guest bedrooms feature antiques and handmade quilts. Some can be adjoined into suites. Breakfast is an adventure in seasonal culinary delights that cover the antique back bar in the dining room. Visit Black Canyon, Gunnison National Park, Grand Mesa, West Elk and Ragged Wilderness areas.

Innkeeper(s): Linda Lentz . $100. 10 rooms with PB and 1 conference room. Breakfast and snacks/refreshments included in rates. Types of meals: Full gourmet bkfst, veg bkfst and early coffee/tea. Beds: KQDT. Modem hook-up, data port, ceiling fan and telephone in room. TV, VCR, fax, copier, spa, library and parlor games on premises. Antiquing, art galleries, bicycling, canoeing/kayaking, cross-country skiing, fishing, golf, hiking, horseback riding, museums, parks, shopping, wineries, dinosaur dig and explore the many activities of the Black Canyon of the Gunnison National Park nearby.

Location: Mountains.

Publicity: *Denver Post and Grand Junction Sentinel.*

Certificate may be used: Anytime, November-April, subject to availability.

Pueblo   E7

Abriendo Inn

300 W Abriendo Ave
Pueblo, CO 81004-1814
(719)544-2703 Fax:(719)542-6544
Internet: www.abriendoinn.com
E-mail: info@abriendoinn.com

Circa 1906. Upon entering this inn, it becomes apparent why it was chosen "Pueblo's Best Weekend Getaway" and "Best Bed and Breakfast Inn for the Colorado Front Range." Special details include curved stained-glass windows, a spiral staircase and parquet floors. Comfortably elegant guest bedrooms feature canopy or brass beds, heart-shaped double whirlpool tubs, cable TV, VCR, microwave and small refrigerator. A typical breakfast served at flexible times, might include a  fruit cup, tomato-basil frittata, nectarine kuchen, cheddar toast, Dutch crumb muffin and beverages. A 24-hour complimentary snack/refreshment center is an added convenience. Enjoy the one acre of park-like grounds and a wraparound porch lined with wicker rockers and chairs for a relaxing change of pace.

Innkeeper(s): Mark and Cassandra Chase . $74-130. 10 rooms, 9 with PB, 1 suite. Breakfast included in rates. Types of meals: Full gourmet bkfst, veg bkfst, early coffee/tea and snacks/refreshments. Beds: KQ. Modem hook-up, data port, cable TV, VCR, reading lamp, refrigerator, ceiling fan, snack bar, clock radio, telephone, desk and whirlpool tub for two in room. Air conditioning. TV, fax, copier, parlor games, fireplace and gift shop on premises. Antiquing, art galleries, beach, bicycling, canoeing/kayaking, cross-country skiing, fishing, golf, hiking, horseback riding, live theater, museums, parks, shopping, sporting events, tennis and water sports nearby.

Location: City.

Publicity: *Pueblo Chieftain, Rocky Mountain News, Denver Post, Colorado Springs Gazette, Sunset Magazine and Boulder Daily Camera.*

"This is a great place with the friendliest people. I've been to a lot of B&Bs; this one is top drawer."

Certificate may be used: Sunday & Monday only, November through March, holidays excluded.

Salida   E5

River Run Inn

8495 Co Rd 160
Salida, CO 81201
(719)539-3818 (800)385-6925 Fax:(801)659-1878
Internet: www.riverruninn.com
E-mail: riverrun@amigo.net

Circa 1895. This gracious brick home, a National Register building, is located on the banks of the Arkansas River, three miles from town. It was once the poor farm, for folks down on their luck who were willing to work in exchange for food and lodging. The house has been renovated to reflect a country-eclectic style and has six guest rooms, most enhanced by mountain views. The location is ideal for anglers, rafters, hikers, bikers and skiers. A 13-bed, third floor is great for groups. A full country breakfast, afternoon cookies and refreshments, evening brandy and sherry are offered daily.

Innkeeper(s): Sally Griego & Brad Poulson. $98-110. 6 rooms with PB and 1 conference room. Breakfast and snacks/refreshments included in rates. Types of meals: Full gourmet bkfst, veg bkfst, early coffee/tea, picnic lunch and dinner. Beds: KQT. Reading lamp in room. TV, VCR, library, parlor games, telephone, fishing and lawn games on premises. Limited handicap access. Antiquing, art galleries, bicycling, canoeing/kayaking, cross-country skiing, downhill skiing, fishing, golf, hiking, horseback riding, live theater, museums, parks, shopping, tennis, water sports, wineries and snowshoeing nearby.

Location: Country, waterfront. Mountain view.

Publicity: *Men's Journal, Denver Post, Colorado Springs Gazette, CBS Denver, The Travel Channel and MSNBC.com.*

"So glad we found a B&B with such character and a great owner as well."

Certificate may be used: Nov. 1-May 31, Sunday through Thursday.

Silverton   F3

The Wyman Hotel & Inn

1371 Greene Street
Silverton, CO 81433
(970)387-5372 (800)609-7845 Fax:(970)387-5745
Internet: www.thewyman.com
E-mail: thewyman@frontier.net

Circa 1902. A stately building renown for its ballroom in the early 1900s, this modern luxury inn is listed in the National Register of Historic Places. Enjoy the smoke-free environment with two common rooms that offer access to a large video library. Well-appointed guest bedrooms are comfortably furnished with antiques and boast spectacular views. Stay in a romantic suite with a whirlpool bath for two. Highly acclaimed gourmet breakfasts are served in the Dining Room accented by the music of Mozart. Sunnyside souffle with roasted potatoes is one of the mouth-watering entrees that may accompany homemade baked goods, fresh fruit and Costa Rican coffee. An elegant, four-course dinner by candlelight features signature dishes such as Veal Piccata and Thai Shrimp and Scallops in Coconut Curry. Rent mountain bikes for a closer look at the San Juan Mountains. Visit Mesa Verde National Park and Anasazi ruins or the Durango and Silverton Narrow Gauge Railroad.

Innkeeper(s): Lorraine & Tom Lewis. $120-215. 17 rooms with PB, 5 suites. Breakfast and afternoon tea included in rates. Types of meals: Full gourmet bkfst, early coffee/tea and snacks/refreshments. Beds: KQ. Data port, TV, VCR, reading lamp, ceiling fan, clock radio, telephone, turn-down service, desk, two-person whirlpools (suites), whirlpool tubs (five rooms), feather beds and down duvets in room. Fax, copier, library, art gallery, videos, wine and cheese social hour and candlelight dinner available at additional charge on premises. Cross-country skiing, fishing, hiking, horseback riding, live theater, parks, shopping, folk and music festival, mountain biking, Jeeping to ghost towns, snowshoeing, sledding and downhill skiing at the new Silverton Mountain nearby.

Location: Mountains.

Publicity: *The Denver Post, The New York Times, Albuquerque Journal, The Gazette, Douglas County News-Press, The Salt Lake Tribune, Austin American Statesman, Outdoor Channel, The Travel Channel, Denver's KUSA News and winner of national award for Best Hospitality and Best Breakfast in U.S. B&Bs.*

"Everything and everyone great, hospitable and helpful. We had to change plans and leave at 6:15 a.m. and could not stay for breakfast so Tom was up at crack of dawn to fix us something. So very beyond

the call and much appreciated!!!"

Certificate may be used: Anytime, November-April, subject to availability, except holidays.

Steamboat Springs   B4

The Inn at Steamboat

3070 Columbine Dr
Steamboat Springs, CO 80487
(970)879-2600 (800)872-2601 Fax:(970)879-9270
Internet: www.inn-at-steamboat.com
E-mail: gzabell@innatsteamboat.com

Circa 1973. Whatever the season, this 34-room inn is near many activities. Skiing is just three blocks away, and in the warm months, guests can hike, bike, go white-water rafting or take a trip through the wilderness on horseback. Most of the guest rooms, which feature country decor, offer views of the ski slopes or surrounding Yampa Valley. In the spring, the grounds are covered with flowers.

Innkeeper(s): Glen and Connie Zabel, Jeanne Morrison. $59-279. 34 rooms, 30 with PB, 4 suites and 1 conference room. Breakfast and afternoon tea included in rates. Types of meals: Cont plus, early coffee/tea and snacks/refreshments. Beds: KQ. Modem hook-up, data port, cable TV, reading lamp, clock radio, telephone, coffeemaker, desk and voice mail in room. Fax, copier, swimming, sauna, parlor games, fireplace, laundry facility and shuttle service to and from the Steamboat ski area during the ski season (8:30 a.m.-5:00 p.m. daily) on premises. Cross-country skiing, downhill skiing, fishing, golf, live theater, parks, shopping, tennis and water sports nearby.

Location: Mountains. At the base of the Steamboat ski area, 4 blocks to the lifts.

"We will treasure the memory of our long weekend at your inn."

Certificate may be used: April 1 to May 31 and Oct. 1 to Nov. 30 (full non-discounted rates apply, some restrictions apply).

Walsenburg   F6

La Plaza Inn

118 West Sixth
Walsenburg, CO 81089
(719)738-5700 (800)352-9237 Fax:(719)738-6220
E-mail: Laplazainn@wmconnect.com

Circa 1907. Stay in the relaxed comfort of this historic stucco inn painted in traditional Southwest colors. Relax in the large well-appointed lobby or second-floor sitting room. Each guest bedroom imparts its own ambiance and is nicely furnished with a mixture of period pieces. Many of the suites feature fully  equipped kitchens. Breakfast is individually served or a buffet is set up in the on-site cafe and bookstore that boasts original 15-foot tin ceilings. Sit in the refreshing shade of the back yard. Enjoy the scenic area by skiing local mountains, hiking nearby trails or engaging in water activities and other outdoor sports.

Innkeeper(s): Martie Henderson. $75-90. 10 rooms with PB, 6 suites and 1 conference room. Breakfast included in rates. Types of meals: Country bkfst, veg bkfst, early coffee/tea and lunch. Restaurant on premises. Beds: KQDT. Modem hook-up, data port, cable TV, VCR, reading lamp, refrigerator, ceiling fan, snack bar, telephone, coffeemaker and desk in room. Air conditioning. Fax, copier, library, parlor games, cafe and bookstore on premises. Antiquing, art galleries, bicycling, canoeing/kayaking, cross-country skiing, fishing, golf, hiking, live theater, museums, parks, shopping, tennis and water sports nearby.

Location: Mountains.

Certificate may be used: Anytime, November-March, subject to availability.

Winter Park C5

Alpen Rose

PO Box 769
Winter Park, CO 80482-0769
(970)726-5039 (866)531-1373 Fax:(970)726-0993
Internet: www.alpenrosebb.com
E-mail: robinana@rkymtnhi.com

Circa 1965. The innkeepers of this European-style mountain B&B like to share their love of the mountains with guests. There is a superb view of the James and Perry Peaks from the large southern deck where you can witness spectacular sunrises and evening alpen glows. The view is enhanced by lofty pines, wild-flowers and quaking aspens. Each of the bedrooms is decorated with treasures brought over from Austria, including traditional featherbeds for the queen-size beds. The town of Winter Park is a small, friendly community located 68 miles west of Denver.

Innkeeper(s): Robin & Rupert Sommerauer. Call for rates. 6 rooms with PB, 1 suite. Breakfast and afternoon tea included in rates. Types of meals: Full gourmet bkfst, veg bkfst, early coffee/tea and snacks/refreshments. Beds: KQDT. Reading lamp and clock radio in room. TV, VCR, fax, copier, spa, library, telephone, fireplace and laundry facility on premises. Antiquing, art galleries, beach, canoeing/kayaking, cross-country skiing, downhill skiing, fishing, golf, hiking, horseback riding, museums, parks, shopping, tennis, water sports, sledding, sleigh rides, dog sleds, ballooning, river rafting, biking, Jeeping, alpine slide and rodeos nearby.

Location: Mountains.

Publicity: *Denver Post, Rocky Mountain News and PBS.*

Certificate may be used: May 25 through Nov. 15, Monday-Thursday.

Bear Paw Inn

871 Bear Paw Dr, PO Box 334
Winter Park, CO 80482
(970)887-1351
Internet: www.bearpaw-winterpark.com
E-mail: bearpaw@rkymtnhi.com

Circa 1989. Secluded, quiet and romantic, this massive award-winning log lodge is exactly the type of welcoming retreat one might hope to enjoy on a vacation in the Colorado wilderness, and the panoramic views of the Continental Divide and Rocky Mountain National Park are just one reason. The cozy interior is highlighted by log beams, massive log walls and antiques. There are two guest rooms, both with a Jacuzzi tub. The master has a private deck with a swing. Guests can snuggle up in feather beds topped with down comforters. Winter Park is a Mecca for skiers, and ski areas are just a few miles from the Bear Paw, as is ice skating, snowmobiling, horse-drawn sleigh rides and other winter activities. For summer guests, there is whitewater rafting, golfing, horseback riding and bike trails. There are 600 miles of bike trials, music festivals and much more.

Innkeeper(s): Rick & Sue Callahan. $170-215. 2 rooms with PB. Breakfast and snacks/refreshments included in rates. Types of meals: Full gourmet bkfst and early coffee/tea. Beds: Q. TV, reading lamp, refrigerator, turn-down service, feather beds, finest linens, Jacuzzi tubs and chocolates in room. VCR, fax, copier, telephone, fireplace, 3-course gourmet breakfast and homemade afternoon treats each day on premises. Antiquing, cross-country skiing, downhill skiing, fishing, live theater, shopping, water sports, hot air balloons, mountain bikes and summer rodeos nearby.

Location: Mountains.

Publicity: *Sunset Magazine, Cape Cod Life, Boston Globe, Los Angeles Times, Continental Airlines Quarterly, Denver Post, Rocky Mountain News, Log Homes Illustrated, Colorado Country Life,* voted "Outstanding Hospitality" by the Colorado Travel Writers and given 10 stars and chosen "Best Date Getaway" by the editors of Denver City Search.

"Outstanding hospitality."

Certificate may be used: October, November, April and May, Sunday-Thursday.

Outpost B&B Inn

PO Box 41
Winter Park, CO 80482
(970)726-5346 (800)430-4538 Fax:(970)726-0126
Internet: www.outpost-colorado.com
E-mail: outpost@coweblink.net

Circa 1972. Rocky mountain peaks, woods and rolling pastures surround this 40-acre spread, which affords views of the Continental Divide. Guests stay in an antique-filled lodge inn. The inn's atrium includes a hot tub. The innkeepers serve a huge, multi-course feast for breakfast. During the winter months, the innkeepers offer free shuttle service to Winter Park and Mary Jane ski areas.

Innkeeper(s): Ken & Barbara Parker. $125. 7 rooms with PB. Breakfast included in rates. Types of meals: Full gourmet bkfst, early coffee/tea, gourmet lunch, picnic lunch, snacks/refreshments and gourmet dinner. Beds: KQDT. Reading lamp, clock radio and desk in room. VCR, fax, spa, library, parlor games, telephone, fireplace and cross-country skiing on premises. Antiquing, cross-country skiing, downhill skiing, fishing, golf, live theater, parks, shopping, water sports, snowmobiling, horseback riding, biking and mountain biking nearby.

Location: Country, mountains. Ski area.

Publicity: *Denver Post.*

Certificate may be used: Sunday-Thursday; April 1-Dec. 1, Jan. 5-Feb. 1, no holidays.

Woodland Park D6

Pikes Peak Paradise

236 Pinecrest Rd
Woodland Park, CO 80863
(719)687-6656 (800)728-8282 Fax:(719)687-9008
E-mail: pppbnb@bemail.com

Circa 1987. This three-story Georgian Colonial with stately white columns rises unexpectedly from the wooded hills west of Colorado Springs. The south wall of the house has large windows to enhance its splendid views of Pikes Peak. A glass door opens from each guest suite onto a private deck or patio with the same riveting view. Eggs Benedict and baked French apple toast are some of the favorites offered for breakfast.

Innkeeper(s): Rayne & Bart Reese. $120-200. 5 rooms, 4 with FP, 5 suites. Breakfast included in rates. Types of meals: Full bkfst. Beds: KQ. Reading lamp, stereo, refrigerator, ceiling fan, clock radio, hot tub/spa, deluxe suites have TV/VCR and four have private hot tubs in room. VCR, fax, spa, parlor games and telephone on premises. Amusement parks, antiquing, bicycling, cross-country skiing, fishing, golf, hiking, horseback riding, live theater, parks, shopping, sporting events, water sports and gambling nearby.

Location: Mountains.

Publicity: *Rocky Mountain News, Denver Post* and Arlington's B&B Journal List.

Certificate may be used: Nov. 1-April 30 (excluding holidays and weekends).

Connecticut

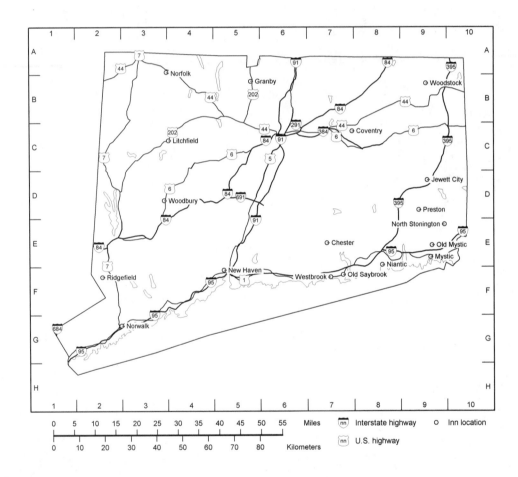

Map legend:
- Interstate highway
- U.S. highway
- Inn location

Miles: 0 5 10 15 20 25 30 35 40 45 50 55
Kilometers: 0 10 20 30 40 50 60 70 80

Locations shown on map:
- Norfolk
- Granby
- Woodstock
- Litchfield
- Coventry
- Jewett City
- Woodbury
- Preston
- North Stonington
- Chester
- Old Mystic
- Mystic
- Niantic
- Ridgefield
- New Haven
- Westbrook
- Old Saybrook
- Norwalk

Chester
E7

The Inn at Chester

318 W Main St
Chester, CT 06412-1026
(860)526-9541 (800)949-7829 Fax:(860)526-4387
Internet: www.innatchester.com
E-mail: innkeeper@innatchester.com

Circa 1778. More than 200 years ago, Jeremiah Parmelee built a clapboard farmhouse along a winding road named the Killingworth Turnpike. The Parmelee Homestead stands as a reflection of the past and is an inspiration for the Inn at Chester. Each of the rooms is individually appointed with Eldred Wheeler Reproductions. The Lincoln Suite has a sitting room with a fireplace. Enjoy lively conversation or live music while imbibing your favorite drink at the inn's tavern, Dunk's Landing. Outside Dunk's Landing, a 30-foot fireplace soars into the rafters. Fine dining is offered in the inn's post-and-beam restaurant.

Innkeeper(s): Sara Sullivan. $195-950. 44 rooms with PB, 2 with FP, 6 suites and 3 conference rooms. Breakfast included in rates. Types of meals: Cont plus, lunch and gourmet dinner. Restaurant on premises. Beds: KQDT. Cable TV, reading lamp, telephone, desk, orthopedic mattresses, Internet amenities and some with French doors in room. Air conditioning. VCR, fax, copier, sauna, bicycles, tennis, library, parlor games and fireplace on premises. Handicap access. Antiquing, cross-country skiing, downhill skiing, fishing, golf, live theater, parks, shopping and water sports nearby.

Location: Country.

Publicity: *New Haven Register, Hartford Courant, Pictorial Gazette, Discover Connecticut, New York Times, Connecticut Magazine and Food Network.*

Certificate may be used: Nov. 1-April 1, Sunday-Thursday.

Coventry
C7

Bird-In-Hand

2011 Main St
Coventry, CT 06238-2034
(860)742-0032 (877)348-0032
Internet: www.thebirdinhand.com
E-mail: info@thebirdinhand.com

Circa 1731. Prepare for a remarkable journey back in time at this former 18th-century tavern. Original wide-board floors, fireplaces and raised paneled walls reflect that era. Romantic canopy beds and Jacuzzi tubs boast added comfort to the guest bedrooms. A secret closet may have harbored runaway slaves during the Underground Railroad. Spacious privacy is offered in the cottage. Conferences and small weddings are accommodated easily. Local universities, Caprilands Herb Farm and Nathan Hale Homestead all are nearby.

Innkeeper(s): Susan Crandall. $90-150. 4 rooms with PB, 3 with FP and 1 cottage. Breakfast included in rates. Types of meals: Country bkfst and early coffee/tea. Beds: QT. Cable TV, VCR, reading lamp, refrigerator, ceiling fan, clock radio, turn-down service and fireplace in room. Air conditioning. Fax, copier, parlor games and telephone on premises. Antiquing, art galleries, beach, canoeing/kayaking, fishing, hiking, live theater, museums, parks, shopping, sporting events, water sports, wineries and casinos nearby.

Location: Country.

Publicity: *Journal Inquirer, Willimantic Chronicle, The Hartford Courant and WFSB.*

"We were delighted then, to find such a jewel in the Bird-In-Hand."

Certificate may be used: From Dec. 1 to May 1, Sunday-Thursday.

Granby
B5

The Dutch Iris Inn B&B

239 Salmon Brook Street
Granby, CT 06035
(860)844-0262 (877)280-0743 Fax:(860)844-0248
Internet: www.dutchirisinn.com
E-mail: info@dutchirisinn.com

Circa 1812. For many years this historic Colonial was used as a summer home. Some of the inn's antiques were the original furnishings, including a Louis XIV couch, Chickering grand piano, fainting couch, four-poster bed and marble-top dresser. Relax in the keeping room by a roaring fire, where the previous owners did the cooking. Several guest bedrooms feature working fireplaces. A customized breakfast menu is savored by candlelight and classical music. Half of the three acres feature perennial and bulb gardens, as well as wild blackberries and blueberries. Sip a cold beverage in a rocking chair on the side porch.

Innkeeper(s): Kevin & Belma Marshall. $99-149. 6 rooms with PB, 4 with FP. Breakfast and snacks/refreshments included in rates. Types of meals: Full bkfst. Beds: KQ. Modem hook-up, cable TV, VCR, reading lamp, clock radio, telephone, voice mail, fireplace, wireless Internet access, fireplace and two with whirlpool tubs in room. Air conditioning. Parlor games on premises. Amusement parks, antiquing, art galleries, beach, bicycling, canoeing/kayaking, cross-country skiing, downhill skiing, fishing, golf, hiking, horseback riding, live theater, museums, parks, shopping, tennis, wineries, private schools: Westminster, Ethel Walker, Avon Olf Farm, Suffield Academy, Loomis Chaffee and Miss Porter's nearby.

Location: Country.

Certificate may be used: Anytime, Sunday-Thursday.

Jewett City
D9

Homespun Farm Bed and Breakfast

306 Preston Rd, Route 164
Jewett City, CT 06351
(860)376-5178 (888)889-6673
Internet: www.homespunfarm.com
E-mail: relax@homespunfarm.com

Circa 1740. The Brewster family, whose great-great grandfather arrived on the Mayflower, owned this Colonial farmhouse for 250 years. Now the Bauers have lovingly renovated the home, which is listed in the National Register. Furnished with antiques and period reproductions, the inn's tasteful decor is accented with an artistic hand-stenciled wood floor and wall border. A sitting room overlooks the golf course and offers gorgeous sunset views. Charming guest bedrooms are well suited for romance, families or business. Luxury abounds with plush robes, candles, aromatherapy personal products, fresh flowers and fine linens on the handmade white oak and pencil post beds. Farm-fresh eggs are part of a scrumptious candlelight breakfast served in the Keeping Room. The extensive grounds, a Certified National Wildlife Federation Backyard Habitat, feature a koi pond, kitchen garden, orchard, grape arbor and flower gardens that welcome birds and butterflies.

Innkeeper(s): Kate & Ron Bauer. $95-140. 2 rooms with PB, 2 with FP, 1 two-bedroom suite. Breakfast and snacks/refreshments included in rates. Types of meals: Full gourmet bkfst, veg bkfst and early coffee/tea. Beds: QT. Cable TV, VCR, reading lamp, clock radio, turn-down service and fireplace in room. Air conditioning. Fax, library, parlor games, telephone and laundry facility on premises. Limited handicap access. Antiquing, art galleries, beach, bicycling, canoeing/kayaking, fishing, golf, hiking, horseback riding, live theater, museums, parks, shopping, sporting events, wineries, Foxwood Casino and Mohegan Sun Casino nearby.

Location: Country.

Publicity: *The New London Day, Ghost Investigator Vol. 3 by Linda Zimmerman, Inn Traveler Magazine "Top 15 B&B in America having most charm" - 2003 and 2004.*

Certificate may be used: Jan. 2 to March 30, Monday-Thursday, Oct. 30 to Dec. 23, Monday through Thursday, no other discounts apply to time frame, subject to availability.

Lisbon   D9

Lonesome Dove Bed and Breakfast

332 South Burnham Hwy
Lisbon, CT 06351
(860)859-9600 (877)793-9880
Internet: www.lonesomedovebnb.com
E-mail: macdore@aol.com

Circa 1989. Peace and tranquility surround this contemporary Cape-style home sitting on three glorious acres. A clean, modern decor is accented by a few well-placed antiques and cherry furnishings. Relax by the fire in the common room. Comfortable guest bedrooms feature robes; one boasts a four-poster bed and fireplace. Sleep on a waterbed in the Master Suite, with a jetted tub and private deck overlooking the stream and woods. After a satisfying breakfast, enjoy the outdoors where a canoe awaits in the pond. Watch for the inn's namesake, the lone mourning dove, one of many varieties of birds often seen here.

Innkeeper(s): Ruth Ann and Leo MacDonald. $95-150. 3 rooms with PB, 2 with FP and 1 conference room. Breakfast included in rates. Types of meals: Country bkfst, veg bkfst, early coffee/tea, afternoon tea and snacks/refreshments. Beds: KQ. Reading lamp, CD player, ceiling fan, clock radio, turndown service and fireplace in room. Central air. TV, spa, parlor games, telephone and fireplace on premises. Antiquing, art galleries, beach, bicycling, canoeing/kayaking, cross-country skiing, fishing, golf, hiking, horseback riding, live theater, museums, parks, shopping, sporting events, tennis, water sports and wineries nearby.

Location: Country. Pond and stream on property.

Publicity: *New London Day.*

Certificate may be used: Anytime, subject to availability.

Litchfield   C4

Abel Darling B&B

PO Box 1502, 102 West St
Litchfield, CT 06759
(860)567-0384 Fax:(860)567-2638
E-mail: abeldarling@hotmail.com

Circa 1782. The spacious guest rooms in this 1782 colonial home offer a light romantic feel and comfortable beds. Breakfast is served in the sunny dining room and includes home-baked breads and muffins. This bed and breakfast is in the heart of the historic district, and nearby is the village green, hosting many restaurants and boutique shops, and the Litchfield countryside.

Innkeeper(s): Colleen Murphy. $85-125. 2 rooms with PB. Breakfast included in rates. Types of meals: Cont plus. Beds: QD. Reading lamp, clock radio, desk and table and chairs in room. VCR, fax, copier, bicycles, library, parlor games and telephone on premises. Antiquing, cross-country skiing, downhill skiing, fishing, golf, live theater, parks, shopping and tennis nearby.

Location: Country, mountains.

Publicity: *Litchfield County Times and New York Times.*

Certificate may be used: Jan. 2-April 30.

Mystic   E9

The Whaler's Inn

20 E Main St
Mystic, CT 06355-2646
(860)536-1506 (800)243-2588 Fax:(860)572-1250
Internet: www.whalersinnmystic.com
E-mail: sales@whalersinnmystic.com

Circa 1901. This classical revival-style inn is built on the historical site of the Hoxie House, the Clinton House and the U.S. Hotel. Just as these famous 19th-century inns offered, the Whaler's Inn has the same charm and convenience for today's visitor to Mystic. Once a booming ship-building center, the town's connection to the sea is ongoing, and the sailing schooners still pass beneath the Bascule Drawbridge in the center of town. More than 75 shops and restaurants are within walking distance.

Innkeeper(s): Richard Prisby. $89-249. 49 rooms with PB and 1 conference room. Types of meals: Cont plus, gourmet lunch and gourmet dinner. Restaurant on premises. Beds: KQD. Reading lamp, desk, cable TV, telephone, voice mail, data port, alarm clock, air conditioning, eight luxury rooms with water views, Jacuzzi tubs and fireplaces in room. TV, telephone and business center on premises. Handicap access. Antiquing, fishing, parks, shopping, water sports, walk to Mystic Seaport and harbor & schooner cruises nearby.

Location: City. Historic downtown Mystic.

Certificate may be used: Nov. 28-March 31, excluding holidays.

New Haven   F5

Three Chimneys Inn at Yale University

C/O JMP
Barrington, NH 03825
(203)789-1201 (800)443-1554 Fax:(203)776-7363
Internet: www.threechimneysinn.com
E-mail: chimneysnh@aol.com

Circa 1870. Gracing the historic Chapel West District, this elegantly restored Painted Lady Victorian mansion is just a block from Yale University. Art museums, boutiques and an assortment of ethnic restaurants are within walking distance. Savor afternoon tea and treats in the library/parlor, and evening wine served fireside. A guest pantry and honor bar offers other snacks and beverages. Work out in the mini exercise facility. Deluxe guest bedrooms feature Georgian and Federal decor, Oriental rugs, antiques, collectibles and four-poster beds with Edwardian privacy drapes. Enjoy reading one of several newspapers delivered daily. Breakfasts are an award-winning affair, and special dietary needs are accommodated with advance notice.

$205-215. 11 rooms with PB and 2 conference rooms. Breakfast included in rates. Types of meals: Full bkfst. Beds: KQ. Modem hook-up, data port, cable TV, VCR, reading lamp, clock radio, desk, EuroShower wands, two-line phone with data port and individual HV/AC in room. Air conditioning. Fax, copier, telephone, fireplace, private on-site parking, space is available for business/social gatherings as well as catering and exercise room on premises. Live theater, parks, shopping, sporting events, dining and museums nearby.

Location: City.

Publicity: *Yankee Magazine editors pick since 1999, The Advocate Business Times, Best of New Haven, Best University B&B National Trust, 4-Star Mobil and National Trust Inn.*

Certificate may be used: Based on availability, void over special events, graduation, parents weekends. May not be used in conjunction with another discount or promotion. All Inn policies and cancellation policies are applicable.

Niantic   F8

Fourteen Lincoln Street, a Chef-Owned Bed & Breakfast

14 Lincoln Street
Niantic, CT 06357
(860)739-6327 Fax:(860)739-6327
Internet: www.14lincolnstreet.com
E-mail: fourteenlincoln@aol.com

Circa 1879. Once a 19th-century New England church, this fully restored bed & breakfast graces a seaside village. A relaxed, elegant decor features oil paintings and antique Oriental carpets that accent comfortable sitting areas. Serene guest chambers in subtle hues boast Jacuzzi tubs and modem hookups. Choose to sleep on the choir loft or sanctuary level in a carved four-poster, pewter knot, ornate Louis XVI or sleigh bed. At this chef-owned B&B, breakfast and afternoon tea are given great gastronomical attention. A bountiful herb-garden inspired breakfast is served with heirloom baked goods and edible flower jellies. Artisan chocolates are made on the premises.

Innkeeper(s): Cheryl Jean. $155-185. 4 rooms with PB. Breakfast and afternoon tea included in rates. Types of meals: Full gourmet bkfst and early coffee/tea. Beds: KQDT. Modem hook-up, cable TV, VCR and telephone in room. Central air. Fax, copier, library, fireplace, lovely outdoor terrace and flower gardens on premises. Antiquing, art galleries, beach, bicycling, fishing, golf, hiking, live theater, museums, parks, shopping, water sports, wineries, Coast Guard Academy and Mystic Aquarium nearby.

Location: Ocean community, waterfront. Seaside village setting.

Certificate may be used: November-April, Sunday-Thursday, subject to availability.

Norfolk   G2

Manor House

69 Maple Ave
Norfolk, CT 06058-0447
(860)542-5690 (866)542-5690 Fax:(860)542-5690
Internet: www.manorhouse-norfolk.com
E-mail: innkeeper@manorhouse-norfolk.com

Circa 1898. Charles Spofford, designer of London's subway, built this home with many gables, exquisite cherry paneling and grand staircase. There are Moorish arches and Tiffany windows. Guests  can enjoy hot-mulled cider after a sleigh ride, hay ride, or horse and carriage drive along the country lanes nearby. The inn was named by "Discerning Traveler" as Connecticut's most romantic hideaway.

Innkeeper(s): Lisa A. Auclair & L. Keith Mullins. $125-250. 9 rooms with PB, 4 with FP, 1 suite and 1 conference room. Breakfast and afternoon tea included in rates. Types of meals: Full gourmet bkfst, early coffee/tea and room service. Beds: KQDT. Reading lamp, ceiling fan, clock radio, desk and three with double whirlpools in room. Fax, library, parlor games, telephone and fireplace on premises. Antiquing, cross-country skiing, downhill skiing, fishing, live theater, parks, shopping, sporting events and water sports nearby.

Location: Mountains.

Publicity: Good Housekeeper, Gourmet, Boston Globe, Philadelphia Inquirer, Innsider, Rhode Island Monthly, Gourmet, National Geographic Traveler and New York Times.

"Queen Victoria, eat your heart out."

Certificate may be used: Weekdays, excluding holidays and month of October.

North Stonington   E9

Antiques & Accommodations

32 Main St
North Stonington, CT 06359-1709
(860)535-1736 (800)554-7829 Fax:(860)535-2613
Internet: www.antiquesandaccommodations.com
E-mail: call@antiquesandaccommodations.com

Circa 1861. Set amongst the backdrop of an acre of herb, edible flower, perennial and cutting gardens, this Victorian treasure offers a romantic location for a weekend getaway. Rooms filled with antiques boast four-poster canopy beds and fresh flowers surrounded by a soft, pleasing decor. Honeymooners or couples celebrating an anniversary are presented with special amenities such as balloons, champagne and heart-shaped waffles for breakfast. Candlelit breakfasts include unique items such as edible flowers along with the delicious entrees. Historic Mystic Seaport and Foxwood's Casino are just minutes from the inn.

Innkeeper(s): Ann & Tom Gray. $110-249. 5 rooms with PB, 2 suites. Breakfast included in rates. Types of meals: Full bkfst and gourmet dinner. Beds: Q. Cable TV, VCR and reading lamp in room. Air conditioning. Antiquing and fishing nearby.

Publicity: Country Inns, Woman's Day, New London Day, Connecticut Magazine and Connecticut Public Radio.

"I loved the great attention to detail and authenticity. A lovely labor of love."

Certificate may be used: Anytime, subject to availability.

Inn at Lower Farm

119 Mystic Rd
North Stonington, CT 06359
(860)535-9075 (866)535-9075 Fax:call to activate
Internet: www.lowerfarm.com
E-mail: info@lowerfarm.com

Circa 1740. Fully restored, this center-chimney Georgian Colonial home sits on more than four acres of gardens and lawns. Soak up the scenic surroundings while relaxing on the porch swing. Enjoy afternoon tea and fresh-baked cookies. Well-appointed guest bedrooms offer a comfortable sleep on four-poster, sleigh or Windsor beds. Some rooms boast fireplaces and can be adjoining. The Travelers Room features a whirlpool tub. Wake up hungry for a bountiful country breakfast in the keeping room. The cattail marsh is a favorite spot for birdwatching.

Innkeeper(s): Mary & Jon Wilska. $95-150. 4 rooms with PB, 3 with FP and 1 conference room. Breakfast, afternoon tea and snacks/refreshments included in rates. Types of meals: Full gourmet bkfst, veg bkfst and early coffee/tea. Beds: Q. Reading lamp, clock radio, desk, fireplace, recliner Queen Anne chairs, individual wall-mounted reading lamps, hair dryer and make-up mirror in room. Central air. TV, VCR, fax, copier, library, parlor games, telephone and Internet hookup available on premises. Antiquing, art galleries, beach, bicycling, canoeing/kayaking, fishing, golf, hiking, horseback riding, live theater, museums, parks, shopping, sporting events, tennis, water sports, wineries, Foxwood and Mohegan Sun Casinos, birdwatching, foliage tour, cider mill and apple and berry picking nearby.

Location: Country. Near Mystic and Stonington, Conn., Westerly, R.I., Foxwoods and Mohegan Sun casinos.

Certificate may be used: November through April, Sunday-Thursday, subject to availability.

Norwalk   G2

Silvermine Tavern

194 Perry Ave
Norwalk, CT 06850-1123
(203)847-4558 (888)693-9967 Fax:(203)847-9171
Internet: www.silverminetavern.com
E-mail: innkeeper@silverminetavern.com

Circa 1790. The Silvermine consists of the Old Mill, the
Country Store, the Coach House and the Tavern itself. Primitive
paintings and furnishings, as well as fami-
ly heirlooms, decorate the inn. Guest
rooms and dining rooms overlook the
Old Mill, the waterfall and swans gliding
across the millpond. Some guest rooms
offer items such as canopy bed or private
decks. In the summer, guests can dine al
fresco and gaze at the mill pond.
Innkeeper(s): Frank Whitman, Jr. $115-150. 10
rooms with PB, 1 suite. Breakfast included in
rates. Types of meals: Cont, lunch and dinner. Restaurant on premises. Beds:
QDT. Reading lamp, clock radio, desk and some with canopied beds in room.
Air conditioning. VCR, fax, copier, parlor games, telephone and fireplace on
premises. Antiquing, fishing, parks and shopping nearby.

Location: Residential area.

Certificate may be used: No Friday nights, no September or October. No
holidays.

Old Mystic   E9

Red Brook Inn

PO Box 237
Old Mystic, CT 06372-0237
(860)572-0349
Internet: www.redbrookinn.com
E-mail: redbrookin@aol.com

Circa 1740. If there was no other reason to visit Mystic, a
charming town brimming with activities, the Red Brook Inn
would be reason enough. The Crary Homestead features three
unique rooms with working fire-
places, while the Haley Tavern
offers seven guest rooms, some
with canopy beds and fireplaces.
Two have whirlpool tubs.
Innkeeper Ruth Keyes has beautiful
antiques decorating her inn.
Guests are sure to enjoy her won-
derful country breakfasts. A special winter dinner takes three
days to complete and she prepares it over an open hearth. In
addition to a full breakfast, afternoon and evening beverages are
provided. The aquarium, Mystic Seaport Museum, a cider mill,
casinos and many shops are only minutes away.
Innkeeper(s): Ruth Keyes. $129-189. 10 rooms with PB, 7 with FP and 3
conference rooms. Breakfast included in rates. Types of meals: Full bkfst.
Beds: QDT. Reading lamp and desk in room. TV, VCR, tennis, library, parlor
games, telephone, fireplace, terrace and parlors on premises. Amusement
parks, antiquing, fishing, live theater, museums, parks, shopping, sporting
events, water sports and casino nearby.

Location: Wooded area.

Publicity: Westerly Sun, Travel & Leisure, Yankee, New York, Country
Decorating, Philadelphia Inquirer, National Geographic Traveler and
Discerning Traveler.

"The staff is wonderful. You made us feel at home. Thank you for
your hospitality."

Certificate may be used: Anytime, subject to availability.

Old Saybrook   F7

Deacon Timothy Pratt Bed & Breakfast Inn C.1746

325 Main Street
Old Saybrook, CT 06475
(860)395-1229 (800)640-1195 Fax:(860)395-4748
Internet: www.pratthouse.net
E-mail: bnbinns@pratthouse.net

Circa 1746. Built prior to the Revolutionary War, this slate blue
house is an outstanding example of center chimney Colonial-
style architecture. Listed in the National Register, the inn's original features include six working fireplaces, hand-hewn beams,
wide board floors, a beehive oven and built-in cupboard. Four-
poster and canopy beds, Oriental rugs and period furnishings
accentuate the New England atmosphere. Fireplaces and Jacuzzi
tubs invite romance and relaxation. On weekends a multi-
course, candlelight breakfast is served in the elegant dining
room. Enjoy homemade muffins or scones, fresh fruit and
entrees such as heart-shaped blueberry pancakes or eggs
Benedict. Among the variety of local historic house museums to
visit, the William Hart house is across the street. The area offers
many shopping and dining opportunities as well as galleries to
explore. Beaches, a state park and river cruises also are available.
Innkeeper(s): Shelley Nobile. $100-220. 7 rooms with PB, 7 with FP, 7 with
HT, 2 total suites, including 1 two-bedroom suite and 1 conference room.
Breakfast, afternoon tea and snacks/refreshments included in rates. Types of
meals: Full gourmet bkfst, veg bkfst and early coffee/tea. Beds: QT. Modem
hook-up, data port, cable TV, VCR, reading lamp, stereo, clock radio, telephone, fireplace, massage therapy (fee), Jacuzzi, queen canopy or four-poster
bed, comfortable sitting area, hair dryer and iron/board in room. Air conditioning. Fax, copier, spa, bicycles, library, parlor games, gift shop, complimentary tea, hot chocolate, spring water, fresh baked cookies, port wine and
guest refrigerator on premises. Antiquing, art galleries, beach, bicycling,
canoeing/kayaking, cross-country skiing, downhill skiing, fishing, golf, hiking,
horseback riding, museums, parks, shopping, sporting events, tennis, wineries, lighthouses, waterfront, dining, park, mini-golf, casinos, spas, playhous-
es, wineries, factory outlet malls, Essex Steam Train & Riverboat, Mystic
Attractions, Goodspeed Opera House, Chamard Vineyards and charming New
England villages nearby.

Location: Country, ocean community. New England shoreline town, historic &
shopping district.

Publicity: Fodor's New England Travel Guide, America's Favorite Inns Book,
Elle Magazine, Coastal Living Magazine, Inn Traveller feature,
Entrepreneur's Business Start-Ups Magazine, Inn Spots & Special Places in
New England, Waterside Escapes by Woodpond Press, Arrington Publishing
Awards: Most Historical Charm, Best Interior Design & Decor and Best
Location for walking to shops & restaurants.

Certificate may be used: November through June, Sunday through Thursday.

Preston   D9

Roseledge Farm B&B

418 Rt 164
Preston, CT 06365-8112
(860)892-4739 Fax:(860)892-4739
E-mail: jrogers981@aol.com

Circa 1720. Hearth-cooked New England breakfasts of eggs,
bacon and homemade breads are served in this colonial inn,
one of the oldest homes in Preston. Wide floor boards original

to the home create a feeling of reverence for the finely maintained historic home. There are pegged mortise and tenon beams and scrolled moldings on the stair treads. Canopy beds with floaty bed curtains add a romantic touch. There is a stone tunnel connecting the street with the barn's basement, and ancient stone walls divide the rolling meadows in view of the inn's four acres. Guests are invited to help with the farm animals, including gathering eggs.

Innkeeper(s): Gail A. Rogers. $85-125. 4 rooms, 3 with PB, 4 with FP, 1 suite and 1 conference room. Breakfast, afternoon tea and dinner included in rates. Types of meals: Full bkfst, early coffee/tea and snacks/refreshments. Beds: QD. Reading lamp, telephone, turn-down service and desk in room. Air conditioning. Fax, child care, parlor games, fireplace, limited pet boarding, farm animals, tea room and antique store on premises. Amusement parks, antiquing, fishing, golf, live theater, parks, shopping, sporting events, tennis, water sports, Yankee baseball stadium and Mystic area nearby.

Location: Country.

Certificate may be used: Jan. 1 to May 1, Sunday-Thursday.

Ridgefield   F2

West Lane Inn

22 West Ln
Ridgefield, CT 06877-4914
(203)438-7323 Fax:(203)438-7325
Internet: www.westlaneinn.com
E-mail: westlanein@aol.com

Circa 1849. Listed in the National Register, this 1849 Victorian mansion combines the ambiance of a country inn with the convenience of a boutique hotel. An enormous front porch is filled with black wrought iron chairs and tables overlooking a manicured lawn on two acres. A polished oak staircase rises to a third-floor landing and lounge. Chandeliers, wall sconces and floral wallpapers accent the intimate atmosphere. Elegant, oversized guest bedrooms feature individual climate control, four-poster beds and upscale amenities like heated towel racks, voice mail, wireless DSL and refrigerators. Two include fireplaces and one boasts a kitchenette. Wake up and enjoy a morning meal in the Breakfast Room before experiencing one of New England's finest towns with a variety of boutiques, museums, antique shops and restaurants.

Innkeeper(s): Maureen Mayer & Deborah Prieger. $125-195. 16 rooms with PB, 2 with FP, 1 suite. Breakfast included in rates. Types of meals: Cont and room service. Beds: Q. Cable TV, VCR, refrigerator, telephone, voice mail, individual climate control, full private baths, heated towel racks, hair dryers, modem and wireless DSL in room. Air conditioning. TV on premises. Antiquing, cross-country skiing, golf, live theater, shopping, award winning restaurants, boutiquing and movies nearby.

Location: New England town.

Publicity: Stanford-Advocate, Greenwich Times and Home & Away Connecticut.

"Thank you for the hospitality you showed us. The rooms are comfortable and quiet. I haven't slept this soundly in weeks."

Certificate may be used: Anytime, Sunday through Thursday, excluding holidays, November through April.

Westbrook   F7

Angels Watch Inn

902 Boston Post Rd
Westbrook, CT 06498-1848
(860)399-8846 Fax:(860)399-2571
Internet: www.angelswatchinn.com
E-mail: info@angelswatchinn.com

Circa 1830. Appreciate the comfortable elegance and tranquil ambiance of this stately 1830 Federal bed and breakfast that is situated on one acre of peaceful grounds in a quaint New England village along the Connecticut River Valley Shoreline. Romantic guest bedrooms are private retreats with canopy beds, fireplaces, stocked refrigerators, strawberries dipped in chocolate, fresh fruit and snack baskets, whirlpools or two-person clawfoot soaking tubs. Maintaining a fine reputation of impeccable standards, the inn caters to the whole person. After breakfast choose from an incredible assortment of spa services that include massage therapy, yoga, intuitive guidance, as well as mind, body and spirit wellness. Go horseback riding then take a sunset cruise. Ask about elopement/small wedding packages and midweek or off-season specials.

Innkeeper(s): Bill & Peggy. $95-185. 5 rooms with PB, 5 with FP, 2 with WP. Breakfast, afternoon tea and snacks/refreshments included in rates. Types of meals: Full gourmet bkfst, veg bkfst, early coffee/tea, picnic lunch, wine and gourmet dinner. Beds: KQT. Data port, cable TV, VCR, reading lamp, stereo, refrigerator, ceiling fan, snack bar, clock radio, turn-down service, desk, hot tub/spa, fireplace, welcome fruit basket, snacks, treats, two have 2-person soaking tub, massage and yoga in room. Air conditioning. Fax, copier, spa, bicycles, library, child care, parlor games, telephone, laundry facility and Internet access on premises. Limited handicap access. Antiquing, art galleries, beach, bicycling, canoeing/kayaking, cross-country skiing, downhill skiing, fishing, golf, hiking, horseback riding, live theater, museums, parks, shopping, sporting events, tennis, water sports and wineries nearby.

Location: Ocean community.

Publicity: The Hartford Courant, New Haven Register, Main Street News, Pictorial and ABC affiliate Positively Connecticut.

Certificate may be used: Sunday-Thursday year-round, holidays and special events excluded. Full season rate apply.

Westbrook Inn B&B

976 Boston Post Rd
Westbrook, CT 06498-1852
(800)342-3162 Fax:(860)399-8023
Internet: www.westbrookinn.com
E-mail: info@westbrookinn.com

Circa 1876. A wraparound porch and flower gardens offer a gracious welcome to this elegant Victorian inn. The innkeeper, an expert in restoring old houses and antiques, has filled the B&B with fine Victorian period furnishings, handsome paintings and wall coverings. Well-appointed guest bedrooms and a spacious two-bedroom cottage provide comfortable accommodations. Some guest rooms include a fireplace, four-poster canopy bed or balcony. A full breakfast features homemade baked goods that accompany a variety of delicious main entrees. Complimentary beverages are available throughout the day. Enjoy bike rides and walks to the beach. Nearby factory outlets and casinos are other popular activities.

Innkeeper(s): Glenn & Chris . $165-195. 9 rooms with PB, 1 cottage and 1 conference room. Breakfast and snacks/refreshments included in rates. Types of meals: Full bkfst, veg bkfst, early coffee/tea and afternoon tea. Beds: KQT. Modem hook-up, data port, cable TV, VCR, reading lamp, refrigerator, clock radio, telephone, coffeemaker, desk, hot tub/spa, fireplace, antiques and cottage has kitchen in room. Central air. Fax, copier, spa, bicycles, library, parlor games, picturesque gardens, gazebo, bistro-style patio, historic front porch and two-person hammock on premises. Handicap access. Antiquing, art galleries, beach, bicycling, canoeing/kayaking, fishing, golf, hiking, horseback riding, live theater, museums, parks, shopping, sporting events, tennis, wineries, boat cruises, casinos, outlet mall and downtown nearby.

Location: Ocean community.

Publicity: *Harbor News, New Haven Register, Middletown Press, Pictorial Newspaper, Arrington's B&B Journal (voted "Most Elegant Inn" - 2004/2005 & "Best Inn with Nearby Attractions" - 2003), NBC (2003) and Comcast Cable.*

Certificate may be used: Nov. 30-April 30, Monday-Thursday.

Woodbury   D3

Hummingbird Hill B&B

891 Main St S
Woodbury, CT 06798
(203)263-3733
E-mail: Humminbgbird@wave-length.net

Circa 1953. Operating as a B&B for five years, this traditional, colonial-style Connecticut home is a testament to the energy of its innkeeper, Sharon Simmons. She and her late husband had often talked about opening a B&B, but it wasn't until his death that she began to read books and attend seminars on the subject. The result is Hummingbird Hill, a cozy and delightful accommodation that will remind you of a stay at your grandmother's. Interiors are in shades of blue and white, and flowers from the garden and candles accent the living room. There are only two rooms with a shared bathroom, but if a guest requires a private bath, the other room won't be rented. Guests have the entire house at their disposal except for the kitchen where the innkeeper prepares the breads, muffins and juices for breakfast. A heated sun porch offers a quiet place to read at any time of the year. An open-air porch and brick patio look out onto the perennial garden, a favorite spot for butterflies, dragonflies, and, of course, the hummingbirds.

Innkeeper(s): Sharon Simmons. $90-120. 2 rooms, 1 with PB. Breakfast included in rates. Types of meals: Cont plus and early coffee/tea. Beds: KT. Reading lamp, clock radio and telephone in room. Air conditioning. TV, VCR and fireplace on premises. Amusement parks, antiquing, art galleries, bicycling, downhill skiing, golf, hiking, museums, shopping and wineries nearby.

Location: Country.

Publicity: *Voices and Republican American.*

Certificate may be used: Anytime, subject to availability.

Longwood

1204 Main St S
Woodbury, CT 06798-3804
(203)266-0800 Fax:(203)263-4479
Internet: www.longwoodcountryinn.com
E-mail: longwood1204@aol.com

Circa 1789. Merryvale, an elegant Colonial inn, is situated in a picturesque New England Village, known as an antique capitol of Connecticut. Guests can enjoy complimentary tea, coffee

and biscuits throughout the day. A grand living room invites travelers to relax by the fireplace and enjoy a book from the extensive collection of classics and mysteries. During the week, guests enjoy an ample breakfast buffet and on weekends, the innkeepers prepare a Federal-style breakfast using historic, 18th-century recipes.

Innkeeper(s): Pat Ubaldi. $115-250. 5 rooms with PB. Breakfast included in rates. Types of meals: Full bkfst. Restaurant on premises. Beds: KQT. Cable TV, reading lamp, clock radio, telephone and desk in room. Air conditioning. Fireplace on premises. Amusement parks, antiquing, cross-country skiing, downhill skiing, fishing and shopping nearby.

Location: Country town.

Publicity: *Voices, Yankee Traveler, Hartford Courant, Newtown Bee, Connecticut Magazine and New York Times.*

"Your hospitality will always be remembered."

Certificate may be used: Jan. 7-Feb. 28, Monday-Thursday, excluding weekend, Valentines and holidays.

Woodstock   B9

Elias Child House B&B

50 Perrin Rd
Woodstock, CT 06281
(860)974-9836 (877)974-9836 Fax:(860)974-1541
Internet: www.eliaschildhouse.com
E-mail: afelice@earthlink.net

Circa 1700. Nine fireplaces warm this heritage three-story colonial home, referred to as "the mansion house" by early settlers. There are two historic cooking hearths, including a beehive oven. Original floors, twelve-over-twelve windows and paneling remain. A bountiful breakfast is served fireside in the dining room and a screened porch and a patio provide nesting spots for reading and relaxing. The inn's grounds are spacious and offer a pool and hammocks. Woodland walks on the 47 acres and antiquing are popular activities.

Innkeeper(s): Anthony Felice, Jr. & MaryBeth Gorke-Felice. $100-135. 3 rooms, 1 with PB, 1 with FP, 1 suite. Breakfast included in rates. Types of meals: Country bkfst and early coffee/tea. Beds: QDT. Reading lamp, clock radio, turn-down service, suite has two fireplaces, sitting room and two baths (one with a clawfoot tub) in room. Air conditioning. VCR, fax, copier, swimming, bicycles, parlor games, telephone, fireplace, hearth-cooking demonstrations and cross-country skiing on premises.

Location: Country.

Publicity: *Time Out New York, Best Fares Magazine, Distinction, Wine Gazette, Car & Driver Magazine, Worcester Telegram and Gazette.*

"Comfortable rooms and delightful country ambiance."

Certificate may be used: Sunday through Thursday, except holidays, Valentine's Day and certain specialty weekends.

Delaware

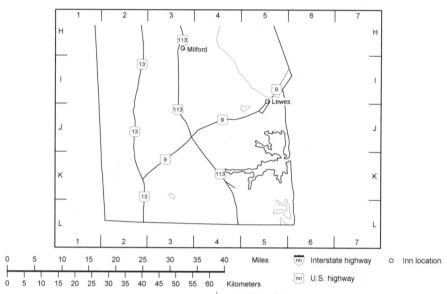

	Miles	
Interstate highway		Inn location
U.S. highway		

Scale: 0 5 10 15 20 25 30 35 40 Miles
0 5 10 15 20 25 30 35 40 45 50 55 60 Kilometers

Lewes 15

The Bay Moon B&B

128 Kings Hwy
Lewes, DE 19958-1418
(302)644-1802 (800)917-2307 Fax:(302)644-1802
E-mail: baymoon@dmv.com

Circa 1887. The exterior of this three-story, cedar Victorian features a front veranda shrouded by the flowers and foliage that also decorate the front walk. The custom-made, hand-crafted beds in the guest rooms are topped with feather pillows and down comforters. Wine is served each evening. The innkeeper offers plenty of amenities. Beach supplies and a heated outdoor shower are helpful for guests who want to enjoy the ocean.

Innkeeper(s): Zina Sweir. $95-150. 4 rooms with PB, 1 suite. Breakfast included in rates. Types of meals: Full bkfst, early coffee/tea and snacks/refreshments. Beds: KQ. Cable TV, VCR, reading lamp, ceiling fan and clock radio in room. Central air. Fax, library, parlor games, telephone, fireplace and outdoor Jacuzzi on premises. Antiquing, fishing, live theater, parks, shopping, sporting events, water sports and beach nearby.
Location: Ocean community. Historic town.
Certificate may be used: Sept. 15-June 15, weekdays Monday-Wednesday only, no holidays.

Milford H3

The Towers B&B

101 NW Front St
Milford, DE 19963-1022
(302)422-3814 (800)366-3814
Internet: www.mispillion.com
E-mail: mispillion@ezol.com

Circa 1783. Once a simple colonial house, this ornate Steamboat Gothic fantasy features every imaginable Victorian architectural detail, all added in 1891. There are 10 distinct styles of gingerbread as well as towers, turrets, gables, porches and bays. Inside, chestnut and cherry woodwork, window seats and stained-glass windows are complemented with American and French antiques. The back garden boasts a gazebo porch and swimming pool. Ask for the splendid Tower Room or Rapunzel Suite.

Innkeeper(s): Daniel & Rhonda Bond. $95-135. 4 rooms with PB, 2 suites. Breakfast included in rates. Beds: QD. Reading lamp, ceiling fan and clock radio in room. Air conditioning. Swimming, telephone and fireplace on premises. Antiquing, fishing, live theater, parks, shopping and water sports nearby.
Location: City, ocean community.
Publicity: *Washington Post, Baltimore Sun, Washingtonian and Mid-Atlantic Country.*
"I felt as if I were inside a beautiful Victorian Christmas card, surrounded by all the things Christmas should be."
Certificate may be used: Any night of the week throughout the year.

Florida

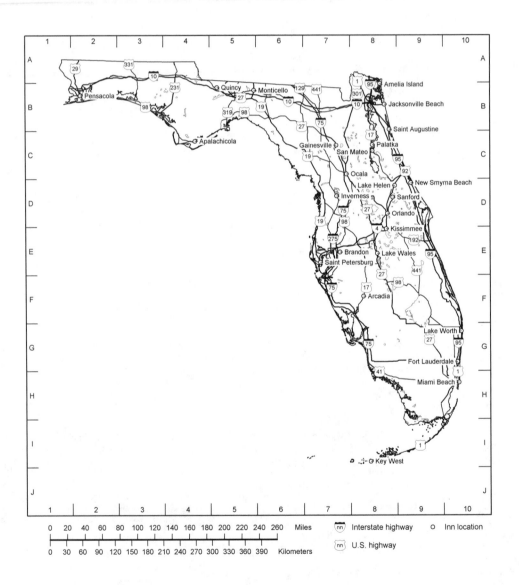

0	20	40	60	80	100	120	140	160	180	200	220	240	260	Miles
0	30	60	90	120	150	180	210	240	270	300	330	360	390	Kilometers

Interstate highway   o Inn location

U.S. highway

Amelia Island   B8

1857 Florida House Inn
PO Box 688, 22 S 3rd St
Amelia Island, FL 32034-4207
(904)261-3300 (800)258-3301 Fax:(904)261-3300
Internet: www.floridahouseinn.com
E-mail: innkeepers@floridahouseinn.com

Circa 1857. Located in the heart of a 50-block historic
National Register area, the Florida House Inn is thought to be
the oldest continuously operating tourist hotel in Florida. The
inn features a small pub, guest parlor, library and a New
Orleans-style courtyard in which guests may enjoy the shade of
200-year-old oaks. Rooms are decorated with country pine and
oak antiques, cheerful handmade rugs and quilts, and 10
rooms offer fireplaces and six Jacuzzi tubs. The Carnegies,
Rockefellers and Ulysses S. Grant have been guests.
$99-219. 15 rooms with PB, 10 with FP, 10 with HT, 1 suite and 1 confer-
ence room. Breakfast included in rates. Types of meals: Full bkfst, early cof-
fee/tea, lunch, picnic lunch and dinner. Restaurant on premises. Beds: KQT.
Cable TV, reading lamp, ceiling fan, clock radio, telephone, desk and 10
Jacuzzi tubs in room. Air conditioning. TV, fax, copier and fireplace on
premises. Handicap access. Antiquing, fishing, live theater and sporting
events nearby.

Location: Village.

Publicity: *Amelia Now, Tampa Tribune, Miami Herald, Toronto Star, Country
Living, Ft. Lauderdale Sun Sentinel, Country Inns, Consumer Reports,
Money Magazine, US News & World Report, Eat Your Way Across the USA
and Gourmet.*

Certificate may be used: Sunday through Thursday.

Apalachicola   C4

Coombs House Inn
80 6th St
Apalachicola, FL 32320-1750
(850)653-9199 Fax:(850)653-2785
Internet: www.coombshouseinn.com
E-mail: coombsstaff@coombshouseinn.com

Circa 1905. This Victorian manor was built for James N.
Coombs, a wealthy lumber baron who served in the Union
Army. Despite his Yankee roots, Coombs was an influential fig-
ure in Apalachicola. The home has been lovingly restored to
reflect its previous grandeur. Co-owner Lynn Wilson is a
renown interior designer and her talents accent the inn's high
ceilings, tiled fireplaces and period antiques. Bright English fabrics decorate windows and Oriental rugs accentuate the hardwood floors.
Innkeeper(s): Pamela Barnes & Anthony Erario. $89-225. 19 rooms with PB
and 1 conference room. Breakfast included in rates. Types of meals: Full
bkfst and early coffee/tea. Beds: KQDT. Cable TV, reading lamp, refrigerator,
ceiling fan, clock radio, telephone, desk and hot tub/spa in room. Air conditioning. Fax, copier, bicycles, beach chairs and umbrellas & towels for beaches on premises. Handicap access. Antiquing, fishing, parks, shopping and
water sports nearby.

Location: City. Island.

Publicity: *Southern Living, Florida Design and Country Inns Magazine.*

Certificate may be used: Dec. 1-Jan. 31, Sunday-Thursday, not on holidays.

Arcadia   F8

Historic Parker House
427 W Hickory St
Arcadia, FL 34266-3703
(863)494-2499 (800)969-2499
Internet: www.historicparkerhouse.com
E-mail: parkerhouse@desoto.net

Circa 1895. Period antiques, including a wonderful clock collection, grace the interior of this turn-of-the-century home,
which was built by a local cattle baron. Along with two charming rooms and a bright, "yellow" suite, innkeepers Shelly and
Bob Baumann added the spacious Blue Room, which offers a
white iron and brass bed and claw-
foot bathtub. An expanded continental breakfast with pastries,
fresh fruits, cereals, muffins and a
variety of beverages is offered
each morning, and afternoon
teas can be prepared on request.
Innkeeper(s): Bob & Shelly Baumann.
$69-85. 4 rooms, 2 with PB, 2 with FP and 1 conference room. Breakfast
and afternoon tea included in rates. Types of meals: Cont plus, early
coffee/tea and room service. Beds: QDT. Cable TV, reading lamp, ceiling fan
and telephone in room. Air conditioning. Parlor games and fireplace on
premises. Antiquing, fishing, parks, shopping, water sports and historical
sites nearby.

Location: City. Small country city.

Publicity: *Tampa Tribune, Desoto Sun Herald, Florida Travel & Life, Miami
Herald (Palm Beach Edition) and WINK-TV News.*

"Everything was first class and very comfortable."

Certificate may be used: May 1 to Dec. 15, Sunday-Friday.

Brandon   E7

Behind The Fence B&B Inn
1400 Viola Dr at Countryside
Brandon, FL 33511-7327
(813)685-8201
Internet: www.floridasecrets.com/fence.htm

Circa 1976. Experience the charm of New England on
Florida's west coast at this secluded country inn surrounded by
tall pines and oaks. Although the frame of the home was built
in the mid-1970s, the innkeepers searched Hillsborough
County for 19th-century and turn-of-the-century artifacts,
including old stairs, doors, windows, a pantry and the back
porch. Guests can stay either in the main house or in a two-
bedroom cottage. All rooms are filled with antique Amish-
county furniture. The innkeepers serve fresh popcorn on cool
nights in front of the fireplace. Breakfast includes fresh fruit,
cereals, juices, coffees and delicious Amish sweet rolls.
Innkeeper(s): Larry & Carolyn Yoss. $79-89. 5 rooms, 3 with PB, 1 suite, 1
cottage and 1 conference room. Breakfast and afternoon tea included in
rates. Types of meals: Cont plus, early coffee/tea and snacks/refreshments.
Beds: DT. Cable TV, reading lamp, refrigerator, clock radio and desk in room.
Air conditioning. VCR, swimming, telephone and fireplace on premises.
Amusement parks, antiquing, canoeing/kayaking, fishing, horseback riding,
parks, shopping, sporting events and water sports nearby.

Location: Subdivision to County Park.

Publicity: *Brandon News, Travel Host and Country Living.*

"One of the best kept secrets in all of Tampa! Thanks again!"

Certificate may be used: Anytime, subject to availability.

Fort Lauderdale   G10

Caledonia Bayshore Villas

4 Phoenix Ave
Kingston 10,
(954)564-6953 Fax:(954)567-3756
Internet: www.caledoniabayshorevillas.com
E-mail: bayshorevillas@bellsouth.net

Enjoy the tranquil surroundings of this intimate boutique hotel
that has been recently refurbished. It is conveniently located
just ten minutes from the airport. Select a studio or one bedroom with a refrigerator and coffeemaker, or stay in one of the
efficiencies that feature a kitchenette. Relax in a lounge by the
pool before taking a refreshing swim. After a continental breakfast, the white sandy beach of Fort Lauderdale is a minute away
and shoppers can be at the mall in less than five minutes.

Innkeeper(s): Karen Lue Roberts. $69-130. 14 rooms with PB and 1 cot-
tage. Types of meals: Cont and early coffee/tea. Beds: KQT. Cable TV,
refrigerator, ceiling fan, clock radio, telephone and coffeemaker in room. Air
conditioning. Swimming and laundry facility on premises. Beach and bicycling nearby.

Location: Ocean community.

Certificate may be used: April 26-Aug. 31, Sunday-Thursday, subject to
availability.

Gainesville   C7

Magnolia Plantation Cottages and Gardens

309 SE 7th Street
Gainesville, FL 32601-6831
(352)375-6653 Fax:(352)338-0303
Internet: www.magnoliabnb.com
E-mail: info@magnoliabnb.com

Circa 1885. This restored French Second Empire Victorian is
in the National Register. Magnolia trees surround the house.
Five guest rooms are filled with family heirlooms. All bathrooms feature clawfoot tubs and candles. There are also private historic cottages available with
Jacuzzis. Guests may enjoy the gardens,
reflecting pond with waterfalls and gazebo. Bicycles are also available.
Evening wine and snacks are included. The inn is two miles from the
University of Florida.

Innkeeper(s): Joe & Cindy Montalto. $90-
250. 5 rooms with PB, 5 with FP and 6
cottages. Breakfast and afternoon tea included in rates. Types of meals: Full
bkfst. Beds: Q. TV, reading lamp, ceiling fan, clock radio, turn-down service,
desk, cottages have Jacuzzi, fireplace, full kitchen and private garden in
room. Air conditioning. VCR, fax, bicycles, library, telephone, fireplace and
cocktail hour on premises. Antiquing, live theater, parks, shopping and sporting events nearby.

Location: City.

Publicity: *Florida Living Magazine and Inn Country USA.*

"This has been a charming, once-in-a-lifetime experience."

Certificate may be used: Sunday-Thursday, all year or anytime, last minute.

Inverness   D7

The Lake House B&B

8604 E Gospel Island Rd
Inverness, FL 34450
(352)344-3586 Fax:(352)344-3586
Internet: www.thelakehouse.org
E-mail: cjenkin5@tampabay.rr.com

Circa 1930. The Lake House was built as a fishing lodge, and
with its location on Big Lake Henderson, offers picturesque
views of woodland and water. Guests usually arrange to be
finished with daytime adventures in time to return to the inn
for sunset views over the lake. A library and a huge stone fireplace are additional gathering places. Guest rooms are furnished in a French Country decor. Miles of paved pathways
entice roller skaters and cyclers to Withlacoochee State Trail
nearby. There are many lakes to choose from for fishing,
water-skiing and boating.

Innkeeper(s): Caroline & Blake Jenkins. $80-100. 5 rooms with PB.
Breakfast included in rates. Types of meals: Cont plus. Beds: KQDT. Cable
TV, reading lamp and ceiling fan in room. Central air. VCR, library, telephone
and fireplace on premises. Amusement parks, antiquing, bicycling,
canoeing/kayaking, fishing, golf, hiking, horseback riding, museums, parks,
shopping, tennis and water sports nearby.

Location: Waterfront.

Publicity: *St. Petersburg Times and Citrus County Chronicle.*

Certificate may be used: Year-round, Monday-Thursday, excluding holidays
and special event weekends.

Jacksonville Beach   B8

Pelican Path B&B By The Sea

11 19th Ave N
Jacksonville Beach, FL 32250-7446
(904)249-1177 (888)749-1177
Internet: www.pelicanpath.com
E-mail: ppbandb@aol.com

Circa 1998. Inspired by San Francisco-style architecture, this
oceanfront inn boasts bay windows on the second and third
floors. Furnished in a modern beach decor, an array of amenities add comfort and pampering while staying for business or
pleasure. Two of the spacious guest bedrooms offer spa tubs
and private balconies featuring a view of the water. A satisfying
breakfast is sure to please. Explore the area on an available
bicycle before driving to some of the local sites. Visit nearby
Kingsley Plantation and Fort Caroline National Monument.

Innkeeper(s): Joan & Tom Hubbard. $115-165. 4 rooms with PB. Breakfast
included in rates. Types of meals: Full gourmet bkfst, veg bkfst and early cof-
fee/tea. Beds: KT. Modem hook-up, cable TV, VCR, reading lamp, refrigerator,
ceiling fan, clock radio, telephone, coffeemaker, desk and hot tub/spa in
room. Central air. Bicycles and small video library on premises. Antiquing, art
galleries, beach, bicycling, canoeing/kayaking, fishing, golf, hiking, horseback
riding, live theater, museums, parks, shopping, sporting events, tennis and
water sports nearby.

Location: Ocean community, waterfront.

Certificate may be used: Sept. 15-Jan. 31, anytime, Sunday-Thursday.

Key West   18

Duval House

815 Duval St
Key West, FL 33040-7405
(305)294-1666 (800)223-8825 Fax:(305)292-1701
Internet: www.duvalhousekeywest.com
E-mail: duvalhs@attglobal.net

Circa 1880. Seven historic houses, painted in island pastel
shades, surround a lush tropical garden and a pool. Located on
an estate in the heart of the historic Old Town, guests relish the
cozy spaces to relax such as the hammock for two, gazebo, sun
decks and private balconies. The inn's white picket fences and
plentiful porches are bordered
by tropical trees, flowers and
vines. A continental-plus break-
fast is served from the pool
house. Rooms have wicker and
antique furniture, Victorian
armoires and Bahamian fans.

Innkeeper(s): Maureen Hance. $110-325. 25 rooms with PB, 4 suites.
Breakfast included in rates. Beds: KQ. Cable TV and telephone in room. Air
conditioning. Swimming and parlor games on premises. Antiquing, shopping,
water sports, spa and historic touring nearby.

Publicity: *Palm Beach Post, Orlando Sentinel, Brides, Vacations,
Honeymoon, St. Petersburg Times and Sun Sentinel.*

"You certainly will see us again."

Certificate may be used: May 1-Dec. 20, Sunday-Thursday only (excluding
holidays and special events).

Westwinds

914 Eaton St
Key West, FL 33040-6923
(305)296-4440 (800)788-4150 Fax:(305)293-0931
Internet: www.westwindskeywest.com
E-mail: frontdesk@westwindskeywest.com

Circa 1900. Hospitality, intimacy and relaxation are the hallmarks of every stay at Westwinds. The Victorian buildings feature tin roofs, clapboard and gingerbread trim. Though situated
in the historic seaport district of Old Town, the gardens are
lush with tropical trees, shrubs and a waterfall. The lounge has
a library, television, refrigerator and Internet access. Choose a
guest bedroom, suite or cottage. Enjoy conversation and meeting new friends over a continental breakfast with fresh fruits,
juices, croissants and local honey. Swim in the heated, in-
ground pool.

Innkeeper(s): Claire Tucker. $80-195. 19 rooms with PB, 5 suites, 1 cottage
and 1 conference room. Breakfast included in rates. Types of meals: Cont.
Beds: KQDT. Reading lamp, ceiling fan, clock radio and telephone in room. Air
conditioning. TV, fax, copier, swimming, bicycles, library, parlor games, laundry facility and gift shop on premises. Handicap access. Art galleries, beach,
bicycling, canoeing/kayaking, fishing, golf, hiking, live theater, museums, shopping, water sports, snorkeling, diving and writers workshops nearby.

Location: City. Historic Seaport District.

Publicity: *NY Times and Conde Nast Traveler.*

Certificate may be used: June-October.

Kissimmee   E8

Wonderland Inn B & B

3601 South Orange Blossom Trail
Kissimmee, FL 34746
(407)847-2477 (877)847-2477 Fax:(407)847-4099
Internet: www.wonderlandinn.com
E-mail: innkeeper@wonderlandinn.com

Circa 1950. Cradled by oaks and orange trees, this brick country inn has been renovated recently to offer gracious Southern
hospitality in a relaxed, elegant setting. Artistically-appointed
guest bedrooms, suites and a romantic honeymoon cottage feature hand-painted garden scenes and nature murals. Generous
amenities include terry cloth robes, refrigerators, coffee makers,
data ports, turndown service and much more. Delve into a
delicious breakfast in the Main House, and gather later for a
sunset wine and cheese hour. Play croquet, and then indulge in
pampering spa services.

Innkeeper(s): Rosemarie Oshaughnessy, Cheyenne Grove & Gretchen. $79-
179. 11 rooms with PB. Types of meals: Full bkfst and early coffee/tea.
Beds: KQD. Modem hook-up, data port, cable TV, VCR, reading lamp, stereo,
refrigerator, ceiling fan, clock radio, telephone, coffeemaker, DVD player, data
port, modem hook-up and VCR in Main house in room. Air conditioning. Fax,
library, parlor games, laundry facility and four-course breakfast on premises.
Limited handicap access. Amusement parks, antiquing, art galleries, beach,
canoeing/kayaking, fishing, golf, hiking, horseback riding, live theater, museums, parks, shopping, water sports and wineries nearby.

Location: Charming Country Inn, Minutes from Disneyworld.

Publicity: *Flordia Magazine, Flordia USA and Tampa Bay.*

Certificate may be used: Anytime, Sept. 1 to Nov. 31, subject to availability,
no other discounts apply when using this promotion.

Lake Helen   D8

Clauser's B&B

201 E Kicklighter Rd
Lake Helen, FL 32744-3514
(386)228-0310 (800)220-0310 Fax:(386)228-2337
Internet: www.clauserinn.com
E-mail: info@clauserinn.com

Circa 1890. This three-story, turn-of-the-century vernacular
Victorian inn is surrounded by a variety of trees in a quiet,
country setting. The inn is listed in the national, state and local
historic registers, and offers eight guest rooms, all with private
bath. Each room features a different type of country decor,
such as Americana, English and country. Guests enjoy hot tub-
bing in the Victorian gazebo or
relaxing on the inn's porches,
which feature rockers, a swing
and cozy wicker furniture. Borrow
a bike to take a closer look at the
historic district. Stetson
University, fine dining and several
state parks are nearby.

Innkeeper(s): Ed & Helene Gracy. $110-150. 8 rooms with PB, 1 with FP.
Breakfast and snacks/refreshments included in rates. Types of meals: Full bkfst
and early coffee/tea. Beds: KQ. Reading lamp, ceiling fan, telephone, desk, hot
tub/spa and private screened porch in room. Air conditioning. VCR, fax, copier,
spa, bicycles, library, parlor games, fireplace and nature trail through forest on
premises. Handicap access. Amusement parks, antiquing, fishing, live theater,
parks, sporting events, water sports and Atlantic beaches nearby.

Location: Small town.

Certificate may be used: April 1-Nov. 30, Sunday-Thursday, excludes holidays.

Lake Wales E8

Chalet Suzanne Country Inn & Restaurant

3800 Chalet Suzanne Dr
Lake Wales, FL 33859-7763
(863)676-6011 (800)433-6011 Fax:(863)676-1814
Internet: www.chaletsuzanne.com
E-mail: info@chaletsuzanne.com

Circa 1924. Situated on 70 acres adjacent to Lake Suzanne, this country inn's architecture includes gabled roofs, balconies, spires and steeples. The superb restaurant has a glowing reputation and offers a six-course candle-light dinner. Places of interest on the property include the Swiss Room, Wine Dungeon, Gift Boutique, Autograph Garden, Chapel Antiques, Ceramic Salon, Airstrip and the Soup Cannery. The inn has been transformed into a village of cottages and miniature chateaux, one connected to the other seemingly with no particular order.

Innkeeper(s): Vita Hinshaw & Family. $169-229. 30 rooms with PB. Breakfast included in rates. Types of meals: Full bkfst, lunch, gourmet dinner and room service. Beds: KDT. Cable TV, reading lamp, refrigerator, clock radio, telephone and desk in room. Air conditioning. TV, VCR, fax, copier, swimming, library and parlor games on premises. Handicap access. Amusement parks, antiquing, fishing, golf, live theater, parks, shopping, sporting events, tennis and water sports nearby.

Location: Waterfront. Rural-lakefront.

Publicity: *National Geographic Traveler, Southern Living, Country Inns, Uncle Ben's 1992 award and Country Inn Cooking.*

"I now know why everyone always says, 'Wow!' when they come up from dinner. Please don't change a thing."

Certificate may be used: Anytime, subject to availability.

Lake Worth G10

Mango Inn

128 N Lakeside Dr
Lake Worth, FL 33460
(561)533-6900 (888)626-4619 Fax:(561)533-6992
Internet: www.mangoinn.com
E-mail: info@mangoinn.com

Circa 1915. After a stay at Mango Inn, you'll want to take the decorator back to your own home and redo everything inside and out. Inside the historic home are eight unique guest rooms, each with luxurious and imaginative décor. From the Seagrape Room with its verdant walls and a bed that includes a picket fence headboard trailed with ivy to the romantic Rose Room with a gingham comforter and rose-covered walls. The poolside cottage is a private retreat with a four-poster bed and French doors that lead out to a private patio. For a longer stay, try the picturesque Little House, a 1,200-square-foot cottage with two bedrooms, two bathrooms, a living room, dining room, full kitchen and laundry facilities. Breakfast treats might include the inn's signature mango-cashew muffins, and the meal is served either by the fireplace in the dining room or on a veranda that looks out to the pool. The innkeepers offer a variety of special packages to add an extra touch of elegance and romance to your stay. The shops of Palm Beach are just a

few miles away, and Lake Worth offers plenty of antique shops.

Innkeeper(s): Erin & Bo Allen. $75-235. 8 rooms with PB and 1 cottage. Breakfast included in rates. Types of meals: Full gourmet bkfst, early coffee/tea and picnic lunch. Beds: Q. Cable TV, VCR, reading lamp, refrigerator, ceiling fan, clock radio and telephone in room. Central air. Fax, swimming, bicycles and fireplace on premises. Limited handicap access. Antiquing, art galleries, beach, bicycling, canoeing/kayaking, fishing, golf, horseback riding, live theater, museums, parks, shopping, sporting events, tennis and water sports nearby.

Certificate may be used: June 1-Dec. 15, Sunday-Thursday, excludes weekends and holidays.

The Parador of the Palm Beaches

1000 S. Federal Hwy
Lake Worth, FL 33460
(561)540-1443 Fax:(561)547-1243
Internet: www.paradorinn.com
E-mail: theparadorinn@aol.com

Circa 1930. Reflecting the definition of parador, this inn, composed of several historic buildings, embraces the concept of converting existing structures into overnight accommodations. The inn exudes a Caribbean decor, and guests can choose from large suites or junior suites with terrazzo, tile and hardwood floors, cedar-beamed ceilings, wide wooden shades and ceiling fans. Enjoy breakfast in the air-conditioned Florida room, in the tropical courtyard or fern garden. Located minutes from the beach only two blocks from the intra-coastal, the inn also has bikes or beach chairs and snorkeling gear available to borrow. A one-person whitewater kayak also is available.

Innkeeper(s): Ed Menzer. $75-150. 7 suites. Breakfast included in rates. Types of meals: KD. Cable TV, reading lamp, refrigerator, ceiling fan, clock radio, coffeemaker and desk in room. Air conditioning. Fax, bicycles, fireplace and laundry facility on premises. Antiquing, art galleries, beach, bicycling, canoeing/kayaking, fishing, golf, hiking, horseback riding, live theater, museums, parks, shopping, tennis, water sports and wineries nearby.

Location: City.

Certificate may be used: Anytime, Sunday-Thursday.

Miami Beach H10

Hotel Ocean

1230 Ocean Drive
Miami Beach, FL 33139
(305)672-2579 Fax:(305)672-7665
Internet: www.hotelocean.com
E-mail: ocean1230@aol.com

Circa 1936. An art deco design is reflected in the architecture, an original fireplace and in the 1930s collectible pieces at this waterfront boutique hotel. Remodeled for the utmost in comfort, state-of-the-art windows are sound proofed. Guest bedrooms and suites are lavishly appointed in a warm Mediterranean style decor and include upscale amenities to pamper and please. Accessed by a private elevator, stay in the Penthouse Suite which features a Jacuzzi and terrace overlooking the Atlantic Ocean. After breakfast take a walking tour of nearby historic landmarks. Shop on famous South Beach.

Innkeeper(s): Anita Haudebert. $250-600. 27 rooms, 14 with PB, 13 suites. Breakfast included in rates. Types of meals: Cont, early coffee/tea, lunch and room service. Restaurant on premises. Beds: KQT. Data port, cable TV, VCR, reading lamp, stereo, refrigerator, clock radio, telephone, turn-down service, desk, voice mail and fireplace in room. Air conditioning. Fax, copier, library, pet boarding, fireplace, laundry facility and gift shop on premises. Limited handicap access. Amusement parks, antiquing, art galleries, beach, bicycling, canoeing/kayaking, fishing, golf, museums, parks, shopping, sporting events, tennis and water sports nearby.

Location: City, waterfront.

Certificate may be used: June 1 until Oct. 30.

Monticello B5

The Cottage B&B

259 West Palmer Mill Road
Monticello, FL 32344
(850)342-3541 (866)342-3541
Internet:
www.bedandbreakfast.com/property/index.aspx?id=614916
E-mail: mjmbandb@yahoo.com

Circa 1914. Amidst peaceful fields and shady oaks, this late Victorian antebellum home boasts a romantic atmosphere. Experience a taste of Europe in the classical Mediterranean-style decor and the three languages spoken fluently by the innkeepers. Breakfast is enjoyed on the elegant patio or dining area. A lighter fare is served daily. For an additional fee, Saturday brunch is offered, and on Sunday a full meal may include the signature puffed apple pancake, rum-raisin French toast and strawberry soup. Lunch and dinner are available by reservation for $12-50 per person. Relax in the garden courtyard with two fountains.

Innkeeper(s): Martha and Jean Michael Cravanzola. $85-150. 2 rooms with PB. Types of meals: Full bkfst, lunch and dinner. Beds: Q. Modem hook-up, cable TV, VCR, stereo, refrigerator, ceiling fan and desk in room. Central air. Library, telephone and fireplace on premises. Amusement parks, antiquing, art galleries, beach, bicycling, canoeing/kayaking, fishing, golf, horseback riding, live theater, museums, parks, shopping, sporting events, tennis, water sports and wineries nearby.

Location: Country.

Certificate may be used: May-August, January and February, Sunday-Thursday as available, except on or near holidays or special events.

New Smyrna Beach D9

Night Swan Intracoastal B&B

512 S Riverside Dr
New Smyrna Beach, FL 32168-7345
(386)423-4940 (800)465-4261 Fax:(386)427-2814
Internet: www.nightswan.com
E-mail: info@nightswan.com

Circa 1906. From the 140-foot dock at this waterside bed & breakfast, guests can gaze at stars, watch as ships pass or perhaps catch site of dolphins. The turn-of-the-century home is decorated with period furnishings, including an antique baby grand piano, which guests are invited to use. Several guest rooms afford views of the Indian River, which is part of the Atlantic Intracoastal Waterway. Seven rooms include a whirlpool tub. The innkeepers have created several special packages, featuring catered gourmet dinners, boat tours or romantic baskets with chocolate, wine and flowers.

Innkeeper(s): Martha & Chuck Nighswonger. $95-175. 15 rooms with PB, 3 total suites, including 2 two-bedroom suites and 1 conference room. Breakfast and snacks/refreshments included in rates. Types of meals: Full bkfst and early coffee/tea. Beds: KQ. Modem hook-up, cable TV, VCR, reading lamp, refrigerator, ceiling fan, clock radio, telephone, desk and seven whirlpool tubs in room. Air conditioning. Fax, library, fireplace and laundry facility on premises. Handicap access. Antiquing, art galleries, beach, bicycling, canoeing/kayaking, fishing, golf, horseback riding, live theater, museums, parks, shopping, tennis and water sports nearby.

Location: Waterfront.

Publicity: *Ft. Lauderdale Sun Sentinel and Florida Living.*

Certificate may be used: June 1-Jan. 30, Sunday-Thursday, except holidays.

Ocala C7

Seven Sisters Inn

820 Se Fort King St
Ocala, FL 34471-2320
(352)867-1170 Fax:(352)867-5266
Internet: www.sevensistersinn.com
E-mail: sistersinn@aol.com

Circa 1888. Gracing the historic district with its stately elegance, this 1888 Queen Anne Victorian bed & breakfast has been meticulously restored and is listed in the National Register. The furnishings and décor of the themed guest bedrooms reflect the four corners of the world. Sleep in a Sultan's bed in India, explore Egyptian artifacts, lounge in French luxury in Paris or experience the harmony of the Orient in China. A three-room suite instills old-fashioned romance with American accents and a canopy bed. Heated towel bars, whirlpool tubs, fireplaces and stone spa showers are delightful amenities included in most rooms. Award-winning recipes are part of a gourmet breakfast served in Monet's Morning Room with crystal, silver, white china and fine linens. Indulge in afternoon tea after a morning bike ride. Ask about candlelit dinners, special events and packages.

Innkeeper(s): Ken Oden & Bonnie Morehardt. $119-269. 14 rooms with PB, 3 with FP, 5 suites and 1 conference room. Breakfast and afternoon tea included in rates. Types of meals: Full gourmet bkfst, picnic lunch and gourmet dinner. Beds: KQT. TV, reading lamp, ceiling fan, clock radio, telephone, turn-down service and desk in room. Air conditioning. Fax, copier, parlor games, fireplace and off-grounds pet boarding available on premises. Antiquing, fishing, golf, live theater, shopping, water sports, national forest and Silver Springs attractions nearby.

Location: City. Historic district.

Publicity: *Southern Living, Glamour, Conde Nast Traveler and Country Inns (one of 12 best).*

Certificate may be used: Sunday-Thursday, no holidays or weekends.

Orlando D8

The Courtyard at Lake Lucerne

211 N Lucerne Circle E
Orlando, FL 32801-3721
(407)648-5188 (800)444-5289 Fax:(407)246-1368
Internet: www.orlandohistoricinn.com
E-mail: info@orlandohistoricinn.com

Circa 1885. This award-winning inn, precisely restored with attention to historical detail, consists of four different architectural styles. The Norment-Parry House is Orlando's oldest home. The Wellborn, an Art-Deco Modern Building, offers one-bedroom suites with kitchenettes. The I.W. Phillips is an antebellum-style manor where breakfast is served in a large reception room with a wide veranda overlooking the courtyard fountains and lush gardens. The Grand Victorian Dr. Phillips House is listed in the National Register of Historic Places. For an enchanting treat, ask for the Turret Room.

Innkeeper(s): Charles Meiner. $89-225. 30 rooms with PB and 1 conference room. Breakfast included in rates. Types of meals: Cont plus. Beds: KQD. Cable TV, reading lamp, refrigerator, clock radio, telephone, desk and hot tub/spa in room. Air conditioning. TV, copier and fireplace on premises. Amusement parks, antiquing, fishing, live theater, shopping, sporting events and water sports nearby.

Location: City.

Publicity: *Florida Historic Homes, Miami Herald, Southern Living and Country Victorian.*

"Best-kept secret in Orlando."

Certificate may be used: Anytime, subject to availability, on regular rate for standard rooms.

Palatka   C8

Azalea House
   220 Madison St
   Palatka, FL 32177-3531
   (386)325-4547
   Internet: www.theazaleahouse.com
   E-mail: azaleahouse@gbso.net

Circa 1878. Located within the Palatka Historic District, this beautifully embellished Queen Anne Victorian is painted a cheerful yellow with complementing green shutters. Bay windows, gables and verandas have discrete touches of royal blue, gold, white and aqua on the gingerbread trim, a true "Painted Lady." There are oak, magnolia and palm trees and an 85-year-old, grafted camellia tree with both pink and white blossoms. Double parlors are furnished with period antiques including an arched, floor-to-ceiling mirror. A three-story heart and curly pine staircase leads to the guest rooms. Breakfast is served on fine china in the formal dining room. Two blocks away is the mile-wide north flowing St. John's River. An unaltered golf course designed by Donald Ross in 1925 is nearby, as well as the Ravine State Botanical Garden. It's 25 minutes to Crescent Beach.

Innkeeper(s): Doug & Jill de Leeuw. $75-135. 6 rooms, 4 with PB. Breakfast and snacks/refreshments included in rates. Types of meals: Full bkfst and early coffee/tea. Beds: Q. Reading lamp, ceiling fan, telephone, turn-down service and alarm clocks in room. Air conditioning. Swimming, fireplace and porch swings on premises. Antiquing, fishing, golf, live theater, parks, shopping and water sports nearby.

Location: City. Historic district.

Publicity: *American Treasures and 2002 B&B Calendar.*

Certificate may be used: June 1 to Sept. 30, all days.

Pensacola   B2

Noble Manor
   110 W Strong St
   Pensacola, FL 32501-3140
   (850)434-9544 (877)598-4634
   Internet: www.noblemanor.com
   E-mail: info2@noblemanor.com

Circa 1905. This two-story home offers Tudor Revival-style architecture. It is set on lavish grounds planted with camellias, azaleas and roses. The inn is decorated with traditional furnishings, antiques and fine art prints, and guests will enjoy a dramatic central staircase and handsome fireplaces. Breakfast is served in the dining room. A front porch and a gazebo with a hot tub are among guests' favorite spots. Pensacola's North Hill Historic District is a historic preservation area. Nearby are Civil War forts and a restored 1800s area.

Innkeeper(s): John & Carol Briscoe. $79-125. 5 rooms with PB, 3 with FP

and 1 conference room. Breakfast and snacks/refreshments included in rates. Types of meals: Cont plus and early coffee/tea. Beds: KQ. Modem hook-up, cable TV, VCR, reading lamp, ceiling fan, clock radio, telephone and desk in room. Central air. Fax, copier, spa, swimming, library, fireplace and laundry facility on premises. Limited handicap access. Antiquing, art galleries, beach, live theater, museums, parks and sporting events nearby.

Location: City. Downtown historic district.

Certificate may be used: Jan. 2-Feb. 28.

Quincy   B5

Allison House Inn
   215 N Madison St
   Quincy, FL 32351
   (850)875-2511 (888)904-2511 Fax:(850)875-2511
   Internet: www.allisonhouseinn.com
   E-mail: innkeeper@tds.net

Circa 1843. Crepe myrtle, azaleas, camellias and roses dot the acre of grounds that welcomes guests to the Allison House. A local historic landmark located in the 36-block historic district, the inn is in a Georgian, English-country style with shutters and an entrance portico. It was built for General Allison, who became Governor of Florida. There are two parlors, and all the rooms are appointed with English antiques. Homemade biscotti is always available for snacking and for breakfast, English muffins and freshly baked breads are offered. Walk around the district and spot the 51 historic homes and buildings. Nearby dining opportunities include the historic Nicholson Farmhouse Restaurant.

Innkeeper(s): Stuart & Eileen Johnson. $85-150. 6 rooms with PB. Breakfast and snacks/refreshments included in rates. Types of meals: Full bkfst. Beds: KQD. Modem hook-up, cable TV, reading lamp, ceiling fan, clock radio, telephone, central air conditioning controls and hair dryers in room. TV, fax and bicycles on premises. Handicap access. Antiquing, art galleries, bicycling, golf, horseback riding, live theater, sporting events and tennis nearby.

Location: City. Small town.

Certificate may be used: June 15-Sept. 15, Sunday-Thursday.

Saint Augustine   B8

Agustin Inn
   29 Cuna St
   Saint Augustine, FL 32084-3681
   (904)823-9559 (800)248-7846 Fax:(904)824-8685
   Internet: www.agustininn.com
   E-mail: agustin@aug.com

Circa 1903. Situated in the historic walking district of our nation's oldest city, this Victorian inn captures the ambiance of old downtown St. Augustine. Innkeepers Robert and Sherri Brackett, members of Historic Inns of St. Augustine and Superior Small Lodging, have furnished the home in comfortable elegance. The twelve guest bedrooms boast mahogany or canopy beds and oval Jacuzzi tubs. Some of the bedrooms have private entrances and terraces where early coffee or tea and evening wine and hors d'oeuvres can be enjoyed while overlooking the fragrant courtyards. Sherri's full homemade breakfasts are satisfying and may feature Belgian waffles with fried apples and bananas, delicious omelets, and home fries with buttermilk biscuits. Venturing out on the cobblestone streets offers a variety of activities and historical sites.

Innkeeper(s): Robert & Sherri Brackett. $89-199. 18 rooms with PB. Breakfast and snacks/refreshments included in rates. Types of meals: Full bkfst and early coffee/tea. Beds: Q. Reading lamp, ceiling fan and Jacuzzi tubs in room. Central air. TV, fax, copier and telephone on premises.

Handicap access. Antiquing, art galleries, beach, fishing, golf, museums, parks and shopping nearby.

Location: Historic District.

Certificate may be used: January, June, July, August and September, Sunday-Thursday, excluding holidays, subject to availability.

Casa De La Paz Bayfront B&B

22 Avenida Menendez
Saint Augustine, FL 32084-3644
(904)829-2915 (800)929-2915
Internet: www.casadelapaz.com
E-mail: innkeeper@casadelapaz.com

Circa 1915. Overlooking Matanzas Bay, Casa de la Paz was built after the devastating 1914 fire leveled much of the old city. An ornate stucco Mediterranean Revival house, it features clay barrel tile roofing, bracketed eaves, verandas and a lush walled courtyard. The home is listed in the National Register of Historic Places. Guest rooms offer ceiling fans, central air, hardwood floors, antiques, a decanter of sherry, chocolates and complimentary snacks.

Innkeeper(s): Sherri & Marshall Crews. $130-500. 7 rooms with PB, 3 with FP and 1 conference room. Breakfast, snacks/refreshments and wine included in rates. Types of meals: Full gourmet bkfst, early coffee/tea and afternoon tea. Beds: KQ. Modem hook-up, data port, cable TV, reading lamp, ceiling fan, snack bar, clock radio, telephone, coffeemaker, hot tub/spa and fireplace in room. Central air. Fax, copier, parlor games and gift shop on premises. Antiquing, art galleries, beach, canoeing/kayaking, fishing, golf, live theater, museums, parks, shopping, sporting events, water sports and wineries nearby.

Location: City, waterfront. Historic town.

Publicity: *Innsider, US Air Magazine, Southern Living, Kiplingers Top 5 Inn, Orlando Sentinel, Sarasota News, Palm Beach Post, PBS, Travel Channel and TLC.*

"We will always recommend your beautifully restored, elegant home."

Certificate may be used: Sunday through Thursday, (holidays and special events excluded), July, August & September, subject to availability.

Castle Garden B&B

15 Shenandoah St
Saint Augustine, FL 32084-2817
(904)829-3839
Internet: www.castlegarden.com
E-mail: castleg@aug.com

Circa 1860. This newly-restored Moorish Revival-style inn was the carriage house to Warden Castle. Among the seven guest rooms are three bridal rooms with in-room Jacuzzi tubs and sunken bedrooms with cathedral ceilings. The innkeepers offer packages including carriage rides, picnic lunches, gift baskets and other enticing possibilities. Guests enjoy a homemade full, country breakfast each morning.

Innkeeper(s): Bruce & Brian Kloeckner. $69-199. 7 rooms with PB, 3 suites. Breakfast included in rates. Types of meals: Full bkfst, early coffee/tea and picnic lunch. Beds: KQT. TV and ceiling fan in room. Air conditioning. Telephone and common sitting room with cable on premises. Antiquing, fishing, golf, live theater, shopping, tennis, water sports and ballooning nearby.

Location: City.

Certificate may be used: Monday through Thursday. Other times if available.

Old City House Inn & Restaurant

115 Cordova St
Saint Augustine, FL 32084-4413
(904)826-0113
Internet: www.oldcityhouse.com
E-mail: relax@oldcityhouse.com

Circa 1873. Strategically located in the center of a city immersed in history, this award-winning inn and restaurant was a former stable. Recently it was locally voted the "best of St. Augustine." A red-tiled roof, coquina walls, veranda and courtyard add to the Spanish atmosphere. Guest bedrooms boast hand-carved, four-poster beds and high-speed Internet. Some rooms feature Jacuzzi tubs. An expansive daily

gourmet breakfast is included. The on-site restaurant is open for lunch and dinner. Unique salads, fresh fish and chicken create the midday menu, while dinner selections boast standards such as Filet Mignon or a more unusual Thai coconut milk beef curry with sesame rice. Choose an appetizer of baked brie, Asian crab cakes or escargot.

Innkeeper(s): James & Ilse Philcox. $89-209. 7 rooms with PB. Breakfast included in rates. Types of meals: Full bkfst, early coffee/tea, gourmet lunch and gourmet dinner. Restaurant on premises. Beds: Q. Cable TV, reading lamp, ceiling fan, clock radio, telephone, hot tub/spa, four-poster hand-carved beds, some with Jacuzzis and high-speed Internet available in room. Air conditioning. TV, VCR, fax, copier and bicycles on premises. Handicap access. Antiquing, fishing, live theater, shopping and water sports nearby.

Location: City.

Publicity: *Florida Times Union, Florida Trend and Ft. Lauderdale Sun Sentinel.*

Certificate may be used: Sunday-Thursday, except holidays.

St. Francis Inn

279 Saint George St
Saint Augustine, FL 32084-5031
(904)824-6068 (800)824-6062 Fax:(904)810-5525
Internet: www.stfrancisinn.com
E-mail: info@stfrancisinn.com

Circa 1791. Long noted for its hospitality, the St. Francis Inn is nearly the oldest house in town. A classic example of Old World architecture, it was built by Gaspar Garcia, who received a Spanish grant to the plot of land. Coquina was the main building material. A buffet breakfast is served. Some rooms have whirlpool tubs and fireplaces. The city of Saint Augustine was founded in 1565.

Innkeeper(s): Joe Finnegan. $109-229. 14 rooms with PB, 8 with FP, 4 suites, 1 cottage and 2 conference rooms. Breakfast included in rates. Types of meals: Full bkfst. Beds: KQDT. Cable TV, reading lamp, refrigerator, ceiling fan, telephone, desk, hot tub/spa and fireplace in room. Air conditioning. TV, fax, copier, swimming, bicycles, parlor games and whirlpool tubs on premises. Antiquing, fishing, parks, shopping, sporting events and water sports nearby.

Location: City.

Publicity: *Orlando Sentinel.*

"We have stayed at many nice hotels but nothing like this. We are really enjoying it."

Certificate may be used: May 1 to Feb. 10, Sunday through Thursday, excluding holiday periods.

Victorian House B&B

11 Cadiz St
Saint Augustine, FL 32084-4431
(904)824-5214 (800)709-5710 Fax:(904)824-7990
Internet: www.victorianhousebnb.com
E-mail: ken@victorianhousebnb.com

Circa 1897. Enjoy the historic ambiance of Saint Augustine at this turn-of-the-century Victorian, decorated to reflect the grandeur of that genteel era. Stenciling highlights the walls, and the innkeepers have filled the guest rooms with canopy beds and period furnishings complementing the heart of pine floors. A full breakfast includes homemade granola, fresh fruit, a hot entree and a variety of freshly made breads.

Innkeeper(s): Ken & Marcia Cerotzke. $99-194. 8 rooms with PB, 4 two-bedroom suites. Breakfast and snacks/refreshments included in rates. Types of meals: Full gourmet bkfst. Beds: KQDT. Cable TV, reading lamp, ceiling fan, clock radio, Laura's suite has a kitchenette with microwave, coffeemaker, toaster and refrigerator in room. Central air. Fax, copier, bicycles, parlor games, telephone and gift shop on premises. Antiquing, art galleries, beach, bicycling, canoeing/kayaking, fishing, golf, hiking, horseback riding, live theater, museums, parks, shopping, tennis, water sports, wineries, fine restaurants, historic sites, the Bayfront, Lightner Museum and Castillo de San Marcos nearby.

Location: City.

Publicity: *Arrington's 2004 B&B Journal (one of the top 15 inns three years in a row).*

Certificate may be used: Jan. 1-Dec. 21, excluding holidays and weekends.

Saint Petersburg   E7

Bayboro House B&B on Old Tampa Bay

1719 Beach Dr SE
Saint Petersburg, FL 33701-5917
(877)823-4955 Fax:(877)823-4955
Internet: www.bayborohouseandb.com
E-mail: bayboro@tampabay.rr.com

Circa 1907. Victorian decor and beautiful antique furnishings fill the Bayboro House, a charming turn-of-the-century manor. The veranda is set up for relaxation with a variety of rockers, swings, wicker chairs and chaise lounges. Breakfasts, served in the formal dining room, feature what every Florida breakfast should, freshly squeezed juices and in-season fruits. Before heading out to one of Saint Petersburg's many restaurants, relax and sip a glass of wine in the parlor.

Innkeeper(s): Sandy & Dave Kelly. $125-249. 5 rooms with PB, 2 suites. Breakfast included in rates. Types of meals: Cont plus. Beds: KQ. Modem hook-up, VCR, reading lamp and ceiling fan in room. Air conditioning. TV, fax, spa, swimming, parlor games, telephone and fireplace on premises. Amusement parks, antiquing, fishing, live theater, parks, shopping, sporting events and water sports nearby.

Location: Waterfront.

Publicity: *Miami Herald, Sun Sentinel and Home Shopping CBS.*

"It was well worth the price, a long weekend that I'll never forget. It was everything that you advertised it to be and so much more. Thanks so much."

Certificate may be used: Anytime, subject to availability.

Best Inn Lee Manor

342 3rd Ave N
Saint Petersburg, FL 33701-3821
(727)894-3248 (866)219-7260 Fax:(727)895-8759
Internet: www.leemanorinn.com
E-mail: info@leemanorinn.com

Circa 1937. Comfortable and convenient, this historic 21-room inn is located downtown. This city oasis is relaxing for the leisure or business traveler. Furnished with antiques, the vintage hotel offers Old World charm and warm hospitality. Each guest bedroom features amenities that include a hair dryer, television, refrigerator and coffee maker with supplies. Danish, fruit, waffles, toast, juice and hot beverages are offered every morning for a complimentary continental breakfast. The Pier, Baywalk, County Courthouse, Tropicana Field, museums, theaters and shops all are nearby.

Innkeeper(s): Kelly & Barry Hekman. $59-139. 21 rooms with PB, 2 suites. Breakfast included in rates. Types of meals: Cont. Beds: QDT. Modem hook-up, data port, cable TV, reading lamp, refrigerator, ceiling fan, clock radio, telephone and coffeemaker in room. Air conditioning. VCR, fax, copier and library on premises. Antiquing, art galleries, beach, bicycling, canoeing/kayaking, fishing, golf, hiking, horseback riding, live theater, museums, parks, shopping, sporting events, tennis and water sports nearby.

Location: City.

Certificate may be used: Anytime, subject to availability.

Inn at the Bay Bed and Breakfast

126 4th Ave NE
Saint Petersburg, FL 33701
(727)822-1700 (888)873-2122 Fax:(727)896-7412
Internet: www.innatthebay.com
E-mail: info@innatthebay.com

Circa 1910. Conveniently located on Tampa Bay, this newly renovated inn is near many of the state's popular attractions. The plush guest bedrooms and suites, themed in regional motifs, showcase Florida. Allergy-free feather beds and whirlpool tubs soothe and rejuvenate. Hospitality is abundant in the provision of thoughtful amenities like fluffy robes, lighted makeup mirrors, cable TV and Internet access. After a delicious breakfast, enjoy reading the daily newspaper in the garden gazebo.

Innkeeper(s): Dennis & Jewly Youschak. $119-270. 12 rooms with PB, 2 with FP and 1 conference room. Breakfast and wine included in rates. Types of meals: Full gourmet bkfst. Beds: KQ. Modem hook-up, data port, cable TV, VCR, reading lamp, CD player, refrigerator, ceiling fan, snack bar, clock radio, telephone, coffeemaker, turn-down service, desk, hot tub/spa, voice mail, fireplace and two suites with fireplaces in room. Central air. Fax, copier, parlor games and gift shop on premises. Handicap access. Amusement parks, antiquing, art galleries, beach, canoeing/kayaking, fishing, golf, hiking, horseback riding, live theater, museums, parks, shopping, sporting events and water sports nearby.

Location: City, ocean community.

Certificate may be used: Anytime, Sunday-Thursday subject to availability, King suite only.

La Veranda Bed & Breakfast

111 5th Ave. N
Saint Petersburg, FL 33701
(727)824-9997 (800)484-8423X8417 Fax:(727)827-1431
Internet: www.laverandabb.com
E-mail: info@laverandabb.com

Circa 1910. Featuring Old World charm in an urban setting, this classic Key West-style mansion is only two blocks from the waterfront. Antiques, Oriental rugs and artwork accent the gracious elegance. Lounge by the fire in the living room or on one of the large wicker-filled wraparound verandas overlooking lush tropical gardens. Romantic one- and two-bedroom suites boast private entrances, as well as indoor and outdoor sitting areas. A gourmet breakfast with Starbucks coffee is served on settings of china, silver and crystal. Corporate services are available with assorted business amenities.

Innkeeper(s): Nancy Mayer. $99-249. 5 rooms, 1 with PB, 4 suites. Breakfast and snacks/refreshments included in rates. Types of meals: Full gourmet bkfst, veg bkfst, early coffee/tea, afternoon tea and room service. Beds: KQT. Cable TV, VCR, reading lamp, CD player, refrigerator, ceiling fan, snack bar, clock radio, telephone, turn-down service, desk and fireplace in room. Air conditioning. Fax, copier, bicycles, library, fireplace and laundry facility on premises. Limited handicap access. Amusement parks, antiquing, art galleries, beach, bicycling, canoeing/kayaking, fishing, golf, hiking, live theater, museums, parks, shopping, sporting events, water sports and wineries nearby.

Location: City.

Publicity: *NY Daily Times and Interstate 75.*

Certificate may be used: Anytime, subject to availability, on rack rate only.

Mansion House B&B

105 5th Ave NE
Saint Petersburg, FL 33701
(727)821-9391 (800)274-7520 Fax:(727)821-6906
Internet: www.mansionbandb.com
E-mail: mansion1@ix.netcom.com

Circa 1901. The first mayor of St. Petersburg once lived here, and the inn is so named in the English tradition that states the home of a mayor shall be known as the mansion house. The home's architecture is Arts and Crafts in style, and has been completely restored, winning awards for beautification and enhancement. The Pembroke Room, in the inn's carriage house, is especially remarkable. Wicker pieces and hand-painted furnishings by Artist Marva Simpson, exposed beams painted a rich teal green, and trails of flowers and ivy decorating the lace-covered windows create the ambiance of an English seaside cottage. The Edinburgh Room is another beauty with its canopy bed topped with luxurious coverings. Guests can walk from the home to a natural harbor, restaurants, popular local parks and the beach. Busch Gardens, museums, an arboretum and a botanical garden are other nearby attractions.

Innkeeper(s): Rose Marie Ray. $119-220. 12 rooms with PB and 4 conference rooms. Breakfast and snacks/refreshments included in rates. Types of meals: Full gourmet bkfst, veg bkfst, early coffee/tea, picnic lunch and afternoon tea. Restaurant on premises. Beds: KQT. Modem hook-up, data port, cable TV, reading lamp, ceiling fan, clock radio, telephone and desk in room. Central air. VCR, fax, copier, library, parlor games, laundry facility, swimming pool and courtyard/garden on premises. Amusement parks, antiquing, art galleries, beach, bicycling, canoeing/kayaking, fishing, golf, hiking, horseback riding, live theater, museums, parks, shopping, sporting events, tennis, water sports and eco-nature tours nearby.

Location: City.

Publicity: *Michelin Green Guide, Frommer's Unofficial Guide to B&Bs of the South and American Bed & Breakfast Book.*

Certificate may be used: June 1-Dec. 15, Sunday to Thursday, excluding holidays, luxury queen, A1Q ($220) or B1Q ($149) rack rate. No discounts or travel agent commissions paid.

San Mateo   C8

Ferncourt B&B

150 Central Ave
San Mateo, FL 32187-0758
(386)328-3633 (888)805-7633
Internet: www.ferncourt.com
E-mail: nico111@bellsouth.net

Circa 1889. This Victorian "painted lady," is one of the few remaining relics from San Mateo's heyday in the early 1900s. Teddy Roosevelt once visited the elegant home. The current owners have restored the Victorian atmosphere with rooms decorated with bright, floral prints and gracious furnishings. Awake to the smells of brewing coffee and the sound of a rooster crowing before settling down to a full gourmet break-

fast. Historic Saint Augustine is a quick, 25-mile drive.

Innkeeper(s): Domenic Nicolosi. $59-149. 5 rooms with PB, 1 two-bedroom suite. Breakfast, afternoon tea and snacks/refreshments included in rates. Types of meals: Cont plus and early coffee/tea. Beds: KQD. Reading lamp, ceiling fan, clock radio and desk in room. Central air. TV, VCR, fax, bicycles, library, parlor games, telephone, fireplace, off-street parking, covered gear storage and large veranda on premises. Antiquing, beach, bicycling, canoeing/kayaking, fishing, golf, hiking, horseback riding, live theater, museums, parks, shopping, sporting events, water sports, off-road vehicle trails, fresh and saltwater fishing, Daytona and eco-tours nearby.

Location: Country. Rural.

"First class operation! A beautiful house with an impressive history and restoration. Great company and fine food."

Certificate may be used: July 15 to Nov. 1, Sunday-Thursday.

Sanford   D8

The Higgins House

420 S Oak Ave
Sanford, FL 32771-1826
(407)324-9238 (800)584-0014 Fax:(407)324-5060
Internet: www.higginshouse.com
E-mail: reservations@higginshouse.com

Circa 1894. This inviting blue Queen Anne-style home features cross gables with patterned wood shingles, bay windows and a charming round window on the second floor. Pine floors, paddle fans and a piano in the parlor, which guests are encouraged to play, create Victorian ambiance. The second-story balcony affords views not only of a charming park and Sanford's oldest church, but of Space Shuttle launches from nearby Cape Canaveral. The Queen

Anne room looks out over a Victorian box garden, while the Wicker Room features a bay window sitting area. The Country Victorian room boasts a 19th-century brass bed. Nature lovers will enjoy close access to Blue Spring State Park, Ocala National Forest, Lake Monroe and the Cape Canaveral National Seashore. And of course, Walt Disney World, Sea World and Universal Studios aren't far away.

Innkeeper(s): Ronald & Phyllis Lloyd. $110-165. 3 rooms with PB. Breakfast and snacks/refreshments included in rates. Types of meals: Full gourmet bkfst, early coffee/tea and picnic lunch. Beds: QD. Reading lamp, ceiling fan and turn-down service in room. Air conditioning. VCR, spa, bicycles, telephone and fireplace on premises. Antiquing, fishing, parks, shopping and water sports nearby.

Location: City. Historic district.

Publicity: *Southern Living, Sanford Herald, Connecticut Traveler, LifeTimes, Orlando Sentinel, Southern Accents, Country Inns and Florida Living.*

"The Higgins House is warm and friendly, filled with such pleasant sounds, and if you love beauty and nature, you're certain to enjoy the grounds."

Certificate may be used: Jan. 30-Dec. 31, Sunday-Thursday, excluding holidays and special events.

Georgia

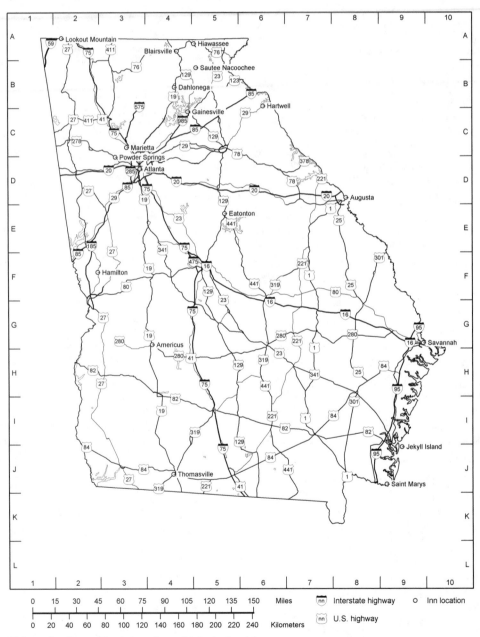

0   15   30   45   60   75   90   105 120 135 150   Miles

0 20 40 60 80 100 120 140 160 180 200 220 240   Kilometers

nn Interstate highway   ○ Inn location

nn U.S. highway

Visit www.iLoveInns.com for photos and more details about each inn.

Americus G4

1906 Pathway Inn B&B

501 S Lee St
Americus, GA 31709-3919
(229)928-2078 (800)889-1466 Fax:(229)928-2078
Internet: www.1906pathwayinn.com
E-mail: info@1906pathwayinn.com

Circa 1906. This turn-of-the-century inn is located along the
Andersonville Trail and not far from the city of Andersonville, a
Civil War village with a museum. Located between Andersonville
and Plains, the home of former President Jimmy Carter, where
you may attend and hear him teach Sunday school. The gracious, wraparound porch is a perfect spot for relaxation. The
innkeepers plan the morning meal to accommodate their guests'
schedules, serving up a candle-lit breakfast with freshly baked
breads using silver, crystal and china. The guest rooms offer
romantic amenities such as whirlpools and snug down comforters. Two of the rooms are named in honor of Jimmy and
Rosalynn Carter. Late afternoons are reserved for wine and
refreshments. Several restaurants are within walking distance.
Innkeeper(s): Angela & Chuck Nolan. $115-135. 5 rooms with PB, 2 with FP.
Breakfast included in rates. Types of meals: Full gourmet bkfst, early coffee/tea,
snacks/refreshments and room service. Beds: KQ. Cable TV, VCR, reading lamp,
ceiling fan, clock radio, telephone, turn-down service, desk and whirlpool tubs
in room. Air conditioning. Fax, copier, parlor games and fireplace on premises.
Antiquing, live theater, parks and federal historic sites nearby.
Location: City.
Certificate may be used: June 1-Aug. 31 and Dec. 1-Jan. 31, Sunday-
Thursday (whirlpool rooms only). Special events and holidays exempt.

Atlanta D3

Beverly Hills Inn

65 Sheridan Dr NE
Atlanta, GA 30305-3121
(404)233-8520 (800)331-8520 Fax:(404)233-8659
Internet: www.beverlyhillsinn.com
E-mail: mit@bhi.com

Circa 1929. Period furniture and polished-wood floors decorate this inn located in the Buckhead neighborhood. There are
private balconies, kitchens and a library with a collection of
newspapers and books. The governor's mansion, Neiman-
Marcus, Saks and Lord & Taylor are five minutes away.

Innkeeper(s): Mit Amin. $99-160. 18
suites. Breakfast included in rates.
Types of meals: Cont plus. Beds: QD.
Cable TV, reading lamp, refrigerator,
clock radio and telephone in room. Air
conditioning. TV and health club privileges on premises. Antiquing, parks
and shopping nearby.
Location: City.
Publicity: *Travel & Leisure, Country Inns, Southern Living, Time and CNN.*
*"Our only regret is that we had so little time. Next stay we will plan
to be here longer."*
Certificate may be used: Anytime, subject to availability.

King-Keith House B&B

889 Edgewood Ave NE
Atlanta, GA 30307
(404)688-7330 (800)728-3879 Fax:(404)584-8408
Internet: www.kingkeith.com
E-mail: kingkeith@mindspring.com

Circa 1890. One of Atlanta's most photographed houses, this
1980 Queen Anne Victorian sits among live oaks and prominent

homes in the restored neighborhood of Inman
Park. Listed in the National Register, it boasts
twelve-foot ceilings and carved fireplaces.
Play the baby grand piano in one of
the elegant public rooms and
stroll through the private gardens.
Enjoy complimentary snacks and
beverages. Romantic guest bed-
rooms offer a variety of pleasing amenities, gorgeous antiques
and some feature clawfoot tubs. The Downstairs Suite includes a
Jacuzzi tub, living room and private entrance off the front porch.
Originally the servant's quarters, the spacious Cottage is a honeymoon favorite with vaulted ceilings, double Jacuzzi and an elegant garden with a fountain. Linger over a gourmet breakfast
served with generous southern hospitality.
Innkeeper(s): Jan & Windell Keith. $90-175. 6 rooms with PB, 1 suite and 1
cottage. Breakfast included in rates. Types of meals: Full gourmet bkfst and
early coffee/tea. Beds: KQDT. Cable TV, reading lamp, refrigerator, ceiling fan,
snack bar, clock radio, telephone, desk, hair dryer and cottage with Jacuzzi and
fireplace in room. Air conditioning. Parlor games on premises. Antiquing, golf,
live theater, parks, shopping, sporting events, tennis and restaurants nearby.
Location: City. Downtown.
Publicity: *Southern Living and Cover Victorian Homes.*
Certificate may be used: Good only Sunday, Monday, Tuesday, Wednesday
and Thursday.

Augusta D8

The Azalea Inn

312-334 Greene St
Augusta, GA 30901
(706)724-3454 (877)292-5324 Fax:(706)724-1033
Internet: www.theazaleainn.com
E-mail: azaleabnb@aol.com

Circa 1895. Three tastefully restored Victorian homes comprise
the Azalea Inn, located in the Olde Town Historic District.
Elegantly furnished suites with 11-foot ceilings also offer fireplaces and large whirlpool tubs.
Breakfast is delivered to your room
in a basket. The inn is within
walking distance to the Riverwalk
on the Savannah River, fine restaurants, museums, antique shops
and unique boutiques.
Innkeeper(s): David Tremaine, Andrew
Harney. $99-179. 21 rooms with PB, 13 with FP, 4 suites. Types of meals:
Cont plus. Beds: KQ. Cable TV, reading lamp, refrigerator, ceiling fan, clock
radio, telephone, desk and whirlpool tubs in room. Air conditioning. Glass-
enclosed sunporches in suites on premises. Handicap access. Antiquing, fishing, golf, live theater, parks, shopping, sporting events, tennis, water sports
and historic sites nearby.
Publicity: *Georgia Journal, Augusta Magazine and S.C. State Newspaper.*
"Third time and loved it!"
Certificate may be used: Sunday-Thursday nights, year-round, excluding holidays and April 1-15.

Queen Anne Inn

406 Greene St
Augusta, GA 30901
(706)723-0045 (877)460-0045 Fax:(706)826-7920
Internet: www.queenanneinnaugusta.com
E-mail: william.mundell@worldnet.att.net

Circa 1890. This inviting three-story inn, filled with marble-
topped antiques, stained glass windows and working fireplaces
offers a special family suite in its handsome turret. Shaded by tall

trees, the inn's veranda is a favorite spot for relaxing after returning from the Savannah River Walk, which starts three blocks away. Rooms are furnished with antique beds such as a Second Empire, an ornate Eastlake and a high-backed sleigh bed. The parlors offer fringed Victorian pieces, Oriental carpets and original paintings. Breakfast is continental, or you can walk down the tree-shaded street to a local cafe, which provides Queen Anne guests a full hot breakfast. Evening in-suite dining is available by selecting room service dinners from quality restaurants working with the inn. The family tower suite offers parents with children a chance to enjoy an elegant inn, yet have quiet quarters for themselves and their young children in a special section of the inn. Best of all, your well-traveled schoolteacher/innkeepers can arrange baby-sitting services for families. A shuttle service is offered as well.

Innkeeper(s): Val & Bill Mundell. $69-99. 7 rooms with PB. TV, VCR, fax, bicycles, library, parking and Jacuzzi on premises. Antiquing, bicycling, canoeing/kayaking, golf, hiking, shopping and museums nearby.
Publicity: *Applause.*

"Thank you so much for taking such good care of my husband on his first trip to Augusta."

Certificate may be used: Year-round, excluding April 1-15 and special events.

Blairsville   A4

Misty Mountain Inn & Cottages

4376 Misty Mountain Ln
Blairsville, GA 30512-5604
(706)745-4786 (888)647-8966 Fax:(706)781-1002
Internet: www.jwww.com/misty
E-mail: mistyinn@alltel.net

Circa 1890. This Victorian farmhouse is situated on a four-acre compound and also features six mountainside cottages located in the woods surrounding the inn. Four spacious guest rooms in the main house have private baths and fireplaces. All are decorated in country antiques with hand-crafted accessories, quilts and green plants. Two cottages boast antique beds and Jacuzzi tubs. The lofted bedroom cottages can comfortably sleep more than two people, offering full baths, living rooms and eat-in kitchens. Flea markets, festivals, antique craft shops, lakes, waterfalls and hiking trails are located nearby.

Innkeeper(s): Peg Shaw. $70-100. 4 rooms with PB, 10 with FP and 6 cottages. Breakfast included in rates. Types of meals: Full bkfst and early coffee/tea. Beds: QT. Reading lamp, ceiling fan, clock radio, desk, fireplace, private balcony or porch and all cottages have fireplace in room. Air conditioning. Fax and telephone on premises. Limited handicap access. Antiquing, bicycling, canoeing/kayaking, fishing, golf, hiking, horseback riding, live theater, museums, parks, shopping, water sports, wineries and Misty Mountain Model Railroad (open to the public for tours May through December) nearby.
Location: Mountains.
Certificate may be used: All except October and holidays.

Dahlonega   B4

Lily Creek Lodge

2608 Auraria Rd
Dahlonega, GA 30533
(706)864-6848 (888)844-2694 Fax:(706)864-6848
Internet: www.lilycreeklodge.com
E-mail: baceks@alltel.net

Circa 1984. Seven forested acres surround Lily Creek Lodge, and guests will enjoy grounds that offer gardens, a secluded

hot tub, a swimming pool with a waterfall and a treehouse where breakfasts can be served. There is a common area indoors with a large stone fireplace, or guests can relax on the deck or in the pavilion out by the pool. A gazebo and swing also are romantic items guests will discover on the lush grounds. Each room has been decorated with a special theme in mind, from the Montana Suite with its oak log bed to the Geisha Suite with its Asian appointments. On arrival, guests are greeted with a selection of port, wine and homemade cookies or other treat. Dahlonega is rich in history, and it is in this historic town that gold was first discovered in the United States. Guests can look for antiques, pan for gold or enjoy the many outdoor activities.

Innkeeper(s): Don & Sharon Bacek. $99-175. 13 rooms with PB, 7 suites and 1 conference room. Breakfast included in rates. Types of meals: Cont plus. Beds: KQ. Some with VCR, kitchens and ceiling fans in room. Air conditioning. VCR, fax, copier, spa, swimming, library, parlor games, telephone, fireplace, bocci court, treehouse, gazebo and walking trails on premises. Antiquing, fishing, golf, hiking, live theater, parks, shopping, water sports, arts, crafts and waterfalls nearby.
Location: Mountains.
Publicity: *New York Times, Nashville Tennessean, Montgomery Alabama Advertiser, Walking Magazine, Dahlonega Nugget, Atlanta Journal Constitution, Piedmont Review, Blue Ridge Country Magazine and Huntsville Alabama Times.*
Certificate may be used: Anytime, Sunday-Thursday, subject to availability, from Jan. 1 to April 30, excluding holidays and special events.

Worley Homestead Inn

168 Main St W
Dahlonega, GA 30533-1005
(706)864-7002

Circa 1845. Two blocks from the historic town square is this beautiful old Colonial Revival inn. Several guest rooms are equipped with fireplaces, adding to the romantic atmosphere and Victorian ambiance. All the rooms have private baths, and feature antique beds. A popular spot for honeymooners and couples celebrating anniversaries, Dahlonega is close to the lures of the Chattahoochee National Forest.

Innkeeper(s): Bill, Francis & Christine. $85-95. 7 rooms. Breakfast and snacks/refreshments included in rates. Types of meals: Full bkfst and early coffee/tea. Cable TV and reading lamp in room. Air conditioning. Telephone and fireplace on premises. Antiquing and shopping nearby.
Location: Small town.
Certificate may be used: January through March, excluding holidays and special events.

Eatonton   E5

The Crockett House

671 Madison Rd
Eatonton, GA 31024-7830
(706)485-2248
Internet: www.bbonline.com/ga/crocketthouse/
E-mail: crocketthouse@communicomm.com

Circa 1895. Century-old pecan, oak, pine and magnolia trees shade this alluring Victorian. The sweeping veranda is lined with rockers and wicker for those who wish to relax and enjoy a gentle Georgia breeze. Guests are welcomed with refreshment, and treated to a gourmet, candlelight breakfast. Rooms are decorated with antiques, and exude an old-fashioned, Southern ambiance. The bed & breakfast is located on the historic Antebellum Trail, which stretches from Athens to Macon, and the inn is about midway between both towns. Atlanta is about an hour and 15 minutes away; Augusta is an hour-and-a-half drive.

Innkeeper(s): Barbara & Glenn Moses. $95-105. 6 rooms with PB, 4 with FP. Breakfast included in rates. Types of meals: Full gourmet bkfst, early coffee/tea and afternoon tea. Beds: KQD. Cable TV, ceiling fan and clock radio in room. Air conditioning. Parlor games on premises. Antiquing, fishing, live theater, parks, shopping, sporting events and water sports nearby.

Location: Small town.

Certificate may be used: Sunday-Thursday, January, February, March & August, excluding special events and based on availability.

Gainesville   C4

Dunlap House

635 Green St N W
Gainesville, GA 30501-3319
(770)536-0200 (800)276-2935 Fax:(770)503-7857
Internet: www.dunlaphouse.com
E-mail: dunlaphouse@mindspring.com

Circa 1910. Located on Gainesville's historic Green Street, this inn offers 9 uniquely decorated guest rooms, all featuring period furnishings. Custom-built king or queen beds and remote-controlled cable TV are found in all of the rooms, several of which have romantic fireplaces. Guests may help themselves to coffee, tea and light refreshments in the inn's common area. Breakfast may be enjoyed in guests' rooms or on the picturesque veranda, with its comfortable wicker furniture. Road Atlanta, Mall of Georgia, Lake Lanier, Brenau University, Riverside Academy and the Quinlan Art Center are nearby.

Innkeeper(s): David & Karen Peters. $85-155. 9 rooms with PB, 2 with FP. Breakfast and snacks/refreshments included in rates. Types of meals: Full bkfst and early coffee/tea. Beds: KQ. Cable TV, reading lamp, clock radio, telephone, desk, laptop computer and phone hook-up in room. Air conditioning. TV and copier on premises. Handicap access. Antiquing, fishing, golf, live theater, parks, shopping, water sports, Road Atlanta Racing and Lake Lanier nearby.

Location: City, mountains.

Publicity: Southern Living, Atlanta Journal Constitution, Country Inns and North Georgia Journal.

Certificate may be used: Jan. 1-March 15, Sunday-Thursday, except Valentine's; July 1-Sept. 20, Sunday-Thursday.

Hamilton   F2

Magnolia Hall B&B

PO Box 326
Hamilton, GA 31811
(706)628-4566
Internet: www.magnoliahallbb.com
E-mail: kgsmag@juno.com

Circa 1890. Fancy gingerbread trim decorates the wide veranda of this two-story Victorian settled in an acre of magnolias and century-old hollies, near the courthouse. Heart-pine floors, tall ceilings, antiques, a grand piano and china, crystal and silver service for breakfast, set the mood for a gracious inn stay. One of the house specialties is Baked Georgia Croissant with fresh peaches and toasted almonds. It's ten miles to Callaway Gardens and 20 miles to Warm Springs.

Innkeeper(s): Dale & Kendrick Smith. $105-125. 5 rooms with PB, 2 suites. Breakfast and snacks/refreshments included in rates. Types of meals: Full gourmet bkfst and early coffee/tea. Beds: QT. Cable TV, VCR, reading lamp, clock radio, turn-down service, desk and refreshments in room. Air conditioning. Parlor games, telephone, fireplace, rockers and porch swing on premises. Handicap access. Amusement parks, antiquing, fishing, golf, parks, shopping, sporting events, tennis, water sports, Wild Animal Park and FDR Home nearby.

Location: Small town, rural setting.

Publicity: Victorian Homes, Georgia Journal, Georgia Magazine and National Geographic Traveler.

Certificate may be used: Jan. 7 to Nov. 12, Monday-Thursday.

Hartwell   B6

Shuler Manor

714 Early Drive
Hartwell, GA 30643
(706)377-3550 (866)377-3550 Fax:(706)377-3551
Internet: www.shulermanor.com
E-mail: bnb@shulermanor.com

Circa 2000. Retreat to two acres of panoramic lakeside bliss at this newly built Federal-style heirloom quality home. Furnished and decorated with a customized style of traditional and contemporary, the foyer leads to a coffered ceiling game parlor with billiards and two great rooms with stone and granite fireplaces, bumper pool and satellite TV. One suite offers transom windows; one suite has a full wall of windows. Six of seven rooms all have fantastic waterfront views. One suite offers a fireplace and Jacuzzi tub. This sheltered peninsula of Lake Hartwell is a perfect refuge to enjoy wildlife, walk nature paths, explore the gardens, sit on the dock or go fishing. A hot tub is a welcome treat for all.

Innkeeper(s): Gary & Theresa Shuler. $65-150. 7 rooms, 4 with PB, 1 with FP, 2 suites, 1 cottage and 1 conference room. Breakfast and snacks/refreshments included in rates. Types of meals: Country bkfst, early coffee/tea and afternoon tea. Beds: KQDT. Modem hook-up, data port, cable TV, VCR, reading lamp, stereo, refrigerator, ceiling fan, snack bar, clock radio, telephone, coffeemaker, turn-down service, desk, one suite with fireplace and Jacuzzi tub in room. Central air. Fax, copier, spa, swimming, library, pet boarding, parlor games, fireplace, laundry facility, game parlor with billiards, 2 great rooms with massive fireplaces, one with bumper pool, TV satellite viewing, outdoor therapeutic hot tub, panoramic views of lake, dock, horseshoes and swimming on premises. Handicap access. Antiquing, art galleries, canoeing/kayaking, fishing, golf, hiking, live theater, museums, parks, shopping, sporting events, wineries, sporting events for Clemson University and/or University of Georgia only 45 minutes drive on game day, 250+ outlet stores, Mall of Georgia and Buford Greenville/Spartanburg nearby.

Location: Waterfront. On Lake Hartwell with a panoramic view of the lake.

Publicity: Hartwell Sun, Anderson Independent Mail and Simply Southern.

Certificate may be used: Sept. 4-April 30, subject to availability.

Hiawassee   A5

Mountain Memories Bed and Breakfast

385 Chancey Drive
Hiawassee, GA 30546-2407
(706)896-8439 (800)335-8439 Fax:(706)896-8439
Internet: www.mountainmemoriesbandb.com
E-mail: mtnmem@brmemc.net

Circa 1960. The mountains of three states are seen from this inn, which also boasts spectacular views of Lake Chatuge. A guest lounge offers an extensive video library to choose from, or select a book to read or a game to play. The tastefully decorated suites and guest bedrooms are very spacious, with private entrances onto large decks or patios. Candles, plush robes and rubber duckies for two-person Jacuzzi tubs encourage romance and relaxation. Breakfast treats may include biscuits and sausage gravy, quiche, fruit, bacon and french toast. Enjoy a late-evening candlelit dessert buffet.

Innkeeper(s): Bill & Too Too Cirlot. $99-165. 6 rooms, 4 with PB, 1 with FP, 1 suite. Breakfast included in rates. Types of meals: Full gourmet bkfst, early coffee/tea and picnic lunch. Beds: KQ. Cable TV, VCR, reading lamp, ceiling fan, clock radio, coffeemaker and fireplace in room. Central air. Fax, library, parlor games, telephone and fireplace on premises. Limited handicap access. Antiquing, art galleries, canoeing/kayaking, fishing, golf, hiking, horseback

riding, live theater, parks, shopping, tennis, water sports and wineries nearby.
Location: Mountains.

Publicity: *North Georgia's most romantic retreat.*

Certificate may be used: Sunday-Thursday, subject to availability, not valid during special events.

Jekyll Island   J9

Jekyll Island Club Hotel

371 Riverview Dr
Jekyll Island, GA 31527-0851
(912)635-2600 (800)535-9547 Fax:(912)635-2818
Internet: www.jekyllclub.com
E-mail: jiclub@technonet.com

Circa 1888. More than 240 acres of grounds surround this venerable Victorian hotel, now a National Historic Landmark. Once the island home to an elite circle of Rockefellers, Pulitzers, Vanderbilts and J. P. Morgan, the entrance hall boasts a boar's head over the fireplace and a polished oak, four-story stairway. Antiques and grand mirrors add to the decor. Guests enjoy the opportunity to dine in the Grand Dining Room with its white columns or play golf, championship croquet or tennis. Furnishings in the well-appointed guest rooms include mahogany beds and armoires and some offer views of the intra-coastal waterway. Additional features such as fireplaces, balconies, suites and Jacuzzi tubs are offered. The Federal Reserve Room, one of the many meeting rooms, was the site where early drafts of the Federal Reserve Act were written.
$89-169. 134 rooms, 113 with PB, 21 suites. Types of meals: Full bkfst, Sun. brunch, early coffee/tea, lunch, picnic lunch, afternoon tea, snacks/refreshments, hors d'oeuvres, gourmet dinner and room service. Restaurant on premises. Beds: KDT. Modem hook-up, cable TV, VCR, reading lamp, clock radio, telephone, desk, voice mail and coffeemakers in room. Air conditioning. Fax, copier, swimming, stable, bicycles, tennis, library, child care, parlor games, gift shop, tours, croquet, golf and fishing on premises. Handicap access. Antiquing, art galleries, beach, bicycling, canoeing/kayaking, fishing, golf, horseback riding, parks, shopping, tennis and water sports nearby.
Location: Waterfront. Historic residential section.

Certificate may be used: Anytime, Sunday-Thursday, subject to availability.

Lookout Mountain   A2

The Chanticleer Inn

1300 Mockingbird Lane
Lookout Mountain, GA 30750
(706)820-2002 (866)424-2684 Fax:(706)820-7976
Internet: www.stayatchanticleer.com
E-mail: info@stayatchanticleer.com

Circa 1934. The local mountain stone exteriors of this inn and the surrounding Country French cottages appear much as they did when first built atop this scenic location. Extensive interior renovations provide modern comfort and technology. Relax by the fire in the large living room and watch a video. An outdoor pool beckons the more active-minded. Hardwood floors, English antiques and a country theme create a pleasant ambiance. Gracious guest bedrooms and suites, some that can be adjoining and several with fireplaces, whirlpool tubs, air and heat controls. Savor a hot Southern-style buffet breakfast. Enjoy five acres of landscaped grounds, patios with benches and a swimming pool.
Innkeeper(s): Kirby & Judy Wahl. $100-295. 17 rooms with PB, 4 with FP, 4 total suites, including 2 two-bedroom suites and 1 three-bedroom suite, 5 cottages and 1 conference room. Breakfast, afternoon tea and snacks/refreshments included in rates. Types of meals: Full bkfst and early coffee/tea. Beds:

KQ. Cable TV, reading lamp, CD player, refrigerator, ceiling fan, clock radio, telephone, desk, hot tub/spa, voice mail, fireplace, down pillows (optional) and Kingsdown mattresses in room. Central air. Fax, copier, swimming, parlor games, gift shop, wedding and banquet facility with full catering, afternoon cookies, tea and coffee on premises. Limited handicap access. Antiquing, art galleries, bicycling, canoeing/kayaking, fishing, golf, hiking, museums, parks, shopping, sporting events, tennis and local spa nearby.
Location: Mountains. Historic, mountaintop community 10 minutes from Chattanooga.

Publicity: *Lookout Mountain Mirror, Chattanooga Times Free Press, Blue Ridge Country Magazine, Southern Living Magazine, Memphis Sentinel, Birmingham and Charlotte papers, local public broadcasting station, Chattanooga Convention and Visitors Bureau Publication.*

Certificate may be used: Anytime, November-May, subject to availability.

Marietta   C3

Sixty Polk Street, A B&B

60 Polk St
Marietta, GA 30064-2349
(770)419-1688 (800)845-7266 Fax:(770)590-7959
Internet: www.sixtypolkstreet.com
E-mail: JMertes@aol.com

Circa 1872. This French Regency Victorian has been completely restored. Period antiques decorate the rooms. Guests are encouraged to enjoy the library or relax in the parlor. Afternoon treats are served in the dining room, and guests are treated to a hearty Southern breakfast. Marietta offers an abundance of antique stores, restaurants and museums, as well as a delightful town square. The inn is just 30 minutes from Atlanta.
Innkeeper(s): Joe & Glenda Mertes. $95-175. 4 rooms with PB, 1 with FP, 1 suite. Breakfast included in rates. Types of meals: Full bkfst. Beds: KQ. TV in room. Library, telephone, fireplace, parlor, front porch with oversized rockers and a screened back porch on premises. Antiquing, golf and live theater nearby.
Location: Historic town.

Publicity: *North Georgian Journal and Victorian Homes Magazine.*

"Better than dreamed of."

Certificate may be used: Sunday-Thursday, anytime, except Thanksgiving and Christmas weeks.

Whitlock Inn

57 Whitlock Ave
Marietta, GA 30064-2343
(770)428-1495 Fax:(770)919-9620
Internet: www.whitlockinn.com
E-mail: alexis@whitlockinn.com

Circa 1900. This cherished Victorian has been restored and is located in a National Register Historic District, one block from the Marietta Square. Amenities even the Ritz doesn't provide are in every room, and you can rock on the front verandas. An afternoon snack also is served. There is a ballroom grandly suitable for weddings and business meetings.
Innkeeper(s): Alexis Edwards. $100-125. 5 rooms with PB and 3 conference rooms. Breakfast included in rates. Types of meals: Cont plus. Beds: KQT. Cable TV, reading lamp, ceiling fan, clock radio, telephone and desk in room. Air conditioning. Fax and copier on premises. Amusement parks, antiquing, live theater, parks, shopping and sporting events nearby.
Location: City.

Publicity: *Marietta Daily Journal.*

"This is the most beautiful inn in Georgia and I've seen nearly all of them."

Certificate may be used: All year, Sunday through Thursday, not available on weekends.

Powder Springs — D3

River Birch B&B

6051 Burnt Hickory Trl
Powder Springs, GA 30127-3062
(770)949-1767 (866)830-6500 Fax:(770)949-1767
E-mail: riverbirchbnb@aol.com

Circa 1975. The entire family, including the family pet, will enjoy this wooded hideaway, surrounded by gardens and trails, yet conveniently located just 25 miles west of historic Atlanta. Choose the luxury of a suite in the country split-level or the privacy of a cottage with antique pine walls and ceilings, a garden tub and full kitchen. Pastoral Georgia can be seen from throughout this B&B, with picturesque views of the pasture. Start each day overlooking the organic gardens from the deck while savoring hearty Southern cuisine and hand-picked blueberries. There are plenty of recreational activities nearby. The Silver Comet Trail, great for bicycling, walking or rollerblading is only five miles away. Shuttle service is offered to and from any station.
Innkeeper(s): Martin & Matha Stone. $85-110. 5 rooms, 3 with PB, 2 cottages and 1 conference room. Breakfast and snacks/refreshments included in rates. Types of meals: Country bkfst, early coffee/tea, picnic lunch, gourmet dinner and room service. Beds: KQT. Refrigerator, ceiling fan, telephone, coffeemaker, desk and hot tub/spa in room. Central air. TV, VCR, fax, copier, spa, stable, library, fireplace and laundry facility on premises. Limited handicap access. Amusement parks, antiquing, art galleries, bicycling, golf, hiking, horseback riding, live theater, museums, parks, shopping, sporting events, tennis and Atlanta zoo nearby.
Location: Country.
Certificate may be used: Anytime, subject to availability.

Saint Marys — J9

Spencer House Inn B&B

200 Osborne Street
Saint Marys, GA 31558-8361
(912)882-1872 (888)800-1872 Fax:(912)882-9427
Internet: www.spencerhouseinn.com
E-mail: info@spencerhouseinn.com

Circa 1872. A white picket fence surrounds this Victorian era house, painted a pleasant pink with white trim on the wide two-level veranda. The Inn is in the St. Marys' Historic District and is on the National Register.
Heart-pine floors, original moldings and high ceilings are features of the rooms. Carefully selected reproductions, fine antiques, coordinated fabrics and rugs have been combined to create a sunny, fresh decor. There are four-poster beds and clawfoot soaking tubs. Breakfast is buffet style with peaches and cream, bread pudding or frittatas as specialties. The Inn is one block to the ferry to Georgia's largest barrier island, Cumberland Island, with 17 miles of white sand beaches, live oak forests, salt marshes and wild horses. Okefenokee National Wildlife Refuge is 45 minutes away.
Innkeeper(s): Mary & Mike Neff. $100-185. 14 rooms with PB, 1 suite. Breakfast included in rates. Types of meals: Full bkfst, early coffee/tea and picnic lunch. Beds: KQDT. Cable TV, reading lamp, ceiling fan, clock radio, telephone, HBO and wireless access in room. Air conditioning. Fax, library, parlor games, elevator, limited handicap access and DSL on premises. Antiquing, fishing, golf, shopping, sporting events, Cumberland Island National Seashore, Okefenokee Swamp, Kings Bay Submarine Base and new waterfront park nearby.

Location: Waterfront. Historic district.
Publicity: *Seabreeze and Water's Edge Magazine.*
"I don't see how it could be improved!"
Certificate may be used: Sunday-Thursday, except holidays and special events, subject to availability.

Sautee Nacoochee — B5

The Stovall House

1526 Hwy 255 N
Sautee Nacoochee, GA 30571
(706)878-3355
Internet: www.stovallhouse.com
E-mail: info@stovallhouse.com

Circa 1837. This house, built by Moses Harshaw and restored in 1983 by Ham Schwartz, has received two state awards for its restoration. The handsome farmhouse has an extensive wraparound porch providing vistas of 26 acres of cow pastures and mountains. High ceilings, polished walnut woodwork and decorative stenciling provide a pleasant backdrop for the inn's collection of antiques. Victorian bathroom fixtures include pull-chain toilets and pedestal sinks. The inn has its own restaurant.
Innkeeper(s): Ham Schwartz. $84-92.
5 rooms with PB. Breakfast included in rates. Types of meals: Cont and dinner. Restaurant on premises. Beds: KQDT. Ceiling fan and clock radio in room. Air conditioning. Library, parlor games, telephone and fireplace on premises. Amusement parks, antiquing, fishing, live theater, parks, shopping and water sports nearby.
Location: Mountains.
Publicity: *Atlanta Journal and GPTV - Historic Inns of Georgia.*
"Great to be home again. Very nostalgic and hospitable."
Certificate may be used: Anytime, subject to availability.

Savannah — G9

Broughton Street Bed & Breakfast

511 E Broughton St
Savannah, GA 31401-3501
(912)232-6633 Fax:(912)447-8980
Internet: www.broughtonst.com
E-mail: savbnb@aol.com

Circa 1883. This historic Victorian townhouse offers two guest rooms and one cottage. Each is decorated with Victorian furnishings, antiques and contemporary artwork. One room includes a Jacuzzi tub and a fireplace. In the afternoons, the innkeepers serve hors d'oeuvres to their guests. Breakfasts feature such items as quiche, homemade Amish bread and fresh fruit.
Innkeeper(s): Miranda Taylor. $125-250. 3 rooms, 2 with PB and 1 cottage. Breakfast, afternoon tea and snacks/refreshments included in rates. Types of meals: Full bkfst. Beds: KQ. Cable TV, VCR, reading lamp, stereo, ceiling fan, clock radio, telephone and turn-down service in room. Air conditioning. Fax, copier, library and fireplace on premises. Antiquing, fishing, golf, live theater, parks, shopping, sporting events, tennis and water sports nearby.
Location: City.
"Our stay was so romantic, we're rejuvenated and ready to take on the world!"
Certificate may be used: January through December, Sunday-Thursday. Tanner Room only.

Thomasville J4

1884 Paxton House Inn

445 Remington Ave
Thomasville, GA 31792-5563
(229)226-5197 Fax:(229)226-9903
Internet: www.1884paxtonhouseinn.com
E-mail: 1884@rose.net

Circa 1884. The picturesque residential neighborhood in the renowned Plantation Region is the perfect setting for this award-winning, historic Gothic Victorian Landmark Home, listed in the National Register. Unique architecture, a grand circular staircase, 12 ornamental fireplaces, 13-foot ceilings, heart-pine floors, a courting window and nine-foot doors reflect remarkable craftsmanship. Museum-quality reproductions, classic antiques, designer fabrics and international collections impart an 18th-century style. Luxurious suites and garden cottages offer upscale amenities that include Egyptian bath towels, terry robes, data ports and sound spas. Breakfast is served with settings of fine china and silver. Indulge in family recipes passed down by generations of Southern chefs. Rock on the wraparound veranda, swim in the indoor lap pool or take a moonlit stroll through the gardens.

Innkeeper(s): Susie M. Sherrod. $165-350. 9 rooms with PB, 3 two-bedroom suites and 2 cottages. Breakfast, afternoon tea and snacks/refreshments included in rates. Types of meals: Full gourmet bkfst, veg bkfst and early coffee/tea. Beds: KQ. Modem hook-up, data port, cable TV, VCR, reading lamp, refrigerator, ceiling fan, clock radio, telephone, coffeemaker, turn-down service, desk, hot tub/spa, private baths with tub/shower, some with wet bar, iron/ironing board, sound spa, hair dryer, terry robes, goose-down pillows, full-length mirror and high-speed wireless Internet in room. Central air. Fax, copier, spa, swimming, library, parlor games, fireplace, gift shop, computer centers, two with fiber optic high-speed-commercial grade connection, lap pool and lemonade social and teas (by reservation) on premises. Amusement parks, antiquing, art galleries, bicycling, fishing, golf, horseback riding, live theater, museums, parks, shopping, sporting events and tennis nearby.

Location: City.

Publicity: *Fodor's (named the South's and America's "Best" B&B Inn), Frommer's (Four Flags), Southern Living, Travel and Leisure, Georgia Journal ("Best B&B Inn" in the Plantation region of Georgia), American Automobile Association, Times Picayune ("Special Inns of the Southeast"), The Sun ("provides us with a true glimpse of Southern living"), St. Louis Times ("the charm of the 1800s still attracts visitors to Thomasville...[Susie Sherrod's] efforts result in a spectacular variety of blossoms"), WALB TV and WCTV.*

Certificate may be used: July-August, Sunday-Thursday, subject to availability, cannot be combined with any other discount program.

Melhana The Grand Plantation

301 Showboat Lane
Thomasville, GA 31792
(229)226-2290 (888)920-3030 Fax:(229)226-4585
Internet: www.melhana.com
E-mail: info@melhana.com

Circa 1825. More than 50 acres surround the historic Melhana Plantation comprised of 30 buildings including the manor, The Hibernia Cottage and a village. There are 30 buildings, all in the National Register. Traditional décor includes furnishings and amenities such as king- and queen-size four-poster beds, desks, paintings, puffy down comforters and handmade duvets. Some accommodations offer marble Jacuzzis and veranda entrances. Most include views of expansive green lawns, the Avenue of Magnolias, camellia gardens, the sunken garden or the plantation's pasture land. The inn's elegantly appointed restaurant has received acclaims from prestigious critics for its Southern cuisine, enhanced by herbs garnered from private kitchen gardens. To fully enjoy the plantation, consider arranging for horseback riding, quail hunting or a carriage ride, but be sure to allow time to linger on the veranda or to enjoy the indoor swimming pool, theater and fitness center.

Innkeeper(s): Charlie & Fran Lewis. $285-450. 38 rooms, 37 with PB, 14 suites, 2 cottages and 3 conference rooms. Breakfast, afternoon tea and snacks/refreshments included in rates. Types of meals: Full gourmet bkfst, gourmet lunch, picnic lunch, gourmet dinner and room service. Restaurant on premises. Beds: KQ. Data port, cable TV, clock radio, telephone, turn-down service, desk, hot tub/spa and voice mail in room. Central air. Fax, copier, swimming, tennis, library, parlor games, fireplace and laundry facility on premises. Limited handicap access. Antiquing, art galleries, beach, canoeing/kayaking, fishing, golf, horseback riding, live theater, parks, tennis, hunting and sporting adventures nearby.

Location: Country.

Certificate may be used: Anytime, subject to availability.

Serendipity Cottage

339 E Jefferson St
Thomasville, GA 31792-5108
(229)226-8111 (800)383-7377 Fax:(229)226-2656
Internet: www.serendipitycottage.com
E-mail: goodnite@rose.net

Circa 1906. Gracing a serene, residential historic district, this bed & breakfast inn is only three blocks from award-winning downtown. The house has been restored for utmost comfort and relaxation and is furnished with antiques and collectibles.

Each pampering guest bedroom offers generous amenities that include an iron, VCR, hair dryer, phone, cable TV, data port, robes, sound spa and turndown service with chocolates. Sip an early-morning hot beverage before savoring a multi-course  breakfast served on the sun porch that overlooks the garden. Ask for a wake-up call, if needed. Homemade cookies, cream sherry and soft drinks provide pleasurable treats.

Innkeeper(s): Kathy & Ed Middleton. $100-135. 4 rooms with PB, 2 with FP. Breakfast included in rates. Types of meals: Full bkfst and early coffee/tea. Beds: QD. Cable TV, VCR, reading lamp, refrigerator, ceiling fan, clock radio, telephone, turn-down service and complimentary sherry in room. Air conditioning. Bicycles, parlor games and fireplace on premises. Antiquing, fishing, live theater, parks, shopping, sporting events and plantation tours nearby.

Location: City.

"Thank you for the wonderful weekend at Serendipity Cottage. The house is absolutely stunning and the food delicious."

Certificate may be used: June 1-Sept. 30, Sunday-Thursday.

Hawaii

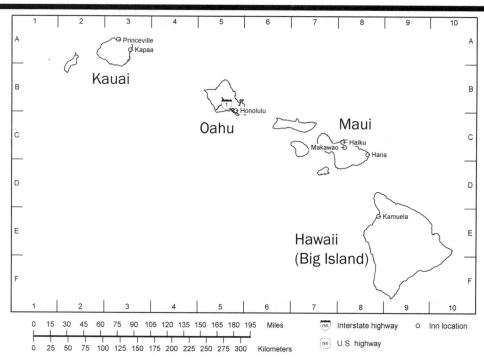

	1	2	3	4	5	6	7	8	9	10	

A — Princeville, Kapaa, Kauai
B — Honolulu, Oahu
C — Maui, Haiku, Makawao, Hana
D
E — Kamuela, Hawaii (Big Island)
F

0 15 30 45 60 75 90 105 120 135 150 165 180 195   Miles

0 25 50 75 100 125 150 175 200 225 250 275 300   Kilometers

Interstate highway   o Inn location

U.S. highway

Hawaii (Big Island)

Kamuela   E8

Kamuela's Mauna Kea View B&B
PO Box 6375
Kamuela, HI 96743-6375
(808)885-8425 Fax:(808)885-6514
Internet: www.stayhawaii.com
E-mail: maunakeaview1@webtv.net

Circa 1988. Guests opt either to stay in a private suite or in a little cottage at this bed & breakfast, which affords views of historic Parker Ranch and its namesake mountain, Mauna Kea. The suite and cottage both offer two bedrooms, a living room, fireplace, kitchenette and bathroom, all comfortably decorated. From the decks on both accommodations, guests enjoy mountain views. The bed & breakfast is located on the Big Island, where guests can enjoy plenty of ocean activities, historic sites, horseback riding and much more.

Innkeeper(s): Richard Mitchell. $77-88. 2 rooms, 1 suite and 1 cottage. Breakfast included in rates. Types of meals: Cont plus. Beds: QDT. Cable TV, reading lamp, ceiling fan, clock radio, telephone, desk, kitchenette and deck in room. Spa and barbecue on premises. Antiquing, downhill skiing, fishing, golf, live theater, parks, shopping, tennis, water sports and white sand beaches nearby.
Location: Mountains.
Publicity: *Coffee Times.*
Certificate may be used: Cottage, Sunday-Wednesday, June and September.

Kauai

Kapaa   A3

Rosewood
872 Kamalu Rd
Kapaa, HI 96746-9701
(808)822-5216 Fax:(808)822-5478
Internet: www.rosewoodkauai.com
E-mail: rosewood@aloha.net

Circa 1900. Inside the inn's historic plantation-style main house, the guest bedroom boasts a country decor and features a served breakfast. Stay in the rustic Thatched Cottage for a truly Polynesian experience, or the Victorian Cottage, offering a kitchen, living and dining area, bedrooms and laundry facilities. Each accommodation includes a welcome basket with tropical fruits, homemade granola with macadamia nuts, fresh-baked muffins, Kona coffee and assorted teas. The one-acre grounds are lush with flowers, plants, a variety of fruit trees and ponds with waterfalls.

Innkeeper(s): Norbert & Rosemary Smith. $40-125. 7 rooms, 4 with PB and 2 cottages. Beds: K. Reading lamp, refrigerator, ceiling fan, clock radio, desk and some with breakfast included in room. VCR, fax, copier, child care, telephone and Internet access on premises. Fishing and water sports nearby.
Location: Mountains, three miles to ocean, stores and restaurants.
Certificate may be used: Anytime.

Princeville   A3

Hale'Aha

PO Box 223370
Princeville, HI 96722
(808)826-6733 (808)826-6733 Fax:(808)826-1558
Internet: www.haleaha.com
E-mail: kauai@pixi.com

Circa 1991. Situated on the gorgeous North Shore on 480 feet of
the Makai Golf Course, this island bed & breakfast offers peaceful
surroundings and scenic views. The Hawaiian name means
House of Gathering, and it is perfectly suited to relax in the spacious living room by the fireplace or on a lanai or rear patio deck.
Cheerful guest bedrooms and suites are decorated in pastels and
some include a whirlpool tub. Enjoy a self-serve breakfast that
may include local fruit, fresh baked bread, pancakes and a
smoothie. Before heading for the beach, take a nap in a hammock
under blue skies amidst the sweet fragrance of tropical breezes.

Innkeeper(s): Gary & Billie Sparks. $115-275. 5 rooms, 3 with PB, 2 suites. Bkfst
included in rates. Types of meals: Full bkfst & early coffee/tea. Beds: KQ. Cable TV,
VCR, CD player, refrigerator, ceiling fan, clock radio, coffeemaker & whirlpool tub in
room. Air conditioning. Telephone & fireplace on premises. Art galleries, beach,
bicycling, canoeing/kayaking, fishing, golf, hiking, horseback riding, live theater,
museums, parks, shopping, tennis & water sports nearby.

Certificate may be used: Anytime, booking less than 30 days of arrival.

Maui

Haiku   C8

Hale Huelo

PO Box 1237, Door of Faith Church R
Haiku, HI 96708-1237
(808)572-8669 Fax:(808)573-8403
Internet: www.maui.net/~halehuel
E-mail: halehuel@maui.net

Circa 1997. This contemporary home boasts stunning views of
the ocean and surrounding rain forest. The modern home features Asian influences in the design. The interior is definitely
Hawaiian, bright tropical prints top the beds and the rooms are
airy and bright. Guests can enjoy the view from their own balcony or perhaps while lounging by the pool. For breakfast, the
innkeepers serve fruit fresh from the many trees on the property, as well as tropical juices, kona coffee and homemade breads.
Hale Huelo is located on the island of Maui, and guests can
spend the day hiking to a volcano, snorkeling, surfing or taking
a helicopter tour of the scenic area.

Innkeeper(s): Doug Barrett & Seiji Kamijo. $85-125. 3 rooms, 2 with PB, 1 suite.
Bkfst included in rates. Types of meals: Cont plus. Beds: Q. Cable TV, VCR, refrigerator, ceiling fan, microwave & coffeemaker in room. Fax, copier, spa, swimming,
library, parlor games, telephone & fireplace on premises. Antiquing, beach, biking, fishing, golf,
live theater, parks, shopping, water sports, biking, hiking & island tours nearby.

Certificate may be used: Anytime, subject to availability.

Hana   C8

Hana Maui Botanical Gardens B&B

PO Box 404, Ulaino Rd
Hana, HI 96713-0404
(808)248-7725 Fax:(808)248-7725
E-mail: joloyce@aol.com

Circa 1976. This Hawaiian country farm features a ranch house
and duplex with two studio apartments set on 27 acres that include
a public botanical garden, fruit trees and flowers. The Flower and
Marine studio have a private bath, kitchen, lanai and carport. Also
offered is Volcano Heart Chalet near Volcano National Park on the
Big Island. The chalet features two keyed rooms, each decorated in

an individual theme, private half baths, a shared shower and a
shared kitchenette and sitting room with a gas fireplace.

Innkeeper(s): Jo Loyce Kaia. $75-100. Call inn for details. Types of meals:
Cont. Beds: QT. Parlor games, telephone, fireplace, no alcohol, no smoking,
free access to 10-acre botanical gardens and fruit picking in season on
premises. Hiking, parks, shopping and swimming nearby.

Certificate may be used: Anytime, subject to availability. Reservations may
be made only one month in advance to qualify for one night free.

Makawao   C8

Banyan Tree House

3265 Baldwin Ave
Makawao, HI 96768-9629
(808)572-9021 Fax:(808)573-5072
Internet: www.hawaii-mauirentals.com
E-mail: banyan@hawaii-mauirentals.com

Circa 1926. Banyan Tree is composed of three bedrooms in a
Hawaiian plantation-style house and four cottages. Ethel Smith
Baldwin, a prominent local citizen who served as secretary of
the Red Cross and founded a flourishing artist organization,
was the most well-known inhabitant of this house. The home
was built by the Maui Agricultural Company, of which
Baldwin's husband was president. The lush setting includes
two acres of gardens, with tree swings and hammocks. Guests
in the main house enjoy a full restaurant kitchen. Three of the
cottages include kitchenettes, and one has a full kitchen. The
house has a full kitchen, spacious living room, fireplace, formal
dining room and a lanai with a view of the ocean. It is popular
for groups, families and workshops. Tropical Hawaii is the decorating theme throughout the rooms and cottages. Beach activities, galleries, shops and restaurants all are nearby.

Innkeeper(s): Suzy Papanikolas. $85-325. 7 rooms, 1 with FP, 4 cottages, 1 guest
house & 1 conference room. Beds: QDT. Refrigerator, telephone & coffeemaker in
room. Fax, copier, spa, swimming, child care, laundry facility, cable TV, VCR, CD
player, library, parlor games & fireplace in Plantation House on premises. Antiquing,
art galleries, beach, bicycling, canoeing/kayaking, fishing, golf, hiking, horseback
riding, live theater, museums, parks, shopping, water sports & wineries nearby.
Location: Six miles from the ocean in the mountains.

Certificate may be used: Anytime, subject to availability, excluding holidays,
Christmas and Easter.

Oahu

Honolulu   B5

The Manoa Valley Inn

2001 Vancouver Dr
Honolulu, HI 96822-2451
(808)947-6019 Fax:(808)946-6168
Internet: www.aloha.net/~wery/
E-mail: manoavalleyinn@aloha.net

Circa 1915. This exquisite home offers the best of two worlds,
a beautiful, country home that is also surrounded by a tropical
paradise. Each restored room features lavish decor with ornate
beds, ceiling fans and period furniture. Little amenities, such as
the his and her robes, create a romantic touch. Breakfasts with
kona coffee, juices, fresh fruits and baked goods are served.
The inn's common rooms offer unique touches. The Manoa
Valley is a perfect location to enjoy Hawaii and is only blocks
away from the University of Hawaii.

Innkeeper(s): Theresa Wery. $99-150. 8 rooms, 5 with PB and 1 cottage.
Breakfast included in rates. Types of meals: Cont. Beds: KQD. TV, ceiling fan,
telephone and daily maid service in room. Fax, copier, billiard room and iron
on premises. Museums and art museums nearby.

Publicity: *Travel Age, Travel Holiday, Travel & Leisure and LA Style.*

"A wonderful place!! Stepping back to a time of luxury!"

Certificate may be used: April, May, September & October. Based on availability, excluding holidays.

Idaho

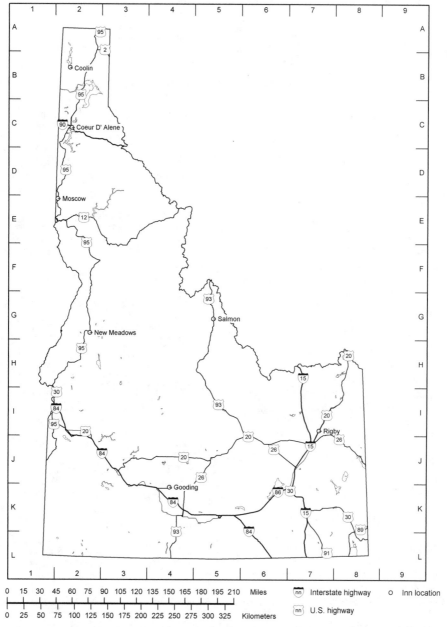

Coeur d' Alene   C2

Baragar House B&B

316 Military Dr
Coeur d' Alene, ID 83814-2137
(208)664-9125 (800)615-8422
Internet: www.baragarhouse.com
E-mail: stay@baragarhouse.com

Circa 1926. Built by a lumber baron, this expansive Craftsman-style bungalow is a pleasurable retreat. Guest bedrooms include the Country Cabin accented with murals of a mountain stream and clouds.
The floral-themed Garden Room has a canopied window seat and antique vanity. The Honeymoon Suite is especially appealing with an oversized bathroom boasting a clawfoot tub under a bay window. Ask about how to sleep under the stars. "Wreck your diet" breakfasts are served daily, though special dietary needs are graciously accommodated. Enjoy the indoor spa and sauna.

Innkeeper(s): Bernie & Carolyn Baragar. $99-139. 3 rooms, 1 with PB. Breakfast and snacks/refreshments included in rates. Types of meals: Full gourmet bkfst, veg bkfst and early coffee/tea. Beds: QD. Cable TV, VCR, reading lamp, refrigerator, ceiling fan, snack bar, clock radio, coffeemaker and desk in room. Air conditioning. Fax, spa, swimming, sauna, tennis, library, parlor games, telephone and laundry facility on premises. Amusement parks, antiquing, art galleries, beach, bicycling, canoeing/kayaking, cross-country skiing, downhill skiing, fishing, golf, hiking, horseback riding, live theater, museums, parks, shopping, tennis, water sports and wineries nearby.

Location: City.

Publicity: *Coeur d'Alene Press and Spokesman Review.*

"Thank you for the hospitality and most exquisite honeymoon setting."

Certificate may be used: Sept. 4-May 29, Sunday-Thursday, subject to availability.

Kingston 5 Ranch B&B

PO Box 2229
Coeur d' Alene, ID 83816
(208)682-4862 (800)254-1852 Fax:(208)682-9445
Internet: www.k5ranch.com
E-mail: info@k5ranch.com

Circa 1930. With the Coeur d'Alene Mountains as its backdrop, this red roofed farmhouse has been renovated with French door and wraparound decks to make the most of its sweeping mountain views and pastoral setting. Innkeepers Walt and Pat Gentry have graced the guest rooms with lace, down

comforters, cozy chairs and romantic touches such as four-poster beds. The suites offer outdoor spas on private decks with mountain views, fireplaces, and baths with whirlpool tubs. The innkeeper is a recipient of several national awards for her recipes. Specialties include Kingston Benedict and stuffed French Toast topped with fresh huckleberry sauce along with freshly baked, prize winning lemon huckleberry muffins. Enjoy activities such as touring two historic gold mines, the Kellogg Gondola, boating or dinner cruises on Lake Coeur d'Alene, ski-ing,, hiking, fishing, bird watching and driving excursions where you may encounter elk, deer, eagles and other wildlife. Often guests find the greatest pleasure to be watching the horses grazing in the pasture or volunteering to pick fresh strawberries, raspberries or loganberries to top an evening desert of vanilla ice cream.

Innkeeper(s): Walter & Pat Gentry. $125-190. 2 rooms, 2 with FP, 2 suites. Breakfast included in rates. Types of meals: Full bkfst and early coffee/tea. Beds: Q. Reading lamp, hot tub/spa, digital clocks, fireplaces, Jacuzzi tub and central heat in room. Air conditioning. TV, VCR, fax, copier, spa, stable, bicycles, telephone, fireplace and kennel one mile off site on premises. Amusement parks, antiquing, cross-country skiing, downhill skiing, fishing, live theater, parks, shopping, water sports, horseback riding, canoeing and mountain biking nearby.

Location: Country, mountains. River/mountains.

Publicity: *A Destination Resort.*

Certificate may be used: Anytime, Monday, Tuesday or Wednesday, based on rate of $189.50/night + tax, excludes February, July & August, all holidays, and holiday periods.

The Roosevelt Inn

105 E Wallace Ave
Coeur d' Alene, ID 83814-2947
(208)765-5200 (800)290-3358 Fax:(208)664-4142
Internet: www.therooseveltinn.com
E-mail: info@therooseveltinn.com

Circa 1905. This turn-of-the-century, red brick home was named for President Roosevelt and is the oldest schoolhouse in town. Roosevelt translates to Rosefield in Dutch, and the innkeepers have created a rosy theme for the inn. The Bell Tower Suite and the Honeymoon Suite are the favorite room requests, but all rooms offer Victorian antiques and some have lake views. Coeur d' Alene has been recognized by National Geographic Magazine as one of the five most beautiful lakes in the world. The area offers the world's longest floating boardwalk and Tubb's Hill Nature Park. A variety of shops and restaurants are within a five minute stroll from the inn. The natural surroundings offer mountain biking, boating, skiing and hiking.

Innkeeper(s): John & Tina Hough. $79-289. 15 rooms, 12 with PB, 3 with FP, 6 total suites, including 4 two-bedroom suites and 2 conference rooms. Breakfast and snacks/refreshments included in rates. Types of meals: Full gourmet bkfst, veg bkfst, early coffee/tea and afternoon tea. Beds: Q. Data port, cable TV, reading lamp, CD player, clock radio, coffeemaker and turn-down service in room. Central air. TV, VCR, fax, copier, spa, sauna, library, parlor games, telephone, fireplace, rose greeting in room and exercise room on premises. Handicap access. Amusement parks, antiquing, art galleries, beach, bicycling, canoeing/kayaking, cross-country skiing, downhill skiing, fishing, golf, hiking, horseback riding, live theater, museums, parks, shopping, sporting events, tennis, water sports and wineries nearby.

Location: City, mountains.

Certificate may be used: Anytime, November-April, subject to availability.

Wolf Lodge Creek B&B

515 S Wolf Lodge Creek Rd
Coeur d' Alene, ID 83814-9416
(208)667-5902 (800)919-9653 Fax:(208)667-1133
Internet: www.wolflodge.com
E-mail: wlcbb@wolflodge.com

Circa 1994. Secluded on the edge of Coeur d'Alene National Forest, this natural wood home is surrounded by covered porches from which guests can enjoy a stunning view. There's an outdoor hot tub for guests to use after a day of hiking, golfing or skiing. There are four rooms and a suite, and each is individually decorated in a country style. All four rooms include a fireplace. The spacious suite includes an oversized tub, balcony and fireplace. Breakfasts are served buffet style, featuring the innkeeper's special granola, homemade breads, muffins, fresh fruit, yogurt, breakfast meats and entrees such as an oatmeal souffle or egg strata. Lake Coeur d'Alene is just a few minutes away, ski areas are within a half-hour drive, but guests can cross-country ski on the home's surrounding 27 acres.

Innkeeper(s): Neva Lindsey. $115-175. 5 rooms with PB, 5 with FP, 1 suite. Breakfast included in rates. Types of meals: Full bkfst. Beds: KQ. Reading lamp and ceiling fan in room. VCR, fax, spa, library, parlor games, telephone and fireplace on premises. Amusement parks, antiquing, cross-country skiing, downhill skiing, fishing, golf, parks, water sports, snowmobiling and horse-back riding nearby.

Location: Mountains.

Publicity: *Northwest Travel.*

"This place is like a little piece of heaven."

Certificate may be used: Sept. 5 through May 15, Sunday through Friday, excluding holidays.

Coolin   B2

Old Northern Inn

PO Box 177, 220 Bayview
Coolin, ID 83821-0177
(208)443-2426 Fax:(208)443-3856
Internet: www.oldnortherninn.com

Circa 1890. This historic inn was built to serve guests riding the Great Northern rail line. Today, travelers come to enjoy trout-filled Priest Lake and all its offerings. The inn is located on the lake shore, and guests enjoy use of a small marina and private beach. There is also a volleyball court, but guests are welcome to simply sit and relax on the spacious deck. The natural surroundings are full of wildlife, and it's not unusual to see deer, caribou and even a moose. The hotel itself is a two-story log and shingle structure, quite at home among the tall cedars. The interior is warm and inviting. There is a common area with a stone fireplace and country furnishings, as well as a view of mountains and the lake. Rooms are decorated with turn-of-the-century antiques, and the suites include a small sitting room. Huckleberry pancakes have been a staple at the inn's breakfast table since the 19th century. In the afternoons, wine, cheese and fruit are served.

Innkeeper(s): Phil & Lorraine Battaglia. $90-140. 6 rooms with PB, 2 suites. Breakfast included in rates. Types of meals: Full bkfst and early coffee/tea. Beds: Q. Reading lamp and desk in room. Fax, copier, swimming, parlor games, telephone and fireplace on premises. Handicap access. Antiquing, fishing, golf, shopping, tennis and water sports nearby.

Location: Waterfront. On Priest Lake.

Publicity: *Seattle Times.*

Certificate may be used: Monday through Thursday nights (Friday, Saturday, Sunday nights excluded), valid from June 1-Oct. 15.

Gooding   K4

Gooding Hotel Bed & Breakfast

112 Main St
Gooding, ID 83330-1102
(208)934-4374 (888)260-6656
Internet: goodingbb.hypermart.net

Circa 1906. An early Gooding settler, William B. Kelly, built this historic hotel, which is the oldest building in town. Each of the guest rooms is named in honor of someone significant in the history of Gooding or the hotel. A buffet breakfast is served

every morning in the William Kelly Room. The area offers many activities, from golfing and fishing to exploring ice caves or visiting wineries and museums.

Innkeeper(s): Dean & Judee Gooding. $64-80. 10 rooms, 2 with PB, 3 suites. Breakfast included in rates. Types of meals: Full gourmet bkfst and room service. Beds: QDT. Reading lamp, ceiling fan, clock radio and desk in room. Air conditioning. Copier, bicycles, parlor games and telephone on premises. Antiquing, cross-country skiing, downhill skiing, fishing, golf, parks, shopping, hunting, snowmobiling, rafting, wineries and museums nearby.

Location: Small town.

Certificate may be used: Labor Day through April 1, upon availability.

Moscow   E2

Paradise Ridge B&B

2455 Blaine Rd
Moscow, ID 83843-7479
(208)882-5292
Internet: www.paradiseridgebb.com
E-mail: paradiseridge@turbonet.com

Circa 1975. Four acres of woods surround this contemporary home, which affords views of buttes and mountains, as well as the town. The decor is a mix of styles, part traditional with a little bit of country. Innkeeper Solveig Miller was a caterer, so she prepares a wonderful breakfast. Huckleberry muffins, scones and oven-puff pancakes are among the homemade offerings.

Innkeeper(s): Jon R. & Solveig L. Miller. $75-105. 3 rooms, 1 with PB, 1 suite. Breakfast included in rates. Types of meals: Full gourmet bkfst, early coffee/tea, gourmet lunch and afternoon tea. Beds: KQ. Ceiling fan in room. Spa on premises. Antiquing, cross-country skiing, fishing, golf, live theater, parks, shopping, sporting events, tennis and water sports nearby.

Location: Forested ridge.

"This certainly rates as one of the best, if not the best, B&B we have stayed in!"

Certificate may be used: Dec. 12 to Jan. 31, any night, except holidays.

New Meadows   G2

Hartland Inn

211 Norris Hwy 95
New Meadows, ID 83654-0215
(208)347-2114 (888)509-7400 Fax:(208)347-2535
Internet: www.hartlandinn.com

Circa 1911. This handsome, three-story house was built by the president of the PIN Railroad. The mansion's pleasant interiors include a sunny sitting room and a formal dining room. Guest rooms offer polished wood floors and ceiling fans, and some include period antiques. Breakfast includes strata, muffins and fruit smoothies. Enjoy the area's mountains, forests, rivers, lakes and scenic drives. The Little Salmon River is three blocks away.

Innkeeper(s): Stephen & JoBeth Mehen. $49-140. 5 rooms, 3 with PB, 4 with FP, 4 suites. Breakfast included in rates. Types of meals: Full bkfst and early coffee/tea. Beds: QD. Cable TV, reading lamp, ceiling fan, telephone, fireplace and four suites have fireplaces in room. Air conditioning. VCR, fax, spa and library on premises. Antiquing, art galleries, bicycling, canoeing/kayaking, cross-country skiing, downhill skiing, fishing, golf, hiking, horseback riding, parks and water sports nearby.

Location: Mountains. Little Salmon River.

Certificate may be used: Sept. 15 to June 15, Sunday-Thursday (holidays excluded).

Rigby 17

Blacksmith Inn

227 N 3900 East
Rigby, ID 83442
(208)745-6208 (888)745-6208 Fax:(208)745-0602
E-mail: theinn@blacksmithinn.com

Circa 1996. This contemporary home features unusual architecture. The inn resembles two dome-shaped buildings connected together, and the home is cedar sided. The inn is new,

so the innkeepers are constantly adding new items. Furnishings and decor are country in style, and quilt-topped beds are tucked beside walls painted with murals of Mountain and Western scenes. Breakfasts are served in a cheerful room with a ceiling fan and plants. Scenery of forests and mountain peaks in the Rigby area is outstanding. Guests can ski, fish and hike, and Rigby also offers antique shops, museums and galleries.

Innkeeper(s): Mike & Karla Black. $75-95. 6 rooms with PB. Breakfast and snacks/refreshments included in rates. Types of meals: Full bkfst and early coffee/tea. Beds: Q. Cable TV, VCR, reading lamp, ceiling fan, clock radio and desk in room. Fax, copier, stable and telephone on premises. Handicap access. Antiquing, cross-country skiing, downhill skiing, fishing, live theater, parks, shopping, sporting events and tennis nearby.

Location: Mountains.

Certificate may be used: Anytime, subject to availability.

Salmon G5

Greyhouse Inn B&B

1115 Hwy 93 South
Salmon, ID 83467
(208)756-3968 (800)348-8097
Internet: www.greyhouseinn.com
E-mail: greyhouse@greyhouseinn.com

Circa 1894. The scenery at Greyhouse is nothing short of wondrous. In the winter, when mountains are capped in white and the evergreens are shrouded in snow, this Victorian appears as a safe haven from the chilly weather. In the summer, the rocky peaks are a contrast to the whimsical house, which looks like something out of an Old West town. The historic home is known around town as the old maternity hospital, but there is nothing medicinal about it now. The rooms are Victorian in style with antique fur-

nishings. The parlor features deep red walls and floral overstuffed sofas and a dressmaker's model garbed in a brown Victorian gown. Outdoor enthusiasts will find no shortage of activities, from facing the rapids in nearby Salmon River to fishing to horseback riding. The town of Salmon is just 12 miles away.

Innkeeper(s): David & Sharon Osgood. $70-90. 7 rooms, 5 with PB, 1 cottage and 2 cabins. Breakfast included in rates. Types of meals: Country bkfst, veg bkfst, early coffee/tea, picnic lunch and dinner. Beds: KQDT. VCR, reading lamp, ceiling fan, clock radio, coffeemaker and desk in room. TV, bicycles, library, parlor games, telephone, gift shop, carriage house and two log cabin rooms on premises. Antiquing, art galleries, bicycling, canoeing/kayaking, cross-country skiing, downhill skiing, fishing, golf, hiking, horseback riding, live theater, museums, parks, shopping, tennis, water sports, float trips, hot springs and mountain biking nearby.

Location: Mountains.

Publicity: *Idaho Statesman Newspaper, PBS and Travel Channel.*

"To come around the corner and find the Greyhouse, as we did, restores my faith! Such a miracle. We had a magical evening here, and we plan to return to stay for a few days. Thanks so much for your kindness and hospitality. We love Idaho!"

Certificate may be used: Sept. 1-May 30.

Illinois

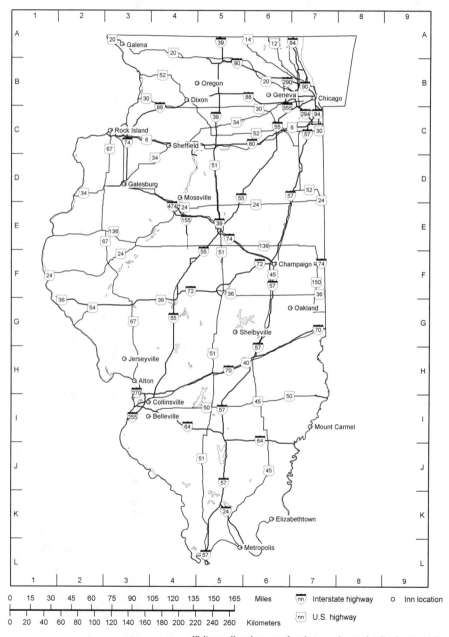

	Miles											
0	15	30	45	60	75	90	105	120	135	150	165	Miles

0   15   30   45   60   75   90   105   120   135   150   165   Miles

0   20   40   60   80   100   120   140   160   180   200   220   240   260   Kilometers

[nn] Interstate highway   ○ Inn location

[nn] U.S. highway

Alton   H3

Beall Mansion, An Elegant B&B

407 East 12th Street
Alton, IL 62002-7230
(618)474-9100 (866)843-2325 Fax:(618)474-9090
Internet: www.beallmansion.com
E-mail: bepampered@beallmansion.com

Circa 1903. An eclectic blend of Neoclassic, Georgian and
Greek Revival styles, the mansion was designed as a wedding
gift by world renown architect, Lucas Pfeiffenberger. Original
woodwork, eleven and a half-foot ceilings, leaded-glass windows, pocket doors, crystal chandeliers and imported marble
and bronze statuary reflect the era's opulence. Elegantly
appointed guest bedrooms are unique in size and decor. Each
includes a private bath with shower and clawfoot tub or
whirlpool for two, imported marble floor and chandelier. Voted
"Illinois Best Bed & Breakfast" by Illinois Magazine's first
Annual Readers Poll.

Innkeeper(s): Jim & Sandy Belote. $97-324. 5 rooms with PB, 2 with FP, 1
suite and 2 conference rooms. Types of meals: Full gourmet bkfst, veg bkfst,
early coffee/tea and room service. Beds: KQD. Modem hook-up, data port,
cable TV, reading lamp, ceiling fan, clock radio, telephone, turn-down service,
desk, hot tub/spa, voice mail, fireplace, two-person whirlpool, iron/board, toiletries, homemade lavender bath salts and high-speed wireless Internet service
in room. Central air. Fax, copier, parlor games, gift shop, veranda, hammock,
badminton, horseshoes and croquet on premises. Amusement parks, antiquing,
art galleries, bicycling, canoeing/kayaking, fishing, golf, hiking, horseback riding,
live theater, museums, parks, shopping, sporting events, tennis, water sports,
wineries, Meeting of the Great Rivers National Scenic Byway, Lewis & Clark
Interpretive Center and Trailsite Number 1 and boat rental nearby.
Location: City. On Millionaire's Row in the historic river town of Alton, Ill, 25
min. from the Gateway Arch & downtown St. Louis, Mo., 90 min. from
Springfield, Ill.
Publicity: *Illinois Magazine, Illinois Now, AAA Midwest Motorist, AAA Home
& Away, BBW Magazine, St. Louis Post Dispatch, Pequot Press, NorthShore
Magazine, The Telegraph, Edwardsville Intelligencer, DeForest Times, The
Daily Journal, Show Me St. Louis, News 4 St. Louis , WBGZ and KWMU.*
Certificate may be used: December-March, Sunday-Thursday night stays.
Reserved at the rack rate. Not available with any other certificate, discount or
coupon. Blackout dates apply, subject to availability. Not valid if booked
through a third party.

Belleville   I3

Swans Court B&B

421 Court St
Belleville, IL 62220-1201
(618)233-0779 (800)840-1058 Fax:(618)277-3150
E-mail: mdixon@isbe.accessus.net

Circa 1883. This home, designated by the Department of the
Interior as a certified historic structure, was once home to
David Baer, known as the "mule king of the world." Baer sold
more than 10,000 mules each year to
British troops in World War I and
to American troops in World
War II. The home is furnished
almost entirely in antiques.
Innkeeper Monty Dixon
searched high and low to fill her
B&B with authentic pieces, creating a nostalgic ambiance. The
library offers a selection of books, games and puzzles for guests
to enjoy. The home is located in a historic neighborhood, within walking distance to shops and restaurants. Belleville is convenient to St. Louis, and there are historic sites, Lewis & Clark
sites and a state park nearby.

Innkeeper(s): Ms. Monty Dixon. $69-96. 4 rooms, 2 with PB, 2 with FP.
Breakfast and snacks/refreshments included in rates. Types of meals: Full
bkfst. Beds: QD. Reading lamp, ceiling fan, clock radio, telephone and folding
tables upon request in room. Air conditioning. VCR, library, parlor games and
fireplace on premises. Handicap access. Antiquing, golf, live theater, shopping, sporting events and tennis nearby.
Location: Town of 45,000.
*"We feel like we have made a new friend. We appreciated all of the
nice little touches, such as the fresh flowers."*
Certificate may be used: Jan. 1-Dec. 20, Monday-Thursday.

Champaign   F6

Golds B&B

2065 County Road 525 E
Champaign, IL 61822-9521
(217)586-4345
Internet: www.culocalbiz.com/goldsbandb
E-mail: reg@prairienet.org

Circa 1874. Visitors to the University of Illinois area may enjoy
a restful experience at this inn, west of town in a peaceful farmhouse setting. Antique country furniture collected by the
innkeepers over the past 25 years is showcased in the inn and
is beautifully offset by early American stenciling on its walls.
Seasonal items from the garden are sometimes used as breakfast fare.

Innkeeper(s): Rita & Bob Gold. $55. 3 rooms, 1 with PB. Breakfast included
in rates. Types of meals: Cont plus and early coffee/tea. Beds: QT. Reading
lamp and clock radio in room. Air conditioning. TV, VCR, telephone and fireplace on premises. Antiquing, fishing, golf, hiking, live theater, museums,
parks, shopping, sporting events and wineries nearby.
Location: Country.
Certificate may be used: Anytime except special event weekends.

Chicago   B7

China Doll Short-Term Rental Apartments

738 West Schubert Avenue
Chicago, IL 60614
(773)525-4967 (866)361-1819 Fax:(773)525-3929
Internet: www.chinadollchicago.com
E-mail: chinadollchicago@yahoo.com

Circa 1895. Everything needed is included for a wonderful visit
to the Windy City. Stay in a self-contained, one-bedroom garden
apartment with exposed brick walls. It is complete with an
entertainment system, fireplace, private Jacuzzi, sauna and a
fully stocked island kitchen with customized breakfast foods per
advance request. A larger accommodation of one to two bedrooms with up to six rooms is available on the second-floor, and
features a private deck in addition to all the same amenities.
Both apartments have an office with computers, high-speed
Internet and other equipment. A laundry room facility is the
only shared amenity. Chinese-Mandarin and English are spoken.
Innkeeper(s): Jim & Yanan Haring. $135-225. 2 rooms with PB, 2 with FP
and 1 conference room. Breakfast, afternoon tea and snacks/refreshments
included in rates. Types of meals: Cont plus. Beds: QDT. Modem hook-up,
data port, cable TV, VCR, reading lamp, stereo, refrigerator, snack bar, clock
radio, telephone, coffeemaker, desk, voice mail and fireplace in room. Air
conditioning. Fax, copier, spa, library, fireplace, laundry facility, sauna and
conference room with projector on premises. Art galleries, beach, bicycling,
cross-country skiing, fishing, golf, hiking, live theater, museums, parks, shopping, sporting events and tennis nearby.
Location: City.
Certificate may be used: Oct. 1 to April 30, Sunday-Thursday, subject to
availability, except Dec. 20 to Jan. 3.

House Of Two Urns

1239 N Greenview Ave
Chicago, IL 60622-3318
(773)235-1408 (800)835-9303 Fax:(773)235-1410
Internet: www.twourns.com
E-mail: twourns@earthlink.net

Circa 1912. This historic townhouse offers guests a unique experience in the Windy City. The house is built in late Victorian style, and innkeeper Kapra Fleming has decorated the B&B in an eclectic style with antiques and family heirlooms. Kapra has included many thoughtful amenities, such as robes, hair dryers, slippers and an alarm clock. Rooms are inviting and tastefully furnished. The spacious loft suite includes a queen and full bed, as well as a private bath. The continental-plus breakfasts include items such as French toast with almonds and bananas or chocolate chip scones. The home is located in the Wicker Park section of Chicago, less than three miles from downtown and six miles from McCormick Center.
Innkeeper(s): Kapra Fleming. $80-155. 4 rooms, 2 with PB, 1 suite. Breakfast included in rates. Types of meals: Cont plus and early coffee/tea. Beds: KQD. Cable TV, VCR, reading lamp, refrigerator, ceiling fan, clock radio, telephone, desk and hair dryer in room. TV, fax, copier, spa, library, parlor games, fireplace, gift shop and limited Internet access on premises. Antiquing, live theater, parks, shopping, sporting events and water sports nearby.
Location: City.
Certificate may be used: Jan. 20 to Feb. 10, Monday-Thursday.

Collinsville   I3

Maggie's B&B

2102 N Keebler Ave
Collinsville, IL 62234-4713
(618)344-8283
E-mail: maggiesbnb@mailstation.com

Circa 1900. A rustic two-acre wooded area surrounds this friendly Victorian inn, once a boarding house. Rooms with 11-foot ceilings are furnished with exquisite antiques and art objects collected on worldwide travels. Downtown St. Louis, the Gateway Arch and the Mississippi riverfront are just 10 minutes away.
Innkeeper(s): Maggie Leyda. $45-100.
4 rooms, 3 with PB, 1 with FP and 1 conference room. Breakfast included in rates. Types of meals: Full bkfst and early coffee/tea. Beds: KQDT. Cable TV, VCR, reading lamp, ceiling fan, clock radio and turn-down service in room. Air conditioning. TV, spa, library, telephone and fireplace on premises. Handicap access. Amusement parks, antiquing, fishing, live theater, parks, shopping and sporting events nearby.
Location: Country.
Publicity: *USA Today, Cooking Light, Collinsville Herald Journal, Innsider, Belleville News, Democrat, Saint Louis Homes & Gardens, Edwardsville Intelligences, St. Louis Business Journal and St. Louis Post Dispatch.*

"We enjoyed a delightful stay. You've thought of everything. What fun!"
Certificate may be used: Anytime, subject to availability.

Dixon   B4

Crawford House Inn

204 E Third St
Dixon, IL 61021
(815)288-3351
Internet: www.crawfordhouseinn.com
E-mail: crwfordinn@cin.net

Circa 1869. In 1869, Joseph Crawford, who counted Abraham Lincoln among his friends, built the Italianate Victorian style

house that now bears his name. His descendants maintained the family home until the 1950s when it was converted into a nursing facility and then lawyer offices. Enjoying life today as a B&B, Crawford House offers its guests a glimpse into small-town America. Three guest rooms have either king- or queen-size feather beds; bathrooms are shared. Breakfasts are served in the dining room and are presented with white linens, china and stemware. Gourmet breakfasts include juice, coffee, an egg entree, fresh baked goods and seasonal fruits. Dixon has just been named "Petunia Capital of the United States," and its streets are lined with colorful beds of the blooms all summer long. At the center of five state parks, the area is popular for cycling. Scenic country roads and paths offer opportunities for walking and horseback riding, as well. Visits can be made to the Ronald Reagan boyhood home, the John Deere Historical Site or local antique stores. Rock River is two blocks away for boating, fishing and canoeing, and across the street is the historical courthouse square where summertime concerts are popular in the evenings. Cross-country skiing and snowmobiling are available during the winter months.
Innkeeper(s): Lyn Miliano. $65-85. 3 rooms, 1 with FP. Breakfast included in rates. Types of meals: Full gourmet bkfst. Beds: KQ. Cable TV, VCR, reading lamp, ceiling fan and clock radio in room. Air conditioning. Library, parlor games and fireplace on premises. Antiquing, bicycling, canoeing/kayaking, fishing, golf, hiking, horseback riding, live theater, museums, parks, shopping, tennis and water sports nearby.
Location: Small town.
Certificate may be used: Anytime, subject to availability.

Elizabethtown   K6

River Rose Inn B&B

1 Main Street, PO Box 78
Elizabethtown, IL 62931-0078
(618)287-8811 Fax:(208)330-8715
Internet: www.shawneelink.com/~riverose
E-mail: riverose@shawneelink.com

Circa 1914. Large, shade trees veil the front of this Greek Gothic home, nestled along the banks of the Ohio River. From the grand front entrance, guests look out to polished woodwork and a staircase leading to shelves of books. Rooms are cheerful and nostalgic, decorated with antiques. Each guest room offers something special. One has a four-poster bed, another offers a fireplace. The Scarlet Room has its own balcony and whirlpool tub, and the Rose Room has a private patio with a swing. The Magnolia Cottage is ideal for honeymooners and includes a whirlpool tub for two, fireplace and a deck that overlooks the river. Breakfasts are served in the dining room where guests can enjoy the water views.
Innkeeper(s): Don & Elisabeth Phillips. $62-109. 5 rooms with PB, 2 with FP and 1 cottage. Breakfast included in rates. Types of meals: Full gourmet bkfst and early coffee/tea. Beds: QT. Modem hook-up, cable TV, VCR, reading lamp, refrigerator, ceiling fan, clock radio, coffeemaker, desk, fireplace and four with whirlpool tub in room. Air conditioning. Fax, copier, spa, swimming, library, parlor games and telephone on premises. Amusement parks, antiquing, beach, bicycling, canoeing/kayaking, fishing, golf, hiking, horseback riding, museums, parks, shopping, water sports, wineries, Metropolis Casino, caves, Shawnee Queen boat rides and festivals nearby.
Location: Waterfront. River town.
Publicity: *Chicago Tribune, Midwest Living, Southern Illinoisan and other various newspapers.*
Certificate may be used: November-January, March, excluding holidays, Sunday-Thursday, some exceptions, subject to availability.

Galena   A3

Aldrich Guest House

900 3rd St
Galena, IL 61036-2627
(815)777-3323 Fax:(815)777-3323
Internet: www.aldrichguesthouse.com
E-mail: jmnadeau@netexpress.net

Circa 1845. This elegant Greek Revival home is listed in the National Register of Historic Places. Victorian antiques decorate the interior. Guest rooms include antiques and handmade quilts. Clawfoot tubs and pedestal sinks in the private bathrooms add to the nostalgic charm of the inn. A multi-course, gourmet breakfast is prepared daily served on fine china and linens. The screened porch overlooks the yard where General Grant once drilled Union soldiers. The home is within walking distance of shops and restaurants.

Innkeeper(s): Jim and Marie Nadeau. $75-150. 5 rooms with PB, 3 with FP. Breakfast included in rates. Types of meals: Full gourmet bkfst and early coffee/tea. Beds: QT. Reading lamp, stereo, ceiling fan, clock radio and desk in room. Air conditioning. VCR, fax, copier, library, parlor games, telephone and fireplace on premises. Handicap access. Antiquing, cross-country skiing, downhill skiing, fishing, golf, live theater, parks, shopping, sporting events, tennis and water sports nearby.
Location: Country.
Publicity: *Chicago Tribune and Telegraph Herald.*

"Thank you for the 'personal touch' you give to your guests."
Certificate may be used: All year, Monday-Thursday, subject to availability.

Annie Wiggins Guest House

1004 Park Avenue
Galena, IL 61036-2622
(815)777-0336
E-mail: bheiken@galenalink.net

Circa 1846. For a nostalgic journey into a bygone era, this Greek Revival mansion is a historical treasure. Built with innovative architecture, Doric and Ionic columns reside with marble fireplaces, brick and woodwork. Several common rooms and a veranda provide places to relax and enjoy panoramic views of the woods and Galena River. The guest bedrooms are resplendently decorated with antiques and touches of yesteryear. Luxurious fine linens, large soaking tubs, candles, private entrances and screened porches are some of the pleasures available.

Innkeeper(s): Bill & Wendy. $125-175. 7 rooms, 6 with PB, 1 suite. Breakfast and afternoon tea included in rates. Types of meals: Full gourmet bkfst and early coffee/tea. Beds: Q. Air conditioning. Library, parlor games and telephone on premises. Antiquing, art galleries, cross-country skiing, downhill skiing, live theater, museums, parks, shopping and wineries nearby.
Location: City.
Certificate may be used: Monday-Thursday, Nov. 5-May 30, except holidays.

Captain Harris Guest House & Honeymoon Cottage

713 S Bench St
Galena, IL 61036-2501
(815)777-4713 (800)996-4799 Fax:(815)777-4713
Internet: www.captainharris.com
E-mail: inquiry@captainharris.com

Circa 1836. One of the area's oldest homes, it was built in the vernacular style and has retained its historical character. Leaded-glass windows made and installed by Frank Lloyd Wright's partner enhance the appeal. Original artwork graces the walls, residing with elegant furnishings of antiques, family heirlooms and historic artifacts. A large suite with fireplace boasts a two-person whirlpool, private entrance and front porch. Guest bedrooms with hardwood floors and Oriental rugs are well decorated with wallpaper, tapestry bedding, Battenburg lace and window treatments. A secluded honeymoon cottage with whirlpool offers VCR, fridge, coffeemaker and front porch. Enjoy a hearty homemade breakfast prepared daily. Please make reservations online or phone the inn.

Innkeeper(s): Warren and Kathy Bell. $85-185. 5 rooms with PB, 3 with FP, 2 with HT, 1 suite and 1 cottage. Breakfast included in rates. Types of meals: Full gourmet bkfst. Beds: Q. Cable TV, VCR, reading lamp, refrigerator, ceiling fan, clock radio, coffeemaker, hot tub/spa, some with fireplace, refrigerator, coffeemaker, 2 with Jacuzzi, VCR, free broadband and TV theater system in room. Central air. Fax, copier, spa, library, parlor games, telephone and laundry facility on premises. Antiquing, art galleries, bicycling, cross-country skiing, downhill skiing, fishing, golf, hiking, horseback riding, live theater, museums, parks, shopping, water sports and wineries nearby.
Location: City.
Certificate may be used: November through April, Sunday through Thursday.

Farmers' Guest House

334 Spring St
Galena, IL 61036-2128
(815)777-3456 (888)459-1847 Fax:(815)777-3514
Internet: www.farmersguesthouse.com
E-mail: farmersgh@galenalink.net

Circa 1867. This two-story brick Italianate building was built as a bakery and served as a store and hotel, as well. Rows of arched, multi-paned windows add charm to the exterior. The rooms are decorated with antiques, lace curtains and floral wallpapers. The accommodations include seven rooms with queen-size beds, one room with a double bed, and two, two-room king Master Suites. There's a bar, featured in the movie "Field of Dreams." A hot tub is offered in the backyard. The inn also has a cabin in the woods available for rent.

Innkeeper(s): Kathie, Jess Farlow. $125-249. 10 rooms with PB, 2 with FP, 2 suites and 1 cabin. Breakfast included in rates. Types of meals: Full bkfst. Beds: KQD. Cable TV, reading lamp, CD player, coffeemaker and hot tub/spa in room. Central air. VCR, fax, library, parlor games, telephone, fireplace, hot tub and evening wine and cheese hour on premises. Antiquing, art galleries, bicycling, cross-country skiing, downhill skiing, golf, hiking, horseback riding, live theater, museums, parks, shopping, wineries and hot air ballooning nearby.
Location: City.
Publicity: *Better Homes & Gardens, Country Discoveries, Comforts at Home, Country Extra and Field of Dreams.*

"Neat old place, fantastic breakfasts."
Certificate may be used: All year, must be Sunday-Monday, Monday-Tuesday, Tuesday-Wednesday or Wednesday-Thursday nights. Based on availability.

The Steamboat House Bed and Breakfast

605 S. Prospect
Galena, IL 61036
(815)777-2317 Fax:(815)776-0712
Internet: www.thesteamboathouse.com
E-mail: glenchar@thesteamboathouse.com

Circa 1855. Truly elegant as well as historic, this brick Gothic Revival, pre-Civil War mansion was built for a renowned Mississippi River steamboat captain. The inn exudes luxury while imparting a welcome, friendly ambiance. Main-floor parlors include a library and billiards room. A central parlor on the second floor offers early-morning Gevalia coffee and tea. Enjoy midweek afternoon treats or wine and cheese on the weekends. Each guest bedroom features a fireplace, heirloom furniture, vintage photographs and original artwork. The formal dining room is set with antique china, crystal and silver for a breakfast that is

sure to please. Relax on the front porch overlooking roses.
Innkeeper(s): Glen and Char Carlson. $90-135. 5 rooms with PB, 5 with FP.
Breakfast, snacks/refreshments and wine included in rates. Types of meals:
Full gourmet bkfst, veg bkfst and early coffee/tea. Beds: QT. Cable TV, VCR,
reading lamp, clock radio, fireplace and heirloom antique furnishings in room.
Central air. Library, parlor games, telephone, billiard room, original parlors,
large covered front porch and LCD TV on premises. Antiquing, art galleries,
bicycling, canoeing/kayaking, cross-country skiing, downhill skiing, fishing,
golf, hiking, horseback riding, live theater, museums, parks, shopping, sporting
events, tennis, water sports, wineries, historic district and trolley tours nearby.
Location: City. Located less than 2 blocks from Main Street Galena.
Certificate may be used: December-February, Monday/Tuesday,
Tuesday/Wednesday, Wednesday/Thursday. Bess or Lene Room, subject to
availability.

Galesburg   D3

Seacord House
624 N Cherry St
Galesburg, IL 61401-2731
(309)342-4107
E-mail: paarentj@galesburg.net

Circa 1891. A former county sheriff and businessman built
this Eastlake-style Victorian, which is located in the town's historic district. The home was named for its builder, Wilkens
Seacord, a prominent local man whose family is mentioned in
Carl Sandburg's autobiography. In keeping with the house's
historical prominence, the innkeepers have tried to maintain its
turn-of-the-century charm. Victorian wallpapers, lacy curtains
and a collection of family antiques grace the guest rooms and
living areas. The bedrooms, however, feature the modern
amenity of waterbeds. For those celebrating romantic occasions, the innkeepers provide heart-shaped muffins along with
regular morning fare.
Innkeeper(s): Gwen and Lyle. $50. 3 rooms. Breakfast included in rates.
Types of meals: Cont plus. Fax on premises.
Certificate may be used: Any day between Nov. 1 and April 1.

Geneva   B6

The Oscar Swan Country Inn
1800 W State St
Geneva, IL 60134-1002
(630)232-0173
Internet: www.oscarswan.com
E-mail: oscarswan@there-is-another-way.com

Circa 1902. This turn-of-the-century Colonial Revival house
rests on seven acres of trees and lawns. Its 6,000 square feet
are filled with homey touches. There is a historic barn on the
property and a
gazebo on the
front lawn. A
pillared
breezeway

connects the round garage to the house. The stone pool is
round, as well. Nina is a retired home economics teacher and
Hans speaks German and was a professor of business adminis-
tration at Indiana University.
Innkeeper(s): Nina Heymann. $88-150. 8 rooms, 4 with PB and 3 confer-
ence rooms. Breakfast included in rates. Types of meals: Full bkfst and lunch.
Beds: KQD. VCR, reading lamp, refrigerator, clock radio and telephone in
room. Air conditioning. TV and fireplace on premises. Antiquing, cross-country skiing, live theater and shopping nearby.
Location: Small town.
Publicity: *Chicago Tribune and Windmill News.*

"Thank you for making our wedding such a beautiful memory. The

accommodations were wonderful, the food excellent."
Certificate may be used: Sunday through Thursday, January, February,
March, April and November.

Jerseyville   H3

The Homeridge B&B
24818 Homeridge Drive
Jerseyville, IL 62052-1127
(618)498-3442
Internet: www.homeridge.com
E-mail: innkeeper@homeridge.com

Circa 1867. This red brick Italianate Victorian features ornate
white trim, a stately front veranda and a cupola where guests
often take in views of sunsets and the surrounding 18 acres.
The home was constructed
by Cornelius Fisher, just
after the Civil War. In
1891, it was purchased by
Senator Theodore
Chapman and remained in

his family until the 1960s. The innkeepers have filled the 14-
room manor with traditional and Victorian furnishings, enhancing the high ceilings and ornate woodwork typical of the era.
Guests are invited to take a relaxing dip in the inn's swimming
pool or enjoy a refreshment on the veranda.
Innkeeper(s): Sue & Howard Landon. $95. 4 rooms with PB. Breakfast
included in rates. Types of meals: Full bkfst, early coffee/tea and afternoon
tea. Beds: KQDT. Reading lamp, ceiling fan, clock radio and desk in room.
Air conditioning. VCR, fax, copier, swimming, bicycles, library, parlor games,
telephone and fireplace on premises. Amusement parks, antiquing, cross-
country skiing, fishing, live theater, parks, shopping, sporting events and
water sports nearby.
Publicity: *Chicago Sun Times, Midwest Living Magazine and St. Louis
Post Dispatch.*

"A most beautiful, entertaining, snow-filled few days."
Certificate may be used: Nov. 1 to March 30, Sunday through Thursday.

Metropolis   L5

Isle of View B&B
205 Metropolis St
Metropolis, IL 62960-2213
(618)524-5838 (800)566-7491
Internet: www.bbonline.com/il/isleofview
E-mail: kimoff@hcis.net

Circa 1889. Metropolis, billed as the "home of Superman," is
not a bustling concrete city, but a quaint, country town tucked
along the Ohio River. The Isle of View, a stunning Italianate
manor, is just a short walk from shops, restaurants and the
Players Riverboat Casino. All the guest rooms
are appointed in Victorian design with
antiques. The Master Suite was originally the home's library and includes
a unique coal-burning fireplace,
canopy bed and two-person
whirlpool tub.
Innkeeper(s): Kim & Gerald Offenburger. $65-125. 5 rooms with PB.
Breakfast included in rates. Types of meals: Full gourmet bkfst and early cof-
fee/tea. Beds: KQD. Cable TV, reading lamp, ceiling fan, telephone and hot
tub/spa in room. Air conditioning. Fireplace on premises. Antiquing, fishing,
live theater, parks, shopping, water sports and riverboat casino nearby.
Location: Small town.

"You may never want to leave."
Certificate may be used: Sunday-Friday, subject to availability.

Mossville   D4

Old Church House Inn

1416 E Mossville Rd, Po Box 295
Mossville, IL 61552
(309)579-2300
Internet: www.bedandbreakfast.com/bbc/p210657.asp
E-mail: churchhouse@prodigy.net

Circa 1869. Take sanctuary at this lovingly restored 1869 brick
Colonial country church situated on Peoria's north side. The
inn offers warm hospitality and comfortable elegance. Relax by
a wood-burning fire with afternoon tea or sit on a
bench among colorful garden blooms. Each guest
bedroom features pampering amenities and distinctive details that may include an antique
carved bedstead, handmade quilts and
lacy curtains. Chocolates are a pleasant treat with turndown service in
the evening.

Innkeeper(s): Dean & Holly Ramseyer. $115.
2 rooms, 1 with PB. Breakfast included in rates. Types of meals: Cont plus,
early coffee/tea, picnic lunch and room service. Beds: Q. Reading lamp, clock
radio and turn-down service in room. Air conditioning. Telephone and fireplace on premises. Antiquing, cross-country skiing, fishing, live theater, shopping, sporting events, water sports and bike trail nearby.
Location: Village.
Publicity: *Chillicothe Bulletin, Journal Star, Country Inns and The
Chicago Tribune.*

*"Your hospitality, thoughtfulness, the cleanliness, beauty, I should just
say everything was the best."*

Certificate may be used: Monday-Thursday all year or anytime with reservations within 48 hours of requested date.

Mount Carmel   I7

Living Legacy Homestead

3759 N 900 Blvd
Mount Carmel, IL 62863-0002
(618)298-2476 (877)548-3276 Fax:(618)298-2476
Internet: www.bbonline.com/il/legacy/
E-mail: llfarm1@earthlink.net

Circa 1870. This turn-of-the-century German homestead
stands on 10 hilltop acres with a panoramic view of the local
area. The eight farm buildings are full of artifacts and equipment that reflect their original functions. These include the
shop and garage, smokehouse, scale shed, machine shed, hen
house, corncrib and feed house and, of course, the outhouse.
The barn hayloft, constructed using wooden pegs, is available
for large group functions. The property was bought in 1902 by
second-generation German immigrants. Their grand-daughter,
innkeeper Edna Schmidt Anderson, was born at the Farmstead
and returned home following her parents' deaths.
Accommodations include the Heritage Room in the farmhouse,
the detached Summer Cottage and some rustic bunk house
rooms with tractor themes: Ford, Oliver, John Deere and Case.
Guests enjoy a full country breakfast in the 1860 Log Room, a
part of the original log cabin, which has exposed interior log
walls. Lunch, dinner, picnics, snacks and refreshments are
available upon request. Guests may choose to study nature,
reflect quietly or go on hikes, picnics and other outdoor activities. An amphitheater made of barn beams offers an exquisite
view of the sunset. The inn is located near the Beall Woods

State Park and Historic New Harmony, Ind. Guests may tour
the grounds by themselves or with a guide.
Innkeeper(s): Edna Schmidt Anderson. $35-75. 4 rooms, 2 with PB, 1 cot-
tage and 1 conference room. Breakfast included in rates. Types of meals: Full
bkfst, early coffee/tea, lunch, picnic lunch, snacks/refreshments and dinner.
Beds: DT. Reading lamp, ceiling fan and clock radio in room. Air conditioning. Library, parlor games, telephone, Amazing Pumpkin Maze 5 acres, "good
old days" Treasures Gift Shop in attic loft and nature walks on premises.
Handicap access. Antiquing, fishing, parks and historic village nearby.
Location: Country.
Certificate may be used: Feb. 1 to Oct. 31, Sunday through Thursday.

Oakland   G6

Inn on The Square

3 Montgomery
Oakland, IL 61943
(217)346-2289 Fax:(217)346-2005
E-mail: innonsq@advant.net

Circa 1878. This inn features hand-carved beams and braided
rugs on wide pine flooring. The Tea Room has oak tables, fresh
flowers and a hand-laid brick fireplace. Guests may wander in
the forest behind the inn or
relax in the library with a
book or jigsaw puzzle. Guest
rooms have oak poster beds
and handmade quilts. The
Pine Room boasts an heir-
loom bed with a carved head-

board. In addition to guest rooms, the inn houses shops selling
ladies apparel, gifts and antiques. The Amish communities of
Arthur and Arcola are 14 miles away.
Innkeeper(s): Linda & Gary Miller. $65. 3 rooms with PB, 1 with FP and 1
conference room. Breakfast included in rates. Types of meals: Full bkfst, early
coffee/tea, lunch and picnic lunch. Restaurant on premises. Beds: D. TV, reading lamp, ceiling fan, clock radio, desk and homemade cookies in room. Air
conditioning. VCR, library, parlor games, telephone and fireplace on premises.
Antiquing, golf, live theater, parks, shopping, sporting events, tennis, water
sports, Amish Community, forest preserve, Lincoln sites and boating nearby.
Location: City. Small town.
Publicity: *Amish Country News, PM, Midwest Living and Country Living.*
Certificate may be used: Anytime, subject to availability. Not available on
graduation weekends, parents weekends or festival weekends.

Oregon   B4

Patchwork Inn

122 N 3rd St
Oregon, IL 61061
(815)732-4113 Fax:(815)732-6557
Internet: www.essex1.com/people/patchworkinn
E-mail: patchworkinn@essex1.com

Circa 1845. Would you like to sleep where Abraham Lincoln
once stayed? This historic inn actually can boast of Mr. Lincoln
having "slept here." The Patchwork Inn is the sort you can
imagine as providing a speaking platform as well from its two-
level veranda across the front facade. Guest rooms feature access
to the veranda, and there are high-ceilings and beds with handmade quilts, the theme of the inn. Guests are pampered at
breakfast with a choice of service in your room, the parlor, sun
room or on the front porch. A walk away is the river, dam and
tree-lined streets filled with historic houses. Guests often enjoy
canoeing on Rock River, picnicking in one of the three state
parks or visiting Ronald Reagan's homestead in Dixon.
Innkeeper(s): Michael & Jean McNamara & Ron Bry. $75-115. 10 rooms

with PB and 1 conference room. Breakfast and snacks/refreshments included in rates. Types of meals: Cont. Beds: DT. Cable TV, reading lamp, telephone and two have whirlpools in room. Air conditioning. Fax, copier, library and parlor games on premises. Limited handicap access. Antiquing, art galleries, bicycling, canoeing/kayaking, cross-country skiing, fishing, golf, hiking, horseback riding, live theater, museums, parks and shopping nearby.
Location: Rural city.
Certificate may be used: Anytime, subject to availability.

Pinehill Inn

400 Mix St
Oregon, IL 61061-1113
(815)732-2067 Fax:(815)732-1348
Internet: www.pinehillbb.com
E-mail: rcar132651@aol.com

Circa 1874. This Italianate country villa is listed in the National Register. Ornate touches include guest rooms with Italian marble fireplaces and French silk-screened mural wallpaper. Outside, guests may enjoy porches, swings and century-old pine trees. Seasonal events include daily chocolate tea parties featuring the inn's own exotic homemade fudge collection.
Innkeeper(s): Ruth Carlson. $80-145. 5 rooms with PB, 3 with FP. Breakfast and snacks/refreshments included in rates. Types of meals: Full gourmet bkfst and early coffee/tea. Beds: QT. Reading lamp, turn-down service and desk in room. Air conditioning. Parlor games, telephone and fireplace on premises. Antiquing, parks, shopping, sporting events and water sports nearby.
Location: City.
Publicity: *Fox Valley Living, Victorian Sampler, Freeport Journal and Passion of the Automobile.*

"We enjoyed our stay at Pine Hill, your gracious hospitality and the peacefulness. Our thanks to you for a delightful stay. We may have to come again, if just to get some fudge."
Certificate may be used: Sunday-Thursday, November through April.

Rock Island   C3

Victorian Inn

702 20th St
Rock Island, IL 61201-2638
(309)788-7068 (800)728-7068 Fax:(309)788-7086
Internet: www.victorianinnbnb.com
E-mail: dparker@victorianinnbandb.com

Circa 1876. Built as a wedding present for the daughter of a Rock Island liquor baron, the inn's striking features include illuminated stained-glass tower windows. Other examples of the Victorian decor are the living room's beveled-plate-glass French doors and the dining room's Flemish Oak ceiling beams and paneling, crowned by turn-of-the-century tapestries. Standing within sight of three other buildings listed in the National Register, the inn's wooded grounds are home to many songbirds from the area. A glassed-in Florida porch is perfect for relaxing during any season and a patio table in the gardens is a great place to enjoy a glass of pink lemonade on warm evenings.
Innkeeper(s): David & Barbara Parker. $75-150. 5 rooms with PB, 2 with FP. Breakfast included in rates. Types of meals: Full gourmet bkfst, early coffee/tea, afternoon tea and snacks/refreshments. Beds: KQDT. Reading lamp, ceiling fan, clock radio and desk in room. Air conditioning. Fax, copier, library, parlor games and fireplace on premises. Antiquing, cross-country skiing, fishing, live theater, parks, sporting events and water sports nearby.
Location: City.
Certificate may be used: Sunday-Thursday, subject to availability, year-round.

Sheffield   C4

Chestnut Street Inn

301 E Chestnut St
Sheffield, IL 61361
(815)454-2419 (800)537-1304
Internet: www.chestnut-inn.com
E-mail: gail@chestnut-inn.com

Circa 1854. Originally built in Italianate style, this mid-19th-century reborn Colonial Revival is the dream-come-true for innkeeper Gail Bruntjen. She spent more than 15 years searching for just the right country home to open a bed & breakfast. With its gracious architectural character and well-organized interior spaces, the Chestnut Street Inn fit the bill. Classic French doors open to a wide foyer with gleaming chandeliers and a floating spindle staircase. Sophisticated chintz fabrics and authentic antiques highlight each room. The  four guest rooms offer down comforters, four-poster beds and private baths. Guests will be delighted by the gourmet selections offered every morning such as broccoli mushroom quiche, homemade breads and fresh fruit, all exquisitely presented by candlelight on fine China and crystal. Afternoon tea and evening snacks are served in the public rooms. Antiquing, shops ,bicycling, hiking, golf and fishing are located nearby.
Innkeeper(s): Gail Bruntjen. $75-175. 4 rooms with PB, 1 with FP, 1 suite and 1 conference room. Breakfast, afternoon tea and snacks/refreshments included in rates. Types of meals: Full bkfst and early coffee/tea. Beds: KQT. Cable TV, VCR, reading lamp, turn-down service and desk in room. Air conditioning. Library, parlor games, telephone and fireplace on premises. Antiquing, bicycling, fishing, golf, parks and shopping nearby.
Location: Village.
Publicity: *The Illinois Review and Illinois Country Living.*

"Without a doubt, the best B&B I've ever been to."
Certificate may be used: Sunday-Thursday, anytime.

Shelbyville   G5

The Shelby Historic House and Inn

816 W Main St
Shelbyville, IL 62565-1354
(217)774-3991 (800)342-9978 Fax:(217)774-2224
Internet: shelbyinn.com
E-mail: kenfry@stewstras.net

This Queen Anne Victorian inn is listed in the National Register of Historic Places. The inn is well known for its conference facilities, and is less than a mile from Lake Shelbyville, one of the state's most popular boating and fishing spots. Guaranteed tee times are available at a neighboring championship golf course. Three state parks are nearby, and the Amish settlement near Arthur is within easy driving distance.
Innkeeper(s): Ken Fry. $65-76. 45 rooms, 6 suites and 1 conference room. Types of meals: Cont. Beds: K. Cable TV, reading lamp, clock radio, telephone and desk in room. Air conditioning. Fax on premises. Handicap access. Antiquing, fishing, live theater, parks, shopping and water sports nearby.
Certificate may be used: Nov. 1 through May 15.

Indiana

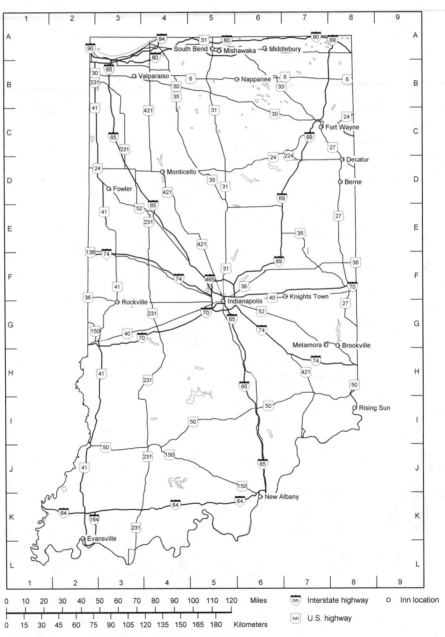

Miles: 0 10 20 30 40 50 60 70 80 90 100 110 120

Kilometers: 0 15 30 45 60 75 90 105 120 135 150 165 180

- [nn] Interstate highway
- [nn] U.S. highway
- ○ Inn location

Visit www.iLoveInns.com for photos and more details about each inn.

Berne   D8

Historic Schug House Inn
706 W Main St
Berne, IN 46711-1328
(260)589-2303
E-mail: schughousebb@onlyinternet.net

Circa 1907. This Queen Anne home was built in 1907 by
Emanuel Wanner. It was constructed for the Schug family,
who occupied the home for 25 years, and whom the innkeepers chose the name of their inn. Victorian features decorate
the home, including inlaid floors, pocket doors and a wraparound porch. Guest rooms boast walnut, cherry and oak furnishings. Fruit, cheeses and pastries are served on antique
china each morning in the dining room. Horse-drawn carriages from the nearby Old Order Amish community often
pass on the street outside.

Innkeeper(s): John Minch. $40-45. 9 rooms with PB and 1 conference room.
Breakfast included in rates. Types of meals: Cont. Beds: KQDT. TV and telephone on premises.

Certificate may be used: Jan. 2-Dec. 20, except July 20-27 and Aug. 23-30.

Brookville   G8

The Hermitage Bed and Breakfast
650 East 8th St
Brookville, IN 47012
(765)647-5182 (877)407-9198
Internet: www.bbonline.com/in/hermitage
E-mail: hermitage@cnz.com

Circa 1835. J. Ottis Adams and T.C. Steele, two renown
Indiana artists, set up their home and art studios on this large
estate that spans 6.5 acres. The Hoosier Group painted here in
the heart of the scenic Whitewater River Valley for several years.
Join Martha for a tour of this 19-room house, and then converse over refreshments in the living room or studios. A library
features a wood-burning fireplace, antique books and magazines. A 112-foot-long veranda with vintage furniture and a
hammock overlooks the picturesque grounds. The adjacent
Town Park and nearby lake offer many outdoor activities. Visit
the historic region of Metamora, a Canal town and South
Central area's covered bridge communities.

Innkeeper(s): Martha Shea. $75. 6 rooms with PB and 1 conference room.
Breakfast and snacks/refreshments included in rates. Types of meals: Full
gourmet bkfst, early coffee/tea and dinner. Beds: KDT. Reading lamp, ceiling
fan, clock radio, turn-down service and desk in room. Air conditioning. TV,
VCR, bicycles, library, parlor games and fireplace on premises. Antiquing,
beach, bicycling, canoeing/kayaking, downhill skiing, fishing, golf, hiking,
horseback riding, parks, shopping, sporting events, tennis, water sports,
wineries, Historic Canal Town and Metamora nearby.

Location: Country. Small town on Whitewater River.

Publicity: *Outdoor Indiana and National Register of Historic Places.*

Certificate may be used: Anytime, subject to availability.

Decatur   D8

Cragwood Inn B&B
303 N 2nd St
Decatur, IN 46733-1329
(219)728-2000
E-mail: cragwood@adamswells.com

Circa 1900. This Queen Anne Victorian with four porches,
gingerbread frosting, a turret and a graceful bay facade was
built by a Decatur banker. Finely carved oak is magnificently
displayed in the paneled ceilings, staircase and pillars of the
parlor. Ornate tin ceilings, beveled leaded-glass windows and a
crystal chandelier are among other highlights. Twin wicker beds
in the Garden Room looks out through a Palladian window.
Two other rooms have their own fireplace.

Innkeeper(s): George & Nancy Craig. $60-65. 4 rooms, 2 with PB, 2 with FP.
Breakfast and snacks/refreshments included in rates. Types of meals: Full
bkfst and early coffee/tea. Beds: QDT. Reading lamp, clock radio and desk in
room. Air conditioning. VCR, library, parlor games, telephone, fireplace and
beautiful flower gardens on premises. Antiquing and parks nearby.

Location: Small town.

Publicity: *Inside Chicago, Great Lakes Getaway and Christmas Victorian Craft.*

*"Your wonderful hospitality, beautiful home and company made my
trip that much more enjoyable."*

Certificate may be used: Sunday-Thursday, all year.

Evansville   K2

Cool Breeze Estate B&B
1240 Se 2nd St
Evansville, IN 47713-1304
(812)422-9635
Internet: www.coolbreezebb.com

Circa 1906. This prairie-style school home is surrounded by
more than an acre of grounds, ideal for those in search of
peace and quiet. Truck and automobile maker Joseph Graham
once lived here, as well as philanthropist Giltner Igleheart.
One room features the wallpaper mural, "Scenic America."
The same mural was chosen by
Jacqueline Kennedy to decorate the White House. The
sunny rooms have names such
as Margaret Mitchell or Bronte.
A zoo, art museum and riverboat casino are among the
nearby attractions.

Innkeeper(s): Katelin & David Hills. $85. 3 rooms with PB, 2 suites and 2
conference rooms. Breakfast included in rates. Types of meals: Full bkfst.
Beds: QD. TV, reading lamp, CD player, clock radio, telephone and desk in
room. Air conditioning. VCR, library, parlor games and fireplace on premises.
Antiquing, live theater, parks, shopping, sporting events, water sports and
university of Southern Indiana nearby.

Publicity: *Evansville Courier and Midwest Living.*

*"It was so much like discovering something wonderful from the past
and disappearing into the warmth of childhood again."*

Certificate may be used: Anytime; no restrictions.

Fort Wayne   C7

The Carole Lombard House B&B

704 Rockhill St
Fort Wayne, IN 46802-5918
(219)426-9896 (888)426-9896

Circa 1895. Jane Alice Peters, a.k.a. Carole Lombard, spent her first six years in this turn-of-the-century home located in Ft. Wayne's historic West-Central neighborhood. The innkeepers named two guest rooms in honor of Lombard and her second husband, Clark Gable. Each of these rooms features memorabilia from the Gable-Lombard romance. A video library with a collection of classic movies is available, including many of Lombard's films. The innkeepers provide information for a self-guided architectural tour of the historic area.

Innkeeper(s): Bev Fiandt. $75-85. 4 rooms with PB. Breakfast included in rates. Types of meals: Full bkfst and early coffee/tea. Beds: KQDT. Cable TV, reading lamp, clock radio and telephone in room. Air conditioning. VCR, bicycles and fireplace on premises. Antiquing, live theater, parks and sporting events nearby.

Location: City.

Publicity: *Playboy and Michigan Living.*

"The elegance and ambience are most appreciated."

Certificate may be used: Sunday-Thursday all year.

Fowler   D3

Pheasant Country B&B

900 E 5th St
Fowler, IN 47944-1518
(765)884-1252 (765)714-2896
E-mail: pheasantcountryinn@yahoo.com

Circa 1940. Situated on a tree-lined brick street in the heart of the small town's historic area east of the Benton County Court House, this English Colonial inn is just 25 minutes northwest of Purdue University. Feel welcomed by the friendly hospitality. Relax amid European antiques in the smoke-free environment that is pleasantly scented with flower and mint aromas. Guest bedrooms feature generous amenities. Wake up to a bountiful breakfast of scones, waffles, egg dishes and beverages while classic music plays in the background. Bicycles are available for leisurely exploring the surrounding scenery.

Innkeeper(s): June Gaylord. $49-89. 4 rooms, 1 with PB. Breakfast, afternoon tea and snacks/refreshments included in rates. Types of meals: Full gourmet bkfst, veg bkfst, early coffee/tea, gourmet lunch, gourmet dinner and room service. Beds: Q. Cable TV/VCR, videos, phone, clock, hair dryer, ironing board, iron, basket of toiletries, fruit basket, fresh flowers, coffeemaker, newspaper, magazines, chocolates, bottled water, central air and ceiling fan in room. Costa Rican coffee, herbal teas, computer, copier, library, gift & antique shop, massage/yoga instructor and bicycles on premises. Art galleries, bicycling, canoeing/kayaking, golf, hiking, horseback riding, live theater, museums, parks, tennis, Purdue sporting events and convocations, antique auctions every weekend, Wabash River, hunting (pheasant, rabbit, turkey and deer) nearby.

Location: Small town.

Publicity: *Benton Review, Lafayette Journal & Courier and Lafayette - WLFI-TV.*

Certificate may be used: Jan. 30 to Dec. 30, Sunday-Saturday.

Indianapolis   G5

Speedway B&B

1829 Cunningham Dr
Indianapolis, IN 46224-5338
(317)487-6531 (800)975-3412 Fax:(317)481-1825
Internet: www.speedwaybb.com
E-mail: speedwaybnb@msn.com

Circa 1906. This two-story white columned inn reflects a plantation-style architecture. The inn is situated on an acre of lawn and trees. The bed & breakfast has a homey decor that includes a wood-paneled common room and elegantly furnished guest rooms. Breakfast includes items such as homemade coffee cake and Danish or sausage and egg casserole. Nearby attractions include President Harrison's home, the Hall of Fame Museum and the largest city park in the nation, Eagle Creek Park.

Innkeeper(s): Pauline Grothe. $65-135. 5 rooms with PB. Breakfast included in rates. Types of meals: Full bkfst. Beds: KQD. Cable TV, reading lamp, clock radio and telephone in room. Air conditioning. VCR, fax, bicycles, parlor games and fireplace on premises. Antiquing, cross-country skiing, fishing, golf, live theater, parks, shopping, sporting events, tennis and water sports nearby.

Location: City.

"It is people like you who have given B&Bs such a good reputation."

Certificate may be used: Monday-Thursday, excluding special events, based upon availability.

The Tranquil Cherub

2164 N Capitol Ave
Indianapolis, IN 46202-1251
(317)923-9036 Fax:(317)923-8676
Internet: www.tranquilcherub.com
E-mail: reservations@tranquilcherub.com

Circa 1890. Visitors to the bustling Indianapolis area will appreciate the quiet elegance of the Tranquil Cherub, a Classical Revival home, five minutes from downtown. Guests may choose from the blue and taupe Wedgwood Room, which offers a mural headboard, or the Gatsby Room highlighted by an Art Deco-era four-poster cannonball bed. The jade-green and navy Rogers Room features stained glass and an oak bedroom set that originated in an old Chicago hotel. Grannies Suite comprises the third floor and is a spacious accommodation with an eclectic selection of antiques. Breakfast is served in the oak-paneled dining room or on a back deck overlooking the lily ponds.

Innkeeper(s): Thom & Barbara Feit. $85-125. 4 rooms, 3 with PB, 2 with FP, 1 suite. Breakfast and snacks/refreshments included in rates. Types of meals: Full gourmet bkfst, veg bkfst and early coffee/tea. Beds: KQT. Data port, cable TV, reading lamp, ceiling fan, snack bar, clock radio, telephone, desk and fireplace in room. Central air. VCR, fax, copier, library, fireplace and gift shop on premises. Antiquing, art galleries, bicycling, golf, hiking, live theater, museums, shopping, sporting events, tennis, wineries and hospital nearby.

Location: City.

Publicity: *Indianapolis Star and Indianapolis Monthly.*

Certificate may be used: Jan. 1 through Dec. 31, Sunday-Thursday. Not valid during special local events.

Knightstown F7

Old Hoosier House

7601 S Greensboro Pike
Knightstown, IN 46148-9613
(765)345-2969 (800)775-5315
E-mail: ktownbb@indy.net

Circa 1840. The Old Hoosier House was owned by the Elisha Scovell family, who were friends of President Martin Van Buren, and the president stayed overnight in the home. Features of the Victorian house include tall, arched windows and a gabled entrance. Rooms are decorated with antiques and lace curtains. Hearty Hoosier breakfasts include such specialties as a breakfast pizza of egg, sausage and cheese, and Melt-Away Puff Pancakes. The inn's eight acres are wooded, and the deck overlooks a pond on the fourth hole of the adjacent golf course.

Innkeeper(s): Jean & John Butler. $70-80. 3 rooms with PB, 1 with FP, 1 suite. Breakfast included in rates. Types of meals: Full bkfst, early coffee/tea, afternoon tea and snacks/refreshments. Beds: KQT. Reading lamp, stereo, refrigerator, ceiling fan, clock radio, telephone and desk in room. Air conditioning. TV, VCR, library and fireplace on premises. Handicap access. Antiquing, fishing, live theater, parks, shopping and sporting events nearby.
Location: Rural, next to 18-hole golf.
Publicity: *Indianapolis Star News, New Castle Courier-Times and Indianapolis Monthly.*

"We had such a wonderful time at your house. Very many thanks."
Certificate may be used: May through October, subject to availability.

Metamora G7

The Thorpe House Country Inn

19049 Clayborne St, PO Box 36
Metamora, IN 47030
(765)647-5425 (888)427-7932
Internet: www.metamora.com/thorpehouse
E-mail: thorpe_house@hotmail.com

Circa 1840. The steam engine still brings passenger cars and the gristmill still grinds cornmeal in historic Metamora. The Thorpe House is located one block from the canal. Rooms feature original pine and poplar floors, antiques, stenciling and country accessories. Enjoy a hearty breakfast selected from the inn's restaurant menu. (Popular items include homemade biscuits, egg dishes and sourdough pecan rolls.) Walk through the village to explore more than 100 shops.

Innkeeper(s): Mike & Jean Owens. $70-125. 5 rooms with PB, 1 suite. Breakfast and snacks/refreshments included in rates. Types of meals: Country bkfst, veg bkfst, early coffee/tea, lunch and picnic lunch. Restaurant on premises. Beds: KDT. Reading lamp, refrigerator, snack bar, clock radio, telephone and coffeemaker in room. Central air. TV, VCR, fax, parlor games, gift shops and pottery studio on premises. Amusement parks, antiquing, art galleries, beach, bicycling, canoeing/kayaking, fishing, golf, hiking, horseback riding, museums, parks, shopping, water sports, flea markets and bird sanctuary nearby.
Location: Restored 1840 canal-town village.
Publicity: *Cincinnati Enquirer, Chicago Sun-Times and Midwest Living.*

"Thanks to all of you for your kindness and hospitality during our stay."
Certificate may be used: April through November, Sunday through Thursday.

Middlebury A6

Bee Hive B&B

Box 1191
Middlebury, IN 46540-1191
(574)825-5023

Circa 1988. This family home is located on 39 acres in the Amish area of Middlebury and was constructed with hand-sawn lumber. Original primitive paintings by Miss Emma Schrock are part of the B&B's collectibles. There is also a collection of antique farm equipment. Guest rooms are in the farmhouse with the exception of Honey Comb Cottage which is a guest house with its own bath. If you'd like to help out with some of the farm chores and are an early riser see if you can coax Herb into letting you help. Afterwards you'll be ready for a full farm breakfast including Treva's home made granola and hearty breakfast casseroles. Ask for advice in discovering the best places to visit in the area.
Innkeeper(s): Herb & Treva Swarm. $65-85. 4 rooms, 1 with PB and 1 cottage. Breakfast included in rates. Types of meals: Country bkfst, early coffee/tea and snacks/refreshments. Beds: QD. TV, VCR, reading lamp, stereo, ceiling fan, clock radio, telephone and coffeemaker in room. Air conditioning. Fax, copier, parlor games and refrigerator on premises. Antiquing, beach, canoeing/kayaking, cross-country skiing, downhill skiing, fishing, golf, hiking, live theater, museums, parks, shopping, sporting events, tennis and Amish heartland tours nearby.
Location: Country.

"What a great place to rest the mind, body and soul."
Certificate may be used: Anytime, subject to availability.

Patchwork Quilt Country Inn

11748 CR 2
Middlebury, IN 46540
(574)825-2417 Fax:(574)825-5172
Internet: www.patchworkquiltinn.com
E-mail: stay@patchworkquiltinn.com

Circa 1875. Located in the heart of Indiana's Amish country, this inn offers comfortable lodging and fine food. Some of the recipes are regionally famous, such as the award-winning Buttermilk Pecan Chicken. All guest rooms feature handsome quilts and country decor, and The Lodge treats visitors to a 5-person hot tub and kitchenette. The smoke-free inn also is host to a gift shop, game room and nature trail.

Innkeeper(s): John & Adrienne Cohoat. $79-179. 15 rooms with PB, 2 suites and 6 conference rooms. Breakfast included in rates. Types of meals: Country bkfst, lunch, picnic lunch, snacks/refreshments and gourmet dinner. Beds: QD. Modem hook-up, TV, reading lamp, refrigerator, clock radio, coffeemaker, three with whirlpool tubs, 1 with hot tub and some with VCR in room. Central air. VCR, fax, copier, library, parlor games, telephone, fireplace, laundry facility, gift shop, game and fitness center, nature trail, meditation cabin, campfire area and movies on premises. Limited handicap access. Amusement parks, antiquing, art galleries, bicycling, canoeing/kayaking, cross-country skiing, downhill skiing, fishing, golf, hiking, horseback riding, live theater, museums, parks, shopping, sporting events, tennis, water sports, wineries and Amish buggy rides and tours nearby.
Location: Country. Amish Country.
Publicity: *Elkhart Truth, Goshen News, Detroit Free Press, Fox 28 TV, WTRE radio and CookingVillage.com.*

Certificate may be used: Anytime except Notre Dame football weekends and other special events.

Tiffany Powell's Bed & Breakfast

523 South Main St
Middlebury, IN 46540-9004
(574)825-5951 Fax:(574)825-2992
Internet: www.tiffanypowells.com
E-mail: tiff@npcc.net

Circa 1914. The porch of this B&B is a favorite spot for guests to sit and watch Amish buggies pass by, especially on Saturday nights. The inn features leaded and beveled glass and original oak floors and woodwork. Guest rooms reflect a fresh country decor with bright handmade quilts sewn by Judy's grandmother. Known locally and acknowledged nationally on the Oprah show for her hospitality, the innkeeper offers a full breakfast. Amish Sausage Casserole is a speciality of the house and is served in the dining room. Shipshewana is seven minutes away, and Amish markets and craft shops are nearby.

Innkeeper(s): Judy Powell. $89. 5 rooms, 3 with PB, 1 with FP. Afternoon tea and snacks/refreshments included in rates. Types of meals: Cont plus and early coffee/tea. Beds: QDT. Cable TV, reading lamp, ceiling fan, clock radio and turn-down service in room. Air conditioning. VCR, bicycles, parlor games, telephone and fireplace on premises. Antiquing, cross-country skiing, fishing, golf, live theater, parks, shopping, sporting events, tennis and water sports nearby.

Location: Small town.

Publicity: *South Bend Tribune, Goshen News and Oprah.*

Certificate may be used: Anytime.

Mishawaka   A5

The Beiger Mansion Inn

317 Lincoln Way E
Mishawaka, IN 46544-2012
(574)256-0365 (800)437-0131 Fax:(574)259-2622
Internet: www.beigermansion.com
E-mail: Ron@BeigerMansion.com

Circa 1903. This Neoclassical limestone mansion was built to satisfy Susie Beiger's wish to copy a friend's Newport, R.I., estate. Palatial rooms that were once a gathering place for local society now welcome guests who seek gracious accommodations. On the premises is a restaurant with a full bar and a pub. Notre Dame, St. Mary's and Indiana University in South Bend are nearby.

Innkeeper(s): Ron Montandon & Dennis Slade. $115-125. 6 rooms with PB, 1 suite. Breakfast included in rates. Types of meals: Full bkfst and gourmet dinner. Restaurant on premises. Beds: Q. Cable TV, reading lamp, clock radio, telephone and desk in room. Air conditioning. TV, VCR, fax, copier and fireplace on premises. Antiquing, fishing, golf, live theater, parks, sporting events and tennis nearby.

Location: City.

Publicity: *Tribune.*

"Can't wait until we return to Mishawaka to stay with you again!"

Certificate may be used: Year-round, except Notre Dame home football and special events.

Monticello   D4

The Victoria B&B

206 S Bluff St
Monticello, IN 47960-2309
(219)583-3440

This Queen Anne Victorian was built by innkeeper Karen McClintock's grandfather. Karen and husband, Steve, have filled the home with family antiques and collectibles, including a whimsical cow collection in the breakfast room. A grand, hand-carved oak staircase greets guests as they arrive. Rooms are decorated in a Victorian country theme, setting off the high ceilings and polished wood floors. The grounds boast old magnolia and maple trees and perennials planted by Karen's grandparents.

Innkeeper(s): Karen McClintock. $55-75. 3 rooms. Breakfast included in rates. Types of meals: Cont plus.

Certificate may be used: Oct. 30 to April 30, Monday-Thursday.

Nappanee   B6

Homespun Country Inn

PO Box 369
Nappanee, IN 46550
(574)773-2034 (800)311-2996 Fax:(574)773-3456
Internet: www.homespuninn.com
E-mail: home@hoosierlink.net

Circa 1902. Windows of stained and leaded glass create colorful prisms at this Queen Anne Victorian inn built in 1902. Quarter-sawn oak highlights the entry and first-floor common rooms. Comfortable antiques and family heirlooms accent the inn. Two parlors offer areas to read, do a jigsaw puzzle or watch satellite TV or a movie. Each guest bedroom displays photos of the home's original occupants. Early risers enjoying a cup of coffee or tea might see a passing horse and buggy while sitting on the porch swing. Breakfast is served in the dining room. Ask about the assortment of special packages and how to add a Homespun Memory Gift Bag to a reservation.

Innkeeper(s): Dianne & Dennis Debelak. $79. 5 rooms with PB. Breakfast and snacks/refreshments included in rates. Types of meals: Full bkfst and early coffee/tea. Beds: QDT. Cable TV, VCR, reading lamp, ceiling fan, clock radio and night lights in room. Air conditioning. Fax, copier, parlor games, telephone and fireplace on premises. Antiquing, golf, live theater, parks, shopping, sporting events and tennis nearby.

Location: Amish heritage.

Publicity: *The Elkhart Truth.*

"We have been telling all our friends about how wonderful your establishment is."

Certificate may be used: Any day January-April. Discount based on regular room rates. No other discount applies.

The Victorian Guest House

302 E Market St
Nappanee, IN 46550-2102
(574)773-4383
Internet: www.victorianb-b.com
E-mail: vghouse@bnin.net

Circa 1887. Listed in the National Register, this three-story Queen Anne Victorian inn was built by Frank Coppes, one of America's first noted kitchen cabinet makers. Nappanee's location makes it an ideal stopping point for those exploring the

heart of Amish country, or visiting the South Bend or chain of lakes areas. Visitors may choose from six guest rooms, including the Coppes Suite, with its original golden oak woodwork, antique tub and stained glass. Full breakfast is served at the antique 11-foot dining room table. Amish Acres is just one mile from the inn.

Innkeeper(s): Bruce & Vickie Hunsberger. $79-119. 6 rooms with PB. Breakfast and afternoon tea included in rates. Types of meals: Full bkfst, early coffee/tea and snacks/refreshments. Beds: QT. Cable TV, reading lamp, ceiling fan, clock radio, telephone and turn-down service in room. Air conditioning. Antiquing, live theater, shopping, sporting events and water sports nearby.

Location: City.

Publicity: *Goshen News.*

Certificate may be used: November-March, Monday-Thursday.

New Albany K6

Honeymoon Mansion B&B & Wedding Chapel

1014 E Main St
New Albany, IN 47150-5843
(812)945-0312 (800)759-7270 Fax:(812)945-6615
Internet: www.honeymoonmansion.com
E-mail: landon@honeymoonmansion.com

Circa 1850. The innkeepers at Honeymoon Mansion can provide guests with the flowers, wedding chapel and honeymoon suite. All you need to bring is a bride or groom. An ordained minister is on the premises and guests can marry or renew their vows in the inn's Victorian wedding chapel. However, one need not be a newlywed to enjoy this bed & breakfast. Canopy beds, stained-glass windows and heart-shaped rugs are a few of the romantic touches. Several suites include marble Jacuzzis flanked on four sides with eight-foot-high marble columns, creating a dramatic and elegant effect. The home itself, a pre-Civil War Italianate-style home listed in the state and national historic registers, boasts many fine period features. Gingerbread trim, intricate molding and a grand staircase add to the Victorian ambiance. Guests are treated to an all-you-can-eat country breakfast with items such as homemade breads, biscuits and gravy, eggs, sausage and potatoes.

Innkeeper(s): Landon Caldwell. $59-190. 12 rooms, 6 with PB, 1 with FP, 6 suites and 2 conference rooms. Breakfast and snacks/refreshments included in rates. Types of meals: Country bkfst and early coffee/tea. Beds: QD. Modem hook-up, cable TV, VCR, reading lamp, stereo, refrigerator, ceiling fan, snack bar, clock radio, coffeemaker, desk, hot tub/spa and fireplace in room. Air conditioning. Fax, copier, parlor games and telephone on premises. Handicap access. Amusement parks, antiquing, art galleries, bicycling, canoeing/kayaking, cross-country skiing, downhill skiing, fishing, golf, hiking, horseback riding, live theater, museums, parks, shopping, sporting events, tennis, water sports, wineries, three state parks, three caves, Culbertson Mansion, riverboat casino, Derby Dinner and Playhouse nearby.

Location: City. Mansion Row.

Publicity: *Courier-Journal, Evening News, Tribune. and WHAS TV.*

Certificate may be used: Anytime, Sunday-Thursday, excluding holidays and Kentucky Derby.

Rising Sun 18

The Jelley House Country Inn

222 S Walnut St
Rising Sun, IN 47040-1142
(812)438-2319
E-mail: jmoore@seidata.com

Circa 1847. This pre-Civil War Colonial changed hands many times before current innkeepers Jeff and Jennifer Moore purchased the place. Antiques decorate the interior, as well as an old pump organ and a baby grand piano. The front porch is lined with comfortable chairs for those who wish to relax. The home is just two blocks from Riverfront Park and the Ohio River, and the innkeepers offer bikes for guests who wish to ride around and explore the area.

Innkeeper(s): Jeff & Jennifer Moore. $65-150. 5 rooms, 1 suite. Breakfast included in rates. Types of meals: Cont plus. Beds: QDT. Cable TV, reading lamp, ceiling fan and clock radio in room. Air conditioning. VCR, bicycles, parlor games, telephone, fireplace and baby grand piano on premises. Antiquing, downhill skiing, fishing, golf, live theater, parks, shopping, sporting events and water sports nearby.

Location: City.

Publicity: *Recorded & News.*

"Beautifully decorated. You have preserved some of the old and new...enjoyed this home atmosphere."

Certificate may be used: Jan. 1-Dec. 30, no holidays, limit one coupon per stay.

Rockville G3

Billie Creek Inn

RR 2, Box 27, Billie Creek Village
Rockville, IN 47872
(765)569-3430 Fax:(765)569-3582
Internet: www.billiecreek.org
E-mail: villagers@ccsdana.net

Circa 1996. Although this inn was built recently, it rests on the outskirts of historic Billie Creek Village. The village is a non-profit, turn-of-the-century living museum, complete with 30 historic buildings and three covered bridges. Guests can explore an 1830s cabin, a farmstead, a general store and much more to experience how Americans lived in the 19th century. The innkeepers take part in the history, dressing in period costume. The inn is decorated in a comfortable, country style. The nine suites include the added amenity of a two-person whirlpool tub. All inn guests receive complimentary admission to Billie Creek Village. Coffee and continental breakfast fare are available around the clock. Special packages include canoeing and bike tours, Civil War Days and covered bridge festivals.

Innkeeper(s): Carol Gum. $49-99. 31 rooms with PB, 9 suites and 2 conference rooms. Breakfast included in rates. Types of meals: Cont. Beds: KD. Cable TV, reading lamp, refrigerator, snack bar, clock radio, telephone, desk and hot tub/spa in room. Air conditioning. VCR, fax, copier, pet boarding, historical village, general store, 7 p.m. player piano concerts nightly, crafts and heated pool mid-April through mid-November on premises. Handicap access. Antiquing, fishing, golf, live theater, parks, shopping, sporting events, tennis and water sports nearby.

Location: Country.

Publicity: *WTWO, WTHI and WBAK.*

Certificate may be used: Year-round, Sunday through Thursday nights except during special events and the Parke County Covered Bridge festival.

Knoll Inn

317 W High St
Rockville, IN 47872
(765)569-6345 (888)569-6345 Fax:(765)569-3445
Internet: www.coveredbridges.com/knoll-inn/
E-mail: knollinn@abcs.com

Circa 1842. This inn, of Greek Revival and Italianate influence, is situated in the historic district. Renovated recently, it offers suites with whirlpool tubs and romantic decor. Farmer's Strada is a favored dish for breakfast, which also includes freshly baked breads and muffins, homemade preserves and fresh fruit such as strawberries and peaches in season. The area offers 32 covered bridges for exploring.

Innkeeper(s): Mark & Sharon Nolin. $95-125. 3 suites and 1 conference room. Breakfast included in rates. Types of meals: Full bkfst and early coffee/tea. Beds: Q. Cable TV, VCR, ceiling fan, hot tub/spa and two suites with whirlpool spas in room. Air conditioning. Spa and telephone on premises. Antiquing, fishing, golf, parks, shopping, sporting events, tennis, water sports and covered bridges nearby.

Location: Small town.

Certificate may be used: Nov. 1 to May 1, Sunday through Wednesday nights. Subject to availability.

Suits Us B&B

514 N College St
Rockville, IN 47872-1511
(765)569-5660 (888)478-4878
E-mail: liannaw@wico.net

Circa 1883. Sixty miles west of Indianapolis is this stately Colonial Revival inn, where Woodrow Wilson, Annie Oakley and James Witcomb Riley were once guests of the Strause Family. The inn offers video library and bicycles. There are 32 covered bridges to visit in the small, surrounding county. Turkey Run State Park is nearby. The Ernie Pyle State Historic Site, Raccoon State Recreation Area and four golf courses are within easy driving distance.

Innkeeper(s): Andy & Lianna Willhite. $60-150. 4 rooms with PB, 1 suite. Breakfast included in rates. Types of meals: Full bkfst and early coffee/tea. Beds: KQD. Cable TV, VCR, reading lamp, stereo, ceiling fan and clock radio in room. Air conditioning. Bicycles, telephone, fireplace and movie library on premises. Antiquing, fishing, golf, parks, shopping and water sports nearby.

Location: City.

Publicity: *Touring America and Traces Historic Magazine.*

Certificate may be used: Nov. 30 to April 30; Sunday-Thursday. Closed Dec. 22 to Jan. 3.

South Bend   A5

Oliver Inn

630 W Washington St
South Bend, IN 46601-1444
(574)232-4545 (888)697-4466 Fax:(574)288-9788
Internet: www.oliverinn.com
E-mail: oliver@michiana.org

Circa 1886. This stately Queen Anne Victorian sits amid 30 towering maples and was once home to Josephine Oliver Ford, daughter of James Oliver, of chilled plow fame. Located in

South Bend's historic district, this inn offers a comfortable library and nine inviting guest rooms, some with built-in fireplaces or double Jacuzzis. The inn is within walking distance of downtown and is next door to the Tippecanoe Restaurant in the Studebaker Mansion.

Innkeeper(s): Richard & Venera Monahan. $95-170. 9 rooms, 7 with PB, 2 with FP, 3 suites and 1 conference room. Breakfast and snacks/refreshments included in rates. Types of meals: Full bkfst and early coffee/tea. Beds: KQ. Cable TV, reading lamp, ceiling fan, telephone, desk, hot tub/spa and several with double whirlpool tubs in room. Air conditioning. Fax, parlor games, fireplace and baby grand with computer disk system on premises. Limited handicap access. Antiquing, canoeing/kayaking, cross-country skiing, fishing, live theater, museums, parks, shopping, sporting events, water sports, fine dining, Amish country and Notre Dame nearby.

Location: City. Lake Michigan (35 miles), Chicago (90 miles).

Certificate may be used: January through December, Sunday-Thursday.

Valparaiso   B3

The Inn at Aberdeen

3158 South SR 2
Valparaiso, IN 46385
(219)465-3753 Fax:(219)465-9227
Internet: www.valpomall.com/theinn
E-mail: inn@innataberdeen.com

Circa 1890. An old stone wall borders this inn, once a dairy farm, horse farm and then hunting lodge. Recently renovated and expanded, this Victorian farmhouse is on more than an acre. An elegant getaway, there's a solarium, library, dining room and parlor for relaxing. The inn offers traditional Queen Anne furnishings in the guest rooms. The Timberlake Suites include fireplaces, two-person Jacuzzi tubs and balconies. The Aberdeen Suite includes a living room and fireplace, while the Alloway Suite offers a living room, kitchenette and a balcony. A conference center on the property is popular for executive meetings and special events, and there is a picturesque gazebo overlooking the inn's beautifully landscaped lawns and English gardens. Golf packages and mystery weekends have received enthusiastic response from guests. There is a golf course, spa and microbrewery adjacent to the inn.

Innkeeper(s): Bill Simon. $99-185. 11 rooms, 10 with FP, 11 suites and 1 conference room. Breakfast and snacks/refreshments included in rates. Types of meals: Full gourmet bkfst and early coffee/tea. Beds: KQ. Cable TV, VCR, reading lamp, ceiling fan, clock radio, telephone, desk and hot tub/spa in room. Air conditioning. Fax, copier, swimming, bicycles, tennis, library, parlor games, fireplace, snack bar and gazebo on premises. Handicap access. Antiquing, cross-country skiing, downhill skiing, fishing, golf, live theater, parks, shopping, sporting events, tennis and water sports nearby.

Location: Rural.

Publicity: *Midwest Living, Chicago Magazine, Chicago Tribune, Country Inns and Indiana Business Magazine ("Best Retreat Site").*

"Every time we have the good fortune to spend an evening here, it is like a perfect fairy tale, transforming us into King and Queen."

Certificate may be used: Sunday through Thursdays only, year-round, excluding holidays and special events.

Iowa

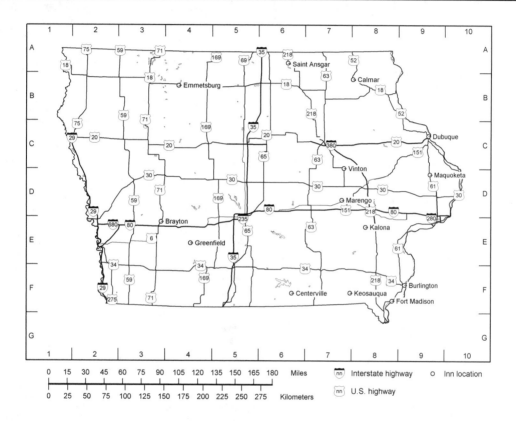

	Miles	Interstate highway	Inn location
	U.S. highway		

Bentonsport   *F8*

Mason House Inn of Bentonsport

21982 Hawk Dr
Bentonsport, IA 52565
(319)592-3133 (800)592-3133
Internet: www.masonhouseinn.com
E-mail: stay@masonhouseinn.com

Circa 1846. A Murphy-style copper bathtub folds down out of the wall at this unusual inn built by Mormon craftsmen, who stayed in Bentonsport for three years on their trek to Utah. More than half of the furniture is original to the home, including a nine-foot walnut headboard and a nine-foot mirror. This is the oldest operating pre-Civil War steamboat inn in Iowa. Guests can imagine the days when steamboats made their way up and down the Des Moines River, while taking in the scenery. A full breakfast is served, but if guests crave a mid-day snack, each room is equipped with its own stocked cookie jar.

Innkeeper(s): Chuck & Joy Hanson. $59-95. 9 rooms with PB, 1 cottage and 1 conference room. Breakfast included in rates. Types of meals: Full bkfst and early coffee/tea. Beds: KQD. Reading lamp and filled cookie jar in room. Air conditioning. Telephone and fireplace on premises. Handicap access. Antiquing, cross-country skiing and shopping nearby.

Location: Rural by river.

Publicity: *Des Moines Register, Decatur Herald & Review, AAA Home & Away and Country Magazine.*

"The attention to detail was fantastic, food was wonderful and the setting was fascinating."

Certificate may be used: Anytime, subject to availability.

Brayton   E3

Hallock House B&B

PO Box 94, 3265 Jay Ave
Brayton, IA 50042-0019
(712)549-2449 (800)945-0663
E-mail: halhsebb@metc.net

Circa 1882. Innkeeper Ruth Barton's great-great uncle, Isaac Hallock, built this Queen Anne Victorian. The home is an architectural gem, featuring high ceilings, ornate woodwork, carved pocket doors and a built-in china cupboard. And as is the Victorian tradition, several porches decorate the exterior. The home is across the street from the site of an old stagecoach stop, which bought an abundance of cattlemen into town, many of whom stayed in the Hallock House. The innkeepers offer stable facilities and an exercise area for guests traveling with horses.

Innkeeper(s): Guy & Ruth Barton. $50. 2 rooms with PB. Breakfast included in rates. Types of meals: Full bkfst. Beds: QD. Reading lamp, ceiling fan and clock radio in room. Air conditioning. VCR, bicycles, pet boarding, telephone and fireplace on premises. Antiquing, fishing, parks and shopping nearby.

Location: Country.

Certificate may be used: Anytime, subject to availability. Reservation required.

Burlington   F9

Schramm House B&B

616 Columbia St
Burlington, IA 52601
(800)683-7117 Fax:(319)754-0373
Internet: www.visit.schramm.com
E-mail: visit@schramm.com

Circa 1866. "Colossal" would be an excellent word to describe this Queen Anne Victorian. The home is an impressive site in this Burlington historic district. The exterior is brick on the first story with clapboard on the second, and a third-story tower is one of the architectural highlights. Inside, the parquet floors and woodwork have been restored to their 19th-century grandeur. The home was built just after the Civil War by a local department store owner. Additions were made in the 1880s. Eventually, the home was converted into apartments, so the innkeepers took on quite a task refurbishing the place back to its original state. The Victorian is decorated with the innkeepers collection of antiques. One particularly appealing guest room includes an exposed brick wall and tin ceiling. Breakfast might begin with a baked pear topped with toasted almonds and a raspberry sauce. From there, freshly baked muffins arrive, followed by an entree, perhaps a frittata or French toast. All courses are served with fine china and crystal. The home is just six blocks from the Mississippi, and don't pass up a walk down the historic Snake Alley.

Innkeeper(s): Sandy & Bruce Morrison. $95-150. 5 rooms with PB. Breakfast included in rates. Types of meals: Full bkfst and early coffee/tea. Beds: Q. Reading lamp, ceiling fan, clock radio, turn-down service, desk, robes and hair dryers in room. VCR, fax, library, parlor games, telephone and fireplace on premises. Antiquing, fishing, golf, parks, shopping and tennis nearby.

Location: Small town historic district.

Publicity: *Hawk Eye.*

Certificate may be used: Anytime, subject to availability.

Calmar   B8

Calmar Guesthouse

103 W North St
Calmar, IA 52132-7605
(563)562-3851
E-mail: lbkruse@acegroup.cc

Circa 1890. This beautifully restored Victorian home was built by John B. Kay, a lawyer and poet. Stained-glass windows, carved moldings, an oak and walnut staircase and gleaming woodwork highlight the gracious interior. A grandfather clock ticks in the living room. In the foyer, a friendship yellow rose is incorporated into the stained-glass window pane. Breakfast is served in the formal dining room. The Laura Ingalls Wilder Museum is nearby in Burr Oak. The Bily Brothers Clock Museum, Smallest Church, Luther College, Niagara Cave, Lake Meyer and Norwegian Museum are located nearby.

Innkeeper(s): Lucille Kruse. $59-65. Call inn for details. Breakfast included in rates. Beds: Q. Cable TV, reading lamp and clock in room. Air conditioning. VCR, bicycles, library, parlor games and telephone on premises. Antiquing, canoeing/kayaking, cross-country skiing, fishing, live theater, parks and shopping nearby.

Location: City.

Publicity: *Iowa Farmer Today, Calmar Courier, Minneapolis Star-Tribune, Home and Away and Iowan.*

"What a delight it was to stay here. No one could have made our stay more welcome or enjoyable."

Certificate may be used: Monday to Thursday, April to October only.

Centerville   F6

One of A Kind

314 W State St
Centerville, IA 52544
(641)437-4540 Fax:(641)437-4540
Internet: www.oneofakindbandb.com
E-mail: jjstuff@sirisonline.com

Circa 1867. This large, three-story brick home with mansard roof and tall bays is the second oldest house in town. The innkeeper has filled the inn with "One of a Kind" craft and decorative items for sale, created on the premises or by local artisans. There is also a tea room, popular for its chicken soup and homemade croissant sandwiches, so of course you can expect a yummy breakfast, as well. Guest quarters are decorated with antiques and reproductions spiced with a variety of collectibles. The largest fish hatchery in the world is a short drive away at Lake Rathbun, but there is plenty to do within walking distance.

Innkeeper(s): Jack & Joyce Stufflebeem. $40-70. 5 rooms, 3 with PB. Breakfast and snacks/refreshments included in rates. Types of meals: Full bkfst, early coffee/tea, lunch, picnic lunch, afternoon tea and gourmet dinner. Beds: QDT. Cable TV, reading lamp, ceiling fan and turn-down service in room. Air conditioning. VCR, fax, copier, parlor games, telephone and tea room on premises. Antiquing, fishing, golf, live theater, parks, shopping, sporting events, tennis and water sports nearby.

Location: Small town.

Certificate may be used: Anytime, subject to availability.

Dubuque C9

The Hancock House

1105 Grove Ter
Dubuque, IA 52001-4644
(563)557-8989 Fax:(563)583-0813
Internet: www.thehancockhouse.com
E-mail: chuckdbq@aol.com

Circa 1891. Victorian splendor can be found at The Hancock House, one of Dubuque's most striking examples of Queen Anne architecture. Rooms feature period furnishings and offer views of the Mississippi River states of Iowa, Illinois and Wisconsin. The Hancock House, listed in the National Register, boasts several unique features, including a fireplace judged blue-ribbon best at the 1893 World's Fair in Chicago. Guests can enjoy the porch swings, wicker furniture and spectacular views from the wraparound front porch.

Innkeeper(s): Chuck & Susan Huntley. $80-175. 9 rooms with PB, 3 with FP, 4 suites. Breakfast included in rates. Types of meals: Full bkfst and early coffee/tea. Beds: Q. Cable TV, reading lamp, clock radio, desk and feather mattress in room. Air conditioning. Fax, copier, parlor games, telephone, fireplace and gift shop on premises. Antiquing, cross-country skiing, downhill skiing, fishing, golf, live theater, parks, shopping, sporting events, tennis, water sports and riverboat casino nearby.

Location: City.

Publicity: *Victorian Sampler (Cover).*

Certificate may be used: Nov. 1 to April 30, Sunday through Thursday.

Lighthouse Valleyview B&B Inn

15931 Lore Mound Rd
Dubuque, IA 52002
(563)583-7327 (800)407-7023
Internet: www.lighthousevalleyview.com
E-mail: lhthse@mcleodusa.net

Circa 1960. Although 12 miles from the nearest body of water, this recently built lighthouse has a gift shop inside. To arrive, guests drive past farms and cornfields. Once inside the building, on clear days they can see views from the top that include three states: Iowa, Illinois and Wisconsin. Other rooms at the hilltop country house are decorated in themes such as Oriental, Safari and Old West. The Nautilus Room offers a collection of decorative lighthouses. There is an indoor pool, hot tub and fireplace for guest use. Coconut Praline French Toast is a favorite breakfast dish.

Innkeeper(s): Jo Ann & Bill Klauer. $75-150. 5 rooms, 3 with PB, 1 with FP, 1 with HT, 1 two-bedroom suite. Breakfast, snacks/refreshments and wine included in rates. Types of meals: Country bkfst, early coffee/tea, picnic lunch and afternoon tea. Beds: KQ. Modem hook-up, cable TV, VCR, reading lamp, stereo, refrigerator, ceiling fan, clock radio, telephone, coffeemaker, hot tub/spa, fireplace and hair dryers in room. Central air. Fax, copier, spa, swimming, sauna, bicycles, library, laundry facility and gift shop on premises. Limited handicap access. Antiquing, art galleries, bicycling, canoeing/kayaking, cross-country skiing, downhill skiing, fishing, golf, hiking, horseback riding, live theater, museums, parks, shopping, sporting events, tennis, water sports, wineries, riverboat gambling and greyhound racing nearby.

Location: Country.

Publicity: *National/international magazines, newspapers and local radio stations.*

Certificate may be used: Anytime, Sunday-Thursday, except holidays.

The Mandolin Inn

199 Loras Blvd
Dubuque, IA 52001-4857
(563)556-0069 (800)524-7996 Fax:(563)556-0587
Internet: www.mandolininn.com
E-mail: innkeeper@mandolininn.com

Circa 1908. This handicapped-accessible three-story brick Edwardian with Queen Anne wraparound veranda boasts a mosaic-tiled porch floor. Inside are inlaid mahogany and rosewood floors, bay windows and a turret that starts in the parlor and ascends to the second-floor Holly Marie Room, decorated in a wedding motif. This room features a seven-piece Rosewood bedroom suite and a crystal chandelier. A gourmet breakfast is served in the dining room with a fantasy forest mural from the turn of the century. There is an herb garden outside the kitchen. Located just 12 blocks away, is the fabulous National Mississippi River Museum and Aquarium. The inn can equally accommodate both business and pleasure travel.

Innkeeper(s): Amy Boynton. $85-150. 8 rooms, 6 with PB and 2 conference rooms. Breakfast included in rates. Types of meals: Full gourmet bkfst and early coffee/tea. Beds: KQ. Cable TV, reading lamp, clock radio and desk in room. Central air. Fax and telephone on premises. Antiquing, cross-country skiing, downhill skiing, live theater, parks, shopping, sporting events and water sports nearby.

Location: City.

"From the moment we entered the Mandolin, we felt at home. I know we'll be back."

Certificate may be used: Nov. 1 through Aug. 31, Sunday through Thursday, except for holidays.

Emmetsburg B4

Queen Marie Victorian B&B

707 Harrison St
Emmetsburg, IA 50536-1351
(712)852-4700 (800)238-9485 Fax:(712)852-3090
Internet: www.nwiowabb.com/queen.htm
E-mail: innkeepr@ncn.net

Circa 1890. Infused with a small-town atmosphere, this showplace Victorian home boasts remarkable woodwork, an open staircase with carved oak and amazing craftsmanship that befits its royal name. Enjoy the warmth of the living room's brass-laced fireplace. Elegant antiques accent the guest bedrooms that are named after their decorative color. After a restful sleep, start the day with a satisfying breakfast. Relax on the front porch swing. The state's Great Lakes area is just minutes away.

Innkeeper(s): Peggy & Paul Osterman. $55-70. 5 rooms, 3 with PB. Breakfast included in rates. Types of meals: Country bkfst, veg bkfst and early coffee/tea. Beds: KQDT. Cable TV, reading lamp, clock radio, turn-down service and desk in room. Central air. Antiquing, bicycling, canoeing/kayaking, cross-country skiing, fishing, golf, parks, shopping, water sports and Nature Center nearby.

Location: City.

Certificate may be used: Anytime, subject to availability, from Oct. 15 to May 15.

Fort Madison — F8

Kingsley Inn

707 Avenue H (Hwy 61)
Fort Madison, IA 52627
(319)372-7074 (800)441-2327 Fax:(319)372-7096
Internet: www.kingsleyinn.com
E-mail: kingsley@interl.net

Circa 1858. Overlooking the Mississippi River, this century-old inn is located in downtown Fort Madison. Though fur-

nished with antiques, all 17 rooms offer modern amenities and private baths (some with whirlpools and fireplaces) as well as river views. A two-bedroom, two-bath suite also is available. There is a restaurant, Alphas on the Riverfront, on the premises.

Innkeeper(s): Alida Willis. $85-185. 17 rooms with PB, 1 suite and 1 conference room. Breakfast included in rates. Types of meals: Full bkfst. Restaurant on premises. Beds: KQD. Cable TV, VCR, reading lamp and wireless Internet in room. Air conditioning. Fax, telephone, elevator and off-street parking on premises. Antiquing, fishing, shopping, historic sites including Nauvoo, IL and casino nearby.

Location: City. On Mississippi River.

Publicity: *Midwest Living, AAA and Rail Fan & Railroad.*

Certificate may be used: Anytime, November-April, subject to availability.

Greenfield — E4

The Brass Lantern

2446 State Hwy 92
Greenfield, IA 50849-9757
(641)743-2031 (888)743-2031 Fax:(515)343-7500
Internet: www.brasslantern.com
E-mail: info@brasslantern.com

Circa 1918. Located on 20 acres, just minutes from the famous bridges of Madison County, this B&B is highlighted by an indoor pool complex with a curving 40-foot pool. Spacious,

luxuriously appointed guest rooms overlook the pool and rolling countryside and share the use of a fully furnished kitchenette. A hearty breakfast is served next door in the formal dining room of the antique-filled 1918 farm house.

Innkeeper(s): Terry & Margie Moore. $100-195. 3 rooms, 2 with PB. Breakfast included in rates. Types of meals: Full bkfst, early coffee/tea and snacks/refreshments. Beds: Q. Cable TV, stereo and telephone in room. Air conditioning. TV, fax and copier on premises. Antiquing, fishing, golf, shopping and hunting nearby.

Location: Country.

"Iowa is a beautiful place and The Brass Lantern is its crown jewel!"
Certificate may be used: Nov. 15-Feb. 15, Monday-Thursday, holidays excluded.

Kalona — E8

Carriage House Bed & Breakfast

1140 Larch Ave
Kalona, IA 52247-9101
(319)656-3824
Internet: www.carriagehousebb.net
E-mail: chouse@kctc.net

For a peaceful getaway, this 15-acre rural setting with neighboring Amish farms is a relaxing choice. Accommodations include the main house and the carriage house, which was built by the host. Gather in the spacious living room, or sit on the porch swing. Comfortable guest bedrooms feature antique furnishings and colorful quilts. A satisfying hearty breakfast is served in the dining room. Play golf at a nearby course, or swim in the local public pool. Buggy rides can be arranged.

Innkeeper(s): Dan & Edie Kemp. Call for rates. Call inn for details. Breakfast included in rates. Types of meals: Country bkfst, veg bkfst, early coffee/tea, picnic lunch, dinner and room service. Antiquing, art galleries, bicycling, fishing, golf, hiking, live theater, museums, parks, shopping, sporting events & tennis nearby.

Publicity: *IA City Press Citizen, Cedar Rapids Gazette and Arrington's Journal.*

Certificate may be used: Anytime, subject to availability.

Keosauqua — F7

Hotel Manning

100 Van Buren St
Keosauqua, IA 52565
(319)293-3232 (800)728-2718 Fax:(319)293-9960
E-mail: hotelman@netins.net

Circa 1899. This historic riverfront inn offers a peek at bygone days. Its steamboat gothic exterior is joined by an interior that strives for historic authenticity. All bedrooms are furnished with

antiques. Lacey-Keosauqua State Park and Lake Sugema are within easy driving distance. Inn guests enjoy a full breakfast. There is a 19-room, modern motel adjacent to the inn.

Innkeeper(s): Ron & Melinda. $40-120. 19 rooms, 11 with PB and 1 conference room. Breakfast included in rates. Beds: QD. Reading lamp and ceiling fan in room. Air conditioning. VCR, fax, copier, parlor games, telephone and 19-room modern motel adjacent on premises. Antiquing, fishing, parks, shopping and nature trails nearby.

Location: Waterfront. Small town on riverfront.

Publicity: *Midwest Living.*

Certificate may be used: Sunday-Thursday, May-October; anytime, November to April.

Maquoketa — D9

Squiers Manor B&B

418 W Pleasant St
Maquoketa, IA 52060-2847
(319)652-6961
Internet: www.squiersmanor.com
E-mail: innkeeper@squiersmanor.com

Circa 1882. Innkeepers Virl and Kathy Banowetz are ace antique dealers, who along with owning one of the Midwest's largest antique shops, have refurbished this elegant, Queen Anne Victorian. The inn is furnished with period antiques that are beyond compare. Guest rooms boast museum-quality pieces such as a Victorian brass bed with lace curtain wings and inlaid mother-of-pearl or an antique mahogany bed with carved birds and flowers. Six guest rooms include whirlpool tubs, and one includes a unique Swiss shower. The innkeepers restored the home's original woodwork, shuttered-windows, fireplaces, gas and electric chandeliers and stained- and engraved-glass windows back to their former glory. They also recently renovated the mansion's attic ballroom into two luxurious suites. The Loft, which is made up of three levels, features pine and wicker furnishings, a sitting room and gas-burning wood stove. On the second level, there is a large Jacuzzi, on the third, an antique queen-size bed. The huge Ballroom Suite boasts 24-foot ceilings, oak and pine antiques, gas-burning wood stove and a Jacuzzi snuggled beside a dormer window. Suite guests enjoy breakfast delivered to their rooms. Other guests feast on an array of mouth-watering treats, such as home-baked breads, seafood quiche and fresh fruits. Evening desserts are served by candlelight.

Innkeeper(s): Virl & Kathy Banowetz. $80-195. 8 rooms with PB, 3 suites. Breakfast included in rates. Types of meals: Full gourmet bkfst. Beds: KQT. Antiquing, cross-country skiing, downhill skiing, fishing, parks, shopping and water sports nearby.

Publicity: *Des Moines Register Datebook and Daily Herald.*

"We couldn't have asked for a more perfect place to spend our honeymoon. The service was excellent and so was the food! It was an exciting experience that we will never forget!"

Certificate may be used: Sunday-Thursday, except in October, Valentine's week, or on holidays.

Marengo   D7

Loy's Farm B&B

2077 KK Ave
Marengo, IA 52301
(319)642-7787
E-mail: lbw20771@ia.net

Circa 1976. This attractive two-story farm home is located just minutes from Iowa's popular Amana Colonies. The inn is the base for a large corn and soybean operation. Loy delights in spoiling her guests with hearty country breakfasts, and arrangements also may be made for farm dinners or picnic baskets upon early reservations.

Innkeeper(s): Loy & Robert Walker. $55-80. 3 rooms, 1 with PB. Breakfast and snacks/refreshments included in rates. Types of meals: Full bkfst & gourmet dinner. Beds: QT. Reading lamp & desk in room. Air conditioning. VCR, copier, parlor games, telephone, fireplace & large recreation room on premises. Antiquing, fishing, live theater, parks, shopping, sporting events, water sports, Tanger Outlet Center, golf, tennis, farm tour, dinner by reservation & hunting nearby.

Location: Country. Heart of Iowa. I-80 exit 216.

Publicity: *Country, Outlook, Cedar Rapids Gazette, Ford Times and Iowa Farmer Today.*

"Thanks again for all your hospitality."

Certificate may be used: Jan. 1 to Dec. 20, Monday through Thursday.

Saint Ansgar   A6

Blue Belle Inn B&B

PO Box 205, 513 W 4th St
Saint Ansgar, IA 50472-0205
(641)713-3113 (877)713-3113
Internet: www.bluebelleinn.com
E-mail: innkeeper@bluebelleinn.com

Circa 1896. This home was purchased from a Knoxville, Tenn., mail-order house. It's difficult to believe that stunning features, such as a tin ceiling, stained-glass windows, intricate wood-

work and pocket doors could have come via the mail, but these original items are still here for guests to admire. Rooms are named after books special to the innkeeper. Four of the rooms include a whirlpool tub for two, and the Never Neverland room has a clawfoot tub. Other rooms offer a skylight, fireplace or perhaps a white iron bed. During the Christmas season, every room has its own decorated tree. The innkeeper hosts a variety of themed luncheons, dinners and events, such as the April in Paris cooking workshop, Mother's Day brunches, the "Some Enchanted Evening" dinner, Murder Mysteries, Ladies nights, Writer's Retreats, quilting seminars and horse-drawn sleigh rides.

Innkeeper(s): Sherrie Hansen. $70-160. 6 rooms, 5 with PB, 2 with FP, 2 suites and 2 conference rooms. Breakfast included in rates. Types of meals: Full gourmet bkfst, early coffee/tea, gourmet lunch, afternoon tea, snacks/refreshments, gourmet dinner and room service. Restaurant on premises. Beds: KQT. TV, VCR, reading lamp, stereo, clock radio, desk and Jacuzzi for two in room. Air conditioning. Fax, library, parlor games, telephone, fireplace, kitchenette, Internet access, piano, treadmill and movies on premises. Antiquing, canoeing/kayaking, fishing, golf, parks, shopping, water sports and hunting nearby.

Location: Small town.

Publicity: *Minneapolis Star Tribune, Post-Bulletin, Midwest Living, Country, AAA Home & Away, Des Moines Register, Country Home, Iowan Magazine, American Patchwork and Quilting and HGTV Restore America.*

Certificate may be used: Nov. 1-April 30, Monday-Thursday nights only, holidays excluded, Dec. 26-31 excluded, subject to availability.

Vinton   C7

Lion & The Lamb B&B

913 2nd Ave
Vinton, IA 52349-1729
(319)472-5086 (888)390-5262 Fax:(319)472-5086
Internet: www.lionlamb.com
E-mail: lionlamb@lionlamb.com

Circa 1892. This Queen Anne Victorian, a true "Painted Lady," boasts a stunning exterior with intricate chimneys, gingerbread trim, gables and turrets. The home still maintains its original pocket doors and parquet flooring, and antiques add to the nostalgic flavor. One room boasts a 150-year-old bedroom set. Breakfasts, as any meal in such fine a house should, are served on china. Succulent French toast topped with powdered sugar and a rich strawberry sauce is a specialty.

Innkeeper(s): John Paul Blix. $75-129. 6 rooms with PB, 2 with FP. Breakfast included in rates. Types of meals: Full bkfst and early coffee/tea. Beds: KQ. TV, reading lamp, ceiling fan and coffeemaker in room. Air conditioning. Parlor games and telephone on premises. Antiquing, cross-country skiing, fishing, golf, live theater, parks, shopping, tennis and water sports nearby.

Location: City.

Publicity: *Cedar Valley Times, Waterloo Courier, Cedar Rapids Gazette, Country Discoveries Magazine and KWWL-Channel 7 Neighborhood News.*

"It is a magical place!"

Certificate may be used: Sunday to Thursday, September to May, excluding holidays and weekends.

Kansas

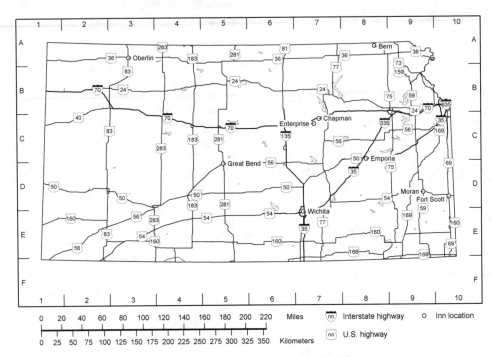

Scale:
| 0 | 20 | 40 | 60 | 80 | 100 | 120 | 140 | 160 | 180 | 200 | 220 | Miles |

| 0 | 25 | 50 | 75 | 100 | 125 | 150 | 175 | 200 | 225 | 250 | 275 | 300 | 325 | 350 | Kilometers |

nn Interstate highway   o Inn location
nn U.S. highway

Bern   A6

Lear Acres B&B
RR 1 Box 31
Bern, KS 66408-9715
(785)336-3903

Circa 1918. A working farm just south of the Nebraska border, Lear Acres is exactly the down-home setting it appears to be. The two-story farmhouse features two spacious guest rooms, all with views of the surrounding countryside. Many of the inn's furnishings are period pieces from the early 1900s. Guests will be greeted by a menagerie of farm pets and animals, adding to the distinctly country atmosphere. The full breakfast features food from the innkeepers' farm and garden.

Innkeeper(s): Toby Lear. $38-45. 2 rooms. Breakfast included in rates. Types of meals: Full bkfst. Reading lamp, refrigerator, ceiling fan, telephone, turn-down service, desk and clock in room. Air conditioning. TV, VCR, fireplace and working farm on premises. Antiquing and casinos nearby.

Location: Country. B&B on a working farm.

Certificate may be used: Anytime, subject to availability.

Chapman   C7

Windmill Inn B&B
1787 Rain Rd
Chapman, KS 67431-9317
(785)263-8755
Internet: www.access-one.com/windmill
E-mail: windmillinn@access-one.com

Circa 1917. The Windmill Inn is a place of memories. Many were created by the innkeeper's grandparents, who built the home. Others are the happy remembrances guests take home. The home is filled with antiques and family heirlooms. Stained glass and a window seat add to the charm. Evening meals or picnic lunches are also available. The wraparound porch offers a relaxing swing, and on starry nights, the outdoor spa is the place to be. Historic Abilene is just a few miles down the road, offering a glimpse of an authentic Old West town, located on the Chisolm Trail.

Innkeeper(s): Tim & Deb Sanders. $80-100. 4 rooms. Breakfast included in rates. Types of meals: Full bkfst.

Certificate may be used: Year-round, Sunday through Thursday, holidays excluded.

Emporia — C8

The White Rose Inn
901 Merchant St
Emporia, KS 66801-2813
(620)343-6336 (800)288-6198
E-mail: whiterose@carrollsweb.com

Circa 1902. Emporia is a Midwest college town, and the White Rose Inn is a mere three blocks from Emporia State University. This Queen Anne Victorian home offers three private suites for its guests, all with a sitting room and queen beds. Each morning, guests will be treated to a different and delicious menu. Guests who so desire may have breakfast in bed, and the innkeepers will happily arrange for a massage, manicure or pedicure. The inn also hosts weddings and family reunions.
Innkeeper(s): Samuel & Lisa Tosti. $59-159. 8 rooms with PB, 4 suites. Breakfast included in rates. Types of meals: Full gourmet bkfst, early coffee/tea, gourmet lunch, picnic lunch, afternoon tea, snacks/refreshments, gourmet dinner and room service. Beds: Q. Cable TV, reading lamp, clock radio and desk in room. Air conditioning. VCR, parlor games and telephone on premises. Antiquing, fishing, live theater, parks and sporting events nearby.
Location: City.
Certificate may be used: Sunday through Thursday, large suites only.

Enterprise — C7

Ehrsam Place Bed and Breakfast Inn
PO BOX 52
Enterprise, KS 67441-0052
(785)263-8747 Fax:(785)263-8548
Internet: www.ehrsamplace.com
E-mail: innkeeper@ehrsamplace.com

Circa 1879. In its early days, this home and the family who lived in it were the talk of the town. The family held an abundance of well-attended parties, and many rumors were spread about why the Ehrsam company safe was kept in the home's basement. Rumors aside, the home features a variety of architectural styles, leaning toward Georgian, with columns gracing the front entrance. The 20-acre grounds are fun to explore, offering a windmill, silo, stables, a carriage house and creek. The innkeepers encourage guests to explore the home as well, which rises three stories. The basement still houses the illusive safe. Rooms are decorated to reflect the area's history. Guests can enjoy breakfast in bed if they choose. With advance notice, the innkeepers will prepare hors d'oeuvres, picnic lunches and dinners for their guests. Candlelight dinners for two also are available, and turn-down service is one of the romantic amenities.
Innkeeper(s): Mary & William Lambert. $55-95. 4 rooms with PB, 3 suites and 1 conference room. Breakfast and snacks/refreshments included in rates. Types of meals: Full gourmet bkfst, veg bkfst, early coffee/tea and gourmet dinner. Beds: Q. Modem hook-up, cable TV, VCR, reading lamp, stereo, ceiling fan, telephone, turn-down service, desk and oversized rooms with sitting area in room. Central air. Fax, bicycles, library, parlor games, laundry facility, gift shop, walking paths and fishing on premises. Antiquing, art galleries, bicycling, fishing, golf, hiking, live theater, museums, parks, shopping, sporting events, tennis, Eisenhower Center, Greyhound Hall of Fame, Milford Lake and Ft. Riley nearby.
Location: Country. 20-acre estate along Smoky Hill River with large wooded area to walk and explore.
Publicity: *Midwest Living and Bed and Breakfast Journal top 15 of 2002.*

"Thank you for history, laughs and most all sharing your treasures with us."
Certificate may be used: All year, if on a weekend, stay must include a Thursday or Sunday night.

Fort Scott — D10

Lyons' Victorian Mansion Bed & Breakfast and Spa
742 S National Ave
Fort Scott, KS 66701-1319
(620)223-3644 (800)784-8378 Fax:(620)223-0062
Internet: www.lyonsmansion.com
E-mail: relax@lyonsmansion.com

Circa 1876. For a business trip, vacation or romantic getaway, this landmark Victorian mansion is a luxurious choice. This gracious home has parlors to gather and Paradise, a full service spa. Spacious guest bedrooms offer King-size beds, refined comfort and modern technology with refreshment centers and dedicated computer lines. The suites feature oversized jetted whirlpools that are made to look like antique clawfoot tubs. Enjoy a hearty breakfast in the grand dining room, unless a breakfast basket delivered to the door is preferred. The grounds are showcased by a gazebo, fish ponds, picnic areas and an enclosed star-lit hot tub. Ask about the creative specialty packages offered.
Innkeeper(s): Pat & Larry Lyons. $79-150. 7 rooms, 6 with PB, 1 suite. Breakfast included in rates. Types of meals: Full bkfst. Three suites with whirlpool in room.
Certificate may be used: Anytime, subject to availability.

Great Bend — D5

Peaceful Acres B&B
RR 5 Box 153
Great Bend, KS 67530-9805
(620)793-7527

Circa 1899. A casual country setting greets guests at Peaceful Acres, a comfortable farmhouse with plenty of calves, chicken, dogs and cats to entertain all visitors, especially children, who are more than welcome here. Activities abound for the youngsters and they also will enjoy the zoo in Great Bend, five miles away. Cheyenne Bottoms and Pawnee Rock are within easy driving distance.
Innkeeper(s): Dale & Doris Nitzel. $35. 2 rooms and 1 conference room. Breakfast included in rates. Types of meals: Full bkfst. Beds: QDT. Reading lamp, ceiling fan, desk and clock in room. Air conditioning. VCR, library, parlor games and telephone on premises. Antiquing, fishing, parks and shopping nearby.
Location: Country.

"Thank you for the charming accommodations. The food was very good and filling, and the place is peaceful, just like the name. We enjoyed the company at breakfast! It felt like staying with family."
Certificate may be used: Anytime available.

Moran — D9

Hedgeapple Acres B&B
4430 Us 54 Hwy
Moran, KS 66755-9500
(620)237-4646
E-mail: hedgeapple@aceks.com

Circa 1974. Nestled on 80-acres of farmland, this country home offers comfortable furnishings and plenty of places to relax. One of the bedchambers boasts a whirlpool tub, while another includes a fireplace. Guests not only enjoy a hearty country breakfast, but supper as well. Spend the day exploring the area, which includes historic Fort Scott, or grab your rod and reel and try out the farm's two stocked ponds.

Innkeeper(s): Jack & Ann Donaldson. $65-85. 4 rooms with PB, 1 with FP and 1 conference room. Breakfast and dinner included in rates. Types of meals: Full bkfst, early coffee/tea, lunch, picnic lunch and snacks/refreshments. Beds: K. Reading lamp and ceiling fan in room. Air conditioning. VCR, parlor games, telephone and fireplace on premises. Handicap access. Antiquing, fishing, golf, live theater, parks, shopping, fishing ponds and walking trails nearby.

Location: Country.

Certificate may be used: Sunday to Thursday, Jan. 10-Nov. 10.

Oberlin   A3

The Landmark Inn at The Historic Bank of Oberlin

PO Box 162
Oberlin, KS 67749
(785)475-2340 (888)639-0003
Internet: www.landmarkinn.com
E-mail: info@landmarkinn.com

Circa 1886. In 1886, this inn served as the Bank of Oberlin, one of the town's most impressive architectural sites. The bank lasted only a few years, though, and went through a number of uses, from county courthouse to the telephone company. Today, it serves as both inn and a historic landmark, a reminder of the past with rooms decorated Victorian style with antiques. One room includes a fireplace; another has a whirlpool tub. In addition to the inviting rooms, there is a restaurant serving dinner specialties such as buttermilk pecan chicken and roasted beef with simmered mushrooms. The inn is listed in the National Register.

Innkeeper(s): Gary Anderson. $69-109. 7 rooms with PB, 1 with FP, 1 suite and 2 conference rooms. Breakfast included in rates. Types of meals: Full gourmet bkfst, early coffee/tea, gourmet lunch, afternoon tea, snacks/refreshments, gourmet dinner and room service. Restaurant on premises. Beds: QD. Cable TV, VCR, reading lamp, ceiling fan, snack bar, clock radio, telephone and desk in room. Air conditioning. Fax, sauna, bicycles, library, parlor games and fireplace on premises. Handicap access. Antiquing, golf, parks, shopping and tennis nearby.

Location: Small town/country.

Publicity: *Kansas Magazine, Dining out in Kansas, Wichita Eagle-Beacon, Salina Journal, Hays Daily News, 2001 Bed & Breakfast Calendar, KSN TV-Wichita, KS, High Plains Public TV and Kansas Public TV Taste of Kansas.*

Certificate may be used: Anytime, January-April, subject to availability.

Wichita   E7

Inn at the Park

3751 E Douglas Ave
Wichita, KS 67218-1002
(316)652-0500 (800)258-1951 Fax:(316)652-0525
Internet: www.innatthepark.com
E-mail: iap@innatthepark.com

Circa 1910. Originally built as a private residence in 1909, the three-story brick mansion and carriage house have been totally renovated to become one of the finest small hotels in the state. The relaxing parkside setting and convenient location is perfect for a distinctive and comfortable stay while traveling on business or for an enchanting romantic getaway. A restored elegance and warm country inn ambiance combine to offer delightful accommodations. Choose from a variety of gorgeous guest bedrooms in the main house, some with stained-glass windows and a fireplace. Sleep on a four-poster, brass, iron, or canopy bed. The Livingston boasts a whirlpool bath. Carriage house rooms include use of a private courtyard and spa. Start the day with a selection of cereals, fresh fruits, baked goods and hot specialty entrees. Visit nearby Old Town and Exploration Place.

Innkeeper(s): Judy Hess and/or Jan Lightner. $89-164. 12 rooms with PB, 8 with FP, 3 suites and 1 conference room. Breakfast included in rates. Types of meals: Cont plus and early coffee/tea. Beds: KQ. Cable TV, VCR, reading lamp, refrigerator, clock radio, telephone, turn-down service and desk in room. Air conditioning. TV, fax, copier and fireplace on premises. Antiquing, live theater, shopping and conference facility nearby.

Location: Residential.

Publicity: *Wichita Business Journal.*

"This is truly a distinctive hotel. Your attention to detail is surpassed only by your devotion to excellent service."

Certificate may be used: All the time.

Kentucky

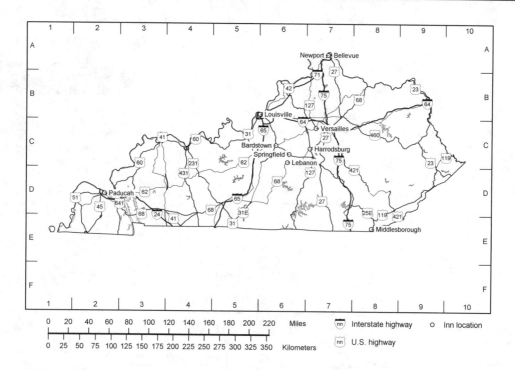

		Miles
		Kilometers

Interstate highway   o   Inn location
U.S. highway

Bardstown   C6

Arbor Rose B&B

209 E Stephen Foster Ave
Bardstown, KY 40004-1513
(502)349-0014 (800)536-0019 Fax:(502)349-7322
Internet: www.arborrosebardstown.com
E-mail: arborrose@bardstown.com

Circa 1820. This late Victorian style home in the National
Register, is located in the historic district a block and a half
from Courthouse Square. Some of the rooms offer fireplaces, all
have cable TV and VCRs. (The inn's fireplaces were made by
Alexander Moore, the master craftsman of "My Old Kentucky
Home.") Full gourmet country breakfasts are served, often on
the outdoor terrace in view of the gardens, Koi pond and fountain. Smoking is not permitted.

Innkeeper(s): Derrick Melzer. $99-139. 5 rooms with PB, 4 with FP and 1
conference room. Breakfast and snacks/refreshments included in rates. Types
of meals: Full gourmet bkfst and early coffee/tea. Beds: KQT. Modem hook-up,
data port, cable TV, VCR, reading lamp, CD player, ceiling fan, clock radio,
telephone, desk and fireplace in room. Central air. Fax, copier, parlor games,
fireplace, hot tub/spa and gift shop on premises. Limited handicap access.
Antiquing, art galleries, golf, hiking, horseback riding, live theater, museums,
parks, shopping, tennis, distilleries and Civil War Monastery nearby.
Location: Historic town.
Publicity: *Kentucky's Best B&B 2001.*

"The food was delicious, our room very attractive and cozy."
Certificate may be used: Nov. 1-June 1, Sunday-Thursday, subject to availability.

Beautiful Dreamer B&B

440 E Stephen Foster Ave
Bardstown, KY 40004-2202
(502)348-4004 (800)811-8312
E-mail: bdreamerbb@yahoo.com

From one of the porches at this Federal-style inn, guests can
view My Old Kentucky Home, the actual house that inspired
the famous Stephen Foster song. Civil War troops camped in
the vicinity of the home, which is located in a historic district.
The home reflects a grandeur of an earlier era. Rooms are furnished elegantly with antiques and reproductions fashioned
from cherrywood. One guest room includes a fireplace and

Jacuzzi tub. Another features a canopy bed and a double Jacuzzi, while a third room offers a plantation, carved, four-poster cherry bed and double Jacuzzi. Guests are encouraged to relax on a porch or in the living room. Refreshments and snacks are available in the upstairs sitting area. Coffee and tea are served prior to breakfast. The morning meal is a hearty affair served family style. Fresh fruit always is available, and home-baked cinnamon or sweet rolls, baked French toast, biscuits and gravy, bacon, country ham or home-seasoned sausage, grits and egg dishes are among the special treats that change daily.

Innkeeper(s): Lynell Ginter. $119-159. 4 rooms with PB, 1 with FP. Breakfast included in rates. Types of meals: Full bkfst and early coffee/tea. Beds: Q. Cable TV, reading lamp, ceiling fan, telephone, hot tub/spa, hair dryers in bathrooms and alarm clock in room. Air conditioning. Parlor games, fireplace and guest refrigerator in common area on premises. Amusement parks, antiquing, fishing, live theater, parks, shopping, water sports, golf and dinner train nearby.
Publicity: Kentucky Standard, Kentucky Living, Evansville Living, Sauver Gourmet Magazine, Unofficial Guide to Bed & Breakfasts, Conde Naste Travel Guide, named "One of Kentucky's Premier B&Bs" by Kentucky Monthly Magazine and Voted Best B&B in Nelson County.

"We've stayed at B&Bs all over the world and Beautiful Dreamer is our favorite by far!"

Certificate may be used: Sunday-Thursday inclusive, January, February, March and November not valid Friday or Saturday, no holidays or special events.

Bellevue   A7

Christopher's B&B
604 Poplar St
Bellevue, KY 41073
(859)491-9354 (888)585-7085
Internet: www.christophersbb.com
E-mail: christbb@fuse.net

Circa 1889. The former home of Bellevue Christian Church, this unique inn sits in one of the area's three historic districts. The spacious building was transformed into a delightful residence and B&B featuring the original hardwood floors and stained-glass windows. Tastefully decorated and furnished in a Victorian style, the gracious guest bedrooms and suite feature Jacuzzi tubs and VCRs.

Innkeeper(s): Brenda Guidugli. $95-169. 3 rooms with PB, 1 suite. Breakfast and snacks/refreshments included in rates. Types of meals: Full bkfst and early coffee/tea. Beds: KQ. Modem hook-up, data port, cable TV, VCR, reading lamp, stereo, refrigerator, ceiling fan, snack bar, clock radio, telephone, coffeemaker, desk, Jacuzzi, ironing board, iron, hair dryer and DVD/VHS movies in room. Central air. Parlor games, fireplace, gift shop, continental plus breakfast (weekdays only) and single/double Jacuzzi tubs on premises. Amusement parks, antiquing, art galleries, fishing, golf, live theater, museums, parks, shopping, sporting events, water sports, Newport Aquarium, Newport on the Levee, Millennium Peace Bell, Riverbend outdoor concerts, Bengals' Paul Brown Stadium, Cincinnati Reds' Great American Ball Park and restaurants with a river view nearby.
Location: City.
Publicity: Midwest Living, The Cincinnati Enquirer, The Kentucky Post, Kentucky Monthly, Arts Across Kentucky, AAA Home Away, City Beat, Kentucky Living, Places To Go, Channel 12 Local News and voted by inngoers in Arrington's Bed and Breakfast Journal 2003 & 2004 Book of Lists as "one of the Top 15 B&Bs/Inns for best design and decor."
Certificate may be used: Anytime, subject to availability.

Harrodsburg   C7

Canaan Land Farm B&B
700 Canaan Land Rd
Harrodsburg, KY 40330-9220
(859)734-3984 (888)734-3984
Internet: www.canaanlandfarm.com
E-mail: info@canaanlandfarm.com

Circa 1795. One of the oldest brick houses in the state, the Benjamin Daniel House is listed in the National Register and sits a mile down a winding historic wagon trail. The 1815 Philemon Waters Log House  offers additional accommodations and two working fireplaces. Guest bedrooms are appointed with antiques, quilts and feather beds. A flock of sheep, goats and other assorted barnyard animals graze the pastures of this historic working farm. Swim in the in-ground pool, soak up the sun in the deck area, relax in the hot tub and nap in a shady hammock. The Farm hosts a variety of retreats. Ask about special weekend packages available.

Innkeeper(s): Mark & Ann Fryer. $85-125. 7 rooms, 6 with PB, 2 with FP. Breakfast included in rates. Types of meals: Full bkfst. Beds: QDT. Reading lamp and desk in room. VCR, spa, swimming, parlor games, telephone and fireplace on premises. Antiquing, fishing, golf, horseback riding, parks, shopping, water sports and historic sites nearby.
Location: Country.
Publicity: Danville Advocate, Lexington Herald Leader and Kentucky Living.

"You truly have a gift for genuine hospitality."
Certificate may be used: November-April, Sunday-Thursday.

Lebanon   C6

Myrtledene B&B
370 N Spalding Ave
Lebanon, KY 40033-1557
(502)692-2223 (800)391-1721
Internet: www.myrtledene.com
E-mail: info@myrtledene.com

Circa 1833. Once a Confederate general's headquarters at one point during the Civil War, this pink brick inn, located at a bend in the road, has greeted visitors entering Lebanon for more than 150 years. When General John Hunt Morgan returned in 1863 to destroy the town, the white flag hoisted to signal a truce was  flown at Myrtledene. A country breakfast usually features ham and biscuits as well as the innkeepers' specialty, peaches and cream French toast.

Innkeeper(s): James F. Spragens. $85. 4 rooms, 2 with PB, 1 with FP and 1 conference room. Breakfast included in rates. Types of meals: Full gourmet bkfst, early coffee/tea and afternoon tea. Beds: DT. Reading lamp, clock radio, turn-down service, Makers Mark bourbon and bourbon chocolates in room. Air conditioning. VCR, library, parlor games, telephone and fireplace on premises. Antiquing, fishing, live theater, parks, shopping and water sports nearby.
Location: City.
Publicity: Lebanon Enterprise, Louisville Courier-Journal, Lebanon/Marion County Kentucky and Sunnyside.

"Our night in the Cabbage Rose Room was an experience of another time, another culture. Your skill in preparing and presenting breakfast was equally elegant! We'll be back!"

Certificate may be used: Anytime except Sept. 27-28.

Louisville   B6

1853 Inn at Woodhaven

401 S Hubbard Ln
Louisville, KY 40207-4074
(502)895-1011 (888)895-1011
Internet: www.innatwoodhaven.com
E-mail: info@innatwoodhaven.com

Circa 1853. This Gothic Revival, painted in a cheerful shade of yellow, is still much the same as it was in the 1850s, when it served as the home on a prominent local farm. The rooms still feature the outstanding carved woodwork, crisscross window designs, winding staircases, decorative mantels and hardwood floors. Guest quarters are tastefully appointed with antiques, suitable for their 12-foot, nine-inch tall ceilings.
Complimentary coffee and tea stations are provided in each room. There are several common areas in the Main House and Carriage House, and guests also take advantage of the inn's porches. Rose Cottage is octagon shaped and features a 25-foot vaulted ceiling, a king bed, fireplace, sitting area, double whirlpool, steam shower and wraparound porch. The National Register home is close to all of Louisville's attractions.
Innkeeper(s): Marsha Burton. $85-225. 8 rooms with PB, 3 with FP, 6 suites and 1 cottage. Breakfast included in rates. Types of meals: Full gourmet bkfst and dinner. Beds: KQ. Cable TV, reading lamp, stereo, ceiling fan, clock radio, telephone, desk, coffee, tea, hot chocolate facility, five with double whirlpools and four with steam showers in room. Air conditioning. Fax, copier, library, parlor games, fireplace and wireless Internet on premises. Handicap access. Amusement parks, antiquing, golf, live theater, parks, shopping, sporting events, tennis and water sports nearby.
Location: City.
Publicity: Courier Journal, New York Times, WAVE and WHAS.
Certificate may be used: Sunday-Thursday, year-round.

Aleksander House

1213 S First St
Louisville, KY 40203
(502)637-4985 (866)637-4985 Fax:(502)635-1398
Internet: www.aleksanderhouse.com
E-mail: alekhouse@aol.com

Circa 1882. French impressionist paintings, French Toile wall coverings in the dining room, gas light fixtures, 12-foot ceilings, fireplaces and walnut woodwork create the pleasant decor of this three-story Italianate Victorian. Ask for Katharine's Room on the third floor and enjoy a four-poster bed, writing desk and settee. Pecan waffles served with glazed peaches and cream or eggs Benedict are popular breakfast entrees. Mystery weekend packages are offered on occasion. The inn is listed in the National Register.
Innkeeper(s): Nancy R Hinchliff. $95-169. 5 rooms, 3 with PB, 2 with FP, 1 suite. Breakfast and snacks/refreshments included in rates. Types of meals: Full gourmet bkfst, veg bkfst and early coffee/tea. Beds: KQDT. Modem hook-up, data port, TV, VCR, reading lamp, refrigerator, ceiling fan, snack bar, clock radio, telephone, coffeemaker, desk, terry cloth robes, irons, ironing boards and hair dryers in room. Central air. Fax, copier, library, pet boarding, parlor games, fireplace and video library on premises. Amusement parks, antiquing, art galleries, bicycling, golf, hiking, horseback riding, live theater, museums, parks, shopping, tennis, wineries and river boating nearby.

Location: City.
Publicity: *Country Inns, Louisville Magazine, Today's Woman Magazine, The Courier-Journal, Country Register and Channel 11-WGN.*
Certificate may be used: Anytime Sunday-Thursday, subject to availability.

Central Park B&B

1353 S Fourth St
Louisville, KY 40208-2349
(502)638-1505 (877)922-1505 Fax:(502)638-1525
Internet: www.centralparkbandb.com
E-mail: centralpar@win.net

Circa 1884. This three-story Second Empire Victorian is listed in the National Register, and it is located in the heart of "Old Louisville," amid America's largest collection of Victorian homes. Enjoy the fine craftsmanship of the home's many amenities, including the reverse-painted glass ceiling of the front porch and the polished woodwork and stained glass. Among its 18 rooms are seven guest rooms, all with private baths and two with whirlpool tubs. There are 11 fireplaces, some with carved mantels and decorative tile. The Carriage House suite has a full kitchen. Antiques are found throughout. Across the street is Central Park; only 3 minutes from downtown and seven minutes from the airport.
Innkeeper(s): Mary & Joseph White. $89-169. 7 rooms with PB, 5 with FP and 1 guest house. Breakfast, snacks/refreshments and wine included in rates. Types of meals: Full gourmet bkfst, early coffee/tea and afternoon tea. Beds: KQ. Modem hook-up, data port, cable TV, VCR, reading lamp, refrigerator, ceiling fan, clock radio, telephone, coffeemaker, desk, hot tub/spa, fireplace, hair dryers, iron/ironing board, DSL, coffee/tea and hot chocolate in room. Central air. Fax on premises. Antiquing, bicycling, golf, live theater, museums, parks, shopping, sporting events, tennis, wineries and fine dining nearby.
Location: City.
Certificate may be used: Jan. 1-Dec. 30, Monday-Thursday.

Gallery House Bed & Breakfast

1386 South Sixth Street
Louisville, KY 40208
(502)635-2550 Fax:(502)635-6204
E-mail: galleryhse@aol.com

Circa 1997. Sitting in the historic district, this newly built Victorian home exudes the ambiance of the era it reflects, yet offers today's modern amenities. Themed guest bedrooms feature original artwork, phones with data ports, cable TV, hair dryers, irons and boards, sound machines and other upscale amenities. The Rose Room also boasts a Delta surround shower and mini refrigerator. An adjacent balcony overlooks Central Park. For complete privacy, stay next door at the quiet, urban Magnolia Cottage. It boasts a fully equipped kitchen, living and dining room, washer and dryer. Breakfast is selected from a menu the night before. Enjoy refreshments each evening.
Innkeeper(s): Leah Stewart & Gordon Moffett. $70-145. 4 rooms, 3 with PB and 1 cottage. Breakfast and snacks/refreshments included in rates. Types of meals: Full gourmet bkfst, veg bkfst, early coffee/tea and dinner. Beds: Q. Modem hook-up, data port, cable TV, reading lamp, ceiling fan, clock radio, telephone, desk and original art in room. Central air. Fireplace on premises. Amusement parks, antiquing, art galleries, golf, hiking, live theater, museums, parks, shopping, sporting events, tennis and wineries nearby.
Location: City, waterfront.
Certificate may be used: Sunday through Thursday, January, July, August, November, December, subject to availability.

Middlesborough
E8

The Ridge Runner B&B
208 Arthur Hts
Middlesborough, KY 40965-1728
(606)248-4299
E-mail: ridgebnb@thefuturenet.net

Circa 1890. Bachelor buttons, lilacs and wildflowers line the white picket fence framing this 20-room brick Victorian mansion. Guests enjoy relaxing in its turn-of-the-century parlor filled with Victorian antiques. Ask for the President's Room and you'll enjoy the best view of the Cumberland Mountains. (The innkeeper's great, great-grandfather hosted President Lincoln the night before his Gettysburg address, and the inn boasts some heirlooms from that home.) A family-style breakfast is provided and special diets can be accommodated if notified in advance. Cumberland Gap National Park is five miles away, and the inn is two miles from the twin tunnels that pass through the Cumberland Gap. Pine Mountain State Park is 12 miles away. Guests also enjoy a visit to the P. 38 restoration project housed at the local airport.

Innkeeper(s): Alan & Susan Meadows and Irma Gall. $70-80. 4 rooms, 2 with PB. Breakfast and snacks/refreshments included in rates. Types of meals: Early coffee/tea. Beds: DT. Reading lamp, ceiling fan, turn-down service and desk in room. Telephone on premises. Antiquing, parks and shopping nearby.

Location: Mountains.

Publicity: *Lexington Herald Leader, Blue Ridge Country, Indianapolis Star, Daily News, Courier Journal and Country Inn.*

Certificate may be used: Nov. 15-April 30, Sunday-Thursday, excluding holidays, weekends (i.e. Thanksgiving, Christmas, Labor Day, etc.). Anytime, subject to availability.

Newport
A7

Cincinnati's Weller Haus B&B
319 Poplar St
Newport, KY 41073-1108
(859)431-6829 (800)431-4287 Fax:(859)431-4332
Internet: www.wellerhaus.com
E-mail: innkeepers@wellerhaus.com

Circa 1880. Set in Taylor Daughter's Historic District and five minutes from downtown Cincinnati, this inn consists of two historic homes. The inn has received awards for preservation, and special features include original woodwork and doors. Secluded gardens are inviting, and there is a wrought iron fence setting off the property. A full breakfast is served by candlelight. Rooms offer antiques and suites feature double Jacuzzi tubs. A sky-lit great room has cathedral ceilings, and an ivy-covered gathering kitchen is open for snacks and drinks. Guests enjoy walking to the Newport Aquarium, Newport on the Levee and the Riverboat Row Restaurants as well as downtown Cincinnati stadiums. Other attractions include live theater and water sports. Business travelers are provided telephones, in room desks, high-speed Internet and a copy machine and fax are on the premises. Private space is available for small meetings. Breakfast can accommodate business schedules.

Innkeeper(s): Valerie & David Brown. $89-180. 5 rooms with PB. Breakfast included in rates. Types of meals: Full bkfst and early coffee/tea. Beds: QDT. Modem hook-up, cable TV, VCR, ceiling fan, telephone, suites have Jacuzzi for two and high-speed Internet access in room. Air conditioning. Amusement parks, antiquing, fishing, live theater, museums, shopping, sporting events and water sports nearby.

Location: City.

Publicity: *Downtowner, Bellevue Community News, Cincinnati Enquirer, Country Inns, Kentucky Monthly and Arrington's Bed & Breakfast Journal & the Book of Lists.*

"You made B&B believers out of us."

Certificate may be used: Anytime, Sunday-Thursday.

Paducah
D2

Paducah Harbor Plaza B&B
201 Broadway St
Paducah, KY 42001-0711
(270)442-2698 (800)719-7799
E-mail: phplaza@apex.net

This striking, five-story brick structure was known as the Hotel Belvedere at the turn of the century. Guests now choose from four guest rooms on the second floor, where they also will find the arch-windowed Broadway Room, with its views of the Market House District and the Ohio River, just a block away. Breakfast is served in this room, which also contains a 1911 player piano. The guest rooms all feature different color schemes and each is furnished with antique furniture and handmade quilts.

Innkeeper(s): Beverly McKinley. $65-85. 4 rooms. Breakfast included in rates. Types of meals: Cont plus. Cable TV, reading lamp, ceiling fan, snack bar, clock radio, telephone and desk in room. Air conditioning. VCR on premises. Antiquing, live theater and shopping nearby.

Location: City.

Certificate may be used: January, February, March, November, December.

Trinity Hills Farm B&B Country Inn-Spa Retreat
10455 Old Lovelaceville Rd
Paducah, KY 42001-9304
(270)488-3999 (800)488-3998
Internet: www.trinityhills.com
E-mail: info@trinityhills.com

Circa 1995. On the edge of a private fishing lake, 12 miles from the city, sits this country home and guesthouse. A pool table and treadmill are in the Dayroom, a popular gathering spot. Guest bedrooms, each with access to a kitchenette, are elegantly furnished and decorated with an interesting mix of collectibles. Suites feature a private fireplace and spa or whirlpool tub. Country Camelot guesthouse includes a heart-shaped Jacuzzi, fireplace, custom stained glass and private decks. Country-style or gourmet fare is enjoyed every morning. Snacks and beverages are available daily and desserts are served on weekend evenings. Corporate meetings and small receptions are often held here. Candlelight dinners and massage therapy by appointment are now

offered. Encounter peacocks, ducks, llamas, pygmy goats, miniature donkeys or an Arabian mare.

Innkeeper(s): Ann & Mike Driver. $95-175. 6 rooms with PB, 5 with FP, 4 suites and 1 guest house. Breakfast included in rates. Types of meals: Full gourmet bkfst and early coffee/tea. Beds: Q. TV, VCR, reading lamp, stereo, refrigerator, ceiling fan, snack bar, clock radio, hot tub/spa, table and chairs and robes in room. Air conditioning. Fax, spa, library, parlor games, telephone, fireplace, treadmill, movie library and wheelchair access on premises. Amusement parks, antiquing, golf, live theater, parks, shopping, sporting events, tennis and water sports nearby.

Location: Country.

Publicity: *Paducah Life, Paducah Sun, Heartland B&Bs, Torchbearer and Paraplegia News.*

Certificate may be used: Monday through Thursday except holidays and AQS Quilt show.

Springfield C6

1851 Historic Maple Hill Manor B&B

2941 Perryville Rd (US 150 EAST)
Springfield, KY 40069-9611
(859)336-3075 (800)886-7546 Fax:(859)336-3076
Internet: www.maplehillmanor.com
E-mail: stay@maplehillmanor.com

Circa 1851. In a tranquil country setting on 14 acres, this Greek Revival mansion with Italianate detail is considered a Kentucky Landmark home and is listed in the National Register of Historic Places. Numerous architectural features include 14-foot ceilings, nine-foot windows, 10-foot doorways and a grand cherry spiral staircase. Guest bedrooms provide spacious serenity, and some boast fireplaces and or Jacuzzis. Enjoy a full country breakfast, and then take a peaceful stroll through flower gardens and the fruit orchard, or relax on a patio swing or porch rocker. The local area has a rich abundance of attractions including Bardstown, Shaker Village, Bourbon, historic Civil War areas and Lincoln Trails. Lexington and Louisville are within an hour's drive.

Innkeeper(s): Todd Allen & Tyler Horton. $100-150. 7 rooms with PB, 2 with FP, 2 with HT, 4 suites and 1 conference room. Breakfast included in rates. Types of meals: Full gourmet bkfst, veg bkfst, early coffee/tea, lunch, picnic lunch, afternoon tea, snacks/refreshments, gourmet dinner and room service. Beds: QDT. TV, VCR, reading lamp, ceiling fan, snack bar, clock radio, coffeemaker, turn-down service, two with Jacuzzi, two with fireplace, designer linens, antique furnishings, rollaway beds available and some with TV/VCR/DVD/CD player (includes movies/music) in room. Central air. Fax, copier, library, parlor games, telephone, fireplace, laundry facility, gift shop, orchard, nature walking paths, flower gardens, snack bar, complimentary homemade evening desserts, alpaca and llama farm, Kentucky Handcrafted Gift Gallery and Murder Mystery events on premises. Limited handicap access. Antiquing, art galleries, bicycling, fishing, golf, hiking, horseback riding, live theater, museums, parks, shopping, tennis, water sports, wineries,

My Old Kentucky Home State Park, Bernheim Forest, Kentucky Railway Museum, Civil War battlefield and museums, Lincoln Homestead and National Museum/birthplace and Kentucky bourbon distilleries nearby.

Location: Country. Rural.

Publicity: *Southern Living, Danville's Advocate-Messenger, Springfield Sun, Cincinnati's Eastside Weekend, Louisville Courier Journal, Lexington Herald-Leader, Arts Across Kentucky, Kentucky Monthly, Arrington's Inn Traveler Magazine, Voted #1 in the US as the B&B with the "most Historical Charm" and voted as "One of Kentucky's Finest B&Bs."*

"Thank you again for your friendly and comfortable hospitality."

Certificate may be used: Anytime, subject to availability.

Versailles C7

1823 Historic Rose Hill Inn

233 Rose Hill
Versailles, KY 40383-1223
(859)873-5957 (800)307-0460
Internet: www.rosehillinn.com
E-mail: innkeepers@rosehillinn.com

Circa 1823. This Victorian mansion, in the National Register, was occupied at different times by both Confederate and Union troops during the Civil War. Near Lexington, the home maintains many elegant features, including original stained-glass windows, 14-foot ceilings and hardwood floors fashioned from timber on the property. The decor is comfortable, yet elegant. Four guest baths include double Jacuzzis. Guests enjoy relaxing in the library, the parlor, or on the porch swing on the veranda. The home's summer kitchen is now a private cottage with a kitchen, two bedrooms and a Jacuzzi. The Cottage and Auntie's Attic are perfect for those

traveling with children or for guests with well-behaved dogs. The innkeepers offer a hearty, full breakfast with specialties such as Mexican eggs, or Banana-filled French toast in the dining room. In summer it's often served on the veranda overlooking the water gardens, lawns and trees where cardinals fly about. Walk to the historic districts, antique shops restaurants and a museum. Additional attractions include Shaker Village, scenic drives past bucolic horse farms, Keeneland Race Track, Kentucky Horse Park and a wildlife sanctuary.

Innkeeper(s): Sharon Amberg . $99-169. 5 rooms with PB, 1 suite and 1 cottage. Breakfast included in rates. Types of meals: Full bkfst and early coffee/tea. Beds: KQDT. TV, VCR, reading lamp, ceiling fan and telephone in room. Library and A/C on premises. Antiquing, fishing, golf, parks, shopping, sporting events, horse farm tours, Kentucky Horse Park, Shaker Village and Keeneland nearby.

Location: Small town near horse farms.

Certificate may be used: Sunday-Thursday, Nov. 1-March 15 (except holidays).

Louisiana

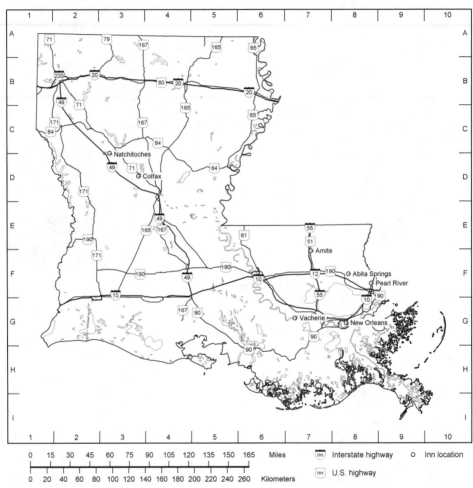

	1	2	3	4	5	6	7	8	9	10	

Miles: 0 15 30 45 60 75 90 105 120 135 150 165

Kilometers: 0 20 40 60 80 100 120 140 160 180 200 220 240 260

[nn] Interstate highway   o Inn location

[nn] U.S. highway

Abita Springs   *F8*

Trail's End Bed & Breakfast

71648 Maple St
Abita Springs, LA 70420-3616
(985)867-9899 (800)897-9907 Fax:(985)871-4339
Internet: www.trailsendbnb.com
E-mail: merle@trailsendbnb.com

Circa 1891. Situated in the center of a small historic town, this Victorian home is aptly named for its location behind the old railroad, which is now the Rails to Trails bike and jogging path. The delightful suite and guest bedrooms are well-appointed, boasting canopy, sleigh and four-poster beds. A satisfying breakfast includes bacon, eggs, grits, toast and fruit. Golf is available on four nearby courses.

Innkeeper(s): Merle & Shelton Mulkey. $75-118. 5 rooms, 4 with PB, 2 with FP, 1 suite. Breakfast and snacks/refreshments included in rates. Types of meals: Full gourmet bkfst, early coffee/tea, picnic lunch & dinner. Beds: QD. Cable TV & ceiling fan in room. Central air. VCR, fax, bicycles, telephone and laundry facility on premises. Amusement parks, antiquing, art galleries, beach, bicycling, golf, live theater, museums, parks, shopping, sporting events, tennis & wineries nearby.

Location: Small town.

Certificate may be used: Anytime, Sunday-Thursday except during special event times, i.e. Mardi Gras, Super Bowl, Sugar Bowl do not apply.

Amite   *F7*

Blythewood Plantation

PO Box 155, 400 Daniel ST
Amite, LA 70422-0155
(985)748-5886 Fax:(985)748-6246

Circa 1885. The grounds surrounding this majestic plantation home were part of a Spanish land grant. The original home, a pre-Civil War manor, burned, but was rebuilt in the late 19th century. The grand rooms include a gas chandelier, leaded-glass doors and walnut mantels, all original features. In true Louisiana style, guests are served a refreshing mint julep upon arrival. Candlelight dinners can be arranged, as can special teas, parties and weddings.

Innkeeper(s): Ipha, Daryl & Beth. $89-189. 9 rooms, 7 with PB and 2 conference rooms. Breakfast included in rates. Types of meals: Full gourmet bkfst, gourmet lunch, picnic lunch, snacks/refreshments and gourmet dinner. Beds: D. Cable TV in room. Air conditioning. VCR and telephone on premises. Handicap access. Antiquing, parks and water sports nearby.
Location: City.
Certificate may be used: Jan. 31-Dec. 30, some restrictions apply.

Colfax   *D3*

Fairmount Plantation

230 Fairmount Plantation Road
Colfax, LA 71417
(318)793-8254 (866)732-2672 Fax:(318)793-8254
Internet: www.fairmountplantation.com
E-mail: fairmount@speedgate.net

Circa 1869. Sheltered by century-old pecan trees in the Red River Valley, this 1869 modified Greek Revival, Creole-cottage home exudes the nostalgia of an 800-acre working cotton plantation. Five glorious acres of landscaped grounds and surrounding pecan orchards are showcased by a Southern Magnolia that blooms from April through June. The front of the property gently slopes into a natural bayou. Upstairs guest bedrooms are furnished with antiques and offer central air and heat. Hors d'oeuvres, an evening buffet and a plantation breakfast are served using typical Louisiana cuisine from Creole to Cajun. Relax on the patio or deck and swim in the sparkling pool.

Innkeeper(s): Judy & Tom Vogel. $100-150. 2 rooms with PB. Breakfast, hors d'oeuvres and dinner included in rates. Beds: DT. Reading lamp, ceiling fan, clock radio, coffeemaker and desk in room. Central air. Fax, copier, swimming, parlor games, telephone and laundry facility on premises. Antiquing, art galleries, fishing, golf, hiking, horseback riding, live theater, museums, parks, shopping and water sports nearby.
Location: Country.
Certificate may be used: Anytime, subject to availability.

Natchitoches   *C3*

Breazeale House B&B

926 Washington St
Natchitoches, LA 71457-4730
(318)352-5630 (800)352-5631
E-mail: wfreeman@cp-tel.net

Circa 1899. This three-story Victorian home boasts a porch accentuated with white columns on the first level and an expansive balcony with balustrades on the second floor. Stained-and leaded-glass windows with white shutters and trim offer an inviting exterior. Eleven fireplaces afford a warm backdrop to the inn's antique Victorian furnishings. A popular

breakfast menu includes crescent rolls with ham and cheese, eggs, muffins and fruit.

Innkeeper(s): Jack & Willa Freeman. $85-100. 5 rooms with PB. Breakfast included in rates. Types of meals: Full bkfst and early coffee/tea. Beds: QDT. Reading lamp, ceiling fan and coffeemaker in room. Air conditioning. TV, fax, swimming, telephone and fireplace on premises. Antiquing, fishing, golf, shopping, sporting events, tennis and water sports nearby.
Certificate may be used: Jan. 6 to Nov. 15, Sunday-Thursday.

New Orleans   *G8*

1800s Mandevilla Bed and Breakfast

7716 St. Charles Ave
New Orleans, LA 70118
(504)862-6396 (800)288-0484 Fax:(504)866-4104
Internet: www.mandevilla.com
E-mail: Marnie-allen@mandevilla.com

Circa 1900. Meticulously restored to offer a luxurious and quiet retreat, this Greek Revival mansion boasts columned double galleries, 12-foot ceilings with ornate crown moldings, marble mantles, crystal chandeliers, elegant period antiques and leaded, stained-glass windows. A business center is available. Delightful guest bedrooms and suites are surrounded by Victorian courtyards with tropical water gardens. Some rooms feature a double Jacuzzi and private balcony. Enjoy breakfast in the dining room or on a tray in-room. Located in the historic University section of the Upper Garden District, the French Quarter is a short, streetcar ride away. Relax in the lush gardens and have a picture taken under the century-old oak tree adorned with Spanish moss. Walk to nearby Audubon Park to play tennis, golf and ride horses or bikes.

$89-159. 5 rooms with PB. Breakfast included in rates. Types of meals: Cont plus. Beds: KQ. Cable TV, ceiling fan, telephone, fireplace, radio, hair dryers, bath amenities and breakfast served on a beautiful tray in room. Air conditioning. Fax, 12-foot ceilings, 18-inch ornate crown moldings, medallions, custom 12-inch cypress baseboard, crystal chandeliers, leaded stained-glass windows and period antiques on premises. Antiquing, art galleries, beach, fishing, golf, hiking, horseback riding, live theater, museums, parks, sporting events, water sports, mansion tours of the garden district, boating and sailing on Lake Pontchartrain, unique cemeteries, "Cities of the Dead" and jogging nearby.
Location: City, ocean community. Universities section of the Upper Garden District.
Publicity: *Travel South and New York Times.*
Certificate may be used: June 1 to Aug. 15, Sunday-Thursday.

1822 Bougainvillea House

924 Gov. Nicholls St.
New Orleans, LA 70116-3106
(504)525-3983 Fax:(504)522-5000
Internet: www.1822bougainvillea.com
E-mail: patkahn@aol.com

Circa 1822. Built by a plantation owner in 1822, this French Quarter guesthouse boasts the romantic mystique of its historical background. Each luxurious suite includes a bedroom, living/dining room, bath, private entrance and either a patio or balcony. Some feature antique furnishings. Dine on culinary delights at famous restaurants nearby, walk along the

levee by the river, shop at the Royal Street boutiques, and plan a visit during Mardi Gras, Creole Christmas or one of the many popular local festivals. Arrange an excursion to the world-class Audubon Zoo, the swamps or take a walking tour of haunted mansions.

Innkeeper(s): Pat Kahn. $90-250. 5 suites. Types of meals: Early coffee/tea. Beds: KQD. Cable TV, reading lamp, refrigerator, ceiling fan, clock radio, telephone, coffeemaker and desk in room. Central air. Fax, copier, bicycles and laundry facility on premises. Amusement parks, antiquing, art galleries, beach, bicycling, fishing, golf, horseback riding, live theater, museums, parks, shopping, sporting events and tennis nearby.

Location: City.

"We love your home and always enjoy our visits here so much!"

Certificate may be used: June, July and August, subject to availability.

1870 Banana Courtyard French Quarter/New Orleans B&B

Box 70556
New Orleans, LA 70172
(504)947-4475 (800)842-4748 Fax:(504)949-5689
Internet: www.bananacourtyard.com
E-mail: bananacour@aol.com

Circa 1870. Everyone feels like an honored guest while staying at this Victorian Creole bed & breakfast extraordinaire. A variety of accommodations are offered, from the main B&B rooms to a romantic 1850s cottage, spacious guest suite, historic townhouse or apartment. Lagniappe means a little something extra, and that is what is offered here. Enjoy a welcome drink, a generous continental breakfast and afternoon beverages. Relaxing is easy in the courtyard on a double hammock. Just outside the gate is the French Quarter, Bourbon Street is only three blocks away.

Innkeeper(s): Mary Ramsey. $55-110. 1 room with PB. Breakfast included in rates. Types of meals: Cont plus. Beds: KQDT. Cable TV, reading lamp, refrigerator, ceiling fan, clock radio, telephone, coffeemaker, turn-down service, desk and fireplace in room. Air conditioning. Fax, library and fireplace on premises. Amusement parks, antiquing, art galleries, bicycling, canoeing/kayaking, fishing, golf, horseback riding, live theater, museums, parks, shopping, sporting events, tennis and water sports nearby.

Location: City. French quarter.

Certificate may be used: Weeknights, off-season.

A Creole House Hotel

1013 Saint Ann St
New Orleans, LA 70116-3012
(504)524-8076 (800)535-7858 Fax:(504)581-3277
Internet: big-easy.org
E-mail: ach5555@aol.com

Circa 1830. Experience classic Southern hospitality at this 1830s townhouse built by a French Creole family, and now listed in the National Register. Enjoy the quiet refuge, authentic ambiance and friendly local flavor located just two blocks from Bourbon Street in the famous French Quarter. Each air-conditioned guest bedroom and suite boasts a different décor from period furnishings to contemporary. Some face one of the delightful courtyards, and others are in the main townhouse. Stay in a two-bedroom suite that features a Jacuzzi. Wake up any time to hot coffee and freshly baked pastries. A very helpful staff will assist with tour planning.

Innkeeper(s): Brent Kovach. $49-189. 29 rooms. Breakfast included in rates. Types of meals: Cont. Beds: KQDT. Reading lamp, clock radio, telephone and desk in room. Air conditioning. Fax, copier and fireplace on premises. Antiquing, fishing, golf, live theater, parks and sporting events nearby.

Certificate may be used: Anytime, subject to availability, excluding special events.

Acadian Orleans Inn

2041 Prytania St
New Orleans, LA 70130
(504)561-8550 (877)566-1411
Internet: www.acadianorleansinn.com
E-mail: mpverhoeven@msn.com

Experience the classic style of "The Big Easy" at this bed & breakfast offering Cajun hospitality. The semi-octagonal bay and transom windows, 12-foot-high ceilings and hand-hewn cypress casings and doors reflect the historic character of the inn. Antiques furnish the elegant guest bedrooms, and some rooms feature clawfoot tubs. A continental breakfast is served daily. Relax on one of the pillared, two-story covered porches, or in the private courtyard with cascading fountain, and watch the world go by. The convenient location is near the Mardi Gras parade route, the French Quarter and the area's many other famous sites.

Innkeeper(s): Mark Verhoeven. Call for rates. Call inn for details.

Certificate may be used: November-February, excludes holidays and special events.

Andrew Jackson Hotel

919 Royal Street, French Quarter
New Orleans, LA 70116-2792
(504)561-5881 (800)654-0224 Fax:(504)596-6769
Internet: www.FrenchQuarterInns.com
E-mail: reservations@FrenchQuarterInns.com

Circa 1860. Encounter the sights and sounds of New Orleans from this historic small hotel situated in the heart of the French Quarter that combines southern style and hospitality. Stay in a balcony suite or a romantic guest bedroom that opens to a tropical gas-lit courtyard that is a classic design of this area. After a late night of music and merriment enjoy a continental breakfast in bed. The staff is trained and available to help make each trip most memorable.

Innkeeper(s): French Quarter Inns. $79-299. 23 rooms with PB, 3 suites and 1 cottage. Breakfast included in rates. Types of meals: Cont and early coffee/tea. Beds: KDT. Cable TV, ceiling fan, telephone and Royal Balcony suites feature views of Royal Street and the Vieux Carre in room. Central air. Tropical courtyard and classic French Quarter fountain on premises. Amusement parks, antiquing, art galleries, bicycling, fishing, horseback riding, live theater, museums, parks, shopping, sporting events, tennis and French Quarter historic district nearby.

Location: City, waterfront. Historic District, French Quarter.

Certificate may be used: Anytime, subject to availability.

Avenue Inn Bed & Breakfast

4125 St. Charles Avenue
New Orleans, LA 70115
(504)269-2640 (800)490-8542 Fax:(504)269-2641
Internet: www.avenueinnbb.com
E-mail: info@avenueinnbb.com

Circa 1891. Set among timeless oaks on famous St. Charles Street is this 1891 Thomas Sully mansion. The inn has high ceilings and hardwood floors, and its 17 guest rooms are furnished with period pieces. Come during Mardi Gras and you can sit on the big front porch and watch the 18 Mardi Gras parades that come down St. Charles Avenue. The French Quarter, Central Business District, Convention Center as well as Tulane and Loyola Universities are all within 1 3/4 miles. Antique shops, restaurants and night spots are within walking distance.

Innkeeper(s): Joe & Bebe Rabhan. $69-299. 17 rooms with PB, 5 with FP. Breakfast included in rates. Types of meals: Cont. Beds: KQD. Modem hookup, data port, cable TV, reading lamp, ceiling fan, clock radio, telephone, desk

and voice mail in room. Central air. VCR, fax, copier, library, parlor games and fireplace on premises. Limited handicap access. Amusement parks, antiquing, art galleries, bicycling, canoeing/kayaking, fishing, golf, live theater, museums, parks, shopping, restaurants, cultural events, sightseeing and day spa nearby.
Location: City.
Certificate may be used: Subject to availability.

Bonne Chance B&B

621 Opelousas Ave
New Orleans, LA 70114
(504)367-0798 Fax:(504)368-4643
Internet: www.bonne-chance.com
E-mail: watsondolores@aol.com

Circa 1890. This recently renovated two-story Eastlake pale pink Victorian with gentle lavender and green trim boasts four balconies and a porch with fretwork and columns. Antique furnishings and Oriental rugs are found throughout, and fully furnished apartments with kitchens are available. A secluded courtyard with fountain and gardens are in the rear of the inn. A free five-minute ferry boat ride takes you to the French Quarter.
Innkeeper(s): Dolores Watson. $85-175. 3 suites. Breakfast included in rates. Types of meals: Cont plus. Beds: Q. Cable TV, reading lamp, refrigerator, ceiling fan, clock radio, telephone, desk and three apartments with fully equipped kitchens in room. Air conditioning. VCR, fax, copier and library on premises. Amusement parks, antiquing, fishing, golf, live theater, parks, shopping, sporting events, tennis and French Quarter nearby.
Location: City.
Publicity: *New Orleans.*
Certificate may be used: June 1-Aug. 31, Dec. 1-31.

Chateau du Louisiane

1216 Louisiana Ave
New Orleans, LA 70115
(504)723-6192 (800)734-0137 Fax:(504)269-2603
Internet: www.chateaulouisiane.com
E-mail: jopreston@cdl.nocoxmail.com

Circa 1885. Built in Greek Revival style, Chateau du Louisiane is located on the edge of New Orleans' famous Garden District. The home, along with the myriad of other historic homes and buildings, is listed in the National Register of Historic Places. Period furnishings decorate the guest rooms, suites and common areas. Each guest room is named after someone famous in Louisiana history, such as Louis Armstrong. The chateau is one mile from the French Quarter, and the St. Charles streetcar stops just three blocks away.
Innkeeper(s): Joanne C. Preston. $99-300. 5 rooms with PB, 2 suites and 2 conference rooms. Breakfast and snacks/refreshments included in rates. Types of meals: Cont plus and early coffee/tea. Beds: KQ. Modem hook-up, data port, cable TV, reading lamp, ceiling fan, clock radio, telephone, voice mail and data ports in room. Central air. Fax, copier, library and parlor games on premises. Antiquing, art galleries, bicycling, fishing, golf, live theater, museums, parks, shopping, sporting events, tennis, water sports, zoo, executive development meetings led by Joanne C. Preston PH.D and RODC nearby.
Location: City.
Certificate may be used: Subject to availability, excludes major events.

Cornstalk Hotel

915 Royal St
New Orleans, LA 70116-2701
(504)523-1515 (800)759-6112 Fax:(504)522-5558
Internet: www.cornstalkhotel.com
E-mail: info@cornstalkhotel.com

Circa 1816. This home belonged to Judge Francois Xavier-Martin, the author of the first history of Louisiana and Louisiana's first State Supreme Court Chief Justice. Andrew

Jackson stayed here and another guest, Harriet Beecher Stowe, wrote Uncle Tom's Cabin after viewing the nearby slave markets. The Civil War followed the widely read publication. Surrounding the inn is a 165-year-old wrought-iron cornstalk fence. Stained-glass windows, Oriental rugs, fireplaces and antiques grace the property. Breakfast and the morning newspaper can be served in your room or set up on the balcony, porch or patio.
Innkeeper(s): Debi & David Spencer. $75-185. 14 rooms with PB. Breakfast included in rates. Types of meals: Cont plus. Beds: KQDT. Modem hook-up, cable TV, reading lamp and telephone in room. Central air. Amusement parks, antiquing, art galleries, bicycling, fishing, golf, hiking, horseback riding, live theater, museums, parks, shopping, sporting events and tennis nearby.
Location: City. In the heart of the French Quarter.
Publicity: *London Sunday Times and Tampa Tribune.*
Certificate may be used: June-August, Sunday-Thursday.

Fairchild House

1518 Prytania St
New Orleans, LA 70130-4416
(504)524-0154 (800)256-8096 Fax:(504)568-0063
Internet: www.fairchildhouse.com
E-mail: info@fairchildhouse.com

Circa 1841. Situated in the oak-lined Lower Garden District of New Orleans, this Greek Revival home was built by architect L.H. Pilie. The house and its guest houses maintain a Victorian ambiance with elegantly appointed guest rooms. Wine and cheese are served upon guests' arrival. Afternoon tea can be served upon request. The bed & breakfast, which is on the Mardi Gras parade route, is 17 blocks from the French Quarter and 12 blocks from the convention center. Streetcars are just one block away, as are many local attractions, including paddleboat cruises, Canal Place and Riverwalk shopping, an aquarium, zoo, the St. Charles Avenue mansions and Tulane and Loyola universities.
Innkeeper(s): Rita Olmo & Beatriz Aprigliano-Ziegler. $75-165. 20 rooms, 17 with PB, 3 suites. Breakfast included in rates. Types of meals: Cont plus. Beds: KQDT. Clock radio, telephone, desk and voice mail in room. Air conditioning. TV, fax and copier on premises. Antiquing, shopping and restaurants nearby.
Location: City.
"Accommodations were great; staff was great ... Hope to see y'all soon!"
Certificate may be used: June 1-Aug. 31. Please call during other seasons.

Hotel Saint Pierre

911 Burgundy Street, French Quarter
New Orleans, LA 70116-3003
(504)524-4401 (800)225-4040 Fax:504-593-9425
Internet: www.FrenchQuarterInns.com
E-mail: reservations@FrenchQuarterInns.com

Circa 1780. Experience the atmosphere and architecture of the French Quarter while staying at this historic collection of Creole cottages. The flavors of Bourbon Street are two blocks away. Select a guest bedroom or suite with a balcony overlooking a lush courtyard and swimming pool. After a continental breakfast with southern-style treats, relax and enjoy the hotel's generous blend of comfortable hospitality. There is so much to see and do in New Orleans and this is the perfect home base.
Innkeeper(s): French Quarter Inns. $69-299. 74 rooms with PB, 3 with FP, 7 suites and 14 cottages. Breakfast included in rates. Types of meals: Cont and early coffee/tea. Beds: KDT. Cable TV, ceiling fan, telephone, hot tub/spa and fireplace in room. Central air. Fax and two swimming pools on premises.

Amusement parks, antiquing, art galleries, bicycling, fishing, golf, live theater, museums, parks, shopping, sporting events, tennis, water sports, historic architecture, national landmarks, fine dining, jazz and live music nearby.

Location: City, waterfront. Historic District, French Quarter.

Certificate may be used: Anytime, subject to availability.

Lafitte Guest House

1003 Bourbon St
New Orleans, LA 70116-2707
(504)581-2678 (800)331-7971 Fax:(504)581-2677
Internet: www.lafitteguesthouse.com
E-mail: lafitte@travelbase.com

Circa 1849. This elegant French manor house has been meticulously restored. The house is filled with fine antiques and paintings collected from around the world. Located in the heart of the French Quarter, the inn is near world-famous restaurants, museums, antique shops and rows of Creole and Spanish cottages. Between 5:30 p.m. and 7 p.m., there is a wine and cheese social hour on Friday and Saturday.

Innkeeper(s): Edward G. Dore & Andrew J. Crocchiolo. $159-229. 14 rooms with PB, 7 with FP, 2 suites. Breakfast included in rates. Types of meals: Cont plus. Beds: KQ. TV, refrigerator, ceiling fan, clock radio, telephone and desk in room. Air conditioning. Fax and copier on premises. Amusement parks, antiquing, fishing, live theater, parks, shopping, sporting events and water sports nearby.

Location: City.

Publicity: *Glamour, Antique Monthly, McCall's, Dixie and Country Living.*

"This old building offers the finest lodgings we have found in the city." — McCall's Magazine

Certificate may be used: Last two weeks of August and first two weeks of December, Sunday through Thursday, subject to availability.

Lamothe House

621 Esplanade Ave
New Orleans, LA 70116-2018
(504)947-1161 (800)367-5858 Fax:(504)943-6536
Internet: new-orleans.org
E-mail: lam5675842@aol.com

Circa 1830. Stay at this 1830s townhouse with Creole-style façade, gracing Esplanade Avenue, a famous street with ancient oaks that shade horse-drawn carriages and some the state's oldest architecture. Furnished with Victorian antiques, decorative fireplaces accent many of the air-conditioned guest bedrooms and suites and some face the lush inner courtyard overlooking the fish pond. A few rooms can be adjoined for those traveling together. More accommodations are offered at the Marigny Guest House, a Creole cottage across the street. Louisiana-roast coffee, fresh-baked pastries and croissants are served for breakfast in the elegant dining room. Sip complimentary sherry in the afternoon. Feel refreshed after a swim in the outdoor pool or soak in the Jacuzzi.

Innkeeper(s): Carol Chauppette. $59-250. 20 rooms with PB, 1 with FP, 9 suites, 2 cottages and 1 conference room. Breakfast included in rates. Types of meals: Cont plus and afternoon tea. Beds: QDT. Cable TV, reading lamp, stereo, ceiling fan, clock radio, telephone, turn-down service and desk in room. Air conditioning. VCR, fax, copier, child care, free parking, swimming pool and Jacuzzi on premises. Amusement parks, antiquing, fishing, live theater, parks, shopping, sporting events and French Quarter nearby.

Location: City. French Quarter.

Publicity: *Southern Living (Cover), Los Angeles Times, Houston Post and Travel & Leisure.*

Certificate may be used: Anytime, subject to availability.

Macarty Park Guest House

3820 Burgundy St
New Orleans, LA 70117
(504)943-4994 (800)521-2790
Internet: www.macartypark.com
E-mail: johnallilo@aol.com

Circa 1899. Relax on the porch swing of this romantic turn-of-the-century home. The parlor is inviting with a beautifully polished carved mantelpiece, balloon curtains and appealing antiques. Guest rooms are tastefully furnished with antiques and reproductions in an elegant uncluttered traditional style and some offer four-poster beds. In addition to the guest rooms, cottages and condos are available. The inn's tropical setting can be enjoyed next to the heated in-ground pool or from the spacious hot tub.

Innkeeper(s): John Alillo & David. $59-225. 8 rooms with PB, 3 with FP, 1 suite and 2 cottages. Breakfast included in rates. Types of meals: Cont plus. Beds: KQDT. Cable TV, reading lamp, clock radio and telephone in room. Air conditioning. Fax, spa and swimming on premises. Antiquing, live theater, shopping, sporting events, tennis and French Quarter nearby.

Location: City.

Certificate may be used: Sunday-Thursday, January, June, August and December.

Maison Perrier B&B

4117 Perrier St
New Orleans, LA 70115
(504)897-1807 (888)610-1807 Fax:(504)897-1399
Internet: www.maisonperrier.com
E-mail: innkeeper@maisonperrier.com

Circa 1892. Experience Southern hospitality and a casually elegant atmosphere at this bed & breakfast located in the Uptown Garden District. The historic Victorian mansion was built in 1892 with renovations carefully preserving ornamental woodwork, fireplace tiles, chandeliers and antique furnishings while adding modern conveniences. Distinctive guest bedrooms and suites with parlors feature stunning beds, romantic touches that include candles and flowers, whirlpool tubs, terry cloth robes, and private balconies. Praline French toast, apple puff pancakes, creole eggs and potato casserole are among the incredible breakfast favorites that begin and end with New Orleans coffee. Relax in the brick courtyards surrounded by tropical plants.

Innkeeper(s): Tracewell Bailey. $89-250. 16 rooms with PB, 10 suites and 4 conference rooms. Breakfast, afternoon tea and snacks/refreshments included in rates. Types of meals: Full gourmet bkfst, veg bkfst, early coffee/tea, picnic lunch and room service. Beds: KQT. Modem hook-up, data port, cable TV, reading lamp, refrigerator, ceiling fan, clock radio, telephone, turn-down service, desk, hot tub/spa, voice mail, fireplace, luxury bath amenities and terry cloth robes in room. Central air. VCR, fax, copier, spa, tennis, library, child care, parlor games, fireplace, laundry facility and gift shop on premises. Limited handicap access. Amusement parks, antiquing, art galleries, beach, bicycling, fishing, golf, live theater, museums, parks, shopping, sporting events, tennis and water sports nearby.

Location: City. Uptown garden district.

Publicity: *Fodors, Frommers and Memphis PBS.*

Certificate may be used: June 1-Sept. 15, Sunday-Thursday, only subject to availability.

Olde Victorian Inn & Spa

914 N Rampart St
New Orleans, LA 70116
(504)522-2446 (800)725-2446 Fax:(504)522-8646
Internet: www.oldevictorianinn.com
E-mail: oldeinn@aol.com

Circa 1842. Experience the romantic 1840s at this two-story Victorian inn in the historic French Quarter. It is one of the area's first homes owned by a free slave before the Civil War. Enjoy tea in the lush tropical courtyard or inside, surrounded by floor to ceiling windows, antiques and plenty of lace and ruffles. Large beds and private baths highlight the elegantly decorated guest bedrooms. Most feature fireplaces and some have balconies. Miss Celie's Spa Orleans provides on-site pampering. Schedule a facial and a couples massage. A gourmet breakfast begins an adventurous day from the front door steps onto Rampart Street.

Innkeeper(s): Keith & Andre West-Harrison. $150-275. 4 rooms with PB. Breakfast included in rates. Types of meals: Full gourmet bkfst, veg bkfst, early coffee/tea and gourmet dinner. Beds: D. Ceiling fan, clock radio, desk, fireplace and clawfoot tubs in room. Central air. TV, VCR, fax, copier, library, telephone and fireplace on premises. Amusement parks, antiquing, art galleries, live theater, museums, parks and shopping nearby.

Location: City.

Publicity: Vogue, Australian Travel Channel and MSN.com.

Certificate may be used: Anytime, subject to availability, excludes special events, Mardi Gras & festivals.

The Queen Anne Hotel

1525 Prytania St
New Orleans, LA 70130-4448
(504)524-0427 (866)240-1625 Fax:(504)522-2977
Internet: www.thequeenanne.com
E-mail: prytaniapk@aol.com

Circa 1890. Located one block from the famous St. Charles Avenue Streetcar line in the Historic Landmark Lower Garden District, this restored Queen Anne Victorian mansion is listed in the National Register. It offers 14-foot cove ceilings, polished hardwood floors and intricately designed fireplace mantels. Original woodwork of red hard pine and Louisiana cypress add to the inn's elegant renovation. Ask for one of the rooms with a balcony that overlooks the graceful 100-year-old oak tree. Guests register at the Prytania Park Hotel a block away. Special offerings include off-street parking and shuttle service to the French Quarter and nearby Convention Center.

Innkeeper(s): Edward Halpern. $149-229. 12 rooms with PB. Breakfast included in rates. Types of meals: Cont. Beds: KQT. Cable TV, reading lamp, ceiling fan, clock radio, telephone, desk, safes, refrigerators and microwaves in room. Air conditioning. Fax and copier on premises. Antiquing, parks, shopping and sporting events nearby.

Location: City. National Historic District.

Certificate may be used: Anytime, subject to availability, excluding special events.

St. Peter Guest House Hotel

1005 Saint Peter St
New Orleans, LA 70116-3014
(504)524-9232 (800)535-7815 Fax:(504)523-5198
Internet: www.crescent-city.org
E-mail: sptlj678z@aol.com

Circa 1800. Comfort and convenience are offered at this popular retreat situated in a quiet area just two blocks from Bourbon Street. This quaint, historic hotel boasts inviting iron-lace balconies with great views and tropical brick courtyards that are so much a part of the French Quarter ambiance. Stay in a spacious, air-conditioned guest bedroom furnished with antiques or choose one with a more contemporary style decor. Wake up to enjoy freshly baked pastries and Louisiana-roast coffee. Ask the 24-hour front desk staff for tour recommendations or help in planning each day's fun and adventure.

Innkeeper(s): Brent Kovach. $59-225. 28 rooms with PB, 11 suites. Breakfast included in rates. Types of meals: Cont plus. Beds: KQDT. Cable TV, reading lamp, ceiling fan, telephone and desk in room. Air conditioning. Fax on premises. Amusement parks, antiquing, fishing, live theater, parks and shopping nearby.

Location: City. French Quarter.

Certificate may be used: Anytime, subject to availability.

Pearl River   F8

Woodridge Bed & Breakfast of Louisiana

40149 Crowe's Landing Rd.
Pearl River, LA 70452
(985)863-9981 (877)643-7109 Fax:(985)863-0820
Internet: www.woodridgebb.com
E-mail: tfotsch@aol.com

Circa 1980. Generous Southern hospitality and comfort mingled with upscale amenities are offered at this Georgian-style home. Each flower-themed guest suite is furnished with antiques and an adjacent access to the balcony. After a restful night's sleep, linger over a big country breakfast with an abundance of homemade breads, a hot entree, meats and seasonal fruits. Shaded by 100-year-old live oak trees, a swing for two is a pleasant interlude. Enjoy the serene gardens with fountains, a bistro and benches to view the dogwood, magnolia, roses and azalea.

Innkeeper(s): Debbi & Tim Fotsch. $65-140. 5 rooms with PB. Breakfast included in rates. Types of meals: Full gourmet bkfst. Beds: QD. Cable TV, reading lamp, refrigerator, ceiling fan and telephone in room. Central air. VCR and fax on premises. Amusement parks, antiquing, art galleries, beach, bicycling, canoeing/kayaking, fishing, golf, hiking, horseback riding, live theater, museums, parks, shopping, sporting events and wineries nearby.

Location: Country.

Certificate may be used: June 1-Aug. 28, subject to availability. Sunday-Thursday during September, subject to availability.

Vacherie   G7

Bay Tree Plantation Bed & Breakfast

3785 Highway 18
Vacherie, LA 70090-7074
(225)265-2109 (800)895-2109 Fax:(225)265-7076
Internet: www.baytree.net
E-mail: info@baytree.net

Circa 1909. Lush green cane fields shield this French Creole cottage that was built in the Greek Revival style on four acres with adjacent Rene House and Dr. Vignes Cottage. On the west bank in St. James Parish, the plantation faces the Great River Road near the Mississippi. Listed in the National Register, the B&B is furnished in elegant antiques. The cottage, guest bedrooms and the master suite feature full and half-tester beds and two-person whirlpool or clawfoot tubs. Some rooms boast fireplaces. Indulge in a satisfying Southern breakfast before embarking on the day's adventures. Relax on the porch, or enjoy a stroll through the flower gardens.

Innkeeper(s): Dinah Laurich. $75-155. 7 rooms with PB, 3 with FP, 3 with HT, 1 two-bedroom suite and 1 cottage. Breakfast included in rates. Types of meals: Country bkfst, veg bkfst and afternoon tea. Beds: QDT. Cable TV, VCR, reading lamp, refrigerator, ceiling fan, clock radio, telephone, coffeemaker, hot tub/spa and fireplace in room. Central air. Fax, copier and spa on premises. Hiking, shopping, plantation tours and swamp tours nearby.

Location: Country, waterfront. Historic Mississippi River.

Publicity: Houston Chronicle Travel Section and Primary Colors.

Certificate may be used: Anytime, Sunday-Thursday only. Weekends included June-September only.

Maine

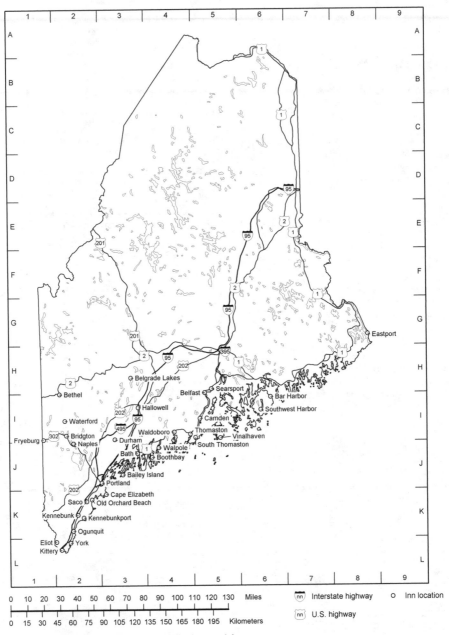

Interstate highway   o Inn location

U.S. highway

Bailey Island   J3

Captain York House B&B

Rt 24, PO Box 298
Bailey Island, ME 04003
(207)833-6224
Internet: www.captainyorkhouse.com
E-mail: athorn7286@aol.com

Circa 1906. Bailey Island is the quaint fisherman's village of
stories, poems and movies. Guests cross the world's only crib-
stone bridge to reach the island, where beautiful sunsets and
dinners of fresh Maine lobster are the norm. This shingled,
turn-of-the-century, Mansard-style B&B was the home of a
famous Maine sea captain, Charles York. Now a homestay-style
bed & breakfast, the innkeepers
have restored the home to its former glory, filling it with many
antiques. Guests at Captain York's
enjoy water views from all the
guest rooms. Wild Maine blueberries often find a significant place on
the breakfast menu.

Innkeeper(s): Alan & Jean Thornton. $70-130. 5 rooms with PB. Breakfast
included in rates. Types of meals: Full bkfst. Beds: QT. Reading lamp in
room. VCR and telephone on premises. Antiquing, live theater, parks, shopping, sporting events, water sports, P. McMilan Museum and Maine Maritime
Museum nearby.

Location: Ocean community.

Publicity: Tri-Town News and Palm Beach Post.

*"Bailey Island turned out to be the hidden treasure of our trip and we
hope to return for your great hospitality again."*

Certificate may be used: Jan. 30 to May 15, Oct. 15-Dec. 15.

Bar Harbor   I6

The Atlantean Inn

26 Ash Place
Bar Harbor, ME 04609
(207)288-5703 (800)722-6671 Fax:(207)288-3115
Internet: www.atlanteaninn.com
E-mail: kgreer@atlanteaninn.com

Circa 1903. Experience a taste of the opulent Victorian era at
this English Tudor-style bed & breakfast, located in historic
downtown. Original watercolors and oil paintings, antique fixtures and furnishings all are placed with care in eye-pleasing
and comfortable arrangements. Hospitality is generous, with
guest bedrooms and suites offering a video library and answering machines. Some feature working fireplaces and Jacuzzis.
Two suites accommodate families with ease. Lobster quiche
and blueberry muffins are two breakfast treats using delicious
regional ingredients. Enjoy the perennial gardens, and relax
under the shade of a maple tree.

Innkeeper(s): Kathleen Greer. $95-285. 8 rooms with PB, 5 with FP, 2
suites. Breakfast and snacks/refreshments included in rates. Types of meals:
Full bkfst and early coffee/tea. Beds: KQDT. Cable TV, VCR, reading lamp,
clock radio, telephone, fireplace suites have refrigerator and several suites
have Jacuzzis in room. Air conditioning. Parlor games and fireplace on
premises. Antiquing, art galleries, beach, bicycling, canoeing/kayaking, fishing, golf, hiking, horseback riding, live theater, museums, parks, shopping,
water sports and whale watching nearby.

Location: Mountains, ocean community.

Certificate may be used: May 23-June 24, Sunday-Thursday, excluding
Memorial Day weekend.

Mira Monte Inn & Suites

69 Mount Desert St
Bar Harbor, ME 04609-1327
(207)288-4263 (800)553-5109 Fax:(207)288-3115
Internet: www.miramonte.com
E-mail: mburns@miramonte.com

Circa 1864. A gracious 16-room Victorian mansion, the Mira
Monte has been renovated in the style of early Bar Harbor. It
features period furnishings, pleasant common rooms, a library
and wraparound porches. Situated on estate grounds, there are
sweeping lawns, paved terraces and many gardens. The inn was
one of the earliest of Bar Harbor's famous summer cottages.
The two-room suites each feature canopy beds, two-person
whirlpools, a parlor with a sleeper sofa, fireplace and kitchenette unit. The two-bedroom suite includes a full kitchen,
dining area and parlor. The suites boast private decks with
views of the gardens.

Innkeeper(s): Marian Burns. $165-265. 16 rooms with PB, 14 with FP, 3
suites. Breakfast and afternoon tea included in rates. Types of meals: Full
bkfst and early coffee/tea. Beds: KQT. Cable TV, VCR, reading lamp, clock
radio, telephone, desk and hot tub/spa in room. Air conditioning. TV, fax,
library, parlor games, fireplace, data ports and Internet access on premises.
Handicap access. Antiquing, fishing, live theater, parks, shopping and Acadia
National Park nearby.

Location: Mountains. Island.

Publicity: Los Angeles Times.

*"On our third year at your wonderful inn in beautiful Bar Harbor.
I think I enjoy it more each year. A perfect place to stay in a perfect environment."*

Certificate may be used: April 26-May 20.

Bath   J3

Fairhaven Inn

118 N. Bath Rd
Bath, ME 04530-0085
(207)443-4391 (888)443-4391 Fax:(207)443-6412
Internet: www.mainecoast.com/fairhaveninn
E-mail: fairhvn@gwi.net

Circa 1790. With its view of the Kennebec River, this site was
so attractive that Pembleton Edgecomb built his Colonial house
where a log cabin had previously stood. His descendants occupied it for the next 125 years. Antiques and country furniture
fill the inn. Meadows and
lawns, and woods of hem-
lock, birch and pine
cover the inn's 16 acres.

Innkeeper(s): Susie & Dave
Reed. $80-130. 8 rooms, 6
with PB, 1 suite and 1 cottage. Breakfast included in rates. Types of meals:
Full gourmet bkfst and early coffee/tea. Beds: KQT. Reading lamp and clock
radio in room. TV, VCR, fax, library, parlor games, telephone and fireplace on
premises. Limited handicap access. Antiquing, art galleries, beach, bicycling,
canoeing/kayaking, cross-country skiing, fishing, golf, hiking, live theater,
museums, parks, shopping, sporting events, tennis and water sports nearby.

Location: Country. River-country setting.

Publicity: The State, Coastal Journal and Times Record.

*"The Fairhaven is now marked in our book with a red star, definitely
a place to remember and visit again."*

Certificate may be used: Sunday-Thursday, Sept. 5-June 30.

The Galen C. Moses House

1009 Washington St
Bath, ME 04530-2759
(207)442-8771 (888)442-8771
Internet: www.galenmoses.com
E-mail: stay@galenmoses.com

Circa 1874. This Victorian mansion is filled with beautiful architectural items, including stained-glass windows, wood-carved and marble fireplaces and a grand staircase. The innkeepers have filled the library, a study, morning room and the parlor with antiques. A corner fireplace warms the dining room, which overlooks the lawns and gardens. Tea is presented in the formal drawing room.
Innkeeper(s): James Haught, Larry Kieft. $99-259. 4 rooms with PB, 1 suite. Breakfast and afternoon tea included in rates. Types of meals: Full gourmet bkfst. Beds: QT. Turn-down service and fans in room. Air conditioning. VCR, bicycles, library, telephone and fireplace on premises. Antiquing, art galleries, beach, bicycling, canoeing/kayaking, cross-country skiing, fishing, golf, hiking, horseback riding, live theater, museums, parks, shopping, tennis, water sports and boats nearby.
Location: City.
Publicity: *Philadelphia, Back Roads USA, Ghost Stories of New England - Susan Smitten, "LC & Co" show and Home & Garden channel - "Restore America."*

"For our first try at B&B lodgings, we've probably started at the top, and nothing else will ever measure up to this. Wonderful food, wonderful home, grounds and wonderful hosts!"
Certificate may be used: Some weekends, November-April, subject to availability.

Pryor House B&B

360 Front St
Bath, ME 04530-2749
(207)443-1146
Internet: www.pryorhouse.com
E-mail: pryorhse@suscommaine.com

Circa 1820. This early Federal house was built by a family of shipbuilders. From its location on the Kennebec River, Elizabeth's provides a relaxing atmosphere with country antiques and "Mr. T," the resident cat. The dining room features stenciled walls and flagstone and brick floors. Choose the Captain's Quarters for a king-size bed, wide-pine flooring, window seat and river view.
Innkeeper(s): Don & Gwenda Pryor. $85-120. 3 rooms with PB, 2 with FP, 1 with WP. Breakfast, afternoon tea and snacks/refreshments included in rates. Types of meals: Full gourmet bkfst, veg bkfst and early coffee/tea. Beds: KQ. TV, reading lamp, clock radio, turn-down service, desk, hot tub/spa and cable TV available in room. Air conditioning. VCR, library, parlor games, telephone and fireplace on premises. Antiquing, art galleries, beach, canoeing/kayaking, downhill skiing, fishing, golf, hiking, live theater, museums, parks, shopping, sporting events, tennis and water sports nearby.
Location: Waterfront. In town.
Publicity: *Times Record.*

"It was truly a warming experience to feel so at home, away from home."
Certificate may be used: Anytime, November-March, subject to availability.

Belfast   H5

The Alden House Bed & Breakfast

63 Church St
Belfast, ME 04915-6208
(207)338-2151 (877)337-8151 Fax:(207)338-2151
Internet: www.thealdenhouse.com
E-mail: info@thealdenhouse.com

Circa 1840. This pre-Civil War, pristinely restored Greek Revival manor was built for prominent Belfast citizen Hiram Alden. Alden was editor of the local paper, town postmaster

and vice-president of American Telegraph. The interior still boasts grand features, such as marble fireplace mantels, tin ceilings and a hand-carved curved staircase. Early risers enjoy the view from the front porch as they sip a cup of freshly ground coffee. Breakfast begins with juice, fresh fruit and muffins, followed by a special entree.
Innkeeper(s): Bruce & Susan Madara. $95-130. 7 rooms, 5 with PB, 1 with FP. Breakfast and afternoon tea included in rates. Types of meals: Full bkfst and early coffee/tea. Beds: QDT. Reading lamp, natural body care products, hair dryers and robes in room. VCR, fax, library, parlor games, telephone and fireplace on premises. Antiquing, cross-country skiing, downhill skiing, fishing, golf, live theater, parks, shopping, tennis and water sports nearby.
Location: City, ocean community.
Publicity: *Bangor Daily News and Waldo Independent.*
Certificate may be used: Nov. 1-May 15.

Belhaven Inn

14 John St
Belfast, ME 04915-6650
(207)338-5435
Internet: www.belhaveninn.com
E-mail: stay@belhaveninn.com

Circa 1851. This 16-room 1851 Federal Victorian stands on an acre in the heart of Belfast, a historic harbor community with roots in shipbuilding. Mullioned windows, pumpkin pine floors and carved mantels are some of the many period features of the inn. A circular staircase leads to the four guest bedrooms, each appointed with period pieces. A three-course country breakfast is served daily on the side porch, weather permitting. It includes items such as fruit cup with yogurt or granola, freshly baked muffins, hot breads and a hot entrée of either eggs, pancakes, crepes or sausage. Locally grown berries and produce are used in season. After breakfast relax on the porch or head into Belfast to explore the many art galleries and shops. Take a ride on the vintage Belfast and Moosehead Train or arrange for a boat to explore the islands in the Penobscot Bay or take a drive and explore the nearby lighthouses.
Innkeeper(s): Anne & Paul Bartels. $85-125. 5 rooms, 3 with PB, 1 suite. Breakfast and snacks/refreshments included in rates. Types of meals: Country bkfst and early coffee/tea. Beds: KQDT. Reading lamp, clock radio, turn-down service and desk in room. TV, VCR, tennis, library, parlor games, telephone, fireplace, badminton and volleyball on premises. Antiquing, art galleries, beach, bicycling, canoeing/kayaking, cross-country skiing, fishing, golf, hiking, horseback riding, live theater, museums, parks, shopping, tennis and wineries nearby.
Location: Country.
Certificate may be used: Jan. 1-June 1, Sunday-Thursday, subject to availability.

The Jeweled Turret Inn

40 Pearl St
Belfast, ME 04915-1907
(207)338-2304 (800)696-2304
Internet: www.jeweledturret.com
E-mail: info@jeweledturret.com

Circa 1898. This grand Victorian is named for the staircase that winds up the turret, lighted by stained- and leaded-glass panels and jewel-like embellishments. It was built for attorney James Harriman. Dark pine beams adorn the ceiling of the den, and the fireplace is constructed of bark and rocks from every state in the Union. Elegant antiques furnish the guest rooms. Guests can relax in one of the inn's four parlors, which are furnished with period antiques, wallpapers, lace and boast fireplaces. Some rooms have a ceiling fan and whirlpool tub or fireplace. The verandas feature wicker and iron bistro sets and views of the historic district. The inn is within walking distance of the town and its shops, restaurants and the harbor.

Innkeeper(s): Cathy & Carl Heffentrager. $105-150. 7 rooms with PB, 1 with FP. Breakfast and afternoon tea included in rates. Types of meals: Full gourmet bkfst and early coffee/tea. Beds: QDT. TV, reading lamp and one with whirlpool tub in room. Telephone and fireplace on premises. Antiquing, cross-country skiing, downhill skiing, fishing, live theater, shopping and water sports nearby.

Location: Small historic coastal town.

Publicity: *News Herald, Republican Journal, Waterville Sentinel, Los Angeles Times, Country Living, Victorian Homes and The Saturday Evening Post.*

"The ambiance was so romantic that we felt like we were on our honeymoon."

Certificate may be used: April, May and November, holidays excluded.

Londonderry Inn

133 Belmont Ave (Rt 3)
Belfast, ME 04915
(207)338-2763 (877)529-9566 Fax:(207)338-6303
Internet: www.londonderry-inn.com
E-mail: info@londonderry-inn.com

Circa 1803. Built in 1803, this Maine farmhouse provides elegant comfort and spacious common areas to relax and enjoy a wonderful vacation. Choose from five delightful guest bedrooms with modern private baths. Wake up each morning to an old-fashioned farmer's breakfast featuring gourmet foods that may include blueberry pancakes and apple walnut muffins served in the large fireplaced country kitchen. Early risers can sip coffee on the screened porch or backyard deck overlooking the garden. Explore six beautiful acres surrounding the inn, pick raspberries in season or catch a glimpse of deer or wild turkeys. Pick a complimentary in-room movie from the extensive video collection of more than 200 films. Visit the area's many historic sites like Fort Knox State Park.

Innkeeper(s): Marsha Oakes. $95-140. 5 rooms with PB. Breakfast and snacks/refreshments included in rates. Types of meals: Country bkfst, early coffee/tea and afternoon tea. Beds: KQD. Cable TV, VCR, reading lamp, refrigerator, clock radio, telephone, twin sleep sofa, bathrobes and hair dryers in room. Fax, copier, library, fireplace, laundry facility, AC, backyard deck, evening dessert, 200+ video/periodical library and laundry facilities (for a nominal fee) on premises. Antiquing, art galleries, beach, bicycling, canoeing/kayaking, downhill skiing, fishing, golf, hiking, live theater, museums, parks, shopping, water sports, wineries, lighthouses, wild blueberries, strawberries and apples nearby.

Location: Country, ocean community. Two miles from downtown Belfast and harbor.

Certificate may be used: October-June, Sunday-Thursday, subject to availability.

Belgrade Lakes   H3

Wings Hill Inn

PO Box 386
Belgrade Lakes, ME 04918-0386
(207)495-2400 (866)495-2400
Internet: wingshillinn.com
E-mail: wingshillinn@earthlink.net

Circa 1800. In a picturesque lakefront village setting, this post and beam farmhouse is an ideal romantic getaway. Relaxation comes easy by the fireplace in the Great Room or the extensive screened wraparound porch overlooking Long Pond. The guest bedrooms boast a comfortable elegance. Hospitality is abundant, as experienced in the optional breakfast basket delivered to the door, or join others in the dining area. Enjoy intimate candlelit dining Sunday-Thursday. Hiking, fishing, boating and

golf are only steps away. Other popular New England sites and activities are an easy drive away.

Innkeeper(s): Christopher & Tracey Anderson. $95-145. 8 rooms with PB. Breakfast and afternoon tea included in rates. Types of meals: Full bkfst and early coffee/tea. Antiquing, cross-country skiing, downhill skiing, fishing, golf, hiking, shopping, sporting events and water sports nearby.

Certificate may be used: November through April, excluding holidays and special events.

Bethel   I2

Chapman Inn

PO Box 1067
Bethel, ME 04217-1067
(207)824-2657 (877)359-1498
Internet: www.chapmaninn.com
E-mail: info@chapmaninn.com

Circa 1865. As one of the town's oldest buildings, this Federal-style inn has been a store, a tavern and a boarding house known as "The Howard." It was the home of William Rogers Chapman,

composer, conductor and founder of the Rubenstein Club and the Metropolitan Musical Society, in addition to the Maine Music Festival. The inn is a convenient place to begin a walking tour of Bethel's historic district.

Innkeeper(s): Sandra & Fred. $25-105. 10 rooms with PB, 2 suites. Breakfast included in rates. Types of meals: Full bkfst, early coffee/tea and afternoon tea. TV, reading lamp, refrigerator, telephone and desk in room. Air conditioning. VCR, fax, sauna, parlor games and fireplace on premises. Antiquing, cross-country skiing, downhill skiing, fishing, golf, live theater, parks, shopping, tennis and water sports nearby.

Location: Mountains. In village.

Certificate may be used: Oct. 15-June 1, Sunday-Friday except holidays.

L'Auberge Country Inn

PO Box 21
Bethel, ME 04217
(207)824-2774 (800)760-2774 Fax:(207)824-0806
Internet: www.laubergecountryinn.com
E-mail: inn@laubergecountryinn.com

Circa 1850. In the foothills of the White Mountains, surrounded by five acres of gardens and woods, this former carriage house was converted to a guest house in the 1920s. Among its seven guest rooms are two spacious suites. The Theater Suite offers a four-poster queen bed and dressing room. The Family Suite can accommodate up to six guests. Mount Abrahms and Sunday River ski areas are just minutes away.

Innkeeper(s): Alexandra & Adam Adler. $69-250. 7 rooms with PB, 1 two-bedroom and 1 three-bedroom suites. Breakfast and afternoon tea included in rates. Types of meals: Country bkfst, veg bkfst, early coffee/tea, picnic lunch, snacks/refreshments, hors d'oeuvres, gourmet dinner and room service. Restaurant on premises. Beds: KQT. Reading lamp, clock radio, turn-down service and desk in room. Air conditioning. TV, VCR, fax, bicycles, library, pet boarding, child care, parlor games, telephone, fireplace, laundry facility and gift shop on premises. Limited handicap access. Amusement parks, antiquing, art galleries, beach, bicycling, canoeing/kayaking, cross-country skiing, downhill skiing, fishing, golf, hiking, horseback riding, live theater, museums, parks, shopping, tennis, water sports, Gould Academy and National Training Laboratories nearby.

Location: Country, mountains. Resort.

Publicity: *Yankee, Gourmet, Canadian Life, Maine Explorers Guide, Fodors, Frommers, Rough Guides, Tripadvisor.com (4 stars) and New York 1 News.*

Certificate may be used: Midweek, non-holiday.

Boothbay   J4

Kenniston Hill Inn

Rt 27, PO Box 125
Boothbay, ME 04537-0125
(207)633-2159 (800)992-2915 Fax:(207)633-2159
Internet: www.kennistonhillinn.com
E-mail: innkeeper@maine.com

Circa 1786. The elegant clapboard home is the oldest inn at
Boothbay Harbor Region and was occupied by the Kenniston family for more than a century. Five of the antique-filled bedrooms
have fireplaces. After a walk through the gardens
or woods, warm up in the parlor next to the
elegant, open-hearthed fireplace.
Boothbay Harbor offers something for everybody, including
whale-watching excursions and
dinner theaters.

Innkeeper(s): Jim & Gerry Botti. $85-130. 10 rooms with PB, 5 with FP and
2 cottages. Breakfast and afternoon tea included in rates. Types of meals:
Country bkfst and early coffee/tea. Beds: KQDT. Reading lamp, ceiling fan
and clock radio in room. Air conditioning. TV, VCR, fax, copier, parlor games,
telephone, fireplace and laundry facility on premises. Antiquing, art galleries,
beach, bicycling, canoeing/kayaking, fishing, golf, hiking, live theater, museums, parks, shopping and tennis nearby.

Location: Ocean community.

Publicity: *Boothbay Register.*

*"England may be the home of the original bed & breakfast, but
Kenniston Hill Inn is where it has been perfected!"*

Certificate may be used: Nov. 1 to June 15, subject to availability.

Bridgton   I2

Tarry-A-While Resort

RR 3, Box 1067, Highland Rd.
Bridgton, ME 04009
(207)647-2522 Fax:(207)647-5512
Internet: www.tarryawhile.com
E-mail: tarryayl@megalink.net

Circa 1897. Tarry-A-While offers a variety of comfortable
accommodations, including a Victorian inn and cottages. There
is also a social hall. The resort is located on a 25-acre hillside
and there are plenty of outdoor activities. Tennis and boating
are included in the rates, and sailing or waterskiing is available.
An 18-hole golf course is a walk away. The inn's dining room,
which overlooks Highland Lake and Pleasant Mountain, serves
"new American" cuisine as you gaze at the sunset.

Innkeeper(s): Marc & Nancy Stretch. $60-135. 27 rooms, 22 with PB.
Breakfast included in rates. Types of meals: Cont. Beds: KQDT. Desk in room.
Air conditioning. Bicycles, tennis, fireplace, golf course, canoes and rowboats
on premises. Antiquing, live theater, shopping, tennis and boats nearby.

Location: Waterfront.

*"Thanks for sharing this magical place with us! What a wonderful
experience."*

Certificate may be used: Anytime, subject to availability.

Camden   I5

Camden Windward House B&B

6 High St
Camden, ME 04843-1611
(207)236-9656 (877)492-9656 Fax:(207)230-0433
Internet: www.windwardhouse.com
E-mail: bnb@windwardhouse.com

Circa 1854. Each guest room at this Greek Revival home has
been individually decorated and features names such as the
Carriage Room, Trisha Romance Room, Brass Room, or Silver
Birch Suite. Expansive views of
Mt. Battie may be seen from its
namesake room. It offers a private
balcony, skylights, cathedral ceilings, sitting area with fireplace, an
extra large TV and a Jacuzzi and
separate shower. All rooms include
antiques and romantic amenities

such as candles and fine linens. The innkeepers further pamper
guests with a hearty breakfast featuring a variety of juices, freshly
ground coffee and teas and a choice of items such as featherbed
eggs, pancakes, French toast or Belgian waffles topped with
fresh Maine blueberries. After the morning meal, guests are sure
to enjoy a day exploring Camden, noted as the village where
"the mountains meet the sea." The inn is open year-round.

Innkeeper(s): Phil & Liane Brookes. $120-280. 8 rooms with PB, 5 with FP,
3 total suites, including 1 two-bedroom suite. Breakfast and afternoon tea
included in rates. Types of meals: Full gourmet bkfst, early coffee/tea and
snacks/refreshments. Beds: KQT. Modem hook-up, cable TV, VCR, reading
lamp, ceiling fan, clock radio, telephone, desk, fireplace, two with Jacuzzi
whirlpool tubs, two with antique clawfoot soaking tubs, phones with data
port, two with private balcony or deck and some with VCRs and/or separate
sitting rooms in room. Air conditioning. Fax, library and parlor games on
premises. Antiquing, art galleries, beach, bicycling, canoeing/kayaking, cross-
country skiing, downhill skiing, fishing, golf, hiking, live theater, museums,
parks, shopping, tennis, water sports and wineries nearby.

Location: Ocean community. Mountains and coastal village.

Certificate may be used: Jan. 2 to May 15, Sunday through Thursday nights.

Captain Swift Inn

72 Elm St
Camden, ME 04843-1907
(207)236-8113 (800)251-0865 Fax:(207)230-0464
Internet: www.swiftinn.com
E-mail: innkeeper@swiftinn.com

Circa 1810. This inviting Federal-style home remains much as
it did in the 19th century, including the original 12-over-12
windows and a beehive oven. The innkeepers have worked diligently to preserve the historic fla-
vor, and the home's original five
fireplaces, handsome wide pine
floors, restored moldings and
exposed beams add to the warm
and cozy interior. Guest rooms
are filled with period antiques
and reproductions and offer

down pillows, handmade quilts and comfortable beds. The
only addition to the home was a new section, which includes
the innkeeper's quarters, a kitchen and a guest room entirely
accessible for guests with wheelchairs. A gourmet, three-course
breakfast includes items that sound decadent, but are truly low
in fat and cholesterol, such as an apple pancake souffle.

Innkeeper(s): Tom & Kathy Filip. $95-155. 4 rooms with PB. Breakfast and afternoon tea included in rates. Types of meals: Full gourmet bkfst and early coffee/tea. Beds: QT. Reading lamp, clock radio and table and chairs in room. Air conditioning. VCR, fax, copier, library, parlor games and telephone on premises. Handicap access. Antiquing, cross-country skiing, downhill skiing, fishing, golf, live theater, parks, shopping, tennis, water sports, schooners, lighthouses and museums nearby.

Publicity: *Maine Boats & Harbors, Boston Patriot Ledger, Tea-Time Journeys, Secrets of Entertaining* and *Wake Up & Smell the Coffee.*

"We came intending to stay for one night and ended up staying for five. . .need we say more!"

Certificate may be used: Anytime, November-April, subject to availability.

The Elms B&B

84 Elm St
Camden, ME 04843-1907
(207)236-6250 (800)755-3567 Fax:(207)236-7330
Internet: www.elmsinn.net
E-mail: info@elmsinn.net

Circa 1806. Captain Calvin Curtis built this Colonial a few minutes' stroll from the picturesque harbor. Candlelight shimmers year round from the inn's windows. A sitting room, library and parlor are open for guests. Tastefully appointed bed chambers scattered with antiques are available in both the main house and the carriage house. A cottage garden can be seen beside the carriage house. A lighthouse theme permeates the decor, and there is a wide selection of lighthouse books, collectibles and artwork.

$99-199. 7 rooms with PB, 4 with FP, 2 with HT. Breakfast, afternoon tea and snacks/refreshments included in rates. Types of meals: Full bkfst and early coffee/tea. Beds: QT. Reading lamp, CD player, ceiling fan, clock radio, telephone, coffeemaker, hot tub/spa and fireplace in room. Air conditioning. Fax, bicycles and parlor games on premises. Antiquing, cross-country skiing, downhill skiing, live theater, parks, shopping, windjammer trips, lighthouses, museums, sailing and hiking nearby.

Location: City.

"If something is worth doing, it's worth doing first class, and your place is definitely first class."

Certificate may be used: Nov. 1 to May 10, all days.

Lord Camden Inn

24 Main St
Camden, ME 04843-1704
(207)236-4325 (800)336-4325 Fax:(207)236-7141
Internet: www.lordcamdeninn.com
E-mail: innkeeper@lordcamdeninn.com

Circa 1893. Lord Camden Inn, housed in a century-old brick building, offers the gentle warmth of a seaside inn with all the comforts and services of a modern downtown hotel. Located in the midst of Camden's fine shops and restaurants, the bustling waterfront and beautiful parks, Lord Camden Inn offers splendid views of the harbor, Camden Hills and the village. Amenities include private baths, cable TV, air conditioning, phones and elevator services.

Innkeeper(s): Stuart & Marianne Smith. $98-228. 31 rooms with PB, 4 suites and 1 conference room. Breakfast included in rates. Types of meals: Full bkfst and early coffee/tea. Beds: KQD. Clock radio, telephone, some microwaves and refrigerators in room. TV, fax, copier and valet service available in high season on premises. Antiquing, cross-country skiing, downhill skiing, fishing, live theater, parks, shopping, water sports, sailing, fine dining, bicycle rentals, kayaking and hiking nearby.

Publicity: *Portland Magazine* and *Thinner.*

Certificate may be used: Oct. 16-May 31, Monday-Sunday.

Cape Elizabeth   K3

Inn By The Sea

40 Bowery Beach Rd
Cape Elizabeth, ME 04107-2599
(207)799-3134 (800)888-4287 Fax:(207)799-4779
Internet: www.innbythesea.com
E-mail: info@innbythesea.com

Circa 1986. This cottage-style resort is like a modern version of the hotels and inns that dotted Maine's coast in its heyday as a summer spot. The inn has its own private boardwalk leading to Crescent Beach. Guests can enjoy swimming, tennis and shuffleboard without leaving the inn's grounds, which also offer a tea garden and gazebo. The well-appointed rooms are elegant, but not imposing, with Chippendale furnishings, light pine and floral chintz. Guests opting for one of the inn's cozy garden suites can grab a book from the inn's library and enjoy it from a rocker on their own private porch. Cuisine at the inn's gourmet Audubon Room is full of memorable items. In the summer months, the inn opens its outdoor pool patio dining service.

Innkeeper(s): Maureen McQuade. $169-639. 43 rooms, 6 with FP, 43 suites and 2 conference rooms. Types of meals: Full bkfst, picnic lunch, gourmet dinner and room service. Restaurant on premises. Beds: KQD. Cable TV, VCR, reading lamp, refrigerator, ceiling fan, clock radio, telephone, coffeemaker, turn-down service, microwaves, high-speed Internet access and corporate desk in room. Fax, copier, outdoor pool, volleyball and shuffleboard on premises. Amusement parks, antiquing, cross-country skiing, downhill skiing, fishing, live theater, parks, shopping, sporting events and water sports nearby.

Location: Ocean community.

Certificate may be used: Anytime, November-April, excluding holidays, subject to availability. Guest must mention gift certificate program when making reservations.

Durham   I3

The Bagley House

1290 Royalsborough Rd
Durham, ME 04222-5225
(207)865-6566 (800)765-1772 Fax:(207)353-5878
Internet: www.bagleyhouse.com
E-mail: bglyhse@aol.com

Circa 1772. Six acres of fields and woods surround the Bagley House. Once an inn, a store and a schoolhouse, it is the oldest house in town. Guest rooms are decorated with colonial furnishings and hand-sewn quilts. For breakfast, guests gather in the country kitchen in front of a huge brick fireplace and beehive oven.

Innkeeper(s): Suzanne O'Connor & Susan Backhouse. $95-175. 8 rooms with PB, 4 with FP and 1 conference room. Breakfast and afternoon tea included in rates. Types of meals: Full bkfst, early coffee/tea, picnic lunch and snacks/refreshments. Beds: KQDT. Reading lamp, refrigerator and desk in room. Fax, telephone, fireplace and blueberry picking on premises. Antiquing, cross-country skiing, downhill skiing, live theater, shopping and sporting events nearby.

Location: Country.

Publicity: *Los Angeles Times, New England Getaways, Lewiston Sun, Springfield Register* and *2001 Yankee Magazine-Editors Pick.*

"I had the good fortune to stumble on the Bagley House. The rooms are well-appointed and the innkeepers are charming."

Certificate may be used: November-June, Sunday-Thursday.

Eastport G8

Weston House

26 Boynton St
Eastport, ME 04631-1305
(207)853-2907 (800)853-2907 Fax:(207)853-0981
Internet: www.westonhouse-maine.com
E-mail: westonhouse@prexar.com

Circa 1810. Jonathan Weston, an 1802 Harvard graduate, built this Federal-style house on a hill overlooking Passamaquoddy Bay. James Audubon stayed here as a guest of the Westons while awaiting passage to Labrador in 1833. Each guest room is furnished with antiques and Oriental rugs. The Weston and Audubon rooms boast views of the bay and gardens. Breakfast menus vary, including such delectables as heavenly pancakes with hot apricot syrup or freshly baked muffins and coddled eggs. Seasonal brunches are served on weekends and holidays. The area is full of outdoor activities, including whale watching. Nearby Saint Andrews-by-the-Sea offers plenty of shops and restaurants.

Innkeeper(s): Jett & John Peterson. $65-85. 3 rooms. Breakfast and afternoon tea included in rates. Types of meals: Full gourmet bkfst and picnic lunch. Beds: KQD. Cable TV, reading lamp, clock radio and desk in room. Parlor games, telephone and fireplace on premises. Fishing, live theater, shopping, tennis, whale watching and nature nearby.

Location: City. Coastal New England village.

Publicity: *Down East, Los Angeles Times, Boston Globe, Boston Magazine* and *New York Times.*

"All parts of ourselves have been nourished."

Certificate may be used: Subject to availability. All months with the exception of the month of August.

Eliot L2

High Meadows B&B

Rt 101
Eliot, ME 03903
(207)439-0590 Fax:(207)439-6343
Internet: www.highmeadowsbnb.com
E-mail: hymedobb@aol.com

Circa 1740. A ship's captain built this house, now filled with remembrances of colonial days. At one point, it was raised and a floor added underneath, so the upstairs is older than the downstairs. It is conveniently located to factory outlets in Kittery, Maine, and great dining and historic museums in Portsmouth, N.H.

Innkeeper(s): Elaine. $80-90. 4 rooms with PB. Breakfast and afternoon tea included in rates. Types of meals: Full bkfst and early coffee/tea. Beds: QDT. Reading lamp in room. Telephone and fireplace on premises. Antiquing, fishing, shopping and water sports nearby.

Location: Country.

Publicity: *Portsmouth Herald and York County Focus.*

"High Meadows was the highlight of our trip."

Certificate may be used: Monday-Thursday; April, May, June.

Fryeburg I1

The Oxford House Inn

105 Main St
Fryeburg, ME 04037-1127
(207)935-3442 (800)261-7206 Fax:(207)935-7046
Internet: www.oxfordhouseinn.com
E-mail: innkeeper@oxfordhouseinn.com

Circa 1913. A picket fence bounded by perennial gardens surrounds this Mission-style home designed by celebrated Maine architect, John Calvin Stevens. Splendid mountain views are enjoyed from the back gardens and from many of the inn's rooms. The guest rooms are cozy and inviting with warm, floral wall coverings, antiques and polished wood floors topped with Oriental rugs. Breakfast is a gourmet treat, and for those who would like to sample more of the innkeeper's cuisine, make a dinner reservation. You'll select from specialties such as champagne poached salmon, rack of lamb with mint chutney, steak au poivre and starters such as escargot, country paté, baked Brie and a Maine crab meat crepe. Guests enjoy the Granite Room lounge for dart games and cocktails, relaxing after canoeing the Saco River or enjoying one of the area's scenic hikes and drives.

Innkeeper(s): John & Phyllis Morris. $95-135. 4 rooms with PB. Breakfast included in rates. Types of meals: Full gourmet bkfst, picnic lunch, gourmet dinner and room service. Restaurant on premises. Beds: KQD. Cable TV, reading lamp and clock radio in room. VCR, fax, copier, parlor games, telephone and fireplace on premises. Antiquing, bicycling, canoeing/kayaking, cross-country skiing, downhill skiing, fishing, golf, hiking, live theater, museums, parks, shopping, tennis and water sports nearby.

Location: Mountains. Village surrounded by mountains, lakes and the Saco River.

Certificate may be used: March, April, May, June, November and December; Sunday-Thursday, no holiday weeks or weekends.

Peace With-Inn Bed & Breakfast

HCR 68, Box 71, Rte 113 North
Fryeburg, ME 04037
(207)935-7363 (866)935-7322
Internet: www.peacewithinn.com
E-mail: info@peacewithinn.com

Circa 1750. Simple pleasures and generous amenities highlight the tranquility and relaxation found at the historic Hardy Farm. Feel welcomed with complimentary refreshments upon check-in. Guest bedrooms feature antiques, fine linens on comfortable beds, Gilchrist and Soames toiletries, luxurious robes, bottled water, fresh flowers, European chocolates and towel heaters. Stay in the Notch room boasting a Select Comfort bed and Jacuzzi for two or choose the first-floor Fireside Room with a gas fireplace. Families appreciate the suite created by adjoining the Meadow and Forest rooms. Wake up hungry to feast on a multiple-course New England-style breakfast. Ask about special packages available. Most personal requests can be arranged from dietary needs to champagne to in-room massage. Enjoy numerous year-round activities.

Innkeeper(s): The Link Family. $90-125. 5 rooms, 4 with PB, 1 with FP, 1 suite. Breakfast and snacks/refreshments included in rates. Types of meals: Full gourmet bkfst, veg bkfst, early coffee/tea, picnic lunch and room service. Beds: Q. Cable TV, VCR, CD player, ceiling fan, clock radio, telephone and hot tub/spa in room. Fax, copier, spa, bicycles, library, parlor games and fireplace on premises. Limited handicap access. Antiquing, beach, bicycling, canoeing/kayaking, cross-country skiing, downhill skiing, fishing, golf, hiking, horseback riding, live theater and shopping nearby.

Location: Country, mountains. Sebago Lake, Lake Winnipesaukee, Maine's "Down East" shoreline.

Certificate may be used: January-May 15, subject to availability.

Hallowell   I3

Maple Hill Farm B&B Inn

11 Inn Road
Hallowell, ME 04347
(207)622-2708 (800)622-2708 Fax:(207)622-0655
Internet: www.MapleBB.com
E-mail: stay@MapleBB.com

Circa 1906. Visitors to Maine's capitol city have the option of staying at this nearby inn, a peaceful farm setting adjacent to a 600-acre state wildlife management area that is available for canoeing, fishing, hiking and hunting. This Victorian Shingle-style inn was once a stagecoach stop and dairy farm. Some rooms include large double whirlpool tubs and fireplaces. The inn, with its 130-acre grounds, easily accommodates conferences, parties and receptions. Guests are welcome to visit the many farm animals. Cobbossee Lake is a five-minute drive from the inn. Nearby downtown Hallowell is listed as a National Historic District and offers antique shops and restaurants.

Innkeeper(s): Scott Cowger & Vince Hannan. $70-185. 8 rooms with PB, 5 with FP and 1 conference room. Breakfast and afternoon tea included in rates. Types of meals: Full bkfst, early coffee/tea and snacks/refreshments. Beds: KQD. TV, VCR, reading lamp, telephone, three with private decks and four with large whirlpool tubs in room. Fireplace on premises. Handicap access. Antiquing, cross-country skiing, live theater, shopping and water sports nearby.

Location: Country.

Publicity: *Family Fun, An Explorer's Guide to Maine, The Forecaster, Portland Press Herald, Kennebec Journal, Maine Times, Travel and Leisure* "Special Hotels" issue as one of 30 Great U.S. Inns and Editor's Pick in the 2002 & 2003 Yankee Magazine Travel Guide to New England.

"You add many thoughtful touches to your service that set your B&B apart from others, and really make a difference. Best of Maine, hands down!" — Maine Times

Certificate may be used: May-October, Sunday-Wednesday. November-April, anytime, but not both Friday and Saturday. Discount is off rack rates. Please inquire.

Kennebunk   K2

The Kennebunk Inn

45 Main St
Kennebunk, ME 04043-1888
(207)985-3351 Fax:(207)985-8865
Internet: www.thekennebunkinn.com
E-mail: info@thekennebunkinn.com

Circa 1799. Built at the turn of the 19th century, Kennebunk Inn has been serving guests since the 1920s. The rooms and suites feature a variety of decor; guests might discover a clawfoot tub or four-poster bed. Games and a selection of books are available for guests, as well as televisions. For a special treat, make dinner reservations at the inn's restaurant, which serves a seasonally changing menu with fresh local seafood and produce. Guests can choose from filet mignon wrapped in puff pastry and topped with Brie cheese or perhaps pan-seared scallops and basil ravioli with a pink peppercorn and white wine cream sauce. Portland Press heralded the inn's restaurant with four stars.

Innkeeper(s): Brian & Shanna O'Hea. $55-155. 27 rooms with PB, 1 with FP, 5 suites and 1 conference room. Breakfast included in rates. Types of meals: Cont plus, early coffee/tea and dinner. Restaurant on premises. Beds: KQDT. Cable TV, VCR, reading lamp, refrigerator, clock radio, telephone and

desk in room. Air conditioning. Fax, copier, library, pet boarding, fireplace and online access on premises. Handicap access. Amusement parks, antiquing, cross-country skiing, fishing, golf, live theater, parks, shopping, sporting events, tennis and water sports nearby.

Publicity: *Down East Magazine.*

Certificate may be used: Anytime, subject to availability. Weekends in July, August and first 2 weekends of December are not available.

Kennebunkport   K2

1802 House

PO Box 646-A
Kennebunkport, ME 04046-1646
(207)967-5632 (800)932-5632 Fax:(207)967-0780
Internet: www.1802inn.com
E-mail: inquiry@1802inn.com

Circa 1802. The rolling fairways of Cape Arundel Golf Course, old shade trees and secluded gardens create the perfect setting for this historic 19th-century farmhouse. Located along the gentle shores of the Kennebunk River, the inn is accentuated by personal service and attention to detail. Romantic guest bedrooms offer four-poster canopy beds, two-person whirlpool tubs and fireplaces. The luxurious three-room Sebago Suite tucked into a private wing is a favorite choice. Homemade specialties and regional delights are part of a gourmet breakfast served in the sunlit dining room. Popular Dock Square is within walking distance for browsing in boutiques and art galleries. Golf packages are available.

Innkeeper(s): Edric & Mary Ellen Mason. $129-369. 6 rooms with PB, 5 with FP, 1 suite. Breakfast and snacks/refreshments included in rates. Types of meals: Full gourmet bkfst, early coffee/tea and picnic lunch. Beds: Q. Cable TV, VCR, reading lamp, CD player, clock radio, turn-down service, fireplace and whirlpool tubs in room. Air conditioning. Fax, parlor games, telephone and gift shop on premises. Antiquing, art galleries, beach, bicycling, canoeing/kayaking, cross-country skiing, fishing, golf, hiking, horseback riding, live theater, museums, parks, shopping, tennis, water sports and wineries nearby.

Location: Country, ocean community.

Publicity: *Down East Magazine, Golf Digest and Modern Bride.*

Certificate may be used: Sunday through Thursday, November and March-April-May.

Captain Fairfield Inn

PO Box 2690
Kennebunkport, ME 04046-2690
(207)967-4454 (800)322-1928 Fax:(207)967-8537
Internet: www.captainfairfield.com
E-mail: jrw@captainfairfield.com

Circa 1813. This romantic country inn is located in the heart of Kennebunkport, a seaside resort. An elegant sea captain's mansion, Captain Fairfield Inn overlooks the scenic Kennebunkport River Green. Shaded by tall trees, and on the National Register, the inn offers an enticing and gracious spot for celebrating anniversaries and honeymoons. Guest rooms are spacious, all with sitting areas, and boast period furnishings such as four-poster and  canopy beds as well as fireplaces and views of the gardens or the neighborhood's historic homes. Down comforters and bouquets of fresh garden flowers are additional amenities. Ask for the Library for a special occasion and you'll enjoy a fireplace and a whirlpool tub for two. Breakfast is a lavish four-course affair and is served next to an open-hearth fireplace in the gathering room or in view of the inn's gardens. Guests enjoy the location's access to the ocean and beaches, boutique shops, art galleries and restaurants. Carriage rides and theater and spa packages are offered. Activities include kayaking, cycling, fishing, whale watching and sailing. Other activities include touring the Brick Store Museum, the Rachel Carson Preserve and the Seashore Trolley Museum.

Innkeeper(s): Janet & Rick Wolf. $110-295. 9 rooms with PB, 6 with FP. Breakfast, afternoon tea and snacks/refreshments included in rates. Types of meals: Full gourmet bkfst and early coffee/tea. Beds: QT. Modem hook-up, data port, reading lamp, ceiling fan, clock radio, telephone, bottled water, hair dryers, iron/ironing board and many with fireplace in room. Air conditioning. Fax, copier, library, parlor games, fireplace, piano, guest refrigerator, ice machine, maps, menus and concierge service on premises. Antiquing, art galleries, beach, bicycling, canoeing/kayaking, cross-country skiing, fishing, golf, hiking, live theater, museums and shopping nearby.

"It couldn't have been nicer...Your breakfasts were delicious and your hospitality unequaled...all in all a wonderful experience."

Certificate may be used: Monday-Thursday nights, November, December, January, February, March, April. Holidays excluded, subject to availability.

Cove House

11 S Maine St
Kennebunkport, ME 04046-6313
(207)967-3704

Circa 1793. This roomy Colonial Revival farmhouse overlooks Chick's Cove on the Kennebunk River. The inn's peaceful setting offers easy access to beaches, shops and the town. Three guest rooms serve visitors of this antique-filled home. Guests enjoy full breakfasts, which often include the inn's famous blueberry muffins, in the Flow Blue dining room. A popular gathering spot is the book-lined living room/library. Bicycles may be borrowed for a leisurely ride around the town. A cozy, secluded cottage with a screened front porch is another lodging option.

Innkeeper(s): Barry Jones. $85-110. 3 rooms with PB and 1 cottage. Breakfast and afternoon tea included in rates. Types of meals: Full bkfst and early coffee/tea. Beds: QT. VCR, bicycles, library, parlor games, telephone and fireplace on premises. Antiquing, cross-country skiing, fishing, live theater, parks, shopping, water sports, whale watching and sailing nearby.

Certificate may be used: Dec. 15-May 15, excluding holiday weekends. Sunday through Thursday.

The Welby Inn

92 Ocean Ave, PO Box 774
Kennebunkport, ME 04046-0774
(207)967-4655 (800)773-4085 Fax:(207)967-8654
Internet: www.welbyinn.com
E-mail: innkeeper@welbyinn.com

Circa 1900. Built as a summer home in this seaport town at the turn of the last century, the inn's Dutch Gambrel architecture is typical of the era. A large common room with Victorian furnishings invites relaxing by the fire or conversing in the window seat. A guest pantry offers beverages and facilities for anytime refreshment. Air-conditioned guest bedrooms feature plush robes and fresh flowers. Sleep in a canopy bed by a fireplace in the Grantham Room overlooking the Kennebunk River, or stay in the cheery James Room with a view of the tidal water. A bountiful breakfast and afternoon tea are served in the dining room and breakfast porch. Stroll to the ocean, or to the shops and restaurants of Dock Square.

Innkeeper(s): Christopher Farr. $99-175. 7 rooms with PB, 1 with FP. Breakfast and afternoon tea included in rates. Types of meals: Full gourmet bkfst and early coffee/tea. Beds: KQDT. Reading lamp and clock radio in room. Air conditioning. TV, VCR, library, parlor games, telephone and fireplace on premises. Amusement parks, antiquing, art galleries, beach, bicycling, cross-country skiing, fishing, golf, live theater, museums, parks, shop-

ping, water sports, art galleries, museums and ocean nearby.
Location: Village.

"I'm glad we found this place before Gourmet Magazine discovers it and the rates increase!"

Certificate may be used: Oct. 15-May 15, Sunday-Thursday, subject to availability.

Kittery   L2

Enchanted Nights B&B

29 Wentworth St
Kittery, ME 03904-1720
(207)439-1489
Internet: www.enchantednights.org

Circa 1890. The innkeepers bill this unique inn as a "Victorian fantasy for the romantic at heart." Each of the guest rooms is unique, from the spacious rooms with double whirlpool tubs and fireplaces to the cozy turret room. A whimsical combination of country French and Victorian decor permeates the interior. Wrought-iron beds and hand-painted furnishings add to the ambiance. Breakfasts, often with a vegetarian theme, are served with gourmet coffee in the morning room on antique floral china.

Innkeeper(s): Nancy Bogenberger & Peter Lamandia. $52-300. 10 rooms with PB, 4 with FP and 2 conference rooms. Breakfast included in rates. Types of meals: Full gourmet bkfst, veg bkfst and early coffee/tea. Beds: KQDT. Cable TV, VCR, reading lamp, refrigerator, ceiling fan, clock radio, microwave, five have whirlpools and four have fireplaces in room. Air conditioning. Telephone and refrigerator on premises. Handicap access. Antiquing, art galleries, beach, bicycling, canoeing/kayaking, golf, hiking, horseback riding, live theater, museums, parks, shopping, sporting events, tennis, water sports, wineries, outlet shopping, historic homes, whale watching and harbor cruises nearby.
Location: City, ocean community.

"The atmosphere was great. Your breakfast was elegant. The breakfast room made us feel we had gone back in time. All in all it was a very enjoyable stay."

Certificate may be used: Nov. 1-April 30, Sunday-Thursday. No holidays.

Lamoine   H6

Capt'n N Eve's Eden

461 Lamoine Beach Road, Rt 184
Lamoine, ME 04605
(207)667-3109 Fax:(207)667-3109
Internet: www.capteve.com
E-mail: evelyn@capteve.com

Circa 1982. Overlook Frenchman's Bay from this modern home on five quiet acres near Acadia National Park. The calm atmosphere makes this bed and breakfast a relaxing place to come back to after sightseeing and enjoying the many nearby activities and historic sites. The sun room boasts views of the ocean and Mt. Desert Island. Wake up after a restful sleep to enjoy breakfast in the dining room. The signature dish is pancakes made with native Maine blueberries. Play tennis, swim, hike or bike on trails.

Innkeeper(s): David and Evelyn Farrell. $40-75. 3 rooms, 1 with PB. Beds: QD. Clock radio in room. TV, VCR, copier, tennis and telephone on premises. Antiquing, art galleries, beach, bicycling, canoeing/kayaking, cross-country skiing, fishing, golf, hiking, horseback riding, live theater, museums, parks, shopping, tennis, water sports and wineries nearby.
Location: Country, waterfront.

Certificate may be used: Anytime, November-March and April-June, subject to availability.

Naples J2

Augustus Bove House

Corner Rts 302 & 114, 11 Sebago Rd
Naples, ME 04055
(207)693-6365 (888)806-6249
Internet: www.naplesmaine.com
E-mail: augbovehouse@pivot.net

Circa 1830. A long front lawn nestles up against the stone foundation and veranda of this house, once known as the Hotel Naples, one of the area's summer hotels in the 1800s. In the 1920s, the inn was host to a number of prominent guests, including Enrico Caruso, Joseph P. Kennedy and Howard Hughes. The guest rooms are decorated in a Colonial style and modestly furnished with antiques. Many rooms provide a view of Long Lake. A fancy country breakfast is provided.

Innkeeper(s): David & Arlene Stetson. $79-200. 10 rooms with PB, 3 suites. Breakfast and afternoon tea included in rates. Types of meals: Full bkfst and early coffee/tea. Beds: KQT. Cable TV and telephone in room. Air conditioning. VCR, fax and spa on premises. Antiquing, cross-country skiing, downhill skiing, fishing, live theater, parks, shopping and water sports nearby.

Location: Waterfront.

Publicity: *Brighton Times, Yankee Magazine and Quality Travel Value Award.*

"Beautiful place, rooms, and people."

Certificate may be used: Void July and August, holidays and first week of October, certain rooms apply.

Inn at Long Lake

P.O. Box 806
Naples, ME 04055
(207)693-6226 (800)437-0328 Fax:(207)693-7132
Internet: www.innatlonglake.com
E-mail: info@innatlonglake.com

Circa 1906. Reopened in 1988, the inn housed the overflow guests from the Lake House resort about 90 years ago. Guests traveled to the resort via the Oxford-Cumberland Canal, and each room is named for a historic canal boat. The cozy rooms offer fluffy comforters and a warm, country decor in a romantic atmosphere.  Warm up in front of a crackling fire in the great room, or enjoy a cool Long Lake breeze on the veranda while watching horses in nearby pastures. The setting is ideal for housing guests for weddings or reunions.

Innkeeper(s): Buddy Marcum. $99-200. 16 rooms with PB, 2 suites and 1 conference room. Breakfast, afternoon tea and snacks/refreshments included in rates. Types of meals: Full bkfst and early coffee/tea. Beds: QDT. TV, VCR, reading lamp, ceiling fan, clock radio, turn-down service and suites have fireplace in room. Air conditioning. Library, telephone and fireplace on premises. Antiquing, cross-country skiing, downhill skiing, fishing, golf, hiking, horseback riding, live theater, parks, shopping and water sports nearby.

Location: Mountains, waterfront.

Publicity: *Bridgton News and Portland Press Herald.*

"Convenient location, tastefully done and the prettiest inn I've ever stayed in."

Certificate may be used: Oct. 16-May 14, Sunday-Thursday.

Ogunquit K2

Hartwell House Inn & Conference Center

312 Shore Rd, PO Box 1950
Ogunquit, ME 03907-0393
(207)646-7210 (800)235-8883 Fax:(207)646-6032
Internet: www.hartwellhouseinn.com
E-mail: info@hartwellhouseinn.com

Circa 1921. Hartwell House offers suites and guest rooms furnished with distinctive early American and English antiques. Many rooms are available with French doors opening to private balconies overlooking sculpted flower gardens. Guests are treated to both a full, gourmet breakfast and afternoon tea. Seasonal dining packages are available. Restaurants, beaches, hiking and outlet shopping is nearby.

$110-265. 11 rooms with PB, 3 suites and 2 conference rooms. Types of meals: Full gourmet bkfst and afternoon tea. Beds: KQ. Reading lamp and refrigerator in room. Air conditioning. Parlor games, telephone and fireplace on premises. Antiquing, cross-country skiing, fishing, live theater, parks, shopping, sporting events, water sports, restaurants, outlet and boutique shopping and beaches nearby.

Location: Ocean community.

Publicity: *Insider.*

"This engaging country inn will be reserved for my special clients."

Certificate may be used: Nov. 1-April 30, excluding holidays and special events.

Yardarm Village Inn

406 Shore Rd, PO Box 773
Ogunquit, ME 03907-0773
(207)646-7006 (888)927-3276 Fax:(207)646-9034
Internet: www.yardarmvillageinn.com
E-mail: yardarm@maine.rr.com

Circa 1874. In the quiet part of town, just south of the entrance to Perkins Cove, this three-story classic New England inn offers a delightful selection of accommodations. The large veranda is the perfect spot for relaxing on a white wicker rocker. Comfortable guest bedrooms and two-room suites are furnished and decorated in a Colonial-country style. Start the day with homemade blueberry muffins, fruit and beverages. Take an afternoon or evening sailboat charter past the three-mile beach or along the rocky coast. The on-site wine and cheese shop is well-stocked to satisfy the most discriminating palate.

Innkeeper(s): Scott & Beverlee. $69-119. 8 rooms with PB, 4 suites. Types of meals: Cont. Beds: KQDT. Cable TV, reading lamp, refrigerator, clock radio and hair dryers in room. Air conditioning. Parlor games, telephone, fireplace, gift shop, private sailboat charters, wine and cheese shop and hand-painted blueberry dinnerware made in Maine on premises. Amusement parks, antiquing, art galleries, beach, bicycling, canoeing/kayaking, fishing, golf, hiking, live theater, museums, parks, shopping, tennis and water sports nearby.

Location: Ocean community.

Certificate may be used: May and October, Sunday-Thursday, excluding holidays.

Old Orchard Beach K2

Atlantic Birches Inn

20 Portland Ave Rt 98
Old Orchard Beach, ME 04064-2212
(207)934-5295 (888)934-5295 Fax:(207)934-3781
Internet: www.atlanticbirches.com
E-mail: info@atlanticbirches.com

Circa 1903. The front porch of this Shingle-style Victorian and 1920s bungalow are shaded by white birch trees. The

houses are a place for relaxation and enjoyment, uncluttered, simple havens filled
with comfortable furnishings.
The guest rooms are decorated with antiques and pastel
wallcoverings. Maine's coast

offers an endless amount of activities, from boating to whale
watching. It is a five-minute walk to the beach and the pier.

Innkeeper(s): Ray & Kim Deleo. $69-135. 10 rooms with PB, 3 two-bed-
room suites. Breakfast included in rates. Types of meals: Cont plus and early
coffee/tea. Beds: KQDT. Modem hook-up, reading lamp, ceiling fan, clock
radio and desk in room. Air conditioning. TV, VCR, fax, copier, swimming,
library, parlor games, telephone, badminton, basketball, horseshoes, volleyball, pool towels and pool lounge chairs on premises. Limited handicap
access. Amusement parks, antiquing, art galleries, beach, bicycling, canoe-
ing/kayaking, fishing, golf, hiking, horseback riding, museums, parks, shopping, sporting events, tennis, water sports, wineries, water park, whale
watching tours, deep sea fishing, hot air ballooning, fireworks, lighthouses,
movie theaters, outlets, cemetery tours, farm stands, tree farms and elk
farm nearby.

Location: Ocean community.

Publicity: *Down East Magazine - Feb 2004.*

*"Your home and family are just delightful! What a treat to stay in
such a warm & loving home."*

Certificate may be used: Any day of the week, Nov. 1 through June 1.

Portland   J3

Inn At ParkSpring

135 Spring St
Portland, ME 04101-3827
(207)774-1059 (800)437-8511 Fax:(207)774-3455
Internet: www.innatparkspring.com
E-mail: john@innatparkspring.com

Circa 1825. Comfortable and casual, this intimate bed and
breakfast was built in the Victorian brick townhome style popular in 1835. Floor-to-ceiling windows, crystal chandeliers, hardwood floors and marble fireplaces reflect traditional period
décor. Guest bedrooms have been recently refurbished and are
tastefully furnished. Stay in the Early American Spring Room
with a sleigh bed and Chippendale secretary desk on an
Oriental rug. The Murphy Room overlooks the courtyard and
boasts a European ambiance. Country elegance is enjoyed in
the Museum Room. The third-floor room features a skylight
and the ground-floor Courtyard Room has a private entrance
and courtyard access. The spacious Gables Room features a
large sitting area. Savor a gourmet breakfast that is sure to satisfy. The ideal downtown location is perfect for local sightseeing
by foot.

Innkeeper(s): Nancy & John Gonsalves. $99-180. 6 rooms with PB.
Breakfast, afternoon tea and snacks/refreshments included in rates. Types of
meals: Full gourmet bkfst and early coffee/tea. Beds: KQT. Modem hook-up,
data port, cable TV, reading lamp, stereo, refrigerator, ceiling fan, clock radio,
telephone, coffeemaker and desk in room. Air conditioning. Fax, copier,
library and parlor games on premises. Antiquing, art galleries, beach, bicycling, canoeing/kayaking, cross-country skiing, downhill skiing, fishing, golf,
hiking, horseback riding, live theater, museums, parks, shopping, sporting
events, tennis, water sports and wineries nearby.

Location: City.

Publicity: *Conde Nast.*

Certificate may be used: Anytime, November-March, subject to availability.

Rumford Point   H2

The Perennial Inn

Jed Martin Rd
Rumford Point, ME 04276
(207)369-0309 Fax:(207)369-8016
Internet: Perennialinn.com
E-mail: info@perennialinn.com

Circa 1884. Encompassing 42 acres of scenic beauty in the
Blue Mountains, this historic 1884 Victorian farmhouse is surrounded by grassy fields, ponds, streams and pine forests. The
renovated New England home with a wraparound porch and
huge red barn offers secluded comfort and convenient access to
Route 2. Read a book from the library in the cheery parlor or
watch a DVD by the fieldstone fireplace in the Gathering
Room. Play pool on a maple table in the billiard parlor.
Genuine hospitality is extended with thoughtful details to pamper and please. Romantic guest bedrooms and a two-room
suite feature wide pine floors, high ceilings, sunny windows
and sitting areas with family heirlooms and fine furnishings. A
hearty country breakfast is served in the dining room. Soak in
the hot tub under the stars.

Innkeeper(s): Jordan & Darlene Ginsberg. $85-175. 7 rooms, 4 with PB, 1
two-bedroom suite. Breakfast, afternoon tea, snacks/refreshments and wine
included in rates. Types of meals: Country bkfst and early coffee/tea. Beds:
QT. Cable TV, VCR, reading lamp, clock radio and desk in room. Air conditioning. Fax, copier, spa, library, pet boarding, parlor games, telephone and
fireplace on premises. Limited handicap access. Amusement parks,
antiquing, art galleries, bicycling, canoeing/kayaking, cross-country skiing,
downhill skiing, fishing, golf, hiking, horseback riding, live theater, parks,
shopping and water sports nearby.

Location: Country, mountains.

Certificate may be used: Sunday-Thursday, May-June and September-Dec. 15.

Saco   K2

Crown 'n' Anchor Inn

121 North St, PO Box 228
Saco, ME 04072-0228
(207)282-3829 (800)561-8865 Fax:(207)282-7495
Internet: crownnanchor.com
E-mail: cna@gwi.net

Circa 1827. This Greek Revival house, listed in the National
Register, features both Victorian baroque and colonial antiques.
Two rooms include whirlpool tubs. A collection of British coro-
nation memorabilia dis-
played throughout the inn
includes 200 items. Guests
gather in the Victorian parlor or the formal library. The
innkeepers, a college librari-
an and an academic book-

seller, lined the shelves with several thousand volumes, including extensive Civil War and British royal family collections and
travel, theater and nautical books. Royal Dalton china, crystal
and fresh flowers create a festive breakfast setting.

Innkeeper(s): John Barclay & Martha Forester. $80-130. 6 rooms with PB, 2
with FP. Breakfast included in rates. Types of meals: Full gourmet bkfst, early
coffee/tea and afternoon tea. Beds: KQDT. Cable TV and two with whirlpools
in room. VCR, library, parlor games, telephone and fireplace on premises.
Amusement parks, antiquing, cross-country skiing, downhill skiing, fishing, live
theater, parks, shopping, sporting events and water sports nearby.

Location: City.

Publicity: *Yankee, Saco, Biddeford, Old Orchard Beach Courier, Country, Portland Press Herald, Editors Choice Southern Maine for 2001 and HGTV.*

"A delightful interlude! A five star B&B."

Certificate may be used: Year-round, Sunday through Thursday with the exception of July and August.

Searsport   H5

1794 Watchtide... by the Sea

190 W Main St, Coastal US Rt. 1
Searsport, ME 04974-3514
(207)548-6575 (800)698-6575 Fax:(207)548-0938
Internet: www.watchtide.com
E-mail: stay@watchtide.com

Circa 1794. Once owned by General Henry Knox, Washington's first Secretary of War, this acclaimed seaside inn has been operating since 1917 and is listed in the National Register. Updated rooms include luxurious amenities such as sheep's wool comforters, luxurious linens, quiet air conditioners, signature pure glycerine soaps, cozy robes, Nan's Crans, Vermont Sweetwater, sound therapy units and all the amenities you'll need. Choose a suite with fireplace and whirlpool tub or an ocean view with two-person Jacuzzi.

Renowned for creating scrumptious meals, the inn's breakfast is served on the 60-foot sunporch overlooking a bird sanctuary and Penobscot Bay. Play croquet on the expansive lawn. Receive a discount at the inn's antique/gift shop. Walk to the beach at Moosepoint State Park. Bar Harbor and Rockland are easy day trips from this central location.

Innkeeper(s): Nancy-Linn Nellis & Jack Elliott. $117-198. 5 rooms, 4 with PB, 1 two-bedroom suite. Breakfast and snacks/refreshments included in rates. Types of meals: Full gourmet bkfst, veg bkfst and early coffee/tea. Beds: KQT. Cable TV, reading lamp, CD player, refrigerator, ceiling fan, clock radio, turn-down service, hot tub/spa, fireplace, robes, hair dryers, sound therapy units, Nan's Crans, Vermont Sweet Water and super quiet Quasar air conditioners in room. Air conditioning. Fax, copier, library, parlor games, telephone, gift shop, guest lounge with large-screen TV, game table, picnic tables, horseshoes, croquet, 60-foot year-round sun porch furnished in wicker with fireplace overlooking Penobscot Bay, sitting room with fireplace, 18-hour refreshment bar and picnic tables overlooking the bay on premises. Antiquing, art galleries, beach, canoeing/kayaking, cross-country skiing, downhill skiing, fishing, golf, hiking, live theater, museums, parks, shopping, sporting events, tennis, water sports, wineries, lighthouses, concerts, whale watching, Acadia National Park and rail and sail trips nearby.

Location: Country. Penobscot Bay.

Publicity: *Yankee Travel Guide Editor's Pick, Yankee Magazine Blue Ribbon Winner, Tastes of New England (Featured Inn May, 2004), Arrington's Book of Lists 2004 (voted the Best to Visit Again and Again), Inn Traveler Magazine, Recommended in Maine...an Explorer's Guide, The Best of New England, Boston Globe, Green Bay Press Gazette, City Line News, Desert News, Asbury Park Press, Berkshire Eagle, Patriot Ledger, Maine Public Broadcasting and Channel 5.*

Certificate may be used: Weekdays Nov. 1-May 1, not including holidays.

Carriage House Inn

120 E. Main Street
Searsport, ME 04974
(207)548-2167 (800)578-2167 Fax:(207)548-2506
Internet: www.carriagehouseinmaine.com
E-mail: info@carriagehouseinmaine.com

Circa 1874. There is a rich history behind this popularly photographed Second Empire Victorian mansion sitting on two acres of landscaped grounds with ocean vistas. It was built in 1874 by a sea captain and later owned by impressionist painter Waldo Peirce whose lifelong friend, Ernest Hemingway, visited often. Play the baby grand piano in the elegant parlor showcasing an original marble fireplace or watch a video by firelight in the nautical den. On the second floor a library/sitting area with bay views extends a peaceful spot to read or listen to a book selection on tape. Guest bedrooms with floor-to-ceiling windows are graciously furnished with 19th-century antiques and artifacts. Honeymooners enjoy the spacious Captain's Quarters with a hand-carved cherry canopy bed, marble-top dresser and bay window. A bountiful breakfast is served in the dining room.

Innkeeper(s): Marcia L. Markwardt. $90-125. 3 rooms with PB. Breakfast, afternoon tea and snacks/refreshments included in rates. Types of meals: Full bkfst, veg bkfst and early coffee/tea. Beds: QD. Reading lamp, CD player, clock radio and desk in room. TV, VCR, fax, library, parlor games, telephone and fireplace on premises. Antiquing, art galleries, beach, bicycling, canoeing/kayaking, cross-country skiing, downhill skiing, fishing, golf, hiking, live theater, museums, parks, shopping and water sports nearby.

Location: Ocean community.

Certificate may be used: Anytime November-May, June-October, Monday-Thursday all subject to availability.

Homeport Inn

RR 1 Box 647
Searsport, ME 04974-9728
(207)548-2259 (800)742-5814 Fax:(207)548-2259
Internet: www.homeportbnb.com
E-mail: hportinn@acadia.net

Circa 1861. Captain John Nickels built this home on Penobscot Bay. On top of the two-story historic landmark is a widow's walk. A scalloped picket fence frames the property. Fine antiques, black marble fireplaces, a collection of grandfather clocks and elaborate ceiling medallions add to the atmosphere. Landscaped grounds sweep out to the ocean's edge. Some rooms have an ocean view. There are Victorian cottages available for weekly rental.

Innkeeper(s): Dr. & Mrs. F. George Johnson. $70-125. 10 rooms, 7 with PB. Breakfast included in rates. Types of meals: Full bkfst. Beds: KQD. Reading lamp and clock radio in room. TV, library and fireplace on premises. Antiquing, art galleries, beach, canoeing/kayaking, cross-country skiing, golf, hiking, live theater, museums, parks, shopping and tennis nearby.

Location: Ocean community, waterfront.

Publicity: *Yankee and Down East.*

"Your breakfast is something we will never forget."

Certificate may be used: Nov. 1 to May 1. Anytime, subject to availability.

South Thomaston   I5

Weskeag at The Water

PO Box 213
South Thomaston, ME 04858-0213
(207)596-6676
Internet: www.weskeag.com
E-mail: weskeag@midcoast.com

Circa 1830. The backyard of this three-story house stretches to the edge of Weskeag River and Ballyhac Cove. Fifty yards from the house, there's reversing white-water rapids, created by the 10-foot tide that narrows into the estuary. Guests often sit by the water's edge to watch the birds and the lobster fishermen. Sea kayakers can launch at the inn and explore the nearby coves and then paddle on to the ocean. The inn's furnishings include a mixture of comfortable antiques. Featherbed eggs are a house specialty.

Innkeeper(s): Gray Smith. $85-135. 8 rooms, 6 with PB. Breakfast included in rates. Types of meals: Full bkfst. Beds: QD. Reading lamp and ceiling fan in room. VCR and telephone on premises. Antiquing, cross-country skiing, downhill skiing, fishing, live theater and shopping nearby.

Location: Ocean community. Tidal saltwater inlet.

Certificate may be used: Oct. 15 through June 15.

Southport   J4

Lawnmeer Inn

PO Box 29
Southport, ME 04576
(800)633-7645
Internet: www.lawnmereinn.com
E-mail: innkeepers@lawnmereinn.com

Circa 1899. This pleasant inn sits by the shoreline, providing a picturesque oceanfront setting. Located on a small, wooded island, it is accessed by a lift bridge. Rooms are clean and homey and there is a private honeymoon cottage in the Smoke House. The dining room is waterside and serves continental cuisine with an emphasis on seafood. Boothbay Harbor is two miles away.

Innkeeper(s): Donna Phelps. $89-199. 30 rooms with PB, 2 suites, 1 cottage and 1 guest house. Breakfast included in rates. Types of meals: Full bkfst, early coffee/tea and gourmet dinner. Restaurant on premises. Beds: KQD. Cable TV, reading lamp, telephone and desk in room. Air conditioning. TV, VCR, fax, parlor games, fireplace and gift shop on premises. Antiquing, art galleries, beach, bicycling, canoeing/kayaking, fishing, golf, live theater, museums, shopping and water sports nearby.

Location: Ocean community, waterfront.

Publicity: *Los Angeles Times and Getaways for Gourmets.*

"Your hospitality was warm and gracious and the food delectable."

Certificate may be used: Sunday-Thursday, May 25 to Columbus Day, when space available, breakfast not included.

Southwest Harbor   I6

The Island House

PO Box 1006
Southwest Harbor, ME 04679-1006
(207)244-5180
Internet: www.islandhousebb.com
E-mail: islandab@downeast.net

Circa 1850. The first guests arrived at Deacon Clark's door as early as 1832. When steamboat service from Boston began in the 1850s, the Island House became a popular summer hotel. Among the guests was Ralph Waldo Emerson. In 1912, the hotel was taken down and rebuilt as two separate homes using much of the woodwork from the original building.

Innkeeper(s): Ann and Charles Bradford. $75-130. 4 rooms with PB and 1 guest house. Breakfast included in rates. Types of meals: Full bkfst and early coffee/tea. Beds: KQDT. TV, reading lamp, clock radio and refrigerator in Carriage House in room. VCR, library, parlor games, telephone, fireplace, cable TV, CD player, telephone and guest house with private bath on premises. Antiquing, art galleries, beach, bicycling, canoeing/kayaking, cross-country skiing, fishing, golf, hiking, horseback riding, live theater, museums, parks, shopping, tennis and water sports nearby.

Location: Ocean community, waterfront. Mountains, ocean.

"Island House is a delight from the moment one enters the door! We loved the thoughtful extras. You've made our vacation very special!"

Certificate may be used: Sunday-Thursday, November through April.

Thomaston   I4

Chestnut Tree B&B

12 Wadsworth St.
Thomaston, ME 04861
(207)354-0089
E-mail: chestnuttreebb@cs.com

Circa 1850. Recently restored, this Federal Colonial home sits on half an acre in the heart of the state's midcoast area. Accented with antiques, the guest lounge is perfect for relaxing over afternoon tea and coffee while reading a book or playing a game of cards. After a good night's sleep in one of the comfortable guest bedrooms, a satisfying breakfast starts the day's delightful activities. Visit nearby Rockland, known as the lobster capital of the world and gateway to Penobscot Bay.

Innkeeper(s): Frank & Diane Cushman . $75-95. 4 rooms with PB. Breakfast and afternoon tea included in rates. Types of meals: Full gourmet bkfst and early coffee/tea. Beds: QT. Cable TV, ceiling fan, clock radio and turn-down service in room. VCR, fax, library and telephone on premises. Antiquing, art galleries, beach, canoeing/kayaking, fishing, golf, hiking and shopping nearby.

Certificate may be used: Sept. 1 to June 30, subject to availability.

Vinalhaven   J5

Payne Homestead at the Moses Webster House

PO Box 216
Vinalhaven, ME 04863-0216
(207)863-9963 (888)863-9963 Fax:(207)863-2295
Internet: www.paynehomestead.com
E-mail: Donna@paynehomestead.com

Circa 1873. Situated on an island, a half-mile from the ferry, this handsome Second Empire French Victorian is at the edge of town. Enjoy a game room, reading nooks and a parlor. The Coral Room boasts a view of Indian Creek, while shadows of Carver's Pond may be seen through the windows of Mama's Room. A favorite selection is the Moses Webster Room that features a marble mantel, tin ceiling and a bay window looking out at the town. Breakfast usually offers fresh fruit platters and egg dishes with either French toast or pancakes. Restaurants and Lane Island Nature Conservancy are close. Take scenic walks past private fishing boats, ponds and shoreline, all part of the hideaway quality noted by National Geographic in "America's Best Kept Secrets."

Innkeeper(s): Lee & Donna Payne. $55-145. 5 rooms, 1 with PB, 1 two-bedroom suite. Breakfast included in rates. Types of meals: Full bkfst and early coffee/tea. Beds: KQDT. TV, VCR, fax, copier, parlor games and telephone on premises. Limited handicap access. Antiquing, bicycling, canoeing/kayaking and parks nearby.

Location: Ocean community. On an island.

Publicity: *National Geographic's "Best kept secrets" and Boston's New England Travel Magazine.*

"Our first stay in a B&B contributed greatly to the perfection of our honeymoon."

Certificate may be used: Sept. 15-June 1, subject to availability.

Waldoboro 14

Broad Bay Inn & Gallery

PO Box 607
Waldoboro, ME 04572-0607
(207)832-6668 (800)736-6769 Fax:(207)832-4632
Internet: www.broadbayinn.com
E-mail: innkeeper@broadbayinn.com

Circa 1830. Sheltered by tall pines, this 1830 Colonial inn sits in a coastal community within walking distance of the Medomak River. Victorian furnishings adorn the guest bedrooms. Sleep in a canopy bed in Sarah's Room. The Lincoln boasts elaborately carved period pieces. Wake up to an elegant breakfast accented with delicious house specialties. Visit the Gallery and Gift Shop open in July and August, featuring the "Union of Maine Visual Artists" including watercolors painted by locals. Plan to attend an art show and workshop. Relax or picnic in the garden and back deck. Open year-round; ask about special packages such as Candlelight Dinner, Sleigh Rides, Theater Tickets and Sail on the Friendship Sloop.

Innkeeper(s): Libby Hopkins. $75-110. 5 rooms, 1 with PB. Breakfast included in rates. Types of meals: Full bkfst, veg bkfst, early coffee/tea and gourmet dinner. Beds: DT. Cable TV, VCR, reading lamp, stereo, clock radio, telephone, desk and voice mail in room. Air conditioning. Fax, copier, library, parlor games, fireplace, old movies, art library, art classes and gift shop on premises. Antiquing, art galleries, beach, bicycling, canoeing/kayaking, cross-country skiing, downhill skiing, fishing, golf, hiking, horseback riding, live theater, museums, parks, shopping, sporting events, tennis and water sports nearby.

Location: Village.

Publicity: *Boston Globe, Ford Times, Courier Gazette, Princeton Packet and Better Homes & Gardens Cookbook.*

"Breakfast was so special - I ran to get my camera. Why, there were even flowers on my plate."

Certificate may be used: May-July, September-January, Sunday through Thursday, excludes holidays.

Walpole J4

Brannon-Bunker Inn

349 S St Rt 129
Walpole, ME 04573
(207)563-5941 (800)563-9225
E-mail: brbnkinn@lincoln.midcoast.com

Circa 1820. This Cape-style house has been a home to many generations of Maine residents, one of whom was captain of a ship that sailed to the Arctic. During the '20s, the barn served as a dance hall. Later, it was converted into comfortable guest rooms. Victorian and American antiques are featured, and there are collections of WWI military memorabilia.

Innkeeper(s): Joe & Jeanne Hovance. $80-90. 7 rooms, 5 with PB, 1 suite. Breakfast included in rates. Types of meals: Cont plus. Beds: QDT. TV, reading lamp, clock radio and desk in room. VCR, library, child care, parlor games, telephone and fireplace on premises. Handicap access. Antiquing, art galleries, beach, bicycling, canoeing/kayaking, fishing, golf, hiking, horseback riding, museums, parks, shopping, tennis and water sports nearby.

Location: Country, Damariscotta river.

Publicity: *Times-Beacon Newspaper.*

"Wonderful beds, your gracious hospitality and the very best muffins anywhere made our stay a memorable one."

Certificate may be used: September through June.

Waterford I2

Kedarburn Inn

Rt 35 Box 61
Waterford, ME 04088
(207)583-6182 (866)583-6182 Fax:(207)583-6424
Internet: www.kedarburn.com
E-mail: inn@kedarburn.com

Circa 1858. The innkeepers of this Victorian establishment invite guests to try a taste of olde English hospitality and cuisine at their inn, nestled in the foothills of the White Mountains in Western Maine. Located in a historic village, the inn sits beside the flowing Kedar Brook, which runs to the shores of Lake Keoka. Each of the spacious rooms is decorated with handmade quilts and dried flowers. Explore the inn's shop and you'll discover a variety of quilts and crafts, all made by innkeeper Margaret Gibson. Ask about special quilting weekends. With prior reservation, the innkeepers will prepare an English afternoon tea.

Innkeeper(s): Margaret & Derek Gibson. $71-125. 7 rooms, 5 with PB, 1 suite. Breakfast included in rates. Types of meals: Full bkfst, early coffee/tea, afternoon tea and snacks/refreshments. Beds: KQDT. Reading lamp, clock radio and desk in room. Air conditioning. VCR, fax, parlor games, telephone and fireplace on premises. Antiquing, cross-country skiing, downhill skiing, fishing, live theater, shopping and water sports nearby.

Location: Mountains.

Publicity: *Maine Times.*

Certificate may be used: November, Sunday-Friday; March, Sunday-Friday; April, Sunday-Friday.

York L2

Apple Blossom B&B

25 Brixham Road
York, ME 03909
(207)351-1727 Fax:(207)363-3520
Internet: www.appleblossombandb.com
E-mail: ablossom@cybertours.com

Circa 1727. Sprawled on 11 acres, this 18th-century Colonial farmhouse offers a peaceful rural setting as well as easy access to nearby historical sites, beaches and outlet malls. Living and dining rooms with fireplaces are pleasant gathering places. Spacious guest bedrooms with pleasant views feature canopy, rice and sleigh beds. Relax with a glass of wine on the screened or wraparound porch. Stroll the lush grounds, and enjoy an evening swim in the pool.

Innkeeper(s): Mary Lou & Bob Erickson. $90-130. 6 rooms with PB. Breakfast, afternoon tea and snacks/refreshments included in rates. Types of meals: Full gourmet bkfst and early coffee/tea. Beds: QDT. Cable TV, reading lamp, clock radio and desk in room. Air conditioning. Swimming, library, telephone and fireplace on premises. Amusement parks, antiquing, art galleries, beach, bicycling, canoeing/kayaking, cross-country skiing, fishing, golf, hiking, horseback riding, live theater, museums, parks, shopping, sporting events and water sports nearby.

Location: Country, ocean community.

Certificate may be used: Anytime, subject to availability.

Maryland

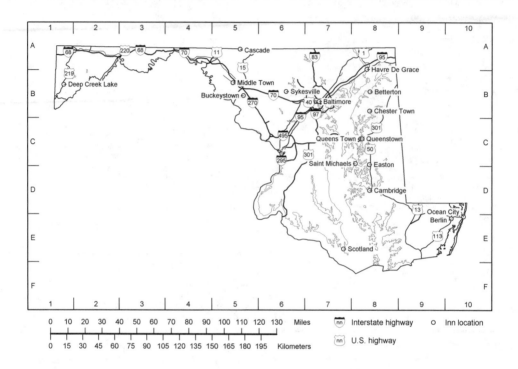

	1	2	3	4	5	6	7	8	9	10
A	68	220 68	70	11	Cascade		83	1 95		
	219				15			Havre De Grace		
B	Deep Creek Lake			Buckeystown	Middle Town	Sykesville	40 Baltimore	Betterton		
					270	70	97	Chester Town		
						95		301		
C					495		Queens Town Queenstown	50		
				295		301	Saint Michaels	Easton		
D								Cambridge	13	Ocean City Berlin
E							Scotland		113	
F										

| 0 | 10 | 20 | 30 | 40 | 50 | 60 | 70 | 80 | 90 | 100 | 110 | 120 | 130 | Miles | (nn) Interstate highway | o Inn location |
| 0 | 15 | 30 | 45 | 60 | 75 | 90 | 105 | 120 | 135 | 150 | 165 | 180 | 195 | Kilometers | (nn) U.S. highway | |

Baltimore   B7

Hopkins Inn
3404 St Paul St
Baltimore, MD 21218
(410)235-8600 (800)537-8483 Fax:(410)235-7051
Internet: www.hopkinsinnbaltimore.com
E-mail: hopkinsinn@bichotels.com

Circa 1920. Major renovations have turned this inn with
Spanish Revival architecture into uptown elegance. Victorian
decor and antique furnishings reside with original artwork in
tasteful luxury. A meeting room and a conference room are
available for business or pleasure. The inviting guest bedrooms
have a cozy ambiance. Start the day with a continental breakfast. Centrally located across from Johns Hopkins University on
renown Homewood Campus, it is close to all the attractions
this area has to offer.

Innkeeper(s): Mr. Jeff Lambert. $89-159. 26 rooms, 15 with PB, 11
suites and 2 conference rooms. Breakfast and afternoon tea included in
rates. Types of meals: Cont plus and early coffee/tea. Beds: QDT. Modem
hook-up, cable TV, reading lamp, clock radio, telephone and desk in room.
Air conditioning. Fax, copier, parlor games, Complimentary continental
breakfast and afternoon cookies and tea served daily, garage parking available at $8 per day, and front desk open 6 AM - 10 PM daily on premises.
Antiquing, art galleries, bicycling, golf, hiking, museums, parks, shopping,
sporting events, Baltimore Inner Harbor, Union Memorial Hospital,
Baltimore Museum of Art, Camden Yards, PSI Net Stadium and
Convention Center nearby.

Location: City. Uptown location adjacent to Johns Hopkins University.

Certificate may be used: Monday-Thursday, for further available dates please
contact innkeeper.

The Inn at Government House
1125 N Calvert St
Baltimore, MD 21202-3801
(410)539-0566 Fax:(410)539-0567

Circa 1883. This is the official guest house for Baltimore's visiting dignitaries, as well as the general public. It is comprised
of two town houses and a Victorian mansion, located in the
Mt. Vernon historic district. Features include chandeliers,
ornate wallpapers and Victorian antiques. Complimentary parking is included.

Innkeeper(s): Jeanie Clark. $125-165. 19 rooms with PB and 2 conference rooms. Breakfast included in rates. Types of meals: Cont, early coffee/tea and afternoon tea. Beds: KQD. Cable TV, reading lamp, clock radio, telephone and desk in room. Air conditioning. Fax, copier, library, parlor games and fireplace on premises. Handicap access. Antiquing, live theater, shopping and sporting events nearby.

Location: City.

Publicity: *Travel.*

Certificate may be used: Subject to availability.

Berlin   E10

Merry Sherwood Plantation

8909 Worcester Hwy
Berlin, MD 21811-3016
(410)641-2112 (800)660-0358 Fax:(410)641-9528
Internet: www.merrysherwood.com
E-mail: info@merrysherwood.com

Circa 1859. This magnificent pre-Civil War mansion is a tribute to Southern plantation architecture. The inn features antique period furniture, hand-woven, Victorian era rugs and a square grand piano. The ballroom, now a parlor for guests, boasts twin fireplaces and pier mirrors. (Ask to see the hidden cupboards behind the fireside bookcases in the library.) Nineteen acres of grounds are beautifully landscaped and feature azaleas, boxwoods and 125 varieties of trees.

Innkeeper(s): Kirk Burbage. $125-175. 8 rooms, 6 with PB, 4 with FP, 1 suite. Breakfast included in rates. Types of meals: Full gourmet bkfst and afternoon tea. Beds: QD. Air conditioning. Telephone and fireplace on premises. Amusement parks, antiquing, fishing, shopping and water sports nearby.

Publicity: *Washington Post, Baltimore Sun and Southern Living.*

"Pure elegance and privacy at its finest."

Certificate may be used: Anytime, Sunday-Thursday.

Betterton   B8

Lantern Inn

115 Ericsson Ave, PO Box 29
Betterton, MD 21610-9746
(410)348-5809 (800)499-7265 Fax:(410)348-2323
Internet: www.lanterninn.com
E-mail: lanterninn@dmv.com

Circa 1904. Framed by a picket fence and a wide two-story front porch, this four-story country inn is located one block from the nettle-free public beach on Chesapeake Bay. Comfortable rooms are furnished with antiques and handmade quilts. The surrounding area is well-known for its wildlife preserves. Antique shops and restaurants are nearby. Kent County offers plenty of cycling possibilities, and there are detailed maps available at the inn for trips that start at the inn and go for 10 to 90 miles. Tennis courts are two blocks away.

Innkeeper(s): Ray & Sandi Sparks. $80-95. 14 rooms, 4 with PB. Breakfast included in rates. Types of meals: Cont plus. Beds: KQDT. Air conditioning. TV, VCR, parlor games, 3 common rooms and 2 with televisions on premises.

Antiquing, fishing, horseback riding and sporting clays nearby.

Location: Small Chesapeake Bay community.

Publicity: *Richland Times-Dispatch, North Carolina Outdoorsman, Washingtonian and Mid-Atlantic Country.*

Certificate may be used: Sunday through Thursday, Jan. 15-Dec. 15, holidays excluded.

Buckeystown   B5

The Inn at Buckeystown

3521 Buckeystown Pike
Buckeystown, MD 21717
(301)874-5755 (800)272-1190 Fax:(301)831-1355
Internet: www.innatbuckeystown.com
E-mail: buckey@frederickmd.com

Circa 1897. Gables, bay windows and a wraparound porch are features of this grand Victorian mansion located on two-and-a-half acres of lawns and gardens (and an ancient cemetery). The inn features a polished staircase, antiques and elegantly decorated guest rooms. Ask for the Victoriana Suite, which boasts a working fireplace and oak decor. A gourmet dinner is served with advance reservation.

High tea and monthly murder mysteries are also offered. The inn also hosts weddings, rehearsals and retreats. The village of Buckeystown is in the National Register.

Innkeeper(s): Janet Wells. $110-250. 8 rooms, 5 with PB. Breakfast and snacks/refreshments included in rates. Types of meals: Full gourmet bkfst, veg bkfst, early coffee/tea and dinner. Restaurant on premises. Beds: QD. Cable TV, reading lamp, refrigerator and desk in room. Air conditioning. TV, VCR, fax, parlor games, telephone, fireplace and tea room on premises. Limited handicap access. Antiquing, art galleries, bicycling, canoeing/kayaking, downhill skiing, fishing, golf, live theater, museums, parks, shopping, sporting events and wineries nearby.

Location: Country.

Publicity: *Mid-Atlantic, Innsider, The Washingtonian, Washington Post, Baltimore Sun, Voted #1 B&B 2003 Frederick Magazine, Channel 9 and Travel Channel.*

"This was one of the best bed and breakfast experiences we have ever had."

Certificate may be used: Anytime, subject to availability, except holidays.

Cambridge   D8

Glasgow B&B Inn

1500 Hambrooks Blvd
Cambridge, MD 21613
(410)228-0575 Fax:(410)221-0297
E-mail: glasgow@dmv.com

Circa 1760. Located along the Choptank River on seven acres, this brick colonial is reached by way of a long tree-lined driveway. The house was built by Dr. William Murray whose son was a friend to Thomas Jefferson and John Quincy Adams. (According to local legend, part of the U.S. Constitution was written here.) The inn is decorated with country colonial antiques and reproductions, enhanced by high ceilings, a mahogany staircase and deep-window seats.

Innkeeper(s): Louiselee Roche & Martha Rayne. $100-150. 7 rooms, 3 with PB, 6 with FP. Breakfast included in rates. Types of meals: Full bkfst. Beds: KQ. TV and telephone in room.

Publicity: *Mid-Atlantic Country and Tidewater Times.*

Certificate may be used: Jan. 1-Dec. 31, Monday-Thursday.

Cascade   A5

The Cascade Inn

14700 Eyler Ave
Cascade, MD 21719-1938
(301)241-4161 (800)362-9526
Internet: www.thecascadeinn.com
E-mail: thecascadeinn@comcast.net

Circa 1890. In the mountain village of Cascade, this gracious shuttered Georgian manor is situated on two acres of trees and wildflowers. Three suites have double whirlpool tubs. There is an outdoor hot tub as well. The Rose Garden Room and Mt. Magnolia suites have fireplaces and porches overlooking the back garden. The inn is appointed with antiques, lace and white  linens, and white wicker. On Sundays, a full breakfast is served. Cascade is located in between Frederick, Md., and Gettysburg, Pa.

Innkeeper(s): Jan and Duane Musgrove. $75-130. 5 rooms, 3 with PB, 2 with FP, 4 total suites, including 1 two-bedroom suite. Breakfast included in rates. Types of meals: Full gourmet bkfst, early coffee/tea and room service. Beds: KQT. Cable TV, VCR, reading lamp, refrigerator, ceiling fan, clock radio, turn-down service, hot tub/spa and fireplace in room. Air conditioning. Copier, spa, library, parlor games and telephone on premises. Limited handicap access. Antiquing, canoeing/kayaking, downhill skiing, fishing, golf, hiking, live theater, parks, shopping, sporting events, water sports, wineries, Near Appalachian Trail, Gettysburg, Antietam and Monocacy Battlefields and Boyd's Bear Outlet nearby.

Location: Mountains.

Publicity: *Warm Welcomes, Baltimore Sun, Frederick News and Washington Post.*

"A wonderful balance of luxury and at-home comfort."

Certificate may be used: Anytime of year, Sunday through Thursday, excluding holidays.

Chestertown   B8

Great Oak Manor

10568 Cliff Rd
Chestertown, MD 21620-4115
(410)778-5943 (800)504-3098 Fax:(410)810-2517
Internet: www.greatoak.com
E-mail: innkeeper@greatoak.com

Circa 1938. This elegant Georgian mansion anchors vast lawns at the end of a long driveway. Situated directly on the Chesapeake Bay, it is a serene and picturesque country estate. A library with fireplace, den and formal parlors are available to guests. With its  grand circular stairway, bayside gazebo, private beach and nearby marina, the Manor is a remarkable setting for events such as weddings and reunions. Chestertown is eight miles away.

Innkeeper(s): Cassandra and John Fedas. $160-280. 12 rooms with PB, 5 with FP, 2 suites and 2 conference rooms. Breakfast and snacks/refreshments included in rates. Types of meals: Full bkfst and early coffee/tea. Beds: KT. TV, VCR, reading lamp, clock radio, telephone and desk in room. Air conditioning. Fax, copier, bicycles, library, parlor games, fireplace, two computer ready rooms and private beach on premises. Limited handicap access. Antiquing, art galleries, canoeing/kayaking, fishing, golf, horseback riding, live

theater, shopping, tennis and Historic Washington College nearby.
Location: Waterfront.

Publicity: *Philadelphia, Diversions, Road Best Traveled, Washingtonian, Country Inns, Southern Living, New Choices, Chesapeake Life and Time Magazine.*

"The charming setting, professional service and personal warmth we experienced at Great Oak will long be a pleasant memory. Thanks for everything!"

Certificate may be used: Dec. 1-March 31, Sunday through Thursday, holidays excluded.

The Inn at Mitchell House

8796 Maryland Pkwy
Chestertown, MD 21620-4209
(410)778-6500
Internet: www.innatmitchellhouse.com
E-mail: innkeeper@innatmitchellhouse.com

Circa 1743. This pristine 18th-century manor house sits as a jewel on 12 acres overlooking Stoneybrook Pond. The guest rooms and the inn's several parlors are preserved and appointed in an authentic Colonial mood, heightened by handsome polished wide-board floors. Eastern Neck Island National Wildlife Refuge, Chesapeake Farms, St. Michaels, Annapolis and nearby Chestertown are all delightful to explore. The Inn at Mitchell House is a popular setting for romantic weddings and small corporate meetings.

Innkeeper(s): Tracy & Jim Stone. $100-140. 5 rooms with PB, 4 with FP. Breakfast included in rates. Types of meals: Full bkfst and early coffee/tea. Beds: KQ. TV, VCR, reading lamp, refrigerator, turn-down service and desk in room. Air conditioning. Telephone and fireplace on premises. Antiquing, fishing, live theater, shopping, sporting events, water sports and private beach nearby.

Location: Country.

Publicity: *Washingtonian, New York Magazine, Glamour, Philadelphia Inquirer, Baltimore Sun, Kent County News, Ten Best Inns in the Country, New York Times, Washington Post and National Geographic Traveler.*

Certificate may be used: Sunday through Thursday, excluding holidays.

Lauretum Inn B&B

954 High St
Chestertown, MD 21620-3955
(410)778-3236 (800)742-3236 Fax:(410)778-3334
Internet: www.chestertown.com/lauretum
E-mail: mshane3400@aol.com

Circa 1881. At the end of a long winding driveway, this massive Queen Anne Victorian commands a hilltop setting on six acres just outside of town. Inviting parlors and a porch are available to guests. Spacious guest rooms overlook the inn's lawns, often visited by deer in the early morning. Peg, the mother of 16 children, once plied the intracoastal waters on her 40-foot boat and can help you plan your stay in the area.

Innkeeper(s): Martha Shane & Walter Schaefer. $65-140. 5 rooms with PB. Breakfast and afternoon tea included in rates. Types of meals: Cont plus and early coffee/tea. Beds: QDT. Reading lamp, clock radio and desk in room. Air conditioning. VCR, telephone and fireplace on premises. Antiquing, fishing, golf, live theater, parks, shopping, sporting events and water sports nearby.

Location: Country. Chesapeake Bay.

Certificate may be used: Jan. 2-March 31, excluding holidays.

Deep Creek Lake   B1

Haley Farm B&B Spa and Retreat Center

16766 Garrett Hwy
Deep Creek Lake, MD 21550-4036
(301)387-9050 (888)231-3276 Fax:(301)387-9050
Internet: www.haleyfarm.com
E-mail: info@haleyfarm.com

Circa 1920. Surrounded by 65 acres of rolling hills and mountains, this farmhouse has been graciously transformed. Chinese carpets, tapestries and European furnishings are some of the innkeepers' many elegant touches. Three luxury suites include a heart-shaped Jacuzzi, king bed, kitchenette and sitting room with a fireplace. There are also six mini-suites and one deluxe guest bedroom. A three-bedroom lakeside cottage includes a boat dock and gorgeous views. Croquet and badminton are set up on the grounds. Other popular activities are fishing in the trout pond, napping in the hammock or picnicking in the gazebo. Be pampered by the spa and sauna with a facial, massage, reflexology or sunless tanning. Ask about retreats and workshops. Located three hours from Washington, DC it is only minutes from the lake, state parks and a ski and golf resort.

$135-215. 10 rooms with PB, 9 with HT, 9 suites. Breakfast included in rates. Types of meals: Full bkfst. Beds: KQ. Ceiling fan and 9 suites with fireplace and Jacuzzis in room. Air conditioning. VCR, spa, bicycles, library, parlor games, telephone and trout pond on premises. Antiquing, cross-country skiing, downhill skiing, fishing, parks, shopping, water sports and white water rafting nearby.

Location: Country, mountains.

"A beautiful setting for a quiet, romantic escape."

Certificate may be used: Monday-Thursday, November-June excluding holidays.

Easton   C8

John S. McDaniel House B&B

14 N Aurora St
Easton, MD 21601-3617
(410)822-3704 (877)822-5702 Fax:(410)822-3704
Internet: www.bnblist.com\md\mcdaniel
E-mail: jsmcdanielhouse@netscape.net

Circa 1865. A wide veranda wraps around this three-story Queen Anne Victorian, complete with octagonal tower and dormers. Located in the historic district, considered to be the "Colonial Capital of the Eastern Shore," it's within walking distance to the classic Avalon Theater, Academy of Art, many good restaurants and unique shops.

Innkeeper(s): Mrs. Mary Lou Karwacki. $105-135. 6 rooms with PB, 1 suite and 1 conference room. Breakfast included in rates. Types of meals: Full gourmet bkfst. Beds: KQ. Cable TV, VCR, ceiling fan, wireless Internet and sitting area in room. Central air. Fax, copier, telephone, fireplace, wraparound porch, large living room, breakfast room and video library on premises. Antiquing, art galleries, beach, bicycling, canoeing/kayaking, golf, hiking, horseback riding, live theater, parks, shopping, tennis and water sports nearby.

Location: Town of Easton.

Publicity: *Public YV - Radio.*

Certificate may be used: Dec. 1-March 15, weekdays and weekends; March 16-Nov. 30 Monday through Thursday night; subject to availability.

Havre De Grace   A8

Vandiver Inn, Kent & Murphy Homes

301 S Union Ave
Havre De Grace, MD 21078-3201
(410)939-5200 (800)245-1655 Fax:(410)939-5202
Internet: www.vandiverinn.com
E-mail: innkeeper@vandiverinn.com

Circa 1886. Three acres surround this three-story historic Victorian mansion. A chandelier lights the entrance. Some of the rooms offer gas fireplaces and clawfoot tubs, and all are furnished with Victorian antiques. For instance, a king-size Victorian bed, original to the house, is one of the features of the Millard E. Tydings Room, also offering a decorative fireplace and sitting area. The innkeeper creates gourmet breakfasts with freshly baked scones or muffins. Spend some time in the garden where a summer gazebo is supported by 12 cedar tree trunks.

Innkeeper(s): Susan Muldoon. $68-185. 17 rooms with PB, 4 with FP. Breakfast included in rates. Types of meals: Full gourmet bkfst, veg bkfst, early coffee/tea, picnic lunch and dinner. Beds: KQDT. Data port, cable TV, reading lamp, clock radio, telephone and desk in room. Central air. Fax, parlor games, fireplace, laundry facility and indoor and outdoor conference rooms on premises. Limited handicap access. Antiquing, art galleries, bicycling, canoeing/kayaking, fishing, golf, hiking, horseback riding, live theater, museums, parks, shopping, tennis, water sports and wineries nearby.

Certificate may be used: Sunday-Thursday, September-April. Not valid on holidays and other blackout dates.

Middletown   B5

Stone Manor

5820 Carroll Boyer Rd
Middletown, MD 21769-6315
(301)473-5454 Fax:(301)371-5622
Internet: www.stonemanor.com
E-mail: themanor@stonemanor.com

Circa 1780. If you're searching for a romantic secluded getaway and hope to be pampered with world-class dining and elegant surroundings, head for this impressive stone estate house. The home is tucked between mountain ranges on 114 acres of picturesque lawns, gardens and working farmland. The interior is intimate and inviting with guest suites decorated in a variety of styles. All include queen-size poster beds and whirlpools baths, and most offer fireplaces and porches that afford tranquil views of flowerbeds, ponds or woods. Be sure and make reservations ahead for the inn's five-course dinners. Recognized by Washingtonian Magazine's "100 Very Best Restaurants", Wine Spectator Magazine and the Distinguished Restaurants of North America, dinner and lunch are available Tuesday through Sunday. The inn was named as one of the Top Ten Inns in America by Country Inns Magazine.

Innkeeper(s): Judith Harne. $150-275. 6 rooms with PB, 4 with FP. Breakfast included in rates. Types of meals: Cont plus, early coffee/tea, gourmet lunch and gourmet dinner. Restaurant on premises. Beds: Q. Turndown service in room. Air conditioning. VCR, fax and copier on premises. Handicap access. Antiquing, cross-country skiing, fishing, live theater, museums, parks, shopping, water sports and Civil War history nearby.

Location: Mountains.

Certificate may be used: January-March, July, August, November, Tuesday-Thursday. Excludes holidays.

Ocean City   E10

An Inn on the Ocean

1001 Atlantic Avenue
Ocean City, MD 21842
(410)289-8894 (888)226-6223 Fax:(410)289-8215
Internet: www.InnOnTheOcean.com
E-mail: innonoc@aol.com

Circa 1938. From the wraparound porch of this inn, guests
can watch birds soar and ocean waters crash upon the shore.
The Inn includes six elegant guest rooms, each individually
decorated with rich fabrics and designer linens. The Hunt and
Tapestry rooms each boast an ocean view. The Oceana Room
includes a private balcony that looks out to the sea. The
Veranda Room has its own oceanfront porch. Some rooms
include a Jacuzzi tub. The gourmet breakfasts include homemade breads, fruit and special egg dishes, such as a frittata.
The Inn is oceanfront, so guests need only walk a few steps to
enjoy the beach and nearby Boardwalk. Golfing, outlet stores,
fishing, water sports, antique shops and harness racing are
other local attractions.

Innkeeper(s): The Barrett's. $130-310. 6 rooms with PB and 1 conference
room. Breakfast and snacks/refreshments included in rates. Types of meals:
Full bkfst and early coffee/tea. Beds: KQ. Cable TV, VCR, reading lamp, ceiling fan, clock radio, Jacuzzi and bathrobes in room. Air conditioning. Fax,
copier, bicycles, parlor games, telephone, fireplace in salon, beach chairs and
umbrellas on premises. Limited handicap access. Amusement parks,
antiquing, art galleries, beach, bicycling, canoeing/kayaking, fishing, golf, hiking, horseback riding, live theater, museums, parks, shopping, sporting
events, tennis and water sports nearby.
Location: Ocean community, waterfront.
Certificate may be used: Jan. 2-Feb. 10, Sunday-Thursday, subject to
availability.

Queenstown   C8

Queenstown Inn Bed & Breakfast

7109 Main St. PO Box 2012
Queenstown, MD 21658-2012
(410)827-3396 (888)744-3407 Fax:(410)827-3397
Internet: www.queenstowninn.com
E-mail: qtbb@dmv.com

Circa 1830. Relaxation is easy at this comfortable inn, built
with an original cast-iron front. Situated near Chesapeake Bay,
take a short walk to a private beach. Boaters are welcome and
can be picked up from a dock a few blocks away. The State
Room is a spacious gathering place with wood stove, brick bar,
stereo and an organ. It opens to a large screened-in porch overlooking flower gardens. Guest bedrooms and a suite are delib-
erately without electronics for a calm setting. A satisfying continental-plus breakfast is served in the Historic Room, which features vintage pictures of the Eastern shore and the inn's past.
Visit the gift shop, an old storefront offering the work of local
artists and craftsmen. Unique gift baskets can be made to
order. An outlet mall and antique center are nearby.

Innkeeper(s): Josh Barns, Micheal Lydon. $95-155. 5 rooms, 4 with PB, 1
suite. Breakfast and snacks/refreshments included in rates. Types of meals:
Cont plus, veg bkfst and early coffee/tea. Beds: QDT. Reading lamp, ceiling
fan and tub with shower in room. Central air. TV, VCR, fax, copier, bicycles,
library, parlor games, telephone, fireplace, laundry facility and gift shop on
premises. Handicap access. Antiquing, art galleries, beach, bicycling, canoe-
ing/kayaking, fishing, golf, hiking, live theater, museums, parks, shopping,
sporting events, tennis, water sports, outlet shopping, Horsehead Wetlands

Center and Wye Island Natural Resources Management area nearby.
Certificate may be used: Monday-Thursday, excluding holidays. Not valid
with other specials.

Saint Michaels   C8

Kemp House Inn

412 Talbot St, PO Box 638
Saint Michaels, MD 21663-0638
(410)745-2243
Internet: www.kemphouseinn.com
E-mail: info@kemphouseinn.com

Circa 1807. This two-story Georgian house was built by
Colonel Joseph Kemp, a shipwright and one of the town forefa-
thers. The inn is appointed in period furnishings accentuated

by candlelight. Guest rooms
include patchwork quilts, a
collection of four-poster rope
beds and old-fashioned night-
shirts. There are several working fireplaces. Robert E. Lee is
said to have been a guest.

Innkeeper(s): Diane M. & Steve Cooper. $95-130. 7 rooms with PB, 4 with
FP and 1 cottage. Breakfast included in rates. Types of meals: Cont plus.
Beds: QDT. Reading lamp in room. Air conditioning. Telephone and fireplace
on premises. Antiquing, fishing, shopping and water sports nearby.
Location: Small town.
Publicity: *Gourmet and Philadelphia*.

*"It was wonderful. We've stayed in many B&Bs, and this was one of
the nicest!"*
Certificate may be used: Sunday through Thursday nights, excluding holidays. Year-round.

Parsonage Inn

210 N Talbot St
Saint Michaels, MD 21663-2102
(410)745-5519 (800)394-5519
Internet: www.parsonage-inn.com
E-mail: parsinn@dmv.com

Circa 1883. A striking Victorian steeple rises next to the wide
bay of this brick residence, once the home of Henry Clay
Dodson, state senator, pharmacist and brickyard owner. The

house features brick detail in a
variety of patterns and inlays, perhaps a design statement for brick
customers. Porches are decorated
with filigree and spindled
columns. Waverly linens, late
Victorian furnishings, fireplaces
and decks add to the creature

comforts. Six bikes await guests who wish to ride to Tilghman
Island or to the ferry that goes to Oxford. Gourmet breakfast is
served in the dining room.

Innkeeper(s): Bill Wilhelm. $100-195. 8 rooms with PB, 3 with FP.
Breakfast included in rates. Types of meals: Full gourmet bkfst. Beds: KQD.
Reading lamp, ceiling fan, clock radio and two with TV in room. Air condi-
tioning. TV, bicycles, telephone and fireplace on premises. Handicap access.
Antiquing, fishing, shopping, water sports and Chesapeake Bay Maritime
Museum nearby.
Location: City. Main St of Historic Town.
Publicity: *Philadelphia Inquirer Sunday Travel, Wilmington and Delaware
News Journal*.

"Striking, extensively renovated."
Certificate may be used: Sunday through Thursday, November until June.

Scotland   E7

St. Michael's Manor B&B

50200 St Michael's Manor Way
Scotland, MD 20687-3107
(301)872-4025 Fax:(301)872-9330
Internet: stmichaels-manor.com
E-mail: stmichaelsman@olg.com

Circa 1805. Sitting on ten scenic acres with a three-acre vineyard, lots of wildlife and an incredible natural beauty, this historic country manor house is located on Long Neck Creek, just
nine miles from St. Mary's
City and 16 miles from
Lexington Park. The estate
offers quiet places to relax.
Guest bedrooms are fur-
nished with period antiques,
beds accented by handmade
quilts and gorgeous views of the water. A bountiful country
breakfast offers a changing menu with seasonal specialties.
Swim in the pool or go canoeing. Take a day trip to
Washington, DC, only sixty miles away.

Innkeeper(s): Joe & Nancy Dick. $60-130. 4 rooms, 1 with PB. Breakfast
included in rates. Types of meals: Full gourmet bkfst, veg bkfst, early
coffee/tea, picnic lunch, afternoon tea and snacks/refreshments. Beds: QDT.
Reading lamp, clock radio, telephone, desk and voice mail in room. Central
air. Fax, copier, swimming, bicycles, library, parlor games, fireplace, laundry
facility, rowboat, canoe, paddleboat and bird watching on premises.
Antiquing, beach, bicycling, canoeing/kayaking, cross-country skiing, fishing,
golf, hiking, live theater, museums, parks, shopping, sporting events, tennis,
water sports, wineries, crabbing and boats nearby.

Location: Country, waterfront. Manor House is located on Long Neck Creek,
one half mile from the Chesapeake Bay.

Publicity: *Washington Post and St. Mary's Co. Enterprise.*

"Your B&B was so warm, cozy and comfortable."

Certificate may be used: Nov. 1-March 31, all nights, Sunday-Saturday.

Sykesville   B6

Inn at Norwood

7514 Norwood Ave
Sykesville, MD 21784
(410)549-7868
Internet: www.innatnorwood.com
E-mail: kelly@innatnorwood.com

Circa 1906. Romance is the trademark of this Colonial Revival
home that sits in the center of Sykesville, a quaint town on the
National Register of Historic Places. The front porch and cozy

parlor are both perfects spots for relaxation. The guest bedrooms and suite are tastefully decorated to reflect the four seasons. They boast two-person Jacuzzi and clawfoot tubs, canopy
and poster beds and some fireplaces. A three-course breakfast
features homemade baked goods such as cinnamon applesauce
cake, a house specialty, fresh fruit, bacon or apple sausage and
an entree. A refreshment bar with snacks and beverages is
always available. Stroll the landscaped grounds with a deck and
tranquil pond.

Innkeeper(s): Kelly & Steve Crum. $90-200. 6 rooms with PB, 4 with FP, 5
with HT. Breakfast and snacks/refreshments included in rates. Types of
meals: Full gourmet bkfst. Beds: KQ. Modem hook-up, data port, cable TV,
VCR, reading lamp, CD player, refrigerator, ceiling fan, snack bar, clock radio,
telephone, coffeemaker, fireplace and four with hot tub in room. Central air.
Fax, copier, bicycles, library and parlor games on premises. Antiquing, bicycling, fishing, golf, hiking, museums and parks nearby.

Location: Country. Small Historic Town.

Publicity: *Baltimore Sun and Carroll County Times.*

Certificate may be used: Anytime, Monday-Thursday, excluding holidays.

Whitehaven   E8

Whitehaven B&B

23844 River St
Quantico, MD 21856
(410)873-3320 (888)205-5921 Fax:(410)873-2162
Internet: www.whitehaven.com
E-mail: whavnbb@dmv.com

Circa 1850. Two historic properties comprise this bed &
breakfast. The Charles Leatherbury House, which dates to
1886, includes two guest rooms, decorated in country
Victorian style. The two rooms share a bath, perfect for couples
traveling together. Book both rooms and you'll enjoy the
utmost of privacy in a historic setting. The Otis Lloyd House,
constructed prior to the Civil War, includes three guest rooms,
each with a private bath. Guests at both houses enjoy a full
breakfast, including farm-fresh eggs and homemade baked
goods. The village of Whitehaven, originally chartered in 1685,
includes 22 buildings listed in the National Register.

Innkeeper(s): Maryen & Mark Herrett. $70-100. 5 rooms, 3 with PB.
Breakfast and snacks/refreshments included in rates. Types of meals: Full
gourmet bkfst and veg bkfst. Beds: KQT. Air conditioning. TV, VCR, fax, copier, bicycles, library, parlor games, fireplace, gas and horseback riding on
premises. Antiquing, art galleries, bicycling, canoeing/kayaking, fishing, golf,
museums, parks and Atlantic beaches nearby.

Location: Country, waterfront. Very small village.

Certificate may be used: Sunday-Thursday, May-October. November-April,
subject to availability.

Massachusetts

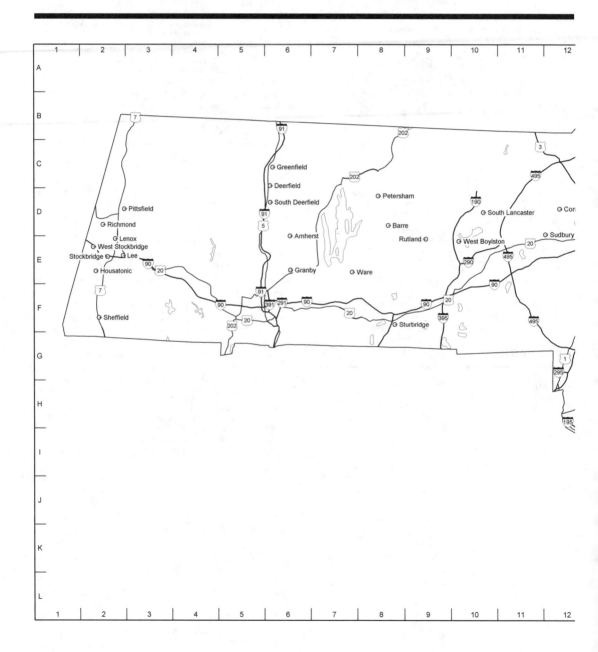

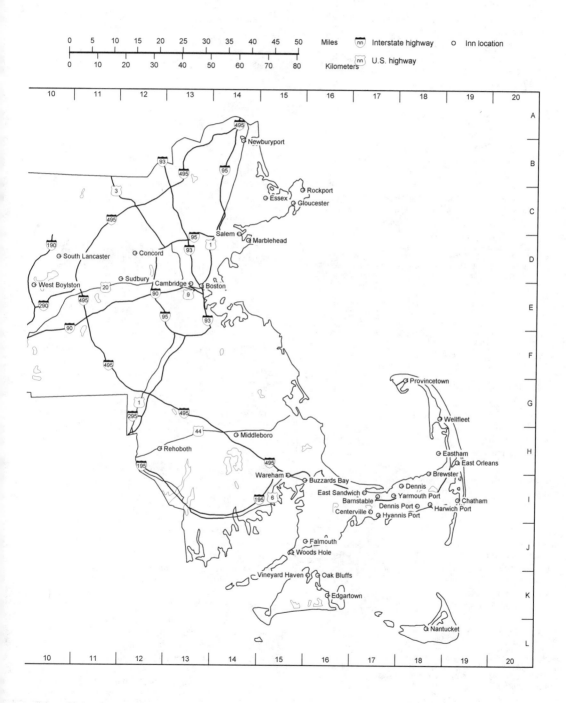

0 5 10 15 20 25 30 35 40 45 50   Miles

0 10 20 30 40 50 60 70 80   Kilometers

Interstate highway   o   Inn location

U.S. highway

Amherst   D6

1886 Todd House

90 Spring Street
Amherst, MA 01002
(413)259-1700 Fax:(413)549-7406
Internet: www.1886toddhouse.com
E-mail: the1886toddhouse@aol.com

Circa 1886. Impressive architectural details and an equally
stunning history permeate this 1886 Queen Anne Victorian,
known locally as the Dell. Emily Dickinson's brother Austin
gave this property situated across the street from the Dickinson
Homestead to Mable Loomis Todd and her husband David
Peck Todd, a noted astronomer and Amherst College professor.
Mable compiled and edited her friend Emily's first three collections of poetry and maintained a 14-year love affair with
Austin. Enjoy viewing the collection of Mable's paintings on
permanent loan from the historical society. The artwork is a fitting accent to the walnut woodwork, Oriental rugs, and carved
antique European period and American Eastlake furnishings.
Stay in one of the gracious and inviting guest bedrooms and
suites. Overlook the English gardens and landscaped grounds
while enjoying a hearty fireside breakfast.

Innkeeper(s): Micki Sanderson/Sanderson Foundation Inc. $75-175. 5 rooms,
3 with PB, 2 with FP, 2 suites. Breakfast and snacks/refreshments included
in rates. Types of meals: Full bkfst and early coffee/tea. Beds: QDT. Modem
hook-up, cable TV, reading lamp, clock radio, fireplace and luxury bedding in
room. Air conditioning. Gardens, lighted parking and art gallery on premises.
Amusement parks, antiquing, art galleries, beach, bicycling, canoeing/kayak-
ing, cross-country skiing, downhill skiing, fishing, golf, hiking, horseback riding, live theater, museums, parks, shopping, sporting events, tennis, water
sports and wineries nearby.
Location: Country. Quiet neighborhood location two blocks from Amherst
Town Common. Connecticut River Valley, 5 College area.
Publicity: Springfield Republican and Hampshire Gazette.
Certificate may be used: November-March & June-July.

Allen House Victorian Inn

599 Main St
Amherst, MA 01002-2409
(413)253-5000
Internet: www.allenhouse.com
E-mail: allenhouse@webtv.net

Circa 1886. This stick-style Queen Anne is much like a
Victorian museum with guest rooms that feature period reproduction wallpapers, pedestal sinks, carved golden oak and
brass beds, painted wooden floors and plenty of antiques.
Among its many other treasures include Eastlake fireplace mantels. Unforgettable breakfasts include specialties such as eggs
Benedict or French toast stuffed
with rich cream cheese.
Afternoon tea is a treat, and the
inn offers plenty of examples of
poetry from Emily Dickinson,
whose home is just across the
street from the inn.

Innkeeper(s): Alan & Ann Zieminski. $75-175. 7 rooms with PB. Breakfast,
afternoon tea and snacks/refreshments included in rates. Types of meals: Full
bkfst and early coffee/tea. Beds: QDT. Modem hook-up, reading lamp, ceiling
fan, clock radio, telephone, desk and down comforters & pillows in room. Air
conditioning. Fax, copier, library, parlor games and fireplace on premises.
Amusement parks, antiquing, cross-country skiing, downhill skiing, fishing, golf,
live theater, parks, shopping, sporting events, tennis and water sports nearby.
Location: Mountains. Small college town.

Publicity: New York Times, Boston Magazine, Bon Appetit, Yankee Travel and
Victorian Homes.

*"Our room and adjoining bath were spotlessly clean, charming, and
quiet, with good lighting. Our meals were delicious and appetizing,
and the casual, family-like atmosphere encouraged discussions among
the guests."*
Certificate may be used: Jan. 1-April 1, Sunday-Thursday.

Barnstable   I17

Ashley Manor Inn

PO Box 856
Barnstable, MA 02630
(508)362-8044 (888)535-2246 Fax:(508)362-9927
Internet: www.ashleymanor.net
E-mail: stay@ashleymanor.net

Circa 1699. This manor house has lived through a succession of
expansions, the first addition built in 1750. The final effect is
wonderful and mysterious. The inn, thought to be a hiding place
for Tories during the Revolutionary War, features a huge open-
hearth fireplace with beehive
oven and a secret passageway connecting the upstairs
and downstairs suites. The
inn is reminiscent of a gracious English country house
and is filled with Oriental
rugs and antiques. All but one of the guest rooms boasts fireplaces, and four have large whirlpool baths. Enjoy complimentary sherry, port and brandy as you relax in the cozy and spacious
living room. Two acres of manicured lawns include a regulation-
size tennis court. Nature lovers will enjoy the landscape, dotted
with cherry and apple trees. The romantic gazebo is the perfect
location to view the fountain garden. A full gourmet breakfast is
served on the brick terrace or fireside in the formal dining room.

Innkeeper(s): Kathy Callahan. $120-225. 6 rooms with PB, 5 with FP, 4 suites.
Breakfast included in rates. Types of meals: Full gourmet bkfst. Beds: KQ. Data
port, reading lamp, clock radio, telephone, coffeemaker, hot tub/spa, voice mail,
fireplace, four with whirlpool baths, flowers, chocolates, beverages and coffee in
room. Air conditioning. Bicycles, tennis, library, parlor games, fireplace and gazebo on premises. Antiquing, art galleries, beach, bicycling, canoeing/kayaking,
fishing, golf, hiking, live theater, museums, parks, shopping and tennis nearby.
Location: Country.
Publicity: Chicago Tribune, Boston Globe, Bon Appetit, Tennis, New York
Times, Pittsburgh Press, Gourmet, GBH and Newsday.

"This is absolutely perfect! So many very special, lovely touches."
Certificate may be used: November-May, Sunday-Thursday, subject to availability and excluding holidays.

Beechwood Inn

2839 Main St, Rt 6A
Barnstable, MA 02630-1017
(508)362-6618 (800)609-6618 Fax:(508)362-0298
Internet: www.beechwoodinn.com
E-mail: info@beechwoodinn.com

Circa 1853. Beechwood is a beautifully restored Queen Anne
Victorian offering period furnishings, some rooms with fireplaces or seasonal ocean views. Its warmth and elegance make
it a favorite hideaway for couples looking for a peaceful and
romantic return to the Victorian era. The inn is named for rare
old beech trees that shade the veranda.

Innkeeper(s): Debbie & Ken Traugot. $110-200. 6 rooms with PB, 3 with
FP. Breakfast and afternoon tea included in rates. Types of meals: Full bkfst
and early coffee/tea. Beds: KQD. TV, VCR, reading lamp, refrigerator, wine

glasses and corkscrew in room. Air conditioning. Fax, copier, bicycles, parlor games, telephone and fireplace on premises. Antiquing, fishing, live theater, parks, shopping, sporting events, water sports, historic sites, whale watching and bird watching nearby.

Location: Ocean community.

Publicity: *National Trust Calendar, New England Weekends, Rhode Island Monthly, Cape Cod Life, Boston Magazine and Yankee Magazine.*

"Your inn is pristine in every detail. We concluded that the innkeepers, who are most hospitable, are the best part of Beechwood."

Certificate may be used: Dec. 1 through March 31, Sunday through Thursday, except holiday periods.

Honeysuckle Hill B&B

591 Old Kings Hwy, Rt 6A
Barnstable, MA 02668-1128
(508)362-8418 (866)444-5522 Fax:(508)362-8386
Internet: www.honeysucklehill.com
E-mail: stay@honeysucklehill.com

Circa 1810. This Queen Anne Victorian, which is listed in the National Register, is set on a picturesque acre with gardens. The interior is decorated with antiques and white wicker furnishings. The hearty breakfasts include items such as Captain's Eggs, homemade granola, fresh fruit and cranberry-orange muffins. Nearby are the dunes of Sandy Neck Beach. Hyannis is 10 minutes away.

Innkeeper(s): Frdddy & Ruth Riley. $100-219. 5 rooms, 4 with PB, 1 suite. Breakfast and snacks/refreshments included in rates. Types of meals: Full gourmet bkfst and early coffee/tea. Beds: QD. Ceiling fan, clock radio, feather beds, fresh flowers and terry cloth robes in room. Air conditioning. TV, VCR, fax, copier, library, parlor games, telephone, fireplace, beach towels, chairs and umbrellas, guest refrigerator, fish pond, porch and gardens on premises. Antiquing, art galleries, beach, bicycling, canoeing/kayaking, fishing, golf, hiking, live theater, museums, parks, shopping, tennis, wineries, ferries and whale watching nearby.

Location: Cape Cod.

Publicity: *Atlanta Constitution, Saint Louis Journal, Prime Time, Cape Cod Travel Guide, Cape Cod Life and Secondhome.*

"The charm, beauty, service and warmth shown to guests are impressive, but the food overwhelms. Breakfasts were divine!"—Judy Kaplan, St. Louis Journal

Certificate may be used: Nov. 1 to April 30, Monday-Thursday.

Lamb and Lion Inn

2504 Main St., Rt. 6A, PO Box 511
Barnstable, MA 02630-0511
(508)362-6823 (800)909-6923 Fax:(508)362-0227
Internet: www.lambandlion.com
E-mail: info@lambandlion.com

Circa 1740. This rambling collection of Cape-style buildings sits on four acres overlooking the Old King's highway. Newly decorated, the inn offers a feeling of casual elegance. The Innkeeper's Pride is a romantic suite with sunken tub, fireplace, kitchenette and a deck overlooking a garden and woods. The Barn-stable is one of the original buildings and now offers three sleeping areas, a living and dining area and French doors to a private patio. A large central courtyard houses a generous sized heated pool and hot tub spa.

Innkeeper(s): Alice Pitcher. $145-250. 10 rooms with PB, 11 with FP, 1 cottage and 1 conference room. Breakfast included in rates. Types of meals: Cont plus. Beds: KQDT. Modem hook-up, cable TV,

VCR, reading lamp, refrigerator, telephone, coffeemaker and fireplace in room. Air conditioning. Fax, copier, spa, swimming, parlor games and fireplace on premises. Antiquing, art galleries, beach, bicycling, canoeing/kayaking, cross-country skiing, fishing, golf, hiking, horseback riding, live theater, museums, parks, shopping, sporting events, tennis, water sports and wineries nearby.

Location: Ocean community.

Certificate may be used: Oct. 31-May 18, Sunday through Friday.

Barre D8

Stevens Farm B&B

Old Coldbrook Rd
Barre, MA 01005
(978)355-2227 Fax:(978)355-2234
Internet: www.stevensfarminn.com
E-mail: stevensfarminn@juno.com

Circa 1789. Guests enjoy an old-fashioned country experience at Stevens Farm. The 18th-century farmhouse has been in the innkeepers' family for nine generations since 1789. Guests can take tours of the 350-acre working farm, enjoy a swimming pool or just relax and enjoy the view from the gazebo. During the winter months, guests can cross-country ski on the property or ice skate on the pond. Colorful, handmade afghans and comfortable antiques decorate the bedchambers. The parlor features Victorian furnishings, an upright piano and a tin ceiling. The innkeeper once worked as a cook and professional baker and prepares the savory full breakfasts. Dinner, featuring items such as Yankee pot roast, homemade bread and cranberry walnut pie, can be arranged. The inn recently received the Governors Hospitality Award.

Innkeeper(s): Richard & Irene Stevens. $75-95. 6 rooms, 1 with PB and 1 conference room. Breakfast and afternoon tea included in rates. Types of meals: Full bkfst, early coffee/tea, picnic lunch, snacks/refreshments and room service. Beds: D. Reading lamp, clock radio and window fans in room. Antiquing, art galleries, bicycling, canoeing/kayaking, cross-country skiing, downhill skiing, fishing, golf, hiking, horseback riding, live theater, museums, shopping, tennis and wineries nearby.

Location: Country.

Certificate may be used: Monday and Tuesday, Jan. 1-March 1.

Boston E13

Charles Street Inn

94 Charles Street
Boston, MA 02114
(617)314-8900 (877)772-8900 Fax:(617)371-0009
Internet: www.charlesstreetinn.com
E-mail: info@charlesstreetinn.com

Circa 1860. Elegantly gracing the historic district of Beacon Hill, this inn was built as a model home in 1860 featuring Second Empire decor. Exquisite luxury resonates from this meticulously renovated and refurbished delight. Each amenity-filled guest bedroom is named after a famous local Victorian who contributed to the arts and is tastefully furnished to reflect that character. Plush comforts include large air-jet whirlpool spa tubs, refrigerators stocked with complimentary beverages, marble fireplaces, stereo CDs, DSL Internet access, Crabtree & Evelyn toiletries, Frette linens, robes and slippers, Turkish rugs, antiques, oil paintings and much more. A deluxe continental breakfast is savored in the privacy of the room. The sights of the city beckon and are even more enjoyable knowing what splendor awaits back at the inn.

Innkeeper(s): Sally Deane & Louise Venden. $225-425. 9 rooms with PB, 9 with FP and 1 conference room. Breakfast and snacks/refreshments included in rates. Types of meals: Cont plus, early coffee/tea, wine and room service.

Beds: KQD. Modem hook-up, data port, cable TV, VCR, reading lamp, stereo, refrigerator, snack bar, clock radio, telephone, coffeemaker, turn-down service, desk, hot tub/spa, voice mail, fireplace and DSL in room. Central air. Fax, copier, library, parlor games and laundry facility on premises. Handicap access. Antiquing, art galleries, bicycling, canoeing/kayaking, live theater, museums, parks, shopping, sporting events and tennis nearby.

Location: City.

Publicity: *Washington Port, Boston Globe, Travel & Leisure, Conde Nast, Johansens Guide to North America, Karen Browns Guide to North American Inns, USA Today, ABC Good Morning America, Travels with Stephanie Abrams and WGBH - American Experience episode about Thomas Edison.*

Certificate may be used: January to March, Sunday-Thursday, excluding holidays.

Brewster   H18

Old Sea Pines Inn

2553 Main St, PO Box 1026
Brewster, MA 02631-1959
(508)896-6114 Fax:(508)896-7387
Internet: www.oldseapinesinn.com
E-mail: innkeeper@oldseapinesinn.com

Circa 1900. Formerly the Sea Pines School of Charm and Personality for Young Women, this turn-of-the-century mansion sits on three-and-one-half acres of trees and lawns. Recently renovated, the inn displays elegant wallpapers and a grand sweeping stairway. On Sunday evenings, mid June through mid September, enjoy a dinner show in conjunction with Cape Cod Repertory Theatre.

Beaches and bike paths are nearby, as are village shops and restaurants.

Innkeeper(s): Michele & Stephen Rowan. $75-150. 24 rooms, 16 with PB, 3 with FP, 2 suites and 2 conference rooms. Breakfast and snacks/refreshments included in rates. Types of meals: Full bkfst, early coffee/tea, afternoon tea and room service. Beds: QDT. Cable TV and reading lamp in room. Air conditioning. TV, telephone and fireplace on premises. Handicap access. Antiquing, fishing, live theater, shopping, water sports and dinner theatre in summer nearby.

Publicity: *New York Times, Cape Cod Oracle, For Women First, Home Office, Entrepreneur, Boston Magazine, Redbook, Travel & Leisure and Better Homes & Gardens-British Edition.*

"The loving care applied by Steve, Michele and staff is deeply appreciated."

Certificate may be used: Weekdays only March 31-May 31 and Oct. 15-Dec. 21.

Buzzards Bay   I16

Hill View Bed and Breakfast

788 Sandwich Rd
Buzzards Bay, MA 02532-2207
(508)888-0214 Fax:(508)888-0214
Internet: www.ahillviewbnb.com
E-mail: reservations@ahillviewbnb.com

Family-owned and operated for generations, this bed and breakfast has been restored and is furnished with period pieces that highlight the refinished oak floors. A private entrance and separate guest area are provided. The Bayberry Room and Blueberry Room boast views of the Sagamore Bridge and Cape Cod Canal. Share the use of a kitchen area with a mini-refrigerator, microwave, toaster and sink. Breakfast is served in the kitchen or on the front enclosed porch. Enjoy easy access to paved bike and walking paths. The beach is minutes away. Martha's Vineyard and Nantucket ferries are nearby. Visit historic Plymouth.

$95-135. 3 rooms with PB. Breakfast included in rates. Types of meals: Cont plus. Beds: QD. Cable TV and clock radio in room. Air conditioning. Fax and copier on premises. Antiquing, art galleries, beach, bicycling, canoeing/kayaking, cross-country skiing, downhill skiing, fishing, golf, hiking, horseback riding, museums, parks, shopping, sporting events, tennis, water sports and wineries nearby.

Certificate may be used: Anyday, January-April.

Cambridge   D13

A Bed & Breakfast In Cambridge

1657 Cambridge St
Cambridge, MA 02138-4316
(617)868-7082 (800)795-7122 Fax:(617)876-8991
Internet: www.cambridgebnb.com
E-mail: doaneperry@yahoo.com

Circa 1897. Located minutes from Harvard Square, this colonial revival house reflects the rich ambiance of the Cambridge historical district. Surround yourself in the finest New England culture, located walking distance from the house. Visit museums, theaters and fine restaurants. Rest under the voluminous trees in the park across the street, or hop on the Red Line for an excursion to Boston. After an active day of sight seeing, return to the warmth of turn-of-the-century antique decor at this three-story home away from home. Enjoy a savory breakfast featuring such delights as home-baked, sesame-orange spice bread and cranberry brody, and spend the afternoon relaxing in an overstuffed chair or Grandmother's cane rockers with some tea or sherry.

Innkeeper(s): Doane Perry. $95-160. 3 rooms. Breakfast and afternoon tea included in rates. Types of meals: Full gourmet bkfst, veg bkfst and early coffee/tea. Beds: KQT. Modem hook-up, data port, cable TV, reading lamp, clock radio, telephone, turn-down service, desk and voice mail in room. Air conditioning. Fax, copier and library on premises. Antiquing, art galleries, beach, bicycling, canoeing/kayaking, cross-country skiing, live theater, museums, parks, shopping, sporting events, tennis and water sports nearby.

Location: City.

Certificate may be used: Jan. 6-Feb. 12, Feb. 24-27, Dec. 9-19.

Irving House at Harvard

24 Irving Street
Cambridge, MA 02138-3007
(617)547-4600 (877)547-4600 Fax:(617)576-2814
Internet: www.irvinghouse.com
E-mail: reserve@irvinghouse.com

Circa 1893. Irving House is located in a historic, turn-of-the-century Colonial Revival and has been receiving guests since the 1940s. The simple, comfortable rooms feature a modern hotel decor, and more than half include a private bath. In the mornings, a continental buffet with fruit, pastries and cereals is set up for guests to enjoy. Harvard Square is just minutes away, and guests can walk to the Red Line stop that goes into Boston.

Innkeeper(s): Rachael Solem & Zoia Krastanova. $90-190. 44 rooms, 32 with PB and 1 conference room. Breakfast and afternoon tea included in rates. Types of meals: Cont plus and early coffee/tea. Beds: QDT. TV, reading lamp, clock radio and desk in room. Central air. Fax, laundry facility, off-street parking and DSL on premises. Limited handicap access. Antiquing, art galleries, bicycling, live theater, museums, parks, shopping, sporting events, tennis and downtown Boston nearby.

Location: City. Harvard University, Harvard Square.

Certificate may be used: November through March, Sunday-Wednesday.

Centerville 117

Long Dell Inn
436 South Main Street
Centerville, MA 02632-3403
(508)775-2750
Internet: www.longdellinn.com
E-mail: stay@longdellinn.com

Circa 1850. Built by a local sea captain in 1850, this classic Greek Revival home with pumpkin pine floors and detailed moldings is listed in the National Register. Relax in the casually elegant living room with floor-to-ceiling windows or on a hammock in the back yard. Afternoon refreshments are provided and a refrigerator and water cooler are available. Well-appointed guest bedrooms in the main house and carriage house feature generous modern amenities. Read the daily newspaper, then meet new friends over breakfast in the sun parlor. Located in a quiet neighborhood, the delights of Cape Cod are within a short walk.

Innkeeper(s): Charlotte & Dick Dornich. $89-145. 6 rooms with PB. Breakfast included in rates. Types of meals: Country bkfst. Beds: KQ. Cable TV, reading lamp, ceiling fan and clock radio in room. Air conditioning. VCR on premises. Antiquing, art galleries, beach, bicycling, canoeing/kayaking, fishing, golf, hiking, horseback riding, museums, parks, shopping, tennis, water sports and wineries nearby.

Location: Country.

Certificate may be used: November through April, anytime.

Chatham 119

Carriage House Inn
407 Old Harbor Rd
Chatham, MA 02633-2322
(508)945-4688 (800)355-8868 Fax:(508)945-8909
Internet: www.thecarriagehouseinn.com
E-mail: info@thecarriagehouseinn.com

Circa 1890. This charming Cape inn offers tasteful, traditional decor and pristine rooms with a light and airy ambiance. The carriage house rooms each include a fireplace and an entrance to an outside sitting area. Breakfast items such as pancakes, French toast, eggs Benedict, homemade muffins and scones, and fresh fruit juices can be enjoyed either in the dining room or on the sun porch. Guests can wander through Chatham's many shops and galleries, or just relax and  enjoy the grounds, which include flower-filled gardens and shaded sitting areas. Beach towels and chairs are furnished for trips to the shore, located within walking distance from the inn.

Innkeeper(s): Jill & James Meyer. $95-195. 6 rooms with PB, 3 with FP. Breakfast, snacks/refreshments and wine included in rates. Types of meals: Full bkfst and early coffee/tea. Beds: Q. Cable TV, reading lamp, CD player, refrigerator, ceiling fan, snack bar, clock radio, telephone, coffeemaker, fireplace, CD alarm clock, hair dryer, iron, ironing board, umbrella, morning newspaper delivered and some available with private entrance in room. Air conditioning. Parlor games, computer with high-speed Internet access, DVDs, CDs and books on premises. Antiquing, art galleries, beach, bicycling, canoeing/kayaking, fishing, golf, hiking, live theater, museums, parks, shopping, tennis and water sports nearby.

Location: Seaside village.

"This might well have been our best B&B experience ever. It was the hosts who made it so memorable."

Certificate may be used: Anytime November-March, excluding holidays, subject to availability.

Old Harbor Inn
22 Old Harbor Rd
Chatham, MA 02633-2315
(508)945-4434 (800)942-4434 Fax:(508)945-7665
Internet: www.chathamoldharborinn.com
E-mail: info@chathamoldharborinn.com

Circa 1932. This pristine New England bed & breakfast was once the home of "Doc" Keene, a popular physician in the area. A meticulous renovation has created an elegant, beautifully appointed inn offering antique furnishings, designer linens  and lavish amenities in an English country decor. A buffet breakfast, featuring Judy's homemade muffins, is served in the sunroom or on the deck. The beaches, boutiques and galleries are a walk away and there is an old grist mill, the Chatham Lighthouse and a railroad museum. Band concerts are offered Friday nights in the summer at Kate Gould Park.

Innkeeper(s): Judy & Ray Braz. $99-269. 8 rooms with PB, 2 with FP, 1 suite. Breakfast, afternoon tea and snacks/refreshments included in rates. Types of meals: Full bkfst and early coffee/tea. Beds: KQT. Cable TV, VCR, reading lamp, CD player, refrigerator, ceiling fan, clock radio, desk, hot tub/spa, fireplace, Jacuzzi in suite, toiletries, welcome package and complementary wireless Internet access in room. Air conditioning. Fax, copier, parlor games, telephone, gift shop, concierge, gift shop, sand chairs, beach umbrellas, beach towels, complementary bottled water, soft drinks, coffee and tea service (7:30 p.m.-8:00 p.m.) on premises. Antiquing, art galleries, beach, bicycling, canoeing/kayaking, fishing, golf, hiking, live theater, museums, parks, shopping, tennis, water sports, art festivals, concerts, Cape Cod League Baseball, nature walks and guided Audubon excursions nearby.

Location: Ocean community. Seaside Village/National Seashore.

Publicity: *Honeymoon, Cape Cod Life, Boston, Cape Cod Travel Guide, Country Inns, Cape Cod Dreams and Off Shore.*

Certificate may be used: Nov. 1-April 30, Sunday-Thursday.

Concord D12

Colonel Roger Brown House
1694 Main St
Concord, MA 01742-2831
(978)369-9119 (800)292-1369 Fax:(978)369-8924
Internet: www.colrogerbrown.com
E-mail: innkeeper@colrogerbrown.com

Circa 1775. This house was the home of Minuteman Roger Brown, who fought the British at the Old North Bridge. The frame for this center-chimney Colonial was being raised on April 19, 1775, the day the battle took place. Some parts of the house were built as early as 1708. Among the many nearby historic sites are Thoreau's Walden Pond, the Concord Museum, the Alcott House, Old North Bridge, Lexington, the National Heritage Museum, Lowell Mills and much more.

Innkeeper(s): Lauri Berlied. $100-185. 5 suites. Breakfast and afternoon tea included in rates. Types of meals: Cont plus. Beds: QDT. Cable TV, reading lamp, refrigerator, snack bar, clock radio, telephone, desk, hot tub/spa, color TV, kitchenette and DSL Internet connection in room. Air conditioning. TV, fax, copier, parlor games, fireplace and data port on premises. Antiquing, cross-country skiing, downhill skiing, fishing, live theater, parks, shopping and water sports nearby.

Location: Town.

Publicity: *Middlesex News, Concord Journal and Washingtonian.*

"The Colonel Roger Brown House makes coming to Concord even more of a treat! Many thanks for your warm hospitality."
Certificate may be used: Nov. 1-April 1, July 1-Aug. 31 on availability.

Hawthorne Inn

462 Lexington Rd
Concord, MA 01742-3729
(978)369-5610 Fax:(978)287-4949
Internet: www.concordmass.com
E-mail: hawthorneinn@concordmass.com

Circa 1870. Share the joy of history, literature, poetry and artwork at this intimate New England bed & breakfast. For 25 years, the inn's ambiance has imparted the spirit of writers and philosophers such as the Alcotts, Emerson, Hawthorne and Thoreau, who once owned and walked the grounds. Antique furnishings, weavings, hardwood floors, a welcoming fireplace and stained-glass windows all exude a wonderful warmth and gentility. Enjoy afternoon tea on a rustic garden bench in the shade of aged trees and colorful plants. The area offers woods to explore, rivers to canoe, a quaint village with museums, infamous Sleepy Hollow Cemetery, and untold treasures.

Innkeeper(s): Marilyn Mudry & Gregory Burch. $135-295. 7 rooms with PB. Breakfast and afternoon tea included in rates. Types of meals: Cont plus. Beds: QDT. Data port, reading lamp, clock radio, telephone and desk in room. Air conditioning. Fax, library, parlor games, fireplace and piano on premises. Antiquing, cross-country skiing, fishing, parks, shopping and author's homes nearby.
Location: Village.
Publicity: *Yankee, New York Times, Los Angeles Times, Le Monde, Early American Life, Evening* and *National Geographic Traveler.*

"Surely there couldn't be a better or more valuable location for a comfortable, old-fashioned country inn."
Certificate may be used: November-March, Saturday-Thursday (no Fridays).

Deerfield   D6

Deerfield Inn

81 Old Main St
Deerfield, MA 01342-0305
(413)774-5587 (800)926-3865 Fax:(413)775-7221
Internet: www.deerfieldinn.com
E-mail: information@deerfieldinn.com

Circa 1884. The village of Deerfield was settled in 1670. Farmers in the area still unearth bones and ax and arrow heads from French/Indian massacre of 1704. Now, 50 beautifully restored 18th- and 19th-century homes line the mile-long main street, considered by many to be the loveliest street in New England. Fourteen of these houses are museums of Pioneer Valley decorative arts and are open year-round to the public. The Memorial Hall Museum, open from May to November, is the oldest museum in New England and full of local antiquities. The inn is situated at the center of this peaceful village, and for those who wish to truly experience New England's past, this is the place. The village has been designated a National Historic Landmark.
Innkeeper(s): Jane & Karl Sabo. $188-255. 23 rooms with PB and 1 conference room. Breakfast and afternoon tea included in rates. Types of meals:

Full bkfst and dinner. Restaurant on premises. Beds: KQT. TV in room. Fax, copier and telephone on premises. Handicap access. Antiquing, cross-country skiing, fishing and live theater nearby.
Publicity: *Travel Today, Colonial Homes, Country Living, Country Inns B&B, Yankee* and *Romantic Homes.*

"We've stayed at many New England inns, but the Deerfield Inn ranks among the best."
Certificate may be used: Sunday-Thursday, based on availability, excluding May, September, October.

Dennis   I18

Isaiah Hall B&B Inn

PO Box 1007
Dennis, MA 02638-6007
(508)385-9928 (800)736-0160 Fax:(508)385-5879
Internet: www.isaiahhallinn.com
E-mail: info@isaiahhallinn.com

Circa 1857. Adjacent to the Cape's oldest cranberry bog is this Greek Revival farmhouse built by Isaiah Hall, a cooper. His grandfather was the first cultivator of cranberries in America and Isaiah designed and patented the original barrel for shipping cranberries. In 1948, Dorothy Gripp, an artist, established the inn. Many examples of her artwork remain. The inn is located in the heart of the Cape and within walking distance to beaches, Dennis village and the Cape Playhouse.
Innkeeper(s): Jerry & Judy Neal. $114-255. 9 rooms, 10 with PB, 1 with FP, 2 suites. Breakfast included in rates. Types of meals: Cont plus and early coffee/tea. Beds: KQDT. Cable TV, reading lamp, clock radio, telephone, desk, hair dryers, robes and antiques in room. Air conditioning. Fax, parlor games, fireplace, gardens and high-speed Internet access available on premises. Antiquing, fishing, golf, live theater, parks, shopping, water sports, whale watching and bike paths nearby.
Publicity: *Cape Cod Life, New York Times, Golf, National Geographic Traveler, Yankee Travel Guide, Hartford Courant,* Best Inn for Relaxing & Unwinding Book of Lists, 2003 Best Hospitality Book of Lists, "Best Mid-Cape B&B" - Silver Award, *Cape Cod Life* and voted "Best Place to Visit Again & Again."

"Your place is so lovely and relaxing."
Certificate may be used: Anytime, November-April, subject to availability.

Dennis Port   I18

Rose Petal B&B

152 Sea St PO Box 974
Dennis Port, MA 02639-2404
(508)398-8470
Internet: www.rosepetalofdennis.com
E-mail: info@rosepetalofdennis.com

Circa 1872. Surrounded by a white picket fence and picturesque gardens, the Rose Petal is situated in the heart of Cape Cod. The Greek Revival-style home was built for Almond Wixon, who was a Mayflower descendant and member of a prominent seafaring family. His homestead has been completely restored and offers guest rooms with spacious private baths. Home-baked pastries highlight a full breakfast served in the dining room. Walk through the historic neighborhood past century-

old homes to Nantucket Sound's sandy beaches.

Innkeeper(s): Gayle & Dan Kelly. $79-125. 3 rooms with PB. Breakfast included in rates. Types of meals: Full gourmet bkfst, early coffee/tea and snacks/refreshments. Beds: QT. Reading lamp, clock radio and turn-down service in room. Air conditioning. TV, parlor games and telephone on premises. Antiquing, art galleries, beach, fishing, golf, live theater, museums, parks, shopping, water sports and whale watching nearby.
Location: Village.

"Perfect. Every detail was appreciated."
Certificate may be used: April and November, Monday-Thursday only.

East Orleans   H19

The Parsonage Inn
202 Main St, PO Box 1501
East Orleans, MA 02643
(508)255-8217 (888)422-8217 Fax:(508)255-8216
Internet: www.parsonageinn.com
E-mail: innkeeper@parsonageinn.com

Circa 1770. Originally a parsonage, this Cape-style home is now a romantic inn nestled in the village of East Orleans and only a mile and a half from Nauset Beach. Rooms are decorated with antiques, quilts, Laura Ashley fabrics and stenciling, and they include the original pine floors and low ceilings. Cooked breakfasts are served either in the dining room or on the brick patio. The innkeepers keep a selection of menus from local restaurants on hand and in the summer season serve appetizers and refreshments each evening while guest peruse their dining choices. The Parsonage is the perfect location to enjoy nature, with the national seashore, Nickerson State Park and whale-watching opportunities available to guests.

Innkeeper(s): Ian & Elizabeth Browne. $90-155. 8 rooms with PB. Breakfast included in rates. Types of meals: Full bkfst, veg bkfst and wine. Beds: QT. Cable TV, reading lamp, refrigerator, clock radio, coffeemaker, all with private en-suite bathrooms, one has a kitchen, all rooms have Queen beds and two also have a twin bed and some have refrigerators in room. Air conditioning. Fax, parlor games, telephone, fireplace, telephone, refrigerator and grand piano on premises. Antiquing, art galleries, beach, bicycling, canoeing/kayaking, fishing, golf, hiking, horseback riding, live theater, museums, parks, shopping, tennis, National Sea Shore, Nauset Beach, Skaket Beach & Flax Pond nearby.
Publicity: *Conde Nast Traveler and Bon Appetit.*

"Your hospitality was as wonderful as your home. Your home was as beautiful as Cape Cod. Thank you!"
Certificate may be used: Anytime, November-April, subject to availability.

Ship's Knees Inn
186 Beach Rd, PO Box 756
East Orleans, MA 02643
(508)255-1312 Fax:(508)240-1351
Internet: www.shipskneesinn.com
E-mail: skinauset@aol.com

Circa 1820. This 180-year-old restored sea captain's home is a three-minute walk to the ocean. Rooms are decorated in a nautical style with antiques. Several rooms feature authentic ship's knees, hand-painted trunks, old clipper ship models and four-poster beds. Some rooms boast ocean views, and the Master Suite has a working fireplace. The inn offers swimming and tennis facilities on the grounds. About three miles away, the innkeepers also offer three rooms, a bedroom effi-

ciency apartment and two heated cottages on the Town Cove. Head into town, or spend the day basking in the beauty of Nauset Beach with its picturesque sand dunes.
Innkeeper(s): Bryan & Hillary. $65-200. 16 rooms, 14 with PB, 1 with FP. Breakfast included in rates. Types of meals: Cont. Beds: KQDT. TV on premises. Amusement parks, antiquing, fishing, live theater, parks, shopping and water sports nearby.
Publicity: *Boston Globe.*

"Warm, homey and very friendly atmosphere. Very impressed with the beamed ceilings."
Certificate may be used: All year, except July, August and holidays.

East Sandwich   I17

Wingscorton Farm Inn
11 Wing Blvd
East Sandwich, MA 02537
(508)888-0534

Circa 1763. Wingscorton is a working farm on 13 acres of lawns, gardens and orchards. It adjoins a short walk to a private ocean beach. This Cape Cod manse, built by a Quaker family, is a historical landmark on what once was known as the King's Highway, the oldest historical district in the United States. All the rooms are furnished with antiques and working fireplaces (one with a secret compartment where runaway slaves hid). Breakfast features fresh produce with eggs, meats and vegetables from the farm's livestock and gardens. Pets and children welcome.

Innkeeper(s): Sheila Weyers & Richard Loring. $175-210. 9 rooms, 7 with FP, 4 suites and 2 cottages. Breakfast included in rates. Types of meals: Full gourmet bkfst. Beds: QDT. TV, reading lamp, refrigerator and clock radio in room. Swimming, library, child care, parlor games, telephone, fireplace and private beach on premises. Antiquing, cross-country skiing, downhill skiing, fishing, live theater, parks, shopping, sporting events and water sports nearby.
Location: Country.
Publicity: *US Air and Travel & Leisure.*

"Absolutely wonderful. We will always remember the wonderful time."
Certificate may be used: January to April 30, Monday, Tuesday, Wednesday, Thursday.

Eastham   H18

Over Look Inn
PO Box 771
Eastham, MA 02642-0771
(508)255-1886 (877)255-1886 Fax:(508)240-0345
Internet: www.overlookinn.com
E-mail: stay@overlookinn.com

Circa 1870. Gracing the Historic District, this Queen Anne Victorian listed in the National Register was originally a sea captain's home in 1870. Relax on a porch rocker or in the backyard hammock. Play pool in the Game Room or read by the fire in the parlor. The Garden Room is perfect for a romantic getaway with a wood-burning fireplace. Furnished in period antiques, the Captain's Room boasts a clawfoot tub. Families appre-

ciate the accommodations in the Carriage House. Enjoy fine Danish hospitality reflected in the generous hot country breakfasts served in the dining room. Ebelskivers, Captain's Eggs, Apple-Cranberry Pancakes, Banana Walnut French Toast and

Parmesan Baked eggs are popular rotating favorites. After exploring this ocean community, converse over afternoon tea. Innkeeper(s): Don & Pam Andersen. $115-240. 11 rooms, 10 with PB, 3 with FP, 4 total suites, including 2 two-bedroom suites and 1 conference room. Breakfast and afternoon tea included in rates. Types of meals: Full bkfst and early coffee/tea. Beds: KQT. Cable TV, reading lamp, refrigerator, ceiling fan, clock radio, telephone, fireplace and hair dryer in room. Air conditioning. VCR, fax, spa, parlor games, gift shop and game room with pool table on premises. Limited handicap access. Antiquing, art galleries, beach, bicycling, canoeing/kayaking, fishing, golf, hiking, horseback riding, live theater, museums, parks, shopping, sporting events, tennis, water sports and wineries nearby.

Location: Ocean community.

"A delightful experience."—Max Nichols, Oklahoma City Journal Record

Certificate may be used: June through September, Sunday-Thursday; Oct. 1-May 31, subject to availability.

Edgartown K16

Ashley Inn

129 Main St, PO Box 650
Edgartown, MA 02539-0650
(508)627-9655 (800)477-9655 Fax:(508)627-6629
Internet: www.ashleyinn.net
E-mail: mail@ashleyinn.net

Circa 1860. A retired whaling captain built this gracious Georgian inn on Martha's Vineyard. Guest rooms are furnished in period antiques, brass and wicker. The inn is just four blocks from the beach, and its Main Street location offers easy access to Edgartown's many fine restaurants and shops. Breakfasts are served in the English tea room, and guests find the inn's grounds perfect for an after-meal stroll. Others like to relax in the hammock or in the comfortable sitting room. A special honeymoon package is available.

Innkeeper(s): Fred Hurley. $125-295. 10 rooms with PB, 1 with FP, 1 suite. Breakfast included in rates. Types of meals: Cont. Beds: KQD. Cable TV and reading lamp in room. Air conditioning. Antiquing, art galleries, beach, bicycling, canoeing/kayaking, fishing, golf, hiking, horseback riding, museums, shopping, tennis, water sports and wineries nearby.

Location: Ocean community.

Certificate may be used: Oct. 23-April 1, Nov. 1-Dec. 31.

Shiretown Inn on the Island of Martha's Vineyard

PO Box 921
Edgartown, MA 02539
(508)627-3353 (800)541-0090 Fax:(508)627-8478
Internet: www.ShiretownInn.com
E-mail: Paradise@ShiretownInn.com

Circa 1795. Listed in the National Register of Historic Places, Shiretown Inn is located in a historic district of whaling captain homes on Martha's Vineyard, the famed island seven miles off the coast of Massachusetts. Ask to stay in one of the inn's two 1795 houses where you can choose a traditionally furnished guest room with a variety of amenities such as a canopy bed and an Oriental rug. More modest rooms are available in the Carriage Houses, and there is a cottage with kitchen and living room that is particularly popular for families with small children. The inn's restaurant offers indoor dining or seating on a garden terrace. There's also a pub. Walk one block to the Chappaquiddick Ferry and the harbor. (Make reservations in advance if you plan to bring your car, as there is limited space on the ferry.) Shops, galleries, restaurants and beaches are near-

by. Cycling, golf, windsurfing, sailing, tennis and horseback riding are also close.

Innkeeper(s): Gene Strimling & Karen Harris. $79-750. 39 rooms with PB, 5 with FP, 5 suites and 1 cottage. Breakfast included in rates. Types of meals: Cont. Restaurant on premises. Beds: KQDT. Cable TV, clock radio and telephone in room. Air conditioning. Fax on premises. Antiquing, fishing, golf, parks, shopping, tennis and water sports nearby.

Certificate may be used: Nov. 1 through May 1, Monday through Thursday except holidays.

Essex C15

George Fuller House

148 Main St, Rt 133
Essex, MA 01929-1304
(978)768-7766 (800)477-0148 Fax:(978)768-6178

Circa 1830. This three-story, Federal-style home is situated on a lawn that reaches to the salt marsh adjoining the Essex River. Original Indian shutters and Queen Anne baseboards remain. Guest accommodations boast Boston rockers, canopy beds and fireplaces. Belgian waffles and praline French toast are a house specialty. Many of the town's 50 antique shops are within walking distance of the inn.

Innkeeper(s): Kathy, Ryan & Michael. $115-225. 7 rooms with PB, 5 with FP. Breakfast and afternoon tea included in rates. Types of meals: Full bkfst. Beds: KQDT. Cable TV, clock radio and telephone in room. Air conditioning. TV, fax and fireplace on premises. Antiquing, cross-country skiing, fishing, live theater, shopping and water sports nearby.

Publicity: *Gloucester Times, Yankee Traveler, Discerning Traveler, Internet and Cape Ann.*

"Thank you for the wonderful time we had at your place. We give you a 5-star rating!"

Certificate may be used: May-October, Sunday-Thursday, subject to availability. November-April, subject to availability, except holidays.

Falmouth J16

The Beach Rose Inn

17 Chase Road
Falmouth, MA 02540
(508)540-5706 (800)498-5706 Fax:(508)540-4880
Internet: www.thebeachroseinn.com
E-mail: innkeepers@thebeachroseinn.com

Circa 1863. Gracing the historic district in a peaceful village setting, this meticulously restored inn is listed in the National Register. The Main Inn, Carriage House and a Housekeeping Cottage offer tastefully decorated accommodations. Antique furnishings mingle well with period reproductions, cheery quilts and fine linens. Some guest bedrooms feature a variety of amenities that may include a whirlpool, fireplace, canopy bed, refrigerator, robes and private entrance. A well-presented breakfast is served in the gathering room or on the sun porch. After a day of exploring Cape Cod, sit and chat in the fireside sitting room.

Innkeeper(s): David and Donna McIlrath. $90-250. 8 rooms with PB, 2 with FP, 1 suite and 1 cottage. Breakfast, afternoon tea and snacks/refreshments included in rates. Types of meals: Full gourmet bkfst and early coffee/tea. Beds: QT. Reading lamp, refrigerator, ceiling fan, clock radio, hot tub/spa and fireplace in room. Air conditioning. TV, VCR, fax, copier, telephone and fireplace on premises. Limited handicap access. Antiquing, art galleries, beach, bicycling, canoeing/kayaking, fishing, golf, hiking, horseback riding, live theater, museums, parks, shopping and water sports nearby.

Location: Country, ocean community. Cape Cod.

Certificate may be used: Oct. 1-April 30, subject to availability, holidays excluded.

Village Green Inn

40 Main St
Falmouth, MA 02540-2667
(508)548-5621 (800)237-1119 Fax:(508)495-2921
Internet: www.villagegreeninn.com
E-mail: vgi40@aol.com

Circa 1804. The inn, listed in the National Register, originally was built in the Federal style for Braddock Dimmick, son of Revolutionary War General Joseph Dimmick. Later, "cranberry king" John Crocker moved the house onto a granite slab foundation, remodeling it in the Victorian style. There are inlaid floors, large porches and gingerbread trim.

Innkeeper(s): Mary B. LeBlanc. $85-225. 5 rooms with PB, 2 with FP, 1 suite. Breakfast and afternoon tea included in rates. Types of meals: Full bkfst, early coffee/tea and snacks/refreshments. Beds: Q. Cable TV, reading lamp, ceiling fan, clock radio, desk, hair dryers and robes in room. Air conditioning. Bicycles, parlor games, telephone and fireplace on premises. Antiquing, fishing, golf, live theater, parks, shopping, water sports and whale watching nearby.

Publicity: *Country Inns, Cape Cod Life, Yankee, London Observer, Escape and New York Magazine.*

"Tasteful, comfortable and the quintessential New England flavor ... You have turned us on to the B&B style of travel and we now have a standard to measure our future choices by."

Certificate may be used: Sunday-Thursday, April, November and December, excluding holidays.

Gloucester   C15

Lanes Cove House

6 Andrews Street
Gloucester, MA 01930
(978)282-4647 Fax:(978)283-1022
Internet: www.lanescovehouse.com
E-mail: lanescove@adelphia.net

Circa 1860. Overlooking picturesque Lanes Cove, this historic Victorian home is only a ten-minute walk to the village beach. Relax and enjoy the year-round scenery from the large deck. Recently renovated for comfort and privacy, guest bedrooms and a suite with a fully equipped kitchen/sitting room boast ocean views and hardwood floors covered with Oriental rugs. An expanded continental breakfast is served in the dining room including a variety of juices, premium coffees and teas, cereals, fresh fruit, yogurt, local breads, scones and muffins with special spreads and toppings. Cape Ann offers numerous activities and sightseeing adventures. For a taste of city life, Boston is only an hour away.

Innkeeper(s): Anna Andella. $110-125. 3 rooms with PB, 1 suite. Breakfast and afternoon tea included in rates. Types of meals: Cont plus and early coffee/tea. Beds: QT. Cable TV, VCR, reading lamp, refrigerator, ceiling fan, clock radio and desk in room. Air conditioning. Parlor games, telephone and fireplace on premises. Antiquing, art galleries, beach, bicycling, canoeing/kayaking, fishing, golf, hiking, horseback riding, live theater, museums, parks, shopping and water sports nearby.

Location: Ocean community.

Certificate may be used: November-April, Sunday-Thursday.

Granby   E6

An Old Indian Trail Bed & Breakfast

664 Amherst Road
Granby, MA 01033
(413)467-3528
Internet: bbonline.com/ma/oit
E-mail: reispd@attbi.com

Circa 1944. This impressive Colonial stone home and cottages are located in a quaint rural setting at the base of the Holyoke Mountain Range. The bed & breakfast offers the best of both worlds with its Amherst location and its proximity to the nearby Five College area of New England. A comfortable blend of contemporary country decor is interspersed with fine artwork throughout the inn. Plenty of good books are found in the living room for relaxed reading. The guest bedrooms, suites and cottages are bright and cheery, some with cozy fireplaces. A wonderful breakfast is served in the dining room of the main house or can be happily delivered. Choose the delicious special of the day from a menu that offers hot and cold selections.

Innkeeper(s): Peter & Dolores Reis. $85-135. 3 rooms with PB, 1 suite and 2 cottages. Breakfast included in rates. Types of meals: Full bkfst. Beds: QD. Modem hook-up, cable TV, VCR, reading lamp, refrigerator, ceiling fan, clock radio, coffeemaker and some with fireplace in room. Fax, copier, telephone and fireplace on premises. Amusement parks, antiquing, art galleries, bicycling, cross-country skiing, fishing, golf, hiking, horseback riding, live theater, museums, parks, shopping, sporting events, tennis, Six Flags, Big E Grounds and Mullin Center nearby.

Location: Country.

Certificate may be used: January-April, Sunday-Thursday, November-December, Sunday-Thursday (excludes holidays).

Greenfield   C6

The Brandt House

29 Highland Ave
Greenfield, MA 01301-3605
(413)774-3329 (800)235-3329 Fax:(413)772-2908
Internet: www.brandthouse.com
E-mail: info@brandthouse.com

Circa 1890. Three-and-a-half-acre lawns surround this impressive three-story Colonial Revival house, situated hilltop. The library and poolroom are popular for lounging, but the favorite gathering areas are the sunroom and the covered north porch. Ask for the aqua and white room with the fireplace, but all the rooms are pleasing. A full breakfast often includes homemade scones and is sometimes available on the slate patio in view of the expansive  lawns and beautiful gardens. A full-time staff provides for guest needs. There is a clay tennis court and nature trails, and in winter, lighted ice skating at a nearby pond. Historic Deerfield and Yankee Candle Company are within five minutes.

Innkeeper(s): Full time staff. $100-225. 9 rooms, 7 with PB, 2 with FP, 1 suite and 1 conference room. Breakfast included in rates. Types of meals: Full bkfst and early coffee/tea. Beds: KQT. Cable TV, reading lamp, refrigerator, ceiling fan, clock radio, telephone, desk, hot tub/spa, refrigerators, two with fireplace and microwave in room. Air conditioning. VCR, fax, copier, tennis, library, parlor games and fireplace on premises. Antiquing, cross-country skiing, downhill skiing, fishing, live theater, parks, shopping, sporting events, water sports, Old Deerfield and Lunt Silver nearby.

Location: Country, mountains.

Certificate may be used: Nov. 1-April 30.

Harwich Port I18

Harbor Breeze of Cape Cod

326 Lower County Rd
Harwich Port, MA 02646-1625
(508)432-0337 (800)455-0247 Fax:(508)432-1276
Internet: www.harborbreezeinn.com
E-mail: harborbreeze@yahoo.com

Circa 1945. Ideally located across the street from picturesque Allens Harbor, this inn is a classic Cape Cod home best enjoyed by couples and families for its casual, friendly atmosphere. A rambling connection of cedar shake additions nestled in an attractive pine setting, surrounds a garden courtyard to form a guest wing. Flowered walkways lead to the private entrances of  guest bedrooms furnished in wicker, wood and country florals. Enjoy ocean breezes while at restful sitting areas and the swimming pool. It is a short walk to Brooks Road Beach on Nantucket Sound.

Innkeeper(s): Jim & Marie David. $99-200. 10 rooms with PB, 1 with FP. Breakfast included in rates. Types of meals: Cont plus and early coffee/tea. Beds: KQT. Cable TV, reading lamp, refrigerator and some with air conditioning and ceiling fans in room. Swimming and telephone on premises. Antiquing, fishing, golf, live theater, parks, shopping, tennis, water sports and whale watching nearby.
Certificate may be used: Nov. 30 to March 31, Monday-Thursday, holidays excluded.

Haydenville D5

Penrose Victorian Inn

133 Main Street
Haydenville, MA 01060
(413)268-3014 (888)268-7711 Fax:(413)268-9232
Internet: www.penroseinn.com
E-mail: zimmer@penroseinn.com

Circa 1820. Experience Victorian elegance at this distinctive Queen Anne that sits on two resplendent acres across from the river. Recently renovated, the inn's antique furnishings and period decor offer a warm hospitality. Common rooms include the music room and parlor. Most of the well-appointed guest bedrooms feature fireplaces. Savor Penrose French toast with fresh seasonal fruit, juice and hot beverages by candlelight. Stroll the perennial and rose gardens with fountain, relax on the porch or go for a swim. Explore Emily Dickens House, Old Deerfield and Calvin Coolidge House, each less than 10 miles away.

Innkeeper(s): Nancy & Dick Zimmer. $95-120. 3 rooms with PB. Breakfast included in rates. Types of meals: Full gourmet bkfst and veg bkfst. Beds: Q. Data port, reading lamp, clock radio, telephone, turn-down service and fireplace in room. Air conditioning. TV, VCR, fax, copier, swimming, library, fireplace and laundry facility on premises. Amusement parks, antiquing, art galleries, bicycling, canoeing/kayaking, cross-country skiing, fishing, golf, hiking, horseback riding, live theater, museums, parks, shopping, sporting events, tennis and water sports nearby.
Location: City. Historic District.
Publicity: Arrington's Bed and Breakfast Journal (voted "Best in the North" and "Best Near a College or University") and Christmas special with Mark Twain House.
Certificate may be used: Anytime, Sunday-Thursday.

Housatonic E2

Christine's Bed-Breakfast & Tearoom

325 N Plain Rd
Housatonic, MA 01236-9741
(413)274-6149 (800)536-1186 Fax:(413)274-6296
Internet: www.christinesinn.com
E-mail: innkeepers@christinesinn.com

Circa 1780. Centrally located between Stockbridge and Great Barrington in the middle of the Berkshires, this country cottage farmhouse has sat at the foothill of Tom Ball Mountain for more than 200 years. Large, open beams, slant ceilings and wide pine floors reflect its original character. Check-in is at the back parlor, once a small barn. High poster and canopy beds highlight the Colonial-style guest bedrooms. A suite features a fireplace and private terrace. Enjoy breakfast crepes with strawberries or baked French toast with peaches and cream in the garden dining room. Afternoon tea is served on the screened-in porch.

Innkeeper(s): Christine Kelsey. $85-195. 4 rooms with PB, 1 with FP, 1 suite. Breakfast and afternoon tea included in rates. Types of meals: Country bkfst, veg bkfst, dinner and room service. Beds: QT. Cable TV, VCR, reading lamp, stereo, ceiling fan, clock radio, telephone, turn-down service, desk and fireplace in room. Air conditioning. Fax, copier, library, parlor games and fireplace on premises. Antiquing, art galleries, bicycling, canoeing/kayaking, cross-country skiing, downhill skiing, fishing, golf, hiking, horseback riding, live theater, museums, parks, shopping, sporting events and tennis nearby.
Location: Country, mountains.
Certificate may be used: Nov. 1-May 20, non-holiday, Sunday-Thursday only.

Hyannis Port I17

The Simmons Homestead Inn

288 Scudder Ave
Hyannis Port, MA 02647
(508)778-4999 (800)637-1649 Fax:(508)790-1342
Internet: www.simmonshomesteadinn.com
E-mail: simmonshomestead@aol.com

Circa 1805. This former sea captain's home features period decor and includes huge needlepoint displays and lifelike ceramic and papier-mache animals that give the inn a country feel. Some rooms boast canopy beds, and each is individually decorated. Traditional full breakfasts are served in the formal dining room. Evening wine helps guests relax after a day of touring the Cape. There is a billiard room on the premises and an outdoor hot tub.

Innkeeper(s): Bill Putman. $140-350. 14 rooms with PB, 2 with FP, 2 suites. Breakfast included in rates. Types of meals: Full bkfst and early coffee/tea. Beds: KQT. Reading lamp, ceiling fan, clock radio and desk in room. VCR, fax, copier, bicycles, library, pet boarding, child care, parlor games, telephone, fireplace, billiard room and modem hook-up on premises. Antiquing, fishing, golf, live theater, parks, shopping, tennis and water sports nearby.
Location: Ocean community. Cape Cod.
Publicity: Bon Appetit, Cape Code Life and Yankee.

"I want to say that part of what makes Cape Cod special for us is the inn. It embodies much of what is wonderful at the Cape. By Sunday, I was completely rested, relaxed, renewed and restored."

Certificate may be used: Anytime, November-June except holiday weekends, subject to availability. July-October, Sunday-Thursday only, subject to availability.

Lee E2

The Parsonage on The Green B&B

20 Park Pl
Lee, MA 01238-1618
(413)243-4364 Fax:(413)243-2372
Internet: www.bbhost.com/parsonageonthegreen
E-mail: parsonage@berkshire.net

Circa 1851. As the former parsonage to the first
Congregational Church (known as having the highest wooden
steeple in the country), this white colonial inn is tucked
behind a white picket fence on a quiet side of the village common. The boughs of an old apple tree shade a pleasant wicker-
filled side veranda. Family heirlooms, 18th-century American
antiques and Oriental rugs are set against polished maple and
oak hardwood floors. An elegant afternoon tea is served graciously from the teacart in the parlor and includes freshly made
sweets such as Victorian lace cookies and scones. Homemade
breads accompany a full breakfast served on fine china in the
candle-lit dining room. Walk to restaurants, galleries and shops.
Stockbridge and Lenox are nearby, as is outlet shopping. One
mile from exit 2 of Mass. Pike.

Innkeeper(s): Barbara & Don Mahony. $80-175. 4 rooms with PB. Breakfast
and afternoon tea included in rates. Types of meals: Full bkfst and early cof-
fee/tea. Beds: QD. Reading lamp, ceiling fan, turn-down service, robes and
hand-dipped chocolates in room. Air conditioning. VCR, bicycles, library, parlor games, telephone, fireplace, piano and newspapers on premises.
Antiquing, bicycling, cross-country skiing, downhill skiing, fishing, golf, hiking, live theater, parks, shopping, sporting events, tennis, water sports and
swimming in Laurel Lake nearby.
Location: Mountains.
Publicity: Berkshire Eagle and Inns and Outs of Collecting.

"Our dream came true, the perfect romantic getaway."
Certificate may be used: Jan. 1 to June 30, Nov. 1 to Dec. 31, excluding
holidays.

Lenox E2

7 Hills Country Inn & Restaurant

40 Plunkett St
Lenox, MA 01240-2795
(413)637-0060 (800)869-6518 Fax:(413)637-3651
Internet: www.sevenhillsinn.com
E-mail: 7hills@berkshire.net

Circa 1911. Descendants of those who sailed on the
Mayflower built this rambling, Tudor-style mansion. The inn's
27 acres of terraced lawns and stunning gardens often serve as
the site for weddings, receptions and meetings. The grounds
include two tennis courts and a swimming pool. Guest rooms
are elegantly appointed with antiques, and the mansion still
maintains its hand-carved fireplaces and leaded glass windows.
In addition to the original elements, some rooms contain the
modern amenities of a jet tub, fireplace and kitchenette. The
inn's chef, whose cuisine has been featured in Gourmet magazine, prepares creative, continental specialties. Seven Hills offers
close access to many attractions in the Berkshires.

Innkeeper(s): Patricia & Jim Eder. $85-350. 58 rooms with PB, 11 with
FP, 2 suites and 4 conference rooms. Breakfast included in rates. Types of
meals: Country bkfst, veg bkfst and gourmet dinner. Restaurant on
premises. Beds: KQDT. Cable TV, reading lamp, clock radio, telephone
and desk in room. Air conditioning. VCR, fax, copier, swimming, tennis,
library, parlor games and fireplace on premises. Handicap access.
Antiquing, art galleries, beach, bicycling, canoeing/kayaking, cross-country skiing, downhill skiing, fishing, golf, hiking, horseback riding, live the-

ater, museums, parks, shopping and water sports nearby.
Location: Mountains.
Publicity: Gourmet, Entrepreneur and Boston Globe.
Certificate may be used: Jan. 1-April 30, all nights; May 1-June 30,
Sunday-Thursday; July 1-Aug. 31, Monday-Wednesday; Sept. 1-Oct. 26,
Sunday-Thursday; Oct. 27-Dec. 15, all nights; Dec. 16-31, Sunday-Thursday.

Birchwood Inn

7 Hubbard St, Box 2020
Lenox, MA 01240-4604
(413)637-2600 (800)524-1646 Fax:(413)637-4604
Internet: www.birchwood-inn.com
E-mail: innkeeper@birchwood-inn.com

Circa 1767. Experience comfortable country elegance at this
Colonial Revival mansion that has welcomed friends since
1767. The inn's antiques, collectibles, quilts, canopy beds
and nine fireplaces create an
idyllic getaway. The inn is
renowned for sumptuous
breakfasts and afternoon tea.
Enjoy Berkshire breezes and
fireflies on the porch in summer, spring blossoms in stone-
fenced gardens, vibrant fall foliage, and the welcome warmth
of the firesides in winter. The oldest home in Lenox, it is a
short walk from its tranquil hilltop setting to the village's
restaurants, galleries and shops.

Innkeeper(s): Ellen Gutman Chenaux. $110-275. 11 rooms with PB, 6 with
FP, 3 suites and 2 conference rooms. Breakfast and afternoon tea included in
rates. Types of meals: Country bkfst and early coffee/tea. Beds: KQT. Modem
hook-up, data port, TV, reading lamp, clock radio, telephone, desk and most
with fireplace in room. Air conditioning. VCR, fax, copier, library, parlor
games, gift shop and fireplaces on premises. Limited handicap access.
Antiquing, art galleries, beach, bicycling, cross-country skiing, downhill ski-
ing, fishing, golf, hiking, live theater, museums, parks, shopping, water
sports, Tanglewood, music and theater festivals and the Norman Rockwell
Museum nearby.
Location: Mountains. Village.
Publicity: Country Inns, Country Living, New York Magazine, Montreal
Gazette, Gourmet Magazine and The Discerning Traveler.
"Thank you for memories that we will cherish forever."
Certificate may be used: Monday-Thursday, Jan. 5-April 15, holidays excluded.

Brook Farm Inn

15 Hawthorne St
Lenox, MA 01240-2404
(413)637-3013 (800)285-7638 Fax:(413)637-4751
Internet: www.brookfarm.com
E-mail: innkeeper@brookfarm.com

Circa 1882. Stay at this gracious Victorian inn named after the
original Brook Farm, a utopian literary commune. It is centrally
located for easy access to all the sites and attractions in the
Berkshires. Afternoon tea and scones are offered in the library,
sometimes accompanied by poetry readings or storytelling.
Gorgeous guest bedrooms that exude a tranquil comfort are
tastefully appointed with antiques and period pieces. A hearty
breakfast buffet starts the day right. Relax in the gardens or
swim in the refreshing pool.

Innkeeper(s): Linda & Phil Halpern. $105-395. 15 rooms with PB, 9 with
FP, 1 suite. Breakfast and afternoon tea included in rates. Types of meals:
Full bkfst and early coffee/tea. Beds: KQT. Modem hook-up, cable TV, VCR,
reading lamp, CD player, refrigerator, ceiling fan, clock radio, telephone, coffeemaker, desk, voice mail, fireplace, fluffy towels, toiletries and 3 with
whirlpools and TV in room. Air conditioning. Fax, copier, swimming, library,
parlor games, butler's pantry, round-the-clock coffee, tea and heated outdoor
pool on premises. Handicap access. Antiquing, art galleries, beach, bicycling,

canoeing/kayaking, cross-country skiing, downhill skiing, fishing, golf, hiking, horseback riding, live theater, museums, parks, shopping, sporting events, tennis, water sports, Tanglewood, concerts, historic homes, Hancock Shaker Village, Norman Rockwell Museum and Shakespeare & Co nearby.

Location: Country, mountains. Berkshire hills.

Publicity: *Berkshire Eagle, Country Inns, Travel & Leisure, Boston Globe, New York Magazine, independenttraveler.com and bedandbreakfast.com.*

"We've been traveling all our lives and never have we felt more at home."
Certificate may be used: November-April, Monday-Thursday.

The Gables Inn

81 Walker St, Rt 183
Lenox, MA 01240-2719
(413)637-3416 (800)382-9401 Fax:(413)637-3416
Internet: www.gableslenox.com
E-mail: gable@berkshire.net

Circa 1885. At one time, this was the home of Pulitzer Prize-winning novelist, Edith Wharton. The Queen Anne-style Berkshire cottage features a handsome eight-sided library and Mrs. Wharton's own four-poster bed. An unusual indoor swimming pool with spa is available in warm weather.

Innkeeper(s): Mary & Frank Newton. $99-250. 17 rooms with PB, 15 with FP, 4 suites. Breakfast included in rates. Beds: Q. Cable TV, VCR, reading lamp, refrigerator, clock radio and desk in room. Air conditioning. Fax, swimming, tennis, telephone and fireplace on premises. Antiquing, cross-country skiing, downhill skiing, fishing, live theater, parks, shopping, sporting events and water sports nearby.

Location: Village.

Publicity: *P.M. Magazine and New York Times.*

"You made us feel like old friends and that good feeling enhanced our pleasure. In essence, it was the best part of our trip."
Certificate may be used: Nov. 1 to May 20, Sunday through Thursday only.

Walker House

64 Walker St
Lenox, MA 01240-2718
(413)637-1271 (800)235-3098 Fax:(413)637-2387
Internet: www.walkerhouse.com
E-mail: walkerhouse.inn@verizon.net

Circa 1804. This beautiful Federal-style house sits in the center of the village on three acres of graceful woods and restored gardens. Guest rooms have fireplaces and private baths. Each is named for a favorite composer such as Beethoven, Mozart or Handel. The innkeepers' musical backgrounds include associations with the San Francisco Opera, the New York City Opera, and the Los Angeles Philharmonic. Walker House concerts are scheduled

from time to time. The innkeepers offer film and opera screenings nightly on a twelve-foot screen. With prior approval, some pets may be allowed.

Innkeeper(s): Peggy & Richard Houdek. $90-220. 8 rooms with PB, 5 with FP and 1 conference room. Breakfast and afternoon tea included in rates. Types of meals: Cont plus and early coffee/tea. Beds: QDT. Reading lamp, clock radio and desk in room. Air conditioning. VCR, fax, copier, library, parlor games, telephone, fireplace, theatre with Internet access and 100-inch screen on premises. Handicap access. Antiquing, cross-country skiing, downhill skiing, fishing, live theater, parks, shopping, water sports and music nearby.

Location: In small village.

Publicity: *Boston Globe, PBS, Los Angeles Times, New York Times and*

Dog Fancy.

"We had a grand time staying with fellow music and opera lovers! Breakfasts were lovely."
Certificate may be used: Nov. 1 to April 30, Sunday through Thursday, excluding holiday periods.

Marblehead   D14

Harborside House B&B

23 Gregory Street
Marblehead, MA 01945
(781)631-1032
Internet: www.harborsidehouse.com
E-mail: stay@harborsidehouse.com

Circa 1850. Enjoy the Colonial charm of this home, which overlooks Marblehead Harbor on Boston's historic North Shore. Rooms are decorated with antiques and period wallpaper. A third-story sundeck offers excellent views. A generous continental breakfast of home-baked breads, muffins and fresh fruit is served each morning in the well-decorated dining room or on the open porch. The village of Marblehead provides many shops and restaurants. Boston and Logan airport are 30 minutes away.

Innkeeper(s): Susan Livingston. $80-95. 2 rooms. Breakfast, afternoon tea and snacks/refreshments included in rates. Types of meals: Cont plus and veg bkfst. Beds: DT. Reading lamp, clock radio and desk in room. TV, bicycles, library, telephone and fireplace on premises. Antiquing, art galleries, bicycling, museums, parks, shopping and water sports nearby.

Location: Waterfront. Historic harbor.

Publicity: *Marblehead Reporter.*

"Harborside Inn is restful, charming, with a beautiful view of the water. I wish we didn't have to leave."
Certificate may be used: January-April, Sunday-Saturday.

Middleboro   H14

On Cranberry Pond B&B

43 Fuller St
Middleboro, MA 02346-1706
(508)946-0768 Fax:(508)947-8221
Internet: www.oncranberrypond.com
E-mail: oncranberrypond@aol.com

Circa 1989. Nestled in the historic "cranberry capital of the world," this 8,000 square-foot modern farmhouse rests on a working cranberry bog. There are two miles of trails to meander, and during berry picking season guests can watch as buckets of the fruit are collected. Rooms are comfortable and well appointed. The Master Suite includes a whirlpool bath for two. A 93-foot deck overlooks the cranberry bog. Innkeeper Jeannine LaBossiere creates gourmet breakfasts and yummy homemade snacks at night. Honeymoons and anniversaries are popular here. There is a spacious conference room with plenty of business amenities. Borrow a fishing rod or one of the innkeeper's mountain bikes for an afternoon's adventure you will long remember. Plymouth, Mass. is nearby and whale watching is a popular activity.

Innkeeper(s): Jeannine LaBossiere & son Tim . $85-240. 6 rooms, 4 with PB, 2 suites and 2 conference rooms. Breakfast and snacks/refreshments included in rates. Types of meals: Full gourmet bkfst, veg bkfst, early coffee/tea, gourmet lunch and room service. Beds: Q. Modem hook-up, data port, cable TV, VCR, reading lamp, CD player, ceiling fan, clock radio, telephone, coffeemaker, ceiling fan, clock radio, telephone, coffeemaker, desk and hot tub in room. Air conditioning. Fax, copier, bicycles and library on premises. Antiquing, art galleries, beach, bicycling, fishing, golf, live theater, museums, parks, shopping, tennis and wineries nearby.

Location: Oversized Cape.

"Your dedication to making your guests comfortable is above and beyond. You are tops in your field."

Certificate may be used: Anytime, subject to availability.

Nantucket   L18

House of The Seven Gables

32 Cliff Rd
Nantucket, MA 02554-3644
(508)228-4706
Internet: www.houseofthesevengables.com
E-mail: walton@nantucket.net

Circa 1880. Originally the annex of the Sea Cliff Inn, one of the island's oldest hotels, this three-story Queen Anne Victorian inn offers 10 guest rooms. Beaches, bike rentals, museums, restaurants, shops and tennis courts are all found nearby. The guest rooms are furnished with king or queen beds and period antiques. Breakfast is served each morning in the guest rooms and often include homemade coffee cake, muffins or Portuguese rolls.

Innkeeper(s): Sue Walton. $100-300. 10 rooms, 8 with PB. Breakfast included in rates. Types of meals: Cont. Beds: KQ. Telephone, fireplace and bird watching on premises. Antiquing, fishing, live theater, shopping and water sports nearby.
Location: The Old Historic District.

"You have a beautiful home and one that makes everyone feel relaxed and at home."

Certificate may be used: Anytime, Sunday-Thursday.

Ivy Lodge

2 Chester St
Nantucket, MA 02554-3505
(508)228-7755
E-mail: IvyNantucket@aol.com

Circa 1790. This 18th-century Colonial has spent much of its life serving the needs of travelers. In the 1800s, the home was used both as an inn and a museum. Today, the home serves as a living museum of American history. The home still includes its colonial, center chimney, pine floors and fireplaces. Guest rooms are decorated with antiques and beds topped with ornate bedspreads and lacy canopies. Vases filled with flowers add extra color. The Brant Point lighthouse is within walking distance of the inn, and the beach is nearby.

Innkeeper(s): Tuge Koseatac. $175-275. 6 rooms. Breakfast included in rates. Types of meals: Cont plus.

Certificate may be used: Oct. 1-30 and May 1-June 15. Excluding holidays and all local festival days and weekends.

The Woodbox Inn

29 Fair St
Nantucket, MA 02554-3798
(508)228-0587
Internet: www.woodboxinn.com
E-mail: woodbox@nantucket.net

Circa 1709. In the heart of the historic district, the Woodbox Inn was built in 1709 by Captain George Bunker. Guest rooms are decorated with antiques and reproductions and some have canopy beds. The six suites offer sitting rooms and fireplaces. Walk to Main Street and enjoy fine boutiques and art galleries. Other activities include biking, tennis, golf, whale watching and sandy beaches for sunning. The inn's award-winning gourmet

dining room features an early American atmosphere with low-beamed ceilings and pine-paneled walls. (Meals are not included in room rates.)

Innkeeper(s): Dexter Tutein. $185-315. 9 rooms with PB, 6 with FP, 6 suites. Types of meals: Full bkfst. Restaurant on premises. Beds: KQDT. Reading lamp, refrigerator, clock radio and desk in room. Telephone and fireplace on premises. Antiquing, fishing, live theater, parks, shopping, tennis and water sports nearby.

Publicity: *Wharton Alumni, Cape Cod Life, Boston Magazine, Wine Spectator, James Beard Foundation and Phantom Gourmet.*

Certificate may be used: Midweek, from mid-October to Jan. 1 and May 1 to Memorial Day, holidays excluded.

Newburyport   B14

Clark Currier Inn

45 Green St
Newburyport, MA 01950-2646
(978)465-8363
Internet: www.clarkcurrierinn.com
E-mail: ccinn1803@yahoo.com

Circa 1803. Once the home of shipbuilder Thomas March Clark, this three-story Federal-style inn provides gracious accommodations to visitors in the Northeast Massachusetts

area. Visitors will enjoy the inn's details added by Samuel McEntire, one of the nation's most celebrated home builders and woodcarvers. Breakfast is served in the dining room or garden room, with an afternoon tea offered in the garden room.

The inn's grounds also boast a picturesque garden and gazebo. Parker River National Wildlife Refuge and Maudslay State Park are nearby, as well as Plum Island beaches.

Innkeeper(s): Bob Nolan. $95-185. 8 rooms with PB. Breakfast and afternoon tea included in rates. Types of meals: Cont plus. Beds: QDT. Reading lamp, CD player, telephone and desk in room. Air conditioning. Parlor games, sherry and fruit are available in the library on premises. Amusement parks, antiquing, cross-country skiing, fishing, live theater, parks, shopping, water sports and many acclaimed and varied restaurants and shops nearby.
Location: City, waterfront. Historic downtown.

"We had a lovely stay in your B&B! We appreciated your hospitality!"

Certificate may be used: Jan. 1 through April 30.

Windsor House

38 Federal St
Newburyport, MA 01950-2820
(978)462-3778 (888)873-5296 Fax:(978)465-3443
Internet: www.bbhost.com/windsorhouse
E-mail: windsorinn@earthlink.net

Circa 1786. This brick Federal-style mansion was designed as a combination home and ship's chandlery (an outfitter and broker for cargo). The Merchant Suite was once the sales room and features a 14-foot ceiling with hand-hewn, beveled beams. The Bridal Suite was once the master suite. The newest suite, England's Rose, is a tribute to Princess Diana. The English innkeepers serve a hearty English-country breakfast and an English tea in the afternoon.

Innkeeper(s): Lord & Lady John & Judith Harris of Penrhyn. $130-165. 4 rooms with PB. Breakfast and afternoon tea included in rates. Types of meals: Full bkfst. Beds: KQD. TV, reading lamp, ceiling fan, telephone, desk, fans, alarm clocks and coffee/tea facilities in room. Air conditioning. VCR, fax, copier and parlor games on premises. Antiquing, cross-country skiing, fishing, golf, live theater, parks, shopping, tennis, water sports, bird watching and wildlife refuge nearby.

Location: City. Historic seaport.

Publicity: *New York Times, Boston Globe, Boston Herald Sunday and Le Monde.*

"You will find what you look for and be met by the unexpected too. A good time!"

Certificate may be used: Nov. 1 to April 30, Sunday through Thursday only, subject to availability. Excludes holidays, discounted winter rates and special events.

Oak Bluffs K16

The Oak Bluffs Inn

P.O. Box 2099
Oak Bluffs, MA 02557
(508)693-7171 (800)955-6235 Fax:(508)693-8787
Internet: www.8009556235.com
E-mail: bmyguest@oakbluffsinn.com

Circa 1870. A widow's walk and gingerbread touches were added to this graceful home to enhance the Victorian atmosphere already prevalent throughout the inn. Rooms are decorated in Victorian style with antiques. Home-baked breads and fresh fruits start off the day. After enjoying the many activities Martha's Vineyard has to offer, return for a scrumptious afternoon tea with scones, tea sandwiches and pastries. Oak Bluffs originally was named Cottage City, and is full of quaint, gingerbread homes to view. Nearby Circuit Avenue offers shopping, ice cream parlors, eateries and the nation's oldest carousel.

Innkeeper(s): Erik & Rhonda Albert. $135-260. 9 rooms with PB. Breakfast included in rates. Types of meals: Cont plus. Beds: QD. Reading lamp, ceiling fan and clock radio in room. Air conditioning. Parlor games, telephone and refrigerator/ice maker on premises. Antiquing, fishing, golf, live theater, parks, shopping, tennis and water sports nearby.

Location: Martha's Vineyard Island.

Certificate may be used: April 29-June 11, Sept. 12-Oct. 31 Sunday-Thursday, excluding holidays.

The Tucker Inn

PO Box 2680
Oak Bluffs, MA 02557-2680
(508)693-1045

Circa 1872. Located on a quiet residential park within walking distance of retail establishments and the town beach, this two-story Victorian Stick/Shingle inn offers visitors to Martha's Vineyard a choice of suites and guest rooms with shared and private baths. The former doctor's residence boasts an attractive veranda that is ideal for reading or relaxing after a busy day exploring the island's  many attractions, or a trip to nearby Chappaquiddick. Public transportation and boat lines are a five-minute walk from the inn.

Innkeeper(s): William Reagan. $35-245. 8 rooms, 5 with PB, 2 suites. Breakfast included in rates. Types of meals: Cont. Beds: QDT. Reading lamp and ceiling fan in room. VCR, telephone and fireplace on premises. Antiquing, fishing, live theater, shopping and water sports nearby.

Location: Residential park.

Certificate may be used: Oct. 1-June 15.

Petersham D8

Winterwood at Petersham

PO Box 176
Petersham, MA 01366-9500
(978)724-8885
Internet: www.winterwoodinn.com
E-mail: winterwoodatpetersham@juno.com

Circa 1842. The town of Petersham is often referred to as a museum of Greek Revival architecture. One of the grand houses facing the common is Winterwood. It boasts fireplaces in almost every room. Private dining is available for groups of up to 70 people. The inn is listed in the National Register.

Innkeeper(s): Jean & Robert Day. $129. 6 rooms with PB, 5 with FP. Breakfast included in rates. Types of meals: Cont plus. Beds: QDT. Reading lamp, clock radio and fireplace in room. Air conditioning. Fax, copier, library, telephone and fireplace on premises. Antiquing, art galleries, bicycling, cross-country skiing, downhill skiing, fishing, golf, hiking and horseback riding nearby.

Location: Country. Town Common.

Publicity: *Boston Globe and Yankee Magazine.*

"Between your physical facilities and Jean's cooking, our return to normal has been made even more difficult. Your hospitality was just a fantastic extra to our total experience."

Certificate may be used: Sunday-Thursday, except months of September and October.

Pittsfield D2

Olde White Horse Inn

378 South St
Pittsfield, MA 01201-6804
(413)442-2512 Fax:(413)443-0490
Internet: www.whitehorsebb.com
E-mail: whitehorsebb@yahoo.com

Circa 1902. Innkeeping runs in the family at the White Horse, which features an elegant Colonial exterior set on an acre of manicured lawn. The current innkeeper's grandparents also were innkeepers, and two rooms are named in honor of them. The Colonial theme continues into the home and to its eight guest rooms, decorated with antiques and beds topped with cozy comforters. The innkeepers' daughters also pitch in and help run the inn; the oldest prepares the breakfasts. The morning meal includes such items as quiche, pancakes, homemade muffins or breads and fresh fruit.

Innkeeper(s): Joe & Linda Kalisz. $85-190. 8 rooms with PB, 2 with FP. Breakfast included in rates. Types of meals: Country bkfst, veg bkfst and early coffee/tea. Beds: QD. Modem hook-up, data port, cable TV, reading lamp, refrigerator, clock radio, telephone, coffeemaker, turn-down service, desk and fireplace in room. Air conditioning. Fax, copier and fireplace on premises. Antiquing, art galleries, beach, bicycling, canoeing/kayaking, cross-country skiing, downhill skiing, fishing, golf, horseback riding, live theater, parks, shopping, sporting events, water sports and wineries nearby.

Location: City.

Certificate may be used: Sunday-Thursday, Nov. 1-April 30.

Provincetown G18

Gabriel's Apartments and Guest Rooms

104 Bradford St
Provincetown, MA 02657-1441
(508)487-3232 (800)969-2643 Fax:(508)487-1605
Internet: www.gabriels.com
E-mail: gabrielsma@aol.com

Circa 1936. Experience Gabriel's heavenly setting and cozy hospitality that have been enjoyed by many since 1979. Restored homes are graced with sky-lit common areas to gather in as a group or an individual. Each guest bedroom and suite is distinguished by the name and character of a famous personality. Most feature fireplaces, many boast Jacuzzi tubs and some include kitchenettes, skylights, sleeping lofts and semi-private porches. Modern amenities include high-speed Internet access and computers, voice mail, VCRs and a video library. Savor a full breakfast each morning. Lounge on a sun deck with afternoon wine and cheese. After a work out in the exercise gym, relax in the sauna or steam room. Soak in one of the two soothing outdoor hot tubs. Conveniently located in the heart of quaint Provincetown, the beach is only one block away.

Innkeeper(s): Gabriel Brooke. $100-300. 22 rooms with PB, 12 with FP, 10 suites and 1 conference room. Breakfast included in rates. Types of meals: Full bkfst and afternoon tea. Beds: QD. Cable TV, VCR, reading lamp, refrigerator, ceiling fan, clock radio, telephone, desk and hot tub/spa in room. Air conditioning. Fax, copier, spa, sauna, bicycles, library, parlor games, fireplace and e-mail on premises. Antiquing, cross-country skiing, fishing, golf, live theater, parks, shopping, tennis, water sports and whale watching nearby.

Location: Ocean community.

Certificate may be used: Nov. 1 to April 1. Most midweeks April, May, June, September, October.

Watership Inn

7 Winthrop St
Provincetown, MA 02657-2116
(508)487-0094 (800)330-9413
Internet: www.watershipinn.com
E-mail: info@watershipinn.com

Circa 1820. This stately manor was built as a home port for a Provincetown sea captain. During the past 10 years, it has been renovated and the original beamed ceilings and polished plank floors provide a background for the inn's antiques and simple decor. Guests enjoy the inn's sun decks and large yard, which offers volleyball and croquet sets.

Innkeeper(s): Richard Conley. $40-215. 15 rooms with PB. Breakfast included in rates. Types of meals: Cont plus. Beds: QDT. Cable TV and refrigerator in room. Antiquing, beach, museums, parks and whale watching nearby.

Publicity: *Boston "In."*

"We found your hospitality and charming inn perfect for our brief yet wonderful escape from Boston."

Certificate may be used: Oct. 1-April 30, excluding holidays and special event periods.

Rehoboth H12

Gilbert's Tree Farm B&B

30 Spring St
Rehoboth, MA 02769-2408
(508)252-6416 Fax:(508)252-6416
Internet: www.gilbertsbb.com
E-mail: jg@gilbertsbb.com

Circa 1835. This country farmhouse sits on 17 acres of woodland that includes an award-winning tree farm. Cross-country skiing and hiking are found right outside the door. If they choose to, guests can even help with the farm chores, caring for horses and gardening. A swimming pool is open during summer. Three antique-filled bedrooms share a second-floor sitting room. There are two first-floor rooms with a working fireplace and private bath. The nearby town of Rehoboth is 360 years old.

Innkeeper(s): Jeanne Gilbert. $70-90. 5 rooms, 2 with PB and 1 conference room. Breakfast, afternoon tea and snacks/refreshments included in rates. Types of meals: Full bkfst and early coffee/tea. Beds: KQDT. Reading lamp, desk and two with fireplace in room. VCR, fax, copier, swimming, stable, bicycles, library, telephone, fireplace and horse boarding only on premises. Antiquing, cross-country skiing, fishing, live theater, parks, shopping, sporting events and water sports nearby.

Location: Country.

Publicity: *Attleboro Sun Chronicle, Country, Somerset Spectator, Country Gazette and Pawtucket Times.*

"This place has become my second home. Thank you for the family atmosphere of relaxation, fun, spontaneity and natural surroundings."

Certificate may be used: Anytime, subject to availability, Sunday through Thursday during the month of January.

Richmond D2

A B&B In The Berkshires

1666 Dublin Rd
Richmond, MA 01254-9620
(413)698-2817 (800)795-7122 Fax:(413)698-3158
Internet: www.abnb.com
E-mail: doaneperry@yahoo.com

Circa 1962. This contemporary home, with its striking gardens, offers easy access to the area's many attractions. Guests choose from three air-conditioned guest rooms, all with cable TV, king or queen beds, phones, private bath, turndown service and VCRs. Bousquet Ski Area, Pleasant Valley Wildlife Sanctuary and Tanglewood all are within  easy driving distance of the inn. Hancock Shaker Village and the Norman Rockwell Museum are other nearby attractions.

Innkeeper(s): Doane Perry. $95-250. 3 rooms with PB. Breakfast and afternoon tea included in rates. Types of meals: Full gourmet bkfst, veg bkfst and early coffee/tea. Beds: KQT. Cable TV, VCR, reading lamp, telephone, turndown service and voice mail in room. Air conditioning. Fax, copier, library, parlor games and fireplace on premises. Limited handicap access. Antiquing, art galleries, beach, bicycling, canoeing/kayaking, cross-country skiing, downhill skiing, fishing, golf, hiking, horseback riding, live theater, museums, parks, shopping, tennis, Kripalu Yoga, Tanglewood, Berkshire Theater Festival, Shakespeare and Company, Edith Wharton, Boston Symphony Orchestra and Hancock Shaker Village nearby.

Location: Country.

Certificate may be used: Nov. 1-Dec. 4, Dec. 8-18, Jan. 19-Feb. 7.

Rockport   C15

Addison Choate Inn

49 Broadway
Rockport, MA 01966-1527
(978)546-7543 (800)245-7543 Fax:(978)546-7638
Internet: www.addisonchoateinn.com
E-mail: info@addisonchoateinn.com

Circa 1851. Antiques and reproductions decorate the interior of this mid-19th-century home. The guest rooms feature antique and wicker furnishings, artwork and polished, pine floors. Freshly ground coffee, homemade baked breads, fruit and cereals are served each morning in the inn's dining room, which still contains the original fireplace with a beehive oven. If weather permits, breakfasts are served on the inn's wraparound porch, offering a view of the garden. Shops, restaurants and art galleries all are nearby.

Innkeeper(s): Cynthia Francis & Ed Cambron. $105-175. 8 rooms with PB, 1 suite and 2 cottages. Breakfast and snacks/refreshments included in rates. Types of meals: Cont plus, early coffee/tea and afternoon tea. Beds: KQT. Cable TV, reading lamp, refrigerator, ceiling fan, clock radio, turn-down service and fireplace in room. Air conditioning. VCR, fax, copier, bicycles, library, parlor games, telephone and fireplace on premises. Antiquing, art galleries, beach, bicycling, canoeing/kayaking, cross-country skiing, fishing, golf, hiking, live theater, museums, parks, shopping and water sports nearby.

Location: Ocean community.

Publicity: Yankee Magazine.

"Our stay was a delight!"

Certificate may be used: Oct. 15-May 15, Sunday-Thursday, subject to availability.

Emerson Inn By The Sea

One Cathedral Avenue
Rockport, MA 01966
(978)546-6321 (800)964-5550 Fax:(978)546-7043
Internet: www.emersoninnbythesea.com
E-mail: info@emersoninnbythesea.com

Circa 1846. This Greek Revival inn's namesake, Ralph Waldo Emerson, once called the place, "thy proper summer home." As it is the oldest continuously operated inn on Cape Ann, decades of travelers agree with his sentiment. The guest rooms are comfortable, yet tastefully furnished, and some boast ocean views. The grounds include a heated, saltwater swimming pool as well as landscaped gardens. Breakfast is included in the rates. Guests also can enjoy dinner at The Grand Cafe, the inn's award winning restaurant.

Innkeeper(s): Bruce & Michele Coates. $95-349. 36 rooms with PB, 2 with FP, 2 two-bedroom suites, 2 cottages and 3 conference rooms. Breakfast and afternoon tea included in rates. Types of meals: Full gourmet bkfst, early coffee/tea, snacks/refreshments and gourmet dinner. Restaurant on premises. Beds: KQDT. Modem hook-up, data port, cable TV, refrigerator, clock radio, telephone, desk, fireplace, 11 with spa tubs and wireless Internet access in room. Air conditioning. TV, VCR, fax, copier, swimming, sauna, parlor games and gift shop on premises. Limited handicap access. Beach, bicycling, canoeing/kayaking, fishing, golf, hiking, live theater, museums and shopping nearby.

Location: Ocean community, waterfront.

Publicity: Yankee Magazine Travel Guide to New England "Must-See" Destination, Arrington's Inn Traveler, The Discerning Traveler, Karen Brown's Guide to New England and TV 40 Springfield.

"We were very impressed with every aspect of the Emerson Inn."

Certificate may be used: November-April, May and October, Sunday-Thursday only, subject to availability.

The Inn on Cove Hill

37 Mount Pleasant St
Rockport, MA 01966-1727
(978)546-2701 (888)546-2701 Fax:(978)546-1095
Internet: www.innoncovehill.com
E-mail: beck@ziplink.net

Circa 1771. Pirate gold found at Gully Point paid for this Georgian Federal-style house. A white picket fence and granite walkway welcome guests. Inside, an exquisitely crafted spiral staircase, random-width, pumpkin-pine floors and hand-forged hinges display the original artisan's handiwork. Furnishings include family heirlooms, four-poster canopy beds, and paintings by area artists. Muffin Du Jour is baked fresh each day by Betsy. Bicycles can be rented, and you can enjoy whale watching, fishing the local waters, or simply exploring the antique shops and village streets.

Innkeeper(s): Betsy Eck. $95-165. 6 rooms with PB, 1 two-bedroom suite. Breakfast included in rates. Types of meals: Cont plus and early coffee/tea. Beds: QDT. Cable TV and reading lamp in room. Central air. TV, library, parlor games, telephone and fireplace on premises. Antiquing, art galleries, beach, bicycling, canoeing/kayaking, fishing, golf, hiking, horseback riding, live theater, museums, parks, shopping, tennis, water sports, wineries, state park, castle and train to Boston nearby.

Location: Ocean community.

Certificate may be used: Anytime, November-May 15.

Sally Webster Inn

34 Mount Pleasant St
Rockport, MA 01966-1713
(978)546-9251 (877)546-9251
Internet: www.sallywebster.com
E-mail: sallywebsterinn@hotmail.com

Circa 1832. William Choate left this pre-Civil War home to be divided by his nine children. Sally Choate Webster, the ninth child, was to receive several first-floor rooms and the attic chamber, but ended up owning the entire home. The innkeepers have filled the gracious home with antiques and period reproductions, which complement the original pumpkin pine floors, antique door moldings and six fireplaces. Shops, restaurants, the beach and the rocky coast are all within three blocks of the  inn. Whale watching, kayaking, antique shops, music festivals, island tours and museums are among the myriad of nearby attractions. In addition to these, Salem is just 15 miles away, and Boston is a 35-mile drive.

Innkeeper(s): John & Kathy Fitzgerald. $80-140. 7 rooms with PB, 1 suite. Breakfast included in rates. Types of meals: Cont plus. Beds: KQDT. Clock radio and guest phone available in room. Air conditioning. TV, copier, parlor games, telephone and fireplace on premises. Antiquing, art galleries, beach, bicycling, canoeing/kayaking, fishing, golf, hiking, horseback riding, live theater, museums, parks, sporting events and water sports nearby.

"All that a bed and breakfast should be."

Certificate may be used: Sunday-Friday, November-March.

Seven South Street Inn

7 South Street
Rockport, MA 01966-1799
(978)546-6708 Fax:(978)546-8444
Internet: www.sevensouthstreetinn.com
E-mail: theinn@sevensouth.net

Circa 1766. Relax in the friendly and gracious atmosphere of this family-owned inn, open year-round. The 1766 Colonial with antiques and reproductions was recently renovated to provide a warm haven of peace and privacy. Gather in the fireside living room, library or sitting room to watch a movie, play games or chat. An outdoor deck is surrounded by colorful, well-kept gardens. Guest bedrooms, a two-room suite and an efficiency suite are inviting accommodations for vacations or extended stays. Enjoy fine linens, towels and robes. Two gourmet breakfast seatings are offered each morning for well-presented, elegant dining that tastes as great as it looks. Swim in the seasonal pool, or ride a bike to explore the scenic area. Make whale watching reservations and visit the local Circles Day Spa.

Innkeeper(s): Debbie & Nick Benn. $79-159. 8 rooms with PB, 1 two-bedroom suite. Breakfast and snacks/refreshments included in rates. Types of meals: Full gourmet bkfst, veg bkfst, early coffee/tea and afternoon tea. Beds: QD. Data port, cable TV, VCR, reading lamp, refrigerator, clock radio, telephone, desk, hair dryers and some with microwave in room. Air conditioning. Swimming, bicycles, library, parlor games and gift shop on premises. Antiquing, art galleries, beach, bicycling, canoeing/kayaking, fishing, golf, hiking, horseback riding, live theater, museums, parks, shopping, tennis and water sports nearby.

Location: Ocean community.

Certificate may be used: Oct. 1 through May 20, subject to availability.

Yankee Clipper Inn

127 Granite St.
Rockport, MA 01966
(978)546-3407 (800)545-3699 Fax:(978)546-9730
Internet: www.yankeeclipperinn.com
E-mail: info@yankeeclipperinn.com

Circa 1929. Sweeping views of the ocean and the rocky shoreline are eye-pleasers at this white clapboard, Art Deco oceanfront mansion and quarter deck. Polished mahogany woodwork and fireplaces reside with fine antiques imparting an old-fashioned, elegant ambiance. Sitting on one-and-a-half acres of breathtaking beauty, every guest bedroom overlooks an expansive vista. Enjoy the heated salt-water pool and New England hospitality.

Innkeeper(s): Randy & Cathy Marks. $129-379. 16 rooms with PB and 1 conference room. Breakfast included in rates. Types of meals: Full gourmet bkfst. Beds: KQDT. Modern hook-up, cable TV, reading lamp, clock radio, telephone, desk, hot tub/spa, some with DVD players and wireless Internet access in room. Central air. Fax, copier, swimming and fireplace on premises. Antiquing, art galleries, beach, bicycling, canoeing/kayaking, fishing, golf, hiking, live theater, museums, parks, shopping, tennis, water sports, whale watching, snorkeling and boat cruises nearby.

Location: Ocean community.

Publicity: *Gloucester Daily Times, Los Angeles Times, North Shore Life, Country Living, Discerning Traveler, Country Inns, Travel Holidays, Arrington's 'Best Ocean View,' Boston Magazine, Channel 5 Chronicle and Great Country Inns.*

"The rooms were comfortable, the views breathtaking from most rooms, and the breakfasts delicious, with prompt and courteous service."

Certificate may be used: Dec. 1-Feb. 28, anytime, subject to availability. March 1-May 30, Sunday-Thursday, subject to availability.

Rutland E9

The General Rufus Putnam House

344 Main St
Rutland, MA 01543-1303
(508)886-0200 Fax:(508)886-4864
Internet: www.rufusputnamhouse.com
E-mail: info@rufusputnamhouse.com

Circa 1750. This historic Georgian Colonial house, listed in the National Register, was the home of General Rufus Putnam, founder of Marietta, Ohio. A memorial tablet on the house states that "to him it is owing ... that the United States is not now a great slaveholding empire." Surrounded by tall maples and a rambling stone house, the inn rests on seven acres of woodlands and meadows. There are eight fireplaces, blue Delft tiles and a beehive oven. Afternoon tea and breakfast are served fireside in the keeping room. The Guest Cottage can sleep up to eight and is perfect for extended stays.

Innkeeper(s): Chris & Marcia Warrington. $100-175. 3 rooms, 1 with PB, 3 with FP, 1 cottage and 1 guest house. Breakfast and snacks/refreshments included in rates. Types of meals: Full bkfst, picnic lunch and afternoon tea. Beds: KQT. TV, reading lamp, clock radio, turn-down service and fireplace in room. Fax, copier, swimming, library, parlor games and telephone on premises. Amusement parks, antiquing, cross-country skiing, downhill skiing, fishing, golf, live theater, parks, shopping, sporting events, tennis and skating nearby.

Location: Country, Gentlemen's farm.

Publicity: *Sunday Telegram, The Land Mark and Washusett People.*

"We were thrilled with the beauty and luxury of this B&B and especially the wonderful hospitality."

Certificate may be used: Jan. 1-March 31, Sunday-Thursday.

Salem D14

Inn on Washington Square

53 Washington Sq
Salem, MA 01970
(978)741-4997
Internet: washingtonsquareinn.com
E-mail: debd731@aol.com

Circa 1850. Overlooking the other historical homes surrounding Salem Common, this Greek Revival house has many original details including wood mouldings and windows. Offering privacy for romance and relaxation, deluxe guest bedrooms feature four-poster or canopy beds, candles, Jacuzzi tubs, a video library for in-room VCRs and one with a fireplace. A breakfast basket of baked goods is delivered to the door. Hot beverages can be made in the personal coffeemakers, or freshly brewed coffee is available in the inn's main sitting area. Perennial gardens and a small koi pond grace the grounds.

Innkeeper(s): Deb D'Alessandro. Call for rates. 3 rooms with PB, 1 with FP. Breakfast included in rates. Types of meals: Cont, early coffee/tea and snacks/refreshments. Beds: KQ. Cable TV, VCR, reading lamp, refrigerator, clock radio and coffeemaker in room. Air conditioning. Antiquing, art galleries, beach, fishing, golf, live theater, museums, parks and shopping nearby.

Location: City, ocean community.

Certificate may be used: Monday-Thursday, Nov. 15-May 1.

The Salem Inn

7 Summer St
Salem, MA 01970-3315
(978)741-0680 (800)446-2995 Fax:(978)744-8924
Internet: www.saleminnma.com
E-mail: reservations@saleminnma.com

Circa 1834. Located in the heart of one of America's oldest cities, the inn's 42 individually decorated guest rooms feature an array of amenities such as antiques, Jacuzzi baths, fireplaces and canopy beds. Comfortable and spacious one-bedroom family suites with kitchenettes, are available. A complimentary continental breakfast is offered. Nearby are fine restaurants, shops, museums, Pickering Wharf and whale watching boats for cruises.
Innkeeper(s): Melinda Contino. $119-295. 41 rooms with PB, 18 with FP, 11 suites. Breakfast included in rates. Types of meals: Cont plus. Beds: KQT. Cable TV, reading lamp, refrigerator, clock radio, telephone, coffeemaker, desk, hot tub/spa and fireplace in room. Air conditioning. Fax on premises. Antiquing, art galleries, beach, bicycling, canoeing/kayaking, fishing, live theater, museums, parks, shopping, sporting events and water sports nearby.
Location: City.
Publicity: *New York Times, Boston Sunday Globe and Country Living Magazine.*
Certificate may be used: Anytime, subject to availability, excluding weekends, May through September.

Sheffield   F2

Birch Hill Bed & Breakfast

254 S Undermountain Rd
Sheffield, MA 01257-9639
(413)229-2143 (800)359-3969 Fax:(413)229-3405
Internet: birchhillbb.com
E-mail: info@birchhillbb.com

Circa 1780. A slice of history is felt at this Colonial home that was built during the American Revolution. Graciously situated on 20 scenic acres in the Berkshires, it is adjacent to the Appalachian Trail. The Chestnut Room has a fantastic view and  invites gathering to play the piano or games in front of the fire, listening to a CD or watching TV. Guest bedrooms and suites offer total relaxation. Some feature sitting areas and fireplaces. Creative, mouth-watering breakfasts begin a day of serendipity. Swim in the pool, try croquet and kayak or canoe in the lake across the street. Bicycles are available to explore the local area.
Innkeeper(s): Wendy & Michael Advocate. $110-215. 7 rooms, 5 with PB, 3 with FP, 1 suite and 1 conference room. Breakfast and afternoon tea included in rates. Types of meals: Full gourmet bkfst, veg bkfst and early coffee/tea. Beds: KDT. Reading lamp, CD player, refrigerator, clock radio and fireplace in room. Central air. TV, VCR, fax, copier, swimming, bicycles, library, child care, parlor games, telephone and fireplace on premises. Amusement parks, antiquing, art galleries, beach, bicycling, canoeing/kayaking, cross-country skiing, downhill skiing, fishing, golf, hiking, horseback riding, live theater, museums, parks, shopping, tennis and water sports nearby.
Location: Country, mountains.

"My experience at your B&B was among the most pleasant I've ever experienced, from the moment I walked in to hear classical music. It was all divine. I can't wait to come back!"
Certificate may be used: Anytime, subject to availability, Sunday-Thursday, excluding July and August.

Staveleigh House

59 Main St
Sheffield, MA 01257-9701
(413)229-2129
Internet: www.staveleigh.com
E-mail: innkeeper@staveleigh.com

Circa 1821. The Reverend Bradford, minister of Old Parish Congregational Church, the oldest church in the Berkshires, built this home for his family. Afternoon tea is served and the inn is especially favored for its splendid breakfast and gracious hospitality. Located next to the town green, the house is in a historic district in the midst of several fine antique shops. It is also near Tanglewood, skiing and all Berkshire attractions.
Innkeeper(s): Ali A. Winston. $115-160. 7 rooms, 5 with PB. Breakfast and afternoon tea included in rates. Types of meals: Full bkfst and early coffee/tea. Beds: KQDT. Reading lamp, ceiling fan, clock radio, turn-down service and desk in room. Air conditioning. Telephone, fireplace and terrycloth bath robes on premises. Handicap access. Antiquing, cross-country skiing, downhill skiing, fishing, live theater, parks, shopping, water sports and art galleries nearby.
Location: Historic district.
Publicity: *Los Angeles Times, Boston Globe and House and Garden Magazine.*
"The hospitality at Staveleigh House is deeper and more thoughtful than any you will find elsewhere." — House & Gardens Magazine
Certificate may be used: Sunday-Thursday, November-March, exclude holidays.

South Deerfield   D6

Deerfield's Yellow Gabled House

111 N Main St
South Deerfield, MA 01373-1026
(413)665-4922 (866)665-4922
Internet: www.yellowgabledhouse.com

Circa 1800. Huge maple trees shade the yard of this historic house, four miles from historic Deerfield and one mile from Route 91. Decorated with antiques, the bed chambers feature coordinating bedspreads and window treatments. One suite includes a sitting room, and canopy beds are another romantic touch. Breakfasts include items such as three-cheese stuffed French toast, an apple puff and fresh fruit topped with a yogurt-cheese sauce. The home is near historic Deerfield, and guests can walk to restaurants. The battle of Bloody Brook Massacre in 1675 occurred at this site, now landscaped with perennial English gardens. Yankee Candle is only one-half mile away and Historic Deerfield is only three miles away.
Innkeeper(s): Edna Julia Stahelek. $80-150. 3 rooms. Breakfast included in rates. Types of meals: Full gourmet bkfst and early coffee/tea. Beds: QT. Cable TV, reading lamp, ceiling fan, clock radio and telephone in room. Air conditioning. VCR on premises. Antiquing, bicycling, cross-country skiing, downhill skiing, fishing, live theater, shopping, sporting events and restaurants nearby.
Location: Western Mass., close to Five College area, Deerfield Academy, Yankee Candle and Magie Wings.
Publicity: *Recorder, Boston Globe and Springfield Republican.*
"We are still speaking of that wonderful weekend and our good fortune in finding you."
Certificate may be used: January, February, and March 30, Sunday-Thursday.

South Lancaster   *D10*

College Town Inn
PO Box 876, Rt 110
South Lancaster, MA 01561
(978)368-7000 (800)369-2717 Fax:(978)365-5426

Circa 1940. This bed and breakfast offers a country location, and guests may choose a room with a private patio or balcony from which to enjoy it. Rooms are furnished with contemporary pieces. In summer, a full breakfast is provided on the patio. Families may prefer the accommodation that has its own kitchen. Nearby are Revolutionary War battlefields, Concord and Longfellow's Wayside Inn.

Innkeeper(s): Jack & Charlotte Creighton. $75-150. 4 rooms with PB, 1 suite and 1 conference room. Breakfast included in rates. Types of meals: Full bkfst. Beds: KQDT. Cable TV, reading lamp, refrigerator, clock radio and telephone in room. Air conditioning. Fax and copier on premises. Antiquing, cross-country skiing, downhill skiing, fishing and golf nearby.

Certificate may be used: Monday-Thursday, no holidays, no weekend, September-April, subject to availability, not to be used in conjunction with other specials.

Stockbridge   *E2*

Seasons on Main B&B
PO Box 634
Stockbridge, MA 01262
(413)298-5419 (888)955-4747 Fax:(413)298-0092
Internet: www.seasonsonmain.com
E-mail: info@seasonsonmain.com

Circa 1862. Seasons on Main was built during the Civil War. The historic Greek Revival home includes a sweeping veranda where guests can relax on wicker chairs and loveseats. The interior is Victorian in style, and two of the rooms include a fireplace. Breakfasts include items such as fresh fruit, muffins or coffeecake and entrees such as baked French toast strata. The inn offers close access to Tanglewood, the Norman Rockwell Museum, Berkshire Botanical Gardens, Edith Wharton's home, hiking, skiing and biking.

Innkeeper(s): Pat O'Neill. $135-250. 4 rooms with PB, 2 with FP. Breakfast and snacks/refreshments included in rates. Types of meals: Full bkfst. Beds: KQD. Cable TV, VCR, reading lamp, refrigerator, clock radio and turn-down service in room. Air conditioning. TV, fax, parlor games, telephone and fireplace on premises. Antiquing, art galleries, bicycling, cross-country skiing, downhill skiing, fishing, golf, hiking, live theater, museums, parks, shopping and tennis nearby.

Location: Country.

Certificate may be used: Jan. 2-April 30, non-holidays. Midweek, Monday-Thursday or stay two nights, get one free on weekends (Thursday, Friday, Saturday, Sunday).

Sturbridge   *F8*

Commonwealth Cottage
PO Box 368
Sturbridge, MA 01566-1225
(508)347-7708
Internet: www.commonwealthcottage.com
E-mail: ccbb@meganet.net

Circa 1873. This 16-room Queen Anne Victorian house, on an acre near the Quinebaug River, is just a few minutes from Old Sturbridge Village. Both the dining room and parlor have fireplaces. The Baroque theme of the Sal Raciti room makes it one of the guest favorites and it features a queen mahogany bed. Breakfast may be offered on the gazebo porch or in the formal dining room. It includes a variety of homemade specialties, such as freshly baked breads and cakes.

Innkeeper(s): Robert & Wiebke Gilbert. $95-145. 3 rooms with PB. Types of meals: Full bkfst, early coffee/tea and snacks/refreshments. Beds: QDT. Reading lamp and ceiling fan in room. Library, parlor games, telephone and fireplace on premises. Antiquing, fishing, live theater, parks, shopping, water sports and museum nearby.
Location: City, country, mountains, ocean community, waterfront. Small town.
Publicity: *Long Island Newsday, Villager, WGGB in Springfield MA and Pax TV-Boston.*

"Your home is so warm and welcoming we feel as though we've stepped back in time. Our stay here has helped to make the wedding experience extra special!"

Certificate may be used: December-August, Sunday-Thursday, holidays, and special events excluded.

Sturbridge Country Inn
PO Box 60, 530 Main St
Sturbridge, MA 01566-0060
(508)347-5503 Fax:(508)347-5319
Internet: www.sturbridgecountryinn.com
E-mail: info@sturbridgecountryinn.com

Circa 1840. Shaded by an old silver maple, this classic Greek Revival house boasts a two-story columned entrance. The attached carriage house now serves as the parlor and displays the original post-and-beam construction and exposed rafters. All guest rooms have individual fireplaces and whirlpool tubs and include breakfast with champagne. They are appointed gracefully in colonial style furnishings, including queen-size and four-posters. A patio and gazebo are favorite summertime retreats. A five-star restaurant and outdoor heated pool are also on the premesis.

Innkeeper(s): Patricia Affenito. $59-179. 13 rooms with PB, 13 with FP, 2 suites and 1 conference room. Breakfast included in rates. Types of meals: Cont, early coffee/tea and room service. Restaurant on premises. Beds: KQ. Cable TV, VCR, reading lamp, refrigerator, ceiling fan, clock radio, telephone, desk and hot tub/spa in room. Air conditioning. TV, fax, copier, spa, swimming, fireplace, restaurant, luxury suites, hair dryer and iron on premises. Antiquing, cross-country skiing, downhill skiing, fishing, live theater, parks, shopping, water sports, casinos and old Sturbridge Village nearby.
Location: Rural.
Publicity: *Southbridge Evening News and Worcester Telegram & Gazette.*
"Best lodging I've ever seen."
Certificate may be used: November-August, Sunday-Thursday. No holidays, no special events. All rooms have a whirlpool tub.

Sudbury   D11

Arabian Horse Inn

277 Old Sudbury Rd
Sudbury, MA 01776-1842
(978)443-7400 (800)272-2426 Fax:(978)443-0234
Internet: www.arabianhorseinn.com
E-mail: info@arabianhorseinn.com

Circa 1880. Secluded on nine wooded acres with a horse farm,
this 1880 Queen Anne Victorian offers the ultimate in privacy
and romance. This inn is the perfect retreat to celebrate birthdays, anniversaries or other special occasions. The three-room
Tanah Suite with a canopy bed, two-person Jacuzzi and fireplace is a honeymoon favorite. A stay in the two-room
Orlandra Suite featuring a draped four-poster bed, two-person
Jacuzzi and huge balcony is also a popular pleaser. A complete
breakfast is made at a flexible time to suit every taste with delicious entrees and accompaniments. Enjoy the meal in the Ye
Old Worlde Café, on the veranda under the pergola or in-room.
Lunch or dinner can be arranged with advance reservation.
Tours are gladly given of the original four-story barn with post
and beam ceiling and huge cupola.

Innkeeper(s): Joan & Richard Beers. $169-319. 3 rooms, 1 with FP, 3
suites. Breakfast and afternoon tea included in rates. Types of meals: Full
gourmet bkfst, early coffee/tea and room service. Beds: K. Cable TV, VCR,
reading lamp, stereo, ceiling fan, clock radio, telephone and desk in room. Air
conditioning. Fax, copier, stable, library, pet boarding, parlor games and fireplace on premises. Amusement parks, antiquing, cross-country skiing, downhill skiing, fishing, golf, live theater, parks, shopping, sporting events, tennis
and water sports nearby.

Location: Country.

Certificate may be used: Anytime, subject to availability.

Hunt House Inn

330 Boston Post Rd.
Sudbury, MA 01776
(978)440-9525 Fax:(978)440-9082
Internet: www.hunthouseinn.com
E-mail: mollyhunthouse@ix.netcom.com

Circa 1850. Well-suited as a bed and breakfast, this early
American farmhouse and barn is located in the King Philip
Historic District. Fully restored, it is furnished with period
antiques and boasts an eclectic decor. The air-conditioned
guest bedrooms feature adjoining rooms. The Executive Suite
includes a sitting area and separate entrance. Breakfast is a
delight every morning, offering combinations of warm muffins,
omelettes and egg dishes, fresh fruit, homemade waffles with
Vermont maple syrup, sausages and an assortment of vegetarian
entrees. Dietary restrictions are accommodated with ease. Visit
the historic sites of nearby Boston.

Innkeeper(s): Molly Davidson. $85-100. 3 rooms with PB, 2 suites and 1
conference room. Breakfast, afternoon tea and snacks/refreshments included
in rates. Types of meals: Full gourmet bkfst, veg bkfst and early coffee/tea.
Beds: QDT. Modem hook-up, TV, reading lamp, snack bar, clock radio and
telephone in room. Air conditioning. VCR, fax and laundry facility on premises. Antiquing, art galleries, beach, canoeing/kayaking, golf, hiking, live theater, museums, parks, shopping, sporting events, tennis and wineries nearby.

Location: City. In 1638 farming and mill community, near historical
Concord, Boston.

Certificate may be used: Monday-Thursday, non holiday.

Vineyard Haven   K16

Clark House

20 Edgartown Rd, PO Box 2108
Vineyard Haven, MA 02568-2108
(508)693-8633 (800)696-8633 Fax:(508)696-6099
E-mail: innkeeper@twinoaksinn.net

Circa 1906. Pastels and floral prints provide a relaxing atmosphere at this Dutch Colonial inn on Martha's Vineyard, which
offers four guest rooms and an apartment with its own kitchen.
The breakfast specialty is apple-
crisp, and guests also enjoy afternoon tea on the enclosed wraparound front porch. The inn is
within walking distance of the
bicycle path, downtown businesses and the ferry, but its location off the main road affords a

more relaxed and sedate feeling for visitors. The family-oriented
inn accommodates family reunions, meetings and weddings,
and its fireplace room is popular with honeymooners.

Innkeeper(s): Steven Perlman/Jennifer Thorman. $85-235. 5 rooms, 3 with
PB, 2 suites and 1 conference room. Breakfast included in rates. Types of
meals: Cont plus, early coffee/tea, afternoon tea and gourmet dinner. Beds:
QDT. Cable TV, reading lamp, ceiling fan, clock radio and desk in room. VCR
and telephone on premises. Antiquing, fishing, live theater, shopping and
water sports nearby.

Publicity: *Detroit Free Press.*

*"We appreciated the wonderful welcome and kind hospitality shown
us for our week's stay on your lovely island."*

Certificate may be used: Nov. 12 to May 15.

Twin Oaks Inn

28 Edgartown Rd
Vineyard Haven, MA 02568
(508)693-1066 (800)339-1066 Fax:(508)696-6099
Internet: www.twinoaksinn.net
E-mail: innkeeper@twinoaksinn.net

Circa 1906. When visiting Martha's Vineyard, Twin Oaks offers
two pleasurable places to choose from that are within walking
distance to the beach, ferry or downtown shops. Stay at the
award-winning Clark House, a classic bed & breakfast or the
Hanover House, an elegant three-diamond country inn just
next door. Gather on one of the porches, the large backyard or
private brick patio and gazebo. Complimentary bikes and high-
speed Internet access are available on a first come first serve
basis. Each of the comfortable guest bedrooms offer Internet
access. Join the "breakfast party" for a bountiful continental-
plus morning meal.

Innkeeper(s): Steve and Judy Perlman. $99-315. 20 rooms. Breakfast
included in rates. Types of meals: Cont plus. Beds: KQD. Cable TV, reading
lamp, refrigerator, ceiling fan and two with fireplace in room. Air conditioning. Fax, copier, parlor games and telephone on premises. Antiquing, art galleries, beach, bicycling, canoeing/kayaking, fishing, golf, hiking, horseback
riding, live theater, museums, parks, shopping, tennis, water sports and
wineries nearby.

Location: Ocean community.

Publicity: *New York Times.*

Certificate may be used: Sept. 16-June 16.

Ware
E7

The Wildwood Inn
121 Church St
Ware, MA 01082-1203
(413)967-7798 (800)860-8098
Internet: www.wildwoodinn.net
E-mail: website@wildwoodbb.net

Circa 1891. This yellow Victorian has a wraparound porch and a beveled-glass front door. American primitive antiques include a collection of New England cradles and heirloom quilts, a saddlemaker's bench and a spinning wheel. The inn's two acres are dotted with maple, chestnut and apple trees. Through the woods, you'll find a river.

Innkeeper(s): Fraidell Fenster & Richard Watson. $60-110. 7 rooms with PB, 1 suite and 2 conference rooms. Breakfast and afternoon tea included in rates. Types of meals: Full bkfst and early coffee/tea. Beds: KQDT. Reading lamp, turn-down service and desk in room. Air conditioning. Library, parlor games, telephone, fireplace and canoe on premises. Handicap access. Amusement parks, antiquing, cross-country skiing, downhill skiing, fishing, hiking, live theater, parks, shopping, sporting events, kayaking and great restaurants nearby.

Location: Small town.

Publicity: *Boston Globe, National Geographic Traveler, Country and Worcester Telegram & Gazette.*

"Excellent accommodations, not only in rooms, but in the kind and thoughtful way you treat your guests. We'll be back!"

Certificate may be used: Anytime, subject to availability, Sunday-Thursday, Nov. 1-April 30, no holidays.

Wareham
I15

Mulberry B&B
257 High St
Wareham, MA 02571-1407
(508)295-0684 (866)295-0684
E-mail: mulberry257@aol.com

Circa 1847. This former blacksmith's house is in the historic district of town and has been featured on the local garden club house tour. Frances, a former school teacher, has decorated the guest rooms in a country style with antiques. A deck, shaded by a tall mulberry tree, looks out to the back garden.

Innkeeper(s): Frances Murphy. $55-85. 3 rooms. Breakfast included in rates. Types of meals: Full bkfst and afternoon tea. Beds: KDT. TV, reading lamp, clock radio and turn-down service in room. Air conditioning. VCR, parlor games and telephone on premises. Antiquing, cross-country skiing, fishing, live theater, parks, shopping, sporting events, water sports and whale watching nearby.

Location: Atlantic Ocean.

Publicity: *Brockton Enterprise and Wareham Courier.*

"Our room was pleasant and I loved the cranberry satin sheets."

Certificate may be used: October through May, except holiday weekends, PC/TC only with certificate.

Wellfleet
G18

Blue Gateways
252 Main St
Wellfleet, MA 02667-7437
(508)349-7530
Internet: www.bluegateways.com
E-mail: info@bluegateways.com

Circa 1712. Built by Squire Higgins in 1712 when George I was on the throne of England and Louis XIV was King of France, this Georgian inn is listed in the National Register. The house always has been a residence, but at times it also has served as a dry and fancy goods store, a pin and needle shop, a dressmaker's shop and a tearoom. Its three bedrooms are appointed with family antiques. The private back yard has an ornamental fish pond. A daily continental breakfast includes delights like juices, fruit, yogurt, specialty homemade granola and fresh to-die-for baked goods. Guest may go beach combing, biking, boating, golfing, hiking, swimming or whale watching. Or they may visit art galleries, museums, wineries or theaters. The inn was featured as Editor's Pick in the 1999 Yankee Magazine's Travel Guide to New England, and it was termed "elegant" in the Cape Cod Travel Guide.

Innkeeper(s): Richard & Bonnie Robicheau. $110-140. 3 rooms with PB. Breakfast included in rates. Types of meals: Cont plus and snacks/refreshments. Beds: KQ. Reading lamp and clock radio in room. Air conditioning. TV, VCR, telephone and fireplace on premises. Antiquing, art galleries, beach, bicycling, canoeing/kayaking, fishing, golf, hiking, horseback riding, live theater, museums, parks, shopping, tennis, water sports, wineries, Audubon and National Seashore nearby.

Location: Country, ocean community.

Certificate may be used: June 1-Aug. 31, Tuesday-Thursday excluding July 3, 4.

The Inn at Duck Creeke
70 Main St, PO Box 364
Wellfleet, MA 02667-0364
(508)349-9333
Internet: www.innatduckcreeke.com
E-mail: info@innatduckcreeke.com

Circa 1815. The five-acre site of this sea captain's house features both a salt-water marsh and a duck pond. The Saltworks house and the main house are appointed in an old-fashioned style with antiques, and the rooms are comfortable and cozy. Some have views of the nearby salt marsh or the pond. The inn is favored for its two restaurants; Sweet Seasons and the Tavern Room. The latter is popular for its jazz performances.

Innkeeper(s): Bob Morrill & Judy Pihl. $65-115. 25 rooms, 17 with PB and 1 conference room. Breakfast included in rates. Types of meals: Cont plus and dinner. Restaurant on premises. Beds: QDT. Some with air conditioning and some with ceiling or oscillating fans in room. Fax, parlor games and fireplace on premises. Antiquing, fishing, live theater, parks, shopping, water sports, National Seashore, Audubon Sanctuary and bike trails nearby.

Location: Close to harbor, beaches.

Publicity: *Italian Vogue, Travel & Leisure, Cape Cod Life, Providence Journal, New York Times, Provincetown, Conde Nast Traveler, British Vogue and Bon a Parte (Denmark).*

"Duck Creeke will always be our favorite stay!"

Certificate may be used: May 1-June 15, Sunday-Thursday.

Stone Lion Inn

130 Commercial Street
Wellfleet, MA 02667
(508)349-9565 Fax:(508)349-9697
Internet: www.stonelioncapecod.com
E-mail: info@stonelioncapecod.com

Circa 1871. Built by a sea captain in the 1800s, this French Second Empire Victorian recently has been renovated and redecorated to offer modern indulgences with an old-fashioned charm. Feel right at home in the comfortable living room with games, puzzles, VCR and videotapes. A large selection of books on local history as well as fiction and non-fiction are available to read. Guest bedrooms are named for Brooklyn neighborhoods where the innkeepers once lived or worked. The Clinton Hill boasts a clawfoot tub and shower and a private deck. A hearty breakfast buffet served in the dining room is sure to please. Vegetarian diets are graciously accommodated with advance notice. An apartment and a cottage provide more space and privacy. The grounds feature fish ponds, fountains, a wisteria-covered gazebo and a hammock.

Innkeeper(s): Janet Lowenstein & Adam Levinson. $90-155. 4 rooms with PB and 1 cottage. Breakfast included in rates. Types of meals: Country bkfst. Beds: Q. Reading lamp, ceiling fan and clock radio in room. Air conditioning. TV, VCR, library, parlor games and telephone on premises. Antiquing, art galleries, beach, bicycling, canoeing/kayaking, fishing, golf, hiking, live theater, parks, shopping, tennis and water sports nearby.

Location: Ocean community.

Publicity: *Conde Nast Traveler (May 2002) and Cape Cod Traveler.*

Certificate may be used: April and October, Sunday-Thursday, November-March, subject to availability, holidays excluded.

West Boylston   E10

The Rose Cottage Bed & Breakfast

24 Worcester St, Rte 12 and 140
West Boylston, MA 01583-1413
(508)835-4034 Fax:(508)835-4034
Internet: www.rosecottagebandb.com
E-mail: rosecottagebandb@msn.com

Circa 1850. This landmark Gothic Revival with its classic gabled roof and gingerbread dormers overlooks Wachusett Reservoir. Elegant antique furnishings complement the white marble fireplaces, gaslight hanging lamps, lavender glass doorknobs, wide-board floors and floor-to-ceiling windows. The delightful guest bedrooms feature vintage quilts, white iron, brass, Art Deco or spool beds,ceiling fans and fluffy towels. With over 20 years of pampering guests, the innkeepers provide a breakfast with signature entrees and regional specialties guests will find delicious. The carriage house is available as a monthly rental— a secluded, fully equipped apartment with a skylight cathedral ceiling.

Innkeeper(s): Michael & Loretta Kittredge. $90. 5 rooms and 1 conference room. Breakfast included in rates. Types of meals: Full gourmet bkfst and early coffee/tea. Beds: DT. Ceiling fan, at additional cost ($20) an extra twin bed can be added+ and some with private bath in room. Air conditioning. Cross-country skiing, downhill skiing, golf, tennis and public pool nearby.

Location: Ten minutes to downtown Worcester, 45 minutes to Boston.

Publicity: *The Telegram Gazette, Item, Landmark and Banner.*

"Your concern, your caring, your friendliness made me feel at home!"

Certificate may be used: January, February and March (subject to availability).

West Stockbridge   E2

Card Lake Inn

PO Box 38
West Stockbridge, MA 01266-0038
(413)232-0272 Fax:(413)232-0294
Internet: www.cardlakeinn.com
E-mail: innkeeper@cardlakeinn.com

Circa 1880. Located in the center of town, this Colonial Revival inn features a popular local restaurant on the premises. Norman Rockwell is said to have frequented its tavern. Stroll around historic West Stockbridge then enjoy the inn's deck cafe with its flower boxes and view of the sculpture garden of an art gallery across the street. Original lighting, hardwood floors and antiques are features of the inn. Chesterwood and Tanglewood are within easy driving distance.

Innkeeper(s): Ed & Lisa Robbins. $100-150. 8 rooms. Breakfast included in rates. Types of meals: Cont and early coffee/tea. Restaurant on premises. Beds: KQ. Ceiling fan and clock radio in room. Air conditioning. VCR and telephone on premises. Amusement parks, antiquing, shopping and sporting events nearby.

Location: Mountains.

Certificate may be used: Anytime excluding holiday weekends and weekends during Tanglewood Season and Foliage.

Woods Hole   J15

Capeside Cottage B&B

320 Woods Hole Rd
Falmouth, MA 02540
(508)548-6218 (800)320-2322 Fax:(508)457-7519
Internet: www.capesidecottage.com
E-mail: capesideseabnb@aol.com

Circa 1942. This is a faithful reproduction of a Cape-style cottage complete with picket fence and rambling roses. An English paddle-tennis court and swimming pool are popular spots in summer. In winter, breakfast is served beside a roaring fire. The inn is the closest bed & breakfast to the ferries to Martha's Vineyard and Nantucket.

Innkeeper(s): Jennifer & Gabriele. $89-175. 6 rooms with PB and 1 cottage. Breakfast included in rates. Types of meals: Full gourmet bkfst and early coffee/tea. Beds: QD. TV, reading lamp, desk and alarm clocks in room. Air conditioning. Fax, swimming, tennis, parlor games, telephone and fireplace on premises. Antiquing, fishing, live theater, shopping and water sports nearby.

Location: Residential.

Publicity: *Cape Cod Standard Times.*

"Our stay at the Marlborough was a little bit of heaven."

Certificate may be used: Nov. 1-May 15, Sunday-Thursday.

Yarmouth Port   I17

Old Yarmouth Inn

223 Main St
Yarmouth Port, MA 02675-1717
(508)362-9962 Fax:(508)362-2995
Internet: www.oldyarmouthinn.com
E-mail: 1696@attbi.com

Circa 1696. The Old Yarmouth originally was built as a stage stop and is one of America's oldest. There is a guest register from the 1860s when it was called the Sears Hotel. Traveling salesmen often stayed here, and according to the register, they sold such items as Henry's Vermont Linament, lightning rods, sewing machines and drilled-eye needles. Today, this venerable inn has rooms with antiques, but also cable television and air conditioning.

Innkeeper(s): Sheila FitzGerald & Arpad Voros. $110-140. 2 rooms with PB and 3 conference rooms. Breakfast included in rates. Types of meals: Cont, gourmet lunch and gourmet dinner. Restaurant on premises. Beds: Q. Cable TV, VCR, reading lamp and clock radio in room. Air conditioning. Fax, copier and fireplace on premises. Antiquing, art galleries, beach, bicycling, fishing, golf, live theater, museums and shopping nearby.

Location: Country.

Publicity: *The Register, Travel News, Cape Cod Travel, Chronicle and WCVB TV.*

Certificate may be used: March 15-June 15 and Nov. 1-Dec. 15, Sunday-Thursday, except holiday weekends.

Olde Captain's Inn on The Cape

101 Main St Rt 6A
Yarmouth Port, MA 02675-1709
(508)362-4496 (888)407-7161
Internet: www.oldecaptainsinn.com
E-mail: general@oldecaptainsinn.com

Circa 1812. Located in the historic district and on Captain's Mile, this house is in the National Register. It is decorated in a traditional style, with coordinated wallpapers and carpets, and there are two suites that include kitchens and living rooms. Apple trees, blackberries and raspberries grow on the acre of grounds and often contribute to the breakfast menus. There is a summer veranda overlooking the property. Good restaurants are within walking distance.

Innkeeper(s): Sven Tilly. $60-120. 3 rooms, 1 with PB, 2 suites. Breakfast included in rates. Types of meals: Cont plus. Beds: QD. Cable TV, reading lamp and clock radio in room. TV on premises. Antiquing, fishing, live theater, shopping, sporting events and water sports nearby.

Location: Historic district.

Certificate may be used: Anytime, Nov. 1-June 1. Sunday through Thursday, June 1-Nov. 1. Excludes holidays.

One Centre Street Inn

1 Center St
Yarmouth Port, MA 02675-1342
(508)362-9951 (866)362-9951 Fax:(508)362-9952
Internet: www.onecentrestreetinn.com
E-mail: sales@onecentrestreetinn.com

Circa 1824. Originally a church parsonage in the 1800s, this Greek Revival-style inn is listed in the National Register of Historic Places. Just one mile from Cape Cod Bay, the inn has an understated elegance that enhances the comfort and conveniences offered, including Cable TV, VCR, CD clock radio, refrigerators in select rooms, and services and amenities for business guests. After a restful night's sleep, indulge in a continental breakfast accompanied by locally roasted gourmet coffee from our own Centre Street Coffee House on the screened porch, garden patios or in the sun-filled dining room while listening to bubbling ponds and soft classical music. Take a bike ride into town or a short stroll to the long boardwalk at Gray's Beach.

Innkeeper(s): Carla and Robert Masse. $150-215. 5 rooms, 3 with PB, 1 with FP, 2 suites. Breakfast included in rates. Types of meals: Full gourmet bkfst, early coffee/tea and afternoon tea. Beds: QDT. Cable TV, VCR, CD player, refrigerator, clock radio, telephone, iron and ironing board in room. Air conditioning. TV, fax, copier, spa, bicycles, parlor games, data port and wireless hookup on premises. Antiquing, art galleries, beach, bicycling, canoeing/kayaking, fishing, golf, hiking, horseback riding, live theater, museums, parks, shopping, tennis, water sports and wineries nearby.

Location: Cape Cod, historic village.

Certificate may be used: Anytime, subject to availability.

Michigan

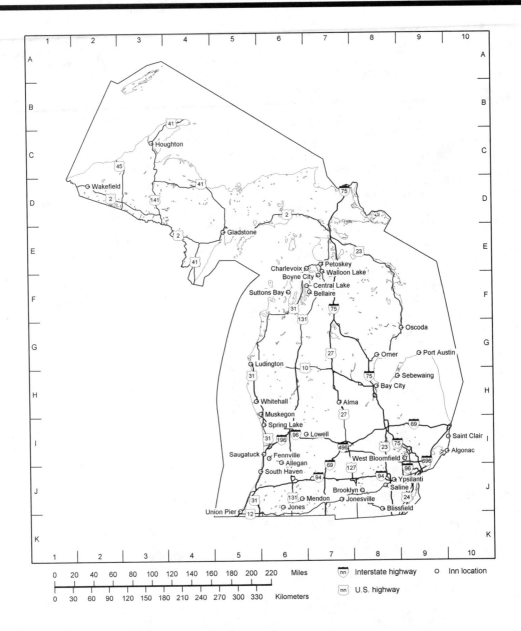

Algonac 19

Linda's Lighthouse Inn

5965 PTE Tremble Rd Box 828
Algonac, MI 48001
(810)794-2992 Fax:(810)794-2992
Internet: www.lindasbnb.com
E-mail: lindasbnb@hotmail.com

Circa 1909. Overlooking Dickerson Island, on the north branch of the St. Clair River, is this two-story Colonial inn, which once aided bootleggers who brought in liquor from Canada during Prohibition. Guests who arrive by boat and use the inn's 100 feet of dockage will have transportation to restaurants provided for them. Guests choose from the Jacuzzi, Lighthouse, Rose and Duck rooms, all featuring feather pillows. St. John's Marsh is less than a half-mile away.

Innkeeper(s): Ron & Linda (Russell) Yetsko. $95-125. 4 rooms with PB. Breakfast and snacks/refreshments included in rates. Types of meals: Full gourmet bkfst, early coffee/tea and picnic lunch. Beds: QD. Reading lamp, ceiling fan, clock radio, telephone, turn-down service, robes and flowers in room. Air conditioning. VCR, copier, bicycles, parlor games and outside hot tub on premises. Antiquing, cross-country skiing, fishing, parks, shopping, water sports, bird watching, hiking and movies nearby.

Location: Waterfront.

Certificate may be used: June 1-Sept. 30, Monday-Thursday, no holidays.

Allegan 16

Castle In The Country Bed and Breakfast

340 M 40 S
Allegan, MI 49010-9609
(269)673-8054 (888)673-8054
Internet: www.castleinthecountry.com
E-mail: info@castleinthecountry.com

Circa 1906. Reflecting its nickname and castle-like appearance, a three-story turret and wide wraparound porch accent this 1906 Queen Anne Victorian adorning five acres of scenic countryside. Gather in one of the several common rooms or sitting areas. A Guest Refreshment Center has a coffee pot and refrigerator. Romantic guest bedrooms and a suite feature fresh flowers, candles, terry robes, handmade bath products, a video library and VCR. Several rooms include whirlpool tubs, fireplaces and CD players. Breakfast is specially prepared and served on fine china and vintage crystal. Innkeepers Herb and Ruth enjoy providing personalized service that ensures a pleasant stay. Ask for an Adventure Map, a helpful tool to enjoy local activities and sites. Many special packages are regularly offered.

Innkeeper(s): Herb & Ruth Boven. $85-205. 5 rooms with PB, 5 with FP, 1 two-bedroom suite. Breakfast included in rates. Types of meals: Full gourmet bkfst, veg bkfst, early coffee/tea, picnic lunch, afternoon tea, snacks/refreshments, wine, dinner and room service. Beds: KQT. Modem hook-up, data port, TV, VCR, reading lamp, stereo, refrigerator, ceiling fan, snack bar, clock radio, turn-down service, desk, hot tub/spa, fireplace, antiques, high-quality linens and fabrics, two-person whirlpool tubs plus separate shower, breakfast by prior arrangement, robes, VHS library, CD library, massage by arrangement, handmade soaps and toiletries in room. Central air. Fax, copier, spa, parlor games, telephone, gift shop, gardens, firepit, wraparound porch and patio on premises. Antiquing, art galleries, beach, bicycling, canoeing/kayaking, cross-country skiing, downhill skiing, fishing, golf, hiking, horseback riding, live theater, museums, parks, shopping, sporting events, tennis, water sports and wineries nearby.

Location: Country.

Publicity: *Arrington's B&B Journal Book of Lists 2002* and on the cover of *Arrington's B&B Journal 2000*.

Certificate may be used: Sunday-Thursday, Nov. 1-May 31 (excluding holidays).

Alma H7

Saravilla

633 N State St
Alma, MI 48801-1640
(989)463-4078
Internet: www.saravilla.com
E-mail: Ljdarrow@saravilla.com

Circa 1894. This 11,000-square-foot Dutch Colonial home with its Queen Anne influences was built as a magnificent wedding gift for lumber baron Ammi W. Wright's only surviving child, Sara. Wright spared no expense building this mansion for his daughter, and the innkeepers have spared nothing in restoring the home to its former prominence. The foyer and dining room boast imported English oak woodwork. The foyer's hand-painted canvas wallcoverings and the ballroom's embossed wallpaper come from France. The home still features original leaded-glass windows, built-in bookcases, window seats and light fixtures. In 1993, the innkeepers added a sunroom with a hot tub that overlooks a formal garden. The full, formal breakfast includes such treats as homemade granola, freshly made coffeecakes, breads, muffins and a mix of entrees.

Innkeeper(s): Linda and Jon Darrow. $90-150. 7 rooms with PB. Types of meals: Full bkfst and room service. Beds: KQT. One with whirlpool tub and three with wood-burning fireplace in room. TV, spa, telephone, fireplace and complimentary beverages and snacks available on premises. Antiquing, cross-country skiing, fishing, live theater and canoeing nearby.

Publicity: *Midwest Living, Michigan Living, Morning Sun, Saginaw News* and *Sault Sunday.*

"I suggest we stay longer next time. We are looking forward to that visit."

Certificate may be used: Sunday-Thursday from Jan. 2 to Dec. 30, excluding holidays.

Bay City H8

Clements Inn

1712 Center Ave M-25
Bay City, MI 48708-6122
(989)894-4600 (800)442-4605 Fax:(989)891-9442
Internet: www.clementsinn.com
E-mail: clementsinn@chartermi.net

Circa 1886. The amber-paned windows and oak ceilings of this three-story Queen Anne Victorian inn are just a few of its impressive features. Built by William Clements, the home joined a number of other impressive estates on Center Avenue, most of which were owned by lumber barons. The inn's well-appointed guest rooms are named for famous authors or fictional characters, continuing a strong tradition started by Clements, a collector of rare books. A winding staircase, original gas lighting fixtures and hand-carved woodwork have impressed many visitors.

Innkeeper(s): Dave & Shirley Roberts. $75-190. 6 rooms with PB, 3 with FP, 2 suites. Breakfast included in rates. Types of meals: Cont. Beds: KQD. Cable TV, VCR, reading lamp, clock radio, telephone, desk and two suites have whirlpool in room. Air conditioning. Fax and parlor games on premises. Antiquing, cross-country skiing, fishing, live theater, parks, shopping, planetarium and birding nearby.

Location: City. Bay City.

Certificate may be used: Sunday-Thursday, Nov. 1-April 30.

Bellaire   F7

Grand Victorian Inn

402 N Bridge St
Bellaire, MI 49615-9591
(231)533-6111
Internet: www.grandvictorian.com
E-mail: innkeeper@grandvictorian.com

Circa 1895. Featured in Country Inns and Midwest Living magazines, this Queen Anne Victorian mansion boasts three original fireplaces, hand-carved mantels, intricate fretwork and numerous architectural details. Relax with a glass of wine before the fire in the formal front parlor, or listen to music while playing cards and games in the back parlor. Guest bedrooms offer an eclectic mix of antique furnishings including Victorian Revival, Eastlake and French Provincial. Soak in an 1890s clawfoot tub, or enjoy the park view from a private balcony. Be pampered with an incredible stay in one of the country's most remarkable and unique inns. The gazebo is a perfect spot to while away the day, or take advantage of the area's many nearby activities.

Innkeeper(s): Ken & Linda Fedraw. $115-135. 4 rooms with PB, 2 with FP. Types of meals: Full gourmet bkfst. Beds: QD. Reading lamp, private bathrooms and coffee and tea service in room. Air conditioning. Telephone and fireplace on premises. Antiquing, cross-country skiing, downhill skiing, fishing, golf, hiking, shopping, water sports, fine dining restaurants and lounging nearby.

Location: City. Northwest Lower Michigan.

Publicity: *Midwest Living, Country Inns, Featured on Nabisco Crackers/Cookies Boxes Promotion, Grand Traverse Magazine and 2003 Book of Lists Award-Arrington's B&B Journal-Most Elegant.*

"We certainly enjoyed our visit to the Grand Victorian. It has been our pleasure to stay in B&Bs in several countries, but never one more beautiful and almost never with such genial hosts."

Certificate may be used: Sunday through Thursday, Sept. 15-June 15.

Blissfield   J8

Hiram D. Ellis Inn

415 W Adrian St Us Hwy 223
Blissfield, MI 49228-1001
(517)486-3155
Internet: www.blissfield.net
E-mail: ellisinn@cass.net

Circa 1883. This red brick Italianate house is in a village setting directly across from the 1851 Hathaway House, an elegant historic restaurant. Rooms at the Hiram D. Ellis Inn feature handsome antique bedsteads, armoires and floral wallpapers. Breakfast is served in the inn's common room, and the innkeeper receives rave reviews on her peach and apple dishes. (There are apple and peach trees on the property.) Bicycles are available for riding around town, or you can walk to the train station and board the murder-mystery dinner train that runs on weekends.

Innkeeper(s): Christine Webster & Frank Seely. $80-100. 4 rooms with PB. Breakfast included in rates. Types of meals: Full bkfst and early coffee/tea. Beds: QD. Cable TV, reading lamp, refrigerator, clock radio, telephone and desk in room. Air conditioning. TV, bicycles and parlor games on premises. Antiquing, cross-country skiing, fishing, golf, live theater, parks and shopping nearby.

Location: Village.

Publicity: *Ann Arbor News and Michigan Living.*

"I have now experienced what it is truly like to have been treated like a queen."

Certificate may be used: Sunday through Thursday, excluding holidays.

Boyne City   F7

Deer Lake Bed & Breakfast

00631 E Deer Lake Rd
Boyne City, MI 49712-9614
(231)582-9039
Internet: www.deerlakebb.com
E-mail: info@deerlakebb.com

Circa 1994. Located in a comfortable, contemporary home, this bed & breakfast offers views from all bedrooms including vistas of lake, pond or forest. Two rooms include private balconies overlooking the lake, and the other three guest quarters share a 40-foot balcony. The house is bright and airy with elegant, country furnishings, French doors and a few lacy touches. Breakfast is served on the sun porch at tables embellished with fine china, crystal and candlelight. For those who enjoy the outdoors, the area offers golf, fishing, swimming, sailing, skiing and much more. For those more creatively inclined, a jewelry class is offered for guests who might enjoy making a 14K gold or sterling ring; jewelry repairs are also available. A variety of massages are available in your room or at a nearby location.

Innkeeper(s): Glenn & Shirley Piepenburg. $95-115. 5 rooms with PB. Breakfast and snacks/refreshments included in rates. Types of meals: Full bkfst and early coffee/tea. Beds: KQT. Reading lamp, ceiling fan, clock radio, turn-down service, iron and ironing board in room. Air conditioning. VCR, swimming, parlor games, telephone, fireplace, sail boat and paddle boat on premises. Antiquing, cross-country skiing, downhill skiing, fishing, parks, shopping, water sports and golf nearby.

Location: Waterfront.

Certificate may be used: Sunday-Thursday, excluding July, August and holidays.

Brooklyn   J8

Dewey Lake Manor

11811 Laird Rd
Brooklyn, MI 49230-9035
(517)467-7122
Internet: www.deweylakemanor.com
E-mail: deweylk@frontiernet.net

Circa 1868. This Italianate house overlooks Dewey Lake and is situated on 18 acres in the Irish Hills. The house is furnished in a country Victorian style with antiques. An enclosed porch is a favorite spot to relax and take in the views of the lake while having breakfast. Favorite pastimes include lakeside bonfires in the summertime and ice skating or cross-country skiing in the winter. Canoe and paddleboats are available to guests.

Innkeeper(s): Barb & Joe Phillips. $80-135. 5 rooms with PB, 5 with FP and 1 conference room. Breakfast included in rates. Types of meals: Full bkfst, early coffee/tea, picnic lunch and snacks/refreshments. Beds: QT. Cable TV, reading lamp, ceiling fan, clock radio, telephone, one with Jacuzzi and five with VCR in room. Air conditioning. Fireplace, VCR in sitting room and baby grand piano in parlor on premises. Antiquing, cross-country skiing, fishing, golf, live theater, shopping, sporting events and water sports nearby.

Location: Waterfront. Country.

Publicity: *Ann Arbor News.*

"I came back and brought my friends. It was wonderful."

Certificate may be used: November through April, subject to availability, special events excluded.

Central Lake   F7

Bridgewalk B&B

2287 S Main, PO Box 399
Central Lake, MI 49622-0399
(231)544-8122
Internet: www.bridgewalkbandb.com

Circa 1895. Secluded on a wooded acre, this three-story Victorian is accessible by crossing a foot bridge over a stream. Guest rooms are simply decorated with Victorian touches, floral prints and fresh flowers. The Garden Suite includes a clawfoot tub. Much of the home's Victorian elements have been restored, including pocket doors and the polished woodwork. Breakfasts begin with such items as a cold fruit soup, freshly baked muffins or scones accompanied with homemade jams and butters. A main dish, perhaps apple-sausage blossoms, tops off the meal.

Innkeeper(s): Janet & Tom Meteer. $85-105. 5 rooms with PB, 1 suite. Breakfast included in rates. Types of meals: Full bkfst and early coffee/tea. Beds: KQT. Reading lamp and ceiling fan in room. Parlor games, telephone and fireplace on premises. Antiquing, cross-country skiing, downhill skiing, fishing, parks, shopping, golf and gourmet restaurants nearby.

Location: Village.

Certificate may be used: Sunday through Thursday nights.

Torchlight Resort

PO Box 267
Central Lake, MI 49622-0267
(231)544-8263
E-mail: knott@torchlake.com

Circa 1940. These one-, three- and four-bedroom cottages are located on the edge of scenic Torch Lake. The cottages, which all boast lake views, include stocked kitchens and barbeque grills, but towels and linens are not provided. The owners offer docking for private boats, and there is a beach and swimming area.

Innkeeper(s): Robert & Glenda Knott. $90-280. 7 cottages with PB. Beds: D. Fishing nearby.

Certificate may be used: First week of May through third week of June and Labor Day through last week of October; seven days a week. On Torch Lake.

Charlevoix   E7

The Inn at Grey Gables

306 Belvedere Ave
Charlevoix, MI 49720-1413
(231)547-2251 (800)280-4667 Fax:(231)547-1944

Circa 1887. Guests at this attractive two-story inn are just a short walk from a public beach. Visitors have their choice of seven rooms, including two suites. The Pine Suite features a kitchen and private entrance, perfect for honeymooners or for those enjoying a longer-than-usual stay. All of the rooms offer private baths and most have queen beds. Guests may opt to relax and enjoy the beautiful surroundings or take advantage of the many recreational activities available in

the Charlevoix area, including Fisherman's Island State Park.

Innkeeper(s): Gary & Kay Anderson. $110-135. 7 rooms, 5 with PB, 2 suites. Breakfast included in rates. Types of meals: Full bkfst. Beds: KQT. Reading lamp, ceiling fan, clock radio and desk in room. Parlor games and telephone on premises. Antiquing, cross-country skiing, downhill skiing, fishing, parks, shopping and water sports nearby.

Location: Country, mountains, ocean community, waterfront. Public beach 1/2 mile.

Publicity: *USA Today.*

Certificate may be used: Nov. 1-May 24, anytime. Sunday-Thursday, June 1-30. Sunday-Thursday, September and Oct. 1-30.

Fennville   I6

The Kingsley House

626 W Main St
Fennville, MI 49408-9442
(269)561-6425 Fax:(269)561-2593
Internet: www.kingsleyhouse.com
E-mail: kingsleyhouse@verizon.net

Circa 1886. Experience the elegance of this Victorian Queen Anne mansion located near the resort towns of Saugatuck, Holland and South Haven. Restored and opened as a bed and breakfast, this relaxing retreat specializes in thoughtful hospitality and generous amenities. Sip lemonade on the wraparound front porch. Savor afternoon tea by the fire in the parlor. Indulge in a treat from the dining room cookie jar. Tastefully appointed and well-decorated guest bedrooms feature an assortment of pleasing comforts. Stay in the Jonathan Room with a two-person Hydromassage tub and gas log fireplace. The Northern Spy is a popular honeymoon suite on the entire third floor, with a double whirlpool tub, fireplace and sitting area in the turret. Royal Doulton china, heirloom silver and vintage linens accent a plentiful gourmet breakfast. Bikes are provided for an easy ride to Hutchins Lake or the winery. Drive to the nearby beaches of Lake Michigan.

Innkeeper(s): Dave Drees. $95-195. 8 rooms with PB, 6 with FP, 4 with HT, 4 suites. Breakfast, afternoon tea and snacks/refreshments included in rates. Types of meals: Full gourmet bkfst, veg bkfst, early coffee/tea and picnic lunch. Beds: KQ. Cable TV, VCR, reading lamp, stereo, ceiling fan, clock radio, desk, hot tub/spa and fireplace in room. Central air. Fax, copier, spa, bicycles, library, parlor games, telephone, outdoor movie theater (seasonal), hammock, porch swing, croquet and afternoon treats/refreshments on premises. Limited handicap access. Amusement parks, antiquing, art galleries, beach, bicycling, canoeing/kayaking, cross-country skiing, downhill skiing, fishing, golf, hiking, horseback riding, live theater, museums, parks, shopping, sporting events, tennis, water sports, wineries and wintertime activities nearby.

Location: Small town.

Publicity: *Country, Glamour, Country Victorian Decorating, Innsider* and *National Geographic Traveler.*

"It was truly enjoyable. You have a lovely home and a gracious way of entertaining."

Certificate may be used: All year, Sunday through Thursday only, no holidays.

Gladstone E5

Kipling House Bed & Breakfast

1716 N Lake Shore Dr
Gladstone, MI 49837-2751
(906)428-1120 (877)905-ROOM
E-mail: info@kiplinghouse.com

Circa 1897. Stay here and learn why this historical Four Square house is named after Rudyard Kipling. Relax on the front porch rockers or by the fire in the parlor. Choose a guest bedroom with a whimsical or elegant decor. The cottage features a sleeping loft and a free-standing fireplace. Gourmet Chef Ralph takes great pride in presenting a splendid candlelight breakfast in the dining room, as well as a tasty dessert in the evenings. The grounds offer a gazebo, deck perennial and water garden. Bikes are available to explore the local Upper Peninsula area. Enjoy nearby Hiawatha National Forest boasting almost one million acres, or visit a restored mining village at Fayette State Park.

Innkeeper(s): Ann & Ralph Miller. $75-150. 6 rooms, 3 with PB and 1 guest house. Breakfast, afternoon tea and snacks/refreshments included in rates. Types of meals: Full gourmet bkfst, early coffee/tea and picnic lunch. Beds: KQD. Modem hook-up, cable TV, VCR, reading lamp, refrigerator, ceiling fan, coffeemaker, turn-down service and fireplace in room. Air conditioning. Copier, bicycles, library, parlor games, telephone, fireplace, laundry facility and gift shop on premises. Antiquing, art galleries, beach, bicycling, canoeing/kayaking, cross-country skiing, downhill skiing, fishing, golf, hiking, museums, parks, shopping and water sports nearby.

Location: City.

Publicity: *Daily Press and WLUC TV.*

Certificate may be used: Anytime, subject to availability.

Houghton C3

Charleston House B&B Inn

918 College Avenue
Houghton, MI 49931-1821
(906)482-7790 (800)482-7404 Fax:(906)482-7068
E-mail: inquiries@charlestonhouseinn.com

Circa 1900. Wide verandas on the first and second stories dominate the exterior of this impressive Colonial Revival-style home, which is painted in a light pink hue with white trim. There are ceiling fans and comfortable wicker furnishings on the verandas, and the second-story porch is a private haven for guests staying in the Daughter's Room. Most of the other bedchambers offer a view of the Portage Canal. Mother's Room makes up for its lack of a view by including a bay window, sitting area and clawfoot tub. The scents of brewing coffee and baking muffins will lure you out of your comfortable bed and down to a breakfast with homemade breads and granola, fresh fruit, yogurt and a special daily entree. The inn overlooks the canal, and Lake Superior is nearby, as is the MTU campus, skiing, shops, restaurants and the downtown area.

Innkeeper(s): John & Helen Sullivan. $98-168. 6 rooms with PB, 2 with FP, 1 suite and 2 conference rooms. Breakfast, snacks/refreshments and wine included in rates. Types of meals: Cont plus and early coffee/tea. Beds: KQT. Cable TV, reading lamp, stereo, refrigerator, ceiling fan, clock radio, telephone, reading lamp, desk and microwave/complimentary soft drinks in room. Air conditioning. Fax, copier, library, parlor games, fireplace, coffee pots and hair dryers on premises. Amusement parks, antiquing, cross-country skiing, downhill skiing, fishing, golf, live theater, parks, shopping, sporting events, tennis and water sports nearby.

Location: City, waterfront. Seven miles from Lake Superior.

Publicity: *Michigan Explorer.*

"The room and the house was the prettiest I've ever seen."

Certificate may be used: Anytime, November-April, subject to availability.

Jones J6

The Sanctuary at Wildwood

58138 M-40
Jones, MI 49061-9713
(269)244-5910 (800)249-5910 Fax:(269)244-9022
Internet: www.sanctuaryatwildwood.com
E-mail: info@sanctuaryatwildwood.com

Circa 1973. Travelers in search of relaxation and a little solitude will enjoy the serenity of this estate, surrounded by 95 forested acres. A stroll down the hiking trails introduces guests to a variety of wildlife, but even inside, guests are pampered by the inn's natural setting. One room, named Medicine Hawk, is adorned with a mural depicting a woodland scene. A mural of a pine forest graces the Quiet Solace room. The Keeper of the Wild Room includes a rustic birch headboard.  Each of the rooms includes a fireplace, Jacuzzi and service bar. There also are three cottage (6 suites), situated around a pond. From the dining and great rooms, guests can watch the abundant wildlife. The innkeeper offers a variety of interesting packages. A heated swimming pool is available during the summer months. Wineries are nearby, and the inn is a half hour from Notre Dame and Shipshewana.

Innkeeper(s): Dick & Dolly Buerkle. $159-219. 11 rooms, 11 with FP, 11 suites, 3 cottages and 1 conference room. Breakfast included in rates. Beds: Q. TV, reading lamp, stereo, refrigerator, snack bar, clock radio, desk, Jacuzzi, fireplace and cottage suites feature Jenn Air kitchenettes in room. Air conditioning. Parlor games, telephone and fireplace on premises. Handicap access. Antiquing, canoeing/kayaking, cross-country skiing, downhill skiing, fishing, golf, horseback riding, shopping and Amish communities nearby.

Location: Rural, wooded countryside.

Publicity: *The Toledo Blade, Chicago Sun Times, Kalamazoo Gazette and South Bend Tribune.*

Certificate may be used: Anytime, November-April, subject to availability, excluding holiday periods.

Jonesville J7

Horse & Carriage B&B

7020 Brown Rd
Jonesville, MI 49250-9720
(517)849-2732 Fax:(517)849-2732
Internet: www.hcbnb.com
E-mail: ccbrown@modempool.com

Circa 1898. Enjoy a peaceful old-fashioned day on the farm. Milk a cow, snuggle shetland sheep, gather eggs and cuddle baby chicks. In the winter, families are treated to a horse-drawn sleigh ride at this 18th-century home, which is surrounded by a 700-acre cattle farm. In the warmer months, horse-drawn carriage rides pass down an old country lane past Buck Lake. The innkeeper's family has lived on the property for more than 150 years. The home itself was built as a one-room schoolhouse. A mix of cottage and Mission furnishings decorate the interior. The Rainbow Room, a perfect place for children, offers twin beds and a playroom. Guests are treated to hearty breakfasts made with farm-fresh eggs, fresh fruits and vegetables served on the porch or fireside.

Innkeeper(s): Keith Brown & family. $85-125. 4 rooms, 2 with PB. Breakfast and snacks/refreshments included in rates. Types of meals: Full gourmet bkfst and early coffee/tea. Beds: KQT. Reading lamp, telephone and desk in room. Air conditioning. Parlor games, fireplace, milk a cow, pet lambs, gather eggs and horse/carriage rides on premises. Antiquing, cross-country skiing, fishing, live theater, parks, shopping, sporting events, water sports, Jackson Space Center, Speedway and County Fair nearby.

Location: Country.

Publicity: *Detroit Free Press, The Toledo Blade, Hillsdale Daily News and MSU Alumni.*

Certificate may be used: Anytime subject to availability.

Munro House B&B Day Spa

202 Maumee St
Jonesville, MI 49250-1247
(517)849-9292 (800)320-3792
Internet: www.munrohouse.com
E-mail: Info@MunroHouse.com

Circa 1834. "The Most Comfortable Lodging in South Central Michigan" is found at this historic 1834 bed & breakfast that was once a station on the Underground Railroad. Relax in an abundance of common areas, play the grand piano, read in the library or watch a video. Enjoy complimentary soft drinks and homemade cookies. Stay in a themed guest bedroom with a gas fireplace and two-person Jacuzzi tub. Wake up to a country-style breakfast. Murder Mystery Dinners, massage/spa services, Chef Night, Romantic Getaways, Holiday Dinners and Intimate Weddings are some of the specialty packages offered.

Innkeeper(s): Mike & Lori Venturini. $109-189. 7 rooms with PB, 5 with FP. Breakfast and snacks/refreshments included in rates. Types of meals: Country bkfst. Beds: Q. Modem hook-up, cable TV, VCR, ceiling fan, clock radio, telephone, desk, two with Jacuzzi tubs and five with fireplace in room. Air conditioning. Fax, copier, library, parlor games, fireplace, 400-title video library, homemade cookies and free soft drinks on premises. Antiquing, golf, horseback riding, live theater and museums nearby.

Location: Village.

"Your home is a wonderful port for the weary traveler. I love it here. The rooms are great and the hospitality unsurpassed."

Certificate may be used: Anytime, except Nascar & Hillsdale College and special events weekends.

Lowell   I6

McGee Homestead B&B

2534 Alden Nash NE
Lowell, MI 49331
(616)897-8142
Internet: www.iserv.net/~mcgeebb
E-mail: mcgeebb@iserv.net

Circa 1880. Just 18 miles from Grand Rapids, travelers will find the McGee Homestead B&B, an Italianate farmhouse with four antique-filled guest rooms. Surrounded by orchards, it is one of the largest farmhouses in the area. Breakfasts feature the

inn's own fresh eggs. Guests may golf at a nearby course or enjoy our hot tub on the screen porch. Lowell is home to Michigan's largest antique mall, and historic covered bridges are found in the surrounding countryside. Travelers who remain on the farm may relax in a hammock or visit a barn full of petting animals.

Innkeeper(s): Chuck & Elaine Brinkert. $58-78. 4 rooms with PB and 1 conference room. Breakfast and snacks/refreshments included in rates. Types of meals: Full bkfst and early coffee/tea. Beds: KQDT. TV, reading lamp and ceiling fan in room. Air conditioning. VCR, library, parlor games, telephone, fire-

place and refrigerator on premises. Antiquing, cross-country skiing, downhill skiing, fishing, parks and shopping nearby.

Location: Country.

Certificate may be used: March 1-Dec. 31, Sunday-Friday.

Ludington   G5

The Inn at Ludington

701 E Ludington Ave
Ludington, MI 49431-2224
(231)845-7055 (800)845-9170
Internet: www.inn-ludington.com
E-mail: innkeeper@inn-ludington.com

Circa 1890. Experience an informal elegance at this Victorian bed and breakfast in the Great Lakes region near Lake Michigan beach that offers a fine blend of the past and the present. Built in 1890, it has been locally awarded for retaining its historical integrity during replicate restoration. Lounge by one of the four fireplaces and savor afternoon refreshments. Choose from one of the six ethnically-themed guest bedrooms. Early risers can enjoy fresh coffee, cereal, yogurt and nut bread. A personally tailored meal is offered at an agreed-upon, pre-determined time. Ask about seasonal getaway or family packages, special events and murder mystery weekends.

Innkeeper(s): Kathy & Ola Kvalvaag. $100-125. 6 rooms with PB, 2 with FP, 2 suites. Breakfast included in rates. Types of meals: Full bkfst and early coffee/tea. Beds: KQD. Cable TV, reading lamp, ceiling fan, clock radio and desk in room. Air conditioning. Copier, library, parlor games, telephone and fireplace on premises. Antiquing, cross-country skiing, fishing, parks, shopping and water sports nearby.

Location: Walk in town to beach.

Publicity: *Ludington Daily News, Detroit Free Press, Chicago Tribune, Country Accents and Michigan Living.*

"Loved the room and everything else about the house."

Certificate may be used: November-April, anytime; May, June, September, October, Sunday-Thursday as available at last minute.

Lamplighter B&B

602 E Ludington Ave
Ludington, MI 49431-2223
(231)843-9792 (800)301-9792 Fax:(231)843-1840
Internet: www.ludington-michigan.com
E-mail: lamplighter@ludington-michigan.com

Circa 1895. This Queen Anne home offers convenient access to Lake Michigan's beaches, the Badger car ferry to Wisconsin and Ludington State Park. A collection of European antiques, original paintings and lithographs decorate the inn. The home's centerpiece, a golden oak curved staircase, leads guests up to their rooms. Two rooms feature whirlpool tubs, one a fireplace. The innkeepers have created a mix of hospitality and convenience that draws both vacationers and business travelers. A full, gourmet breakfast is served each morning. The innkeepers are fluent in German.

Innkeeper(s): Jane & Bill Carpenter. $115-145. 5 rooms with PB, 1 with FP. Breakfast included in rates. Types of meals: Full gourmet bkfst and early coffee/tea. Beds: Q. Cable TV, reading lamp, clock radio, telephone, turn-down service and two with Jacuzzi in room. Air conditioning. VCR, fax, copier, parlor games, fireplace, gazebo and terrace on premises. Amusement parks, antiquing, cross-country skiing, fishing, golf, parks, shopping, tennis and water sports nearby.

Location: City.

"For my husband's first bed and breakfast experience, it couldn't have been better."

Certificate may be used: November through May, Sunday through Thursday, holidays excluded.

The Ludington House

501 E Ludington Ave
Ludington, MI 49431-2220
(231)845-7769 (800)827-7869
Internet: www.ludingtonhouse.com
E-mail: gypsyginger@webtv.net

Enjoy the opulence of the Victorian era at this 19th-century home, which was built by a lumber baron. Grand rooms with high ceilings, stained glass and polished oak floors are enhanced by a country collection of period antiques. A showpiece carved, winding staircase and Italian mantels are other notable architectural features. An antique wedding gown decorates the Bridal Suite. The innkeepers will prepare a picnic lunch, and there are bicycles for guest use. The innkeepers also offer murder-mystery packages.

Innkeeper(s): Virginia Boegner. $80-120. 8 rooms. Breakfast included in rates. Types of meals: Full bkfst.

Certificate may be used: November to Memorial Day excluding Valentine's Day, Memorial Day and New Year's Eve. Also excludes whirlpool tub rooms.

Mendon   J6

The Mendon Country Inn

PO Box 98
Mendon, MI 49072-9502
(269)496-8132 (800)304-3366 Fax:(269)496-8403
Internet: www.rivercountry.com/mci/
E-mail: vasame@aol.com

Circa 1873. This two-story stagecoach inn was constructed with St. Joseph River clay bricks fired on the property. There are eight-foot windows, high ceilings and a walnut staircase. Country antiques are accentuated with woven rugs, collectibles and bright quilts. There are nine antique-filled guest rooms and nine suites which include a fireplace and Jacuzzi tub. Depending on the season, guests may also borrow a tandem bike or arrange for a canoe trip. Special events are featured throughout the year. The inn's Golden Getaway package includes lodging, a dinner for two and special activity, which might be golfing, a river canoe trip, skiing or perhaps a relaxing massage. A rural Amish community and Shipshewana are nearby.

Innkeeper(s): Geff & Cheryl Clarke. $79-149. 18 rooms with PB, 14 with FP, 9 suites, 2 cottages and 1 conference room. Breakfast included in rates. Types of meals: Full bkfst and early coffee/tea. Beds: QD. TV, reading lamp, ceiling fan, clock radio, desk, hot tub/spa and most rooms with fireplaces in room. Air conditioning. Fax, sauna, bicycles, library, parlor games, telephone, fireplace and canoeing on premises. Handicap access. Antiquing, cross-country skiing, downhill skiing, fishing, shopping and canoeing nearby.

Location: Waterfront. Rural country.

Publicity: *Insider, Country Home, Country Magazine and Midwest Living.*

"A great experience. Good food and great hosts. Thank you."

Certificate may be used: Sunday-Thursday throughout the year, plus November-May on weekends, excluding special event weekends.

Muskegon   H6

Port City Victorian Inn, Bed & Breakfast

1259 Lakeshore Dr
Muskegon, MI 49441-1659
(231)759-0205 (800)274-3574 Fax:(231)759-0205
Internet: www.portcityinn.com
E-mail: pcvicinn@gte.net

Circa 1877. Old world elegance characterizes this Queen Anne Victorian mansion gracing the bluff of Muskegon Lake. The front parlor boasts curved leaded-glass windows with views of the harbor. A paneled grand entryway is accented by the carved posts and spindles of an oak staircase leading up to a TV room and rooftop balcony overlooking the state park. Luxurious honeymoon suites boasts two-person whirlpool baths, and romantic guest bedrooms include desks, modems, refrigerators and ice buckets. Early risers sip morning coffee while reading the local newspaper. A hot breakfast can be delivered to the room, enjoyed in the formal dining room or served in the 14-window sunroom. Ask about special packages available.

Innkeeper(s): Barbara Schossau & Fred Schossau. $80-155. 5 rooms with PB, 2 with FP, 3 suites. Breakfast included in rates. Types of meals: Country bkfst, early coffee/tea, snacks/refreshments and room service. Beds: Q. Modem hook-up, data port, cable TV, VCR, reading lamp, CD player, refrigerator, ceiling fan, clock radio, telephone, coffeemaker, turn-down service, desk, double whirlpool tubs, fireplace, hair dryers, robes and lake views in room. Central air. Fax, copier, bicycles, parlor games and fireplace on premises. Amusement parks, antiquing, art galleries, beach, bicycling, canoeing/kayaking, cross-country skiing, fishing, golf, hiking, live theater, museums, parks, shopping, sporting events, tennis, water sports, Lake Michigan, Muskegon Lake and Port City Princess cruise ship nearby.

Location: City, waterfront.

Publicity: *Muskegon Chronicle, Detroit Free Press, Arrington's Bed & Breakfast Journal and Arrington's Bed & Breakfast Journal's award "Best In The Midwest."*

"The inn offers only comfort, good food and total peace of mind."

Certificate may be used: Anytime, November-April, subject to availability.

Omer   G8

Rifle River B&B

500 Center Ave
Omer, MI 48749
(517)653-2543
E-mail: jao517@aol.com

A gathering of maple trees shades this historic home, located in the heart of Omer. The town, which was founded just after the Civil War, has seen a multitude of disasters, and this sturdy home has stood through its fair share of floods, tornadoes and fires. The innkeepers offer four rooms decorated with antiques. Waterbeds and Jacuzzi tubs are relaxing amenities. The home, as its name might suggest, is only two blocks from the Rifle River, which offers fishing and canoeing.

Innkeeper(s): Judy O'Boyle. $49-55. 4 rooms. Breakfast included in rates. Types of meals: Cont.

Certificate may be used: Sept. 10-Nov. 1 and March 25-May 15.

Oscoda   G9

Huron House Bed & Breakfast

3124 N US-23
Oscoda, MI 48750
(989)739-9255 Fax:(989)739-0195
Internet: www.huronhouse.com
E-mail: huron@huronhouse.com

Circa 1950. From this romantic setting you can enjoy strolls along the beach, sunrise over the lake, or a soak in a private hot tub. The waterside inn offers warmly decorated guest rooms with antiques, handsome beds, wallpapers, and a variety of amenities including decks, fireplaces and Jacuzzi tubs. Breakfast is brought to your room in the morning. Plan a drive, cycling excursion or hiking trip on the scenic 22-mile River Road National Scenic Byway along the AuSable River.

Innkeeper(s): Denny & Martie Lorenz. $130-185. 14 rooms, 13 with FP, 14 suites. Breakfast included in rates. Types of meals: Cont plus. Beds: K. Cable TV, CD player, refrigerator, ceiling fan, clock radio, coffeemaker, hot tub/spa and fireplace in room. Air conditioning. Spa and fireplace on premises. Antiquing, beach, canoeing/kayaking, cross-country skiing, fishing, golf, hiking, horseback riding, parks, shopping and water sports nearby.

Location: Waterfront.

Publicity: *Midwest Living.*

Certificate may be used: Sunday-Thursday, Nov. 1-May 1.

Petoskey   E7

Terrace Inn

PO Box 266
Petoskey, MI 49770-0266
(231)347-2410 (800)530-9898 Fax:(231)347-2407
Internet: www.theterraceinn.com
E-mail: info@theterraceinn.com

Circa 1911. This Victorian inn is located on what began as a Chautauqua summer resort, surrounded by more than 400 Victorian cottages. Terrace Inn was built in 1911, and most of its furnishings are original to the property. Guests will enjoy stunning views of Lake Michigan and Little Traverse Bay, and they can enjoy the shore at the private Bay View beach. In keeping with the surrounding homes, the guest rooms are decorated in a  romantic-country cottage style. To take guests back in time, there are no televisions or telephones in the rooms. This historic resort town offers many attractions, from swimming and watersports to hiking to summer theater. During the summer season, the inn's restaurant (open all year) and outdoor veranda are great spots for dinner.

Innkeeper(s): Mo and Patty Rave. $59-159. 43 rooms with PB, 1 suite and 2 conference rooms. Breakfast included in rates. Types of meals: Cont plus, Sun. brunch, lunch, snacks/refreshments and dinner. Restaurant on premises. Beds: QDT. Reading lamp, 10 have A/C and suite with hot tub in room. TV, VCR, bicycles, tennis, library, parlor games, telephone, fireplace, beach and cross-country skiing on premises. Limited handicap access. Antiquing, art galleries, beach, bicycling, canoeing/kayaking, cross-country skiing, downhill skiing, fishing, golf, hiking, horseback riding, live theater, museums, parks, shopping, tennis, water sports, wineries and Chautauqua nearby.

Location: Small resort town.

Publicity: *Oakland Press & Observer Eccentric, Midwest Living, Michigan Magazine and Detroit News.*

Certificate may be used: Sept. 7-June 15, Sunday-Thursday.

Port Austin   G9

Lake Street Manor

8569 Lake St
Port Austin, MI 48467
(989)738-7720 (888)273-8987
Internet: hometown.aol.com/lakestreetmanor

Circa 1875. As history has shown, the homes of lumber barons are often some of the most luxurious. This Victorian, with its peak roofs and gingerbread trim is no exception. The Culhane family, who made their fortune in the timber business, used this home as their summer retreat. In the 1930s, it was rented out as a summer guest house, and today the innkeeper, Carolyn, has once again opened the doors to visitors. The rooms have charming names: The Garden Basket Room, the Wedding Ring Room and the Raspberry Wine Room, to name a few. The Parlor Room, which includes a bay window, is accessed by double pocket doors, a characteristic feature in Victorian homes. The Bay Room, which is one of the inn's common rooms, includes a hot tub in front of a wood-burning stove.

Innkeeper(s): Carolyn and Jack. $65-85. 5 rooms, 3 with PB. Breakfast included in rates. Types of meals: Cont plus and room service. Beds: D. Cable TV, VCR, reading lamp and ceiling fan in room. Spa, bicycles, parlor games, telephone, woodstove, stereo, BBQ, yard games and hot tub on premises. Antiquing, cross-country skiing, fishing, golf, live theater, parks, shopping, tennis, water sports, horseback riding and canoe rental nearby.

Location: City. Lake Huron.

Certificate may be used: May 1-Oct. 31, Sunday-Thursday, no holidays.

Saint Clair   I10

William Hopkins Manor

613 N Riverside Ave
Saint Clair, MI 48079-5417
(810)329-0188 Fax:(810)329-6239
Internet: www.laketolake.com
E-mail: whmanor@aol.com

Circa 1876. This three-story Second Empire Victorian, encompasses 10,000 square feet and comes complete with tower, slate mansard roof, dormers, porches and an elaborate wrought iron fence. Its riverfront location across the street from the St. Clair River affords the pastime of watching freighters and barges pass by. Guest rooms feature reproductions and antiques, and some rooms have fireplaces. A billiard room and two parlors are available for relaxing. Breakfast is served family style in the dining room. The Historic St. Clair Inn, a five-minute walk away, offers an interesting dining option.

Innkeeper(s): Sharon Llewellyn & Terry Mazzarese. $80-100. 5 rooms, 1 with PB, 1 with FP. Breakfast included in rates. Types of meals: Full bkfst, veg bkfst and early coffee/tea. Beds: QD. Reading lamp and clock radio in room. Air conditioning. Fireplace and CD players on premises. Antiquing, art galleries, beach, canoeing/kayaking, fishing, golf, horseback riding, live theater, museums, parks, shopping and water sports nearby.

Location: Small town.

Publicity: *Southern Sunrise, Midwest Living, The Voice, Between the Lines, Detroit Free Press and Detroit News.*

Certificate may be used: Monday through Thursday. For other available dates, please contact innkeeper.

Saline J8

The Homestead B&B

9279 Macon Rd
Saline, MI 48176-9305
(734)429-9625

Circa 1851. The Homestead is a two-story brick farmhouse situated on 50 acres of fields, woods and river. The house has 15-inch-thick walls and is furnished with Victorian antiques and family heirlooms. This was a favorite camping spot for Native Americans while they salted their fish, and many arrowheads have been found on the farm. Activities include long walks through meadows of wildflowers and cross-country skiing in season. It is 40 minutes from Detroit and Toledo and 10 minutes from Ann Arbor.

Innkeeper(s): Shirley Grossman. $70-75. 5 rooms and 1 conference room. Breakfast and snacks/refreshments included in rates. Types of meals: Full bkfst and early coffee/tea. Beds: DT. TV and reading lamp in room. Air conditioning. VCR, telephone and fireplace on premises. Antiquing, cross-country skiing, parks, shopping and sporting events nearby.

Location: Country.

Publicity: *Ann Arbor News, Country Focus and Saline Reporter.*

"We're spoiled now and wouldn't want to stay elsewhere! No motel offers deer at dusk and dawn!"

Certificate may be used: Jan. 2-June 1, Sunday to Friday & Sept. 1-Dec. 30, Sunday to Friday.

Saugatuck I6

Bayside Inn

618 Water St Box 186
Saugatuck, MI 49453
(269)857-4321 Fax:(269)857-1870
Internet: www.baysideinn.net
E-mail: info@baysideinn.net

Circa 1926. Located on the edge of the Kalamazoo River and across from the nature observation tower, this downtown inn was once a boathouse. The common room now has a fireplace and view of the water. Each guest room has its own deck. The inn is near several restaurants, shops and beaches. Fishing for salmon, perch and trout is popular.

Innkeeper(s): Kathy Wilson. $85-250. 10 rooms with PB, 4 with FP, 4 suites and 1 conference room. Breakfast included in rates. Types of meals: Cont plus. Beds: KQ. Cable TV, VCR, reading lamp, refrigerator and telephone in room. Air conditioning. TV, fax, copier, spa and fireplace on premises. Antiquing, cross-country skiing, fishing, live theater, shopping and water sports nearby.

Location: City.

"Our stay was wonderful, more pleasant than anticipated, we were so pleased. As for breakfast, it gets our A 1 rating."

Certificate may be used: November through March, Monday through Thursday excluding holidays.

Twin Oaks Inn

PO Box 818, 227 Griffith St
Saugatuck, MI 49453-0818
(269)857-1600 (800)788-6188 Fax:(269)857-7440
E-mail: twinoaks@sirus.com

Circa 1860. This large Queen Anne Victorian inn was a boarding house for lumbermen at the turn of the century. Now an old-English-style inn, it offers a variety of lodging choices, including a

room with its own Jacuzzi. There are many diversions at Twin Oaks, including a collection of videotaped movies numbering more than 700. Guests may borrow bicycles or play horseshoes on the inn's grounds.

Innkeeper(s): Willa Lemken. $105-145. 6 rooms with PB and 1 conference room. Types of meals: Full bkfst, early coffee/tea and snacks/refreshments. Beds: KQ. Cable TV, VCR, reading lamp, stereo, clock radio, desk and hot tub/spa in room. Air conditioning. Parlor games, telephone and fireplace on premises. Antiquing, cross-country skiing, fishing, live theater, parks, shopping and water sports nearby.

Location: Downtown small village.

Certificate may be used: Nov. 1-April 30, Sunday through Thursday.

Sebewaing H9

Antique Inn

4 N. Center St.
Sebewaing, MI 48759
(989)883-9424 (888)883-9424
Internet: www.antiqueinn.com
E-mail: antique@avci.net

Circa 1895. Renovated and restored, this historic red brick building of Romanesque design is now home to the bed & breakfast upstairs and an antique store downstairs. Each spacious guest bedroom is a private hideaway with stained-glass windows and antique furnishings. Sleep late, if desired, and then enjoy a buffet breakfast served in the parlor. Bikes are available to explore the town. Ask about packages for special occasions.

Innkeeper(s): Dana Roof. $65-85. 4 rooms with PB. Breakfast and snacks/refreshments included in rates. Types of meals: Cont plus, early coffee/tea and picnic lunch. Beds: D. Modem hook-up, cable TV, VCR, reading lamp and telephone in room. Central air. Bicycles, library, child care, parlor games and gift shop on premises. Antiquing, beach, bicycling, canoeing/kayaking, cross-country skiing, fishing, golf, hiking, horseback riding, museums, parks, shopping and water sports nearby.

Location: Village.

Publicity: *Local newspapers and regional antique guides.*

Certificate may be used: Anytime, Sunday-Thursday.

South Haven J5

Old Harbor Inn

515 Williams St
South Haven, MI 49090-1480
(269)637-8480 (800)433-9210 Fax:(269)637-9496
Internet: www.oldharborinn.com
E-mail: info@oldharborinn.com

Circa 1987. Whether staying in a Harbor View, Deluxe, Grand Room or Master Suite, the hospitality, comfortable accommodations, thoughtful amenities and splendid views create a delightful nautical atmosphere at this captivating inn. Select a room with a Jacuzzi, fireplace, kitchenette, private balcony or adjoining deck. A light continental breakfast is served daily. Swim in the indoor pool and soak in the hot tub. On the inn's lower level, York's Landing serves pizza, snacks and drinks. Explore downtown or walk to the beach.

Innkeeper(s): Robin Smith. $79-249. 44 rooms with PB, 3 with FP, 6 suites. Breakfast included in rates. Types of meals: Cont. Restaurant on premises. Beds: KQT. Cable TV, VCR, reading lamp, refrigerator, ceiling fan, clock radio, telephone, coffeemaker, turn-down service, desk and fireplace in room. Air conditioning. Fax, copier, spa, child care and laundry facility on premises. Limited handicap access. Antiquing, art galleries, beach, bicycling, canoeing/kayaking, cross-country skiing, downhill skiing, fishing, golf, hiking, horseback riding, live theater, museums, parks, shopping, tennis and wineries nearby.

Location: Waterfront.

Certificate may be used: Anytime, November-April, subject to availability.

The Seymour House

1248 Blue Star Hwy
South Haven, MI 49090-9696
(269)227-3918 Fax:(269)227-3010
Internet: www.seymourhouse.com
E-mail: seymour@cybersol.com

Circa 1862. Less than half a mile from the shores of Lake Michigan, this pre-Civil War, Italianate-style home rests upon 11 acres of grounds, complete with nature trails. The Austrian Room, popular with honeymoon-ers, includes a double Jacuzzi tub. Poached pears with raspberry sauce, but-termilk blueberry pancakes and locally made sausages are a few of the items that  might appear on the breakfast menu. The inn is midway between Saugatuck and South Haven, which offer plenty of activities. Beaches, Kal-Haven Trail, shopping, horseback riding and winery tours are among the fun destination choices.

Innkeeper(s): Friedl Scimo. $85-145. 5 rooms with PB, 2 with FP and 1 cabin. Breakfast and afternoon tea included in rates. Types of meals: Full gourmet bkfst and early coffee/tea. Beds: KQD. TV, VCR, reading lamp, ceiling fan, clock radio and two with Jacuzzi in room. Air conditioning. Fax, copier, swimming, library, parlor games, telephone and fireplace on premises. Antiquing, cross-country skiing, downhill skiing, fishing, golf, live theater, parks, shopping and water sports nearby.

Location: Country setting.

Publicity: *Country and Michigan Living.*

"As one who comes from the land that invented B&Bs, I hope to say that this is a truly superb example."

Certificate may be used: Jan. 1-March 31, Monday-Thursday, holidays excluded.

Victoria Resort B&B

241 Oak St
South Haven, MI 49090-2302
(269)637-6414 (800)473-7376
Internet: www.victoriaresort.com
E-mail: info@victoriaresort.com

Circa 1925. Less than two blocks from a sandy beach, this Classical Revival inn offers many recreational opportunities for its guests, who may choose from bicycling, beach and pool swimming, basketball and tennis, among others. The inn's 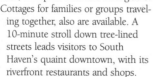 rooms provide visitors several options, including cable TV, fireplaces, whirlpool tubs and ceiling fans. Cottages for families or groups travel-ing together, also are available. A 10-minute stroll down tree-lined streets leads visitors to South Haven's quaint downtown, with its riverfront restaurants and shops.

Innkeeper(s): Bob & Jan. $59-190. 9 rooms with PB, 4 with FP, 2 suites and 7 cottages. Breakfast included in rates. Types of meals: Full bkfst. Beds: KQ. Cable TV, VCR, reading lamp, refrigerator, ceiling fan, clock radio, telephone, desk and six with whirlpool in room. Air conditioning. Fax, swimming, bicycles, tennis, library, fireplace and basketball on premises. Antiquing, cross-country skiing, downhill skiing, fishing, parks, shopping, water sports and horseback riding nearby.

Location: City.

Certificate may be used: Sept. 9-May 21.

Spring Lake   I6

Hideaway Acres, LLC

1870 Pontaluna Rd
Spring Lake, MI 49456
(231)798-7271 (800)865-3545 Fax:(231)798-6414
Internet: www.bbonline.com/mi/hideawayacres/

Circa 1979. This bed & breakfast is located on 25 acres. There is a tennis court, a whirlpool, sauna and indoor pool to keep guests busy, but travelers are welcome to simply sit and relax in front of the stone fireplace or stroll the wooded grounds. The Royal Suite is a romantic haven with a fireplace and Jacuzzi tub. Three other rooms also include Jacuzzi tubs. Although there is plenty to do at the inn, the area has many lake-related activities, shops, museums and state parks to visit.

Innkeeper(s): Debbie Stowers. $119-169. 5 rooms with PB, 1 with FP, 1 suite and 2 conference rooms. Breakfast included in rates. Types of meals: Cont, early coffee/tea and snacks/refreshments. Beds: Q. Cable TV, VCR, reading lamp, stereo, clock radio, telephone and hot tub/spa in room. Air conditioning. Fax, spa, swimming, sauna, tennis, parlor games, fireplace and indoor pool on premises. Amusement parks, antiquing, cross-country skiing, downhill skiing, fishing, golf, live theater, parks, shopping, sporting events and water sports nearby.

Publicity: *Travel News.*

Certificate may be used: Jan. 2-April 30, Nov. 1-Dec. 29, Sunday-Thursday (no holidays).

Suttons Bay   F6

Korner Kottage B&B

503 N St Josephs Ave, PO Box 174
Suttons Bay, MI 49682-0174
(231)271-2711 Fax:(231)271-2712
Internet: www.kornerkottage.com
E-mail: info@kornerkottage.com

Circa 1920. The lake stone screened porch of this restored vin-tage home reflects an idyllic quaintness. Located in a Nordic village on Leelanau Peninsula, it is within view of the bay and downtown. Relax in an inviting living room. Cheery guest bed-rooms are clean and crisp with ironed bed linens. Enjoy a hearty breakfast in the dining room before taking a short walk to the public beach or unique shops.

Innkeeper(s): Sharon Sutterfield. $120-155. 3 rooms with PB. Types of meals: Full bkfst. Beds: KQ. Cable TV, refrigerator and refrigerator in room. Air conditioning. TV and telephone on premises. Antiquing, art galleries, beach, golf, live theater, shopping, casinos, dining, marina and National Parks nearby.

Publicity: *The Detroit News.*

"Thank you very much for making our stay here in your home a very pleasant experience."

Certificate may be used: November through March, holidays excluded and Dec. 22 through Jan. 2.

Union Pier   J5

Pine Garth Inn

PO Box 347, 15970 Lake Shore Dr
Union Pier, MI 49129-0347
(269)469-1642 Fax:(269)469-0418
Internet: www.pinegarth.com
E-mail: relax@pinegarth.com

Circa 1905. The seven rooms and five guest cottages at this charming bed & breakfast inn are decorated in a country style and each boasts something special. Some have a private deck

and a wall of windows that look out to Lake Michigan. Other rooms feature items such as an unusual twig canopy bed, and several have whirlpool tubs. The deluxe cottages offer two queen-size beds, a wood-burning fireplace, VCR, cable TV and an outdoor tub on a private deck with a gas grill. Rates vary for the cottages. The inn has its own private beach and there are sand dunes, vineyards, forests and miles of beaches in the area.

Innkeeper(s): Nessa & Denise. $140-205. 7 rooms with PB, 1 with FP and 5 guest houses. Breakfast included in rates. Types of meals: Full gourmet bkfst, afternoon tea and snacks/refreshments. Beds: Q. VCR, reading lamp, ceiling fan and clock radio in room. TV, fax, copier, swimming, bicycles, library, parlor games, telephone and fireplace on premises. Shopping nearby.

Location: Waterfront.

Publicity: *Midwest Living, St. Louis News and Channel 16 South Bend.*

"Your warm and courteous reception, attentiveness and helpfulness will never be forgotten."

Certificate may be used: Nov. 1 to May 15, Sunday through Thursday, excluding holidays.

The Inn at Union Pier

PO Box 222, 9708 Berrien Street
Union Pier, MI 49129-0222
(269)469-4700 Fax:(269)469-4720
Internet: www.innatunionpier.com
E-mail: theinn@qtm.net

Circa 1920. Set on a shady acre across a country road from Lake Michigan, this inn features unique Swedish ceramic wood-burning fireplaces, a hot tub and sauna, a veranda ringing the house and a large common room with comfortable overstuffed furniture and a grand piano. Rooms offer such amenities as private balconies and porches, whirlpools, views of the English garden and furniture dating from the early 1900s. Breakfast includes fresh fruit and homemade jams made of fruit from surrounding farms.

Innkeeper(s): Bill & Joyce Jann. $155-230. 16 rooms with PB, 12 with FP, 2 with HT, 2 suites and 1 conference room. Breakfast and snacks/refreshments included in rates. Types of meals: Full gourmet bkfst and early coffee/tea. Beds: KQT. Ceiling fan, clock radio, telephone and wood-burning fireplace in room. Air conditioning. VCR, fax, copier, spa, swimming, sauna, bicycles, library, parlor games and fireplace on premises. Handicap access. Antiquing, art galleries, bicycling, cross-country skiing, hiking, parks, sporting events, water sports, wineries and wine tasting nearby.

Location: Lake Michigan.

Publicity: *Chicago, Midwest Living, W, Country Living, Travel & Leisure, Bride's, Chicago Tribune, "Chicagoing" on WLS-TV and Romantic-Inns-The Travel Channel.*

"The food, the atmosphere, the accommodations, and of course, the entire staff made this the most relaxing weekend ever."

Certificate may be used: Oct. 1-May 25, Sunday through Thursday only, no holidays.

Wakefield   D2

Regal Country Inn

1602 E Hwy 2
Wakefield, MI 49968-9581
(906)229-5122 Fax:(906)229-5755
Internet: www.regalcountryinn.com
E-mail: regalinn@charterinternet.com

Circa 1973. Choose from four types of accommodations at this quaint, smoke-free bed & breakfast. Historical rooms feature antique furnishings, scrapbooks and literature documenting nearby towns. Relax on rocker/recliners in a comfortable study bedroom. The Victorians include quilt-topped beds. Country rooms are ideal for families. Savor treats from the 1950s as well as a limited menu and delicious desserts at the inn's Old Tyme Ice Cream Parlour and Soda Fountain. Room service and meals are offered for an added charge. Gather for conversation in the Fireside Room. Hike, fish, ski, golf, snowmobile, visit waterfalls and lighthouses in this scenic Upper Peninsula region. Cultural events and local festivals are held throughout the year.

Innkeeper(s): Richard Swanson. $45-139. 18 rooms with PB. Breakfast included in rates. Types of meals: Cont, early coffee/tea, picnic lunch, afternoon tea, dinner and room service. Restaurant on premises. Beds: QD. Cable TV, VCR and reading lamp in room. Central air. Fax, copier, sauna, bicycles, parlor games and fireplace on premises. Antiquing, art galleries, beach, bicycling, canoeing/kayaking, cross-country skiing, downhill skiing, fishing, golf, hiking, horseback riding, live theater, museums, parks, shopping and tennis nearby.

Location: City. On the edge of the old mining and logging community of Wakefield, the western gateway to the Porcupine Mountains Wilderness State Park.

Publicity: *Detroit Free Press.*

"Thanks for all your efforts in making our stay here wonderful. What a delightful inn! This is my first time staying at a B&B and I'm hooked! The town is a real gem, too. You are a great host and truly know how to keep your guests happy."

Certificate may be used: Jan. 1-March 15, Sunday-Thursday only. Nov. 25-Dec. 25, Sunday-Thursday only. Not available July 1-6. Other times, anytime subject to availability. Cannot be used with any other discounts. Only one discount per stay.

Walloon Lake   E7

Masters House B&B

2253 N Shore Dr
Walloon Lake, MI 49796
(231)535-2227
Internet: www.sphills.com

Circa 1890. This bed & breakfast once served as the location for the town's first telephone company. There are six comfortably decorated rooms, two with private bath. The home is within walking distance of the beach, shops and restaurants in town.

Innkeeper(s): Joe Breidenstein. $60-120. 6 rooms, 2 with PB and 1 cottage. Breakfast included in rates. Types of meals: Cont plus. Beds: KQDT. Reading lamp and clock radio in room. VCR and telephone on premises. Antiquing, cross-country skiing, downhill skiing, fishing, live theater, water sports, snowmobiling and hunting (game and mushrooms) nearby.

Location: Resort village.

Certificate may be used: Anytime, subject to availability, midweek most likely.

West Bloomfield I9

The Wren's Nest Bed & Breakfast

7405 West Maple Rd.
West Bloomfield, MI 48322
(248)624-6874 Fax:(248) 624-9869
Internet: www.thewrensnestbb.com
E-mail: thewrensnest@comcast.net

Circa 1840. Stay at this delightful farmhouse adjacent to a woodland in a country setting. It is surrounded by professionally landscaped grounds that are accented by numerous birdhouses created by the innkeeper, a plethora of perennial and annual flower beds and a heritage vegetable garden with more than 60 varieties of heirloom tomatoes. Watch TV by the fire or play piano in the living room. Relax on one of the two sun porches. Feel at home in one of the comfortable guest bedrooms. Start each morning with a full-course breakfast made from scratch with fresh ingredients and no preservatives. Personal dietary needs are accommodated with advance notice. This historic bed and breakfast is available for special events, adult or children's tea gatherings and other parties.

Innkeeper(s): Irene Scheel. $95-115. 6 rooms, 3 with PB, 1 guest house and 1 conference room. Breakfast, afternoon tea and snacks/refreshments included in rates. Types of meals: Full gourmet bkfst, veg bkfst and room service. Beds: KQDT. Modem hook-up, data port, cable TV, VCR, reading lamp, stereo, refrigerator, ceiling fan, snack bar, clock radio, telephone, coffeemaker, turn-down service, desk, voice mail and fireplace in room. Central air. Fax, copier, library, laundry facility, heirloom vegetables in the summer and pygmy goats on premises. Limited handicap access. Antiquing, art galleries, beach, bicycling, cross-country skiing, downhill skiing, fishing, golf, hiking, horseback riding, live theater, museums, parks, shopping, sporting events, tennis, water sports, theatres and malls nearby.

Location: City, country.

Publicity: *Detroit News, The West Bloomfield Eccentric, Midwest Living, Japanese Free Press and WDIV 4 Detroit.*

Certificate may be used: Anytime, Sunday-Thursday.

Whitehall H5

White Swan Inn

303 S Mears Ave
Whitehall, MI 49461-1323
(231)894-5169 (888)948-7926
Internet: www.whiteswaninn.com
E-mail: info@whiteswaninn.com

Circa 1884. Maple trees shade this sturdy Queen Anne home, a block from White Lake. A screened porch filled with white wicker and an upstairs coffee room are leisurely retreats.

Parquet floors in the dining room, antique furnishings and chandeliers add to the comfortable decor. Chicken and broccoli quiche is a favorite breakfast recipe. Cross the street for summer theater or walk to shops and restaurants nearby.

Innkeeper(s): Cathy & Ron Russell. $95-155. 4 rooms with PB, 2 with FP. Breakfast and snacks/refreshments included in rates. Types of meals: Full bkfst and early coffee/tea. Beds: KQDT. Cable TV, VCR, reading lamp, ceiling fan, clock radio, desk, fireplace and one suite with whirlpool tub in room. Air conditioning. Fax, copier, parlor games, telephone, gift shop and beverage center on premises. Amusement parks, antiquing, art galleries, beach, bicycling, canoeing/kayaking, cross-country skiing, fishing, golf, hiking, horseback riding, live theater, museums, parks, shopping, sporting events, tennis, water sports, thoroughbred racing and seasonal festivals nearby.

Location: Small resort town.

Publicity: *White Lake Beacon, Muskegon Chronicle, Michigan Travel Ideas, Bed, Breakfast and Bike Midwest, Book of Lists, Arrington's B&B Journal, Cookbook-Great Lakes, Great Breakfasts, WKAR TV - "Best of Bed & Breakfast," Cookbook-Inn Time for Breakfast and Voted by inngoers-Best in the Midwest 2003.*

"What a great place to gather with old friends and relive past fun times and create new ones."

Certificate may be used: Jan. 5-Dec. 15, Sunday-Thursday.

Ypsilanti J8

Parish House Inn

103 S Huron St
Ypsilanti, MI 48197-5421
(734)480-4800 (800)480-4866 Fax:(734)480-7472
Internet: www.parishhouseinn.com
E-mail: parishinn@aol.com

Circa 1893. This Queen Anne Victorian was named in honor of its service as a parsonage for the First Congregational Church. The home remained a parsonage for more than 50 years after its construction and then served as a church office and Sunday school building. It was moved to its present site in Ypsilanti's historic district in the late 1980s. The rooms are individually decorated with Victorian-style wallpapers and antiques. One guest room includes a two-person Jacuzzi tub. Those in search of a late-night snack need only venture into the kitchen to find drinks and the cookie jar. For special occasions, the innkeepers can arrange trays with flowers, non-alcoholic champagne, chocolates, fruit or cheese. The terrace overlooks the Huron River.

Innkeeper(s): Mrs. Chris Mason. $95-150. 8 rooms with PB, 3 with FP and 1 conference room. Breakfast and snacks/refreshments included in rates. Types of meals: Full gourmet bkfst, early coffee/tea, picnic lunch and afternoon tea. Beds: QDT. Cable TV, VCR, reading lamp, ceiling fan, clock radio, telephone and desk in room. Air conditioning. Fax, library, parlor games and fireplace on premises. Handicap access. Amusement parks, antiquing, cross-country skiing, fishing, live theater, parks, shopping, sporting events and water sports nearby.

Location: City.

Publicity: *Detroit Free Press and Midwest Living.*

Certificate may be used: December through May, Sunday through Thursday.

Minnesota

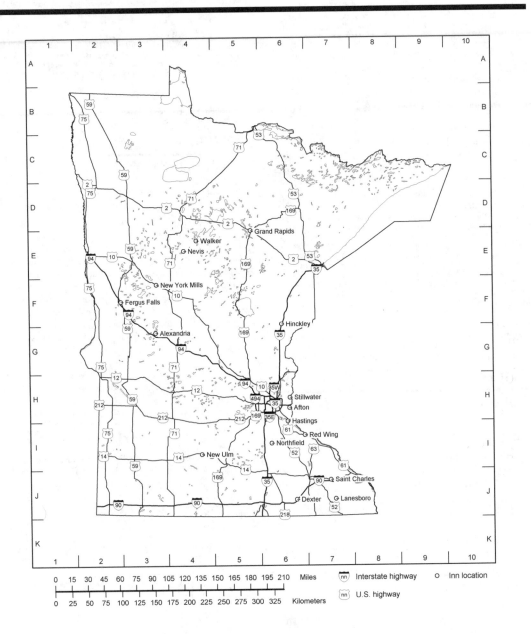

Miles		
0 15 30 45 60 75 90 105 120 135 150 165 180 195 210		

Kilometers		
0 25 50 75 100 125 150 175 200 225 250 275 300 325		

[nn] Interstate highway   o Inn location

[nn] U.S. highway

Afton   H6

The Historic Afton House Inn

PO Box 326
Afton, MN 55001
(651)436-8883 (877)436-8883 Fax:(651)436-6859
Internet: www.aftonhouseinn.com
E-mail: reservations@aftonhouseinn.com

Circa 1867. Located on two acres of waterfront on the St.
Croix River, this historic inn reflects an old New England-style
architecture. Guest rooms offer Jacuzzi tubs, fireplaces, waterfront balconies and are decorated with
American country antiques. A
restaurant on the premises provides candlelight dining in the
Wheel Room. (Ask for Banana
Foster, or any flaming dessert—
a house specialty.) Or you
might prefer to dine in the Catfish Saloon & Cafe, which has a
more casual menu. Champagne Brunch cruises are offered on
the Grand Duchess May-October. Three charter vessels are
available for private cruises for weddings, birthdays, anniversaries, corporate getaways or for groups of 10-350. Visit the
inn's web site for online availability.

Innkeeper(s): Gordy & Kathy Jarvis. $65-275. 25 rooms with PB, 19 with
FP, 3 total suites, including 2 two-bedroom suites and 2 conference rooms.
Breakfast included in rates. Types of meals: Full bkfst, Sun. brunch, gourmet
lunch, gourmet dinner and room service. Restaurant on premises. Beds: KQ.
Modem hook-up, data port, cable TV, VCR, ceiling fan, clock radio, telephone, desk, hot tub/spa and most with gas fireplace in room. Central air.
Fax, copier, spa and gift shop on premises. Handicap access. Antiquing, art
galleries, beach, bicycling, cross-country skiing, downhill skiing, fishing, golf,
hiking, horseback riding, live theater, museums, parks, shopping, tennis,
water sports and wineries nearby.

Location: Country.

Publicity: *St. Paul Pioneer Press, Woodbury Bulletin, Hudson Star Observer
and Stillwater Gazette.*

Certificate may be used: Anytime, Sunday-Thursday.

Alexandria   G3

Cedar Rose Inn

422 7th Ave W
Alexandria, MN 56308
(320)762-8430 (888)203-5333 Fax:(320)762-8044
Internet: www.cedarroseinn.com
E-mail: aggie@cedarroseinn.com

Circa 1903. Diamond-paned windows, gables, a wraparound
porch with a swing for two and stained glass enhance the exteri-
or of this handsome three-story Tudor Revival home in the
National Register. Located in what was once referred to as the
"Silk Stocking District," the home was built by the town's mayor.
Arched doorways, Tiffany chandeliers, a glorious open staircase,
maple floors and oak woodwork set the atmosphere. There's a
library, a formal dining room and a parlor with fireplace and window seat. Request the Noah P. Ward room and enjoy the king-
size bed and double whirlpool with mood lights for a special celebration. Wake to the aroma of freshly baked caramel rolls,
scones or cinnamon buns. Entrees of sausage and quiche are
favorites. In the evening, enjoy watching the sunset over Lake
Winona. Private hiking trails are available for guests or enjoy a
day of lake activities, shopping, antiquing or horseback riding.

Innkeeper(s): Aggie & Florian Ledermann. $85-140. 4 rooms with PB, 1 with

FP, 2 suites. Breakfast and snacks/refreshments included in rates. Types of
meals: Full bkfst, early coffee/tea, picnic lunch, afternoon tea and room service. Beds: KQ. Reading lamp, CD player, refrigerator, clock radio, desk and
fireplace in room. Central air. Sauna, library, parlor games and telephone on
premises. Antiquing, beach, bicycling, canoeing/kayaking, cross-country skiing, downhill skiing, fishing, golf, hiking, horseback riding, live theater, museums, parks, shopping, tennis, water sports and wineries nearby.

Location: City.

*"The Cedar Rose Inn was more than we imagined it would be. We
felt like royalty in your beautiful dining room."*

Certificate may be used: Anytime, subject to availability.

Dexter   J6

Ice Haus B&B

65150 220th St
Dexter, MN 55926
(507)584-0101 (888)ICE-HAUS Fax:(507)584-2260
Internet: www.icehaus.com
E-mail: icehaus@icehaus.com

Circa 1995. Part of a 22-acre working farm complex boasting
an historic barn, the contemporary main house was built using
environmentally safe methods and materials. Family heirlooms
accent modern furnishings. Enjoy self-serve tea and evening
snacks. Guest bedrooms feature terry robes to lounge in comfort. Ask for the romantic Bridal Suite with two-person
whirlpool tub. Breakfast may include the popular Ice Haus
Skillet made with eggs, cheese, potatoes, mixed vegetables and
country gravy. Explore the wooded grounds with a creek,
wildlife sanctuary and wildflower-filled meadow.

Innkeeper(s): Shirley & Mike Adams. $65-125. 4 rooms with PB. Breakfast,
afternoon tea and snacks/refreshments included in rates. Types of meals: Full
gourmet bkfst, veg bkfst, early coffee/tea, picnic lunch and gourmet dinner.
Beds: KQD. Data port, cable TV, VCR, reading lamp, clock radio and turn-
down service in room. Central air. Fax, copier, telephone, fireplace and gift
shop on premises. Handicap access. Antiquing, bicycling, cross-country skiing, golf, horseback riding, museums, parks, shopping and tennis nearby.

Location: Country.

Certificate may be used: Anytime, subject to availability.

Fergus Falls   F3

Bakketopp Hus

20517 Hillcrest Rd
Fergus Falls, MN 56537-9649
(218)739-2915 (800)739-2915
E-mail: ddn@prtel.com

Circa 1976. From the decks of this wooded home, guests can
enjoy the scenery of Long Lake and catch glimpses of wildlife.
Antiques, handmade quilts and down comforters decorate the
cozy guest rooms. Guest accommodations include one room
with a private spa and one with a draped canopy bed. Another
room is near a fireplace. A bounty of nearby outdoor activities
are sure to please nature lovers. Antique shops and restaurants
are nearby.

Innkeeper(s): Dennis & Judy Nims. $75-110. 3 rooms with PB. Breakfast,
afternoon tea and snacks/refreshments included in rates. Types of meals: Full
gourmet bkfst and early coffee/tea. Beds: Q. Reading lamp, clock radio, desk
and hot tub/spa in room. Central air. TV, VCR, parlor games, telephone and
fireplace on premises. Amusement parks, antiquing, cross-country skiing,
fishing, live theater, parks, shopping and water sports nearby.

Location: Waterfront.

Publicity: *Minneapolis Tribune and Minnesota Monthly.*

Certificate may be used: Sunday through Thursday for months of March,
November, December, January, February.

Grand Rapids   E5

Morning Glory Bed and Breakfast

726 NW 2nd Ave
Grand Rapids, MN 55744
(218)326-3978 (866)926-3978
Internet: www.morningglorybandb.com
E-mail: morningglory@grandrapids-mn.com

Circa 1960. The many activities of downtown are just a few blocks away from this comfortable two-story brick bed and breakfast. Relax by the wood-burning fireplace in the living room that also has a piano, library, game area and terrace door leading to a private patio with a garden fountain. Cookies and beverages are always available. On the weekends wine and appetizers are also served. Each air-conditioned guest suite features a sitting room. The romantic Champagne and Roses Suite includes a two-person whirlpool and two-sided gas fireplace. In the cheery breakfast room continental-plus fare is offered weekdays and a three-course meal is served on weekends. Play championship golf, hike the Mesabi Trail or take a drive through the Chippewa National Forest on the Edge of the Wilderness Scenic Byway.

Innkeeper(s): Karen and Ron Herbig. $80-120. 4 rooms, 2 with FP, 4 suites. Breakfast and snacks/refreshments included in rates. Types of meals: Full gourmet bkfst, veg bkfst, early coffee/tea and dinner. Beds: QD. Modem hook-up, cable TV, VCR, reading lamp, CD player, ceiling fan, clock radio, telephone, desk, hot tub/spa and fireplace in room. Central air. Copier, library and parlor games on premises. Antiquing, art galleries, beach, bicycling, canoeing/kayaking, cross-country skiing, fishing, golf, hiking, live theater, museums, parks, shopping, tennis and water sports nearby.
Location: City.
Certificate may be used: Anytime, November-March, subject to availability.

Hastings   H6

Thorwood & Rosewood Historic Inns

315 Pine St
Hastings, MN 55033-1137
(651)437-3297 (888)846-7966 Fax:(651)437-4129
Internet: www.thorwoodinn.com
E-mail: mrthorwood@aol.com

Circa 1880. This Queen Anne Victorian has several verandas and porches. Grained cherry woodwork and fireplaces add elegance to the inn. All but two of the 15 rooms have fireplaces. In the Mississippi Under the Stars Room, a skylight shines down on the teak whirlpool tub. This 900-square-foot suite features tapestries, paisleys and a copper soaking tub as well as a round shower. The innkeepers serve a formal, five-course afternoon tea on Wednesday and Sundays, which guests can enjoy with a prior reservation.

Innkeeper(s): Dick & Pam Thorsen. $97-277. 14 rooms with PB, 12 with FP, 3 suites and 3 conference rooms. Breakfast and snacks/refreshments included in rates. Types of meals: Full bkfst, early coffee/tea, gourmet lunch, picnic lunch, gourmet dinner and room service. Beds: QDT. TV, VCR, reading lamp, stereo, refrigerator, snack bar, telephone, desk and fireplace in room. Central air. Fax, copier, library, parlor games, fireplace, laundry facility and gift shop on premises. Handicap access. Amusement parks, antiquing, cross-country skiing, downhill skiing, golf, live theater, shopping, sporting events, nine hole golf course and mall of America nearby.
Location: Small town.
Publicity: *Travel Holiday, Midwest Living and Glamour.*
Certificate may be used: Nov. 1-Sept. 30, Sunday-Thursday except holidays.

Hinckley   F6

Dakota Lodge B&B

40497 Hwy 48
Hinckley, MN 55037-9418
(320)384-6052
Internet: www.dakotalodge.com
E-mail: daklodge@pinenet.com

Circa 1976. Designed for comfort and privacy on six scenic acres, the lodge boasts a rustic exterior and a gracious interior. Well-appointed guest bedrooms feature whirlpool tubs and fireplaces. A graciously furnished two-bedroom cottage also is available. Start the day with a satisfying breakfast. A variety of nearby activities include a 32-mile bike trail, casino and antique shops.
Innkeeper(s): Sue Davidson, Steve Johnson. $89-145. 5 rooms with PB, 4 with FP and 1 cottage. Breakfast included in rates. Types of meals: Full bkfst and early coffee/tea. Beds: KQ. Reading lamp and ceiling fan in room. Air conditioning. VCR, fax, copier, library, parlor games, telephone and fireplace on premises. Antiquing, cross-country skiing, fishing, parks and water sports nearby.
Location: Country.
Certificate may be used: All year, Sunday-Thursday, excluding holidays. Subject to availability.

Lanesboro   J7

Stone Mill Suites

PO Box 407
Lanesboro, MN 55949
(507)467-8663 (866)897-8663 Fax:(507)467-2470
Internet: www.stonemillsuites.com
E-mail: stonemillsuites@hotmail.com

Circa 1885. Combining a historical heritage with modern conveniences, this nineteenth-century stone building was built using limestone quarried from the area's surrounding bluffs. The original clay ceilings and stair railings accent the decor. Themed suites and guest bedrooms reflect local history and its undeniable charm. Relaxing amenities feature a fireplace, whirlpool tub, microwave and refrigerator. Children are welcome, ask about family packages. A generous continental breakfast may include English muffins, bakery items from Lanesboro Pasteries, cereal, fruit, beverages and French toast topped with strawberries, blueberries and whipped cream. A variety of museums and the Laura Ingalls Wilder Site are all within a 30-minute drive.
$80-140. 10 rooms with PB, 4 with FP, 7 suites. Breakfast included in rates. Types of meals: Cont plus and early coffee/tea. Beds: KQDT. Modem hook-up, data port, cable TV, VCR, reading lamp, refrigerator, ceiling fan, clock radio, telephone, coffeemaker, desk, hot tub/spa, fireplace and microwave in room. Air conditioning. Fax and parlor games on premises. Handicap access. Antiquing, art galleries, bicycling, canoeing/kayaking, cross-country skiing, fishing, golf, hiking, live theater, museums, parks, shopping and wineries nearby.
Location: Historic Bluff Country.
Publicity: *MN Monthly, Midwest Getaway, Wisconsin State Journal and Minneapolis Star Tribune.*
Certificate may be used: Anytime, Sunday-Thursday.

Nevis   E4

The Park Street Inn

106 Park St
Nevis, MN 56467-9704
(218)652-4500 (800)797-1778
Internet: www.parkstreetinn.com
E-mail: psi@eot.com

Circa 1912. This late Victorian home was built by one of Minnesota's many Norwegian immigrants, a prominent business-

man. He picked an ideal spot for the home, which overlooks Lake Belle Taine and sits across from a town park. The suite includes an all-season porch and a double whirlpool tub. The Grotto Room, a new addition, offers an oversize whirlpool and a waterfall. Oak lamposts light the foyer, and the front parlor is highlighted by a Mission oak fireplace. Homemade fare such as waffles, pancakes, savory meats, egg dishes and French toast are served during the inn's daily country breakfast. Bicyclists will appreciate the close access to the Heartland Bike Trail, just half a block away.
Innkeeper(s): Irene & Len Hall. $75-125. 4 rooms with PB, 1 suite. Breakfast included in rates. Types of meals: Full bkfst, early coffee/tea and picnic lunch. Beds: KQD. Reading lamp and hot tub/spa in room. VCR, spa, bicycles, library, telephone and fireplace on premises. Amusement parks, antiquing, cross-country skiing, fishing, golf, parks, shopping and water sports nearby.
Location: Small town.

"Our favorite respite in the Heartland, where the pace is slow, hospitality is great and food is wonderful."
Certificate may be used: Sept. 15 to May 15, anytime, except holidays.

New Ulm 14

Deutsche Strasse (German Street) B&B
404 South German Street
New Ulm, MN 56073
(507)354-2005 (866)226-9856
Internet: www.deutschestrasse.com
E-mail: info@deutschestrasse.com

Overlooking the Minnesota River Valley, this stately 1884 home located in the historic district blends Craftsman or Arts and Crafts architecture with a Victorian flair. Common rooms offer a variety of relaxing settings. Play games in the formal dining room, watch the fish in the huge aquarium, sit by the candlelit fireplace in the living room, or play the piano in the Welcome Room. Guest bedrooms exude Old World charm and are furnished with antiques and decorative accents. Breakfast is served on fine crystal and china in the All-Season Sun Porch. Accompanied by the inn's special blend coffee, signature dishes may include homemade granola, German sautéed apples with cinnamon-swirl French toast and Deutsche Strasse Potato Hash.
Innkeeper(s): Gary and Ramona Sonnenberg. Call for rates. Call inn for details.
Certificate may be used: Anytime, November-March, subject to availability.

New York Mills F3

Whistle Stop Inn B&B
107 E Nowell
New York Mills, MN 56567-9704
(218)385-2223 (800)328-6315
Internet: www.whistlestopbedandbreakfast.com
E-mail: whistlestop@wcta.net

Circa 1903. A choo-choo theme permeates the atmosphere at this signature Victorian home. Antiques and railroad memorabilia decorate guest rooms with names such as Great Northern or Burlington Northern. The Northern Pacific room includes a bath with a clawfoot tub. For something unusual, try a night in the beautifully restored 19th-century Pullman dining car. It is paneled in mahogany and features floral carpeting as well as a double whirlpool, TV, VCR, refrigerator and fireplace. A caboose

offers a queen-size Murphy bed, whirlpool, TV, VCR and refrigerator. A second Pullman car with the same amenities has just been added and it features a gas-burning fireplace.
Innkeeper(s): Roger & Jann Lee. $75-140. 5 rooms with PB. Breakfast included in rates. Types of meals: Full bkfst, early coffee/tea and afternoon tea. Beds: QD. Cable TV, reading lamp, refrigerator, ceiling fan, clock radio, telephone, desk, hot tub/spa and microwave in room. Bicycles on premises. Antiquing, cross-country skiing, golf, parks, shopping, tennis, snow-mobiling trails and cultural center nearby.
Publicity: USA Weekend, Minneapolis Tribune, Fargo Forum, ABC-Fargo, WDAY, Fargo, Channel 14 and Fergus Falls.
Certificate may be used: Year-round, Sunday-Thursday, excluding holidays.

Northfield 16

Archer House
212 Division St S
Northfield, MN 55057-2074
(507)645-5661 (800)247-2235 Fax:(507)645-4295
Internet: www.archerhouse.com
E-mail: guestservice@archerhouse.com

Circa 1877. Archer House is a stunning historic hotel, featuring impressive French Second Empire architecture. The hotel has been serving guests for more than a century, and the most recent restorations including rebuilding the front portico, constructed by looking at old pictures of the hotel. Many rooms offer whirlpool or clawfoot tubs, and some offer a view of the Cannon River. Northfield has many attractions, its historical society museum is located in a former bank. It was at this bank that infamous Jesse James' criminal career came to an abrupt halt; his robbery attempt thwarted by local townsfolk.
Innkeeper(s): Laurie Hatfield - Director of Guest Services. $75-140. 36 rooms with PB, 2 two-bedroom suites. Types of meals: Early coffee/tea and room service. Restaurant on premises. Beds: QDT. Cable TV, ceiling fan, telephone, desk, suites have whirlpool and home-baked cookies in room. Air conditioning. VCR, fax, copier, two distinctive restaurants, charming coffee cafe, beauty salon, comfortable lounge and unique retail shops on premises. Antiquing, cross-country skiing, golf, live theater, parks, tennis, bike trail, shopping, college sporting events, library, historical society museum and the grand event center nearby.
Certificate may be used: Anytime, Sunday-Thursday, November, December, January.

Red Wing 16

The Candlelight Inn
818 W 3rd St
Red Wing, MN 55066-2205
(651)388-8034 (800)254-9194
Internet: www.candlelightinn-redwing.com
E-mail: info@candlelightinn-redwing.com

Circa 1877. Listed in the Minnesota historic register, this modified Italianate Victorian was built by a prominent Red Wing businessman. The interior woodwork of Candlelight Inn is an impressive sight. Butternut, cherry, oak and walnut combine throughout the house to create the rich parquet floors and stunning grand staircase. A crackling fire in the library welcomes guests and its leather furnishings and wide selection of books make this a great location for relaxation. The wrap-around-screened porch offers comfortable wicker furnishings. Each of the guest rooms includes a fireplace, and three rooms also feature a whirlpool tub. Homemade scones, fresh peaches with custard sauce and wild rice quiche are some of the gourmet breakfast dishes. The Mississippi River town of Red

Wing features many historic homes and buildings, as well as shops, restaurants and the restored Sheldon Theater. Hiking and biking trails are nearby, as well as Treasure Island Casino.

Innkeeper(s): Lynette and Zig Gudrais. $109-199. 5 rooms with PB, 5 with FP. Breakfast and snacks/refreshments included in rates. Types of meals: Full bkfst, early coffee/tea and picnic lunch. Beds: Q. Reading lamp, clock radio and hot tub/spa in room. Air conditioning. Library, parlor games, telephone and fireplace on premises. Antiquing, bicycling, cross-country skiing, downhill skiing, golf, hiking, live theater, museums, parks, shopping, water sports, wineries and casino nearby.

Location: City.

Publicity: *Minnesota Monthly and Minneapolis-St. Paul Magazine.*

"Thanks very much for a very enjoyable stay. Your hospitality is wonderful and the breakfasts were the highlight of the wonderful meals we enjoyed this weekend. Thank you for sharing the history of this home and providing all the interesting suggestions of things to do and see in the area. A return visit will be a must!"

Certificate may be used: Nov. 1 to May 31, anytime, Sunday-Thursday.

Saint Charles   J7

Victorian Lace Inn B&B and Tea Room

1512 Whitewater Ave
Saint Charles, MN 55972-1234
(507)932-4496
Internet: www.bluffcountry.com
E-mail: viclaceskv@prodigy.net

Circa 1869. This newly restored brick Victorian features a pleasant front porch where guests often linger to watch an occasional Amish buggy pass by. Lace curtains and antique furnishings are features of the guest rooms.

Innkeeper(s): Sharon Vreeman. $75-85. 4 rooms. Breakfast included in rates. Types of meals: Full gourmet bkfst, early coffee/tea, gourmet lunch, afternoon tea and gourmet dinner. Beds: QD. Reading lamp and clock in room. Air conditioning. Library, parlor games and telephone on premises. Antiquing, cross-country skiing, fishing, golf, live theater, parks, shopping, tennis and water sports nearby.

"They have thought of everything."

Certificate may be used: January-December, Sunday-Thursday, except holidays.

Stillwater   H6

Cover Park Manor

15330 58th St N
Stillwater, MN 55082-6508
(651)430-9292 (877)430-9292 Fax:(651)430-0034
Internet: www.coverpark.com
E-mail: coverpark@coverpark.com

Circa 1850. Cover Park, a historic Victorian home, rests adjacent to its namesake park on an acre of grounds. Two guest rooms offer a view of the park and the St. Croix River. Each room includes a fireplace and a whirlpool tub. Amenities include items such as refrigerators, stereos and TVs. In addition to the whirlpool and fireplace, Adell's Suite includes a king-size white iron bed, a sitting room and a private porch. Breakfasts include fresh fruit, one-half-dozen varieties of freshly baked pastries and special entrees. The manor is one mile from historic Stillwater's main street.

Innkeeper(s): Chuck & Judy Dougherty. $95-195. 4 rooms with PB, 4 with FP, 2 suites. Breakfast and snacks/refreshments included in rates. Types of meals: Full gourmet bkfst, early coffee/tea, picnic lunch, afternoon tea and room service. Beds: KQ. Cable TV, reading lamp, stereo, refrigerator, clock radio, telephone, desk and hot tub/spa in room. Air conditioning. Fax, copier, parlor games and fireplace on premises. Handicap access. Amusement parks, antiquing, cross-country skiing, downhill skiing, fishing, golf, live theater,

parks, shopping, sporting events, tennis and water sports nearby.

Publicity: *Pioneer Press, Star Tribune, Country Magazine and Courier.*

Certificate may be used: Jan. 2-Aug. 15, Monday-Thursday, not on holidays.

James A. Mulvey Residence Inn

622 W Churchill
Stillwater, MN 55082
(651)430-8008 (800)820-8008
Internet: www.jamesmulveyinn.com
E-mail: truettldem@aol.com

Circa 1878. A charming river town is home to this Italianate-style inn, just a short distance from the Twin Cities, but far from the metro area in atmosphere. Visitors select from seven guest rooms, many decorated Victorian style. The three suites have Southwest, Art Deco or Country French themes, and there are double Jacuzzi tubs and fireplaces. The inn, just nine blocks from the St. Croix River, is a popular stop for couples celebrating anniversaries. Guests enjoy early coffee or tea service that precedes the full breakfasts. A handsome great room in the vine-covered Carriage House invites relaxation. Antiquing, fishing and skiing are nearby, and there are many picnic spots in the area.

Innkeeper(s): Truett & Jill Lawson. $179-219. 7 rooms with PB, 7 with FP, 3 suites. Breakfast and afternoon tea included in rates. Types of meals: Full gourmet bkfst and early coffee/tea. Beds: QD. Reading lamp, clock radio, hot tub/spa and double whirlpool Jacuzzi tubs in room. Air conditioning. Bicycles, parlor games and telephone on premises. Antiquing, cross-country skiing, downhill skiing, fishing, live theater, parks, shopping, water sports and Mall of America nearby.

Location: City.

Publicity: *Cover of Christian B&B Directory and Bungalow Magazine.*

Certificate may be used: Anytime, Sunday-Thursday.

Walker   E4

Peacecliff

7361 Breezy Point Road NW
Walker, MN 56484-9579
(218)547-2832

Circa 1957. Innkeepers Dave and Kathy Laursen are Minnesota natives, and after years away, returned to their home state and opened this serene, waterfront B&B. The English Tudor affords views of Lake Leech from most of its rooms, which are decorated with a mix of traditional and Victorian furnishings. The Laursens are nature lovers, having trekked across miles of mountain trails and scenic areas. They are happy to point out nearby recreation sites, including the North Country Trail, a 68-mile journey through Chippewa National Forest. There are also 150 miles of paved bike trails to enjoy.

Innkeeper(s): Dave & Kathy Laursen. $65-125. 5 rooms, 2 with PB, 1 with FP, 1 suite. Breakfast included in rates. Types of meals: Full gourmet bkfst, early coffee/tea and gourmet dinner. Beds: KQDT. Reading lamp and clock radio in room. VCR, telephone and fireplace on premises. Amusement parks, antiquing, cross-country skiing, fishing, live theater, parks, shopping, water sports and bike trails nearby.

Location: Waterfront.

Certificate may be used: Sunday-Thursday, except holidays.

Mississippi

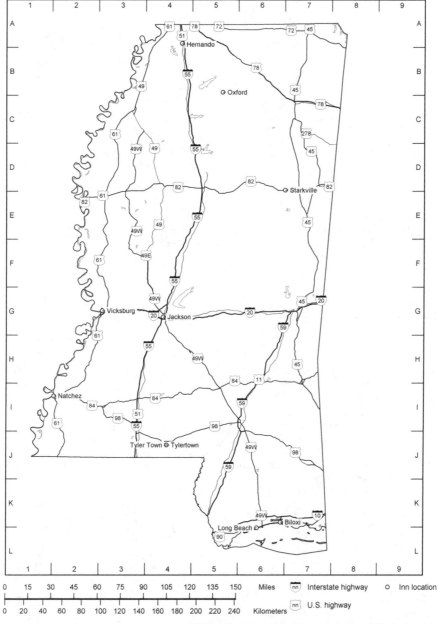

1	2	3	4	5	6	7	8	9

Scale:
0 | 15 | 30 | 45 | 60 | 75 | 90 | 105 | 120 | 135 | 150   Miles

0 | 20 | 40 | 60 | 80 | 100 | 120 | 140 | 160 | 180 | 200 | 220 | 240   Kilometers

Interstate highway   Inn location

U.S. highway

Biloxi   K6

The Santini-Stewart House Bed and Breakfast Inn
964 Beach Blvd
Biloxi, MS 39530-3740
(228)436-4078 (800)686-1146 Fax:(228)392-9193
E-mail: jad39530@cs.com

Circa 1837. This pre-Civil War home is named not for its first resident, but for the residents that lived there for the longest time. The Santini family lived in this historic home for more than a century. The B&B is not only listed on the National Register of Historic Places, but also with the Civil War Preservation Trust. Each room is decorated with a different theme. One room features a Western motif, one is African in style, the third is decorated with an Oriental flair and the fourth has European decor. In addition to the guest rooms in the main house, the innkeepers also offer a private honeymoon cottage with a Jacuzzi tub, wet bar and king-size bed. A full, Southern-style breakfast is served in the formal dining room on a table set with fine china, sterling silver and crystal. Among the nearby attractions are Jefferson Davis' home, Beauvoir. Charter boats, sunset cruises, walking tours, a lighthouse, NASA and outlet shops are other options.

Innkeeper(s): James A & Patricia S Dunay. $75-175. 5 rooms with PB, 2 with FP, 1 cottage and 1 conference room. Breakfast and afternoon tea included in rates. Types of meals: Full bkfst and early coffee/tea. Beds: KQ. Modem hook-up, data port, cable TV, reading lamp, clock radio, telephone, coffeemaker, turn-down service and hot tub/spa in room. Air conditioning. Spa, bicycles, parlor games, fireplace, laundry facility, BBQ grills and picnic area on premises. Amusement parks, antiquing, art galleries, beach, bicycling, canoeing/kayaking, fishing, golf, live theater, museums, parks, shopping, sporting events, water sports and motorcoach luncheon tours nearby.
Location: City, ocean community.

Certificate may be used: Sunday-Thursday, October-February, excluding holidays.

Hernando   A4

Sassafras Inn
785 Hwy 51 S
Hernando, MS 38632-8149
(662)429-5864 (800)882-1897 Fax:(601)429-4591
Internet: www.memphis.to
E-mail: sassyinn@memphis.to

Circa 1985. This modern inn offers guests to the state's Northwest corner a delightful respite from their travels or from the hustle and bustle of Memphis, 10 miles south. An impressive indoor swimming pool and spa are guest favorites and visitors also enjoy the cabana room for reading or lounging, or the recreation room with billiards, darts and ping pong. A romantic honeymoon cottage also is available. Arkabutla Lake is an easy drive from the inn.

Innkeeper(s): Dennis & Francee McClanahan. $75-225. 4 rooms, 3 with PB, 1 suite and 1 cottage. Breakfast, afternoon tea and snacks/refreshments included in rates. Types of meals: Full bkfst and early coffee/tea. Beds: QD. Cable TV, VCR, reading lamp, stereo, refrigerator, ceiling fan, snack bar, clock radio, telephone, turn-down service, desk and hot tub/spa in room. Air conditioning. TV, fax, copier, spa, swimming, library, parlor games, fireplace, indoor pool, basketball and billiards on premises. Antiquing, parks and water sports nearby.

Publicity: Memphis Commercial Appeal, DeSoto Times, Claridon Ledger, Los Angeles Times and WHBQ Romantic Getaways.

Certificate may be used: All year, Sunday through Thursday, no holidays.

Jackson   G4

Fairview Inn
734 Fairview St
Jackson, MS 39202-1624
(601)948-3429 (888)948-1908 Fax:(601)948-1203
Internet: www.fairviewinn.com
E-mail: fairview@fairviewinn.com

Circa 1908. Elegant and romantic canopied beds are among the enticements at this magnificent Colonial Revival mansion. Designed by an associate of Frank Lloyd Wright, the home boasts unforgettable polished hardwood floors, a beautiful marble floor, fine furnishings and tasteful decor. The innkeepers, Carol and William Simmons, pamper guests with a plentiful cook-to-order breakfast and fresh flowers and have hosted many a wedding reception and party. Underneath the shade of ancient oaks and graceful magnolia trees, an inviting deck offers a quiet space to reflect or enjoy conversation. History buffs will appreciate William's knowledge of Mississippi's past. There are helpful business amenities here, including in-room data ports. The inn has been hailed for its hospitality and cuisine by Country Inns magazine and the James Beard Foundation.

Innkeeper(s): Carol & William Simmons. $115-290. 18 rooms with PB and 4 conference rooms. Breakfast included in rates. Types of meals: Full gourmet bkfst, early coffee/tea, gourmet lunch, snacks/refreshments and gourmet dinner. Beds: KQ. Cable TV, reading lamp, snack bar, clock radio, telephone, turn-down service and desk in room. Air conditioning. VCR, fax, copier, library, fireplace, voice mail and data ports on premises. Handicap access. Antiquing, live theater, parks, shopping, sporting events and tennis nearby.

Publicity: Country Inns, Travel & Leisure, Southern Living, "Most Outstanding Inn North America 2003" by Conde Nast Johansen and ETV Documentary.

"Fairview Inn is southern hospitality at its best." — Travel and Leisure

Certificate may be used: Jan. 1 to Dec. 31, except for Thanksgiving and Christmas Day.

Long Beach   L6

Red Creek Inn, Vineyard & Racing Stable
7416 Red Creek Rd
Long Beach, MS 39560-8804
(228)452-3080 (800)729-9670 Fax:(228)452-4450
Internet: redcreekinn.com
E-mail: info@redcreekinn.com

Circa 1899. This inn was built in the raised French cottage-style by a retired Italian sea captain, who wished to entice his bride to move from her parents' home in New Orleans. There are two swings on the 64-foot front porch and one swing that hangs from a 300-year-old oak tree. Magnolias and ancient live oaks, some registered with the Live Oak Society of the Louisiana Garden Club, on four acres. The inn features a parlor, six fireplaces, ceiling fans and antiques, including a Victorian organ, wooden radios and a Victrola. The inn's suite includes a Jacuzzi tub.

Innkeeper(s): Karl & Toni Mertz. $49-134. 6 rooms, 5 with PB, 1 with FP, 1 suite and 1 conference room. Breakfast included in rates. Types of meals: Cont plus and early coffee/tea. Beds: QDT. TV and reading lamp in room. Air conditioning. VCR, fax, copier, library, parlor games, telephone and fireplace on premises. Amusement parks, antiquing, fishing, golf, live theater, parks, shopping, water sports and casinos nearby.

Location: Country.

Publicity: *Jackson Daily News, Innviews, Men's Journal, The Bridal Directory, TV Channel 13 and Mississippi ETV.*

"We loved waking up here on these misty spring mornings. The Old South is here."

Certificate may be used: Sunday-Thursday, May-August and anytime September-April (depending upon availability). Holidays usually excluded.

Natchez   I2

The Burn

712 N Union St
Natchez, MS 39120-2951
(601)442-1344 (800)654-8859 Fax:(601)445-0606
Internet: www.theburnbnb.com
E-mail: book@theburnbnb.com

Circa 1834. Sitting on a high bluff with two acres of terraced gardens that include dogwoods, azaleas and camellias, this Greek Revival mansion is located only five blocks from the Mississippi River and historic downtown. Owned by the original family for 101 years, this Antebellum bed & breakfast inn is listed in the National Register and showcases a freestanding spiral staircase. Lavish Southern hospitality is imparted now. Wine and refreshments are served upon arrival. Experience an intimate and romantic ambiance featuring period antique furnishings. After savoring a full plantation breakfast enjoy a memorable home tour. Relax in the outdoor cloistered brick patio boasting a courtyard fountain and pool.

Innkeeper(s): Ty & Sonja Taylor. $125-200. 9 rooms with PB, 2 suites and 1 conference room. Breakfast and snacks/refreshments included in rates. Types of meals: Country bkfst, veg bkfst and early coffee/tea. Beds: KQD. Modem hook-up, data port, cable TV, reading lamp, ceiling fan, clock radio, telephone, coffeemaker, desk and fireplace in room. Central air. Fax, copier, swimming, library, fireplace, laundry facility, Internet and gift shop on premises. Limited handicap access. Antiquing, art galleries, bicycling, canoeing/kayaking, fishing, golf, hiking, horseback riding, live theater, museums, parks, shopping, tennis, water sports and wineries nearby.

Location: City.

Publicity: *Country Inns and Bon Appetit.*

"We are still basking in the pleasures we found at The Burn."

Certificate may be used: Sunday through Thursday only, March, April, October and all holidays excluded.

Monmouth Plantation

36 Melrose Ave
Natchez, MS 39120-4005
(601)442-5852 (800)828-4531 Fax:(601)446-7762
Internet: www.monmouthplantation.com
E-mail: luxury@monmouthplantation.com

Circa 1818. Monmouth was the home of General Quitman who became acting Governor of Mexico, Governor of Mississippi, and a U.S. Congressman. In the National Historic Landmark, the inn features antique four-poster and canopy beds, turndown service and an evening cocktail hour. Guests Jefferson Davis and Henry Clay enjoyed the same acres of gardens, pond and walking paths available today. Elegant, five-course Southern dinners are served in the beautifully appointed dining room and parlors.

Innkeeper(s): Ron & Lani Riches. $155-375. 31 rooms with PB, 18 with FP, 16 suites, 6 cottages and 1 conference room. Breakfast included in rates. Types of meals: Full bkfst, early coffee/tea and dinner. Restaurant on premises. Beds: KQDT. Cable TV, reading lamp, CD player, clock radio, turn-down service and desk in room. Air conditioning. TV, VCR, fax, copier, telephone and fireplace on premises. Antiquing and shopping nearby.

Publicity: *Conde Nast Traveler.*

"The best historical inn we have stayed at anywhere."

Certificate may be used: January-February, June-July, August, November-December, Sunday-Thursday, subject to availability.

Myrtle Corner

600 State St
Natchez, MS 39120
(601)455-5999 (866)488-5999 Fax:(601)304-4065
Internet: www.myrtlecorner.com
E-mail: myrtlecorner@hotmail.com

Circa 1897. The exterior of Myrtle Corner appears as a fanciful confection of light pink with snow-white trim along the streets of historic downtown Natchez. Antiques and reproductions decorate the interior. The Magnolia Suite includes two bedrooms, a gas-log fireplace and bathroom with a Jacuzzi tub. A carved mahogany, four-poster bed graces the Myrtle and Cypress rooms. The Raintree room has a marble bath. Guests are greeted with a bottle of wine. Each morning, a full breakfast is served in the formal dining room with traditional Southern items such as biscuits and grits and gourmet treats such as eggs Benedict or pecan waffles.

Innkeeper(s): Layne Taylor and Don Vesterse. $110-330. 4 rooms with PB, 4 with FP, 1 suite. Breakfast included in rates. Types of meals: Full gourmet bkfst and early coffee/tea. Beds: KQT. Cable TV, reading lamp, ceiling fan, clock radio, desk, hot tub/spa and fireplace in room. Central air. VCR, fax, copier, telephone, fireplace, laundry facility, private planted courtyard and galleries on premises. Antiquing, art galleries, bicycling, fishing, golf, hiking, live theater, museums, parks, shopping, tennis, water sports and wineries nearby.

Location: City. Historic Garden District.

Publicity: *Country Roads and WYES TV-12 New Orleans.*

Certificate may be used: June-September, Sunday-Thursday, except holidays. November-February, Sunday-Thursday, except holidays.

Oxford   B5

Oliver-Britt House

512 Van Buren Ave
Oxford, MS 38655-3838
(662)234-8043
E-mail: oliv6448@bellsouth.net

Circa 1905. White columns and a picturesque veranda highlight the exterior of this Greek Revival inn shaded by trees. English country comfort is the emphasis in the interior, which includes a collection of antiques. On weekends, guests are treated to a Southern-style breakfast with all the trimmings.

Innkeeper(s): Glynn Oliver & Mary Ann Britt. $60-95. 5 rooms with PB. Types of meals: Early coffee/tea. Beds: KQ. Cable TV, reading lamp, ceiling fan, clock radio and desk in room. Air conditioning. Telephone and full breakfast (weekends only) on premises. Antiquing, parks, shopping and sporting events nearby.

Location: City.

Certificate may be used: Anytime, subject to availability.

Starkville   D7

The Cedars B&B

2173 Oktoc Rd
Starkville, MS 39759-9251
(662)324-7569

Circa 1836. This historic plantation offers a glimpse of life in the 19th-century South. The late Colonial/Greek Revival structure was built primarily by slaves, with construction lasting two years. The inn's 183 acres boast fishing ponds, pasture and woods, and guests love to explore, hike and ride horses. Four guest rooms are available, two with private bath. Visitors enjoy the inn's collection of 19th- and early 20th-century horse and farm equipment.

Noxubee Wildlife Refuge and the Tombigbee National Forest are within easy driving distance.

Innkeeper(s): Erin Scanlon. $50-65. 4 rooms, 2 with PB, 4 with FP and 2 conference rooms. Breakfast and snacks/refreshments included in rates. Types of meals: Full bkfst, early coffee/tea and picnic lunch. Beds: DT. Reading lamp, desk and refrigerator by request in room. Air conditioning. Parlor games, telephone and fireplace on premises. Antiquing, fishing, live theater, parks, shopping, sporting events and water sports nearby.
Location: 19th-century plantation.
Certificate may be used: Anytime based on availability.

Tylertown   J4

Merry Wood B&B, Vacation Sanctuary

5439 Marcia Ave
New Orleans, LA 70124
(504)222-1415 (866)222-1415 Fax:(504)222-1449
Internet: www.merrywoodcottages.com
E-mail: merrywoodcottage@aol.com

Circa 1940. A quiet "comfortable wilderness" surrounds this country cottage and two guest houses that offer flexible accommodations, a tranquil pond and river frontage with a private beach. Decorated in vintage furnishings, the old-fashioned ambiance is enhanced by antique footed tubs, quilts, brick floors, period-style stoves and tin ceilings. Modern amenities include electric security gates, satellite TV, VCR, central air and heat, microwaves and ceiling fans. Hair dryers, robes and fine linens are additional luxuries. Enjoy a satisfying breakfast of farm-fresh coddled eggs, homemade biscuits and gravy, Mayhaw jelly, Southern cheese grits, vegetarian sausage, fruit with cream and granola topping and beverages. Bikes are available. Guided nature walks, spa services, yoga/tai chi classes and canoeing can be arranged.

Innkeeper(s): Drs. Merry & Ryck Caplan. $130-180. 5 rooms, 4 with PB, 5 with FP, 2 suites, 1 cottage, 2 guest houses and 2 conference rooms. Breakfast and snacks/refreshments included in rates. Types of meals: Full gourmet bkfst, veg bkfst, early coffee/tea, gourmet lunch, picnic lunch, afternoon tea, gourmet dinner & room service. Beds: KT. Modem hook-up, data port, cable TV, VCR, reading lamp, stereo, refrigerator, ceiling fan, snack bar, clock radio, telephone, coffeemaker, turn-down service, desk, fireplace, terrycloth robes, hair dryers, iron & ironing board in room. Central air. Fax, copier, swimming, bicycles, library, parlor games, fireplace, laundry facility, exercise room, reading room, canoes, BBQ, picnic supplies, beach supplies, organic vegetable & flower garden for guest use, river trails & spa services on premises. Limited handicap access. Amusement parks, antiquing, art galleries, beach, bicycling, canoeing/kayaking, fishing, golf, hiking, horseback riding, live theater, museums, parks and shopping nearby.
Location: Country, waterfront. River frontage with private beach.

Publicity: *Country Roads, St. Charles Magazine, Natural Awakenings and WWLTV.*
Certificate may be used: Jan. 1-March 31, Sunday through Thursday, subject to availability.

Vicksburg   G3

Anchuca

1010 First East St
Vicksburg, MS 39183
(601)661-0111 (888)686-0111 Fax:(601)661-0111
Internet: www.anchucamansion.com
E-mail: reservations@anchucamansion.com

Circa 1832. This early Greek Revival mansion rises resplendently above the brick-paved streets of Vicksburg. It houses magnificent period antiques and artifacts. Confederate President Jefferson Davis once addressed the townspeople from the balcony while his brother was living in the home after the Civil War. The turn-of-the-century guest cottage has been transformed into an enchanting hideaway and rooms in the mansion are appointed with formal decor and four-poster beds. A swimming pool and Jacuzzi are modern amenities.

Innkeeper(s): Thomas Pharr & Christopher Brinkley. $95-175. 8 rooms with PB, 4 with FP, 3 suites. Breakfast included in rates. Types of meals: Full gourmet bkfst, veg bkfst, early coffee/tea, gourmet lunch, picnic lunch, afternoon tea, snacks/refreshments, gourmet dinner and room service. Beds: KQT. Cable TV, reading lamp, clock radio, coffeemaker, turn-down service, hot tub/spa, mini refrigerator stocked with snacks and beverages and coffee center in room. Central air. Fax, spa, swimming, library, parlor games, telephone, fireplace and laundry facility on premises. Antiquing, fishing, golf, museums, parks, shopping, sporting events, tennis and National Military Park nearby.
Location: City.
Publicity: *Times Herald, Southern Living, Innsider, Country Inns, Smithsonian, Conde Nast and Johansens.*

"The 'Southern Hospitality' will not be forgotten. The best Southern breakfast in town."
Certificate may be used: Anytime, Sunday-Thursday.

Stained Glass Manor - Oak Hall

2430 Drummond St
Vicksburg, MS 39180-4114
(601)638-8893 (888)VIC-KBNB Fax:(601)636-3055
Internet: www.vickbnb.com
E-mail: vickbnb@magnolia.net

Circa 1902. Billed by the innkeepers as "Vicksburg's historic Vick inn," this restored, Mission-style manor boasts 40 stained-glass windows, original woodwork and light fixtures. Period furnishings create a Victorian flavor. George Washington Maher, who employed a young draftsman named Frank Lloyd Wright, probably designed the home, which was built from 1902 to 1908. Lewis J. Millet did the art for 36 of the stained-glass panels. The home's first owner, Fannie Vick Willis Johnson, was a descendent of the first Vick in Vicksburg. All but one guest room has a fireplace, and all are richly appointed with antiques, reproductions and Oriental rugs. "New Orleans" breakfasts begin with cafe au lait, freshly baked bread, Quiche Lorraine and other treats.

Innkeeper(s): Bill & Shirley Smollen. $99-185. 5 rooms with PB, 3 with FP, 1 cottage, 1 guest house, 1 cabin and 3 conference rooms. Breakfast included in rates. Types of meals: Full gourmet bkfst. Beds: KQDT. Modem hook-up, cable TV, VCR, clock radio, telephone, desk, fireplace and cast iron claw-foot tubs in room. Air conditioning. Fax, sauna, library, parlor games, fireplace and laundry facility on premises. Antiquing, art galleries, bicycling, fishing, golf, hiking, horseback riding, live theater, museums, parks, shopping, tennis, home tours and historic sites nearby.
Location: City. Historic City.
Certificate may be used: Anytime, Sunday-Thursday, subject to availability, excluding holiday weekends, Valentines Day, etc.

Missouri

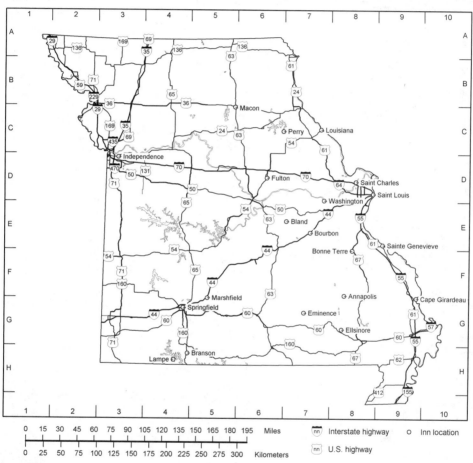

0 15 30 45 60 75 90 105 120 135 150 165 180 195   Miles

0 25 50 75 100 125 150 175 200 225 250 275 300   Kilometers

nn Interstate highway   o Inn location

nn U.S. highway

Annapolis   F8

Rachel's B&B

202 West Second
Annapolis, MO 63620
(573)598-4656 (888)245-7771 Fax:(573)598-3439
Internet: www.rachelsbb.com
E-mail: info@rachelsbb.com

Circa 1921. Formerly the Bolch Mansion, now this renovated Arts and Craft-style B&B is named after the innkeepers' youngest daughter. Annapolis' oldest home, with original glass doorknobs, woodwork, built-in book cases and country ele-gance, sits on one acre surrounded by mountains and hills. Perfect for a remote romantic getaway, enjoy two-person Jacuzzis, bath salts, robes, fireplace, soft music, romantic in-room videos and private decks. Some rooms are specifically family friendly. In the common room an antique rocking horse is available. There is a large video selection. Enjoy the land-scaped grounds with garden pond, goldfish and waterfall, then relax in the outdoor hot tub.

Innkeeper(s): Joe & Sharon Cluck. $65-140. 6 rooms with PB, 4 with FP, 5 total suites, including 1 two-bedroom suite and 1 conference room. Breakfast and snacks/refreshments included in rates. Types of meals: Full gourmet bkfst, veg bkfst, early coffee/tea, picnic lunch and gourmet dinner. Restaurant on premises. Beds: KQDT. Cable TV, VCR, reading lamp, stereo, refrigerator, ceiling fan, clock radio, turn-down service, desk, hot tub/spa, fireplace, hot tub and snuggly robes in room. Central air. Fax, copier, spa, swimming, library, parlor games, telephone and laundry facility on premises. Handicap access. Antiquing, beach, bicycling, canoeing/kayaking, fishing, golf, hiking, horseback riding, live theater, museums, parks, shopping and water sports nearby.

Location: Country, mountains. Two hours south of St. Louis.

Publicity: *Journal Banner, Mountain Echo News, Mustang Club, Top 15 handicap accessible B&B by B&B Journal Book of List for 2001, Bed & Breakfast and Bikes, Best for Rest and Relaxation 2003, Inn Travelers Magazine (fall 2004) and KTJJ.*

Certificate may be used: Anytime, Sunday-Thursday.

Bland E7

Caverly Farm & Orchard B&B

100 Cedar Ridge Lane
Bland, MO 65014
(573)646-3732 Fax:(573)646-5274
E-mail: caverlydn@socket.net

Circa 1850. Built prior to the Civil War, this farmhouse has been renovated completely. The innkeepers preserved many original features, and to keep the home authentic, they used original accents within the home. Guest rooms are decorated in Colonial style and include family antiques. Take a stroll around the inn's 50-plus acres, and you'll find woods, a pond, a variety of birds and perhaps a deer or two. Breakfasts include items such as farm-fresh cheesy eggs with chives, Canadian bacon, fresh fruit and homemade breads served with homemade preserves and jams. The home is within an hour's drive of antique shops, craft stores, farm auctions, wineries and the state capital, Jefferson City. Hermann, a historic town about 45 miles away, is an interesting place to visit, especially during its famous Oktoberfest.

Innkeeper(s): David & Nancy Caverly. $55-60. 3 rooms with PB. Breakfast included in rates. Types of meals: Country bkfst, veg bkfst and early coffee/tea. Beds: QDT. Reading lamp, ceiling fan, clock radio and desk in room. Central air. TV, VCR, library, parlor games and telephone on premises. Limited handicap access. Antiquing, canoeing/kayaking, fishing, golf, hiking, museums, shopping and wineries nearby.

Location: Country.

Publicity: *Southern Living, St. Louis Post Dispatch, High Performance People and Country Magazine.*

Certificate may be used: Jan. 15-Dec. 15, Sunday through Saturday.

Bonne Terre F8

Victorian Veranda

207 E School St
Bonne Terre, MO 63628
(573)358-1134 (800)343-1134
Internet: www.victorianveranda.com
E-mail: info@victorianveranda.com

Circa 1868. A veranda encircles this blue and white Queen Anne and there are finely crafted decorative details such as porch columns and dentil work. Furnishings in the dining room are country-style enhanced by light floral wallpaper, fine wood paneling and woodwork around the doors, all painted white. Egg casseroles, potatoes and coffee cakes are served here. There are eight state parks in the area and Cherokee Landing offers canoe trips along the river.

Innkeeper(s): Galen & Karen Forney. $85-125. 4 rooms with PB, 1 with FP, 1 suite. Breakfast, afternoon tea and snacks/refreshments included in rates. Types of meals: Full gourmet bkfst, early coffee/tea, picnic lunch and room service. Beds: Q. Reading lamp, stereo, refrigerator, ceiling fan, snack bar, clock radio, telephone and desk in room. Air conditioning. VCR, parlor games and fireplace on premises. Antiquing, fishing, golf, live theater, parks, shopping, sporting events, tennis, water sports and scuba diving/cave nearby.

Location: Small town.

Certificate may be used: Jan. 2 to Dec. 23, Sunday-Thursday.

Bourbon E7

Meramec Farm Cabins & Trail Riding Vacations, LLC

208 Thickety Ford
Bourbon, MO 65441
(573)732-4765
Internet: www.wine_mo.com/meramec.html
E-mail: mfarmbnb@fidnet.com

Circa 1883. This farmhouse inn and cedar guest cabin are found on a working cattle operation, little more than an hour's drive from St. Louis. Seven generations have lived and worked the farm, which boasts 460 acres. Visitors stay in the 1880s farmhouse or the cabin, built from cedar cut on the farm. The inn's proximity to the Meramec River and Vilander Bluffs provides excellent views and many outdoor activities. Spring visitors are treated to the sight of baby calves. Meramec Caverns and several state parks are nearby.

Innkeeper(s): Carol Springer. $75. 2 cabins. Types of meals: Full bkfst, early coffee/tea, picnic lunch and gourmet dinner. Beds: QDT. Reading lamp, refrigerator, ceiling fan, clock radio and desk in room. Air conditioning. Telephone, fireplace, BBQ, picnic tables and porches on premises. Antiquing and fishing nearby.

Location: Country.

Publicity: *Midwest Motorist, St. Louis Post-Dispatch and St. Louis.*

Certificate may be used: Anytime, Sunday-Thursday, Nov. 1-April 1, subject to availability.

Branson H4

Aunt Sadie's Garden Glade

163 Fountain St
Branson, MO 65616-9194
(417)335-4063 (800)944-4250 Fax:(417)336-6772
Internet: www.auntsadies.com
E-mail: auntsadies@aol.com

Circa 1965. Tranquil surroundings highlight this romantic bed and breakfast. Secluded cabins offer assorted comforts such as hot tubs or whirlpools, refrigerators, microwaves, coffee makers, fireplaces, TVs and VCRs. In the main house a hearty country breakfast is served family style every morning. Anticipate savoring fresh fruit, hot biscuits and gravy, meat dishes, an egg entree, fresh pastry and of course, hot coffee or tea.

Innkeeper(s): Dick & Linda Hovell. $95-150. 4 cabins, 3 with FP. Breakfast and snacks/refreshments included in rates. Types of meals: Full bkfst and early coffee/tea. Beds: KQ. Cable TV, VCR, ceiling fan, telephone and hot tub or whirlpool in room. Air conditioning. TV, copier and parlor games on premises.

Location: Mountains.

Certificate may be used: Jan. 30-Sept. 1, Sunday-Thursday.

Branson Hotel B&B Inn

214 W Main St
Branson, MO 65616-2724
(417)335-6104 (800)933-0651 Fax:(417)339-3224
Internet: www.bransonhotelbb.com
E-mail: info@bransonhotelbb.com

Circa 1903. A picket fence frames the Branson Hotel, a Four Square style Victorian and a Branson Historic Landmark. Adirondack chairs fill the fieldstone veranda and the front balcony, affording guests the pleasure of visiting and enjoying the view. As Branson's oldest commercial structure, important gatherings here played a significant part in the history of Branson, and the novel "Shepherd of the Hills" was written here. A harvest table in the glass-enclosed dining room is laden with hearty gourmet breakfast offerings including bacon quiche, cinnamon spiced pears and broiled grapefruit.

Innkeeper(s): Randy & Cynthia Parker. $75-99. 7 rooms with PB. Breakfast and snacks/refreshments included in rates. Types of meals: Full gourmet bkfst, early coffee/tea and room service. Beds: KQ. Modem hook-up, data port, cable TV, reading lamp, ceiling fan, clock radio, telephone and robes in room. Central air. Fax and gift shop on premises. Amusement parks, antiquing, fishing, golf, hiking, horseback riding, live theater, museums, parks, shopping, tennis, water sports and wineries nearby.
Location: City. Historic downtown.
Publicity: *Southern Living, Midwest Living, Glamour and Automobile Magazine.*
Certificate may be used: Jan. 2-May 15, subject to availability.

Cape Girardeau   G9

Bellevue B&B

312 Bellevue St
Cape Girardeau, MO 63701-7233
(573)335-3302 (800)768-6822 Fax:(573)332-7752
Internet: www.flinthills.com:80/~atway/mo/bellevue.html
E-mail: info@bellevue-bb.com

Circa 1891. Within three blocks of Mississippi River front Park, this Queen Anne Victorian with gables and bay windows is in the local historic register. The house is painted deep hunter green with taupe and cranberry trim, emphasizing the historic craftsmanship of its gables, bay windows, balustrades, cornices and stained glass windows. A glider and two wicker rocking chairs sit on the front porch. Inside, the original woodwork remains as well as several sets of original pocket doors and fireplaces. Ask for the Parkridge Room where a six-foot high antique headboard is the focal point or for the Shea Lorraine or Dearborn rooms, both with large whirlpool tubs. There's a fireplace on the patio for evening get-togethers. SEMO University is nearby.

Innkeeper(s): Marsha Toll. $75-125. 4 rooms with PB. Breakfast included in rates. Types of meals: Full bkfst. Beds: Q. Cable TV, ceiling fan, whirlpool and some with phones in room. Air conditioning.
Location: City.
Certificate may be used: Sunday-Friday, Jan. 1-April 30, November-December.

Ellsinore   G8

Alcorn Corner B&B

Hcr 3 Box 247
Ellsinore, MO 63937
(573)322-5297

Circa 1904. Surrounded by 20 acres, this simple Victorian farmhouse is the kind of bed & breakfast guests will enjoy sharing with their children. There are farm animals, and the innkeeper, a former teacher, is like a grandma to families. Early American furnishings are found in the two guest rooms, and a family-style breakfast with three menu choices is offered.

Innkeeper(s): Virgie Alcorn Evans. $35-50. 2 rooms. Beds: DT. Reading lamp and turn-down service in room. VCR, library, telephone and fireplace on premises. Antiquing, parks, shopping and museums nearby.
Location: Country.
Certificate may be used: May 25 to Nov. 15, Monday-Friday, excluding holidays.

Eminence   G7

Old Blue House B&B

PO Box 117
Eminence, MO 65466-0117
(573)226-3498
Internet: www.missouri2000.net/oldbluehouse
E-mail: oldbluehouseb-b@webtv.net

Circa 1800. This old two-story frame house once was home to a beauty shop, grocery store and pharmacy. There are antiques throughout and framed prints, much of which is for sale. The garden is shaded by maple and magnolia trees and there are peonies, lilacs and roses. Breakfast is continental plus. However, if you'd like a country breakfast with sausage, gravy, scrambled eggs and homemade biscuits there is an extra charge. Eminence is located in the Ozark National Scenic Riverway.

Innkeeper(s): Wanda L. Pummill. $65-90. 3 rooms with PB. Breakfast and snacks/refreshments included in rates. Types of meals: Full bkfst and early coffee/tea. Beds: D. Cable TV, reading lamp, ceiling fan and desk in room. Air conditioning. Parlor games and telephone on premises. Antiquing, beach, bicycling, canoeing/kayaking, fishing, golf, hiking, horseback riding, parks, shopping, water sports and cross-country trail rides nearby.
Location: City.
Publicity: *St. Louis Post Dispatch, Midwest Living, B&B Guest House and Inns of Missouri.*
Certificate may be used: Jan. 1 to Dec. 31, Sunday-Thursday only, no holidays or holiday weekends.

Fulton   D6

Romancing The Past Victorian B&B

830 Court St
Fulton, MO 65251
(573)592-1996 Fax:(573)592-1999
Internet: www.romancingthepast.com
E-mail: innkeeper@sockets.net

Circa 1867. A porch wraps around this pristine Victorian home and offers white wicker furnishings. There's a hammock and hot tub with gazebo in the garden. Finely crafted and restored fretwork, brackets and bay windows decorate the exterior. Polished woodwork, a gracious staircase and parquet floors are highlighted with well-chosen Victorian antiques. The Victorian Rose Room features a private balcony. The Renaissance Suite boasts a fainting couch and carved walnut canopy bed, a sitting room and a large bath decorated in the Neoclassical style. In fact, luxurious baths are the inn's hallmark, as is evidenced by the award-winning spa bathroom in the Miss James Study, and there are both indoor and outdoor spas and aromatherapy.

Innkeeper(s): Jim & ReNee Yeager. $100-170. 3 rooms, 4 with PB, 3 with FP. Breakfast included in rates. Types of meals: Full gourmet bkfst, early coffee/tea, picnic lunch and snacks/refreshments. Beds: Q. Reading lamp, stereo, ceiling fan, clock radio, telephone, turn-down service, desk and clock in room. VCR, fax, copier, spa, bicycles, library, parlor games, fireplace, CD player, TV and evening desserts on premises. Antiquing, fishing, golf, live theater, parks, shopping, sporting events, tennis, UMC and bike trails nearby.
Location: City. Small town, beautiful historic neighborhood.
Publicity: *Awards for Best Spa Bath and Best Interior Design in Arrington's Bed and Breakfast Journal.*
Certificate may be used: Monday-Thursday, no holidays.

Independence   D3

Serendipity B&B

116 S Pleasant St
Independence, MO 64050
(816)833-4719 (800)203-4299 Fax:(816)833-4719
Internet: www.bbhost.com/serendipitybb
E-mail: serendipitybandb@aol.com

Circa 1887. This three-story brick home offers guests the ultimate Victorian experience. Antique furnishings and period
appointments create an authentic period ambiance. Victorian
children's books and toys, antique pictures, china figurines and
a collection of antique colored glassware add to the home's
charm. Stereoscopes and music box tunes are other special
touches. A full breakfast is served by candlelight in the formal
dining room. Outside gardens include arbors, Victorian gazing
balls, birdhouses, birdbaths, a hammock, swing and fountain.
If time and weather permit, guests may request a ride in an
antique car and tour of the house.
Innkeeper(s): Susan & Doug Walter. $45-85. 6 rooms with PB. Types of
meals: Full bkfst. Beds: KQD. Air conditioning. TV, VCR, fax and copier on
premises. Amusement parks, antiquing, fishing, golf, live theater, parks, shopping, sporting events, tennis, water sports, historic sites and casinos nearby.
Location: City.

"It was so special to spend time with you and to share your lovely home."
Certificate may be used: Anytime, subject to availability.

Woodstock Inn B&B

1212 W Lexington Ave
Independence, MO 64050-3524
(816)833-2233 (800)276-5202 Fax:(816)461-7226
Internet: www.independence-missouri.com
E-mail: woodstock@independence-missouri.com

Circa 1900. This home, originally built as a doll and quilt factory, is in the perfect location for sightseeing in historic
Independence. Visit the home of Harry S Truman or the
Truman Library and Museum. The Old Jail Museum is another
popular attraction. A large country breakfast is served each
morning featuring malted Belgian waffles and an additional
entree. Independence is less than 30 minutes from Kansas City,
where you may spend the day browsing through the shops at
Country Club Plaza or Halls' Crown Center.
Innkeeper(s): Todd & Patricia Justice. $75-189. 11 rooms with PB, 2 suites.
Breakfast included in rates. Types of meals: Full bkfst and early coffee/tea.
Beds: KQD. Cable TV, VCR, reading lamp, stereo, refrigerator, clock radio,
telephone, coffeemaker, turn-down service, desk, hot tub/spa, voice mail and
fireplaces in room. Air conditioning. Fax and parlor games on premises.
Handicap access. Amusement parks, antiquing, art galleries, fishing, golf, live
theater, museums, parks, shopping and sporting events nearby.
Location: City.
Publicity: *Country, San Francisco Chronicle, Independence Examiner, Kansas
City Star and New York Times.*

"Pleasant, accommodating people, a facility of good character."
Certificate may be used: Dec. 1-Feb. 28, anytime except during holidays and
special events. Subject to availability.

Lampe   H4

Grandpa's Farm B&B

4738 W State Hwy 86
Lampe, MO 65681
(417)779-5106 (800)280-5106
Internet: www.grandpasfarmbandb.com
E-mail: keithpat@inter-linc.net

Circa 1891. This limestone farmhouse in the heart of the
Ozarks offers guests a chance to experience country life in a
relaxed farm setting. Midway between Silver Dollar City and
Eureka Springs, Ark., and close to Branson, the inn boasts several lodging options, including a duplex with suites and a honeymoon suite. The innkeepers are known for their substantial
country breakfast and say guests enjoy comparing how long the
meal lasts before they eat again. Although the inn's 116 acres
are not farmed extensively, domesticated farm animals are on
the premises.
Innkeeper(s): Keith & Pat Lamb. $65-95. 4 suites. Breakfast included in
rates. Types of meals: Full bkfst. Beds: KQ. Reading lamp, refrigerator, ceiling
fan, clock radio, desk and hot tub/spa in room. Air conditioning. VCR, fax,
spa, parlor games, telephone, fireplace and RCA satellite dish with 32-inch
TV screen on premises. Handicap access. Amusement parks, antiquing, fishing, live theater, parks, shopping, water sports, country western shows and
Passion Plays in Branson & Eureka Springs nearby.
Location: Country.
Certificate may be used: All months except June, July, August, October, no
major holidays.

Louisiana   C7

Eagle's Nest

221 Georgia
Louisiana, MO 63353-1715
(573)754-9888 Fax:(573)754-5406
Internet: www.theeaglesnest-louisiana.com
E-mail: reflectionsofmo@big-river.net

Circa 1859. Experience small-town America just a block from
the Mississippi River at this inn that was originally an old bank.
Four adjacent historic buildings are being restored for expan-
sion to include a cooking school and conference facilities.
Lavish guest bedrooms and suites feature Jacuzzi tubs and
plush robes. Linger over a scrumptious breakfast in the Bistro.
Overlook the garden while relaxing in the private guest lounge
with an afternoon beverage and fresh cookies from the bakery.
Soak in the solarium hot tub for a truly stress-free stay.
Innkeeper(s): Karen Stoeckley & Staff. $85-125. 14 rooms with PB, 3 suites
and 2 conference rooms. Breakfast and snacks/refreshments included in
rates. Types of meals: Full gourmet bkfst, veg bkfst, gourmet lunch, picnic
lunch, afternoon tea and gourmet dinner. Restaurant on premises. Beds: Q.
Data port, cable TV, reading lamp, ceiling fan, clock radio, telephone, desk
and hot tub/spa in room. Central air. Spa, library, parlor games, fireplace and
gift shop on premises. Handicap access. Antiquing, art galleries, bicycling,
canoeing/kayaking, fishing, golf, hiking, horseback riding, museums, parks,
shopping, tennis and wineries nearby.
Location: City. Located in downtown historic Louisiana Mo., just one block
from the Mississippi River.
Certificate may be used: Jan. 15 to Nov. 30, any days, subject to availability.

Macon   C5

The Phillips Place Bed & Breakfast

705 Jackson Street
Macon, MO 63552
(660)385-3535
Internet: www.phillipsplacebandb.com
E-mail: info@phillipsplaceband.com

Circa 1899. Adorning a corner acre with a huge arbor and
swing, this Georgian Revival was built with locally made yellow
brick and features Victorian details and décor. Fully restored, it
boasts original fretwork, leaded glass and an oak, maple, cherry
and walnut parquet floor. Relax on wicker rockers on the wide
front porch. Sit by the oak fireplace in the large oval living
room with window seats in the alcoves. Stay in the Ruby Suite
spanning the full length of the main house, or the first-floor

Turner Suite. A columned breezeway leads to the two-story carriage house. Take the hayloft steps or iron spiral staircase to the West Suite or the East Suite which has a fully equipped kitchen and opens to a balcony. A bountiful breakfast is served in the formal octagonal dining room, garden room or outside courtyard. Savor Scott's homemade biscuits and gravy and Gooey Overnight Almond French Toast. The spa includes a lap pool, sauna, hot tub, exercise equipment and massage therapy.

Innkeeper(s): Scott & Carol Phillips. $99-159. 4 suites and 1 conference room. Breakfast, brunch and snacks/refreshments included in rates. Types of meals: Country bkfst, veg bkfst, early coffee/tea, lunch and dinner. Beds: KQ. Modem hook-up, data port, cable TV, VCR, reading lamp, CD player, refrigerator, ceiling fan, clock radio, telephone, coffeemaker, turn-down service, desk and voice mail in room. Central air. Fax, copier, spa, sauna, parlor games and laundry facility on premises. Antiquing, bicycling, canoeing/kayaking, fishing, golf, hiking, live theater, museums, parks, shopping, tennis and water sports nearby.
Location: Small town.
Certificate may be used: Anytime, subject to availability. Must advise of this offer when calling for reservation.

St. Agnes Hall B&B

502 Jackson St
Macon, MO 63552-1717
(660)385-2774 Fax:(660)385-7372
Internet: www.saintagneshall.com
E-mail: info@saintagneshall.com

Circa 1846. This two-and-a-half story brick home boasts a rather unique history. As a stop along the Underground Railroad, it served as a "safe-house" for many slaves seeking freedom in the North. During the Civil War, it was used as Union headquarters. Eventually in the 1880s, the home was converted into a boarding house and day school for young women. In 1895, the home was renovated and used as a private residence. It was the boyhood home of U.S. Sen. James Preston Kem. Antiques and collectibles decorate the interior, all surrounded by Victorian decor.

Innkeeper(s): Scott & Carol Phillips. $68-98. 4 rooms with PB, 2 with FP, 1 suite. Breakfast included in rates. Types of meals: Full bkfst and early coffee/tea. Beds: KQ. Cable TV, reading lamp, ceiling fan and clock radio in room. Air conditioning. VCR, fax, copier, parlor games, telephone and fireplace on premises. Antiquing, fishing, golf, parks, shopping, water sports, swimming and fine dining nearby.
Location: City.
Certificate may be used: Sunday-Friday, excluding special events.

Marshfield   G5

The Dickey House B&B, Ltd.

331 S Clay St
Marshfield, MO 65706-2114
(417)468-3000 (800)450-7444 Fax:(417)859-2775
Internet: www.dickeyhouse.com
E-mail: info@dickeyhouse.com

Circa 1913. This Greek Revival mansion is framed by ancient oak trees and boasts eight massive two-story Ionic columns. Burled woodwork, beveled glass and polished hardwood floors accentuate the gracious rooms. Interior columns soar in the parlor, creating a suitably elegant setting for the innkeeper's outstanding collection of antiques. A queen-size canopy bed, fireplace and sunporch are featured in the Heritage Room. Some rooms offer amenities such as Jacuzzi tubs and

a fireplace. All rooms include cable TV and a VCR. The innkeepers also offer a sun room with a hot tub.

Innkeeper(s): Larry & Michaelene Stevens. $75-165. 7 rooms, 3 with PB, 4 suites. Breakfast included in rates. Types of meals: Full bkfst. Beds: KQD. Cable TV, VCR, reading lamp, ceiling fan, clock radio, telephone and four with double Jacuzzi in room. New sun room with therapeutic hot tub on premises. Handicap access.
Location: Small town.
Certificate may be used: Jan. 10 to April 30, Sunday-Thursday.

Perry   C6

Kennedy's Red Barn Inn

22748 Joanna Dr
Perry, MO 63462
(573)565-9612 (866)565-9612 Fax:(775)416-3984
Internet: www.redbarninn.com
E-mail: redbarn@redbarninn.com

Circa 1848. Country living is at its best at this old Missouri red barn that has been restored as a delightful home on Mark Twain Lake. Beamed ceilings, an antique staircase, rustic wood floors and lots of room inside and out instill a relaxing ambiance. The main floor includes a gift shop, sitting room, library and dining room where a hearty breakfast is served. Guest bedrooms feature quilt-covered brass beds, lace curtains, antiques and wicker. A red heart whirlpool tub with bath products enhances a romantic setting. After a workout in the exercise room, an outdoor aroma-scented hot tub feels great.

Innkeeper(s): Jack & Rebecca Kennedy. $50-60. 3 rooms. Breakfast and snacks/refreshments included in rates. Types of meals: Country bkfst, early coffee/tea and afternoon tea. Beds: QD. Ceiling fan, clock radio and desk in room. Central air. TV, VCR, fax, copier, spa, bicycles, library, telephone, fireplace, laundry facility and gift shop on premises. Amusement parks, antiquing, art galleries, beach, bicycling, canoeing/kayaking, fishing, golf, hiking, horseback riding, live theater, museums, parks, shopping, tennis and water sports nearby.
Location: Country. Mark Twain Lake.
Publicity: *Courier Post and Lake Gazette.*
Certificate may be used: November-January, anytime.

Saint Charles   D8

Lococo House II Bed & Breakfast

1309 N. Fifth Street
Saint Charles, MO 63301
(636)946-0619 Fax:(636)940-7134
Internet: www.lococohouse.com
E-mail: Rhonaloc@aol.com

Circa 1907. A classic two-story brick Queen Anne, this home away from home is comfortably furnished with family heirlooms intermingled with flea-market finds. Relax in the unpretentious parlor. Oak-mantled fireplaces are accented by emerald green glass brick. Guest bedrooms offer privacy and whirlpool tubs. Feel fueled for the day with a breakfast that may include the signature Lococo House French Toast. Day tours to nearby wineries through the scenic river valley are available. Ask about the cyclist's shuttle package for Katy Trail riders.

Innkeeper(s): Rhona & Leo Lococo. $95. 5 rooms, 2 with PB. Breakfast and snacks/refreshments included in rates. Types of meals: Country bkfst, veg bkfst, early coffee/tea, afternoon tea and room service. Beds: DT. Modem hook-up, data port, cable TV, VCR, reading lamp, stereo, refrigerator, ceiling fan, telephone and hot tub/spa in room. Air conditioning. Fax, copier, spa, library, parlor games, laundry facility and gift shop on premises. Antiquing, art galleries, bicycling, fishing, golf, museums, parks, shopping, sporting events and wineries nearby.
Location: City.
Certificate may be used: Anytime, Sunday-Thursday.

Saint Louis　　　　D8

Eastlake Inn Bed & Breakfast

703 N Kirkwood Rd
Saint Louis, MO 63122-2719
(314)965-0066　Fax:(314)966-8615
Internet: www.eastlakeinn.com
E-mail: info@eastlakeinn.com

Circa 1920. Tall trees shade this colonial-style inn on one acre of grounds. Eastlake antiques are found throughout along with an antique doll collection. Guest rooms include the Garden Room with a queen Eastlake bed and a view of the perennial gardens. The Magnolia Room has a fireplace and a double whirlpool tub. A full breakfast is offered in the dining room under the lights of a chandelier. Dishes include items such as peach French toast, maple sausage, and fruit from the local farmer's market. The inn's two golden retrievers may enjoy a garden tour with you or stroll through the pleasant neighborhood on a walk to Mudd Grove.

Innkeeper(s): Lori & Dean Murray. $70-165. 3 rooms, 2 with PB, 1 with FP, 1 suite. Breakfast included in rates. Types of meals: Full gourmet bkfst and early coffee/tea. Beds: KQD. Modem hook-up, data port, cable TV, VCR, reading lamp, ceiling fan, clock radio, telephone, coffeemaker, turn-down service, hot tub/spa and fireplace in room. Central air. Fax, copier, library, parlor games and fireplace on premises. Amusement parks, antiquing, art galleries, bicycling, canoeing/kayaking, downhill skiing, fishing, golf, hiking, horseback riding, live theater, museums, parks, shopping, sporting events, tennis and wineries nearby.

Location: Historic town.

Certificate may be used: Jan. 1-March 31, Sunday-Thursday, subject to availability.

Lehmann House B&B

10 Benton Pl
Saint Louis, MO 63104-2411
(314)422-1483　Fax:(314)241-1597
E-mail: Lehmann.House.Bed.Breakfast@worldnet.att.net

Circa 1893. This National Register manor's most prominent resident, former U.S. Solicitor General Frederick Lehmann, hosted Presidents Taft, Theodore Roosevelt and Coolidge at this gracious home. Several key turn-of-the-century literary figures also visited the Lehmann family. The inn's formal dining room, complete with oak paneling and a fireplace, is a stunning place to enjoy the formal breakfasts. Antiques and gracious furnishings dot the well-appointed guest rooms. The home is located in St. Louis' oldest historic district, Lafayette Square.

Innkeeper(s): Marie & Michael Davies. $100. 2 rooms with PB, 2 with FP. Breakfast included in rates. Types of meals: Full bkfst and early coffee/tea. Beds: KQDT. Reading lamp, ceiling fan and clock radio in room. Air conditioning. Swimming, tennis, library, parlor games, telephone and fireplace on premises. Amusement parks, antiquing, live theater, parks, shopping, sporting events, museums, zoos and botanical gardens nearby.

Location: City.

Publicity: *St. Louis Post Dispatch and KTVI-St. Louis.*

"Wonderful mansion with great future ahead. Thanks for the wonderful hospitality."

Certificate may be used: Nov. 1-March 30, Sunday-Thursday only, holidays and special events excluded.

Sainte Genevieve　　　　E9

Inn St. Gemme Beauvais

78 N Main St
Sainte Genevieve, MO 63670-1336
(573)883-5744　(800)818-5744　Fax:(573)883-3899
Internet: www.bbhost.com/innstgemme
E-mail: stgemme@brick.net

Circa 1848. This three-story, Federal-style inn is an impressive site on Ste. Genevieve's Main Street. The town is one of the oldest west of the Mississippi River, and the St. Gemme Beauvais is the oldest operating Missouri bed & breakfast. The rooms are nicely appointed in period style, but there are modern amenities here, too. The Jacuzzi tubs in some guest rooms are one relaxing example. There is an outdoor hot tub, as well. The romantic carriage house includes a king-size bed, double Jacuzzi tub and a fireplace. Guests are pampered with all sorts of cuisine, including full breakfasts served at individual candle-lit tables with a choice of eight entrees. Later, tea, drinks, hors d'oeuvres and refreshments are also served.

Innkeeper(s): Janet Joggerst. $89-179. 9 rooms with PB, 1 with FP, 6 suites and 1 conference room. Breakfast, afternoon tea and snacks/refreshments included in rates. Types of meals: Full gourmet bkfst. Beds: KQD. Cable TV, reading lamp, stereo, ceiling fan, clock radio, desk and hot tub/spa in room. Air conditioning. VCR, fax, copier, parlor games, telephone and fireplace on premises. Antiquing, golf, parks, shopping and historic area nearby.

Location: Historic town 60 miles south of St. Louis.

Certificate may be used: Sunday through Thursday, Nov. 1-April 30.

Main Street Inn

221 N Main St
Sainte Genevieve, MO 63670-0307
(573)883-9199　(800)918-9199　Fax:(573)839-9911
Internet: www.rivervalleyinns.com
E-mail: info@mainstreetinnbb.com

Circa 1882. This exquisite inn is one of Missouri's finest bed & breakfast establishments. Built as the Meyer Hotel, the inn has welcomed guests for more than a century. Now completely renovated, each of the individually appointed rooms includes amenities such as bubble bath and flowers. Rooms are subtly decorated. Beds are topped with vintage quilts and tasteful linens. Three rooms include a whirlpool tub. The morning meal is prepared in a beautiful brick kitchen, which features an unusual blue cookstove, and is served in the elegant dining room. The menu changes from day to day, apricot filled French toast with pecan topping is one of the inn's specialties.

Innkeeper(s): Ken & Karen Kulberg. $95-139. 8 rooms with PB, 1 with FP and 1 conference room. Breakfast and snacks/refreshments included in rates. Types of meals: Full gourmet bkfst and early coffee/tea. Beds: QDT. Modem hook-up, cable TV, VCR, reading lamp, refrigerator, ceiling fan, telephone, desk, hot tub/spa and fireplace in room. Central air. TV, fax, copier, library, parlor games and gift shop on premises. Antiquing, art galleries, bicycling, fishing, golf, hiking, museums, parks, shopping, tennis, wineries and historic sites nearby.

Location: City. Historic village.

Certificate may be used: Jan. 15-Dec. 15, Sunday-Thursday.

Southern Hotel

146 South Third Street
Sainte Genevieve, MO 63670
(573)883-3493　(800)275-1412　Fax:(573)883-9612
Internet: www.southernhotelbb.com
E-mail: mike@southernhotelbb.com

Circa 1790. Located at the square in historic Sainte Genevieve, the Southern Hotel is a landmark and was known for providing the best accommodations between Natchez and St. Louis, as well as good food, gambling and pool. Guests now enjoy two parlors, a dining room and a game room on the first floor where a quilt is always underway. Guest rooms offer country Victorian furnishings along with whimsical collectibles. Highlights include a rosewood tester bed, a unique iron

bed, several hand-painted headboards and a delicately carved Victorian bed. The clawfoot tubs are hand-painted. Guests also can browse the studio shop as they stroll through the gardens or relax on the long front porch.

Innkeeper(s): Mike & Barbara Hankins. $93-138. 8 rooms with PB, 4 with FP and 2 conference rooms. Breakfast included in rates. Types of meals: Full gourmet bkfst, early coffee/tea and snacks/refreshments. Beds: KQD. Reading lamp, ceiling fan, clock radio, fireplace and clock radios in room. Central air. Fax, copier, bicycles, parlor games, telephone, fireplace and gift shop on premises. Antiquing, art galleries, bicycling, fishing, golf, hiking, museums, parks, shopping, tennis and wineries nearby.

Location: City.

Publicity: *Midwest Living, Southern Living, Country Inns, PBS, Country Inn Cooking, 25 Most Romantic B&B/Inn 2002 and in the top 15 B&B/Inn Best Cook Book 2003.*

"I can't imagine ever staying in a motel again! It was so nice to be greeted by someone who expected us. We felt right at home."

Certificate may be used: Anytime, Sunday-Thursday.

Springfield   G4

Virginia Rose B&B
317 E Glenwood St
Springfield, MO 65807-3543
(417)883-0693 (800)345-1412
E-mail: vrosebb@sisna.com

Circa 1906. Three generations of the Botts family lived in this home before it was sold to the current innkeepers, Virginia and Jackie Buck. The grounds still include the rustic red barn.

Comfortable, country rooms are named after Buck family members and feature beds covered with quilts. The innkeepers also offer a two-bedroom suite, the Rambling Rose, which is decorated in a sportsman theme in honor of the nearby Bass Pro. Hearty breakfasts are served in the dining room, and the innkeepers will provide low-fat fare on request.

Innkeeper(s): Jackie & Virginia Buck. $70-120. 4 rooms, 2 with PB, 1 suite. Breakfast included in rates. Types of meals: Full bkfst, early coffee/tea, picnic lunch and snacks/refreshments. Beds: KQT. Reading lamp, clock radio, telephone and turn-down service in room. Air conditioning. VCR, fax and parlor games on premises. Amusement parks, antiquing, fishing, live theater, parks, shopping, sporting events and water sports nearby.

Location: City.

Publicity: *Auctions & Antiques, Springfield Business Journal, Today's Women Journal and Springfield News-leader.*

"The accommodations are wonderful and the hospitality couldn't be warmer."

Certificate may be used: Sunday through Thursday, Jan. 7-Dec. 13, subject to availability and excluding holidays.

Walnut Street Inn
900 E Walnut St
Springfield, MO 65806-2603
(417)864-6346 (800)593-6346 Fax:(417)864-6184
Internet: www.walnutstreetinn.com
E-mail: stay@walnutstreetinn.com

Circa 1894. This three-story Queen Anne gabled house has cast-iron Corinthian columns and a veranda. Polished wood floors and antiques are featured throughout. Upstairs you'll find the gathering room with a fireplace. Ask for the McCann guest room with two bay windows, or one of the five rooms with a double Jacuzzi tub. A full breakfast is served, including

items such as strawberry-filled French toast.

Innkeeper(s): Gary & Paula Blankenship. $89-169. 12 rooms with PB, 10 with FP, 2 suites. Breakfast included in rates. Types of meals: Full gourmet bkfst, early coffee/tea and afternoon tea. Beds: KQD. Cable TV, VCR, reading lamp, CD player, refrigerator, ceiling fan, clock radio, telephone, coffeemaker, turn-down service, desk, beverage bars and modem in room. Air conditioning. Fax and copier on premises. Handicap access. Amusement parks, antiquing, fishing, live theater, parks, shopping, sporting events and water sports nearby.

Location: City.

Publicity: *Southern Living, Women's World, Midwest Living, Victoria, Country Inns, Innsider, Glamour, Midwest Motorist, Missouri, Saint Louis Post, Kansas City Star and USA Today.*

"Rest assured your establishment's qualities are unmatched and through your commitment to excellence you have won a life-long client."

Certificate may be used: Sunday-Thursday, excluding holidays and certain dates.

Washington   D7

Schwegmann House
438 W Front St
Washington, MO 63090-2103
(636)239-5025 (800)949-2262
Internet: www.schwegmannhouse.com
E-mail: cathy@schwegmannhouse.com

Circa 1861. John F. Schwegmann, a native of Germany, built a flour mill on the Missouri riverfront. This stately three-story home was built not only for the miller and his family, but also to provide extra lodging for overnight customers who traveled long hours to the town. Today, weary travelers enjoy the formal gardens and warm atmosphere of this restful home. Patios overlook the river, and the gracious rooms are decorated with antiques and handmade quilts. The new Miller Suite boasts a tub for two and breakfast can be delivered to their door. Guests enjoy full breakfasts complete

with house specialties such as German apple pancakes or a three-cheese strata accompanied with homemade breads, meat, juice and fresh fruit. There are 11 wineries nearby, or guests can visit one of the historic districts, many galleries, historic sites, antique shops, excellent restaurants and riverfront park located nearby.

Innkeeper(s): Catherine & Bill Nagel. $110-160. 9 rooms with PB, 1 suite. Breakfast and snacks/refreshments included in rates. Types of meals: Full gourmet bkfst and early coffee/tea. Beds: QD. Reading lamp, ceiling fan, telephone and desk in room. Air conditioning. Parlor games and fireplace on premises. Antiquing, Missouri River Wine Country and Katy Bike Trail nearby.

Location: City, waterfront. Missouri River.

Publicity: *St. Louis Post-Dispatch, West County Journal, Midwest Living, Country Inns, Midwest Motorist and Ozark.*

"Like Grandma's house many years ago."

Certificate may be used: Jan. 1-April 30, Monday-Thursday.

Montana

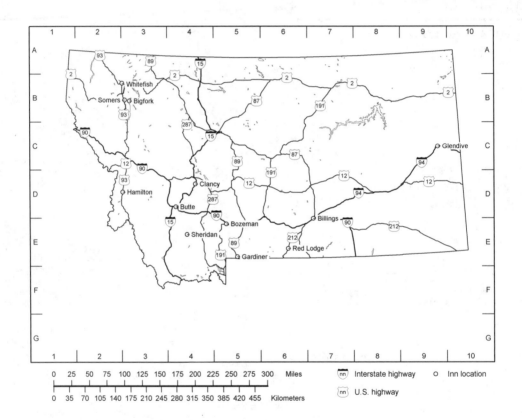

Visit www.iLoveInns.com for photos and more details about each inn.

Bigfork   B3

Burggraf's Countrylane Inn

Rainbow Drive on Swan Lake
Bigfork, MT 59911
(406)837-4608 (800)525-3344 Fax:(406)837-2468
Internet: www.countrylanebandb.net
E-mail: nburggraf@yahoo.com

Circa 1984. This contemporary log home on Swan Lake, minutes from Flathead Lake in the Rockies, offers fine accommodations in one of America's most beautiful settings. Upon arrival, visitors enjoy chilled wine and fresh fruit. Ceiling fans, clock radios and turndown service are amenities. Picnic baskets are available and would be ideal for taking along on a paddle boat lake excursion. Guests enjoy complimentary use of canoes, lawn croquet and barbecue grills by the lake. In addition, there is a small rental cabin, and rental fishing equipment are available, and all will enjoy the inn's seven scenic acres.

Innkeeper(s): Natalie & RJ Burggraf. $105-130. 6 rooms with PB. Breakfast included in rates. Types of meals: Full gourmet bkfst and early coffee/tea. Beds: KQT. Cable TV, VCR, reading lamp, refrigerator, ceiling fan and clock radio in room. Fax, copier, swimming, library, pet boarding, parlor games, telephone and fireplace on premises. Handicap access. Antiquing, cross-country skiing, downhill skiing, fishing, live theater, parks, shopping, sporting events and water sports nearby.

Certificate may be used: May, June, September, weekdays only.

Billings   D7

Josephine Bed & Breakfast

514 N 29th St
Billings, MT 59101-1128
(406)248-5898 (800)552-5898
Internet: www.thejosephine.com
E-mail: info@thejosephine.com

Circa 1910. Enjoy a smoke-free visit at this historic home with a large pillared wraparound porch. Common areas include a cozy parlor with upright piano, TV/VCR, and a comfy study offering board games, books, a desk and phone with dataport. The elegant and comfortable guest bedrooms and suites feature custom stenciling, wicker and waterfall furniture, a whirlpool and clawfoot tub, antiques and modem friendly phones. A gourmet candlelight breakfast is served in the dining room on Blue Willow china. Complimentary newspapers, snacks and beverages are provided.

Innkeeper(s): (L) . $65-160. 5 rooms with PB, 2 suites. Breakfast and snacks/refreshments included in rates. Types of meals: Full gourmet bkfst, veg bkfst, early coffee/tea and room service. Beds: QD. Modem hook-up, data port, cable TV, VCR, reading lamp, refrigerator, ceiling fan, snack bar, clock radio, telephone, coffeemaker, desk and Castle Suite has whirlpool in room. Air conditioning. Library, parlor games, guest computer with rapid Internet, guest passes to health club, complimentary snacks and beverages on premises. Antiquing, art galleries, canoeing/kayaking, cross-country skiing, downhill skiing, fishing, golf, hiking, live theater, museums, parks, shopping, sporting events and tennis nearby.

Location: City.

Certificate may be used: Oct. 1-March 31.

Bozeman   E5

Cottonwood Inn Bed & Breakfast

13515 Cottonwood Canyon Rd
Bozeman, MT 59730
(406)763-5452 (888)879-4667 Fax:(406)763-5639
Internet: www.cottonwood-inn.com
E-mail: info@cottonwood-inn.com

Circa 1995. Honeymooners appreciate the scenic, five-acre mountain location of this custom bed & breakfast featuring stained glass and log accents of cedar and redwood. Guest bedrooms boast a Western decor, ranging from lodgepole and whitewashed pine to white wicker and brass, with some antiques added in. Breakfast cuisine may include Southwestern souffle and bacon, puff pastry filled with fresh berries and topped with hot English custard, breads, juice and hot beverages. Relax on the deck amidst annual and perennial gardens and fields of alpine wildflowers.

Innkeeper(s): Joe & Debbie Velli. $85-129. 5 rooms with PB, 1 with FP, 1 suite. Breakfast, afternoon tea and snacks/refreshments included in rates. Types of meals: Full gourmet bkfst, veg bkfst and early coffee/tea. Beds: QD. Reading lamp, ceiling fan, clock radio, turn-down service and terry cloth robes in room. TV, VCR, fax, copier, spa, library, parlor games, telephone, fireplace, laundry facility and gift shop on premises. Limited handicap access. Antiquing, art galleries, bicycling, canoeing/kayaking, cross-country skiing, downhill skiing, fishing, golf, hiking, horseback riding, live theater, museums, parks, shopping, sporting events, tennis and water sports nearby.

Location: Mountains.

Certificate may be used: Sunday-Thursday, Oct. 15-April 30, subject to availability.

Lindley House

202 Lindley Pl
Bozeman, MT 59715-4833
(406)587-8403 (800)787-8404 Fax:(406)582-8112
Internet: www.avicom.net/lindley
E-mail: lindley@avicom.net

Circa 1889. The beautiful Montana scenery is a perfect backdrop for this romantic bed & breakfast listed in the National Register. The pampering begins in the guest rooms, which offer  plenty of soft, down comforters, feather pillows, fluffy robes and a collection of soaps and oils for a long soak in the tub. Each of the rooms is distinct and memorable. The Marie Antoinette Suite boasts a fireplace, sitting room, clawfoot tub and balcony. The Garden Room offers French Provencal decor with a private garden entrance. Other rooms include items such as wicker furnishings, bay windows, lacy curtains, dramatic wall coverings, a French bistro table or brass bed. The gourmet breakfasts, which feature special treats such as crepes, souffles and a variety of breads, yogurt and cereals, are a perfect start to the day.

Innkeeper(s): Stephanie Volz. $75-250. 6 rooms with PB, 3 suites. Breakfast and afternoon tea included in rates. Types of meals: Full bkfst. Beds: KQT. Antiquing, cross-country skiing, fishing, live theater, shopping and water sports nearby.

"Elegant, but comfortable. Beautifully restored, wonderful attention to detail."

Certificate may be used: Nov. 1 through April 30, Monday through Thursday.

Silver Forest Inn

15325 Bridger Canyon Rd
Bozeman, MT 59715-8278
(406)586-1882 (877)394-9357 Fax:(406)582-0492
Internet: www.silverforestinn.com
E-mail: info@silverforestinn.com

Circa 1932. This historic log home was originally built as a summer artist colony and school of drama. It later served as a hunting lodge. The unusual turret, stone and massive pine log construction makes for a unique accommodation and the secluded setting adds to the experience. Ask to stay in the Turret Room for an expansive view overlooking Bridger Mountains. It boasts a queen-size log bed. (The bath is shared.) A family suite is offered for families with children. Breakfast specialties include blueberry/cream cheese French toast, fresh fruit and chicken sausage.

Innkeeper(s): Lorraine & Mike Conn. $75-130. 6 rooms, 4 with PB. Breakfast and snacks/refreshments included in rates. Types of meals: Full gourmet bkfst and early coffee/tea. Beds: KQT. Reading lamp, clock radio and desk in room. TV, VCR, fax, telephone, fireplace, spa and DVD on premises. Antiquing, bicycling, canoeing/kayaking, cross-country skiing, downhill skiing, fishing, golf, hiking, horseback riding, museums, parks and shopping nearby.

Location: Mountains. Ski resorts.

Certificate may be used: October-November, Sunday-Thursday, April-May, Sunday-Thursday.

Voss Inn

319 S Willson Ave
Bozeman, MT 59715-4632
(406)587-0982 Fax:(406)585-2964
Internet: www.bozeman-vossinn.com
E-mail: vossinn@bridgeband.com

Circa 1883. The Voss Inn is a restored two-story Victorian mansion with a large front porch and a Victorian parlor. Antique furnishings include an upright piano and chandelier. Two of the inn's six rooms include air conditioning. A full breakfast is served, with freshly baked rolls kept in a unique warmer that's built into an ornate 1880s radiator.

Innkeeper(s): Bruce & Frankee Muller. $105-125. 6 rooms with PB, 3 with FP, 1 suite and 1 conference room. Breakfast and afternoon tea included in rates. Types of meals: Full gourmet bkfst, veg bkfst, early coffee/tea and gourmet dinner. Beds: KQT. Modem hook-up, data port, reading lamp, clock radio, telephone, desk and fireplace in room. Air conditioning. TV, fax, copier, library, parlor games and gift shop on premises. Antiquing, art galleries, bicycling, canoeing/kayaking, cross-country skiing, downhill skiing, fishing, golf, hiking, horseback riding, live theater, museums, parks, shopping, sporting events, tennis, golf, hunting, hiking and biking nearby.

Location: City.

Publicity: *Sunset, Cosmopolitan, Gourmet, Countryside and Country Inns.*

"First class all the way."

Certificate may be used: Sunday-Thursday, January-April and October-Dec. 15, subject to availability.

Butte   D4

Copper King Mansion

219 W Granite St
Butte, MT 59701-9235
(406)782-7580
Internet: www.copperkingmansion.com
E-mail: information@copperkingmansion.com

Circa 1884. This turn-of-the-century marvel was built, as the name indicates, by W.A. Clark, one of the nation's leading copper barons. In the early 1900s, Clark made millions each month hauling copper out of Butte's vast mines. Stained-glass windows, gold leafing on the ceilings and elaborate woodwork are just a few of the opulent touches. Clark commissioned artisans brought in from Germany to carve the intricate staircase, which graces the front hall. The mansion is decked floor to ceiling in antiques collected by the innkeeper's mother and grandmother, who purchased the home from Clark's relatives. A three-room master suite includes two fireplaces, a lavish bedroom, a sitting room and a huge bathroom with a clawfoot tub.

Innkeeper(s): John Thompson & Erin Sigl. $65-100. 4 rooms. Breakfast included in rates. Types of meals: Full bkfst.

Publicity: *Sunset Magazine.*

Certificate may be used: January, February, March, April, October, November, December.

Clancy   D4

Elkhorn View B&B

88 Howard Beer Rd.
Clancy, MT 59634
(406)442-1224 Fax:(406)442-5575
Internet: www.elkviewbb.com
E-mail: elkviewbb@hotmail.com

Circa 2001. Recently custom built from 14-inch diameter logs, this lodge sits on 440 park-like acres with hiking, biking and cross-country ski trails. Exposed trusses, a 32-foot high ceiling, slate floors and massive stone fireplaces create a spacious place to relax. The great room boasts a 61-inch satellite TV. Each guest bedroom is decorated with a theme that reflects the land or culture. Explore the outdoors after a satisfying breakfast or make a reservation for a massage. Enjoy the view from the deck while soaking in the hot tub. A sauna and exercise room is also available.

Innkeeper(s): Zac and Lana Titus. $125-145. 4 rooms with PB and 1 conference room. Breakfast, afternoon tea and snacks/refreshments included in rates. Types of meals: Full gourmet bkfst, veg bkfst, early coffee/tea, lunch and dinner. Beds: QD. Modem hook-up, reading lamp, clock radio, telephone, turn-down service, robes, toiletries and reading material in room. Air conditioning. TV, VCR, fax, copier, spa, sauna, bicycles, library, fireplace and laundry facility on premises. Handicap access. Antiquing, art galleries, bicycling, canoeing/kayaking, cross-country skiing, downhill skiing, fishing, golf, hiking, horseback riding, live theater, museums, parks, shopping, sporting events, tennis and water sports nearby.

Location: Country, mountains. Located just 10 miles outside of Helena, convenient yet secluded.

Publicity: *KTVH.*

Certificate may be used: Anytime, Sunday-Thursday.

Gardiner E5

Yellowstone Suites B&B
506 4th St
Gardiner, MT 59030
(406)848-7937 (800)948-7937
Internet: www.yellowstonesuites.com
E-mail: bandb@montanadsl.net

Circa 1904. This three-story stone Victorian home is located just three blocks from the historic Roosevelt Arch, the original gateway to Yellowstone Park. Seasonal activities for the adventure-minded include whitewater rafting, fishing, horseback riding, hiking and canoeing in the summer and snowshoeing, snowmobiling and cross-country skiing in the winter. The road from Gardiner to Cooke City travels through the northern range where antelope, bison, elk, deer, big-horn sheep and wolves are commonly seen. At the end of the day, relax in a rocking chair on the inn's spacious, covered veranda, or soak in the hot tub.

Innkeeper(s): Carolyn and Carol. $49-108. 4 rooms, 2 with PB, 1 suite and 1 conference room. Breakfast and snacks/refreshments included in rates. Types of meals: Full gourmet bkfst, veg bkfst and early coffee/tea. Beds: QT. Cable TV, VCR, reading lamp, refrigerator, ceiling fan, snack bar, clock radio, telephone, coffeemaker and hot tub/spa in room. Air conditioning. Spa, library, parlor games, landscaped garden and covered porch veranda on premises. Art galleries, canoeing/kayaking, cross-country skiing, fishing, hiking, horseback riding, museums, parks and shopping nearby.

Location: Country, mountains. Yellowstone National Park.

Publicity: *Sunset Magazine.*

Certificate may be used: Sept. 20 to May 24.

Glendive C9

The Hostetler House B&B
113 N Douglas St
Glendive, MT 59330-1619
(406)377-4505 (800)965-8456 Fax:(406)377-8456
E-mail: hostetler@midrivers.com

Circa 1912. Casual country decor mixed with handmade and heirloom furnishings are highlights at this Prairie School home. The inn features many comforting touches, such as a romantic hot tub and gazebo, enclosed sun porch and sitting room filled with books and videos. One room has a private bath; the two guest rooms that share a bath are furnished by Dea, an interior decorator. The full breakfasts  may be enjoyed on Grandma's china in the dining room or on the sun porch. The historic Bell Street Bridge and the Yellowstone River are one block from the inn, and downtown shopping is two blocks away. Makoshika State Park, home of numerous fossil finds, is nearby.

Innkeeper(s): Craig & Dea Hostetler. $50-65. 3 rooms. Breakfast included in rates. Types of meals: Full gourmet bkfst and early coffee/tea. Beds: QDT. Reading lamp, ceiling fan and air conditioning in room. VCR, fax, spa, bicycles, library, parlor games, telephone and secretarial service on premises. Antiquing, cross-country skiing, fishing, live theater, parks, shopping, sporting events, water sports and fossil and agate hunting nearby.

Location: City. Small town.

Publicity: *Ranger Review/Circle Banner.*

"Warmth and loving care are evident throughout your exquisite home. Your attention to small details is uplifting. Thank you for a restful sojourn."
Certificate may be used: Anytime.

Hamilton D3

Deer Crossing B&B
396 Hayes Creek Rd
Hamilton, MT 59840-9744
(406)363-2232 (800)763-2232
Internet: www.deercrossingmontana.com
E-mail: deercrossing@montana.com

Circa 1980. This Western-style ranch bed & breakfast is located on 25 acres of woods and pastures. One suite includes a double Jacuzzi tub and another has a private balcony. In addition to the suites and guest rooms, travelers also can opt to stay in the bunkhouse, a historic homestead building with a wood-burning stove. A new creekside log cabin includes a covered porch, fireplace and full kitchen especially appealing to families with small children or long-term guests who want to regroup while enjoying a scenic setting. The area offers many activities, including horseback riding, hiking, fly fishing and historic sites.

Innkeeper(s): Mary Lynch. $99-149. 5 rooms with PB, 2 suites and 2 cabins. Breakfast and snacks/refreshments included in rates. Types of meals: Full bkfst and early coffee/tea. Beds: KQDT. TV, reading lamp, stereo, clock radio and desk in room. VCR, child care, parlor games, telephone, fireplace, satellite dish and fireplace on premises. Antiquing, cross-country skiing, downhill skiing, parks, shopping and water sports nearby.

Location: Mountains. Ranch, 50 miles south of Missoula.

Publicity: *Country Magazine, Montana Handbook*, named "Best Bed & Breakfast in the Bitterroot" and *Horse and Rider.*

"It is so nice to be back after three years and from 5,000 miles away!"
Certificate may be used: Oct. 1 to May 1, any day of the week.

Red Lodge E6

Willows Inn
PO Box 886
Red Lodge, MT 59068-0886
(406)446-3913
Internet: www.bbhost.com/willowsinn
E-mail: willowinn@earthlink.net

Circa 1909. Dreams do come true at this three-story Queen Anne Victorian with gingerbread trim and white picket fence. An assortment of common rooms are accented with original wood molding, leaded-glass windows and boast reading nooks, a TV parlor with extensive videos and a living room. One storybook cottage offer privacy. Antique furnishings and specialty bath products highlight the well-appointed guest bedrooms. Savor a gourmet breakfast and Elven's tasty afternoon refreshments in the cheery wicker-filled dining room. Relax on comfy chairs and enjoy the mountain view from the large front porch that overlooks the colorful flowerbeds and manicured lawn. Stroll down Main Street and stop for lunch or dinner cuisine at Bridge Creek Backcountry Kitchen and Wine Bar.

Innkeeper(s): Carolyn, Kerry & Elven Boggio. $65-85. 5 rooms, 3 with PB and 2 cottages. Breakfast and snacks/refreshments included in rates. Types of meals: Full gourmet bkfst and veg bkfst. Beds: KQDT. VCR, reading lamp, ceiling fan and cottages with television in room. Air conditioning. TV, sauna, bicycles, library, parlor games, telephone, cable TV and CD player on premises. Antiquing, art galleries, bicycling, canoeing/kayaking, cross-country skiing, downhill skiing, fishing, golf, hiking, horseback riding, museums, parks, shopping and tennis nearby.

Location: Mountains.

Publicity: *The Billings Gazette, Innsider, Travel & Leisure, National Geographic Traveler, Gourmet, Country, Forbes, Los Angeles Times and New York Times.*

"It was heavenly. The bed was comfortable and we loved the decor."

Certificate may be used: October-June (excluding Christmas Dec. 24-31).

Sheridan   E4

Montana Mountain Inn

3209 Hwy 287, PO Box 396
Sheridan, MT 59749
(406)842-7111 (866)842-7111 Fax:(406)842-7114
E-mail: Mtmountaininn@aol.com

Circa 1898. A Victorian mansion with a three-story turret and original spiral staircase, this inn has recently been refurbished to offer true Western-style casual elegance and maximum comfort. Secluded suites suit a variety of tastes and meet most every need. A nutritious breakfast will start the day's adventures. Discover seven acres of gardens, ponds, lush landscaped grounds and spectacular mountain views. After a day of hiking, fishing or horseback riding, enjoy the soothing hot tub.

Innkeeper(s): Victoria/Nicholas Nedelcove. $59-98. 7 suites. Breakfast included in rates. Types of meals: Country bkfst, early coffee/tea, picnic lunch and snacks/refreshments. Beds: QT. Cable TV, VCR, reading lamp, ceiling fan, clock radio, telephone, coffeemaker, hot tub/spa and voice mail in room. Fax, copier, spa, stable, library, pet boarding, parlor games, fireplace, laundry facility and trout pond on premises. Limited handicap access. Antiquing, art galleries, bicycling, canoeing/kayaking, cross-country skiing, downhill skiing, fishing, hiking, horseback riding, museums, parks, shopping, sporting events, water sports, hunting, float trips, river rafting and cattle drives nearby.

Location: Country, mountains. Heart of the Ruby Valley, surrounded by Tobacco Root and Ruby Mountains.

Certificate may be used: March-June, any day of the week.

Somers   B3

Outlook Inn Bed & Breakfast

PO Box 177
Somers, MT 59932-0177
(406)857-2060 (888)857-VIEW
Internet: www.outlookinnbandb.com
E-mail: outlook@digisys.net

Circa 1998. Surrounded by scenic beauty, this Flathead Valley lodge overlooks the lake and the Rocky Mountains. Relax by the river-rock fireplace. A common room includes thoughtful use of a microwave, refrigerator, TV, phone, modem hookup, games and a small library. Each of the Montana-themed guest bedrooms features a log deck. The Gone Fishing room offers a jetted tub. The romantic Honeymoon in the Rockies boasts a double-headed shower. Huckleberry pancakes and flathead monster potatoes are hearty breakfast favorites. Enjoy seven acres of spectacular views and a variety of activities.

Innkeeper(s): Todd & Michelle Ahern. $65-95. 4 rooms with PB, 4 with FP. Breakfast included in rates. Types of meals: Full gourmet bkfst, veg bkfst and early coffee/tea. Beds: Q. Modem hook-up, cable TV, VCR, reading lamp, refrigerator, clock radio, telephone, hot tub/spa and fireplace in room. Library, parlor games, fireplace and laundry facility on premises. Antiquing, art galleries, beach, bicycling, canoeing/kayaking, cross-country skiing, downhill skiing, fishing, golf, hiking, horseback riding, live theater, museums, parks, shopping, tennis, water sports and wineries nearby.

Location: Country. Next to water.

Publicity: *Denver Post, Daily and Interlake.*

Certificate may be used: Monday-Thursday from October to May.

Whitefish   B2

Good Medicine Lodge

537 Wisconsin Ave
Whitefish, MT 59937-2127
(406)862-5488 (800)860-5488 Fax:(406)862-5489
Internet: www.goodmedicinelodge.com
E-mail: info@goodmedicinelodge.com

Circa 1974. This modern lodge is fashioned from cedar wood. Guest rooms feature natural cedar walls and ceilings with exposed cedar beams. The décor is Western in style with comfortable furnishings. Two rooms include a fireplace. Breakfast includes a large European-style buffet with homemade baked goods, granola, sliced meats, cheeses, juices and freshly brewed coffee. The lodge is located in a mountain setting near to Glacier Park, golf courses, skiing, watersports and much more.

Innkeeper(s): Betsy & Woody Cox. $90-185. 9 rooms with PB, 2 with FP, 1 with WP, 2 two-bedroom suites and 1 conference room. Breakfast, snacks/refreshments and wine included in rates. Types of meals: Full gourmet bkfst, hors d'oeuvres and room service. Beds: KQT. Data port, reading lamp, CD player, ceiling fan, clock radio, telephone, desk, hot tub/spa, fireplace and wireless DSL in room. Central air. TV, VCR, fax, copier, spa, library, parlor games and laundry facility on premises. Limited handicap access. Amusement parks, antiquing, art galleries, beach, bicycling, canoeing/kayaking, cross-country skiing, downhill skiing, fishing, golf, hiking, horseback riding, parks, sporting events, tennis and water sports nearby.

Location: City, mountains. Mountains near Glacier National Park.

Publicity: *"Mountain Sports and Living" Inn of the Month and "Travel America Magazine" top ten most romantic inns.*

Certificate may be used: Oct. 1-May 31.

Kandahar-The Lodge at Big Mountain

PO Box 278
Whitefish, MT 59937
(406)862-6098 (800)862-6094 Fax:(406)862-6095
Internet: www.kandaharlodge.com
E-mail: info@kandaharlodge.com

Circa 1983. Surrounded by alpine splendor, this European-style chalet is in the center of a year-round recreational wonderland. The mountain inn features an upscale rustic decor with comfortable furnishings. Relax in the large lobby with a wood-burning fireplace and big screen TV or gather in the Snug Bar to tell fish stories. A variety of guest accommodations include hotel-style rooms, studios with kitchens that convert into a two-room suite and loft units with pine paneling, leather furniture and down comforters. Cafe Kandahar, the intimate candle-lit restaurant, offers a breakfast and fine dining with an award-winning wine list. Enjoy the large outdoor Jacuzzi, sauna and steam room. A groomed ski run starts at the back door.

Innkeeper(s): Jennifer Fisher & Jim Lockwood. $99-399. 50 rooms, 49 with PB, 1 suite and 1 conference room. Breakfast included in rates. Types of meals: Full bkfst, early coffee/tea and dinner. Restaurant on premises. Beds: KQ. Data port, cable TV, refrigerator, ceiling fan, clock radio, telephone, coffeemaker, microwave and loft rooms have air conditioning in room. VCR, fax, copier, spa, sauna, fireplace, laundry facility, steam room, full service lounge, exercise room and massage services on premises. Art galleries, beach, bicycling, canoeing/kayaking, cross-country skiing, downhill skiing, fishing, golf, hiking, live theater, museums, parks, shopping, tennis, water sports, Glacier National Park and Flathead Lake and Canadian border nearby.

Location: Mountains. Located in beautiful Big Mountain Resort near Whitefish, Montana and close to Glacier Park.

Publicity: *Mountain Living.*

Certificate may be used: June 1-30, Sept. 1-30, Nov. 26-Dec. 18.

Nebraska

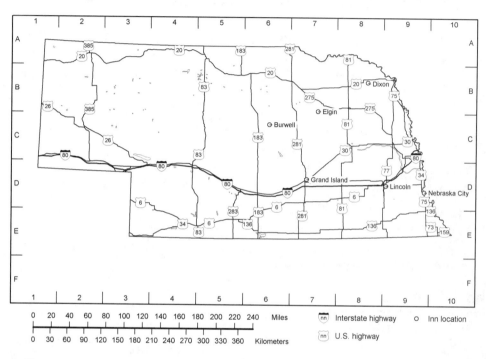

0 20 40 60 80 100 120 140 160 180 200 220 240 Miles

0 30 60 90 120 150 180 210 240 270 300 330 360 Kilometers

(nn) Interstate highway   o Inn location

(nn) U.S. highway

Burwell   C6

Autumn Leaf B&B
RR 2 Box 21
Burwell, NE 68823-9004
(308)346-4366 Fax:(308)346-9108
Internet: www.geocities.com/autumnleafbb
E-mail: autumnleafbb@yahoo.com

Located in the scenic "Gateway to the Sandhills" less than a mile
to North Loup River, this spacious monolithic dome is ideal for a
rustic and homey bed and breakfast experience. Relax in the sitting area with a fireplace, television and a selection of children's
videos. Take the spiral staircase up to a roomy loft. Enjoy a comfortable night's rest in one of the three guest bedrooms. The
breakfast nook in the kitchen includes an extra microwave and
purified water. Laundry service, kennels and a small amount of
meat storage are available. Ask about hunting packages.
$65-75. 4 rooms.

Certificate may be used: Anytime, November-March, subject to availability.
April-October, Sunday-Thursday.

Dixon   B8

The George Farm
57759 874 Road
Dixon, NE 68732-3024
(402)584-2625
E-mail: dixonmom@nntc.net

Circa 1926. Two miles off Highway 20, west of Sioux City, lies
this air-conditioned farmhouse furnished in country decor.
Although in a rural setting, the farm offers a wide array of activities within easy driving distance. Wayne State College is nearby,
as are an abundance of local crafts and antique establishments.
Marie, an avid antiquer, can provide help for those searching the
area for special items. Relax with a stroll through the farm's 640
acres, or just enjoy some peace and quiet in the library. The inn
accepts children and pets, with prior arrangement.
Innkeeper(s): Marie George. $40-55. 6 rooms. Breakfast included in rates.
Types of meals: Full bkfst. Beds: QD. Reading lamp, clock radio and desk in
room. Air conditioning. VCR, parlor games and telephone on premises.
Location: Country.

Certificate may be used: Year-round except second weekend in July and first
weekend of pheasant hunting season (usually first weekend of November).

Elgin   B7

Plantation House

401 Plantation St RR 2 Box 17
Elgin, NE 68636-9301
(402)843-2287 (888)446-2287 Fax:(402)843-2287
Internet: www.plantation-house.com
E-mail: plantation@gpcom.net

Circa 1916. This historic mansion sits adjacent to Elgin City Park, and guests will marvel at its beauty and size. Once a small Victorian farmhouse, the Plantation House has evolved into a 20-room Greek Revival treasure. Visitors will be treated to a tour and a large family-style breakfast, and may venture to the park to play tennis or horseshoes.  The antique-filled guest rooms include the Stained Glass Room, with a queen bed and available twin-bed anteroom, and the Old Master Bedroom, with clawfoot tub and pedestal sink.

Innkeeper(s): Kyle & Deb Warren. $60-75. 5 rooms with PB, 1 cottage and 2 conference rooms. Breakfast included in rates. Types of meals: Full bkfst and early coffee/tea. Beds: QT. Reading lamp, ceiling fan and clock radio in room. Air conditioning. VCR, fax, copier, library, parlor games, telephone and fireplace on premises. Antiquing, fishing, parks, shopping and historical parks and sites nearby.

Location: Edge of small town.

Publicity: *Omaha World Herald, Norfolk Daily News, Home & Away, Midwest Living and Nebraska Life.*

"Gorgeous house! Relaxing atmosphere. Just like going to Mom's house."

Certificate may be used: Jan. 30 to April 30, Sunday-Friday. Oct. 1 to Nov. 15, Sunday-Friday.

Grand Island   D7

Kirschke House B&B

1124 W 3rd St
Grand Island, NE 68801-5834
(308)381-6851 (866)330-6851
Internet: www.kirschkehouse.com

A steeply sloping roofline and a two-story tower mark this distinctive, vine-covered brick Victorian house. Meticulously restored, there are polished wood floors, fresh wallpapers and  carefully chosen antiques. The Roses Roses Room is a spacious accommodation with a lace canopy bed, wicker rocking chair and accents of roses and vines. In the old brick wash house is a wooden hot tub. In winter and spring, the area is popular for viewing the migration of sandhill cranes and whooping cranes.

Innkeeper(s): Lois Hank. Call for rates. Call inn for details.

Certificate may be used: Anytime, subject to availability.

Lincoln   D9

The Atwood House B&B

740 S 17th St
Lincoln, NE 68508-3708
(402)438-4567 (800)884-6554 Fax:(402)477-8314
Internet: www.atwoodhouse.com
E-mail: larry@atwoodhouse.com

Circa 1894. Located two blocks from the state capitol, this 7,500-square-foot mansion, in the Neoclassical Georgian Revival style, features four massive columns. Interior columns are repeated throughout such as on the dressing room vanity, on the staircase and on the parlor fireplace. Classically appointed, the parlor and entranceway set an elegant yet inviting tone. Guest suites are large and feature spacious sitting rooms, fireplaces, massive bedsteads and Oriental carpets. The 800-square-foot bridal suite consists of three rooms, and it includes a fireplace, a carved walnut bed and a large whirlpool tub set off by columns. Breakfast is served on bone china with Waterford crystal and sterling flatware.

Innkeeper(s): Ruth & Larry Stoll. $85-179. 4 rooms, 2 with FP, 4 suites, 1 cottage and 1 conference room. Breakfast and snacks/refreshments included in rates. Types of meals: Full gourmet bkfst, veg bkfst and early coffee/tea. Beds: KQ. Modem hook-up, cable TV, VCR, reading lamp, stereo, refrigerator, ceiling fan, clock radio, telephone, coffeemaker, turn-down service, desk, hot tub/spa, fireplace and three with two-person whirlpool in room. Central air. Fax, copier and library on premises. Antiquing, bicycling, cross-country skiing, fishing, golf, horseback riding, live theater, parks, shopping, sporting events, tennis and water sports nearby.

Location: City.

Publicity: *Lincoln Journal Star, Channel 8 local (ABC), Channel 10/11 local (CBS), KLIN and AM1400.*

"Such a delightful B&B! It is such a nice change in my travels."

Certificate may be used: Jan. 2 to April 30, Monday-Thursday for the Beals, Atwood or Carriage House suite.

Nebraska City   D9

Whispering Pines

RR 2
Nebraska City, NE 68410-9802
(402)873-5850
Internet: www.bbonline.com/ne/whispering/
E-mail: wppines@alltel.net

Circa 1892. An easy getaway from Kansas City, Lincoln or Omaha, Nebraska City's Whispering Pines offers visitors a relaxing alternative from big-city life. Fresh flowers in each bedroom greet guests at this two-story brick Italianate, furnished with Victorian and country decor. Situated on more than six acres of trees, flowers and ponds, the inn is a birdwatcher's delight. Breakfast is served formally in the dining room, or guests may opt to eat on the deck with its view of the garden and pines. The inn is within easy walking distance to Arbor Lodge, home of the founder of Arbor Day.

Innkeeper(s): W.B. Smulling. $55-80. 5 rooms, 2 with PB. Breakfast included in rates. Types of meals: Full gourmet bkfst.

Certificate may be used: Jan. 2 to Dec. 15, Sunday-Thursday.

Nevada

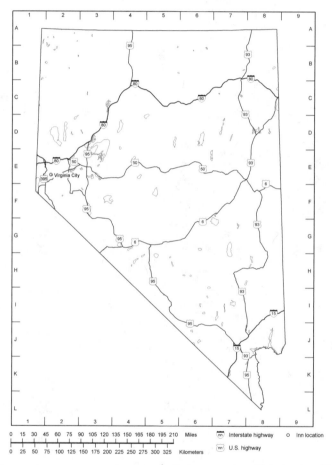

Virginia City   E2

Chollar Mansion
565 S D St
Virginia City, NV 89440
(775)847-9777

Circa 1861. Built in 1861, this National Register home is the perfect spot to immerse yourself into the mining mystique when the home served as a mining office. The innkeepers are knowledgeable about the mine's history and enjoy touring guests to the 164-square-foot underground vault where the company's bullion was stored. There's a paymaster's booth next to the kitchen, a men's and ladies' parlor, a library, and a formal dining room where breakfast is served (full breakfasts are provided in the winter and a continental breakfast is offered at other times of the year). Furnishings include antiques that highlight the inn's detailed Victorian craftsmanship. A cottage on the property, decorated in country style, is popular with families who have children. Other accommodations include a suite with a private bath and two rooms that share a bath between them. Guests enjoy views through Six Mile Canyon for up to 140-180 miles across to the mountain ranges on clear days.

Innkeeper(s): Kenneth & Kay Benton. Call for rates. 4 rooms with PB. Types of meals: Full bkfst. TV and ceiling fan in room.

Certificate may be used: Jan. 1 to Feb. 28, upon availability.

New Hampshire

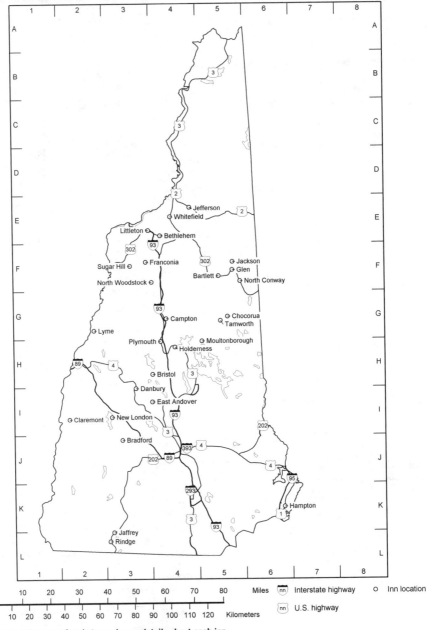

	Miles		Interstate highway		Inn location

U.S. highway

Visit www.iLoveInns.com for photos and more details about each inn.

Bartlett   F5

The Bartlett Inn

Rt 302, PO Box 327
Bartlett, NH 03812
(603)374-2353 (800)292-2353 Fax:(603)374-2547
Internet: www.bartlettinn.com
E-mail: stay@bartlettinn.com

Circa 1885. One mile from White Mountain National Forest, near Crawford Notch State Park and Mount Washington, stands an 1885 Stick Victorian Inn cottage on two-and-a-half acres. The inn has appeared in numerous publications, including Outside Magazine, because of its proximity to the wilderness. Guests may choose among 16 bedrooms and 10 cottages. A full country breakfast offers courses such as custom omelets, crepes, waffles, ham and bacon. After a day enjoying the wilderness by hiking, canoeing or mountain biking, guests may relax in a rocking chair on the front porch, swing in the hammock or enjoy the stars as they soak in the hot tub. Moose, deer, fox and coyote have been spotted in nearby areas.

Innkeeper(s): Miriam Habert & Nick Jacques. $79-175. 16 rooms, 10 with PB, 4 with FP and 10 cottages. Breakfast included in rates. Types of meals: Country bkfst and early coffee/tea. Beds: D. Cable TV, refrigerator and coffeemaker in room. Air conditioning. VCR, fax, spa, library, parlor games, telephone and fireplace on premises. Limited handicap access. Antiquing, art galleries, bicycling, canoeing/kayaking, cross-country skiing, downhill skiing, fishing, golf, hiking, horseback riding, live theater, museums, parks, shopping, tennis and water sports nearby.

Location: Country, mountains.

Publicity: *Outside Magazine, Adventure Journal, Boston Herald, Backcountry, NH Explorers Guide, Family Camping and New Hampshire Handbook.*

"Walking through your door felt like stepping back in time."

Certificate may be used: Sunday-Thursday nights, excluding August, Oct. 1-15, Dec. 15-Jan. 1.

Bethlehem   E4

The Mulburn Inn

2370 Main St, Rt 302
Bethlehem, NH 03574
(603)869-3389 (800)457-9440
Internet: www.mulburninn.com
E-mail: info@mulburninn.com

Circa 1908. This English Tudor mansion was once the summer estate of the Woolworth family. The home was built by notable architect Sylvanius D. Morgan, whose inspired design includes many intricate details. The home's romantic ambiance entices a multitude of visitors, and it is within these idyllic walls that Cary Grant and Barbara Hutton enjoyed their honeymoon. Today, guests also have use of a hot tub.

Innkeeper(s): Christina Ferraro & Alecia Loveless. $85-175. 7 rooms with PB. Breakfast included in rates. Types of meals: Full gourmet bkfst. Beds: KQ. Reading lamp, clock radio and desk in room. Air conditioning. TV, VCR, fax, spa, library, parlor games, telephone and fireplace on premises. Antiquing, bicycling, canoeing/kayaking, cross-country skiing, downhill skiing, fishing, golf, live theater, parks, shopping, tennis, water sports and romantic getaways nearby.

Location: Mountains.

Publicity: *Cover of Yankee B&B Guide, NECN This is Your Dream House, The Today Show and Home & Garden Channel.*

"You have put a lot of thought, charm, beauty and warmth into the inn. Your breakfasts were oh, so delicious!!"

Certificate may be used: Jan. 1-Sept. 10, Sunday-Thursday; Oct. 25-Dec. 24, Sunday-Thursday.

Bradford   J3

Candlelite Inn

5 Greenhouse Ln
Bradford, NH 03221-3505
(603)938-5571 (888)812-5571 Fax:(603)938-2564
Internet: www.candleliteinn.com
E-mail: candlelite@conknet.com

Circa 1897. Nestled on three acres of countryside in the valley of the Lake Sunapee region, this Victorian inn has all of the grace and charm of an era gone by. The inn offers a gazebo porch perfect for sipping lemonade on a summer day. On winter days, keep warm by the parlor's fireplace, while relaxing with a good book. Enjoy a three-course gourmet breakfast, including dessert, in the sun room overlooking the pond. Country roads invite fall strolls, cross-country skiing and snowshoeing.

Innkeeper(s): Les & Marilyn Gordon. $95-140. 6 rooms with PB, 1 with FP, 2 suites and 1 conference room. Breakfast and snacks/refreshments included in rates. Types of meals: Full gourmet bkfst, early coffee/tea and picnic lunch. Beds: Q. Reading lamp, ceiling fan, clock radio, some with sitting areas, glass front gas stove, large shower heads and hair dryers in room. Air conditioning. Parlor games, telephone, fireplace, gift shop, piano, afternoon refreshments into the evening, stocked guest refrigerator, porches and pond on premises. Antiquing, bicycling, canoeing/kayaking, cross-country skiing, downhill skiing, fishing, golf, hiking, horseback riding, live theater, museums, shopping, sporting events and tennis nearby.

Location: Country, mountains.

Publicity: *Taste of New England, Congressional Record, Country Extra Magazine, Arrington's Book of Lists, Accord Publishing B&B calendar, New Hampshire Magazine, Best Recipes from American Country Inns and Bed & Breakfasts—Volume III, Hospitality News and Voted 2001 Inn of the Year.*

Certificate may be used: Sunday through Thursday, excluding holidays, November-May.

Bristol   H4

Henry Whipple House

75 Summer Street
Bristol, NH 03222
(603)744-6157 Fax:(603)744-6569
Internet: www.thewhipplehouse.com
E-mail: info@thewhipplehouse.com

Circa 1904. Centrally located in scenic New England, this Queen Anne is a grand example of a typical Victorian-era home. Stained-glass windows, oak woodwork, chandeliers and hardwood floors all add to the historic charm. Bedchambers in the main house and two carriage house suites are furnished with antiques, candles, personal spa amenities and plush towels. Several rooms feature bronze-engraved fireplaces. Locally grown produce and high-quality meats from Edwards of Surrey, Virginia are used to make a gourmet breakfast of homemade scones or baked goods, eggs Benedict, potato cakes with warm apple sauce, asparagus frittata, crispy bacon and gruyere omelets, tipsy orange French toast and apple pecan pancakes. Enjoy the year-round beauty and activities available nearby.

Innkeeper(s): Sandra Heaney. $90-175. 8 rooms, 6 with PB, 2 with FP, 2 suites. Breakfast included in rates. Types of meals: Full gourmet bkfst, veg bkfst and early coffee/tea. Beds: KQDT. Modem hook-up, cable TV, VCR, reading lamp, stereo, refrigerator, ceiling fan, clock radio, coffeemaker and fireplace in room. Air conditioning. Fax, copier, library, parlor games and telephone on premises. Amusement parks, antiquing, art galleries, beach, bicycling, canoeing/kayaking, cross-country skiing, downhill skiing, fishing, golf, hiking, horseback riding, live theater, museums, parks, shopping and water sports nearby.

Location: Country, mountains.

Certificate may be used: April 1-May 25, Oct. 20-Dec. 15.

Pleasant View Bed and Breakfast

22 Hemp Hill Road
Bristol, NH 03222
(603)744-5547 (888)909-2700 Fax:(603)744-9757
Internet: www.pleasantviewbedandbreakfast.com
E-mail: theinnwench@metrocast.net

Gracing the heart of the state's Lakes Region on a scenic rural road, this bed and breakfast was built as a farmhouse prior to 1832 for a local blacksmith with land extending to the shores of Newfound Lake. Relax in country elegance in the great room or on the patio. Play games or read a book from the library by a warm fire. Comfortable guest bedrooms include turndown service. After a satisfying breakfast take a bike ride to enjoy the surrounding beauty.

$95-115. 6 rooms with PB. Breakfast included in rates. Types of meals: Full bkfst and early coffee/tea. Beds: KQD. Data port, cable TV, reading lamp, clock radio, turn-down service and desk in room. Fax, copier, bicycles, library, parlor games, telephone and fireplace on premises. Antiquing, art galleries, beach, bicycling, canoeing/kayaking, cross-country skiing, downhill skiing, fishing, golf, hiking, horseback riding, live theater, museums, parks, shopping, water sports and wineries nearby.

Location: Country.

Certificate may be used: Anytime, Sunday-Thursday.

Campton   G4

Colonel Spencer Inn

3 Colonel Spencer Rd
Campton, NH 03223
(603)536-3438
Internet: www.colonelspencerinn.com

Circa 1764. This pre-Revolutionary Colonial boasts Indian shutters, gleaming plank floors and a secret hiding place. Joseph Spencer, one of the home's early owners, fought at Bunker Hill and with General Washington. Within view of the river and the mountains, the inn is now a cozy retreat with warm Colonial decor. A suite with a kitchen is also available.

Innkeeper(s): Carolyn & Alan Hill. $45-65. 7 rooms with PB, 1 suite. Breakfast and snacks/refreshments included in rates. Types of meals: Full bkfst. Beds: D. Reading lamp and fans in room. TV, parlor games, telephone and fireplace on premises. Antiquing, cross-country skiing, downhill skiing, fishing, live theater, parks, shopping, sporting events, water sports and water parks nearby.

Location: Country, mountains.

"You have something very special here, and we very much enjoyed a little piece of it!"

Certificate may be used: Anytime except holiday weekends and weekends in October.

Mountain-Fare Inn

Mad River Rd, PO Box 553
Campton, NH 03223
(603)726-4283 Fax:(603)726-8188
Internet: www.mountainfareinn.com
E-mail: mtnfareinn@cyberportal.net

Circa 1830. Located in the White Mountains between Franconia Notch and Squam Lake, this white farmhouse is surrounded by flower gardens in the summer and unparalleled foliage in the fall. Mountain-Fare is an early 19th-century village inn in an ideal spot from which to enjoy New Hampshire's many offerings. Each season brings with it different activities, from skiing to biking and hiking or simply taking in the beautiful scenery. Skiers will enjoy the inn's lodge atmosphere during the winter, as well as the close  access to ski areas. The inn is appointed in a charming New Hampshire style with country-cottage decor. There's a game room with billiards and a soccer field for playing ball. The hearty breakfast is a favorite of returning guests.

Innkeeper(s): Susan & Nick Preston. $85-145. 10 rooms with PB. Breakfast and afternoon tea included in rates. Types of meals: Full bkfst. Beds: QDT. Reading lamp and clock radio in room. TV, VCR, sauna, telephone, fireplace, game room with billiards and soccer field on premises. Antiquing, cross-country skiing, downhill skiing, fishing, hiking, live theater, parks, sporting events and water sports nearby.

Location: Mountains. New Hampshire White Mountains.

Publicity: *Ski, Skiing and Snow Country.*

"Thank you for your unusually caring attitude toward your guests."

Certificate may be used: Sunday through Thursday nights except Dec. 15-Jan. 2 and Sept. 15-Oct. 20.

Chocorua   G5

Brass Heart Inn

PO Box 370
Chocorua, NH 03817-0370
(603)323-7766 (800)833-9509 Fax:(603)323-7531
Internet: www.thebrassheartinn.com
E-mail: info@thebrassheartinn.com

Circa 1787. The main building of Harte's, home to a prosperous farm family for over 150 years, is Federal style. It became a guest house in the 1890s. An old apple orchard and sugar house remain, and there's a kitchen garden. A rocky brook still winds through the rolling fields, and in the adjacent woods, there's a natural swimming hole. Guest rooms are furnished in antiques and replicas.

Innkeeper(s): Don & Joanna Harte. $70-240. 14 rooms, 5 with PB, 1 with FP, 4 suites, 3 cottages and 1 conference room. Breakfast included in rates. Types of meals: Full gourmet bkfst. Restaurant on premises. Beds: KQDT. Reading lamp, refrigerator, clock radio, coffeemaker, turn-down service and fireplace in room. TV, fax, copier, library, parlor games, telephone and gift shop on premises. Limited handicap access. Antiquing, art galleries, beach, bicycling, canoeing/kayaking, cross-country skiing, downhill skiing, fishing, golf, hiking, horseback riding, live theater, museums, shopping, tennis and water sports nearby.

Location: Country.

Publicity: *Esquire, Boston Globe, Seattle Times, Los Angeles Times, WRCH, WPKQ and WMagic.*

"Delicious food, delightful humor!"

Certificate may be used: Jan. 2 through May, Thursday before Memorial Day. Sunday-Thursday.

Riverbend Inn Bed & Breakfast

P. O. Box 288
Chocorua, NH 03817
(603)323-7440 (800)628-6944 Fax:(603)323-7554
Internet: www.riverbendinn.com
E-mail: info@riverbendinn.com

Circa 1968. Sitting on 15 scenic acres, this secluded country estate is conveniently located between the White Mountains and Lakes Region. Recently renovated, a luxurious decor is accented by antique furnishings. Enjoy afternoon drinks by the fire. Air conditioned guest bedrooms feature cotton linens, mahogany beds, terry robes and cable TV. One room boasts a private deck and entrance. Breakfast is a multi-course delight that may include

favorites like fresh fruit compote and maple yogurt with roasted granola or grapefruit sections with rum-raisin sauce, cinnamon plum cake or cranberry-bran muffins, eggs florentine or Creme Brulee French Toast. Wander through the gorgeous gardens, meadows and be refreshed by the Chocorua River that runs through the grounds. Relax on the deck or in a hammock.
Innkeeper(s): Craig Cox, Jerry Weiss. $79-199. 10 rooms, 6 with PB. Breakfast and snacks/refreshments included in rates. Types of meals: Full gourmet bkfst. Beds: KQD. Cable TV, reading lamp, luxurious all-cotton bed linens and plush terry robes in room. Air conditioning. Fax, copier, library, parlor games, telephone, fireplace, hammocks, yoga/meditation room and massage available on premises. Antiquing, art galleries, bicycling, canoeing/kayaking, cross-country skiing, downhill skiing, fishing, golf, hiking, horseback riding, live theater, museums, parks, shopping, water sports and sled dog races nearby.
Location: Country, mountains, waterfront. Babbling brook frontage.
Publicity: *New Hampshire Magazine (June 2004 cover).*

"We can't wait to see all four seasons here. Thank you for all the extra touches."
Certificate may be used: Anytime, November-May, subject to availability.

Claremont   I2

Goddard Mansion B&B

25 Hillstead Rd
Claremont, NH 03743-3317
(603)543-0603 (800)736-0603 Fax:(603)543-0001
Internet: www.goddardmansion.com
E-mail: info@goddardmansion.com

Circa 1905. This English-style manor house and adjacent gar-den tea house is surrounded by seven acres of lawns and gar-dens. Each of the guest rooms is decorated in a different style. One features French Country decor, another sports a Victorian look. The living room with
its fireplace, window seats and baby grand piano is a perfect place to relax. Homemade breakfasts, made using natural ingre-

dients and fresh produce, include items such as souffles, pan-cakes, freshly baked muffins and fruit. The hearty breakfasts are served in the wood paneled dining room highlighted by an antique Wurlitzer jukebox.
Innkeeper(s): Debbie Albee. $75-135. 10 rooms, 3 with PB, 1 suite and 2 conference rooms. Breakfast included in rates. Types of meals: Full gourmet bkfst. Beds: KQDT. TV, reading lamp, clock radio, telephone, turn-down ser-

vice and some with desks in room. Air conditioning. VCR, fax, bicycles, library, parlor games, fireplace, child care and Internet connection on premises. Antiquing, cross-country skiing, downhill skiing, fishing, live theater, parks, shopping and canoeing and kayaking on Connecticut River nearby.
Location: Mountains. Rural.
Publicity: *Eagle Times, Yankee (editors pick), Boston Globe and Manchester Union Leader.*

"A perfect romantic getaway spot."
Certificate may be used: Anytime, subject to availability.

Danbury   H3

The Inn at Danbury

67 N.H. Route 104
Danbury, NH 03230
(603)768-3318 Fax:(603)768-3773
Internet: www.innatdanbury.com
E-mail: alex@innatdanbury.com

Circa 1870. Multilingual innkeeper Alexandra imparts a New England hospitality with a European flair at this cozy yet ram-bling country inn on five wooded acres. The original 1850 roadside farmhouse has evolved into comfortable accommoda-tions with a carriage house and historic wing. Sit by the locally quarried mica stone fireplace in the living room, read a book from the secluded library, converse on the wraparound four-seasons porch, play games in the front game room or relax in the upstairs common room. All the suites and guest bedrooms feature scenic views and either a modern rustic or historically preserved decor. The Alpenglow Bistro dining room offers din-ners and Sunday brunch. An adjacent sunroom opens onto a patio and English gardens.
Innkeeper(s): Alex Graf. Call for rates. Call inn for details. Types of meals: Dinner. Reading lamp, ceiling fan and clock radio in room. VCR, child care, telephone and fireplace on premises. Antiquing, cross-country skiing, down-hill skiing, live theater and shopping nearby.
Location: Mountains. Rural town.
Certificate may be used: Anytime, excluding holidays, some weekends and February.

East Andover   J4

Highland Lake Inn B&B

32 Maple St
East Andover, NH 03231-0164
(603)735-6426 Fax:(603)735-5355
Internet: www.highlandlakeinn.com
E-mail: highlandlakeinn@msn.com

Circa 1767. This early Colonial-Victorian inn overlooks three mountains, and all the rooms have views of either the lake or the mountains. Many guest rooms feature handmade quilts and some have four-poster beds. Guests may relax with a book from the inn's library in front of the sit-ting room fireplace or walk the seven-acre grounds and enjoy old apple and maple trees, as well as the shoreline of the lake. Adjacent to a 21-acre nature conservancy, there are scenic trails and a stream to explore. Highland Lake is stocked with bass and also has trout. Fresh fruit salads, hot entrees, and homemade breads are featured at breakfast.
Innkeeper(s): Steve & Judee Hodges. $90-130. 10 rooms with PB, 2 with FP. Breakfast and snacks/refreshments included in rates. Types of meals: Full gourmet bkfst, veg bkfst and early coffee/tea. Beds: KQT. Reading lamp, ceil-

ing fan, clock radio, desk and fireplace in room. TV, VCR, fax, swimming, library, parlor games, telephone and gift shop on premises. Limited handicap access. Antiquing, art galleries, beach, bicycling, canoeing/kayaking, cross-country skiing, downhill skiing, fishing, golf, hiking, live theater, museums, shopping, water sports, NASCAR Track and Greyhound Racing nearby.

Location: Country, mountains.

Publicity: *Intertown, Neighbors, Valley Business Journal and WMUR Channel 9.*

"New Hampshire at its most magical."

Certificate may be used: May-October, Sunday-Thursday; November-April, subject to availability.

Franconia   F3

Franconia Inn

1300 Easton Rd
Franconia, NH 03580-4921
(603)823-5542 (800)473-5299 Fax:(603)823-8078
Internet: www.franconiainn.com
E-mail: info@franconiainn.com

Circa 1934. Beautifully situated on 117 acres below the White Mountain's famous Franconia Notch, this white clapboard inn is three stories high. An oak-paneled library, parlor, rathskeller

lounge and two verandas offer relaxing retreats. The inn's rooms are simply decorated in a pleasing style and there is a special honeymoon suite with private Jacuzzi. Bach, classic wines

and an elegant American cuisine are featured in the inn's unpretentious dining room. There's no shortage of activity here. The inn offers four clay tennis courts, horseback riding, a heated swimming pool, croquet, fishing, cross-country ski trails and glider rides among its outdoor amenities.

Innkeeper(s): Alec Morris. $103-188. 34 rooms, 29 with PB, 3 with FP, 4 suites, 1 cottage and 1 conference room. Breakfast included in rates. Types of meals: Full gourmet bkfst, early coffee/tea, picnic lunch and gourmet dinner. Restaurant on premises. Beds: KQDT. Reading lamp, clock radio and desk in room. TV, VCR, copier, spa, swimming, bicycles, tennis, child care, parlor games, telephone, fireplace, sleighs and ice skating on premises. Amusement parks, antiquing, cross-country skiing, downhill skiing, fishing, live theater, parks, shopping and sporting events nearby.

Location: Country, mountains.

Publicity: *Philadelphia Inquirer, Boston Globe, Travel & Leisure and Powder.*

"The piece de resistance of the Franconia Notch is the Franconia Inn."—Philadelphia Inquirer

Certificate may be used: Midweek, Sunday-Thursday, non-holiday, June, November-March.

Glen   F5

Bernerhof Inn

Rt 302, PO Box 240
Glen, NH 03838-0240
(603)383-9132 (800)548-8007 Fax:(603)383-0809
Internet: www.bernerhofinn.com
E-mail: stay@bernerhofinn.com

Circa 1880. Built in the late 19th century for travelers passing through Crawford Notch, this historic Victorian Inn was named by the Zumsteins, its proprietors known for providing fine accommodations, musical enjoyment and outstanding food. Today's innkeepers continue this hospitable commitment offering creative gourmet cuisine in the dining room and casual fare in the Black Bear Pub. Elegantly decorated guest

bedrooms are non-smoking, some feature brass beds, antiques, stained glass, spa tub Jacuzzis and a fireplace. Novice and experienced chefs alike enjoy learning tricks of the trade at A Taste of the Mountains Cooking School. Located in the foothills of the White Mountains, a variety of outdoor activities are easily accessible.

Innkeeper(s): George & June Phillips. $99-189. 9 rooms with PB, 3 with FP, 2 two-bedroom suites. Breakfast included in rates. Types of meals: Full gourmet bkfst, early coffee/tea, picnic lunch and gourmet dinner. Restaurant on premises. Beds: KQ. Cable TV, VCR, reading lamp, refrigerator, ceiling fan, clock radio, telephone, hot tub/spa, most with two-person spa/tub Jacuzzi, one with fireplace and one with sauna in room. Air conditioning. Fax, copier, spa, sauna, library and parlor games on premises. Amusement parks, antiquing, bicycling, canoeing/kayaking, cross-country skiing, downhill skiing, fishing, golf, hiking, horseback riding, live theater, parks, shopping, rock climbing, ice climbing and snow shoeing nearby.

Location: Mountains.

Publicity: *Yankee Magazine, Boston Globe, Bon Appetit, Good Housekeeping, Skiing, Gault Millau, Country New England Inns and Weekends for Two in New England: 50 Romantic Getaways Inn Spots & Special Places in New England.*

"When people want to treat themselves, this is where they come."

Certificate may be used: Nov. 1 to June 15; Sunday-Thursday, non-holiday week.

Covered Bridge House B&B

Rt 302
Glen, NH 03838
(603)383-9109 (800)232-9109 Fax:(603)383-8089
Internet: www.coveredbridgehouse.com
E-mail: info@coveredbridgehouse.com

Circa 1910. The two-acre grounds at this inn boast the only privately owned covered bridge with a gift shop inside. The bridge, which dates to 1850, houses the inn's gift shop. The grounds also include a private beach area that rests along side a river where guests can go swimming or tubing. Guest rooms are decorated in a country Colonial style with quilts, floral comforters and stenciled walls. Breakfasts include fresh fruit, homemade muffins and made-to-order eggs or perhaps French toast. In warmer weather breakfast is served on the patio.

Innkeeper(s): Dan & Nancy Wanek. $59-109. 6 rooms, 4 with PB. Breakfast included in rates. Types of meals: Full bkfst and early coffee/tea. Beds: KQT. Reading lamp, ceiling fan and clock radio in room. Air conditioning. Spa, swimming and telephone on premises. Amusement parks, antiquing, cross-country skiing, downhill skiing, fishing, golf, live theater, parks, shopping, tennis and water sports nearby.

Location: Mountains, waterfront.

Certificate may be used: Nov. 1 to May 31, Sunday-Thursday excluding holidays.

Hampton   K6

The Victoria Inn

430 High St
Hampton, NH 03842-2311
(603)929-1437 (800)291-2672
Internet: www.thevictoriainn.com
E-mail: Nyhans@thevictoriainn.com

Circa 1875. Elegance and style are featured at this Queen Anne Victorian inn just a half-mile from the ocean. A romantic gazebo, spacious guest rooms and Victorian furnishings throughout the inn add to its considerable charm. The Honeymoon Suite and Victoria Room are popular with those seeking privacy and luxury. Guests may borrow the inn's bicycles for a relaxing ride or read a book in its deluxe morning room. Common areas include the living room and the sitting room, with its cozy fireplace.

Innkeeper(s): John & Pamela Nyhan. $100-150. 6 rooms with PB, 3 total suites, including 1 two-bedroom suite. Breakfast included in rates. Types of meals: Full bkfst, early coffee/tea and afternoon tea. Beds: KQ. Modem hook-up, cable TV, reading lamp, ceiling fan, clock radio, telephone and turn-down service in room. Air conditioning. VCR, fax, copier, bicycles, library, parlor games and fireplace on premises. Amusement parks, antiquing, beach, bicycling, cross-country skiing, downhill skiing, fishing, golf, hiking, live theater, parks, shopping, sporting events and water sports nearby.

Location: Ocean community.

Certificate may be used: Nov. 1-April 30.

Holderness   H4

The Inn on Golden Pond

Rt 3, PO Box 680
Holderness, NH 03245
(603)968-7269 Fax:(603)968-9226
Internet: www.innongoldenpond.com
E-mail: innkeepers@innongoldenpond.com

Circa 1879. Framed by meandering stone walls and split-rail fences more than 100 years old, this inn is situated on 50 acres of woodlands. Most rooms overlook picturesque countryside. Nearby Squam Lake was the setting for the film "On Golden Pond." An inviting, 70-foot screened porch provides a place to relax during the summer.

Innkeeper(s): Bill & Bonnie Webb. $105-175. 6 rooms with PB, 2 suites. Breakfast included in rates. Types of meals: Country bkfst and early coffee/tea. Beds: KQT. Reading lamp, clock radio and turn-down service in room. Air conditioning. TV, fax, library, parlor games, telephone, fireplace and gift shop on premises. Antiquing, art galleries, beach, bicycling, canoeing/kayaking, cross-country skiing, downhill skiing, fishing, golf, hiking, horseback riding, live theater, museums, parks, shopping, sporting events, tennis and water sports nearby.

Location: Country.

Publicity: *Boston Globe, Baltimore Sun and Los Angeles Times.*

"Another sweet flower added to my bouquet of life."

Certificate may be used: Sunday-Thursday year-round. Not available in October or on holidays.

Jackson   F5

Inn at Ellis River

P.O. Box 656
Jackson, NH 03846
(603)383-9339 (800)233-8309 Fax:(603)383-4142
Internet: www.ellisriverhouse.com
E-mail: innkeeper@erhinn.com

Circa 1893. Andrew Harriman built this farmhouse, as well as the village town hall and three-room schoolhouse where the innkeepers' children attended school. Classic antiques and Laura Ashley prints decorate the guest rooms and riverfront "honeymoon" cottage, and each window reveals views of magnificent mountains, or spectacular Ellis River. In 1993, the innkeepers added 18 rooms, 11 of which feature fireplaces and six offer two-person Jacuzzis. They also added three suites, a heated, outdoor pool, an indoor Jacuzzi, sauna and a cozy pub.

Innkeeper(s): Frank Baker & Lyn Norris-Baker. $110-250. 20 rooms with PB, 14 with FP, 4 suites, 1 cottage and 1 conference room. Breakfast and snacks/refreshments included in rates. Types of meals: Full gourmet bkfst,

veg bkfst, early coffee/tea, picnic lunch, afternoon tea, hors d'oeuvres and dinner. Beds: KQD. Cable TV, reading lamp, telephone, hot tub/spa and fireplace in room. Air conditioning. Fax, spa, swimming, sauna, parlor games and gift shop on premises. Limited handicap access. Amusement parks, antiquing, cross-country skiing, downhill skiing, fishing, live theater, parks, shopping, sporting events and water sports nearby.

Location: Mountains. River frontage.

Publicity: *Philadelphia Inquirer.*

"We have stayed at many B&Bs all over the world and are in agreement that the beauty and hospitality of Ellis River House is that of a world-class bed & breakfast."

Certificate may be used: Midweek, Sunday-Thursday; January, March, April, May and November (non-holiday periods).

Dana Place Inn

Rt 16, Pinkham Notch Rd
Jackson, NH 03846
(603)383-6822 (800)537-9276 Fax:(603)383-6022
Internet: www.danaplace.com
E-mail: reservations@danaplace.com

Circa 1860. The original owners received this Colonial farmhouse as a wedding present. The warm, cozy atmosphere of the inn is surpassed only by the spectacular mountain views. During autumn, the fall leaves explode with color, and guests can

enjoy the surroundings while taking a hike or bike ride through the area. The beautiful Ellis River is the perfect place for an afternoon of fly-fishing or a picnic. After a scrumptious country breakfast, winter guests can step out the door and into skis for a day of cross-country skiing.

Innkeeper(s): The Levine Family. $99-195. 35 rooms with PB. Breakfast and afternoon tea included in rates. Types of meals: Full bkfst, picnic lunch, gourmet dinner and room service. Restaurant on premises. Beds: KQDT. Reading lamp and desk in room. VCR, fax, copier, spa, swimming, tennis, library, parlor games, telephone, fireplace, hiking, indoor heated pool and Jacuzzi on premises. Amusement parks, antiquing, cross-country skiing, downhill skiing, fishing, golf, live theater, parks, shopping, water sports and White Mountain attractions nearby.

Location: Mountains.

Publicity: *Travel & Leisure, Inn Spots, Bon Appetit and Country Journal.*

"We had such a delightful time at Dana Place Inn. We will recommend you to everyone."

Certificate may be used: Midweek, year-round, excluding February, August, Sept. 20-Oct. 20 and holiday periods.

Jaffrey   L3

The Benjamin Prescott Inn

Rt 124 E, 433 Turnpike Rd
Jaffrey, NH 03452
(603)532-6637 (888)950-6637 Fax:(603)532-6637
Internet: www.benjaminprescottinn.com
E-mail: innkeeper@benjaminprescottinn.com

Circa 1853. Colonel Prescott arrived on foot in Jaffrey in 1775 with an ax in his hand and a bag of beans on his back. The family built this classic Greek Revival many years later. Now, candles light the windows, seen from the stonewall-lined lane adjacent to the inn. Each room bears the name of a Prescott family member and is furnished with antiques.

Innkeeper(s): Bob & Alice Seidel. $75-160. 10 rooms with PB, 3 suites. Breakfast included in rates. Types of meals: Country bkfst and early coffee/tea. Beds: KQDT. Modem hook-up, TV, reading lamp, ceiling fan, clock radio, telephone, desk, toiletries and private label glycerine soaps in room. Fax, copier, library, parlor games, fireplace, open cookie jar in winter and tea (on request) on premises. Limited handicap access. Antiquing, art galleries, bicycling, canoeing/kayaking, cross-country skiing, downhill skiing, fishing, golf, hiking, horseback riding, live theater, museums, parks, shopping, national Shrine, lectures and concerts nearby.

Location: Country.

"We have a candle glowing in the window just for you."
Certificate may be used: Dec. 1-July 31, Sunday-Thursday.

Jefferson   E4

Applebrook B&B

Rt 115A, PO Box 178
Jefferson, NH 03583-0178
(603)586-7713 (800)545-6504
Internet: www.applebrook.com
E-mail: vacation@applebrook.com

Circa 1797. Panoramic views surround this large Victorian farmhouse nestled in the middle of New Hampshire's White Mountains. Guests can awake to the smell of freshly baked muffins made with locally picked berries. A comfortable, fire-lit sitting room boasts stained glass, a goldfish pool and a beautiful view of Mt. Washington. The romantic Nellie's Nook, includes a king-size bed and a balcony with views of the mountains and a two-person spa.  Test your golfing skills at the nearby 18-hole championship course, or spend the day antique hunting. A trout stream and spring-fed rock pool are nearby. Wintertime guests can ice skate or race through the powder at nearby ski resorts or by way of snowmobile, finish off the day with a moonlight toboggan ride. After a full day, guests can enjoy a soak in the hot tub under the stars, where they might see shooting stars or the Northern Lights.

Innkeeper(s): Sandra Conley. $60-125. 14 rooms, 8 with PB and 1 conference room. Breakfast included in rates. Types of meals: Full bkfst and early coffee/tea. Beds: KQDT. Reading lamp, ceiling fan, desk and hot tub/spa in room. Library, parlor games, telephone and fireplace on premises. Amusement parks, antiquing, cross-country skiing, downhill skiing, fishing, live theater, parks, shopping and water sports nearby.

Location: Mountains.

Publicity: *Outside, PriceCostco Connection, New Hampshire Outdoor Companion and Outdoor.*

"We came for a night and stayed for a week."
Certificate may be used: May 15-Oct. 15, Sunday-Thursday.

Jefferson Inn

Rt 2
Jefferson, NH 03583
(603)586-7998 (800)729-7908 Fax:(603)586-7808
Internet: www.jeffersoninn.com
E-mail: jeffinn@ncia.net

Circa 1896. A turret, gables and wraparound verandas characterize this romantic 19th-century Victorian home. Cradled in the White Mountain National Forest, the inn overlooks

Jefferson Meadows to Franconia Notch, Mt. Washington and the northern Presidential range. Each of the guest bedrooms and family suites boast a distinctively unique decor and offers privacy. Indulge in a leisurely full  breakfast. Swim in the spring-fed pond across the street. During winter, it transforms into an ice skating rink. A horse-drawn wagon and sleigh rides are available. Afternoon beverages and homemade baked goods are served in the afternoon. The Weathervane Summer Theater provides nightly entertainment. Biking and golf are nearby.

Innkeeper(s): Mark & Cindy Robert and Bette Bovio. $75-175. 11 rooms with PB, 2 suites. Breakfast, afternoon tea and snacks/refreshments included in rates. Types of meals: Full gourmet bkfst and early coffee/tea. Beds: KQDT. Data port, TV, reading lamp, refrigerator and turn-down service in room. Fax, library, parlor games, telephone and laundry facility on premises. Limited handicap access. Amusement parks, antiquing, art galleries, bicycling, canoeing/kayaking, cross-country skiing, downhill skiing, fishing, golf, hiking, horseback riding, live theater, parks, shopping, tennis, moose tours, snowmobiling and horse drawn sleigh rides nearby.

Location: Country, mountains.

"Marvelous breakfast and a warm, comfortable atmosphere."
Certificate may be used: November-March, any day of the week, excluding Valentine's weekend holiday.

Littleton   E3

Beal House Inn & Fine Dining Restaurant

2 W Main St
Littleton, NH 03561-3502
(603)444-2661 (866)616-BEAL Fax:(603)444-6224
Internet: www.bealhouseinn.com
E-mail: info@bealhouseinn.com

Circa 1833. This Main Street landmark is centrally located in the White Mountains for year-round enjoyment. Refurbished and elegantly furnished with antiques, the suites feature four-poster and canopy beds, fireplaces, Jacuzzis and clawfoot tubs. Relax in luxury with down comforters, bathrobes, coffeemakers, CD players and satellite TV. A feta and fresh spinach frittata with home-baked wheat bread, banana buttermilk pancakes served with local maple syrup, or other delicious recipes may be served for breakfast. Enjoy the pleasant interlude of afternoon tea. The inn's award winning restaurant offers an  extensive menu for fine dining.

Innkeeper(s): Jose Luis & Catherine Pawelek. $125-245. 8 rooms with PB, 4 with FP, 5 total suites, including 1 two-bedroom suite and 1 conference room. Breakfast and afternoon tea included in rates. Types of meals: Full gourmet bkfst, gourmet dinner and room service. Restaurant on premises. Beds: KQD. Modem hook-up, data port, cable TV, VCR, reading lamp, stereo, refrigerator, ceiling fan, clock radio, telephone, coffeemaker, desk, fireplace, hair dryer and bathrobes in room. Central air. Fax, copier, library, pet boarding, parlor games, gift shop, pet-friendly suite with separate back entrance, private deck and enclosed yard on premises. Limited handicap access. Antiquing, art galleries, bicycling, canoeing/kayaking, cross-country skiing, downhill skiing, fishing, golf, hiking, horseback riding, live theater, museums, parks, shopping, tennis, water sports and sleigh rides nearby.

Location: Mountains. Near Vermont border, west side of White Mountains.

Publicity: *Boston Globe, USA Today, American Historic Country Inns, Glamour, NHToDo, New Hampshire Adventures, Le Soleil, Star Ledger, Miami Herald, Yankee, Courier, Ammonoosuc Times, New Hampshire Magazine and WMUR/Channel 9.*

"These innkeepers know and understand people, their needs and wants. Attention to cleanliness and amenities, from check-in to check-out, is a treasure."

Certificate may be used: Sunday-Thursday, except fall foliage and holidays.

Lyme   G2

The Dowds' Country Inn

PO Box 58
Lyme, NH 03768
(603)795-4712 (800)482-4712 Fax:(603)795-4220
Internet: www.dowdscountryinn.com
E-mail: reservations@dowdscountryinn.com

Circa 1780. This 18th-century inn offers pure New England elegance. The historic home, surrounded by a plentiful six acres, rests on The Common in this charming historic village. The grounds include a duck pond, fountain and gardens- a perfect setting for the many parties and weddings held at the inn. The guest rooms are decorated in a warm, inviting style, many feature stencilled walls or country artwork. The innkeepers serve made-to-order breakfasts and an opulent afternoon tea. The staff will gladly help you plan a day trip to enjoy the charm of the surrounding village and nearby places of interest.

Innkeeper(s): Tami Dowd. $125-230. 22 rooms with PB, 3 suites and 2 conference rooms. Breakfast and afternoon tea included in rates. Types of meals: Country bkfst. Beds: QT. Modem hook-up, reading lamp, clock radio, telephone, turn-down service and desk in room. Air conditioning. VCR, fax, copier, library and gift shop on premises. Handicap access. Antiquing, art galleries, beach, bicycling, canoeing/kayaking, cross-country skiing, downhill skiing, fishing, golf, hiking, horseback riding, live theater, museums, parks, shopping, sporting events, tennis and water sports nearby.

Location: Country, mountains.

Certificate may be used: Nov. 1 through April 1, excluding holidays and group reservations, subject to availability.

Moultonborough   H5

Olde Orchard Inn

RR 1 Box 256
Moultonborough, NH 03254-9502
(603)476-5004 (800)598-5845 Fax:(603)476-5004
Internet: www.oldeorchardinn.com
E-mail: innkeeper@oldeorchardinn.com

Circa 1790. Sitting on the outskirts of this rural town in the northern part of the state's Lakes Region, this quiet and informal inn is surrounded by 12 acres of fields. Musicians are invited to play the piano or Hammond organ. Nine distinct guest bedrooms retain the ambiance of the 18th-century farmhouse. All feature air conditioning and private baths, some boast whirlpool tubs and fireplaces. Wake up to savor a full country candlelit breakfast made with ingredients from the orchard and locally roasted coffee. Read in a lawn chair by the pond or relax with a refreshing beverage on the porch and watch the sun set. Lake Winnipesaukee is less than a mile down a quiet road. Four-season activities and sophisticated dining are nearby.

Innkeeper(s): Clark & Jo Hills. $75-185. 9 rooms with PB, 3 with FP. Breakfast included in rates. Types of meals: Country bkfst, veg bkfst, early coffee/tea and snacks/refreshments. Beds: QDT. TV, reading lamp, clock radio, desk, hot tub/spa, fireplace, three with whirlpools, fresh flowers and fine robes in room. Air conditioning. VCR, fax, spa, library, parlor games, telephone, fireplace, piano, Hammond organ, sauna and gazebo on premises. Handicap access. Antiquing, art galleries, beach, bicycling, canoeing/kayaking, cross-country skiing, downhill skiing, fishing, golf, hiking, horseback riding, live theater, museums, parks, shopping, tennis and water sports nearby.

Location: Country. Mountains, lake.

Publicity: *Merideth News.*

"What a wonderful getaway we had at your lovely inn. We're so glad we found you on the Internet."

Certificate may be used: Nov. 1-May 15, holidays excluded (Maiden's Blush & Fireside rooms only).

New London   I3

Colonial Farm Inn

Rt 11, PO Box 1053
New London, NH 03257-1053
(603)526-6121 (800)805-8504 Fax:(603)641-0314
E-mail: colonialfarm@fcgnetworks.net

Circa 1836. The village of New London holds what should be the world's most popular festival, the Chocolate Fest. The innkeepers at Colonial Farm won the award for top confection, a tangy chocolate-almond pate. The historic home, an example of a center-chimney Colonial, is decorated in a tasteful, period style with a mix of antiques and pieces such as four-poster beds. A memorable breakfast is served, and guests would be wise to save at least one night for dinner at the inn. The dining rooms, with exposed beams and plank floorboards, are cozy and romantic, and the food has drawn many compliments. Specialties include crostini with chicken liver pate and prosciutto, roasted red and green peppers with goat cheese, tenderloin of beef with a burgundy-shallot sauce or, perhaps, chicken stuffed with homemade boursin cheese and walnuts.

Innkeeper(s): Robert & Kathryn Joseph. $85-95. 5 rooms with PB and 1 conference room. Breakfast included in rates. Types of meals: Full bkfst and gourmet dinner. Restaurant on premises. Beds: QDT. Reading lamp in room. Air conditioning. VCR, bicycles, library, parlor games, telephone, fireplace, antique shop and pond on premises. Handicap access. Antiquing, cross-country skiing, downhill skiing, fishing, live theater, parks, shopping, sporting events and water sports nearby.

Location: Country.

Publicity: *New York Times.*

Certificate may be used: Jan. 1-Dec. 31, excluding weekends in the summer. Excluding weekends of April 24, Oct. 2 and Oct. 9.

North Conway   F5

1785 Inn & Restaurant

PO Box 1785
North Conway, NH 03860-1785
(603)356-9025 (800)421-1785 Fax:(603)356-6081
Internet: www.the1785inn.com
E-mail: the1785inn@aol.com

Circa 1785. The main section of this center-chimney house was built by Captain Elijah Dinsmore of the New Hampshire Rangers. He was granted the land for service in the American Revolution. Original hand-hewn beams, corner posts, fireplaces, and a brick oven are still visible and operating. The inn is located at the historical marker popularized by the White Mountain School of Art in the 19th century.

Innkeeper(s): Becky & Charlie Mallar. $69-219. 17 rooms, 12 with PB, 1 suite and 1 conference room. Breakfast included in rates. Types of meals: Country bkfst, early coffee/tea, afternoon tea, snacks/refreshments, gourmet dinner and room service. Restaurant on premises. Beds: KQDT. Cable TV, VCR, reading lamp, refrigerator, ceiling fan, snack bar, clock radio, coffeemaker and turn-down service in room. Air conditioning. Fax, copier, swimming, library, parlor games, telephone, fireplace, cross-country skiing and nature trails on premises. Limited handicap access.

Amusement parks, antiquing, art galleries, beach, bicycling, canoeing/kayaking, cross-country skiing, downhill skiing, fishing, golf, hiking, horseback riding, live theater, museums, parks, shopping, tennis, water sports, walking, gardens, nature trails, rock climbing and ice climbing nearby.

Location: Mountains.

Publicity: *Country, Bon Appetit, Travel & Leisure, Ski, Travel Holiday, Connecticut, Better Homes & Gardens and The Wedding Story.*

"Occasionally in our lifetime is a moment so unexpectedly perfect that we use it as our measure for our unforgettable moments. We just had such an experience at The 1785 Inn."

Certificate may be used: Anytime, November-June, subject to availability.

Cabernet Inn

Rt 16, Box 489
North Conway, NH 03860
(603)356-4704 (800)866-4704 Fax:(603)356-5399
Internet: www.cabernetinn.com
E-mail: info@cabernetinn.com

Circa 1842. Built prior to the Civil War, this historic home features a deep burgundy exterior highlighted by hunter green shutters and trim. Window boxes filled with flowers add a touch more color. The one-acre grounds are shaded by trees and colored by a variety of flowers. More than half of the guest rooms include a fireplace, and some have double whirlpool tubs. In the afternoons, homemade treats are served, and in the mornings, guests enjoy a full country breakfast with items such as eggs, French toast, pancakes, bacon, sausages and fresh seasonal fruits.

Innkeeper(s): Bruce & Jessica Zarenko. $90-225. 11 rooms with PB, 6 with FP. Breakfast and afternoon tea included in rates. Types of meals: Country bkfst and early coffee/tea. Beds: Q. Reading lamp, ceiling fan, hot tub/spa and antiques in room. Air conditioning. TV, VCR, fax, parlor games, telephone and fireplace on premises. Limited handicap access. Antiquing, art gallery, bicycling, canoeing/kayaking, cross-country skiing, downhill skiing, fishing, golf, hiking, horseback riding, live theater, parks and shopping nearby.

Location: Mountains.

Certificate may be used: November-June, Sunday-Thursday, subject to availability.

Cranmore Mt. Lodge

859 Kearsarge Rd, PO Box 1194
North Conway, NH 03860-1194
(603)356-2044 (800)356-3596 Fax:(603)356-4498
Internet: www.north-conway.com
E-mail: thelodge@northconway.com

Circa 1860. Babe Ruth was a frequent guest at this old New England farmhouse when his daughter was the owner. There are many rare Babe Ruth photos displayed in the inn and one guest room is still decorated with his furnishings. The barn on the property is held together with wooden pegs and contains dorm rooms.

Innkeeper(s): Jean & Kevin Flanagan. $110-275. 24 rooms with PB, 3 suites. Breakfast included in rates. Types of meals: Full bkfst and early coffee/tea. Beds: KQDT. Data port, cable TV, refrigerator, ceiling fan and telephone in room. Air conditioning. TV, VCR, fax, copier, spa, swimming, tennis, parlor games and fireplace on premises. Amusement parks, antiquing, cross-country skiing, downhill skiing, fishing, live theater, parks, shopping and water sports nearby.

Location: Mountains.

Publicity: *Ski, Snow Country, Montreal Gazette and Newsday.*

"Your accommodations are lovely, your breakfasts delicious."

Certificate may be used: Nov. 1-Sept. 15, Sunday through Thursday, excluding holidays and school vacation.

Old Red Inn & Cottages

PO Box 467
North Conway, NH 03860-0467
(603)356-2642 (800)338-1356 Fax:(603)356-6626
Internet: www.oldredinn.com
E-mail: oldredinn@adelphia.net

Circa 1810. Guests can opt to stay in an early 19th-century home or in one of a collection of cottages at this country inn. The rooms are decorated with handmade quilts and stenciling dots the walls. Several rooms include four-poster or canopy beds. Two-bedroom cottages feature a screened porch. A hearty, country meal accompanied by freshly baked breads, muffins and homemade preserves starts off the day. The inn is near many of the town's shops, restaurants and outlets.

Innkeeper(s): Dick & Terry Potochniak. $98-178. 17 rooms, 15 with PB, 1 suite and 10 cottages. Breakfast included in rates. Types of meals: Full bkfst and early coffee/tea. Beds: QDT. Cable TV, reading lamp and refrigerator in room. Air conditioning. Fax, copier, swimming, telephone and fireplace on premises. Amusement parks, antiquing, cross-country skiing, downhill skiing, fishing, golf, live theater, parks, shopping, sporting events, tennis and water sports nearby.

Location: Mountains.

Certificate may be used: Jan. 2-June 20, Sunday-Thursday, (inn rooms only), non-holiday or vacation weeks.

Victorian Harvest Inn

28 Locust Ln, Box 1763
North Conway, NH 03860
(603)356-3548 (800)642-0749 Fax:(603)356-8430
Internet: www.victorianharvestinn.com
E-mail: help@victorianharvestinn.com

Circa 1853. Mountain views, personalized attention and tranquility are available at this tastefully restored Victorian inn that sits on a hill in the Mt. Washington Valley. Relax in the library while listening to Beethoven, Bach or Vivaldi. Many guest bedrooms feature fireplaces and Jacuzzis. Breakfast may include Belgian waffles, Dutch pannekoukan, Italian frittatas, down-home pancakes or omelettes. Swim in the pool and enjoy the gardens. Nearby outlet shopping, hiking trails, horseback riding and kayaking beckon the more adventuresome.

Innkeeper(s): David & Judy Wooster. $90-220. 8 rooms with PB. Breakfast and afternoon tea included in rates. Types of meals: Full gourmet bkfst. Air conditioning. VCR, fax, copier, swimming, library, parlor games, telephone and fireplace on premises. Antiquing, canoeing/kayaking, cross-country skiing, downhill skiing, golf, hiking, horseback riding, live theater, parks, shopping, water sports, tubing and outlet shopping nearby.

Location: Mountains.

Certificate may be used: Sunday-Thursday, November-June, no holiday weeks.

North Woodstock   F4

Wilderness Inn B&B

Rfd 1, Box 69, Rts 3 & 112
North Woodstock, NH 03262-9710
(603)745-3890 (888)777-7813
Internet: www.thewildernessinn.com
E-mail: info@thewildernessinn.com

Circa 1912. Surrounded by the White Mountain National Forest, this charming shingled home offers a picturesque getaway for every season. Guest rooms, all with private baths, are furnished with antiques and Oriental rugs. The innkeepers also offer

family suites and a private cottage with a fireplace, Jacuzzi and a view of Lost River. Breakfast is a delightful affair with choices ranging from fresh muffins to brie cheese omelets, French toast topped with homemade apple syrup, crepes or specialty pancakes. For the children, the innkeepers create teddy bear pancakes or French toast. If you wish, afternoon tea also is served.
Innkeeper(s): Michael & Rosanna Yarnell. $65-170. 8 rooms, 7 with PB and 1 cottage. Breakfast included in rates. Types of meals: Full gourmet bkfst. Beds: QDT. TV, cottage has fireplace and two-person Jacuzzi in room.

"The stay at your inn, attempting and completing the 3D jig-saw puzzle, combined with those unforgettable breakfasts, and your combined friendliness, makes the Wilderness Inn a place for special memories."
Certificate may be used: All midweek except holidays and July-October.

Plymouth   H4

Federal House Inn

POB 147
Plymouth, NH 03264
(603)536-4644 (866)536-4644
Internet: www.federalhouseinnnh.com
E-mail: info@federalhouseinnnh.com

Circa 1835. As the name suggests, this bed & breakfast is a historic, brick Federal-style in the foothills of the White Mountains. In the afternoons, gather by the wood-burning stove in the parlor or on the patio for a wine-and-cheese social with the innkeepers. Home-baked cookies or other treats also are offered. Spacious suites boast views of Tenney Mountain. Guest bedrooms feature canopy, sleigh or four-poster beds, luxurious linens, Caswell-Massey toiletries and turndown service with handmade gourmet chocolates. A generous New England breakfast buffet is the perfect start to a new day. Spa and beach towels are available for the large Jacuzzi overlooking the gardens.
Innkeeper(s): Jeff Demoura and Jody "Jon" Dickerson. $99-175. 5 rooms. Breakfast, afternoon tea and snacks/refreshments included in rates. Types of meals: Full gourmet bkfst and early coffee/tea. Beds: Q. Reading lamp, stereo, clock radio, turn-down service, desk and fireplace in room. Air conditioning. TV, VCR, fax, copier, spa, library, telephone and fireplace on premises. Antiquing, art galleries, beach, bicycling, canoeing/kayaking, cross-country skiing, downhill skiing, fishing, golf, hiking, horseback riding, museums, parks, shopping, sporting events, tennis and water sports nearby.
Location: Mountains.
Certificate may be used: January-August and November-January (no September and October). Subject to availability, Sunday-Thursday.

Rindge   L3

Woodbound Inn

62 Woodbound Rd
Rindge, NH 03461
(603)532-8341 (800)688-7770 Fax:(603)532-8341
Internet: www.woodbound.com
E-mail: woodbound@aol.com

Circa 1819. Vacationers have enjoyed the Woodbound Inn since its opening as a year-round resort in 1892. The main inn actually was built in 1819, and this portion offers 19 guest rooms, all appointed with classic-style furnishings. The innkeepers offer more modern accommodations in the Edgewood Building, and there are eleven cabins available. The one- and two-bedroom cabins rest along the shore of Lake Contoocook. The inn's 162 acres include a private beach, fishing, hiking, nature trails, tennis courts, a volleyball court, a game room and a golf course. There is a full service restaurant, a cocktail lounge and banquet facilities on premises. If for some reason one would want to venture away from the inn, the region is full of activities, including ski areas,

more golf courses and Mount Monadnock.
Innkeeper(s): Rick Kohlmorgen. $89-139. 48 rooms, 45 with PB, 13 cabins and 5 conference rooms. Breakfast included in rates. Types of meals: Full bkfst, lunch and dinner. Restaurant on premises. Beds: QDT. Clock radio, telephone, desk and cabins are lakefront with fireplaces in room. Air conditioning. VCR, copier, swimming, tennis, library, parlor games and fireplace on premises. Handicap access. Amusement parks, antiquing, cross-country skiing, downhill skiing, fishing, live theater, parks, shopping and water sports nearby.
Location: Mountains.
Certificate may be used: Jan. 2-May 15, Oct. 20-Dec. 29.

Snowville   G5

Snowvillage Inn

146 Stewart Rd, PO Box 68
Snowville, NH 03832
(603)447-2818 (800)447-4345 Fax:(603)447-5268
Internet: www.snowvillageinn.com
E-mail: info@snowvillageinn.com

Circa 1915. Peacefully sitting on a secluded hillside with panoramic views of the entire Presidential mountain range, this Victorian inn is a wonderful blend of Apine flair and New England charm. In the Main House, built by author Frank Simonds, enjoy many common rooms to gather in, there are books to read by the fireplace, or watch a gorgeous sunset on the front porch. Each of the comfortable guest bedrooms in the Chimney House and Carriage House are named after a writer, in honor of the inn's heritage. Discover more breathtaking vistas, fireplaces and antique furnishings. Renown for its elegant country dining, breakfast is a satisfying culinary delight. Explore the award-winning gardens and nature trails.
Innkeeper(s): Kevin, Caitlin & Maggie Flynn. $99-249. 18 rooms with PB, 4 with FP. Breakfast included in rates. Types of meals: Full gourmet bkfst and gourmet dinner. Restaurant on premises. Beds: KQD. Reading lamp, clock radio, telephone, desk and fireplace in room. Fax, copier, library, parlor games, fireplace, cross-country skiing and showshoeing on premises. Limited handicap access. Antiquing, art galleries, bicycling, canoeing/kayaking, cross-country skiing, downhill skiing, fishing, golf, hiking, horseback riding, live theater, museums and water sports nearby.
Location: Mountains.
Publicity: *Yankee Magazine, Wine Spectator, Boston Globe, Bon Appetit, WMUR New Hampshire and Food Network.*
Certificate may be used: Jan. 1-Sept. 13, Nov. 1-Dec. 20, Sunday-Thursday, not available during foliage.

Sugar Hill   F3

A Grand Inn-Sunset Hill House

231 Sunset Hill Rd
Sugar Hill, NH 03585
(603)823-5522 (800)786-4455 Fax:(603)823-5738
Internet: www.sunsethillhouse.com
E-mail: innkeeper@sunsethillhouse.com

Circa 1882. This Second Empire luxury inn has views of five mountain ranges. Three parlors, all with cozy fireplaces, are favorite gathering spots. Afternoon tea is served here. The inn's lush grounds offer many opportunities for recreation or relaxing, and guests often enjoy special events here, such as the Fields of Lupine Festival. The Cannon Mountain Ski Area and Franconia Notch State Park are nearby, and there is 30 kilometers of cross-country ski trails at the inn. Be sure to inquire about golf and ski packages. In the fall, a Thanksgiving package allows guests to help decorate the inn for the holidays as well as enjoy Thanksgiving dinner together. NH Magazine just named Sunset Hill House — A Grand Inn the "Very Best in NH for a Spectacular Meal."

Innkeeper(s): Lon, Nancy, Mary Pearl & Adeline Henderson. $100-350. 28 rooms with PB and 3 conference rooms. Breakfast included in rates. Types of meals: Full bkfst, early coffee/tea, picnic lunch, snacks/refreshments and dinner. Restaurant on premises. Beds: KQDT. Reading lamp, clock radio, desk, suites with fireplaces and/or whirlpools and many with ceiling fans in room. Fax, parlor games, telephone, fireplace, tavern, golf course and clubhouse on premises. Antiquing, cross-country skiing, downhill skiing, fishing, live theater, parks, shopping, water sports and golf course nearby.

Location: Mountains.

Publicity: *Yankee Travel Guide, Courier, Caledonia Record, Boston Globe, Portsmouth Herald, Manchester Union Leader, Journal Enquirer, Sunday Telegraph, Boston Herald, New Hampshire Magazine, GeoSaison, National Geographic, Traveller, Small Meeting Marketplace, BBW Magazine, Ski Magazine, Peoples Places and Plants Magazine and Korean Times.*

"I have visited numerous inns and innkeepers in my 10 years as a travel writer, but have to admit that few have impressed me as much as yours and you did."

Certificate may be used: Anytime, Sunday-Thursday, not including foliage season or holidays.

Sugar Hill Inn

po Box 954
Franconia, NH 03580
(603)823-5621 (800)548-4748 Fax:(603)823-5639
Internet: www.sugarhillinn.com
E-mail: info@sugarhillinn.com

Circa 1789. Set on 16 acres in the White Mountains, this rambling 1798 country colonial farmhouse is surrounded by gardens and rolling lawns. The inn has six Cottage rooms, four Classic rooms and five Luxury rooms, for a total of 15 guest rooms. Some have fireplaces and whirlpool tubs. Virgin pine flooring, hand-hewn beams and rippled glass windows speak of elegance of days gone by. Handmade quilts and pillows, stenciled walls and antiques create delightful period decor. Start the day with a three-course breakfast including courses like omelettes, blueberry pancakes or eggs Benedict. Then set out to see the countryside. The inn is near Dartmouth College, the Ariel Mountain Tramway and the Cog Railway as well as the New England Ski Museum and Robert Frost's Home. Outdoor activities include hiking, biking, ice skating, fishing, tennis and golf. Dinner, afternoon tea and picnic lunches are available upon request.

Innkeeper(s): Judy & Orlo Coots. $100-380. 15 rooms with PB, 11 with FP, 3 with WP and 6 cottages. Breakfast and afternoon tea included in rates. Types of meals: Full gourmet bkfst, veg bkfst, early coffee/tea, picnic lunch and gourmet dinner. Restaurant on premises. Beds: KQDT. Cable TV, reading lamp, clock radio, coffeemaker, desk, hot tub/spa & fireplace in room. Air conditioning. TV, VCR, fax, copier, parlor games, telephone, gift shop and spa room with massages and facials on premises. Amusement parks, antiquing, art galleries, beach, bicycling, canoeing/kayaking, cross-country skiing, downhill skiing, fishing, golf, hiking, horseback riding, live theater, museums, parks, shopping, tennis & water sports nearby.

Location: Mountains.

Publicity: *Boston Globe, Arrington's Inn Traveler, Fodor's, Frommers and Yankee Magazine.*

Certificate may be used: May 1-July 31, Sunday-Thursday. Dec. 1-March 31, Sunday-Thursday, no holidays.

Tamworth   G5

A B&B at Whispering Pines

Rt 113A & Hemenway Rd
Tamworth, NH 03886
(603)323-7337 Fax:call for #
Internet: www.WhisperingPinesNH.com
E-mail: erickson@ncia.net

Circa 1900. Two farmhouses were joined more than a century ago to become what is now a delightful bed & breakfast that sits on 22 wooded acres in the quiet corner of the Mt. Washington Valley. Sheltered by tall pines, the tranquil setting offers a peaceful getaway and the inn provides generous hospitality. Relax on the wicker-filled, screened-in porch or in the quaint living room with an antique soapstone stove. Each guest bedroom boasts a view of the gardens or woods. Linger over a hearty breakfast served in the large country kitchen. Cross-country ski or snowshoe from the back door to connect with Tamworth Outing Club Trails and Hemenway State Forest. Ask about special packages that are available.

Innkeeper(s): Karen & Kim Erickson. $75-135. 4 rooms, 2 with PB. Breakfast and snacks/refreshments included in rates. Types of meals: Country bkfst, veg bkfst and early coffee/tea. Beds: KQD. Reading lamp, clock radio, telephone, coffeemaker and guest sitting room has fireplace/wood burning stove in room. Library, parlor games, fireplace, gift shop, guest refrigerator, screened-in guest porch, guest living room, coffeemaker and refreshments on premises. Amusement parks, antiquing, art galleries, beach, bicycling, canoeing/kayaking, cross-country skiing, downhill skiing, fishing, golf, hiking, horseback riding, live theater, parks, shopping, tennis and water sports nearby.

Location: Country, mountains. Foothills of the White Mountains, next to a state forest.

Publicity: *Summer Week.*

Certificate may be used: March-May; November-December; and Sunday-Thursday, July-Sept. 13.

Whitefield   E4

Spalding Inn & Club

Mountain View Rd
Whitefield, NH 03598
(603)837-2572 (800)368-8439 Fax:(603)837-3062
Internet: www.spaldinginn.com
E-mail: spaldinginn@ncia.net

Circa 1865. Guests have enjoyed New England hospitality at this charming country inn since 1865. Guest rooms are located in the main inn and in the carriage house. There are several private cottages as well, each with one or more bedrooms, a living room, fireplace and private bath. French country decor and antiques create a romantic atmosphere. The

inn is noted for its cuisine, but the dining room's mountain views are memorable, too. Breakfasts won't leave you hungry, a variety of country goodies are prepared. Dinners, served by candlelight, feature a menu which changes daily. The innkeepers offer a variety of packages, with golf, tennis, family vacation and theater-lovers as themes.

Innkeeper(s): Walter Loope. $99-350. 36 rooms with PB, 6 with FP, 6 suites, 6 cottages and 2 conference rooms. Breakfast included in rates. Types of meals: Full bkfst, early coffee/tea, afternoon tea and dinner. Restaurant on premises. Beds: KQT. TV, VCR, reading lamp, ceiling fan, telephone, desk, fireplace and cottages have fireplace and kitchen in room. Fax, copier, swimming, tennis, library, parlor games, gift shop, golf, four clay tennis courts, swimming pool, satellite TV in main lodge and billiard room on premises. Limited handicap access. Amusement parks, antiquing, art galleries, bicycling, fishing, golf, hiking, live theater, parks, tennis, four clay tennis courts and fitness center nearby.

Location: Mountains.

Publicity: *Travel.*

"A special spot in an enchanting setting."

Certificate may be used: June 15-July 15, Sept. 1-15, Oct. 15-30; Sunday-Friday.

New Jersey

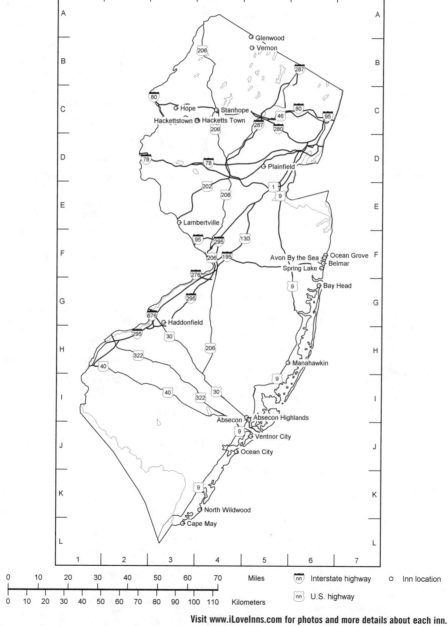

	1	2	3	4	5	6	7	
A								A
B								B
C								C
D								D
E								E
F								F
G								G
H								H
I								I
J								J
K								K
L								L

Glenwood
Vernon
206
287
80
Hope
Stanhope
Hackettstown
Hacketts Town
206
46
80
95
287
280
78
78
Plainfield
202
1
206
9
Lambertville
95
295
130
Avon By the Sea
Ocean Grove
206
195
Belmar
Spring Lake
9
Bay Head
276
295
676
Haddonfield
295
30
206
322
Manahawkin
40
9
40
322
30
Absecon
Absecon Highlands
9
Ventnor City
Ocean City
9
North Wildwood
Cape May

0	10	20	30	40	50	60	70	Miles

0	10	20	30	40	50	60	70	80	90	100	110	Kilometers

nn Interstate highway   o Inn location

nn U.S. highway

Absecon 15

Dr. Jonathan Pitney House

57 North Shore Rd
Absecon, NJ 08201
(609)569-1799 (888)774-8639 Fax:(609)569-9224
Internet: www.pitneyhouse.com
E-mail: drpitney@pitneyhouse.com

Circa 1799. A picket fence surrounds this recently renovated Italianate and Colonial inn. It was the home of Dr. Pitney, considered the Father of Atlantic City. Some of the inn's rooms feature Colonial decor, while others are in a Victorian motif. There are clawfoot tubs, whirlpools, ceiling fans and fireplaces. Breakfast is offered gourmet-style and features an entree, freshly baked breads and cakes. Nearby is Atlantic City, Smithville, a winery, beaches, boardwalk, the convention center and a bird sanctuary.

Innkeeper(s): Don Kelly . $100-250. 10 rooms with PB, 10 with FP, 3 with WP, 3 suites. Breakfast and afternoon tea included in rates. Types of meals: Full gourmet bkfst and early coffee/tea. Beds: QD. Cable TV, VCR, ceiling fan and desk in room. Air conditioning. Fax, library, parlor games, telephone and fireplace on premises. Handicap access. Antiquing, fishing, golf, parks, shopping, sporting events, tennis, water sports and casinos nearby.

Certificate may be used: Anytime, November-April, subject to availability.

Absecon Highlands 15

White Manor Inn

739 S 2nd Ave
Absecon Highlands, NJ 08205-9542
(609)748-3996 Fax:(609)652-0073
E-mail: info@whitemanorinn.com

Circa 1932. This quiet country inn was built by the innkeeper's father and includes unique touches throughout, many created by innkeeper Howard Bensel himself, who became a master craftsman from his father's teachings and renovated the

home extensively. Beautiful flowers and plants adorn both the lush grounds and the interior of the home. Everything is comfortable and cozy at this charming B&B, a relaxing contrast to the glitz of nearby Atlantic City.

Innkeeper(s): Anna Mae & Howard R. Bensel Jr. $65-105. 7 rooms, 5 with PB, 1 suite and 1 conference room. Breakfast and snacks/refreshments included in rates. Types of meals: Cont plus and early coffee/tea. Beds: QDT. Ceiling fan in room. Air conditioning. Parlor games and telephone on premises. Amusement parks, antiquing, fishing, live theater, parks, shopping, sporting events, water sports, golf, bird watching and casinos nearby.

Location: Country.

"We felt more like relatives than total strangers. By far the most clean inn that I have seen — spotless!"

Certificate may be used: Nov. 1-April 30, Monday through Thursday.

Avon By The Sea F6

The Avon Manor B&B Inn

109 Sylvania Ave
Avon By The Sea, NJ 07717-1338
(732)776-7770
Internet: www.avonmanor.com
E-mail: gregmav@aol.com

Circa 1907. The Avon Manor was built as a private summer residence in the Colonial Revival style. The handsome facade is graced by a 100-foot wraparound veranda. Light, airy bedrooms are decorated with antiques, wicker and period pieces. Guests breakfast in a sunny dining room or on the veranda.

Innkeeper(s): Greg Dietrich. $75-175. 9 rooms, 7 with PB, 1 suite. Breakfast and afternoon tea included in rates. Types of meals: Full bkfst. Beds: KQT. TV and reading lamp in room. Air conditioning. Child care and fireplace on premises. Amusement parks, antiquing, fishing, live theater, shopping, sporting events and water sports nearby.

Certificate may be used: Oct. 1 to May 10, not valid holidays or special events.

Bay Head G6

Bay Head Harbor Inn Bed & Breakfast

676 Main Avenue
Bay Head, NJ 08742-5346
(732)899-0767 Fax:(732)899-0148
Internet: www.bayhead.org/harborinn
E-mail: bayheadharbor@aol.com

Circa 1890. This three-story Shingle-style inn, just a block from the beach and the bay, boasts several rooms with porches. The inn is decorated with folk art and country antiques. Afternoon tea and evening snacks are served. Walk to fine restaurants, unique shops and Twilight Lake.

Innkeeper(s): Janice & Dan Eskesen. $100-190. 9 rooms. Breakfast, afternoon tea and snacks/refreshments included in rates. Types of meals: Cont plus and early coffee/tea. Beds: QDT. Reading lamp and clock radio in room. Air conditioning. TV, parlor games, telephone, fireplace, refrigerator and reading material/areas on premises. Amusement parks, antiquing, fishing, golf, parks, shopping, tennis, water sports and fine and casual dining nearby.

Certificate may be used: Sept. 15-April 15, subject to availability. Sunday through Thursday, with two-night minimum.

Belmar F6

The Inn at The Shore Bed & Breakfast

301 4th Ave
Belmar, NJ 07719-2104
(732)681-3762 Fax:(732)280-1914
Internet: www.theinnatheshore.com
E-mail: tomvolker@optonline.net

Circa 1880. This child friendly country Victorian actually is near two different shores. Both the ocean and Silver Lake are within easy walking distance of the inn. From the inn's wraparound porch, guests can view swans on the lake. The innkeepers decorated their Victorian home in period style. The inn's patio is set up for barbecues.

Innkeeper(s): Rosemary & Tom Volker. $135-225. 10 rooms, 4 with PB, 4 with FP and 1 conference room. Breakfast, afternoon tea and snacks/refreshments included in rates. Types of meals: Full gourmet bkfst. Beds: KQDT. Modem hook-up, data port, cable TV, VCR, reading lamp, CD player, ceiling fan, clock radio, telephone, voice mail, fireplace, modem, whirlpool tubs, fireplaces and guest pantry in room. Central air. Fax, copier, bicycles, library, parlor games, aquarium, patio with gas grill, guest pantry with refrigerator and microwave on premises. Amusement parks, antiquing, art galleries, beach, bicycling, canoeing/kayaking, fishing, golf, hiking, horseback riding, live theater, museums, parks, shopping, sporting events, tennis and water sports nearby.

Location: Ocean community.

"You both have created a warm, cozy and comfortable refuge for us weary travelers."

Certificate may be used: Anytime, subject to availability.

Cape May   L3

The Abbey Bed & Breakfast
34 Gurney St at Columbia Ave
Cape May, NJ 08204
(609)884-4506 (866)884-8800 Fax:(609)884-2379
Internet: www.abbeybedandbreakfast.com
E-mail: theabbey@bellatlantic.net

Circa 1869. This historic inn consists of two buildings, one a Gothic Revival villa with a 60-foot tower, Gothic arched windows and shaded verandas. Furnishings include floor-to-ceiling mirrors, ornate gas chandeliers, marble-topped dressers and beds of carved walnut, wrought iron and brass. The cottage adjacent to the villa is a classic Second Empire-style cottage with a mansard roof. A full breakfast is served in the dining room in spring and fall and on the veranda in the summer. Late afternoon refreshments and tea are served each day at 5 p.m. The beautiful inn is featured in the town's Grand Christmas Tour, and public tours and tea are offered three times a week in season.

Innkeeper(s): Jay & Marianne Schatz. $85-250. 14 rooms with PB, 2 suites and 2 conference rooms. Breakfast and afternoon tea included in rates. Types of meals: Full bkfst and early coffee/tea. Beds: KQD. Reading lamp, ceiling fan, some with air conditioning, all with small refrigerator and antiques in room. Parlor games, beach passes, beach chairs, on- and off-site parking and house telephone for local and long distance toll calls on premises. Antiquing, art galleries, beach, bicycling, canoeing/kayaking, fishing, golf, hiking, horseback riding, live theater, museums, parks, shopping, tennis, wineries, birding, free zoo, nature center, nature walks and Cape May Point State Park nearby.

Location: Ocean community. National Historic District.

Publicity: *Richmond Times-Dispatch, New York Times, Glamour, Philadelphia Inquirer, National Geographic Traveler, Smithsonian* and *Victorian Homes Magazine.*

"Staying with you folks really makes the difference between a 'nice' vacation and a great one!"

Certificate may be used: Sunday or Monday through Thursday; April, May, June and October, except Victorian week.

Abigail Adams B&B By The Sea
12 Jackson St
Cape May, NJ 08204-1418
(609)884-1371 (888)827-4354
Internet: www.abigailadamsinn.com
E-mail: info@abigailadamsinn.com

Circa 1888. This charming Victorian is only 100 feet from the beach which affords refreshing sea breezes and ocean views. There is a free-standing circular staircase, as well as original fire-places and woodwork throughout. The decor is highlighted with flowered chintz and antiques, and the dining room is hand-stenciled. A full breakfast features the inn's homemade baked sweets.

Innkeeper(s): Kate Emerson. $85-215. 6 rooms, 4 with PB. Breakfast included in rates. Types of meals: Full bkfst and afternoon tea. Beds: QD. TV, ceiling fan and clock radio in room. Air conditioning. Telephone and fireplace on premises. Amusement parks, antiquing, fishing, live theater and water sports nearby.

"What a wonderful time. Comfortable & homey."

Certificate may be used: Oct. 15-May 15, Sunday-Thursday, excluding holidays.

Albert Stevens Inn
127 Myrtle Ave
Cape May, NJ 08204-1237
(609)884-4717 (800)890-2287 Fax:(609)884-8320
Internet: www.albertstevensinn.com
E-mail: albertstevensinn@hotmail.com

Circa 1898. Dr. Albert Stevens built this Queen Anne Free Classic house for his home and office. Carved woodwork and Victorian antiques enhance the delightful architectural details. The floating staircase and tower lead to spacious air-conditioned guest bedrooms. Enjoy a complete breakfast as well as afternoon tea and refreshments. Relax in the comfortably heated sunroom, or on the inviting veranda. The outside hot tub offers to soothe and rejuvenate. Free on-site parking is convenient for shopping, restaurants and the beach a short walk away. Beach towels and chairs are gladly provided.

Innkeeper(s): Jim & Lenanne Labrusciano. $90-220. 10 rooms, 7 with PB, 1 with FP, 3 three-bedroom suites. Breakfast, afternoon tea and wine included in rates. Types of meals: Full bkfst and early coffee/tea. Beds: KQD. Cable TV, VCR, reading lamp, refrigerator, ceiling fan, clock radio and fireplace in room. Air conditioning. Fax, copier, spa, parlor games, telephone, hot tub and on-site parking on premises. Amusement parks, antiquing, art galleries, beach, bicycling, canoeing/kayaking, fishing, golf, live theater, museums, parks, shopping, tennis, water sports, wineries and bird watching nearby.

Location: City, ocean community.

Publicity: *The Jersey Shore, Mid-Atlantic Country, Atlantic City Press, Cape May Star and Wave, The Herald, Washington Post, The New York Times, Philadelphia Inquirer* and *NBC News.*

Certificate may be used: Nov. 1-April 30, Sunday-Thursday, except weeks that contain a holiday.

Bedford Inn
805 Stockton Ave
Cape May, NJ 08204-2446
(609)884-4158 (866)215-9507 Fax:(609)884-6320
Internet: www.bedfordinn.com
E-mail: info@bedfordinn.com

Circa 1880. The Bedford, decked in gingerbread trim with verandas on both of its two stories, has welcomed guests since its creation in the 19th century. Electrified gaslights, period wallcoverings and rich, Victorian furnishings create an air of nostalgia. The inn is close to many of Cape May's shops and restaurants, as well as the beach, which is just half a block away. Guests are pampered with breakfasts of quiche, gourmet egg dishes, French toast and freshly baked breads.

Innkeeper(s): Cindy, James and Kurt Schmucker. $100-245. 10 rooms, 3 suites. Breakfast included in rates. Types of meals: Full bkfst and afternoon tea. Beds: KQDT. Cable TV, VCR and alarm clock in room. Air conditioning. Library, telephone, fireplace, refrigerator, free limited driveway parking, hot beverage service 24/7, phone line for computer hook-up and small collection of VHS tapes at no charge on premises. Antiquing, fishing, live theater, parks, water sports, house tours, trolley tours, restaurants and beach nearby.

Location: Ocean community.

Certificate may be used: April, May & October, midweek only, Monday through Thursday, excluding Memorial Day and Columbus Day.

Captain Mey's B&B Inn

202 Ocean St
Cape May, NJ 08204-2322
(609)884-7793 (800)981-3702 Fax:(609)884-7793
Internet: www.captainmeys.com
E-mail: innkeeper@snip.net

Circa 1890. Built in 1890 by homeopathic physician Dr. Walter H. Phillips, today this Victorian bed & breakfast inn is named after Captain Cornelius J. Mey, sent to explore this coast by the Dutch West India Company, and whose name as discoverer was given to the local shores. The Dutch heritage is reflect-

ed in the table-top Persian rugs, Delft Blue China, imported lace curtains and European antiques. Relax on the wicker-filled wraparound sun and shade veranda with hanging ferns. Meticulously restored, the dining room features chestnut oak Eastlake paneling, a leaded glass bay window and fireplace. Stay in a luxury guest bedroom with a romantic whirlpool tub for two. Linger over a hearty country breakfast with candlelight and classical music. Relax in Captain Mey's Courtyard with a good book or a picnic lunch.

Innkeeper(s): George & Kathleen Blinn. $85-235. 7 rooms with PB, 2 with HT, 1 two-bedroom suite. Breakfast and afternoon tea included in rates. Types of meals: Full bkfst. Beds: QT. TV, reading lamp, refrigerator, ceiling fan, clock radio, some with two-person whirlpool tubs, hair dryers, iron and iron board in room. Air conditioning. Fax, parlor games, telephone, fireplace, Internet access, beach chairs and beach towels on premises. Amusement parks, antiquing, art galleries, beach, bicycling, canoeing/kayaking, fishing, golf, horseback riding, live theater, museums, parks, shopping, tennis, water sports, wineries, horse & carriage rides, trolly rides, bird watching, lighthouse and ferry nearby.

Location: Ocean community.

Publicity: Georgraphia atlas New Jersey, "featured cover" Americana, Country Living, New Jersey Monthly, WKYW News (CBS) Philadelphia, WNJN (N.J. Network News Trenton), New Jersey Country Roads Magazine and Traveller.

"The innkeepers pamper you so much you wish you could stay forever."

Certificate may be used: April to May & mid-October to Dec. 20, Monday-Thursday, excluding weekends, holidays and special events. Good for second-floor rooms only.

The Carroll Villa B&B

19 Jackson St
Cape May, NJ 08204-1417
(609)884-9619 Fax:(609)884-0264
Internet: www.carrollvilla.com
E-mail: cvres@eticomm.net

Circa 1882. This Victorian hotel is located one-half block from the ocean on the oldest street in the historic district of Cape May. Breakfast at the Villa is a memorable event, featuring dishes acclaimed by the New York Times and Frommer's. Homemade fruit breads, Italian omelets and Crab Eggs Benedict are a few specialties. Meals are served in the Mad Batter Restaurant on a European veranda, a secluded garden terrace or in the sky-lit Victorian dining room. The restaurant serves breakfast, lunch, dinner and cocktails daily. The decor of this inn is

decidedly Victorian with period antiques and wallpapers.

Innkeeper(s): Mark Kulkowitz & Pamela Ann Huber. $75-190. 22 rooms with PB and 2 conference rooms. Breakfast included in rates. Types of meals: Full bkfst, lunch and dinner. Beds: QD. TV, VCR, ceiling fan, clock radio and telephone in room. Air conditioning. Fax, copier and fireplace on premises. Amusement parks, antiquing, fishing, live theater, parks and shopping nearby.

Location: City.

Publicity: Atlantic City Press, Asbury Press, Frommer's, New York Times and Washington Post.

"Mr. Kulkowitz is a superb host. He strives to accommodate the diverse needs of guests."

Certificate may be used: Sept. 20-May 20, Sunday through Thursday, no holidays, weekends or Christmas week.

The Duke of Windsor Inn

817 Washington St
Cape May, NJ 08204-1651
(609)884-1355 (800)826-8973
Internet: www.dukeofwindsorinn.com
E-mail: innkeeper@dukeofwindsorinn.com

Circa 1896. This Queen Anne Victorian was built by Delaware River boat pilot Harry Hazelhurst and his wife, Florence. They were both six feet tall, so the house was built with large open rooms and doorways, and extra-wide stairs. The inn has a carved, natural oak open staircase with stained-glass windows at top and bottom. Five antique chandeliers grace the dining room. Parking is available on premises.

Innkeeper(s): Patricia Joyce. $125-235. 10 rooms with PB. Breakfast and afternoon tea included in rates. Types of meals: Full bkfst and early coffee/tea. Beds: QDT. Ceiling fan in room. Air conditioning. Telephone, fireplace, off-street parking, outside hot and cold shower and refrigerator available for guest use on premises. Antiquing, fishing, live theater, parks, shopping and water sports nearby.

Publicity: Philadelphia Magazine, New Jersey Countryside Magazine, Endless Vacation and Shape.

"Breakfast at a.m. and tea at p.m. were delicious and relaxing. We can't wait to come back."

Certificate may be used: Nov. 1-May 31, Sunday-Thursday, excluding holidays.

Fairthorne B&B

111 Ocean St
Cape May, NJ 08204-2319
(609)884-8791 (800)438-8742 Fax:(609)898-6129
Internet: www.fairthorne.com
E-mail: fairthornebnb@aol.com

Circa 1892. Antiques abound in this three-story Colonial Revival. Lace curtains and a light color scheme complete the charming decor. There is a new, yet historic addition to the B&B. The innkeepers now offer guest quarters (with fireplaces) in The Fairthorne Cottage, a restored 1880s building adjacent to the inn. The signature breakfasts include special daily entrees along with an assortment of home-baked breads and muffins. A light afternoon tea also is served with refreshments. The proximity to the beach will be much appreciated by guests, and the innkeepers offer the use of beach towels, bicycles and sand chairs. The nearby historic district is full of fun shops and restaurants.

Innkeeper(s): Diane & Ed Hutchinson. $190-275. 8 rooms with PB, 1 suite. Breakfast and afternoon tea included in rates. Types of meals: Full bkfst and early coffee/tea. Beds: KQ. Reading lamp, refrigerator, ceiling fan and clock radio in room. Air conditioning. Fax, telephone and fireplace on premises. Antiquing, fishing, live theater, parks, shopping, water sports and historic lighthouse & Victorian architectural tours nearby.

Location: City. In historic district.

Publicity: *New Jersey Countryside, The Discerning Traveler, Arrington's and NJ Golf.*

"I feel as if I have come to stay with a dear old friend who has spared no expense to provide me with all that my heart can desire! ... I will savor the memory of your hospitality for years to come. Thanks so much."

Certificate may be used: Nov. 1-May 31, Sunday-Thursday, except holidays.

Gingerbread House

28 Gurney St
Cape May, NJ 08204
(609)884-0211
Internet: gingerbreadinn.com
E-mail: info@gingerbreadinn.com

Circa 1869. The Gingerbread is one of eight original Stockton Row Cottages, summer retreats built for families from Philadelphia and Virginia. It is a half-block from the ocean and breezes waft over the wicker-filled porch. The inn is listed in the National Register. It has been meticulously restored and decorated with period antiques and a fine collection of paintings. The inn's woodwork is especially notable, guests enter through handmade teak double doors. Innkeeper(s): Fred & Joan Echevarria. $90-260. 6 rooms, 3 with PB, 1 suite. Breakfast and afternoon tea included in rates. Types of meals: Full bkfst. Beds: QD. Air conditioning. Telephone and fireplace on premises. Antiquing, fishing, live theater, parks, shopping, water sports, birding and Victorian homes nearby.

Location: Ocean community.

Publicity: *Philadelphia Inquirer, New Jersey Monthly and Atlantic City Press Newspaper.*

"The elegance, charm and authenticity of historic Cape May, but more than that, it appeals to us as 'home.'"

Certificate may be used: Oct. 14-May 25, Monday-Thursday.

The Henry Sawyer Inn

722 Columbia Ave
Cape May, NJ 08204-2332
(609)884-5667 (800)449-5667 Fax:(609)884-9406
Internet: www.henrysawyerinn.com

Circa 1877. This fully restored, three-story peach Victorian home boasts a gingerbread embellished veranda, brick-colored shutters and brown trim. Inside, the parlor features Victorian antiques, a marble fireplace, polished wood floors, an Oriental rug, formal wallcoverings, a crystal chandelier and fresh flowers. Guest rooms have been decorated with careful attention to a romantic and fresh Victorian theme, as well. One room includes a whirlpool tub, one includes a private porch, and another a fireplace. Innkeeper(s): Mary & Barbara Morris. $85-250. 5 rooms with PB, 1 with FP, 2 suites. Breakfast and afternoon tea included in rates. Types of meals: Full bkfst and early coffee/tea. Beds: KQT. Cable TV, reading lamp, ceiling fan, clock radio, small refrigerator and one with whirlpool or private porch in room. Air conditioning. VCR, fax, telephone, fireplace and parking on premises. Antiquing, fishing, golf, live theater, parks, shopping, tennis, water sports, carriage and Victorian trolley nearby.

Location: City, ocean community.

Certificate may be used: Anytime, November-April, subject to availability.

The King's Cottage

9 Perry St
Cape May, NJ 08204-1460
(609)884-0415 (877)258-1876 Fax:(609)884-1113
Internet: www.kingscottage.com
E-mail: kingscottage@snip.net

Circa 1878. Enjoy the beautiful ocean views as you relax on antique wicker on the wraparound verandas at this architectural gem, designed by Frank Furness. The railings boast ceramic tiles that were part of a Japanese exhibition from the Philadelphia Centennial of 1876, and a measured drawing is recorded in the Library of Congress. Most of the guest rooms afford ocean views and two offer private verandas. All feature unique period decor and antiques. Breakfasts are served in the formal dining room on tables set with china, crystal and silver. Innkeeper(s): Roseann Baker & Barbara Preminger. $100-235. 9 rooms with PB, 1 with FP, 1 suite. Breakfast, afternoon tea and snacks/refreshments included in rates. Types of meals: Full gourmet bkfst, veg bkfst and early coffee/tea. Beds: Q. Reading lamp in room. Air conditioning. Telephone, private veranda with some accommodations and on-site parking on premises. Amusement parks, antiquing, art galleries, beach, bicycling, canoeing/kayaking, fishing, golf, hiking, horseback riding, live theater, museums, parks, shopping, tennis, water sports, wineries, dolphin watching, lighthouse and casinos nearby.

Location: Ocean community, waterfront.

Publicity: *Victorian Affair, Atlantic City Press, Newark Star, New Jersey Savy Living and Cape May Videos.*

"Thanks so much for your warm and inviting hospitality. I never expected to feel so at home at a bed and breakfast. Your personal touch made this a memorable experience and not just "a place to stay." The views and ocean breezes were more than you described. Truly great."

Certificate may be used: October-December, February-May, Sunday-Thursday, excludes holidays, subject to availability. Must mention ad when calling to book with coupon.

The Mission Inn

1117 New Jersey Ave
Cape May, NJ 08204-2638
(609)884-8380 (800)800-8390 Fax:(609)884-4191
Internet: www.missioninn.net
E-mail: info@missioninn.net

Circa 1912. Renown for being the town's only house built with Spanish-style architecture and Mission-style decor, this historic inn is located in a gorgeous seashore setting. Tyrone Power, Errol Flynn and Robert Preston are some of the notables who have stayed here. Relax on oversized comfortable furnishings by the fireplace in the Great Room. After a good nights rest, an artistically presented  and abundant breakfast may include seasonal fruits, homemade breads and muffins, stuffed French toast, peppered ham, sausage patties or smoked bacon. The patio and veranda are resplendent with colorful flowers and indigenous fruit-bearing trees. Bikes are available for further exploring. Beach towels and chairs are also provided. Innkeeper(s): Susan Babineau-Roberts. $89-255. 8 rooms with PB, 3 with FP. Breakfast and snacks/refreshments included in rates. Types of meals: Full gourmet bkfst and early coffee/tea. Beds: K. Cable TV, reading lamp, ceiling fan, clock radio and some with fireplaces and/or Jacuzzi tub and/or spa therapy shower in room. Air conditioning. VCR, bicycles, library, parlor games, fireplace, on-site parking, beach towels and beach chairs on premises. Antiquing, art galleries, beach, bicycling, canoeing/kayaking, fishing, golf, hiking, horseback riding, live theater, museums, parks, shopping, tennis, water sports and wineries nearby.

Location: Ocean community.

Publicity: *Cape May County Herald, Atlantic City Press, Bright Side Newspaper, Cape May Chamber of Commerce (both local and county guidebook), KOOL 98.3 (Atlantic and Cape May Counties), Arrington's 2003 Book of Lists voted "Best on Eastern Seaboard" and 2004 Book of Lists voted "Best Interior Design and Decor."*

"Cape May's best kept secret."

Certificate may be used: Sunday through Thursday, January-April 30, subject to availability, holidays excluded.

The Queen Victoria

102 Ocean St
Cape May, NJ 08204-2320
(609)884-8702
Internet: www.queenvictoria.com
E-mail: doug@queenvictoria.com

Circa 1881. This nationally acclaimed inn, a block from the ocean and shops in the historic district, is comprised of two beautiful Victorian homes, restored and furnished with antiques. "Victorian Homes" magazine featured 23 color photographs of The Queen Victoria, because of its décor and luxurious amenities. Guest rooms offer handmade quilts, antiques, air conditioning, mini-refrigerators and all have private baths. Luxury suites and many rooms have a whirlpool tub and some with handsome fireplace. Afternoon tea is enjoyed while rocking on the porch in summer or before a warm fireplace in winter. Breakfast is hearty buffet style and the inn has its own cookbook. The innkeepers keep a fleet of complimentary bicycles available for guests and there are beach chairs and beach towels as well. The inn is open all year with special Christmas festivities and winter packages.

Innkeeper(s): Doug & Anna Marie McMain. $100-300. 21 rooms with PB, 6 suites. Breakfast and afternoon tea included in rates. Types of meals: Full bkfst and early coffee/tea. Beds: Q. TV, reading lamp, refrigerator, clock radio and some with phones in room. Air conditioning. Bicycles and fireplace on premises. Amusement parks, antiquing, beach, golf, parks, water sports and historic tours nearby.

Publicity: *Philadelphia Inquirer and Travel channel.*

Certificate may be used: Monday through Thursday, November through March, except holidays and Christmas week.

Queen's Hotel

601 Columbia Ave
Cape May, NJ 08204-2305
(609)884-1613
Internet: www.queenshotel.com
E-mail: doug@queenvictoria.com

Circa 1876. This elegant Victorian hotel is located just a block from the beach in the center of Cape May's historic district. Period decor graces the luxurious guest rooms. The feeling is both romantic and historic. Many of the rooms and suites offer double whirlpool tubs or glass-enclosed marble showers. Other amenities include hair dryers, TV, heated towel bar, air conditioning, coffeemakers and mini refrigerators. Some have private balconies and ocean views. A continental breakfast buffet is included in the rates. Restaurants and cafes are within walking distance or you can ask for the continental breakfast tray for a small charge. The hotel's staff includes professional concierge service. Shops are one block away. There are bicycles on the premises to explore the town and scenic water views.

Innkeeper(s): Doug & Anna Marie McMain. $90-280. 11 rooms with PB, 1 with FP, 1 suite. Breakfast included in rates. Types of meals: Cont. Beds: Q. Cable TV, reading lamp, refrigerator, ceiling fan, clock radio, telephone, hair

dryer, coffeemaker and heated towel bar in room. Air conditioning. Bicycles on premises. Amusement parks, antiquing, bicycling, fishing, golf, live theater, parks, water sports and historic tours nearby.

Location: City.

Publicity: *Philadelphia Inquirer.*

Certificate may be used: Monday through Thursday, November through March, except holidays and Christmas week.

Rhythm of The Sea

1123 W. Beach Ave
Cape May, NJ 08204-2628
(609)884-7788
Internet: www.rhythmofthesea.com
E-mail: rhythm@algorithms.com

Circa 1915. The apt name of this oceanfront inn describes the soothing sounds of the sea that lull many a happy guest into a restful night's sleep. Watching sunsets, strolling the beach, bird watching and whale watching are popular activities. Many of the features of a Craftsman home are incorporated in this seaside inn, such as light-filled spacious rooms, adjoining dining and living areas and gleaming natural wood floors. Mission oak furnishings compliment the inn's architecture. For guests seeking an especially private stay, ask for the three-room suite and arrange for a private dinner prepared by the innkeeper Wolfgang Wendt, a European trained chef. Full breakfasts are provided each morning. Guests are given complimentary beach towels and chairs. There is free parking and complimentary use of bicycles.

Innkeeper(s): Robyn & Wolfgang Wendt. $198-365. 7 rooms with PB, 2 with FP, 1 suite. Breakfast and snacks/refreshments included in rates. Types of meals: Full bkfst and dinner. Beds: Q. Reading lamp and clock radio in room. Air conditioning. VCR, bicycles, telephone and fireplace on premises. Amusement parks, antiquing, fishing, live theater, shopping and water sports nearby.

Location: Ocean community.

Publicity: *Atlantic City Press, New Jersey Monthly and POV.*

"Your home is lovely, the atmosphere is soothing."

Certificate may be used: October-April, Sunday-Thursday, not valid on holidays or with any other promotional offer.

White Dove Cottage

619 Hughes St
Cape May, NJ 08204-2317
(609)884-0613 (800)321-3683
Internet: www.whitedovecottage.com

Circa 1866. The beautiful octagonal slate on the Mansard roof of this Second Empire house is just one of the inn's many handsome details. Bright sunny rooms are furnished in American and European antiques, period wallpapers, paintings, prints and handmade quilts. Suites with fireplaces or Jacuzzi tub are available. Located on a quiet, gas-lit street, the inn is two blocks from the beach, restaurants and shops.

Innkeeper(s): Alison Bjork and Joan Bjork. $90-250. 4 rooms with PB, 2 suites. Breakfast and afternoon tea included in rates. Types of meals: Full gourmet bkfst and early coffee/tea. Beds: KQD. Clock radio, two suites with fireplace and Jacuzzi in room. Parlor games, telephone and fireplace on premises. Antiquing, fishing, live theater, shopping and water sports nearby.

Location: Seashore resort.

Publicity: *Bride.*

Certificate may be used: Sept. 15 through June 15, Sunday through Thursday. Exclude Christmas week and Victorian Week.

Glenwood   A5

Apple Valley Inn
967 County Rt, 517
Glenwood, NJ 07418
(973)764-3735 Fax:(973)764-1050
Internet: www.applevalleyinn.com
E-mail: appleinn@warwick.net

Circa 1804. This three-story Colonial farmhouse is set on three acres with its own apple orchard and in-ground pool. A brook running next to the house is a great trout-fishing spot. The innkeeper is an avid antique collector and guest rooms (named after varieties of apples) include American antiques. Try the Red Delicious room. Across the street is a popular pick-your-own-fruit farm. Check with the innkeeper to find when the strawberries, peaches, cherries and apples are ripe so you can gather your favorites. Mountain Creek, ski slopes and the Appalachian Trail are five minutes away.

Innkeeper(s): Lee Petroski. $80-120. 7 rooms, 2 with PB. Breakfast and afternoon tea included in rates. Types of meals: Full bkfst, early coffee/tea and picnic lunch. Beds: DT. Reading lamp and ceiling fan in room. Air conditioning. VCR, fax, copier, swimming, bicycles, library, parlor games, telephone and fireplace on premises. Amusement parks, antiquing, cross-country skiing, downhill skiing, fishing, hiking, live theater, parks, shopping, sporting events and Appalachian Trail nearby.

Location: Mountains.

Publicity: *Cleveland Plain Dealer, Appalachian Trail News, New Jersey Herald and Country Living.*

Certificate may be used: Anytime, Sunday-Thursday.

Hackettstown   C4

The Everitt House, A Victorian Bed & Breakfast
200 High Street
Hackettstown, NJ 07840
(908)684-1307 Fax:(908)684-8049
Internet: www.everitthouse.com
E-mail: dsamuel146@aol.com

Circa 1876. Named in honor of its first owner, an influential man and former mayor, this Second Empire Victorian with Mansard roof is located in the town's historic district, only one hour from New York City. The formal living room is the perfect place to plan the day's activities. Guest bedrooms feature sitting areas and a warm and appealing atmosphere. The bountiful morning meal, which may include stuffed pancakes, chocolate croissants and a frittata, can only be overshadowed by the picturesque views from the glass-enclosed breakfast room. Enjoy snacks and beverages available any time. Manicured lawns, colorful flowers, rose and rock gardens all combine to create a park-like setting. The Delaware Water Gap is a 30-minute drive.

Innkeeper(s): David & Mary Samuel. $115-150. 4 rooms with PB, 1 suite and 1 conference room. Breakfast included in rates. Types of meals: Full gourmet bkfst, early coffee/tea, afternoon tea and snacks/refreshments. Beds: KQD. Data port, cable TV, reading lamp, ceiling fan, clock radio and telephone in room. Air conditioning. Fax and copier on premises. Antiquing, bicy-

cling, canoeing/kayaking, fishing, golf, hiking, horseback riding, live theater, parks, shopping and wineries nearby.

Location: Country.

Publicity: *WRNJ Radio.*

Certificate may be used: All year, Sunday through Thursday, excludes holidays.

Haddonfield   G3

Haddonfield Inn
44 West End Ave
Haddonfield, NJ 08033-2616
(856)428-2195 (800)269-0014 Fax:(856)354-1273
Internet: www.haddonfieldinn.com
E-mail: innkeeper@haddonfieldinn.com

Circa 1865. This three-story Victorian house, complete with gabled roofs, a turret and veranda, is in the National Trust. Its location is historic Haddonfield, said by Philadelphia Magazine to be the most picturesque village in the Delaware Valley. Handsome heritage homes, fine museums, symphony orchestras, theater and more than 200 shops and restaurants are nearby. Parlors are furnished with antiques and chandeliers, and the guest rooms offer whirlpools and fireplaces, each in the theme of a European country or other culture. Upon arrival, guests are offered snacks and beverages. In the morning, a gourmet breakfast is served before a flickering fireplace in the dining room or on the wraparound veranda overlooking the inn's lawns. For guest convenience, there is an elevator, and the innkeeper provides concierge service. The inn is popular for small meetings and special events. Walk to the train to visit Philadelphia (17 minutes away) and connect to stadiums, the airport and Amtrak.

Innkeeper(s): Nancy & Fred Chorpita. $140-215. 8 rooms with PB, 1 suite. Breakfast and snacks/refreshments included in rates. Types of meals: Full gourmet bkfst. Beds: KQ. Modem hook-up, cable TV, snack bar, telephone, hot tub/spa and voice mail in room. Central air. Spa, swimming, tennis, fireplace, Internet access and golf on premises. Handicap access. Amusement parks, golf, museums, parks, sporting events, tennis, swimming and health clubs nearby.

Location: City.

Certificate may be used: Sunday through Thursday, holidays excluded. Hong Kong, Safari and Dub Lynn rooms only.

Hope   C3

The Inn at Millrace Pond
PO Box 359
Hope, NJ 07844-0359
(908)459-4884 (800)746-6467 Fax:(908)459-5276
Internet: www.innatmillracepond.com
E-mail: millrace@epix.net

Circa 1769. The former grist mill buildings house an authentically restored Colonial inn, set in the rolling hills of Northwestern New Jersey. Decorated in the Colonial period, many of the rooms feature original wide-board floors, antiques and Oriental rugs. Rooms in the limestone Grist Mill, a building listed in the National Register of Historic Places, boast handcrafted American primitive reproductions and braided rugs. The inn's restaurant features the original millrace room, complete with running water. A former

wheel chamber has a staircase that leads to the Tavern Room with its own walk-in fireplace and grain chute.

Innkeeper(s): Cordie & Charles Puttkammer. $130-175. 17 rooms with PB, 1 with FP, 1 suite and 1 conference room. Breakfast included in rates. Types of meals: Cont plus and snacks/refreshments. Restaurant on premises. Beds: Q. Cable TV, reading lamp, clock radio, telephone and desk in room. Air conditioning. TV, fax, copier, bicycles and fireplace on premises. Handicap access. Amusement parks, antiquing, cross-country skiing, fishing, parks, shopping and tennis court on property nearby.

Location: Within historic district.

"The most interesting thing of all is the way these buildings have been restored."

Certificate may be used: All year, Sunday through Thursday, excludes holidays.

Lambertville   E3

Chimney Hill Farm Estate & The Ol' Barn Inn

207 Goat Hill Rd
Lambertville, NJ 08530
(609)397-1516 (800)211-4667 Fax:(609)397-9353
Internet: www.chimneyhillinn.com
E-mail: info@chimneyhillinn.com

Circa 1820. Chimney Hill, in the hills above the riverside town of Lambertville, is a grand display of stonework, designed with both Federal and Greek Revival-style architecture. The inn's sunroom is particularly appealing, with its stone walls, fireplaces and French windows looking out to eight acres of gardens and fields. All eight of the guest rooms in the estate farmhouse  include fireplaces, and some have canopied beds. The Ol' Barn has four suites with fireplaces, Jacuzzis, steam rooms, guest pantries, spiral staircases and loft bedrooms. The innkeepers offer adventure, romance and special interest packages for their guests, and the inn is also popular for corporate retreats. There are plenty of seasonal activities nearby, from kayaking to skiing. New Hope is the neighboring town and offers many charming restaurants and shops, as well.

Innkeeper(s): Terry & Richard Anderson. $130-395. 12 rooms, 8 with PB, 10 with FP, 4 suites and 2 conference rooms. Breakfast and snacks/refreshments included in rates. Types of meals: Country bkfst and early coffee/tea. Beds: KQD. Modem hook-up, data port, cable TV, reading lamp, refrigerator, ceiling fan, snack bar, clock radio, telephone, coffeemaker, desk, fireplace and Jacuzzi in room. Air conditioning. Fax, copier, parlor games, gift shop and wireless Internet access on premises. Limited handicap access. Antiquing, art galleries, bicycling, canoeing/kayaking, fishing, golf, hiking, horseback riding, live theater, museums, parks, shopping, tennis and wineries nearby.

Location: Country.

Publicity: *Country Inns* (Cover), *Colonial Homes Magazine, Country Roads Magazine, NY Times, NJ Magazine,* and *New Jersey Network.*

"We would be hard pressed to find a more perfect setting to begin our married life together."

Certificate may be used: Jan. 3-Dec. 20, Monday-Thursday. No holidays, no October dates.

York Street House

42 York St
Lambertville, NJ 08530-2024
(609)397-3007 (888)398-3199 Fax:(609)397-6700
Internet: www.yorkstreethouse.com
E-mail: innkeeper@yorkstreethouse.com

Circa 1909. Built by early industrialist George Massey as a 25th wedding anniversary present for his wife, the gracious manor house is situated on almost an acre in the heart of the historic district. Common rooms are warmed by Mercer Tile fireplaces and an original Waterford Crystal chandelier. A winding three-story staircase leads to well-appointed guest bedrooms with period furnishings. Looking out on the lawn and sitting porch, breakfast is served in the dining room, showcasing built-in leaded-glass china and large oak servers. Art galleries, antique shops and restaurants are nearby. Enjoy mule-drawn barges and carriage rides. New Hope, Penn. is a short walk across the Delaware River Bridge, with many quaint shops.

Innkeeper(s): Laurie and Mark Weinstein. $100-215. 6 rooms with PB, 3 with FP and 1 conference room. Breakfast and snacks/refreshments included in rates. Types of meals: Full gourmet bkfst, veg bkfst, early coffee/tea and picnic lunch. Beds: KQT. Cable TV, reading lamp, ceiling fan, clock radio, desk, fireplace and Jacuzzi in room. Air conditioning. VCR, fax, copier, parlor games and telephone on premises. Antiquing, art galleries, bicycling, canoeing/kayaking, cross-country skiing, fishing, golf, hiking, horseback riding, live theater, museums, parks, shopping, sporting events, water sports and wineries nearby.

Location: Small town.

Certificate may be used: Sunday to Thursday.

Manahawkin   H5

Goose N. Berry Inn

190 N Main St
Manahawkin, NJ 08050-2932
(609)597-6350 Fax:(609)597-6918
Internet: www.goosenberryinn.com
E-mail: info@goosenberryinn.com

Circa 1868. This Queen Anne Victorian, built by an English merchant, has been painstakingly restored and redecorated. Period antiques decorate the guest rooms, each of which has its own personal flair. The Capstan Room features a nautical Victorian theme with paintings in honor of the area's seafaring tradition. Another room is decorated with antique needlepoint samplers, some a century old. There are plenty of places to  relax, including a library stocked with books. Guests enjoy a wide variety of items during the gourmet buffet breakfast, baked French toast, fresh fruit, homemade breads, egg dishes and gourmet coffee are among the options. The innkeepers have snacks available throughout the day. For those celebrating a special occasions, the innkeepers can prepare a tray with champagne, chocolates or perhaps wine and cheese. The Times-Beacon newspapers voted the inn as the "most romantic getaway" two years in a row.

Innkeeper(s): Mirtha & Mike Kopec. $75-175. 5 rooms with PB, 1 suite and 1 conference room. Breakfast, afternoon tea and snacks/refreshments included in rates. Types of meals: Full gourmet bkfst, early coffee/tea, gourmet lunch and picnic lunch. Beds: D. Reading lamp, turn-down service and alarms available in room. Air conditioning. Bicycles, parlor games and canoe on premises. Amusement parks, antiquing, fishing, live theater, parks, shopping, water sports, gambling & casino shows, Atlantic City and wineries nearby.

Certificate may be used: Sept. 15-May 15 except holiday periods and special events.

North Wildwood   K4

Candlelight Inn

2310 Central Ave
North Wildwood, NJ 08260-5944
(609)522-6200 (800)992-2632 Fax:(609)522-6125
Internet: www.candlelight-inn.com
E-mail: info@candlelight-inn.com

Circa 1905. Candlelight Inn offers ten guest rooms in a restored Queen Anne Victorian. The home is decorated with an assortment of period pieces. Among its antiques are a Victorian sofa dating to 1855 and an 1890 Eastlake piano. Breakfasts begin with a fresh fruit course, followed by fresh breads and a daily entrée, such as waffles, pancakes or a specialty egg dish. Candlelight Inn is about eight miles from the historic towns of Cape May and Cold Spring Village.

Innkeeper(s): Bill & Nancy Moncrief. $125-250. 10 rooms with PB, 2 with FP, 3 suites. Breakfast and afternoon tea included in rates. Types of meals: Full bkfst, early coffee/tea and snacks/refreshments. Beds: KQT. Cable TV, reading lamp, refrigerator, ceiling fan, clock radio, coffeemaker, desk, fireplace and four with double whirlpool tubs in room. Central air. Fax, copier, telephone, fireplace and hot tub on premises. Limited handicap access. Amusement parks, antiquing, art galleries, beach, bicycling, fishing, golf, live theater, museums, parks, shopping, tennis and water sports nearby.

Location: Ocean community.

Publicity: *Select Registry.*

Certificate may be used: November-April (excluding holidays), Sunday-Thursday.

Ocean City   J4

Serendipity B&B

712 E 9th St
Ocean City, NJ 08226-3554
(609)399-1554 (800)842-8544 Fax:(609)399-1527
Internet: www.serendipitynj.com
E-mail: info@serendipitynj.com

Circa 1912. The beach and the boardwalk are less than half a block from this renovated Dutch Colonial bed & breakfast for a perfect weekend escape or vacation. Stay in a guest bedroom decorated in pastels and furnished with wicker. Healthy full breakfasts are served in the dining room or, in the summer, on a vine-shaded veranda. Choose from six entrees daily, including vegetarian and high protein selections. Relax on the garden veranda or soak in the spa/hot tub.

Innkeeper(s): Clara & Bill Plowfield. $83-195. 6 rooms, 4 with PB. Breakfast and snacks/refreshments included in rates. Types of meals: Full bkfst. Beds: KQDT. Cable TV, VCR, reading lamp, ceiling fan, bathrobes and bottled water in room. Air conditioning. Parlor games, telephone, fireplace, dressing rooms with showers and beach towels, beach chairs, guest refrigerator, microwave, video library and outdoor hot tub on premises. Amusement parks, antiquing, fishing, live theater, parks, shopping, water sports, ocean beach and boardwalk nearby.

Location: Ocean community.

Publicity: *Philadelphia Inquirer Magazine and "Best Weekend Escape"*

Awarded by Arrington's Bed & Breakfast Journal 2004 Book of Lists.

"Serendipity is such a gift. For me it's a little like being adopted during vacation time by a caring sister and brother. Your home is a home away from home. You make it so."

Certificate may be used: November-April, Sunday-Thursday. No holidays. May not be combined with any other offers.

Ocean Grove   J4

The Cordova

26 Webb Ave
Ocean Grove, NJ 07756-1334
(732)774-3084 Fax:(732)897-1666
Internet: www.thecordova.com
E-mail: info@thecordova.com

Circa 1885. This century-old Victorian community was founded as a Methodist retreat. Ocean-bathing and cars were not allowed on Sunday until a few years ago. There are no souvenir shops along the white sandy beach and wooden boardwalk. The inn has hosted Presidents Wilson, Cleveland and Roosevelt, who were also speakers at the Great Auditorium with its 5,500 seats. Guests have use of the kitchen, lounge, picnic and barbecue areas, thus making this a popu-  lar place for family reunions, retreats, showers and weddings. Ask about the inn's special events. Three suites and two cottage apartments also are available. The Cordova was chosen by New Jersey Magazine as one of the seven best places on the Jersey Shore.

Innkeeper(s): Nicole Mesler and Luis Velasquez. $55-189. 17 rooms, 7 with PB, 3 suites and 2 cottages. Breakfast included in rates. Types of meals: Cont plus. Beds: KQDT. VCR, tennis, library and telephone on premises. Antiquing, fishing, shopping, tennis, music concerts, garden tours and dances nearby.

Publicity: *New Jersey, Asbury Park Press, St. Martin's Press and "O'New Jersey" by Robert Heide and John Gilman.*

"Warm, helpful and inviting, homey and lived-in atmosphere."

Certificate may be used: Anytime between Sept. 15-May 15 (except holidays) and Sunday through Thursday in the summer months.

The Manchester Inn B&B and Secret Garden Restaurant

25 Ocean Pathway
Ocean Grove, NJ 07756-1645
(732)775-0616
Internet: www.themanchesterinn.com
E-mail: thenjinn@aol.com

Circa 1875. Enjoy cool ocean breezes while you lounge on the front porch of this quaint Victorian, which is featured in the town's annual Victorian Holiday House Tour each December. The full-service restaurant has bright, flowery decor and offers plenty of choices for breakfast, lunch and dinner. Ocean Grove is an ideal spot to bask in the Victorian tradition. The beach is only one block and the inn looks out onto Ocean Parkway, one of Ocean Grove's finest streets. The town itself offers many festivals throughout the year, plus a variety of interesting shops to explore.

Innkeeper(s): Margaret & Clark Cate. $75-155. 35 rooms, 23 with PB, 2 two-bedroom suites and 1 conference room. Breakfast included in rates. Types of meals: Full gourmet bkfst, veg bkfst and Sun. brunch. Restaurant on premises. Beds: KQDT. Ceiling fan and some with private porches in room. Air conditioning. TV, VCR, fax, copier, parlor games, telephone and full breakfast on premises. Amusement parks, antiquing, art galleries, beach, bicycling, fishing, golf, live theater, museums, parks, shopping, sporting events, tennis, water sports and Great Auditorium nearby.

Location: Ocean community. Historic seaside town.

Publicity: *Times, Cablevision feature and WWOR*.

Certificate may be used: Anytime, subject to availability.

Plainfield   D5

Pillars of Plainfield B&B

922 Central Ave
Plainfield, NJ 07060
(908)753-0922 (888)PIL-LARS
Internet: www.pillars2.com
E-mail: info@pillars2.com

Circa 1870. Victorian and Georgian influences are mingled in the design of this grand historic mansion, which boasts majestic columns and a wraparound porch. An acre of well-manicured grounds and gardens surrounds the home, which is located in Plainfield's Van Wyck Historic District. Guest rooms and suites are appointed with traditional furnishings, and each room has its own special decor. The romantic Van Wyck Brooks Suite includes a fireplace and a canopy bed topped with a down quilt. A wicker table and chairs are tucked into the bay window alcove of the Clementine Yates room. Another spacious room includes a full kitchen. Business travelers will appreciate the private in-room phones with voice mail and wi-fi. Swedish home cooking highlights the morning meal, which is accompanied by freshly ground coffee. Plainfield, the first inland settlement in New Jersey, offers many historic attractions, including the Drake House Museum.

Innkeeper(s): Chuck & Tom Hale. $114-250. 7 rooms with PB, 2 with FP. Breakfast and snacks/refreshments included in rates. Types of meals: Full bkfst, veg bkfst and early coffee/tea. Beds: QT. Modem hook-up, data port, cable TV, VCR, reading lamp, ceiling fan, clock radio, telephone, coffeemaker, turn-down service, desk and voice mail in room. Air conditioning. Fax, copier, library, parlor games, fireplace and laundry facility on premises. Amusement parks, antiquing, art galleries, beach, golf, hiking, live theater, museums, parks, shopping, sporting events and tennis nearby.

Location: City.

Certificate may be used: Sunday night free with Saturday night booked at standard rates, does not apply to holiday weekends. No other discounts apply. Direct booking required.

Spring Lake   F6

The Normandy Inn

21 Tuttle Ave
Spring Lake, NJ 07762-1533
(732)449-7172 (800)449-1888 Fax:(732)449-1070
Internet: www.normandyinn.com
E-mail: normandy@bellatlantic.net

Circa 1888. In a picturesque seaside town, this historic Italianate Villa with Queen Anne details is just half a block from the ocean. Listed in the National Register, the Colonial Revival and Neoclassicism interior reflect its traditionally elegant Victorian heritage. Relax in spacious double parlours or play the 1886 trumpet-legged grand piano. Fine antiques adorn air-conditioned guest bedrooms. Some rooms feature cozy fireplaces, canopy beds and Jacuzzis. Choose from a selection of hearty country breakfast entrees to savor in the dining room. The inn's exceptional service, romantic ambiance and central

location make it the perfect all-season getaway.

Innkeeper(s): The Valori family. $135-396. 17 rooms with PB, 7 with FP, 2 suites and 1 conference room. Breakfast and afternoon tea included in rates. Types of meals: Full gourmet bkfst, early coffee/tea, picnic lunch and snacks/refreshments. Beds: KQDT. Modem hook-up, data port, cable TV, VCR, reading lamp, refrigerator, clock radio, telephone, coffeemaker, desk, Jacuzzi tubs and fireplace in room. Central air. Fax, copier, bicycles, library, parlor games, fireplace and gift shop on premises. Amusement parks, antiquing, art galleries, beach, bicycling, canoeing/kayaking, fishing, golf, hiking, horseback riding, live theater, museums, parks, shopping, sporting events, tennis and water sports nearby.

Location: Ocean community.

Publicity: *New York Times*.

"The cozy and delicious accommodations of your inn were beyond expectations."

Certificate may be used: Oct. 1 to April 30, Sunday through Thursday, subject to availability.

Sea Crest By The Sea

19 Tuttle Ave
Spring Lake, NJ 07762-1533
(732)449-9031 (800)803-9031 Fax:(732)974-0403
Internet: www.seacrestbythesea.com
E-mail: capt@seacrestbythesea.com

Circa 1885. You can hear the surf from most rooms in this Victorian mansion, located an hour from New York city or Philadelphia. Guests will be pampered with Egyptian cotton and Belgian-lace linens, queen-size feather beds, fresh flowers and classical music. Six rooms have Jacuzzis for two and there are eight with fireplaces. Tunes from a player piano announce afternoon tea at 4 p.m.—a good time to make dinner reservations at one of the area's fine restaurants. In the morning family china, crystal and silver add to the ambiance of a full gourmet breakfast. Bicycles are available and the beach is a half block away.

Innkeeper(s): Barbara & Fred Vogel. $300-450. 8 rooms with PB, 8 with FP, 5 suites and 1 conference room. Breakfast and afternoon tea included in rates. Types of meals: Full gourmet bkfst. Beds: Q. Cable TV, VCR, reading lamp, CD player, refrigerator, ceiling fan, clock radio, telephone, hot tub/spa, Jacuzzis for two, fireplace, robes, hair dryers and slippers in room. Central air. Fax, copier, bicycles, parlor games, fireplace, gift shop, evening cordials, passes to premier health fitness club and beach gear on premises. Amusement parks, antiquing, art galleries, beach, bicycling, canoeing/kayaking, fishing, golf, hiking, live theater, museums, parks, shopping, tennis, water sports and Atlantic Beach nearby.

Location: Ocean community.

Publicity: *New York Times, Gourmet, Victoria, Star Ledger and New York Magazine*.

"This romantic storybook atmosphere is delightful! A visual feast."

Certificate may be used: Oct. 1-May 15, Sunday-Thursday, subject to availability (excluding holiday periods).

Spring Lake Inn

104 Salem Ave
Spring Lake, NJ 07762-1040
(732)449-2010 Fax:(732)449-4020
Internet: www.springlakeinn.com
E-mail: springlakeinn@aol.com

Circa 1888. Only a block from the beach, this historic Victorian inn boasts an informal seaside atmosphere. Relax on the 80-foot, rocker-lined porch or fireside in the parlor. Well-decorated guest bedrooms and suites offer a variety of peaceful settings including the Turret, surrounded by four windows, and the Tower View suite with sleigh bed and ocean views. Enjoy a leisurely breakfast served in the spacious dining room featuring a 12-foot ceiling. Walk to the town center, with more than 60 shops to explore.

Innkeeper(s): Barbara & Andy Seaman. $99-499. 16 rooms with PB, 8 with FP, 2 suites and 2 conference rooms. Breakfast and snacks/refreshments included in rates. Types of meals: Full gourmet bkfst, Sun. brunch, early coffee/tea and afternoon tea. Beds: QD. Modem hook-up, cable TV, VCR, reading lamp, stereo, refrigerator, ceiling fan, snack bar, clock radio, desk, hot tub/spa, fireplace, beach chairs, beach badges, beach towels and ocean views in room. Air conditioning. Fax, copier, swimming, library, parlor games, telephone and gift shop on premises. Limited handicap access. Amusement parks, antiquing, art galleries, beach, bicycling, canoeing/kayaking, fishing, golf, hiking, horseback riding, live theater, museums, parks, shopping, sporting events, tennis, water sports and wineries nearby.

Location: Ocean community. Two blocks from the lake and one block from the ocean. The town center is within walking distance.

Publicity: *Asbury Press and NJ 12.*

Certificate may be used: Oct. 1 to May 15, subject to availability.

Stanhope   C4

Whistling Swan Inn
110 Main St
Stanhope, NJ 07874-2632
(973)347-6369 Fax:(973)347-3391
Internet: www.whistlingswaninn.com
E-mail: wswan@worldnet.att.net

Circa 1905. This Queen Anne Victorian has a limestone wraparound veranda and a tall, steep-roofed turret. Family antiques fill the rooms and highlight the polished ornate woodwork, pocket doors and winding staircase. It is a little more than a mile from Waterloo Village and the International Trade Center.

Innkeeper(s): Liz & Ron Armstrong. $99-219. 9 rooms with PB, 1 suite and 1 conference room. Breakfast included in rates. Types of meals: Full bkfst. Beds: Q. Data port, cable TV, VCR, reading lamp, ceiling fan, clock radio, telephone, desk, iron and hair dryer in room. Air conditioning. Fax, copier, bicycles, parlor games, fireplace, tubs for two and Victorian garden on premises. Antiquing, fishing, live theater, parks, shopping, sporting events, water sports, golf, hiking and boating nearby.

Location: Mountains. Rural village.

Publicity: *Sunday Herald, New York Times, New Jersey Monthly, Mid-Atlantic Country, Star Ledger, Daily Record, Philadelphia, Country and Chicago Sun Times.*

"Thank you for your outstanding hospitality. We had a delightful time while we were with you and will not hesitate to recommend the inn to our listening audience, friends and anyone else who will listen!"— Joel H. Klein, Travel Editor, WOAI AM

Certificate may be used: Thursday, Friday and Sunday from January through April, excluding holidays.

Ventnor City   J5

Carisbrooke Inn
105 S Little Rock Ave
Ventnor City, NJ 08406-2840
(609)822-6392 Fax:(609)822-2563
Internet: www.carisbrookeinn.com
E-mail: info@carisbrookeinn.com

Circa 1918. Relaxation is easy at this enticing seaside bed & breakfast just a few steps away from the world-famous boardwalk and only one mile from Atlantic City. Delight in the ocean

view from the front deck or the tranquility of the back patio. Afternoon refreshments are enjoyed in the sunny Main Parlor, or by the warmth of a winter fire. Pleasant guest bedrooms feature comfortable amenities and the romantic accents of plants, fresh flowers and lacy curtains. The innkeepers offer a huge breakfast that may include homemade waffles and fresh berries, banana pecan pancakes, Italian frittata with fresh herbs and cheese, Quiche Lorraine and French toast, accompanied by fruit and just-baked muffins and breads. Beach towels and tags are provided for fun in the sun at the shore.

Innkeeper(s): John and Julie Battista. $95-315. 8 rooms with PB. Breakfast and snacks/refreshments included in rates. Types of meals: Full gourmet bkfst and early coffee/tea. Beds: KQD. Cable TV, reading lamp, clock radio and fresh flowers in room. Air conditioning. Fax, copier, parlor games, telephone, fireplace, complimentary tea/coffee/snacks in main parlor, beach tags and towels and chairs (in season) on premises. Amusement parks, antiquing, beach, bicycling, fishing, golf, live theater, parks, shopping, tennis, water sports and casinos nearby.

Location: City, ocean community.

"You have a beautiful, elegant inn. My stay here was absolutely wonderful."

Certificate may be used: Feb. 1-June 30, Sunday-Friday; Sept. 15-Nov. 30, Sunday-Friday. Based on availability.

Vernon   B5

Alpine Haus B&B
217 State Rt 94
Vernon, NJ 07462
(973)209-7080 Fax:(973)209-7090
Internet: www.alpinehausbb.com
E-mail: alpinehs@warwick.net

Circa 1887. A private hideaway in the mountains, this former farmhouse is more than 100 years old. The renovated Federal-style inn with Victorian accents offers comfortable guest bedrooms named after mountain flowers with a decor reflecting that theme. Antiques also highlight the inn. The adjacent Carriage House has two suites with four-poster beds, stone fireplace and Jacuzzi. A generous country breakfast is enjoyed in the dining room or a continental breakfast on the second-story covered porch with majestic views. The family room and formal sitting room with fireplace are wonderful gathering places for games or conversation. Located next to Mountain Creek Ski and Water Park.

Innkeeper(s): Jack & Allison Smith. $110-225. 10 rooms with PB, 3 with FP, 2 suites. Breakfast included in rates. Types of meals: Country bkfst, veg bkfst, early coffee/tea and snacks/refreshments. Beds: QDT. Modem hook-up, data port, cable TV, VCR, reading lamp, refrigerator, clock radio, telephone, coffeemaker, desk, hot tub/spa, Internet access and two suites with fireplace and Jacuzzi in room. Central air. Fax, parlor games and fireplace on premises. Handicap access. Antiquing, art galleries, canoeing/kayaking, cross-country skiing, downhill skiing, fishing, golf, hiking, horseback riding, museums, parks, shopping, water sports and wineries nearby.

Location: Country, mountains.

Certificate may be used: Sunday-Thursday, excluding weeks of Christmas and New Year's and holiday weekends. Friday and Saturday between March 15 and May 30 and Nov. 1-Dec. 13, excludes holiday weekends. Cannot be combined with any other offer.

New Mexico

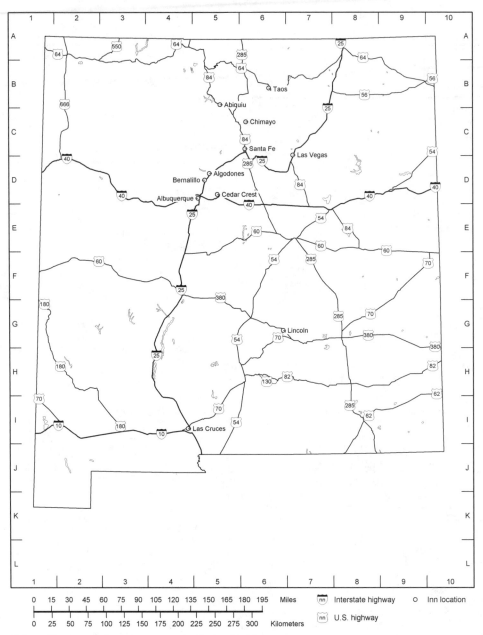

Visit www.iLoveInns.com for photos and more details about each inn.

Abiquiu   B5

Casa del Rio

PO Box 702
Abiquiu, NM 87510
(505)753-2035 (800)920-1495
Internet: www.casadelrio.net
E-mail: casadelrio@newmexico.com

Circa 1988. These authentic adobe guest houses are filled with local handmade crafts, rugs, bed coverings and furniture. Bathrooms boast handmade Mexican tile, and rooms are decorated in traditional New Mexico style with kiva fireplaces. The

patio windows afford a view of cliffs above the Rio Chama, which is just a short walk away. Casa del Rio is near

many attractions, including Indian pueblos, the many museums of Ghost Ranch, galleries and an abundance of outdoor activities. The property is halfway between Taos and Santa Fe.

Innkeeper(s): Eileen Sopanen-Vigil. $100-135. 3 rooms with PB, 1 with FP and 1 guest house. Breakfast included in rates. Types of meals: Full bkfst and veg bkfst. Beds: KQT. Reading lamp, refrigerator, clock radio, turn-down service, fireplace and patio in room. Fax, copier, telephone and gift shop on premises. Bicycling, cross-country skiing, downhill skiing, fishing, golf, hiking, museums, parks, shopping, wineries, birding, swimming, rock climbing and rafting nearby.

Location: Country, mountains, waterfront.

Certificate may be used: November-April 15, Sunday-Thursday, excluding major holidays.

Albuquerque   D5

Brittania & W.E. Mauger Estate B&B

701 Roma Ave NW
Albuquerque, NM 87102-2038
(505)242-8755 (800)719-9189 Fax:(505)842-8835
Internet: www.maugerbb.com
E-mail: maugerbb@aol.com

Circa 1897. Now an elegantly restored Victorian, this former boarding house is listed in the National Register. Guest bedrooms offer amenities that include satellite television, refrigerators, a basket with snacks,

voice mail and European down comforters on the beds. The inn is located four blocks from the convention center/business district and Historic Route 66. Old Town is less than one mile

away. There are many interesting museums to visit locally, featuring topics from Native American culture to the atomic age.

Innkeeper(s): Mark Brown & Keith Lewis. $89-209. 8 rooms with PB, 2 guest houses and 1 conference room. Breakfast included in rates. Types of meals: Full bkfst and snacks/refreshments. Beds: KQDT. TV, reading lamp, refrigerator, ceiling fan, snack bar, clock radio, telephone, desk, voice mail, coffeemaker, iron and hair dryer in room. Air conditioning. Amusement parks, antiquing, live theater and shopping nearby.

Location: City. Downtown Albuquerque.

Publicity: *Albuquerque Journal, Phoenix Home and Garden, Albuquerque Monthly, National Geographic Traveler, New Mexico Business Week and Golf Digest.*

"Because of your hospitality, kindness and warmth, we will always compare the quality of our experience by the W.E. Mauger Estate."

Certificate may be used: Nov. 15-March 1, except Thanksgiving and Christmas, Sunday-Thursday. Friday and Saturday subject to availability.

Casa Del Granjero & El Rancho Guest House

414 C De Baca Ln Nw
Albuquerque, NM 87114-1600
(505)897-4144 (800)701-4144 Fax:(505)792-3118
Internet: www.innewmexico.com
E-mail: granjero@prodigy.net

Circa 1890. Innkeepers Victoria and Butch Farmer, who appropriately named their home Casa del Granjero, or "the farmer's house," have designed their bed & breakfast to reflect Southwestern style with a hint of old Spanish flair. The adobe's guest rooms all include a rustic, kiva fireplace. Cuarto Allegre is the largest suite in the main house, and it includes a canopy bed covered in lace and French doors that open onto a small porch. Cuarto del Rey affords a mountain view and includes Mexican furnishings and handmade quilts. Cuarto de Flores also has quilts, Mexican tile and French doors leading to a private porch. The innkeepers have a hot tub room for guest use in a special garden area. The innkeepers also have restored a historic adobe ranch house across the road. The accommodations here include three suites and a guest room with a double bed. A kitchen, common area and wood-burning stove also are located in this house. A variety of baked goods, New Mexican-style recipes and fresh fruit are served each morning in the dining room or on the portal. Several recipes have been featured in a cookbook.

Innkeeper(s): Victoria & Butch Farmer. $79-179. 7 rooms with PB, 7 with FP, 5 suites. Breakfast included in rates. Types of meals: Full bkfst, picnic lunch, gourmet dinner and room service. Beds: KQT. Antiquing, cross-country skiing, downhill skiing, fishing, golf, hiking, live theater, shopping and water sports nearby.

Publicity: *Hidden SW.*

"Wonderful place, wonderful people. Thanks so much."

Certificate may be used: January through April, May through December from Sunday through Thursday. Holidays and special events excluded.

Hacienda Antigua Inn

6708 Tierra Dr NW
Albuquerque, NM 87107-6025
(505)345-5399 (800)201-2986 Fax:(505)345-3855
Internet: www.haciendantigua.com
E-mail: info@haciendantigua.com

Circa 1790. In the more than 200 years since this Spanish Colonial-style hacienda was constructed, the current innkeeper is only the fifth owner. Once a stagecoach stop on the El Camino Real, it also served as a cantina and mercantile store. It was built by Don Pablo Yrisarri, who was sent by the King of Spain to search the area for gold. The home is elegant, yet maintains a rustic, Spanish charm with exposed beams, walls up to 30 inches thick, brick floors and adobe fireplaces. Along with a sitting room and kiva fireplace, the Don Pablo Suite includes a "ducking door" that leads onto the courtyard. Other rooms have clawfoot tubs, antique iron beds or a private patio. The cuisine is notable and one of the inn's recipes appeared in Culinary Trends magazine. Guests might sample a green chile souffle along with bread pudding and fresh fruit. The inn has been featured on the TV series "Great Country Inns."

Innkeeper(s): Bob Thompson. $149-300. 8 rooms with PB, 7 with FP, 4 suites. Breakfast included in rates. Types of meals: Full bkfst and early coffee/tea. Beds: KQT. Reading lamp, refrigerator, ceiling fan, clock radio and telephone in room. Air conditioning. TV, VCR, fax, spa, swimming and fireplace on premises. Amusement parks, antiquing, cross-country skiing, downhill skiing, fishing, golf, live theater, parks, shopping, sporting events, tennis, hiking, biking and balloon fiesta nearby.

Location: Semi-rural.

Publicity: *Culinary Trends, Cavalcade of Enchantment and Great Country Inns.*

Certificate may be used: Jan. 3 through Feb. 28.

Algodones   D5

Hacienda Vargas

PO Box 307
Algodones, NM 87001-0307
(505)867-9115 (800)261-0006 Fax:(505)867-0640
Internet: www.haciendavargas.com
E-mail: stay@haciendavargas.com

Circa 1840. Nestled among the cottonwoods and mesas of the middle Rio Grande Valley, between Albuquerque and Santa Fe, Hacienda Vargas has seen two centuries of Old West history. It

once served as a trading post for Native Americans as well as a 19th-century stagecoach stop between Santa Fe and Las Cruces. The grounds contain an adobe chapel, courtyard and gardens. The main house features five kiva fireplaces, Southwest antiques, Spanish tile, a library and suites with private Jacuzzis.

Innkeeper(s): Cynthia & Richard Spence. $79-149. 7 rooms with PB, 6 with FP, 4 suites. Breakfast included in rates. Types of meals: Full bkfst. Beds: QT. Reading lamp, ceiling fan, clock radio, desk and suites have spa in room. Air conditioning. Parlor games, telephone and fireplace on premises. Antiquing, downhill skiing, fishing, live theater, shopping, sporting events, Golf MECCA and car racing nearby.

Location: Valley.

Publicity: *Albuquerque Journal (Country Inns), Vogue and San Francisco Chronicle.*

"This is the best! Breakfast was the best we've ever had!"

Certificate may be used: Sunday-Thursday except holidays or Balloon Fiesta.

Bernalillo   D5

La Hacienda Grande

21 Barros Rd
Bernalillo, NM 87004
(505)867-1887 (800)353-1887 Fax:(505)771-1436
Internet: www.lahaciendagrande.com
E-mail: lhg@swcp.com

Circa 1711. The rooms in this historic adobe inn surround a central courtyard. The first European trekked across the grounds as early as 1540. The land was part of a 1711 land grant from Spain, and owned by descendants of the original family until the innkeepers purchased it. The decor is Southwestern, and each bedchamber is filled with beautiful, handcrafted furnishings. One includes an iron high-poster bed and Jacuzzi tub, and others offer a kiva fireplace. Breakfasts are served in a dining room decorated with wood beams and a brick floor.

Innkeeper(s): Troy & Melody Scott. $109-139. 6 rooms with PB, 5 with FP and 1 conference room. Breakfast included in rates. Types of meals: Full bkfst and early coffee/tea. Beds: KQDT. Reading lamp, clock radio and sitting areas and TV on request in room. Air conditioning. VCR, fax, copier, library, parlor games, telephone, fireplace and phone on premises. Antiquing, cross-country skiing, downhill skiing, fishing, live theater, parks, shopping, sporting events and water sports nearby.

Location: City, country, mountains.

Certificate may be used: All dates except holiday weeks and Albuquerque Balloon Festival (first Saturday in October for 10 days).

Cedar Crest   D5

Elaine's, A B&B

p.o. box 444
Cedar Crest, NM 87008-0444
(505)281-2467 (800)821-3092 Fax:(505)281-1384
Internet: www.elainesbnb.com
E-mail: elaine@elainesbnb.com

Circa 1979. Ideally located on the historic Turquoise Trail adjacent to the Cibola National Forest, this three-story log home is situated on four acres of evergreens in the forests of the Sandia Peaks. Over one hundred varieties of birds, including three types of hummingbirds, visit the property. Enchanting moun-

tain views from one of the three balconies are unforgettable. Furnished with European country antiques, several of the guest bedrooms feature private fireplaces and Jacuzzis. Start the day off right with a substantial breakfast of favorite comfort foods. Visit the historic sites, shops and galleries in Albuquerque and Santa Fe, only minutes away from this secluded inn.

Innkeeper(s): Elaine O'Neil. $89-139. 5 rooms, 2 with FP, 5 suites. Breakfast included in rates. Types of meals: Full gourmet bkfst, veg bkfst, early coffee/tea and snacks/refreshments. Beds: KQ. Reading lamp, ceiling fan, hot tub/spa, fireplace, European country antiques and several with Jacuzzi in room. Air conditioning. TV, VCR, fax, copier, spa, library, parlor games, telephone, over 100 varieties of birds, views of the mountains, three balconies, flagstone patios and garden on premises. Amusement parks, antiquing, art galleries, bicycling, cross-country skiing, downhill skiing, golf, hiking, horseback riding, museums, parks, shopping and wineries nearby.

Location: Mountains. Four acres of evergreens in the forests of the Sandia Peaks.

Publicity: *Fodor's, L.A. Times, Albuquerque Journal, New Mexico Magazine, Fort Worth Star-Telegram, Washington Post, Pittsburgh-Gazette and St. Petersburg Times.*

"Fabulous! Mystical in the spring snow!"

Certificate may be used: Jan. 15-April 15, excluding holidays.

Chimayo   C6

Casa Escondida

PO Box 142
Chimayo, NM 87522
(505)351-4805 (800)643-7201 Fax:(505)351-2575
Internet: www.casaescondida.com
E-mail: info@casaescondida.com

Circa 1970. Secluded on six acres in an historic mountain village, this Adobe-style inn features Spanish Colonial architecture. Tongue and groove ceilings, heavy beams known as vigas, French doors, wood, brick and Saltillo tile floors all add to the warm ambiance. The air is scented with the fragrance of pinon wood from kiva fireplaces. A library offers quiet entertainment.

Inviting guest bedrooms include bathrobes to relax in. Some rooms boast gorgeous views, oversized tubs, fireplaces, private access to a deck or patio, and can be made into an adjoining suite. Enjoy a leisurely gourmet breakfast in the sunny dining room, or alfresco. Surrounded by trees, an outside hot tub is the perfect spot to relax.

Innkeeper(s): Belinda Bowling. $85-145. 8 rooms, 5 with PB, 2 with FP, 1 suite and 1 guest house. Breakfast, afternoon tea and snacks/refreshments included in rates. Types of meals: Full bkfst and early coffee/tea. Beds: QT. Refrigerator, ceiling fan, fireplace, kitchenette, wood-burning stove, oversized tub, private deck and private patio in room. Air conditioning. Fax, copier, spa, library, parlor games, telephone, guest phone and laptop hook-up on premises. Limited handicap access. Art galleries, bicycling, canoeing/kayaking, cross-country skiing, downhill skiing, fishing, golf, hiking, horseback riding, live theater, museums, parks, shopping, wineries, hot air ballooning, ancient ruins, Indian pueblos, rafting, bird watching, southwest cooking classes, casinos, concerts, Cumbre & Toltec Scenic Railroad, Lensic Performing Arts Center, Santa Fe Southern Railway, Santa Fe Horse Park, Santa Fe Farmers Market and Santa Fe Community College Planetarium nearby.

Location: Country, mountains.

Certificate may be used: November-February. Reservation is subject to room availability. Blackout periods being the week of Thanksgiving, Dec. 22-Jan.1 and Valentine's Day weekend.

Las Cruces   I4

Lundeen Inn of The Arts

618 S Alameda Blvd
Las Cruces, NM 88005-2817
(505)526-3326 (888)526-3326 Fax:(505)647-1334
Internet: www.innofthearts.com
E-mail: lundeen@innofthearts.com

This restored Mexican territorial inn, in the historic district, combines an inn with a fine arts gallery. An enormous great room features polished wood floors, an 18-foot ceiling of pressed tin, paladian windows and art, of course. Many of the inn's special features have been designed by innkeeper Jerry, an architect. Guest rooms have themes centered around New Mexican and Native American artists. For instance, the Georgia O'Keeffe room features calla lilies on the fireplace mantel and is decorated in gray, white and black.

Innkeeper(s): Jerry & Linda Lundeen. $72-125. 7 rooms with PB, 3 with FP and 1 conference room. Breakfast included in rates. Types of meals: Full bkfst. Beds: KQDT. Cable TV, reading lamp, refrigerator, ceiling fan, clock radio, telephone and desk in room. Air conditioning. Fax, copier, pet boarding and fireplace on premises. Handicap access. Golf, parks and shopping nearby.

Location: City.

Publicity: Country Inns and New Mexico Magazine.

Certificate may be used: June 1-Oct. 1.

T.R.H. Smith Mansion B&B

909 N Alameda Blvd
Las Cruces, NM 88005-2124
(505)525-2525 (800)526-1914 Fax:(505)524-8227
Internet: www.smithmansion.com
E-mail: smithmansion@zianet.com

Circa 1914. Surrounded by park-like grounds with tall pecan and sycamore trees, this beautifully preserved Prairie-style 5,700-square-foot mansion has a somewhat notorious past. The home was designed by prominent Southwest architect Henry Trost, and built by banker/embezzler TRH Smith. It was rumored to have served as a bordello and to have buried treasure somewhere within its walls. Four well-appointed guest bedrooms offer a variety of styles including Latin American,

European, Southwest and Pacific Rim. Each one features both cable TV and a professional computer with DSL for always-on Internet and e-mail access. In the dining or garden rooms enjoy a hearty German-style breakfast of fresh fruit, home-baked breads, an egg entrée, imported meats and cheeses along with fresh-ground coffees and teas made from herbs grown on the grounds.

Innkeeper(s): Marlene & Jay Tebo. $85-150. 4 rooms with PB, 1 with FP. Breakfast included in rates. Types of meals: Full gourmet bkfst. Beds: KQ. Reading lamp, clock radio and desk in room. Parlor games, telephone and fireplace on premises. Antiquing, golf, live theater, parks, shopping, sporting events and tennis nearby.

Publicity: Las Cruces Sun-News, Las Cruces Bulletin, Gateway Magazine and New Mexico Magazine.

Certificate may be used: Jan. 1-Dec. 31, Sunday through Friday.

Las Vegas   C7

Carriage House B&B

925 6th St
Las Vegas, NM 87701-4306
(505)454-1784 (888)221-9689
Internet: www.newmexicocarriagehouse.com
E-mail: carriagebb@desertgate.com

Circa 1893. A prominent local attorney built this historic Queen Anne Victorian home. The innkeepers offer five comfortable guest rooms, and pamper their guests with a full breakfast and afternoon tea. Las Vegas has an amazing Wild West past, and there are more than 900 buildings in town that are listed in the National Register.

Innkeeper(s): Anne & John Bradford. $75-95. 12 rooms, 4 with PB. Breakfast included in rates. Types of meals: Cont plus, early coffee/tea and afternoon tea. Beds: Q. Ceiling fan in room. TV, fax, telephone and afternoon tea available by reservation on premises. Antiquing, art galleries, cross-country skiing, downhill skiing, fishing, golf, hiking, museums, parks, shopping and wineries nearby.

Location: City, mountains.

Publicity: Red Dawn.

Certificate may be used: Sept. 15 to June 15, Sunday-Thursday, subject to availability.

Plaza Hotel

230 Plaza
Las Vegas, NM 87701
(505)425-3591 (800)328-1882 Fax:(505)425-9659
Internet: www.plazahotel-nm.com
E-mail: lodging@plazahotel-nm.com

Circa 1882. This brick Italianate Victorian hotel, once frequented by the likes of Doc Holliday, Big Nose Kate and members of the James Gang, was renovated in 1982. A stencil pattern found in the dining room inspired the selection of Victorian wallpaper borders in the guest rooms, decorated with period furnishings. Guests also have access to a business center and T-1 internet.

Innkeeper(s): Wid & Kak Slick. $59-146. 37 rooms with PB, 4 suites and 1 conference room. Breakfast included in rates. Types of meals: Cont. Restaurant on premises. Beds: KQD. Cable TV, reading lamp, telephone and desk in room. Air conditioning. TV, copier and business center and T-1 Internet on premises. Handicap access. Antiquing, cross-country skiing, fishing, parks, water sports and hot springs nearby.

Location: City.

Certificate may be used: All week, Nov. 1-May 1.

Lincoln   G6

Casa De Patron B&B Inn

PO Box 27, Hwy 380 E
Lincoln, NM 88338-0027
(505)653-4676 (800)524-5202 Fax:(505)653-4671
Internet: www.casaptron.com
E-mail: patron@pvtnetworks.net

Circa 1860. This historic adobe once was used to imprison
Billy the Kid and played an integral part in the colorful frontier
days of Lincoln County. Shaded courtyards and walled garden
add to the authentic Old West atmosphere, and the comfortable
rooms are supplemented by
two contemporary adobe
casitas. Cleis plays the inn's
pipe organ and arranges soap-
making workshops for guests.

Innkeeper(s): Jeremy & Cleis
Jordan. $84-117. 7 rooms with
PB, 2 with FP, 2 cottages and 1 conference room. Breakfast included in
rates. Types of meals: Full bkfst. Beds: KQT. Reading lamp, handmade soap,
candy, some snacks/refrigerator and one with double Jacuzzi tub in room.
VCR, fax, copier, parlor games, telephone and fireplace on premises.
Handicap access. Downhill skiing, hiking, museums, parks, shopping and
casinos nearby.

Location: Mountains. Country.

Publicity: *Bedrooms & Baths, Ruidoso News, Roswell Daily Record,
Adventure West Magazine, Tampa Tribune/Times, Recommended Romantic
Inns, Country, Southern Living, True West, Historic Traveler, Albuquerque
Journal, Preservation News, Young Guns, Set, Travelin', Rocky Mountain
News and Milwaukee Journal.*

"The time with you at Casa de Patron is truly a treasure to me."

Certificate may be used: All year (Sunday through Thursday) with blackout
dates: Memorial Day weekend, July 4th weekend, Thanksgiving week and
Christmas-New Year's week, first weekend in August.

Santa Fe   C6

Alexander's Inn

529 E Palace Ave
Santa Fe, NM 87501-2200
(505)986-1431 (888)321-5123 Fax:(505)982-8572
Internet: www.alexanders-inn.com
E-mail: alexandinn@aol.com

Circa 1903. Twin gables and a massive front porch are prominent features of this Craftsman-style brick and wood inn.
French and American country decor, stained-glass windows and

a selection of antiques
create a light Victorian
touch. The inn also fea-
tures beautiful gardens
of roses and lilacs. The
exquisite Southwest
adobe casitas are a favorite for families and romantic getaways.
Breakfast is often served in the backyard garden. Home-baked
treats are offered to guests in the afternoon.

Innkeeper(s): Carolyn Lee. $85-195. 8 rooms with PB, 5 with FP, 1 suite
and 4 cottages. Breakfast and afternoon tea included in rates. Types of
meals: Full gourmet bkfst and early coffee/tea. Beds: KQT. Cable TV, VCR,
reading lamp, refrigerator, clock radio, telephone, desk and hot tub/spa in
room. Fax, spa, library, child care, parlor games and fireplace on premises.
Antiquing, cross-country skiing, downhill skiing, fishing, live theater, parks,
shopping, water sports, museums and Pueblos nearby.

Location: City.

Publicity: *New Mexican, Glamour, Southwest Art and San Diego Union Tribune.*

*"Thanks to the kindness and thoughtfulness of the staff, our three
days in Santa Fe were magical."*

Certificate may be used: Nov. 1-Feb. 28, Sunday-Thursday, no holidays.

Don Gaspar Inn

623 Don Gaspar Avenue
Santa Fe, NM 87505
(505)986-8664 (888)986-8664 Fax:(505)986-0696
Internet: www.dongaspar.com
E-mail: info@dongaspar.com

Circa 1912. This lush, peaceful hideaway is located within one
of Santa Fe's first historic districts. Within the Compounds surrounding adobe walls are brick pathways meandering through
beautiful gardens, emerald lawns, trees and a courtyard fountain. The elegant Southwestern decor is an idyllic match for the
warmth and romance of the grounds. For those seeking privacy,
the innkeepers offer the Main House, a historic Mission-style
home perfect for a pair of romantics or a group as large as six.
The house has three bedrooms, two bathrooms, a fully
equipped kitchen and two wood-burning fireplaces. In addition
to the main house, there are three suites in a Territorial-style
home with thick walls and polished wood floors. There also are
two private casitas, each with a gas-burning fireplace. The
Fountain Casita includes a fully equipped kitchen, while the
Courtyard Casita offers a double whirlpool tub. All accommodations include a TV, telephone, microwave and refrigerators.

Innkeeper(s): Aggie, Trudi and Ana. $115-295. 10 rooms with PB, 8 with
FP, 3 suites and 3 guest houses. Breakfast included in rates. Types of meals:
Full bkfst. Beds: KQ. TV, VCR, reading lamp, refrigerator, ceiling fan, clock
radio, telephone, coffeemaker, hot tub/spa, voice mail and fireplace in room.
Air conditioning. Fax, copier, fireplace, laundry facility, gardens, courtyard,
fountain and two casitas on premises. Handicap access. Antiquing, art galleries, bicycling, cross-country skiing, fishing, golf, hiking, horseback riding,
live theater, museums, parks, shopping and tennis nearby.

Location: Mountains.

Publicity: *Sunset, Conde Nast Traveler, Fodors and PBS.*

"Everything was simply perfect."

Certificate may be used: Nov. 1-March 1, Sunday-Thursday, holidays excluded.

The Madeleine (formerly The Preston House)

106 Faithway St
Santa Fe, NM 87501
(505)982-3465 (888)877-7622 Fax:(505)982-8572
Internet: www.madeleineinn.com
E-mail: madeleineinn@aol.com

Circa 1886. This gracious 19th-century home is the only
authentic example of Queen Anne architecture in Santa Fe.
This home displays a wonderful Victorian atmosphere with
period furnishings, quaint wallpapers and beds covered with
down quilts. Afternoon tea is a must, as Carolyn serves up a
mouth-watering array of cakes, pies, cookies
and tarts. The Madeleine, which is located
in downtown Santa Fe, is within walking
distance of the Plaza.

Innkeeper(s): Carolyn Lee. $70-180. 8
rooms, 6 with PB, 4 with FP and 2 cottages. Breakfast and afternoon tea included
in rates. Types of meals: Full bkfst and early
coffee/tea. Beds: KQDT. Cable TV, reading
lamp, refrigerator, ceiling fan, clock radio,

telephone and desk in room. Fax, copier and fireplace on premises. Antiquing, cross-country skiing, downhill skiing, fishing, live theater, parks and shopping nearby.

Location: City, mountains.

Publicity: *Country Inns.*

"We were extremely pleased — glad we found you. We shall return."

Certificate may be used: Sunday-Thursday nights, November-February, no holidays.

Taos   B6

Adobe & Pines Inn

PO Box 837
Ranchos De Taos, NM 87557-0837
(505)751-0947 (800)723-8267 Fax:(505)758-8423
Internet: www.newmex.com/adobepines
E-mail: mail@adobepines.com

Circa 1832. Set on several acres of pine, orchard and pasture-covered land near Taos, this restored adobe hacienda provides a peaceful, romantic getaway. A stream running through the grounds adds to the tranquility. Rooms feature Southwestern details, kiva fireplaces, down comforters and pillows. A sepa-

rate guest cottage includes a canopy bed, whirlpool bath, two fireplaces and a kitchen. Exotic evening hors d'oeuvres and gourmet breakfasts are enjoyed by guests. A flower-filled, stone-walled courtyard affords magnificent views of Taos Mountain.

Innkeeper(s): David & KayAnn Tyssee, Cathy Ann Connelly. $95-195. 9 rooms with PB, 8 with FP, 6 suites, 4 cottages and 1 guest house. Breakfast and snacks/refreshments included in rates. Types of meals: Full gourmet bkfst, veg bkfst and early coffee/tea. Beds: KQ. Cable TV, VCR, reading lamp, stereo, refrigerator, ceiling fan, clock radio, coffeemaker, desk and hot tub/spa in room. Air conditioning. Fax, copier, library, pet boarding, parlor games, telephone, fireplace and laundry facility on premises. Limited handicap access. Antiquing, art galleries, bicycling, canoeing/kayaking, cross-country skiing, downhill skiing, fishing, golf, hiking, horseback riding, live theater, museums, parks, shopping, tennis and wineries nearby.

Location: Country, mountains. High desert.

Publicity: *Yellow Brick Road, Denver Post, Los Angeles Times and San Francisco Examiner.*

"The Adobe & Pines Inn warms your soul and your senses with traditional New Mexican decor, hospitality and comfort."

Certificate may be used: Anytime, Sunday-Thursday.

Casa Encantada

PO Box 6460
Taos, NM 87571
(505)758-7477 (800)223-TAOS Fax:(505)737-5085
Internet: www.casaencantada.com
E-mail: encantada@newmex.com

Circa 1930. Located only a few blocks from the historic Taos plaza, this historic adobe rests in a quiet neighborhood behind soft adobe walls. Secluded gardens, courtyards and patios add

to the serenity. Most guest accommodations include a fireplace, and all have been individually decorated with original local art. Some have kitchenettes. The Santa Fe Suite is popular for anniversaries and special occasions. It includes a living room with fireplace, dressing area, and king bedroom. The Anasazi offers Taos character with a sun room, loft bedroom, living room and gas kiva. The Casita, once the hacienda's chapel, is the most spacious suite and with Southwest style offers two queen bedrooms, two kiva fireplaces, a kitchenette, bath, laundry and a private courtyard. Skiing, shopping, galleries, restaurants and much more are all nearby.

Innkeeper(s): Sharon Nicholson. $100-185. 9 rooms with PB, 6 with FP, 6 suites and 1 conference room. Breakfast included in rates. Types of meals: Full gourmet bkfst and early coffee/tea. Beds: KQ. Cable TV, VCR, reading lamp, refrigerator, ceiling fan, clock radio and desk in room. Fax, copier, library, telephone and fireplace on premises. Antiquing, cross-country skiing, downhill skiing, fishing, golf, live theater, parks, shopping, sporting events, tennis and water sports nearby.

Location: Mountains.

Certificate may be used: Jan. 6-Dec. 15, Sunday-Friday.

Dobson House

PO Box 1584
El Prado, NM 87529-1584
(505)776-5738
Internet: www.new-mexico-bed-and-breakfast.com
E-mail: dobhouse@newmex.com

Circa 1996. This adobe inn is the perfect beginning for spiritual renewal. The 6,000-square-foot house is located in a rift valley on a hill overlooking the Rio Grande Gorge. Featured on the Discovery Channel, it was built with recycled materials, 34 tons of Colorado sandstone and 28,000 pounds of dry cement so that it blends into its desert surroundings. The suites have separate sitting and sleeping areas and private patios bordered by terraced gardens. Breakfast is served in the round room with ponderosa pine and glass walls with a panoramic mountain view. Enjoy delightful dishes such as fresh fruit, organic chicken apple sausages, cheese artichoke omelettes and Texas pecan biscuits. Climb Mt. Wheeler, take a llama trek, raft the river or soak in the nearby hot springs. In the still of the evening, explore the wonder of the sky through a 16-inch telescope.

Innkeeper(s): Joan & John Dobson. $110-130. 2 suites. Breakfast and snacks/refreshments included in rates. Types of meals: Full gourmet bkfst, veg bkfst, early coffee/tea and picnic lunch. Beds: Q. Reading lamp, sofa and table in room. Library, parlor games, telephone, private patio for each room and gift shop on premises. Art galleries, bicycling, canoeing/kayaking, cross-country skiing, downhill skiing, fishing, golf, hiking, horseback riding, museums, shopping, water sports and wineries nearby.

Location: Mountains.

Publicity: *Denver Post, Dallas Morning News, Ski Magazine, Albuquerque Journal, Great Destinations - Santa Fe & Taos, Unofficial Guide to B&Bs and Country Inns in Southwest, Natural Homes Magazine, Wall St. Journal-European Edition and Discovery Channel.*

Certificate may be used: Sunday-Thursday, November-May 15, excluding holidays.

New York

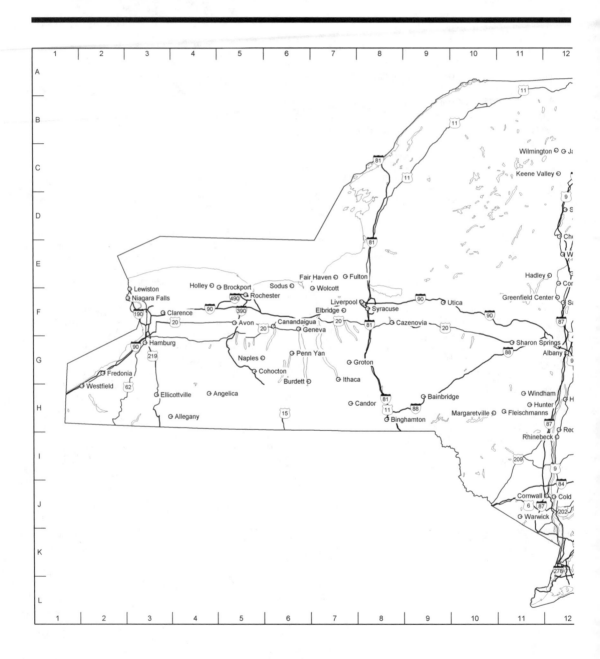

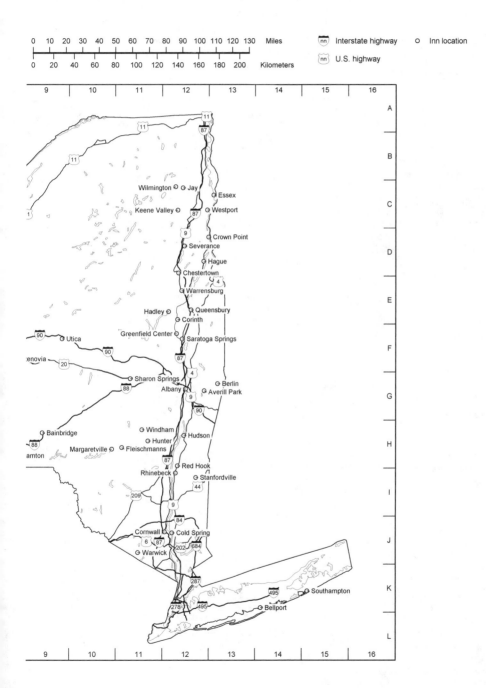

Adirondack D12

Adirondack Pines Bed & Breakfast & Guest House

1257 Valentine Road
Adirondack, NY 12808
(518)494-5249 Fax:(518)494-5299
Internet: www.adirondackpines.com
E-mail: stay@adirondackpines.com

Circa 1837. Surrounded by year-round scenic beauty, there is much to experience while staying at this historic 1837 Country Farmhouse, just two minutes from Schroon Lake's beach and boat launch. Relax in the living room with cable TV. Antiques and handmade quilts accent the pleasant décor of the air-conditioned guest bedrooms. The Master Suite boasts wide plank flooring, a refrigerator, gas stove and a two-person Jacuzzi tub. The spacious Balsam Room offers a Queen and a twin bed. A small room with a twin bed accommodates a fourth person. Linger over a candlelit country breakfast in the dining room by the wood stove. A private, newly renovated three-bedroom house with a gas fireplace is also available. Soak up nature while strolling the 100 acres of grounds. Ski nearby Gore Mountain or hike Pharaoh Mountain for breathtaking views.

Innkeeper(s): Dan & Nancy Lindsley-Freebern. $65-125. 3 rooms, 2 with PB, 1 with FP and 1 guest house. Breakfast and snacks/refreshments included in rates. Types of meals: Country bkfst. Beds: KQDT. Cable TV, VCR, refrigerator, clock radio, coffeemaker, two-person Jacuzzi tub and gas freestanding fireplace in room. Air conditioning. Fax, copier, parlor games, telephone and fireplace on premises. Amusement parks, antiquing, art galleries, beach, bicycling, canoeing/kayaking, cross-country skiing, downhill skiing, fishing, hiking, horseback riding, museums, shopping, water sports and wineries nearby.

Location: Country, mountains.

Certificate may be used: Anytime, Sunday-Thursday and Nov. 30 to Dec. 20, subject to availability.

Albany G12

Mansion Hill Inn & Restaurant

115 Philip St at Park Avenue
Albany, NY 12202-1747
(518)465-2038 Fax:(518)434-2313
Internet: www.mansionhill.com
E-mail: inn@mansionhill.com

Circa 1861. This Victorian houses guest rooms and apartment suites on the top two floors and a restaurant on the street level. Originally the home of brush maker Daniel Brown, it later served as a bulk grocery store. It is located in the historic district just around the corner from the Governor's Executive Mansion in the Mansion Neighborhood. It is a few minutes' walk to the State Capitol and the downtown Albany business district.

Innkeeper(s): Maryellen, Elizabeth & Stephen Stofelano Jr. $95-155. 8 rooms with PB and 1 conference room. Breakfast included in rates. Types of meals: Full gourmet bkfst, gourmet lunch, gourmet dinner and room service. Restaurant on premises. Beds: Q. Cable TV, reading lamp, clock radio, telephone and desk in room. Air conditioning. TV, VCR, fax, copier, pet boarding, child care and fireplace on premises. Antiquing, fishing, live theater, parks, shopping and sporting events nearby.

Location: City.

Publicity: Hartford Courant, Albany Review, Hudson Valley Magazine, Albany Times Union and Nation's Business.

"Rooms were beautiful and comfortable down to the shower curtain."

Certificate may be used: Available year-round on Fridays, Saturdays and Sundays; subject to availability and reservation.

Pine Haven B&B

531 Western Ave
Albany, NY 12203-1721
(518)482-1574
Internet: www.pinehavenbedandbreakfast.com
E-mail: pinehavenb@aol.com

Circa 1896. This turn-of-the-century Victorian is located in Pine Hills, an Albany historic district. In keeping with this history, the innkeepers have tried to preserve the home's 19th-century charm. The rooms offer old-fashioned comfort with Victorian influences. The Capitol Building and other historic sites are nearby.

Innkeeper(s): Janice Tricarico. $114. 5 rooms with PB, 2 with FP. Breakfast included in rates. Types of meals: Cont plus and early coffee/tea. Beds: QDT. Cable TV, reading lamp, clock radio, telephone and desk in room. Air conditioning. Parlor games, fireplace and free off-street parking on premises. Antiquing, cross-country skiing, live theater, parks, shopping and sporting events nearby.

Location: City.

Certificate may be used: Year-round, anytime, subject to availability.

Allegany H3

Gallets House B&B

1759 Four Mile Rd
Allegany, NY 14706-9724
(716)373-7493 Fax:(716)806-0384
Internet: www.galletshouse.com
E-mail: info@galletshouse.com

Circa 1896. Built by the innkeeper's great uncle Joseph Gallets, who was an oil producer, lumberman and farmer, this historic Victorian home features a third-floor museum with original family photos and heirlooms to browse through. Relax by the fireplaces in the parlor and common room. Enjoy refreshments on the 100-foot porch. Elegant air-conditioned guest bedrooms feature private baths and robes. Two rooms boast whirlpool tubs. Perfect for families and pets, the Carriage House Apartment has three bedrooms, two baths and a full kitchen. Fruits, homemade breads and biscuits are a prelude to sumptuous hot entrees and Joan's memorable French toast or apple cinnamon pancakes for breakfast in the formal dining room. The B&B is near ski resorts, Allegany State Park, St. Bonaventure University, golf courses and a main snowmobile trail. Ask about romance packages and monthly murder mysteries.

Innkeeper(s): Joan & Gary Boser. $85-140. 6 rooms with PB, 2 with FP, 1 guest house and 1 conference room. Breakfast and snacks/refreshments included in rates. Types of meals: Full gourmet bkfst, early coffee/tea and afternoon tea. Beds: KQD. Modem hook-up, cable TV, reading lamp, CD player, ceiling fan, clock radio, telephone, desk and two with whirlpool tubs in room. Air conditioning. Fax, copier, spa and fireplace on premises. Limited handicap access. Antiquing, art galleries, bicycling, canoeing/kayaking, cross-country skiing, downhill skiing, fishing, golf, hiking, horseback riding, live theater, museums, parks, shopping, sporting events, snowmobile trails and snow tubing nearby.

Location: Country, mountains.

Certificate may be used: March-November, Sunday-Thursday, excluding holidays, subject to availability.

Angelica H4

Angelica Inn
64 E Main St. Box 686
Angelica, NY 14709-8710
(585)466-3063
E-mail: npetito@hotmail.com

Circa 1882. Located in the Allegany foothills, the Angelica Inn features stained glass, crystal chandeliers, parquet floors, an oak staircase, carved woodwork, antique furnishings and scented rooms. Guest rooms offer such amenities as fireplaces, a porch and a breakfast alcove area.

Innkeeper(s): Cynthia & Nicholas Petito. $75-125. 6 rooms with PB, 3 with FP and 1 conference room. Breakfast included in rates. Types of meals: Full bkfst. Beds: KQ. Cable TV, refrigerator, ceiling fan and desk in room. Antiquing, cross-country skiing, fishing, golf, parks and casino nearby.
Location: Country. Historic village, rural.

"Victorian at its best!"
Certificate may be used: Sunday through Thursday, Jan. 30 to June 1.

Averill Park G12

La Perla at the Gregory House, Country Inn & Restaurant
Rt 43 PO Box 401
Averill Park, NY 12018-0401
(518)674-3774 Fax:(518)674-8916
Internet: www.gregoryhouse.com
E-mail: info@gregoryhouse.com

Circa 1830. Stockbroker Elias Gregory built what is now the restaurant, as his Colonial home in the 1800s. The newer B&B inn, just twelve years old, blends well with the original house to retain the ambiance of its Victorian heritage. Gather by the dramatic fireplace in the common room which boasts vaulted ceilings, comfy furniture and a big-screen TV. The decor of each well-appointed guest bedroom is inviting. Award-winning La Perla offers Italian continental cuisine and is personally run by innkeeper Alfonso. This rural country town is surrounded by the Adirondacks, Berkshires, Hudson River, Saratoga and Albany with a variety of historic and scenic attractions.

Innkeeper(s): Anna Maria & Alfonso Acampora. $100-125. 12 rooms with PB and 1 conference room. Breakfast included in rates. Types of meals: Cont. Restaurant on premises. Beds: QDT. TV, reading lamp, clock radio, telephone and desk in room. Air conditioning. VCR, fax, copier and fireplace on premises. Amusement parks, antiquing, cross-country skiing, downhill skiing, fishing, live theater, parks, shopping, sporting events and water sports nearby.
Location: Village.
Publicity: *Hudson Valley, Albany Times Union, Schenectady Gazette, Courier and Sunday Record.*

"We experienced privacy and quiet, lovely surroundings indoors and out, excellent service and as much friendliness as we were comfortable with, but no more."
Certificate may be used: November-April, Sunday-Thursday.

Avon F5

Avon Inn
55 E Main St
Avon, NY 14414-1438
(585)226-8181 Fax:(585)226-8185
Internet: www.avoninn.com
E-mail: laminn57@aol.com

Circa 1820. This Greek Revival mansion, in both the state and national historic registers, has been providing lodging for more than a century. After 1866, the residence was turned into a health center that provided water cures from the local sulphur springs. The guest registry included the likes of Henry Ford, Thomas Edison and Eleanor Roosevelt. Though the inn is no longer a health spa, guests can still relax in the garden with its towering trees and fountain or on the Grecian-pillared front porch. A full-service restaurant and conference facilities are on the premises.

Innkeeper(s): Linda Moran. $75-115. 14 rooms with PB. Breakfast included in rates. Types of meals: Cont. Restaurant on premises. Beds: KQD. Clock radio, telephone and desk in room. Air conditioning. TV, fax and copier on premises. Amusement parks, antiquing, cross-country skiing, downhill skiing, fishing, golf, museums, parks and shopping nearby.
Certificate may be used: Not valid with a Saturday, May 1-Nov. 15.

White Oak Bed and Breakfast
277 Genesee Street
Avon, NY 14414
(585)226-6735
Internet: whiteoakbandb.com
E-mail: avon-bnb@frontiernet.net

Circa 1860. Built as a summer home in the 1860s, this distinctive Second Empire Victorian with a mansard roof and wraparound porch has been recently renovated to retain its original charm and traditional decor. A private den/parlor with TV/VCR and board games is a convenient gathering place. Well-placed period furnishings accent the guest bedrooms and spacious Pine Suite. Enjoy the expansive view from the dining room while savoring home-baked breads, fresh fruit, and perhaps a broccoli cheddar omelette with home fries and bacon for breakfast. The one acre of gardens, with flowers for every season, include private sitting areas to chat. Visit nearby Genesee Country Village or take day trips to explore the scenic Finger Lakes Region.

Innkeeper(s): Barbara Herman. Call for rates. 3 rooms with PB. Breakfast and snacks/refreshments included in rates. Types of meals: Country bkfst, veg bkfst, early coffee/tea and picnic lunch. Beds: QD. Antiquing, art galleries, bicycling, fishing, golf, hiking, horseback riding, live theater, museums, parks, shopping and wineries nearby.
Certificate may be used: Anytime, subject to availability.

Bainbridge H9

Berry Hill Gardens B&B
242 Ward Loomis Rd.
Bainbridge, NY 13733
(607)967-8745 (800)497-8745 Fax:(607)967-2227
Internet: www.berryhillgardens.com
E-mail: info@berryhillgardens.com

Circa 1820. Surrounded by flower and herb gardens, this farmhouse presides over 180 acres. Guest rooms are furnished in antiques and decorated with bunches of fresh and dried flowers. Organic gardens provide 100 varieties of annuals and perennials. There are tulips, poppies, lilacs, sweet peas and in May, the fruit trees are in bloom. A full country breakfast is served. By advance reservation you can arrange for a sleigh ride or horse-drawn wagon to take you

through the woods and meadows of the Berry Hill Farm, or you may stroll through the gardens and woods on your own.
Innkeeper(s): Jean Fowler & Cecilio Rios. $75-125. 5 rooms, 2 with PB, 1 suite, 1 cottage and 1 guest house. Types of meals: Country bkfst and early coffee/tea. Beds: QDT. Reading lamp, ceiling fan, clock radio and desk in room. TV, VCR, fax, copier, swimming, parlor games and telephone on premises. Antiquing, art galleries, bicycling, canoeing/kayaking, cross-country skiing, fishing, golf, hiking, horseback riding, live theater, museums, parks, shopping, sporting events, tennis and water sports nearby.
Publicity: *Country Living Gardener Magazine-August 2001 and Binghamton Press and Sun.*

"The house is just wonderful and our rooms were exceptionally comfortable."
Certificate may be used: Jan. 2-April 30, anytime. May 1-Dec. 20, Sunday through Thursday only. Holidays and special events excluded.

Bellport K14

Great South Bay Inn

160 S Country Rd
Bellport, NY 11713-2516
(631)286-8588 Fax:(631)286-2460
Internet: www.libedandbreakfast.com
E-mail: info@libedandbreakfast.com

Circa 1890. Long Island's south shore is home to this Cape Cod-style inn filled with turn-of-the-century antiques. Six guest

rooms are available, four with private baths and all featuring original wainscoting. Favorite relaxing spots include the private garden and the parlor with its welcoming fireplace. During the summer months, guests enjoy taking the ferry over to the village's private beach or simply, frequenting one of the local restaurants, which are open all year. The innkeepers are fluent in French and pride themselves on serving guests' individual needs, whether you are on business travel or on vacation. Fire Island National Seashore and the Wertheim National Wildlife Refuge are nearby.
Innkeeper(s): Judy Mortimer. $99-135. 6 rooms, 4 with PB, 1 with FP, 1 suite. Breakfast included in rates. Types of meals: Full bkfst. Beds: QDT. Cable TV, VCR, reading lamp, ceiling fan, clock radio and desk in room. Air conditioning. Fax, copier, telephone and fireplace on premises. Amusement parks, antiquing, fishing, golf, live theater, parks, shopping, tennis and water sports nearby.
Certificate may be used: Mid-January to mid-April, Rooms 5 & 6. Other rooms depending on availability.

Berlin G13

Sedgwick Inn

Rt 22, Box 250
Berlin, NY 12022
(518)658-2334 Fax:(518)658-3998
Internet: www.sedgwickinn.com
E-mail: sedgwickin@aol.com

Circa 1791. The Sedgwick Inn sits on 12 acres in the Taconic Valley in the Berkshire Mountains. The main house features guest rooms, the low-ceilinged Coach Room Tavern and a glass-

enclosed dining porch facing an English garden. A Colonial-style motel behind the main house sits beside a rushing brook. A converted carriage house with a hardwood dance floor and hand-hewn beams

serves as a gift shop with prints, paintings, sculptures and a selection of unusual crafts and gourmet items.
Innkeeper(s): Chad & Diane Niedzwiecki. $85-165. 11 rooms with PB, 1 suite and 1 conference room. Breakfast included in rates. Types of meals: Full bkfst, lunch, gourmet dinner and room service. Restaurant on premises. Beds: KQD. Cable TV, reading lamp, ceiling fan, clock radio and telephone in room. TV, VCR, fax and fireplace on premises. Antiquing, cross-country skiing, downhill skiing, fishing, golf, live theater, parks and water sports nearby.
Publicity: *Berkshire Eagle, Hudson Valley Magazine, Albany Times Union, Good Housekeeping and US Air.*

"We were absolutely enchanted. We found this to be a charming place, a rare and wonderful treat."
Certificate may be used: Monday-Thursday, year-round. Subject to availability.

Binghamton H8

The Mansion on Asbury Court

9 Asbury Court
Binghamton, NY 13905
(607)772-2959 Fax:(607)722-3052
Internet: www.mansiononasbury.com
E-mail: jaustin52@stny.rr.com

Circa 1881. Painstakingly restored to retain its historic prominence since 1881, this 21-room Queen Anne Victorian mansion boasts comfortable surroundings in a smoke-free environment. Relax on the covered porch. Sit and admire the original oil painting of General Jones that hangs over one of the 11 fireplaces. A conference room and high-tech amenities assist with business-related activities. Select a guest bedroom with a whirlpool tub and a fireplace. After breakfast go shopping on Clinton Street, known as Antique Row in Binghamton. A recreation park is just one block away with tennis, swimming, basketball and a carousel. Customized wedding packages and airport pick-up can be arranged.
Innkeeper(s): Steve and Joanne Austin. $75-105. 4 rooms, 2 with PB, 4 with FP, 1 with WP and 1 conference room. Breakfast included in rates. Types of meals: Full gourmet bkfst, early coffee/tea, snacks/refreshments and room service. Beds: Q. Modem hook-up, reading lamp, refrigerator, ceiling fan, clock radio, coffeemaker, hot tub/spa, hair dryer and massage by appointment in room. Fax, copier, spa, parlor games, swimming, tennis and basketball on premises. Antiquing, art galleries, canoeing/kayaking, cross-country skiing, downhill skiing, fishing, golf, hiking, horseback riding, live theater, museums, parks, shopping, sporting events, tennis, water sports, wineries, BC Open, Chris Thater Memorial Race, opera and free carousel nearby.
Location: City.
Certificate may be used: Sunday-Thursday, not BU graduation weekend, subject to availability.

Bloomfield F5

A Wolfpack Bed N' Breakfast

6700 State Rt 5 & 20
Bloomfield, NY 14469
(585)657-4863 Fax:(585)657-4576
Internet: www.wolfpack-bnb.com
E-mail: wlfpkbnb@rochester.rr.com

Circa 1820. Relatives of President Taft built this Colonial farmhouse, now restored and a peaceful place to stay while exploring the picturesque and historic Finger Lakes region. The guest bedrooms are decorated in a comfortable country charm. Most feature a fireplace and Jacuzzi for two to inspire romance. The Carriage House, perfect for family retreats, has a full kitchen, dining area, living room and private deck. A hearty breakfast is prepared to please. Enjoy gently swinging in the gazebo loveseat, while planning the day's events.

Innkeeper(s): Robin Grentus & Michael. $95-165. 3 rooms with PB and 1 cottage. Breakfast and snacks/refreshments included in rates. Types of meals: Country bkfst and early coffee/tea. Beds: KQT. Reading lamp, ceiling fan, clock radio, fireplace and two with Jacuzzi in room. Air conditioning. TV, VCR, fax, copier, library, parlor games, telephone and fireplace on premises. Amusement parks, antiquing, art galleries, beach, cross-country skiing, downhill skiing, fishing, golf, hiking, horseback riding, live theater, museums, parks, shopping, water sports and wineries nearby.

Location: Country.

Certificate may be used: Anytime, subject to availability.

Brockport   E5

The Portico B&B

3741 Lake Rd N
Brockport, NY 14420-1415
(585)637-0220

Circa 1850. Named for its three porches, called porticos, this Greek Revival inn is situated amid blue spruce, maple and sycamore trees in a historic district. Tall columns and a cupola add to its charm. The interior features three fireplaces. Three antique-filled guest rooms are available to visitors, who enjoy a full Victorian breakfast and kettledrum, also known as afternoon tea. The inn is listed in the National Register, as are several other structures in town. The surrounding area offers many attractions, including the Cobblestone Museum, Darien Lake Amusement Park, George Eastman House and Strasenburgh Planetarium. Several colleges, golf courses and parks are nearby. In winter, sleigh rides also are available nearby.

Innkeeper(s): Anne Klein. $70-80. 3 rooms with PB, 3 with FP. Breakfast included in rates. Types of meals: Full bkfst and early coffee/tea. Reading lamp and turn-down service in room. VCR, telephone and fireplace on premises. Amusement parks, antiquing, cross-country skiing, downhill skiing, live theater, shopping, sporting events and sleigh rides nearby.

Location: Suburban - Country.

Certificate may be used: Anytime, Sunday-Thursday.

The Victorian B&B

320 S Main St
Brockport, NY 14420-2253
(585)637-7519 Fax:(585)637-7519
Internet: www.victorianbandb.com
E-mail: sk320@aol.com

Circa 1890. Within walking distance of the historic Erie Canal, this Queen Anne Victorian inn is located on Brockport's Main Street. Visitors select from five second-floor guest rooms, all with phones, private baths and TVs. Victorian furnishings are found throughout the inn. A favorite spot is the solarium, with its three walls of windows and fireplace, perfect for curling up with a book or magazine. Two first-floor sitting areas with fireplaces also provide relaxing havens for guests. Lake Ontario is just 10 miles away, and visitors will find much to explore in Brockport and Rochester. Brockport is home to the State University of New York and Niagara Falls is an hour away.

Innkeeper(s): Sharon Kehoe. $79-120. 5

rooms with PB. Breakfast and afternoon tea included in rates. Types of meals: Full bkfst. Beds: KQDT. Cable TV, reading lamp, clock radio, telephone, desk and Jacuzzi tub in room. Air conditioning. VCR, fax, fireplace and e-mail access on premises. Antiquing, cross-country skiing, live theater, shopping and sporting events nearby.

Location: Village on Erie Canal.

"Memories of another time; hospitality of another era."

Certificate may be used: Anytime, subject to availability.

Burdett   G6

The Red House Country Inn

4586 Picnic Area Rd
Burdett, NY 14818-9716
(607)546-8566 Fax:(607)546-4105
Internet: www.redhousecountryinn.com
E-mail: redhsinn@aol.com

Circa 1844. Nestled within the 16,000-acre Finger Lakes National Forest, this old farmstead has an in-ground swimming pool, large veranda overlooking groomed lawns, flower gardens and picnic areas. Pet Samoyeds and goats share the seven acres. Next to the property are acres of wild blueberry patches and stocked fishing ponds. The Red House is near Seneca Lake, world-famous Glen Gorge, and Cornell University.

$89-129. 5 rooms, 4 with PB, 1 with FP. Breakfast and afternoon tea included in rates. Types of meals: Full bkfst and early coffee/tea. Beds: QDT. Reading lamp and clock radio in room. Telephone and fireplace on premises. Antiquing, cross-country skiing, fishing, live theater, parks, shopping, sporting events, water sports and wineries nearby.

Location: National forest.

Publicity: *New York Alive, Discerning Traveler and New York Magazine.*

"An Inn-credible delight. What a wonderful place to stay and a difficult place to leave. It doesn't get any better than this."

Certificate may be used: November-April, Sunday-Thursday.

Canandaigua   F6

Habersham Country Inn B&B

6124 State Route 5 And 20
Canandaigua, NY 14424-7938
(585)394-1510 (800)240-0644
Internet: www.habershaminn.com
E-mail: bandb@rochester.rr.com

Circa 1843. A vast, sweeping front lawn and 11 peaceful acres surround this pre-Civil War home. Guests can relax on the front porch with Muff and Josie, the innkeepers' adorable canine friends, or, when there's a chill in the air, rest near the crackling fireplace of the living room. There are five guest rooms, including a suite with a two-person Jacuzzi. Bristol Ski Mountain, museums, galleries, Seneca Park Zoo, horse racing, antique shopping and sporting activities are among the local attractions. Tour the many wineries in the fingerlakes region.

Innkeeper(s): Raymond & Sharon Lesio. $89-185. 5 rooms, 3 with PB. Breakfast and snacks/refreshments included in rates. Types of meals: Full gourmet bkfst and veg bkfst. Beds: QDT. Modem hook-up, cable TV, VCR, reading lamp and clock radio in room. Central air. Fax, parlor games, telephone and fireplace on premises. Antiquing, art galleries, beach, canoeing/kayaking, downhill skiing, fishing, golf, hiking, live theater, museums, parks, shopping, water sports and wineries nearby.

Location: Country.

Certificate may be used: November through April, Tuesday through Thursday.

Candor H7

The Edge of Thyme, A B&B Inn

6 Main St
Candor, NY 13743-1615
(607)659-5155 (800)722-7365 Fax:(607)659-5155
Internet: www.edgeofthyme.com
E-mail: innthyme@twcny.rr.com

Circa 1840. Originally the summer home of John D. Rockefeller's secretary, this two-story Georgian-style inn offers gracious accommodations a short drive from Ithaca. The inn sports many interesting features, including an impressive stairway,
marble fireplaces, parquet floors, pergola (arbor) and windowed porch with leaded glass. Guests may relax in front of the inn's fireplace, catch up with reading in its library or watch television  in the sitting room. An authentic turn-of-the-century full breakfast is served, and guests also may arrange for special high teas.

Innkeeper(s): Prof. Frank & Eva Mae Musgrave. $80-135. 5 rooms, 3 with PB, 2 suites. Breakfast included in rates. Types of meals: Full gourmet bkfst, veg bkfst, early coffee/tea and afternoon tea. Beds: KQDT. Reading lamp, ceiling fan, clock radio and desk in room. Air conditioning. TV, VCR, fax, library, child care, parlor games, telephone, fireplace, gift shop and high tea by appointment on premises. Antiquing, art galleries, cross-country skiing, downhill skiing, fishing, golf, hiking, horseback riding, live theater, museums, parks, shopping, sporting events and wineries nearby.

Location: Village.

Publicity: *Historic Inns of the Northeast, 17 newspapers across the US by a freelance writer concentrating on the Finger Lakes, The Ithaca Journal, The Press and Sun Bullitan.*

Certificate may be used: Sunday through Thursday. Not valid in May, excluding specific weekends.

Cazenovia F8

Brae Loch Inn

5 Albany St
Cazenovia, NY 13035-1403
(315)655-3431 Fax:(315)655-4844
Internet: www.braelochinn.com
E-mail: braeloch1@aol.com

Circa 1805. Hunter green awnings accentuate the attractive architecture of the Brae Loch. Since 1946 the inn has been owned and operated by the same family. A Scottish theme is evident throughout, including in the inn's restaurant. Four of the oldest rooms have fireplaces (non-working). Stickley, Harden and antique furniture add to the old-world atmosphere, and many rooms offer canopy beds. Guest rooms are on the second floor above the restaurant.

Innkeeper(s): Jim & Val Barr. $85-155. 12 rooms with PB and 1 conference room. Breakfast included in rates. Types of meals: Cont and gourmet dinner. Restaurant on premises. Beds: KQDT. Cable TV, reading lamp, clock radio, telephone, desk and three with Jacuzzis in room. Air conditioning. Fax, copier and fireplace on premises. Antiquing, cross-country skiing, downhill skiing, fishing, golf, parks, shopping, sporting events, tennis, water sports and swimming nearby.

Location: Small village by lake.

Publicity: *The Globe and Mail, Traveler Magazine and CNY.*

"Everything was just perfect. The Brae Loch and staff make you feel as if you were at home."

Certificate may be used: Anytime, Sunday-Thursday.

Chestertown D12

The Chester Inn B&B

Box 163
Chestertown, NY 12817
(518)494-4148
Internet: www.thechesterinn.com
E-mail: icecream@netheaven.com

Circa 1830. There are 14 acres of meadow surrounding this completely restored early Greek Revival home. Yellow with white trim, there are two front porches, bordered by lilacs, that stretch across the house. Barns, a smoke house and an ancient family cemetery rests on the property. Inside, the inn's grand hall has hand-grained woodwork and mahogany railings. Country Victorian antiques combined with Laura Ashley fabrics, replica wallpapers and down comforters are features. Breakfast specialties such as skillet corn bread and vegetable souffle with pan-fried potatoes are served by candlelight. A block away is the Main Street Ice Cream Parlor & Restaurant and Miss Hester's Emporium Gift Shop owned by the innkeepers.

Innkeeper(s): Bruce & Suzanne Robbins. $89-159. 4 rooms with PB, 2 suites. Breakfast and afternoon tea included in rates. Types of meals: Full bkfst and early coffee/tea. Beds: QDT. Reading lamp, ceiling fan, clock radio and one with fireplace in room. Air conditioning. VCR, parlor games and telephone on premises. Amusement parks, antiquing, cross-country skiing, downhill skiing, fishing, golf, live theater, parks, shopping, sporting events, tennis and water sports nearby.

Location: Mountains. Small village.

Publicity: *Adirondack Guide, Glens Falls Post Star, WRGB, Schenectady and New York.*

"We'll shout your praises!"

Certificate may be used: March 1 to May 23, Sunday-Thursday (Charles Fowler Room); Oct. 10 to Dec. 20, Sunday-Thursday (Charles Fowler Room).

Friends Lake Inn

963 Friends Lake Rd
Chestertown, NY 12817
(518)494-4751 Fax:(518)494-4616
Internet: www.friendslake.com
E-mail: friends@friendslake.com

Circa 1860. This Mission-style inn offers its guests elegant accommodations, fine dining and an award-winning wine list. Overlooking Friends Lake, the inn provides easy access to the entire Adirondack area. Guests are welcome to borrow a canoe for a lake outing and use the inn's private beach or in-ground swimming pool. Guest rooms are well-appointed and most include four-poster beds. Many have breathtaking lake views or Jacuzzis. Three rooms have a wood-burning fireplace. An outdoor sauna is a favorite spot after a busy day of recreation. The 25km Tubbs Snowshoe Center is on site with wilderness trails and rentals. Trails are available for hiking as well.

Innkeeper(s): Sharon & Greg Taylor. $295-425. 17 rooms with PB. Breakfast and dinner included in rates. Types of meals: Country bkfst, picnic lunch and room service. Restaurant on premises. Beds: KQ. Reading lamp, clock radio and turn-down service in room. Air conditioning. VCR, fax, copier, parlor games, telephone, fireplace, pool, beach and sauna on premises. Amusement parks, antiquing, cross-country skiing, downhill skiing, fishing, live theater, museums, parks, shopping, sporting events and water sports nearby.

Location: Mountains.

Publicity: *Country Inns and New York Times.*

"Everyone here is so pleasant, you end up feeling like family!"

Certificate may be used: Any Sunday-Thursday, excluding holidays, subject to availability.

Clarence
F3

Asa Ransom House

10529 Main St, Rt 5
Clarence, NY 14031-1684
(716)759-2315 (800)841-2340 Fax:(716)759-2791
Internet: www.asaransom.com
E-mail: innfo@asaransom.com

Circa 1853. Set on spacious lawns, behind a white picket fence, the Asa Ransom House rests on the site of the first grist mill built in Erie County. Silversmith Asa Ransom constructed an inn and grist mill here in response to the Holland Land

Company's offering of free land to anyone who would start and operate a tavern. A specialty of the dining room is "Veal Perrott" and "Pistachio Banana Muffins."

Innkeeper(s): Robert & Abigail Lenz. $98-175. 9 rooms with PB, 8 with FP, 2 suites and 1 conference room. Breakfast included in rates. Types of meals: Full bkfst, early coffee/tea and dinner. Restaurant on premises. Beds: KQT. Reading lamp, stereo, clock radio, telephone, turn-down service, desk and old radio tapes in room. Air conditioning. TV, fax, copier, library, parlor games and fireplace on premises. Handicap access. Antiquing, cross-country skiing, live theater, parks and shopping nearby.
Location: Village.
Publicity: *Toronto Star, Buffalo News, Prevention Magazine, Country Living, Country Inns and Inn Country USA.*

"Popular spot keeps getting better."
Certificate may be used: March-June, September-Dec. 15, Sunday-Thursday.

Cohocton
G5

Ambroselli's Villa Serendip

10849 State Route 371
Cohocton, NY 14826
(585)384-5299 Fax:(585)384-9228
Internet: www.villaserendip.com
E-mail: inhost@yahoo.com

Circa 1860. Country Victorian elegance awaits at this Italianate villa surrounded by rolling hills and scenic splendor. Non-smoking guest bedrooms and suites easily accommodate families and honeymooners alike. Cupid's Retreat with a canopy bed and fireplace is perfect for a private romantic getaway. The first-floor Victorian Bride's Dream features a four-poster rice bed and bay window alcove. The Empire Suite offers spaciousness and extra beds as well as a sitting room with a large screen television and VCR. Oven-baked bananas, French toast with glazed pecans, muffins, skillet potatoes with sausage and rosemary, and scrambled eggs with three cheeses are popular breakfast favorites. Visit Canandaigua Lake, Corning Glass Factory and award-winning wineries.

Innkeeper(s): Fran Ambroselli. $95-225. 5 rooms with PB, 2 suites. Breakfast included in rates. Types of meals: Full gourmet bkfst, veg bkfst, early coffee/tea, afternoon tea and snacks/refreshments. Beds: KQ. Modem hook-up, cable TV, VCR, reading lamp, refrigerator, ceiling fan, clock radio, telephone, turn-down service, fireplace and hot tub in room. Parlor games, fireplace and Jacuzzi suite on premises. Handicap access. Antiquing, beach, cross-country skiing, downhill skiing, fishing, golf, hiking, horseback riding, live theater, museums, parks, shopping, wineries, Mountain Ski Resort, Swain Ski Resort, Letworth State Park, Stony Brook State Park, Corning Museum of Glass and Keuka Lake nearby.
Location: Country, mountains.
Certificate may be used: Anytime, subject to availability.

Cold Spring
J12

Pig Hill Inn

73 Main St
Cold Spring, NY 10516-3014
(845)265-9247 Fax:(845)265-4614
Internet: www.pighillinn.com
E-mail: pighillinn@aol.com

Circa 1808. The antiques at this stately three-story inn can be purchased, and they range from Chippendale to chinoiserie style. Rooms feature formal English and Adirondack decor with special touches such as four-poster or brass beds, painted rockers and, of course, pigs. The lawn features a tri-level garden. The delicious breakfasts can be shared with guests in the Victorian conservatory, dining room or garden, or it may be served in the privacy of your room. The inn is about an hour out of New York City, and the train station is only two blocks away.

Innkeeper(s): Natalie Rush. $120-220. 9 rooms, 5 with PB, 6 with FP and 1 conference room. Breakfast included in rates. Types of meals: Full bkfst. Beds: KQDT. Telephone on premises. Antiquing, live theater, shopping, sporting events and great restaurants nearby.
Location: Small Hudson River town.
Publicity: *National Geographic, Woman's Home Journal, Country Inns and Getaways for Gourmets.*

"Some of our fondest memories of New York were at Pig Hill."
Certificate may be used: Sunday-Thursday, excluding holidays.

Corinth
E12

Agape Farm B&B and Paintball

4839 Rt 9N
Corinth, NY 12822-1704
(518)654-7777 Fax:(518)654-7777
Internet: www.geocities.com/agapefarm
E-mail: agapefarmbnb@adelphia.net

Circa 1870. Amid 33 acres of fields and woods, this Adirondack farmhouse is home to chickens and horses, as well as guests seeking a refreshing getaway. Visitors have their choice of six guest rooms, all with ceiling fans, phones, private baths and views of the tranquil surroundings. The inn's wraparound porch lures many visitors, who often enjoy a glass of icy lemonade. Homemade breads, jams, jellies and muffins are part of the full breakfast served here, and

guests are welcome to pick berries or gather a ripe tomato from the garden. A trout-filled stream on the grounds flows to the Hudson River, a mile away.

Innkeeper(s): Fred & Sigrid Koch. $79-175. 6 rooms with PB and 1 conference room. Breakfast and snacks/refreshments included in rates. Types of meals: Full gourmet bkfst, veg bkfst and early coffee/tea. Beds: KQDT. Reading lamp, ceiling fan, clock radio, telephone and desk in room. TV, VCR, fax, swimming, child care, parlor games, laundry facility and downstairs HC room and bath on premises. Handicap access. Amusement parks, antiquing, art galleries, beach, bicycling, canoeing/kayaking, cross-country skiing, downhill skiing, fishing, golf, hiking, horseback riding, museums, parks, shopping, sporting events, tennis and water sports nearby.
Location: Country. Saratoga Region.

"Clean and impeccable, we were treated royally."
Certificate may be used: Sept. 15 to June 1.

Cornwall H6

Cromwell Manor Inn B&B

174 Angola Rd
Cornwall, NY 12518
(845)534-7136
Internet: www.cromwellmanor.com
E-mail: cmi@hvc.rr.com

Circa 1820. Listed in the National Register of Historic Places, this stunning Greek Revival mansion sits on seven lush acres with scenic Hudson Valley views. It is elegantly furnished with

period antiques and fine reproductions. The Chimneys Cottage, built in 1764, offers romantic guest bedrooms with a country decor. Savor a bountiful gourmet breakfast before a

stroll in the garden. The inn extends afternoon hospitality, while boasting spa and fitness facilities. After a day of exploring, relax by the fireside or indulge in the Jacuzzi.

Innkeeper(s): Jack & Cynthia Trowell. $165-370. 13 rooms, 10 with PB, 7 with FP, 3 total suites, including 1 two-bedroom suite and 1 conference room. Breakfast and afternoon tea included in rates. Types of meals: Full gourmet bkfst, early coffee/tea, picnic lunch, snacks/refreshments and room service. Beds: KQDT. Modem hook-up, reading lamp, CD player, refrigerator, snack bar, clock radio, telephone, turn-down service, desk, hot tub/spa and fireplace in room. Central air. TV, VCR, fax, copier and parlor games on premises. Handicap access. Antiquing, art galleries, bicycling, canoeing/kayaking, cross-country skiing, downhill skiing, fishing, golf, hiking, horseback riding, live theater, museums, parks, shopping, sporting events, tennis, water sports, wineries, Hudson Valley Mansions, Woodbury Common Premium Outlets, Storm King Art Center, Renaissance Festival, West Point sports and mountain biking nearby.

Location: Country, mountains. Hudson River Valley.

Publicity: *USA Today, Marie Claire Maison, New York Times, Wall Street Journal, Hudson Valley Magazine, Montreal Gazette, Washington Post, New York Magazine, Philadelphia Inquirer, Fox, CBS Early Show and Top 10 Inns of NY.*

Certificate may be used: Anytime, Sunday-Thursday, subject to availability, holidays excluded.

Crown Point D12

Crown Point Bed & Breakfast

PO Box 490
Crown Point, NY 12928
(518)597-3651 Fax:(518)597-4451
Internet: www.crownpointbandb.com
E-mail: mail@crownpointbandb.com

Circa 1886. In the heart of the Adirondacks, this Queen Anne Victorian Painted Lady sits on five-and-a-half partially wooded acres. Recently renovated, stained-glass windows, eight varieties of wood flooring and paneling, pocket doors, four carved stone fireplaces and a Baldwin icebox are original details that blend perfectly with floral wallpapers, Oriental rugs, and fine antiques to enhance the luxurious ambiance. Each custom-decorated guest bedroom and suite features comfortable slippers, robes, shower massage, hair dryers and gourmet truffles with turn-down service. A satisfying breakfast is served on English bone china with vintage glassware. Three porches and a side sitting lawn with bistro tables invite relaxation amidst a fountain and flower gardens.

Innkeeper(s): Hugh & Sandy Johnson. $80-165. 6 rooms with PB. Breakfast included in rates. Types of meals: Full gourmet bkfst, veg bkfst, early

coffee/tea and picnic lunch. Beds: QDT. Reading lamp, ceiling fan, turn-down service, desk, hot tub/spa, robes, slippers, shower massage, hair dryers and gourmet truffles in room. TV, fax, copier, bicycles, parlor games, telephone, gift shop and fireplaces on premises. Antiquing, art galleries, beach, bicycling, canoeing/kayaking, fishing, golf, hiking, live theater, museums, parks, shopping, tennis and water sports nearby.

Location: Country, mountains.

Publicity: *Mineville.*

Certificate may be used: Nov. 1-May 1.

Elbridge F7

Fox Ridge Farm B&B

4786 Foster Rd
Elbridge, NY 13060-9770
(315)673-4881
Internet: www.foxridgebb.com
E-mail: stay@foxridgebb.com

Circa 1910. Guests shouldn't be surprised to encounter deer or other wildlife at this secluded country home surrounded by woods. The innkeepers have transformed the former farmhouse into an inn with rooms boasting quilts, a four-poster bed and views of the woods or flower garden. Enjoy breakfasts in front of a fire in the large country kitchen. The innkeepers are happy to accommodate dietary needs. Snacks and refreshments always are available for hungry guests in the evening. Nearby Skaneateles Lake offers swimming, boating and other outdoor activities. Dinner cruises, touring wineries and antique shopping are other popular activities.

Innkeeper(s): Marge & Bob Sykes. $55-95. 3 rooms, 1 with PB. Breakfast and snacks/refreshments included in rates. Types of meals: Full gourmet bkfst and early coffee/tea. Beds: QD. Reading lamp, clock radio and desk in room. VCR, parlor games, telephone, fireplace, grand piano and wood stove on premises. Antiquing, cross-country skiing, downhill skiing, fishing, live theater, parks, shopping, sporting events and water sports nearby.

Location: Rural.

"If I could, I would take Marge Sykes home to Seattle with us. We stayed 7 days for a family reunion. Great company, marvelous hosts and the most delicious breakfasts everyday."

Certificate may be used: Nov. 1 to May 15, Sunday-Thursday, excluding holidays.

Ellicottville H3

The Jefferson Inn of Ellicottville

3 Jefferson St, PO Box 1566
Ellicottville, NY 14731-1566
(716)699-5869 (800)577-8451 Fax:(716)699-5758
Internet: www.thejeffersoninn.com
E-mail: info@thejeffersoninn.com

Circa 1835. The Allegheny Mountains provide a perfect backdrop for this restored Victorian home built by Robert H. Shankland, an influential citizen who owned the local newspaper, along with other enterprises. The home's

100-foot wraparound Greek Revival porch was added in the 1920s and patterned after the summer home of President Woodrow Wilson. A full breakfast is served to B&B guests. (There are two separate efficiency units

offered to visitors with children or pets.) The only bed & breakfast within the village, it is located in the center of town where you'll enjoy following the tree-lined streets to restaurants and shops.

Innkeeper(s): Jim Buchanan & Donna Gushue. $79-199. 7 rooms with PB, 3 with FP, 1 suite. Breakfast included in rates. Types of meals: Full gourmet bkfst, early coffee/tea and picnic lunch. Beds: KQT. Modem hook-up, cable TV, reading lamp, clock radio, telephone, coffeemaker, desk and fireplace in room. Central air. TV, VCR, fax, spa, library and parlor games on premises. Handicap access. Antiquing, art galleries, bicycling, cross-country skiing, downhill skiing, fishing, golf, hiking, horseback riding, museums, parks, shopping, tennis and casino nearby.

Location: Village.

Publicity: *Arrington's Bed and Breakfast Journal, Book of Lists, Genesse Country Magazine, Buffalo Spree Magazine, Olean Chronicle and Ellicottville News.*

"Even though we just met, we are leaving with the feeling we just spent the weekend with good friends."

Certificate may be used: April-June, Sunday to Thursday and November Sunday to Thursday.

Essex   C13

The Stone House
PO Box 43
Essex, NY 12936-0043
(518)963-7713 Fax:(518)963-7713

Circa 1826. Just a two-minute walk from the ferry that traverses Lake Champlain, this stately Georgian stone house offers a tranquil English country setting. Breakfast may be eaten in the elegant dining room or on the garden terrace, and guests also enjoy an evening snack and glass of wine by candlelight on the inn's porch. The charming hamlet of Essex, listed in the National Register, is waiting to be explored, and visitors may do so by borrowing one of the inn's bicycles. Antiquing, fine dining and shopping are found in town, and Lake Champlain and nearby Lake George provide many recreational activities.

Innkeeper(s): Sylvia Hobbs. $75-150. 4 rooms, 2 with PB, 1 suite and 1 cottage. Breakfast, afternoon tea and snacks/refreshments included in rates. Types of meals: Cont plus and early coffee/tea. Beds: QDT. Reading lamp, refrigerator, clock radio and turn-down service in room. TV, VCR, bicycles, library, telephone and CD player on premises. Antiquing, fishing, golf, live theater, parks, shopping, tennis and water sports nearby.

Location: Mountains. Lake Champlain.

"Without a doubt, the highlight of our trip!"

Certificate may be used: May-June, September-October, Sunday to Friday.

Fair Haven   E7

Black Creek Farm B&B
PO Box 390
Fair Haven, NY 13064-0390
(315)947-5282
E-mail: ksarber@redcreek.net

Circa 1888. Pines and towering birch trees frame this Victorian farmhouse inn, filled with an amazing assortment of authentic antiques. Set on 20 acres, Black Creek Farm is a refreshing escape from big-city life. Guests enjoy relaxing in a hammock on the porch or by taking a stroll along the peaceful back roads. A hearty country breakfast features seasonal fruit raised on the grounds as well as home baked date-nut, banana-nut or pumpkin-raisin bread. A new  pond-side guest house is an especially popular accommodation for honeymooners and families, offering complete privacy. It features a gas fireplace and double shower. Bring your own breakfast makings and enjoy breakfast sitting on the patio or

the porch which overlooks the pond, with ducks and geese, bass and perch. Sometimes turkey or deer may be seen in the meadow. There's a peddle boat on the pond in summer. In winter sledding and snowmobiling are popular. The B&B is two miles from Lake Ontario, Fair Haven Beach State Park and minutes away from Sterling Renaissance Festival.

Innkeeper(s): Bob & Kathy Sarber. $60-125. 3 rooms with PB. Types of meals: Full bkfst and early coffee/tea. Beds: Q. Air conditioning. VCR, bicycles, parlor games, pedal boat, satellite dish and movies available on premises. Cross-country skiing, fishing, water sports and snowmobiling nearby.

Location: Country.

Certificate may be used: Oct. 30-Dec. 15 and Jan. 8-March 15.

Frost Haven B&B Inn
14380 West Bay Rd, PO Box 241
Fair Haven, NY 13064-0241
(315)947-5331

This Federal-style inn near Lake Ontario offers a relaxing getaway for residents of nearby Rochester and Syracuse. Four guest rooms are available, all furnished with Victorian stylings and featuring bath robes and ceiling fans. Guests enjoy a full breakfast before beginning a busy day of antiquing, fishing, sightseeing, swimming or sunbathing. Fair Haven Beach State Park is nearby, and Fort Ontario is within easy driving distance.

Innkeeper(s): Jean & Glen Spry. $66. 7 rooms. Reading lamp and ceiling fan in room. VCR and telephone on premises. Antiquing nearby.

Location: Village.

Certificate may be used: Weekends July through Labor Day excluded.

Fleischmanns   H11

River Run
Main St, Box 9
Fleischmanns, NY 12430
(845)254-4884
Internet: www.catskill.net/riverrun
E-mail: riverrun@catskill.net

Circa 1887. The backyard of this large three-story Victorian gently slopes to the river where the Bushkill and Little Red Kill trout streams meet. Inside, stained-glass windows surround the inn's common areas, shining on the oak-floored dining room and the book-filled parlor. The parlor also includes a fireplace and a piano. Adirondack chairs are situated comfortably on the front porch. Tennis courts, a pool, park, theater and restaurants are within walking distance, as is a country auction held each Saturday night. The inn is two and a half hours out of New York City, 35 minutes west of Woodstock, and accessible by public transportation. Also, the inn was the recipient of the "Catskill Service Award" for best accommodations in the Belleayre Region for 1998, 1999 and 2000.

Innkeeper(s): Ben & Melissa Fenton. $70-125. 8 rooms, 4 with PB, 1 suite. Breakfast and afternoon tea included in rates. Types of meals: Cont plus and early coffee/tea. Beds: KQDT. TV and reading lamp in room. VCR, bicycles, library, parlor games, telephone, fireplace, refrigerator, two-bedroom and two-bath suite on premises. Antiquing, cross-country skiing, downhill skiing, fishing, golf, hiking, horseback riding, live theater, parks, shopping, tennis, water sports, auctions and flea and farmers markets nearby.

Location: Mountains.

Publicity: *New York Magazine, Boston Globe, Catskill Mountain News, Kingston Freeman, New York Times, New York Daily News, Philadelphia Inquirer, Inn Country USA and Newsday.*

"We are really happy to know of a place that welcomes all of our family."

Certificate may be used: Weekends March 1-May 20, Nov. 1-Dec. 20; weekdays (Sunday-Thursday) all year (all holiday periods excluded).

Fredonia   G2

Brookside Manor B & B

3728 Route 83
Fredonia, NY 14063-9740
(716)672-7721 (800)929-7599
Internet: bbonline.com/ny/brookside/
E-mail: brookbnb@yahoo.com

Circa 1875. Just six minutes from the historic village of
Fredonia, in the heart of the Chautauqua Wine Trail, this
Gothic Victorian Manor graces more than five partially wooded
acres. Relax in the parlor or use the meeting/function rooms on
the main floor. The inviting curved staircase with walnut banister leads to the well-appointed guest bedrooms that are accented with family heirlooms. Savor a complete breakfast in the
sun-filled dining room enhanced with fresh flowers, china, and
fine linens. Explore the glorious flower gardens or visit the
many local attractions. Swimming, fishing and boating are popular activities at Lake Erie and Cassadaga Lake.

Innkeeper(s): Andrea Andrews & Dale Mirth. $79-89. 4 rooms with PB.
Breakfast included in rates. Types of meals: Full gourmet bkfst and veg bkfst.
Beds: QD. Cable TV, ceiling fan, clock radio and telephone in room. Air con-
ditioning. VCR, parlor games and fireplace on premises. Amusement parks,
antiquing, art galleries, beach, bicycling, canoeing/kayaking, cross-country
skiing, downhill skiing, fishing, golf, hiking, horseback riding, live theater,
museums, parks, shopping, sporting events, tennis and wineries nearby.
Location: Rural.
Certificate may be used: Anytime, Jan. 2-April 30, except Chautauqua Wine
Trail events (2 weekends) and Valentine's Day weekend.

The White Inn

52 E Main St
Fredonia, NY 14063-1822
(716)672-2103 (888)FRE-DONI Fax:(716)672-2107
Internet: www.whiteinn.com
E-mail: res@whiteinn.com

Circa 1919. Pleasantly blending the delightful ambiance of yesteryear with the modern elegance of today, this traditional
Victorian inn sits in the center of a thriving cultural and histori-

cal community. Great attention is
given to detail, and the qualities
of service and warmth are a top
priority. Meticulously restored,
distinctive guest bedrooms provide comfort and style. The
Presidential Suite boasts a fireplace and whirlpool tub. Linger
over a leisurely breakfast. Known for its American cuisine, the
inn offers fine dining, cocktails and casual fare in the lounge or
on the 100-foot-long veranda.

Innkeeper(s): Robert Contiguglia & Kathleen Dennison. $69-179. 23 rooms
with PB, 2 with FP, 11 suites and 4 conference rooms. Breakfast included in
rates. Types of meals: Full bkfst, lunch and gourmet dinner. Restaurant on
premises. Beds: KQD. Cable TV, reading lamp, clock radio, telephone and
desk in room. Air conditioning. VCR, fax, copier and fireplace on premises.
Antiquing, golf, live theater, parks, shopping and wineries nearby.
Location: City.
Publicity: *Upstate New York Magazine, Country Living, US Air Magazine and
Buffalo News.*
Certificate may be used: Anytime, November-April, excluding holidays and
holiday weekends, subject to availability.

Fulton   E7

Battle Island Inn

2167 State Route 48 N
Fulton, NY 13069-4132
(315)593-3699 Fax:(315)592-5071
Internet: www.battle-island-inn.com
E-mail: battleislandinn@usadatanet.net

Circa 1840. Topped with a gothic cupola, this family farmhouse
overlooks the Oswego River and a golf course. There are three
antique-filled parlors. Guest accommodations are furnished in a
variety of styles including Victorian and Renaissance Revival.

There are four wooded acres with
lawns and gardens. Guests are
often found relaxing on one of
the inn's four porches and enjoying the views. The Honeymoon
suite features a canopy bed, full
bath and private Jacuzzi.

Innkeeper(s): Diane Bednarek and Jim
Sokolowski. $75-125. 4 rooms with PB, 1 suite. Breakfast included in rates.
Types of meals: Full gourmet bkfst and early coffee/tea. Beds: KQ. Cable TV,
reading lamp, ceiling fan, clock radio, telephone and desk in room. TV, VCR,
fax, copier, fireplace and refrigerator on premises. Handicap access. Cross-
country skiing, fishing, golf, live theater, parks, shopping, water sports and
fort nearby.
Location: Country.
Publicity: *Lake Effect, Palladium Times, Travel, Journey, Oswego County
Business and Valley News.*
"We will certainly never forget our wonderful weeks at Battle Island Inn."
Certificate may be used: Sunday-Thursday.

Geneva   F6

Geneva On The Lake

1001 Lochland Rd, Rt 14S
Geneva, NY 14456
(315)789-7190 (800)343-6382 Fax:(315)789-0322
Internet: www.genevaonthelake.com
E-mail: info@genevaonthelake.com

Circa 1911. This opulent world-class inn is a replica of the
Renaissance-era Lancellotti Villa in Frascati, Italy. It is listed in
the National Register. Although originally built as a residence, it
became a monastery for Capuchin monks. Now it is one of the
finest resorts in the U.S.
Renovated under the direction of award-winning
designer William Schickel,
there are 10 two-bedroom
suites, some with views of
the lake. Here, you may
have an experience as fine as Europe can offer, without leaving
the country. Some compare it to the Grand Hotel du Cap-Ferrat
on the French Riviera. The inn has been awarded four diamonds
from AAA for more than two decades. Breakfast is available daily
and on Sunday, brunch is served. Dinner is served each
evening, and in the summer lunch is offered on the terrace.

Innkeeper(s): William J. Schickel. $138-770. 29 rooms with PB, 3 with FP,
23 suites and 3 conference rooms. Breakfast included in rates. Types of
meals: Cont, gourmet dinner and room service. Restaurant on premises.
Beds: KQDT. TV, CD player, refrigerator, clock radio, telephone, turn-down
service and desk in room. Air conditioning. VCR, fax, copier, swimming, bicycles, parlor games, fireplace, sailing, fishing, lawn games and boats on

premises. Antiquing, cross-country skiing, downhill skiing, live theater, parks, shopping, sporting events, water sports and wineries nearby.

Location: Waterfront.

Publicity: *Travel & Leisure, Bon Appetit, Country Inns, The New York Times, Bride's, Catholic Register, Pittsford-Brighton Post, New York, Glamour, Gourmet, Washingtonian, Toronto Star, Globe & Mail and Rochester Democrat & Chronicle.*

"The food was superb and the service impeccable."

Certificate may be used: Sunday through Thursday, Nov. 1 through April 30.

Greenfield Center   F12

The Wayside Inn & Meeting Center

PO Box 3274
Saratoga Springs, NY 12866
(518)893-7249 (800)893-2884 Fax:(518)893-2884
Internet: www.waysidein.com
E-mail: waysidein@aol.com

Circa 1786. This Federal-Era inn and meeting center provides a unique atmosphere to visitors of the Saratoga Springs area. Situated on 10 acres amidst a brook, herb gardens, ponds and willows, the inn originally served as a stagecoach tavern. Many interesting pieces, gathered during the innkeepers' many years living abroad, highlight the inn's interior. Visitors select from the Colonial American, European, Far Eastern and Middle Eastern rooms. Migrating birds are known to frequent the inn's picturesque pond.

Innkeeper(s): Karen & Dale Shook. $75-195. 4 rooms with PB, 2 with FP, 1 cottage and 2 conference rooms. Breakfast included in rates. Types of meals: Full gourmet bkfst, veg bkfst, early coffee/tea, gourmet lunch, picnic lunch, afternoon tea, snacks/refreshments and gourmet dinner. Restaurant on premises. Beds: KQ. Modem hook-up, cable TV, VCR, reading lamp, CD player, refrigerator, ceiling fan, clock radio, coffeemaker, desk, hot tub/spa and fireplace in room. Air conditioning. Fax, copier, spa, swimming, sauna, library, parlor games, telephone, fireplace, gift shop, koi ponds, Arts Center - Herb Gardens, perennial garden, pond stream orchard and gazebo on premises. Limited handicap access. Amusement parks, antiquing, art galleries, beach, bicycling, canoeing/kayaking, cross-country skiing, downhill skiing, fishing, golf, hiking, horseback riding, live theater, museums, parks, shopping, sporting events, tennis, water sports and wineries nearby.

Location: Mountains.

Publicity: *Daily Gazette, Saratogian, Albany Times-Union, Capital District Business Review, Saratoga Business Journal, Glens Falls Business Journal, Hudson Valley Magazine and Adirondack Life Magazine.*

Certificate may be used: January-June, September, December; Sunday, Monday, Tuesday, Wednesday, Thursday. Space available.

Groton   G7

Benn Conger Inn

206 W Cortland St
Groton, NY 13073-1008
(607)898-5817 (888)871-0220 Fax:(607)898-5818
Internet: www.benncongerinn.com
E-mail: benncongerinn@yahoo.com

Circa 1920. Once home to namesake Benn Conger, founder of Smith-Corona typewriters and Dutch Schultz, notorious bootlegger, this majestic inn overlooks a picturesque village in the heart of the Finger Lakes. Sitting on 20 park-like acres, it includes a mansion reminiscent of Tara in "Gone With The Wind," as well as a delightful Victorian cottage. Spacious guest bedrooms and suites are a stunning collaboration of interior design, architecture and thoughtful amenities. Several feature whirlpool tubs, fireplaces and large porches. Choose from American or European menu selections for breakfast in the Morning Room or on the Terrace. Chef/owner Peter prepares

renown Mediterranean cuisine for dinner, and offers an award-winning wine selection. He and his wife, innkeeper Alison instill an elegant ambiance steeped in tradition and hospitality.

Innkeeper(s): Alison van der Meulen. $90-250. 10 rooms, 9 with PB, 7 with FP, 1 suite. Breakfast and afternoon tea included in rates. Types of meals: Full gourmet bkfst, early coffee/tea, picnic lunch, snacks/refreshments, gourmet dinner and room service. Restaurant on premises. Beds: KQDT. Modem hook-up, data port, cable TV, reading lamp, ceiling fan, clock radio, telephone, turn-down service, desk, hot tub/spa, digital TV and Music Choice in room. Air conditioning. Fax, copier, spa, bicycles, library, pet boarding, parlor games, fireplace and laundry facility on premises. Limited handicap access. Antiquing, art galleries, beach, bicycling, canoeing/kayaking, cross-country skiing, downhill skiing, fishing, golf, hiking, horseback riding, live theater, museums, parks, shopping, sporting events, tennis, water sports and wineries nearby.

Location: Country. 20-acre village near Ithaca.

Publicity: *Syracuse New Times, Herald American, Ithaca Journal, Ithaca Times and Cortland Standard.*

Certificate may be used: Anytime, subject to availability. Anytime, Sunday-Thursday, not available Memorial Day weekend, College, University-related weekends or major holidays.

Hadley   E12

Saratoga Rose Inn & Restaurant

4724 Rockwell St
Hadley, NY 12835-0238
(518)696-2861 (800)942-5025 Fax:(518)696-5319
Internet: www.saratogarose.com
E-mail: saratogarose@adelphia.net

Circa 1885. This romantic Queen Anne Victorian offers a small, candle-lit restaurant perfect for an evening for two. Breakfast specialties include Grand Marnier French toast and Eggs Anthony. Rooms are decorated in period style. The Queen Anne Room, decorated in blue, boasts a wood and tile fireplace and a quilt-covered bed. The Carriage House features an iron canopy bed, skylight, TV, fireplace and private deck with a Jacuzzi while the Garden Room offers a private sunporch and outside deck with a Jacuzzi spa. Each of the rooms features something special. Guests can take in the mountain view or relax on the veranda while sipping a cocktail.

Innkeeper(s): Nancy Merlino, Chef Anthony. $160-190. 6 rooms with PB, 6 with FP. Breakfast included in rates. Types of meals: Full gourmet bkfst and gourmet dinner. Beds: KD. Ceiling fan, clock radio, hot tub/spa and four with private hot tubs in room. Air conditioning. VCR, telephone and fireplace on premises. Amusement parks, antiquing, cross-country skiing, downhill skiing, fishing, live theater, parks, shopping and sporting events nearby.

Location: Mountains, waterfront.

Publicity: *Getaways for Gourmets.*

"A must for the inn traveler."

Certificate may be used: November-May, Monday-Thursday, may exclude holidays, upon availability.

Hague   D12

Trout House Village Resort

PO Box 510, Lake Shore Dr
Hague, NY 12836-0510
(518)543-6088 (800)368-6088 Fax:(518)543-6124
Internet: www.trouthouse.com
E-mail: info@trouthouse.com

Circa 1920. On the shores of beautiful Lake George is this resort inn, offering accommodations in the inn, authentic log cabins or cottages. Many of the guest rooms in the inn boast lake views,

while the log cabins offer jetted tubs and fireplaces. The guest quarters are furnished comfortably. The emphasis here is on the abundance of outdoor activities. Outstanding cross-country skiing, downhill skiing and snowmobiling are found nearby. The inn furnishes bicycles, canoes, kayaks, paddle boats, rowboats, sleds, shuffleboard, skis and toboggans. Summertime evenings offer games of capture-the-flag and soccer. Other activities include basketball, horseshoes, ping pong, a putting green and volleyball.
Innkeeper(s): Scott & Alice Patchett. $59-350. 42 rooms, 9 with PB, 15 with FP, 3 cottages, 17 cabins and 2 conference rooms. Beds: QDT. Modem hook-up, cable TV, VCR, reading lamp, CD player, refrigerator, clock radio, telephone, coffeemaker, desk, hot tub/spa, voice mail and hair dryer in room. Fax, copier, spa, swimming, bicycles, child care, parlor games, fireplace, canoes, rowboats, kayaks, shuffleboard, basketball, horseshoes, ping-pong, BBQ grills, volleyball and putting green on premises. Handicap access. Amusement parks, antiquing, art galleries, beach, bicycling, canoeing/kayaking, cross-country skiing, downhill skiing, fishing, golf, hiking, horseback riding, live theater, museums, parks, shopping, tennis, water sports and child care nearby.
Location: Waterfront. Adirondack mountains.

"My wife and I felt the family warmth at this resort. There wasn't that coldness you get at larger resorts."
Certificate may be used: Sept. 15-June 5, except holiday weekends.

Hamburg   G3

Sharon's Lake House B&B
4862 Lake Shore Rd
Hamburg, NY 14075-5542
(716)627-7561

Circa 1935. This historic lakefront house is located 10 miles from Buffalo and 45 minutes from Niagara Falls. Overlooking Lake Erie, the West Lake Room and the Upper Lake Room provide spectacular views. The home's beautiful furnishings offer additional delights.
Innkeeper(s): Sharon & Vince Di Maria. $110. 2 rooms, 1 with PB. Breakfast included in rates. Types of meals: Full gourmet bkfst and gourmet dinner. Beds: D. Cable TV, reading lamp, CD player, ceiling fan, clock radio and telephone in room. VCR, fax, spa, swimming, bicycles, library, parlor games, fireplace, hot tub room and computer room at an hourly rate available on premises. Antiquing, art galleries, beach, bicycling, canoeing/kayaking, cross-country skiing, downhill skiing, fishing, golf, hiking, live theater, museums, parks, shopping, water sports and wineries nearby.
Location: Waterfront.

"Spectacular view, exquisitely furnished."
Certificate may be used: Anytime, all year.

Holley   E4

Rosewood Bed & Breakfast
68 Geddes Street
Holley, NY 14470-1145
(585)638-6186 Fax:(585)638-7568
Internet: www.rosewoodbnb.com
E-mail: rosewdbnb@aol.com

Circa 1891. Restoring this splendid Victorian home was a labor of love that resulted in a glorious transformation of comfort and elegance. Double parlors offer a working fireplace and a grand piano. An extensive music and video collection provides listening and viewing entertainment. Pour through the books in the upstairs library that boasts a reading nook. Guest bedrooms feature antique canopy and four-poster featherbeds, a soaking tub surrounded by red marble, vintage linens, Damask wallpaper and stylized painting. Start the day with fresh berry ambrosia, cherry coffee cake, asparagus quiche, herb-roasted potatoes and beverages. Enjoy the large wraparound porch and the rose and

perennial gardens. Browse in the gift shop for antique treasures like lace pillows, linens, silver and jewelry.
Innkeeper(s): Karen Cook & Roy Nichols. $69-89. 5 rooms, 2 with PB. Breakfast included in rates. Types of meals: Full gourmet bkfst, veg bkfst and early coffee/tea. Beds: QT. Reading lamp and ceiling fan in room. Air conditioning. TV, VCR, fax, bicycles, library, parlor games, telephone, fireplace and gift shop on premises. Amusement parks, antiquing, art galleries, beach, bicycling, canoeing/kayaking, fishing, golf, hiking, museums, parks, shopping and wineries nearby.
Location: Village.
Certificate may be used: January-March, except Valentine's Day.

Hudson   H12

The Inn at Blue Stores
2323 Rt 9
Hudson, NY 12534-0099
(518)537-4277 Fax:(518)537-4277
Internet: www.innatbluestores.com
E-mail: ptrob@valstar.net

Circa 1908. A rural Hudson Valley setting may seem an unusual place for a Spanish-style inn, but this former gentlemen's farm now provides a unique setting for those seeking a relaxing getaway. Visitors will enjoy the inn's clay tile roof and stucco exterior, along with its impressive interior, featuring black oak woodwork, leaded-glass entry and stained glass. Visitors are treated to full breakfasts and refreshing afternoon teas. The spacious porch and swimming pool are favorite spots for relaxing and socializing.

Innkeeper(s): Linda & Robert Saulpaugh. $99-215. 5 rooms, 2 with PB, 1 suite. Breakfast included in rates. Types of meals: Full gourmet bkfst, early coffee/tea and afternoon tea. Beds: KQT. TV, VCR, reading lamp, clock radio and desk in room. Air conditioning. Fax, swimming, parlor games, telephone and fireplace on premises. Antiquing, art galleries, bicycling, canoeing/kayaking, cross-country skiing, fishing, golf, hiking, horseback riding, live theater, museums, parks, shopping, tennis, wineries, historic sites, OLANA, Hyde Park and Clermont Mills Estate nearby.
Location: Country.
Publicity: *Hudson Valley.*
Certificate may be used: Dec. 1-April 30, Monday-Thursday, except holidays.

Hunter   H11

The Redcoat's Country Inn & Restaurant
50 Dale Lane
Hunter, NY 12427
(518)589-9858
Internet: www.redcoatsonline.com
E-mail: info@redcoatsonline.com

Circa 1910. Styled as a charming English country inn, this delightful four-story lodging sits on 15 acres in the northern Catskill Mountains in the center of the Game Preserve. Relax on the front porch or outdoor deck. Elegant cuisine is served in the dinner restaurant that is open to the public. Gather by the stone fireplace in the lounge and linger over a great meal in one of the two cozy dining rooms. Playing golf and skiing are favorite seasonal activities.

Innkeeper(s): Steve and Carol Fink. $99-139. 14 rooms, 7 with PB. Types of meals: Full gourmet bkfst. Beds: DT. Reading lamp in room. Fireplace on premises. Antiquing,

cross-country skiing, downhill skiing, fishing, golf, hiking and shopping nearby.
Location: Catskill Mountains.
Publicity: *New York Times, Ski Magazine and Golf Magazine.*
"Loved the place even more than last time."
Certificate may be used: April-June, Monday-Thursday, subject to availability.
Nov. 1-15, Monday-Thursday, subject to availability.

Ithaca   G7

La Tourelle Country Inn
1150 Danby Rd, Rt 96B
Ithaca, NY 14850-9406
(607)273-2734 (800)765-1492 Fax:(607)273-4821
Internet: www.latourelleinn.com
E-mail: info@latourelleinn.com

Circa 1986. This white stucco European-style country inn is
located on 70 acres three miles from town, allowing for wildflower walks, cross-country skiing and all-season hiking.
Adjacent Buttermilk Falls State
Park provides stone paths, water-
falls and streams. The inn is dec-
orated with a hint of European
decor and includes fireplace
suites and tower suites. For an
extra fee, a continental breakfast
arrives at your door in a basket,
French Provincial style, and guests often tote it to the patio or
gazebo to enjoy views of the rolling countryside. There is also a
tennis court available.
Innkeeper(s): Leslie Leonard. $99-250. 34 rooms with PB, 1 with FP and 1
conference room. Types of meals: Cont, early coffee/tea and gourmet dinner.
Restaurant on premises. Beds: KQ. Cable TV, VCR, reading lamp, refrigerator,
clock radio, telephone, coffeemaker, desk, high-speed Internet and refrigerator
in room. Air conditioning. Copier, tennis, fireplace, hiking trails and fishing
ponds on premises. Handicap access. Antiquing, cross-country skiing, downhill skiing, fishing, live theater, parks, shopping, sporting events and water
sports nearby.
Location: 70 acres hillside, country.
Certificate may be used: Sunday through Thursday not including holidays or
college specialty days. No weekends. Based on availability.

Log Country Inn - B&B of Ithaca
PO Box 581
Ithaca, NY 14851-0581
(607)589-4771 (800)274-4771 Fax:(607)589-6151
Internet: www.logtv.com/inn
E-mail: wanda@logtv.com

Circa 1969. As the name indicates, this bed & breakfast is
indeed fashioned from logs and rests in a picturesque country
setting surrounded by 65 wooded acres. The cozy rooms are
rustic with exposed beams and country furnishings. There is
also a Jacuzzi, fireplace and sauna. The decor is dotted with a
European influence, as is the morning meal. Guests enjoy a full
breakfast with blintzes or Russian pancakes. The innkeeper welcomes children and pets.
Innkeeper(s): Wanda Grunberg. $45-200. 5 rooms, 3 with PB, 1 suite.
Breakfast and afternoon tea included in rates. Types of meals: Full bkfst.
Beds: QDT. Cable TV, reading lamp and telephone in room. VCR, fax, spa,
sauna and Jacuzzi on premises. Antiquing, cross-country skiing, fishing, hik-
ing, parks, shopping, sporting events, water sports, wineries and wine vineyards nearby.
Location: On the edge of state forest.
Certificate may be used: Jan. 15-May 1, Sunday-Thursday.

Stone Quarry House
26 Quarry Road
Ithaca, NY 14850
(607)272-0556
Internet: stonequarryhouse.com
E-mail: nnorton@mac.com

Circa 1880. Sitting on a reclaimed stone quarry, this 1880
farmhouse and newly built carriage house sits 300 yards from a
one-room schoolhouse still in use. The inn features Arts and
Crafts décor with Stickley and Amish furniture accented by
hand-knotted Persian carpets. Two guest bedrooms in the main
house each boast whirlpool tubs surrounded by granite, wood
floors and skylights. The one-bedroom apartment offers a fully
equipped kitchen, a dining area, washer and dryer. Luxurious
comfortable surroundings include a great selection of current
books and an outdoor hot tub. The quiet hillside setting boasts
a flagstone walk with stone bench and finch feeder, a meadow,
fragrant cutting gardens and a fountain. Sit in an Adirondack
chair by the spring-fed pond or take an invigorating dip in the
cool water. Dine in the famous Moosewood Restaurant and ask
about the town's best new places to eat.
Innkeeper(s): Buzz Dolph and Nancy Norton. $110-175. 4 rooms with PB, 1
with FP, 2 suites, 1 cottage and 1 guest house. Types of meals: Full gourmet
bkfst. Beds: KQ. Modem hook-up, data port, cable TV, VCR, reading lamp,
CD player, refrigerator, ceiling fan, clock radio, telephone, coffeemaker, hot
tub/spa, voice mail, fireplace, washer and dryer, dishwasher, full kitchen and
dining area, Stickley and Amish furniture, hand-knotted Persian carpets and
library in room. Central air. Spa, swimming, library, parlor games and laundry
facility on premises. Limited handicap access. Antiquing, art galleries, bicycling, canoeing/kayaking, cross-country skiing, downhill skiing, fishing, golf,
hiking, horseback riding, live theater, museums, parks, shopping, sporting
events, tennis, water sports, wineries, Paleontolgy Research Institute -
Museum of the Earth, Sapsucker Woods Ornithology Lab, Friends of the
Library book sale, Angelhart Barn Sale, Grassroots Music Festival, Ithaca
Festival and Finger Lakes Wine Trail nearby.
Location: Country. Two miles from Cornell University and four miles from
Ithaca College. Quiet setting with pond and open meadow hillside.
Publicity: *Hideaways Spring/Summer 2004.*
Certificate may be used: Anytime, Sunday-Thursday.

Jay   C12

Book and Blanket B&B
Rt 9N, PO Box 164
Jay, NY 12941-0164
(518)946-8323
Internet: www.adirondackinns.com/bookandblanket/
E-mail: bookinnjay@aol.com

Circa 1860. This Adirondack bed & breakfast served as the
town's post office for many years and also as barracks for state
troopers. Thankfully, however, it is now a restful bed & breakfast catering to the literary set. Guest rooms are named for
authors and there are books in every nook and cranny of the
house. Guests may even take a book home with them. Each of
the guest rooms is comfortably furnished. The inn is a short
walk from the Jay Village Green and the original site of the
Historic Jay covered bridge.
Innkeeper(s): Kathy, Fred, Sam & Zoe the Basset Hound. $70-90. 3 rooms,
1 with PB. Breakfast, afternoon tea and snacks/refreshments included in
rates. Types of meals: Full bkfst, veg bkfst and early coffee/tea. Beds: QDT.
Reading lamp and clock radio in room. TV, VCR, library, parlor games, telephone, fireplace and whirlpool tub on premises. Antiquing, art galleries,
beach, bicycling, canoeing/kayaking, cross-country skiing, downhill skiing,
fishing, golf, hiking, parks, sporting events, tennis, water sports, Olympic
venues i.e. bobsled, luge, ski jump and ice skating nearby.
Location: Country, mountains, waterfront. Small hamlet.
Certificate may be used: Jan. 15 to June 20, Sunday-Thursday.

Keene Valley   C12

Trail's End Inn

Trail's End Rd, HC 01, Box 103
Keene Valley, NY 12943
(518)576-9860 (800)281-9860 Fax:(518)576-9235
Internet: www.trailsendinn.com
E-mail: innkeeper@trailsendinn.com

Circa 1902. This charming mountain inn is in the heart of the
Adirondack's High Peaks. Surrounded by woods and adjacent
to a small pond, the inn offers spacious guest rooms with
antique furnishings and country quilts. All-you-
can-eat morning meals in the glassed-
in breakfast room not only provide
a lovely look at the countryside,
but often a close-up view of various bird species. Fresh air and
gorgeous views abound, and visitors enjoy invigorating hikes, trout
fishing and fine cross-country skiing. Downhill skiers will love
the challenge of nearby White Mountain, with the longest verti-
cal drop in the East.

Innkeeper(s): Paul & Kristen Morrison. $49-125. 10 rooms, 6 with PB, 3
with FP, 2 suites and 1 cottage. Breakfast included in rates. Types of meals:
Full bkfst, early coffee/tea and picnic lunch. Beds: KQDT. Reading lamp, telephone, desk and guest kitchenette in room. VCR, fax, copier, library, child
care, parlor games and fireplace on premises. Antiquing, cross-country skiing,
downhill skiing, fishing, golf, parks, shopping, tennis, water sports, 1980
Olympic headquarters in Lake Placid, rock climbing, ice climbing and major
hiking trails nearby.

Location: Mountains.

Publicity: Outside, Mid-Atlantic and Lake Placid News.

"Felt like home. What a treasure we found."

Certificate may be used: Jan. 1-June 15 and Oct. 15-Dec. 31; Sunday
through Thursday, excluding holiday periods.

Lewiston   F3

The Little Blue Angel House

115 Center St
Lewiston, NY 14092-1537
(716)754-4963

Circa 1906. Located in the heart of the village's main street,
this Colonial inn offers charming accommodations and convenient access to area activities. Three unique guest rooms are
available, including a Chinese-themed room with a king bed
and a Victorian-style room with a queen bed. The inn's decor
includes antiques, collectibles and contemporary art. Ten minutes away are the American and Canadian Falls.

Innkeeper(s): Mary & Ken. $65-175. 3 rooms, 1 with PB, 1 suite. Breakfast
included in rates. Types of meals: Full gourmet bkfst. Beds: KQT. Cable TV,
reading lamp, ceiling fan and clock radio in room. Air conditioning. VCR,
spa, telephone and fireplace on premises. Amusement parks, antiquing,
cross-country skiing, fishing, live theater, parks, shopping and sporting
events nearby.

Location: Rural historic village.

Certificate may be used: Nov. 1-April 30, any day except holidays and special events.

Liverpool   F8

Ancestor's Inn at The Bassett House

215 Sycamore St
Liverpool, NY 13088
(888)866-8591
Internet: www.ancestorsinn.com
E-mail: innkeeper@ancestorsinn.com

Circa 1862. Early local residents, George and Hannah Bassett
built this Italianate home. The innkeepers call the home
Ancestor's Inn because guest rooms are named after a special
relative. Valentine's Room includes a double whirlpool tub. A
hearty, full breakfast is served each morning. Homemade granola, pastries and breads accompany the daily breakfast entree.
Complimentary beverages are available in a guest refrigerator.

Innkeeper(s): Mary & Dan Weidman. $70-115. 4 rooms with PB. Breakfast
included in rates. Types of meals: Full gourmet bkfst, early coffee/tea and afternoon tea. Beds: Q. TV, VCR, reading lamp, ceiling fan and clock radio in room.
Air conditioning. Library, parlor games, telephone, fireplace, movies available
and porch on premises. Antiquing, cross-country skiing, golf, live theater, parks,
shopping, sporting events, water sports and New York State Fair nearby.

Certificate may be used: Nov. 1 to May 1, Sunday-Thursday, holidays excluded.

Margaretville   H10

Margaretville Mountain Inn B&B and Village Suites

1478 Margaretville Mountain Rd
Margaretville, NY 12455-9735
(845)586-3933
Internet: www.margaretvilleinn.com
E-mail: mmibnb@catskill.net

Circa 1886. Reminiscent of the Victorian era, this home rests on
the site of the nation's first cauliflower farm. The owners have
restored the slate roof, elaborate exterior
woodwork and decorative interior woodwork. A full breakfast is served in the formal
dining room on English china, or guests can
enjoy the morning meal on the veranda,
which overlooks the Catskill Mountains. The
surrounding area offers a variety of activities
including antique shopping, ice skating, golf,
tennis, swimming, boating, fishing and hiking. The innkeepers offer ski packages.

Innkeeper(s): Carol & Peter Molnar. $65-300. 6 rooms with PB, 2 suites.
Breakfast included in rates. Types of meals: Full gourmet bkfst. Beds: KQDT. TV,
suites with fireplace, full kitchen and porch and patio in room. Fax and telephone
on premises. Cross-country skiing, downhill skiing, hiking and swimming nearby.

Publicity: Spotlight and NY Wedding.

*"Truly a step back in time to all that was charming, elegant and
wholesome—right here in the 20th century."*

Certificate may be used: Sunday-Thursday, non-holidays. Weekends only in
March, April and May.

Naples   G5

Monier Manor

154 N. Main Street
Naples, NY 14512
(585)374-6719 Fax:(585)374-9103
Internet: www.moniermanor.com
E-mail: monierma@rochester.rr.com

Circa 1850. Luxurious comfort is experienced at this showcase Victorian Italianate mansion that sits on more than two
scenic acres in the village. Bruce and Donna have recently fin-

ished extensive renovations. Their personal collection of Persian rugs adorns the refinished wood floors. New windows provide a sound and climate barrier, and the décor has been professionally designed. Relax by the upscale marble fireplace in the parlor or sip a glass of wine in the cupola overlooking the valley and mountains. Lavish guest bedrooms are incredibly large and feature many pleasurable refinements. Enjoy remote control fireplaces, satellite television with in-room movies, CD players and immense private bathrooms. Gourmet breakfasts are served in the very formal dining room. A guest refrigerator, microwave and coffeemaker are on the second floor. A nearby winery and local shops are an easy walk. Soak in the outdoor hot tub.

Innkeeper(s): Bruce & Donna Scott. $105-165. 4 rooms with PB, 4 with FP. Breakfast, afternoon tea and snacks/refreshments included in rates. Types of meals: Full bkfst and early coffee/tea. Beds: Q. Cable TV, reading lamp, clock radio and fireplace in room. Central air. Fax, spa, library, parlor games, telephone, refrigerator and snack bar located in main guest hallway upstairs on premises. Amusement parks, antiquing, art galleries, cross-country skiing, downhill skiing, fishing, golf, hiking, live theater, museums, parks, shopping, water sports and wineries nearby.

Location: Wine country.

Certificate may be used: Anytime, November-March, subject to availability, excluding holidays and holiday weekends.

Niagara Falls   F3

Cameo Inn

3881 Lower River Rd, Rt 18-F
Niagara Falls, NY 14174
(716)745-3034
Internet: www.cameoinn.com
E-mail: cameoinn@adelphia.net

Circa 1860. This Colonial Revival inn offers a restful setting ideal for those seeking a peaceful getaway. The inn's three secluded acres add to its romantic setting, as does an interior that features several fireplaces. Visitors select from three suites, which feature private sun rooms, or two guest rooms that share a bath. Popular spots with guests include the library, great room and solarium. Fort Niagara and several state parks are nearby, and the American and Canadian Falls are within easy driving distance of the inn. The inn is actually located about eight miles north of Niagara Falls near the village of Youngstown.

Innkeeper(s): Gregory Fisher. $75-175. 5 rooms. Breakfast included in rates. Types of meals: Full bkfst. Beds: QDT. TV in room. Air conditioning. Amusement parks, antiquing, cross-country skiing, downhill skiing, fishing, live theater, shopping, sporting events and water sports nearby.

Publicity: *Country Folk Art, Esquire, Journey, Seaway Trail, Waterways and Buffalo News.*

"I made the right choice when I selected Cameo."

Certificate may be used: Anytime Nov. 15-April 30; Sunday-Thursday, May 1-Nov. 14, holidays and special event periods excluded. All subject to availability.

The Cameo Inn

4710 Lower River Rd, Rt 18-F
Niagara Falls, NY 14174
(716)745-3034
Internet: www.cameoinn.com
E-mail: info@cameoinn.com

Circa 1875. This classic Queen Anne Victorian inn offers a breathtaking view of the lower Niagara River. Located on the Seaway Trail, the inn offers convenient access to sightseeing in this popular region. The inn's interior features family heirlooms

and period antiques, and visitors choose from four guest rooms, including a three-room suite overlooking the river. Breakfast is served buffet-style, and the entrees, which change daily, may include German oven pancakes or Grand Marnier French toast. Area attractions include Old Fort Niagara, outlet malls and several state parks.

Innkeeper(s): Gregory Fisher. $65-115. 4 rooms, 2 with PB, 1 suite. Breakfast included in rates. Types of meals: Full bkfst. Beds: QDT. Cable TV, reading lamp and ceiling fan in room. TV, telephone and fireplace on premises. Amusement parks, antiquing, cross-country skiing, downhill skiing, fishing, live theater, shopping, sporting events and water sports nearby.

Publicity: *Country Folk Art, Esquire, Journey, Seaway Trail, Waterways and Buffalo News.*

"I made the right choice when I selected Cameo."

Certificate may be used: Anytime Nov. 15-April 30; Sunday through Thursday May 1-Nov. 14. Holidays and special event periods excluded. All subject to availability.

Penn Yan   G6

Fox Inn

158 Main St
Penn Yan, NY 14527-1201
(315)536-1100 (800)901-7997
Internet: www.foxinnbandb.com
E-mail: cliforr@aol.com

Circa 1820. Experience the pleasant elegance of a fine, historic home at this Greek Revival Inn. Furnished with Empire antiques, the accommodations include a living room with marble fireplace, sun porch, parlor with billiards table and formal rose gardens. Five guest rooms and one two-bedroom suite each have private baths. The gourmet breakfast provides a selection of six different types of pancakes served with fresh blueberries or raspberries and four varieties of French toast. Located near the Windmill Farm Market, the largest farm market in New York, you can spend a casual day shopping or visiting nearby museums or wineries. Or, enjoy more active alternatives such as biking, hiking and picnicking or boating on Keuka Lake.

Innkeeper(s): Cliff & Michele Orr. $109-173. 6 rooms with PB, 1 with FP, 1 suite and 1 conference room. Breakfast included in rates. Types of meals: Full gourmet bkfst and early coffee/tea. Beds: QD. Cable TV, VCR, clock radio, telephone, turn-down service and hot tub/spa in room. Air conditioning. Library, parlor games, fireplace and billiard table on premises. Amusement parks, antiquing, art galleries, beach, bicycling, canoeing/kayaking, cross-country skiing, downhill skiing, fishing, golf, hiking, horseback riding, live theater, museums, parks, shopping, tennis, water sports and wineries nearby.

Publicity: *Inn Times "Top 50 Inns in America Award."*

Certificate may be used: Anytime, December-April, subject to availability.

The Wagener Estate B&B

351 Elm St
Penn Yan, NY 14527-1446
(315)536-4591 Fax:(315)531-8142
Internet: www.wagenerestate.com
E-mail: wagener-estate@wagenerestate.com

Circa 1794. Nestled in the Finger Lakes area on four shaded acres, this 15-room house features a wicker-furnished veranda where guests can relax in solitude or chat with others. Some of the early hand-hewn framing and the original brick fireplace and oven can be seen in the Family Room at the north end of the house. Most of the land, which is known as Penn Yan, was once owned by the original occupants of the home, David Wagener and his wife, Rebecca. David died in 1799, leaving

this property to his son, Squire Wagener, who is considered to be the founder of Penn Yan. Some rooms include air conditioning and a television. Gift certificates are available.

Innkeeper(s): Lisa & Ken Greenwood. $75-95. 6 rooms, 4 with PB. Breakfast included in rates. Types of meals: Full bkfst. Beds: KQDT. Some with TV in room. Parlor games on premises. Antiquing, cross-country skiing, fishing, parks, water sports and wineries nearby.

Publicity: *Finger Lakes Times, Chronicle Express and New York Times.*

"Thanks so much for the wonderful hospitality and the magnificent culinary treats."

Certificate may be used: Dec. 1 to April 15, Sunday-Friday.

Queensbury   E12

The Crislip's B&B

693 Ridge Rd
Queensbury, NY 12804-6901
(518)793-6869
E-mail: nedbc1938@att.net

Circa 1802. This Federal-style house was built by Quakers and was once owned by the area's first doctor, who used it as a training center for young interns. There's an acre of lawns and annual gardens and a Victorian Italianate veranda overlooks the Green Mountains. The inn is furnished with 18th-century antiques and reproductions, including four-poster canopy beds and highboys. There's a keeping room with a huge fireplace. Historic stone walls flank the property.

Innkeeper(s): Ned & Joyce Crislip. $75-90. 3 rooms with PB. Breakfast included in rates. Types of meals: Full bkfst and early coffee/tea. Beds: KD. Reading lamp in room. Air conditioning. Telephone and fireplace on premises. Amusement parks, antiquing, cross-country skiing, downhill skiing, fishing, live theater, parks, shopping, sporting events, water sports and civic center nearby.

Location: Mountains.

Certificate may be used: November through May, Sunday-Thursday.

Red Hook   H12

The Grand Dutchess

7571 Old Post Rd
Red Hook, NY 12571-1403
(845)758-5818 Fax:(845)758-3143
Internet: www.granddutchess.com
E-mail: grandut@worldnet.att.net

Circa 1874. This Second Empire Victorian was originally built as the Hoffman Inn. It later served as the town school, a speakeasy and then a lonely hearts club. Twin parlors behind etched-glass and wood sliding doors feature hardwood floors, antique chandeliers, arched marble fireplaces with massive carved mirrors, Oriental rugs and heirloom antiques. Lace curtains decorate the floor-to-ceiling windows. Most of the rooms have queen-size beds and private baths and are located at the corners of the home to maximize the use of natur-

al light. A full breakfast of homemade breads, a main dish, cereal and fruit is offered. For young guests, the innkeeper will prepare chocolate chip pancakes.

Innkeeper(s): Elizabeth Pagano & Harold Gruber. $95-155. 6 rooms, 4 with PB, 1 suite and 1 conference room. Breakfast included in rates. Types of meals: Full gourmet bkfst, early coffee/tea and snacks/refreshments. Beds: KQDT. Reading lamp and clock radio in room. Air conditioning. VCR, fax, copier, library, parlor games and telephone on premises. Antiquing, cross-country skiing, fishing, golf, live theater, parks, shopping, tennis, historic homes and Rhinebeck Aerodrome nearby.

Location: City, country, mountains, ocean community, waterfront. Town.

Publicity: *Northeast, Gazette Advertiser, Poughkeepsie Journal and "The Eleanor Affair" an award-winning short film.*

"This place is outrageous! We love this place!"

Certificate may be used: Jan. 2-March 31, subject to availability. April 1-Jan. 1, Sunday-Thursday, subject to availability.

Rhinebeck   I12

Olde Rhinebeck Inn

340 Wurtemburg Rd
Rhinebeck, NY 12572
(845)871-1745 Fax:(845)876-8809
Internet: www.rhinebeckinn.com
E-mail: innkeeper@rhinebeckinn.com

Circa 1745. Located on three acres, this is a beautifully maintained early colonial farmhouse. The original buttermilk blue finishes remain and there is original hardware throughout. The innkeeper provides fine linens, antiques, fresh flowers and a breakfast that is served in the historic dining room. Offerings include sweet potato frittata, baked French pear and apple butter maple pecan muffins. Ther is a bass-stocked pond on the property.

Innkeeper(s): Jonna Paolella. $195-295. 4 rooms with PB, 1 with WP. Breakfast included in rates. Types of meals: Full bkfst and afternoon tea. Beds: Q. Reading lamp and satellite TV in room. Air conditioning. VCR, fax, parlor games, telephone and fireplace on premises. Antiquing, golf, parks and shopping nearby.

Location: Country. three miles south of historic village.

Publicity: *Country Living.*

Certificate may be used: Sunday-Thursday, Nov. 1-May 15.

Rochester   F5

428 Mount Vernon

428 Mount Vernon Ave
Rochester, NY 14620-2710
(585)271-0792 (800)836-3159
Internet: www.428mtvernon.com

Circa 1917. Victorian furnishings and decor grace the interior of this stately Irish manor house. Set on two lush acres of shade trees and foliage, this secluded spot is perfect for guests in search of relaxation. Guests can create their morning meals from a varied breakfast menu. The inn is adjacent to Highland Park, great walking park and conservatory.

Innkeeper(s): Philip & Claire Lanzatella. $125. 7 rooms with PB and 1 conference room. Breakfast included in rates. Types of meals: Full gourmet bkfst and early coffee/tea. Beds: QDT. Cable TV, reading lamp, ceiling fan, clock radio, telephone, turn-down service and desk in room. Air conditioning. Parlor games and fireplace on premises. Antiquing, cross-country skiing, live theater, parks, shopping, Annual Lilac Festival, University of Rochester and Rochester Institute of Technology and Museum nearby.

Location: City.

"Everything was wonderful, they took care in every detail."

Certificate may be used: Jan. 15-April 1, Sunday-Thursday.

A B&B at Dartmouth House

215 Dartmouth Street
Rochester, NY 14607-3202
(585)271-7872 (800)724-6298 Fax:(585)473-0778
Internet: www.DartmouthHouse.com
E-mail: stay@DartmouthHouse.com

Circa 1905. The lavish, four-course breakfasts served daily at this beautiful turn-of-the-century Edwardian home are unforgettable. Innkeeper and award-winning, gourmet cook Ellie Klein starts off the meal with special fresh juice, which is served in the parlor. From this point, guests are seated at the candlelit dining table to enjoy a series of delectable dishes, such as poached pears, a mouth-watering entree, a light, lemon ice and a rich dessert. And each of the courses is served on a separate pattern of Depression Glass. If the breakfast isn't enough, Ellie and husband, Bill, an electrical engineer, have stocked the individually decorated bathrooms with  fluffy towels and bathrobes and guests can soak in inviting clawfoot tubs. Each of the bedchambers boasts antique collectibles and fresh flowers. The inn is located in the prestigious turn-of-the-century Park Avenue Historical and Cultural District. The entire area is an architect's dream. Museums, colleges, Eastman School of Music, Highland Park, restaurants and antique shops are among the many nearby attractions.

Innkeeper(s): Ellie & Bill Klein. $125-150. 4 rooms with PB, 1 two-bedroom suite. Breakfast, afternoon tea and snacks/refreshments included in rates. Types of meals: Full gourmet bkfst, veg bkfst and early coffee/tea. Beds: KQT. Modem hook-up, data port, cable TV, VCR, reading lamp, refrigerator, ceiling fan, clock radio, telephone, coffeemaker, desk, WiFi DSL, fluffy robes, movie library, lighted makeup mirrors, new pillowtop mattresses, lots of pillows and comfortable chairs in room. Central air. Fax, copier, bicycles, library, parlor games and fireplace on premises. Amusement parks, antiquing, art galleries, beach, bicycling, canoeing/kayaking, cross-country skiing, fishing, golf, hiking, live theater, museums, parks, shopping, tennis, water sports, wineries, George Eastman International Museum of Photography, Park Avenue, Memorial Art Gallery, Rochester Museum and Science Center, boutiques, cafes and book sellers nearby.
Location: City. Cultural & historic district.
Publicity: *Democrat & Chronicle, DAKA, Genesee Country, Seaway Trail, Oneida News, Travelers News, Country Living* and *The New York Times Travel Section.*

"The food was fabulous, the company fascinating, and the personal attention beyond comparison. You made me feel at home instantly."

Certificate may be used: Jan. 31-April 1, Monday through Thursday, two-night minimum stay.

The Edward Harris House B&B Inn

35 Argyle Street
Rochester, NY 14607
(585)473-9752 (800)419-1213 Fax:(585)473-9752
Internet: www.edwardharrishousebb.com
E-mail: ehhbb@aol.com

Circa 1896. Acclaimed as one of the finest early examples of architect Claude Bragdon's work, this Georgian mansion is a restored Landmark home. Its history only enhances the rich warmth, and the immense size reflects a cozy ambiance. Relax in a leather chair in the traditional library. Antiques and collectibles combine well with florals and chintz for a touch of romance. Two guest bedrooms and the Garden Suite boast fireplaces. Four-poster rice beds and hand-painted furniture add to the individual decorating styles. A gourmet candlelight breakfast is served in the formal dining room on crystal and china or on the brick garden patio. The night before, choose a main entree from a seasonal menu offering seven or eight items. Enjoy afternoon tea on the wicker-filled front porch. A plethora of historic sites, including The George Eastman House and Strong Museum, are within a one-mile range.

Innkeeper(s): Susan Alvarez. $125-150. 5 rooms, 4 with PB, 3 with FP, 2 suites and 1 conference room. Breakfast included in rates. Types of meals: Full gourmet bkfst, veg bkfst, early coffee/tea, afternoon tea, snacks/refreshments and room service. Beds: KQDT. Data port, cable TV, reading lamp, stereo, refrigerator, ceiling fan, clock radio, telephone, coffeemaker, turn-down service, desk and fireplace in room. Air conditioning. VCR, fax, copier, library, parlor games, fireplace, laundry facility and small kitchen on guest room level on premises. Limited handicap access. Amusement parks, antiquing, art galleries, beach, bicycling, canoeing/kayaking, cross-country skiing, downhill skiing, fishing, golf, hiking, horseback riding, live theater, museums, parks, shopping, sporting events, tennis, water sports and wineries nearby.
Location: City. Nestled within the Arts/Cultural District of Rochester.
Certificate may be used: Anytime, subject to availability.

Saratoga Springs   F12

Apple Tree B&B

49 W High St
Ballston Spa, NY 12020-1912
(518)885-1113 Fax:(518)885-9758
Internet: www.appletreebb.com
E-mail: mail@appletreebb.com

Circa 1878. A pond, waterfall and a garden decorate the entrance to this Second Empire Victorian, which is located in the historic district of Ballston Spa, a village just a few minutes from Saratoga Springs. Guest rooms feature Victorian and French-country decor, and each  has antiques and whirlpool tubs. Guests enjoy fresh fruit, homemade baked goods, a selection of beverages and a daily entree during the breakfast service.

Innkeeper(s): Dolores & Jim Taisey. $100-175. 5 rooms with PB. Breakfast included in rates. Types of meals: Full bkfst and early coffee/tea. Beds: Q. Cable TV, VCR, reading lamp, refrigerator, clock radio and whirlpool in room. Central air. Parlor games, telephone and fireplace on premises. Amusement parks, antiquing, cross-country skiing, downhill skiing, fishing, live theater, parks, shopping, sporting events, water sports and Saratoga Race Course nearby.
Location: Village (historic district).
Publicity: *Country Folk Art Magazine.*
Certificate may be used: Midweek, Sunday-Thursday, January-April.

Country Life B&B

67 Tabor Road
Saratoga Springs, NY 12834
(518)692-7203 (888)692-7203 Fax:(518)692-9203
Internet: www.countrylifebb.com
E-mail: stay@countrylifebb.com

Circa 1829. Near the Battenkill River in the Adirondack foothills, this Flat Front farmhouse sits on 118 acres surrounded by rolling hills. Filled with antiques and traditional furnishings, romantic guest bedrooms feature comfortable terry robes, sherry and candy. A free breakfast is a delicious way to begin the day. Relax on three acres of groomed lawn with flower gardens, a two-person hammock and a porch swing. The bridge across an old mill stream leads to woodland trails. Swim in the ponds with two waterfalls and a rock slide.

Innkeeper(s): Wendy & Richard Duvall. $85-175. 4 rooms with PB. Breakfast and snacks/refreshments included in rates. Types of meals: Country bkfst, veg bkfst and early coffee/tea. Beds: KQ. TV, reading lamp, ceiling fan, clock radio, turn-down service, terry cloth robes, sherry, candy, extra blankets and pillows in room. Air conditioning. Fax, swimming, bicycles, library, child care, parlor games, telephone, fireplace and coffeemaker on premises. Limited handicap access. Antiquing, art galleries, beach, bicycling, canoeing/kayaking, cross-country skiing, downhill skiing, fishing, golf, hiking, horseback riding, live theater, museums, parks and shopping nearby.

Location: Country, mountains. In the Adirondack foothills, near Saratoga Springs.

Publicity: *Long Island Newsday, Inn Times, NY Times, Country Extra, Long Island Lifestyles Magazine, Washington County Magazine, Glens Falls Business News, ABC TV-Weekend Report and CBS-TV This Morning.*

Certificate may be used: Anytime, November to May, subject to availability. Can not be combined with any other special offers.

Westchester House B&B

102 Lincoln Ave, PO Box 944
Saratoga Springs, NY 12866-4536
(518)587-7613 (800)581-7613 Fax:(518)583-9562
Internet: www.westchesterhousebandb.com
E-mail: innkeepers@westchesterhousebandb.com

Circa 1885. This gracious Queen Anne Victorian has been welcoming vacationers for more than 100 years. Antiques from four generations of the Melvin family grace the high-ceilinged rooms.

Oriental rugs top gleaming wood floors, while antique clocks and lace curtains set a graceful tone. Guests gather on the wraparound porch, in the parlors or gardens for an afternoon refreshment of old-fashioned lemonade. Most attractions are within walking distance.

Innkeeper(s): Bob & Stephanie Melvin. $180-350. 7 rooms with PB and 1 conference room. Breakfast and afternoon tea included in rates. Types of meals: Cont plus and early coffee/tea. Beds: KQT. Reading lamp, ceiling fan, clock radio, telephone, desk, data port and voice mail in room. Air conditioning. TV, fax, copier, library and baby grand piano on premises. Antiquing, cross-country skiing, fishing, live theater, parks, shopping, sporting events, water sports, opera, ballet, horse racing, race track and Saratoga Performing Arts Center nearby.

Location: City. Upstate New York small town.

Publicity: *Getaways for Gourmets, Albany Times Union, Saratogian, Capital, Country Inns, New York Daily News, WNYT, Newsday and Hudson Valley.*

"I adored your B&B and have raved about it to all. One of the most beautiful and welcoming places we've ever visited."

Certificate may be used: Sunday-Thursday, April-June 15, September, November, excluding holiday weekends.

Severance D12

The Red House

PO Box 125
Severance, NY 12872-0125
(518)532-7734
Internet: www.lakeparadoxclub.com
E-mail: redhouselpc@aol.com

Circa 1850. Twenty feet from the banks of Paradox Brook, on the West end of Paradox Lake, is this two-story farmhouse inn that boasts a multitude of recreational offerings for its guests, including swimming, tennis, boating and fishing. The inn features three guest rooms, one with private bath. The inn's full breakfasts include homemade breads and regional specialties. Be sure to plan a day trip to Fort Ticonderoga and ride the ferry

across Lake Champlain to Vermont. Hiking and cross-country skiing are available nearby

Innkeeper(s): Helen Wildman. $80-100. 3 rooms, 1 with PB. Breakfast included in rates. Types of meals: Full bkfst. Beds: KQT. Reading lamp, clock radio, telephone and desk in room. Parlor games and fireplace on premises. Golf, hiking and canoeing nearby.

Location: Country, mountains. By brook.

"Thanks for your wonderful hospitality, we'll definitely be back again."

Certificate may be used: Anytime, subject to availability.

Sharon Springs G11

Edgefield

P.O. Box 152
Sharon Springs, NY 13459-0152
(518)284-3339
Internet: www.sharonsprings.com/edgefield.htm
E-mail: dmwood71@hotmail.com

Circa 1865. This home has seen many changes. It began as a farmhouse, a wing was added in the 1880s, and by the turn of the century, sported an elegant Greek Revival facade. Edgefield is one of a collection of nearby homes used as a family compound for summer vacations. The rooms are decorated with traditional furnishings in a formal English-country style. In the English tradition, afternoon tea is presented with cookies and tea sandwiches. Sharon Springs includes many historic sites, and the town is listed in the National Register.

Innkeeper(s): Daniel Marshall Wood. $125-185. 5 rooms with PB. Breakfast, afternoon tea, hors d'oeuvres and wine included in rates. Types of meals: Full gourmet bkfst and early coffee/tea. Beds: QT. Reading lamp, ceiling fan, clock radio, turn-down service and desk in room. Air conditioning. Library, fireplace, antique furnishings and veranda on premises. Antiquing, cross-country skiing, golf, hiking, live theater, museums, parks, shopping, water sports, wineries and Glimmerglass Opera nearby.

Location: Village.

Publicity: *Conde Nast Traveler (Oct. 2003), Colonial Homes Magazine, Philadelphia Inquirer and Boston Globe.*

"Truly what I always imagined the perfect B&B experience to be!"

Certificate may be used: Sept. 8-30, Oct. 20-June 30, Sunday-Thursday.

Sodus E6

Maxwell Creek Inn

7563 Lake Rd
Sodus, NY 14551-9309
(315)483-2222 (800)315-2206
Internet: www.maxwellcreekinn-bnb.com
E-mail: mcinnbnb@att.net

Circa 1846. Located on the shores of Lake Ontario, this historic cobblestone house rests on six acres and is surrounded by a woodland wildlife preserve and apple orchards. On the Seaway Trail near Sodus Bay, the property includes a historic grist mill and is rumored to have been a part of the Underground Railroad. Stroll through the apple orchards to the lake or enjoy the fishing stream, tennis courts and hiking trails. Maxwell Creek's spacious accommodations are comprised of five guest rooms in the main house, including a honeymoon

suite. The Cobblestone Cottage, an original carriage house, offers two efficiency suites popular for families and groups. Guests are treated to a full breakfast served by candlelight in a rustic wood-paneled dining room warmed by a unique fireplace.

Innkeeper(s): Patrick & Belinda McElroy. $93-168. 7 rooms with PB, 2 suites and 1 cottage. Breakfast included in rates. Types of meals: Full gourmet bkfst. Beds: KQDT. Reading lamp and desk in room. Tennis, library, parlor games, telephone, fishing creek and hiking on premises. Amusement parks, antiquing, canoeing/kayaking, cross-country skiing, downhill skiing, fishing, hiking, parks, shopping, water sports, fall foliage train rides and snowmobiling nearby.

Location: Waterfront. Country-resort.

Publicity: *Atlanta Journal and Newman Times.*

"The best food I've ever tasted."

Certificate may be used: Anytime, November-April, subject to availability.

Southampton   K15

1 Evergreen On Pine

89 Pine St
Southampton, NY 11968-4945
(631)283-0564 (877)824-6600 Fax:(631)287-1741
Internet: www.evergreenonpine.com

Circa 1860. Guests enjoy a short walk to the beach from this two-and-a-half-story cottage, tucked behind an arched hedge and shaded by tall trees. Located in the middle of the village, the bed and breakfast offers guests a front porch and a patio for relaxing. Guest rooms are comfortable and welcoming. Breakfast is continental style and features cereal, muffins and fruit. Nearby Main Street is lined with unique shops and restaurants and a number of antique shops. Visit the area's wineries or glean fresh local produce from the popular fruit and vegetable stands when not strolling the beach.

Innkeeper(s): Stephanie & Michael Hunn. $100-450. 5 rooms with PB, 1 suite. Breakfast included in rates. Types of meals: Cont and early coffee/tea. Beds: QD. Cable TV, refrigerator, ceiling fan, clock radio, telephone and coffeemaker in room. Air conditioning. Fax, copier and fireplace on premises. Antiquing, art galleries, beach, bicycling, canoeing/kayaking, fishing, golf, hiking, horseback riding, live theater, museums, parks, shopping and wineries nearby.

Location: Country, ocean community.

Certificate may be used: October to May, Sunday-Thursday.

Mainstay

579 Hill St
Southampton, NY 11968-5305
(631)283-4375 Fax:(631)287-6240
Internet: www.themainstay.com
E-mail: elizmain@hamptons.com

Circa 1870. This Colonial has served as a guest house, country store and now a bed & breakfast with eight guest rooms. Antiques, including iron beds, decorate the bedchambers. One suite includes a clawfoot tub. A decanter of sherry has been placed in each guest room. Several walls feature hand-painted murals. There is a swimming pool for guest use, as well as beach access.

Innkeeper(s): Elizabeth Main. $100-450. 8 rooms with PB, 2 suites. Breakfast included in rates. Types of meals: Cont. Beds: KQDT. Reading lamp and ceiling fan in room. Fax, telephone and fireplace on premises. Antiquing, fishing, golf, live theater, parks, shopping, tennis and water sports nearby.

Location: Ocean community.

Publicity: *New York Times.*

Certificate may be used: Anytime, November-March, subject to availability.

Stanfordville   I12

Lakehouse Inn on Golden Pond

Shelley Hill Rd
Stanfordville, NY 12581
(845)266-8093 Fax:(845)266-4051
Internet: www.lakehouse-rhinebeck.com
E-mail: judy@lakehouse-rhinebeck.com

Circa 1990. Romance abounds at this secluded contemporary home, which is surrounded by breathtaking vistas of woods and Golden Pond. Rest beneath a canopy flanked by lacy curtains as you gaze out the window. Enjoy a long, relaxing bath, or take a stroll around the 22-acre grounds. Each guest room includes a fireplace and whirlpool tub, and most include decks. The decor is a mix with a hint of Victorian, some Asian influences and modern touches that highlight the oak floors and vaulted pine ceilings. The innkeepers start off the day with a gourmet breakfast delivered to your room in a covered basket. Historic mansions and wineries are among the nearby attractions.

Innkeeper(s): Judy & Rich Kohler. $125-675. 10 rooms with PB, 7 with FP, 7 suites. Breakfast included in rates. Beds: KQ. VCR, reading lamp, CD player, refrigerator, ceiling fan, clock radio, telephone and hot tub/spa in room. Air conditioning. TV, fax, copier, parlor games, fireplace and video library on premises. Antiquing, cross-country skiing, fishing, live theater, parks, shopping, sporting events, water sports and boating nearby.

Location: Waterfront.

Publicity: *Newsday, New York Post, New York Magazine and Country Living.*

Certificate may be used: Monday, Tuesday, Wednesday, excluding holidays.

Syracuse   F8

Bed and Breakfast at Giddings Garden

290 West Seneca Tnpke.
Syracuse, NY 13207-2639
(315)492-6389 (800)377-3452
Internet: www.giddingsgarden.com
E-mail: giddingsb-b@webtv.net

Circa 1810. Once a prestigious tavern, this two-hundred-year-old Federal-style inn has been restored to include the many original chandeliers and rich douglas fir floors while adding upscale details and amenities. Spacious guest bedrooms feature handpicked antique furnishings and collectibles. Marble baths and floor-to ceiling mirrored showers add to the elegance. Savor a creative gourmet breakfast and enjoy refreshments any time at the complimentary guest station with well-stocked refrigerator and microwave. Sip a glass of wine on the old stone patio or stroll the one-acre grounds that are accented by beautifully landscaped gardens, fish ponds and park benches. Downtown and the university are just five minutes away. Skaneateles Lake and the many wineries of the Finger Lakes are also nearby.

Innkeeper(s): Pat & Nancie Roberts. $90-225. 5 rooms with PB, 2 with FP, 1 with HT, 1 two-bedroom suite and 1 guest house. Breakfast and snacks/refreshments included in rates. Types of meals: Full gourmet bkfst, veg bkfst and early coffee/tea. Beds: Q. Modem hook-up, cable TV, VCR, reading lamp, CD player, refrigerator, snack bar, clock radio, telephone, coffeemaker, desk, hot tub/spa, fireplace, HBO, Internet access, VCR/DVD in West Wing, some with microwave, fax and copier in room. Air conditioning. Fax, copier, complimentary refreshment center, free local calls, off-street parking, concierge services and early and/or bagged breakfast available on premises. Antiquing, cross-country skiing, downhill skiing, fishing, golf, hiking, horseback riding, live theater, museums, parks, shopping, sporting events, tennis, water sports, wineries, Coors Light Baloon Fest, Jazz Fest, Blues Fest, Rosamond Gifford Zoo and Skaneateles Music Festival nearby.

Location: City.

Publicity: *Onondaga Historical Home Tour (featured home).*

Certificate may be used: Jan. 30 to Dec. 20, Sunday-Friday subject to availability, holidays excluded.

Troy   G12

Olde Judge Mansion B&B

3300 6th Ave
Troy, NY 12180-1206
(518)274-5698 (866)653-5834
Internet: www.oldejudgemansion.com
E-mail: ojm@nycap.rr.com

Circa 1892. Experience the Victorian splendor of oak woodwork, 12-foot ceilings, pocket doors and embossed tin walls at this Gothic Italianate built in 1892. In the oak archway entry, view the photos displayed of historic Troy. Gather in the formal parlor to converse by the glow of kerosene lamps. An inviting Lazy Boy is perfect for video watching in the TV room. A sunny sitting room features reading materials and a chest stocked with forgotten conveniences. Kitchen privileges and laundry facilities are available. A stained-glass Newel Post Lamp on the ornate staircase leads to the comfortable guest bedrooms which are all on the second floor. Enjoy a casual, self-serve expanded continental breakfast buffet in the dining room. Shoot pool, play traditional feather, baseball or electric darts in the recreation/game room.

Innkeeper(s): Christina A. Urzan. $46-65. 5 rooms, 3 with PB. Breakfast, afternoon tea and snacks/refreshments included in rates. Types of meals: Full bkfst and early coffee/tea. Beds: KQDT. Cable TV, VCR, ceiling fan, clock radio, telephone and broadband hook-up in room. Air conditioning. Fax, parlor games, laundry facility and Jacuzzi in shared bathroom on premises. Antiquing, fishing, golf, museums, parks, shopping, tennis and year-round ice skating nearby.

Location: City.

Publicity: *Onondaga Historical Home Tour (featured home).*

Certificate may be used: Anytime.

Utica   F9

Adam Bowman Manor

197 Riverside Dr
Utica, NY 13502-2322
(315)738-0276 Fax:(315)738-0276
E-mail: bargood@msn.com

Circa 1823. The founder of Deerfield, George Weaver, built this graceful brick Federal house for his daughter. It is said to have been a part of the Underground Railroad (there's a secret tunnel) and is in the National Register. Handsomely landscaped grounds include a fountain, a gazebo, tall oaks and borders of perennials. The late Duke and Dutchess of Windsor were guests here and there are rooms named for them. The Duke's room has French-country furniture, a hand-painted fireplace and a King bed. Enjoy the Drawing Room and library, and in the morning guests are offered a full breakfast in the elegantly appointed dining room.

Innkeeper(s): Marion & Barry Goodwin. $40-75. 4 rooms, 2 with PB, 2 with FP. Breakfast included in rates. Types of meals: Full bkfst. Beds: KQD. Reading lamp, clock radio and desk in room. Air conditioning. VCR, fax, library, parlor games, telephone and fireplace on premises. Antiquing, cross-country skiing, downhill skiing, golf, live theater, parks, shopping, tennis and water sports nearby.

Location: City.

"Great company, good food and new friends for us."

Certificate may be used: Anytime except months of May, September and October.

Warrensburg   E12

The Cornerstone Victorian B&B

3921 Main St, Route 9
Warrensburg, NY 12885-1149
(518)623-3308 Fax:(518)623-3979
Internet: www.cornerstonevictorian.com
E-mail: stay@cornerstonevictorian.com

Circa 1904. Replete with gleaming woodwork and polished interior columns, this large wood and stone Victorian home has a wraparound porch overlooking Hackensack Mountain. Inside are stained-glass windows, Victorian furnishings, three terracotta fireplaces and a beautiful cherry staircase. Awake each morning to a candlelight breakfast complete with homemade morning cakes, Louise's famous granola and other gourmet entrees. Simply ask the innkeepers, with their 25-year experience in the hospitality field, and they can help you plan your leisure activities in the Lake George/Adirondack and Saratoga Springs area.

Innkeeper(s): Doug & Louise Goettsche. $85-175. 5 rooms with PB, 1 with FP and 1 conference room. Breakfast included in rates. Types of meals: Full bkfst and early coffee/tea. Beds: Q. Ceiling fan and hair dryer in room. Air conditioning. VCR, fax, copier and bicycles on premises. Amusement parks, antiquing, cross-country skiing, downhill skiing, fishing, golf, hiking, live theater, museums, parks, shopping, tennis and water sports nearby.

Location: Mountains.

Certificate may be used: Sunday-Thursday nights, excluding peak season, holiday periods and special rates.

Country Road Lodge B&B

115 Hickory Hill Rd
Warrensburg, NY 12885-3912
(518)623-2207 Fax:(518)623-4363
Internet: www.countryroadlodge.com
E-mail: mail@countryroadlodge.com

Circa 1929. Originally built for a local businessman as a simple "camp," this bed & breakfast has expanded to offer comfortable accommodations. At the end of a short country road in a secluded setting on the Hudson River, 40 acres of woodlands and fields are surrounded by a state forest preserve. Common rooms boast panoramic views of the river and the Adirondack Mountains. After a restful night's sleep, enjoy homemade bread and muffins in the dining room while selecting from the breakfast menu. Nature walks, bird watching, hiking and cross-country skiing are just out the front door.

Innkeeper(s): Sandi & Steve Parisi. $72-82. 4 rooms, 2 with PB, 1 two-bedroom suite. Breakfast included in rates. Types of meals: Country bkfst, veg bkfst and early coffee/tea. Beds: KQT. Reading lamp and ceiling fan in room. Air conditioning. Library, parlor games, telephone, wood burning stove in common room, 24-hour hot and cold beverage counter, screened gazebo and Adirondack lawn chairs on premises. Amusement parks, antiquing, art galleries, beach, bicycling, canoeing/kayaking, cross-country skiing, downhill skiing, fishing, golf, hiking, horseback riding, live theater, museums, parks, shopping, tennis, whitewater rafting, snowshoeing, scenic drives, lake cruises, Colonial history sites and garage sales nearby.

Location: Country, mountains, waterfront.

Publicity: *North Jersey Herald & News, New York Times, Adirondack Journal and Christian Science Monitor.*

"Homey, casual atmosphere. We really had a wonderful time. You're both wonderful hosts and the Lodge is definitely our kind of B&B! We will always feel very special about this place and will always be back."

Certificate may be used: Anytime, Sunday-Thursday, excluding holidays. Not valid with other discount programs.

The Merrill Magee House

3 Hudson St PO Box 391
Warrensburg, NY 12885-0391
(518)623-2449 (888)664-4661 Fax:(518)623-3990
Internet: www.merrillmageehouse.com
E-mail: mmhinn1@capital.net

Circa 1834. This stately Greek Revival home offers beautiful
antique fireplaces in every guest room. The Sage, Rosemary,
Thyme and Coriander rooms feature sitting areas. The decor is
romantic and distinctly
Victorian. Romantic getaway
packages include candlelight
dinners. The local area hosts
art and craft festivals, an
antique car show, white-water
rafting and Gore Mountain
Oktoberfest. Tour the Adirondacks from the sky during
September's balloon festival or browse through the world's
largest garage sale in early October.

Innkeeper(s): Pam Converse. $125-165. 10 rooms with PB, 10 with FP, 1
guest house and 1 conference room. Breakfast included in rates. Types of
meals: Full gourmet bkfst, veg bkfst, early coffee/tea, picnic lunch and
gourmet dinner. Restaurant on premises. Beds: KQT. Reading lamp, clock
radio and fireplace in room. Central air. TV, VCR, swimming, library, parlor
games and telephone on premises. Handicap access. Amusement parks,
antiquing, art galleries, beach, bicycling, canoeing/kayaking, cross-country
skiing, downhill skiing, fishing, golf, hiking, horseback riding, live theater,
museums, parks, shopping, sporting events, tennis and water sports nearby.
Location: Country, mountains.

"A really classy and friendly operation—a real joy."
Certificate may be used: Oct. 15 to June 15, Monday-Friday.

Warwick   J11

Glenwood House B&B and Cottage Suites

49 Glenwood Rd
Warwick, NY 10969
(845)258-5066
Internet: www.glenwoodhouse.com
E-mail: info@glenwoodhouse.com

Circa 1855. Built prior to the Civil War, this restored Victorian
farmhouse is secluded on more than two picturesque acres in
New York's Pochuck Valley. The spacious front veranda is filled
with comfortable wicker furnishings, inviting guests to relax
and enjoy the country setting. Guest rooms are decorated with
a romantic flair. Three rooms include canopied beds. Deluxe
cottage suites include a whirlpool tub for two and a fireplace.
Seasonal, farm-fresh fruits start off the breakfast service, which
might include an entrée such as Texas-style French toast or buttermilk pancakes accompanied by bacon or sausage. The home
is close to ski areas, golf courses, wineries, historic home tours
and antique stores. The Appalachian Trail, Hudson River and
Greenwood Lake are other nearby attractions.

Innkeeper(s): Andrea & Kevin Colman. $110-295. 7 rooms with PB, 2 with FP,
3 suites and 2 cottages. Breakfast included in rates. Types of meals: Country
bkfst. Beds: KQD. Modem hook-up, cable TV, VCR, reading lamp, CD player,
refrigerator, ceiling fan, clock radio, desk, hot tub/spa, fireplace and Jacuzzi for
two in room. Air conditioning. Copier, spa, library, parlor games and telephone
on premises. Antiquing, art galleries, beach, downhill skiing, fishing, golf, hiking, horseback riding, live theater, parks, shopping, tennis, water sports, wineries, Mountain Creek Ski Resort and Water Park, Appalachian Trail, Holly Trail,
Artist's Open Studio Tour, Walkill River Wildlife Refuge and Famous Black Dirt
Region and 'Onion Capital of The World' nearby.
Location: Country, mountains.
Certificate may be used: Anytime, Sunday-Thursday, non-holiday.

Westfield   H2

Westfield House

7573 E Main Rd
Westfield, NY 14787
(877)299-7496 Fax:(716)326-2543
Internet: www.westfieldhousebnb.com
E-mail: whouse@adelphia.net

Circa 1840. This brick home was built as a homestead on a
large property of farmland and vineyards. The next owner constructed the impressive Greek Revival addition. The home also
served guests as a tea room and later as a family-style eatery.
Guests will enjoy the elegance of the past, which has been
wonderfully preserved at Westfield House. Breakfasts are served
on fine china and silver in the home's formal dining room.
Wintertime guests enjoy their morning meal in front of a warm
fire. Each of the rooms offers something special. The Hopson
Room includes a four-poster bed and high ceilings while the
Rowan Place boasts Gothic crystal windows that look out to
the maple trees. The Garden Room is another good choice and
features a handsome sleigh bed.

Innkeeper(s): Kathleen Grant and Marianne Heck. $75-130. 7 rooms with
PB, 2 suites and 1 conference room. Breakfast included in rates. Types of
meals: Full bkfst and snacks/refreshments. Beds: KQDT. TV, reading lamp,
refrigerator, clock radio and desk in room. Air conditioning. VCR, parlor
games and telephone on premises. Antiquing, cross-country skiing, downhill
skiing, fishing, golf, live theater, parks, water sports and Chautauqua
Institute nearby.
Location: Vineyards.
Publicity: *Canadian Leisure Ways and Seaway Trail.*

*"Your accommodations and hospitality are wonderful! Simply out-
standing. The living room changes its character by the hour."*
Certificate may be used: September to June, based on availability.

The William Seward Inn

6645 S Portage Rd
Westfield, NY 14787-9602
(716)326-4151 (800)338-4151 Fax:(716)326-4163
Internet: www.williamsewardinn.com
E-mail: wmseward@cecomet.net

Circa 1821. This two-story Greek Revival estate stands on a
knoll overlooking Lake Erie. Secretary of State Seward was a
Holland Land Company agent before becoming governor of
New York. He later served as Lincoln's Secretary of State and is
known for the Alaska Purchase. George Patterson bought
Seward's home and also became governor of New York. Most of
the mansion's furnishings are dated 1790 to 1870 from the
Sheraton-Victorian period.

Innkeeper(s): James & Debbie Dahlberg. $70-185. 12 rooms with PB, 2
with FP. Breakfast included in rates. Types of meals: Full bkfst and gourmet
dinner. Beds: KQT. TV, reading lamp, clock radio, desk, 4 with double Jacuzzi
and some with ceiling fans in room. Air conditioning. Fax, library, parlor
games, telephone and fireplace on premises. Handicap access. Amusement
parks, antiquing, cross-country skiing, downhill skiing, fishing, parks, shopping and water sports nearby.
Location: Country.
Publicity: *Intelligencer, Evening Observer, New York-Pennsylvania Collector,
Upstate New York Magazine, Pittsburgh Post-Gazette, Toronto Globe & Mail,
Lake Erie Magazine and Seaway Trail Magazine.*

*"The breakfasts are delicious. The solitude and your hospitality are
what the doctor ordered."*
Certificate may be used: Anytime, except Friday-Saturday, June 20 through
October, some holiday weekends.

Westport C12

The Victorian Lady

PO Box 88
Westport, NY 12993-0088
(518)962-2345 Fax:(518)962-2345
Internet: www.victorianladybb.com
E-mail: victorianlady@westelcom.com

Circa 1856. This Second Empire home features all the delicate elements of a true "Painted Lady," from the vivid color scheme to the Eastlake porch that graces the exterior. Delicate it's not, however, having stood for more than a century. Its interior is decked in peri-od style with antiques from this more gracious era. A proper afternoon tea is served, and breakfasts are served by can-dlelight. More than an acre of 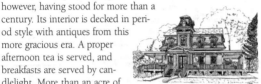 grounds, highlighted by English gardens, surround the home. Lake Champlain is a mere 100 yards from the front door.

Innkeeper(s): Doris & Wayne Deswert. $125-140. 4 rooms with PB. Breakfast and afternoon tea included in rates. Types of meals: Full gourmet bkfst and early coffee/tea. Beds: KQT. Reading lamp, ceiling fan, clock radio and desk in room. VCR, fax, copier, library, parlor games and telephone on premises. Antiquing, cross-country skiing, downhill skiing, fishing, golf, live theater, parks, shopping, tennis and water sports nearby.

Location: Historic village.

Publicity: Victorian Homes Magazine.

Certificate may be used: Anytime, May 29 to Oct. 15, subject to availability.

Wilmington C12

Willkommen Hof

Rt 86, PO Box 240
Wilmington, NY 12997
(518)946-7669 (800)541-9119 Fax:(518)946-7626
Internet: www.lakeplacid.net/willkommenhof
E-mail: willkommenhof@whiteface.net.

Circa 1910. This turn-of-the-century farmhouse served as an inn during the 1920s, but little else is known about its past. The innkeepers have created a cozy atmosphere, perfect for relaxation after a day exploring the Adirondack Mountain area. A large selection of books and a roaring fire greet  guests who choose to settle down in the reading room. The innkeepers also offer a large selection of movies. Relax in the sauna or outdoor spa or sim-ply enjoy the comfort of your bedchamber.

Innkeeper(s): Heike & Bert Yost. $50-165. 8 rooms, 3 with PB, 1 suite. Breakfast and afternoon tea included in rates. Types of meals: Full bkfst and dinner. Restaurant on premises. Beds: KQDT. TV, VCR, reading lamp, refriger-ator, ceiling fan, clock radio, coffeemaker, hot tub/spa and fireplace in room. Fax, copier, spa, sauna, library, parlor games, telephone and baby grand piano on premises. Amusement parks, antiquing, art galleries, beach, bicycling, canoeing/kayaking, cross-country skiing, downhill skiing, fishing, golf, hiking, horseback riding, live theater, museums, shopping and water sports nearby.

Location: Mountains.

"Vielen Dank! Alles war sehr schoen and the breakfasts were delicious."

Certificate may be used: Midweek, non-holiday, year-round.

Windham H11

Albergo Allegria B&B

#43 Route 296, PO Box 267
Windham, NY 12496-0267
(518)734-5560 Fax:(518)734-5570
Internet: www.albergousa.com
E-mail: mail@albergousa.com

Circa 1892. Two former boarding houses were joined to create this luxurious, Victorian bed & breakfast whose name means "the inn of happiness." Guest quarters, laced with a Victorian theme, are decorated with period wallpapers and antique fur-nishings. One master suite includes an enormous Jacuzzi tub. There are plenty of relaxing options at Albergo Allegria, including an inviting lounge with a large fireplace and over-stuffed couches. Guests also can choose from more than 300 videos in the innkeeper's movie  collection. Located just a few feet behind the inn are the Carriage House Suites, each of which includes a double whirlpool tub, gas fireplace, king-size bed and cathedral ceil-ings with skylights. The innkeepers came to the area originally to open a deluxe, gourmet restaurant. Their command of cui-sine is evident each morning as guests feast on a variety of home-baked muffins and pastries, gourmet omelettes, waffles and other tempting treats. The inn is a registered historic site.

Innkeeper(s): Leslie & Marianna Leman. $73-299. 21 rooms with PB, 8 with FP, 9 suites. Breakfast included in rates. Types of meals: Full gourmet bkfst. Beds: KQT. Cable TV, VCR, reading lamp, refrigerator, ceiling fan, clock radio, telephone and desk in room. Air conditioning. Fax, copier, bicycles, parlor games, fireplace, afternoon tea on Saturdays, 24-hour guest pantry with soft drinks and hot beverages and sweets on premises. Handicap access. Amusement parks, antiquing, bicycling, cross-country skiing, downhill skiing, fishing, hiking, parks, shopping, tennis, water sports, bird watching and waterfalls nearby.

Location: Mountains.

Publicity: Yankee.

Certificate may be used: Anytime, Sunday-Thursday, non-holidays.

B & B Windham Chalet

292 South St, PO Box 418
Windham, NY 12496
(518)734-6335
Internet: www.windhamchalet.com
E-mail: info@windhamchalet.com

Circa 1865. Located just across the road from Ski Windham and nestled between two golf courses, this farmhouse-style inn offers countryside and mountain views to its guests, as well as personalized hospitality. Breakfast may be enjoyed in the din-ing room or outside on a picturesque deck complete with the sounds of a babbling brook. Guests also enjoy a large living room, wood-burning fireplace and a sauna. The Catskills pro-vide many other tourist attractions, including caverns, fairs and ethnic festivals, as well as shopping, antiquing and sport-ing activities. The innkeeper welcomes couples and families with children.

Innkeeper(s): Emilce Cacace. $75-170. 5 rooms, 4 with PB. Breakfast and afternoon tea included in rates. Types of meals: Cont plus. Beds: KQDT. Data port, cable TV, VCR, reading lamp, stereo, refrigerator, clock radio, turn-down service, fireplace, theme rooms, hair dryers, shampoo, conditioner, lotion, toothpaste and robes in room. Air conditioning. Sauna, bicycles, parlor

games, telephone, gift shop, outdoor hot tub, high-speed Internet access, book library and DVD movies on premises. Amusement parks, antiquing, art galleries, bicycling, canoeing/kayaking, cross-country skiing, downhill skiing, fishing, golf, hiking, horseback riding, live theater, museums, parks, shopping, water sports, ski slopes and snowboarding nearby.
Location: Mountains. Walking distance to Windham Mountain Slopes.

"Your warm and cozy home is surpassed only by your warm and friendly smile. Breakfast - Wow - it can't be beat!"

Certificate may be used: April through November except holidays and holiday weekends.

Country Suite B&B

Rt 23 W, PO Box 700
Windham, NY 12496-0700
(518)734-4079 Fax:(518)734-9149
Internet: www.countrysuite.com
E-mail: ctrysuite@aol.com

Circa 1865. This carefully restored country farmhouse in the Catskill Mountains two miles from Ski Windham, offers large lawns and a picturesque gazebo. Five guest rooms, all with private baths and king or queen beds, are available to visitors. The inn's country-style furnishings include antiques and family heirlooms. A full gourmet breakfast is offered. After a busy day of exploring the area's historic sites, boutiques and antique shops or enjoying boating, golfing, tennis and other activities, guests often gather in the inn's comfortable living room to relax.
Innkeeper(s): Lorraine Seidel & Sondra Clark. $109-189. 5 rooms with PB. Breakfast included in rates. Types of meals: Full gourmet bkfst. Beds: KQ. Fireplace on premises. Antiquing and downhill skiing nearby.
Location: Country, mountains. Catskills.

"Country elegance with a distinctly urban flair. A treasure to be discovered over and over again."

Certificate may be used: April through Nov. 1, Sunday-Thursday.

Point Lookout Mountain Inn

The Mohican Trail, RT 23
Windham, NY 12439
(518)734-3381 Fax:(518)734-6526
Internet: www.pointlookoutinn.com
E-mail: pointlookoutinn1@aol.com

Circa 1965. Renown internationally for its panoramic five-state view, this cliffside country inn is a landmark in the Northern Catskill Mountains. Gather to play games in the Great Room, read a book on the balcony or enjoy the peaceful courtyard. Newly redecorated guest bedrooms offer comfort and style while boasting incredible vistas during sunrise, moonrise or sunset. The first meal of the day is the popular "Raid the Refrigerator" breakfast,

conveniently indulged when desired. After a day of visiting local historic sites, hiking, golf or skiing, the hot tub and in-house massage therapy offer total relaxation.
Innkeeper(s): Ron and Laurie Landstrom. $75-175. 14 rooms with PB and 1 conference room. Breakfast included in rates. Types of meals: Full gourmet bkfst, veg bkfst, early coffee/tea, gourmet lunch, picnic lunch, afternoon tea, snacks/refreshments, gourmet dinner and room service. Restaurant on premises. Beds: QDT. Cable TV, reading lamp, ceiling fan and clock radio in room. VCR, fax, copier, parlor games, telephone, fireplace and 180 mile view of five states on premises. Handicap access. Amusement parks, antiquing, art galleries, bicycling, canoeing/kayaking, cross-country skiing, downhill skiing, fishing, golf, hiking, horseback riding, live theater, museums, parks, shopping, sporting events, tennis, water sports and wineries nearby.
Location: Country.
Publicity: *Hudson Valley Magazine* and *Ski Magazine*.

"Just wanted to thank you, once again, for a great time."

Certificate may be used: Sunday-Thursday, non-holidays.

Wolcott F7

Bonnie Castle Farm B&B

PO Box 188
Wolcott, NY 14590-0188
(315)587-2273 (800)587-4006 Fax:(315)587-4003
Internet: www.virtualcities.com/ons/ny/r/nyr9701.htm
E-mail: empgap@zlink.net

Circa 1887. This large, waterfront home is surrounded by expansive lawns and trees, which overlook the east side of Great Sodus Bay, a popular resort at the turn of the century. Accommodations include a suite and large guest rooms with water views. Other rooms feature wainscoting and cathedral ceilings. A full, gourmet breakfast includes a cereal bar, fresh fruit and juices and an assortment of entrees such as Orange Blossom French toast, sausages, a creamy potato casserole and fresh-baked pastries topped off  with teas and Irish creme coffee. Guests can visit many nearby attractions, such as the Renaissance Festival, Erie Canal and Chimney Bluffs State Park.
Innkeeper(s): Eric & Georgia Pendleton. $99-165. 8 rooms with PB, 1 suite. Breakfast included in rates. Types of meals: Full gourmet bkfst. Beds: KQD. Cable TV, VCR, ceiling fan and clock radio in room. Air conditioning. TV, fax, copier, spa, swimming, telephone and fireplace on premises. Antiquing, cross-country skiing, downhill skiing, fishing, live theater, parks, shopping, sporting events and water sports nearby.
Location: Country, waterfront. Rural.

"We love Bonnie Castle. You have a magnificent establishment. We are just crazy about your place. Hope to see you soon."

Certificate may be used: Anytime except Friday and Saturday from May 15-Sept. 15.

North Carolina

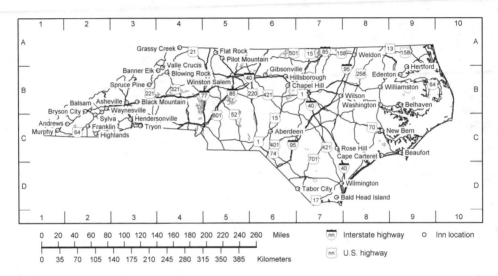

	1	2	3	4	5	6	7	8	9	10

Grassy Creek, Flat Rock, Pilot Mountain, Banner Elk, Valle Crucis, Blowing Rock, Spruce Pine, Winston Salem, Gibsonville, Hillsborough, Chapel Hill, Weldon, Hertford, Edenton, Williamston, Balsam, Asheville, Black Mountain, Bryson City, Waynesville, Wilson, Washington, Belhaven, Andrews, Sylva, Hendersonville, Murphy, Franklin, Tryon, Aberdeen, New Bern, Highlands, Rose Hill, Cape Carteret, Beaufort, Wilmington, Tabor City, Bald Head Island

0 20 40 60 80 100 120 140 160 180 200 220 240 260 Miles

0 35 70 105 140 175 210 245 280 315 350 385 Kilometers

(nn) Interstate highway   o Inn location

(nn) U.S. highway

Aberdeen   C6

The Inn at Bryant House

214 N Poplar St
Aberdeen, NC 28315-2812
(910)944-3300 (800)453-4019 Fax:(910)944-8898
Internet: innatbryanthouse.com
E-mail: lsteele@eclipsetel.com

Circa 1913. This Colonial Revival inn has been completely
restored to its original Southern splendor. Pastel colors flow
through the entire house, and the sitting, dining and living
rooms open to one another for easy access. Breakfast is served
in the dining or garden room. With advance notice, lunches
and dinners can be served for small business meetings, wedding parties, family gatherings, club activities and weekend
retreats. The Pinehurst area is known for its quiet rolling hills
and more than 30 championship-quality golf courses.

Innkeeper(s): Lee & Sharon Steele. $70-105. 9 rooms, 8 with PB. Breakfast
included in rates. Types of meals: Full bkfst. Beds: QDT. Reading lamp in
room. Air conditioning. VCR, telephone and fireplace on premises. Antiquing,
golf, live theater and shopping nearby.

Location: Historic district.

Certificate may be used: Any time of the year, when available.

Andrews   C2

Hawkesdene House B&B Inn and Cottages

PO Box 670
Andrews, NC 28901
(828)321-6027 (800)447-9549 Fax:(828)321-5007
Internet: www.hawkesdene.com
E-mail: hawke@dnet.net

Circa 1994. Want to take a llama trek to a hidden waterfall,
pan for gold and sapphires or experience a sunset dinner atop a
mountain gazebo? Located in a remote cove of the North
Carolina Mountains, this inn offers 20 wooded acres to
explore. The bright interiors satisfy the soul and lead the eye to
picturesque countryside views, as well. Sample breakfast dishes
include stuffed French toast, a fruit smoothie and freshly made
muffins all served in the dining room. Bring your own groceries
for visits in the pristine cottages. A stream runs through the
property. Plan to stay long enough to enjoy fly-fishing, horseback riding, whitewater rafting, canoeing and porch rocking.

Innkeeper(s): Mark & Melissa Harris. $85-125. 9 rooms, 4 with PB, 1 suite
and 4 cottages. Breakfast included in rates. Types of meals: Full gourmet
bkfst and early coffee/tea. Beds: KQDT. Cable TV, VCR, reading lamp, ceiling
fan and clock radio in room. Central air. Fax, copier, library, parlor games,
telephone, fireplace, laundry facility, gift shop and llama trek suppers on
premises. Handicap access. Antiquing, bicycling, canoeing/kayaking, fishing,
golf, hiking, horseback riding, live theater, museums, parks, water sports,
gem mining and service railway nearby.

Location: Mountains.

Certificate may be used: Anytime, subject to availability.

Asheville B3

1900 Inn on Montford

296 Montford Ave
Asheville, NC 28801-1660
(828)254-9569 (800)254-9569 Fax:(828)254-9518
Internet: www.innonmontford.com
E-mail: info@innonmontford.com

Circa 1900. This National Register home was one of a few local homes designed by Richard Sharpe Smith, the supervising architect for the nearby Biltmore Estate. The simple exterior and pleasing Arts & Crafts style is flanked by a wide veranda for relaxing and enjoying the neighborhood. English and American antiques fill the elegant inn. Well-appointed guest bedrooms feature King-size beds and fireplaces. Some have whirlpool tubs, and one boasts a clawfoot tub. A secluded, deluxe five-room whirlpool suite also offers a sitting room and private entrance with balcony.

Breakfasts include a special fruit dish such as baked banana souffle, a daily entree and dessert. The inn hosts a social hour from 6-7 p.m. daily. Spend the day touring historic homes, or hike and raft in nearby wilderness areas.

Innkeeper(s): Ron and Lynn Carlson. $125-345. 5 rooms with PB, 5 with FP, 1 suite. Breakfast and snacks/refreshments included in rates. Types of meals: Full gourmet bkfst and early coffee/tea. Beds: KQ. Modem hook-up, data port, cable TV, VCR, reading lamp, CD player, refrigerator, ceiling fan, clock radio, telephone, desk, fireplace, high-speed Internet access (wired or wireless), coffee or tea delivered to your door at 8 a.m. and the 1,000-square-foot Zelda's Retreat has a 7-body jet shower with steam bath in room. Air conditioning. Fax, copier, library, coffee/tea 24 hours a day, complimentary soda and water on premises. Antiquing, art galleries, bicycling, canoeing/kayaking, downhill skiing, fishing, golf, hiking, horseback riding, live theater, museums, parks, shopping, sporting events, tennis, water sports, wineries, Biltmore Estate and Chimney Rock nearby.
Location: City.
Publicity: *Health Magazine, Jan/Feb 2003, Charlotte Taste Magazine, Asheville Magazine, Knoxville NBC affiliate and Asheville WLOS ABC affiliate.*
Certificate may be used: Jan. 5-Sept. 30, Sunday-Thursday, except holidays.

Albemarle Inn

86 Edgemont Rd
Asheville, NC 28801-1544
(828)255-0027 (800)621-7435 Fax:(828)236-3397
Internet: www.albemarleinn.com
E-mail: info@albemarleinn.com

Circa 1907. In the residential Grove Park area, this AAA four-diamond elegant Greek Revival Mansion graces almost an acre of landscaped grounds. The inn features an exquisite carved-oak staircase and period furnishings. Enjoy late afternoon refreshments on the veranda overlooking award-winning English gardens or fireside in the parlor. Spacious guest bedrooms and suites boast fine linens, antique clawfoot tubs and showers, televisions and phones. Some rooms include a whirlpool tub and a fireplace. A sumptuous candlelight breakfast is served at individual tables in the dining room or on the plant-filled sun porch. Gourmet dishes may include poached cinnamon pears, stuffed French toast with orange sauce and sausages. Inspired by the singing

birds, composer Bela Bartok wrote his third piano concerto while staying here. The inn is a member of Select Registry.
Innkeeper(s): Cathy & Larry Sklar. $165-295. 11 rooms with PB, 1 with FP, 2 suites. Breakfast and snacks/refreshments included in rates. Types of meals: Full gourmet bkfst, early coffee/tea and afternoon tea. Beds: KQDT. Modem hook-up, cable TV, reading lamp, ceiling fan, clock radio, telephone, coffeemaker, turn-down service and suite has 2-person marble whirlpool tub in room. Air conditioning. Parlor games and fireplace on premises. Antiquing, art galleries, bicycling, canoeing/kayaking, downhill skiing, fishing, golf, hiking, horseback riding, live theater, museums, parks, shopping, sporting events, tennis, wineries, golf and Biltmore Estate nearby.
Location: City, mountains. Residential area.
Publicity: *AAA Four-Diamond Award, National Geographic Traveler, Travel Holiday, Charleston Living & Home Design and WLOS TV (ABC).*

"Most outstanding breakfast I've ever had. We were impressed to say the least!"

Certificate may be used: Sunday-Thursday, Jan. 2-June 30, Aug. 1-Sept. 30, Nov. 1-Dec. 12, except holidays, subject to availability, not to be combined with any other promotions.

Beaufort House Victorian B&B

61 N Liberty St
Asheville, NC 28801-1829
(828)254-8334 (800)261-2221 Fax:(828)251-2082
Internet: www.beauforthouse.com
E-mail: rob@beauforthouse.com

Circa 1894. In the Queen Anne Victorian style, this inn rests on two acres of beautifully landscaped grounds, including a tea garden. Offering views of the mountains, the full wraparound porch is festooned with gingerbread trim. Most guest rooms feature Jacuzzi tubs. Ask for the Sarah Davidson Suite where light streams through a handsome fan window onto a king-size canopy bed decked in white Battenburg Lace. There is a sitting area with wing back chairs and a Queen Anne desk. Guests are pampered with a lavish, gourmet breakfast.
Innkeeper(s): Robert & Jacqueline Glasgow. $125-285. 11 rooms. Breakfast and afternoon tea included in rates. Types of meals: Full gourmet bkfst, early coffee/tea and picnic lunch. Beds: KQ. Cable TV, VCR, reading lamp, refrigerator, ceiling fan, snack bar, clock radio, telephone, desk and CD in room. Air conditioning. Fax, parlor games and fireplace on premises. Amusement parks, antiquing, downhill skiing, fishing, golf, live theater, parks, shopping, sporting events and tennis nearby.
Location: City, mountains.
Certificate may be used: Jan. 2-March 14, midweek stay only. Excludes holidays.

Biltmore Village Inn

119 Dodge St.
Asheville, NC 28803
(828)274-8707 (866)274-8779
Internet: www.biltmorevillageinn.com
E-mail: info@biltmorevillageinn.com

Circa 1892. As the gentle breeze blows, enjoy the mountain views from the porch of this historic Queen Anne Victorian. The inn is a county landmark listed in the National Register. Collections of paintings and antique furnishings appropriately reside together. Afternoon tea is served fireside in the parlor for a relaxing respite. Spacious guest bedrooms boast canopy and poster beds, double whirlpool tubs and fireplaces. A satisfying breakfast offers specialties like Caribbean pears, orange raspberry croissants in almond custard, and parmesan souffle with an apple and bacon confit. The enchanting grounds are graced with flowering bushes and trees, boxwoods and perennial gardens.
Innkeeper(s): Owen Sullivan and Ripley Hotch. $175-285. 5 rooms with PB, 5 with FP, 1 suite and 1 cottage. Breakfast and afternoon tea included in rates. Types of meals: Full gourmet bkfst, veg bkfst and early coffee/tea. Beds: KQ. Modem hook-up, data port, cable TV, VCR, reading lamp, refriger-

ator, clock radio, telephone, coffeemaker, desk, hot tub/spa and fireplace in room. Central air. Fax, copier, spa, library, parlor games and fireplace on premises. Limited handicap access. Antiquing, art galleries, canoeing/kayaking, fishing, golf, hiking, horseback riding, live theater, museums, parks, shopping, tennis, water sports and wineries nearby.
Location: Mountains.
Certificate may be used: January-July, Sunday-Thursday.

Carolina B&B

177 Cumberland Ave
Asheville, NC 28801-1736
(828)254-3608 (888)254-3608
Internet: www.carolinabb.com
E-mail: info@carolinabb.com

Circa 1901. Architect Richard Sharp Smith, whose credits include creating homes for such tycoons as George Vanderbilt, designed this home in Asheville's historic Montford district. Bay windows and porches decorate Carolina's exterior. Inside, rooms feature pine floors, high ceilings and many fireplaces. Guest rooms are furnished with antiques and unique collectibles. The expansive breakfasts include fresh breads, fruits, egg dishes and breakfast meats.

Innkeeper(s): Sue Birkholz & David Feinstein. $95-200. 7 rooms, 6 with PB, 6 with FP and 1 cottage. Breakfast and wine included in rates. Types of meals: Full gourmet bkfst, veg bkfst, picnic lunch and afternoon tea. Beds: KQT. Modem hook-up, data port, cable TV, VCR, reading lamp, refrigerator, ceiling fan, clock radio, desk and fireplace in room. Air conditioning. Fax, copier, spa, library, parlor games and laundry facility on premises. Antiquing, art galleries, bicycling, canoeing/kayaking, cross-country skiing, downhill skiing, fishing, golf, hiking, horseback riding, live theater, museums, parks, shopping, sporting events, tennis, water sports, wineries and Biltmore Estate nearby.
Location: City, mountains.
Publicity: *Orange County Register, Asheville Citizen-Times, Charlotte and Mid-Atlantic Country.*

"It was like a dream, exactly as we pictured the perfect honeymoon. Excellent host & hostess, very helpful and informative as to local area. Food was wonderful. Rated an A-plus."
Certificate may be used: January-August, Sunday-Thursday, excluding all holidays.

Corner Oak Manor

53 Saint Dunstans Rd
Asheville, NC 28803-2620
(828)253-3525 (888)633-3525
Internet: www.corneroakmanor.com
E-mail: info@corneroakmanor.com

Circa 1920. Surrounded by oak, maple and pine trees, this English Tudor inn is decorated with many fine oak antiques and handmade items. Innkeeper Karen Spradley has hand-stitched something special for each room, and the house features handmade items by local artisans. Breakfast delights include entrees such as Blueberry Ricotta Pancakes, Four Cheese and Herb Quiche and Orange French Toast. When you aren't enjoying local activities, you can sit on the shady deck, relax in the Jacuzzi, play a few songs on the piano or curl up with a good book.

Innkeeper(s): Karen & Andy Spradley. $125-195. 4 rooms with PB and 1 cottage. Breakfast included in rates. Types of meals: Full gourmet bkfst. Beds: Q. Reading lamp, refrigerator, ceiling fan and one cottage with fireplace in room. Air conditioning. Parlor games, telephone, fireplace and outdoor Jacuzzi on premises. Antiquing, fishing, live theater, parks and shopping nearby.

Location: Quiet neighborhood, 1/2 mile from Biltmore Estate.
"Great food, comfortable bed, quiet, restful atmosphere, you provided it all and we enjoyed it all!"
Certificate may be used: January-March anytime except holidays, April-September & November, Sunday-Thursday only. No holidays, October & December excluded.

Katherine's Bed & Breakfast

43 Watauga Street
Asheville, NC 28801
(828)236-9494 (888)325-3190 Fax:(828)236-2218
Internet: www.katherinesbandb.com
E-mail: lstrongman@earthlink.net

Circa 1904. Honored with The Griffin Award by the preservation society, this 2.5 story Queen Anne Vernacular boasts Colonial Revival details. Innkeeper Ineke's talent for historical restoration, skill in creating a rich, high style and taste for international travel is reflected in the elegant and comfortable decor. Each guest bedroom offers picture-perfect furnishings, air conditioning, robes, down comforter, fireplace and a welcoming teddy bear. The Pine Room boasts a canopy bed, clawfoot tub, hand-stenciled walls and bay window accented with lace and silk. Mahogany pieces in the spacious Sandalwood Room are highlighted by red and camel tones with a blue porcelain collection. Linger over a sumptuous morning meal in the cheery breakfast room before exploring the local area.

Innkeeper(s): Ineke Strongman & Michael Pewther. $110-185. 6 rooms with PB and 1 conference room. Breakfast and snacks/refreshments included in rates. Types of meals: Full gourmet bkfst, early coffee/tea and picnic lunch. Beds: KQD. TV, VCR, reading lamp, stereo, refrigerator, ceiling fan, clock radio, telephone and turn-down service in room. Central air. Fax, tennis, library and gift shop on premises. Antiquing, art galleries, bicycling, canoeing/kayaking, cross-country skiing, downhill skiing, fishing, golf, hiking, horseback riding, live theater, museums, parks, shopping, tennis, water sports and wineries nearby.
Location: City, mountains.
Publicity: *Charlotte Parent Magazine.*
Certificate may be used: Subject to availability, Sunday-Thursday, August and September.

Wright Inn & Carriage House

235 Pearson Dr
Asheville, NC 28801-1613
(828)251-0789 (800)552-5724 Fax:(828)251-0929
Internet: www.wrightinn.com
E-mail: info@wrightinn.com

Circa 1899. A true landmark that is timeless in the old-fashioned graciousness and modern conveniences offered, this gabled Queen Anne boasts an award-winning restoration and lavish gardens. Gather in the Coleman Parlor and the Drawing Room with period decor, fireplaces and inviting activities. Romantic suites and guest bedrooms feature distinctive designs; several feature fireplaces and high-speed Internet. The three-bedroom Carriage House is perfect for larger groups or families. Enjoy a gourmet breakfast and an afternoon social hour. Relax on the large wraparound porch and gazebo.

Innkeeper(s): Vicki & Mark Maurer. $140-325. 10 rooms with PB, 4 with FP. Breakfast included in rates. Types of meals: Full gourmet bkfst, early coffee/tea and afternoon tea. Beds: KQDT. Cable TV, reading lamp, clock radio and telephone in room. Central air. Fax, library, parlor games, fireplace, afternoon social hour is included in rates, high-speed Internet and cable TV

on premises. Hiking, shopping and water sports nearby.
Location: City. Historic Montford District, Biltmore Estate.
Certificate may be used: January-June, subject to availability, July-December, Sunday-Thursday.

Bald Head Island   D7

Theodosia's B&B
2 Keelson Row
Bald Head Island, NC 28461
(910)457-6563 (800)656-1812 Fax:(910)457-6055
Internet: www.theodosias.com
E-mail: stay@theodosias.com

Circa 1817. For a romantic getaway or a quiet retreat, this historic barrier island at the mouth of the Cape Fear River offers a tranquil beauty. Exquisite accommodations are found at this modern Victorian bed & breakfast inn that boasts a southern elegant decor. Stay in the main inn, Carriage House, or three-story Cottage. Delightful guest bedrooms feature splendid views of the harbor, river, marshes and lighthouse from balconies. In the dining room, breakfast entrees may include favorites such as Eggs Benedict, Caramel Soaked French Toast, Egg Souffle and Belgian Waffles. Relax on porch rockers or swings, explore the sites and trips to the beach by bike or electric golf cart. Enjoy use of the golf course, tennis courts and other club facilities. Chat with new friends over afternoon refreshments. Weddings and special events are popular at this idyllic setting. Innkeeper Gary is also a minister, available for planning and performing a wedding ceremony.
Innkeeper(s): Thompson & Brandy Higgins. $170-275. 13 rooms with PB, 1 suite. Breakfast and snacks/refreshments included in rates. Types of meals: Full bkfst. Beds: KQD. Cable TV, reading lamp, clock radio, telephone and desk in room. Air conditioning. Fax, bicycles and fireplace on premises. Handicap access. Fishing, golf, parks, tennis and water sports nearby.
Location: Ocean community, waterfront.
Publicity: *The Thomasville Times, Southern Living, Raleigh News and Observer, Charlotte Observer, Money Magazine and Coastal Living.*
Certificate may be used: Oct. 15-March 31, Sunday-Thursday.

Balsam   B2

Balsam Mountain Inn
PO Box 40
Balsam, NC 28707-0040
(828)456-9498 (800)224-9498 Fax:(828)456-9298
Internet: www.balsaminn.com
E-mail: balsaminn@earthlink.net

Circa 1905. This inn, just a quarter mile from the famed Blue Ridge Parkway, is surrounded by the majestic Smoky Mountains. The inn was built in the Neoclassical style and overlooks the scenic hamlet of Balsam. The inn is listed in the National Register of Historic Places and is designated a Jackson County Historic Site. It features a mansard roof and wraparound porches with mountain views. A complimentary full breakfast is served daily, and dinner also is available daily.
Innkeeper(s): Sharon White and Kim Shailer. $120-180. 50 rooms with PB, 8 suites. Breakfast included in rates. Types of meals: Full gourmet bkfst, early coffee/tea, picnic lunch and gourmet dinner. Restaurant on premises. Beds: KD. Reading lamp and desk in room. Fax, copier, parlor games, fireplace, hiking trails and wildflower walks on premises. Handicap access. Antiquing, downhill skiing, fishing, parks, shopping, whitewater rafting, hiking and Blue Ridge Pkwy nearby.
Location: Mountains.

"What wonderful memories we have of this beautiful inn."
Certificate may be used: Sunday through Thursday, November through June & September, excluding holiday periods.

Banner Elk   B4

Beech Alpen Inn
700 Beech Mountain Pkwy
Banner Elk, NC 28604-8015
(828)387-2252 Fax:(704)387-2229

Circa 1968. This rustic inn is a Bavarian delight affording scenic vistas of the Blue Ridge Mountains. The innkeepers offer accommodations at Top of the Beech, a Swiss-style ski chalet with views of nearby slopes. The interiors of both properties are inviting. At the Beech Alpen, several guest rooms have stone fireplaces or French doors that open onto a balcony. Top of the Beech's great room is a wonderful place to relax, with a huge stone fireplace and comfortable furnishings. The Beech Alpen Restaurant serves a variety of dinner fare.
Innkeeper(s): Brenda Fisher. $49-149. 25 rooms with PB, 4 with FP. Breakfast included in rates. Types of meals: Cont, early coffee/tea and gourmet dinner. Restaurant on premises. Beds: KQD. Cable TV in room. Fax, copier, parlor games, telephone and fireplace on premises. Antiquing, cross-country skiing, downhill skiing, fishing, live theater, parks, shopping and sporting events nearby.
Location: Mountains.
Certificate may be used: Sunday-Thursday, Jan. 3-Dec. 14.

Hummingbird Lodge B&B
8778 NC Hwy 194 South
Banner Elk, NC 28604-9136
(828)963-7210 Fax:(828)898-8339
E-mail: hummingbird@aczonline.net

Circa 1991. Perched on the side of a mountain, on more than five acres, Hummingbird Lodge is an Appalachian log home constructed of red cedar. There is a spacious, open dining room that overlooks the valley as well as an outside breakfast terrace. Breakfast specialties include dishes such as eggs Benedict, hash brown casseroles, homemade breads and blueberry pancakes. A variety of ski resorts are nearby such as Ski Beech on Beech Mountain and Sugar Mountain. The Banner Elk area also offers river rafting, trout fishing, golf, gemstone mining and horseback riding. Be sure not to miss Grandfather Mountain Park and its mile-high swinging bridge.
Innkeeper(s): Randy & Susan Hutchings. $99-140. 4 rooms, 3 with PB, 1 suite. Breakfast included in rates. Types of meals: Full bkfst. Beds: QT. Reading lamp, ceiling fan, clock radio and turn-down service in room. VCR, fax, copier, parlor games, telephone, fireplace and hiking trails on premises. Amusement parks, antiquing, downhill skiing, fishing, golf, live theater, parks, shopping, sporting events, tennis, water sports, hiking and horseback riding nearby.
Location: Mountains.
Certificate may be used: Jan. 1-Dec. 31, Sunday-Thursday.

Beaufort   C9

Pecan Tree Inn B&B
116 Queen St
Beaufort, NC 28516-2214
(252)728-6733 (800)728-7871 Fax:(252)728-3909
Internet: www.pecantree.com
E-mail: innkeeper@pecantree.com

Circa 1866. A few steps from the scenic yacht harbor, this landmark inn is located in the heart of the historic district. Built in 1866, the Victorian architecture is enhanced by light-filled bay windows, antique furnishings and handsome, uncluttered decor. Sleep well in distinctive yet comfortable guest bedrooms. The romantic Queen Anne bridal suite and the Beaufort Suite feature

King-size canopy beds and two-person Jacuzzi tubs. Relax on one of the three porches or stroll through the renowned flower and herb gardens. Innkeepers David and Allison DuBuisson will personalize each stay to help you discover all that this delightful seaport has to offer.

$90-175. 7 rooms with PB, 2 suites. Breakfast included in rates. Types of meals: Cont plus and early coffee/tea. Beds: KQ. Cable TV, reading lamp, ceiling fan, clock radio and two King/two-person Jacuzzi suites in room. Air conditioning. Bicycles, library, parlor games and telephone on premises. Antiquing, bicycling, fishing, shopping, water sports, beaches, shelling, boating, kayaking, ecological excursions, jogging and historic tours nearby.
Location: Waterfront.
Publicity: *Charlotte Observer, Raleigh News & Observer, Rocky Mount Telegram, Southern Getaway, Conde Nast, State, Southern Living, Birds and Blooms, Charlotte News, Observer, Carolina Gardner, Cruising Guide to Coastal North Carolina, ABC - Greenville NC and Video - NC's Best 50 Inns.*
Certificate may be used: Nov. 1 through March 31, Sunday through Thursday.

Belhaven   B9

River Forest Manor

738 E Main St
Belhaven, NC 27810-1622
(252)943-2151 (800)346-2151 Fax:(252)943-6628
Internet: www.riverforestmanor.com
E-mail: manor@riverforestmarina.com

Circa 1899. Both Twiggy and Walter Cronkite have passed through the two-story, pillared rotunda entrance of this white mansion located on the Atlantic Intracoastal Waterway. Ornate, carved ceilings, cut and leaded-glass windows and crystal chandeliers grace the inn. Antiques are found throughout. Each evening a smorgasbord buffet features more than 50 items from the inn's kitchen.
Innkeeper(s): Melba, Axson Jr. & Mark Smith. $65-95. 12 rooms with PB. Breakfast included in rates. Types of meals: Full bkfst and dinner. Restaurant on premises. Beds: KQD. Cable TV, reading lamp and telephone in room. Air conditioning. TV, VCR, fax, copier and fireplace on premises. Antiquing, fishing, water sports, beach and Wildlife Center nearby.
Location: Waterfront. Intracoastal Waterway.
Publicity: *Southern Living, National Geographic, North Carolina Accommodations, Country Inns, State and Historical Inns.*

"River Forest Manor is our favorite place in east North Carolina."
Certificate may be used: April 1 through 30, Sunday through Thursday.

Black Mountain   B3

Red Rocker Inn

136 N Dougherty St
Black Mountain, NC 28711-3326
(828)669-5991 (888)669-5991
Internet: www.redrockerinn.com
E-mail: info@redrockerinn.com

Circa 1896. Voted as the best B&B in Asheville, Black Mountain and all of Western North Carolina for the past five years, this three-story inn sits on one acre of pristinely landscaped grounds. Located just 14 miles east of Asheville and the famous Biltmore Estate, discover why the Atlanta Journal named this inn one of its "Top 12 Favorites in the Southeast." Elegant, air-conditioned guest bedrooms exude an inviting ambiance. Many feature fireplaces and whirlpool tubs. Each morning sit down to a heaping Southern breakfast that is sure to satisfy. Stroll through gorgeous gardens with a view of the mountains or relax in front of a roar-

ing fire. Red rockers line the expansive wraparound porch, a perfect spot to enjoy tea and hand-dipped macaroons. Special dining packages are available year-round which include homemade specialties and award-winning desserts.
Innkeeper(s): The Lindberg family. $95-175. 17 rooms with PB, 3 with FP. Breakfast, afternoon tea and snacks/refreshments included in rates. Types of meals: Full bkfst, early coffee/tea and dinner. Restaurant on premises. Beds: KQD. Reading lamp, ceiling fan, desk and five with whirlpool tubs in room. Air conditioning. Fax, library, parlor games, telephone and fireplace on premises. Antiquing, downhill skiing, fishing, golf, live theater, parks, shopping, tennis and water sports nearby.
Location: Mountains.
Certificate may be used: Feb. 1 to March 15, Sunday-Thursday; Nov. 15 to Dec. 20, Sunday-Thursday.

Blowing Rock   B4

Blowing Rock Victorian Inn

PO Box 283
Blowing Rock, NC 28605-0283
(828)295-0034 Fax:(828)263-0200
Internet: www.blowingrockvictorianinn.com
E-mail: info@blowingrockvictorianinn.com

Circa 1932. Located in the heart of Blowing Rock, a short walk from Main Street's shops and a variety of restaurants, this elegantly restored inn offers gables, balconies, porches and a turret, all set off with white trim and borders of white impatiens. A fetching Victorian flower garden adds to the appeal and draws passers-by to pause and take in the picture-perfect scene. Baskets of flowers hang from the balconies, and each suite has a private entrance, ceiling fan, deluxe bath, luxurious comforter and small refrigerator.

Two rooms have large Jacuzzi baths as well as separate showers and there are four rooms with fireplaces. Spacious decks offer large rockers overlooking the garden. Blowing Rock has been a Blue Ridge resort for more than 100 years and is named for a rock that hangs over a cliff.
Innkeeper(s): Scott Seaman. $119-199. 6 rooms with PB. Breakfast and wine included in rates. Types of meals: Full bkfst and early coffee/tea. Beds: KQ. Cable TV, reading lamp, ceiling fan, snack bar, fireplace, refrigerator and two-person Jacuzzi tubs in room. Air conditioning. Telephone on premises. Amusement parks, antiquing, canoeing/kayaking, cross-country skiing, downhill skiing, fishing, golf, hiking, horseback riding, live theater, parks, shopping, sporting events, tennis, water sports and craft shows nearby.
Location: Mountains.
Certificate may be used: Jan. 3-April 30, Sunday through Thursday.

Bryson City   B2

Randolph House Country Inn

223 Fryemont Rd, PO Box 816
Bryson City, NC 28713-0816
(828)488-3472 (800)480-3472
Internet: www.randolphhouse.com

Circa 1895. Randolph House is a mountain estate tucked among pine trees and dogwoods, near the entrance of Great Smoky Mountain National Park. Antiques, some original to the house, fill this National Register home. Each guest room is appointed in a different color scheme. The house provides an unforgettable experience, not the least of which is the gourmet dining provided on the terrace or in the dining room.
Innkeeper(s): Bill & Ruth Randolph Adams. $75-150. 7 rooms, 3 with PB, 4

with FP, 1 cottage and 1 conference room. Breakfast included in rates. Types of meals: Country bkfst and dinner. Restaurant on premises. Beds: KQD. Reading lamp and desk in room. Air conditioning. TV, library, parlor games, telephone and fireplace on premises. Limited handicap access. Amusement parks, antiquing, bicycling, canoeing/kayaking, fishing, golf, hiking, horseback riding, parks, shopping and tennis nearby.
Location: Mountains.
Publicity: *New York Times and Tourist News.*

"Very enjoyable, great food."

Certificate may be used: June and September from Sunday through Thursday for bed and breakfast.

Cape Carteret   C8

Harborlight Guest House
332 Live Oak Dr
Cape Carteret, NC 28584
(252)393-6868 (800)624-VIEW
Internet: www.harborlightnc.com
E-mail: info@harborlightnc.com

Circa 1963. This three-story home rests on a peninsula just yards from Bogue Sound and the Intracoastal Waterway. In-room amenities might include a massive whirlpool tub, a claw-foot tub or fireplace, and each of the guest suites feature a beautiful water view. The décor is done in a modern, coastal style. Multi-course, gourmet breakfasts begin with fresh juices, coffee, tea and an appetizer, perhaps a stuffed mushroom. From there, guests enjoy a fresh fruit dish followed by a creative entrée. All of which is served in suite or deckside. Museums, an aquarium, historic sites, Hammocks Beach State Park and harbor tours are among the attractions. Fort Macon State Park affords guests an opportunity to view a restored Civil War fort. Popular beaches and horseback riding are just minutes away.
Innkeeper(s): Debbie Mugno & Bob Pickens. $150-300. 7 rooms, 5 with FP, 5 with HT, 7 suites and 1 conference room. Breakfast included in rates. Types of meals: Full gourmet bkfst, early coffee/tea, snacks/refreshments and room service. Beds: KQT. Cable TV, VCR, reading lamp, CD player, refrigerator, ceiling fan, clock radio, coffeemaker, desk, robes and slippers for stays of two nights or more, two-person jetted whirlpool tubs and 6 suites with Jacuzzi tub in room. Fax, copier, video library and Internet access on premises. Handicap access. Antiquing, art galleries, beach, bicycling, canoeing/kayaking, fishing, golf, hiking, horseback riding, live theater, museums, parks, shopping, tennis, water sports and island excursions nearby.
Location: Ocean community, waterfront.
Publicity: *Southern Living, The State Magazine, Carolina Style Magazine and Coastal Living.*
Certificate may be used: Nov. 1-Feb. 28, Sunday-Thursday, excluding holidays. Only certain suites available for this special.

Chapel Hill   B6

The Inn at Bingham School
PO Box 267
Chapel Hill, NC 27514-0267
(919)563-5583 (800)566-5583 Fax:(919)563-9826
Internet: www.chapel-hill-inn.com
E-mail: fdeprez@aol.com

Circa 1790. This inn served as one of the locations of the famed Bingham School. This particular campus was the site of a liberal arts preparatory school for those aspiring to attend the University at Chapel Hill. The inn is listed as a National Trust property and has garnered awards for its restoration. The property still includes many historic structures

including a 1790s log home, an 1801 Federal addition, an 1835 Greek Revival home, the headmaster's office, which was built in 1845, and a well house, smokehouse and milk house. Original heart of pine floors are found throughout the inn. Guests can opt to stay in the Log Room, located in the log cabin, with a tight-winder staircase and fireplace. Other possibilities include Rusty's Room with two antique rope beds. The suite offers a bedroom glassed in on three sides. A mix of breakfasts are served, often including pear almond Belgian waffles, quiche or souffles.
Innkeeper(s): Francois & Christina Deprez. $85-135. 5 rooms with PB, 4 with FP, 1 suite, 1 cottage and 1 conference room. Breakfast and snacks/refreshments included in rates. Types of meals: Full gourmet bkfst and early coffee/tea. Beds: QD. Reading lamp, clock radio, telephone, desk, hair dryers and robes in room. Air conditioning. VCR, fax, library, parlor games, fireplace, trails and hammocks on premises. Antiquing, fishing, live theater, parks, shopping, sporting events and water sports nearby.
Location: Country. 11 miles west of Chapel Hill.
Publicity: *Southern Inns, Mebane Enterprise, Burlington Times, Times News and Washington Post.*
Certificate may be used: Dec. 1-March 31, Sunday-Thursday only.

Edenton   B9

The Lords Proprietors' Inn
300 N Broad St
Edenton, NC 27932-1905
(252)482-3641 (800)348-8933 Fax:(252)482-2432
Internet: www.lordspropedenton.com
E-mail: stay@edentoninn.com

Circa 1801. Since 1982 this elegant inn has been welcoming guests. Located in the historic district, three houses on the grounds feature guest bedrooms and suites with wood-burning fireplaces and double whirlpool tubs. Dining is in a separate building on a garden patio. On Tuesday through Saturday gourmet dinners are prepared by Chef Kevin Yokley. On Albemarle Sound, Edenton was one of the Colonial capitals of North Carolina. Guided walking tours of area museum homes begin at the nearby visitor's center.
Innkeeper(s): Arch & Jane Edwards. $155-260. 16 rooms with PB, 2 with FP, 2 suites and 1 conference room. Breakfast included in rates. Types of meals: Full bkfst, early coffee/tea and gourmet dinner. Beds: KQT. Cable TV and VCR in room. Air conditioning. TV, fax and child care on premises. Handicap access. Antiquing, fishing, shopping, swimming and golf nearby.
Location: Historic waterfront town.
Publicity: *Virginia Pilot, Washington Post, House Beautiful, Southern Living, Mid-Atlantic Country, Metro Magazine and PBS - Inn Country USA & Inn Country Chefs.*

"One of the friendliest and best-managed inns I have ever visited."

Certificate may be used: Anytime, except holidays and special weekends (i.e. Christmas candlelight tour, etc).

Trestle House Inn
632 Soundside Rd
Edenton, NC 27932-9668
(252)482-2282 (800)645-8466 Fax:(252)482-7003
Internet: www.trestlehouseinn.com
E-mail: thinn@coastalnet.com

Circa 1968. Trestle House is located on a six acres with a lake and a pond filled with large-mouth bass. The interior is unique as it features beams that were actually trestles that once belonged to the Southern Railway Company. Rooms are named for different birds, such as the Osprey and Mallard rooms. Two

rooms have a sleigh bed. The morning meal includes home-made breads, breakfast casseroles and fresh orange juice.
Innkeeper(s): Peter L. Bogus. $90-125. 5 rooms with PB, 1 suite. Breakfast included in rates. Types of meals: Full gourmet bkfst. Beds: KQDT. Modem hook-up, data port, cable TV, reading lamp, ceiling fan, clock radio, telephone and desk in room. Central air. VCR, swimming, library, parlor games and fireplace on premises. Amusement parks, antiquing, art galleries, beach, bicycling, canoeing/kayaking, fishing, golf, hiking, live theater, museums, parks, shopping, tennis and water sports nearby.
Location: Waterfront.
Publicity: *North Carolina Traveler and WITN.*

"We have stayed at many B&B, but yours is special because it brings us close to nature. Your breakfasts are wonderful and relaxing while eating and watching wildlife in their natural habitat!"
Certificate may be used: Nov. 1-March 31, excluding holidays and holiday weekends.

Flat Rock   A5

Highland Lake Inn - A Country Retreat
PO Box 1026
Flat Rock, NC 28731
(828)693-6812 (800)635-5101 Fax:(828)696-8951
Internet: www.HLInn.com
E-mail: btaylor@HLInn.com

Circa 1900. A great place for families, this country farm setting features acres of activities. Besides a visit to the goat barn or watching for the resident peacock, canoe the lake, hike, swim, bike, play volleyball or horseshoes. The inn offers romantic guest bedrooms, some with whirlpool tubs or French doors leading to a porch with rockers. A rustic lodge with cozy rooms and private baths boasts a river rock fireplace in the lobby, billiards and table tennis in the recreation room. There are ten cabin rooms. Cottages with two to four bedrooms have kitchen facilities and some include a washer, dryer and large outside deck. The restaurant boasts an award-winning wine list and meals are made with fresh organic ingredients from the gardens. Explore local Carl Sandburg's home or Flat Rock Playhouse and historic sites in nearby Hendersonville. The Biltmore Estate is 28 miles away.
Innkeeper(s): Jack & Linda Grup. $89-399. 63 rooms, 36 with PB, 17 with FP, 1 suite, 16 cottages, 10 cabins and 3 conference rooms. Breakfast included in rates. Types of meals: Country bkfst, gourmet lunch, picnic lunch and gourmet dinner. Restaurant on premises. Beds: KQT. Modem hook-up, data port, cable TV, reading lamp, refrigerator, ceiling fan, clock radio, telephone, coffeemaker, desk, voice mail and some with fireplace in room. Air conditioning. VCR, fax, copier, swimming, bicycles, tennis, parlor games, fireplace, gift shop, variety of conference facilities, yoga studio and in-room massage (by appointment) on premises. Limited handicap access. Antiquing, art galleries, bicycling, canoeing/kayaking, fishing, golf, hiking, horseback riding, live theater, parks, shopping and wineries nearby.
Location: Country, mountains. Western North Carolina.
Publicity: *Southern Living, The Southern Gardener, Wine Spectator Magazine (recipient of "Award of Excellence" for having one of the best restaurant wine lists in the world) and PBS.*
Certificate may be used: December-March.

Franklin   C2

Buttonwood Inn
50 Admiral Drive
Franklin, NC 28734-1981
(828)369-8985 (888)368-8985
E-mail: innkeeperbwbb@myexcel.com

Circa 1920. Trees surround this two-story batten board house located adjacent to the Franklin Golf Course. Local crafts and handmade family quilts accent the country decor. Wonderful breakfasts are served here—often eggs Benedict, baked peaches

and sausage and freshly baked scones with homemade lemon butter. On a sunny morning, enjoy breakfast on the deck and savor the Smoky Mountain vistas. Afterward, you'll be ready for white-water rafting, hiking and fishing.
Innkeeper(s): Liz Oehser. $65-105. 4 rooms with PB. Breakfast and afternoon tea included in rates. Types of meals: Full bkfst and early coffee/tea. Beds: KDT. Ceiling fan and clock radio in room. Telephone on premises. Antiquing, fishing, parks and shopping nearby.
Location: Mountains. County city line.
Certificate may be used: Sunday-Thursday, except October, no weekends or holidays.

Gibsonville   B6

Burke Manor Inn
303 Burke Street
Gibsonville, NC 27249
(336)449-6266 (888)BUR-KE11 Fax:(336)449-9440
Internet: www.burkemanor.com
E-mail: info@burkemanor.com

Circa 1906. Blending the warmth of exceptional hospitality with prestigious service, this historic Victorian bed & breakfast inn features luxurious surroundings, quality reproductions and a comfortable atmosphere. Lavish suites include upscale amenities for the leisure and business traveler alike. Breakfast reflects the quality of food that has given the inn's restaurant a reputation for fine dining. Play tennis, then swim in the heated pool or soak tired muscles in the hot tub. The 3.5 acres provide a peaceful setting for beautiful garden weddings. It is an easy walk from the inn to downtown sites and shops.
Innkeeper(s): Vernon & Lynn Brady. $89-199. 7 rooms with PB, 1 suite and 2 conference rooms. Breakfast and snacks/refreshments included in rates. Types of meals: Full gourmet bkfst, veg bkfst and early coffee/tea. Beds: KQ. Modem hook-up, cable TV, reading lamp, stereo, ceiling fan, snack bar, clock radio, telephone, desk, hot tub/spa, voice mail, high thread count pressed linens, plush robes, candles, heated pool and breakfast in room. Central air. Fax, copier, swimming, tennis, parlor games, 4,800-square-foot wedding reception pavilion and gift shop on premises. Limited handicap access. Amusement parks, antiquing, art galleries, bicycling, canoeing/kayaking, fishing, golf, hiking, live theater, museums, parks, shopping, sporting events, tennis and water sports nearby.
Location: City.
Publicity: *Times News ("Best Bed and Breakfast"), Alamance Chamber of Commerce ("Retailer of the Year"), Greensboro News and Record, Burlington Times News, Crossroads Journal, WFMY TV 2, WBAG and WBAG 1150AM.*
Certificate may be used: Anytime, Sunday-Thursday.

Grassy Creek   A4

River House
1896 Old Field Creek Rd
Grassy Creek, NC 28631
(336)982-2109
Internet: www.riverhousenc.com
E-mail: riverhouse@skybest.com

Circa 1870. On 180 acres, with a mile of riverfront on the North Fork of the New River in the Blue Ridge Mountains of Ashe County, this year-round country inn and restaurant is ideal for romantic getaways, weddings, honeymoons, reunions, vacations, retreats and seminars. Relax by a warm log fire or on  front porch rockers. Choose from guest bedrooms with hot tubs, gas-log fireplaces and porches or stay in one of the secluded cabins by the millpond, river's edge or a log cabin among the trees. A gourmet breakfast is included and served in the renowned restaurant where dinner is offered nightly with libations and an international wine list. Play tennis on one of the full-sized courts, hike or bike. Fishing, tubing and canoeing are also popular available activities.

Innkeeper(s): Gayle Winston. $115-175. 9 rooms with PB, 6 with FP, 4 suites, 1 cottage, 2 cabins and 3 conference rooms. Breakfast included in rates. Types of meals: Full gourmet bkfst, early coffee/tea, gourmet lunch, picnic lunch, afternoon tea, gourmet dinner and room service. Restaurant on premises. Beds: KQT. Reading lamp, refrigerator, ceiling fan, clock radio, desk, hot tub/spa and whirlpool tubs in room. VCR, fax, copier, spa, swimming, tennis, library, parlor games, telephone and fireplace on premises. Antiquing, canoeing/kayaking, cross-country skiing, downhill skiing, fishing, golf, hiking, live theater, parks, shopping, sporting events, tennis and water sports nearby.
Location: Mountains, waterfront.
Certificate may be used: Anytime, Sunday-Thursday, excluding June, July, August and October.

Hendersonville   C3

Claddagh Inn
755 N Main St
Hendersonville, NC 28792-5079
(828)697-7778 (800)225-4700 Fax:(828)697-8664
Internet: www.claddaghinn.com/
E-mail: innkeepers@claddaghinn.com

Circa 1888. Claddagh has been host for more than 90 years to visitors staying in Hendersonville. The wide, wraparound veranda is filled with rocking chairs, while the library is filled with inviting books. Many of North Carolina's finest craft and antique shops are just two blocks from the inn. Carl Sandburg's house and the Biltmore Estate are nearby, and within a short drive are spectacular sights in the Great Smoky Mountains.

Innkeeper(s): Vanessa Mintz. $79-169. 16 rooms, 14 with PB, 3 with FP, 2 suites and 1 conference room. Breakfast included in rates. Types of meals: Full bkfst and early coffee/tea. Beds: KQDT. Data port, cable TV, VCR, reading lamp, CD player, ceiling fan, clock radio, telephone, turn-down service, desk, voice mail and fireplace in room. Air conditioning. Fax, copier, tennis, library, parlor games, refrigerator and TV on premises. Antiquing, fishing, live theater, parks, shopping, water sports, tennis and golf nearby.
Location: City, mountains.
Publicity: *Country Inn, Blue Ridge Country and Southern Living.*

"Excellent food, clean, home-like atmosphere."
Certificate may be used: Anytime, subject to availability.

Echo Mountain Inn
2849 Laurel Park Hwy
Hendersonville, NC 28739-8925
(828)693-9626 (888)324-6466 Fax:(828)697-2047
Internet: www.echoinn.com
E-mail: info@echoinn.com

Circa 1896. Sitting on top of Echo Mountain, this large stone and wood inn has spectacular views, especially from the dining room and many of the guest rooms. Rooms are decorated with antiques and reproductions and many include a fireplace. The historic town of Hendersonville is three miles away. Gourmet

dining includes an added touch of the city lights below. Guests may want to partake in refreshments of their choice served in the inn's fireside tavern.

Innkeeper(s): Peter & Shirley Demaras. $75-175. 37 rooms with PB, 8 with FP, 2 suites and 1 conference room. Breakfast included in rates. Types of meals: Cont, early coffee/tea, lunch, picnic lunch, gourmet dinner and room service. Restaurant on premises. Beds: KQDT. Cable TV, stereo, refrigerator & telephone in room. Air conditioning. Fireplace on premises. Antiquing, downhill skiing, fishing, golf, live theater & shopping nearby.

Location: Mountains.
"It was quite fabulous and the food entirely too rich."
Certificate may be used: January-September, November-December, Sunday-Thursday. Holidays, holiday weeks and special events excluded.

Melange Bed & Breakfast
1230 5th Ave W
Hendersonville, NC 28739-4112
(828)697-5253 (800)303-5253 Fax:(828)697-5751
Internet: www.melangebb.com
E-mail: mail@melangebb.com

Circa 1920. Classical gardens and fountains bordered by hemlock hedges and century-old trees accent this stately New England Colonial home with an elegant European flair. Listed in the National Register, it is furnished with antiques and boasts an eclectic melange of French Mediterranean decor. Luxurious guest bedrooms are named after their color scheme and feature posh wall and window coverings, colorful Anatolian rugs, Turkish bathrobes, refrigerators and feather beds with down comforters. The romantic, two-bedroom Rose Suite includes a Jacuzzi, big screen TV, surround stereo/CD as well as a large living and sitting area. Stay in the art deco Green Room with private porch and wood fireplace. Gourmet breakfasts are a delightful experience served alfresco in the rose garden patio or by candlelight in the greenhouse room.

Innkeeper(s): Lale & Mehmet Ozelsel. $105-185. 5 rooms, 4 with PB, 1 suite and 1 conference room. Breakfast, afternoon tea and snacks/refreshments included in rates. Types of meals: Full gourmet bkfst, veg bkfst, gourmet lunch, picnic lunch and room service. Beds: KQD. Modem hook-up, cable TV, VCR, reading lamp, stereo, refrigerator, ceiling fan, clock radio, coffeemaker, desk, hot tub/spa, fireplace, DVD and balcony in room. Central air. Fax, copier, library, parlor games, telephone, fireplace, gardens and patio/porch on premises. Limited handicap access. Antiquing, art galleries, bicycling, canoeing/kayaking, fishing, golf, hiking, horseback riding, live theater, museums, parks, shopping, tennis and wineries nearby.
Location: City, mountains.
Publicity: *Hendersonville Times News.*
Certificate may be used: Anytime, Monday-Thursday, Jan. 4-April 2.

The Waverly Inn
783 N Main St
Hendersonville, NC 28792-5079
(828)693-9193 (800)537-8195 Fax:(828)692-1010
Internet: www.waverlyinn.com
E-mail: waverlyinn@ioa.com

Circa 1898. In the National Register, this three-story Victorian and Colonial Revival house has a two-tiered, sawn work trimmed porch and widow's walk. A beautifully carved Eastlake staircase and an original registration desk grace the inn. There are four-poster canopy beds and clawfoot tubs. Breakfast is served in the handsome dining room. The Waverly is the oldest surviving inn in Hendersonville.

Innkeeper(s): John & Diane Sheiry, Darla Olmstead. $109-225. 13 rooms with PB, 1 suite. Breakfast and snacks/refreshments included in rates. Types of meals: Full bkfst and picnic lunch. Beds: KQDT. Cable TV, reading lamp, ceiling fan, clock radio, telephone and desk in room. Air conditioning. Fax and parlor games on premises. Antiquing, cross-country skiing, fishing, live theater, parks, shopping and hiking nearby.
Location: In town near mountains.
Publicity: *New York Times, Country, Blue Ridge Country, Vogue, Southern Living and Travel South.*

"Our main topic of conversation while driving back was what a great time we had at your place."
Certificate may be used: January, February, March, anytime. November, December, April, May, September, Sunday-Thursday.

Hertford   B9

1812 on The Perquimans B&B Inn

385 Old Neck Road
Hertford, NC 27944
(252)426-1812

Circa 1790. William and Sarah Fletcher were the first residents of this Federal-style plantation home, and the house is still in the family today. The Fletchers were Quakers and the first North Carolina residents to offer to pay the way for workers who wished to return to Africa. The farm rests along the banks of the Perquimans River, and the grounds retain many original outbuildings, including a brick dairy, smokehouse and a 19th-century frame barn. In the National Register of Historic Places, the inn is appropriately appointed with antiques highlighting the restored mantels and woodwork. A lovely, pastoral retreat.
Innkeeper(s): Peter & Nancy Rascoe. $80-85. 5 rooms. Breakfast included in rates. Types of meals: Full bkfst. Beds: KQD.
Certificate may be used: All year, except for weekends in April, May, September, October and major holidays.

Highlands   C2

Colonial Pines Inn Bed and Breakfast

541 Hickory St
Highlands, NC 28741
(828)526-2060 (866)526-2060
Internet: www.colonialpinesinn.com
E-mail: sleeptight@colonialpinesinn.com

Circa 1937. Secluded on a hillside just half a mile from Highlands' Main Street, this inn offers relaxing porches that boast a mountain view. The parlor is another restful option, offering a TV, fireplace and piano. Rooms, highlighted by knotty pine, are decorated with an eclectic mix of antiques. The guest pantry is always stocked with refreshments for those who need a little something in the afternoon. For breakfast, freshly baked breads accompany items such as a potato/bacon casserole and baked pears topped with currant sauce. In addition to guest rooms and suites, there are two cottages available, each with a fireplace and kitchen.
Innkeeper(s): Chris & Donna Alley. $85-165. 8 rooms, 6 with PB, 1 with FP, 3 total suites, including 2 two-bedroom suites, 1 cottage & 1 guest house. Breakfast, afternoon tea & snacks/refreshments included in rates. Types of meals: Full gourmet bkfst & early coffee/tea. Beds: KQDT. Data port, cable TV, VCR, reading lamp, CD player, refrigerator, ceiling fan, snack bar, telephone & fireplace in room. Fax on premises. Antiquing, art galleries, canoeing/kayaking, downhill skiing, fishing, golf, hiking, horseback riding, live theater, shopping & tennis nearby.
Location: Mountains.
Publicity: *Greenville News, Atlanta Journal, Highlander, Atlanta Constitution and Birmingham News.*

"There was nothing we needed which you did not provide."
Certificate may be used: Anytime, November-April, subject to availability, excluding holidays.

Hillsborough   B6

Hillsborough House Inn

209 E Tryon St # 880
Hillsborough, NC 27278-2527
(919)644-1600 (800)616-1660 Fax:(919)644-1308
Internet: www.hillsborough-inn.com
E-mail: inn.keeper@rtmx.net

Circa 1790. This Italianate-style house, on seven wooded acres, sits back on a spacious, well-tended lawn, the site for croquet, hide-and-seek games and picnics for the Webb family

for more than 140 years. In the Hillsborough Historic District, the inn boasts an 80-foot-long veranda and an 1850 addition. The decor is both elegant and eclectic, such as the 10-foot-high papier-mache cactus that rests next to an English sideboard from the 1800s. A favorite guest room features a high queen bed draped from the ceiling with yards of white voile. Your hostess is an artist and has her studio here.
Innkeeper(s): Lauri & Kirk Michel. $130-200. 6 rooms, 5 with PB, 4 with FP, 1 suite, 1 cottage and 1 conference room. Types of meals: Full bkfst, early coffee/tea and gourmet dinner. Beds: KQT. Reading lamp, CD player, ceiling fan, clock radio and fireplace in room. Central air. TV, VCR, fax, copier, spa, swimming, library, parlor games, telephone, fireplace and gift shop on premises. Antiquing, art galleries, golf, hiking, horseback riding, museums, shopping, sporting events and water sports nearby.
Location: Small town historic district.
Publicity: *Durham Morning Herald, News of Orange County, Southern Accents, Mid-Atlantic Country and Raleigh News & Observer.*

"What a marvelous discovery! Creative genius everywhere."
Certificate may be used: Sunday-Thursday, Dec. 1-March 1 excluding holidays, subject to availability.

Murphy   C1

Huntington Hall B&B

272 Valley River Ave
Murphy, NC 28906-2829
(828)837-9567 (800)824-6189 Fax:(828)837-2527
Internet: bed-breakfast-inn.com/
E-mail: huntington@webwork2.com

Circa 1881. This two-story country Victorian home was built by J.H. Dillard, the town mayor and twice a member of the House of Representatives. Clapboard siding and tall columns accent the large front porch. An English country theme is highlighted throughout. Afternoon refreshments and evening turndown service are included. Breakfast is served on the sun porch. Murder-mystery, summer-theater, and white-water-rafting packages are available.
Innkeeper(s): Curt & Nancy Harris. $75-125. 5 rooms with PB. Breakfast included in rates. Types of meals: Full gourmet bkfst and early coffee/tea. Beds: KQD. Cable TV, reading lamp, ceiling fan, clock radio, turn-down service and desk in room. Air conditioning. TV, VCR, fax, copier, library, parlor games, telephone and fireplace on premises. Antiquing, fishing, live theater, parks, shopping, tennis and water sports nearby.
Location: Mountains. Small town.
Publicity: *Atlanta Journal, Petersen's 4-Wheel and New York Times.*

"A bed and breakfast well done."
Certificate may be used: Sunday-Thursday any month.

New Bern   C8

Harmony House Inn

215 Pollock St
New Bern, NC 28560-4942
(252)636-3810 (800)636-3113 Fax:(252)636-3810
Internet: www.harmonyhouseinn.com
E-mail: stay@harmonyhouseinn.com

Circa 1850. Long ago, this two-story Greek Revival was sawed in half and the west side moved nine feet to accommodate new hall-

ways, additional rooms and a staircase. A wall was then built to divide the house into two sections. The rooms are decorated with antiques, the innkeeper's collection of handmade crafts and other collectibles. Two of the suites include a heart-shaped Jacuzzi tub. Offshore breezes sway blossoms in the lush garden. Cross the street to an excellent restaurant or take a picnic to the shore.
Innkeeper(s): Ed & Sooki Kirkpatrick. $89-160. 10 rooms with PB, 3 suites and 2 conference rooms. Breakfast included in rates. Types of meals: Full bkfst and early coffee/tea. Beds: KQT. Modem hook-up, data port, cable TV, reading lamp, ceiling fan, clock radio and telephone in room. Central air. Fax, copier, parlor games and gift shop on premises. Antiquing, art galleries, beach, bicycling, golf, live theater, museums, parks and shopping nearby.

"We feel nourished even now, six months after our visit to Harmony House."
Certificate may be used: Year-round, Sunday through Thursday. Weekends November through February on a space available basis, excluding holidays and special events.

Meadows Inn a Colonial B&B

212 Pollock St.
New Bern, NC 28560
(252)634-1776 (877)551-1776 Fax:(252)634-1776
Internet: www.meadowsinn-nc.com
E-mail: meadowsinnbnb@earthlink.net

Circa 1847. In the heart of the historic district, this Greek Revival/Federal-style home is considered to be the town's first inn. Boaters enjoy the close proximity to the dock of the Neuse and Trent Rivers with the Intercoastal Waterway only 30 miles away. The Gathering Room is a favorite place to play the baby grand piano or work on a puzzle. Hot and cold beverages always are available. Themed guest bedrooms are spacious and comfortable with non-working fireplaces. Ask about a romantic package in the Victorian Room, or choose the family-friendly two-room suite on the third floor. The morning meal may include quiche, breakfast pizza, scrambled egg enchiladas, or baked French toast to enjoy with fresh fruit, hot breads or muffins and juice.
Innkeeper(s): John & Betty Foy. $89-160. 7 rooms with PB, 1 suite and 1 conference room. Breakfast included in rates. Types of meals: Full bkfst, early coffee/tea and afternoon tea. Beds: QDT. Cable TV, reading lamp, ceiling fan, telephone and fireplace in room. Air conditioning. Fax, copier, parlor games, CD player and refrigerator on premises. Antiquing, art galleries, beach, bicycling, canoeing/kayaking, fishing, golf, hiking, parks and wineries nearby.
Location: City. Confluence of the Neuse and Trent Rivers, 30 miles to Intercoastal Waterway.
Certificate may be used: Anytime, November-April, subject to availability.

Ocean Isle   C8

Goose Creek B&B

1901 Egret St SW
Ocean Isle, NC 28469
(910)754-5849 (800)275-6540 Fax:(910)754-5849
Internet: www.goosecreekbb.com
E-mail: info@goosecreekbb.com

Circa 1984. This contemporary-style home located on a wooded acre offers four comfortable guest rooms. With more than 2,000 square feet of decks and porches, there are plenty of places to relax. The home rests on the banks of Goose Creek and includes its own fishing pier. The area boasts over thirty golf courses, and the Intracoastal Waterway, from which Goose Creek flows, is nearby. Ocean Isle Beach is an eight-minute drive.
Innkeeper(s): Peggy & Jim Grich. $70-150. 3 rooms with PB. Breakfast included in rates. Types of meals: Cont plus. Beds: Q. TV, VCR, reading lamp and ceiling fan in room. Air conditioning. Fax, copier, telephone and fireplace on premises. Antiquing, fishing, golf, tennis, water sports and bird watching nearby.
Location: Waterfront.
Certificate may be used: Jan. 1-May 15, Sunday-Thursday; Oct. 1-Nov. 30, Sunday-Thursday.

Pilot Mountain   A5

The Blue Fawn B&B

3052 Siloam Rd, PO Box 986
Pilot Mountain (Siloam), NC 27041
(336)374-2064
E-mail: bluefawnbb@surry.net

Circa 1892. This Greek Revival-style house, with its four two-story columns, is bordered by an old stone fence. Located 10 minutes from town, the Blue Fawn B&B offers a friendly stay in  a small tobacco farming community. There are three porches, and one is off the second-story guest rooms, which are decorated comfortably with many quilts. Spinach blue cheese strudel, Irish soda bread and fruit or homemade biscuits served with sausage gravy, fried potatoes and baked garlic cheese grits are some of the breakfast offerings. It's a tenth of a mile to the Yadkin River.
Innkeeper(s): Geno & Terri Cella. $65-85. 3 rooms with PB, 1 suite. Breakfast, afternoon tea and snacks/refreshments included in rates. Types of meals: Full gourmet bkfst, early coffee/tea, picnic lunch and room service. Beds: KQDT. Cable TV, reading lamp, refrigerator, ceiling fan, clock radio, turn-down service, desk, second-story porch off rooms and quilts in room. Air conditioning. VCR, bicycles, library, telephone and three porches on premises. Antiquing, fishing, live theater, parks, shopping, water sports, golf, horseback riding and hiking nearby.
Location: Country.
Publicity: *Mt. Airy News.*
Certificate may be used: January-December.

Rose Hill   C7

Six Runs Plantation, Inc

2794 Register Sutton Road
Rose Hill, NC 28458
(910)532-4810

Circa 1828. A rice plantation 200 years ago and a hunting preserve for 20 years, the rustic lodge of pegged heart pine and juniper logs offers deluxe accommodations. The decor is Colonial, with leather Chippendale and Queen Anne furnishings. The large log great room features exposed beams, an open fire, grand piano and satellite TV. There is a fireplace in the lounge, and the formal dining room is spacious and perfect for conferences. The namesake, Six Runs River, weaves through 1,000 acres enhancing the natural habitat of game including quail, ducks and deer. Walking trails, an indoor Jacuzzi, sun porch and decks provide relaxing interludes.
Innkeeper(s): Becky Edwards. $125-160. 8 rooms, 5 with PB, 1 with FP. Breakfast included in rates. Types of meals: Cont, picnic lunch, snacks/refreshments and gourmet dinner. Canoeing/kayaking, fishing, hiking, bird watching, dirt bike trails, wildflowers, hunting, sporting clays and historic battlefields nearby.
Certificate may be used: Anytime.

Spruce Pine   B3

Richmond Inn B&B

51 Pine Ave
Spruce Pine, NC 28777-2733
(828)765-6993 Fax:(707)356-4880
Internet: www.richmond-inn.com
E-mail: innkeeper@richmond-inn.com

Circa 1939. The scent of freshly baked muffins and steaming coffee serves as a pleasing wake-up call for guests staying at this country mountain home. More than an acre of wooded grounds surround the inn, which overlooks the Toe River valley. Rooms are decorated with family heirlooms and antiques. Several guest rooms include four-poster beds. Crackling flames from the stone fireplace warm the living room, a perfect place to relax. The innkeepers keep a guest refrigerator in the butler's pantry.

Innkeeper(s): Maggie Haskell & Family. $65-125. 8 rooms with PB, 1 with FP, 2 suites. Breakfast included in rates. Types of meals: Full bkfst and early coffee/tea. Beds: QT. Reading lamp, ceiling fan, clock radio, desk and Jacuzzi in suite in room. VCR, fax, telephone and fireplace on premises. Antiquing, cross-country skiing, downhill skiing, golf, parks, shopping, gem mining and crafts nearby.

Location: Mountains.

Certificate may be used: January-April, Sunday-Thursday.

Sylva C2

Mountain Brook

208 Mountain Brook Rd #19
Sylva, NC 28779-9659
(828)586-4329
Internet: www.mountainbrook.com
E-mail: AHI@mountainbrook.com

Circa 1931. Located in the Great Smokies, Mountain Brook in western North Carolina consists of 14 cabins on a hillside amid rhododendron, elm, maple and oak trees. The resort's 200-acre terrain is crisscrossed with brooks and waterfalls, contains a trout-stocked pond and nature trail. Two cabins are constructed with logs from the property, while nine are made from native stone. They feature fireplaces, full kitchens, porch swings and some have Jacuzzi's.

Innkeeper(s): Gus, Michele, Maqelle McMahon. $90-140. 12 cottages with PB, 12 with FP. Types of meals: Early coffee/tea. Beds: KD. Reading lamp, refrigerator and clock radio in room. Game room and spa/sauna bungalow on premises. Handicap access. Amusement parks, antiquing, downhill skiing, fishing, golf, live theater, shopping, sporting events, tennis, water sports, casino, Great Smokies National Park, railroad and nature trail nearby.

Location: Mountains. Rural.

Publicity: *Brides Magazine, Today and The Hudspeth Report.*

"The cottage was delightfully cozy, and our privacy was not interrupted even once."

Certificate may be used: Feb. 1 to Oct. 1, Nov. 1 to Dec. 20, holidays excluded.

Tabor City D7

Four Rooster Inn

403 Pireway Rd/Rt 904
Tabor City, NC 28463-2519
(910)653-3878 (800)653-5008 Fax:(910)653-3878
Internet: www.4roosterinn.com
E-mail: info@4roosterinn.com

Circa 1949. This inn is surrounded by more than an acre of lush grounds, featuring camellias and azaleas planted by the innkeeper's father. Antiques, fine linens and tables set with china and crystal await to pamper you. Afternoon tea is served in the parlor. The innkeepers place a tray with steaming fresh coffee or tea and the newspaper beside your guest room door in the morning. After a good night's sleep and coffee, guests settle down to a lavish, gourmet Southern breakfast, served in

the inn's formal dining room. Sherried fruit compote, warm yam bread and succulent French toast stuffed with cheese are just a few of the possible items guests might enjoy. Myrtle Beach offers outlet shopping, beaches, and more than 100 golf courses, the first of which is just four miles from the inn.

Innkeeper(s): Gloria & Bob Rogers. $75-95. 4 rooms, 2 with PB. Breakfast, afternoon tea and snacks/refreshments included in rates. Types of meals: Full gourmet bkfst and early coffee/tea. Beds: QD. Reading lamp, clock radio, telephone, turn-down service and desk in room. Air conditioning. VCR, parlor games and fireplace on premises. Amusement parks, antiquing, fishing, live theater, parks, shopping, sporting events, water sports and outlets nearby.

"Such a fine place, we crowed over their outstanding hospitality, beautiful antiques and excellent food." — Southern Living Magazine

Certificate may be used: Anytime, Sunday-Thursday, room assignment to best available determined on day of arrival.

Tryon C3

Foxtrot Inn

PO Box 1561, 210 Fox Trot Lane
Tryon, NC 28782-1561
(828)859-9706 (888)676-8050
Internet: www.foxtrotinn.com
E-mail: wim@foxtrotinn.com

Circa 1915. Located on six acres in town, this turn-of-the-century home features mountain views and large guest rooms. There is a private two bedroom guest cottage with its own kitchen and a hanging deck. The rooms are furnished with antiques. The Cherry Room in the main house has a four-poster, queen-size canopy bed with a sitting area overlooking the inn's swimming pool. The Oak Suite includes a wood-paneled sitting room with cathedral ceiling. A cozy fireplace warms the lobby.

Innkeeper(s): Wim Woody. $85-150. 4 rooms with PB, 2 suites and 1 cottage. Breakfast included in rates. Types of meals: Full bkfst. Beds: QDT. Reading lamp, clock radio and desk in room. Air conditioning. Swimming, parlor games, telephone and fireplace on premises. Antiquing, fishing, parks, shopping and water sports nearby.

Location: Mountains.

Certificate may be used: Anytime, subject to availability.

Mimosa Inn

Mimosa Inn Dr
Tryon, NC 28782
(828)859-7688
E-mail: jimsott@msn.com

Circa 1903. The Mimosa is situated on the southern slope of the Blue Ridge Mountains. With its long rolling lawns and large columned veranda, the inn has been a landmark and social gathering place for almost a century. Breakfasts are served either in the dining room or on the columned veranda.

Innkeeper(s): Jim & Stephanie Ott. $95. 10 rooms with PB and 1 conference room. Breakfast included in rates. Types of meals: Full bkfst and early coffee/tea. Beds: QT. Reading lamp in room. Air conditioning. Library, parlor games, telephone and fireplace on premises. Amusement parks, antiquing, fishing, live theater, parks and shopping nearby.

Location: Mountains.

"Thanks for your hospitality. We could just feel that Southern charm."

Certificate may be used: January-March, Sunday-Thursday. April-December, Monday-Thursday, except holidays and special events.

Tryon Old South B&B

27 Markham Rd
Tryon, NC 28782-3054
(828)859-6965 (800)288-7966 Fax:(828)859-6965
Internet: www.tryonoldsouth.com
E-mail: pat@tryonoldsouth.com

Circa 1910. This Colonial Revival inn is located just two blocks from downtown and Trade Street's antique and gift shops. Located in the Thermal Belt, Tryon is known for its pleasant, mild weather. Guests don't go away hungry from innkeeper Pat Grogan's large Southern-style breakfasts. Unique woodwork abounds in this inn and equally as impressive is a curving staircase. Behind the property is a large wooded area and several waterfalls are just a couple of miles away. The inn is close to Asheville attractions.

Innkeeper(s): Tony & Pat Grogan. $75-105. 4 rooms with PB and 2 guest houses. Breakfast included in rates. Types of meals: Full bkfst, early coffee/tea and wine. Beds: KQD. TV, reading lamp and clock radio in room. Air conditioning. VCR, fax, copier, parlor games, telephone and fireplace on premises. Limited handicap access. Antiquing, art galleries, fishing, golf, hiking, horseback riding, live theater, museums, parks, shopping, wineries and waterfalls nearby.
Location: Mountains. Small town.
Certificate may be used: Anytime except for the months of August, September and October.

Valle Crucis   B4

The Mast Farm Inn

PO Box 704
Valle Crucis, NC 28691
(828)963-5857 (888)963-5857 Fax:(828)963-6404
Internet: www.mastfarminn.com
E-mail: stay@mastfarminn.com

Circa 1812. Listed in the National Register of Historic Places, this 18-acre farmstead includes a main house and ten outbuildings, one of them a log cabin built in 1812. The inn features a wraparound porch with rocking chairs, swings and a view of the mountain valley. Fresh flowers gathered from the garden add fragrance throughout the inn. Rooms are furnished with antiques, quilts and mountain crafts. In addition to the inn rooms, there are seven cottages available, some with kitchens.

Before breakfast is served, early morning coffee can be delivered to your room. Organic home-grown vegetables are featured at dinners, included in a contemporary regional cuisine.

Innkeeper(s): Wanda Hinshaw & Kay Philipp. $125-295. 15 rooms, 8 with PB, 4 with FP, 3 with HT, 7 cottages and 2 guest houses. Breakfast included in rates. Types of meals: Full gourmet bkfst, veg bkfst, early coffee/tea and gourmet dinner. Restaurant on premises. Beds: KQT. Modem hook-up, data port, reading lamp, CD player, refrigerator, ceiling fan, clock radio, telephone, coffeemaker, hot tub/spa, fireplace and the two cottages have a kitchen in room. Central air. Fax, copier, spa, parlor games and gift shop on premises. Handicap access. Antiquing, art galleries, bicycling, canoeing/kayaking, downhill skiing, fishing, golf, hiking, horseback riding, live theater, parks, shopping, water sports, river sports, Blue Ridge Pkwy and Grandfather Mt nearby.
Location: Country, mountains.
Publicity: *Travel & Leisure, Cooking Light, Blue Ridge Country, Southern Living, New York Times, Our State, Carolina Gardener, Charlotte Taste and Appalachian Voice.*

"We want to live here!"
Certificate may be used: May and September only.

Washington   B8

The Moss House Bed & Breakfast

129 Van Norden St
Washington, NC 27889-4846
(252)975-3967 (888)975-3393 Fax:(252)975-1148
Internet: www.themosshouse.com
E-mail: info@themosshouse.com

Circa 1902. High ceilings and heart pine floors impart a light and airy ambiance to this Victorian home that is steeped in family history and filled with heirlooms and original artwork. The B&B is owned and operated by the great-granddaughter of Mr. & Mrs. Frank A. Moss, its builders. Fresh flowers and greenery cut from the gardens are thoughtful details in the elegant guest bedrooms. A satisfying Southern gourmet breakfast is served. Listed in the National Register and located in the historic district at the start of the self-guided walking tour, it is also one block from the Pamlico River, and a short walk to downtown shops, restaurants and a sailboat marina.

Innkeeper(s): Mary Havens Cooper. $85-95. 4 rooms with PB, 1 suite. Breakfast included in rates. Types of meals: Full gourmet bkfst and early coffee/tea. Beds: KQT. Modem hook-up, cable TV, reading lamp, ceiling fan, clock radio and telephone in room. Central air. Fax, copier and parlor games on premises. Antiquing, art galleries, canoeing/kayaking, golf, hiking, museums, parks, shopping, tennis, water sports, wineries, sailing charters and sailing school nearby.
Location: Historic small town.
Publicity: *Sail Magazine, Coastal Living and Washington Daily News.*

"We really enjoyed the comfortable atmosphere and the food was delectable."
Certificate may be used: Anytime, November-April, Sunday-Thursday, subject to availability.

Waynesville   B2

Adger House Bed & Breakfast

127 Balsam Drive
Waynesville, NC 28786
(828)452-0861 (866)234-3701 Fax:(828)452-0847
Internet: www.adgerhouse.com
E-mail: info@adgerhouse.com

Circa 1906. Cradled by three wooded acres, this neo-classical revival home has retained much of its original architectural details. High ceilings, hardwood floors and paneled wainscoting complement the period antiques and reproductions. There is ample room to roam, whether enjoying afternoon refreshments in the Eagle's Nest Parlor, reading in a well-stocked library or relaxing in the sunroom. Oversize guest bedrooms are splendidly furnished. Choose a room with a fireplace, loft or double shower. A generous breakfast is served in the Adgerwood Room or al fresco on the patio. Stroll the gardens, or visit the quaint historic village nearby.

Innkeeper(s): Leslie & Bruce Merrell. $95-150. 5 rooms with PB, 2 with FP. Breakfast and afternoon tea included in rates. Types of meals: Full gourmet bkfst, early coffee/tea and snacks/refreshments. Beds: KQT. Reading lamp, ceiling fan, clock radio, turn-down service and fireplace in room. TV, library, parlor games and telephone on premises. Limited handicap access. Antiquing, art galleries, bicycling, canoeing/kayaking, downhill skiing, fishing, golf, hiking, horseback riding, museums, parks, shopping and water sports nearby.
Location: Mountains.
Certificate may be used: Anytime, subject to availability.

Belle Meade Inn

1534 S Main St
Waynesville, NC 28786-1319
(828)456-9333 (888)621-0686 Fax:(828)456-6633
Internet: www.thebellemeade.com
E-mail: bellemeadeinn2@aol.com

Circa 1908. Located near Asheville in the mountains of the Western part of the state, this Craftsman-style home was named Belle Meade, a French phrase meaning "beautiful meadow." Chestnut woodwork provides the background for antiques and traditional furnishings. A fieldstone fireplace is featured in the living room. The Great Smoky Mountain Railroad ride is nearby.
Innkeeper(s): Rick Silveira & Janice Vangundy Silveira. $80-110. 4 rooms with PB, 2 with FP. Breakfast and afternoon tea included in rates. Types of meals: Full bkfst and early coffee/tea. Beds: QD. Reading lamp, ceiling fan, clock radio and Direct TV/HBO in room. Air conditioning. VCR, fax, copier, parlor games, telephone, fireplace and veranda with rocking chairs on premises. Amusement parks, antiquing, cross-country skiing, downhill skiing, fishing, golf, live theater, parks, shopping, sporting events and tennis nearby.
Location: Mountains.
Publicity: *Blue Ridge Magazine, Asheville Citizen Times* and *St. Petersburg Times.*

"Immaculately clean. Distinctively furnished. Friendly atmosphere."
Certificate may be used: Sunday-Thursday, April 1-Oct. 31.

Herren House

94 East St
Waynesville, NC 28786-3836
(828)452-7837 (800)284-1932
Internet: www.herrenhouse.com
E-mail: herren@brinet.com

Circa 1897. Pink and white paint emphasize the Victorian features of this two-story inn with wraparound porch. Inside, the Victorian decor is enhanced with the innkeepers' paintings and handmade furniture. Soft music and candlelight set the tone for breakfast, which often features the inn's homemade chicken sausage and a baked egg dish along with freshly baked items such as apricot scones. (Saturday evening dinners are available by prior arrangement.) A garden gazebo is an inviting spot with an overhead fan and piped in music. A block away are galleries, antique shops and restaurants. The Great Smoky Mountains National Park and the Blue Ridge Parkway begin a few minutes from the inn.
Innkeeper(s): Jackie & Frank Blevins. $85-150. 6 rooms with PB. Breakfast, afternoon tea and snacks/refreshments included in rates. Types of meals: Full gourmet bkfst and early coffee/tea. Beds: KQT. Cable TV, VCR, reading lamp, ceiling fan and desk in room. Air conditioning. Fax, copier, library, parlor games, telephone and gourmet dinner served at additional charge Saturday evenings on premises. Handicap access. Antiquing, cross-country skiing, downhill skiing, fishing, golf, live theater, parks, shopping and water sports nearby.
Location: Mountains.

"The two of you have mastered the art of sensory pleasures! Nothing was left unattended."
Certificate may be used: November-May, Sunday-Thursday.

Mountain Creek Inn

146 Chestnut Walk Dr
Waynesville, NC 28786-5381
(828)456-5509 (800)557-9766
Internet: www.mountaincreekbb.com
E-mail: mountaincreekbb@msn.com

Circa 1950. From its floor-to-ceiling windows, this hilltop lodge affords views of mountains and woods and is surrounded by more than five, peaceful acres. Meander through the gardens or take a leisurely stroll on a nature path. The innkeepers found their bed & breakfast while trekking through the Smoky Mountains on a tandem bicycle. If weather permits, the full gourmet breakfast is served on the deck. For an additional charge, picnic lunches and romantic getaway packages for two can be prepared.
Innkeeper(s): Guy & Hylah Smalley. $95-135. 7 rooms with PB. Breakfast and afternoon tea included in rates. Types of meals: Full gourmet bkfst, early coffee/tea, gourmet lunch, picnic lunch and snacks/refreshments. Beds: KQ. Reading lamp and turn-down service in room. Air conditioning. Library, telephone and fireplace on premises. Handicap access. Amusement parks, antiquing, bicycling, cross-country skiing, downhill skiing, fishing, hiking, live theater, parks, shopping and water sports nearby.
Location: Mountains.
Certificate may be used: Jan. 2-May 15, Sunday-Thursday. No holidays.

Weldon   A8

Weldon Place Inn

500 Washington Ave
Weldon, NC 27890-1644
(252)536-4582 (800)831-4470 Fax:(252)536-4582
E-mail: weldonplaceinn@email.com

Circa 1914. Blueberry buckle and strawberry blintzes are a pleasant way to start your morning at this Colonial Revival home. Located in a National Historic District, it is two miles from I-95. Wedding showers and other celebrations are popular here. There are beveled-glass windows, canopy beds and Italian fireplaces. Most of the inn's antiques are original to the house, including a horse-hair stuffed couch with its original upholstery. Select the Romantic Retreat package and you'll enjoy sweets, other treats, a gift bag, sparkling cider, a whirlpool tub and breakfast in bed.
Innkeeper(s): Bill & Cathy Eleczko. $60-89. 4 rooms with PB. Breakfast included in rates. Types of meals: Full bkfst and early coffee/tea. Beds: D. Cable TV, reading lamp, clock radio and coffeemaker in room. Air conditioning. VCR and telephone on premises. Antiquing, fishing, live theater and shopping nearby.
Location: Historic small town.
Certificate may be used: Anytime, based upon availability.

Williamston   B8

Big Mill Bed & Breakfast

1607 Big Mill Rd
Williamston, NC 27892-8032
(252)792-8787
Internet: www.bigmill.com
E-mail: info@bigmill.com

Circa 1918. Originally built as a small arts and crafts frame house, the many renovations conceal its true age. The historic farm outbuildings that include the chicken coop, smokehouse, pack house, tobacco barns and potato house, were built on on-site heart pine and cypress trees that were felled and floated down the streams of this 250-acre woodland estate. The Corncrib guest bedroom is in the pack house that originally housed mules. Each of the guest bedrooms feature climate control, stenciled floors, faux-painted walls, hand-decorated tiles on the wet bar and a private entrance. The suite also boasts a stone fireplace and impressive view. The countryside setting includes a three-acre lake with bridges, fruit orchard, vegetable and flower gardens. Eighty-year-old pecan trees planted by Chloe's parents provide nuts for homemade treats as well as shade for the inn.

Innkeeper(s): Chloe Tuttle. $58-75. 4 rooms with PB, 1 with FP, 1 suite, 1 cottage and 1 conference room. Breakfast included in rates. Types of meals: Cont and picnic lunch. Beds: QDT. TV, VCR, reading lamp, refrigerator, ceiling fan, telephone, desk, private entrances, individual climate control, wet bars, kitchenettes with sinks, refrigerators, toaster ovens and coffee pots in room. Air conditioning. Fax, bicycles, parlor games, fireplace, laundry facility, lake fishing and off-street parking for any size vehicle on premises. Limited handicap access. Antiquing, bicycling, canoeing/kayaking, fishing, golf, hiking, horseback riding, sporting events, water sports, horse shows, nature trails, nature preserves, boating access, Roanoke River Refuge, Gardner's Creek camping platforms and Bob Martin Agriculture Center nearby.

Location: Country. Carolina countryside.

Publicity: *WRAL-TV.*

Certificate may be used: December-February, subject to availability, excluding Valentine's Day, applies to nightly rates only.

Wilmington   D7

C.W. Worth House B&B

412 S 3rd St
Wilmington, NC 28401-5102
(910)762-8562 (800)340-8559 Fax:(910)763-2173
Internet: www.worthhouse.com
E-mail: relax@worthhouse.com

Circa 1893. This beautifully detailed three-story Queen Anne Victorian boasts two turrets and a wide veranda. From the outside, it gives the appearance of a small castle. The inn was renovated around 1910, and it retains many of the architectural details of the original house, including the paneled front hall. Victorian decor is found throughout the inn, including period antiques. The Rose Suite offers a king four-poster bed, sitting room and bath with a clawfoot tub and separate shower. Guests are treated to gourmet breakfasts. Freshly baked muffins and entrees such as eggs Florentine, rosemary and goat cheese strata and stuffed French toast are served. A second-story porch overlooks the garden with dogwood, ponds and pecan trees.

Innkeeper(s): Margi & Doug Erickson. $120-150. 7 rooms with PB. Breakfast and snacks/refreshments included in rates. Types of meals: Full gourmet bkfst and early coffee/tea. Beds: KQT. Data port, reading lamp, ceiling fan, clock radio, telephone, desk and one with two-person whirlpool in room. Central air. TV, VCR, fax, copier, parlor games and wireless high-speed Internet access on premises. Antiquing, art galleries, beach, canoeing/kayaking, fishing, golf, live theater, museums, parks, shopping, sporting events, water sports, wineries, performing arts, fine dining, carriage rides, historic home tours and walking tours nearby.

Location: City.

Publicity: *History Channel.*

Certificate may be used: Sunday-Thursday, excluding holidays.

Graystone Inn

100 S 3rd St
Wilmington, NC 28401-4503
(910)763-2000 (888)763-4773 Fax:(910)763-5555
Internet: www.graystoneinn.com
E-mail: reservations@graystoneinn.com

Circa 1906. If you are a connoisseur of inns, you'll be delighted with this stately mansion in the Wilmington Historic District and in the National Register. Recently chosen by American Historic Inns as one of America's Top Ten Romantic Inns, towering columns mark the balconied grand entrance. Its 14,000 square feet of magnificent space includes antique furnishings,

art and amenities. A staircase of hand-carved red oak rises three stories. Guests lounge in the music room, drawing room and library. A conference room and reception area with a fireplace and sitting area are on the third floor, once a grand ballroom. The elegant guest rooms are often chosen for special occasions, especially the 1,300-square-foot Bellevue, which offers a sitting room, king bed, sofa and handsome period antiques.

Innkeeper(s): Paul & Yolanda Bolda. $159-329. 7 rooms with PB, 6 with FP, 2 suites and 1 conference room. Breakfast included in rates. Types of meals: Full gourmet bkfst and early coffee/tea. Beds: KQ. Data port, TV, reading lamp, ceiling fan, clock radio, telephone, turn-down service, desk, computer jacks and many with four-poster beds in room. Air conditioning. Fax, copier, library, parlor games, fireplace, weight training room and PC data ports on premises. Antiquing, fishing, golf, live theater, parks, shopping, sporting events, tennis, water sports and museums nearby.

Location: City.

Publicity: *Country Inns, TV series Young Indiana Jones, Matlock, Dawsons Creek, Movie Rambling Rose, Mary Jane's Last Dance and Cats Eye.*

Certificate may be used: Nov. 1-March 31.

Rosehill Inn Bed & Breakfast

114 S 3rd St
Wilmington, NC 28401-4556
(910)815-0250 (800)815-0250 Fax:(910)815-0350
Internet: www.rosehill.com
E-mail: rosehill@rosehill.com

Circa 1848. Architect Henry Bacon Jr., most famous for designing the Lincoln Memorial in Washington, D.C., lived here in the late 19th century. Located in the largest urban historic district in the country, this Neoclassical Victorian was

completely renovated in 1995. The guest rooms are spacious and decorated in period furnishings. Breakfast treats include eggs Benedict with Cajun Crab Hollandaise and stuffed French toast with orange syrup.

Innkeeper(s): Laurel Jones. $99-229. 6 rooms with PB. Breakfast included in rates. Types of meals: Full gourmet bkfst and early coffee/tea. Beds: KQD. Modem hook-up, data port, cable TV, VCR, reading lamp, clock radio, telephone, desk, data port and iron and ironing board in room. Fax on premises. Antiquing, fishing, golf, live theater, parks, shopping, sporting events, tennis, water sports, battleship memorial and beaches nearby.

Location: Historic district.

Publicity: *Southern Living, Wilmington Star News, Wilmington Magazine, Washington Post, Insiders Guide to Wilmington, Atlanta Sun, Philadelphia Inquirer and Oprah Winfrey "The Wedding."*

Certificate may be used: Dec. 1 to Feb. 28 (excluding Feb. 13-15), Sunday-Thursday.

Wilson   B7

Miss Betty's B&B Inn

600 West Nash St
Wilson, NC 27893-3045
(252)243-4447 (800)258-2058 Fax:(252)243-4447
Internet: www.missbettysbnb.com
E-mail: info@missbettysbnb.com

Circa 1858. Located in a gracious setting in the downtown historic district, the inn is comprised of several restored historic homes, chief of which is the two-story National Register Italianate building called the Davis-Whitehead Harris House. Here there are 12-foot high ceilings, heart-pine and oak floors and wonderful collections of antiques. Breakfast is served in the Victorian dining room of the main house, with its walnut antique furniture and clusters of roses on the wallpaper. All the extras, such as lace tablecloths and hearty meals, conjure up the Old South. Smoking is allowed on the outside porches — there are six of them — and the deck. Four golf courses, numerous tennis courts and many fine restaurants are nearby. Wilson is known as the antique capitol of North Carolina.

Innkeeper(s): Betty & Fred Spitz. $60-80. 14 rooms with PB, 11 with FP, 3 suites. Breakfast included in rates. Types of meals: Full bkfst. Beds: KQDT. Cable TV, reading lamp, ceiling fan, clock radio, telephone and desk in room. Air conditioning. TV, fax, copier, parlor games and fireplace on premises. Handicap access. Live theater and sporting events nearby.
Location: Midway between Maine and Florida, along the main North-South Route I-95.
Publicity: Wilson Daily Times-1996, The Philadelphia Enquirer-1999, Southern Living-1997, Mid-Atlantic Country-1995, Our State/NC-1995 and Washington Post-1998.

"Yours is second to none. Everything was perfect. I can see why you are so highly rated."

Certificate may be used: Call for availability, guest rooms 2 and 3 in Main House.

Winston-Salem   B5

Augustus T. Zevely Inn

803 S Main St
Winston-Salem, NC 27101-5332
(336)748-9299 (800)928-9299 Fax:(336)721-2211
Internet: www.winston-salem-inn.com
E-mail: ctheall@dddcompany.com

Circa 1844. The Zevely Inn is the only lodging in Old Salem. Each of the rooms at this charming pre-Civil War inn have a view of historic Old Salem. Moravian furnishings and fixtures permeate the decor of each of the guest quarters, some of which boast working fireplaces. The home's architecture is reminiscent of many structures built in Old Salem during the second quarter of the 19th century. The formal dining room and parlor have

wood burning fireplaces. The two-story porch offers visitors a view of the period gardens and a beautiful magnolia tree. A line of Old Salem furniture has been created by Lexington Furniture Industries, and several pieces were created especially for the Zevely Inn.

Innkeeper(s): Larry Arnold. $80-205. 12 rooms with PB, 3 with FP, 1 suite. Breakfast and snacks/refreshments included in rates. Beds: KQDT. Cable TV, reading lamp, refrigerator, clock radio, telephone, desk and whirlpool tub in room. Air conditioning. Fax, copier, parlor games and fireplace on premises. Antiquing, live theater, shopping, sporting events and Old Salem Historic District nearby.
Location: City.
Publicity: Washington Post Travel, Salem Star, Winston-Salem Journal, Tasteful, Country Living, National Trust for Historic Preservation, Homes and Gardens, Homes Across America, Southern Living, Heritage Travel, Top 25 Historic Inns & Hotels and Home & Gardens Network Show.

"Colonial charm with modern conveniences, great food. Very nice! Everything was superb."

Certificate may be used: November, December, January, February on Sunday, Monday, excluding seasonal events.

Summit Street Inns

434 Summit at W 5th
Winston-Salem, NC 27101
(336)777-1887 (800)301-1887 Fax:(336)777-0518
Internet: www.bbinn.com
E-mail: innkeeper@bbinn.com

Circa 1887. Located in a historic urban residential neighborhood, this inn is comprised of two adjacent Victorian homes. Both homes are listed in the National Register and boast such features as wraparound porches, gabled roofs, ornate entrances, beautiful windows and high ceilings. Guest rooms are decorated with Victorian antiques, and each includes a double whirlpool tub. The innkeepers provide many thoughtful amenities, such as stocked mini-refrigerators,

microwaves, coffeemakers, stereos, TVs with VCRs and free movies, irons, bathrobes and hair dryers. There is a Nautilus exercise room and a billiards room. Two gourmet restaurants in historic homes are only two blocks away.

Innkeeper(s): Constance Creasman. $89-209. 10 rooms with PB, 5 with FP. Breakfast included in rates. Types of meals: Full bkfst, early coffee/tea, lunch, gourmet dinner and room service. Beds: K. Cable TV, VCR, reading lamp, stereo, refrigerator, ceiling fan, clock radio, telephone, desk, hot tub/spa, towel warmer and hair dryer in room. Air conditioning. TV on premises. Antiquing, live theater, parks, shopping and sporting events nearby.
Location: City.
Publicity: Winston-Salem Journal, Charlotte Observer, Mid-Atlantic Country, Southern Living, Southern Accents, USA Today and American Way.

"I have never seen anything like the meticulous and thorough attention to detail." — Dannye Romine, The Charlotte Observer

Certificate may be used: Sunday-Monday.

North Dakota

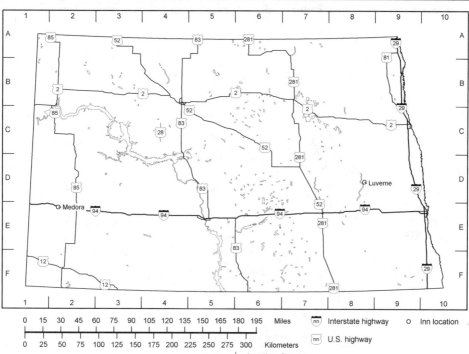

0 15 30 45 60 75 90 105 120 135 150 165 180 195 Miles   [nn] Interstate highway   o Inn location

0 25 50 75 100 125 150 175 200 225 250 275 300 Kilometers   [nn] U.S. highway

Luverne   D8

Volden Farm

11943 County Rd 26
Luverne, ND 58056
(701)769-2275 Fax:(701)769-2610
Internet: www.ndbba.com/vf.htm
E-mail: voldenfarm-bb@broadvu.com

Circa 1926. Perennial gardens and a hedge of lilacs surround this redwood house with its newer addition. A favorite room is the North Room with a lace canopy bed, an old pie safe and a Texas Star quilt made by the host's grandmother. Guests enjoy soaking in the clawfoot tub while looking out over the hills. There are two libraries, a music room and game room. The innkeepers also offer lodging in the Law Office, which dates to 1885 and is a separate little prairie house ideal for families. A stream, bordered by old oaks and formed by a natural spring, meanders through the property. The chickens here lay green and blue eggs. Dinner is available by advanced arrangement. Hiking, birdwatching, snowshoeing and skiing are nearby.

Innkeeper(s): JoAnne Wold. $60-95. 4 rooms, 3 with PB & 1 cottage. Breakfast and snacks/refreshments included in rates. Types of meals: Full gourmet bkfst, early coffee/tea, picnic lunch and gourmet dinner. Beds: KDT. Reading lamp, refrigerator, clock radio and desk in room. Bicycles, library, parlor games, telephone and fireplace on premises. Antiquing, cross-country skiing, downhill skiing, fishing, hiking, golf, canoeing, snowshoeing & bird watching nearby.

Location: Country.
Publicity: *Fargo Forum, Horizons, Grand Forks Herald, Mid-West Living and Getaways.*

"Very pleasant indeed! JoAnne makes you feel good. There's so much to do, and the hospitality is amazing!"
Certificate may be used: Anytime, holidays excluded.

Medora   E2

The Rough Riders Hotel B&B

Medora, ND
Medora, ND 58645
(701)623-4444 (800)633-6721 Fax:(701)623-4494
E-mail: medora@medora.com

Circa 1865. This old hotel has the branding marks of Teddy Roosevelt's cattle ranch as well as other brands stamped into the rough-board facade out front. A wooden sidewalk helps to maintain the turn-of-the-century cow-town feeling. Rustic guest rooms are above the restaurant and are furnished with homesteader antiques original to the area. In the summer, an outdoor pageant is held complete with stagecoach and horses. In October, deer hunters are accommodated. The hotel, along with two motels, is managed by the non-profit Theodore Roosevelt Medora Foundation.

Innkeeper(s): Randy Hatzenbuhler. $45-58. 9 rooms with PB. Breakfast included in rates.
Certificate may be used: Oct. 1-May 1.

Ohio

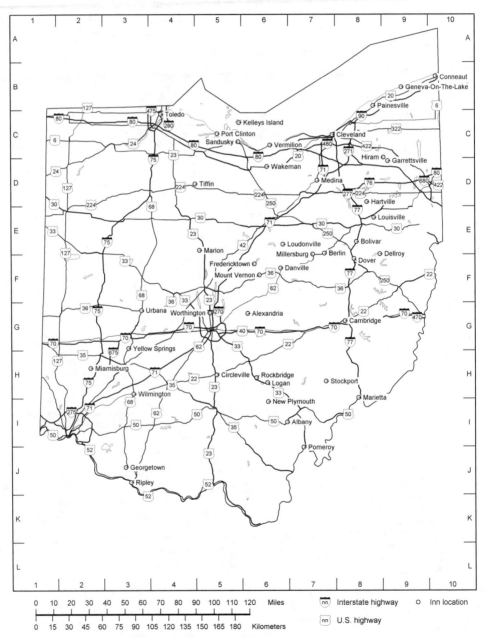

0 10 20 30 40 50 60 70 80 90 100 110 120 Miles

0 15 30 45 60 75 90 105 120 135 150 165 180 Kilometers

(nn) Interstate highway   o Inn location

(nn) U.S. highway

Albany   I6

Albany House

9 Clinton St
Albany, OH 45710
(740)698-6311 (888)212-8163

Circa 1860. Located seven miles from Ohio University in a quaint village setting, this inn is filled with antiques, quilts, Oriental rugs and collectibles. A new addition includes an indoor pool, fireplace, showers and changing room.
Innkeeper(s): Sarah & Ted Hutchins. $75-135. 7 rooms with PB and 1 conference room. Breakfast and snacks/refreshments included in rates. Types of meals: Full gourmet bkfst and early coffee/tea. Beds: QDT. Antiquing, fishing, live theater, parks, shopping and water sports nearby.
Publicity: *Post, A. News, S.E. Ohio Magazine, Midwest and Bike.*
Certificate may be used: Weekdays, Sunday-Thursday; weekends if available.

Alexandria   G6

WillowBrooke Bed 'n Breakfast

4459 Morse Road
Alexandria, OH 43001
(740)924-6161 (800)722-6372 Fax:(740)924-0224
Internet: www.willowbrooke.com
E-mail: wilbrk@aol.com

Circa 1980. There are no worries at this English Tudor Manor House and Guest Cottage located in a secluded 34-acre wooded setting. Furnished in a traditional decor, spacious guest bedrooms and romantic suites offer extensive amenities that pamper and please like feather beds or pillowtop mattresses, candlelight, whirlpool tubs, kitchens and balconies or patios. Families are welcome to stay in the Garden Suite or Guest House. For breakfast, choose from three juices along with French toast and strawberries, scrambled eggs and ham. Enjoy year-round use of the outdoor hot tub, and browse the gift shop for glass oil candles and crystal table accessories.
Innkeeper(s): Sandra Gilson. $100-150. 6 rooms with PB, 3 with FP, 3 suites and 1 guest house. Breakfast included in rates. Types of meals: Full bkfst and early coffee/tea. Beds: KQ. Modem hook-up, cable TV, VCR, reading lamp, stereo, refrigerator, ceiling fan, clock radio, telephone, coffeemaker, turn-down service, desk, hot tub/spa and fireplace in room. Central air. Fax, copier, spa, sauna, parlor games, fireplace, gift shop with Firelight oil candles, crystal table setting accessories and outdoor five-person hydrotherapy hot tub on premises. Limited handicap access. Antiquing, art galleries, beach, bicycling, canoeing/kayaking, fishing, golf, hiking, horseback riding, live theater, museums, parks, shopping, sporting events, tennis and wineries nearby.
Location: Country. Located 1/4 mile back into the woods.
Certificate may be used: Anytime, Monday-Thursday, subject to availability.

Berlin   E7

Donna's Premier Lodging B&B

PO Box 307
Berlin, OH 44610
(330)893-3068 (800)320-3338 Fax:(330)893-0037
Internet: www.donnasofberlin.com
E-mail: info@donnasb-b.com

Circa 1991. Romantic accommodations on a secluded six-acre wooded hillside include stately Victorian chalets, inviting log cabins, private cottages, villas and bridal suites. The natural setting and luxurious amenities instill a peaceful relaxation. Play pool in a chalet rec room. Snuggle by a fireplace or indulge in the intimacy of a two-person Jacuzzi. Beautifully landscaped grounds offer spots to sit by the 75-foot waterfall, stream and fountain combination. Nature lovers enjoy the serenity of a starlit stroll. Visit nearby Amish Country or go antiquing. Ask about midweek and special sweetheart packages.
Innkeeper(s): Johannes & Donna Marie Schlabach. $99-369. 16 rooms with PB, 16 with FP, 2 suites, 2 cottages and 7 cabins. Types of meals: Country bkfst and veg bkfst. Beds: KQ. Cable TV, VCR, reading lamp, stereo, refrigerator, ceiling fan, clock radio, telephone, coffeemaker, hot tub/spa, fireplace, Jacuzzi, mood lighting, 3 with billiards, 9 with kitchenette, 7 with full kitchen and Romancing the Stone cabin with waterfall in room. Central air. Fax, copier, parlor games, gift shop, landscaped grounds with waterfall/stream/pond combination, picnic table and hammock on premises. Limited handicap access. Antiquing, canoeing/kayaking, golf, horseback riding, museums, shopping, tennis, wineries, buggy rides and sleigh rides nearby.
Location: Country.
Publicity: *Country Traveler, Amish Heartland, Country Living Magazine, and Neil Zurker's "One Tank Trips" TV 27.*
Certificate may be used: November-May, Sunday-Thursday, Honeymoon/Anniversary Villa only.

Bolivar   E8

Springhouse Bed & Breakfast

10903 St. Route 212, NE
Bolivar, OH 44612
(330)874-4255 (800)796-9100 Fax:(330)874-1106
Internet: www.springhousebnb.com
E-mail: bnb@wilkshire.net

Circa 1857. Overlooking picturesque Tuscarawas River Valley, this peaceful six-acre estate is composed of a main house and seven outbuildings in the middle of 50 acres of trees and cornfields. The historic Modern Greek Revival home, a smokehouse and springhouse are listed in the National Register. Antique furnishings and country accents highlight 11-foot ceilings, massive woodwork and original floors. Spacious guest bedrooms and the Bell Tower Suite boast comfort and luxury. Lounge in a plush robe on a canopy or brass bed. A candlelight breakfast is served with soft music playing. Stroll the gardens, relax by the pond or stone fountain, soak in the hot tub or sit on the balcony.
Innkeeper(s): Tim & Elise Shuff. $85-150. 5 rooms, 4 with PB, 1 suite. Breakfast and snacks/refreshments included in rates. Types of meals: Full gourmet bkfst, veg bkfst, early coffee/tea and picnic lunch. Beds: KQD. Data port, TV, VCR, reading lamp, refrigerator, ceiling fan, snack bar, clock radio, telephone, coffeemaker, turn-down service, desk, plush robes, blow dryers and satellite dish in room. Central air. Fax, copier, spa, library and parlor games on premises. Limited handicap access. Antiquing, bicycling, canoeing/kayaking, fishing, golf, hiking, horseback riding, museums, parks, shopping, wineries, Canton Pro-Football Hall of Fame (15 minutes), "Trumpet in the Land" outdoor drama (20 minutes) and Amish Country nearby.
Location: Country.
Publicity: *Akron Beacon Journal.*
Certificate may be used: Anytime, Sunday-Thursday.

Cambridge   G8

Colonel Taylor Inn B&B and Gift Shop

633 Upland Rd
Cambridge, OH 43725
(740)432-7802 Fax:(740)435-3152
Internet: www.coltaylorinnbb.com
E-mail: coltaylr@coltaylorinnbb.com

Circa 1878. The namesake who built this Victorian Painted
Lady was a Civil War veteran and congressman. The spacious
mansion imparts an intimate ambiance. The Grand Foyer showcases a carved staircase, oak paneling, 11-foot ceilings, hardwood floors and stained-glass windows. A large sitting room
boasts a big screen TV and table games. The parlor and library
provide quiet places to read or chat. The inns boasts 11 fireplaces, and one of the guest bedrooms even has a fireside
whirlpool tub in the bath. Apple French toast, sausage, coffee
cake and fresh fruit is one of the delightful breakfasts served
daily. The historic downtown district is seven blocks away.

Innkeeper(s): Jim & Patricia Irvin. $135-195. 4 rooms with PB, 4 with FP, 1
suite and 2 conference rooms. Breakfast included in rates. Types of meals: Full
gourmet bkfst, early coffee/tea and afternoon tea. Beds: Q. Cable TV, reading
lamp, ceiling fan, clock radio, fireplace and one with bathroom whirlpool
tub/fireplace in room. Central air. TV, VCR, library, parlor games, fireplace,
large-screen TV, two parlors, formal dining room and three porches on premises. Antiquing, art galleries, beach, bicycling, cross-country skiing, fishing, golf,
hiking, horseback riding, live theater, museums, parks, shopping, water sports,
wineries, glass factories, potteries, festivals and concerts nearby.

Location: Small town historic area.

Publicity: *Arrington's Bed & Breakfast Journal, Inn Traveler* and voted "Best in
the USA" & awarded "The Inn with the most Hospitality" 2003 by inngoers.

Certificate may be used: Anytime, Sunday-Thursday.

Circleville   H5

Penguin Crossing B&B

3291 State Route 56 West
Circleville, OH 43113-9622
(740)477-6222 (800)736-4846 Fax:(740)420-6060
Internet: www.penguin.cc
E-mail: innkeepers@penguin.cc

Circa 1820. This romantic country getaway on 300 acres offers
heart-shaped personal Jacuzzis for two, antique appointed
rooms, gourmet hot chocolate served fireside, candlelight
breakfasts and room amenities
such as a wood-burning fireplace
or brass bed. Bright colors and
original walnut woodwork add to
the decor in this 1820s brick
farmhouse, once a stagecoach
stop. As the name might suggest,
the inn has a collection of pen-
guins on display. In the evenings, guests enjoy moon-lit walks
along the old country lane and in the daytime, exploring the
inn's farmland, watching the kittens playing in the barn, or
cycling to downtown Circleville, four miles away. Breakfasts
include a selection of natural foods, and the innkeeper is happy
to cater to special dietary needs.

Innkeeper(s): Allan Colgan & Carol Jones. $100-225. 5 rooms with PB, 2
with FP. Breakfast included in rates. Types of meals: Full bkfst and early cof-
fee/tea. Beds: KQ. TV, VCR, reading lamp, telephone, desk and four with
Jacuzzi in room. Air conditioning. Fax, library and fireplace on premises.

Handicap access. Antiquing, fishing, horseback riding, live theater, parks,
shopping, sporting events and water sports nearby.

Location: Country.

"If I had to describe this home in one word, it would be — enchanting."

Certificate may be used: Anytime, subject to availability.

Cleveland   C7

Brownstone Inn-Downtown

3649 Prospect Ave
Cleveland, OH 44115
(216)426-1753 Fax:(216)431-0648
Internet: www.brownstoneinndowntown.com
E-mail: ryates1@mindspring.com

Circa 1874. A bright blue door welcomes guests at the front of
this inn, which is actually located in a historic brownstone in
downtown Cleveland. The inn was built just a few years after
the Civil War and is listed as a National Landmark Row House
and listed in the National Register. Victorian appointments and
antiques decorate the inn's interior. The guest rooms range
from the opulent Bridal Suite to cozier rooms with double
beds. The suite includes a fireplace and private bath. There is a
kitchenette, which guests may use to fix that midnight snack.

Innkeeper(s): Mr Robin Yates. $85-105. 5 rooms, 1 with PB, 1 with FP.
Breakfast included in rates. Types of meals: Full bkfst and early coffee/tea.
Beds: QD. Reading lamp, CD player, refrigerator, ceiling fan, clock radio, telephone, coffeemaker and desk in room. Central air. Fax and fireplace on
premises. Antiquing, art galleries, beach, bicycling, fishing, golf, hiking, live
theater, museums, parks, shopping and tennis nearby.

Location: City.

Certificate may be used: January and February.

Glendennis B&B

2808 Bridge Ave
Cleveland, OH 44113
(216)589-0663
E-mail: glendennis@rmrc.net

Circa 1862. Built in 1862 in the Victorian Greek Revival style
of architecture, the restored interior of this historic bed and
breakfast is furnished with antiques. Browse through the gift
shop. The air-conditioned guest bedroom features amenities to
enhance business or pleasure. A refrigerator, coffeemaker, desk,
voice mail, and modem hookup are included. Turndown service is also provided. Wake up to enjoy a satisfying breakfast.
The popular West Side Market is just one-quarter mile away.

Innkeeper(s): Dave & Emily Dennis. $110. 1 suite. Breakfast included in
rates. Types of meals: Cont, veg bkfst and early coffee/tea. Beds: D. Modem
hook-up, TV, reading lamp, refrigerator, clock radio, telephone, coffeemaker,
turn-down service, desk and voice mail in room. Central air. Library, child
care, parlor games, laundry facility, private garages and gift shop on premises. Amusement parks, antiquing, art galleries, beach, bicycling,
canoeing/kayaking, cross-country skiing, downhill skiing, fishing, golf, hiking,
horseback riding, live theater, museums, parks, shopping, sporting events,
tennis, water sports and wineries nearby.

Location: City.

Publicity: *Gourmet Magazine* and HGTV *"If Walls Could Talk."*

Certificate may be used: November through March.

Conneaut   B10

Campbell Braemar

390 State St
Conneaut, OH 44030-2510
(440)599-7362

Circa 1927. This little Colonial Revival house is decorated in a Scottish style, and a Scottish breakfast is provided. Guests are invited to use the kitchen for light cooking as the hosts live next door. Wineries, golf, fishing, sandy beaches of Lake Erie and hunting are nearby. The innkeepers also offer a fully furnished apartment with two large bedrooms, a living room, cable TV and a fully equipped kitchen.

Innkeeper(s): Mary & Andrew Campbell. $78-98. 3 rooms. Breakfast and afternoon tea included in rates. Types of meals: Full bkfst and early coffee/tea. Beds: KQD. Reading lamp and clock radio in room. Air conditioning. Telephone and fireplace on premises. Antiquing, fishing, parks and water sports nearby.

Certificate may be used: Monday-Friday, January through June, September through December, except holidays.

Danville   F6

Red Fox Country Inn

26367 Danville Amity Rd, PO Box 717
Danville, OH 43014-0746
(740)599-7369 (877)600-7310
Internet: www.redfoxcountryinn.com
E-mail: sudsimp@aol.com

Circa 1830. This inn, located on 15 scenic central Ohio acres, was built originally to house those traveling on the Danville-Amity Wagon Road and later became a farm home. Amish woven rag rugs and country antiques decorate the guest rooms. Some of the furnishings belonged to early owners, and some date to the 18th century. Four rooms include Amish-made oak beds and the fifth an 1880s brass and iron double bed. Breakfasts include fresh pastries, fruits, coffee and a variety of delectable entrees. Special dietary needs usually can be accommodated. There are books and games available in the inn's sitting room, and guests also are invited to relax on the front porch. Golfing, canoeing, fishing, horseback riding, hiking, biking, skiing and Mohican State Park are nearby, and the inn is 30 minutes from the largest Amish community in the United States.

Innkeeper(s): Sue & Denny Simpkins. $65-105. 5 rooms with PB. Breakfast included in rates. Beds: QD. Reading lamp and clock radio in room. Air conditioning. Library, telephone and great place for retreats on premises.

Location: Small town.

Publicity: *Dealers Automotive, Columbus Dispatch, Mount Vernon News and Cincinnati Enquirer.*

"Our dinner and breakfast were '5 star.' Thank you for the gracious hospitality and special kindness you showed us."

Certificate may be used: Weekdays all year-round. Weekends Jan. 1-March 31. Excludes holidays and events at area colleges.

The White Oak Inn

29683 Walhonding Rd, Sr 715
Danville, OH 43014-9681
(740)599-6107
Internet: www.whiteoakinn.com
E-mail: info@whiteoakinn.com

Circa 1915. Large oaks and ivy surround the wide front porch of this three-story farmhouse situated on 13 green acres. It is located on the former Indian trail and pioneer road that runs along the Kokosing River, and an Indian mound has been discovered on the property. The inn's woodwork is all original white oak, and guest rooms are furnished in antiques. Visitors often shop for maple syrup, cheese and handicrafts at nearby Amish farms. Three cozy fireplace rooms and two cottages provide the perfect setting for romantic evenings.

Innkeeper(s): Yvonne & Ian Martin. $95-205. 12 rooms with PB, 6 with FP and 1 conference room. Breakfast and snacks/refreshments included in rates. Types of meals: Full bkfst, early coffee/tea and gourmet dinner. Beds: KQDT. Reading lamp, ceiling fan, clock radio, telephone, TV jacks and three with whirlpool tub in room. Air conditioning. Library, parlor games, fireplace, guest refrigerator and piano on premises. Antiquing, fishing, horseback riding, parks, shopping, water sports and Amish area/museums nearby.

Location: Rural.

Publicity: *Ladies Home Journal, Columbus Monthly, Cleveland Plain Dealer, Country, Glamour, Columbus Dispatch, Midwest Living and PBS - Country Inn Cooking.*

"The dinner was just fabulous and we enjoyed playing the antique grand piano."

Certificate may be used: Sunday to Thursday nights, year-round.

Dellroy   E8

Whispering Pines Bed and Breakfast

PO Box 340
Dellroy, OH 44620
(330)735-2824 (866)4LAKEVU Fax:(330)735-7006
Internet: www.atwoodlake.com
E-mail: whisperingpines@atwoodlake.com

Circa 1880. Blissful memories are made at this Victorian Italianate inn sitting on seven lush acres of rolling hills. Exquisitely furnished with antiques and period pieces, the decor is relaxing and elegant. Romantic guest bedrooms and honeymoon suite offer gorgeous lake views, fluffy robes and CD players to enhance any mood. Some feature fireplaces, private balconies and Jacuzzis. Breakfast is such a delight, the frequently requested mouth-watering recipes are now in a cookbook. Each season brings an eye-pleasing adventure to the surrounding area for an ultimate getaway, perfect for any occasion.

Innkeeper(s): Bill & Linda Horn. $150-225. 9 rooms with PB, 7 with FP. Breakfast, afternoon tea and snacks/refreshments included in rates. Types of meals: Full gourmet bkfst, veg bkfst and early coffee/tea. Beds: KQ. Reading lamp, CD player, refrigerator, ceiling fan, snack bar, clock radio, hot tub/spa, fireplace and seven with 2-person spa tub in room. Central air. Fax, spa, parlor games and telephone on premises. Antiquing, art galleries, beach, bicycling, canoeing/kayaking, fishing, golf, hiking, horseback riding, live theater, museums, parks, shopping, tennis, water sports and wineries nearby.

Location: Country, waterfront.

Certificate may be used: Dec. 1-April 30, Sunday-Thursday.

Dover   F8

Olde World Bed & Breakfast & Tea Room

2982 State Route 516 NW
Dover, OH 44622-7247
(330)343-1333 (800)447-1273 Fax:(330)364-8022
Internet: www.oldeworldbb.com
E-mail: owbb@tusco.net

Circa 1881. A quaint atmosphere is imparted at this red brick Victorian farmhouse. The tea parlor features beautifully preserved woodwork found in the pocket doors and fireplace mantel. Themed guest bedrooms and a suite include Parisian, Alpine, Mediterranean and the signature Victorian decor which boasts a carved bed and clawfoot tub. Enjoy an elegant breakfast in the floral-wallpapered dining room with chandelier. The meal may include Swiss eggs, rhubarb muffins, cream scones and grilled local whole hog sausage. Queen's tea is served every Wednesday through Saturday afternoon. The veranda is a favorite retreat while munching on warm, homemade cookies. The Amish countryside and an abundance of antiquing opportunities are nearby.

Innkeeper(s): Jonna Cronebaugh. $85-125. 4 rooms with PB, 1 suite and 1 conference room. Breakfast included in rates. Types of meals: Full gourmet bkfst, lunch, afternoon tea, snacks/refreshments, wine, dinner and room service. Beds: KQ. TV, VCR, reading lamp, CD player, clock radio, fireplace and robes in room. Central air. Fax, spa, parlor games, telephone, gift shop and tea room that serves lunch (Wednesday-Saturday) on premises. Antiquing, canoeing/kayaking, fishing, golf, hiking, horseback riding, live theater, shopping, tennis, water sports, wineries, Amish Country, historical Indian sites, Warther museum, Riverfront Antique Mall, Trumpet in the Land outdoor drama, Zoar Village and Ohio Erie Canal Towpath nearby.

Location: Country.

Publicity: *Ohio Magazine, Columbus Dispatch, Canton Repository, Cleveland Plain Dealer, Ohio Pass Magazine, Home & Away and Country Discovers.*

Certificate may be used: November-April, Sunday-Thursday, subject to availability.

Fredericktown   F6

Heartland Country Resort

3020 Township Rd 190
Fredericktown, OH 43019
(419)768-9300 (800)230-7030 Fax:(419)768-9133
Internet: www.heartlandcountryresort.com
E-mail: heartbb@bright.net

Circa 1996. Peacefully secluded among shady woodlands and rolling hills, this upscale country resort and relaxing retreat is a sprawling haven on more than one hundred acres. The newly constructed log home offers a private setting and luxurious comfort. The refurbished main farmhouse boasts a screened porch and spacious deck. A pool table, games and puzzles are enjoyed in the recreation  room. A video library provides a large selection of movies. Stay in a deluxe guest suite with cathedral ceilings, two-person Jacuzzis, full kitchens or kitchenettes, private entrances and porches. Start the day with a scrumptious breakfast. A variety of wrangling and horseback riding activities are available for everyone, from beginners to the experienced. Explore nearby Amish country, Mohican and Malabar State Parks and Kingwood Garden Center.

Innkeeper(s): Dorene Henschen. $150-175. 3 suites. Breakfast and afternoon tea included in rates. Types of meals: Cont plus, picnic lunch, dinner and room service. Beds: QT. TV, VCR, reading lamp, ceiling fan, clock radio, telephone, coffeemaker, desk, hot tub/spa, fireplace, suites have Jacuzzi and hot tub on screened porch in room. Central air. Fax, spa, stable, library, pet boarding, parlor games, laundry facility, pool table, wrangler activities, chickens, horses, cattle, golden retrievers and cats on premises. Antiquing, canoeing/kayaking, cross-country skiing, downhill skiing, fishing, golf, hiking, horseback riding, water sports, Amish Country, birding, mid-Ohio raceway, Mohican and Malabar farm state parks and Kingwood garden center nearby.

Location: Country.

Publicity: *Columbus Dispatch, Country Extra, One Tank Trips, Getaways, Home and Away and Ohio Magazine.*

"Warm hospitality . . . Beautiful surroundings and pure peace & quiet. What more could one want from a B&B in the country? Thank you for an excellent memory!"

Certificate may be used: Anytime, November-April, subject to availability.

Garrettsville   D9

Blueberry Hill B&B

11085 North St (Rt 88)
Garrettsville, OH 44231
(330)527-5068
E-mail: darling@apk.net

Although this restored Victorian is just minutes from downtown Garrettsville, the landscaped grounds create a secluded, pastoral setting. Relax in front of a wood-burning fireplace or stroll through nearby woods. Rooms are decorated in Laura Ashley prints with Victorian touches and the innkeepers own an impressive collection of artwork.  The home is located on the outskirts of one of the largest Amish towns in the United States, and it is near both Hiram College and Kent State University.

Innkeeper(s): Deborah Darling. $100. 2 rooms. Breakfast included in rates. Types of meals: Cont.

Certificate may be used: All year, Monday through Thursday, except holidays.

Geneva on the Lake   B9

The Lakehouse Inn

5653 Lake Road E
Geneva on the Lake, OH 44041
(440)466-8668 Fax:(440)466-2556
Internet: www.thelakehouseinn.com
E-mail: inquiries@thelakehouseinn.com

Circa 1940. In a quaint lakefront location, this inn offers a variety of accommodations that boast a nautical/country décor. Stay "bed and breakfast style" in standard guest bedrooms or Jacuzzi suites with fireplaces, DVD players, microwaves and refrigerators. Renovated cottages include a living room, fully equipped kitchen, bath and one or two bedrooms. Linens, towels, paper goods and cleaning supplies are not provided. The secluded Beach House features a living and dining area, kitchen, Jacuzzi bath, two-person shower, spacious bedroom and outdoor deck. Enjoy the central air and heat as well as panoramic views of Lake Erie and the Geneva Marina.

Innkeeper(s): Andrea Fagnilli. $70-225. 18 rooms with PB, 4 with FP, 4 with WP, 3 total suites, including 4 two-bedroom suites, 8 cottages, 1 guest house and 1 conference room. Breakfast included in rates. Types of meals: Full bkfst, veg bkfst, early coffee/tea, snacks/refreshments, wine and dinner. Beds: KQDT. Cable TV, CD player, refrigerator, ceiling fan, clock radio, telephone, fireplace, Jacuzzi tub and high-speed wireless Internet in room. Air conditioning. VCR, fax, copier, swimming, parlor games, gift shop, lakefront winery, lakefront decks, horseshoes, croquet and bocce ball on premises. Amusement parks, antiquing, beach, bicycling, canoeing/kayaking, fishing, golf, hiking, museums, parks, shopping, tennis, water sports, wineries, Geneva-on-the-Lake summer resort, historic Ashtabula Harbor and covered bridges nearby.

Location: Waterfront.

Certificate may be used: Anytime, November-March, subject to availability.

Georgetown J3

Bailey House
112 N Water St
Georgetown, OH 45121-1332
(937)378-3087
Internet: www.baileyhousebandb.com
E-mail: baileyho@bright.net

Circa 1830. The stately columns of this three-story Greek Revival house once greeted Ulysses S. Grant, a frequent visitor during his boyhood when he was sent to buy milk from the Bailey's. A story is told that Grant accidentally overheard that the Bailey boy was leaving West Point. Grant immediately ran through the woods to the home of Congressman Thomas Hamer and petitioned an appointment in Bailey's place which he received,  thus launching his military career. The inn has double parlors, pegged oak floors and Federal-style fireplace mantels. Antique washstands, chests and beds are found in the large guest rooms.

Innkeeper(s): Nancy Purdy. $60-70. 4 rooms, 1 with PB, 2 with FP. Breakfast included in rates. Types of meals: Full bkfst and early coffee/tea. Beds: QD. Reading lamp, clock radio, telephone, desk, fireplace (two rooms) and desk (one room) in room. Air conditioning. Library, parlor games, fireplace and herb garden on premises. Antiquing, fishing, golf, parks, shopping, tennis, water sports, private tours of U.S. Grant Home, historic sites and John Ruthven Art Gallery nearby.

Location: Historic District town.

"Thank you for your warm hospitality, from the comfortable house to the delicious breakfast."

Certificate may be used: Sunday-Thursday, Jan. 2 to Sept. 10.

Hartville D8

Ivy & Lace
415 S Prospect Ave
Hartville, OH 44632-9401
(330)877-6357
E-mail: suzbnb@juno.com

Circa 1920. Large trees shade the exterior of Ivy & Lace, a historic home built in the Mission and four-square architectural styles, both of which were popular when the property was being constructed. Hartville's blacksmith built this home. Guest rooms feature antique furnishings, including a few pieces from the innkeepers' family. Rates include a full breakfast, and the artfully presented morning specialties include garnishes of

fresh flowers or fresh fruit. Crepes and French toast are among the entrees. Guests can walk from the home to the Town Square with its charming shops. French and Flea markets, Quail Hollow State Park, Pro Football Hall of Fame and First Ladies Library are popular attractions in the area.

Innkeeper(s): Sue & Paul Tarr. $65-75. 3 rooms, 1 with PB. Breakfast included in rates. Types of meals: Full bkfst. Beds: QDT. Cable TV, reading lamp, refrigerator, ceiling fan, clock radio and phones can be arranged in room. Air conditioning. TV, parlor games and fireplace on premises. Antiquing, cross-country skiing, golf, live theater, museums, parks, shopping and sporting events nearby.

Location: Village.

Certificate may be used: Jan. 1-April 30, Sunday-Saturday (seven days).

Hiram C9

The Lily Ponds B&B
PO Box 322, 6720 Wakefield Rd
Hiram, OH 44234-0322
(330)569-3222 (800)325-5087 Fax:(330)569-3223
Internet: www.lilypondsbedandbreakfast.com
E-mail: lilypondsbb@aol.com

Circa 1940. This homestay is located on 20 acres of woodland dotted with rhododendron and mountain laurel. There are two large ponds and an old stone bridge. Your hostess works with a tour company and has traveled around the world. The inn's decor includes her collections of Eskimo art and artifacts and a variety of antiques. Pecan waffles served with locally harvested maple syrup are a favorite breakfast. Guests enjoy borrowing the canoe or hiking the inn's trails. Six Flags is a 15-minute drive away.

Innkeeper(s): Marilane Spencer. $75-95. 3 rooms with PB. Breakfast included in rates. Types of meals: Full bkfst and early coffee/tea. Beds: KQT. Cable TV, reading lamp, clock radio and terry cloth robes in room. Air conditioning. TV, VCR, bicycles, library, child care, parlor games, telephone, fireplace, canoeing and skiing on premises. Amusement parks, antiquing, canoeing/kayaking, cross-country skiing, downhill skiing, fishing, golf, parks, shopping, water sports, Six Flags and Sea World nearby.

Location: Village, on pond.

Publicity: *Local newspaper, Record-Courier and Record-News.*

"We felt like we were staying with friends from the very start."

Certificate may be used: Anytime, subject to availability.

Kelleys Island C5

Himmelblau B&B
337 Shannon Way
Kelleys Island, OH 43438
(419)746-2200
Internet: www.himmelblauhouse.com
E-mail: kinkeepr@aol.com

Circa 1893. This secluded Queen Anne Victorian on the Eastern Shore of Kelleys Island rests on more than eight acres of lake front lawns and cedar groves. Its front yard tree swing and slate blue and white gabled entrance offer an inviting introduction to a pleasant stay. Once the summer home of an Ohio governor, the property was also an early 1900s vineyard. Inside are a screened porch and a second-floor reading corner, which offers expansive Lake Erie views. A favorite activity of guests is to walk along the pristine shoreline at sunrise. The more adventurous enjoy snorkeling around an old shipwreck yards from the shoreline. Watching for white-tail deer after a moonlight

swim, sunbathing and stargazing are popular activities, as well.
Innkeeper(s): Marvin Robinson. $95-150. 4 rooms, 1 with PB. Breakfast
included in rates. Types of meals: Full gourmet bkfst. Beds: KQD. Reading
lamp, ceiling fan and fireplace in room. Air conditioning. TV, VCR, swimming,
bicycles, library, parlor games and fireplace on premises. Amusement parks,
antiquing, art galleries, beach, bicycling, canoeing/kayaking, fishing, hiking,
parks, shopping, water sports and wineries nearby.

Location: Waterfront.

Certificate may be used: April, May, June, September, October, Sunday-Thursday.

The Inn on Kelleys Island

PO Box 489
Kelleys Island, OH 43438-0011
(419)746-2258
E-mail: innki20@yahoo.com

Circa 1876. With a private deck on the shore of Lake Erie, this
waterfront Victorian offers an acre of grounds. Built by the
innkeeper's ancestor, Captain Frank Hamilton, the house features a black marble fireplace and
a porch with a spectacular Lake
Erie view. The Pilot House is a
room with large windows looking
out to the lake. The inn is close
to the ferry and downtown with
restaurants, taverns and shops.

Innkeeper(s): Lori & Pat Hayes. $79-99.
4 rooms. Breakfast included in rates. Types of meals: Cont and early coffee/tea.
Beds: Q. Reading lamp and ceiling fan in room. VCR, telephone and fireplace
on premises. Amusement parks, antiquing, fishing and shopping nearby.

Location: Waterfront.

Certificate may be used: Sunday-Thursday during months of May, June,
September and October; excluding holidays and festivals.

Logan   H6

The Inn At Cedar Falls

21190 SR 374
Logan, OH 43138
(740)385-7489 (800)653-2557 Fax:(740)385-0820
Internet: www.innatcedarfalls.com
E-mail: innatcedarfalls@hockinghills.com

Circa 1987. This sophisticated inn, complete with traditional
rooms along with separate cottages and cabins, was constructed on 75 acres adjacent to Hocking Hills State Parks and one-
half mile from the waterfalls. The kitchen and dining rooms are
in a 19th-century log house.
Accommodations in the two-
story barn-shaped building are
simple and comfortable, each
furnished with antiques. There
are six fully equipped log cabins
and twelve cozy cottages available, each individually decorated. The

cabins include a kitchen and living room with a gas-log stove;
some have a whirlpool tub. The cottages feature under-the-
counter refrigerators, gas-log stoves and whirlpool tubs. There
also is a meeting room equipped with a wood-burning stove.
Verandas provide sweeping views of woodland and meadow.
The grounds include organic gardens for the inn's gourmet dinners, and animals that have been spotted include red fox, wild
turkey and white-tail deer.
Innkeeper(s): Ellen Grinsfelder & Terry Lingo. $85-245. 27 rooms with PB,

18 with FP, 12 cottages, 6 cabins and 1 conference room. Breakfast included
in rates. Types of meals: Full gourmet bkfst, veg bkfst, early coffee/tea, lunch,
picnic lunch and gourmet dinner. Restaurant on premises. Beds: KQT.
Reading lamp, refrigerator, clock radio, coffeemaker, desk, whirlpool tub, cabins and cottages with gas-log stoves and ceiling fans in room. Air conditioning. Fax, copier, parlor games and fireplace on premises. Handicap access.
Antiquing, bicycling, canoeing/kayaking, cross-country skiing, fishing, golf,
hiking, horseback riding, live theater, parks and shopping nearby.

Location: Surrounded on 3 sides by the Hocking Hills State Park.

Publicity: *Country Living, Ohio Magazine, Columbus Dispatch, Country, Post,
Channel 4 and Ed Johnson.*

"Very peaceful, relaxing and friendly. Couldn't be nicer."

Certificate may be used: Anytime, subject to availability, year-round, Sunday-
Thursday only, except holidays.

Loudonville   E6

Blackfork Inn

303 N Water St
Loudonville, OH 44842-1273
(419)994-3252
Internet: www.blackforkinn.com
E-mail: bfinn@bright.net

Circa 1865. A Civil War businessman, Philip Black, brought
the railroad to town and built the Blackfork. Its well-preserved
Second Empire style has earned it a place in the National
Register. Noted preservationists have restored the inn with care
and it is filled with a collection of Ohio antiques. Located in a
scenic Amish area, the inn specializes in three-course Amish-
style breakfasts with local produce. The innkeepers also offer
two large three-room suites in a restored 1847 house; one suite
includes a gas fireplace. Ask the innkeepers about arranging a
personal tour of Amish homes.
Innkeeper(s): Sue & Al Gorisek. $70-135. 8 rooms with PB, 2 suites.
Breakfast included in rates. Types of meals: Country bkfst, veg bkfst and
early coffee/tea. Beds: KQDT. Reading lamp, CD player and desk in room.
Central air. Bicycles, library, parlor games and masseuse on call on premises.
Antiquing, art galleries, beach, bicycling, canoeing/kayaking, cross-country
skiing, downhill skiing, fishing, golf, horseback riding, live theater, museums,
parks, shopping, sporting events, tennis, water sports and wineries nearby.

Location: Country small village.

Certificate may be used: Anytime, Sunday-Thursday.

Louisville   E8

The Mainstay B&B

1320 E Main St
Louisville, OH 44641-1910
(330)875-1021
Internet: www.bbonline.com/oh/mainstay
E-mail: mainstay@cannet.com

Circa 1886. Built by a Civil War veteran, this Victorian still
has the original fish scale on its gables, and inside, it features
carved-oak woodwork and oak doors. Guests are treated to a
complimentary basket of fruit and cheese in their air-conditioned rooms. Outside are flower gar-
dens with birdbaths and a water
fountain. Nearby colleges are
Malone, Walsh, Mount Union and
Kent State University.

Innkeeper(s): Mary & Joe Shurilla. $95. 3
rooms with PB. Breakfast and snacks/refresh-
ments included in rates. Types of meals: Full
bkfst and early coffee/tea. Beds: QDT.

Reading lamp, clock radio and whirlpools in room. Air conditioning. VCR, parlor games, telephone and fireplace on premises. Antiquing, downhill skiing and parks nearby.

Location: City.

Certificate may be used: Sunday through Thursday, no holidays or Pro Football H.O.F. week.

Marietta   H8

The Buckley House

332 Front St
Marietta, OH 45750-2913
(740)373-3080 (888)282-5540
E-mail: dnicholas@wscc.edu

Circa 1879. Conveniently located in the downtown historic district, this Southern-style home features impressive views of Muskingum Park, Lookout Point and Valley Gem, a traditional stern-wheel boat. After a peaceful night's rest in the well-appointed guest bedrooms, begin a new day with a delicious breakfast. A New Orleans-style garden with gazebo and fish pond grace the grounds that include a spa. Ponder fond memories while relaxing on the double porches or decks. The coveted Pineapple Award for excellence was bestowed on this inn by the Ohio Bed and Breakfast Association.

Innkeeper(s): Dell & Alf Nicholas. $85-95. 3 rooms with PB. Breakfast included in rates. Types of meals: Full bkfst and early coffee/tea. Beds: KDT. Reading lamp and ceiling fan in room. Central air. VCR, fax, spa, library, parlor games, telephone and fireplace on premises. Antiquing, fishing, live theater, parks, shopping and water sports nearby.

Location: City.

Certificate may be used: Nov. 15-March 31, Monday-Thursday.

Marion   E5

Hide Away Country Inn

1601 SR 4
Bucyrus, OH 44820-9587
(419)562-3013 (800)570-8233 Fax:(419)562-3003
Internet: www.hideawayinn.com
E-mail: innkeeper@hideawayinn.com

Circa 1938. Experience a refreshing getaway while staying at this remarkable inn. Because of the inn's outrageous service, even the business traveler will feel rejuvenated after embarking on a rendezvous with nature here. Exquisite guest suites feature private Jacuzzis, fireplaces and amenities that pamper. Savor a leisurely five-course breakfast. Enjoy fine dining in the restaurant, or ask for an intimate picnic to be arranged. A productive conference room instills a personal quiet and inspires the mind.

Innkeeper(s): Steve & Debbie Miller. $87-287. 12 rooms with PB, 7 with FP, 8 suites, 2 guest houses and 2 conference rooms. Breakfast included in rates. Types of meals: Full gourmet bkfst, early coffee/tea, gourmet lunch, picnic lunch, afternoon tea, snacks/refreshments, gourmet dinner and room service. Restaurant on premises. Beds: KQD. TV, VCR, ceiling fan, snack bar, telephone, turn-down service, voice mail, fireplace, satellite TV and Jacuzzi in room. Air conditioning. Fax, copier, swimming, bicycles, library and child care on premises. Amusement parks, antiquing, bicycling, downhill skiing, fishing, golf, hiking, horseback riding, live theater, parks, shopping, sporting events, water sports and Baja boats nearby.

Location: Waterfront.

Publicity: *New York Times, Columbus Dispatch, Ohio Country Journal, Akron Beacon Journal, Cleveland Plain Dealer, Travel & Leisure, Neil Zurcker One Tank-Trips-Cleveland, Akron WKBN, Del's Folks and Del's Feasts Cleveland and Cleveland WKYC.*

Certificate may be used: Sunday-Thursday, excluding holidays and special event dates.

Medina   D7

C.M. Spitzer House

504 West Liberty
Medina, OH 44256
(330)725-7289 (888)777-1379
Internet: www.spitzerhouse.com
E-mail: spitzer@apk.net

This Queen Anne Victorian with distinctive Stick-style detailing would be a happy addition to the Painted Ladies series of architectural books with its three stories, stained-glass windows, variety of gables and many colors. A beautiful cherry staircase and cherry and oak woodwork are backgrounds for the inn's antiques, lacey linens and featherbeds. Ask for the Honeymoon suite for a pink heart-shaped Jacuzzi for two. Breakfast is served in the dining room. Afterwards, stroll through the blooming Victorian garden. Medina is a restored Victorian town in the National Register of Historic Places.

Innkeeper(s): Dale & Janet Rogers. Call for rates. Call inn for details.

Certificate may be used: Anytime January through April except holidays.

Miamisburg   H2

English Manor B&B

505 E Linden Ave
Miamisburg, OH 45342-2850
(937)866-2288 (800)676-9456
Internet: www.englishmanorbandb.com
E-mail: englishmanor@englishmanorbandb.com

Circa 1924. This is a beautiful English Tudor mansion situated on a tree-lined street of Victorian homes. Well-chosen antiques combined with the innkeepers' personal heirlooms added to the inn's polished floors, sparkling leaded-and-stained-glass windows and shining silver, make this an elegant retreat. Breakfast is served in the formal dining room. Fine restaurants, a water park, baseball, air force museum and theater are close by, as is The River Corridor bikeway on the banks of the Great Miami River.

Innkeeper(s): Julie & Larry Chmiel. $79-95. 5 rooms and 1 conference room. Breakfast included in rates. Types of meals: Full bkfst. Clock radio, telephone and turn-down service in room. Air conditioning. VCR and fireplace on premises. Amusement parks, antiquing, live theater, shopping and sporting events nearby.

Location: City.

Certificate may be used: Sunday-Thursday all year, upon availability.

Millersburg   F7

Hotel Millersburg

35 West Jackson Street
Millersburg, OH 44654
(330)674-1457 (800)822-1457 Fax:(330)674-4487
Internet: www.hotelmillersburg.com
E-mail: hotelmillersburg@valkyrie.net

Circa 1847. Built in the state's earliest frontier, this hotel is the area's oldest large building and was a welcome improvement over the era's stagecoach inns. Listed in the National Register, extensive renovations have retained its historical integrity while adding modern refinements. The pristine exterior and rooms with tin ceilings reflect yesterday's virtues while an elaborate fire safety system and private bathrooms offer today's comforts. Smoking and non-smoking guest bedrooms feature air conditioning, cable TV and a coffeemaker. Handmade Amish quilts grace many of the beds. Two-room suites include a large sitting room. Dine in the Tavern with an ornate brass and oak bar and a full menu with daily specials and Certified Angus Beef. The Courtyard boasts live entertainment and fresh grilled meats. The elegant Formal Dining Room is perfect to reserve for private banquets or parties.

Innkeeper(s): Bill Robinson. $35-109. 24 rooms with PB, 2 suites and 1 conference room. Types of meals: Lunch and dinner. Restaurant on premises. Beds: QDT. Private bath, air conditioning, cable TV with remote, coffeemaker, telephone and daily housekeeping service in room. TV, fax, copier, parlor games and telephone on premises. Antiquing, bicycling, canoeing/kayaking, fishing, golf, hiking, horseback riding and shopping nearby.

Location: Country.

Certificate may be used: Sunday through Thursday, Nov. 15-Sept. 30.

Mount Vernon   F6

Locust Grove Ranch B&B

12480 Dunham Rd.
Mount Vernon, OH 43050
(740)392-6443
Internet: www.locustgroveranch.com
E-mail: cindy@locustgroveranch.com

Circa 2000. Newly built to reflect Federal-style architecture, this ranch spans 75 rolling acres with woods and a meandering creek. An inviting ambiance is highlighted by the country décor, central air conditioning and warm hospitality. Read by the fireplace in the Great Room or play the baby grand piano. The library is perfect for small gatherings. Spacious guest bedrooms offer pleasant amenities and pampering touches like turndown service. In-room massage can be arranged. Breakfast is fuel for the day when you are served golden wheat waffles with apple pecan syrup, seasoned home fries, fresh berry bowl and cinnamon maple buns. Explore the country roads on a bike, go horseback riding or swim in the pool. Volleyball, horseshoes and bocce ball are also popular activities as well as tractor rides.

Innkeeper(s): Cindy & Marwood Hallett. $79-109. 3 rooms with PB, 1 with FP. Breakfast and snacks/refreshments included in rates. Types of meals: Country bkfst, veg bkfst, early coffee/tea, picnic lunch and afternoon tea. Beds: Q. Modem hook-up, data port, reading lamp, clock radio, telephone, turn-down service and fireplace in room. Central air. VCR, copier, swimming, stable, bicycles, library, parlor games, laundry facility, horse boarding and in-room massage on premises. Antiquing, art galleries, bicycling, canoeing/kayaking, downhill skiing, fishing, golf, hiking, horseback riding, parks, shopping, sporting events, tennis and Mid-Ohio sports car course nearby.

Location: Country.

Publicity: *Heart of Ohio Tour.*

Certificate may be used: Nov. 1 to April 30, any day. May 1 to Oct. 31, Sunday to Thursday.

New Plymouth   I6

Ravenwood Castle

65666 Bethel Rd
New Plymouth, OH 45654-9707
(740)596-2606 (800)477-1541
Internet: www.ravenwoodcastle.com
E-mail: ravenwood@hocking.net

Circa 1995. Although this is a newer construction, the architect modeled the inn after a 12th-century, Norman-style castle, offering a glimpse back at Medieval England. A Great Hall with  massive stone fireplace, dramatic rooms and suites with antique stained-glass windows and gas fireplaces make for a unique getaway. The castle, which overlooks Vinton County's Swan township, is surrounded by 50 acres of forest and large rock formations and is reached by a half-mile private road. There is a seasonal tea room and gift shop on the premises.

Innkeeper(s): Jim & Sue Maxwell. $105-275. 6 rooms with PB, 2 suites and 7 cottages. Breakfast included in rates. Types of meals: Full bkfst, early coffee/tea, picnic lunch, afternoon tea, snacks/refreshments, gourmet dinner and room service. Restaurant on premises. Beds: KQD. Ceiling fan and desk in room. Air conditioning. TV, VCR, fax, copier, parlor games, telephone and pub on premises. Handicap access. Antiquing, fishing, shopping, water sports, caves and waterfalls nearby.

Location: Forested.

Publicity: *Columbus Dispatch, Cincinnati Enquirer, Midwest Living, USA Today, Honeymoon, Ohio Magazine, Milwaukee Journal Sentinel, Copley News Service, PBS-TV* and *"Country Inn Cooking with Gail Greco."*

"The atmosphere is romantic, the food excellent, the hospitality super!"

Certificate may be used: Nov. 1-March 31, Sunday-Thursday, except holidays and Christmas week.

Painesville   B8

Fitzgerald's Irish B & B

47 Mentor Ave
Painesville, OH 44077-3201
(440)639-0845
Internet: www.fitzgeraldsbnb.com
E-mail: info@fitzgeraldsbnb.com

Circa 1937. Warm Irish hospitality is extended at this 1937 French Tudor home situated in the historic district. It was recently restored as a landmark of craftsmanship with its castle-like design, unusual turret, slate roof, ornate staircase, hardwood floors and elaborate 11-foot fireplace. Watch satellite TV in the sitting room, play games and relax by the fire in the large gathering room. Lounge on the sun porch overlooking the park-like grounds and frequent birds. Air-conditioned guest bedrooms include pleasing amenities. Sleep on a four-poster or sleigh bed. The third-floor Bushmills Room features a microwave, refrigerator, VCR, CD player, Jacuzzi tub and Roman shower. Savor a full breakfast on weekends and holidays and a generous continental breakfast during the week. Popular trails and beaches of the Great Lakes region are nearby.

Innkeeper(s): Debra & Tom Fitzgerald. $85-140. 4 rooms, 3 with PB. Breakfast included in rates. Types of meals: Full bkfst and early coffee/tea. Beds: Q. Modem hook-up, TV, VCR, reading lamp, CD player, refrigerator, ceiling fan, clock radio, telephone, coffeemaker, desk and hot tub/spa in room. Central air. Parlor games and fireplace on premises. Amusement parks, antiquing, art galleries, beach, bicycling, canoeing/kayaking, cross-country skiing, downhill skiing, fishing, golf, hiking, horseback riding, live theater, museums, parks, shopping, sporting events, tennis, water sports and wineries nearby.

Location: City.

Publicity: *New Herald, The Cleveland Plain Dealer, Midwest Irish News, Arrington's 2003 & 2004 Book of Lists winner of top 15 B&Bs for interior design and decor and WVIZ the Cleveland PBS station.*

Certificate may be used: Sunday-Thursday, Sept. 12-April 29.

Rider's 1812 Inn

792 Mentor Ave
Painesville, OH 44077-2516
(440)354-8200 Fax:(440)350-9385
Internet: www.ridersinn.com
E-mail: ridersinn@ncweb.com

Circa 1812. In the days when this inn and tavern served the frontier Western Reserve, it could provide lodging and meals for more than 100 overnight guests. Restored in 1988, the pub features an original fireplace and wavy window panes. Most of the inn's floors are rare, long-needle pine. A passageway in the cellar is said to have been part of the Underground Railroad. An English-style restaurant is also on the premises. Guest rooms are furnished with antiques. Breakfast in bed is the option of choice.

Innkeeper(s): Elaine Crane & Gary Herman, Bob Beauvais- General Manager. $75-101. 10 rooms, 9 with PB, 1 suite and 3 conference rooms. Breakfast included in rates. Types of meals: Full gourmet bkfst, veg bkfst, early coffee/tea, lunch, picnic lunch, afternoon tea, dinner and room service. Beds: KQDT. Cable TV, reading lamp, CD player, refrigerator, ceiling fan, snack bar, clock radio, telephone, turn-down service, desk and voice mail in room. Central air. Fax, copier, library, pet boarding, child care, parlor games, fireplace and laundry facility on premises. Limited handicap access. Antiquing, art galleries, beach, cross-country skiing, fishing, golf, horseback riding, live theater, museums, parks, shopping, sporting events, tennis and wineries nearby.

Location: College town, County Seat.

Publicity: *Business Review, News-Herald, Midwest Living, WEWS, Haunted Ohio V and Channel 5.*

Certificate may be used: Sept. 1-May 1, Sunday-Friday.

Pomeroy   J7

Holly Hill Inn

114 Butternut Ave
Pomeroy, OH 45769-1295
(740)992-5657

Circa 1836. This gracious clapboard inn with its many shuttered windows is shaded by giant holly trees. Original window panes of blown glass remain, as well as wide-board floors, mantels and fireplaces. The family's antique collection includes a crocheted canopy bed in the Honeymoon Room overlooking a working fireplace. Dozens of antique quilts are displayed and for sale. Guests are invited to borrow an antique bike to ride through the countryside.

Innkeeper(s): George Stewart. $59-89. 4 rooms, 2 with FP and 1 conference room. Breakfast included in rates. Types of meals: Full bkfst. Beds: DT. Cable TV, VCR, stereo, clock radio, telephone and desk in room. Fireplace on premises. Antiquing, shopping and sporting events nearby.

Publicity: *Sunday Times-Sentinel.*

"Your inn is so beautiful, and it has so much historic charm."

Certificate may be used: Sunday through Thursday. Some weekends, based on availability. Not special weekends and holidays.

Port Clinton   C5

SunnySide Tower Bed & Breakfast Inn

3612 NW Catawba Rd
Port Clinton, OH 43452-9726
(419)797-9315 (888)831-1263
Internet: www.sunnysidetower.com
E-mail: ssidetowr@cros.net

Circa 1879. One of Catawba Island's original landmarks, this classic Victorian farmhouse is the innkeeper's ancestral family home. The hilltop inn and tower with a fourth-story widow's watch sits on 19 acres of wooded nature trails, herb gardens and landscaping. A glacial rock fireplace is showcased in the great room, or relax in the sunroom, a screened porch with wicker furniture. Distinctive country antique guest bedrooms feature comfortable period furnishings. Appetites are awakened with the aroma of gourmet coffee and teas accompanying a country breakfast. Share a romantic moment in a double hammock, or soak in the hot tub. The area offers easy access to a variety of Lake Erie activities and several state parks.

Innkeeper(s): John Davenport. $69-159. 10 rooms, 4 with PB and 1 conference room. Breakfast included in rates. Types of meals: Country bkfst. Beds: KQD. Reading lamp, ceiling fan and clock radio in room. Central air. TV, parlor games, telephone, fireplace, laundry facility, hot tub and children's play area on premises. Handicap access. Amusement parks, antiquing, art galleries, beach, bicycling, canoeing/kayaking, fishing, golf, hiking, live theater, museums, parks, shopping, tennis, water sports, wineries, basketball courts, baseball/soccer fields and sledding hill nearby.

Location: Half-mile from water.

Certificate may be used: Anytime Sunday-Thursday, subject to availability, October through May.

Ripley   J3

Baird House B&B

201 N 2nd St
Ripley, OH 45167-1002
(937)392-4918

Circa 1825. A lacy wrought-iron porch and balcony decorate the front facade of this historic house, while the second-floor porch at the rear offers views of the Ohio River, 500 feet away. There are nine marble fireplaces and an enormous chandelier in the parlor. A full breakfast is served.

Innkeeper(s): Patricia Kittles. $125-150. 3 rooms, 2 with PB, 3 with FP, 1 suite. Breakfast included in rates. Types of meals: Full gourmet bkfst, early coffee/tea, afternoon tea and snacks/refreshments. Beds: KDT. Reading lamp, stereo, ceiling fan, clock radio, telephone, turn-down service, desk and electric blankets in winter in room. Air conditioning. Fireplace, organ, swings and porches on premises. Antiquing, shopping and sporting events nearby.

Location: City. Ohio River.

Publicity: *Ohio Magazine.*

"Thanks for a wonderful memory."

Certificate may be used: Anytime, subject to availability.

The Signal House

234 N Front St
Ripley, OH 45167-1015
(937)392-1640 Fax:(937)392-1640
Internet: www.thesignalhouse.com
E-mail: signalhouse@webtv.net

Circa 1830. This Greek Italianate home is said to have been used to aid the Underground Railroad. A light in the attic told Rev. John Rankin, a dedicated abolitionist, that it was safe to transport slaves to freedom. Located within a 55-acre historical district, guests can take a glance back in time, exploring museums and antique shops. Twelve-foot ceilings with ornate plaster-work grace the parlor, and guests can sit on any of three porches anticipating paddle-wheelers traversing the Ohio River.

Innkeeper(s): Vic & Betsy Billingsley. $95-150. 2 rooms, 1 two-bedroom suite. Breakfast and snacks/refreshments included in rates. Types of meals: Full bkfst and early coffee/tea. Beds: QD. Reading lamp, ceiling fan, clock radio and desk in room. Central air. TV, VCR, fax, copier, library, parlor games, telephone and fireplace on premises. Antiquing, bicycling, fishing, golf, hiking, museums, parks, shopping, tennis, water sports, wineries, auctions, fishing tournaments and downtown Cincinnati nearby.

Location: Waterfront.

Publicity: *Cincinnati Enquirer, Ohio Columbus Dispatch, Ohio Off the Beaten Path, Cincinnati Magazine, Cincinnati Post, Dayton Daily News, Ohio Magazine, Cleveland Plain Dealer, Maysville Ledger Independent, Particular Places II, Channel 12, WKRC- "One Tank Trip" and Husband's first car in "Lost in Yonkers."*

Certificate may be used: Monday-Thursday.

Rockbridge   H6

Glenlaurel Inn

14940 Mt Olive Rd
Rockbridge, OH 43149-9736
(740)385-4070 (800)809-7378 Fax:(740)385-9669
Internet: www.glenlaurelinn.com
E-mail: michael@glenlaurelinn.com

Circa 1994. Innkeeper Michael Daniels created Glenlaurel to be like a Scottish country home. A creek, with a waterfall, meanders through the 133-acre grounds, which are covered with woods. There are four rooms in the main house, three suites in the nearby carriage, and guests also can select from 13 different cottages tucked on the property. The guest quarters are romantic and elegant done in a European-country style. Bathrobes, luxurious linens, soft comforters, down-filled pillows, whirlpool tubs and fireplaces are among the possible amenities. The cottages are especially idyllic, each includes a double-sided fireplace that warms both the bedchamber and living room. Each night, Saturdays excepted, a five-course dinner is an option for guests. On Saturday night, a vast seven-course meal is available.

Innkeeper(s): Michael Daniels. $119-299. 4 rooms with PB, 14 with FP, 3 suites, 13 cottages and 1 conference room. Breakfast included in rates. Types of meals: Full gourmet bkfst, picnic lunch, afternoon tea and gourmet dinner. Restaurant on premises. Beds: KQ. Reading lamp, stereo, refrigerator, ceiling fan, telephone, desk, hot tub/spa and welcome snacks in room. Air conditioning. Fax, copier, spa, library, parlor games and fireplace on premises. Handicap access. Antiquing, fishing, golf, parks, shopping and water sports nearby.

Location: Woods & waterfalls.

Publicity: *Lancaster Eagle-Gazette.*

"With a staff eager to help us and make us feel welcome, we leave today spoiled, satisfied and eager to return."

Certificate may be used: Monday through Thursday, except during October.

Sandusky   C5

Wagner's 1844 Inn

230 E Washington St
Sandusky, OH 44870-2611
(419)626-1726 Fax:(419)626-0002
Internet: www.lrbcg.com/wagnersinn
E-mail: wagnersinn@sanduskyohio.com

Circa 1844. This inn originally was constructed as a log cabin. Additions and renovations were made, and the house evolved into Italianate style accented with brackets under the eaves and black shutters on the second-story windows. A wrought-iron fence frames the house, and there are ornate wrought-iron porch rails. A billiard room and screened-in porch are available to guests. The ferry to Cedar Point and Lake Erie Island is within walking distance.

Innkeeper(s): Barb Wagner. $80-100. 3 rooms with PB, 2 with FP. Breakfast included in rates. Types of meals: Cont plus. Beds: Q. Reading lamp, clock radio, desk and fireplace in room. Central air. TV, library, parlor games, telephone and TV on premises. Amusement parks, antiquing, fishing, golf, hiking, museums, parks, shopping, tennis, Lake Erie Islands and golf nearby.

Location: City.

Publicity: *Lorain Journal and Sandusky Register.*

"This B&B rates in our Top 10."

Certificate may be used: Nov. 1 to April 1, Sunday-Thursday.

Stockport   H7

Stockport Mill

1995 Broadway Ave
Stockport, OH 43787
(740)559-2822 Fax:(740)559-2236
Internet: www.stockportmill.com
E-mail: mill@stockportmill.com

Circa 1906. Stay at this century-old restored grain mill on the Muskingum River for a truly authentic historic experience combined with everything desired for a romantic getaway, business retreat or stress-free change of pace. Each of the four floors offers an assortment of common areas and accommodations. Browse the main lobby, an inviting library and the gift gallery showcasing local craftsman and artists. The Massage Therapy Room was the original grain bin. Themed guest bedrooms are named and decorated as a tribute to the local region and its prominent people. Stay in a luxurious suite with a two-person whirlpool spa and private balcony. Riverboat Rooms feature clawfoot tubs, southern views of the river and private terraces. Ask about special packages and scheduling events at the Boathouse Banquet Hall.

Innkeeper(s): Susan Kaster & Teresa Coleman. $65-300. 14 rooms with PB, 1 with FP, 7 with HT, 6 suites and 1 conference room. Types of meals: Full bkfst, lunch, snacks/refreshments and dinner. Restaurant on premises. Beds: KQ. TV, reading lamp, ceiling fan, clock radio, telephone, coffeemaker, hot tub/spa, satellite dish and refrigerator in one suite in room. Air conditioning. VCR, fax, copier, library, parlor games, gift shop, satellite dish, VCR and massage therapy by appointment on premises. Limited handicap access. Antiquing, canoeing/kayaking, fishing, golf, live theater, museums, parks, shopping, walk track, boat launching, swimming pool and bowling nearby.

Location: Country, waterfront.

Certificate may be used: Anytime, November-March, subject to availability, suites only (2nd or 3rd floor). Does not include Valentines Day or holidays.

Tiffin **D5**

Fort Ball Bed & Breakfast

25 Adams St
Tiffin, OH 44883-2208
(419)447-0776 (888)447-0776 Fax:(419)448-8415
Internet: www.fortball.com
E-mail: ftballbanb@friendlynet.com

Circa 1894. The prominent front turret and wraparound porch are classic details of this Queen Anne Revival house built by John King, builder of the Tiffin Court House and College Hall at Heidelberg College. The innkeepers dedicated more than a year restoring this turn-of-the-century Victorian to its original elegant state. The renovation yielded rich hardwood flooring, wood paneling and many additional architectural details like the elaborate woodwork in the parlor, front entryway and sitting room. Guest rooms are comfortably decorated to accommodate business travelers, families or honeymooners, and offer private and shared baths while some feature whirlpool tubs for two. Breakfast can be enjoyed in the dining room with its elegantly restored woodwork. The inn is within walking distance of the downtown business district, restaurants, antiques, shopping, museums and theater.

Innkeeper(s): Lenora Livingston. $65-105. 4 rooms, 2 with PB. Breakfast and snacks/refreshments included in rates. Types of meals: Full bkfst and early coffee/tea. Beds: KQDT. TV, VCR, reading lamp, ceiling fan, clock radio, telephone and hot tub/spa in room. Air conditioning. Fax, library, parlor games and fireplace on premises. Amusement parks, antiquing, golf, live theater, parks, tennis and historical sites nearby.

Location: City.

Publicity: *Advertiser-Tribune*.

Certificate may be used: Jan. 10 to Nov. 10, Sunday-Friday, excluding holidays.

Toledo **C4**

The William Cummings House B&B

1022 N Superior St
Toledo, OH 43604
(419)244-3219 (888)708-6998 Fax:(419)244-3219
E-mail: BnBToledo@aol.com

Circa 1857. This Second Empire Victorian, which is listed in the National Register, is located in the historic Vistula neighborhood. The inn's fine appointments, collected for several years, include period antiques, Victorian chandeliers, mirrors, wallcoverings and draperies. The hosts are classical musicians of renown. Sometimes the inn is the location for chamber music, poetry readings and other cultural events.

Innkeeper(s): Lowell Greer, Lorelei Crawford. $40-90. 3 rooms, 1 suite. Breakfast and snacks/refreshments included in rates. Types of meals: Cont plus. Beds: KQDT. TV, VCR, reading lamp, ceiling fan, clock radio, desk, fresh flowers, robes and house chocolates in room. Air conditioning. Fax, copier, library, parlor games, telephone, video library and refrigerator on premises. Amusement parks, antiquing, fishing, live theater, parks, shopping, sporting events, water sports, Toledo Art Museum, Toledo Zoo and science center nearby.

Location: City.

"We will never forget our wedding night at your B&B. We'll try to be in the area next anniversary."

Certificate may be used: Oct. 1 through May 31, Sunday-Thursday.

Urbana **G3**

Northern Plantation B&B

3421 E RR 296
Urbana, OH 43078
(937)652-1782 (800)652-1782

Circa 1913. This Victorian farmhouse, located on 100 acres, is occupied by fourth-generation family members. (Marsha's father was born in the downstairs bedroom in 1914.) The Homestead Library is decorated traditionally and has a handsome fireplace, while the dining room features a dining set and a china cabinet made by the innkeeper's great-grandfather. Most of the guest rooms have canopy beds. A large country breakfast is served. On the property is a fishing pond, corn fields, soybeans and woods with a creek. Nearby are Ohio Caverns and Indian Lake.

$85-105. 4 rooms, 1 with PB. Breakfast included in rates. Types of meals: Full bkfst and snacks/refreshments. Beds: KD. Reading lamp and clock radio in room. Air conditioning. VCR, library, parlor games, telephone and fireplace on premises. Antiquing, cross-country skiing, parks, shopping and Pratt Castle nearby.

Location: Country.

Certificate may be used: Any day, except holidays.

Vermilion **C6**

Gilchrist Guesthouse

5662 Huron St
Vermilion, OH 44089-1000
(440)967-1237

Circa 1885. Captain J.C. Gilchrist, owner of the largest fleet of ships on the Great Lakes, built this charming 1885 Victorian, which is listed in the National Register. From the wraparound porch, guests can relax and enjoy the view. The grounds, nestled near Lake Erie's southern shore, are surrounded by gracious old buckeye trees. Guest rooms are filled with antiques. The innkeepers transformed the second-story ballroom into a comfortable common room filled with games and a TV. The large, continental breakfasts feature sweet rolls and muffins from Vermilion's century-old family bakery. The innkeepers also offer kitchen suites for those planning longer stays. The home is only 400 feet from city docks and the beach, and a two-block walk takes guests into the downtown area with its many shops and restaurants. A maritime museum and historic lighthouse are next door.

Innkeeper(s): Dan & Laura Roth. $85-115. 4 rooms. Breakfast included in rates. Types of meals: Cont plus.

Certificate may be used: Nov. 30 to May 15, excluding Saturday and holidays.

Wakeman   D6

Melrose Farm B & B

727 Vesta Rd
Wakeman, OH 44889-9392
(419)929-1867 (877)929-1867
Internet: www.melrosefarmbb.com
E-mail: melrose@accnorwalk.com

Circa 1867. Experience a slower pace at this secluded 19th
century farmhouse surrounded by a country setting. Antique
furnishings accent the period charm and decor. Borrow a book
from the library to read by the fire or in the garden. Relax on
the screened-in porch. Families appreciate the playroom for
children and the large yard. Well-appointed guest bedrooms
and suites provide restful retreats. After a satisfying breakfast,
bikes are available to explore the scenic area. Other sightseeing
adventures might include visiting the Rock and Roll Hall of
Fame or watching the Indians play baseball in nearby
Cleveland. Cedar Point Amusement Park and Amish Country
are easy day trips.

Innkeeper(s): Abe & Eleanor Klassen. $85. 3 rooms with PB, 2 with FP, 2
suites. Breakfast, afternoon tea and snacks/refreshments included in rates.
Types of meals: Full gourmet bkfst, veg bkfst, early coffee/tea and picnic
lunch. Beds: QDT. Modem hook-up, reading lamp, ceiling fan, clock radio,
desk and fireplace in room. Central air. TV, VCR, bicycles, tennis, library, parlor games, telephone, fireplace and gift shop on premises. Amusement parks,
antiquing, art galleries, beach, bicycling, fishing, golf, hiking, museums,
parks, sporting events, tennis and wineries nearby.

Location: Country.

Certificate may be used: Anytime, Sunday-Thursday.

Wilmington   H3

Cedar Hill B&B In The Woods

4003 St, Rt 73 W
Wilmington, OH 45177
(937)383-2525 (877)722-2525
Internet: bbonline.com/oh/cedarhill
E-mail: cedarhillbb@hotmail.com

Circa 1992. The guest rooms on the second floor of this carriage house overlook the trees of its 10 wooded acres. A spacious common room features a limestone fireplace with a large
open hearth. Trails meander through the woods where you may
spot deer, raccoon and other wildlife. Hearty breakfast menus
highlight the mornings. The inn is 10 minutes from
Waynesville, the antique capital of Ohio. David Smith's Shaker-
design studio is nearby.

Innkeeper(s): Joan & Rick McCarren. $85-125. 3 rooms with PB. Types of
meals: Full bkfst, early coffee/tea and snacks/refreshments. Beds: D. Reading
lamp, clock radio and desk in room. Air conditioning. TV and telephone on
premises. Amusement parks, antiquing, live theater, shopping and sporting
events nearby.

Location: Woods.

Certificate may be used: Anytime, November-April, subject to availability.

Worthington   G5

The Worthington Inn

649 High St
Worthington, OH 43085-4144
(614)885-2600 Fax:(614)885-1283
Internet: www.worthingtoninn.com
E-mail: reservations@worthingtoninn.com

Circa 1831. One of the area's most significant landmarks, this
extensively restored and expanded inn features architecture and
decor that reflects Early American Colonial, Federalist and
Victorian styles. Considered a distinguished small hotel, expect
to find luxurious accommodations, attentive service and generous upscale amenities. Each well-appointed suite and guest
bedroom boasts authentic American antiques. Meals are
enjoyed in the on-site Seven Seas Restaurant, highly acclaimed
for its cuisine and extensive wine list. An intimate pub offers a
more casual ambiance and live entertainment. The Van Loon
Ballroom is perfect for weddings, meetings or special events.
Executive services with cutting-edge technology easily meet
business needs. Shop at specialty stores just an inviting stroll
from this quaint, historic location.

$150-260. 26 rooms, 22 with PB, 4 suites and 5 conference rooms. Breakfast
included in rates. Types of meals: Full gourmet bkfst, lunch, snacks/refresh-
ments, dinner and room service. Restaurant on premises. Beds: QD. Data port,
cable TV, reading lamp, clock radio, telephone, turn-down service, desk and
voice mail in room. Air conditioning. Fax, copier and gift shop on premises.
Limited handicap access. Amusement parks, antiquing, art galleries, bicycling,
golf, hiking, live theater, parks, shopping and sporting events nearby.

Location: City. Suburban, historic community, with easy access from
major freeways.

Publicity: *Country Inns, Columbus Dispatch, Columbus Monthly, Ohio and
Midwest Living.*

Certificate may be used: Anytime, subject to availability.

Yellow Springs   G3

Arthur Morgan House Bed & Breakfast

120 W Limestone St
Yellow Springs, OH 45387-1803
(937)767-1761
Internet: www.arthurmorganhouse.com
E-mail: post@arthurmorganhouse.com

Circa 1921. Just steps from downtown, this modern stucco bed
and breakfast was built for a local notable in 1921 and now provides smoke-free, pet-free accommodations. Play games at a
table in the living room. Browse through the books and crafts
from southern Africa for sale in the small shop. The second-floor
sunroom features a reading nook with views of the wooded
backyard. Comfortable guest bedrooms on the second and third
floors boast oak floors, air conditioning and wireless Internet.
Breakfast is made with organically grown ingredients, cage-free
eggs and locally roasted coffee. The Little Miami Scenic Bike
Path runs through the village that has more than fifty gift shops.

Innkeeper(s): Susanne Oldham. $85-95. 6 rooms with PB. Breakfast includ-
ed in rates. Types of meals: Full bkfst. Beds: KQT. Reading lamp, clock radio,
turn-down service and DSL in room. Air conditioning. Library, parlor games,
telephone and DSL on premises. Limited handicap access. Antiquing, art galleries, bicycling, canoeing/kayaking, cross-country skiing, hiking, live theater,
museums, parks, shopping, tennis, water sports, music and film nearby.

Location: Village.

Certificate may be used: Monday-Thursday nights.

Oklahoma

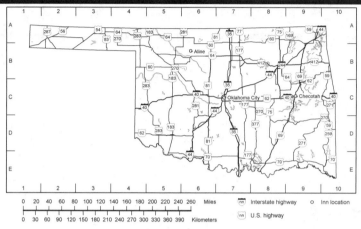

Aline
B6

Heritage Manor
33 Heritage Road
Aline, OK 73716-9118
(580)463-2563 (800)295-2563
Internet: www.1aj.org
E-mail: heritage@pldi.net

Circa 1903. This inn provides a way to enjoy and experience the ambiance of the turn of the century. Explore and relax in the inn's peaceful gardens and 80-acre wildlife habitat and watch song birds, butterflies, long-haired cattle, donkeys, llamas and ostriches. The inn invites visitors to enjoy its more than 5,000-volume library and more than a 100 channels on Dish TV. Guests can walk the suspension bridge to two roof-top decks and a widow's walk to view the stars and sunsets. There is also an out-door hot tub for soaking. Dine in the parlor, gazebo, courtyard or tree-top-level deck where the choice of time and menu is entirely up to the guest.
Innkeeper(s): A.J. & Carolyn Rexroat. $55-150. 4 rooms, 2 suites and 2 conference rooms. Breakfast and snacks/refreshments included in rates. Types of meals: Full bkfst, early coffee/tea, gourmet lunch, picnic lunch, afternoon tea and gourmet dinner. Beds: QD. Cable TV, reading lamp, telephone and desk in room. Air conditioning. VCR, spa, library, parlor games and fireplace on premises. Handicap access. Antiquing, fishing, live theater, parks, shopping, sporting events and water sports nearby.
Location: Country.
Publicity: *Country, Enid Morning News, Daily Oklahoman, Cherokee Messenger, Republican and Fairview Republican and Discover Oklahoma.*
Certificate may be used: Anytime available.

Checotah
C9

Sharpe House
301 Nw 2nd St
Checotah, OK 74426-2240
(918)473-2832

Circa 1911. Built on land originally bought from a Creek Indian, this Southern plantation-style inn was a teacherage—the rooming house for single female teachers. It is furnished with heirlooms from the innkeepers' families and hand-crafted

accessories. The look of the house is antebellum, but the specialty of the kitchen is Mexican cuisine. Family-style evening meals are available upon request. Checotah is located at the junction of I-40 and U.S. 69. This makes it the ideal base for your day trips of exploration or recreation in Green Country.
Innkeeper(s): Kay Kindt. $35-50. 3 rooms with PB, 1 suite. Breakfast included in rates. Types of meals: Full bkfst and early coffee/tea. Beds: D. Cable TV, reading lamp and ceiling fan in room. Air conditioning. Library, child care, parlor games, telephone and fireplace on premises. Amusement parks, antiquing, fishing, parks, shopping and water sports nearby.
Location: Small town, Lake Eufaula.
Certificate may be used: Anytime, space available.

Oklahoma City
C7

The Grandison at Maney Park
1200 N Shartel Ave
Oklahoma City, OK 73103-2402
(405)232-8778 (800)240-4667
Internet: www.bbonline.com/ok/grandison
E-mail: grandison@juno.com

Circa 1904. This spacious Victorian has been graciously restored and maintains its original mahogany woodwork, stained glass, brass fixtures and a grand staircase. Several rooms include a Jacuzzi, and all have their own unique decor. The Treehouse Hideaway includes a Queen bed that is meant to look like a hammock and walls are painted with a blue sky and stars. The Jacuzzi tub rests beneath a skylight. The home is located north of downtown Oklahoma City in a historic neighborhood listed in the National Register.
Innkeeper(s): Claudia & Bob Wright. $75-150. 9 rooms with PB. Breakfast and snacks/refreshments included in rates. Types of meals: Full bkfst, early coffee/tea and room service. Beds: KQT. TV, VCR, ceiling fan, telephone and seven with Jacuzzis in room. Air conditioning. Fax, copier, workout room, video library, gift shop and special packages on premises. Handicap access. Antiquing, live theater, parks and sporting events nearby.
Location: City.
Publicity: *Daily Oklahoman, Oklahoma Pride, Oklahoma Gazette, Discover Oklahoma, Tulsa People Magazine, Travel & Leisure, Country Discoveries Magazine, Discover Oklahoma and Oklahoma Living.*
"Like going home to Grandma's!"
Certificate may be used: Anytime, Sunday-Thursday.

Oregon

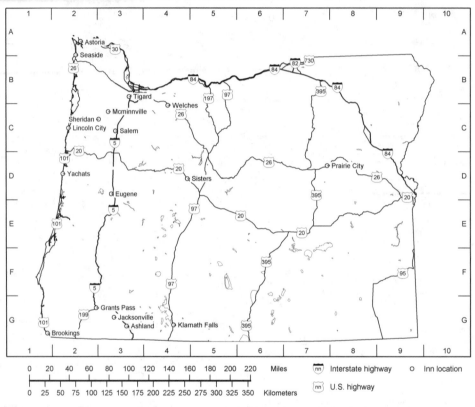

Ashland G3

Chanticleer B&B Inn

120 Gresham St
Ashland, OR 97520-2807
(541)482-1919 (800)898-1950
Internet: www.ashlandbnb.com

Circa 1920. This clapboard, Craftsman-style house has been totally renovated and several rooms added. The inn is light and airy and decorated with antiques. Special features include the open hearth fireplace and bricked patio garden.

Innkeeper(s): Howie Wilcox and Ellen Campbell. $110-195. 6 rooms with PB, 1 with FP, 1 suite. Breakfast included in rates. Types of meals: Full gourmet bkfst and early coffee/tea. Beds: QT. TV, reading lamp, clock radio, telephone and desk in room. Air conditioning. Fireplace on premises. Antiquing, cross-country skiing, downhill skiing, live theater, shopping and sporting events nearby.
Location: Village/town.

Publicity: *Country Home* and *Pacific Northwest.*

"Chanticleer has set the standard by which all others will be judged."
Certificate may be used: Nov. 1-March 31, excluding weekends and holidays.

McCall House

153 Oak Street
Ashland, OR 97520
(541)482-9296 (800)808-9749 Fax:(541)482-2125
Internet: www.mccallhouse.com
E-mail: mccall@mccallhouse.com

Circa 1883. Experience a blend of elegant Victorian splendor, rich history and splendid hospitality at this restored Italianate mansion that sits between the Siskiyou and Cascade Mountains just one block from the Oregon Shakespeare Festival. Relax in the refined double parlor that features some of the original furnishings. Luxurious guest bedrooms and a suite have been enhanced with modern amenities and boast an assortment of pleasures that may include antiques, fireplaces, sitting areas and clawfoot tubs. The Carriage House North and South are cottages with two private quarters that have refrigerators, microwaves and coffeemakers. After a generous breakfast explore nearby Lithia Park and Ashland's Plaza.

Innkeeper(s): Nola O'Hara. $100-225. 10 rooms with PB, 4 with FP, 1 suite and 1 conference room. Breakfast and snacks/refreshments included in rates. Types of meals: Full gourmet bkfst, veg bkfst, early coffee/tea, afternoon tea and wine. Beds: KQT. Modem hook-up, data port, cable TV, VCR, reading lamp, refrigerator, ceiling fan, clock radio, telephone, coffeemaker, turn-down service, desk, voice mail and fireplace in room. Central air. Fax, copier, library, parlor games and gift shop on premises. Limited handicap access. Antiquing, art galleries, bicycling, canoeing/kayaking, cross-country skiing, downhill skiing, fishing, golf, hiking, horseback riding, live theater, museums, parks, shopping, tennis, wineries, Oregon Shakespeare Festival, Britt Music Festival and Historical Society and Museum nearby.

Location: Mountains. Small town.

Certificate may be used: Anytime, November-March, subject to availability.

Mt. Ashland Inn

550 Mt Ashland Ski Rd
Ashland, OR 97520-9745
(541)482-8707 (800)830-8707
Internet: www.mtashlandinn.com
E-mail: stay@mtashlandinn.com

Innkeepers Chuck and Laurel Biegert truly have mastered the art of innkeeping. It doesn't hurt that the two "keep" a spectacular mountain cedar log lodge surrounded by a pine forest. During chilly months, a fire crackles in the front room's magnificent stone fireplace. Guests trample in after a day on the slopes ready to enjoy a soak in the outdoor spa and sauna under a night sky sparkling with stars. Guest rooms and suites are appointed with elegant, yet comfortable furnishings. Quilts, antiques, double whirlpool tubs and wonderful views are just some of the surprises guests will discover. The Biegerts go all out during the holiday season, and from November to New Year's, the inn participates in the town's Festival of Lights. But winter isn't the only season to visit the inn, the area offers hiking, fishing, shopping, galleries, museums and more. No matter what time of year, guests are treated to a divine breakfast. The cuisine at Mount Ashland has been featured in several cookbooks, including Bon Appetit.

Innkeeper(s): Chuck & Laurel Biegert. $136-200. 5 rooms, 5 with FP, 5 suites and 1 conference room. Breakfast included in rates. Types of meals: Full gourmet bkfst, early coffee/tea, gourmet lunch, picnic lunch, snacks/refreshments, hors d'oeuvres and wine. Beds: KQT. Reading lamp, CD player, refrigerator, clock radio, desk, hot tub/spa, fireplace, thick Turkish cotton robes, hair dryer and microwave in room. Spa, sauna, parlor games, telephone, gift shop, complimentary snowshoes and cross-country skis on premises. Antiquing, art galleries, bicycling, canoeing/kayaking, cross-country skiing, downhill skiing, fishing, golf, hiking, horseback riding, live theater, museums, parks, shopping, water sports and wineries nearby.

Location: Mountains. Three miles from alpine skiing.

Publicity: Log Home Living, Country Living, Bon Appetit, Glamour, Pacific Northwest, Edward Carter's Travels, Snow Country, Oregon, Glamour, Travel & Leisure, Country Living and Log Home Living.

"I've wondered where my dreams go when I can't remember them. Now I know they come here, among the snow, trees, valley, dogs, wind, sun, and dance at night around the Lodge."

Certificate may be used: Oct. 15 through May 31, excluding holiday periods, Sunday through Thursday.

Wolfe Manor Inn

586 B St
Ashland, OR 97520
(541)488-3676 (800)801-3676 Fax:(541)488-4567
Internet: www.wolfemanor.com
E-mail: wolfebandb@aol.com

Circa 1910. A glass door with sidelights welcomes guests to this massive Craftsman-style home. A grand parlor/ballroom with original lighting fixtures and fine woodwork is the combination sitting area and dining room. Bedrooms offer views of the mountains or the inn's pleasantly landscaped lawns and gardens. Guests often enjoy relaxing on the inn's porches.

Innkeeper(s): Sybil & Ron Maddox. $89-150. 5 rooms with PB. Breakfast and snacks/refreshments included in rates. Types of meals: Full gourmet bkfst, veg bkfst and early coffee/tea. Beds: QD. Reading lamp, ceiling fan and clock radio in room. Central air. TV, fax, copier, library, telephone, refrigerator, snack bar and coffeemaker on premises. Antiquing, art galleries, bicycling, canoeing/kayaking, cross-country skiing, downhill skiing, fishing, golf, hiking, horseback riding, live theater, museums, parks, shopping, tennis, water sports and wineries nearby.

Location: City.

Publicity: Getaways Magazine, PNW "Best Places to Stay" and Conde Nast Magazine.

Certificate may be used: Oct. 15 through April 15, Sunday through Thursday.

Astoria A2

Franklin Street Station Bed & Breakfast

1140 Franklin Ave
Astoria, OR 97103-4132
(503)325-4314 (800)448-1098 Fax:(801)681-5641
Internet: www.franklin-st-station-bb.com
E-mail: franklinststationbb@yahoo.com

Circa 1900. Sit out on the balcony and take in views of the Columbia River and beautiful sunsets from this 1900 Victorian-style inn. Ornate craftsmanship and antique furnishings, right down to the clawfoot bathtubs, transport visitors into the past. The six guest rooms are named Starlight Suite, Sweet Tranquility, the Hide-away,the Magestic, Magnolia Retreat and Enchanted Haven. The full breakfast includes dishes like fruit, waffles and sausage. The Flavel House Museum and Heritage Museum within walking distance, and the Astoria Column and Fort Clatsop are a short drive from the inn.

Innkeeper(s): Sharon Middleton, Rebecca Greenway. $75-135. 7 rooms, 5 with PB, 1 with FP, 3 suites. Breakfast and snacks/refreshments included in rates. Types of meals: Full bkfst, veg bkfst and early coffee/tea. Beds: Q. Cable TV, VCR, reading lamp, stereo, refrigerator, clock radio, telephone, coffeemaker, fireplace, clawfoot tubs and balconies in room. Copier, library, parlor games and fireplace on premises. Antiquing, art galleries, beach, fishing, golf, hiking, horseback riding, live theater, museums, parks, shopping, wineries and swimming nearby.

Location: City.

Publicity: LA Times.

Certificate may be used: Oct. 15-Jan. 15, anytime.

Grandview B&B

1574 Grand Ave
Astoria, OR 97103-3733
(503)325-0000 (800)488-3250
Internet: www.pacifier.com/~grndview/
E-mail: grandviewbnb@freedom.usa.com

Circa 1896. To fully enjoy its views of the Columbia River, this Victorian house has both a tower and a turret. Antiques and white wicker furnishings contribute to the inn's casual, homey

feeling. The Bird Meadow Room is particularly appealing to bird-lovers with its birdcage, bird books and bird wallpaper. Breakfast, served in the main-floor turret, frequently includes smoked salmon with bagels and cream cheese.

Innkeeper(s): Charleen Maxwell. $61-105. 9 rooms, 7 with PB, 3 with FP, 2 suites. Breakfast and snacks/refreshments included in rates. Types of meals: Full bkfst. Beds: QT. Parlor games, telephone and fireplace on premises. Antiquing, fishing, live theater, parks, shopping, water sports, historic homes tour, old-fashioned trolley, river walk, aqua center, movie complex and forts nearby.

Location: City.

Publicity: *Pacific Northwest Magazine, Northwest Discoveries, Los Angeles Times, Oregonian and Daily Astorian.*

"I have travelled all over the world and for the first time I found in the country of the computers such a romantic house with such poetic rooms at the Grandview Bed & Breakfast. Thanks." - MD from Paris, France

Certificate may be used: Nov. 1-May 17, holidays okay except two weekends in February may be excluded.

Brookings   G1

Chetco River Inn/Lavender Farm

21202 High Prairie Rd
Brookings, OR 97415-8200
(541)251-0087
Internet: www.chetcoriverinn.com
E-mail: chetcoriverinn@starband.net

Circa 1987. Situated on 40 wooded acres and the Chetco River, this modern bed & breakfast offers a cedar lodge exterior and a marble- and antique-filled interior. A collection of crafts, Oriental rugs and leather sofas add to your enjoyment. Breakfast and goodies served to guests include the addition of the farm's honey. Enjoy the sounds of the rushing river without interruption, or stroll through the acres of lavender. (Because it's 18 miles from Brookings, the property is out of the summer coastal fog.) Hiking the many inviting trails, exploring the Kalmiopsis Wilderness area and steelhead fishing are the favorite activities.

Innkeeper(s): Sandra Brugger. $125-145. 5 rooms with PB and 1 cottage. Breakfast included in rates. Types of meals: Full gourmet bkfst, early coffee/tea, picnic lunch and gourmet dinner. Beds: KT. Reading lamp and views in room. Library, parlor games, telephone, fireplace, darts, horseshoes and other outdoor games on premises. Antiquing, fishing, golf, live theater, parks, shopping and water sports nearby.

Location: Riverfront in mountain.

Publicity: *Country, Oregon Coast, Medford Newspaper, Tribune and Sunset.*

Certificate may be used: Anytime, Sunday-Thursday, subject to availability, except holidays and weekends.

Sea Dreamer Inn

15167 McVay Ln
Brookings, OR 97415
(541)469-6629 (800)408-4367
Internet: www.seadreamerinn.com
E-mail: pennybnb@wbtv.net

Circa 1912. Curry County's oldest Country Victorian home, this inn overlooks the famous lily fields to the ocean beyond. Sit on the front porch and whale watch. Inside, play games by

the fire, or munch a homemade cookie while perusing the library books. After a comfortable night's rest, enjoy a delicious breakfast served in the formal dining room. Walk the spacious grounds with flowers, landscaped lawns and shade trees that enhance the private ambiance. Bikes are available to further explore the local area.

Innkeeper(s): Penny Wallace & Don Roy. $50-80. 4 rooms, 1 with PB. Breakfast and snacks/refreshments included in rates. Types of meals: Full gourmet bkfst, veg bkfst and early coffee/tea. Beds: QDT. Cable TV, reading lamp, ceiling fan, telephone, turn-down service and desk in room. Bicycles, child care and fireplace on premises. Antiquing, art galleries, beach, bicycling, canoeing/kayaking, fishing, golf, hiking, horseback riding, live theater, museums, parks, shopping, water sports and wineries nearby.

Location: Country, mountains, ocean community.

Certificate may be used: Sept. 4-April 30, subject to availability.

South Coast Inn B&B

516 Redwood St
Brookings, OR 97415-9672
(541)469-5557 (800)525-9273 Fax:(541)469-6615
Internet: www.southcoastinn.com
E-mail: innkeeper@southcoastinn.com

Circa 1917. Enjoy panoramic views of the Pacific Ocean at this Craftsman-style inn designed by renowned San Francisco architect Bernard Maybeck. All rooms are furnished with antiques, ceiling fans, CD player, VCRs and TVs. Two guest rooms afford panoramic views of the coastline and there is a separate cottage. A floor-to-ceiling stone fireplace and beamed ceilings make the parlor a great place to gather with friends. There are sun decks and a strolling garden. The Brookings area offers something for everyone. Outdoor activities include hiking, boating, golfing, digging for clams or simply enjoying a stroll along the spectacular coastline. Concerts, galleries, museums, antiques, specialty shops and fine restaurants all can be found within the area.

Innkeeper(s): Sheldon & Gro Lent. $99-139. 4 rooms with PB and 1 cottage. Breakfast included in rates. Types of meals: Full gourmet bkfst and early coffee/tea. Beds: KQ. Cable TV, VCR, reading lamp, ceiling fan, clock radio, desk, hair dryers in baths and 1 with gas fireplace/stove in room. Fax, spa, sauna, library, parlor games, telephone, fireplace and continental breakfast in cottage on premises. Antiquing, fishing, live theater, parks, shopping and water sports nearby.

Location: City, ocean community.

"Thank you for your special brand of magic. What a place!"

Certificate may be used: November-April, except holidays.

Eugene   D3

Campbell House, A City Inn

252 Pearl St
Eugene, OR 97401-2366
(541)343-1119 (800)264-2519 Fax:(541)343-2258
Internet: www.campbellhouse.com
E-mail: campbellhouse@campbellhouse.com

Circa 1892. Fully restored, this gracious Victorian inn sits on one acre of landscaped beauty. Classic elegance and comfort combine with generous hospitality and service to ensure a pleasant visit. Suites and guest bedrooms feature private covered balconies or a patio with pond. Gas fireplaces, jetted or clawfoot tubs and four-poster beds are featured in some rooms. For more space, stay in Celeste

Cottage, a full-size house next door. Hunger is far from the mind after a satisfying breakfast each morning. Downtown is within a short walk. Ride the riverside bike paths, or jog the renowned Pre's Trail. Enjoy wine or cider in the evenings.
Innkeeper(s): Myra Plant. $92-349. 19 rooms with PB, 8 with FP, 1 suite and 2 conference rooms. Breakfast included in rates. Types of meals: Full bkfst, early coffee/tea and room service. Beds: KQDT. Cable TV, VCR, reading lamp, refrigerator, ceiling fan, snack bar, telephone, turn-down service, desk and jetted or clawfoot tubs in room. Air conditioning. Fax, copier, library, parlor games, fireplace and complimentary evening wine and beverages on premises. Handicap access. Antiquing, bicycling, fishing, golf, hiking, live theater, parks, shopping, sporting events, water sports and rock climbing nearby.
Location: City. On Skinner's Butte.
Publicity: Oregon Business, American Travels, B&B Innkeepers Journal, Eugene Register Guard, Country Inns, Oregonian, Sunset, Good Evening Show and KVAL & KAUW News.

"I guess we've never felt so pampered! Thank you so much. The room is beautiful! We had a wonderful getaway."
Certificate may be used: January-March (not valid during events, holidays or conferences).

Kjaer's House In Woods

814 Lorane Hwy
Eugene, OR 97405-2321
(541)343-3234 (800)437-4501
E-mail: Eunicekjaer@hotmail.com

Circa 1910. This handsome Craftsman house on two landscaped acres was built by a Minnesota lawyer. It was originally accessible by streetcar. Antiques include a square grand piano of

rosewood and a collection of antique wedding photos. The house is attractively furnished and surrounded by flower gardens.
Innkeeper(s): George & Eunice Kjaer. $65-80. 2 rooms with PB and 1 conference room. Breakfast included in rates. Types of meals: Full gourmet bkfst and early coffee/tea. Beds: Q.
Reading lamp and clock radio in room. TV, VCR, library, parlor games and telephone on premises. Antiquing, fishing, live theater, parks, shopping and sporting events nearby.
Location: City.
Publicity: Register Guard and Oregonian.

"Lovely ambiance and greatest sleep ever. Delicious and beautiful food presentation."
Certificate may be used: Nov. 1-May 10, Sunday-Friday.

The Oval Door

988 Lawrence St
Eugene, OR 97401-2827
(541)683-3160 (800)882-3160
Internet: www.ovaldoor.com
E-mail: chef@ovaldoor.com

Circa 1990. This recently constructed New England farm-style house comes complete with wraparound porch. It is located in a residential neighborhood 15 blocks from the University of Oregon. A welcoming parlor boasts a fireplace and plush furniture. Guest rooms feature ceiling fans and antiques. There is both a whirlpool room with music and a library. Breakfast can be made to order for special dietary needs, but the regular gourmet offerings are especially good. Homemade breads and local fruits and berries are also featured. Arrive in time to enjoy afternoon tea and freshly baked cookies or sweets.
Innkeeper(s): Nicole Wergeland, Melissa Coray. $75-195. 4 rooms with PB. Beds: QT. TV, VCR, reading lamp, ceiling fan, clock radio, telephone, turn-down service and desk in room. Fax, library, parlor games and fireplace on premises.

Location: City.
Certificate may be used: November-April, Sunday-Thursday. Not valid during special events, holidays or conferences.

Pookie's B&B on College Hill

2013 Charnelton St
Eugene, OR 97405-2819
(541)343-0383 (800)558-0383 Fax:(541)431-0967
Internet: www.pookiesbandblodging.com
E-mail: pookiesbandb@aol.com

Circa 1918. Pookie's is a charming Craftsman house with "yester-year charm." Surrounded by maple and fir trees, the B&B is located in an older, quiet neighborhood. Mahogany and oak antiques decorate the rooms. The innkeeper worked for many years in the area as a concierge and can offer you expert help with excursion planning or business needs.
Innkeeper(s): Pookie & Doug Walling. $80-115. 3 rooms, 2 with PB, 1 suite. Breakfast included in rates. Types of meals: Full bkfst and early coffee/tea. Beds: KQT. Cable TV, reading lamp, ceiling fan, clock radio, telephone and desk in room. VCR, fax, copier and parlor games on premises. Antiquing, fishing, live theater, parks, shopping, sporting events, water sports and baseball stadium nearby.
Location: City.
Publicity: Oregon Wine.

"I love the attention to detail. The welcoming touches: flowers, the 'convenience basket' of necessary items . . . I'm happy to have discovered your lovely home."
Certificate may be used: Jan. 15-May 1, Sunday-Wednesday, suite only.

Grants Pass　　　　　　　　　G2

Lawnridge House

1304 N W Lawnridge Ave
Grants Pass, OR 97526-1218
(541)476-8518
E-mail: lawnhouse@yahoo.com

Circa 1909. This inn, a graceful, gabled clapboard house is shaded by 200-year-old oaks. The home features spacious rooms with comfortable antiques, canopy beds and beamed ceilings. Mini refrigerators, TVs and VCRs are among the amenities. A family suite accommodates up to six people and includes one or two bedrooms, a sitting room and bathroom. The innkeeper serves

Northwest regional cuisine for the full breakfasts. The Rogue River is five minutes away, and the Ashland Shakespearean Festival is a 45-minute drive.
Innkeeper(s): Barbara Head. $85-95. 4 rooms with PB, 2 suites. Breakfast included in rates. Types of meals: Full bkfst. Beds: KQ. Reading lamp, refrigerator and desk in room. Air conditioning. Parlor games, telephone and fireplace on premises. Antiquing, fishing, live theater and water sports nearby.
Location: City.
Publicity: Grants Pass Courier, This Week and CBS TV.

"Thank you for your incredible friendliness, warmth, and energy expended on our behalf! I've never felt so nestled in the lap of luxury - what a pleasure!"
Certificate may be used: Jan. 6-May 15, space available basis only same day, no advance reservations. Ask for special Canadian discounts.

Weasku Inn

5560 Rogue River Hwy
Grants Pass, OR 97527
(541)471-8000 (800)493-2758 Fax:(541)471-7038
Internet: www.weasku.com
E-mail: info@weasku.com

Circa 1924. Built as a secluded fishing lodge, this historic inn once hosted the likes of President Herbert Hoover, Zane Grey, Walt Disney, Clark Gable and Carole Lombard. It is said that after Lombard's death, Gable spent several weeks here lamenting the loss of his beloved wife. A complete restoration took place in the late 1990s, reviving the inn back to its former glory. The log exterior, surrounding by towering trees and 10 fragrant acres, is a welcoming site. Inside, crackling fires from the inn's rock fireplaces warm the common rooms. Vaulted ceilings and exposed log beams add a cozy, rustic touch to the pristine, airy rooms all decorated in Pacific Northwest style. Many rooms include a whirlpool tub and river rock fireplace, and several offer excellent views of the Rogue River, which runs through the inn's grounds. In addition to the inn rooms, there are riverfront cabins, offering an especially romantic setting. In the evenings, guests are treated to a wine and cheese reception, and in the mornings, a continental breakfast is served. The staff can help plan many activities, including fishing and white-water rafting trips.
Innkeeper(s): Sue Price. $110-295. 17 rooms with PB, 12 with FP, 3 suites, 12 cabins and 1 conference room. Breakfast and snacks/refreshments included in rates. Types of meals: Cont plus. Beds: KQT. Data port, cable TV, reading lamp, ceiling fan, clock radio, telephone and hot tub/spa in room. Central air. Fax, parlor games and fireplace on premises. Handicap access. Antiquing, canoeing/kayaking, fishing, golf, hiking, live theater, museums, parks, shopping, water sports, wineries, jet boat excursions and wildlife park nearby.
Location: On the Rogue River.
Publicity: *Travel & Leisure Magazine, LA Magazine, Sunset and SF Magazine.*
Certificate may be used: Anytime, Sunday-Thursday, subject to availability.

Jacksonville   G3

Historic Orth House B&B

105 W Main St, PO Box 1437
Jacksonville, OR 97530
(541)899-8665 (800)700-7301 Fax:(541)899-9146
Internet: www.orthbnb.com
E-mail: orthbnb@orthbnb.com

Circa 1880. Surrounded by a white picket fence and a half acre of landscaped grounds, this historic, two-story brick
Italianate home was built during the Gold Rush and is now listed in the National Register. Large guest bedrooms feature period furnishings and claw-foot tubs. After a satisfying breakfast, stroll among the blooming flower gardens.
Innkeeper(s): Lee & Marilyn Lewis. $95-250. 4 rooms, 3 with PB, 1 two-bedroom suite. Breakfast included in rates. Types of meals: Full bkfst. Beds: KQT. Reading lamp, ceiling fan and clock radio in room. Air conditioning. Fax, copier and telephone on premises. Antiquing, art galleries, downhill skiing, fishing, golf, live theater, museums, parks, shopping, wineries, Britt Music Festival and Ashland Shakespeare Festival nearby.
Location: City, mountains. City/Rural.
Publicity: *American Profile and Country Discoveries.*
Certificate may be used: Anytime, November-April, subject to availability.

Touvelle House

PO Box 1891
Jacksonville, OR 97530-1891
(541)899-8938 (800)846-8422 Fax:(541)899-3992
Internet: www.touvellehouse.com
E-mail: touvelle@wave.net

Circa 1916. This Craftsman inn is two blocks away from the main street of this old Gold Rush town. The common areas of this Craftsman inn include The Library, which has a TV and VCR; The Great Room, featuring a large-stoned fireplace; The Sunroom, which consists of many windows; and The Dining Room, featuring an intricate built-in buffet. Guests can relax on either of two spacious covered verandas.
Innkeeper(s): Steven Harris. $110-195. 6 rooms with PB, 1 suite. Breakfast included in rates. Types of meals: Full bkfst. Beds: KQDT. Antiquing, cross-country skiing, downhill skiing, fishing, live theater, water sports and festival nearby.
Publicity: *ABC News.*

"The accommodations are beautiful, the atmosphere superb, the breakfast and other goodies delightful, but it is the warmth and caring of the host that will make the difference in this B&B!! "
Certificate may be used: Jan. 1-April 30, Nov. 1-Dec. 20, Sunday-Thursday night, except holidays.

Klamath Falls   G4

Thompsons' B&B

1420 Wild Plum Ct
Klamath Falls, OR 97601-1983
(541)882-7938
Internet: www.thompsonsbandb.com
E-mail: thompsonbandb@charter.net

Circa 1987. The huge picture windows in this comfortable retreat look out to a spectacular view of Klamath Lake and nearby mountains. Innkeeper Mary Pohll has a collection of dolls and clowns. Popular Moore Park is next door, providing a day of hiking, picnicking or relaxing at the marina. The inn is a perfect site to just relax and enjoy the view. Bird watching is a must, as the inn is home to pelicans, snow geese, bald eagles and many varieties of wild ducks.
Innkeeper(s): Mary & Bill Pohll. $84-110. 4 rooms with PB. Breakfast included in rates. Types of meals: Full bkfst and early coffee/tea. Beds: K. Cable TV, reading lamp, refrigerator, clock radio, telephone and desk in room. Air conditioning. TV and parlor games on premises. Antiquing, parks and water sports nearby.
Location: City, mountains.

"Hospitality as glorious as your surroundings."
Certificate may be used: Anytime November-April, subject to availability.

Lincoln City   C2

Brey House

3725 NW Keel Ave
Lincoln City, OR 97367
(541)994-7123
Internet: www.breyhouse.com
E-mail: breysinn@webtv.net

Circa 1941. The innkeepers at this three-story, Cape Cod-style house claim that when you stay with them it's like staying with Aunt Shirley and Uncle Milt. Guest rooms include some with ocean views and private entrances, and the Deluxe Suite offers a living room with fireplace, two baths and a kitchen. The Admiral's Room on the third floor has knotty pine walls, a skylight, fireplace and the best view.

Innkeeper(s): Milt & Shirley Brey. $90-160. 4 rooms with PB, 3 with FP, 2 suites. Breakfast included in rates. Types of meals: Full gourmet bkfst and early coffee/tea. Beds: KQ. Cable TV, VCR, reading lamp, refrigerator, ceiling fan, clock radio, desk and hot tub/spa in room. Parlor games, telephone and fireplace on premises. Antiquing, fishing, golf, live theater, parks, shopping, tennis, water sports and Indian casino nearby.

Location: City, ocean community.

Certificate may be used: September-June, Sunday-Friday. No Saturdays, no holiday weekends.

Coast Inn B&B

4507 SW Coast Ave
Lincoln City, OR 97367-1528
(541)994-7932 (888)994-7932 Fax:(541)994-7935
Internet: www.oregoncoastinn.com
E-mail: coastinn@oregoncoastinn.com

Circa 1939. A short walk from Siletz Bay with its herd of seals, this 4,000-square-foot house is 300 feet from the beach. A serene decor and mission-style furnishings provide a comfortable area to read a good book from the B&Bs library. Enjoy the sights and sounds of the Pacific from a window-wrapped botanical sunroom and deck. Writing journals are placed in the light and airy guest bedrooms and suites featuring luxury beds with down comforters, plush robes and a small refrigerator stocked with bottled water and fruit drinks. One romantic suite's amenities include a gas fireplace, microwave, flat screen TV with DVD and a vintage bathtub. Healthy gourmet breakfasts with fresh Oregon berries and peaches are served in the dining room, accented with vibrant art quilt designs. Small pets are allowed in one room with prior arrangement.

Innkeeper(s): Rosie Huntemann. $100-150. 4 rooms with PB, 1 with FP, 2 suites. Breakfast and snacks/refreshments included in rates. Types of meals: Full gourmet bkfst, early coffee/tea, gourmet dinner and room service. Beds: Q. Cable TV, refrigerator, one bathtub and some with microwaves in room. TV, VCR, fax, copier, library and Internet access on premises. Antiquing, fishing, golf, live theater, parks, tennis, water sports, Oregon Coast Aquarium, factory outlet shopping, beachcombing, whale watching and lighthouses nearby.

Location: Ocean community.

Publicity: *Oregonian & L C Newsguard.*

Certificate may be used: October through April, Sunday-Friday; May through September, Sunday-Thursday, no holidays.

McMinnville   C3

Youngberg Hill Vineyards & Inn

10660 SW Youngberg Hill Rd
McMinnville, OR 97128-8560
(503)472-2727 (888)657-8668 Fax:(503)472-1313
Internet: www.youngberghill.com
E-mail: youngberghill@netscape.net

Circa 1989. This inn's motto of "Come for the Wine — Savor the View" perfectly tells the guest what they are in store for. Enjoy estate-grown wine and wine tasting while taking in the spectacular views of Willamette Valley in the heart of the wine country that surround this Craftsman-style farmhouse set on 50 acres. Elegant adult accommodations provide the perfect romantic getaway. Relax in the library, tasting room or game room. Spacious suites and guest bedrooms are luxuriously furnished with a French Country decor. In the dining room, Youngberg Hill-blend coffee starts the morning repast of hot muffins, local fruit and a three-item entree that could include strawberry blintzes, braised sausage in homemade pear chutney and provincial potatoes. Special dietary needs will be addressed. Enjoy the region's many scenic activities.

Innkeeper(s): Nicolette & Wayne Bailey. $139-239. 7 rooms with PB, 3 with FP, 3 suites and 1 conference room. Breakfast included in rates. Types of meals: Full gourmet bkfst, veg bkfst, early coffee/tea and afternoon tea. Beds: KQ. Reading lamp, clock radio, turn-down service, irons, ironing boards, fireplace and wireless Internet access in room. Central air. Fax, copier, library, parlor games, telephone, fireplace, wine tasting, gift shop and event site designed especially for weddings on premises. Limited handicap access. Antiquing, art galleries, bicycling, fishing, golf, hiking, horseback riding, live theater, museums, parks, shopping, sporting events, tennis and wineries nearby.

Location: Country.

Publicity: *Bon Appetit, Sunset Magazine, Travel & Leisure Magazine* and *National Geographic Traveler.*

"This is Nirvana! Second time here and certainly not the last."

Certificate may be used: Anytime, November-April, subject to availability. Guest must declare coupon at time of reservation request.

Prairie City   D7

Strawberry Mountain Inn

67845 Highway 26
Prairie City, OR 97869-9000
(541)820-4522 (800)545-6913 Fax:(541)820-4522
Internet: www.strawberrymountaininn.com
E-mail: lindaharrington600@msn.com

Circa 1910. Vistas of Strawberry Mountain are a highlight of a getaway to this peaceful inn, set on three acres of farmland. The home, the largest in Grant County, was built by a man who bred and raised horses for the U.S. Cavalry. The interior is spacious and comfortable, a place where guests are made to feel at home. There is a library offering a wide selection of books, and guests can relax on the front porch or enjoy a game of chess in the parlor. A deep-dish apple puff pancake or croissant French toast might appear on the breakfast table, served by candlelight while classical melodies play out in the background.

Innkeeper(s): Linda & Bill Harrington. $85-120. 5 rooms, 4 with PB. Breakfast included in rates. Types of meals: Full gourmet bkfst, veg bkfst and gourmet dinner. Beds: KQDT. Cable TV, VCR, reading lamp and ceiling fan in room. Air conditioning. Fax, copier, spa, stable, library, parlor games, telephone, laundry facility, gift shop, guest common area with library, video library, music and game table on premises. Antiquing, art galleries, bicycling, canoeing/kayaking, cross-country skiing, fishing, golf, hiking, horseback riding, museums, parks, shopping, tennis, water sports, wildlife viewing, birdwatching, fossil beds, ghost towns, gold panning, white water rafting, flea markets and local festivals nearby.

Location: Country, mountains. Walking distance to village dining and shopping.

Publicity: *Northwest Best Places, Eastern Oregonian, Oregonia Travel Section: A Secret Too Good To Keep* and *Southern Oregon Public Television* documentary on the *Journey Through Time Scenic ByWay: Inns on the ByWay.*

Certificate may be used: Nov. 15 to March 15, excluding holidays. Anytime, subject to availability, if certificate is mentioned at time of reservation only.

Salem   C3

A Creekside Garden Inn

333 Wyatt Ct NE
Salem, OR 97301-4269
(503)391-0837
Internet: www.salembandb.com
E-mail: rickiemh@open.org

Circa 1938. Each room in this Mt. Vernon Colonial replica of George Washington's house has a garden theme. Consider the Picket Fences room. This gracious view room features a fireplace, Queen-size plus daybed, antique toys and a private bath. The four other upstairs guest rooms offer similar themes. There are regular evening movie screenings complete with popcorn in the common room. The extensive gardens offer guests an opportunity to stroll along historic Mill Creek or enjoy a round of croquet in the spacious backyard, weather permitting. Hazelnut waffles, confetti hash and oatmeal custard are a few of the breakfast specialties. The inn is just two blocks from the Court-Chemeketa Historic District.

Innkeeper(s): Ms. Rickie Hart. $65-95. 5 rooms, 3 with PB, 1 with FP. Breakfast and snacks/refreshments included in rates. Types of meals: Full gourmet bkfst and early coffee/tea. Beds: QT. Reading lamp and desk in room. VCR, bicycles, parlor games, telephone and fireplace on premises. Amusement parks, antiquing, golf, live theater, parks, shopping, sporting events, wine country tours and wineries nearby.
Location: City.
Publicity: *Statesman Journal, Sunset, The Oregonian, The Christian Science Monitor and Carlton Food Network (United Kingdom).*

"We all agreed that you were the best hostess yet for one of our weekends!"
Certificate may be used: Nov. 15 to May 1, no holidays.

Seaside   A2

A Riverside Inn Bed & Breakfast

430 S Holladay Dr
Seaside, OR 97138-6730
(503)738-8254
Internet: ariversideinn.com
E-mail: ariversideinn@earthlink.com

Circa 1907. Gracing the Necanicum River on the picturesque North Coast, this historic inn was built in 1907 and has been completely renovated. The Victorian atmosphere is accented with antiques, artwork, books and fresh flowers. Stay in a guest bedroom or suite with a separate entrance or a cottage-style room with open beam ceilings and skylights. Self-contained units are also available with fully-equipped kitchens, living and dining areas. Breakfast and afternoon High Tea are available in the Lord Wicklow dining room with advance reservations. Fish, feed the ducks or relax on the riverfront deck. The beach is an easy three-and-a-half-block walk. Stroll along the seafront Promenade at this popular, year-round family resort community.

$49-149. 12 rooms with PB. Beds: KQT. TV, VCR, refrigerator, coffeemaker, suite has kitchenette, sitting room and private entrance in room. Air conditioning. Antiquing, art galleries, beach, bicycling, canoeing/kayaking, fishing, golf, hiking, horseback riding, live theater, museums, parks, tennis, water sports, wineries and seasonal pool nearby.
Location: Ocean community, waterfront.
Certificate may be used: Anytime, subject to availability. Must call ahead for a reservation and mention the coupon.

Custer House B&B

811 1st Ave
Seaside, OR 97138-6803
(503)738-7825 (800)738-7852 Fax:(503)738-4324
Internet: www.clatsop.com/custer
E-mail: custerbb@seasurf.com

Circa 1900. Wicker furnishings and a clawfoot tub are features of one of the rooms in this farmhouse-style B&B. It is located four blocks from the ocean and two blocks from the Seaside Convention Center. Your host is retired from the Air Force. Enjoy exploring the area's historic forts and beaches.

Innkeeper(s): Larry Weday & Ali Winchester. $70-85. 6 rooms with PB, 3 cottages and 1 conference room. Breakfast included in rates. Types of meals: Full bkfst. Beds: QT. Reading lamp, clock radio and desk in room. VCR, bicycles, parlor games, telephone and fireplace on premises.

Antiquing, fishing, live theater, parks, shopping and water sports nearby.
Location: City, ocean community.
Publicity: *Oregon Adventures.*
Certificate may be used: Oct. 15-May 15.

The Guest House B&B

486 Necanicum Dr
Seaside, OR 97138
(503)717-0495 (800)340-8150 Fax:(503)717-9385
E-mail: guest-house@moriah.com

Circa 1981. Across the street from the city historic museum, this B&B is situated behind a picket fence. Although the inn is of contemporary construction, all the guest rooms here offer antique beds and historical touches such as old area photos. Breakfast is served in the dining room where guests enjoy views of the Necanicum River. The Lewis and Clark Trail ends in the town of Seaside. The house is two blocks from the beach and near shops, restaurants and many outdoor activities. Portland is an hour and a half away, and Seattle is about three and a half hours from Seaside.

Innkeeper(s): Nancy & Ken Bailey. $60-95. 4 rooms with PB, 1 with FP. Breakfast and snacks/refreshments included in rates. Types of meals: Full bkfst and early coffee/tea. Beds: QDT. Cable TV, reading lamp, stereo, ceiling fan and clock radio in room. Fax, spa, library, pet boarding, parlor games, telephone and fireplace on premises. Amusement parks, antiquing, fishing, golf, live theater, parks, shopping, tennis and water sports nearby.
Certificate may be used: Anytime, subject to availability, except for major holidays.

Sheridan   C3

Bethell Lodging B&B In Wine Country

17950 Highway 22
Sheridan, OR 97378
(503)623-1300 (866)842-2686
Internet: www.bethell-lodging.com
E-mail: Boylans@bethell-lodging.com

Circa 1957. Ten acres of forest and gardens surround this third-generation family home and private cottage. Choose a complimentary bottle of wine upon check-in. The inn is child-friendly and offers handicap access. The cottage in the forest provides complete privacy, a fireplace and a kitchenette. Enjoy breakfast in the dining area near the large stone fireplace. A variety of French toast entrees, egg dishes, homemade muffins and jams with berries  from the garden are served. Allergy and dietary restrictions are easily accommodated. At the end of the day, soak in the outdoor covered hot tub secluded by tall firs and meadows.

Innkeeper(s): Boylan Family. $100-200. 2 rooms, 1 with PB, 1 with FP and 1 cottage. Breakfast and afternoon tea included in rates. Types of meals: Full bkfst and veg bkfst. Beds: K. Modem hook-up, cable TV, VCR, reading lamp, CD player, refrigerator, ceiling fan, clock radio, telephone, coffeemaker and fireplace in room. Air conditioning. Spa on premises. Handicap access. Antiquing, art galleries, beach, bicycling, fishing, golf, horseback riding, museums, parks, shopping and wineries nearby.
Location: Country. Forest setting 20 miles from Salem.

"Your lovely home and warm hospitality was a serene interlude."
Certificate may be used: Anytime, subject to availability.

Sisters   D4

Aspen Meadow Lodge

68733 Junipine Lane
Sisters, OR 97759
(541)549-4312 (866)549-4312 Fax:(541)549-4213
Internet: www.sisterslodging.com

Experience and appreciate the beauty of nature at this peaceful
retreat on nine pristine acres bordered by scenic and serene
Squaw Creek with an abundance of Aspen and Ponderosa.
Enjoy bird and wildlife watching from the wraparound deck or
looking through the many windows of the Great Room that
also boasts a huge rock fireplace. Self-sustaining lodge guest
bedrooms feature private entrances, refrigerators, microwaves,
TVs, robes, a video library and comfortable beds topped with
colorful quilts. Ask about pet-friendly rooms. A hearty country
breakfast is sure to satisfy. There is easy access to the upper
deck outdoor hot tub. Numerous golf courses are nearby and
the quaint town is a mile and a half away.
$89-119. 5 rooms with PB. TV, VCR, refrigerator, private entrance, satellite
and access to video library in room. Outdoor hot tub, video library, coffee/tea
makers, microwaves and robes on premises. Antiquing, golf, hiking, shopping
and USGA Aspen Lakes Golf Course nearby.
Certificate may be used: November through April, subject to availability.

Tigard   B3

The Woven Glass Inn

14645 Sw Beef Bend Rd
Tigard, OR 97224-1342
(503)590-6040
E-mail: wovenglass@wovenglassinn.com

Circa 1938. This comfortable farmhouse is surrounded by more
than an acre of grounds, including a sunken garden. The French
Room includes a four-poster, king bed and a private deck.
Guests staying in the Garden Suite enjoy a view of the garden.
Beds in both guest rooms include fluffy down pillows and fine
linens. The inn is 20 minutes from Portland, and the area offers
a variety of wineries to visit. There is a friendly cat in residence.
Innkeeper(s): Paul & Renee Giroux. $65-75. 2 rooms with PB, 2 with FP, 1
suite. Breakfast included in rates. Types of meals: Full bkfst. Beds: KQ. Reading
lamp, clock radio, telephone, turn-down service, desk and fans in room.
Library, parlor games, fireplace and sitting room with limited kitchen facilities
on premises. Amusement parks, antiquing, cross-country skiing, downhill skiing, fishing, golf, live theater, parks, shopping, sporting events, tennis, water
sports, alpaca farm, ballooning, bicycling, water parks and rivers nearby.
Location: Country.
Publicity: *Wine Press.*

*"We needed a little rest and relaxation and we found it here. We
loved everything."*
Certificate may be used: Oct. 1-April 30, Sunday-Thursday.

Welches   C4

Old Welches Inn B&B

26401 E Welches Rd
Welches, OR 97067-9701
(503)622-3754 Fax:(503)622-5370
Internet: www.lodging-mthood.com
E-mail: innmthood@cs.com

Circa 1890. This two-story Colonial building, was originally
the first hotel to be built in the Mt. Hood area. Reconstructed
in the '30s, the building now has shutters and French windows. The inn's two acres offer a plethora of flower beds and
views of the Salmon River and Hunchback Mountain. Rooms
are named for wildflowers and
include antiques. If traveling
with children or friends try
Lilybank, a private cottage which
overlooks the first hole of Three
Nines. There are two bedrooms,
two baths and a kitchen and a
river rock fireplace.
Innkeeper(s): Judith & Ted Mondun. $96-163. 4 rooms and 1 cottage.
Breakfast and snacks/refreshments included in rates. Types of meals: Full
bkfst and early coffee/tea. Beds: QD. Reading lamp and turn-down service in
room. VCR, fax, pet boarding, parlor games, telephone and fireplace on
premises. Antiquing, cross-country skiing, downhill skiing, fishing, golf, parks,
shopping, sporting events and tennis nearby.
Location: Mountains.
Publicity: *Oregonian, Sunset and Northwest Best Places.*
Certificate may be used: March 1-31, Nov. 1-20, subject to availability.

Yachats   D2

Sea Quest

95354 Hwy 101 S
Yachats, OR 97498-9713
(541)547-3782 (800)341-4878 Fax:(541)547-3719
E-mail: seaquest@newportnet.com

Circa 1990. This 6,000-square-foot cedar and glass house is
only 100 feet from the ocean, located on two-and-one-half
acres. Each guest room has a Jacuzzi tub and outside entrance.
The second-floor breakfast room is distinguished by wide views
of the ocean, forest and Ten Mile
Creek. Guests are often found
relaxing in front of the home's
floor-to-ceiling brick fireplace. More adventuresome
guests may enjoy the
Oregon coast and nearby aquariums.
Innkeeper(s): George & Elaine. $150-245. 5 rooms with PB. Breakfast
included in rates. Types of meals: Full bkfst and early coffee/tea. Beds: Q.
Reading lamp, CD player and hot tub/spa in room. Fax, spa, sauna, library,
parlor games, telephone and fireplace on premises. Antiquing, fishing, parks,
shopping, water sports, horseback riding, Oregon Coast Aquarium, Cape
Perpetual and Devil's Churn nearby.
Location: Ocean community, waterfront.
Certificate may be used: Jan. 5 to May 5, Sunday-Thursday, no holidays.

Pennsylvania

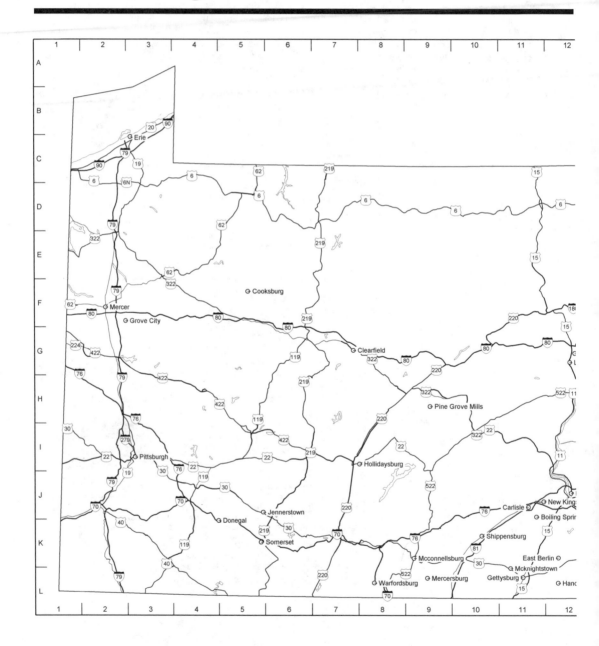

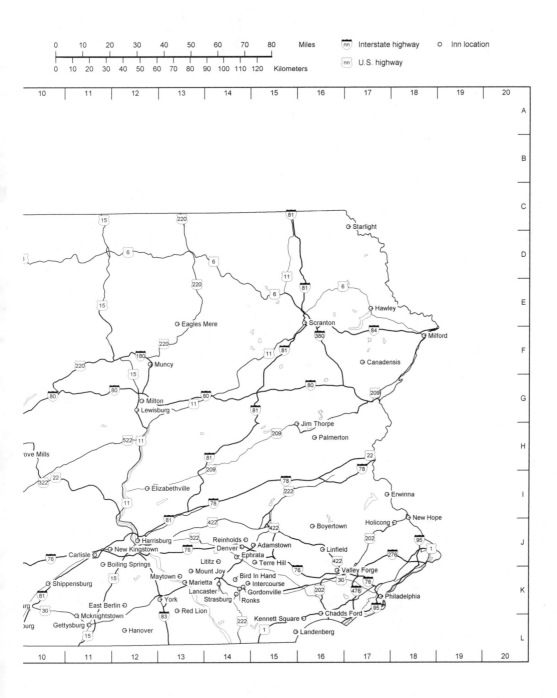

Miles
Interstate highway ○ Inn location
U.S. highway

Adamstown J15

Adamstown Inn

62 W Main St
Adamstown, PA 19501
(717)484-0800 (800)594-4808
Internet: www.adamstown.com
E-mail: stay@adamstown.com

Circa 1830. This restored Victorian with its 1850s pump organ found in the large parlor and other local antiques, fits right into this community known as one of the antique capitals of America (3,000 antique dealers). Other decorations include family heirlooms, Victorian wallpaper, handmade quilts and lace curtains. For outlet mall fans, Adamstown is 10 miles from Reading, which offers a vast assortment of top-quality merchandise.

Innkeeper(s): Tom & Wanda Berman. $70-169. 4 rooms with PB, 1 suite. Breakfast, afternoon tea and snacks/refreshments included in rates. Types of meals: Cont plus and early coffee/tea. Beds: KQ. Reading lamp, ceiling fan, clock radio, desk, hot tub/spa, fireplace and two with Jacuzzi in room. Air conditioning. TV, copier, library, parlor games, telephone and fireplace on premises. Amusement parks, antiquing, fishing, live theater, parks and shopping nearby.
Location: Lancaster County's Amish Country.
Publicity: Country Victorian, Lancaster Intelligencer, Reading Eagle, Travel & Leisure, Country Almanac, Lancaster Magazine and Chester County Magazine.

"Your warm hospitality and lovely home left us with such pleasant memories."
Certificate may be used: Nov. 1-April 15, Sunday through Thursday.

Bird-in-Hand K14

Mill Creek Homestead B&B

2578 Old Philadelphia Pike
Bird-in-Hand, PA 17505-9796
(717)291-6419 (800)771-2578 Fax:(717)291-2171
Internet: www.millcreekhomestead.com
E-mail: valfone@yahoo.com

Circa 1793. This 18th-century fieldstone farmhouse is one of the oldest homes in Bird-in-the-Hand. Located in the Pennsylvania Dutch Heartland, the inn is decorated for comfort with Amish influences represented throughout. There are four guest rooms with private baths and fireplaces or stoves. Guests are invited to lounge by the outdoor pool or sit on the porch and watch the horse-drawn buggies go by. A full breakfast is served in the formal dining room, while afternoon refreshments are in the common rooms. The inn is within walking distance of shops, museums, farmers market, antiques and crafts.

Innkeeper(s): Vicki & Frank Alfone. $109-195. 4 rooms with PB. Breakfast, afternoon tea and snacks/refreshments included in rates. Types of meals: Full bkfst and early coffee/tea. Beds: QT. Reading lamp, stereo, ceiling fan, clock radio, turn-down service, fireplace, robes and hair dryers in room. Central air. TV, VCR, swimming, library, parlor games, telephone and gift shop on premises. Amusement parks, antiquing, art galleries, bicycling, fishing, golf, hiking, live theater, museums, parks, shopping, tennis, water sports and wineries nearby.

Location: Country, rural.
Publicity: Country Inns and Lancaster County Magazine.

"Thank you for sharing your wonderful home with us. I knew this place would be perfect!"
Certificate may be used: Tuesday-Thursday, Jan. 2-April 30, excluding holidays.

Boiling Springs J11

Gelinas Manor Victorian B&B

219 Front Street
Boiling Springs, PA 17007
(717)258-6584 (888)789-9411 Fax:(717)245-9328
Internet: www.gelinas-manor.com
E-mail: Relax@gelinas-manor.com

Circa 1869. One of the first homes in the quiet historic village by the lake, this 1869 Victorian is listed in the National Register. Enjoy comfortable accommodations and a satisfying breakfast before embarking on the day's activities. The well-stocked lake and crystal-clear Yellow Breeches Creek are considered some of the country's best trout fishing areas. The nearby Fly Shop features locally tied flys, fishing gear, clothing and gifts as well as offering experienced tips for any interested fisherman. The famous Allenberry Resort and Playhouse is minutes away for fine dining and entertainment in the evening. Visit the sites of Gettysburg within a 30-minute drive, or savor the flavors of Hershey in an hour. The inn is about 1½ hours away from Pennsylvania Dutch Country in Lancaster County.
Innkeeper(s): Lee & Kitty Gelinas. $60-125. 4 rooms, 3 with PB, 1 two-bedroom suite. Breakfast included in rates. Types of meals: Full gourmet bkfst. Beds: QDT. Cable TV, refrigerator, ceiling fan, clock radio, telephone and turn-down service in room. Air conditioning. Fax, copier, library and fireplace on premises. Amusement parks, antiquing, art galleries, cross-country skiing, downhill skiing, fishing, golf, hiking, live theater, museums, parks, shopping, sporting events and tennis nearby.
Location: Historic Village.
Certificate may be used: Anytime, November-March, subject to availability.

Boyertown J16

The Enchanted Cottage

22 Deer Run Rd, Rd 4
Boyertown, PA 19512-8312
(610)845-8845
Internet: www.choice-guide.com/pa/enchanted
E-mail: pete.mcconnell@choicebedandbreakfast.com

Circa 1984. This timber and stone cottage looks much like one might imagine the woodcutter's tiny house in the fairy tale "Hansel and Gretel." Ivy covers the front of the main house, which guests reach via a little brick path. Inside, exposed wood beams, a bay window and a wood stove create a cozy, romantic ambiance in the living room. The first floor also includes a kitchenette. Upstairs, guests will find a quilt-topped double bed and a bathroom with a clawfoot tub. The innkeepers live in a nearby home where gourmet breakfasts are served. The cottage is near many attractions, including historic sites such as the Daniel Boone Home, Dupont Estate, Longwood Gardens, museums, Amish farms and a restored iron making village. Outlet shopping in Reading is a popular activity.
Innkeeper(s): Peg & Richard Groff. $100-110. 2 rooms, 1 with PB and 1 cottage. Breakfast and snacks/refreshments included in rates. Types of meals: Full gourmet bkfst, early bkfst and early coffee/tea. Beds: D. Reading lamp, refrigerator, ceiling fan, snack bar, telephone, coffeemaker, kitchenette and fireplace in room. Air conditioning. TV, library and fireplace on premises.

Amusement parks, antiquing, art galleries, downhill skiing, golf, hiking, museums, shopping, tennis, wineries, many historic sights & sites and auctions nearby.

Publicity: *Boyertown Area Times, Allentown News, Pottstown Mercury, Reading Times and New York Times.*

"The Enchanted Cottage is a place you've seen in dreams."

Certificate may be used: April 1-Sept. 30, Monday-Thursday, other dates as available.

Canadensis   F17

Brookview Manor Inn

RR 2 Box 2960, Route 447
Canadensis, PA 18325
(570)595-2451 (800)585-7974 Fax:(570)595-7154
Internet: www.thebrookviewmanor.com
E-mail: innkeepers@thebrookviewmanor.com

Circa 1901. By the side of the road, hanging from a tall evergreen, is the welcoming sign to this forest retreat on six acres adjoining 250 acres of woodland and hiking trails. The expansive wraparound porch overlooks a
small stream. There are brightly decorated common rooms and eight
fireplaces. Ten guest rooms include
two with Jacuzzis and two deluxe
suites. The carriage house has three
additional rooms. One of the inn's
dining rooms is surrounded by original stained glass, a romantic location
for the inn's special six-course dinners prepared by an award
winning New York chef now on staff. The innkeepers like to
share a "secret waterfall" within a 30-minute walk from the inn.

Innkeeper(s): Gaile & Marty Horowitz. $130-250. 10 rooms with PB, 8 with FP, 2 suites. Breakfast included in rates. Types of meals: Full gourmet bkfst, early coffee/tea, afternoon tea and dinner. Beds: KQ. TV, VCR, reading lamp, two rooms with Jacuzzi and suites have sitting rooms and private porches in room. Air conditioning. Fax, copier, telephone, fireplace, swing, wraparound porch overlooking small stream, hiking, gourmet dinner available by reservation and scheduled murder mystery weekends on premises. Amusement parks, antiquing, cross-country skiing, downhill skiing, fishing, live theater, parks, shopping, water sports and hiking nearby.

Location: Mountains.

Publicity: *Mid-Atlantic Country, Bridal Guide, New York Times and Pocono Record.*

"Thanks for a great wedding weekend. Everything was perfect."

Certificate may be used: Sunday to Thursday, subject to availability, not on holiday or special event weeks.

The Merry Inn

Rt 390
Canadensis, PA 18325-0757
(570)595-2011 (800)858-4182
Internet: www.pbcomputerconsulting.com/themerryinn
E-mail: merryinn@ezaccess.net

Circa 1942. Set in the picturesque Pocono Mountains, this bed & breakfast is a 90-minute drive from the metropolitan New York and Philadelphia areas. The turn-of-the-century, mountainside home was built by two sisters and at one time
was used as a boarding
house. Current owners
and innkeepers Meredyth
and Chris Huggard have
decorated their B&B
using an eclectic mix of

styles. Each guest room is individually appointed, with styles ranging from Victorian to country. Guests enjoy use of an outdoor Jacuzzi set into the mountainside. Bedrooms are set up to accommodate families, and children are welcome here.

Innkeeper(s): Meredyth & Christopher Huggard. $80-95. 6 rooms with PB. Breakfast included in rates. Types of meals: Full bkfst. Beds: KQDT. Cable TV, VCR, reading lamp and clock radio in room. Parlor games, telephone, fireplace and Jacuzzi (outdoor) on premises. Antiquing, cross-country skiing, downhill skiing, fishing, live theater, parks, shopping, water sports and golf nearby.

Location: Mountains.

Certificate may be used: Anytime midweek, weekends Nov. 15-April 15. No holidays.

Carlisle   J11

Carlisle House

148 South Hanover St
Carlisle, PA 17013-3420
(717)249-0350 Fax:(717)249-0458
Internet: www.thecarlislehouse.com
E-mail: info@thecarlislehouse.com

Circa 1750. Blending a rich history with modern comforts, excellent standards and high-tech amenities for business or leisure, this elegant bed and breakfast offers a memorable stay. Chat with new acquaintances in the sitting room. Relax on the veranda or downstairs patio. Enjoy 24-hour access to the fully equipped kitchen with complimentary fruits and beverages. Guest bedrooms feature period décor and furnishings. Some include a private entrance, fireplace and Jacuzzi bath. The Hydrangea Room becomes a suite when adding loft rooms. The spacious Rose Room boasts an original clawfoot tub. Savor an award-winning country breakfast. Conveniently situated in the heart of the state, Gettysburg battlefields, Hershey's Chocolate World, and Lancaster's Amish Country are some of the many day trips available.

Innkeeper(s): Alan & Mary Duxbury. $90-160. 8 rooms with PB, 3 with WP. Breakfast and snacks/refreshments included in rates. Types of meals: Country bkfst and early coffee/tea. Beds: QD. Data port, cable TV, reading lamp, CD player, refrigerator, clock radio, telephone, coffeemaker, turn-down service, desk and voice mail in room. Air conditioning. Fax, copier, library and parlor games on premises. Amusement parks, antiquing, art galleries, fishing, golf, hiking, museums, parks, shopping and sporting events nearby.

Location: City.

Certificate may be used: Anytime, Sunday-Thursday.

Pheasant Field B&B

150 Hickorytown Rd
Carlisle, PA 17013-9732
(717)258-0717 (877)258-0717
Internet: www.pheasantfield.com
E-mail: stay@pheasantfield.com

Circa 1800. Located on 10 acres of central Pennsylvania farmland, this brick, two-story Federal-style farmhouse features wooden shutters and a covered front porch. Rooms include a TV and telephone. An early 19th-century stone barn is on the property, and horse boarding is available. The Appalachian Trail is less than a mile away. Fly-fishing is popular at Yellow Breeches and Letort Spring. Dickinson College and Carlisle Fairgrounds are other
points of interest.

Innkeeper(s): Dee Fegan. $90-
175. 7 rooms with PB, 1 with
FP and 1 conference room.
Breakfast and snacks/refresh-

ments included in rates. Types of meals: Full bkfst and early coffee/tea. Beds: KQT. Cable TV, VCR, reading lamp, refrigerator, ceiling fan, clock radio, telephone, desk and fireplace in room. Central air. Fax, stable, tennis, library, parlor games, laundry facility, labyrinth and piano on premises. Limited handicap access. Amusement parks, antiquing, art galleries, cross-country skiing, downhill skiing, fishing, golf, hiking, live theater, museums, parks and sporting events nearby.

Location: Country.

Publicity: *Outdoor Traveler and Harrisburg Magazine.*

"You have an outstanding, charming and warm house. I felt for the first time as being home."

Certificate may be used: January and March.

Chadds Ford   K16

Hamanassett B&B
PO Box 366
Chadds Ford, PA 19017-0366
(610)459-3000 (877)836-8212 Fax:(610)558-7366
Internet: www.hamanassett.com
E-mail: visitus@hamanassett.com

Circa 1856. Located in Brandywine Valley, this Federalist mansion offers romantic accommodations with thoughtful extras. Inside the impressive three-story manor there is a spacious living room with wood-burning fireplace and a baby grand piano. A billiards room features fireside contemporary and antique games as well as a pool table. Relax in the cozy solarium with separate sitting areas. Appealing guest bedrooms provide upscale amenities that pamper and please. A Rosewood half-tester bed is showcased in the Windsor Room. The carriage house is perfect for children and pets. Candlelight gourmet breakfasts are served in the formal dining room that boasts a floor-to-ceiling fireplace and looks out on spacious lawns, trees and a stone terrace. A guest refrigerator is stocked with snacks and beverages.

Innkeeper(s): Ashley & Glenn Mon. $130-400. 6 rooms with PB, 1 with FP, 2 suites and 1 guest house. Breakfast, afternoon tea and snacks/refreshments included in rates. Types of meals: Full gourmet bkfst and veg bkfst. Beds: KQT. Data port, cable TV, VCR, reading lamp, CD player, refrigerator, ceiling fan, clock radio, telephone, coffeemaker, desk, fireplace, robes and hair dryer in room. Air conditioning. Fax, copier, library, parlor games, gift shop and special dietary needs accommodated on premises. Antiquing, art galleries, canoeing/kayaking, fishing, golf, hiking, horseback riding, live theater, museums, parks, shopping, sporting events, wineries, Brandywine Valley attractions and gardens nearby.

Location: Country. Brandywine Valley.

Publicity: *Philadelphia, Back Roads USA, Mid-Atlantic Country, Philadelphia and Its Countryside and voted "One of the Most Romantic B&Bs in North America."*

"For our first try at B&B lodgings, we've probably started at the top, and nothing else will ever measure up to this. Wonderful food, wonderful home, grounds and wonderful hostess!"

Certificate may be used: Sunday-Thursday, November through March, excluding holidays. May not be used with any other promotions.

Pennsbury Inn
883 Baltimore Pike
Chadds Ford, PA 19317-9305
(610)388-1435 Fax:(610)388-1436
Internet: www.pennsburyinn.com
E-mail: info@pennsburyinn.com

Circa 1714. Listed in the National Register, this country farmhouse with hand-molded Flemish Bond brick facade was built originally with Brandywine Blue Granite rubble stone and later enlarged. Retaining its colonial heritage with slanted doorways,

winding wood staircases and huge fireplaces, it boasts modern conveniences. There are elegant public sitting areas such as the living room, music room, library with an impressive book collection and breakfast in the dining room. The comfortable guest bedrooms feature antique feather beds and unique architectural details. The eight-acre estate boasts formal gardens that include a fish pond and reflection pool in a serene woodland setting.

Innkeeper(s): Cheryl. $100-225. 7 rooms, 6 with PB, 1 suite and 3 conference rooms. Breakfast, afternoon tea and snacks/refreshments included in rates. Types of meals: Country bkfst, veg bkfst and early coffee/tea. Beds: KQDT. Modem hook-up, data port, cable TV, reading lamp, CD player, clock radio, telephone, turn-down service, desk and three with decorative fireplaces in room. Central air. VCR, fax, copier, library, parlor games and fireplace on premises. Antiquing, art galleries, bicycling, canoeing/kayaking, golf, hiking, live theater, museums, parks, shopping, sporting events, tennis and wineries nearby.

Location: City.

Certificate may be used: Sunday through Thursday, January, February, March, July, August, september, October, November and December. Not valid April, May or June.

Choconut   C14

Addison House B&B
RR #1, Box 1586
Friendsville, PA 18818
(570)553-2682
Internet: www.1811addison.com
E-mail: info@1811addison.com

Circa 1811. Addison House was built by one of Choconut's earliest settlers, an Irish immigrant who purchased the vast homestead for just under a dollar an acre. The early 19th-century house is built in Federal style, but its interior includes many Victorian features, from the rich décor to the hand-carved marble fireplaces. A creek rambles through the 260-acre property, and guests will enjoy the secluded, wilderness setting. In the guest rooms, fluffy comforters top antique beds and floral wallcoverings add to the country Victorian ambiance. Breakfasts begin with items such as fresh berries with cream, followed by a rich entrée. The innkeepers are happy to help guests plan their days. The area offers a multitude of outdoor activities, as well as historic sites, antique shops, covered bridges and much more.

Innkeeper(s): Dennis & Gloria McLallen. $65-95. 3 rooms, 1 suite. Breakfast included in rates. Types of meals: Full gourmet bkfst, early coffee/tea and afternoon tea. Beds: D. Turn-down service, ice water and chocolates in room. Central air. TV, VCR, swimming, library, parlor games, telephone and fireplace on premises. Antiquing, art galleries, bicycling, canoeing/kayaking, cross-country skiing, fishing, golf, hiking, live theater, museums, parks, shopping, sporting events, wineries, zoo and house tours by appointment nearby.

Location: Country, mountains. Farm, horses.

Certificate may be used: Jan. 1-Dec. 31.

Clearfield   G7

Christopher Kratzer House
101 E Cherry St
Clearfield, PA 16830-2315
(814)765-5024 (888)252-2632
E-mail: bbaggett@uplink.net

Circa 1840. This inn is the oldest home in town, built by a carpenter and architect who also started Clearfield's first newspaper. The innkeepers keep a book of history about the house and town for interested guests. The interior is a mix of antiques from different eras, many are family pieces. There are collections of art and musical instruments. Two guest rooms afford views of the Susquehanna River. Refreshments and a glass of wine are served in the afternoons. The inn's Bridal Suite Special includes complimentary champagne, fruit and snacks, and breakfast may be served in the privacy of your room. Small wedding receptions, brunches and parties are hosted at the inn.

Innkeeper(s): Bruce & Ginny Baggett. $65-90. 4 rooms, 2 with PB. Breakfast, afternoon tea and snacks/refreshments included in rates. Types of meals: Full gourmet bkfst and early coffee/tea. Beds: KQT. Cable TV, reading lamp, ceiling fan, clock radio, telephone and desk in room. Air conditioning. Library, parlor games and fireplace on premises. Antiquing, cross-country skiing, fishing, live theater, parks, shopping, sporting events, hiking, biking and playground across street nearby.

Location: Mountains. Small town.

Publicity: *Local PA newspapers.*

"Past and present joyously intermingle in this place."

Certificate may be used: Anytime, subject to availability.

Cooksburg   F5

Clarion River Lodge

HC 1 Box 22d
Cooksburg, PA 16217-9704
(814)744-8171 (800)648-6743 Fax:(814)744-8553
E-mail: e.oday@penn.com

Circa 1964. This lodge is a rustic retreat above the Clarion River and surrounded by Cook Forest. Its pegged-oak flooring, oak beams, pine ceiling, wild cherry and butternut paneling and fieldstone fireplace add to the lodge's natural character. A distinctive glassed-in breezeway leads from the main building to the guest wing. Rooms are decorated with modern Scandinavian decor. Dinner and continental breakfast packages available.

Innkeeper(s): Ellen O'Day. $72-129. 20 rooms with PB and 1 conference room. Breakfast included in rates. Types of meals: Cont. Beds: KQ. Cable TV, reading lamp, refrigerator, clock radio, telephone and desk in room. Air conditioning. TV, VCR, fax and fireplace on premises. Antiquing, fishing, live theater, parks and shopping nearby.

Location: River.

Publicity: *Pittsburgh Press and Pittsburgh Women's Journal.*

"If your idea of Paradise is a secluded rustic retreat surrounded by the most beautiful country this side of the Rockies, search no more."

Certificate may be used: November-April, Sunday-Thursday, no holidays.

Denver   J14

Cocalico Creek B&B

224 S Fourth St
Denver, PA 17517
(717)336-0271 (888)208-7334
Internet: www.cocalicocrk.com
E-mail: cocalicocrk@dejazzd.com

Circa 1927. Casual elegance is found at this tranquil retreat in a country setting. Overlooking gardens and pastures, the B&B is accented with sounds of splashing ducks in the creek or ponds or an occasional buggy passing by. Comfortably decorated guest bedrooms, most with a view and some with a fireplace, are named for local wildlife. Blending traditional and antique furnishings, the rooms are enhanced with wallpaper, lace curtains and Oriental rugs. Enjoy a four-course breakfast made with many local seasonal ingredients, served in the candlelit dining room. Dietary requests are accommodated. Relax inside by the large stone fireplace or on the stenciled porch with wicker furniture. Schedule an in-room massage or dinner at an Amish home.

Innkeeper(s): Charlene Sweeney. $99-125. 4 rooms with PB, 2 with FP. Breakfast and snacks/refreshments included in rates. Types of meals: Full bkfst, veg bkfst and early coffee/tea. Beds: Q. Reading lamp, clock radio,

turn-down service, heated beds, robes, hair dryer and two with fireplace in room. Air conditioning. TV, VCR, library, telephone, fireplace, gift shop, TV, stereo, board/card games and puzzles on premises. Amusement parks, antiquing, art galleries, bicycling, cross-country skiing, fishing, golf, hiking, horseback riding, live theater, museums, parks, shopping, sporting events, tennis and wineries nearby.

Location: Small town.

Certificate may be used: Anytime, Sunday-Thursday.

Donegal   K4

Lesley's Mountain View Country Inn

10 Mountain View Rd
Donegal, PA 15628
(724)593-6349 (800)392-7773
Internet: www.shol.com/mtviewbb
E-mail: mtview@lhtc.net

Circa 1855. Six wooded acres surround this Georgian-style farmhouse, a county historic landmark. The innkeepers own Donegal antiques and have selected many fine 18th- and 19th-century pieces to furnish the inn. There is a large barn on the property. Guests enjoy the rural setting for its outstanding views of the Laurel Mountains. Fallingwater, a famous Frank Lloyd Wright house, is 20 minutes away.

Innkeeper(s): Lesley O'Leary. $150-210. 8 rooms with PB. Breakfast included in rates. Types of meals: Full bkfst, early coffee/tea and snacks/refreshments. Restaurant on premises. Beds: QD. TV and telephone in room. Air conditioning. Steinway grand piano and restaurant for fine dining on premises. Amusement parks, antiquing, cross-country skiing, downhill skiing, fishing, live theater and shopping nearby.

Location: Falling water-Frank Lloyd Wright.

Certificate may be used: Anytime except holiday weekends and month of October.

Eagles Mere   E13

Crestmont Inn

Crestmont Dr
Eagles Mere, PA 17731
(570)525-3519 (800)522-8767
Internet: www.crestmont-inn.com
E-mail: crestmnt@epix.net

Circa 1914. Eagles Mere has been a vacation site since the late 19th century and still abounds with Victorian charm. The Crestmont Inn is no exception. The rooms are tastefully decorated with flowers and elegant furnishings. Suites include two-person whirlpool tubs. A hearty country breakfast is served each morning, and guests also are treated to a five-course dinner in the candle-lit dining room. Savor a variety of mouth-watering entrees and finish off the evening with scrumptious desserts such as fresh fruit pies, English trifle or Orange Charlotte. The cocktail lounge is a perfect place to mingle and enjoy hors d'oeuvres, wines and spirits. The inn grounds offer tennis and shuffleboard courts. The Wyoming State Forest borders the property, and golfing is just minutes away.

Innkeeper(s): Elna & Fred Mulford. $128-198. 14 rooms with PB, 3 with HT. Breakfast included in rates. Types of meals: Country bkfst, afternoon tea, snacks/refreshments, hors d'oeuvres, wine and dinner. Restaurant on premises. Beds: KQD. Modem hook-up, cable TV, VCR, reading lamp, clock radio, telephone and hot tub/spa in room. Central air. Fax, copier, tennis, library, parlor games and fireplace on premises. Limited handicap access. Antiquing, art galleries, beach, bicycling, canoeing/kayaking, cross-country skiing, fishing, golf, hiking, horseback riding, live theater, museums, parks, shopping, tennis, water sports and wineries nearby.

Location: Mountains. Endless mountain 2,200 feet.

Certificate may be used: Monday through Thursday.

East Berlin K12

Bechtel Victorian Mansion B&B Inn

400 W King St
East Berlin, PA 17316
(717)259-7760 (800)579-1108
Internet: www.bbonline.com/pa/bechtel/
E-mail: bechtelvictbb@aol.com

Circa 1897. The town of East Berlin, near Lancaster and 18 miles east of Gettysburg, was settled by Pennsylvania Germans prior to the American Revolution. William Leas, a wealthy banker, built this many-gabled romantic Queen Anne mansion, now listed in the National Register. The inn is furnished with an abundance of museum-quality antiques and collections. Rooms are decorated in country Victorian style with beautiful quilts and comforters, lace, dolls and teddy bears.

Innkeeper(s): Richard & Carol Carlson. $100-150. 7 rooms with PB, 2 suites. Breakfast included in rates. Types of meals: Full bkfst, early coffee/tea and snacks/refreshments. Beds: KQD. Reading lamp and turn-down service in room. Air conditioning. TV, VCR, parlor games, telephone and fireplace on premises. Amusement parks, antiquing, bicycling, downhill skiing, fishing, golf, hiking, live theater, museums, shopping and wineries nearby.

Location: Historic district-German town.

Publicity: *Washington Post and Richmond Times.*

Certificate may be used: Nov. 30-Aug. 31, Sunday through Thursday, excludes holidays and special events.

Elizabethville I12

The Inn at Elizabethville

30 W Main St, PO Box 646
Elizabethville, PA 17023
(717)362-3476 (866)362-3476 Fax:(717)362-1444
Internet: innatelizabethville.com
E-mail: dwchin@epix.net

Circa 1883. This comfortable, two-story house was owned by a Civil War veteran and founder of a local wagon company. The sitting room features an unusual fireplace with cabinets and painted decorations. County auctions, local craft fairs and outdoor activities entice guests. Comfortable living rooms, porches and a sun parlor are available for relaxation.

Innkeeper(s): David Chin. $40-60. 7 rooms with PB. Breakfast, afternoon tea and snacks/refreshments included in rates. Types of meals: Full gourmet bkfst, early coffee/tea, gourmet lunch, gourmet dinner and room service. Beds: QDT. Reading lamp, ceiling fan, clock radio, telephone and four with cable TV in room. Air conditioning. TV, VCR, fax, fireplace, laundry facility, complimentary beverages, freshly baked pastries and hot water for tea/instant coffee on premises. Antiquing, art galleries, fishing, golf, parks, shopping, tennis, water sports, wineries, Amish store and farmers' market (Friday nights only) nearby.

Location: City.

Publicity: *Harrisburg Patriot-News and Upper Dauphin Sentinel.*

Certificate may be used: Anytime, subject to availability.

Ephrata J14

Doneckers, The Inns

318-324 N State St
Ephrata, PA 17522
(717)738-9502 Fax:(717)738-9554
E-mail: inns@doneckers.com

Circa 1777. Jacob Gorgas, a devout member of the Ephrata Cloister and a clock maker, noted for crafting 150 eight-day Gorgas grandfather clocks, built this stately Dutch Colonial-style home. Guests can opt to stay in one of three antique-filled homes. The 1777 House, which includes 12 rooms, features hand-stenciled walls, suites with whirlpool baths, fireplaces, original stone masonry and an antique tiled floor. The home served as a tavern in the 1800s and an elegant inn in the early 1900s. The Homestead includes four rooms, some with fireplaces and amenities such as Jacuzzis, sitting areas and four-poster beds. The Guesthouse

features a variety of beautifully decorated rooms each named and themed in honor of local landmarks or significant citizens. All guests enjoy an expansive breakfast with freshly squeezed juice, fruits, breakfast cheeses and other delicacies. The homes are part of the Donecker Community, which features upscale fashion stores, furniture galleries and a restaurant within walking distance of the 1777 House.

Innkeeper(s): Kelly Snyder. $79-210. 35 rooms, 33 with PB, 8 with FP, 15 with HT. Breakfast included in rates. Types of meals: Cont plus, gourmet lunch and gourmet dinner. Restaurant on premises. Beds: KQDT. Cable TV, reading lamp, CD player, refrigerator, clock radio, telephone, hot tub/spa and fireplace in room. Central air. VCR, fax, copier and parlor games on premises. Limited handicap access. Amusement parks, antiquing, art galleries, golf, live theater, museums, parks, shopping, sporting events and wineries nearby.

Location: Small town.

Publicity: *Daily News and Country Inns.*

"A peaceful refuge."

Certificate may be used: Sunday-Thursday, except holidays, year-round.

Erie C3

Spencer House B&B

519 W 6th St
Erie, PA 16507-1128
(814)454-5984 (800)890-7263 Fax:(814)456-5091
Internet: www.spencerhouse.net
E-mail: spencerhousebnb@aol.com

Circa 1876. This romantic Victorian mansion sits on Millionaire's Row in historic Erie. The original woodwork, 12-foot ceilings and pocket shutters reflect the distinctive quality of yesteryear. Peruse the well-stocked library. Some of the guest bedrooms feature fireplaces and clawfoot tubs. The Tree Top Room offers a floor-to-ceiling canopy bed and reading nook. Enjoy a relaxing rocking chair on the wraparound porch.

Innkeeper(s): Laurie Lawrence. $85-159. 8 rooms, 7 with PB, 2 with FP, 3 total suites, including 1 two-bedroom suite. Breakfast and snacks/refreshments included in rates. Types of meals: Full bkfst and early coffee/tea. Beds: KQDT. Cable TV, VCR, reading lamp, ceiling fan, clock radio, telephone, desk, hot tub/spa, fireplace, bathrobes and toiletries in room. Air conditioning. Fax, copier, bicycles, parlor games, coffee and tea and snacks offered throughout the day on premises. Amusement parks, antiquing, art galleries, beach, bicycling, canoeing/kayaking, cross-country skiing, downhill skiing, fishing, golf, hiking, live theater, museums, parks, shopping, sporting events, tennis, water sports and wineries nearby.

Location: City.

Certificate may be used: Sept. 1-Dec. 31, Feb. 1-April 30, Sunday-Thursday.

Erwinna   I17

Evermay-On-The-Delaware

River Rd, PO Box 60
Erwinna, PA 18920
(610)294-9100 Fax:(610)294-8249
Internet: www.evermay.com
E-mail: moffly@evermay.com

Circa 1700. Twenty-five acres of Bucks County at its best — rolling green meadows, lawns, stately maples and the silvery Delaware River, surround this three-story manor. Serving as an inn since 1871, it has hosted such guests as the Barrymore family. Rich walnut wainscoting, a grandfather clock and twin fireplaces warm the parlor, scented by vases of roses or gladiolus. Antique-filled guest rooms overlook the river or gardens.

Innkeeper(s): Bill & Danielle Moffly.
$145-275. 18 rooms with PB, 1 suite, 2 cottages and 2 conference rooms. Breakfast and afternoon tea included in rates. Types of meals: Cont plus, picnic lunch and gourmet dinner. Restaurant on premises. Beds: KQ. Reading lamp, telephone and turn-down service in room. Air conditioning. VCR, fax, copier, library, parlor games and fireplace on premises. Antiquing, cross-country skiing, fishing, live theater, parks, shopping, sporting events and water sports nearby.

Location: Waterfront. Rural Bucks County.
Publicity: *New York Times, Philadelphia, Travel & Leisure, Food and Wine, Child, Colonial Homes and USAir Magazine.*

"It was pure perfection. Everything from the flowers to the wonderful food."

Certificate may be used: Sunday-Thursday, excluding holidays.

Golden Pheasant Inn on the Delaware

763 River Rd
Erwinna, PA 18920-9254
(610)294-9595 (800)830-4474 Fax:(610)294-9882
Internet: www.goldenpheasant.com
E-mail: barbara@goldenpheasant.com

Circa 1857. The Golden Pheasant is well established as the location of a wonderful, gourmet restaurant, but it is also home to six charming guest rooms decorated by Barbara Faure. Four-poster canopy beds and antiques decorate the rooms, which offer views of the canal and river. The fieldstone inn was built as a mule-barge stop for travelers heading down the Delaware Canal. The five-acre grounds resemble a French-country estate, and guests can enjoy the lush surroundings in a plant-filled greenhouse dining room. There are two other dining rooms, including an original fieldstone room with exposed beams and stone walls with decorative copper pots hanging here and there. The restaurant's French cuisine, prepared by chef Michel Faure, is outstanding. One might start off with Michel's special pheasant pate, followed by a savory onion soup baked with three cheeses. A mix of greens dressed in vinaigrette cleanses the palate before one samples roast duck in a luxurious raspberry, ginger and rum sauce or perhaps a sirloin steak flamed in cognac.

Innkeeper(s): Barbara & Michel Faure. $95-225. 6 rooms with PB, 4 with FP, 1 suite, 1 cottage and 3 conference rooms. Breakfast included in rates. Types of meals: Cont plus, early coffee/tea, picnic lunch, snacks/refresh-

ments, gourmet dinner and room service. Restaurant on premises. Beds: Q. Reading lamp, CD player, refrigerator, ceiling fan, clock radio, telephone, coffeemaker, desk, hot tub/spa and fireplace in room. Air conditioning. Fax, copier, swimming, library, parlor games and canal path for walking on premises. Limited handicap access. Antiquing, art galleries, bicycling, canoeing/kayaking, cross-country skiing, fishing, golf, hiking, horseback riding, live theater, museums, parks, shopping, tennis, water sports, wineries, historic Doylestown, New Hope and Washington Crossing nearby.

Location: Country.
Publicity: *The Philadelphia Inquirer, New York Times, Philadelphia Magazine, Food Network and Fox.*

"A more stunningly romantic spot is hard to imagine. A taste of France on the banks of the Delaware."

Certificate may be used: Sunday-Thursday, excluding holidays.

Etters   K13

Canna Country Inn

393 Valley Rd
Etters, PA 17319-8916
(717)938-6077 Fax:(717)938-5898
Internet: www.cannainnbandb.com
E-mail: cannainnbandb@aol.com

Circa 1840. Originally a Pennsylvania Dutch Country barn in the early 1840s, this massive bed and breakfast sits on three acres in the rolling hills. Among the huge wood timbers and exposed stone of the rustic decor are all the upscale modern amenities desired for a relaxing getaway or to maintain job responsibilities. Relax with evening refreshments by the rock fireplace in the living area or on the back deck. Guest bedrooms include Internet access, air conditioning, phone and TV. A two-bedroom suite also features a DVD and CD player. Enjoy a hearty country breakfast served in the formal dining room. Work out in the exercise room and utilize the business center. Explore the park-like setting of the partially wooded grounds with a stream.

Innkeeper(s): Joan E. Tily. $64-105. 6 rooms, 5 with PB, 1 suite and 1 conference room. Breakfast, afternoon tea and snacks/refreshments included in rates. Types of meals: Full bkfst. Beds: KQ. Modem hook-up, data port, cable TV, reading lamp, CD player, ceiling fan, clock radio and desk in room. Central air. VCR, fax, copier, telephone, fireplace, laundry facility, exercise room, business center, meeting room and banquet facilities on premises. Limited handicap access. Amusement parks, antiquing, art galleries, bicycling, canoeing/kayaking, cross-country skiing, downhill skiing, fishing, golf, hiking, horseback riding, live theater, museums, parks, shopping, sporting events, tennis, water sports and wineries nearby.

Location: Country.
Publicity: *Harrisburg Magazine and York Dispatch.*
Certificate may be used: Anytime, subject to availability.

Gettysburg   L11

The Gaslight Inn

33 E Middle St
Gettysburg, PA 17325
(717)337-9100 (800)914-5698
Internet: www.thegaslightinn.com
E-mail: info@thegaslightinn.com

Circa 1872. Gaslights illuminate the brick pathways leading to this 130-year-old Italianate-style, expanded farmhouse. The inn boasts two elegant parlors separated by original pocket doors, a spacious dining room and a first-floor guest room with wheelchair access that opens to a large, brick patio. An open switchback staircase leads to the second- and third-floor guest rooms, all individually decorated in traditional and European furnish-

ings. Some of the rooms feature covered decks,fireplaces, whirlpool tubs and steam showers for two. Guests are invited to enjoy a hearty or heart-healthy breakfast and inn-baked cookies and brownies and refreshments in the afternoon. Winter weekend packages are available and carriage rides, private guides and a variety of activities can be arranged with the help of the innkeepers.

Innkeeper(s): Denis & Roberta Sullivan. $110-195. 9 rooms with PB, 6 with FP. Breakfast and snacks/refreshments included in rates. Types of meals: Full gourmet bkfst, veg bkfst and early coffee/tea. Beds: KQT. Cable TV, VCR, reading lamp, ceiling fan, clock radio, telephone, desk, hot tub/spa, fireplace and steam baths in room. Central air. Spa, library, parlor games and spa facilities on premises. Handicap access. Antiquing, art galleries, bicycling, cross-country skiing, downhill skiing, fishing, golf, hiking, horseback riding, live theater, museums, parks, shopping, tennis, water sports and historic educational tours and lectures nearby.

Location: Small town, historic site.

Publicity: *Tyler Texas Times, Hanover Sun, Los Angeles Times, Southern Living and Country Inns.*

Certificate may be used: Dec. 1 to March 31, Sunday-Thursday, except New Year's Eve and Valentine's Day.

James Gettys Hotel

27 Chambersburg St
Gettysburg, PA 17325
(717)337-1334 Fax:(717)334-2103
Internet: www.jamesgettyshotel.com
E-mail: info@jamesgettyshotel.com

Circa 1803. Listed in the National Register, this newly renovated four-story hotel once served as a tavern through the Battle of Gettysburg and was used as a hospital for soldiers. Outfitted with cranberry colored awnings and a gold painted entrance, the hotel offers a tea room, nature store and gallery on the street level. From the lobby, a polished chestnut staircase leads to the guest quarters. All accommodations are suites with living rooms appointed with home furnishings, and each has its own kitchenette. Breakfasts of home-baked scones and coffee cake are brought to your room.

Innkeeper(s): Stephanie McSherry. $135-165. 11 suites. Breakfast included in rates. Types of meals: Cont. Beds: QD. Cable TV, reading lamp, refrigerator, clock radio, telephone, coffeemaker and turn-down service in room. Air conditioning. VCR and fax on premises. Handicap access. Amusement parks, antiquing, art galleries, bicycling, cross-country skiing, downhill skiing, fishing, golf, hiking, horseback riding, museums, parks, shopping, tennis and wineries nearby.

Location: Small historic town.

Certificate may be used: Monday through Thursday, excluding holidays and special events, Jan. 1-Dec. 30.

Keystone Inn B&B

231 Hanover St
Gettysburg, PA 17325-1913
(717)337-3888

Circa 1913. Furniture maker Clayton Reaser constructed this three-story brick Victorian with a wide-columned porch hugging the north and west sides. Cut stone graces every door and window sill, each with a keystone. A chestnut staircase ascends the full three stories, and the interior is decorated with comfortable furnishings, ruffles and lace.

Innkeeper(s): Wilmer & Doris Martin. $89-129. 5 rooms with PB, 1 suite. Breakfast and afternoon tea included in rates. Types of meals: Full bkfst and early coffee/tea. Beds: KQDT. TV, reading lamp and desk in room. Air conditioning. Library, parlor games and telephone on premises. Amusement parks, antiquing, cross-country skiing, downhill skiing, fishing, live theater, parks, shopping, Civil War Battlefield and historic sites nearby.

Location: Small town.

Publicity: *Lancaster Sunday News, York Sunday News, Hanover Sun, Allentown Morning Call, Gettysburg Times, Pennsylvania and Los Angeles Times.*

"We slept like lambs. This home has a warmth that is soothing."

Certificate may be used: November-April, Monday-Thursday.

Gordonville   K14

1766 Osceola Mill House

313 Osceola Mill Rd
Gordonville, PA 17529-9713
(717)768-3758 (800)878-7719
Internet: www.lancaster-inn.com
E-mail: elalahr@epix.net

Circa 1766. In a quaint historic setting adjacent to a mill and a miller's cottage, this handsome limestone mill house rests on the banks of Pequea Creek. There are deep-set windows and wide pine floors. Guest bedrooms and the keeping room feature working fireplaces that add to the warmth and charm. Breakfast fare may include tasty regional specialties like locally made Pennsylvania Dutch sausage, and Dutch babies- an oven-puffed pancake filled with fresh fruit. Amish neighbors farm the adjacent fields, their horse and buggies enhance the picturesque ambiance.

Innkeeper(s): John & Elaine Lahr. $82-149. 5 rooms with PB, 4 with FP. Types of meals: Full gourmet bkfst. Beds: Q. TV and VCR on premises.

Publicity: *The Journal, Country Living, Washington Times, Gourmet and BBC.*

"We had a thoroughly delightful stay at your inn. Probably the most comfortable overnight stay we've ever had."

Certificate may be used: January-March, Sunday-Thursday, subject to availability, excludes holidays and special events, can not be combined with any other offers, discounts or gift certificates.

Grove City   F2

Snow Goose Inn

112 E Main St
Grove City, PA 16127
(724)458-4644 (800)317-4644
Internet: www.bbonline.com/pa/snowgoose
E-mail: msgoose1@earthlink.net

Circa 1895. This home was built as a residence for young women attending Grove City College. It was later used as a family home and offices for a local doctor. Eventually, it was transformed into an intimate bed & breakfast, offering four cozy guest rooms. The interior is comfortable, decorated with antiques and touches country with stenciling, collectibles and a few of the signature geese on display. Museums, shops, Amish farms, colleges and several state parks are in the vicinity, offering many activities.

Innkeeper(s): Orvil & Dorothy McMillen. $70. 4 rooms with PB. Breakfast and snacks/refreshments included in rates. Types of meals: Full gourmet bkfst and early coffee/tea. Beds: QD. Reading lamp, stereo, refrigerator and clock radio in room. Air conditioning. VCR, parlor games, telephone and fireplace on premises. Amusement parks, antiquing, cross-country skiing, downhill skiing, fishing, golf,

live theater, parks, shopping, sporting events, tennis and water sports nearby.
Location: City.
Publicity: *Allied News.*

"Your thoughtful touches and homey atmosphere were a balm to our chaotic lives."
Certificate may be used: All year.

Hanover   L12

The Beechmont B&B Inn
315 Broadway
Hanover, PA 17331-2505
(717)632-3013 (800)553-7009 Fax:(717)632-2769
Internet: www.thebeechmont.com
E-mail: innkeeper@thebeechmont.com

Circa 1834. Feel welcomed by centuries of charm at this gracious Georgian inn, a witness to the Battle of Hanover, Civil War's first major battle on free soil. A 130-year-old magnolia tree shades the flagstone patio, and wicker furniture invites a lingering rest on the front porch. The romantic Magnolia Suite features a marble fireplace and queen canopy bed. The inn is noted for its sumptuous breakfasts.
Innkeeper(s): Kathryn & Thomas White. $85-150. 7 rooms with PB, 3 with FP, 3 suites. Breakfast and snacks/refreshments included in rates. Types of meals: Full gourmet bkfst and early coffee/tea. Beds: QD. Cable TV, ceiling fan, clock radio, telephone, desk and fireplace in room. Air conditioning. Fax, copier, library and parlor games on premises. Antiquing, bicycling, cross-country skiing, fishing, golf, hiking, horseback riding, live theater, parks, shopping, sporting events, water sports and wineries nearby.
Location: City.
Publicity: *Evening Sun and York Daily Record.*

"I had a marvelous time at your charming, lovely inn."
Certificate may be used: Sunday-Thursday, Dec. 1-March 31, excluding holidays.

Harrisburg   J12

Abide With Me B&B
2601 Walnut St
Harrisburg, PA 17103-1952
(717)236-5873
Internet: www.abidebb.com
E-mail: adamsdj@pa.net

Circa 1870. A city historical site, this B&B is a brick Second Empire Victorian. There are three stories with shuttered windows, a large bay and a rounded front veranda. Oak, parquet and wide-plank floors and fireplaces add to the interest inside. Modestly furnished, the B&B offers some antiques and country pieces. The Harrisburg State Capital is a mile-and-a-half away.
Innkeeper(s): Don & Joyce Adams. $65. 4 rooms. Breakfast included in rates. Types of meals: Full gourmet bkfst and early coffee/tea. Beds: QDT. Air conditioning. VCR, parlor games, telephone and fireplace on premises. Amusement parks, antiquing, fishing, live theater, parks, shopping, sporting events and water sports nearby.
Location: City.
Certificate may be used: Anytime available except Auto Show week in October.

Hawley   E17

Academy Street B&B
528 Academy St
Hawley, PA 18428-1434
(570)226-3430
Internet: www.academybb.com
E-mail: manrojas@ptd.net

Circa 1863. This restored Civil War Victorian home boasts a mahogany front door with the original glass paneling, two large fireplaces (one in mosaic, the other in fine polished marble) and a living room with a polished marble mantel and yellow pine floor. Original woodwork and a fireplace are in the light-filled dining room where guests are served a full gourmet breakfast. Other treats include late-night sweets in the rooms or offered in the parlor room.
Innkeeper(s): Michele & Manuel Rojas. $85-115. 7 rooms, 4 with PB. Breakfast and snacks/refreshments included in rates. Types of meals: Early coffee/tea. Beds: QDT. Cable TV, VCR, reading lamp and CD player in room. Air conditioning. TV and telephone on premises. Amusement parks, antiquing, fishing, horseback riding, live theater, parks, shopping and water sports nearby.
Publicity: *Wayne Independent and Citizens' Voice.*

"Truly wonderful everything!"
Certificate may be used: Monday through Thursday, non-holiday.

Holicong   J18

Barley Sheaf Farm
5281 York Rd, Rt 202 Box 10
Holicong, PA 18928
(215)794-5104 Fax:(215)794-5332
Internet: www.barleysheaf.com
E-mail: info@barleysheaf.com

Circa 1740. Situated on part of the original William Penn land grant, this beautiful stone house with ebony green shuttered windows and mansard roof is set on 30 acres of farmland. Once owned by noted playwright George Kaufman, it was the gathering place for the Marx Brothers, Lillian Hellman and S.J. Perlman. The bank barn, pond and majestic old trees round out a beautiful setting.
Innkeeper(s): Peter Suess. $105-285. 15 rooms with PB, 6 with FP, 7 suites and 3 conference rooms. Breakfast and afternoon tea included in rates. Types of meals: Full bkfst and early coffee/tea. Beds: KQD. Reading lamp, telephone, desk and Jacuzzis in room. Air conditioning. VCR, fax, copier, swimming, parlor games and fireplace on premises. Handicap access. Amusement parks, antiquing, cross-country skiing, downhill skiing, fishing, live theater, parks, shopping, water sports and museums nearby.
Location: Country.
Publicity: *Country Living, Romantic Inns of America and CNC Business Channel.*
Certificate may be used: Sunday through Thursday, no holidays.

Hollidaysburg   I8

Hoenstine's B&B
418 N Montgomery St
Hollidaysburg, PA 16648-1432
(814)695-0632 (888)550-9655 Fax:(814)696-7310
E-mail: hoenstine@mindspring.com

Circa 1830. This inn is an antique-lover's dream, as it boasts many pieces of original furniture. Stained-glass windows and the 10-foot-high ceilings add to the atmosphere. Breakfast is served

in the home's formal dining room. The B&B is within walking distance of shops, restaurants and the downtown historic district.

Innkeeper(s): Barbara Hoenstine. $50-80. 4 rooms, 1 with PB. Breakfast included in rates. Types of meals: Full bkfst. Beds: QDT. Cable TV, VCR, reading lamp, ceiling fan, clock radio and desk in room. Fax, copier, library, parlor games and telephone on premises. Amusement parks, antiquing, cross-country skiing, downhill skiing, fishing, golf, live theater, parks, shopping, sporting events, tennis, water sports and hiking trails nearby.

Location: Mountains. Small town.

"Thank you for a truly calm and quiet week. This was our first B&B experience and it won't be our last."

Certificate may be used: Monday-Friday all year, Saturday and Sunday based on availability.

Intercourse   K14

Carriage Corner

3705 E Newport Rd, PO Box 371
Intercourse, PA 17534-0371
(717)768-3059 (800)209-3059 Fax:(717)768-0691
Internet: www.carriagecornerbandb.com
E-mail: gschuit@dejazzd.com

Circa 1979. Located in the heart of Amish farmland, this two-story Colonial rests on a pastoral acre. Homemade, country breakfasts are served, often including innkeeper Gordon Schuit's special recipe for oatmeal pancakes. A five-minute walk will take guests into the village where they'll find Amish buggies traveling down the lanes and more than 100 shops displaying local crafts, pottery, quilts and furniture, as well as art galleries. The  innkeepers can arrange for dinners in an Amish home, buggy rides and working Amish farm tours. Longwood Gardens, Hershey's Chocolate World and Gettysburg are also nearby.

Innkeeper(s): Gordon & Gwen Schuit. $68-89. 5 rooms with PB and 1 conference room. Breakfast included in rates. Types of meals: Country bkfst and early coffee/tea. Beds: Q. Cable TV and clock radio in room. Central air. VCR, fax, library, parlor games, telephone and fireplace on premises. Amusement parks, antiquing, art galleries, bicycling, live theater, museums, parks, shopping, wineries, hub of Amish farmland, Amish dinners arranged, buggy rides, working Amish farm tours, Strasburg Steam Railroad, Railroad Museum of PA, "Daniel" at Sight and Sound, festivals and auctions, craft and quilt fairs, farmers' markets and roadside stands, Longwood Gardens, Hershey's Chocolate World and Gettysburg nearby.

Location: Country. Amish farmland.

Certificate may be used: January and February, excluding holiday weekends. March-May, November, December, Sunday through Wednesday, excluding special events.

Jennerstown   J5

The Olde Stage Coach B&B

1760 Lincoln Hwy, PO Box 337
Jennerstown, PA 15547
(814)629-7440
Internet: www.oldestagecoachbandb.com
E-mail: carol@oldestagecoachbandb.com

Circa 1752. This renovated two-story Country Victorian farmhouse, located in the Laurel Mountains on historical Lincoln Highway, once served as a stagecoach rest stop. The yellow

house has white trim and a wraparound porch overlooking the inn's acre. The common room features Victorian antiques, and guest rooms offer a fresh country decor. Blueberry French toast is a specialty of the innkeepers as well as home-baked breads and apple pancakes. The immediate area boasts the Mountain Playhouse, three golf courses within three miles, trout streams and lakes, hiking, skiing and outlet shopping — something for all generations.

Innkeeper(s): Carol & George Neuhof. $75-85. 4 rooms with PB. Breakfast and snacks/refreshments included in rates. Types of meals: Full bkfst and early coffee/tea. Beds: QDT. Reading lamp, ceiling fan and clock radio in room. VCR, library, telephone and wraparound porch with swing on premises. Amusement parks, antiquing, cross-country skiing, downhill skiing, fishing, golf, live theater, parks, shopping and Nascar racing nearby.

Certificate may be used: Sunday-Thursday, Jan. 3-November, except special holidays.

Jim Thorpe   H15

Harry Packer Mansion

Packer Hill, PO Box 458
Jim Thorpe, PA 18229
(570)325-8566
Internet: www.murdermansion.com
E-mail: mystery@murdermansion.com

Circa 1874. This extravagant Second Empire mansion was used as the model for the haunted mansion in Disney World. It was constructed of New England sandstone, and local brick and stone trimmed in cast iron. Past ornately carved columns on the front veranda, guests enter 400-pound, solid walnut doors. The opulent interior includes marble mantels, hand-painted ceilings and elegant antiques. Murder-mystery weekends are a mansion specialty.

Innkeeper(s): Robert & Patricia Handwerk. $150-250. 12 rooms with PB, 3 suites and 3 conference rooms. Breakfast included in rates. Types of meals: Full gourmet bkfst. Beds: Q. Reading lamp, refrigerator, clock radio, turn-down service and desk in room. Air conditioning. TV, parlor games, telephone, fireplace and Murder Mystery Weekends on premises. Antiquing, cross-country skiing, downhill skiing, fishing, parks, shopping and water sports nearby.

Location: Mountains.

Publicity: *Philadelphia Inquirer, New York, Victorian Homes, Washington Post, Conde Nast Traveler* and winner Best Murder Mystery by Arringtons *Book of Lists.*

"What a beautiful place and your hospitality was wonderful. We will see you again soon."

Certificate may be used: Sunday through Thursday night except for holidays, May 1-Nov. 1.

The Inn at Jim Thorpe

24 Broadway
Jim Thorpe, PA 18229
(570)325-2599 (800)329-2599 Fax:(570)325-9145
Internet: www.innjt.com
E-mail: innjt@ptd.net

Circa 1848. This massive New Orleans-style structure, now restored, hosted some colorful 19th-century guests, including Thomas Edison, John D. Rockefeller and Buffalo Bill. All rooms are appointed with Victorian furnishings and have private baths with pedestal sinks and marble floors. The suites include fireplaces and whirlpool tubs. Also on the premises are a Victorian dining Room, Irish pub and a conference center. The inn is situated in the heart of Jim Thorpe, a quaint Victorian town that was known at the turn of the century as the "Switzerland of America." Historic mansion tours, museums and art galleries are nearby, and mountain biking and whitewater rafting are among the outdoor activities.

Innkeeper(s): David Drury. $99-299. 34 rooms with PB, 11 suites and 2 conference rooms. Breakfast included in rates. Types of meals: Cont plus, lunch, dinner and room service. Beds: KQ. Cable TV, reading lamp, clock radio, telephone, 11 suites with whirlpools and some with fireplaces in room. Air conditioning. Fax, copier, fireplace, game room, exercise room and elevator on premises. Handicap access. Antiquing, art galleries, bicycling, canoeing/kayaking, downhill skiing, fishing, golf, hiking, horseback riding, museums, parks, shopping and wineries nearby.

Publicity: *Philadelphia Inquirer, Pennsylvania Magazine and Allentown Morning Call.*

"We had the opportunity to spend a weekend at your lovely inn. Your staff is extremely friendly, helpful, and courteous. I can't remember when we felt so relaxed, we hope to come back again soon."

Certificate may be used: Sunday-Thursday excluding holidays and Christmas week and the month of August.

The VictoriAnn B&B

68 Broadway
Jim Thorpe, PA 18229-2022
(570)325-8107 (888)241-4460 Fax:(570)325-8107
Internet: www.thevictoriann.com
E-mail: victori@ptdprolog.net

Circa 1860. Historic Millionaire's Row is the site of this Victorian, which is painted a deep red hue with blue trim. Innkeeper Louise Ogilvie preserves the 19th-century ambiance throughout the home, decorating the place with Victorian furnishings and bright wallpapers. Some rooms are European in style and share a bath. The two suites include a private bath. The grounds include a garden. Louise's history is as fascinating as the historic home's past. She was an actress and cabaret singer in New York and was proprietor of a renowned nightclub in San Juan, Puerto Rico.

Innkeeper(s): Louise Ogilvie. $75-150. 8 rooms, 4 with PB, 2 suites and 1 conference room. Breakfast included in rates. Types of meals: Full bkfst. Beds: KQDT. Cable TV, reading lamp, ceiling fan, clock radio, telephone and turn-down service in room. Air conditioning. VCR, fax, copier, library and fireplace on premises. Antiquing, cross-country skiing, downhill skiing, fishing, golf, parks, shopping, tennis and water sports nearby.

Location: Mountains, waterfront.

Publicity: *Times News.*

"We never thought our weekend would turn out to be such a wonderful adventure. Thank you for opening your inn to us."

Certificate may be used: Jan. 1-30, Sunday through Thursday; March, April, Sunday-Thursday; Nov. 1-30, Sunday through Thursday.

Kennett Square   L16

Kennett House Bed and Breakfast

503 W State St
Kennett Square, PA 19348-3028
(610)444-9592 (800)820-9592 Fax:(610)444-7633
Internet: www.kennetthouse.com
E-mail: innkeeper@kennetthouse.com

Circa 1910. This granite American four-square home features an extensive wraparound porch, a front door surrounded by leaded-glass windows and magnificent chestnut woodwork. Beyond the foyer are two downstairs parlors with fireplaces, while a second-floor parlor provides a sunny setting for afternoon tea. Rooms are furnished with period antiques and Oriental carpets. An elegant

gourmet breakfast is served each morning.

Innkeeper(s): Carol & Jeff Yetter. $125-175. 4 rooms with PB, 1 suite. Breakfast and snacks/refreshments included in rates. Types of meals: Full gourmet bkfst and early coffee/tea. Beds: Q. Cable TV, reading lamp, ceiling fan and high-speed Internet access in room. Central air. VCR, fax, copier, library, parlor games, telephone and fireplace on premises. Antiquing, art galleries, bicycling, canoeing/kayaking, fishing, golf, hiking, horseback riding, live theater, museums, parks, shopping, sporting events, wineries, longwood Gardens, Brandywine Valley attractions and Amish country nearby.

Location: Historic small town.

"Truly an enchanting place."

Certificate may be used: No holidays or holiday weekends. Jan. 1-Feb. 28, all week; March 1-Dec. 31, Sunday-Thursday only.

Lancaster   K14

1725 Historic Witmer's Tavern Inn & Museum

2014 Old Philadelphia Pike
Lancaster, PA 17602-3413
(717)299-5305
Internet: www.witmerstavern.com
E-mail: witmerstavern@cs.com

Circa 1725. This pre-Revolutionary War inn is the oldest and most complete Pennsylvania inn still lodging travelers in the original building. On the National Register of Historic Places, the property has been restored to its original, pioneer style with hand-fashioned hardware and "bubbly" glass nine-over-six windows. Guest rooms feature antiques, fresh flowers, quilts and wood-burning fireplaces.

Revolutionary and Colonial dignitaries like Washington, Lafayette, Jefferson and Adams were entertained here. The Witmers provisioned hundreds of immigrants as they set up Conestoga Wagon trains headed for western and southern homestead regions. Amish farmland is adjacent to and in the rear of the inn, and a lovely park is located nearby. The innkeeper, native to the area, can provide an abundance of local information. He can also plan extra touches for a special occasion. Guests can make appointments for therapeutic massage, reflexology, aromatherapy and reiki sessions. The inn offers Pandora's Antique Shop in the building housing antique quilts, paintings, prints, furnishings and unique collectibles.

Innkeeper(s): Brant Hartung. $70-110. 7 rooms, 2 with PB, 6 with FP. Breakfast included in rates. Types of meals: Cont plus. Beds: D. Reading lamp, desk and six rooms with wood-burning fireplaces in room. Air conditioning. Parlor games, telephone and fireplace on premises. Amusement parks, antiquing, fishing, golf, live theater, shopping, sporting events, tennis, water sports, nature preserves, wineries and Amish farms and villages nearby.

Location: Country. Rural neighborhood.

Publicity: *Stuart News, Pennsylvania, Antique, Travel & Leisure, Mid-Atlantic, Country Living, Early American Life, Colonial Homes and USA Today.*

"Your personal attention and enthusiastic knowledge of the area and Witmer's history made it come alive and gave us the good feelings we came looking for."

Certificate may be used: December-April, Sunday through Thursday only, excluding all holidays.

The King's Cottage, A B&B Inn

1049 E King St
Lancaster, PA 17602-3231
(717)397-1017 (800)747-8717 Fax:(717)397-3447
Internet: www.kingscottagebb.com
E-mail: info@kingscottagebb.com

Circa 1913. This Spanish Mission Revival house features a red-tile roof and stucco walls, common in many stately turn-of-the-century houses in California and New Mexico. Its elegant interiors include a sweeping staircase, a library with marble fireplace, stained-glass windows and a solarium. The inn is appointed with Oriental rugs and antiques and fine 18th-century English reproductions. Three  guest rooms have Jacuzzi/whirlpool tubs and four have fireplaces. The formal dining room provides the location for gourmet morning meals.

Innkeeper(s): Janis Kutterer and Ann Willets. $150-260. 8 rooms with PB and 1 guest house. Breakfast and afternoon tea included in rates. Types of meals: Full bkfst. Beds: KQ. Cable TV, reading lamp, clock radio, telephone, turn-down service, desk, VCR or DVD and some with whirlpools in room. Parlor games and fireplace on premises. Amusement parks, antiquing, fishing, golf, live theater, shopping, sporting events, outlet shopping, Amish dinners and quilts nearby.
Location: Residential neighborhood.
Publicity: *Country, USA Weekend, Bon Appetit, Intelligencer Journal, Times, New York Magazine, Forbes, Washingtonian, Long Island Wine Gazette and Discerning Traveler.*

"I appreciate your attention to all our needs and look forward to recommending your inn to friends."
Certificate may be used: November-July, Monday-Thursday.

New Life Homestead B&B

1400 E King St, Rt 462
Lancaster, PA 17602-3240
(717)396-8928
Internet: www.newlifebnb.com
E-mail: carolg@newlifebnb.com

Circa 1912. This two-and-a-half story brick home is situated within one mile of Amish Farms, and it's less than two miles from the city of Lancaster. Innkeepers Carol and Bill Giersch, both Mennonites, host evening discussions about the culture and history of Amish and Mennonite people. Carol's homemade breakfasts are made with local produce.

Innkeeper(s): Carol Giersch. $65-85. 3 rooms, 2 with PB, 1 suite. Breakfast included in rates. Types of meals: Full bkfst and snacks/refreshments. Beds: QDT. TV, VCR and telephone on premises. Amusement parks, antiquing, fishing, live theater, shopping and sporting events nearby.
Location: Suburban.
Publicity: *Keystone Gazette and Pennsylvania Dutch Traveler.*

"Reminded me of my childhood at home."
Certificate may be used: January, February, March, anytime.

O'Flaherty's Dingeldein House B&B

1105 E King St
Lancaster, PA 17602-3233
(717)293-1723 (800)779-7765 Fax:(717)293-1947
Internet: www.800padutch.com/ofhouse.html
E-mail: nancy@dingeldeinhouse.com

Circa 1910. This Dutch Colonial home was once residence to the Armstrong family, who acquired fame and fortune in the tile floor industry. Springtime guests will brighten at the sight of

this home's beautiful flowers. During winter months, innkeepers Jack and Sue Flatley deck the halls with plenty of seasonal decorations. Breakfast by candlelight might include fresh-baked muffins, fruits, the innkeepers' special blend of coffee and mouth-watering omelets, pancakes or French toast. Cozy rooms include comfortable furnishings and cheery wall coverings. With advance notice, the innkeepers can arrange for guests to enjoy dinner at the home of one of their Amish friends.

Innkeeper(s): Danny & Nancy Whittle. $95-120. 6 rooms with PB, 1 suite. Breakfast included in rates. Types of meals: Full gourmet bkfst and early coffee/tea. Beds: QT. Reading lamp, ceiling fan, clock radio and desk in room. Air conditioning. VCR, fax, copier, library, parlor games, telephone and fireplace on premises. Amusement parks, antiquing, fishing, live theater, parks, shopping and sporting events nearby.
Location: Residential.
Publicity: *Gourmet.*

Certificate may be used: All year except June, July, August and October, Sunday through Thursday. Weekends, January and February.

Landenberg   L15

Cornerstone B&B Inn

300 Buttonwood Rd
Landenberg, PA 19350-9398
(610)274-2143 Fax:(610)274-0734
Internet: www.cornerstoneinn.net
E-mail: corner3000@aol.com

Circa 1704. The Cornerstone is a fine 18th-century country manor house filled with antique furnishings. Two fireplaces make the parlor inviting. Wing chairs, fresh flowers and working fireplaces add enjoyment to the guest rooms. Award-winning perennial gardens, a water garden and swimming pool are additional amenities.

Innkeeper(s): Linda Chamberlin & Marty Mulligan. $100-250. 9 rooms, 5 with FP, 1 suite and 8 cottages. Breakfast included in rates. Types of meals: Full bkfst and early coffee/tea. Beds: KQT. Cable TV, reading lamp and clock radio in room. Air conditioning. VCR, fax, telephone and fireplace on premises. Amusement parks, antiquing, live theater, parks, shopping and sporting events nearby.
Location: Country.

Certificate may be used: Sunday-Thursday, Jan. 2-Dec. 15. No holiday weekdays.

Lewisburg   G12

Brookpark Farm B&B

145 Brookpark Circle
Lewisburg, PA 17837-9653
(570)523-0220
E-mail: ctmoyer@chilitech.net

Circa 1914. Twenty-five acres surround this three-story brick house. The innkeepers operate the Pennsylvania House Gallery in their enormous barn on the property. The inn, therefore, includes traditional, transitional and country designs from these furniture collections including cherry, pine and mahogany woods.

Innkeeper(s): Crystale & Todd Moyer. $85-105. 7 rooms, 3 suites and 2 conference rooms. Breakfast included in rates. Types of meals: Full gourmet bkfst and early coffee/tea. Restaurant on premises. Beds: Q. Reading lamp and clock radio in room. Air conditioning. Parlor games and telephone on premises. Amusement parks, antiquing, fishing, live theater, parks, shopping and sporting events nearby.
Location: Country.

Certificate may be used: Anytime, subject to availability.

Linfield J16

Shearer Elegance

1154 Main St
Linfield, PA 19468-1139
(610)495-7429 (800)861-0308 Fax:(610)495-7814
Internet: www.shearerelegance.com
E-mail: shirley@shearerelegance.com

Circa 1897. This stone Queen Anne mansion is the height of Victorian opulence and style. Peaked roofs, intricate trim and a stenciled wraparound porch grace the exterior. Guests enter the home via a marble entry, which boasts a three-story staircase. Stained-glass windows and carved mantels are other notable features. The Victorian furnishings and decor complement the ornate workmanship, and lacy curtains are a romantic touch. The bedrooms feature hand-carved, built-in wardrobes. The grounds are dotted with gardens. The inn is located in the village of Linfield, about 15 minutes from Valley Forge.

Innkeeper(s): Shirley & Malcolm Shearer. $100-155. 7 rooms with PB, 3 suites and 3 conference rooms. Types of meals: Full bkfst and early coffee/tea. Beds: KQ. Cable TV, VCR, reading lamp, stereo, refrigerator, ceiling fan, clock radio and desk in room. Air conditioning. Fax, copier, library, parlor games and telephone on premises. Amusement parks, antiquing, downhill skiing, fishing, golf, live theater, parks, shopping, sporting events, tennis and outlets nearby.

Location: Country.

Publicity: *Reading, Norristown, Pottstown and Local.*

"Thank you for creating such a beautiful place to escape reality."
Certificate may be used: Jan. 2 to Nov. 10.

Lititz J14

The Alden House

62 E Main St
Lititz, PA 17543-1947
(717)627-3363 (800)584-0753
Internet: www.aldenhouse.com
E-mail: inn@aldenhouse.com

Circa 1850. For more than 200 years, breezes have carried the sound of church bells to the stately homes lining Main Street. This Federal-style brick home in the center of the historic district

is within an easy walk to the country's first pretzel factory, unique shops, fine restaurants, chocolate factory and museums. Relax on one of the many porches. Spacious guest bedrooms and suites are furnished with distinctive antiques. Old-fashioned hospitality includes a gourmet breakfast.

Innkeeper(s): Bob & Shirley McCarthy. $90-130. 5 rooms with PB, 1 with FP, 3 suites. Breakfast included in rates. Types of meals: Full gourmet bkfst, early coffee/tea and snacks/refreshments. Beds: Q. Cable TV, VCR, clock radio and desk in room. Air conditioning. Telephone and off-street parking on premises. Amusement parks, antiquing, live theater, parks and shopping nearby.

Location: Small, historic town.

Publicity: *Mobile Travel Guide, American Historic Inns, Official Vacation Guide Lancaster County, Christian Bed and Breakfast Directory, Stash Tea Guide Bed and Breakfast Inns, San Francisco Chronicle, Lititz 2003 and Lititz Record Express.*

"Thanks for all the personal touches and for the warmth. We appreciated the wonderful breakfasts—all the touches of home!"
Certificate may be used: November through April, Sunday to Thursday, except holiday weeks.

The Lititz House B&B

301 N Broad St
Lititz, PA 17543
(717)626-5299 (800)464-6764
Internet: www.casualcornersbnb.com
E-mail: stay@lititzhouse.com

Circa 1904. Experience small-town charm in the heart of Pennsylvania Dutch Country mingled with elegant touches for enjoyment and comfort. Gather in the second-floor sitting room for conversation, evening wine and brandy and early morning coffee. Watch TV, read or use a data port connection to access the Internet. Air-conditioned guest bedrooms with a private entrance are tastefully decorated and furnished with antiques. Some of the many breakfast favorites include French coffee cake, blueberry buckle, Belgian waffles and egg strata. Browse the Gift Gallery featuring an assortment of crafts and treasures to buy. Relax on the large wraparound front porch or the backyard swing amidst the the flower and herb garden.

Innkeeper(s): Pat & Jim Erven. $85-130. 5 rooms, 3 with PB, 1 suite. Breakfast included in rates. Types of meals: Full gourmet bkfst, veg bkfst, early coffee/tea, snacks/refreshments, hors d'oeuvres and wine. Beds: QD. Reading lamp, ceiling fan and turn-down service in room. Air conditioning. Parlor games, telephone and fireplace on premises. Amusement parks, antiquing, art galleries, bicycling, golf, hiking, live theater, museums, parks, shopping, tennis and wineries nearby.

Location: Lancaster County.

Certificate may be used: Anytime, November-April, subject to availability.

Marietta K13

Railroad House Restaurant B&B

280 W Front St
Marietta, PA 17547-1405
(717)426-4141
Internet: www.therailroadhouse.com

Circa 1820. The Railroad House, a sprawling old hotel, conjures up memories of the days when riding the rail was the way to travel. The house was built as a refuge for weary men who were working along the Susquehanna River. When the railroad finally made its way through Marietta, the rail station's waiting room and ticket office were located in what's now known as the Railroad House.

The restored rooms feature antiques, Oriental rugs, Victorian decor and rustic touches such as exposed brick walls. The chefs at the inn's restaurant create a menu of American and continental dishes using spices and produce from the beautifully restored gardens. The innovative recipes have been featured in Bon Appetit. The innkeepers also host a variety of special events and weekends, including murder mysteries and clambakes serenaded by jazz bands. Carriage rides and special walking tours of Marietta can be arranged.

Innkeeper(s): Richard & Donna Chambers. $89-129. 8 rooms with PB, 1 cottage and 1 conference room. Breakfast included in rates. Types of meals: Full gourmet bkfst, early coffee/tea, gourmet lunch, picnic lunch, afternoon tea, snacks/refreshments and gourmet dinner. Restaurant on premises. Beds:

QDT. Reading lamp, refrigerator, clock radio and desk in room. Air conditioning. Copier, bicycles, parlor games, telephone, fireplace, gardens and yard games on premises. Amusement parks, antiquing, downhill skiing, fishing, live theater, parks, shopping, sporting events, water sports and music box museum nearby.

Location: Small town.

Certificate may be used: Anytime.

Maytown   K13

Maytown Manor B&B

25 W High St, PO Box 275
Maytown, PA 17550
(717)426-2116 (866)426-2116 Fax:(717)426-2116
Internet: www.maytownmanorbandb.com
E-mail: innkeepers@maytownmanorbandb.com

Circa 1880. Known locally as the Hiestand Estate, this Federal-style brick house was recently professionally restored. Traditional and antique furnishings enhance a peaceful ambiance. The parlor is a delightful gathering place to read by the fire, play the piano, or enjoy conversation. The spacious guest bedrooms are comfortable, with thoughtful amenities for a pleasant stay. Breakfast is a satisfying repast in the formal dining room. An inviting porch swing is perfect for relaxing. The sunlit back patio leads to colorful flower gardens and a manicured lawn. Share the company of innkeepers Jeff and Julie during afternoon tea.

Innkeeper(s): Jeff & Julie Clouser. $90-95. 3 rooms with PB. Breakfast, afternoon tea and snacks/refreshments included in rates. Types of meals: Full bkfst and early coffee/tea. Beds: QD. Cable TV, ceiling fan and clock radio in room. Central air. TV, VCR, tennis, library, parlor games, telephone and fireplace on premises. Amusement parks, antiquing, art galleries, bicycling, downhill skiing, golf, hiking, live theater, museums, parks, shopping, sporting events, tennis and wineries nearby.

Location: Small village.

Publicity: *Marietta Traveler, Mount Joy/Elizabethtown Merchandiser, Lancaster County Magazine, Donegal Performing Arts Program, Mayfest Program, Millersville Art Auction, 2003 Best Breakfast and 2002 Best Room of the Year.*

Certificate may be used: November-April, Sunday-Thursday, subject to availability.

Mc Knightstown   L11

Country Escape

275 Old Rt 30
Mc Knightstown, PA 17343-0195
(717)338-0611 (800)484-32444371 Fax:(717)334-5227
Internet: www.countryescape.com
E-mail: merry@countryescape.com

Circa 1867. This country Victorian, a brick structure featuring a porch decked in gingerbread trim, rests on the route that Confederate soldiers took on their way to nearby Gettysburg. The home itself was built just a few years after the Civil War. There are three comfortable guest rooms decorated in country style. For an extra fee, business travelers can use the inn's typing, copying, faxing or desktop publishing services. There is also

a children's play area outside. A traditional American breakfast is served, with such hearty items as eggs, pancakes, bacon and sausage. The inn offers close access to the famous battlefield, as well as other historic sites.

Innkeeper(s): Merry Bush & Ross Hetrick. $65-125. 3 rooms, 1 with PB, 1 two-bedroom suite. Breakfast and snacks/refreshments included in rates. Types of meals: Country bkfst, veg bkfst and early coffee/tea. Beds: Q. Reading lamp and clock radio in room. Air conditioning. TV, VCR, fax, copier, parlor games, telephone, fireplace, children's play area and gardens on premises. Antiquing, art galleries, bicycling, downhill skiing, fishing, golf, hiking, horseback riding, live theater, museums, parks, shopping, wineries, crafts and Gettysburg battlefield nearby.

Location: Country. Country/rural.

Publicity: *Gettysburg Times and Hanover Evening Sun.*

Certificate may be used: Jan. 1 through May 15 and Aug. 1 through Dec. 30, Monday through Thursday.

McConnellsburg   K9

The McConnellsburg Inn

131 W Market St
McConnellsburg, PA 17233-1007
(717)485-5495 Fax:(717)485-5495
Internet: www.innernet.net/mconburgin/
E-mail: Mconburgin@innernet.net

Circa 1903. Located in the historic district, this turn-of-the-century inn was built for a retired Union officer of the Civil War. Guest bedrooms include four-poster canopy beds. Gettysburg, East Broad Top Railroad, Cowans Gap State Park and Buchanan State Forest are nearby, as are Great Cove Golf Course and Whitetail Ski Resort.

Innkeeper(s): Kathryn Beckman. $70-85. 3 rooms with PB. Breakfast included in rates. Types of meals: Cont. Beds: Q. Modem hook-up, cable TV, reading lamp and clock radio in room. Air conditioning. Telephone on premises. Antiquing, cross-country skiing, downhill skiing, fishing, golf, water sports, nature photography, hiking and country auctions nearby.

Location: Tuscarora Mountains.

Publicity: *Pennsylvania.*

Certificate may be used: Nov. 1-March 15, Sunday-Thursday.

Mercer   F2

The John Orr Guest House

320 E Butler St
Mercer, PA 16137
(724)662-0839 (877)849-0839 Fax:(724)662-3883
Internet: www.jorrbandb.com
E-mail: innkeeper@jorrbandb.com

Circa 1905. A prominent local businessman built this turn-of-the-20th-century home, which is constructed in Greek Revival style. The home has been restored, leaving in place the original woodwork and other architectural features. Guest rooms and common areas include period-style furnishings and some antiques. The front porch is set up for those who wish to relax, offering comfortable wicker chairs and a porch swing. The innkeepers serve a full breakfast with items such as stuffed French toast, Belgian waffles, a hearty egg casserole and scones. Mercer is a quaint Victorian town with many historic homes, fine restaurants and attractions to visit.

Innkeeper(s): Ann & Jack Hausser. $70-85. 3 rooms with PB, 2 with FP. Breakfast and snacks/refreshments included in rates. Types of meals: Full bkfst, veg bkfst and early coffee/tea. Beds: QD. Reading lamp, ceiling fan and clock radio in room. Central air. TV, VCR, fax, copier, telephone, fireplace, CD player, stereo and refrigerator on premises. Antiquing, bicycling, fishing, golf, museums, parks, shopping, lakes and Amish crafts nearby.

Location: Small town at I-79 & I-80.

Certificate may be used: All year, Sunday through Friday.

Mercersburg   L9

The Mercersburg Inn

405 S Main St
Mercersburg, PA 17236-9517
(717)328-5231 Fax:(717)328-3403
Internet: www.mercersburginn.com
E-mail: sandy@mercersburginn.com

Circa 1909. Situated on a hill overlooking the Tuscorora
Mountains, the valley and village, this 20,000-square-foot
Georgian Revival mansion was built for industrialist Harry
Byron. Six massive columns mark the entrance, which opens to
a majestic hall featuring chestnut wainscoting and an elegant
double stairway and rare scagliola (marbleized) columns. All
the rooms are furnished with antiques and reproductions. A
local craftsman built the inn's four-poster, canopied king-size
beds. Many of the rooms have their own balconies and a few
have fireplaces. Thursday through Sunday evening, the inn's
chef prepares noteworthy, elegant dinners, which feature an
array of seasonal specialties.

Innkeeper(s): Walt & Sandy Filkowski. $135-275. 15 rooms with PB, 3 with
FP and 1 conference room. Breakfast included in rates. Types of meals: Full
gourmet bkfst, picnic lunch and gourmet dinner. Restaurant on premises.
Beds: KQT. Reading lamp, telephone and desk in room. Air conditioning.
VCR, bicycles, parlor games and fireplace on premises. Antiquing, cross-
country skiing, downhill skiing, fishing, golf, live theater, shopping and water
sports nearby.

Location: Mountains. Cumberland Valley.

Publicity: *Mid-Atlantic Country, Washington Post, The Herald-Mail, Richmond
News Leader, Washingtonian, Philadelphia Inquirer and Pittsburgh.*

"Elegance personified! Outstanding ambiance and warm hospitality."
Certificate may be used: Sunday-Thursday, non-holidays.

Milford   F18

Cliff Park Inn & Golf Course

155 Cliff Park Rd
Milford, PA 18337-9708
(570)296-6491 (800)225-6535 Fax:(570)296-3982
Internet: www.cliffparkinn.com
E-mail: info@cliffparkinn.com

Circa 1820. This historic country inn is located on a 600-acre
family estate, bordering the Delaware River. It has been in the
Buchanan family since 1820. Rooms are spacious with individual climate control, telephone and Victorian-style furnishings.
Cliff Park features both a full-service restaurant and golf school.
The inn's golf course, established in 1913, is
one of the oldest in the United
States. Cliff Park's picturesque
setting is popular for country
weddings and private business
conferences. Both B&B or MAP
plans are offered.

Innkeeper(s): Jamie & Yvonne Klausmann. $93-160. 18 rooms with PB and
1 conference room. Breakfast included in rates. Types of meals: Full bkfst,
lunch, picnic lunch and dinner. Restaurant on premises. Beds: KQDT. TV, fax
and telephone on premises. Handicap access. Cross-country skiing and water
sports nearby.

*"Cliff Park Inn is the sort of inn I look for in the English countryside.
It has that authentic charm that comes from history."*
Certificate may be used: Nov. 1-May 20, Sunday-Thursday.

Milton   G12

Pau-Lyn's Country B&B

1160 Broadway Rd
Milton, PA 17847-9506
(570)742-4110
Internet: www.welcome.to/paulyns
E-mail: paulyns@uplink.net

Circa 1850. This Victorian brick home offers a formal dining
room with a fireplace and antique musical instruments. This
restful haven offers a porch and patio overlooking the large
lawn. Nearby are working farms and dairies, covered bridges,
mountains, rivers and valleys.

Innkeeper(s): Paul & Evelyn Landis. $70-80. 7 rooms. Breakfast included in
rates. Types of meals: Full bkfst. Beds: QDT. Reading lamp and clock radio in
room. Air conditioning. Telephone, fireplace and large lawn and patio on
premises. Amusement parks, antiquing, bicycling, golf, hiking, shopping,
museums, underground railroad and little league museum and field nearby.

Location: Near small town.

Certificate may be used: Year-round, Sunday through Thursday, some weekends. All depends on availability.

Tomlinson Manor B&B

250 Broadway
Milton, PA 17847-1706
(570)742-3657
Internet: www.sunlink.net/~tmbandb/
E-mail: tmbandb@evenlink.com

Circa 1927. In the Georgian style, this appealing three-story
stone manor was designed by Dr. Charles Tomlinson, a local
physician and amateur architect. Shutters border the small-
paned windows, and there are gardens all around. All the
rooms, including the library, are furnished with antiques. Next
door to the B&B is a dinner theater.

Innkeeper(s): Mike & Nancy Slease. $65. 3 rooms. Breakfast included in
rates. Types of meals: Full bkfst. Reading lamp and clock radio in room. Air
conditioning. VCR, telephone and fireplace on premises. Antiquing, live theater, shopping and sporting events nearby.

Location: Town.

Certificate may be used: Anytime, except college weekends.

Mount Joy   K13

Cedar Hill Farm

305 Longenecker Rd
Mount Joy, PA 17552-8404
(717)653-4655 Fax:(717)653-9242
Internet: www.cedarhillfarm.com
E-mail: cedarhillbnb@comcast.net

Circa 1817. Situated on 70 acres overlooking Chiques Creek,
this stone farmhouse boasts a two-tiered front veranda affording pastoral views of the surrounding fields. The host was born
in the house and is the third generation to have lived here
since the Swarr family first purchased it in 1878. Family heirlooms and antiques include an elaborately carved walnut bedstead, a marble-topped wash-
stand and a "tumbling block"
quilt. In the kitchen, a copper
kettle, bread paddle and baskets
of dried herbs accentuate the
walk-in fireplace, where guests
often linger over breakfast.

Cedar Hill is a working poultry and grain farm.

Innkeeper(s): Russel & Gladys Swarr. $85-105. 5 rooms with PB. Breakfast included in rates. Types of meals: Full bkfst and early coffee/tea. Beds: KQDT. Central air. VCR, fax, parlor games, telephone, Internet access, picnic table and meadows and stream on premises. Amusement parks, antiquing, cross-country skiing, fishing, live theater, parks, shopping, sporting events, water sports and Amish country nearby.

Location: Country. Midway between Lancaster and Hershey.

Publicity: *Women's World, Lancaster Farming, Philadelphia, New York Times, Ladies Home Journal and Lancaster County Heritage.*

"Dorothy can have Kansas, Scarlett can take Tara, Rick can keep Paris — I've stayed at Cedar Hill Farm."

Certificate may be used: Nov. 1-April 1, Sunday through Thursday, holidays excluded.

Hillside Farm Bed & Breakfast

607 Eby Chiques Road
Mount Joy, PA 17552-8819
(717)653-6697 (888)249-3406 Fax:(717)653-9775
Internet: www.hillsidefarmbandb.com
E-mail: innkeeper@hillsidefarmbandb.com

Circa 1860. This comfortable farm has a relaxing homey feel to it. Rooms are simply decorated and special extras such as handmade quilts and antiques add an elegant country touch. Two

guest cottages each offer a king bed, whirlpool tub for two, fireplace, wet bar and deck overlooking a bucolic meadow. The home is a true monument to the cow. Dairy antiques, cow knick-knacks and antique milk bottles abound. Some of the bottles were found during the renovation of the home and its grounds. Spend the day hunting for bargains in nearby antique shops, malls and factory outlets, or tour local Amish and Pennsylvania Dutch attractions. The farm is a good vacation spot for families with children above the age of 10.

Innkeeper(s): Gary Lintner. $90-215. 5 rooms with PB, 3 with FP, 1 suite and 2 cottages. Breakfast included in rates. Types of meals: Country bkfst, veg bkfst, early coffee/tea and snacks/refreshments. Beds: KQT. TV, VCR, reading lamp, stereo, refrigerator, ceiling fan, snack bar, clock radio, coffeemaker and fireplace in room. Central air. Fax, copier, spa, library, parlor games, telephone and gift shop on premises. Amusement parks, antiquing, art galleries, bicycling, fishing, golf, hiking, live theater, museums, parks, shopping, tennis and wineries nearby.

Location: Country.

Publicity: *Washingtonian Magazine.*

Certificate may be used: November through March, Sunday through Thursday, subject to availability, rooms only.

The Victorian Rose Bed & Breakfast

214 Marietta Ave
Mount Joy, PA 17552-3106
(717)492-0050 (888)313-7494
Internet: www.thevictorianrosebandb.com
E-mail: victorianrosebb@juno.com

Circa 1897. Central to Hershey and Gettysburg battlefield, The Victorian Rose in Mount Joy is an elegant but comfortable place from which to explore beautiful Lancaster County. Enjoy the stately guest rooms and a number of elegant areas including the library and a formal living room. Guests are treated to innkeeper Doris Tyson's home-baked treats for breakfast, and to her homemade candies at other times. Pennsylvania Dutch Country is just 12 miles from the inn.

Innkeeper(s): Doris L. Tyson. $75-95. 4 rooms, 3 with PB. Breakfast included in rates. Types of meals: Full gourmet bkfst. Beds: Q. TV, VCR, reading

lamp, ceiling fan and clock radio in room. Air conditioning. Fax, copier, library, telephone and fireplace on premises. Amusement parks, antiquing, fishing, golf, live theater, museums, parks, shopping and wineries nearby.

Location: Town.

Publicity: *Lancaster Historic Preservation Trust Featured Home 2001 tour and PA Dutch Visitor & Convention Bureau of Authentic B&B Association.*

Certificate may be used: November-May, Sunday-Thursday, subject to availability.

Muncy F12

The Bodine House B&B

307 S Main St
Muncy, PA 17756-1507
(570)546-8949 Fax:(570)546-0607
E-mail: Bodine@pcspower.net

Circa 1805. This Federal-style townhouse, framed by a white picket fence, is in the National Register. Antique and reproduction furnishings highlight the inn's four fireplaces, the parlor, study and library. A favorite guest room features a walnut canopy bed, hand-stenciled and bordered walls, and a framed sampler by the innkeeper's great-great-grandmother. Candlelight breakfasts are served beside the fireplace in a gracious Colonial dining room. Also available is a guest cottage with kitchenette.

Innkeeper(s): David & Marie Louise Smith. $70-125. 3 rooms with PB, 1 with FP and 1 cottage. Breakfast included in rates. Types of meals: Full bkfst, early coffee/tea and afternoon tea. Beds: QDT. Cable TV, reading lamp and turn-down service in room. Air conditioning. TV, VCR, fax, bicycles, library, telephone, fireplace and afternoon tea (by request) on premises. Antiquing, canoeing/kayaking, cross-country skiing, fishing, parks, shopping and sporting events nearby.

Location: Village.

Publicity: *Colonial Homes and Philadelphia Inquirer.*

"What an experience, made special by your wonderful hospitality."

Certificate may be used: Sunday through Thursday, year-round, subject to availability.

New Hope I18

Aaron Burr House Inn & Conference Center

80 W Bridge St
New Hope, PA 18938-1303
(215)862-2570 Fax:(215)862-3937
Internet: aaronburrhouse.com
E-mail: stay@new-hope-inn.com

Circa 1870. Aaron Burr hid in this Bucks County house after his infamous duel with Alexander Hamilton. The home also is one of the Wedgwood Collection inns. A Victorian Shingle style, it is in the National Register. Its three stories, including the spacious parlor, are appointed with antiques and reproductions. Guest rooms offer amenities such as private baths, tele-

phones and TVs, and many have two-person whirlpool tubs and fireplaces. Within walking distance are fine restaurants, shops and art galleries. The grounds offer two gazebos, stately old trees, a screened-in flagstone patio and a barn perfect for bicycle storage.

Innkeeper(s): Carl Glassman & Nadine Silnutzer. $95-255. 12 rooms with PB, 6 with FP, 6 suites, 1 cottage and 3 conference rooms. Breakfast, afternoon tea and snacks/refreshments included in rates. Types of meals: Cont plus, early coffee/tea and room service. Beds: KQT. Reading lamp, stereo, refrigerator, ceiling fan, clock radio, telephone, turn-down service, desk, whirlpools and some with fireplace and canopy beds in room. Air conditioning. VCR, fax, swimming, tennis, pet boarding and parlor games on premises. Handicap access. Antiquing, cross-country skiing, downhill skiing, fishing, live theater, parks, shopping, sporting events, water sports and covered bridge nearby.

Location: Art colony/village.

Publicity: *The Intelligencer Record, Bucks County Courier Times, Time Magazine, CNN Travel Show and 4 platinum bars from Inspected Inns of New Hope.*

Certificate may be used: Monday-Thursday, December-April, holidays excluded.

The Whitehall Inn

1370 Pineville Rd
New Hope, PA 18938-9495
(215)598-7945 (800)598-9021 Fax:(215)598-0378
E-mail: whitehall@hotmail.com

Circa 1794. This white-plastered stone farmhouse is located on 13 country acres studded with stately maple and chestnut trees. Inside, a winding walnut staircase leads to antique-furnished guest rooms that offer wide pine floors, wavy-glass windows, high ceilings and some fireplaces. An antique clock collection, Oriental rugs and late Victorian furnishings are found throughout. Afternoon tea, evening chocolates and candlelight breakfasts served with heirloom china and sterling reflect the inn's many amenities. There are stables on the property and horseback riding may be arranged.

Innkeeper(s): Mike Wass. $140-220. 5 rooms with PB. Breakfast and afternoon tea included in rates. Types of meals: Full bkfst and early coffee/tea. Beds: Q. Reading lamp, clock radio, turn-down service, desk, fireplace and deep-soaking tubs in room. Air conditioning. Fax, copier, swimming, library, parlor games, telephone and heated outdoor pool on premises. Amusement parks, antiquing, cross-country skiing, live theater and shopping nearby.

Location: Country.

Certificate may be used: January-September, Monday-Thursday.

New Kingstown   J11

Kanaga House B&B Inn

6940 Carlisle Pike, PO Box 92
New Kingstown, PA 17072
(717)766-8654 (877)9KA-NAGA Fax:(717)697-3908
Internet: www.kanagahouse.com
E-mail: stay@kanagahouse.com

Circa 1775. Stay in this restored 1775 stone house while visiting the area's many tourist attractions such as Gettysburg Civil War Battlefield, Hershey Chocolate World, Lancaster Dutch Country or Harrisburg (the state capital). The well-appointed guest bedrooms offer canopy beds, and one boasts a fireplace. Tree-studded grounds and a large gazebo are perfect for weddings. The first-floor rooms and catering staff also enhance business meetings and retreats. Walk the nearby Appalachian Trail, or fly fish in the Yellow Breeches and Letort Springs.

Innkeeper(s): Mary Jane & Dave Kretzing. $85-125. 6 rooms with PB, 1 with FP and 1 conference room. Breakfast included in rates. Types of meals: Full bkfst and early coffee/tea. Beds: Q. TV, reading lamp, refrigerator, clock radio, telephone and desk in room. Air conditioning. VCR, copier, fireplace and gazebo with table and chairs on premises. Amusement parks, antiquing, downhill skiing, live theater and shopping nearby.

Location: Rural setting.

Certificate may be used: Oct. 15 to March 31, Sunday-Thursday only, excluding holidays.

Palmerton   H16

The Roth House

4285 Little Gap Rd
Palmerton, PA 18071
(610)824-5341 Fax:(610)826-4220
Internet: bbonline.com/pa/roth
E-mail: bdvda86652@aol.com

Circa 1825. There is much to enjoy at this country bed & breakfast in the quaint village of Little Gap. Quality craftsmanship and an appealing decor combine to provide comfortable accommodations. The spacious living room and dining area are wonderful gathering places. Themed guest bedrooms offer a romantic getaway. The Roth Suite features a Jacuzzi, champagne and chocolates. A generous breakfast usually includes homemade bread, fresh fruit, meat and a main entree. The inn sits on one acre at the foot of the picturesque Pocono Mountains, and guests can relax on the gracious front porch or take a tranquil stroll by the creek. Bikes are available for exploring the area. Ask about seasonal ski packages.

Innkeeper(s): Barb & Mar Costenbader. $85-145. 4 rooms with PB. Breakfast and snacks/refreshments included in rates. Types of meals: Country bkfst. Beds: Q. Cable TV, ceiling fan, clock radio, coffeemaker and hot tub/spa in room. Air conditioning. VCR and bicycles on premises. Amusement parks, antiquing, bicycling, canoeing/kayaking, cross-country skiing, downhill skiing, fishing, golf, hiking, horseback riding, museums, parks, shopping and wineries nearby.

Location: Country, mountains.

Publicity: *The Pocono Record.*

Certificate may be used: April-June, Sunday-Thursday, subject to availability.

Philadelphia   K17

Gaskill House Bed & Breakfast

312 Gaskill Street
Philadelphia, PA 19147
(215)413-0669
Internet: www.gaskillhouse.com
E-mail: gaskillbnb@aol.com

Circa 1828. Located in the heart of Society Hill's Historic District, this urban oasis is listed in the National Register. A double townhouse built with Federal architecture, the home has been restored recently. Equipped with modern comforts, the gracious furnishings and decor of the 18th century have been retained. Elegant guest bedrooms offer spacious tranquility, whirlpool baths, fireplaces and and abundance of useful amenities. A made-to-order American breakfast is a welcome way to start the day. Guests can explore the many sites of the city.

Innkeeper(s): Guy Davis. $120-200. 4 rooms with PB, 3 with FP. Breakfast included in rates. Types of meals: Full bkfst. Beds: Q. Modem hook-up, cable TV, VCR, reading lamp, CD player, ceiling fan, telephone, desk, hot tub/spa and fireplace in room. Central air. Fax, copier, spa, library, fireplace and laundry facility on premises. Antiquing, art galleries, bicycling, live theater, museums, parks, shopping and sporting events nearby.

Location: City.

Publicity: *Philadelphia Magazine.*

Certificate may be used: Anytime, subject to availability.

Rittenhouse Square B&B

1715 Rittenhouse Square
Philadelphia, PA 19103
(215)546-6500 (877)791-6500 Fax:(215)546-8787
Internet: www.rittenhousebb.com
E-mail: innkeeper@rittenhousebb.com

Circa 1911. Experience elegant luxury at this comfortably renovated carriage house, internationally renown for business or pleasure. Impressive art, impeccable decor, lavish furnishings and extraordinary service are the hallmarks of this inn. The guest bedrooms are spectacular, tranquil retreats. Distinctive amenities include CD players, triple sheeting, turndown service, computer workstations, plush robes and marble bathrooms. Enjoy breakfast in The Cafe and early evening wine and snacks in the gorgeous lobby.

Innkeeper(s): Harriet S. Seltzer. $209-299. 10 rooms with PB, 1 with FP, 2 suites and 1 conference room. Breakfast and snacks/refreshments included in rates. Types of meals: Cont plus. Beds: KQD. Modem hook-up, data port, cable TV, CD player, telephone, coffeemaker, turn-down service, voice mail and fireplace in room. Central air. Fax, copier, parlor games, fireplace and laundry facility on premises. Limited handicap access. Antiquing, art galleries, museums, shopping and sporting events nearby.

Location: City.

Certificate may be used: Anytime, subject to availability, Sunday-Thursday.

Pine Grove Mills   H9

The Chatelaine Bed & Breakfast

PO Box 10268 Calder Square
State College, PA 16805
(814)238-2028 (800)251-2028 Fax:(814)238-1699
Internet: www.chatelainebandb.com
E-mail: kkeeper0@adelphia.net

Circa 1841. Pass by the border of heirloom perennials and a welcoming signpost, through the double canopy of stately pine to this vintage farmhouse. A formal yet comfortable sitting room features deep sofas, chairs and luxurious hassocks. Distinctive antiques furnish elegantly decorated guest bedrooms and a suite. Generous amenities include robes, soda, ice and glasses. Enjoy cordials from bedside decanters. A breakfast feast is a lighthearted, whimsical affair in the dining room amidst an extensive china collection. Take a break from the B&B's peaceful serenity to visit nearby historic sites.

Innkeeper(s): Mae McQuade. Call for rates. 4 rooms with PB, 1 suite. Breakfast and snacks/refreshments included in rates. Types of meals: Full bkfst and early coffee/tea. Beds: KQT. Cable TV, reading lamp and desk in room. Air conditioning. Library, parlor games and telephone on premises. Antiquing, art galleries, bicycling, canoeing/kayaking, cross-country skiing, downhill skiing, golf, hiking, live theater, museums, parks, shopping, sporting events, tennis, water sports and wineries nearby.

Location: Country.

Publicity: *Pennsylvania Hospitality Innkeeper of the Year for 2003.*

Certificate may be used: Anytime, subject to availability.

Pittsburgh   I3

The Priory

614 Pressley St
Pittsburgh, PA 15212-5616
(412)231-3338 Fax:(412)231-4838
Internet: www.edgpgh
E-mail: edgpgh@stargate.net

Circa 1888. The Priory, now a European-style hotel, was built to provide lodging for Benedictine priests traveling through Pittsburgh. It is adjacent to Pittsburgh's Grand Hall at the Priory in historic East Allegheny. The inn's design and maze of rooms and corridors give it a distinctly Old World flavor. All rooms are decorated with Victorian furnishings.

Innkeeper(s): John and Suzanne Graf. $119-155. 24 rooms with PB, 3 suites and 1 conference room. Breakfast included in rates. Types of meals: Cont plus. Beds: KQD. Handicap access.

Publicity: *Pittsburgh Press, US Air, Country Inns, Innsider, Youngstown Vindicator, Travel & Leisure, Gourmet, Mid-Atlantic Country and National Geographic Traveler.*

"Although we had been told that the place was elegant, we were hardly prepared for the richness of detail. We felt as though we were guests in a manor."

Certificate may be used: December-March, excludes New Year's Eve and Valentine's Day.

Red Lion   K13

Red Lion Bed & Breakfast

101 S Franklin St
Red Lion, PA 17356
(717)244-4739 Fax:(717)246-9202
Internet: www.redlionbandb.com
E-mail: staywithus@redlionbandb.com

Circa 1920. Explore one of the more popular regions of the state while staying at this unpretentious and quiet three-story brick, Federal-style home. Snuggle up next to the fireplace in the living room with a book from the well-stocked collection of reading material. Sip a cool iced tea on the enclosed sun porch or outside garden patio. Half of the six quaint and comfortable guest bedrooms offer a full bath and queen-size bed. Twin beds and cots are also available for families or groups traveling together. Breakfasts are substantial with quiche, pancakes, stuffed French toast, fresh baked rolls and muffins served alongside fruit or granola. The town has antique and craft shops and is within a 45-minute drive of vineyards, the Amish country of Lancaster, Hershey and the Gettysburg Battlefield.

Innkeeper(s): George & Danielle Sanders. $65-85. 6 rooms, 3 with PB and 1 conference room. Breakfast included in rates. Types of meals: Full bkfst. Beds: QT. TV, VCR, ceiling fan and clock radio in room. Air conditioning. Library, parlor games, telephone, fireplace, off-street parking and modem hook-up on premises. Amusement parks, antiquing, canoeing/kayaking, fishing, golf, hiking, horseback riding, live theater, parks, water sports and wineries nearby.

Location: Small town.

Certificate may be used: Anytime, subject to availability.

Reinholds   J14

Barnyard Inn B&B and Carriage House

2145 Old Lancaster Pike
Reinholds, PA 17569
(717)484-1111
Internet: www.barnyardinn.com
E-mail: pam@barnyardinn.com

Overlooking the countryside on two-and-a-half wooded acres, this restored German schoolhouse is furnished with family heirlooms and antiques. The huge living room is accented with a corner fireplace and carved wooden mantle. French doors lead to the elegant dining room boasting a crystal chandelier. Well-appointed guest bedrooms and a suite are named after the barnyard of animals found in the mobile petting zoo behind the inn. The Carriage House is a more private and

spacious three-room suite with an equipped kitchen.
Innkeeper(s): Pam Pozniak. Call for rates. Call inn for details.
Certificate may be used: Nov. 15 through March 15, Sunday through Thursday, excluding holidays.

Brownstone Colonial Inn

590 Galen Hall Rd
Reinholds, PA 17569-9420
(717)484-4460 (877)464-9862 Fax:(717)484-4460
Internet: www.brownstonecolonialinn.com
E-mail: info@brownstonecolonialinn.com

Circa 1790. Early German Mennonite settlers built this sandstone farmhouse in 1790. It graces seven scenic acres amidst Amish countryside. Feel relaxed and pampered at this fully restored inn. Guest bedrooms and a suite boast random-width plank floors, locally handcrafted period-authentic furniture, sleigh or pencil post beds and antique Shaker peg boards. Enjoy a hearty country breakfast in the homestead's original smokehouse with brick floor, ceiling beams and open hearth fireplace. Start the day with fresh juices, homemade pastries and jams, a hot entree and fruits grown on-site. Stroll by the fish pond and gardens, or walk the nearby nature trails. An abundance of outlet and antique malls as well as historical and cultural sites are minutes away.
Innkeeper(s): Brenda & Mark Miller. $85-115. 3 rooms, 2 with PB, 1 suite. Breakfast and snacks/refreshments included in rates. Types of meals: Full bkfst, early coffee/tea and afternoon tea. Beds: QDT. Modem hook-up, reading lamp, clock radio and desk in room. Central air. VCR, telephone and fireplace on premises. Amusement parks, antiquing, cross-country skiing, fishing, golf, hiking, horseback riding, live theater, museums, parks, shopping, sporting events, water sports and wineries nearby.
Location: Country.

"We can't wait to tell friends and family about your paradise."
Certificate may be used: December-March, Monday-Wednesday.

Ronks   K14

Candlelight Inn B&B

2574 Lincoln Hwy E
Ronks, PA 17572-9771
(717)299-6005 (800)772-2635 Fax:(717)299-6397
Internet: www.candleinn.com
E-mail: candleinn@aol.com

Circa 1920. Located in the Pennsylvania Dutch area, this Federal-style house offers a side porch for enjoying the home's acre and a half of tall trees and surrounding Amish farmland. Guest rooms feature Victorian decor. Three rooms include a Jacuzzi tub and fireplace. The inn's gourmet breakfast, which might include a creme caramel French toast, is served by candlelight. The innkeepers are professional classical musicians. Lancaster is five miles to the east.
Innkeeper(s): Tim & Heidi Soberick. $85-169. 7 rooms with PB, 3 with FP, 3 with HT. Breakfast included in rates. Types of meals: Full gourmet bkfst. Beds: KQT. Reading lamp, clock radio, desk, amaretto, robes, three with Jacuzzi and fireplaces in room. Air conditioning. Fax, parlor games, telephone, fireplace, badminton and croquet on premises. Amusement parks, antiquing, cross-country skiing, downhill skiing, fishing, live theater, parks, shopping, sporting events and water sports nearby.
Location: Country. Suburban-surrounded by farms.
Publicity: *Lancaster Daily News, Pennsylvania Dutch Traveler* and *Pennsylvania Intelligencer Journal.*
Certificate may be used: December through April, excluding holidays, Sunday through Thursday.

Scranton   E16

The Weeping Willow Inn

308 N Eaton Rd
Tunkhannock, PA 18657-1706
(570)836-7257
Internet: www.weepingwillowinn.com
E-mail: weepingwillow@emcs.net

Circa 1836. This Colonial, set on 22 acres, is filled with beautiful antiques and an elegant traditional decor. The home's original pine floor is topped with Oriental rugs. Breakfasts, with a fresh fruit parfait and perhaps apple-cinnamon French toast, are served by candlelight. The nearby Susquehanna River and mountains provide ample activities, from hiking to fishing and canoeing. Antique and craft shops also are plentiful in the area.
Innkeeper(s): Patty & Randy Ehrenzeller. $75-95. 3 rooms with PB. Breakfast included in rates. Types of meals: Full bkfst. Beds: QD. Reading lamp, clock radio, telephone and turn-down service in room. Air conditioning. Parlor games and fireplace on premises. Antiquing, cross-country skiing, downhill skiing, fishing, golf, parks, shopping, tennis and water sports nearby.
Location: Mountains.
Publicity: *WNEP TV and local travel agency.*
Certificate may be used: Tuesday through Thursday, no holidays, Dec. 1 through April 30.

Shippensburg   K10

Field & Pine B&B

2155 Ritner Hwy
Shippensburg, PA 17257-9756
(717)776-7179
Internet: www.cvbednbreakfasts.com/field
E-mail: fieldpine@aol.com

Circa 1790. Local limestone was used to build this stone house, located on the main wagon road to Baltimore and Washington. Originally, it was a tavern and weigh station. The house is surrounded by stately pines, and sheep graze on the inn's 80 acres. The bedrooms are hand-stenciled and furnished with quilts and antiques.
Innkeeper(s): Mary Ellen & Allan Williams. $75-90. 3 rooms, 1 with PB, 1 with FP, 1 suite. Breakfast and snacks/refreshments included in rates. Types of meals: Full gourmet bkfst and early coffee/tea. Beds: QDT. TV, reading lamp, stereo, clock radio, turn-down service and desk in room. Air conditioning. VCR, telephone and fireplace on premises. Antiquing, fishing, parks and shopping nearby.
Location: Country.
Publicity: *Central Pennsylvania Magazine.*

"Our visit in this lovely country home has been most delightful. The ambiance of antiques and tasteful decorating exemplifies real country living."
Certificate may be used: Sunday through Thursday, year-round. Plus weekends subject to availability in January, February and March.

Somerset   K5

Quill Haven Country Inn
1519 North Center Ave
Somerset, PA 15501-7001
(814)443-4514 (866)784-5522 Fax:(814)445-1376
Internet: www.quillhaven.com
E-mail: quill@quillhaven.com

Circa 1918. Set on three acres that were once part of a chicken and turkey farm, this historic Arts & Crafts-style home offers guest rooms, each individually appointed. The Bridal Suite includes a four-poster wrought iron bed and sunken tub in the bath. The Country Room includes a decorative pot-bellied stove. Antiques, reproductions and stained-glass lamps decorate the rooms. Guests are treated to a full breakfast with items such as baked grapefruit or apples, homemade breads and entrees such as stuffed French toast or a specialty casserole of ham, cheese and potatoes. Guests can spend the day boating or swimming at nearby Youghiogheny Reservoir, take a whitewater-rafting trip, bike or hike through the scenic countryside, ski at one of three ski resorts in the area or shop at antique stores, outlets and flea markets. Frank Lloyd Wright's Fallingwater is another nearby attraction.
Innkeeper(s): Carol & Rowland Miller. $85-115. 4 rooms with PB. Breakfast and snacks/refreshments included in rates. Types of meals: Full bkfst and early coffee/tea. Beds: KQ. Cable TV, VCR, reading lamp, ceiling fan, clock radio, turn-down service and heated mattress pad in room. Air conditioning. Library, parlor games, telephone, outdoor hot tub, common room with fireplace and mini kitchenette on premises. Amusement parks, antiquing, bicycling, canoeing/kayaking, cross-country skiing, downhill skiing, fishing, golf, hiking, horseback riding, live theater, parks, shopping, tennis, water sports, wineries, Seven Springs, Hidden Valley and Laurel Highlands nearby.
Location: Country, mountains.
Publicity: *Westsylvania Magazine.*

"What a beautiful memory we will have of our first B&B experience! We've never felt quite so pampered in all our 25 years of marriage."
Certificate may be used: Anytime, March-September, subject to availability.

Starlight   C17

The Inn at Starlight Lake
PO Box 27
Starlight, PA 18461-0027
(570)798-2519 (800)248-2519 Fax:(570)798-2672
Internet: www.innatstarlightlake.com
E-mail: theinn@unforgettable.com

Circa 1909. Acres of woodland and meadow surround the last surviving railroad inn on the New York, Ontario and Western lines. Originally a boarding house, the inn was part of a little village that had its own store, church, blacksmith shop and creamery. Platforms, first erected to accommodate tents for the summer season, were later replaced by three small cottage buildings that now include a suite with a double whirlpool. A modern three-bedroom house is  available for family reunions and conferences. The inn is situated on the 45-acre, spring-fed Starlight Lake, providing summertime canoeing, swimming, fishing and sailing. (No motorboats are allowed on the lake.) Breakfast is served in the lakeside dining area where dinner is also available.

Innkeeper(s): Jack & Judy McMahon. $165-195. 26 rooms, 20 with PB, 1 with FP, 1 suite, 3 cottages, 1 guest house and 1 conference room. Breakfast and dinner included in rates. Types of meals: Full gourmet bkfst, veg bkfst, early coffee/tea, gourmet lunch, picnic lunch and snacks/refreshments. Restaurant on premises. Beds: KQDT. Reading lamp and ceiling fan in room. TV, fax, copier, bicycles, tennis, library, parlor games, fireplace and laundry facility on premises. Limited handicap access. Antiquing, bicycling, canoeing/kayaking, downhill skiing, fishing, golf, horseback riding, live theater, tennis and water sports nearby.
Location: Mountains.
Publicity: *New York Times, Philadelphia Inquirer, Newsday, Discerning Traveler, Freeman and Travel Network.*
Certificate may be used: Jan. 3 to Dec. 15, Sunday to Friday, except when a holiday falls on that day.

Strasburg   K14

Strasburg Village Inn
1 W Main St, Centre Sq
Strasburg, PA 17579
(717)687-0900 (800)541-1055
Internet: strasburg.com
E-mail: foraroom@strasburg.com

Circa 1788. Located on historic Strasburg's Centre Square, this brick inn offers guests a glimpse of early Americana, in the center of the Amish country. Despite the old-fashioned charm, two suites offer the romantic, albeit modern, amenity of Jacuzzi tubs. The inn is adjacent to the Strasburg Country Store and Creamery, the town's oldest operating store. The shop offers a variety of baked goods, a 19th-century soda fountain, a deli with homemade ice cream, penny candy and plenty of collectibles. Guests are treated to a full breakfast at The Creamery. The inn is surrounded by many Pennsylvania Dutch sites, including Amish farms, antique stores and historic villages. Sight and Sound Theater, the Strasburg Railroad and Dutch Wonderland Amusement Park are nearby.
Innkeeper(s): Ruth Frankfort. $70-150. 10 rooms with PB, 2 suites. Breakfast included in rates. Types of meals: Full bkfst and early coffee/tea. Restaurant on premises. Beds: KQD. Cable TV and reading lamp in room. Air conditioning. Telephone and restaurant on premises. Several outlet malls nearby.
Location: City.
Certificate may be used: Sunday-Thursday, Nov. 1-May 21, excluding holidays.

Terre Hill   J15

The Artist's Inn & Gallery
PO Box 26
Terre Hill, PA 17581
(717)445-0219 (888)999-4479
Internet: www.artistinn.com
E-mail: info@artistinn.com

Circa 1853. Four-course breakfasts and warm and inviting guest rooms are offered at this Federal-style inn. Watch Amish buggies clip clop by from the Victorian veranda and listen to the chimes from the church across the way. Then plan your day with the help of innkeepers Jan and Bruce, avid adventurers who cross-country ski and explore the area's best offerings to share insights with guests. There's an art gallery with works by the resident artist. Guest accommodations are inviting with antiques, gas fireplaces, hardwood floors and decorative painting, wallpapers and borders. The Rose Room offers a Jacuzzi bath. The Garden Suite offers a whirlpool bath for two, massage shower, fireplace, king-size featherbed, private balcony and sitting room. Breakfasts feature breads such as scones or muffins, fruit parfaits, crepes or egg dishes and a luscious dessert—perhaps a pie, cake or tart.

Innkeeper(s): Jan & Bruce Garrabrandt. $115-189. 3 rooms with PB, 3 with FP, 2 suites. Breakfast and snacks/refreshments included in rates. Types of meals: Full gourmet bkfst, veg bkfst, early coffee/tea and afternoon tea. Beds: KQ. Reading lamp, ceiling fan, turn-down service, hot tub/spa, hair dryers, robes, feather beds, CD players, clock radios and whirlpool baths in room. Central air. Library, parlor games, telephone, fireplace and art gallery on premises. Limited handicap access. Amusement parks, antiquing, art galleries, bicycling, cross-country skiing, fishing, golf, hiking, live theater, museums, parks, shopping, tennis and wineries nearby.

Location: Small town.

Certificate may be used: Sunday-Thursday, November through April.

Valley Forge   K16

The Great Valley House of Valley Forge

1475 Swedesford Road
Malvern, PA 19355
(610)644-6759
Internet: www.greatvalleyhouse.com
E-mail: info@greatvalleyhouse.com

Circa 1691. This 300-year-old Colonial stone farmhouse sits on four acres just two miles from Valley Forge Park. Boxwoods line the walkway, and ancient trees surround the house. Each of the three antique-filled guest rooms is hand-stenciled and features a canopied or brass bed topped with handmade quilts. Guests enjoy a full breakfast before a 14-foot fireplace in the "summer kitchen," the oldest part of the house. On the grounds are a swimming pool, walking and hiking trails and the home's original smokehouse.

Innkeeper(s): Pattye Benson. $85-115. 3 rooms with PB. Breakfast included in rates. Types of meals: Full gourmet bkfst and early coffee/tea. Beds: QDT. Cable TV, reading lamp, refrigerator, clock radio, telephone, turn-down service, desk and free high-speed Internet access in room. Air conditioning. TV, fax, swimming, parlor games, fireplace and grand piano on premises. Antiquing, cross-country skiing, fishing, live theater, parks, shopping, sporting events and water sports nearby.

Location: Rural/suburban setting.

Publicity: *Main Line Philadelphia, Philadelphia Inquirer, Washington Post, New York Times, Suburban Newspaper, Travel cable network, Network TV and commercial site.*

"As a business traveler, Patty's enthusiasm and warm welcome makes you feel just like you're home."

Certificate may be used: Nov. 1-April 30, both nights must be Sunday-Thursday, excludes holidays.

Warfordsburg   L8

Buck Valley Ranch, LLC

1344 Negro Mountain Rd
Warfordsburg, PA 17267-9667
(717)294-3759 (800)294-3759 Fax:(717)294-6413
E-mail: bvranch@nb.net

Circa 1930. Trail riding is a popular activity on the ranch's 64 acres in the Appalachian Mountains of South Central Pennsylvania. State game lands and forests border the ranch. The guest house, decorated in a ranch/cowboy style, is a private farmhouse that can accommodate eight people. Meals are prepared using homegrown vegetables and locally raised meats. Rates also include horseback riding.

Innkeeper(s): Nadine & Leon Fox. $125. 4 rooms. Breakfast, snacks/refreshments and dinner included in rates. Types of meals: Full gourmet bkfst, early coffee/tea and gourmet lunch. Beds: DT. Reading lamp in room. Air conditioning. Fax, copier, spa, swimming, sauna, stable, parlor games and telephone on premises. Amusement parks, antiquing, cross-country skiing, downhill skiing, fishing, golf, parks, shopping, water sports, C&O Canal, steam train rides and trail rides nearby.

Location: Country, mountains.

Publicity: *Washington Post, Pittsburgh Press, PA bride, Baltimore Sun and Potomac.*

Certificate may be used: Jan. 1-Dec. 31, Sunday-Thursday, excluding weekends and holidays.

York   K13

Friendship House B&B

728 E Philadelphia St
York, PA 17403-1609
(717)843-8299
E-mail: friendshiphome@juno.com

Circa 1897. A walk down East Philadelphia Street takes visitors past an unassuming row of 19th-century townhouses. The Friendship House is a welcoming site with its light blue shutters and pink trim. Innkeepers Becky Detwiler and Karen Maust have added a shot of Victorian influence to their charming townhouse B&B, decorating with wallcoverings and lacy curtains. A country feast is prepared some mornings with choices ranging from quiche to French toast accompanied with items such as baked apples, smoked sausage and homemade breads. Most items are selected carefully from a nearby farmer's market. A cozy gathering place is in the living room with its gas log fireplace.

Innkeeper(s): Becky Detwiler & Karen Maust. $70. 3 rooms, 2 with PB, 1 suite. Breakfast and snacks/refreshments included in rates. Types of meals: Full bkfst. Beds: Q. Air conditioning. VCR and telephone on premises. Antiquing, golf, live theater, parks, shopping and museums nearby.

Location: Dutch Country.

Certificate may be used: Jan. 2-March 31.

Rhode Island

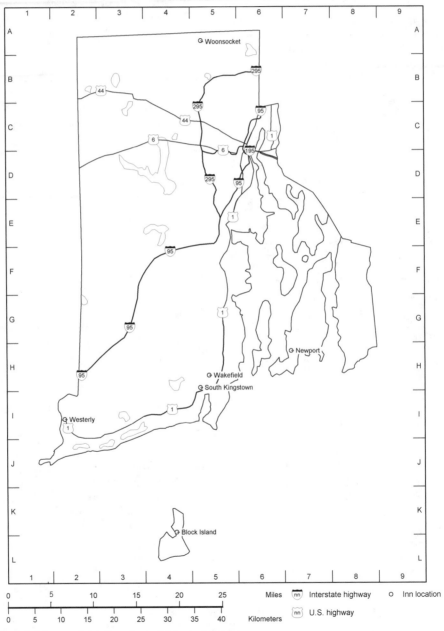

Woonsocket

Newport

Wakefield
South Kingstown

Westerly

Block Island

Miles		Interstate highway
		U.S. highway
Kilometers		Inn location

Block Island K4

The Bellevue House

PO Box 1198, High St
Block Island, RI 02807-1198
(401)466-2912 Fax:(401)466-2912
Internet: www.blockisland.com/bellevue
E-mail: bellevue@riconnect.com

Circa 1882. Offering a hilltop perch, meadow-like setting and ocean views, this Colonial Revival farmhouse inn in the Block Island Historic District has served guests for more than a century. A variety of accommodations includes six guest rooms, one with private bath, four suites and two cottages. The Old Harbor Ferry, restaurants and shops are just a five-minute walk from the inn. Guests may  use ferries from New London, Conn., Montauk Point, N.Y., and Point Judith, R.I., to reach the island. Beaches, Block Island National Wildlife Reserve and Rodmans Hollow Nature Area are nearby. Children are welcome.

Innkeeper(s): Kelly Leone. $65-285. 6 rooms, 4 suites and 2 cottages. Breakfast included in rates. Types of meals: Cont. Beds: KQD. Reading lamp in room. Library, telephone, gas grills and picnic tables on premises. Fishing, parks, shopping and water sports nearby.

Location: 12 miles from mainland Rhode Island.

Certificate may be used: Sunday through Thursday, May 20-June 21, Sept. 11-Oct. 11.

Blue Dory Inn

PO Box 488, Dodge St
Block Island, RI 02807-0488
(401)466-5891 (800)992-7290 Fax:(401)466-9910
Internet: www.blockislandinns.com
E-mail: rundezvous@aol.com

Circa 1887. This Shingle Victorian inn on Crescent Beach offers many guest rooms with ocean views. The Cottage, The Doll House and The Tea House are separate structures for those desiring more room or privacy. Antiques and Victorian touches are featured throughout. Year-round car ferry service, taking approximately one hour, is found at Point Judith, R.I. The island also may be reached by air on New England Airlines or by charter. Mohegan Bluffs Scenic Natural Area is nearby.

Innkeeper(s): Ann Law. $65-495. 12 rooms with PB, 3 suites, 4 cottages and 1 conference room. Breakfast and afternoon tea included in rates. Types of meals: Cont plus and early coffee/tea. Beds: KQDT. Reading lamp, CD player, telephone, desk, most with air conditioning, VCRs and cable TV in room. TV, VCR, fax, copier, swimming, child care and parlor games on premises. Antiquing, beach, fishing, live theater, parks, shopping and water sports nearby.

Location: Ocean community.

"The Blue Dory is a wonderful place to stay. The room was lovely, the view spectacular and the sound of surf was both restful and tranquil."

Certificate may be used: Midweek Sept. 15-June 15, Sunday through Thursday.

The Sheffield House, A Bed & Breakfast Inn

PO Box 1387, High St
Block Island, RI 02807
(401)466-2494 (866)466-2494 Fax:(401)466-7745
Internet: www.thesheffieldhouse.com
E-mail: info@thesheffieldhouse.com

Circa 1888. Step off the ferry and step into a bygone era at this Queen Anne Victorian, which overlooks the Old Harbor district. Relax on one of the front porch rockers or enjoy the fragrance as you stroll through the private garden. Guest rooms are furnished with antiques and family pieces; each is individually decorated.

Innkeeper(s): Nancy Sarah. $55-205. 6 rooms, 4 with PB. Breakfast and afternoon tea included in rates. Types of meals: Full gourmet bkfst. Beds: Q. Reading lamp, refrigerator, ceiling fan, clock radio and some have small library in room. TV, VCR, fax, copier, library, parlor games, telephone, fireplace, laundry facility and outdoor shower on premises. Limited handicap access. Antiquing, art galleries, beach, bicycling, canoeing/kayaking, fishing, hiking, horseback riding, shopping, water sports, ocean, nature hikes and restaurants nearby.

Location: Ocean community.

Certificate may be used: Oct. 15-May 15, Sunday-Thursday.

Newport H7

Agincourt Inn

120 Miantonomi Ave
Newport, RI 02842-5450
(401)847-0902 (800)352-3750 Fax:(401)848-6529
Internet: www.agincourtinn.com
E-mail: randy@shadowlawn.com

Circa 1856. This elegant, three-story Stick Victorian inn, listed in the National Register, offers a glimpse of fine living in an earlier age. The innkeepers' attention to detail is evident throughout, with French crystal chandeliers, stained-glass windows and parquet floors in the library as a few of the highlights. Parlors are found on each of the inn's floors. Newport's many attractions, including the Art Museum, sailing and the world famous Newport mansions are just a short drive from the inn.

Innkeeper(s): Randy & Selma Fabricant. $79-250. 8 rooms, 8 with FP, 8 suites. Breakfast included in rates. Types of meals: Full bkfst. Beds: KQ. Cable TV, VCR, reading lamp, refrigerator, clock radio and fireplace in room. Air conditioning. Fax, library, parlor games and telephone on premises. Antiquing, art galleries, beach, bicycling, canoeing/kayaking, fishing, golf, hiking, horseback riding, live theater, museums, parks, shopping, sporting events, tennis, water sports, wineries, mansions and sailing nearby.

Location: Ocean community.

Publicity: *Newport Daily News, Providence Journal, West Essex Tribune, Victorian Homes, Travel Channel (haunted inns) and Mr. Smith.*

"A dream come true! Thanks for everything! We'll be back."

Certificate may be used: Jan. 20-April 30, Monday-Thursday, no holidays, festivals.

Beech Tree Inn

34 Rhode Island Ave
Newport, RI 02840-2667
(401)847-9794 (800)748-6565 Fax:(401)847-6824
Internet: www.beechtreeinn.com
E-mail: cmquilt13@cox.net

Circa 1897. This inn's location in historic Newport offers close access to the famous local mansions, and the turn-of-the-century home is within walking distance of the harbor. Most of the guest rooms include a fireplace. Special furnishings include canopy or poster beds, and suites offer the added amenity of a whirlpool tub. The innkeepers provide a breakfast feast, and guests enjoy made-to-order fare that might include eggs, pancakes, waffles, omelettes, ham, bacon and more. Snacks, such as freshly baked cookies, are always on hand to curb one's appetite.

Innkeeper(s): Cindy Mahood. $99-350. 5 rooms with PB, 3 with FP, 1 suite, 1 guest house and 1 conference room. Breakfast, afternoon tea and snacks/refreshments included in rates. Types of meals: Full bkfst and early coffee/tea. Beds: KQ. Cable TV, reading lamp, refrigerator, ceiling fan, telephone, desk, fireplaces, Jacuzzi and clock in room. Air conditioning. Fax, copier, fireplace and free parking on premises. Antiquing, cross-country skiing, downhill skiing, fishing, golf, live theater, parks, shopping, sporting events, tennis and water sports nearby.

Location: City. Quiet residential.

Certificate may be used: During off season (November-April), midweek, Sunday-Thursday.

The Burbank Rose B&B

111 Memorial Blvd W
Newport, RI 02840-3469
(401)849-9457 (888)297-5800
Internet: www.burbankrose.com
E-mail: theburbankrose@yahoo.com

Circa 1850. The innkeepers of this cheery, yellow home named their B&B in honor of their ancestor, famed horticulturist Luther Burbank. As a guest, he probably would be taken by  the bright, flowery hues that adorn the interior of this Federal-style home. Rooms, some of which afford harbor views, are light and airy with simple decor. The innkeepers serve afternoon refreshments and a substantial breakfast buffet. The home is located in Newport's Historic Hill district and within walking distance of shops, restaurants and many of the seaside village's popular attractions.

Innkeeper(s): Brian Cole. $69-199. 3 rooms with PB, 2 suites. Breakfast included in rates. Types of meals: Cont. Beds: QT. Reading lamp and clock radio in room. Air conditioning. VCR, parlor games and telephone on premises. Antiquing, fishing, live theater, shopping, water sports, sailing, golf and tennis nearby.

Location: City, ocean community, waterfront.

Certificate may be used: Nov. 1-April 30, Sunday-Thursday.

Cliffside Inn

2 Seaview Ave
Newport, RI 02840-3627
(401)847-1811 (800)845-1811 Fax:(401)848-5850
Internet: www.cliffsideinn.com
E-mail: innkeeper@legendaryinnsofnewport.com

Circa 1876. The governor of Maryland, Thomas Swann, built this Newport summer house in the style of a Second Empire Victorian. It features a mansard roof and many bay windows. The rooms are decorated in a Victorian motif. Suites have marble baths, and all rooms have fireplaces. Fourteen rooms have a double whirlpool tub. The Cliff Walk is located one block from the inn.

Innkeeper(s): Stephan Nicolas. $245-625. 16 rooms with PB, 16 with FP, 8 suites and 1 cottage. Breakfast and afternoon tea included in rates. Types of meals: Full gourmet bkfst and early coffee/tea. Restaurant on premises. Beds: KQ. Cable TV, VCR, reading lamp, stereo, ceiling fan, clock radio, telephone, turn-down service, desk, LCD TV, complimentary high-speed wireless Internet access, twice daily maid service and handcrafted artisan chocolates in room. Air conditioning. Fax, parlor games, fireplace, tea shot, parlor breakfast and movie libraries on premises. Antiquing, fishing, live theater, shopping and water sports nearby.

Location: Ocean community.

Publicity: *Conde Naste, Boston, New York Times, Zagat Survey, Bride's Magazine, Frommer's, Discerning Traveler* and *Good Morning America.*

"...it captures the grandeur of the Victorian age."

Certificate may be used: January to March, Sunday-Thursday, holidays and school vacation weeks excluded, subject to availability.

Fair Street Guest House

28 Fair St
Newport, RI 02840-3442
(401)849-4046 (888)701-1431 Fax:(401)847-1084
Internet: www.fairstreetguesthouse.com
E-mail: dhooley@c21edpariseau.com

Circa 1880. This 1880 Victorian inn on the National Historic Register is located in Newport Historic District just blocks from the waterfront. It's within blocks of a number of well-known sites, including St. Mary's Church, where Jack and Jacqueline Kennedy were married, Banister's Wharf and Christie's Landing. It has seven guest rooms decorated with furniture from the Victorian era. Breakfast is served in the dining room, on the enclosed porch or in the garden, and offers such dishes as muffins, bagels with cream cheese, cereal and fruit.

Innkeeper(s): Denise Hooley. $99-225. 7 rooms with PB. Breakfast included in rates. Types of meals: Cont plus and early coffee/tea. Beds: KQDT. Cable TV, reading lamp, ceiling fan and clock radio in room. Central air. VCR, fax, telephone and fireplace on premises. Antiquing, art galleries, beach, bicycling, canoeing/kayaking, golf, hiking, horseback riding, live theater, museums, parks, shopping, tennis, water sports and wineries nearby.

Location: City, ocean community.

Certificate may be used: Nov. 1 through April 15, Sunday-Friday.

Hammett House Inn

505 Thames St
Newport, RI 02840-6723
(401)846-0400 (800)548-9417 Fax:(401)274-2690
Internet: hammetthouseinn.com
E-mail: Check-In@HammettHouseInn.Com

Circa 1758. After a gracious welcome, enjoy the warm, relaxed ambiance of this historic three-story Georgian Federal home. Built in 1785, it boasts post and beam construction and beaded clapboard exterior. Completely renovated with thoughtful attention to detail, the tranquil intimate setting and comfortable surroundings instill a sense of timelessness. Air-conditioned guest bedrooms feature antique furnishings and a touch of romance. Many include harbor views. Walk to nearby shops, restaurants and the waterfront.

Innkeeper(s): Marianne Spaziano. $95-195. 5 rooms with PB. Breakfast included in rates. Types of meals: Cont plus and gourmet dinner. Restaurant on premises. Beds: Q. Cable TV, reading lamp and clock radio in room. Air conditioning. TV, fax and telephone on premises. Antiquing, fishing, live theater, parks, shopping, water sports and Newport mansion tours nearby.

Location: City.

Certificate may be used: Anytime Nov. 16-April 1; April-June, Tuesday-Thursday only.

Inntowne Inn

6 Mary St
Newport, RI 02840-3028
(401)846-9200 (800)457-7803 Fax:(401)846-1534
Internet: www.inntowneinn.com
E-mail: innkeeper@msn.com

Circa 1935. This Colonial-style inn is an elegant spot from which to enjoy the seaside town of Newport. Waverly and Laura Ashley prints decorate the individually appointed guest rooms, some of which have four-poster or canopy beds. The innkeeper serves an expanded continental breakfast with items such as fresh fruit, quiche and ham and cheese croissants. Afternoon tea also is served. A day in Newport offers many activities, including touring the Tennis Hall of Fame, taking a cruise through the harbor, shopping for antiques or perhaps taking a trek down Cliff Walk, a one-and-a-half-mile path offering the ocean on one side and historic mansions on the other. Parking is included in the rates.

Innkeeper(s): Carmella Gardner. $130-224. 26 rooms with PB, 1 suite. Afternoon tea included in rates. Types of meals: Cont plus. Beds: KQDT. Reading lamp and telephone in room. Air conditioning. VCR, fax, copier, parlor games and parking included in rates on premises. Antiquing, parks and shopping nearby.

"Thank you for your excellent service with a smile."

Certificate may be used: Nov. 1 to Feb. 28, Sunday through Thursday.

Jailhouse Inn

13 Marlborough St
Newport, RI 02840-2545
(401)847-4638 (800)427-9444 Fax:(401)849-0605
Internet: www.historicinnsofnewport.com
E-mail: vacation@jailhouse.com

Circa 1772. Listed in the National Register, this renovated inn was built in 1772 as a Colonial jail. Comfort, convenience and a stylish decor permeate the atmosphere today. Bright and cheery guest bedrooms and spacious suites offer air conditioning, tasteful furnishings, compact refrigerators and cable TV. Wake up to a continental breakfast buffet before exploring the harbor shops and restaurants only one block away. Relax on the porch with afternoon tea. Visit nearby historic Fort Adams. White Horse Tavern is across the street.

Innkeeper(s): Bryan Stovall. $55-280. 23 rooms with PB, 4 suites. Breakfast and afternoon tea included in rates. Types of meals: Cont and early coffee/tea. Beds: KQ. Modem hook-up, data port, cable TV, reading lamp, refrigerator, clock radio, telephone and desk in room. Air conditioning. Fax on premises. Limited handicap access. Antiquing, art galleries, beach, bicycling, canoeing/kayaking, fishing, golf, hiking, horseback riding, live theater, museums, parks, shopping, tennis, water sports and wineries nearby.

Location: City.

"I found this very relaxing and a great pleasure."

Certificate may be used: Nov. 10-May 10, Sunday through Friday.

The Melville House

39 Clarke St
Newport, RI 02840-3023
(401)847-0640 Fax:(401)847-0956
Internet: www.melvillehouse.com
E-mail: innkeeper@ids.net

Circa 1750. During the American Revolution this attractive National Register Colonial inn once housed aides to General Rochambeau. Reflecting its historic heritage, the interior decor features early American furnishings. Stay in the spacious Fireplace Suite. A full breakfast is served each morning that may include homemade scones, muffins or coffee cakes and stuffed French toast, pepper frittata or whole wheat pancakes. Take a pleasant walk from this 1750 inn to the waterfront and local sites.

Innkeeper(s): Bob & Priscilla Peretti. $110-175. 6 rooms with PB, 1 suite. Breakfast and afternoon tea included in rates. Types of meals: Full bkfst and early coffee/tea. Beds: KDT. Air conditioning. Fax, bicycles, parlor games, telephone and fireplace on premises. Antiquing, fishing, live theater, parks, shopping and water sports nearby.

Location: City.

Publicity: *Country Inns*, "Lodging Pick" for Newport, *Good Housekeeping* and *New York Post*.

"Comfortable with a quiet elegance."

Certificate may be used: Nov. 1-April 30, Sunday-Thursday, no holidays.

Victorian Ladies Inn

63 Memorial Blvd
Newport, RI 02840-3629
(401)849-9960
Internet: www.victorianladies.com
E-mail: info@victorianladies.com

Circa 1851. Innkeepers Donald and Helene have created a comfortable and welcoming atmosphere at this restored three-story Victorian inn and cottage. Intimate and inviting, this traditional New England bed & breakfast features spacious guest bedrooms furnished with period pieces, fine reproductions, rich fabrics and wallcoverings. Linger over a gracious breakfast in the dining room. Stroll through the award-winning gardens, walk over the small bridge and gaze at the koi pond. Relax in the living room while planning activities for the day. Walk to nearby beaches, the Colonial town and harbor front.

Innkeeper(s): Donald & Helene O'Neill. $125-275. 11 rooms with PB, 1 with FP. Breakfast included in rates. Types of meals: Full gourmet bkfst and veg bkfst. Beds: KQ. Cable TV, VCR, reading lamp, clock radio, telephone, desk and one with fireplace in room. Central air. Library, parlor games and fireplace on premises. Antiquing, art galleries, beach, bicycling, canoeing/kayaking, fishing, golf, hiking, horseback riding, live theater, museums, parks, shopping, tennis, water sports and wineries nearby.

Location: Ocean community.

Publicity: *Country Inns, Glamour, Bride Magazine, L.A. Times, Country Victorian, Yankee Magazine, Newport Life Magazine* and Voted Best Hotel/B&B by Newport Voters for 5 years.

"We want to move in!"

Certificate may be used: Feb. 15 to Dec. 15, Sunday-Thursday, (months of July and August excluded).

South Kingstown H5

Admiral Dewey Inn

668 Matunuck Beach Rd
South Kingstown, RI 02879-7053
(401)783-2090 (800)457-2090
Internet: www.admiraldeweyinn.com
E-mail: admiraldeweyinn@cox.net

Circa 1898. Although the prices have risen a bit since this inn's days as a boarding house (the rate was 50 cents per night), this Stick-style home still offers hospitality and comfort. The National Register inn is within walking distance of

Matunuck Beach. Guests can enjoy the sea breeze from the inn's wraparound porch. Period antiques decorate the guest rooms, some of which offer ocean views.

Innkeeper(s): Joan Lebel. $100-150. 10 rooms, 8 with PB. Breakfast included in rates. Types of meals: Cont plus, early coffee/tea and picnic lunch. Beds: QDT. VCR, fax, copier, parlor games, telephone and fireplace on premises. Antiquing, fishing, live theater, parks, shopping and water sports nearby.

Location: Ocean community. Free access to town beach.

Publicity: *Yankee Traveler and Rhode Island Monthly.*

Certificate may be used: Oct. 1 to May 1 (holiday weekends excluded). No weekends.

Wakefield   H5

Brookside Manor
380-B Post Rd
Wakefield, RI 02879
(401)788-3527 Fax:(401)788-3530
Internet: www.brooksidemanor.net
E-mail: allyson@brooksidemanor.net

Circa 1690. Both architecturally and historically, this Colonial manor house fits in the category of great country homes. Formerly part of a large estate, it has been converted into a luxurious inn. The original one-and-a-half-story, post and beam structure with hearth and chimney still stands. Enjoy public gathering rooms splendidly decorated and furnished with antiques and Oriental rugs. Dramatic guest bedrooms offer an escape to a relaxing yet refined elegance. Homemade sausage, scones, fruit and a frittata are typical af the breakfasts served. Eight acres of professionally landscaped gardens are bordered by brick and stone terraces. A pond and brook add a park-like setting.

Innkeeper(s): Allyson Huskisson & Bob Vitale. $150-250. 5 rooms with PB, 5 with FP. Breakfast, afternoon tea and snacks/refreshments included in rates. Types of meals: Full gourmet bkfst, veg bkfst, early coffee/tea and gourmet dinner. Beds: KQT. Modem hook-up, cable TV, reading lamp, clock radio, telephone, turn-down service, desk, voice mail and fireplace in room. Central air. Fax, copier, library, parlor games and fireplace on premises. Amusement parks, antiquing, art galleries, beach, bicycling, canoeing/kayaking, fishing, golf, hiking, horseback riding, live theater, museums, parks, shopping, sporting events, tennis, water sports and wineries nearby.

Location: Country.

Publicity: *The Italian Travel Magazine, Dove, Harper & Queens and Country Living.*

Certificate may be used: Nov. 1-May 14, Monday-Thursday.

Westerly   I2

Grandview B&B
212 Shore Rd
Westerly, RI 02891-3623
(401)596-6384 (800)447-6384 Fax:(401)596-3036
Internet: grandviewbandb.com
E-mail: info@grandviewbandb.com

Circa 1910. An impressive wraparound stone porch highlights this majestic Shingle Victorian inn, which also boasts a lovely ocean view from its hilltop site. The inn features 9 guest

rooms, a family room with cable TV, a spacious living room with a handsome stone fireplace, and a sun porch where visitors enjoy a hearty breakfast buffet. Antiquing, fishing, golf, swimming and tennis are found nearby as are Watch Hill, Mystic and Newport. The Foxwoods and Mohegan Sun casinos also are nearby.

Innkeeper(s): Patricia Grand. $85-115. 9 rooms, 4 with PB, 1 suite. Breakfast included in rates. Types of meals: Cont plus and early coffee/tea. Beds: KQDT. Reading lamp, refrigerator, ceiling fan, clock radio, 6 with ceiling fans, air conditioning and table fans in room. TV, VCR, fax, copier, library, parlor games, telephone, fireplace and large video library on premises. Antiquing, art galleries, beach, bicycling, canoeing/kayaking, fishing, golf, hiking, live theater, museums, parks, shopping, tennis, water sports, wineries and casinos nearby.

Location: Ocean community.

Certificate may be used: Anytime, November-April, subject to availability.

Woonsocket   A5

Pillsbury House Bed & Breakfast
341 Prospect Street
Woonsocket, RI 02895
(401)766-7983 (800)205-4112
Internet: www.pillsburyhouse.com
E-mail: rogerwnri@prodigy.net

Circa 1875. On an historic street in the fashionable North End, this restored Victorian mansion is one of the area's oldest. Boasting original parquet floors, high ceilings and furnished with antiques and period pieces, a grand elegance is imparted. Sit by the fire in the evenings or on the shaded porch during the day. A guest kitchenette on the second floor includes a microwave, refrigerator stocked with beverages, hair dryer and ironing board. Tastefully decorated guest bedrooms and a suite offer comfort and character. Breakfast in the gracious dining room is a satisfying meal with fresh fruit, homemade baked goods and a hot entree. Located in the heart of the Blackstone River Valley National Heritage Corridor, there is much to see and do.

Innkeeper(s): Susan & Roger Bouchard. $95-135. 4 rooms with PB. Breakfast included in rates. Types of meals: Full bkfst and veg bkfst. Beds: KQDT. Clock radio in room. Air conditioning. TV, VCR, fax, telephone, fireplace, complimentary juices, beer and water available in second floor refreshment area on premises. Antiquing, canoeing/kayaking, live theater, museums, parks, shopping, wineries, commuter train station to Boston 20 minutes away, 59 minute train ride to South Station and Museum of Work & Culture nearby.

Location: City.

Certificate may be used: Sunday through Thursday, year-round.

South Carolina

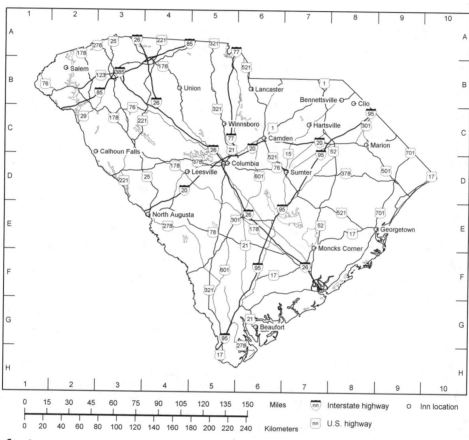

| | | | Interstate highway | | Inn location |
| nn | Interstate highway | | nn | U.S. highway | |

0 15 30 45 60 75 90 105 120 135 150   Miles
0 20 40 60 80 100 120 140 160 180 200 220 240   Kilometers

Beaufort   G6

The Beaufort Inn

PO Box 1257, 809 Port Republic St
Beaufort, SC 29901-1257
(843)521-9000 Fax:(843)521-9500
Internet: www.beaufortinn.com
E-mail: bftinn@hargray.com

Circa 1897. Every inch of this breathtaking inn offers something
special. The interior is decorated to the hilt with lovely furnishings, plants, beautiful rugs and warm, inviting tones. Rooms
include four-poster and canopy beds combined with the modern
amenities such as fireplaces, wet bars and stocked refrigerators.
Enjoy a complimentary full breakfast at the inn's gourmet restaurant. The chef offers everything from a light breakfast of fresh fruit,
cereal and a bagel to heartier treats such as pecan peach pancakes
and Belgium waffles served with fresh fruit and crisp bacon.

Innkeeper(s): Associated Luxury Inns of Beaufort. $145-350. 21 rooms with
PB, 9 with FP, 6 suites and 1 conference room. Breakfast included in rates.
Types of meals: Full gourmet bkfst, early coffee/tea, gourmet dinner and room
service. Restaurant on premises. Beds: KQ. Data port, cable TV, VCR, reading
lamp, refrigerator, ceiling fan and telephone in room. Air conditioning. Fax
and copier on premises. Antiquing, fishing, live theater, parks, shopping and
water sports nearby.

Location: Historic Landmark District.

Publicity: Beaufort, Southern Living,
Country Inns, Carolina Style, US Air and
Town & Country.

Certificate may be used: December,
January and February, Sunday through
Wednesday night only. Good only for four
rooms which have a rate of $195 or higher.

The Cuthbert House Inn B&B

1203 Bay St
Beaufort, SC 29902-5401
(843)521-1315 (800)327-9275 Fax:(843)521-1314
Internet: www.cuthberthouseinn.com
E-mail: cuthbert@hargray.com

Circa 1790. This 18th-century waterfront mansion, listed in the National Register, boasts a veranda overlooking Beaufort Bay. The home was built during Washington's presidency, and General W.T. Sherman was once a guest here. The home has been lovingly restored to its original grandeur. Rich painted walls are highlighted by fine molding. Hardwood floors are topped with Oriental rugs and elegant 19th-century furnishings. The morning meal is served in a breakfast room that overlooks the water. The surrounding area offers plenty of activities in every season, and for those celebrating a new marriage, a honeymoon suite is available.

Innkeeper(s): Gary & Sharon Groves. $155-265. 7 rooms with PB, 2 suites. Breakfast and snacks/refreshments included in rates. Types of meals: Country bkfst. Beds: KQ. Data port, cable TV, VCR, CD player, refrigerator, clock radio, telephone, voice mail, hair dryer, robes and some with fireplace or whirlpool in room. Air conditioning. Fax, bicycles, library, off-street parking and loaner beach towels and chairs on premises. Antiquing, fishing, parks, water sports, Parris Island USMC Depot, Ace Basin Tours and National Historic District tours nearby.

Location: Waterfront. Beaufort Bay-waterfront.

Publicity: *Beaufort Gazette, Atlanta Journal-Constitution, Glamour, Travel & Leisure, Delta Airlines Sky Magazine, Shape Magazine, Coastal Living, House & Garden Channel, White Squall and Top 10 Most Romantic Inns for 2002.*

Certificate may be used: Jan. 6 to Feb. 28, Sunday-Thursday.

Bennettsville   B8

Breeden Inn, Cottages & Retreat on Main

404 E Main St
Bennettsville, SC 29512
(843)479-3665 (888)335-2996 Fax:(843)479-7998
Internet: www.breedeninn.com
E-mail: info@breedeninn.com

Circa 1886. Three historic buildings in a village-like setting comprise this inn: the 1886 Southern mansion, the Carriage House and the Garden Cottage. One especially bountiful cotton crop paid for the construction of the mansion, which local attorney Thomas Bouchier presented to his bride as a wedding gift. The Main House exterior is graced with more than two dozen columns. The interior of each house features many interesting and varied architectural details. Suites and guest bedrooms delight with exquisite linens, antiques, collectibles, needlework and art. A satisfying morning meal is served in the dining room, breakfast parlor or on the veranda. Porch swings, rockers and ceiling fans are an inviting setting while overlooking the backyard wildlife habitat with trees and woodlands beyond.

Innkeeper(s): Wesley & Bonnie Park. $130-150. 10 rooms with PB, 9 with FP, 3 two-bedroom suites, 2 cottages, 2 guest houses and 1 conference room. Breakfast and snacks/refreshments included in rates. Types of meals: Full bkfst, veg bkfst and early coffee/tea. Beds: QDT. Data port, cable TV, VCR, reading lamp, refrigerator, ceiling fan, snack bar, clock radio, telephone, desk, voice mail, fireplace, one suite with sunken whirlpool, private phone lines, data port, hair dryer, iron/ironing board, full-length mirror, alarm clock, plush bed linens including down comforter and feather bed and fresh cut florals from the gar-

dens of the inn in room. Central air. Fax, copier, swimming, bicycles, parlor games, laundry facility, gift shop, in-ground swimming pool, period Koi pond, antique/collectibles shop, hammock, binoculars/field guide books for birding, bicycles, volleyball, piano, refreshment drink upon arrival, two parlors, gathering room, two laundry rooms and two fully equipped period kitchens on premises. Antiquing, art galleries, bicycling, fishing, golf, live theater, museums, parks, shopping, tennis, local antiquing, 600-acre Lake Wallace, walking trails, swimming, historic touring, birding, volleyball and board games nearby.

Location: Small Southern county seat town. Population 10,000.

Publicity: *Pee Dee, Sandlapper, South Carolina's Official Travel Guide: South Carolina Smiles, pictured on the official map for the state of S.C. and The National Wildlife Federation .*

"We were absolutely speechless at how lovely and comfortable our room was. Every detail was exquisite, especially the bedding. We had a wonderful romantic weekend. It was just what we were looking for and more. The gardens, your porches, the delicious food and your warm and friendly ways. Staying here was the highlight of our trip."

Certificate may be used: Year-round. Excludes special event dates and holidays.

Historic District Inns of Bennettsville

PO Box 826
Bennettsville, SC 29512
(843)479-2066 (800)248-0128 Fax:(843)479-2393
Internet: www.historicdistrictinns.com
E-mail: weamia@msn.com

Circa 1900. Three luxury inns: The Manse, The Ellerbe House and Hugh McColl Inn are situated in the quaint Historic District. All elegantly furnished with antiques, spacious suites offer sitting rooms, fireplaces and kitchens. Comfortable guest bedrooms feature thick comforters, fluffy pillows and plush linens. Continental breakfast is delivered to the room, and lunch is available in the on-site restaurant. This quiet but corporate-savvy town is centrally located to Myrtle Beach, S.C.; Pinehurst, N.C.; renown golf courses; and featured on the South Carolina Cotton Trail.

Innkeeper(s): Mary Altman. $75-125. 12 rooms with PB, 6 suites and 1 cottage. Beds: KQDT.

Certificate may be used: May 1 to Dec. 31, Sunday-Saturday.

Calhoun Falls   C2

Latimer Inn

PO Box 295
Calhoun Falls, SC 29628-0295
(864)391-2747 Fax:(864)391-2747
Internet: www.latimerinn.com
E-mail: latimerinn@wctel.net

Circa 1907. Thirty-seven acres surround this three-story Colonial inn. There is a tree-shaded porch and a balcony that stretches across the second story offering views out over the grounds. Some guest rooms offer high ceilings and whirlpool tubs and all have television and private baths. Guests may use the washer and dryer, fish cleaning area, boat hookups and the gas grill on the patio. A continental breakfast is provided. Calhoun Falls State Park is a mile away.

Innkeeper(s): Harrison & Anne Sawyer. $49-129. 17 rooms with PB, 1 with FP, 3 suites and 1 conference room. Types of meals: Full gourmet bkfst, gourmet dinner and room service. Beds: QDT. Cable TV, VCR, reading lamp, stereo, refrigerator, ceiling fan, snack bar, clock radio, telephone and hot tub/spa in room. Air conditioning. Fax, copier, spa, swimming, tennis, parlor games and fireplace on premises. Antiquing, fishing, golf, live theater, parks, shopping, sporting events, tennis, water sports, historical Abbeville and SC nearby.

Location: Historical Abbeville.

"We felt very welcome, enjoyed our stay, and will return."

Certificate may be used: Anytime, subject to availability.

Camden C6

A Camden, SC Bed & Breakfast

127 Union St
Camden, SC 29020-2700
(803)432-2366
Internet: www.camdenscbandb.com
E-mail: jerixon@tech-tech.com

Circa 1920. In a peaceful and convenient part of town, a furnished Gardener's Cottage provides the perfect place to relax and be refreshed. Stay from two nights to two months for a vacation, business trip, equine or sporting event. Leave all cares behind as southern comforts include tableware and linens, cable TV and Internet access. Pets are welcome. Explore the many activities and scenic sites of the area.

Innkeeper(s): Janie Erickson. $99-190. 3 rooms, 2 with FP, 3 suites and 2 cottages. Breakfast included in rates. Types of meals: Full gourmet bkfst, early coffee/tea, snacks/refreshments and room service. Beds: KQT. Reading lamp and turn-down service in room. Air conditioning. Fax, telephone, fireplace and Internet access on premises. Antiquing, fishing, golf, live theater, parks, shopping, tennis and water sports nearby.
Location: Historic town.

"It was great being pampered by you."
Certificate may be used: July 1-Aug. 1, Sunday-Thursday.

Candlelight Inn

1904 Broad St
Camden, SC 29020-2606
(803)424-1057
E-mail: candlelightinncamden@yahoo.com

Circa 1928. Two acres of camellias, azaleas and oak trees surround this Cape Cod-style home. As per the name, the innkeepers keep a candle in each window, welcoming guests to this homey bed & breakfast. The decor is a delightful and tasteful mix of country, with quilts, hand-crafted samplers, poster beds, family antiques and traditional furnishings. Each of the rooms is named for someone significant in the innkeeper's life, and a picture of the special person decorates each room. Guests will enjoy the hearty breakfast, which changes daily. Several of innkeeper Jo Ann Celani's recipes have been featured in a cookbook, and one recipe won a blue ribbon at the Michigan State Fair.

Innkeeper(s): Jo Ann & George Celani. $90-125. 3 rooms with PB, 1 suite. Breakfast and snacks/refreshments included in rates. Types of meals: Full bkfst and early coffee/tea. Beds: QT. TV, reading lamp, clock radio, telephone, turn-down service and desk in room. Air conditioning. Library, parlor games and fireplace on premises. Antiquing, art galleries, fishing, golf, live theater, parks, shopping, tennis and two steeplechase races nearby.
Location: Historic town.
Publicity: Chronicle-Independent, Sandlapper and Southern Inns and B&Bs.

"You have captured the true spirit of a bed & breakfast."
Certificate may be used: Based on availability excluding race weekends.

Clio B8

Henry Bennett House

301 Red Bluff St
Clio, SC 29525-3009
(843)586-9290
Internet: www.bennetthouse.com
E-mail: info@bennetthouse.com

A huge veranda, decorated with whimsical gingerbread trim, rambles around the exterior of this Victorian, which was built by a cotton farmer. A turret and widow's walk also grace the home. Clawfoot tubs and working fireplaces are some of the amenities found in the comfortable guest rooms. The area offers several golf courses and antiquing.

Innkeeper(s): Connie Hodgkinson. $55. 3 rooms. Breakfast included in rates. Types of meals: Full bkfst.
Certificate may be used: April-October.

Columbia D5

Chesnut Cottage B&B

1718 Hampton St
Columbia, SC 29201-3420
(803)256-1718 (888)308-1718
Internet: www.chestnutcottage.com
E-mail: ggarrett@sc.rr.com

Circa 1850. This inn was originally the home of Confederate General James Chesnut and his wife, writer Mary Boykin Miller Chesnut. She authored "A Diary From Dixie," written during the Civil War but published posthumously in 1905. The white frame one-and-a-half-story house has a central dormer with an arched window above the main entrance. The small porch has four octagonal columns and an ironwork balustrade. Hearty breakfasts are served in the privacy of your room, on the porch or in the main dining room. The innkeepers can provide you with sightseeing information, make advance dinner reservations, as well as cater to any other special interests you might have.

Innkeeper(s): Gale Garrett. $95-225. 5 rooms with PB, 3 with FP, 1 two-bedroom suite. Breakfast and snacks/refreshments included in rates. Types of meals: Country bkfst, veg bkfst, early coffee/tea and room service. Beds: KQ. Modem hook-up, data port, cable TV, VCR, reading lamp, stereo, refrigerator, ceiling fan, snack bar, clock radio, telephone, coffeemaker, turn-down service, desk and fireplace in room. Central air. Fax and copier on premises. Antiquing, art galleries, fishing, hiking, live theater, museums, parks, shopping, sporting events and water sports nearby.
Location: City.
Publicity: Sandlapper, London Financial Times, State Newspaper and TV show.

"You really know how to pamper and spoil. Chesnut Cottage is a great place to stay."
Certificate may be used: All year, Sunday through Thursday.

Georgetown E8

Live Oak Inn B&B

515 Prince St
Georgetown, SC 29440
(843)545-8658 (888)730-6004 Fax:(843)545-8948
Internet: www.liveoakinn.com
E-mail: info@liveoakinn.com

Circa 1905. Said to have lived five centuries, two live oaks spread their branches over this recently renovated Victorian. Some of the turn-of-the-century treasures in the home are its grand carved stairway, its columned entry and inlaid hardwood floors. There's a whirlpool in most of the guest rooms, and furnishings include family antiques and collections. (Sam's Rooms features quilts made by the family's grandmothers.)

Innkeeper(s): Fred & Jackie Hoelscher. $115-150. 3 rooms with PB, 3 with FP. Breakfast and snacks/refreshments included in rates. Types of meals: Full gourmet bkfst and early coffee/tea. Beds: KQDT. Modem hook-up, cable TV, VCR, reading lamp, ceiling fan, clock radio, telephone, desk, hot tub/spa and fireplace in room. Central air. Fax, copier, bicycles, library, parlor games and laundry facility on premises. Amusement parks, antiquing, art galleries, beach, bicycling, canoeing/kayaking, fishing, golf, hiking, live theater, museums, parks, shopping, sporting events, tennis, water sports and wineries nearby.

Location: Ocean community.

Publicity: *Southern Living, Sandlapper, Sun News, Charlotte Observer, A Taste of Charlotte, Georgetown Times and Southern Style.*

Certificate may be used: Anytime, November-April, subject to availability.

The Shaw House B&B

613 Cypress Ct
Georgetown, SC 29440-3349
(843)546-9663
E-mail: marydshaw@aol.com

Circa 1972. Near Georgetown's historical district is the Shaw House. It features a beautiful view of the Willowbank marsh, which stretches out for more than 1000 acres. Sometimes giant turtles come up and lay eggs on the lawn. Guests enjoy rocking on the inn's front and back porches and identifying the large variety of birds that live here. A Southern home-cooked breakfast often includes grits, quiche and Mary's heart-shaped biscuits.

Innkeeper(s): Mary & Joe Shaw. $65-90. 3 rooms with PB. Breakfast included in rates. Types of meals: Full bkfst, early coffee/tea and snacks/refreshments. Beds: KQ. Cable TV, reading lamp, stereo, ceiling fan, clock radio, telephone, turn-down service and desk in room. Air conditioning. TV, bicycles, library and fireplace on premises. Amusement parks, antiquing, fishing, live theater, parks, shopping and water sports nearby.

Location: City.

Publicity: *Charlotte Observer and Country.*

"Your home speaks of abundance and comfort and joy."

Certificate may be used: Sunday-Friday, anytime available.

Hartsville   C7

Missouri Inn B&B

314 E Home Ave
Hartsville, SC 29550-3716
(843)383-9553 Fax:(843)383-9553
Internet: www.missouri-inn.biz
E-mail: stay@missouriinn.com

Circa 1901. It is from the third owners of this Federal-style inn that it derives its name. The home was at that time owned by the innkeepers' grandparents, F.E. and Emily Fitchett, and "Missouri" was the nickname given to Emily by her son-in-law. The entire house, including the five guest rooms, are decorated with antiques, and features wallpaper original to the home. The full breakfasts are hearty and homemade. The home, located in the town historic district, is across the street from Coker College and four blocks from downtown Hartsville.

Innkeeper(s): Kyle & Kenny Segars. $75-85. 5 rooms with PB, 3 with FP. Breakfast included in rates. Types of meals: Full gourmet bkfst, early coffee/tea, lunch, afternoon tea and gourmet dinner. Beds: KQT. Cable TV, reading lamp, ceiling fan, clock radio, telephone, desk, robes, flowers, mints

and heated towel racks in room. Air conditioning. VCR, fax, copier, library, parlor games and fireplace on premises. Handicap access. Antiquing, fishing, golf, parks, tennis and water sports nearby.

Location: Small town, Historic District.

Certificate may be used: All days except Nascar weekends (March 20-22 and Labor Day weekend).

Lancaster   B6

Kilburnie, the Inn at Craig Farm

1824 Craig Farm Road
Lancaster, SC 29720
(803)416-8420 Fax:(803)416-8429
Internet: www.kilburnie.com
E-mail: jtromp@infoave.net

Circa 1828. The area's oldest surviving antebellum home, this Greek Revival was saved from demolition, moved to this 400-acre estate and extensively restored. Listed in the National Register, its historic and architectural significance is seen in the intricate details found in the public rooms. Experience Southern hospitality accented by European charm in a quiet and secluded setting with a classic elegance. Each guest bedroom and suite boasts a fireplace, as do two bathrooms. An unsurpassed two-course breakfast may include fresh-baked bread and muffins, a fruit appetizer of Poached Pears with Blueberries or Southern Pecan Peaches and a main entree of Oven-Shirred Eggs or Herbed Goat Cheese Omelette. Relax on one of the piazza rockers after a stroll on the nature path through the wildlife backyard habitat with bridges spanning the woodlands.

Innkeeper(s): Johannes Tromp. $125-175. 5 rooms with PB, 7 with FP, 1 suite and 1 conference room. Breakfast included in rates. Types of meals: Full gourmet bkfst and gourmet dinner. Beds: KQ. Modem hook-up, cable TV, VCR, reading lamp, clock radio, telephone, turn-down service, desk, hot tub/spa and fireplace in room. Central air. Fax, copier, library, fireplace and laundry facility on premises. Amusement parks, antiquing, golf, parks and shopping nearby.

Location: Country.

Publicity: *Sandlapper Magazine and Winner of the 2003 South Carolina Heritage Tourism Award.*

Certificate may be used: Anytime, Sunday-Thursday, except holidays.

Leesville   D4

The Able House Inn

244 E Columbia Ave
Leesville, SC 29070-9284
(803)532-2763 Fax:(803)532-2763
E-mail: ablehouse@pbtcomm.net

Circa 1939. This elegant, white brick home was built by a local druggist. Relax in the tastefully decorated living room or lounge on a comfy wicker chair among the large plants in the sunroom. Guest rooms, named after various relatives, boast beautiful amenities such as a canopied bed or window seats. Jennifer's Room opens into a sitting room with a window seat so large, some guests have snuggled down for a restful night's sleep instead of the large, brass and enamel four-poster bed.

Innkeepers offer guests snacks/refreshments in the evening and turndown service each night. Wake to freshly ground coffee before taking on the day. During the warmer months, innkeepers offer guests the use of their swimming pool.

Innkeeper(s): Jack & Annabelle Wright. $85-95. 5 rooms with PB, 1 suite. Breakfast and snacks/refreshments included in rates. Types of meals: Cont plus and early coffee/tea. Beds: QD. Cable TV, reading lamp, ceiling fan, clock radio, telephone, turn-down service and desk in room. Air conditioning. VCR, fax, copier, swimming, parlor games and fireplace on premises. Antiquing, fishing, golf, live theater, shopping, sporting events, tennis and water sports nearby.

Location: City.

Publicity: Sandlapper and State Newspaper.

"Thank you for the warm Southern welcome. Your place is absolutely beautiful, very inviting. The food was extraordinary!"

Certificate may be used: Sept. 1 to April 1.

Marion   C8

Montgomery's Grove

408 Harlee St
Marion, SC 29571-3144
(843)423-5220 (877)646-7721
Internet: www.bbonline.com/sc/montgomery

Circa 1893. The stunning rooms of this majestic Eastlake-style manor are adorned in Victorian tradition with Oriental rugs, polished hardwood floors, chandeliers and gracious furnishings. High ceilings and fireplaces in each room complete the elegant look. Guest rooms are filled with antiques and magazines or books from the 1890s. Hearty full breakfasts are served each day, and candlelight dinner packages can be arranged. Guests will appreciate this inn's five acres of century-old trees and gardens. The inn is about a half-hour drive to famous Myrtle Beach and minutes from I-95.

Innkeeper(s): Coreen & Richard Roberts. $90-120. 5 rooms, 3 with PB, 1 suite. Breakfast included in rates. Types of meals: Full bkfst, lunch, picnic lunch, afternoon tea and gourmet dinner. Beds: KQ. Antiquing, fishing, live theater and water sports nearby.

Publicity: Pee Dee Magazine, Sandlapper, Marion Star, Palmetto Places TV and Country Living.

Certificate may be used: Anytime except Labor Day weekend.

Moncks Corner   E7

Rice Hope Plantation Inn Bed & Breakfast

206 Rice Hope Dr
Moncks Corner, SC 29461-9781
(843)761-4832 (800)569-4038 Fax:(843)884-5020
Internet: www.ricehope.com
E-mail: lou@ricehope.com

Circa 1840. Resting on 285 secluded acres of natural beauty, this historic mansion sits among oaks on a bluff overlooking the Cooper River. A stay here is a visit to yesteryear, where it is said to be 45 short minutes and three long centuries from downtown Charleston. Formal gardens boast a 200-year-old camellia and many more varieties of trees and plants, making it a perfect setting for outdoor weddings or other special occasions. Nearby attractions include the Trappist Monastery at Mepkin Plantation, Francis Marion National Forest and Cypress Gardens.

Innkeeper(s): Jamie Edens. $85-165. 5 rooms with PB and 1 conference room. Breakfast included in rates. Types of meals: Full bkfst and early coffee/tea. Beds: KQD. TV, reading lamp, ceiling fan, clock radio and coffeemaker in room. Air conditioning. Copier, tennis, library, parlor games, telephone and fireplace on premises. Antiquing, art galleries, beach, bicycling,

canoeing/kayaking, fishing, golf, museums, parks, shopping and tennis nearby.

Location: Country, waterfront. Riverfront.

Publicity: "W" Fasion Magazine photo shoot, Green Power commercial, Japanese TV Documentary, Travel Channel, Haunted Inns and film location for "Consenting Adults" with Kevin Costner.

Certificate may be used: Sunday-Thursday, all year.

North Augusta   E4

Rosemary & Lookaway Halls

804 Carolina Ave
North Augusta, SC 29841
(803)278-6222 (800)642-9259 Fax:(803)278-4877
Internet: www.augustainns.com
E-mail: innkeeper@sandhurstestate.com

Circa 1902. These historic homes are gracious examples of Southern elegance and charm. Manicured lawns adorn the exterior of both homes, which appear almost as a vision out of "Gone With the Wind." The Rosemary Hall boasts a spectacular heart-of-pine staircase. The homes stand as living museums, filled to the brim with beautiful furnishings and elegant decor, all highlighted by stained-glass windows, chandeliers and lacy touches. Some guest rooms include Jacuzzis, while others offer verandas. A proper afternoon tea is served each afternoon at Rosemary Hall. The Southern hospitality begins during the morning meal. The opulent gourmet fare might include baked orange-pecan English muffins served with Canadian bacon or, perhaps, a Southern strata with cheese and bacon. The catering menu is even more tasteful, and many weddings, showers and parties are hosted at these inns.

Innkeeper(s): Sandra Croy. $125-225. 23 rooms with PB and 2 conference rooms. Breakfast and snacks/refreshments included in rates. Types of meals: Full bkfst and early coffee/tea. Beds: KQDT. Cable TV, reading lamp, clock radio, telephone, turn-down service and desk in room. Air conditioning. Fax, copier and fireplace on premises. Handicap access. Antiquing, fishing, parks, shopping, sporting events and water sports nearby.

Location: City.

Publicity: Conde' Naste preferred hotel and inn and Top 10 Bed and Breakfast in South Carolina.

Certificate may be used: Sunday-Thursday, excluding holidays and special events.

Salem   B2

Sunrise Farm B&B

325 Sunrise Dr
Salem, SC 29676-3444
(864)944-0121 (888)991-0121
Internet: www.bbonline.com/sc/sunrisefarm
E-mail: sfbb@bellsouth.net

Circa 1890. Situated on the remaining part of a 1,000-acre cotton plantation, this country Victorian features large porches with rockers and wicker. Guest rooms are furnished with period antiques, thick comforters, extra pillows and family heirlooms. The "corn crib" cottage is located in the original farm structure used for storing corn. It has a fully equipped kitchen, sitting area and bedroom with tub and shower. The June Rose Garden Cottage includes a river rock fireplace and full kitchen, as well as pastoral and mountain views. The inn offers a full breakfast, snacks and country picnic baskets. Children and pets are welcome.

Innkeeper(s): Barbara Laughter. $95-130. 4 rooms with PB and 2 cottages. Breakfast and snacks/refreshments included in rates. Types of meals: Full bkfst and picnic lunch. Beds: Q. TV, VCR, ceiling fan and free movies in

room. Air conditioning. Telephone, fireplace, llamas, miniature horses, goats, a pot belly pig, cats and dog on premises. Antiquing, fishing, parks, sporting events, water sports and boating nearby.
Location: Country, mountains.
Publicity: *National Geographic Traveler, Southern Living, Country Extra and Palmetto Places.*
Certificate may be used: Dec. 1-Feb. 28, Sunday-Thursday, cottages only.

Sumter   D7

Magnolia House
230 Church St
Sumter, SC 29150-4256
(803)775-6694 (888)666-0296

Circa 1907. Each room of this Greek Revival home with its five fireplaces is decorated in antiques from a different era. Also gracing the inn are inlaid oak floors and stained-glass windows. Sumter's historic district includes neighborhood heroes such as George Franklin Haynesworth, who fired the first shot of The War Between the States. Guests may enjoy an afternoon refreshment in the formal backyard garden. Breakfast is served in the large dining room with massive French antiques.

Innkeeper(s): Pierre & Liz Tremblay. $95-145. 5 rooms, 4 with PB, 1 suite. Breakfast included in rates. Types of meals: Full bkfst and early coffee/tea. Beds: QDT. TV, reading lamp, ceiling fan, clock radio, telephone, turn-down service and desk in room. Air conditioning. VCR, parlor games, fireplace and English gardens with fountains on premises. Antiquing, bicycling, canoeing/kayaking, fishing, golf, live theater, parks and shopping nearby.
Location: City.
Certificate may be used: Weekends only except holidays and special events.

Union   B4

The Inn at Merridun
100 Merridun Pl
Union, SC 29379-2200
(864)427-7052 (888)892-6020 Fax:(864)429-0373
Internet: www.merridun.com
E-mail: info@merridun.com

Circa 1855. Nestled on nine acres of wooded ground, this Greek Revival inn is in a small Southern college town. During spring, see the South in its colorful splendor with blooming azaleas, magnolias and wisteria. Sip an iced drink on the inn's marble verandas and relive memories of a bygone era. Soft strains of Mozart and Beethoven, as well as the

smell of freshly baked cookies and country suppers, fill the air of this antebellum country inn. In addition to a complimentary breakfast, guest will enjoy the inn's dessert selection offered every evening.
Innkeeper(s): Peggy Waller & JD, the inn cat. $99-125. 5 rooms with PB and 3 conference rooms. Breakfast included in rates. Types of meals: Full gourmet bkfst, early coffee/tea, gourmet lunch, picnic lunch, afternoon tea and gourmet dinner. Beds: KQT. Reading lamp, ceiling fan, clock radio, telephone, desk, TV/VCR and hair dryers in room. Air conditioning. Fax, copier, library, parlor games, fireplace, refrigerator on each floor for guest use, evening dessert and Miss Fannie's Tea Room on premises. Amusement parks, antiquing, fishing, parks, shopping, sporting events and water sports nearby.
Location: City.
Publicity: *Charlotte Observer, Spartanburg Herald, Southern Living, Atlanta Journal-Constitution, Sandlapper Magazine, SCETV, Prime Time Live, BBC Documentary and Marshall Tucker Band Music Video.*
Certificate may be used: Jan. 15-Nov. 15, Monday-Thursday.

Winnsboro   C5

Songbird Manor
116 N Zion St
Winnsboro, SC 29180-1140
(803)635-6963 (888)636-7698 Fax:(803)635-6963
Internet: www.bbonline.com/sc/songbird
E-mail: songbirdmanor@msn.com

Circa 1912. Influential local businessman Marcus Doty built this home, which features William Morris-style architecture. Doty made sure his home was a showplace from the beveled-glass windows to the molded plaster ceilings with extensive oak and chestnut woodwork. It was also the first home in the county to include indoor plumbing. Three of the guest rooms include the home's original clawfoot or pedestal tubs. All of the guest rooms have a fireplace. The gracious veranda is the location for afternoon refreshments and breakfast in good weather. Although

enjoying a lazy day on the inn's swings and rocking chairs is a favorite pastime, you may opt to bicycle through the Winnsboro's historic district or enjoy the area's abundance of outdoor activities, from hunting to fishing to golf.
Innkeeper(s): Susan Yenner. $65-110. 5 rooms with PB, 5 with FP, 1 suite. Breakfast included in rates. Types of meals: Full gourmet bkfst, picnic lunch and dinner. Beds: KQT. Cable TV, reading lamp, ceiling fan, clock radio, telephone and turn-down service in room. Air conditioning. VCR, fax, bicycles, library and parlor games on premises. Antiquing, fishing, museums, parks and water sports nearby.
Location: City.
Publicity: *Sandlapper and Herald Independent.*
"We had a very restful two-night stay in a beautiful surrounding."
Certificate may be used: Jan. 2-March 31, subject to availability.

South Dakota

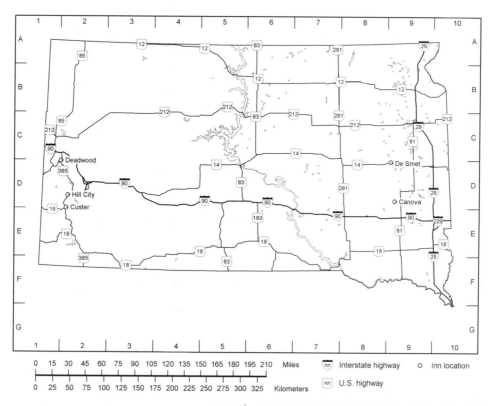

| | 1 | 2 | 3 | 4 | 5 | 6 | 7 | 8 | 9 | 10 |

0   15   30   45   60   75   90   105 120 135 150 165 180 195 210   Miles

0   25   50   75   100 125 150 175 200 225 250 275 300 325   Kilometers

Interstate highway   ○ Inn location

U.S. highway

Canova   D9

B&B at Skoglund Farm

24375 438 Avenue
Canova, SD 57321-9726
(605)247-3445

Circa 1917. This is a working farm on the South Dakota prairie. Peacocks stroll around the farm along with cattle, chickens, emu and other fowl. Guests can enjoy an evening meal with the family. The innkeepers offer special rates for families with children. The farm's rates are $30 per adult, $25 per teenager and $20 per child. Children age five and younger stay for free.

Innkeeper(s): Alden & Delores Skoglund.
$60. 4 rooms. Breakfast and dinner includ-

ed in rates. Types of meals: Full bkfst, early coffee/tea and snacks/refreshments. Beds: QDT. TV, reading lamp and clock radio in room. VCR, library and telephone on premises. Antiquing, fishing, parks, shopping, sporting events and water sports nearby.

Location: Country.

"Thanks for the down-home hospitality and good food."

Certificate may be used: Anytime, subject to availability.

Custer   D2

Custer Mansion B&B

35 Centennial Dr
Custer, SD 57730-9642
(605)673-3333 (877)519-4948 Fax:(605)673-6696
Internet: www.custermansionbb.com
E-mail: cusmanbb@gwtc.net

Circa 1891. Situated on one and a half acres of gardens and aspens, this two-story Gothic Victorian was built by one of the original Black Hills homesteaders. Architectural features include

Eastlake stick trim, seven gables and stained-glass windows. Antiques fill the guest bedrooms and honeymoon or anniversary suites and family suites. Enjoy a hearty breakfast of fresh fruits, home-baked goods, meats, creative egg dishes, pancakes, waffles and French toast before venturing out for a day of activities in the Black Hills. Conveniently located, all area attractions are close by. After a day of sightseeing, relax in the outdoor hot tub. Pastries and hot and cold beverages are always available.

Innkeeper(s): Bob & Patricia Meakim. $65-125. 6 rooms, 5 with PB, 1 suite. Breakfast, afternoon tea and snacks/refreshments included in rates. Types of meals: Full gourmet bkfst, veg bkfst and early coffee/tea. Beds: KQDT. Cable TV, VCR, reading lamp, ceiling fan, clock radio and hot tub/spa in room. Air conditioning. Spa, library, parlor games and telephone on premises. Antiquing, art galleries, beach, bicycling, canoeing/kayaking, fishing, golf, hiking, horseback riding, live theater, museums, parks, shopping, tennis and water sports nearby.

Location: Country. Black Hills.

Publicity: *Country Extra Magazine, National Historic Society, Midwest Living Magazine and Classic American Home.*

Certificate may be used: Oct. 11 to April 30, anytime, subject to availability.

De Smet   D9

Prairie House Manor B&B

RR 2, Box 61A
DeSmet, SD 57231-9428
(605)854-9131 (800)297-2416 Fax:(605)854-9001
Internet: www.prairiehousemanor.com
E-mail: info@prairiehousemanor.com

Circa 1894. Laura Ingalls Wilder wrote about the first owner of this house in her novel, "The Long Winter." The homey, country bed & breakfast offers rooms with items such as white iron beds, pedestal sinks and hardwood floors topped with rag rugs. Wilder was a resident of DeSmet, and the town features a church her father helped to build, as well as a schoolhouse where the author once taught. In addition to the six rooms in the main house, the innkeepers also offer a sportsman facility that is popular in the fall for pheasant hunters. Stay there in the summer to enjoy the great fishing at Lake Thompson, the state's new park. There's a game cleaning shed and freezers. The cottage has its own fully equipped kitchen and is self catering.

Innkeeper(s): Larry & Connie Cheney. $69-89. 6 rooms with PB. Breakfast included in rates. Types of meals: Full bkfst and early coffee/tea. Beds: KQDT. Cable TV, VCR, reading lamp, ceiling fan and clock radio in room. Air conditioning. Fax, bicycles, library, parlor games, telephone and one sportsman facility on premises. Antiquing, cross-country skiing, fishing, golf, live theater, parks, shopping, tennis, water sports and Laura Ingalls Wilder author's museum tours nearby.

Location: City. Small town of 1,200.

Publicity: *Plainsman.*

"It was so much fun to stay in the prettiest house on the prairie."

Certificate may be used: All year, Sunday through Thursday, call for reservations.

Deadwood   D2

Black Hills Hideaway B&B

HCR 73, Box 1129 (FS #247)
Deadwood, SD 57732-9712
(605)578-3054 Fax:(605)578-2028
Internet: www.enetis.net/~hideaway
E-mail: hideaway@enetis.net

Circa 1975. Guests enjoy the privacy of 67 wooded acres and views of mountain peaks at this bed & breakfast. The eight guest rooms are tucked into a mountain chalet-style home with cathedral ceilings and natural wood interior. The home is located on what was a wagon trail in the late 19th century. The decor is comfortable and there's a huge brick fireplace to enjoy. Each guest room has its own theme, including Western and European themes with antiques. Most rooms have a fireplace, deck and whirlpool or hot tubs. The innkeepers also offer a housekeeping cabin south of Pactola Lake. The home is about 40 miles from Mt. Rushmore and the Crazy Horse Monument. A gold mine, the Passion Play, Spearfish Canyon and other attractions are nearby. Deadwood, a historic national landmark, is 7 miles away.

Innkeeper(s): Ned & Kathy Bode. $109-179. 8 rooms with PB, 7 with FP. Breakfast and snacks/refreshments included in rates. Types of meals: Full bkfst, early coffee/tea and dinner. Beds: KQ. VCR, reading lamp, ceiling fan, clock radio, turn-down service, hot tub/spa and most with fireplace in room. Fax, copier, bicycles, parlor games, telephone, fireplace and robes on premises. Antiquing, cross-country skiing, downhill skiing, fishing, golf, hiking, gambling, snowmobiling and gold mines nearby.

Location: Mountains.

Certificate may be used: Sept. 16-May 15, Sunday-Thursday, subject to availability.

Hill City   D2

High Country Ranch B&B Trail Rides

12172 Deerfield Rd
Hill City, SD 57745
(605)574-9003 (888)222-4628 Fax:(605)574-9003
Internet: www.highcountryranch.com
E-mail: hcranch@rapidnet.com

Circa 1994. Ten cabins set on a grassy meadow offer skylights and private decks. Some have full kitchens, and there are special honeymoon and anniversary accommodations. The inn's special use permit allows guests to enjoy the Black Hills National Forest on horseback with half-day and full-day rides available. The dining room looks like a covered wagon. The ranch is close to Mount Rushmore.

Innkeeper(s): Larry and Bonnie McCaskell. $65-225. 10 cabins, 1 with FP. Breakfast included in rates. Types of meals: Full bkfst and early coffee/tea. Beds: Q. Cable TV, VCR, reading lamp, refrigerator, ceiling fan, clock radio and hot tub/spa in room. Air conditioning. Fax, copier, spa, stable, parlor games and telephone on premises. Handicap access. Cross-country skiing, downhill skiing, fishing, golf, live theater, parks, shopping, tennis, water sports, deer and turkey hunting, horseback riding and Mt. Rushmore nearby.

Location: Guest ranch.

Publicity: *Minnesota Monthly.*

Certificate may be used: Sept. 25-May 1.

Tennessee

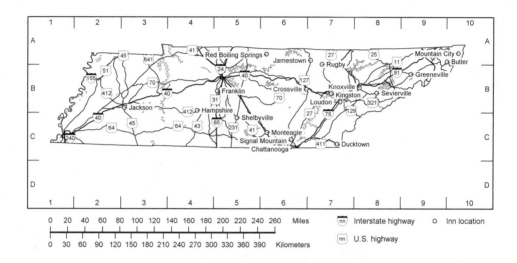

	1	2	3	4	5	6	7	8	9	10	

```
0  20  40  60  80  100 120 140 160 180 200 220 240 260   Miles
0  30  60  90  120 150 180 210 240 270 300 330 360 390   Kilometers
```

nn Interstate highway   o Inn location
nn U.S. highway

Butler   A10

Iron Mountain Inn B&B & Creekside Chalet

PO Box 30
Butler, TN 37640
(423)768-2446 (888)781-2399
Internet: www.ironmountaininn.com
E-mail: ironmtn@preferred.com

Circa 1998. Above the clouds on more than 140 acres, this light-filled log home offers breathtaking mountain views. Guest bedrooms feature private balconies and whirlpool tubs. Ask for the Memories or Equestrian with a steam shower. Coffee and sweets are delivered to the door before a full breakfast is served downstairs with tempting dishes such as crepes, Belgian waffles, souffles and omelettes. White-water rafting, horseback riding, fly-fishing or boating on Watauga Lake are favorite activities. This is the perfect location for a romantic wedding or elopement. The innkeeper will help plan a hassle-free, dream-fulfilled day within a budget. Ask about the year-round Sweetheart Special romantic getaway. Pampering includes an in-room massage or a private hideaway in the Creekside Chalet with a hot tub under the stars.

Innkeeper(s): Vikki Woods. $125-300. 4 rooms with PB. Breakfast, afternoon tea and snacks/refreshments included in rates. Types of meals: Veg bkfst and early coffee/tea. Beds: KQT. Modem hook-up, data port, reading lamp, ceiling fan, clock radio, turn-down service, whirlpools and breakfast in bed with reservation in room. Central air. Fax, copier, library, parlor games,

fireplace and laundry facility on premises. Antiquing, art galleries, canoeing/kayaking, cross-country skiing, downhill skiing, fishing, golf, hiking, horseback riding, live theater, water sports, Appalachian Trail, outlet shopping, ghost tours by boat and country auctions nearby.

Location: Mountains. Backs up to National Forest bordered by two creeks.

Publicity: *Awarded #1 Best Place to Stay, Elizabethton Star, USA Today, Johnson City Press, The Tennessee Magazine, Log Home, Country Magazine, Marquee Magazine and PBS.*

Certificate may be used: Anytime, November-April, subject to availability.

Chattanooga   C6

Mayor's Mansion Inn and Restaurant

801 Vine St
Chattanooga, TN 37403-2318
(423)265-5000 Fax:(423)265-5555
Internet: www.mayorsmansioninn.com
E-mail: info@mayorsmansioninn.com

Circa 1889. This former mayor's mansion of Tudor and Romanesque design was presented with the 1997 award for Excellence in Preservation by the National Trust. The interior of this gracious home boasts 16-foot ceilings and floors patterned

from three different woods. The large entrance hall features carved cornices, a coiffured ceiling and a fireplace. Every room offers something special, from Tiffany windows and beveled glass to the mansion's eight fireplaces and luxurious ballroom. The cornerstone of the Fortwood Historic District, Chattanooga's finest historic residential area, the mansion also has received the coveted City Beautiful Award.

Innkeeper(s): Carmen & Gene Drake. $150-295. 11 rooms with PB, 4 with FP, 3 suites. Breakfast included in rates. Types of meals: Full bkfst and gourmet dinner. Restaurant on premises. Beds: KQD. Data port, cable TV, VCR, reading lamp, CD player, snack bar, clock radio, telephone, turn-down service and desk in room. Air conditioning. Fax, copier, library, parlor games and fireplace on premises. Amusement parks, antiquing, fishing, live theater, parks, shopping, sporting events and water sports nearby.

Location: City.

Publicity: *Chattanooga News Free, Nashville Tennessean, Southern Accents, National Geographic, Preservation Magazine, Traveler, News Free Press, Blue Ridge Magazine, PBS, CBS and NBC.*

Certificate may be used: Sunday-Thursday, except May, October, Valentine's Day and other special times.

Crossville   B6

An-Jen Inn

8654 Hwy 127 North
Crossville, TN 38571
(931)456-0515
Internet: www.anjenbb.com
E-mail: anjenbb@multipro.com

Circa 1910. Innkeeper Sandra Monk-Goldston's family has lived on this 25-acre spread for seven generations. She was born in the turn-of-the-century house that now serves as a six-room bed & breakfast. She named her inn after two nieces, Andrea and Jennifer, and they each have a room named after them, as well. The inn is decorated in a nostalgic Victorian theme, with antiques and family pieces. In addition to the inn, Sandra operates the Fantasy Wedding Chapel in a adjacent building that resembles a tiny country church.

Innkeeper(s): Sandra & Ron Goldston. $85. 6 rooms. Breakfast included in rates. Types of meals: Full bkfst, early coffee/tea, lunch and dinner. Beds: D. Cable TV, VCR, reading lamp, stereo, refrigerator, ceiling fan, clock radio, telephone, turn-down service, desk and hot tub/spa in room. Air conditioning. Spa, swimming, fireplace and wedding chapel on premises. Amusement parks, antiquing, fishing, golf, live theater, parks, shopping, sporting events, tennis and water sports nearby.

Location: Country, mountains.

Publicity: *Tennessee Living.*

Certificate may be used: January-December, Monday-Thursday, except major holidays, $85 per night, two people per room.

Ducktown   C7

The White House B&B

104 Main St, PO Box 668
Ducktown, TN 37326-0668
(423)496-4166 (800)775-4166 Fax:(423)496-9778
Internet: www.bbonline.com/tn/whitehouse
E-mail: mardan@tds.net

Circa 1898. This Queen Anne Victorian boasts a wraparound porch with a swing. Rooms are decorated in traditional style with family antiques. Innkeepers pamper their guests with Tennessee hospitality, a hearty country breakfast and a mouth-watering sundae bar in the evenings. The innkeepers also help guests plan daily activities, and the area is bursting with possibilities. Hiking, horseback riding, panning for gold and driving tours are only a few choices. The Ocoee River is the perfect

place for a river float trip or take on the challenge of roaring rapids. The river was selected as the site of the 1996 Summer Olympic Whitewater Slalom events.

Innkeeper(s): Dan & Mardee Kauffman. $75-85. 3 rooms. Breakfast, afternoon tea and snacks/refreshments included in rates. Types of meals: Full gourmet bkfst and early coffee/tea. Beds: QT. Reading lamp, ceiling fan, clock radio and central heat in room. Central air. VCR, fax, library, parlor games, telephone and fireplace on premises. Antiquing, fishing, golf, parks, shopping and water sports nearby.

Location: Mountains. Small town in the mountains.

Publicity: *Southern Living.*

"From the moment we walked into your home, we sensed so much hospitality and warmth. You took such good care of us in every way and lavished so much love on us - and the food!!! Oh, my goodness!!! We'll just have to come back!"

Certificate may be used: Sunday through Thursday, April-November. Everyday, December through March. Holidays and special events excluded.

Franklin   B5

Namaste Acres Country Ranch Inn

5436 Leipers Creek Rd
Franklin, TN 37064-9208
(615)791-0333
Internet: www.namasteacres.com
E-mail: namastebb@aol.com

Circa 1993. This handsome Dutch Colonial is directly across the street from the original Natchez Trace. As the B&B is within walking distance of miles of hiking and horseback riding trails. Each of the suites includes private entrances and features individual themes. One room boasts rustic, cowboy decor with a clawfoot tub, hand-crafted furnishings, log and rope beds, and rough sawn lumber walls. The innkeepers chose the name Namaste from an Indian word, and carry an Indian theme in one of the guest rooms. Namaste Acres is just 12 miles outside of historic Franklin, which offers plenty of shops, a self-guided walking tour, Civil War sites and the largest assortment of antique dealers in the United States.

Innkeeper(s): Bill & Lisa Winters. $85-95. 3 rooms. Types of meals: Full bkfst. Beds: Q. Spa, swimming and guided trail rides on premises.

Publicity: *Southern Living, Western Horseman and Horse Illustrated.*

Certificate may be used: Year-round, Sunday-Thursday only. No holidays.

Greeneville   B9

Nolichuckey Bluffs

295 Kinser Park Lane
Greeneville, TN 37743-4748
(423)787-7947 (800)842-4690 Fax:(423)787-9247
Internet: www.usit.net/cabins
E-mail: cabins@usit.net

Circa 1997. Nolichuckey Bluffs is composed of five cabins located on 16 wooded acres overlooking the river. Redbud Cabin, for instance, offers two bedrooms, a kitchen, dining area, living room and private Jacuzzi. Six can sleep here, and there are generously sized decks, a fireplace and air conditioning. A full breakfast is served in the new country store. Best of all is the hot tub/gazebo perched high on the blufftop over the river.

Innkeeper(s): Patricia & Brooke Sadler. $90-130. 5 rooms with PB, 5 with FP. Breakfast included in rates. Types of meals: Full bkfst and snacks/refreshments. Beds: KQDT. TV, VCR, reading lamp, refrigerator, ceiling fan, clock radio, telephone, desk and hot tub/spa in room. Air conditioning. Fax, copier, bicycles, library, parlor games and canoes on premises. Antiquing, fishing, golf, parks, shopping and tennis nearby.

Location: Mountains.

Certificate may be used: Anytime, subject to availability.

Hampshire   B4

Ridgetop B&B

Hwy 412 W, PO Box 193
Hampshire, TN 38461-0193
(931)285-2777 (800)377-2770
E-mail: natcheztrace@worldnet.att.net

Circa 1979. This contemporary Western cedar house rests on 20 cleared acres along the top of the ridge. A quarter-mile below is a waterfall. Blueberries grow in abundance on the property and guests may pick them in summer. These provide the filling for luscious breakfast muffins, waffles and pancakes year-round. There are 170 acres in all, mostly wooded. Picture windows and a deck provide views of the trees and wildlife: flying squirrels, birds, raccoons and deer. The inn is handicap-accessible. The innkeepers will help guests plan excursions on the Natchez Trace, including biking trips.

Innkeeper(s): Bill & Kay Jones. $75-95. 3 rooms, 1 with FP, 1 cottage and 1 cabin. Breakfast included in rates. Types of meals: Full bkfst and early coffee/tea. Beds: DT. Reading lamp, refrigerator, ceiling fan, clock radio and desk in room. Air conditioning. Telephone and fireplace on premises. Handicap access. Antiquing, fishing, parks, shopping, water sports and antebellum homes nearby.

Location: Countryside.

Publicity: *Columbia Daily Herald.*

"What a delightful visit! Thank you for creating such a peaceful, immaculate, interesting environment for us!"

Certificate may be used: Nov. 15-March 1, excluding holidays and holiday weekends.

Jackson   B3

Highland Place B&B Inn

519 N Highland Ave
Jackson, TN 38301-4824
(731)427-1472
Internet: www.highlandplace.com
E-mail: relax@highlandplace.com

Circa 1911. Whether traveling for business or pleasure, a stay at this elegant Colonial Revival mansion will relax and inspire. Conveniently located in a quiet downtown historical district, the perfect blend of old and new furnishings provide luxurious comfort and modern convenience. Spacious barely describes the 10-foot-wide hallways, high ceilings, marble fireplace and many exquisite common rooms to gather in and dine together. An audio center enhances the gracious ambiance, and a video library offers further entertainment. The impressive guest bedrooms are well-appointed. Special attention is given to meet personal or corporate needs.

Innkeeper(s): Cindy & Bill Pflaum. $125-195. 4 rooms with PB, 2 with FP, 1 two-bedroom suite and 1 conference room. Breakfast included in rates. Types of meals: Full gourmet bkfst, early coffee/tea, afternoon tea, wine and gourmet dinner. Beds: KQT. Modem hook-up, data port, cable TV, VCR, reading lamp, stereo, ceiling fan, clock radio, desk and fireplace in room. Central air. Library, telephone and Internet access on premises. Antiquing, art galleries, bicycling, fishing, golf, live theater, parks, shopping, sporting events and tennis nearby.

Location: City.

Certificate may be used: Jan. 15-Dec. 15, Sunday-Saturday.

Jamestown   A7

Wildwood Lodge B&B, Cabins and Stables

3636 Pickett Park Hwy
Jamestown, TN 38556-5881
(931)879-9454 Fax:(801)382-3750
Internet: www.wildwoodlodge.ws
E-mail: wildwoodbed@twlakes.net

Circa 1990. Cradled by 27 acres of lush, wooded grounds with rolling hills and wildflower trails, this modern three-story lodge offers friendly, relaxed comfort. Lounge on extensive decks and hammocks or stroll amongst the gardens. Gather in the sitting room and browse the large library assortment. Inviting guest bedrooms feature warm, wood paneling, natural crafted furnishings, and hand-stitched quilts. Cabins and the Acorn Cottage are also available. Meet new friends over a hearty country breakfast. Visit the stables to go horseback riding or fish in the stocked pond.

Innkeeper(s): Reg and Julia Johnson, Clare Jung. $60-90. 19 rooms, 10 with PB, 1 cottage and 3 cabins. Breakfast included in rates. Types of meals: Country bkfst, veg bkfst, early coffee/tea, picnic lunch and gourmet dinner. Restaurant on premises. Beds: KQDT. TV, VCR, reading lamp, ceiling fan, clock radio, coffeemaker, desk and film library in room. Central air. Fax, copier, spa, stable, library, parlor games, telephone, fireplace, laundry facility and stocked fishing pond on premises. Limited handicap access. Antiquing, bicycling, canoeing/kayaking, fishing, golf, hiking, horseback riding, live theater, parks, shopping, tennis, water sports and wineries nearby.

Location: Country. National Park.

Certificate may be used: Anytime, Sunday-Thursday, not available in October or first 2 weeks of August.

Kingston   B7

Whitestone Country Inn

1200 Paint Rock Rd
Kingston, TN 37763-5843
(865)376-0113 (888)247-2464 Fax:(865)376-4454
Internet: www.whitestoneinn.com
E-mail: moreinfo@whitestoneinn.com

Circa 1995. This regal farmhouse sits majestically on a hilltop overlooking miles of countryside and Watts Bar Lake. The inn is surrounded by 360 acres, some of which borders a scenic lake where guests can enjoy fishing or simply communing with nature. There are eight miles of hiking trails, and the many porches and decks are perfect places to relax. The inn's interior is as pleasing as the exterior surroundings. Guest rooms are elegantly  appointed, and each includes a fireplace and whirlpool tub. Guests are treated to a hearty, country-style breakfast, and dinners and lunch are available by reservation. The inn is one hour from Chattanooga, Knoxville and the Great Smoky Mountains National Park.

Innkeeper(s): Paul & Jean Cowell. $150-270. 21 rooms with PB, 21 with FP and 2 conference rooms. Breakfast included in rates. Types of meals: Full bkfst, picnic lunch and dinner. Restaurant on premises. Beds: KQ. Cable TV, VCR, reading lamp, stereo, ceiling fan, clock radio, telephone, turn-down service, desk and hot tub/spa in room. Air conditioning. Fax, copier, spa, library, parlor games and fireplace on premises. Handicap

access. Antiquing, fishing, golf, shopping and water sports nearby.
Location: Country, mountains, waterfront. Lake.

"Not only have you built a place of beauty, you have established a sanctuary of rest. An escape from the noise and hurry of everyday life."
Certificate may be used: Jan. 1 to March 31, Sunday-Thursday.

Knoxville   B8

Maplehurst Inn
800 W Hill Ave
Knoxville, TN 37902
(865)523-7773 (800)451-1562
Internet: www.maplehurstinn.com
E-mail: sonny@maplehurstinn.com

Circa 1917. This townhouse, located in the downtown neighborhood of Maplehurst, is situated on a hill that overlooks the Tennessee River. A parlor with fireplace and piano invites guests to mingle in the evening or to relax quietly with a book. The inn's favorite room is the Penthouse with king bed, cherry furnishings and a sky lit Jacuzzi. The Anniversary Suite offers a double Jacuzzi and canopy bed. A light informal breakfast is served in the Garden Room overlooking the river, while breakfast casseroles, country potatoes, quiches and breads are offered buffet-style in the dining room. Check there for brownies and cookies if you come back in the middle of the day. The inn is within two blocks of the Convention Center and City Hall as well as several fine restaurants. The University of Tennessee and Neyland Stadium are nearby.

Innkeeper(s): Sonny & Becky Harben. $79-149. 11 rooms with PB, 1 suite. Breakfast and snacks/refreshments included in rates. Types of meals: Full gourmet bkfst, veg bkfst and early coffee/tea. Beds: KD. Cable TV, VCR, reading lamp, ceiling fan, clock radio, telephone, desk and some with Jacuzzi in room. Air conditioning. Laundry facility on premises. Antiquing, canoeing/kayaking, live theater, museums and parks nearby.
Location: City.
Certificate may be used: Anytime, subject to availability.

Loudon   B7

The Mason Place B&B
600 Commerce St
Loudon, TN 37774-1101
(865)458-3921 Fax:(865)458-6092
Internet: www.themasonplace.com
E-mail: thempbb@aol.com

Circa 1865. In the National Register, Mason Place is acclaimed for its award-winning restoration. In the Greek Revival style, the inn has a red slate roof and graceful columns. Three porches overlook three acres of lawns, trees and gardens. Inside, guests are welcomed to a grand entrance hall and tasteful antiques. There are 10 working fireplaces in the mansion's 7,000 square feet. Guests enjoy the Grecian swimming pool, gazebo and wisteria-covered arbor. A favorite honeymoon getaway has been created from the old smokehouse. It features brick walls and floors, a library loft, feather bed, wood burning Franklin fireplace and a tin bathtub (once featured in the movie Maverick).

Innkeeper(s): Bob & Donna Siewert. $96-135. 5 rooms with PB, 5 with FP. Breakfast included in rates. Types of meals: Full gourmet bkfst, early coffee/tea, picnic lunch and afternoon tea. Beds: Q. Reading lamp, clock radio and desk in room. Air conditioning. Fireplace, horseshoe and croquet on premises. Amusement parks, antiquing, fishing, parks, shopping, tennis, wineries and white water rafting nearby.
Location: City. Quaint Civil War town of 5,000.

Publicity: *Country Inn, Country Side, Country Travels, Tennessee Cross Roads, Antiquing in Tennessee, Knox-Chattanooga, Oak Ridge and Detroit Magazine.*

"Absolutely wonderful in every way. You are in for a treat! The best getaway ever!"
Certificate may be used: January, February, March, Sunday-Thursday.

Monteagle   C6

Adams Edgeworth Inn
Monteagle Assembly
Monteagle, TN 37356
(931)924-4000 Fax:(931)924-3236
Internet: www.adamsedgeworthinn.com
E-mail: innjoy@blomand.net

Circa 1896. Built in 1896 this National Register Victorian inn recently has been refurbished in a country-chintz style. Original paintings, sculptures and country antiques are found throughout. Wide verandas are filled with wicker furnishings and breezy hammocks, and there's an award-winning chef who will prepare delicious candle-lit dinners. You can stroll through the 96-acre Victorian village that surrounds  the inn and enjoy rolling hills, creeks and Victorian cottages. Waterfalls, natural caves and scenic overlooks are along the 150 miles of hiking trails of nearby South Cumberland State Park.

Innkeeper(s): Wendy Adams. $125-275. 10 rooms with PB, 10 with FP, 3 suites and 1 conference room. Breakfast included in rates. Types of meals: Full bkfst and gourmet dinner. Beds: KQD. Phone, air-conditioning and ceiling fan and some with TV in room. VCR, fax, copier, telephone and fireplace on premises. Antiquing, fishing, hiking, live theater, parks, shopping, sporting events, spelunking and historic architecture nearby.
Location: Mountains.

Publicity: *Country Inns, Chattanooga News Free Press, Tempo, Gourmet, Victorian Homes, Brides, Tennessean, Southern Living, National Geographic, Inn Country, PBS Crossroads, ABC TV, CBS TV and Travel Channel.*

Certificate may be used: January, February, March, November and December, Sunday-Thursday (except special events such as Valentine's, New Year's, etc. and subject to availability).

Mooresburg   B8

Home Place
132 Church Lane
Mooresburg, TN 37811
(423)921-8424 (800)521-8424 Fax:(423)921-8003
Internet: www.homeplacebb.com
E-mail: prisrogers@charter.net

Circa 1850. In a tranquil country setting cradled by trees, the architecture looks like a large New England home, but was actually built as a log cabin. It continues to be owned by the prominent Rogers family for all these generations. A casual and comfortable place to stay, the inn has antiques and heirlooms that add to the pleasant decor. Thoughtful attention is given to providing amenities such as a beverage-filled guest refrigerator. The family room features a gift shop selling the inn's locally made, private label soaps, candles and many other regional items.

Innkeeper(s): Priscilla Rogers. $45-65. 4 rooms, 2 with PB, 3 with FP and 1 conference room. Breakfast included in rates. Types of meals: Full bkfst, veg bkfst and early coffee/tea. Beds: KQDT. Cable TV, VCR, reading lamp and telephone in room. Central air. Fax, spa and fireplace on premises. Limited handicap access. Amusement parks, antiquing, fishing, golf, museums, parks, shopping, sporting events, tennis and water sports nearby.

Location: Country, mountains.

Certificate may be used: Anytime, subject to availability.

Mountain City   A10

Prospect Hill B&B Inn

801 W Main St (Hwy 67)
Mountain City, TN 37683
(423)727-0139 (800)339-5084
Internet: www.prospect-hill.com
E-mail: stay@prospect-hill.com

Circa 1889. This three-story shingle-style Victorian manor garners a great deal of attention from passersby with its appealing architecture and commanding hilltop location. Romantic rooms offer tall arched windows, 11-foot ceilings and spectacular views. Fashioned from handmade bricks, it was once home to Major Joseph Wagner, who, like many of his neighbors in far northeastern Tennessee, served on the Union side. The restored home features five guest rooms. A 1910 oak Craftsman dining set complements the oak Stickley furniture (circa 1997) that decorates the living room. Fireplaces, whirlpools and stained glass add luxury to the guest rooms. Prospect Hill boasts views of the Appalachian and Blue Ridge Mountains. From the front window, guests can see three states: Tennessee, Virginia and North Carolina. The inn is within an hour of the Blue Ridge Parkway, Appalachian Trail and Roan and Grandfather mountains, and the Virginia Creeper Trail.

Innkeeper(s): Judy & Robert Hotchkiss. $89-169. 5 rooms with PB, 4 with FP and 1 conference room. Breakfast and snacks/refreshments included in rates. Types of meals: Full gourmet bkfst, veg bkfst and early coffee/tea. Beds: KQT. Modem hook-up, data port, cable TV, VCR, reading lamp, ceiling fan, snack bar, clock radio, telephone, turn-down service, desk, fireplace, historic stained glass, balcony or porch, private entrance, bed for one child, scenic views and garden in room. Central air. Fax, copier, library, laundry facility and gift shop on premises. Limited handicap access. Antiquing, bicycling, canoeing/kayaking, cross-country skiing, downhill skiing, fishing, golf, hiking, horseback riding, live theater, museums, parks, shopping, water sports, wineries, mountain views, scenery, stables, swimming, fly fishing, outlets and drive-in movies nearby.

Location: Country, mountains. Small town America.

Publicity: *Marquee Magazine, Old-House Journal, Haunted Inns of the Southeast, USA Today (sleep with a ghost), Arrington's (named Most Romantic Hideaway 2004), Arrington's (Named Best Southern Inn 2004), Voted Most Romantic Hideaway (Arrington's-2003) and Best Southern Inn.*

"The most wonderful thing I'll always remember about our stay is, by far, the wonderful home we came back to each night."

Certificate may be used: Sunday to Thursday, except October and NASCAR weekends.

Red Boiling Springs   A6

Armours Hotel

321 E Main St
Red Boiling Springs, TN 37150-2322
(615)699-2180 Fax:(615)699-5111
Internet: www.armourshotel.com
E-mail: armourshotel@yahoo.com

Circa 1924. As Tennessee's only remaining mineral bathhouse, this two-story, National Historic Register house is tucked away in the rolling hills of the Cumberland Plateau. Whether resting in one of the 23 antique-furnished guest rooms, listening to the babbling creek from the second-floor veranda, strolling under covered bridges, or simply enjoying the sunrise in a rocking chair on the porch before breakfast, tranquillity awaits each guest. Spend the afternoon in the gazebo with your favorite book from the library next door, or get in a game of tennis at the park across the street before dinner.

Innkeeper(s): Reba Hilton. $59-149. 21 rooms, 18 with PB, 3 suites. Breakfast and dinner included in rates. Types of meals: Country bkfst and lunch. Beds: KQDT. Reading lamp, clock radio, desk and bath house (mineral and steam) in room. Air conditioning. TV, VCR, fax, copier, spa, telephone, fireplace and massage room on premises. Limited handicap access. Antiquing, fishing, golf, hiking, horseback riding, parks, tennis, water sports and wineries nearby.

Location: Country.

Publicity: *Southern Living, Tennessean and Country Crossroads.*

Certificate may be used: January through April.

Rugby   A7

Newbury House at Historic Rugby

Hwy 52, PO Box 8
Rugby, TN 37733-0008
(423)628-2441 (888)214-3400 Fax:(423)628-2266
Internet: www.historicrugby.org
E-mail: rugbytn@highland.net

Circa 1880. Mansard-roofed Newbury House first lodged visitors traveling to this English village when author and social reformer Thomas Hughes founded Rugby. Filled with authentic Victorian antiques, the inn includes some furnishings that are original to the colony. There are also several restored cottages on the property, and there is a two-room suite with a queen bed, two twin beds and a private bathroom.

Innkeeper(s): Historic Rugby. $66-90. 6 rooms, 4 with PB, 1 suite and 2 cottages. Breakfast included in rates. Types of meals: Full bkfst, early coffee/tea, lunch, picnic lunch and dinner. Restaurant on premises. Beds: QDT. Reading lamp, ceiling fan and desk in room. Air conditioning. Library, parlor games, telephone, fireplace and veranda on premises. Antiquing, fishing, parks, shopping, water sports, hiking, historic village and building tours nearby.

Location: Tiny village on Cumberland Pl.

Publicity: *New York Times, Americana, USA Weekend, Tennessean, Southern Living, Atlanta Journal-Constitution, Victorian Homes and A&E History Channel.*

"I love the peaceful atmosphere here and the beauty of nature surrounding Rugby."

Certificate may be used: June 1-Sept. 30 and Nov. 1-April 30, excluding Friday and Saturday nights.

Sevierville B8

Huckleberry Inn

1754 Sandstone Way
Sevierville, TN 37876-8816
(865)607-5913 (800)704-3278
Internet: www.rimstarintl.com
E-mail: hberryinn@aol.com

Circa 1992. Located on 25 acres outside Pigeon Forge, this finely built log home was purchased from its original builders. Beautifully crafted stone fireplaces, queen beds and whirlpool baths are features. Guests enjoy the screened porches, views of the Great Smoky Mountains and five-course breakfasts.

Innkeeper(s): Karan Bailey. $69-99. 3 rooms with PB, 2 with FP. Breakfast and snacks/refreshments included in rates. Types of meals: Full bkfst. Beds: Q. Reading lamp, clock radio and refreshments in room. Air conditioning. VCR, fax, parlor games, telephone and fireplace on premises. Handicap access. Amusement parks, antiquing, downhill skiing, fishing, golf, live theater, parks, shopping, sporting events and water sports nearby.

Location: Mountains.

Publicity: *Smoky Mountain News and Log Home Living.*

Certificate may be used: Sunday-Thursday, January-May, excluding holidays.

Shelbyville C5

Cinnamon Ridge B&B

799 Whitthorne St
Shelbyville, TN 37160-3501
(931)685-9200 (877)685-9200 Fax:(931)684-0978
Internet: www.bbonline.com/tn/cinnamon/
E-mail: cinnamonridge@cafes.net

Circa 1927. Tennessee offers many reasons to visit, not the least of which is this hospitable home. The light scent of cinnamon permeates the home, which is decorated with antiques in a mix of Colonial and Traditional styles. Innkeeper Pat Sherrill loves to pamper guests, especially with food. The full breakfasts are accompanied by candlelight and soft, soothing music. Pat serves afternoon teas and has created a few special events, including her Chocolate Lovers' Paradise, where guests enjoy a variety of cocoa-laden delicacies.

Innkeeper(s): Bill & Pat Sherrill. $65-75. 5 rooms with PB and 1 conference room. Breakfast, afternoon tea and snacks/refreshments included in rates. Types of meals: Full bkfst and early coffee/tea. Beds: KD. Cable TV, reading lamp, ceiling fan, clock radio, telephone, desk and central heat in room. Central air. VCR, fax, bicycles and fireplace on premises. Amusement parks, antiquing, fishing, live theater, parks, shopping and water sports nearby.

Location: City. Rolling hills, historic area.

Certificate may be used: Jan. 7-Nov. 13, Sunday through Wednesday.

Signal Mountain C6

Roost Guest House

1607 Anderson Pike
Signal Mountain, TN 37377-3523
(423)886-7509
E-mail: robinpaint@earthlink.net

Circa 1997. Located on two peaceful wooded acres, this guest house features exposed barn beams, a skylight, cathedral ceilings and picture windows. The décor is rustic with custom cabinetry and paintings of local artists. Amenities include a dishwasher, microwave, refrigerator, TV and VCR, breakfast nook and sitting room. Families enjoy staying here when visiting for reunions and weddings. Breakfasts are made to order. Choices range from vegetarian to all-American to heart healthy. Galleries, one-of-a-kind shops and cafes are close by.

Innkeeper(s): Robin Howe Townsend. $95. 2 rooms, 1 with PB. Breakfast included in rates. Types of meals: Full bkfst and early coffee/tea. Beds: QDT. TV, VCR, reading lamp, refrigerator, clock radio, telephone and coffeemaker in room. Air conditioning. Fireplace, basketball, play yard and gardens on premises. Antiquing, art galleries, hiking, live theater, museums, parks and sporting events nearby.

Location: Private secluded mountain setting just minutes from Chattanooga.

Certificate may be used: All year, Sunday-Friday, holidays excluded.

Texas

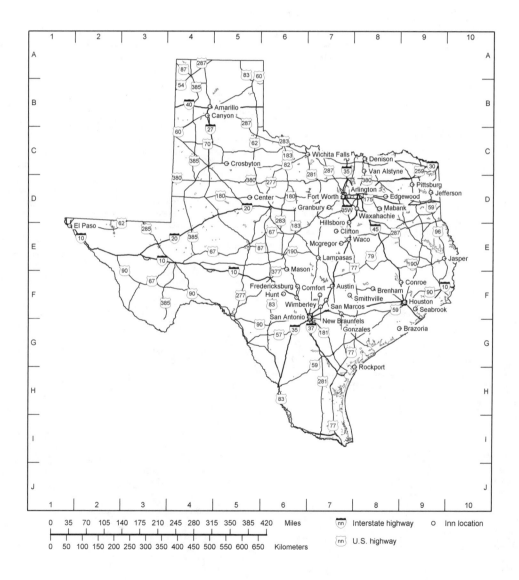

Amarillo   B4

Parkview House B&B

1311 S Jefferson St
Amarillo, TX 79101-4029
(806)373-9464 Fax:(806)373-3166
Internet: members.aol.com/parkviewbb
E-mail: parkviewbb@aol.com

Circa 1908. Ionic columns support the wraparound wicker-
filled front porch of this Prairie Victorian. Antique mahogany,
oak and walnut furnishings highlight the inviting interior.
Gather by the fireplace in the eclectic country kitchen with a
hot beverage. Themed guest bed-
rooms and a cozy cottage feature
fabric-draped bedsteads and a
romantic ambiance. A delicious
continental-plus breakfast is
served in the formal dining room.
Herb and rose gardens are accented by statuary and gazing balls.

Relax on the tree-shaded porch, or enjoy the tranquility of the
Koi pond. Borrow a bicycle to explore the neighborhood. Shop
along Historic Route 66, hike in Palo Duro Canyon or watch an
award-winning outdoor musical play, to name just a few of the
many area attractions and cultural activities. At the end of the
day, soak in the hot tub under a canopy of stars.

Innkeeper(s): Carol & Nabil Dia. $75-135. 5 rooms, 3 with PB, 1 suite and
1 cottage. Breakfast included in rates. Types of meals: Full gourmet bkfst,
early coffee/tea and snacks/refreshments. Beds: QD. TV, reading lamp, clock
radio, hot tub/spa, some ceiling fans, desks and telephones in room. Air conditioning. VCR, fax, bicycles, parlor games, telephone and fireplace on
premises. Amusement parks, antiquing, bicycling, hiking, horseback riding,
live theater, parks, shopping, tennis, water sports and bird watching nearby.
Location: City.
Publicity: *Lubbock Avalanche, Amarillo Globe News, Accent West, Sunday
Telegraph Review and Channel 7.*

*"You are what give B&Bs such a wonderful reputation. Thanks very
much for the wonderful stay! The hospitality was warm and the
ambiance incredible."*

Certificate may be used: Anytime, Monday to Thursday, excluding some
holidays and weekends, based on availability. American Historic Inns must
be mentioned.

Arlington   D7

The Sanford House Bed & Breakfast

506 N Center St
Arlington, TX 76011-7145
(817)861-2129 (877)204-4914 Fax:(817)861-2030
Internet: www.thesanfordhouse.com
E-mail: chriss@thesanfordhouse.com

Circa 1997. Metroplex residents consider this premier bed &
breakfast in the historic downtown area to be their favorite local
getaway. The frame two-story house is decorated in French
Country and offers well-appointed guest bedrooms named after
famous composers. Stay in the hunter green and burgandy
Beethoven room with a marble gas fireplace. In both the Strauss
and Bach rooms, double doors lead out to a veranda overlooking the garden gazebos, waterfalls and arbors. Private cottages
instill romance and pampering. Relax by firelight on the leather
sofa in the living area. The oversized bathroom includes a garden tub and separate shower. Sleep soundly in the bedroom's

sleigh bed. Breakfast is a delicious feast with favorites like
seafood crepes, quiche, hash brown casserole, biscuits and
gravy. Swim in the pool or visit the on-site spa and salon. An
abundance of entertaining attractions are within easy reach.

Innkeeper(s): Mike & Chris Speights. $99-200. 12 rooms with PB, 5 with FP,
4 cottages and 1 conference room. Breakfast and snacks/refreshments included in rates. Types of meals: Full gourmet bkfst, veg bkfst, early coffee/tea,
afternoon tea and gourmet dinner. Beds: KQT. Data port, cable TV, VCR,
reading lamp, stereo, refrigerator, ceiling fan, snack bar, clock radio, telephone, coffeemaker, desk, hot tub/spa, voice mail and fireplace in room.
Central air. Fax, copier, spa, swimming, library, parlor games, fireplace, laundry facility and Sanford Spa & Salon on premises. Handicap access.
Amusement parks, antiquing, art galleries, bicycling, hiking, live theater,
museums, parks, shopping and sporting events nearby.
Location: City. Only blocks from the Arlington Entertainment District, Six
Flags, Hurricane Harbor and Arlington Ballpark.
Certificate may be used: Anytime, Sunday-Thursday.

Austin   F7

Austin Governors' Inn

611 W 22nd St
Austin, TX 78705-5115
(512)477-0711 (800)871-8908 Fax:(512)476-4769
Internet: www.governorsinnaustin.com
E-mail: governorsinn@earthlink.net

Circa 1897. This Neoclassical Victorian is just a few blocks
from the University of Texas campus and three blocks from the
State Capitol. Guests can enjoy the view of two acres of trees
and foliage from the porches that decorate each story of the
inn. The innkeepers have decorated the guest rooms with
antiques and named them after former Texas governors. Several
of the bathrooms include clawfoot tubs.

Innkeeper(s): Lisa Wiedemann. $59-139. 10 rooms with PB, 5 with FP and 1
conference room. Breakfast, afternoon tea and snacks/refreshments included in
rates. Types of meals: Full gourmet bkfst, early coffee/tea and picnic lunch.
Beds: KQ. Cable TV, reading lamp, ceiling fan, clock radio, telephone, turn-
down service, desk, hair dryers and robes in room. Air conditioning. VCR, fax,
copier, parlor games and fireplace on premises. Handicap access. Antiquing,
fishing, live theater, parks, shopping, sporting events and water sports nearby.
Location: City.
Publicity: *USA Today, Instyle, Voted best B&B in 1997, 1998, 1999, 2000,
2001 by the Austin Chronicle and Romantic Inns of America.*

Certificate may be used: May 1-Sept. 30, Sunday-Thursday, not valid on
holidays.

Carrington's Bluff

1900 David St
Austin, TX 78705-5312
(512)479-0638 (888)290-6090 Fax:(512)478-2009
Internet: www.carringtonsbluff.com
E-mail: phoebe@carringtonsbluff.com

Circa 1877. Situated on a tree-covered bluff in the heart of
Austin, this inn sits next to a 500-year-old oak tree. The
innkeepers combine down-home hospitality with English
charm. The house is filled with English and American antiques
and handmade quilts. Rooms are carefully decorated with dried
flowers, inviting colors and antique beds, such as the oak barley twist bed in the Martha Hill Carrington Room. After a
hearty breakfast, relax on a 35-foot-long porch that overlooks
the bluff. The Austin area is booming with things to do.

Innkeeper(s): Phoebe & Jeff Williams. $89-149. 8 rooms with PB and 1 con-
ference room. Breakfast and snacks/refreshments included in rates. Types of
meals: Full gourmet bkfst and early coffee/tea. Beds: KQDT. Cable TV, reading
lamp, ceiling fan, clock radio, telephone and desk in room. Air conditioning.
TV, VCR, fax, copier, library, child care, parlor games and fireplace on premises. Amusement parks, antiquing, fishing, live theater, parks, shopping, sporting events and water sports nearby.

Location: City.
Publicity: *PBS Special.*

"Victorian writer's dream place."
Certificate may be used: Anytime, subject to availability.

Woodburn House B&B

4401 Avenue D
Austin, TX 78751-3714
(512)458-4335 (888)690-9763 Fax:(512)458-4319
Internet: www.woodburnhouse.com
E-mail: woodburnhouse@yahoo.com

Circa 1909. This stately home was named for Bettie Hamilton Woodburn, who bought the house in 1920. Hamilton's father was once the provisional governor of Texas and a friend of

Abraham Lincoln. The home once was slated for demolition and saved in 1979 when George Boutwell bought the home for $1 and moved it to its present location. Guests will be taken immediately by the warmth of the home surrounded by old

trees. The home is furnished with period antiques. Breakfasts are served formally in the dining room.
Innkeeper(s): Herb & Sandra Dickson. $90-140. 5 rooms, 4 with PB, 1 two-bedroom suite. Breakfast included in rates. Types of meals: Full gourmet bkfst and early coffee/tea. Beds: KQT. Modem hook-up, data port, cable TV, reading lamp, stereo, ceiling fan, clock radio, telephone, desk, two-person whirlpool, double vanity, sitting room with sofa and suite has TV/VCR in room. Central air. VCR, fax and massage en suite (with reservation) on premises. Antiquing, bicycling, fishing, hiking, live theater, parks, shopping, sporting events, tennis, museums-Elisabet Ney, Bob Bullock and LBJ Library nearby.
Location: City. Central Austin.
Publicity: *Austin Chronicle, Dallas Morning News, USA Today and Hard Promises.*
"The comfort, the breakfasts and the hospitality were excellent and greatly appreciated."
Certificate may be used: Sunday-Thursday, no holidays, excluding February, March, April, October & November.

Brazoria   G8

Roses & The River

7074 County Road 506
Brazoria, TX 77422
(979)798-1070 (800)610-1070 Fax:(979)798-1070
Internet: www.roses-and-the-river.com
E-mail: hosack@roses-and-the-river.com

Circa 1980. This Texas farmhouse rests beside the banks of the San Bernard River. There is a sweeping veranda lined with rockers, and the two-acre grounds are well landscaped with an impressive rose garden. Each of the three guest rooms has been decorated with a rose theme. Rooms are named New Dawn, Rainbow's End and Rise 'n Shine. Two rooms view the river and one views the rose gardens. Breakfasts include unique treats such as a "blushing orange cooler," baked Alaska grapefruit, homemade sweet rolls and savory egg dishes. The area offers many attractions, including two wildlife refuges, Sea Center Texas, where guests can learn about marine life, the Center for the Arts and Sciences and several historical sites.
Innkeeper(s): Mary Jo & Dick Hosack. $125-150. 3 rooms with PB. Breakfast included in rates. Types of meals: Full gourmet bkfst, veg bkfst, early coffee/tea and hors d'oeuvres. Beds: Q. Cable TV, VCR, reading lamp, ceiling fan, clock radio, telephone, coffeemaker and desk in room. Central air. Fax, copier, library, fireplace and laundry facility on premises. Amusement

parks, antiquing, beach, fishing, golf, live theater, museums, parks, shopping, water sports and wineries nearby.
Location: Country, waterfront.
Publicity: *Brazosport Facts.*
Certificate may be used: Anytime, subject to availability.

Brenham   F8

Mariposa Ranch B&B

8904 Mariposa Ln
Brenham, TX 77833-8906
(979)836-4737 (877)647-4774
Internet: www.mariposaranch.com
E-mail: info@mariposaranch.com

Circa 1865. Several buildings comprise the inn: a Victorian, an 1820 log cabin, a quaint cottage, a farmhouse and a 1836 Greek Revival home. Guests relax on the veranda, stroll through the Live Oaks or explore the ranch's 100 acres of fields and meadows. The inn is furnished with fine antiques. Ask for the Texas Ranger Cabin and enjoy a massive stone fireplace, sofa, clawfoot tub and loft with queen bed. Jennifer's Suite boasts a king

canopy bed and two fireplaces. The "Enchanted Evening" package offers champagne, fruit, flowers, candlelight, candy and an optional massage. Guests can select a room with a Jacuzzi for two or a clawfoot tub for additional luxury.
Innkeeper(s): Johnna & Charles Chamberlain. $79-250. 11 rooms with PB, 7 with FP, 2 suites, 5 cottages, 1 guest house, 4 cabins and 2 conference rooms. Breakfast included in rates. Types of meals: Full bkfst, veg bkfst, early coffee/tea, gourmet lunch, picnic lunch, snacks/refreshments, gourmet dinner and room service. Beds: KQDT. TV, VCR, reading lamp, CD player, refrigerator, ceiling fan, clock radio, hot tub/spa and fireplace in room. Central air. Fax, copier, library, parlor games, telephone, fireplace and laundry facility on premises. Antiquing, fishing, golf, live theater, parks, shopping, tennis and water sports nearby.
Location: Country. Texas hill country.
Publicity: *Southern Living, Texas Monthly, "D" Magazine and Austin American.*
Certificate may be used: Anytime, Sunday-Thursday, except holidays, special events or spring break.

Canyon   B4

Historical Hudspeth House

1905 4th Ave
Canyon, TX 79015-4023
(806)655-9800 (800)655-9809 Fax:(806)655-7457
Internet: www.hudspethinn.com
E-mail: jaokill@netscape.com

Circa 1909. Artist Georgia O'Keefe was once a guest at this three-story prairie home, which serves as a bed & breakfast. The home boasts many impressive architectural features, including an expansive entry with stained glass and a grandfather clock. The parlor boasts 12-foot ceilings and antiques, other rooms include chandeliers and huge fireplaces. Guests can arrange to have a candlelight dinner in their room.
Innkeeper(s): John & Connie Okill. $75-150. 8 rooms with PB, 5 with FP, 2 suites and 2 conference rooms. Breakfast included in rates. Types of meals: Early coffee/tea. Beds: KQ. Cable TV, reading lamp, ceiling fan, clock radio, telephone and five with fireplaces in room. Air conditioning. Fax, copier, spa and fireplace on premises. Amusement parks, antiquing, live theater, parks and sporting events nearby.
Location: City.
Publicity: *Southern Living and Valentine Getaways.*
Certificate may be used: January, March, September, October, Sunday-Thursday only.

Center   D5

Pine Colony Inn

500 Shelbyville St
Center, TX 75935-3732
(936)598-7700 (866)731-7700
Internet: www.pinecolonyinn.com
E-mail: pinecolony@classicnet.net

Circa 1945. This inn is a restored hotel with more than 8,000 square feet of antique-filled rooms. Artwork from local artist Woodrow Foster adorns the walls. These limited-edition prints are framed and sold by the innkeepers. The town is located between Toledo Bend, which has one of the largest man-made

lakes in the United States, and Lake Pinkston, where the state record bass (just under 17 pounds) was caught in 1986. Ask the innkeepers about all the little-out-of-the-way places to see either by foot, bicycle or car.

Innkeeper(s): Marcille Hughes. $55-75. 12 rooms with PB, 5 suites. Breakfast included in rates. Types of meals: Full bkfst and early coffee/tea. Beds: KQD. Cable TV, VCR, reading lamp, stereo, refrigerator, ceiling fan, clock radio, telephone, turn-down service, desk, kitchenette, microwave, French doors and balcony in room. Air conditioning. TV, fax, stable, gift shop, art gallery, framing shop and high-speed Internet on premises. Handicap access. Amusement parks, antiquing, art galleries, golf, hiking, horseback riding, museums, parks, shopping, sporting events, water sports, bass fishing, Big Thicket National Preserve and Angelina National Forest nearby.
Location: City.
Publicity: *Inn Traveler.*
Certificate may be used: All days except Thanksgiving Day, Christmas Eve and New Year's Eve. All other days are acceptable.

Clifton   E7

Heart Cottage Bed & Breakfast

178 CR 3242
Clifton, TX 76634
(254)675-3189
Internet: www.heartcottage.com
E-mail: heartcottagebnb@htcomp.net

Circa 1909. Boasting panoramic views of rolling prairie land, this contemporary-styled Victorian guest house features heart-shaped architectural details. The signature heart theme also is found in decorative touches and collections. A vaulted ceiling in the living area and sleeping loft enhances spaciousness. Books, games, a satellite TV and videos are provided. A fully equipped kitchen includes breakfast items to enjoy as desired. Relax on an Adirondack chair on the wood porch after visiting the local sites.

Innkeeper(s): Vivian Ender. $110-145. 1 cottage. Breakfast and snacks/refreshments included in rates. Types of meals: Cont plus. Beds: QT. Cable TV, VCR, reading lamp, refrigerator, ceiling fan, clock radio, coffeemaker, fully equipped kitchen, parlor games and videos in room. Air conditioning. Antiquing, art galleries, canoeing/kayaking, fishing, golf, live theater, museums, parks, shopping, tennis and water sports nearby.
Location: Country. 15 minutes from President George W. Bush's ranch.
Certificate may be used: Anytime, Sunday-Thursday.

Comfort   F6

Idlewilde

115 Hwy 473
Comfort, TX 78013
(830)995-3844
E-mail: idlewilde@omniglobal.net

Circa 1902. Known as a "Haven in the Hills" this Western-style farmhouse and surrounding grounds were a girls' summer camp for more than sixty years. Experience a quiet privacy in one of the two air-conditioned cottages that feature kitchenettes and wood-burning stoves. The innkeepers offer a

morning meal in the main house dining area or wherever desired, even breakfast in bed. Tennis courts, a pool and a pavilion provide pleasant diversions.

Innkeeper(s): Hank Engel & Connie Engel & Nicholas Engel. $85-115. 2 cottages. Breakfast included in rates. Types of meals: Full bkfst and picnic lunch. Beds: Q. Amusement parks, antiquing, fishing, golf, shopping, sporting events and water sports nearby.
Publicity: *Austin Chronicle and Hill Country Recorder.*
Certificate may be used: Any night, year-round, except holidays.

Conroe   F9

Heather's Glen . . . A B&B & More

200 E Phillips St
Conroe, TX 77301-2646
(936)441-6611 (800)665-2643 Fax:(936)441-6603
Internet: www.heathersglen.com
E-mail: heathersbb@aol.com

Circa 1900. This turn-of-the-century mansion still maintains many of its original features, such as heart-of-pine flooring, gracious staircases and antique glass windows. Verandas and covered porches decorate the exterior, creating ideal places to relax. Guest rooms are decorated in a romantic, country flavor. One room has a bed draped with a lacy canopy, and five rooms include double Jacuzzi tubs. Antique shops, an outlet mall and Lake Conroe are nearby, and the home is within an hour of Houston.

Innkeeper(s): Ed & Jamie George. $90-250. 13 rooms, 8 with PB, 3 with FP and 3 conference rooms. Breakfast, afternoon tea and snacks/refreshments included in rates. Types of meals: Full gourmet bkfst and early coffee/tea. Beds: QD. Cable TV, reading lamp, CD player, refrigerator, ceiling fan, clock radio, telephone, turn-down service, desk and hot tub/spa in room. Air conditioning. Fax, copier, parlor games and fireplace on premises. Handicap access. Amusement parks, antiquing, downhill skiing, fishing, live theater, parks, shopping, sporting events, water sports and auctions weekly nearby.
Location: City, country.
Publicity: *HGTV-If Walls Could Talk.*
Certificate may be used: Jan. 1-Dec. 31, Monday-Thursday, subject to availability.

Crosbyton   C5

Smith House Inn

306 W Aspen St
Crosbyton, TX 79322-2506
(806)675-2178
Internet: www.smithhousebnb.com
E-mail: smithhousebnb@texasonline.net

Circa 1921. Built as a boarding house, this inn proudly shares much of its original furnishings in its transformation to a bed

& breakfast inn. A guest register that dates to 1921 is fun to peruse and the original player piano still is the focal point of entertainment in the parlor. The dining room, with capacity for 35, is the location for a full Texan breakfast of homemade bread, meat and egg dishes. A variety of rooms include the Bridal suite with private sitting room and large bath.

Innkeeper(s): Terry & Karen Ellison. $60-125. 11 rooms, 7 with PB, 1 suite and 2 conference rooms. Breakfast included in rates. Types of meals: Full bkfst. Beds: KQDT. Air conditioning. VCR, parlor games and telephone on premises. Antiquing, fishing, parks and water sports nearby.

Location: Country. Ranching.

Certificate may be used: Weekdays and weekend if one weekday is included, i.e. Sunday/Monday or Thursday/Friday, year-round.

Denison C8

Inn of Many Faces Victorian Bed & Breakfast

412 W Morton St
Denison, TX 75020-2422
(903)465-4639 Fax:(903)465-3328
Internet: www.innofmanyfaces.com
E-mail: theinn@sbcglobal.net

Circa 1897. Resplendently sitting in the middle of towering pecan trees on two wooded acres, this restored Queen Anne Victorian provides rest and relaxation. A collection of whimsical faces are displayed throughout the house and gardens. Themed guest bedrooms offer spacious accommodations. The Katy Room is a romantic retreat that boasts a fireplace and whirlpool bath. The Cabbage Rose Room overlooks the lawn and gardens, gazebo and gold fish pond. In the morning, savor fresh fruit, a baked entree, breakfast meats, hot breads and muffins. Located near Lake Texoma allows for easy access to boating and fishing. Play golf on one of several area courses, shop for antiques or browse local art galleries.

Innkeeper(s): Charlie & Gloria Morton. $109-139. 4 rooms with PB, 2 with FP and 1 conference room. Breakfast and snacks/refreshments included in rates. Types of meals: Full gourmet bkfst, veg bkfst and early coffee/tea. Beds: KQD. Cable TV, VCR, reading lamp, ceiling fan, clock radio, hot tub/spa and fireplace in room. Central air. Fax, copier, parlor games, telephone, fireplace and massages available on premises. Antiquing, art galleries, fishing, golf, hiking, horseback riding, live theater, museums, parks, shopping, sporting events, tennis, water sports and wineries nearby.

Location: City.

Publicity: *Dallas Morning News, Texas Highways, Herald Democrat and McKinney Courier-Gazette.*

Certificate may be used: Anytime, Sunday-Thursday.

Edgewood D8

Crooked Creek Farm B&B

621 VZCR 3110
Edgewood, TX 75117-4620
(903)896-1284 (800)766-0790
Internet: www.cantonfleamarket.com/crookedcreek/

Circa 1977. This traditional brick house, which is found in a rural community of 1,300, is nestled on the edge of the East Texas timberline. Not far from the Greater Dallas area, the farm covers more than 100 acres where cattle graze and hay is grown and baled. Trees, a creek, nature trails, and four fishing ponds are on the property. A hearty country breakfast may feature ham and bacon, eggs, seasoned hash browns, biscuits and gravy as well as a fruit dish served with home baked sweet breads. The menu varies daily. In town, Heritage Park Museum

offers turn-of-the-century restored buildings furnished to represent the rural life of a century ago.

Innkeeper(s): Dorthy Thornton. $75. 6 rooms. Breakfast included in rates. Types of meals: Full bkfst and early coffee/tea. Beds: KQDT. Reading lamp, ceiling fan and clock radio in room. Air conditioning. VCR, outdoor games, fishing and complimentary evening desserts with coffee or soft drinks on premises. Antiquing, golf, shopping, Tyler Rose Garden, Caldwell Zoo and state of the art fish hatchery nearby.

Location: Country.

"What a wonderful time we spent at your B&B. We were spoiled, entertained and well fed. Can't wait to come back."

Certificate may be used: All year, except Canton Texas "First Monday Trade Days" weekend each month.

El Paso E1

Sunset Heights B&B

717 W Yandell Dr
El Paso, TX 79902-3837
(915)544-1743 Fax:(915)544-5119

Circa 1905. This luxurious inn is accentuated by palm trees and Spanish-style arches. Inside, bedrooms are filled with antiques and boast brass and four-poster beds. Breakfast is a five- to eight-course feast prepared by innkeeper Richard Barnett. On any morning, a guest might awake to sample a breakfast with Southwestern flair, including Eggs Chillquillas and pit-smoked Machakas, a combination of smoked beef, avocado and onion. Juice, fresh coffee, tea, dessert and fresh fruits top off the meal, which might begin with caviar and quiche. Enjoy the morning meal in the dining room or spend breakfast in bed.

Innkeeper(s): Mrs. Mel Martinez. $75-150. 5 rooms with PB, 1 with FP, 1 suite, 1 cottage and 1 conference room. Breakfast included in rates. Types of meals: Full gourmet bkfst, picnic lunch and gourmet dinner. Beds: KQD. Cable TV, VCR, reading lamp, refrigerator, ceiling fan, clock radio, telephone and turn-down service in room. Air conditioning. TV, fax, copier, spa, swimming and parlor games on premises. Amusement parks, antiquing, parks, shopping and sporting events nearby.

Location: City.

Publicity: *Southwest Profile and Pony Soldiers.*

Certificate may be used: Year-round, except weekends and holidays.

Fort Worth D7

Azalea Plantation B & B

1400 Robinwood Dr
Fort Worth, TX 76111-4950
(817)838-5882 (800)687-3529
Internet: www.azaleaplantation.com
E-mail: Rmlinnartz@aol.com

Circa 1948. Called the best-kept secret in the metro-plex, this historic plantation-style home is surrounded by two acres of magnolias, azaleas and majestic oaks. It proudly features pristine Southern hospitality and pays special attention to small details and personal touches that pamper. Antiques highlight the Victorian decor and ambiance. An elegant parlor with a warm fire is an inviting place to review local dining guides and menus. Romantic guest bedrooms and suites include whirlpool baths, CD players and terry robes. Gaze at the collection of chintz china in the dining room where a bountiful breakfast is served buffet style. The grounds and gardens offer yard games and sitting areas in the gazebo and wooden swing.

Innkeeper(s): Martha & Richard Linnartz. $125-159. 5 rooms, 2 with PB, 2 suites and 1 conference room. Breakfast included in rates. Types of meals: Full gourmet bkfst, veg bkfst, early coffee/tea and snacks/refreshments. Beds: KQD. Modem hook-up, TV, reading lamp, stereo, refrigerator, ceiling fan, clock radio, coffeemaker, turn-down service, hot tub/spa and 2 rooms in main house with balconies overlooking the front yard fountain in room. Central air. Fax, library, parlor games, telephone, fireplace, romantic gazebo in side meadow, rear parking and walking path through beautiful park on premises. Amusement parks, antiquing, art galleries, beach, fishing, golf, horseback riding, live theater, museums, parks, sporting events and wineries nearby.
Location: City. Minutes from downtown Fort Worth.
Certificate may be used: Anytime, Sunday-Thursday.

MD Resort Bed & Breakfast

601 Old Base Road
Fort Worth, TX 76078
(817)489-5150 Fax:(817)489-5036
Internet: www.mdresort.com
E-mail: innkeeper@mdresort.com

Circa 2001. Stay at a home away from home at this antique-filled country lodge and working ranch on 37 T-shaped acres. Enjoy a large meeting room, living room with big screen TV, game room and limited access to the full kitchen. Each of the guest bedrooms is decorated in a theme, such as German, Western, Victorian or safari, to name just a few. A full home-cooked breakfast will satisfy the heartiest of appetites. A completely furnished barn apartment also is available. The large spa and swimming pool are especially refreshing interludes after a nature walk. Lunch and dinner are served by reservation. A laundry room is accessible when needed.

Innkeeper(s): Wendy or Marcus. $69-279. 14 rooms, 12 with PB, 3 suites, 1 cottage, 1 cabin and 1 conference room. Breakfast included in rates. Types of meals: Country bkfst, lunch, picnic lunch, snacks/refreshments, dinner and room service. Beds: KQ. Modem hook-up, cable TV, VCR, reading lamp, refrigerator, ceiling fan, clock radio, coffeemaker and wireless high-speed Internet access in room. Central air. Fax, copier, spa, swimming, stable, library, pet boarding, parlor games, telephone, fireplace, laundry facility, gift shop and recreation room with pool table on premises. Handicap access. Amusement parks, antiquing, art galleries, bicycling, fishing, golf, hiking, horseback riding, live theater, museums, parks, shopping, sporting events, water sports, Texas Motor Speedway and Exotic Feline Sanctuary nearby.
Location: City, country. 37-acre working ranch, in the country and close to the city.
Publicity: *Wise County Messenger and Times Record.*
Certificate may be used: Sunday-Thursday, except on holidays or TMS (Texas Motor Speedway) weekends. Cannot be combined with any other offers.

Miss Molly's Bed & Breakfast, Inc

109 1/2 W Exchange Ave
Fort Worth, TX 76106-8508
(817)626-1522 (800)996-6559 Fax:(817)625-2723
Internet: www.missmollyshotel.com
E-mail: missmollys@travelbase.com

Circa 1910. An Old West ambiance permeates this hotel, which once was a house of ill repute. Miss Josie's Room, named for the former madame, is decked with elaborate wall and ceiling coverings and carved oak furniture. The Gunslinger Room is filled with pictures of famous and infamous gunfighters. Rodeo memorabilia decorates the Rodeo Room, and twin iron beds and a pot belly stove add flair to the Cowboy's Room. Telephones and TV sets are the only things missing from the rooms, as the innkeeper hopes to preserve the flavor of the past.
Innkeeper(s): Dawn Street. $125-200. 7 rooms, 1 with PB, 1 suite. Breakfast included in rates. Types of meals: Full bkfst and early coffee/tea. Restaurant on premises. Beds: DT. Reading lamp and ceiling fan in room. Air conditioning. Fax, copier, parlor games and telephone on premises. Amusement parks, antiquing, live theater, shopping, sporting events and stockyards National Historic district nearby.

Publicity: *British Bulldog, Arkansas Gazette, Dallas Morning News, Fort Worth Star-Telegram, Continental Profiles, Fort Worth Gazette and Eyes Of Texas.*
Certificate may be used: Year-round, Sunday through Thursday excluding holidays and Stockyards annual special event dates.

Texas White House B&B

1417 8th Ave
Fort Worth, TX 76104-4111
(817)923-3597 (800)279-6491 Fax:(817)923-0410
Internet: www.texaswhitehouse.com
E-mail: txwhitehou@aol.com

Circa 1910. A spacious encircling veranda shaded by an old elm tree, graces the front of this two-story home located within five minutes of downtown, TCU, the zoo and many other area attractions. The inn's parlor and living room with fireplace and gleaming hardwood floors are the most popular spots for relaxing when not lingering on the porch. Guest rooms are equipped with phones and television, and early morning coffee is provided before the inn's full breakfast at a time convenient to your personal schedule. Suites include hot tub, sauna and fireplace. Baked egg casseroles and freshly made breads are served to your room or in the dining room. The owners are Fort Worth experts and keep abreast of cultural attractions and are happy to help with reservations and planning. The inn is popular with business travelers — secretarial services are available, etc. — during the week and appealing to couples on weekends.
Innkeeper(s): Grover & Jamie McMains. $105-205. 5 rooms with PB and 1 conference room. Breakfast and snacks/refreshments included in rates. Types of meals: Full gourmet bkfst, early coffee/tea and room service. Beds: Q. Modem hook-up, data port, cable TV, VCR, reading lamp, ceiling fan, clock radio, telephone, coffeemaker, turn-down service and desk in room. Central air. Fax, fireplace and laundry facility on premises. Antiquing, art galleries, golf, live theater, museums and parks nearby.
Location: City.
Certificate may be used: Sunday-Thursday, no holidays. Nights must be consecutive; May 1-Sept. 30.

Fredericksburg   F6

Alte Welt Gasthof (Old World Inn)

PO Box 628
Fredericksburg, TX 78624
(830)997-0443 (888)991-6749 Fax:(830)997-0040
Internet: www.texas-bed-n-breakfast.com
E-mail: stay@texas-bed-n-breakfast.com

Circa 1915. Located on the second floor above a Main Street shop, Alte Welt is in a Basse Block building in the historic district. The entryway opens to an antique-filled foyer. A three-room suite offers a white sofa, silver accents including a silver, tin ceiling, wood floors and an antique iron four-poster bed draped in soft gauze. An armoire with TV and a small refrigerator and microwave add convenience. The innkeeper collects antique, crocheted and embroidered linens for the guest rooms. There is a spacious deck with hot tub adjoining one of the suites. Together, the two suites can accommodate as many as 6 people, so it is popular with families and small groups, who enjoy the freedom of simply going downstairs to Main Street and all its boutiques, shops and restaurants.
Innkeeper(s): Ron & Donna Maddux. $150-165. 2 suites. Breakfast included in rates. Types of meals: Cont and early coffee/tea. Beds: Q. Cable TV, reading lamp, refrigerator, ceiling fan, clock radio, telephone, desk, hot tub/spa, microwave and coffee bar in room. Air conditioning. Antiquing, fishing, golf, parks, shopping, tennis, museums and hunting nearby.
Certificate may be used: Jan. 2 to Feb. 5 and Sept. 3-23, Sunday-Thursday, suite No. 1 only.

Gonzales   F7

Boothe House B&B

706 Saint George St.
Gonzales, TX 78629
(830)672-7509 (877)245-0011
Internet: www.bbonline.com/tx/boothehouse
E-mail: aldawn@the-cia.net

Circa 1913. Restoration of this Neoclassical Colonial home has been a labor of love. Great attention was given to the historic preservation of details like paint colors, design and materials used. Even the landscaping was returned to its original beauty with antique roses and a fish pond. The vintage-filled guest bedrooms, two with working fireplaces, adjoin a sitting room that can connect suites. A gourmet, organic breakfast is seasoned with herbs from the garden. The owner makes muffins, cinnamon rolls, scones, crepes, jams, preserves, salsa and granola in addition to various hot entrees. Enjoy swimming in the full-size pool and visiting the many local sites.

Innkeeper(s): Dawn & Al O'Donnell. $95-140. 4 rooms with PB, 2 with FP, 2 suites and 1 cottage. Breakfast and snacks/refreshments included in rates. Types of meals: Full gourmet bkfst, early coffee/tea, picnic lunch and gourmet dinner. Beds: QD. Cable TV, VCR, reading lamp, refrigerator, clock radio, coffeemaker and fireplace in room. Central air. Swimming, parlor games, telephone and fireplace on premises. Limited handicap access. Antiquing, bicycling, canoeing/kayaking, fishing, golf, hiking, live theater, museums, parks and shopping nearby.

Location: City.

Publicity: *Texas Highways and Texmoto.*

Certificate may be used: January-March, Sunday-Thursday and August, Sunday-Thursday.

St. James Inn

723 Saint James St
Gonzales, TX 78629-3411
(830)672-7066 Fax:(830)672-7787
Internet: www.stjamesinn.com
E-mail: email@stjamesinn.com

Circa 1914. A premiere bed & breakfast ideally located in the original Old Town Historic District, this three-story home was built by a cattle baron and encompasses 10,000 square feet. A casual elegance is found throughout the inn, featuring the hardwood floors, a tiled solarium and parlor. The cheerfully decorat-

ed guest bedrooms and suite with fireplaces and porches encourage relaxation. Feast on a sumptuous four-course gourmet breakfast. Enjoy a fun day in the local rural setting that is often compared to scenic European areas.

Innkeeper(s): Ann & J.R. Covert. Call for rates. 5 rooms with PB, 5 with FP, 1 suite and 1 conference room. Breakfast and afternoon tea included in rates. Types of meals: Full gourmet bkfst and early coffee/tea. Beds: KQ. TV in room. Antiquing, fishing, golf, museums, parks, shopping and walking and driving tours nearby.

Location: Downtown.

Publicity: *Gonzales Inquirer, Houston Chronicle, Victoria Advocate, Austin American Statesman and San Antonio Express-News.*

"We had a wonderful weekend. It's a marvelous home and your hospitality is superb. We'll be back."

Certificate may be used: Feb. 1-Sept. 15, guest pays for breakfast.

Granbury   D7

Dabney House B&B

106 S Jones St
Granbury, TX 76048-1905
(817)579-1260 (800)566-1260
Internet: www.flash.net/~safe-dabney
E-mail: safe-dabney@flash.net

Circa 1907. Built during the Mission Period, this Craftsman-style country manor boasts original hardwood floors, stained-glass windows and some of the original light fixtures. The parlor and dining rooms have large, exposed, wooden beams and the ceilings throughout are 10-feet high. The Dabney Suite has a

private entrance into an enclosed sun porch with rattan table and chairs that allow for a private breakfast or a candlelight dinner by advance reservation. The bedroom of this suite is furnished with a four-post tester bed with drapes and an 1800 wardrobe.

Innkeeper(s): John & Gwen Hurley. $75-110. 4 rooms with PB, 1 suite. Breakfast and snacks/refreshments included in rates. Types of meals: Full bkfst. Beds: Q. Reading lamp, ceiling fan, clock radio and desk in room. Air conditioning. VCR, spa, library, parlor games, telephone, hot tub, evening beverage and dinner available with 48 hour notice on premises. Antiquing, fishing, live theater, parks, shopping and water sports nearby.

Location: Small town.

Publicity: *Fort Worth Star Telegram and Dallas Morning News.*

Certificate may be used: Year-round, Sunday night through Friday night. Excludes holidays and festivals (no Saturday night).

Hillsboro   D7

Tarlton House B&B Retreat Center

211 N Pleasant St
Hillsboro, TX 76645-2115
(254)582-7216 (800)823-7216 Fax:(254)582-3776

Circa 1895. Steeply pitched gables punctuate the roof line of this light blue and white Queen Anne Victorian. A veranda curves around the front and side. The entrance door contains 123 pieces of beveled glass, and when the morning sunlight filters through, rainbows sparkle over the carved oak stairway and woodwork of the interior. There are seven coal fireplaces and twelve-foot ceilings. Original English antiques collected by the Rhoads, Whites & Lovelace families of the inn's owners fill its 21 rooms.

Innkeeper(s): Pat & Bill Lovelace. $65-118. 8 rooms with PB, 3 with FP, 2 suites and 1 conference room. Breakfast and snacks/refreshments included in rates. Types of meals: Full gourmet bkfst, veg bkfst, early coffee/tea and dinner. Beds: KDT. TV, VCR, reading lamp, ceiling fan, clock radio, desk and fireplace in room. Air conditioning. Fax, library, parlor games, telephone and fireplace on premises. Antiquing, fishing, golf, horseback riding, museums, parks and shopping nearby.

Location: City.

Publicity: *Southern Living, Fort Worth Star and Waco Tribune.*

"We appreciated your warm hospitality, the beauty of your home and all that delicious food!"

Certificate may be used: Anytime, subject to availability.

Houston   F9

Palms on West Main

807 W Main St #1
Houston, TX 77006
(713)522-7987 Fax:(713)522-3150
Internet: www.palmsonwestmain.com
E-mail: meadeandsmith@pdq.net

Circa 1914. Centrally located in Houston's historic museum district, this early 20th-century Dutch Colonial home can be found in the same neighborhood where Howard Hughes grew up, possessing unique architecture and mature trees. The inn's host, Tom Meade, a member of the Greater Houston Preservation Alliance, has restored many original designs of the house and enjoys providing ample information on Houston's history and attractions. Private access to each suite is located off the "Key West" deck, filled with tropical plants and fountains. Fireplaces and individual design distinguish each room. With many activities in the Houston area, guests get prepared each morning with a country breakfast delivered to their room offering ham frittata, apple cinnamon muffins, fresh fruit, juice and coffee.

Innkeeper(s): Tom Meade, Rick Smith. $99. 3 rooms, 2 with FP, 3 suites. Breakfast included in rates. Types of meals: Full bkfst. Beds: KQ. Cable TV, VCR, reading lamp, ceiling fan, telephone and desk in room. Air conditioning. Fax, bicycles and fireplace on premises. Amusement parks, antiquing, art galleries, bicycling, golf, live theater, museums, parks, shopping and sporting events nearby.

Location: City.

Certificate may be used: Anytime, Sunday-Thursday.

Robin's Nest

4104 Greeley St
Houston, TX 77006-5609
(713)528-5821 (800)622-8343 Fax:(713)529-4821
Internet: www.therobin.com
E-mail: robin@therobin.com

Circa 1898. Robin's Nest is the oldest home in Houston's historic Montrose District. A two-story wooden Queen Anne Victorian, the historic home features original pine hardwoods, tall windows, high ceilings and a wraparound veranda. Luxurious fabrics, all custom sewn, warm the interior, which also boasts wall murals. The home originally was a dairy farm and now rests on an urban lot surrounded by dozens of rose bushes and azaleas. Located in the city's museum and arts district, the inn offers close proximity to downtown Houston, theaters and gourmet restaurants. Galveston and Johnson Space Center are about an hour away.

Innkeeper(s): Robin Smith. $89-175. 5 rooms with PB and 1 conference room. Breakfast included in rates. Types of meals: Full bkfst. Beds: QT. Cable TV, refrigerator, ceiling fan, telephone and baths in room. Air conditioning. TV on premises. Amusement parks, antiquing, fishing, live theater, museums, shopping, sporting events and water sports nearby.

Location: City. Inside 610 Loop very near downtown, George R. Brown Convention Center and Texas Medical Center.

Publicity: *Houston Home and Garden, Houston Business Journal, Woman's Day, Houston Metropolitan, Houston Post, Southern Living, Texas Monthly, Houston Chronicle, Inside Houston and Houston Press "Best Houston B&B 2002."*

"Fanciful and beautiful, comfortable and happy. We saw a whole new side of Houston, thanks to you."

Certificate may be used: Sunday-Thursday, all year.

Hunt   F6

Roddy Tree Ranch

PO Box 820
Hunt, TX 78024-0820
(830)367-2871 (800)309-9868 Fax:(830)367-2872
Internet: www.roddytree.com
E-mail: cabins@roddytree.com

Circa 1940. Experience the rustic elegance of these cedar and rock cottages on fifty tranquil acres along the Guadalupe River in Texas Hill Country. The campground resort ambiance and dude ranch-like setting are perfect for peaceful getaways or family vacations. Stay in a nicely decorated one-to-four bedroom cottage with antique furnishings, climate control, fully equipped kitchens, video library and barbecue grills. Some include a porch, deck, fireplace, living room or sitting area. A covered pavilion boasts a jukebox and picnic tables. Swim in the pool or in the river, fish in the catch and release pond, play badminton, volleyball or horseshoes and go for a nature walk. Take out a canoe or paddleboat. Kids love the playscape and playground area. Browse through nearby shops. Visit San Antonio and the Alamo within an hour's drive.

Innkeeper(s): Keith & Gretchen Asbury. $100-300. 16 cottages with PB, 8 with FP and 1 conference room. Types of meals: Full gourmet bkfst, veg bkfst, picnic lunch and room service. Beds: KQDT. Modem hook-up, TV, VCR, reading lamp, CD player, refrigerator, ceiling fan, clock radio, coffeemaker and fireplace in room. Central air. Fax, copier, swimming, stable, child care, parlor games, telephone, gift shop and fireplace on premises. Handicap access. Amusement parks, antiquing, art galleries, bicycling, canoeing/kayaking, fishing, golf, hiking, horseback riding, live theater, museums, parks, shopping, tennis, water sports and wineries nearby.

Location: Country, waterfront.

Publicity: *Kerrville Daily Times, West Kerr Current, HGTV and KLRN San Antonio.*

Certificate may be used: September-May (off-season), Sunday-Thursday, subject to availability.

Jasper   E9

Swann Hotel

250 N Main St
Jasper, TX 75951-4114
(877)489-9717 Fax:(409)489-9010
Internet: www.swannhotel.com
E-mail: swannhotel104@hotmail.com

Circa 1901. Known for its historic elegance and classic Southern hospitality, this restored Victorian is surrounded by a quiet community in the East Texas Pineywoods. Originally built in 1901 as a family home, 14 years later a widow and mother of six established it as a hotel that became popular for its comfort, service and fine dining. Those traits continue today. Carefully decorated guest bedrooms provide a calm respite after a day of sightseeing. Start each morning with a complimentary gourmet breakfast. Savor the hotel's excellent cuisine in Miss Genie's Dining Room. Toledo Bend and Lake Sam Rayburn are a short drive.

Innkeeper(s): Mary & Jerry Silmon. $79. 6 rooms, 4 with PB and 1 conference room. Breakfast included in rates. Types of meals: Full gourmet bkfst and gourmet dinner. Restaurant on premises. Beds: QDT. Ceiling fan in room. Central air. TV, VCR, library, pet boarding, telephone and gift shop on premises. Limited handicap access. Antiquing, art galleries, canoeing/kayaking, fishing, golf, hiking, tennis and water sports nearby.

Certificate may be used: Anytime, Sunday-Thursday.

Jefferson   D9

McKay House

306 E Delta St
Jefferson, TX 75657-2026
(903)665-7322 (800)468-2627
Internet: www.mckayhouse.com
E-mail: innkeeper@mckayhouse.com

Circa 1851. For more than 15 years, the McKay House has been widely acclaimed for its high standards, personal service and satisfied guests. Both Lady Bird Johnson and Alex Haley

have enjoyed the gracious Southern hospitality offered at the McKay House. The Greek Revival cottage features a front porch with pillars. Heart-of-pine floors, 14-foot ceilings and documented wallpapers complement antique furnishings. A full "gentleman's" breakfast is served in the garden conservatory by the gable fireplace. Orange French toast, home-baked muffins and shirred eggs are a few of the house specialties. In each of the seven bedchambers you find a Victorian nightgown and old-fashioned nightshirt laid out for you. History abounds in Jefferson, considered the "Williamsburg of the Southwest."

Innkeeper(s): Hugh Lewis. $89-149. 7 rooms with PB, 6 with FP and 1 cottage. Breakfast included in rates. Types of meals: Full gourmet bkfst and early coffee/tea. Beds: KQD. Cable TV, ceiling fan, clock radio, telephone, suites and Internet also in room. Air conditioning. Parlor games, fireplace and refrigerator in common rooms on premises. Antiquing, fishing, live theater, parks, shopping and water sports nearby.
Location: City.
Publicity: *Southern Accents, Dallas Morning News, Country Home and Bride.*

"The facilities of the McKay House are exceeded only by the service and dedication of the owners."

Certificate may be used: Sunday through Thursday, not including spring break or festivals/holidays; space available, reserved one week in advance please.

Old Mulberry Inn

209 E Jefferson St
Jefferson, TX 75657-2017
(903)665-1945 (800)263-5319 Fax:(903)665-9123
Internet: www.oldmulberryinn.com
E-mail: mulberry@jeffersontx.com

Circa 1996. Nineteenth-century charm meets modern-day comfort in this plantation-style home. The property sits atop "Quality Hill" in the town which once was a busy river port in the 1800s. The wide-plank heart-pine flooring, from a cotton gin near Dallas, provides a soft backdrop to the inn's antiques. Relax on the sofa in the library to gaze at clouds painted on the ceiling 30 feet overhead. In the morning, enjoy coffee and biscotti on one of three porches. Then move to the dining room and partake of a three-course breakfast, featuring such delicacies as yogurt parfait, artichoke quiche and mulberry almond coffee cake.

Innkeeper(s): Donald & Gloria Degn. $79-169. 5 rooms with PB and 1 conference room. Breakfast included in rates. Types of meals: Full gourmet bkfst, early coffee/tea and snacks/refreshments. Beds: KQ. Cable TV, VCR, reading lamp, CD player, ceiling fan, clock radio, upscale toiletries and one with two-person Jacuzzi in room. Central air. Fax, copier, library, parlor games, telephone, fireplace and video library on premises. Antiquing, canoeing/kayaking, fishing, golf, live theater, museums, water sports and casinos nearby.
Location: Small town.

Publicity: *Southern Living, Dallas Morning News, Texas Highways, Houston Chronicle, LA Times, Shreveport News, AAA 3 diamond award since 1999, Best Recipes from American Country Inns and Bed and Breakfasts and Texas Bed & Breakfast Cookbook.*
Certificate may be used: Anytime, Sunday-Friday, except holiday/special event weekends. Anytime, January and August.

Lampasas   E7

Historic Moses Hughes Ranch

7075 W FM 580
Lampasas, TX 76550-3662
(512)556-5923
Internet: www.moseshughesranch.com
E-mail: musee-solomon@earthlink.net

Circa 1856. Nestled among ancient oaks in the heart of the Texas Hill Country, this native stone ranch house rests on 45 acres that include springs, a creek, wildlife and other natural beauty. The ranch was built by Moses Hughes, the first white settler and founder of Lampasas.

He and his wife decided to stay in the area after her health dramatically improved after visiting the springs. Guests can join the innkeepers on the stone patio or upstairs wooden porch for a taste of Texas Hill Country life.

Innkeeper(s): Al & Beverly Solomon. $80-100. 3 rooms with PB and 1 cottage. Breakfast included in rates. Types of meals: Cont. Beds: QD. Reading lamp in room. Air conditioning. VCR, library, telephone, fireplace and creek & springs on premises. Antiquing, fishing, hiking, parks, water sports, birding and caves nearby.
Location: Ranch.
Publicity: *Spiegel Catalog, Dallas Morning News, Discover, Texas Highway, CBS, ABC and Texas Film Commission.*

"What a delightful respite! Thank you for sharing your very interesting philosophies and personalities with us at this very special B&B. We hate to leave."

Certificate may be used: Year-round, Sunday-Thursday, no holidays.

Mabank   D8

Bird House Bed & Breakfast

103 E Kaufman St
Mabank, TX 75147-9710
(903)887-1242 (888)474-5225 Fax:(903)887-7698
Internet: www.bbonline.com/tx/birdhouse
E-mail: come2relax@aol.com

Circa 1995. In a 100-year-old small town, this newer inn was built for comfort while imparting the warm ambiance of an old farmhouse. Sound-insulated walls retain privacy and quiet. The tastefully decorated guest bedrooms feature family heirlooms and antiques, custom furnishings made by innkeeper John, and coordinating linens and curtains. A wholesome breakfast is served with a creative flair. Family friendly, the inn has a large fenced-in back yard.

Innkeeper(s): John & Janette Bird. $74-97. 4 rooms with PB. Breakfast included in rates. Types of meals: Full gourmet bkfst, early coffee/tea and room service. Beds: KQ. Cable TV, VCR, reading lamp, refrigerator, ceiling fan, clock radio, telephone, coffeemaker and desk in room. Central air. Fax, copier, fireplace and laundry facility on premises. Handicap access. Antiquing, beach, fishing, golf, parks, shopping, tennis and water sports nearby.
Location: Country.
Certificate may be used: Anytime, subject to availability.

Mason E6

Hasse House and Ranch

PO Box 1648
Mason, TX 76856
(888)414-2773
E-mail: laverne@hctc.net

Circa 1883. Guests may explore the 320-acre Hasse ranch, which is a working ranch where deer, wild turkey, antelope, quail and a bounty of wildflowers and bluebonnets are common sights. After purchasing the land, Henry Hasse and his wife lived in a log cabin on the property before building the sandstone home 23 years later. Three generations of Hasses have lived here, and today it is owned by a great-granddaughter who restored the home in 1980. The house is located in  the small German village of Art, Texas, which is located six miles east of Mason. The innkeepers rent the two-bedroom National Register home out to only one group or guest at a time, host free. The home is filled with period furniture and accessories, yet offers the modern convenience of an on-site washer and dryer and a fully stocked kitchen. The ranch grounds include a two-mile nature trail perfect for nature lovers.

Innkeeper(s): Laverne Lee. $85. 2 rooms with PB. Types of meals: Cont plus. Beds: D. TV, reading lamp, refrigerator, ceiling fan, snack bar, coffeemaker, dishwasher and microwave in room. Air conditioning. Library, parlor games, washer, dryer, stove, microwave and patio on premises. Handicap access. Antiquing, parks, shopping, water sports, bicycle routes, 2-mile nature trail on ranch, bird-watching and wildflower viewing nearby.

Location: 320-acre ranch.

Publicity: *San Angelo, TX Special and "Eyes of Texas."*

"We enjoyed every aspect of our stay; the atmosphere, sense of history, rustic setting with a touch of class. We would love to return the same time next year!"

Certificate may be used: Throughout the year, except for major holidays.

Mason Square B&B

134 Ft McKavett, PO Box 298
Mason, TX 76856-0298
(325)347-6398 (800)369-0405
E-mail: hinck5415@hctc.net

Circa 1901. A fine collection of framed, historically significant maps of Texas and the Southwest that span centuries of discovery and settlement are throughout the guest rooms and hallway of this inn. Located on the second floor of a historic commercial building, the B&B has original pressed-tin ceilings, Victorian woodwork and doors, stained-glass transoms and oak floors. Guests can step outside for a stroll down memory lane as the inn is part of the courthouse square with buildings dating from 1879. Several antique shops, galleries and some local businesses have occupied the same buildings for generations.

Innkeeper(s): Brent & Monica Hinckley. $60-70. 3 rooms. Breakfast included in rates. Types of meals: Cont plus. Reading lamp, ceiling fan, clock radio and desk in room. Air conditioning. VCR and telephone on premises. Antiquing nearby.

Location: City.

Certificate may be used: All times, except holidays.

McGregor E7

Lighthouse Bed & Breakfast

421 S Harrison St
McGregor, TX 76657-1562
(254)840-2589 (800)616-0603 Fax:(254)840-3988
Internet: www.thelighthousebandb.com
E-mail: stay@thelighthousebandb.com

Circa 1894. The romantic charm of the past is highlighted at this recently restored Queen Anne Victorian. The inn's gingerbread trim and wraparound porch with swing and rockers are welcoming first impressions. Grace and elegance are reflected in the six generations of family heirloom antiques and furnishings. The appealing guest bedrooms feature a variety of comforts that may include clawfoot tubs, fireplaces, VCRs, canopy and brass beds. A candle-lit breakfast is served family-style on fine china with silver settings and vintage linens. The stained-glass garden gazebo is showcased on a landscaped lawn.

Innkeeper(s): Jerry & Jan Walters. $80-150. 13 rooms with PB, 2 with FP, 1 suite. Breakfast and snacks/refreshments included in rates. Types of meals: Full bkfst and early coffee/tea. Beds: KQD. Modem hook-up, cable TV, VCR, reading lamp, ceiling fan, clock radio, telephone, desk and fireplace in room. Central air. TV, spa, library, parlor games, fireplace and laundry facility on premises. Antiquing, art galleries, fishing, golf, hiking, horseback riding, live theater, museums, parks, shopping, sporting events and tennis nearby.

Location: Suburban.

Certificate may be used: Jan. 2-Dec. 30, Sunday-Thursday.

New Braunfels F7

Aunt Nora's Countryside Inn

120 Naked Indian Trail
New Braunfels, TX 78132-1865
(830)905-3989 (800)687-2887
Internet: www.auntnoras.com
E-mail: info@auntnoras.com

Circa 1983. Romance the Texas Hill Country in New Braunfels, Canyon Lake, Gruene near the Guadalupe River. The Country Victorian decor and quality handcrafted furniture provide comfort and style. Each guest suite offers several spacious rooms, including a kitchen. To add to the pampering, an excellent breakfast is delivered to the door each morning, ready to satisfy. Spectacular views can be seen from the private deck or porch overlooking the meadows. Picnic tables in the courtyard, small ponds with waterfalls and a hot tub surrounded by mountain hills and fresh air are pleasurable treats to enjoy. A small intimate wedding in the gazebo is complete with a pastor available to perform the ceremony.

Innkeeper(s): Jack & Kathy Tipton. $115-175. 4 cottages with PB. Breakfast included in rates. Types of meals: Full bkfst. Beds: QT. TV, VCR, reading lamp, refrigerator, ceiling fan, coffeemaker and hot tub/spa in room. Air conditioning. Spa, telephone and laundry facility on premises. Amusement parks, antiquing, beach, canoeing/kayaking, fishing, golf, live theater, museums, parks, shopping, tennis, water sports, wineries, Schlitterbahn, Natural Bridge Caverns, Sea World and Fiesta Texas nearby.

Location: Country. Texas hill country.

Publicity: *San Antonio Wedding Pages 2002 & 2003, Dallas Morning News, San Antonio Express and "Show Me Texas."*

Certificate may be used: Aug. 15 through February, Sunday through Wednesday, excluding holidays and special events.

Gruene Mansion Inn

1275 Gruene Rd
New Braunfels, TX 78130-3003
(830)629-2641 Fax:(830)629-7375
Internet: www.gruenemansioninn.com
E-mail: frontdesk@gruenemansioninn.com

Circa 1872. Overlook the Guadalupe River from the porches of this Victorian mansion located on three acres in Hill Country, adjacent to the state's oldest dance hall. The inn has been designated a Historic Landmark and is listed in the National Register. The Mansion, barns, corn crib, carriage house and other outbuildings have all been refurbished to offer quiet and private guest bedrooms, cottages and guest houses. A rustic Victorian elegance is the ambiance and style of decor that blends antiques, fine fabrics and wall coverings. Savor breakfast entrees that boast a Mexican flair and flavor. For a day trip, visit the Alamo, 30 miles away.

Innkeeper(s): Jackie Walcott. $119-219. 30 rooms with PB, 1 cottage and 1 conference room. Breakfast included in rates. Beds: KQDT. Cable TV, reading lamp, refrigerator, ceiling fan, clock radio, coffeemaker and fireplace in room. Central air. Fax, copier, telephone, porch with rocking chairs looking at Guadalupe River and gift shop on premises. Handicap access. Amusement parks, antiquing, art galleries, bicycling, canoeing/kayaking, fishing, golf, hiking, horseback riding, live theater, museums, parks, shopping, sporting events, tennis, water sports, wineries and oldest dance hall in Texas nearby.

Location: Hill country of Texas.

Publicity: *San Antonio Express News, Austin American Statesmen and New Braunfels Herald Zietung.*

Certificate may be used: January-February, Sunday-Thursday, Sunday Hauses only; September, Sunday-Thursday, Sunday Hauses only.

Old Hunter Rd Stagecoach Stop B&B

5541 FM 1102 (Hunter Rd)
New Braunfels, TX 78132
(830)620-9453 (800)201-2912
Internet: www.stagecoachbedandbreakfast.com
E-mail: stagecoach@satx.rr.com

Circa 1850. Listed in the National Register, these historic hand-hewn log cabins, along with the main house, were used as a stagecoach stop for 15 years. Filled with Texas antiques, the romantic cabins offer porches, lace and in-season fragrant rose and herb bouquets. Request the LBJ Room and sleep in the former president's grandfather's cedar poster bed. Breakfast is served before the dining room fireplace and may include lemon pancakes with peppered bacon, Belgian waffles, homemade Rose jams and fresh-baked breads. The innkeeper, a landscape designer specializing in xeroscapes, has planted the three acres of gardens with antique roses and other gorgeous plants.

Innkeeper(s): Bettina & Jeff Messinger. $105-180. 4 rooms with PB. Breakfast included in rates. Types of meals: Full gourmet bkfst, veg bkfst and early coffee/tea. Beds: Q. Modem hook-up, data port, cable TV, reading lamp, CD player, ceiling fan, clock radio, telephone, coffeemaker, turn-down service, desk and hot tub/spa in room. Central air. Fax, copier, spa, swimming, bicycles, library, parlor games and fireplace on premises. Art galleries, beach, bicycling, canoeing/kayaking, fishing, golf, hiking, horseback riding and museums nearby.

Location: Country. Texas hill country.

Certificate may be used: January, February, September, October, November, December; Tuesday, Wednesday, Thursday.

Pittsburg D9

Carson House Inn & Grille

302 Mount Pleasant St
Pittsburg, TX 75686-1335
(903)856-2468 (888)302-1878 Fax:(903)856-0709
Internet: www.carsonhouse.com
E-mail: mailus@carsonhouse.com

Circa 1878. The city's oldest occupied home, this bed & breakfast with manicured lawns, a Koi pond and patio, also features a highly acclaimed restaurant. The interior was built using more than one mile of curly pine. The milled lumber, known for its interesting grain pattern, came from diseased trees, now thought to be extinct. The Carson Room boasts a sleigh bed, sitting area and private entrance. It adjoins the Abernathy Room with a brass bed. The Camp Room offers a relaxing two-person whirlpool tub. The private Carson and Barnes Railroad Car, decorated with artifacts, is a fitting tribute to local history. A refrigerator, two-person shower and a Jacuzzi just outside make this a perfect retreat. A cooked-to-order breakfast is made when desired.

Innkeeper(s): Eileen & Clark Jesmore. $85-145. 8 rooms, 6 with PB, 1 suite and 1 cottage. Breakfast included in rates. Types of meals: Full gourmet bkfst, veg bkfst, gourmet lunch, snacks/refreshments, gourmet dinner and room service. Restaurant on premises. Beds: KQD. Modem hook-up, data port, cable TV, VCR, reading lamp, refrigerator, ceiling fan, clock radio, telephone, coffeemaker, turn-down service, desk, hot tub/spa and voice mail in room. Central air. Fax, fireplace and laundry facility on premises. Antiquing, bicycling, fishing, golf, hiking, horseback riding, live theater, museums, parks, shopping and water sports nearby.

Location: City.

Publicity: *Dallas Morning News, Gourmet Magazine, Texas Parks & Wildlife and Romantic America.*

Certificate may be used: Anytime, subject to availability.

Rockport H8

Anthony's By Sea Bed & Breakfast

732 S Pearl St
Rockport, TX 78382-2420
(361)729-6100 (800)460-2557 Fax:(361)729-2450
Internet: www.anthonysbythesea.com
E-mail: info@anthonysbythesea.com

Circa 1997. This quiet, casual retreat is hidden away beneath huge oak trees, near the ocean in an area known as the Texas Riviera. Choose from comfortably furnished single rooms or suites with private baths and sitting areas. Separate guest house has a fully equipped kitchen, spacious living area and sleeps up to six, making it ideal for families and small groups. A sparkling pool and covered lanai provide the most popular areas for relaxing or enjoying the gourmet breakfasts. Located within walking distance of Rockport Beach, a variety of water activities are available, as well as local shopping, restaurants and museums.

Innkeeper(s): Smitty & Beth. $105. 6 rooms, 4 with PB, 1 suite, 1 guest house and 1 conference room. Breakfast included in rates. Types of meals: Full gourmet bkfst and early coffee/tea. Beds: KQD. Cable TV, VCR, reading lamp, refrigerator, ceiling fan and clock radio in room. Central air. Fax, swimming, pet boarding, parlor games, laundry facility and pets allowed on premises. Limited handicap access.

Location: City, ocean community.

Publicity: *New York Times.*

Certificate may be used: Anytime, November-March, subject to availability.

San Antonio   F7

B&B on The River

129 Woodward Pl
San Antonio, TX 78204-1120
(210)225-6333 (800)730-0019 Fax:(210)271-3992
Internet: www.hotx.com/sa/bb/
E-mail: innonriver@hotmail.com

Circa 1916. Located in a restored river home, the inn is encir-
cled by an iron fence and shaded by a tall pecan tree. There are
gables and a wraparound porch. Inside are polished pine floors
and tall ceilings. Antiques, Jacuzzi tubs, fireplaces and private
porches are among the guest room offerings. A third-floor penthouse offers French doors opening to a private balcony. There
is a large Jacuzzi and king-size bed. Stroll to the Riverwalk for
scenic shopping, restaurants and entertainment. The
Convention Center is four blocks away. The innkeeper is a bal-
loonist and offers balloon rides by prior arrangements.

Innkeeper(s): A.D. Zucht. $69-175. 12 rooms with PB, 2 with FP. Breakfast
included in rates. Types of meals: Full bkfst. Beds: KQT. Cable TV, reading
lamp, ceiling fan, clock radio, telephone, one with refrigerator and 4 with spa
in room. Air conditioning. Fax, copier, Internet access and outdoor patio overlooking river on premises. Antiquing, live theater, parks, shopping, river and
museums nearby.

Location: City.

Certificate may be used: Anytime, subject to availability.

Brackenridge House

230 Madison
San Antonio, TX 78204-1320
(210)271-3442 (800)221-1412 Fax:(210)226-3139
Internet: www.brackenridgehouse.com
E-mail: benniesueb@aol.com

Circa 1901. Each of the guest rooms at Brackenridge House is
individually decorated. Clawfoot tubs, iron beds and a private
veranda are a few of the items that guests might discover.
Several rooms include kitchenettes. Blansett Barn, often rented
by families or those on an extended stay, includes two bedrooms, a bathroom, a full kitchen and living and dining areas.
Many of San Antonio's interesting sites are nearby. The San
Antonio Mission Trail begins just a block away, and trolleys will
take you to the Alamo, the River Walk, convention center and
more. Coffeehouses, restaurants and antique stores all are within walking distance. Small pets are welcome in Blansett Barn.

Innkeeper(s): Bennie & Sue Blansett. $110-250. 6 rooms with PB, 2 suites
and 1 cottage. Breakfast included in rates. Types of meals: Full gourmet bkfst
and early coffee/tea. Beds: KQD. Modem hook-up, data port, cable TV, VCR,
reading lamp, refrigerator, ceiling fan, clock radio, telephone, coffeemaker,
desk, microwave, iron, ironing board and hair dryer in room. Air conditioning.
Fax, copier, spa and parlor games on premises. Amusement parks, antiquing,
fishing, golf, live theater, parks, shopping, sporting events and tennis nearby.

Location: City. 1/2 mile to Alamo & Riverwalk.

Publicity: *San Antonio Express News, Huntington Beach Herald, New York
Times and Seattle Times.*

"Innkeeper was very nice, very helpful."

Certificate may be used: All year, no holidays or fiesta, Monday-Thursday.

Christmas House B&B

2307 McCullough
San Antonio, TX 78212
(210)737-2786 (800)268-4187 Fax:(210)734-5712
Internet: www.christmashousebnb.com
E-mail: christmashsb@earthlink.net

Circa 1908. Located in Monte Vista historic district, this two-
story white inn has a natural wood balcony built over the front
porch. The window trim is in red and
green, starting the Christmas theme of the
inn. (There's a Christmas tree decorated all
year long.) Guest rooms open out to
pecan-shaded balconies. The Victorian
Bedroom offers pink and mauve touches
mixed with the room's gold and black
decor. The Blue & Silver Room is handicap
accessible and is on the first floor. Antique
furnishings in the inn are available for sale.

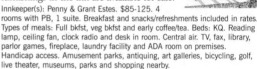

Innkeeper(s): Penny & Grant Estes. $85-125. 4
rooms with PB, 1 suite. Breakfast and snacks/refreshments included in rates.
Types of meals: Full bkfst, veg bkfst and early coffee/tea. Beds: KQ. Reading
lamp, ceiling fan, clock radio and desk in room. Central air. TV, fax, library,
parlor games, fireplace, laundry facility and ADA room on premises.
Handicap access. Amusement parks, antiquing, art galleries, bicycling, golf,
live theater, museums, parks and shopping nearby.

Location: City.

Publicity: *Fort Worth Star Telegram.*

*"What a treat to rise to the sweet smell of candied pecans and a
tasty breakfast."*

Certificate may be used: Sunday-Thursday, not on holidays or during Fiesta.

Noble Inns

107 Madison
San Antonio, TX 78204-1319
(210)225-4045 (800)221-4045 Fax:(210)227-0877
Internet: www.nobleinns.com
E-mail: stay@nobleinns.com

Circa 1894. Two historic homes, both designated city historic
structures, comprise the Noble Inns collection. Both are located in the King William Historic District. The Jackson House is
a brick and limestone Victorian. It offers a conservatory of
stained and leaded glass enclosing a heated spa. Breakfast is
served in the dining room and there is a parlor. The Pancoast
Carriage House provides individual suites with full kitchens
and stocked continental breakfasts. There is a swimming pool
as well as spa. Both inns are furnished with Victorian-era
antiques. There are fireplaces, marble baths, clawfoot tubs or
whirlpools. Fresh flowers and fluffy monogrammed robes greet
guests when they enter their rooms. Transportation in a classic
1960 Rolls Royce Silver Cloud II is available upon request. Call
ahead for rates.

Innkeeper(s): Don & Liesl Noble. $120-250. 9 rooms with PB, 9 with FP, 4
with HT, 4 suites. Breakfast and afternoon tea included in rates. Types of
meals: Full bkfst, veg bkfst and early coffee/tea. Beds: KQ. Data port, cable
TV, reading lamp, ceiling fan, clock radio, telephone and turn-down service
in room. Air conditioning. Fax, spa, library, parlor games, fireplace and voice
mail on premises. Antiquing, live theater, parks, shopping and sporting
events nearby.

Location: City.

Certificate may be used: Jan. 3 to Feb. 12, Monday-Thursday and June 1-
Aug. 28, Monday-Thursday, holidays and special events excluded.

San Marcos   F7

Crystal River Inn

326 W Hopkins St
San Marcos, TX 78666-4404
(512)396-3739 (888)396-3739 Fax:(512)396-6311
Internet: www.crystalriverinn.com
E-mail: info@crystalriverinn.com

Circa 1883. Tall white columns accent this Greek Revival inn that features a fireside dining room with a piano and wet bar. Innkeepers encourage a varied itinerary, including sleeping until noon and having breakfast in bed to participating in a hilarious murder mystery. Rock the afternoon away on the veranda or curl up by the fireplace in a guest bedroom by the headwaters of crystal-clear San Marcos River. Clawfoot tubs, four-poster and canopied beds add to the pleasing ambiance. Shop at the state's largest outlet mall that features more than 200 designer stores.

Innkeeper(s): Mike, Cathy & Sarah Dillon. $90-160. 13 rooms with PB, 4 with FP, 3 suites, 1 cabin and 1 conference room. Breakfast included in rates. Types of meals: Full bkfst, early coffee/tea, lunch and dinner. Beds: KQDT. Cable TV, reading lamp, stereo, refrigerator, ceiling fan, clock radio, telephone and desk in room. Air conditioning. Fax, copier, bicycles, child care, fireplace, gardens, fish pond and veranda on premises. Handicap access. Amusement parks, antiquing, fishing, golf, live theater, parks, shopping, sporting events and water sports nearby.

Location: City. Small town.

Publicity: *Texas Monthly, USA Today, Country Inns, Southern Living, Dallas Morning News, Houston Chronicle, Boston Globe and Texas Highways.*

"Thanks for a smashing good time! We really can't remember having more fun anywhere, ever!"

Certificate may be used: Sunday-Thursday, year-round, except for holiday weeks (Thanksgiving, Memorial Day, July 4th, etc.).

Seabrook   F9

Pelican House B&B Inn

1302 First St
Seabrook, TX 77586-3802
(281)474-5295 Fax:(281)474-7840
Internet: www.pelicanhouse.com
E-mail: pelicanhouse@usa.net

Circa 1902. An acre of lawns with live oak and pecan trees stretch to the banks of Old Seabrook's Back Bay from this cozy white country house. Just beyond a white picket fence, the inn's salmon shutters and inviting front porch welcome guests. Inside, there are two dining areas and a sitting room. Bed chambers feature Queen-size beds and a nautical, whimsical decor. Stuffed french toast with apricot glaze is a favorite morning entree. In April and September, great white pelicans assemble on the bay and fish for mullet. Ospreys and other shore birds are seen most of the year. Within walking distance are antique shops and restaurants. The Nasa Space Center is three miles away and the Kemah Boardwalk is just a short drive.

Innkeeper(s): Suzanne Silver. $110-120. 4 rooms with PB. Breakfast included in rates. Types of meals: Full gourmet bkfst. Beds: Q. Reading lamp, ceiling fan, clock radio and desk in room. Air conditioning. VCR, fax, copier, parlor games and telephone on premises. Antiquing, fishing, golf, parks, shopping, tennis and water sports nearby.

Location: Waterfront.

Publicity: *Houston Life and Texas Highways.*

Certificate may be used: Monday-Thursday, all year.

Smithville   F7

The Katy House Bed & Breakfast

201 Ramona St, PO Box 803
Smithville, TX 78957-0803
(512)237-4262 (800)843-5289 Fax:(512)237-2239
Internet: www.katyhouse.com
E-mail: thekatyh@onr.com

Circa 1909. Shaded by tall trees, the Katy House's Italianate exterior is graced by an arched portico over the bay-windowed living room. Long leaf pine floors, pocket doors and a graceful stairway accent the completely refurbished interior. The inn is decorated almost exclusively in American antique oak and railroad memorabilia. A 1909 caboose is being restored to be used as a guest room. Historic Main Street is one block away with a fine collection of antique shops. Guests usually come back from walking tours with pockets full of pecans found around town. Smithville was the hometown location for the movie "Hope Floats."

Innkeeper(s): Bruce & Sallie Blalock. $95-125. 5 rooms with PB, 1 suite and 2 cottages. Breakfast included in rates. Types of meals: Full bkfst and early coffee/tea. Beds: Q. TV, VCR and ceiling fan in room. Air conditioning. Antiquing, fishing, parks and shopping nearby.

Location: Small town.

Publicity: *Texas Country Reporter.*

Certificate may be used: Sunday through Thursday, except holidays.

Van Alstyne   C8

Durning House B&B

205 W Stephens, PO Box 1173
Van Alstyne, TX 75495-1173
(903)482-5188

Circa 1900. Decorated with American oak and antiques, the inn has been host to many events, including weddings, office parties, Christmas parties, club meetings and murder-mystery dinners. Three life-size pigs grace the east garden. The innkeepers have published a cookbook titled "Hog Heaven" that includes more than 400 recipes featured at the inn. Your hosts also appear regularly on a TV show preparing recipes from "Hog Heaven."

Innkeeper(s): Brenda Hix & Sherry Heath. $110-135. 2 rooms. Types of meals: Cont and dinner. Restaurant on premises. Beds: QD. Reading lamp, stereo, refrigerator, ceiling fan, clock radio, desk and Jacuzzi in room. Air conditioning. Fireplace and massage therapy on premises. Handicap access. Antiquing, fishing, live theater, shopping, sporting events and water sports nearby.

Location: Small town.

Certificate may be used: Jan. 30-Nov. 20, Sunday-Friday.

Waco   E7

The Judge Baylor House

908 Speight Ave
Waco, TX 76706-2343
(254)756-0273 (888)522-9567 Fax:(254)756-0711
Internet: www.eyeweb.com/jbaylor
E-mail: jbaylor@iamerica.net

Circa 1940. This home was built by the head of the chemistry department at Baylor University, which is just one block away. There are five well-appointed guest rooms, each decorated with

English antiques. Each room has something special. In one room, guests will discover French doors leading out to a patio. In another, there is a poster bed and hand-painted pedestal sink. Aside from the university and Elizabeth

Barrett & Robert Browning Library, the home is near the Brazos Riverwalk, Lake Waco, the Texas Sports Hall of Fame, antique shops, historic homes and more.

Innkeeper(s): Bruce & Dorothy Dyer. $72-105. 5 rooms, 4 with PB, 1 suite. Breakfast and afternoon tea included in rates. Types of meals: Full bkfst and early coffee/tea. Beds: KQT. Ceiling fan, clock radio and desk in room. Air conditioning. VCR, fax, copier, library, parlor games, telephone and fireplace on premises. Antiquing, fishing, golf, live theater, parks, shopping, sporting events and tennis nearby.

Location: City.

Publicity: *Fort Worth Star-Telegram, Dallas Morning News, Arrington's B&B Journal and Country Extra.*

Certificate may be used: Sunday through Thursday.

Waxahachie   D8

The BonnyNook

414 W Main St
Waxahachie, TX 75165-3234
(972)938-7207 Fax:(972)937-7700
Internet: www.bonnynook.com
E-mail: vaughn@hyperusa.com

Circa 1887. Each of the five guest rooms at this Queen Anne "Painted Lady" is filled with plants and antiques from around the world. The Sterling Room, a large octagon-shaped chamber, features a hand-carved mahogany canopy bed. The Morrow Room boasts a 100-year-old sleigh bed and an antique clawfoot

tub with a shower. Three of the guest baths offer whirlpool tubs. Bon Appetit featured BonnyNook as part of an article on bed & breakfasts. The hearty breakfasts feature such notable items as blueberry pudding coffeecake or Southern crepes filled with veg-

etables and eggs. Innkeeper Bonnie Franks keeps a special Coffee Nook filled with teas, coffee, hot cocoa and a refrigerator for her guests. Don't forget to ask about the inn's special cookies. BonnyNook is only two blocks from antique shops, boutiques and restaurants. Gourmet, six-course meals are available by reservation. Massage also is available by reservation.

Innkeeper(s): Vaughn & Bonnie Franks. $85-125. 5 rooms with PB. Breakfast and snacks/refreshments included in rates. Types of meals: Full bkfst, early coffee/tea and gourmet dinner. Beds: KQD. Reading lamp, ceiling fan, clock radio, telephone, desk, hot tub/spa and some with Jacuzzis in room. Air conditioning. Fax, copier, parlor games, coffee nook with refrigerator and ice buckets/ice on premises. Antiquing, parks and shopping nearby.

Location: Small town.

Publicity: *Texas Highways, Dallas Morning News, Forbes, Texas People & Places and Bon Appetit.*

"This was a wonderful retreat from the everyday hustle and bustle and we didn't hear a phone ring once!"

Certificate may be used: Sunday-Thursday.

Wichita Falls   C6

Harrison House B&B

2014 11th St
Wichita Falls, TX 76301-4905
(940)322-2299
Internet: www.hhbb.com
E-mail: hhbbweddings@aol.com

This prairie-style inn features 10-foot ceilings, narrow-board oak floors, a hand-carved mantelpiece, gumwood paneling and detailed molding. The home was built by oilman, developer and philanthropist N.H. Martin. After the discovery of oil on the family ranch in nearby Jolly, Martin and his partner went on to build the Country Club Estates. They donated the land on which Hardin Junior College

(now Midwestern State University) was built. The inn also caters to special occasions and as many as 200 guests can be accommodated for a stand-up buffet.

Innkeeper(s): Suzanne Staha. $55-125. 4 rooms, 1 suite. Breakfast included in rates. Reading lamp, ceiling fan, clock radio and desk in room. Air conditioning. VCR, telephone and fireplace on premises. Antiquing and shopping nearby.

Location: City.

Certificate may be used: All year, Sunday-Thursday.

Wimberley   F7

Southwind

2701 FM 3237
Wimberley, TX 78676-5511
(512)847-5277 (800)508-5277
Internet: www.southwindbedandbreak.com
E-mail: southwind701@att.net

Circa 1985. Located three miles northeast of the quaint village of Wimberley, this early Texas-style inn sits on 25 wooded acres along with three secluded rustic cedar cabins, each with Jacuzzi tub, kitchen, fireplace and porch. Roam the unspoiled acres and discover deer crossing your path and armadillos, raccoons and foxes skittering just beyond your footsteps. During the wet season, enjoy clear natural springs with access to the swimming hole. The inn offers a library/lounge with a fireplace, or you can take advantage of the panoramic valley views from the porch hot tub or from one of the rocking chairs. The parlor is a cool retreat in the summer and provides a warm fireplace in winter weather. Two cabins feature wheelchair access. Cabin guests are invited to enjoy the inn, library and hot tub. Gourmet dinners may be enjoyed by advance reservation.

$80-105. 6 rooms with PB, 4 with FP. Breakfast included in rates. Types of meals: Full gourmet bkfst and early coffee/tea. Beds: KQ. Reading lamp, ceiling fan and desk in room. Air conditioning. Spa, library, parlor games, telephone and fireplace on premises. Handicap access. Amusement parks, antiquing, canoeing/kayaking, fishing, hiking, live theater, parks, shopping, sporting events, water sports, massage therapist on call by request and swimming nearby.

Location: Rural Texas Hill Country.

Certificate may be used: Sunday through Thursday nights only, except holidays and April, June and July.

Utah

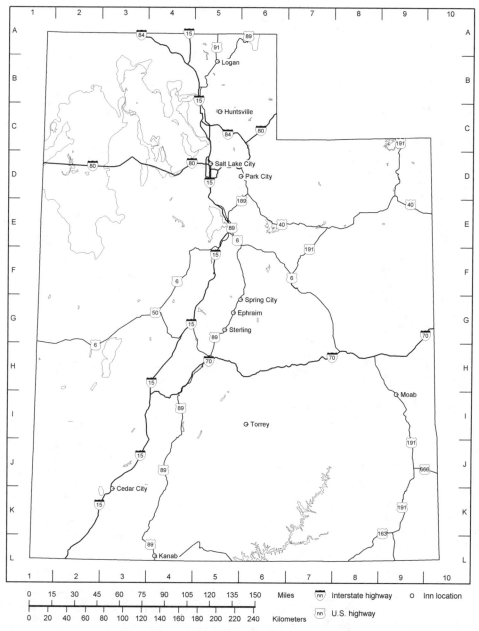

	1	2	3	4	5	6	7	8	9	10	

Logan

Huntsville

Salt Lake City
Park City

Spring City
Ephraim
Sterling

Moab

Torrey

Cedar City

Kanab

0 15 30 45 60 75 90 105 120 135 150   Miles

0 20 40 60 80 100 120 140 160 180 200 220 240   Kilometers

Interstate highway   Inn location

U.S. highway

Cedar City   K3

A Garden Cottage Bed & Breakfast

16 North 200 West
Cedar City, UT 84720
(435)586-4919 (866)586-4919
Internet: www.thegardencottagebnb.com
E-mail: romance@thegardencottagebnb.com

Circa 1920. Taste the gracious ambiance of Merrie Olde England at this quaint English cottage across from the Utah Shakespearean Festival. At the top of a winding staircase, antique-filled guest bedrooms feature Victorian furnishings and handmade vintage linens with embroidery and lace. A pleasing breakfast usually includes home-baked breads, fresh fruit, quiche, juice smoothies, hot chocolate, tea, cider and coffee. The B&B is surrounded by an award-winning, old-fashioned garden to enjoy. Arrington's Bed and Breakfast Journal recently named the inn as one of the Top 15 B&B/Country Inns.

Innkeeper(s): Gary & Diana Simkins. $99-109. 5 rooms with PB. Breakfast included in rates. Types of meals: Full bkfst and early coffee/tea. Beds: QT. Data port and reading lamp in room. Central air. TV, VCR and fireplace on premises. Antiquing, art galleries, bicycling, cross-country skiing, downhill skiing, fishing, golf, hiking, horseback riding, live theater, museums, parks, shopping, sporting events, tennis, water sports, Utah Shakespearean Festival, Zion National Park, Bryce Canyon National Park, Cedar Breaks National Monument, Utah Summer Games and Brian Head Ski Resort nearby.

Location: Mountains. Small rural town in the mountains.
Publicity: *The Spectrum Newspaper and Cedar City Magazine.*
Certificate may be used: Anytime, Nov. 1-May 31.

Bard's Inn

150 S 100 W
Cedar City, UT 84720-3276
(435)586-6612

Circa 1910. This handsome bungalow features stained-glass windows, a wide front porch and a second-story porch. The Katharina Room has an antique, high-back queen bed and a twin-size walnut sleigh bed. Homemade pastries and fruit are served on the porch or in the formal dining room.

Innkeeper(s): Jack & Audrey Whipple. $85. 7 rooms with PB. Breakfast included in rates. Types of meals: Full bkfst. Beds: QT. Reading lamp in room. Air conditioning. Antiquing, cross-country skiing, downhill skiing, live theater, parks, shopping and sporting events nearby.

Location: City.
Certificate may be used: Oct. 16 to May 15, based on availability.

Cherished Memories Bed & Breakfast

170 N. 400 W.
Cedar City, UT 84720
(435)867-6498 (866)867-6498
Internet: www.cherishedmemoriesbnb.com
E-mail: memories@cherishedmemoriesbnb.com

Circa 1906. Built with adobe brick and trimmed in gingerbread and lattice, this 1906 Victorian home is furnished with unusual pieces and distinctive antiques. Formerly known as the Paxman Summer House, it has been recently renovated to pamper and please. The warm and inviting parlor invites conversation. Relax on spacious front and rear porches. Air-conditioned

guest bedrooms are delightfully decorated and feature comfortable Queen pillowtop beds. After a restful sleep, linger over a satisfying breakfast in the elegant formal dining room. Historic downtown and the Utah Shakespearean Festival are just two blocks away. Take a shuttle to Brian Head Ski Resort or plan a scenic day trip to Bryce Canyon or Zion National Parks. Box lunches can be arranged.

Innkeeper(s): Larry & Rae Overson. $95-110. 4 rooms with PB. Breakfast included in rates. Types of meals: Full gourmet bkfst, early coffee/tea, picnic lunch and room service. Beds: QT. Reading lamp and ceiling fan in room. Air conditioning. TV, VCR, parlor games and telephone on premises. Limited handicap access. Antiquing, art galleries, bicycling, cross-country skiing, downhill skiing, fishing, golf, hiking, horseback riding, live theater, museums, parks, shopping, sporting events, tennis and water sports nearby.

Location: Country.
Certificate may be used: November to May.

Storybook Cottage, A Bed and Breakfast

218-S 100 West
Cedar City, UT 84720
(435)586-8057 (866)586-8057 Fax:(435)586-9838
Internet: www.storybookbnb.com
E-mail: don@storybookbnb.com

Circa 1926. Recently renovated, this Tudor-Storybook home was built in 1926 and boasts an early 20th-century décor and intimate ambiance. Sit by the fire with a book selection from the library, watch a video or play a game. Stay in one of the three air-conditioned guest bedrooms that feature data ports, modem hookups, ceiling fans and desks. After a satisfying breakfast relax in the garden on the patio. Zion and Bryce National Parks are wonderful day trips to experience.

Innkeeper(s): Pam & Don McMurray. $110-125. 3 rooms with PB. Breakfast included in rates. Types of meals: KQ. Modem hook-up, data port, reading lamp, ceiling fan and desk in room. Central air. TV, VCR, fax, copier, library, parlor games, telephone and fireplace on premises. Bicycling, downhill skiing, fishing, golf and live theater nearby.

Location: Mountains.
Certificate may be used: Anyday from Nov. 1 through June 15.

Stratford Bed & Breakfast

161 South 200 West
Cedar City, UT 84720
(435)867-5280 (877)530-5280
Internet: www.stratfordbb.com
E-mail: marybeth@stratfordbb.com

Circa 1934. Just two blocks from Main Street, this whimsical bed & breakfast adorns a quiet, tree-lined neighborhood in the historic downtown area. Sit on the inviting front porch with a glass of lemonade overlooking the hummingbirds in the garden. Watch cable TV or a video in the parlor. After sleeping under a quilt in a comfortable bed, read the morning paper before breakfast. Enjoy a family-style meal in front of the bay window of the breakfast room that includes fruit, an entree and just-baked breads with homemade jams and jellies. Take a shady one-block stroll to the Utah Shakespeare Festival.

Innkeeper(s): Mary Beth Cook. $85-120. 4 rooms with PB, 1 suite. Breakfast and snacks/refreshments included in rates. Types of meals: Full bkfst and early coffee/tea. Beds: KQT. Modem hook-up, data port, ceiling fan, feather beds and iron/ironing board in room. Central air. TV, VCR, telephone, fireplace and backyard picnic area on premises. Limited handicap access. Antiquing, art galleries, bicycling, cross-country skiing, downhill skiing, fishing, golf, hiking, live theater, museums, parks, Utah Shakespearean Festival, Neil Simon Festival, Zion National Park, Cedar Breaks National Park and Brian Head Ski Resort nearby.

Location: City.

Certificate may be used: Anytime, subject to availability.

Ephraim   G5

Ephraim Homestead

135 W 100 N (43-2)
Ephraim, UT 84627-1131
(435)283-6367
Internet: www.sanpete.com

Circa 1880. Three buildings comprise this Mormon pioneer homestead. The Granary, circa 1860, is furnished in Mormon pioneer items and resembles a museum reproduction with its fireplace, cast-iron cookstove, rustic kitchen, antique beds and cradle. The barn offers two rustic rooms on the top floor, while the Victorian Gothic house, fashioned of adobe, is furnished in Eastlake antiques. It features Scandinavian/Victorian stencilings in its two tiny guest rooms located up steep stairs off the kitchen. Apple muffins and French toast are prepared on the wood stove for guests.

Innkeeper(s): Sherron Andreasen. $55-95. 2 rooms and 1 cottage. Breakfast included in rates. Types of meals: Full bkfst and snacks/refreshments. Reading lamp, stereo, refrigerator, telephone, desk, antique parlor and cookstoves in room. Air conditioning. Fireplace, garden, swings, porches and patio on premises. Antiquing, cross-country skiing, live theater, shopping and sporting events nearby.

Location: Near mountains.

Certificate may be used: All year, excluding third and fourth weeks of June and major holidays.

Huntsville   C5

Jackson Fork Inn LLC

7345 E 900 S
Huntsville, UT 84317-9778
(801)745-0051 (800)255-0672
Internet: www.jacksonforkinn.com
E-mail: vjfi@softcom.net

Circa 1938. Surrounded by scenic mountains, pine and aspen trees, the location in the Ogden Valley Recreation Area is ideal for nature enthusiasts. The inn is named after the large hayfork that hauled hay into the loft of this former modern dairy barn and hangs on display outside. Two-story guest bedrooms are cozy and comfortable boasting lofts and spiral staircases. Several rooms include two-person whirlpool tubs. A self-serve continental breakfast is prepared each day with muffins and fresh coffee. A first-floor restaurant offers fish, chicken, steak, pasta and vegetarian dishes. Skiers appreciate the nearby Powder Mountain, Nordic Valley and Snowbasin ski resorts.

Innkeeper(s): Vicki Petersen. $75-125. 7 rooms with PB. Breakfast included in rates. Types of meals: Cont. Restaurant on premises. Beds: Q. Reading lamp and ceiling fan in room. Air conditioning. TV, fireplace and full breakfast on Sunday on premises. Cross-country skiing, downhill skiing, fishing, parks, shopping and water sports nearby.

Location: Mountains.

Certificate may be used: Anytime, subject to availability.

Kanab   L4

Viola's Garden Bed & Breakfast

250 North 100 West
Kanab, UT 84741
(435)644-5683
Internet: www.violas-garden.com
E-mail: nileen@violas-garden.com

Ordered from a 1912 Sears and Roebuck's catalog, this home has been lovingly restored by descendants of the original owners. The formal parlor boasts a hand-painted ceiling. Relax in the cafe sun room. An eclectic Victorian decor highlights the guest bedrooms. The Rose Garden Room features a clawfoot tub. Cherry and Apple Blossom rooms share a large deck overlooking the hot tub, while the Lilac Room includes a private balcony. Savor every mouthful of a delicious breakfast served in the formal dining room.

Innkeeper(s): Von & Nileen Whitlock. $75-125. Call inn for details.

Certificate may be used: January-April, subject to availability.

Logan   B5

Logan House Inn

168 N 100 E
Logan, UT 84321-4610
(435)752-7727 (800)478-7459 Fax:(435)752-0092
Internet: www.loganhouseinn.com
E-mail: loganhouse@loganhouseinn.com

Circa 1898. Located in the Logan Historic District, the white pillars and gabled entrance to this Georgian manor is a foretaste of an exceptional lodging experience. There is a third-floor ballroom and a reception area includes a glass conservatory with a baby grand piano. It opens to a large wraparound veranda and lush courtyard. Ask for The Library for book-lined walls, a draped four-poster queen-size bed, fireplace and whirlpool. If you prefer the bridal suite, otherwise known as The Master Suite, you'll enjoy leaded glass windows, a king bed, balcony, sitting porch and a bath with whirlpool tub. In the morning, the inn's full breakfast might include stuffed French toast with raspberry sauce, breakfast rolls and fruit.

Innkeeper(s): Rod & Marion Vaughn. $79-225. 6 rooms with PB, 3 with FP, 3 suites and 1 conference room. Breakfast included in rates. Types of meals: Full bkfst. Beds: KQD. Cable TV, VCR, reading lamp, ceiling fan, clock radio, telephone and computer hookup in room. Air conditioning. Parlor games and fireplace on premises. Handicap access. Antiquing, cross-country skiing, downhill skiing, fishing, live theater, shopping, sporting events, water sports and opera festival nearby.

Certificate may be used: Oct. 15 to March 15, all days of the week.

Moab   I9

Cali Cochitta Bed & Breakfast Inn

110 S 200 East
Moab, UT 84532
(435)259-4961 (888)429-8112 Fax:(435)259-4964
Internet: www.moabdreaminn.com
E-mail: calicochitta@moabdreaminn.com

Circa 1870. This two-story sandstone brick Victorian is in Red Rock Country, which is known for its beautiful panoramas. Innkeeper Kim's beautiful garden has a fountain and is lit by torches at night. She grows both flowers and herbs. The inn is decorated with period Victorian pieces and is full of music and candlelight at night. It has five guest bedrooms including one suite and one cottage. Innkeeper David Boger has 20 years in food management at country clubs and fine restaurants and has catered for international organizations and dignitaries including President George Bush. He cooks with fresh herbs from Kim's garden. Breakfasts include such gourmet fare as crab quiche, homemade blueberry muffins, banana bread, coffee cakes and fresh seasonal berries with the inn's secret Grand Marnier sauce. Other culinary requests, from picnic lunches to candlelight dinners, can be accommodated upon request. The inn is near Arches and Canyonlands National Park and not far from the town of Moab. Guests may enjoy antiquing, shopping touring museums and visiting wineries. Or they may go bicycling, canoeing, fishing, golfing, hiking or horseback riding. David and Kim suggest that guests get up early at least one morning during their stay, and sit on the front porch with a cup of coffee, tea or juice and soak in the magnificent Southern Utah sunrise.

Innkeeper(s): David & Kim Boger. $69-130. 5 rooms with PB, 1 suite and 1 cottage. Breakfast, afternoon tea and snacks/refreshments included in rates. Types of meals: Full gourmet bkfst, early coffee/tea, lunch, picnic lunch and gourmet dinner. Beds: QDT. Cable TV, reading lamp, ceiling fan, clock radio, turn-down service and desk in room. Central air. Spa, library, child care, parlor games and telephone on premises. Handicap access. Antiquing, art galleries, bicycling, canoeing/kayaking, cross-country skiing, fishing, golf, hiking, horseback riding, live theater, museums, parks, shopping, tennis, water sports, wineries, rock climbing and river rafting nearby.

Location: City.

Publicity: *PBS.*

Certificate may be used: January, February excluding holidays and special events. Sunday through Wednesday, subject to availability.

Park City   **D6**

The 1904 Imperial Hotel-A B&B

221 Main St, PO Box 1628
Park City, UT 84060-1628
(435)649-1904 (800)669-8824 Fax:(435)645-7421
Internet: www.1904imperial.com
E-mail: stay@1904imperial.com

Circa 1904. Too much of a good thing can be wonderful. That's what they'll tell you at the Imperial, a historic turn-of-the-century hotel decorated in a "Western" Victorian style. Several guest rooms include amenities like clawfoot or Roman tubs and sitting areas. A few overlook Park City's historic Main Street. The inn's largest suite includes a bedroom and a spiral staircase leading up to a cozy loft area. There are ski lockers and a Jacuzzi on-site. Transportation to area ski lifts are located nearby.

Innkeeper(s): Tish Fowler. $80-245. 10 rooms with PB, 2 suites. Breakfast included in rates. Types of meals: Full bkfst and snacks/refreshments. Beds: KQT. Cable TV, reading lamp, clock radio, telephone and desk in room. Fax, copier, parlor games and fireplace on premises. Antiquing, cross-country skiing, downhill skiing, fishing, live theater, parks, shopping, sporting events and water sports nearby.

Location: Mountains.

Certificate may be used: April 15-June 15; Sept. 15-Nov. 15, space available.

The Old Miners' Lodge - A B&B Inn

615 Woodside Ave, PO Box 2639
Park City, UT 84060-2639
(435)645-8068 (800)648-8068 Fax:(435)645-7420
Internet: www.oldminerslodge.com
E-mail: stay@oldminerslodge.com

Circa 1889. This originally was established as a miners' boarding house by E. P. Ferry, owner of the Woodside-Norfolk silver mines. A two-story Victorian with Western flavor, the lodge is a significant structure in the Park City National Historic District. Just on the edge of the woods is a deck and a steaming hot tub.

Innkeeper(s): Susan Wynne & Liza Simpson. $75-275. 12 rooms with PB, 3 suites and 3 conference rooms. Breakfast and snacks/refreshments included in rates. Types of meals: Full bkfst and early coffee/tea. Beds: KQDT. Reading lamp, refrigerator, ceiling fan, turn-down service, robes and clock in room. Fax, copier, spa, library, parlor games, telephone and fireplace on premises. Antiquing, cross-country skiing, downhill skiing, fishing, live theater, parks and shopping nearby.

Location: Mountains.

Publicity: *Boston Herald, Los Angeles Times, Detroit Free Press, Washington Post, Ski, Bon Appetit and ESPN.*

"This is the creme de la creme. The most wonderful place I have stayed at bar none, including ski country in the U.S. and Europe."

Certificate may be used: April 15-June 15 or Sept. 15-Nov. 15, any days of the week. June 15-Sept. 15, any stay Sunday-Thursday. Not weekends.

Old Town Guest House

Box 162
Park City, UT 84060
(435)649-2642 (800)290-6423#3710 Fax:(435)649-3320
Internet: www.oldtownguesthouse.com
E-mail: Dlovci@cs.com

Circa 1900. Centrally located, this historic inn is perfect for hikers, skiers and bikers to enjoy all that the mountains offer. Experience convenience and affordability accented with adventure and inspiration. Some of the comfortable guest bedrooms and suites feature lodge-pole pine furnishings and a jetted tub or fireplace. A Park City Breakfast is included and sure to please hungry appetites. The innkeepers' motto of "play hard, rest easy" is pleasantly fulfilled. Assistance is offered in making the most of any stay. Refuel with afternoon snacks and relax in the hot tub.

Innkeeper(s): Deb Lovci. $59-209. 4 rooms with PB, 1 with FP, 1 suite. Breakfast, afternoon tea and snacks/refreshments included in rates. Types of meals: Country bkfst, veg bkfst and early coffee/tea. Beds: QT. Modem hookup, data port, cable TV, VCR, reading lamp, stereo, refrigerator, ceiling fan, snack bar, clock radio, telephone, desk, hot tub/spa, voice mail, fireplace, robes and Internet access in room. Fax, spa, parlor games, laundry facility, ski boot dryers, video library, afternoon snacks, bike storage, ski storage, computer and day packs on premises. Antiquing, art galleries, bicycling, canoeing/kayaking, cross-country skiing, downhill skiing, fishing, golf, hiking, horseback riding, live theater, museums, parks, shopping, tennis, Park City Mountain Resort (walking distance), Deer Valley (free shuttle), The Canyons (free shuttle) and snowshoeing nearby.

Location: Mountains. Ski areas and mountain biking trails.

Publicity: *Utah Outdoor Magazine, Utah Outdoors July 2002 and voted inn "with best activities."*

Certificate may be used: May-Dec. 15, subject to availability.

Woodside Inn

PO Box 682680
Park City, UT 84068
(435)649-3494 (888)241-5890 Fax:(435)649-2392

Circa 2000. In classic mountain style, this newly built wood-and-stone bed & breakfast is decorated in a blend of contemporary and antique furnishings. Snacks and refreshments are served in the afternoon. Well-appointed guest bedrooms and a suite offer comfort and style. Generous amenities boast a double Jacuzzi tub with separate shower, DVD and CD players, fine linens, down comforters, robes, appliances for personal grooming and slate water fountains. A hearty breakfast may include fruit smoothies, apple pancakes and egg souffles. Ski and luggage storage is available.

Innkeeper(s): Bob McCallister. $89-289. 6 rooms, 5 with PB, 1 suite. Breakfast and snacks/refreshments included in rates. Types of meals: Full bkfst and early coffee/tea. Beds: KQT. Modem hook-up, data port, cable TV, reading lamp, CD player, ceiling fan, clock radio, telephone, desk, hot tub/spa and DVD players in room. Air conditioning. Fax, copier, parlor games, fireplace, elevator and guest refrigerator on premises. Handicap access. Art galleries, bicycling, canoeing/kayaking, cross-country skiing, downhill skiing, fishing, golf, hiking, horseback riding, live theater, museums, parks, shopping, tennis and water sports nearby.

Location: Mountains.

Certificate may be used: April-Dec. 15 any days of week. Not available Dec. 15-March 31.

Salt Lake City   D5

The Anton Boxrud B&B

57 S 600 E
Salt Lake City, UT 84102-1006
(801)363-8035 (800)524-5511 Fax:(801)596-1316
Internet: www.antonboxrud.com
E-mail: info@antonboxrud.com

Circa 1901. One of Salt Lake City's grand old homes, this Victorian home with eclectic style is on the register of the Salt Lake City Historical Society. The interior is furnished with antiques from around the country and Old World details. In the sitting and dining rooms, guests will find chairs with intricate carvings, a table with carved swans for support, embossed brass door knobs and stained and beveled glass. There is an out-door hot tub available to guests. The inn is located just a half-block south of the Utah Governor's Mansion in the historic district. A full homemade breakfast and evening snack are provided.

Innkeeper(s): Jane Johnson. $69-140. 7 rooms, 5 with PB, 1 suite. Breakfast included in rates. Types of meals: Full bkfst, early coffee/tea, snacks/refreshments and gourmet dinner. Beds: KQT. Reading lamp, clock radio and desk in room. Telephone and fireplace on premises. Amusement parks, antiquing, cross-country skiing, downhill skiing, fishing, live theater, shopping, sporting events and water sports nearby.

Location: City.

Publicity: *Salt Lake Tribune.*

"Made us feel at home and well-fed. Can you adopt us?"

Certificate may be used: Anytime.

Haxton Manor

943 East South Temple
Salt Lake City, UT 84102
(801)363-4646 Fax:(801)363-4686
Internet: www.haxtonmanor.com
E-mail: innkeepers@haxtonmanor.com

Circa 1906. Built by pioneers, this historic inn prominently sits in the distinct Avenues District. Victorian splendor is reflected in the gables and wraparound porch. The authentic Boar's Head pub, decor and furnishings are reminiscent of an English manor house. The living room invites conversation by the beehive fireplace. Elegant guest bedrooms and suites feature fine amenities and service. The Sussex and Windsor suites boast two-person jetted tubs and fireplaces. Speaker phones, voice mail and computer data ports are added conveniences. A generous continental breakfast is served in the intimate dining room. Enjoy a variety of complimentary beverages at any time. An exercise bike is set up for the fitness-minded.

Innkeeper(s): Buffi and Douglas King. $100-170. 7 rooms with PB, 2 with FP. Breakfast, afternoon tea and snacks/refreshments included in rates. Types of meals: Country bkfst and early coffee/tea. Beds: QT. Data port, cable TV, VCR, reading lamp, ceiling fan, clock radio, telephone, turn-down service, desk, voice mail, most with jetted tubs, fireplace and wireless Internet access in room. Central air. Fax, library, parlor games, fireplace and limited health/workout facilities on premises. Limited handicap access. Antiquing, bicycling, cross-country skiing, downhill skiing, golf, hiking, live theater, museums, parks, shopping, sporting events and tennis nearby.

Location: City. Beautiful central location in historic district on a huge corner lot.

Publicity: *British Hospitality House at the 2002 Salt Lake games.*

Certificate may be used: Anytime, subject to availability.

Saltair B&B

164 S 900 E
Salt Lake City, UT 84102-4103
(801)533-8184 (800)733-8184 Fax:(801)595-0332
Internet: www.saltlakebandb.com
E-mail: saltair@saltlakebandb.com

Circa 1903. The Saltair is the oldest continuously operating bed & breakfast in Utah and offers a prime location to enjoy Salt Lake City. The simply decorated rooms include light, airy window dressings, charming furnishings and special touches. Breakfasts, especially the delicious Saltair Eggs Benedict topped with avocado, sour creme and salsa, are memorable. The inn is within walking distance to four historic districts and only one mile from Temple Square and the Governor's Mansion. Day trips include treks to several national and state parks and the Wasatch Front ski areas.

Innkeeper(s): Nancy Saxton & Jan Bartlett. $79-149. 7 rooms, 4 with PB. Breakfast and snacks/refreshments included in rates. Types of meals: Full gourmet bkfst and early coffee/tea. Beds: QT. Reading lamp, clock radio and fresh flowers in room. Air conditioning. VCR, fax, spa, parlor games and telephone on premises. Antiquing, cross-country skiing, downhill skiing, fishing, live theater, parks, shopping, sporting events and water sports nearby.

Location: City.

Publicity: *Mobil, Logan Sun and Sunset.*

"Your swing and Saltair Muffins were fabulous."

Certificate may be used: April-July, September-November, Dec. 1-15.

Wildflowers B&B

936 E 1700 S
Salt Lake City, UT 84105-3329
(801)466-0600 (800)569-0009 Fax:(801)484-7832
E-mail: lark2spur@aol.com

Circa 1891. Holding true to its name, the grounds surrounding this Victorian home are covered with all sorts of flowers ranging from wild geraniums to coreopsis to meadow rue. The outside beauty only serves to complement the magnificence on the inside of this historic residence. Hand-carved staircases, stained-glass windows, clawfoot bathtubs and original chandeliers make up just some of the touches that will make a stay here memorable. Situated in the heart of Salt Lake City, this home offers all the comfort one could ask for and the convenience of being just a few minutes away from skiing or a trip downtown. Like this classic residence, 10 nearby homes are also listed in the National Register of Historic Places.

Innkeeper(s): Jeri Parker & Cill Sparks. $70-125. 5 rooms with PB, 2 suites and 1 conference room. Breakfast included in rates. Types of meals: Full gourmet bkfst. Beds: KQD. Cable TV, VCR, reading lamp, refrigerator, ceiling fan, clock radio, telephone and desk in room. Air conditioning. Fax, copier, bicycles, parlor games, fireplace and art on premises. Amusement parks, antiquing, cross-country skiing, downhill skiing, fishing, live theater, parks, shopping, sporting events, water sports and museums nearby.

Location: City. 5 minutes to mountains.

Publicity: *Salt Lake Tribune.*

"Service above and beyond my expectations with people that I'll remember."

Certificate may be used: Not February, March, holidays. All other times depending on availability.

Spring City   G6

The Garden, Bed & Breakfast Inn

PO Box 425
Spring City, UT 84662
(435)462-9285 (877)537-2337
Internet: www.bedsandroses.com
E-mail: info@BedsAndRoses.com

Circa 1994. Nature enthusiasts will adore this 20-acre retreat situated at the base of Horseshoe Mountain. Continuous awe-inspiring views include gorgeous sunsets and a bright canopy of stars. The comfortable guest bedrooms feature kitchenettes with popcorn for movie watching. Enjoy a full hot breakfast delivered to your door. Choose from popular homemade wheat waffles with all the trimmings or traditional fare of eggs, bacon, sausage, home fries, French toast and a fruit medley with bagels and cream cheese. The inn boasts farm animals and an assortment of wildlife. Equestrian facilities are available.

Innkeeper(s): Phyllis & Bud Snedecor. $65-135. 3 rooms with PB. Breakfast and snacks/refreshments included in rates. Types of meals: Full gourmet bkfst, veg bkfst, early coffee/tea, picnic lunch and room service. Beds: Q. Modem hook-up, cable TV, VCR, reading lamp, stereo, clock radio, telephone, coffeemaker, desk, fireplace, table for two, Eve's Garden Room has a large jetted tub, Lilac Room has kitchenette with microwave, sink and large refrigerator in room. Fax, copier, stable, library, laundry facility, wood stove in the parlor, fire pit, hammock, stream, hiking trails, animals and view on premises. Handicap access. Antiquing, art galleries, bicycling, cross-country skiing, fishing, golf, hiking, horseback riding, live theater, museums, parks, shopping, tennis, wineries, local artists, handmade violins, furniture, pottery, blacksmithing and old home tours and maps (and driving CD) of local historical areas nearby.

Location: Country, mountains.

Certificate may be used: Anytime, Sunday-Thursday.

Sterling   G5

Cedar Crest Inn

819 Palisade Rd
Sterling, UT 84665
(435)835-6352
E-mail: cedar@heavenlyplace.com

Circa 1903. Several structures comprise the Cedar Crest Inn, including the Swiss-style Lindenhaus, named for a giant linden tree adjacent to the home. The tree was brought to America from Germany as a seedling. Guests also can opt to stay in Linderhof, which offers three beautiful suites. The third structure on this 18-acre property is the popular Cedar Crest Restaurant, which serves a variety of gourmet entrees, including lobster, chicken Cordon Bleu and Filet Mignon. The grounds are beautiful, and on cold nights, guests can stay indoors and watch a favorite movie. The innkeepers have a selection of more than 300.

Innkeeper(s): Ron & Don Kelsch. $59-89. 8 rooms with PB, 2 suites. Breakfast included in rates. Types of meals: Full gourmet bkfst, early coffee/tea and gourmet dinner. Restaurant on premises. Beds: KQD. Cable TV, VCR, reading lamp, refrigerator, clock radio and desk in room. Air conditioning. Spa, bicycles, parlor games, telephone and fireplace on premises. Antiquing, cross-country skiing, parks, shopping and water sports nearby.

Location: Mountains.

Certificate may be used: April 1-Aug. 30, Saturday-Thursday. Excludes holidays and special events. Does not include breakfast on weekday mornings or rooms Friday night.

Torrey   I6

SkyRidge Inn Bed and Breakfast

PO Box 750220
Torrey, UT 84775-0220
(435)425-3222 Fax:(435)425-3222
Internet: www.skyridgeinn.com
E-mail: info@skyridgeinn.com

Circa 1994. Located on 75 acres, this gabled, three-story territorial style inn offers views of Capitol Reef National Park, Dixie National Forest and Torrey Valley. Antiques, art and upscale furnishings fill the rooms. Some guest chambers feature a hot tub, jetted tub and private deck. Breakfast is served in the dining room overlooking forested Boulder Mountain. Wilderness tours via horseback or four-wheel drive may be arranged. The natural arches, sheer canyon walls and multi-colored cliffs and domes of Capitol Reef National Park are five minutes away. Guests are welcome to pick fruit from the Park's ancient orchards during summer and fall.

Innkeeper(s): Shauna and Jerry Agnew. $104-172. 6 rooms with PB and 1 conference room. Breakfast and snacks/refreshments included in rates. Types of meals: Full gourmet bkfst. Beds: KQT. TV, VCR, reading lamp, CD player, refrigerator, ceiling fan, clock radio, telephone, coffeemaker, turn-down service, desk, hot tub/spa, private decks, patio, coffee service and robes in room. Air conditioning. Fax, spa, library, parlor games, fireplace and refrigerator on premises. Antiquing, art galleries, bicycling, fishing, hiking, horseback riding, museums, parks, shopping, Capitol Reef National Park, Grand Staircase National Park and Dixie National Forest nearby.

Location: Country. Capitol Reef National Park - 3 miles.

Publicity: *National Geographic Traveler, Sunset Magazine* and *Travel and Leisure Magazine.*

Certificate may be used: Anytime, November-March, subject to availability.

Vermont

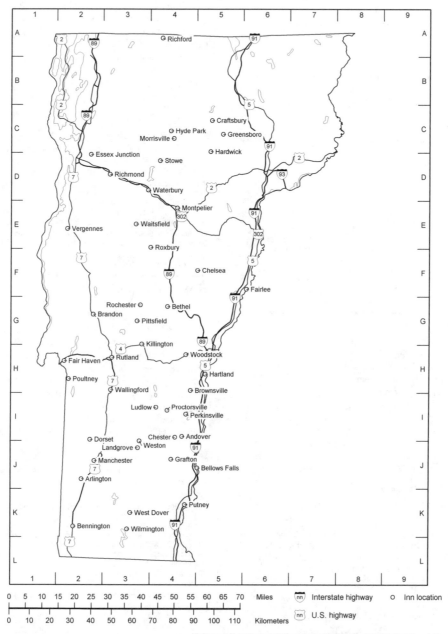

A1 ⊙ Richford
A2 [89]
A2 [2]
A6 [91]

B2 [2]
B2 [89]
B5 ⊙ 5

C5 ⊙ Craftsbury
C4 ⊙ Hyde Park
C5 ⊙ Greensboro
C4 Morrisville ⊙
C5 ⊙ Hardwick
C6 [91]
C7 [2]

D2 ⊙ Essex Junction
D4 ⊙ Stowe
D2 ⊙ Richmond
D4 ⊙ Waterbury
D4 [2]
D6 [93]

E4 Montpelier
E4 [302]
E6 [302]
E3 ⊙ Waitsfield
E2 ⊙ Vergennes
E4 ⊙ Roxbury
E2 [7]

F4 [89]
F4 ⊙ Chelsea
F6 [5]
F6 ⊙ Fairlee
F5 [91]

G3 Rochester ⊙
G4 ⊙ Bethel
G2 ⊙ Brandon
G3 ⊙ Pittsfield
G5 [89]

H2 ⊙ Fair Haven
H3 ⊙ Rutland
H3 [4]
H4 ⊙ Killington
H5 ⊙ Woodstock
H5 [5]
H5 ⊙ Hartland
H2 ⊙ Poultney
H3 [7]
H3 ⊙ Wallingford
H5 ⊙ Brownsville

I4 Ludlow ⊙
I4 ⊙ Proctorsville
I5 ⊙ Perkinsville

J3 ⊙ Dorset
J4 Chester ⊙ ⊙ Andover
J3 Landgrove ⊙ Weston
J5 [91]
J3 ⊙ Manchester
J4 ⊙ Grafton
J3 [7]
J5 ⊙ Bellows Falls
J2 ⊙ Arlington

K5 ⊙ Putney
K4 ⊙ West Dover
K2 ⊙ Bennington
K4 ⊙ Wilmington
K5 [91]
K2 [7]

| 0 | 5 | 10 | 15 | 20 | 25 | 30 | 35 | 40 | 45 | 50 | 55 | 60 | 65 | 70 | Miles |

| 0 | 10 | 20 | 30 | 40 | 50 | 60 | 70 | 80 | 90 | 100 | 110 | Kilometers |

[nn] Interstate highway   ⊙ Inn location

[nn] U.S. highway

Andover 14

Historic Rowells Inn

1834 Simonsville Rd
Andover, VT 05143
(802)875-3658 (800)728-0842 Fax:(802)875-3680
Internet: www.rowellsinn.com
E-mail: innkeep@rowellsinn.com

Circa 1820. Experience the heritage of New England hospitality at this Greek Revival brick inn that is listed in the National Register. Built as a stagecoach stop and part of the Underground Railroad, historic details and lavish antiques combine with generous service in a splendid setting. Rockers on the front porch and a fire in the parlor or Sun Room provide comfortable relaxation. The Tavern Room, an English-style pub is ideal for working on puzzles with new friends and a cold drink. Authentically furnished guest bedrooms and suites feature canopy feather beds, fresh flowers, air conditioning or ceiling fans. Some boast clawfoot tubs, wood-burning fireplaces and balcony access. The country breakfasts are always a satisfying delight. Dinner service is available. Play horseshoes, badminton or croquet on the one and a half acres with flower gardens and a small fish pond.

Innkeeper(s): Michael Brengolini, Susan McNulty. $89-175. 7 rooms with PB, 2 with FP, 2 suites and 1 conference room. Breakfast and snacks/refreshments included in rates. Types of meals: Country bkfst, veg bkfst, early coffee/tea, picnic lunch, afternoon tea and gourmet dinner. Restaurant on premises. Beds: KQDT. Reading lamp, ceiling fan, clock radio, desk and fireplace in room. Air conditioning. TV, VCR, fax, copier, library, parlor games, telephone and fireplace on premises. Handicap access. Antiquing, art galleries, bicycling, canoeing/kayaking, cross-country skiing, downhill skiing, fishing, golf, hiking, horseback riding, live theater, museums, parks, shopping, tennis, water sports, wineries, foliage and bird watching nearby.

Location: Country.

Certificate may be used: April-June, subject to availability. July-August, Sunday-Thursday.

Arlington J2

Hill Farm Inn

458 Hill Farm Rd
Arlington, VT 05250-9311
(802)375-2269 (800)882-2545 Fax:(802)375-9918
Internet: www.hillfarminn.com
E-mail: stay@hillfarminn.com

Circa 1790. One of Vermont's original land grant farmsteads, Hill Farm Inn has welcomed guests since 1905 when the widow Mettie Hill opened her home to summer vacationers.

The farm is surrounded by 50 peaceful acres that border the Battenkill River. Guests can relax and enjoy the simple life and visit the inn's sheep, goats and chickens or soak in the 360-degree views of the mountains. Accommodations are charming and cozy, and summer guests have the option of staying in one of four cabins. A large, country breakfast of homemade fare starts off each day.

Innkeeper(s): Al & Lisa Gray. $80-185. 15 rooms with PB, 3 with FP, 6 suites and 4 cabins. Breakfast and afternoon tea included in rates. Types of meals: Full bkfst. Beds: KQDT. Cable TV, VCR, reading lamp, refrigerator, ceiling fan, clock radio and two kitchenettes in room. Air conditioning. Fax, copier, parlor games, telephone, fireplace and farm animals on premises. Amusement parks, antiquing, art galleries, bicycling, cross-country skiing,

downhill skiing, fishing, golf, hiking, horseback riding, live theater, museums, parks, shopping and families welcome nearby.

Location: Country, mountains. One mile of river frontage.

Publicity: *Providence Journal, Boston Globe, Innsider and Country.*

"I have already taken the liberty of changing the meaning of relaxation in the dictionary to 'Hill Farm Inn.' Thank you. . . It was great."

Certificate may be used: Nov. 1-Sept. 15, Sunday-Thursday; excluding holiday periods.

Ira Allen House

6311 Rte 7A
Arlington, VT 05250-9317
(802)362-2284 (888)733-8666 Fax:(802)362-2284
Internet: www.iraallenhouse.com
E-mail: stay@iraallenhouse.com

Circa 1770. Built by Ethan Allen's brother, this Colonial Revival inn is a state historic site. Hand-blown glass panes, hand-hewn beams, handmade bricks and wide-board floors provide evidence of the inn's longevity. Surrounded by farms and forest, the inn's setting is perfect for those searching for some peace and quiet. Plenty of recreational activities also are found nearby, including fine trout fishing, swimming and canoeing in the Battenkill River on the property.

Innkeeper(s): Sandy & Ray Walters. $110-140. 5 suites. Breakfast included in rates. Types of meals: Full bkfst. Reading lamp in room. Air conditioning. VCR, telephone and fireplace on premises. Antiquing, canoeing/kayaking, cross-country skiing, downhill skiing, live theater and shopping nearby.

Location: Mountains.

Certificate may be used: Year-round except foliage season (last week September-last week October) and holidays, Sunday through Thursday.

Bellows Falls J5

River Mist B&B

7 Burt St
Bellows Falls, VT 05101-1401
(802)463-9023 (888)463-9023 Fax:(802)463-9002
Internet: www.river-mist.com
E-mail: rivermistbnb@aol.com

Circa 1895. The scenic village of Bellows Falls is home to this late 19th-century Queen Anne Victorian inn, with its inviting wraparound porch and country Victorian interior. Guests may relax in any of three sitting rooms or in front of the fireplace. Enjoy a day of antiquing, skiing or just wandering around the picturesque environs. Be sure to take a ride on the Green Mountain Flyer before leaving town.

Innkeeper(s): Roger Riccio & Verone Reynolds. $99-150. 4 rooms with PB, 2 with FP. Breakfast included in rates. Types of meals: Full gourmet bkfst, early coffee/tea and afternoon tea. Beds: QT. Cable TV, VCR, reading lamp, ceiling fan, turn-down service and fireplace in room. Air conditioning. Fax, parlor games, telephone and fireplace on premises. Amusement parks, antiquing, art galleries, bicycling, canoeing/kayaking, cross-country skiing, downhill skiing, fishing, golf, hiking, horseback riding, live theater, parks, shopping, sporting events, tennis, water sports and wineries nearby.

Location: Village.

Certificate may be used: December through February, Sunday through Thursday.

Bennington   K2

Alexandra B&B

Rt 7A Orchard Rd
Bennington, VT 05201
(802)442-5619 (888)207-9386 Fax:(802)442-5592
Internet: www.alexandrainn.com
E-mail: alexandr@sover.net

Circa 1859. Located on two acres at the edge of town,
Alexandra is a Colonial-style inn. There are king or queen beds
in all the rooms, as well as fireplaces and views of Bennington
Monument and the Green Mountains. Each bath offers water
jets and showers. A full gourmet breakfast is served. Bennington
College and the business district are five minutes from the inn.
Innkeeper(s): Alex Koks & Andra Erickson. $100-150. 13 rooms with PB, 12
with FP, 7 suites and 1 conference room. Breakfast included in rates. Types
of meals: Full gourmet bkfst and early coffee/tea. Beds: KQ. Modem hook-up,
cable TV, VCR, reading lamp, clock radio, telephone, desk and hot tub/spa in
room. Air conditioning. Fax and copier on premises. Limited handicap access.
Antiquing, art galleries, bicycling, canoeing/kayaking, cross-country skiing,
downhill skiing, fishing, golf, hiking, horseback riding, live theater, museums,
parks, shopping, tennis, water sports and wineries nearby.
Location: Town.
Certificate may be used: Jan. 2-July 1, weekdays only.

South Shire Inn

124 Elm St
Bennington, VT 05201-2232
(802)447-3839 Fax:(802)442-3547
Internet: www.southshire.com
E-mail: relax@southshire.com

Circa 1887. Built in the late 1800s, this inn boasts a mahogany-
paneled library, soaring 10-foot ceilings, and three of the guest
rooms include one of the home's original fireplaces. Guest rooms
feature antiques and Victorian décor. Rooms in the restored carriage house include both a fireplace and a whirlpool tub. Guests
are pampered with both a full breakfast, as well as afternoon tea.
Local attractions include the Bennington Museum, antique
shops, craft stores, covered bridges and skiing.
Innkeeper(s): George & Joyce Goeke. $110-190. 9 rooms with PB, 7 with
FP, 1 suite. Breakfast and afternoon tea included in rates. Types of meals:
Full bkfst, veg bkfst and early coffee/tea. Beds: KQD. Cable TV, VCR, reading
lamp, ceiling fan, clock radio, telephone and whirlpool tubs in room. Central
air. Fax, copier, library, parlor games, fireplace and guest refrigerator on
premises. Antiquing, art galleries, bicycling, canoeing/kayaking, cross-country
skiing, downhill skiing, fishing, golf, hiking, horseback riding, live theater,
museums and shopping nearby.
Location: Mountains.
Certificate may be used: Sunday-Thursday, Nov. 1-May 31, excluding holidays and special events.

Bethel   G4

Greenhurst Inn

88 North Rd
Bethel, VT 05032-9404
(802)234-9474 (800)510-2553
Internet: www.greenhurstinn.com
E-mail: crfollo@msn.com

Circa 1890. In the National Register of Historic Places,
Greenhurst is a gracious Victorian mansion built for the
Harringtons of Philadelphia. Overlooking the White River, the
inn's opulent interiors include etched windows once featured
on the cover of Vermont Life. There are eight masterpiece fireplaces and a north and south parlor.

Innkeeper(s): Lyle Wolf. $50-100. 13 rooms, 7 with
PB, 4 with FP. Breakfast included in rates.
Types of meals: Cont plus and early cof-
fee/tea. Beds: QDT. Reading lamp,
clock radio and desk in room. TV,
VCR, library, parlor games, tele-
phone and fireplace on premises.
Antiquing, cross-country skiing,
downhill skiing, fishing, live theater, parks, shopping and water sports nearby.
Publicity: *Best Country Inns of New England, Victorian Homes, Washington
Post, Boston Globe, Bride's Magazine, Los Angeles Times, Time, New York
Times, Vermont Life and The Man Who Corrupted Hadleyburg.*
"The inn is magnificent! The hospitality unforgettable."
Certificate may be used: Sunday through Thursday except Sept. 15-Oct. 15.

Brandon   G2

12 Franklin Street B&B

12 Franklin Street
Brandon, VT 05733
(802)247-6672
Internet: www.12franklinstreet.com
E-mail: relax@12franklinstreet.com

Circa 1850. An intimate ambiance is imparted at this recently
renovated Federal-style bed & breakfast. Situated in the western part of the state, the inn offers seasonal activities enhanced
by the scenic beauty. It is easy to feel comfortable in the
relaxed, smoke-free atmosphere with three guest bedrooms. Sip
morning coffee or tea on the porch while breakfast is prepared.
Mouth-watering quiche, fresh-baked breads and muffins, fruit,
and "the best French toast on the East Coast" await a hungry
appetite. Special dietary restrictions are accommodated gladly.
Innkeeper(s): Linda Healy & Jim Schamber. $65-105. 3 rooms. Breakfast
included in rates. Types of meals: Full bkfst and early coffee/tea. Beds: KQDT.
Reading lamp and clock radio in room. Air conditioning. TV, VCR, fax, telephone, porch and off-street parking on premises. Antiquing, art galleries,
canoeing/kayaking, cross-country skiing, fishing, golf, hiking, museums,
parks, shopping, Lake Dunmore and Lake Champlain nearby.
Location: Mountains. Small village.
Publicity: *Rutland Business Journal and Albany Times Union.*
Certificate may be used: Nov. 1 to June 30, Sunday-Thursday.

Churchill House Inn

3128 Forest Dale Rd, Rte 73 E
Brandon, VT 05733-9202
(802)247-3078 (877)297-2831 Fax:(802)247-0113
Internet: www.churchillhouseinn.com
E-mail: innkeeper@churchillhouseinn.com

Circa 1871. Caleb Churchill and his son, Nathan, first built a
three-story lumber mill, a grist mill and a distillery here, all
water powered. Later, with their milled lumber, they constructed this 20-room house. Because of its location, it became a
stagecoach stop and has served generations of travelers with
comfortable accommodations. The inn is adjacent to Green
Mountain National Forest, and excellent hiking, biking, skiing
and fishing are just steps away. The inn serves a four-course
dinner and a full breakfast.
Innkeeper(s): Linda & Richard Daybell. $90-220. 9 rooms with PB.
Breakfast and dinner included in rates. Types of meals: Full bkfst and picnic
lunch. Beds: QDT. Antiquing, cross-country skiing, downhill skiing, parks,
shopping and water sports nearby.
Publicity: *Country and Yankee.*
*"We felt the warm, welcoming, down-home appeal as we entered the
front hall. The food was uncommonly good — home cooking with a
gourmet flair!"*
Certificate may be used: January-September, Monday-Thursday, subject
to availability.

The Gazebo Inn

On Rt 7 (25 Grove St)
Brandon, VT 05733
(802)247-3235 (888)858-3235
Internet: www.brandon.org/gazebo.htm
E-mail: gazebo@sover.net

Circa 1865. Cozy elegance is found year-round at this classic
New England clapboard home, which is listed in the National
Register. Located in the foothills of the Green Mountain
National Forest, the inn abounds with pastoral scenes and
panoramic vistas. Furnished with Victorian antiques, common
rooms include a library with TV/VCR, parlor, reading alcove and
screened porch. Distinctive guest bedrooms offer air conditioning and feather beds with down comforters. Mother-daughter
hostesses Donna and Lindsay provide a four-course scrumptious
breakfast and daily refreshments. There is much to enjoy with
two acres of private landscaped grounds and a gazebo. Walk
into town or swim or boat at Lake Dunmore, only 10 minutes
away. During winter try cross-country skiing at Blueberry Hill.

Innkeeper(s): Donna & Lindsay Taylor. $85-125. 4 rooms with PB. Breakfast
and snacks/refreshments included in rates. Types of meals: Full gourmet bkfst
and veg bkfst. Beds: QDT. Reading lamp, turn-down service, Wake-up calls,
hair dryers, plush robes, plush linens 400 count and feather beds in room.
Air conditioning. TV, VCR, library, parlor games, telephone, fireplace and
wood burning stove on premises. Handicap access. Antiquing, art galleries,
beach, bicycling, canoeing/kayaking, cross-country skiing, downhill skiing,
fishing, golf, hiking, horseback riding, live theater, museums, shopping, water
sports, swimming, summer concerts and fine dining nearby.

Location: Small town/village.

*"Thank you for your New England-style hospitality. We had a won-
derful time. We will try to make this an annual event."*

Certificate may be used: November-April, Friday and Saturday evenings,
except for holiday weekends.

Lilac Inn

53 Park St
Brandon, VT 05733-1121
(802)247-5463 (800)221-0720 Fax:(802)247-5499
Internet: www.lilacinn.com
E-mail: lilacinn@sover.net

Circa 1909. For some, the scenery is enough of a reason to
visit Vermont. For those who need more, try the Lilac Inn. The
restored inn's beautiful furnishings, polished woodwork and
fireplaces add to the ambiance.
Canopy beds dressed with fine
linens, flowers, whirlpool tubs
and sitting areas grace the guest
rooms. A full, gourmet breakfast
is included in the rates. The inn
is a popular site for unforgettable
romantic weddings. The landscaped, two-acre grounds include
ponds, a gazebo and hundreds of perennials and annuals.
Flowers decorate the ground's stone walls.

Innkeeper(s): Shelly & Doug Sawyer. $140-325. 9 rooms with PB, 3 with FP
and 4 conference rooms. Breakfast included in rates. Types of meals: Country
bkfst and gourmet dinner. Restaurant on premises. Beds: QT. Cable TV, reading lamp, CD player, ceiling fan, clock radio, desk and fireplace in room. Air
conditioning. Fax, copier, library and telephone on premises. Handicap
access. Antiquing, art galleries, beach, bicycling, canoeing/kayaking, cross-
country skiing, downhill skiing, fishing, golf, hiking, horseback riding, live
theater, museums, parks, shopping, water sports and Warren Kimble nearby.

Location: Small town.

Publicity: *Yankee and Vermont & Country Inns.*

"Tasteful, charming and personable."

Certificate may be used: Anytime, subject to availability.

Rosebelle's Victorian Inn

PO BOX 370, Rt 7
Brandon, VT 05733-0370
(802)247-0098 (888)767-3235 Fax:(802)247-4552
Internet: www.rosebelles.com
E-mail: rosebelle@adelphia.net

Circa 1839. Experience the year-round romantic charm of this
elegant French Second Empire Victorian inn with mansard roof,
Italianate porch and artistic filigree. Listed in the National
Register and part of the Underground Railroad, this lovingly
restored inn has an impressive histo-
ry spanning from 1839. Favorite
gathering spots include the comfortable common rooms and the
wicker-filled porch. Delightful
guest bedrooms are furnished
with authentic period pieces and
boast plush amenities. Sit at individ-
ual tables to savor a scrumptious gourmet breakfast accompanied by Vermont Cabot butter, maple syrup and locally made
jams. Stroll through the lush one-acre grounds and flower gardens to encounter butterflies and hummingbirds. Browse the
gift boutique for treasures to take home. The innkeepers speak
French, offer gift certificates and special packages.

Innkeeper(s): Ginette & Norm Milot. $95-125. 5 rooms with PB. Breakfast
included in rates. Types of meals: Full bkfst. Beds: QDT. Ceiling fan and clock
radio in room. VCR, parlor games, telephone, fireplace, storage barn for bikes
and skis on premises. Antiquing, cross-country skiing, downhill skiing, fishing, live theater, parks, shopping, sporting events, water sports, hiking, snow
shoeing, Bluegrass Festival and underground railroad site nearby.

Location: Mountains. Historic town/village.

"You have captured a beautiful part of our history."

Certificate may be used: Jan. 30 to Sept. 1, Sunday-Thursday, except holiday weekends-Memorial Day, 4th of July, Labor Day, Valentine week. Call for
possible weekend availability.

Brownsville   H4

Mill Brook B&B

P.O. Box 410
Brownsville, VT 05037-0410
(802)484-7283
Internet: www.millbrookbb.com
E-mail: k@millbrookbb.com

Circa 1878. Once known as the House of Seven Gables, Mill
Brook has been in constant use as a family home and for a
while, a boarding house for mill loggers. Old German Fraktur
paintings decorate the woodwork and there are three sitting
rooms for guests. Antique furnishings are found throughout.
Popular activities in the area include hang gliding, bike tours
and canoeing.

Innkeeper(s): K. Carriere. $80-140. 5 rooms, 2 with PB, 3 suites. Breakfast
included in rates. Types of meals: Full bkfst, early coffee/tea and
snacks/refreshments. Beds: QDT. TV, reading lamp, ceiling fan and telephone
in room. VCR on premises. Antiquing, cross-country skiing, downhill skiing,
live theater, shopping and sporting events nearby.

Location: Country, mountains. Rural village.

"Splendid hospitality. Your B&B was beyond our expectation."

Certificate may be used: March-August and November, Monday-Thursday,
excluding holidays.

Chelsea   F5

Shire Inn

Main St, PO Box 37
Chelsea, VT 05038
(802)685-3031 (800)441-6908 Fax:(802)685-3871
Internet: www.shireinn.com
E-mail: keepers@shireinn.com

Circa 1832. Granite lintels over the windows and a sunburst
light over the entry highlight this Adams-style brick home. The
romantic inn, which is located in a 210-year-old historic village,
has a grand spiral staircase ascend-
ing from wide-plank pumpkin pine
floors in the entryway. Guest
rooms include antique canopied
beds, tall windows and 10-foot
ceilings. Most have wood-burning fireplaces. Included on the

property's 23 acres are granite post fencing, perennial gardens
dating from the 19th century, and a broad, rocky stream
spanned by a farm bridge. On most evenings a five-course
gourmet dinner is available.

Innkeeper(s): Jay & Karen Keller. $105-155. 6 rooms with PB, 4 with FP.
Breakfast included in rates. Types of meals: Full bkfst, early coffee/tea and
afternoon tea. Beds: KQD. Reading lamp and desk in room. Fax, copier, bicycles, library, parlor games, telephone and fireplace on premises. Antiquing,
cross-country skiing, downhill skiing, fishing, hiking, live theater, parks, shopping and water sports nearby.

Location: Country village.

Publicity: *Country Inn Review, Vermont Life and PBS.*

*"What an inn should be! Absolutely delicious food - great hospitality!
The rooms are filled with romance."*

Certificate may be used: Anytime except Sept. 10-Oct. 20 and holidays,
subject to availability.

Chester   I4

Hugging Bear Inn & Shoppe

244 Main St
Chester, VT 05143
(802)875-2412 (800)325-0519
Internet: huggingbear.com
E-mail: georgette@huggingbear.com

Circa 1850. Among the 10,000 teddy bear inhabitants of this
white Victorian inn, several peek out from the third-story windows of the octagonal tower. There is a teddy bear shop on the
premises and children and adults can
borrow a bear to take to bed with
them. Rooms are decorated with
antiques and comfortable furniture. A bear puppet show is
often staged during breakfast.

Innkeeper(s): Georgette Thomas. $65-
165. 6 rooms with PB. Breakfast included in rates. Types of meals: Country
bkfst and early coffee/tea. Beds: KQDT. Reading lamp and teddy bear in
room. Air conditioning. TV, VCR, parlor games, telephone, fireplace, 10,000
teddy bears and library on premises. Antiquing, cross-country skiing, downhill
skiing, fishing, golf, parks, shopping and swimming nearby.

Location: Mountains.

Publicity: *Rutland Daily Herald, Exxon Travel, Teddy Bear Review, Teddy Bear
Scene and Boston Globe.*

Certificate may be used: Monday through Thursday, November through May
except holiday weeks (Christmas to New Year's and Presidents' weeks).

The Inn at Cranberry Farm

61 Williams River Rd
Chester, VT 05143
(802)463-1339 (800)854-2208
Internet: www.cranberryfarminn.com
E-mail: paulansue@msn.com

Circa 1992. This contemporary post-and-beam inn in the
Green Mountains provides a peaceful and romantic getaway. Its
guest rooms feature views of the farmland, meadows, rivers and
woods of the surrounding area.
Breakfasts are enjoyed in the
dining room and often feature
Vermont French toast with
local maple syrup. For those
choosing to relax at the inn,
the loft library and patio are
popular locations.

Innkeeper(s): Susan Morency & Paul Florindo. $130-245. 11 rooms with PB
and 1 conference room. Breakfast included in rates. Types of meals: Full
bkfst, early coffee/tea and snacks/refreshments. Reading lamp and clock radio
in room. Telephone and fireplace on premises. Cross-country skiing, downhill
skiing and shopping nearby.

Location: Country, mountains.

Publicity: *Vermont, Bellows Falls Town Crier and Retirement.*

Certificate may be used: Feb. 1-Sept. 10, Sunday-Thursday; Nov. 1-Dec. 22,
Sunday-Friday, subject to availability.

Craftsbury   C5

Craftsbury Inn

Main St, Box 36
Craftsbury, VT 05826-0036
(802)586-2848 (800)336-2848
Internet: www.craftsburyinn.com
E-mail: cburyinn@together.net

Circa 1850. Bird's-eye maple woodwork and embossed tin
ceilings testify to the history of this mid-19th-century Greek
Revival inn, which also features random-width floors with
square nails. The foundation and porch
steps were made of bull's-eye granite,
quarried in town. The living room fireplace once graced the first post office in
Montpelier. Guest rooms sport country
antiques and handmade quilts. The dining room is open to the public for dinner by advance reservation and features
French inspired American cuisine.

Innkeeper(s): Bill & Kathy Maire. $80-175. 10 rooms, 6 with PB and 1 con-
ference room. Breakfast included in rates. Types of meals: Full bkfst and
gourmet dinner. Restaurant on premises. Beds: DT. Reading lamp in room.
VCR, parlor games, telephone and fireplace on premises. Antiquing, cross-
country skiing, downhill skiing, fishing, shopping and water sports nearby.

Location: Village.

Publicity: *Boston Globe and New York Times.*

"Very comfortable - the dining was a special treat!"

Certificate may be used: Sunday through Thursday, January-December,
except during foliage season.

Dorset I2

Marble West Inn

PO Box 847, Dorset West Rd
Dorset, VT 05251-0847
(802)867-4155 (800)453-7629 Fax:(802)867-5731
Internet: www.marblewestinn.com
E-mail: marwest@sover.net

Circa 1840. This historic Greek Revival inn boasts many elegant touches, including stenciling in its entrance hallways done by one of the nation's top craftspeople. Guests also will enjoy

Oriental rugs, handsome marble fireplaces and polished dark oak floors. Visitors delight at the many stunning views enjoyed at the inn, including Green Peak and Owl's Head mountains, flower-filled gardens and meadows and two trout-stocked ponds. Emerald Lake State Park is nearby.

Innkeeper(s): Paul Quinn. $89-179. 8 rooms with PB, 4 with FP, 1 suite. Breakfast and afternoon tea included in rates. Types of meals: Full bkfst. Beds: KQDT. Reading lamp and desk in room. Library, parlor games, telephone and fireplace on premises. Antiquing, cross-country skiing, downhill skiing, fishing, live theater, parks, shopping, water sports, designer outlet shopping, horseback riding, art galleries, biking, golf, tennis and fine dining nearby.
Location: Mountains.

"A charming inn with wonderful hospitality. The room was comfortable, immaculate, and furnished with every imaginable need and comfort."
Certificate may be used: Jan. 1-Sept. 1, Nov. 1-Dec. 15, Sunday-Thursday.

Essex Junction D2

The Inn at Essex

70 Essex Way
Essex Junction, VT 05452-3383
(802)878-1100 (800)727-4295 Fax:(802)878-0063
Internet: www.innatessex.com
E-mail: innfo@innatessex.com

Circa 1989. Elegant furnishings and decor, each in a different style, grace the guest rooms at this luxurious Colonial inn, which carries a four-diamond rating. Several guest suites include whirlpool tubs and 50 of the rooms include wood-burning fireplaces. The two restaurants are operated by New England Culinary Institute, one a gourmet restaurant and the other a more casual tavern. The inn also includes a swimming pool, library, country store, bakery and a golf course.

Innkeeper(s): Jim Glanville. $179-499. 120 rooms. Breakfast included in rates. Types of meals: Full bkfst. Beds: KQD. Cable TV, coffeemaker, iron, ironing board, hair dryer and pay-per-view movies in room. Golf course, hiking, antiques, skiing and outdoor pool on premises.
Certificate may be used: November-July, Sunday-Thursday.

Fair Haven H2

Maplewood Inn

Rt 22A S
Fair Haven, VT 05743
(802)265-8039 (800)253-7729 Fax:(802)265-8210
Internet: www.maplewoodinn.com
E-mail: stay@maplewoodinn.net

Circa 1843. This beautifully restored Greek Revival house, which is in the National Register, was once the family home of the founder of Maplewood Dairy, Isaac Wood. Period antiques

and reproductions grace the inn's spacious rooms and suites. Some rooms boast fireplaces and all have sitting areas. A porch wing, built around

1795, was a tavern formerly located down the road. Overlooking three acres of lawn, the inn offers an idyllic setting.
Innkeeper(s): Scott Rose. $80-145. 5 rooms with PB, 4 with FP, 2 suites and 1 conference room. Breakfast included in rates. Beds: QD. Cable TV, reading lamp, refrigerator, clock radio, telephone and desk in room. Air conditioning. TV, fax, copier, library, parlor games, fireplace, hot beverage bar and snacks on premises. Amusement parks, antiquing, cross-country skiing, downhill skiing, fishing, live theater, parks, shopping, sporting events and water sports nearby.
Location: Rural countryside.
Publicity: *New England Getaways, Country, Americana and Innsider.*

"Your inn is perfection. Leaving under protest."
Certificate may be used: Jan. 3-April 30 and Nov. 1-Dec. 23, Sunday-Thursday.

Fairlee F6

Silver Maple Lodge & Cottages

520 US Rt 5 South
Fairlee, VT 05045
(802)333-4326 (800)666-1946
Internet: www.silvermaplelodge.com
E-mail: scott@silvermaplelodge.com

Circa 1790. This old Cape farmhouse was expanded in the 1850s and became an inn in the '20s when Elmer & Della Batchelder opened their home to guests. It became so successful that several cottages, built from lumber on the property, were added. For 60 years, the Batchelder family continued the operation. They misnamed the lodge, however, mistaking silver poplar trees on the property for what they thought were silver maples. Guest rooms are decorated with many of the inn's original furnishings, and the new innkeepers have carefully restored the rooms and added several bathrooms. A screened-in porch surrounds two sides of the house. Three of the cottages include working fireplaces and one is handicap accessible.
Innkeeper(s): Scott & Sharon Wright. $69-99. 16 rooms, 14 with PB, 3 with FP and 8 cottages. Breakfast included in rates. Types of meals: Cont. Beds: KQDT. TV, reading lamp, refrigerator, clock radio and desk in room. VCR, copier, bicycles, parlor games, telephone and fireplace on premises. Handicap access. Antiquing, cross-country skiing, downhill skiing, fishing, live theater, parks, shopping and water sports nearby.
Location: Country.
Publicity: *Boston Globe, Vermont Country Sampler, Travel Holiday, Travel America and New York Times.*

"Your gracious hospitality and attractive home all add up to a pleasant experience."
Certificate may be used: Sunday-Thursday, Oct. 20-Sept. 20.

Gaysville G4

Cobble House Inn

PO Box 49
Gaysville, VT 05746-0049
(802)234-5458
Internet: www.cobblehouseinn.com
E-mail: unwind@cobblehouseinn.com

Circa 1864. One of the grandest homes in the area, this Victorian mansion commands a breathtaking view of the Green

Mountains. The White River flows just below, enticing the more adventurous to spend the day tubing, canoeing or fishing for salmon and trout. Enjoy breakfast and afternoon treats. Perennial gardens grace the spacious grounds. Advance notice is needed for dinner, which can be served on the porch in a majestic setting or in the cozy dining room.

Innkeeper(s): Tony Caparis. $115-130. 4 rooms with PB. Breakfast included in rates. Types of meals: Full gourmet bkfst and dinner. Beds: Q. Telephone and clawfoot tubs in room. Wood stove, flannel sheets, ornate carved beds, locally produced maple syrup available for purchase, snowshoeing, horseshoe pits and volleyball on premises. Antiquing, art galleries, bicycling, canoeing/kayaking, cross-country skiing, downhill skiing, fishing, golf, hiking, live theater, museums, parks, tennis, water sports, bike tours, swimming and tubing nearby.

Location: Country, mountains. White river.

Publicity: *Vermont Country Sampler, Syracuse Alumni Magazine, Vermont Life, Women's Day and Vermont.*

"My favorite place!"

Certificate may be used: Anytime, subject to availability.

Grafton   J4

Grafton Homestead, LLC

PO Box 102
Grafton, VT 05146
(802)843-1111 Fax:(802)843-1111
Internet: www.graftonhomestead.com
E-mail: vacation@graftonhomestead.com

Circa 1800. Rest and relaxation come easy at this historic Cape Cod Colonial in an idyllic location. Furnished with country antiques and cottage-style decor, the large private suite boasts a separate entrance and a full kitchen and imparts a feeling of being secluded. Enjoy views of the woodlands and a short walk to the pristine village. Visit the local cheese factory, plan a fall foliage trip and taste fresh Vermont maple syrup.

Innkeeper(s): Jennifer Karpin. $100-122. 2 rooms, 1 with PB, 1 suite. Types of meals: Cont. Beds: QD. VCR, reading lamp, refrigerator, clock radio, telephone, coffeemaker and desk in room. Library, parlor games and laundry facility on premises. Antiquing, art galleries, bicycling, cross-country skiing, downhill skiing, fishing, golf, hiking, horseback riding, museums, parks, shopping, tennis and covered bridges nearby.

Location: Country, mountains.

Certificate may be used: Jan. 2-Aug. 31, Monday-Thursday.

Greensboro   C5

Highland Lodge

1608 Craftsbury Road
Greensboro, VT 05841-8085
(802)533-2647 Fax:(802)533-7494
Internet: www.highlandlodge.com
E-mail: Highland.Lodge@verizon.net

Circa 1865. With a private beach and 120 acres to enjoy, guests rarely have trouble finding a way to pass the time at this lodge. The lodge is located in a mid-19th-century farmhouse, and visitors either room here in country guest rooms or in a collection of cottages. The cottages have from one to three bedrooms, a living room, bathroom and a porch. All guests are welcome to use the lodge's common areas or simply relax on the porch, but there's sailing, swimming, fishing, boating and nature trails. In the winter, the lodge grooms 60 kilometers of

cross-country ski trails and has a ski shop renting all the necessary gear. The breakfast choices include French toast, waffles, pancakes, eggs or muffins, and at dinner, guests choose from four entrees accompanied by salad, homemade bread and dessert.

Innkeeper(s): Wilhelmina & David Smith. $230-300. 11 cottages with PB. Breakfast and dinner included in rates. Types of meals: Full bkfst, early coffee/tea, lunch, picnic lunch and afternoon tea. Restaurant on premises. Beds: QDT. Reading lamp and refrigerator in room. Fax, copier, swimming, bicycles, tennis, library, child care, parlor games, telephone, fireplace, sailing, cross-country skiing and Internet access on premises. Handicap access. Antiquing, downhill skiing, golf, live theater and nature trail nearby.

Location: Mountains, waterfront. Rural countryside in Green Mountain foothills.

Publicity: *New England Skiers Guide, Vermont Magazine, Hardwick Gazette, Rural New England Magazine, Better Homes & Gardens, Providence Sunday Journal, Yankee, Vermont Life and US Air Attache.*

"We had a great time last weekend and enjoyed everything we did— hiking, climbing, swimming, canoeing and eating."

Certificate may be used: During the months of January, March, June, September and October.

Hardwick   C5

Somerset House B&B

130 Highland Ave, PO Box 1098
Hardwick, VT 05843-1098
(802)472-5484 (800)838-8074
Internet: www.somersethousebb.com

Circa 1894. After having been away for two years in England, the innkeepers returned home to Vermont and settled in this gracious Victorian house to provide lodging for those visiting this beautiful part of the country. The home is located in the heart of the village and set amid lawns and flower gardens. Breakfast is served in the dining room.

Innkeeper(s): Judy & Roger Waible. $79-99. 4 rooms. Breakfast included in rates. Types of meals: Full gourmet bkfst. Beds: QT. Reading lamp in room. Library, parlor games, telephone and fireplace on premises. Antiquing, bicycling, cross-country skiing, downhill skiing, fishing, hiking, horseback riding, live theater, shopping and water sports nearby.

Location: Village.

"We found a treasure. C'est super fun."

Certificate may be used: Anytime except June-October and holidays.

Hartland   H5

Sumner Mansion

4 Station Road
Hartland, VT 05048
(802)436-3386 (888)529-8796 Fax:(802)436-3386
Internet: www.sumnermansion.com
E-mail: Sumnerm@vermontel.net

Circa 1807. Considered one of the state's finest examples of Federal architecture, this mansion is listed in the National Register. The Colonial atmosphere with Queen Anne decor is accented by generous hospitality. Common rooms invite relaxation, games and conversation. Distinctive, air-conditioned guest bedrooms and the David Sumner Suite feature 10-foot ceilings, canopy beds and working fireplaces. A bountiful country breakfast buffet may be filling enough until afternoon refreshments in the grand dining room. A personalized itinerary is provided for daily excursions.

Innkeeper(s): Mary Louise & Ron Thorburn. $96-150. 5 rooms, 3 with PB, 2 with FP, 1 suite and 2 conference rooms. Breakfast and afternoon tea included in rates. Types of meals: Full gourmet bkfst, veg bkfst, early coffee/tea, lunch and room service. Beds: KQ. Data port, reading lamp, CD player, clock radio and turn-down service in room. Air conditioning. TV, VCR, fax, copier, stable, bicycles, library, pet boarding, child care, parlor games, telephone, fireplace and laundry facility on premises. Handicap access. Antiquing, art galleries, bicycling, canoeing/kayaking, cross-country skiing, downhill skiing, fishing, golf, hiking, horseback riding, live theater, museums, parks, shopping, tennis and National Parks nearby.

Location: Mountains.

Publicity: *Valley News and Rutland Herald.*

Certificate may be used: Sunday through Thursday nights, all year.

Hyde Park   C4

Fitch Hill Inn

258 Fitch Hill Rd
Hyde Park, VT 05655-7363
(802)888-3834 (800)639-2903 Fax:(802)888-7789
Internet: www.fitchhillinn.com
E-mail: bnbinnsinquiry@fitchhillinn.com

Circa 1797. Sitting on three and a half acres of hilltop land, this quiet 1797 Federalist-style home overlooks the picturesque Green Mountains. Surrounding the inn are numerous flower-filled gardens and woods to enjoy strolling through. Guest bedrooms share a period-furnished living room with a wood stove, a TV room and a movie library. The second-floor honeymoon New Hampshire Suite features a sleigh bed, gas fireplace, two-person jetted tub and a wet bar with sink, refrigerator and microwave. A ground-floor suite includes a butler's kitchen, whirlpool tub and private entrance with deck. All the rooms boast wonderful garden and mountain views. A full hot breakfast is served in the dining room. It is easy to enjoy the tranquility of this 18th-century home with a three-level deck and year-round hot tub. Relax on one of the two covered porches with a spectacular vista.

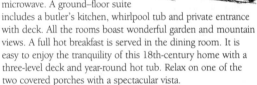

Innkeeper(s): Julie & John Rohleder. $85-205. 6 rooms with PB, 2 with FP, 2 suites. Breakfast included in rates. Types of meals: Full bkfst, early coffee/tea and afternoon tea. Beds: QD. Cable TV, VCR, reading lamp, stereo, refrigerator, ceiling fan, clock radio, telephone, desk, hot tub/spa and some with Jacuzzi in room. Air conditioning. Library, parlor games, fireplace and hot tub on premises. Amusement parks, antiquing, cross-country skiing, downhill skiing, fishing, live theater, parks and water sports nearby.

Location: Mountains.

Publicity: *Stowe Reporter, Morrisville News Dispatch, Out & About, Eco-Traveller, Country Living, Bon Appetit and Yankee Magazine.*

Certificate may be used: March, April, May, except Memorial Day weekend, and November, except Thanksgiving weekend.

Killington   G3

The Cascades Lodge & Restaurant

Killington Village, 58 Old Mill Rd
Killington, VT 05751-9710
(802)422-3731 (800)345-0113 Fax:(802)422-3351
Internet: www.cascadeslodge.com
E-mail: info@cascadeslodge.com

Circa 1980. Breathtaking views and modern amenities are found at this contemporary three-story country lodge in the heart of the Green Mountains. Guests enjoy an exercise area, indoor pool with sundeck, sauna and whirlpool. A bar and award-winning restaurant are on the premises, and the inn's amenities make it an ideal spot for meetings, reunions or weddings. Within walking distance is an 18-hole golf course and the Killington Summer Theater.

Innkeeper(s): Bob, Vickie & Andrew MacKenzie. $79-299. 46 rooms with PB, 6 suites. Breakfast included in rates. Types of meals: Full bkfst, early coffee/tea, picnic lunch, gourmet dinner and room service. Restaurant on premises. Beds: QD. Cable TV, clock radio, telephone and desk in room. VCR, fax, copier, spa, sauna, parlor games and fireplace on premises. Handicap access. Antiquing, cross-country skiing, downhill skiing, fishing, live theater, parks and shopping nearby.

Location: Mountains. Walk to slopes and golf.

Certificate may be used: Anyday, May 1 to Nov. 1, space available.

Cortina Inn & Resort

103 US Route 4
Killington, VT 05751
(802)773-3333 (800)451-6108 Fax:(802)775-6948
Internet: www.cortinainn.com
E-mail: cortina1@aol.com

Circa 1966. This property combines the amenities of a resort hotel with the ambiance of a country inn. Guests can reserve room packages that include breakfast; the cuisine is highly recommended. The brunches include carved meats and homemade breads along with traditional breakfast fare. Dinner is a special occasion with delicious appetizers and unique main dishes. Each of the rooms is individually decorated and includes original artwork. Some suites feature Jacuzzis and wet bars. The inn boasts an indoor swimming pool, exercise room and a masseur to soothe worn muscles.

Innkeeper(s): Ted Bridges. $119-199. 96 rooms with PB, 14 with FP, 7 suites and 3 conference rooms. Breakfast and afternoon tea included in rates. Types of meals: Full gourmet bkfst, early coffee/tea, picnic lunch, snacks/refreshments, gourmet dinner and room service. Restaurant on premises. Beds: KQD. Modem hook-up, data port, cable TV, reading lamp, clock radio, telephone, coffeemaker, desk, voice mail, some with fireplace, hot tub/spa, refrigerator and VCR in room. Air conditioning. TV, VCR, fax, copier, spa, swimming, sauna, bicycles, tennis, library, parlor games, fireplace, laundry facility and gift shop on premises. Handicap access. Amusement parks, antiquing, art galleries, bicycling, canoeing/kayaking, cross-country skiing, downhill skiing, fishing, golf, hiking, horseback riding, museums, tennis and wineries nearby.

Location: Mountains.

Publicity: *Travel Agent East Magazine, New York Post, Ski Magazine and Travel Channel.*

Certificate may be used: Anytime, Sunday-Thursday, Dec. 25-Jan. 3, Feb. 13-21.

The Peak Chalet

PO Box 511, 184 South View Path
Killington, VT 05751-0511
(802)422-4278
Internet: www.thepeakchalet.com
E-mail: peakchalet@aol.com

Circa 1978. This contemporary chalet-style inn is located in the heart of the Killington Ski Resort. That convenience is matched by the inn's elegant accommodations and attention to detail. Guest rooms feature either a four-poster, iron, panel or sleigh bed, all queen-size. The living room, with its impressive stone fireplace and view of the Green Mountains, is a favorite gathering spot for those not on the slopes.

Innkeeper(s): Greg & Diane Becker. $64-127. 5 rooms, 4 with PB. Breakfast included in rates. Types of meals: Cont plus. Beds: QT. Reading lamp in room. VCR, telephone and fireplace on premises. Antiquing, bicycling, cross-country skiing, downhill skiing, fishing, golf, live theater, parks, shopping, tennis and water sports nearby.

Location: Mountains.

Certificate may be used: Jan. 1-Sept. 20 and Oct. 15-Dec. 20, Sunday-Thursday, holidays excluded.

The Vermont Inn

Rt 4
Killington, VT 05751
(802)775-0708 (800)541-7795 Fax:(802)773-5810
Internet: www.vermontinn.com
E-mail: relax@vermontinn.com

Circa 1840. Surrounded by mountain views, this rambling red and white farmhouse has provided lodging and superb cuisine for many years. Exposed beams add to the atmosphere in the living

and game rooms. The award-winning dining room provides candlelight tables beside a huge fieldstone fireplace.

Innkeeper(s): Megan & Greg Smith. $50-185. 18 rooms with PB, 5 with FP, 2 with HT. Breakfast and after-noon tea included in rates. Types of meals: Full bkfst, early coffee/tea and gourmet dinner. Beds: QDT. Ceiling fan, clock radio, two with Jacuzzi tub and 5 with fireplace in room. Air conditioning. VCR, fax, copier, spa, swimming, sauna, tennis, library, parlor games, telephone, fireplace and screened porch on premises. Handicap access. Antiquing, cross-country skiing, downhill skiing, fishing, live theater, parks, shopping and water sports nearby.
Location: Mountains.
Publicity: *New York Daily News, New Jersey Star Leader, Rutland Business Journal, Bridgeport Post Telegram, New York Times, Boston, Vermont and Asbury Park Press.*

"We had a wonderful time. The inn is breathtaking. Hope to be back."
Certificate may be used: Jan. 1-Sept. 15, Sunday-Thursday.

Landgrove   J3

The Landgrove Inn

132 Landgrove Rd
Landgrove, VT 05148
(802)824-6673 (800)669-8466 Fax:(802)824-6790
Internet: www.landgroveinn.com
E-mail: vtinn@sover.net

Circa 1810. This rambling inn is located along a country lane in the valley of Landgrove in the Green Mountain National Forest. Breakfast and dinner are served in the newly renovated and stenciled dining room. Evening sleigh or hay rides often are arranged. Or guests can relax in the gathering room with fireplace and pub. Rooms vary in style and bedding arrangements, including some newly decorated rooms with country decor, so inquire when making your reservation.

Innkeeper(s): Tom & Maureen Checchia. $80-225. 18 rooms, 16 with PB and 1 conference room. Breakfast included in rates. Types of meals: Full bkfst, afternoon tea and dinner. Restaurant on premises. Beds: KQD. Reading lamp and some with fireplace and hot air massage tub in room. VCR, fax, copier, tennis, parlor games, telephone, fireplace, heated pool, fishing pond and hiking trails on premises. Antiquing, cross-country skiing, downhill skiing, fishing, live theater, parks and shopping nearby.
Location: Rural country.

"A true country inn with great food — we'll be back."
Certificate may be used: May 20-Sept. 20 and Dec. 20-April 1, Sunday through Thursday, non-holidays.

Ludlow   I4

The Andrie Rose Inn

13 Pleasant St
Ludlow, VT 05149
(802)228-4846 (800)223-4846 Fax:(802)228-7910
Internet: www.andrieroseinn.com
E-mail: andrie@mail.tds.net

Circa 1829. This village Colonial was named for Andrie Rose, who operated a guest house here during the 1950s. Recently, the inn has been polished to a shine and lavishly appointed with antiques, wallpapers, down comforters and whirlpool tubs. A Vermont country candlelight breakfast is served. This is the closest inn to the access road of Okemo Mountain and the ski shuttle stops at the inn. The guest house offers four luxury family suites with fireplaces and canopy beds.

Innkeeper(s): Michael & Irene Maston. $90-330. 16 rooms, 9 with PB, 7 with FP, 7 suites. Breakfast and snacks/refreshments included in rates. Types of meals: Country bkfst, veg bkfst, early coffee/tea, gourmet dinner and room service. Restaurant on premises. Beds: KQD. Modem hook-up, cable TV, VCR, reading lamp, stereo, refrigerator, ceiling fan, clock radio, telephone, turn-down service, hot tub/spa and suites have fireplace in room. Air conditioning. Fax, copier, spa, bicycles, library, parlor games, fireplace, laundry facility, gift shop and restaurant service on Friday & Saturday on premises. Limited handicap access. Antiquing, art galleries, beach, bicycling, canoeing/kayaking, cross-country skiing, downhill skiing, fishing, golf, hiking, horseback riding, live theater, museums, parks, shopping, tennis and water sports nearby.
Publicity: *Country Inns magazine, USA Today, New York magazine, Inn Times and Getaways - Boston.*

"Thank you for a truly relaxing, delicious and romantic getaway."
Certificate may be used: May-Sept. 14, Sunday-Thursday & Nov. 1-20, Sunday-Thursday, subject to availability (family suites excluded, applies to Main Lodge and Solitude Building only).

Echo Lake Inn

PO Box 154
Ludlow, VT 05149-0154
(802)228-8602 (800)356-6844 Fax:(802)228-3075
Internet: echolakeinn.com
E-mail: echolkinn@aol.com

Circa 1840. An abundance of year-round activities at an ideal location in the state's central mountain lakes region make this authentic Victorian inn a popular choice. Built as a summer hotel in 1840, its rich heritage includes visits from many historic figures. Relax in the quiet comfort of the living room with its shelves of books and a fireplace or gather for refreshments in The Pub. The assortment of guest bedrooms, suites and condos ensure perfect accommodations for varied needs. Some

boast two-person Jacuzzi tubs and fireplaces. Dining is a treat, with the fine country restaurant highly acclaimed for its excellent food, attentive service and casual ambiance. Tennis, badminton and volleyball courts are adjacent to the large swimming pool. Take out a canoe or rowboat from the dock on crystal-clear Echo Lake or fly fish the Black River.

Innkeeper(s): Peter & Joanne Modisette. $109-380. 23 rooms with PB, 1 suite. Breakfast included in rates. Types of meals: Full bkfst, early coffee/tea, gourmet dinner and room service. Restaurant on premises. Beds: QDT. Reading lamp, ceiling fan and desk in room. Fax, spa, swimming, sauna, tennis, library, parlor games, telephone, fireplace, fine dining, children's paddling pool, all-weather surface, back board and night lighting, house racquets and balls, volleyball and badminton on premises. Antiquing, beach, canoeing/kayaking, cross-country skiing, downhill skiing, fishing, golf, hiking, horseback riding, live theater, shopping, water sports, wineries, Okemo Skiing, one of Vermont's best trout fishing rivers, fly fishing and rowing nearby.

Location: Mountains.

Publicity: *Vermont, Bon Appetit, Gourmet, Vermont Magazine ("turn-of-the-century charm with modern luxury") and Restaurants of New England.*

"Very special! We've decided to make the Echo Lake Inn a yearly tradition for our family."

Certificate may be used: April 1-Sept. 20, Oct. 20-Dec. 12, Jan. 1-March 31, Sunday-Thursday, non-holiday.

Manchester   J2

Manchester Highlands Inn

216 Highland Ave, Box 1754
Manchester, VT 05255
(802)362-4565 (800)743-4565 Fax:(802)362-4028
Internet: www.highlandsinn.com
E-mail: relax@highlandsinn.com

Circa 1898. This Queen Anne Victorian mansion sits proudly on the crest of a hill overlooking the village. From the three-story turret, guests can look out over Mt. Equinox, the Green Mountains and the valley below. Feather beds and down comforters adorn the beds in the guest rooms. Many with canopy beds and fireplaces. A game room with billiards and a stone fireplace are popular in winter, while summertime guests enjoy the outdoor pool, croquet lawn and veranda. Gourmet country breakfasts and home-baked afternoon snacks are served.

Innkeeper(s): Patricia & Robert Eichorn. $110-185. 15 rooms with PB. Breakfast and afternoon tea included in rates. Types of meals: Full gourmet bkfst. Beds: KQDT. Reading lamp, clock radio and several rooms with gas fireplaces in room. Air conditioning. TV, VCR, fax, swimming, library, parlor games, telephone, fireplace, game room, guest bar, bottomless cookie jar and Saturday wine & hors d'oeuvres on premises. Antiquing, bicycling, canoeing/kayaking, cross-country skiing, downhill skiing, fishing, golf, hiking, horseback riding, live theater, parks, shopping, ice skating and sleigh rides nearby.

Location: Mountains.

Publicity: *Bennington Banner, Gourmet, Toronto Sun, Vermont Magazine, Asbury Park Press, Vermont Weathervane, Yankee Traveler, Boston Globe, Cat Fanciers Magazine, NY Times and Miami Herald.*

"We couldn't believe such a place existed. Now, we can't wait to come again."

Certificate may be used: Jan. 6-June 15, Monday-Thursday only. Non-holiday periods.

Wilburton Inn

PO Box 468
Manchester, VT 05254-0468
(802)362-2500 (800)648-4944 Fax:(802)362-1107
Internet: www.wilburton.com
E-mail: wilbuinn@sover.net

Circa 1902. Shaded by tall maples, this three-story brick mansion sits high on a hill overlooking the Battenkill Valley, which is set against a majestic mountain backdrop. In addition to the mansion, the inn offers four villas and a five-bedroom reunion house. Carved moldings, mahogany paneling, Oriental carpets and leaded-glass windows are complemented by carefully chosen antiques.

The inn's 20 acres provide three tennis courts, a pool, green lawns, sculpture gardens and panoramic views. Country weddings are a Wilburton Inn's specialty. Gourmet dining is served in the billiard room with European ambiance. Gleneagles golf courses provide the inn with golf privileges.

Innkeeper(s): Georgette Levis. $105-235. 35 rooms, 8 with FP and 1 conference room. Breakfast included in rates. Types of meals: Full gourmet bkfst, afternoon tea, gourmet dinner and room service. Restaurant on premises. Beds: KQ. TV in room. Air conditioning. Fax, copier, parlor games and telephone on premises. Antiquing, cross-country skiing, downhill skiing, fishing, golf, live theater and water sports nearby.

Publicity: *Great Escapes TV, Travelhost, Getaways For Gourmets, Country Inns, Bed & Breakfast, Gourmet, Best Places to Stay In New England and New York Times July 2002.*

"Simply splendid! Peaceful, beautiful, elegant. Ambiance & ambiance!"

Certificate may be used: All April, any day, all month.

Montpelier   E4

Betsy's B&B

74 E State St
Montpelier, VT 05602-3112
(802)229-0466 Fax:(802)229-5412
Internet: www.BetsysBnB.com
E-mail: BetsysBnB@adelphia.net

Circa 1895. Within walking distance of downtown and located in the state's largest historic preservation district, this Queen Anne Victorian with romantic turret and carriage house features lavish Victorian antiques throughout its interior. Bay windows, carved woodwork, high ceilings, lace curtains and wood floors add to the authenticity. The full breakfast varies in content but not quality, and guest favorites include orange pancakes.

Innkeeper(s): Jon & Betsy Anderson. $70-110. 12 rooms with PB, 5 two-bedroom suites. Breakfast included in rates. Types of meals: Full bkfst. Beds: QDT. Data port, cable TV, reading lamp, clock radio, telephone, desk and voice mail in room. Air conditioning. VCR, fax, copier, parlor games, fireplace, laundry facility and refrigerator on premises. Antiquing, cross-country skiing, downhill skiing, fishing, live theater, parks, shopping and water sports nearby.

Location: City. Residential in small city.

Certificate may be used: Nov. 1-April 30, holiday weekends excluded.

Morrisville   C4

Village Victorian B & B

107 Union St
Morrisville, VT 05661-6061
(802)888-8850 (866)266-4672
Internet: www.villagevictorian.com
E-mail: philip@villagevictorian.com

Circa 1890. In a typical New England setting, this 1890s Victorian imparts warmth and peace to all who stay here. Sitting in a quiet village in the Lamoille Valley, it is located just seven miles from Stowe. Relax on the porches and patios, or walk through the gardens. Play games by the fire in the living room, read a book or practice the piano. Elegant air-conditioned guest bedrooms offer a variety of pleasant amenities from robes to a video library. Stay in the third-floor Aster Suite with vaulted ceilings, sitting room and Jacuzzi tub. Breakfast in the dining room always includes a taste of Vermont with seasonal fruit, Cabot cheese and yogurt, Sugarwoods Farm Pure Maple Syrup and Green Mountain Coffee Roasters fresh-ground coffee. A laundry

facility, microwave, refrigerator, iron and board are available.
Innkeeper(s): Philip and Ellen Wolff. $80-160. 4 rooms with PB, 1 suite. Breakfast included in rates. Types of meals: Full bkfst. Beds: Q. Cable TV and VCR in room. Air conditioning. TV, fax, library, parlor games, telephone, fireplace, laundry facility, gift shop, refrigerator, soda, microwave and video library on premises. Antiquing, art galleries, beach, bicycling, canoeing/kayaking, cross-country skiing, downhill skiing, fishing, golf, hiking, horseback riding, live theater, museums, parks, shopping, sporting events, tennis, water sports and wineries nearby.
Location: Village in the Lamoille Valley.
Certificate may be used: Oct. 25-Dec. 9, March 15-May 15.

Northfield   E4
The Northfield Inn

228 Highland Ave
Northfield, VT 05663-5663
(802)485-8558
Internet: www.TheNorthfieldInn.com
E-mail: TheNorthfieldInn@aol.com

Circa 1901. A view of the Green Mountains can be seen from this Victorian inn, which is set on a mountainside surrounded by gardens and overlooking an apple orchard and pond. The picturesque inn also affords a view of the village of Northfield and historic Norwich University. Rooms are decorated with antiques and Oriental rugs, and bedrooms feature European feather bedding and brass and carved-wood beds. Many outdoor activities are available on the three-acre property, including croquet, horseshoes, ice skating and sledding. Visitors may want to take a climb uphill to visit the Old Slate Quarry or just relax on one of the porches overlooking the garden with bird songs, wind chimes and gentle breezes.
Innkeeper(s): Aglaia Stalb. $95-179. 12 rooms with PB, 2 suites. Breakfast and snacks/refreshments included in rates. Types of meals: Full bkfst. Beds: QDT. Cable TV, reading lamp, ceiling fan, clock radio, telephone and central cooling system available in room. TV, VCR, bicycles, library, parlor games, fireplace, lounge and fitness center on premises. Antiquing, cross-country skiing, downhill skiing, fishing, golf, hiking, live theater, parks, shopping, sporting events, water sports, sledding, flying, fairs, auctions. Veteran's and Labor Day Festivals and Parade, Vermont Quilt Festival and 5 covered bridges in Northfield nearby.
Location: Mountains.
Publicity: *Conde Nast Traveler and Gentlemen's Quarterly.*

"There's no place like here."
Certificate may be used: Nov. 1-April 30 weekdays only, as available.

Perkinsville   I4
The Inn at Weathersfield

1342 Route 106
Perkinsville, VT 05151
(802)263-9217 Fax:(802)263-9219
Internet: www.weathersfieldinn.com
E-mail: stay@weathersfieldinn.com

Circa 1792. Perfectly suited for a quiet getaway, this stately Georgian-style inn with post and beam interior was built in 1792 and thought to have been a stop on the Underground Railroad. Decorated in a rustic elegance, each guest bedroom and suite includes cozy robes and slippers. Many feature fireplaces, four-poster beds, CD stereos, whirlpool or clawfoot tubs and private rooftop decks. Choose a hot, made-to-order breakfast from a menu. Roam the 21 wooded acres with a pond, walking trails, gardens, back roads and an outdoor starlit amphitheater. The candlelit dining room offers New Vermont cuisine, and lighter fare is available in the Pub on select nights. Relax by the fire in the study after a full day of skiing. A computer provides high-speed Internet access for guest use.

Innkeeper(s): Jane and David Sandelman. $140-210. 12 rooms with PB, 6 with FP, 3 suites and 1 conference room. Breakfast, afternoon tea and snacks/refreshments included in rates. Types of meals: Full gourmet bkfst, veg bkfst, early coffee/tea, picnic lunch and gourmet dinner. Restaurant on premises. Beds: KQDT. Modem hook-up, cable TV, reading lamp, stereo, clock radio, desk, fireplace, robes and slippers in room. VCR, fax, copier, sauna, stable, library, pet boarding, parlor games, fireplace, high-speed Internet, gift shop and full service restaurant on premises. Antiquing, art galleries, bicycling, canoeing/kayaking, cross-country skiing, downhill skiing, fishing, golf, hiking, horseback riding, live theater, museums, parks and shopping nearby.
Location: Country, mountains. Set on 21 wooded acres.
Certificate may be used: Sunday-Thursday excluding Sept. 15- Nov. 1, Christmas week, Presidents week.

Pittsfield   G3
Casa Bella Inn

P.O. Box 685
Pittsfield, VT 05762
(802)746-8943 (877)746-8943 Fax:(802)746-8395
Internet: www.casabellainn.com
E-mail: info@casabellainn.com

Circa 1835. Originally built as a stagecoach stop, this full-service country inn sits in a scenic mountain valley and exudes a New England ambiance with accents of Tuscany. It has been recently renovated to provide modern comfort and a relaxed, casual atmosphere. Sit on one of the two-story porches overlooking the village green. In-room massage services are available. Savor a full breakfast after a restful sleep in a well-appointed guest bedroom. The warm hospitality continues with afternoon refreshments. Northern Italian cuisine is featured in the on-site restaurant that seats 30. Visit the Green Mountain National Forest and go tubing in the White River. Experience the many winter activities available at nearby Killington Ski Resort. The fall colors are a must-see annual event.
Innkeeper(s): Franco & Susan Cacozza. $90-115. 8 rooms with PB. Breakfast and afternoon tea included in rates. Types of meals: Full gourmet bkfst, snacks/refreshments and gourmet dinner. Restaurant on premises. Beds: QDT. Reading lamp and clock radio in room. Parlor games and telephone on premises. Antiquing, art galleries, bicycling, canoeing/kayaking, cross-country skiing, downhill skiing, fishing, golf, hiking, horseback riding, parks, shopping, tennis, water sports, fly fishing and snowmobiling nearby.
Location: Country, mountains.
Certificate may be used: May-August, Sunday-Thursday, subject to availability, excludes holidays.

Poultney   H2
Bentley House B&B

399 Bentley Ave
Poultney, VT 05764
(802)287-4004 (800)894-4004
Internet: www.thebentleyhouse.com
E-mail: towerhal@sover.net

Circa 1895. This three-story peaked turret Queen Anne inn is located next to Green Mountain College. Stained glass, polished woodwork and original fireplace mantels add to the Victorian atmosphere, and the guest rooms are furnished with antiques of the period. A sitting room adjacent to the guest rooms has its own fireplace.
Innkeeper(s): Denise & Bob DiMaio. $55-85. 5 rooms with PB, 1 suite. Types of meals: Full bkfst. Beds: Q. Clock radio in room. Bicycles, parlor games, telephone, fireplace, guest kitchenette and cable TV on premises. Antiquing, cross-country skiing, fishing, parks, shopping and water sports nearby.
Location: Mountains. Small rural college town.
Publicity: *Rutland Herald and Rutland Business Journal.*

"Your beautiful home was delightful and just the best place to stay!"
Certificate may be used: Nov. 1-April 30, Sunday-Saturday.

Proctorsville   I4

Golden Stage Inn

PO Box 218
Proctorsville, VT 05153
(802)226-7744 (800)253-8226 Fax:(802)226-7882
Internet: www.goldenstageinn.com
E-mail: goldenstageinn@tds.net

Circa 1788. The Golden Stage Inn was a stagecoach stop built
shortly before Vermont became a state. It served as a link in the
Underground Railroad and was the home of Cornelia Otis
Skinner. Cornelia's Room still offers its original polished wide-
pine floors and view of Okemo
Mountain, and now there's a
four-poster cherry bed, farm animal border, wainscoting and a
comforter filled with wool from
the inn's sheep. Outside are
gardens of wildflowers, a little
pen with two sheep, a swimming pool and blueberries and
raspberries for the picking. Breakfast offerings include an often-
requested recipe, Golden Stage Granola. Home-baked breakfast
dishes are garnished with Johnny-jump-ups and nasturtiums
from the garden. Guests can indulge anytime by reaching into
the inn's bottomless cookie jar. The inn offers stay & ski packages at Okemo Mountain with 48 hours advance notice, and
it's a 20 minute drive to Killington access.

Innkeeper(s): Sandy & Peter Gregg. $69-250. 10 rooms, 8 with PB, 1 with
FP, 1 two-bedroom suite. Breakfast, afternoon tea and snacks/refreshments
included in rates. Types of meals: Country bkfst, veg bkfst and dinner. Beds:
KQDT. TV, reading lamp, clock radio and fireplace in room. Central air. VCR,
fax, copier, swimming, library, parlor games, telephone and one handicapped-
equipped room on premises. Handicap access. Antiquing, cross-country skiing, downhill skiing, fishing, golf, live theater and shopping nearby.

Location: Country, mountains.

Publicity: *Journal Inquirer, Gourmet and Los Angeles Times.*

"The essence of a country inn!"

Certificate may be used: Sunday-Thursday, year-round; excludes fall foliage
and premium times. Cannot be combined with other offers.

Putney   K4

The Putney Inn

PO Box 181
Putney, VT 05346-0181
(802)387-5517 (800)653-5517 Fax:(802)387-5211
Internet: www.putneyinn.com
E-mail: info@putneyinn.com

Circa 1790. The property surrounding this New England farmhouse was deeded to an English Army Captain by King George
in 1790. The grounds' first home burned in a fire, and this inn
was constructed on the original foundation. Eventually it
became a Catholic seminary, and then an elegant country inn.
Rooms are located in a 1960s building, adjacent to the main
historic farmhouse. The rooms are decorated in a Colonial style
with antiques. The inn's dining
room, headed by renown chef
Ann Cooper, features New
England cuisine. The ingredients
are fresh and locally produced,
and might include appetizers
such as smoked salmon on

Johnnycakes with an apple cider vinaigrette. Entrees such as a
mixed grill of local venison and game hen flavored by an apple-
horseradish marinade follow. Craft and antique shops, hiking,
skiing and biking are among the local activities.

Innkeeper(s): Randi Ziter. $78-158. 25 rooms with PB and 4 conference rooms.
Breakfast included in rates. Types of meals: Full gourmet bkfst, veg bkfst, early
coffee/tea, gourmet lunch, picnic lunch, afternoon tea, snacks/refreshments, hors
d'oeuvres, wine and gourmet dinner. Restaurant on premises. Beds: Q. Modem
hook-up, data port, cable TV, reading lamp, clock radio, telephone, coffeemaker
and desk in room. Air conditioning. VCR, fax, copier and full dining restaurant
on premises. Handicap access. Amusement parks, antiquing, art galleries, bicycling, canoeing/kayaking, cross-country skiing, downhill skiing, fishing, golf, hiking, horseback riding, live theater, parks, shopping, tennis, water sports, wineries, national forest and nature hikes nearby.

Location: Country. Walk to village and river.

Publicity: *Chicago Tribune, Boston Herald, Culinary Arts, US Air, Travel &
Leisure, Vermont Life, Vermont Magazine and Dine-Around.*

Certificate may be used: November through April. Holidays excluded.
May through June, Sunday through Thursday. Not in conjunction with any
other promotion.

Richford   A4

Grey Gables Mansion

122 River Street
Richford, VT 05476
(802)848-3625 Fax:(802)848-3629
Internet: www.greygablesmansion.com
E-mail: info@greygablesmansion.com

Circa 1888. A stately balloon frame, classic asymmetrical multi-
gables and ornate exterior highlight this 1888 Queen Anne
Victorian listed in the National Register. Hand-carved woodwork,
molded cornices, walnut and mahogany grand staircases grace
the interior. Sit by the fire to watch TV in the library that boasts a
video collection, games and books. Each of the lavish guest bedrooms feature colorful stained-glass windows, wood floors, cable
TV and Gilchrist & Soames toiletries. Families appreciate the
available Kids Room. Breakfast favorites may include blueberry
pancakes with Vermont maple syrup, eggs Benedict, fruit, cereals,
breads and muffins. Enjoy baked treats with afternoon tea while
watching the Missisquoi River flow by from the front porch. Ski
nearby Jay Peak, Mount Sutton or Stowe. Located on the
Canadian border, Montreal is an hour away.

Innkeeper(s): Pam Montgomery. $79-139. 6 rooms, 5 with PB. Breakfast and
afternoon tea included in rates. Types of meals: Country bkfst. Beds: QDT.
Cable TV, reading lamp, ceiling fan, clock radio and hair dryers in room. VCR,
fax, library, parlor games and video library on premises. Antiquing, bicycling,
canoeing/kayaking, cross-country skiing, downhill skiing, fishing, golf, hiking,
parks and shopping nearby.

Location: Mountains. In small New England town in Mountain Valley.

Certificate may be used: Anytime, Sunday-Thursday, not available on holidays, subject to availability.

Richmond   D3

The Richmond Victorian Inn

P.O. Box 652
Richmond, VT 05477
(802)434-4410 (888)242-3362 Fax:(802)434-4411
Internet: www.richmondvictorianinn.com
E-mail: innkeeper@richmondvictorianinn.com

Circa 1850. This Queen Anne Victorian, with a three-story
tower, is accented with green shutters, a sunburst design, fish
scale shingles and a gingerbread front porch. The Tower Room
is filled with white wicker, delicate flowered wallpaper and an
antique brass bed. The Gold Room features a Queen-size bed

and a Jacuzzi, while the Pansy Room features an antique bed, white walls and a stenciled pansy border. There are hardwood floors and leaded-glass windows throughout. From the tree-shaded porch, enjoy the inn's lawns and flower gardens after a full breakfast.

Innkeeper(s): Frank & Joyce Stewart. $90-150. 6 rooms with PB. Breakfast and snacks/refreshments included in rates. Types of meals: Full gourmet bkfst, veg bkfst, early coffee/tea and afternoon tea. Beds: QDT. Reading lamp, clock radio, antique furnishings, cozy quilts, down comforters and plush robes in room. TV, VCR, fax, library, parlor games, telephone and British-style afternoon tea (Sundays from 2-5 p.m. September-Mother's Day) on premises. Antiquing, art galleries, beach, bicycling, canoeing/kayaking, cross-country skiing, downhill skiing, fishing, golf, hiking, live theater, museums, parks, shopping, sporting events, water sports, wineries, artists' studios, Audubon Center, Huntington Gorge and Little River State Park nearby.

Location: Country, mountains. Small Vermont town, 12 miles east of Burlington.

Publicity: *Hartford Courant (2003), Out and About in Vermont 5th Ed., Rogers (2004), Best Recipes of American Country Inns and Bed and Breakfasts - Maynard (2004).*

"I have stayed at many B&Bs, but by far this is the most wonderful experience. The hospitality was #1, the food was A+. Rooms very comfortable. ... I felt like family. Hope our paths cross again."

Certificate may be used: November-April, non-holidays, subject to availability and prior booking. May not be combined with other promotions.

Rochester   G3

Liberty Hill Farm

511 Liberty Hill Rd
Rochester, VT 05767
(802)767-3926 Fax:(802)767-6056
Internet: www.libertyhillfarm.com
E-mail: beth@libertyhillfarm.com

Circa 1825. A working dairy farm with a herd of registered Holsteins, this farmhouse offers a country setting and easy access to recreational activities. The inn's location, between the White River and the Green Mountains, is ideal for outdoor enthusiasts and animal lovers. Stroll to the barn, feed the calves or climb up to the hayloft and read or play with the kittens. Fishing, hiking, skiing and swimming are popular pastimes of guests, who are treated to a family-style dinner and full breakfast, both featuring many delicious homemade specialties.

Innkeeper(s): Robert & Beth Kennett. $150. 7 rooms. Breakfast and dinner included in rates. Types of meals: Full bkfst and early coffee/tea. Beds: QDT. Reading lamp, clock radio and desk in room. VCR, swimming, library, child care, parlor games, telephone, working dairy farm and private beach for swimming and fishing on premises. Antiquing, art galleries, beach, bicycling, canoeing/kayaking, cross-country skiing, downhill skiing, fishing, golf, hiking, live theater, museums, parks, shopping, sporting events, water sports and wineries nearby.

Location: Lakefront in the country and mountains.

Publicity: *New York Times, Boston Globe, Vermont Life, Family Circle, Family Fun, Woman's Day, Country Home, Boston Chronicle, Yankee and Good Morning America.*

"We had a wonderful time exploring your farm and the countryside. The food was great."

Certificate may be used: Jan. 1 to May 20, Sunday-Thursday nights.

Roxbury   E4

Johnnycake Flats Inn

47 Carrie Howe Rd
Roxbury, VT 05669
(802)485-8961
Internet: www.johnnycakeflats.com
E-mail: jcflats@tds.net

Circa 1806. Johnnycake Flats is an unpretentious and delightfully small bed and breakfast that offers guests a quiet escape from the hectic pace of metropolitan life. The guest rooms in this registered historical site include family antiques, Shaker baskets and handmade quilts. The innkeepers can help you identify local wildflowers and birds. In winter, enjoy cross-country skiing or snowshoeing and come home to sip hot cider beside the fire.

Innkeeper(s): Debra & Jim Rogler. $115-125. 3 rooms, 1 with PB. Breakfast and afternoon tea included in rates. Types of meals: Cont plus and early coffee/tea. Beds: DT. Reading lamp and clock radio in room. Bicycles, library, telephone, fireplace and snowshoes on premises. Antiquing, bicycling, cross-country skiing, downhill skiing, fishing, live theater, parks, shopping, sporting events, water sports and snowshoeing nearby.

Location: Country, mountains.

Publicity: *Local area newspapers.*

"You've nurtured a bit of paradise here, thanks for the lovely stay."

Certificate may be used: Anytime, subject to availability.

Rutland   H3

The Inn at Rutland

70 N Main St
Rutland, VT 05701-3249
(802)773-0575 (800)808-0575 Fax:(802)775-3506
Internet: www.innatrutland.com
E-mail: relax@innatrutland.com

Circa 1889. This distinctive Victorian mansion is filled with many period details, from high, plaster-worked ceilings to leather wainscotting in the dining room. Leaded windows and interesting woodwork are found throughout. Guest rooms have been decorated to maintain Victorian charm without a loss of modern comforts. A wrap around porch and common rooms are available to guests. Located in central Vermont, The Inn at Rutland is only 15 minutes from the Killington and Pico ski areas.

Innkeeper(s): Steven & Leslie Brenner. $90-205. 11 rooms with PB, 2 with FP. Breakfast and afternoon tea included in rates. Types of meals: Full gourmet bkfst and veg bkfst. Beds: KQD. Cable TV, reading lamp, ceiling fan, clock radio, telephone, hair dryers and some with fireplace in room. Air conditioning. TV, library, parlor games, fireplace and wraparound front porch with great views on premises. Antiquing, art galleries, bicycling, canoeing/kayaking, cross-country skiing, downhill skiing, fishing, golf, hiking, horseback riding, live theater, museums, parks, shopping, tennis, water sports and museums nearby.

Location: City, mountains. Views of valley and mountains.

"A lovely page in the 'memory album' of our minds."

Certificate may be used: March-Mid September, Sunday-Thursday, November-mid December, Sunday-Thursday. Rooms available, Washington, Windham, Franklin, Orleans.

Stowe D4

1066 Ye Olde England Inne

433 Mountain Rd
Stowe, VT 05672-4628
(802)253-7558 (800)477-3771 Fax:(802)253-8944
Internet: www.oldeenglandinne.com
E-mail: englandinn@aol.com

Circa 1890. Originally a farmhouse, Ye Olde England Inne has acquired a Tudor facade, interior beams and stone work. Each guest room is different. One cozy room includes hunter green carpeting and cheerful wallcoverings with red flowers. A matching comforter tops the lace canopy bed and a massive wardrobe further decorates the room. Other rooms are more traditional style. The suites and cottages include a whirlpool tub, and many offer a mountain view and a private porch from which to enjoy it. The inn has a variety of getaway packages. A popular honeymoon package includes French champagne, a complete spa treatment and in winter, a sleigh ride. Mr. Pickwick's, which resembles an English pub, is an ideal spot to relax and enjoy ale or a glass or wine. The inn also offers Copperfields, where guests can enjoy a romantic dinner. Guests can spend their days hiking, skiing, relaxing by the inn's pool or exploring Stowe.
Innkeeper(s): Christopher & Linda Francis. $98-375. 30 rooms with PB, 13 with FP, 12 suites and 1 conference room. Breakfast included in rates. Types of meals: Full gourmet bkfst, gourmet lunch and afternoon tea. Restaurant on premises. Beds: QDT. Cable TV, reading lamp, stereo, refrigerator, ceiling fan, clock radio and telephone in room. Air conditioning. TV, fax, copier, spa and fireplace on premises. Antiquing, cross-country skiing, downhill skiing, live theater, parks, shopping and sporting events nearby.
Location: Mountains.
Publicity: *National Geographic Traveler and Channel 5 TV in Boston.*
Certificate may be used: Midweek, non-holiday, subject to advance reservations and availability.

Brass Lantern Inn B&B

717 Maple St
Stowe, VT 05672-4250
(802)253-2229 (800)729-2980 Fax:(802)253-7425
Internet: www.brasslanterninn.com
E-mail: info@brasslanterninn.com

Circa 1810. This rambling farmhouse and carriage barn rests at the foot of Mt. Mansfield. A recent award-winning renovation has brought a new shine to the inn, from the gleaming plank floors to the polished woodwork and crackling fireplaces and soothing whirlpool tubs. Quilts and antiques fill the guest rooms, and many, like the Honeymoon Room, have their own fireplace, whirlpool tub and mountain view. A complimentary afternoon and evening tea is provided along with a full Vermont-style breakfast. A new two-bedroom cottage is now available, as well. The inn is a multi-time winner of the Golden Fork Award from the Gourmet Dinners Society of North America.
Innkeeper(s): Andy Aldrich. $95-225. 9 rooms with PB, 6 with FP, 6 with WP, 1 cottage and 1 conference room. Breakfast and afternoon tea included in rates. Types of meals: Country bkfst, veg bkfst and early coffee/tea. Beds: Q. Modem hook-up, data port, TV, VCR, reading lamp, stereo, clock radio, telephone, desk, hot tub/spa, fireplace, six with whirlpool tubs, fireplace and mountain views in room. Air conditioning. Fax, copier, library, parlor games, gift shop, gardens, patio and green hotel on premises. Antiquing, art galleries, beach, bicycling, canoeing/kayaking, cross-country skiing, downhill skiing, fishing, golf, hiking,

horseback riding, live theater, museums, parks, shopping, sporting events, tennis, water sports, wineries, tours, historic district, sleigh/surrey rides, dog sled, snowshoe, Ben & Jerry's, cider mill, glass blowing and covered bridges nearby.
Location: Village/country.
Publicity: *Vermont, Vermont Life, Innsider, Discerning Traveler, Ski, Arrington's B&B Journal, Yankee, Ski Year and Vermont B&B Innkeeper of the Year 2001.*
"The little things made us glad we stopped."
Certificate may be used: Midweek and limited weekends during April, May and to mid-June; late October, November and to mid-December excluding holidays.

Hob Knob Inn & Restaurant

2364 Mountain Road R
Stowe, VT 05672
(802)253-8549 (800)245-8540 Fax:(802)253-6721
Internet: www.hobknobinn.com
E-mail: info@hobknobinn.com

Circa 1938. Surrounded by a forest of poplar, white birch, pine and maple trees, this historic ski lodge from the 1930s sits on ten hillside acres with gardens, ponds and wide lawns. The original building features a lounge where appetizers and beverages are served and a dining room. Stay in one of the two guest bedrooms with fireplaces and a suite with a Jacuzzi tub, kitchen and fireplace. On a nearby wooded knoll a rustic cabin offers spacious privacy with a fieldstone fireplace and a small kitchen. Stay in one of the rooms in the secluded newer lodge with amazing views of Mount Mansfield. Most have patios or balconies. Linger over breakfast then go for a hike or play golf at Stowe Country Club. Take a refreshing swim in the pool.
Innkeeper(s): Bob & Barbara Fisher. $75-235. 20 cabins with PB, 20 with FP, 20 with HT, 1 and 3 total suites, including 2 two-bedroom suites, 1 guest house and 1 conference room. Breakfast included in rates. Types of meals: Country bkfst, early coffee/tea, wine and dinner. Beds: KQ. Cable TV, reading lamp, refrigerator, clock radio, telephone, coffeemaker, desk and fireplace in room. Air conditioning. Fax, copier and swimming on premises. Antiquing, art galleries, bicycling, canoeing/kayaking, cross-country skiing, downhill skiing, fishing, golf, hiking, horseback riding, live theater, museums, shopping, tennis, water sports, wineries and gondola rides nearby.
Location: Mountains.
Publicity: *Stowe Reporter.*
Certificate may be used: Oct. 24-Dec. 17 and April 1-June 17, subject to availability.

Honeywood Inn

4583 Mountain Rd
Stowe, VT 05672
(802)253-4846 (800)821-7891 Fax:(802)253-7050
Internet: www.honeywoodinn.com
E-mail: honeywd@aol.com

Circa 1980. Stowe needs no introduction to its famous outdoor resort facilities. The Honeywood Inn is perfectly situated to take advantage of these activities in every season of the year. Cross-country ski trails leave right from the front door, and during the warm months, a 5.3-mile bike and walking path winds through some of Vermont's most splendid scenery, crossing wooden bridges and working farms. The inn resembles a Swiss chalet, while the interior decor has a homey, country feel. Some guest rooms feature canopy, brass or sleigh beds; others boast a spa. If the night is star filled, an outdoor hot tub makes a fun nightcap. In the morning, a light breakfast of fresh fruit, homemade muffins and cereal is followed by a more substantial one of waffles with homemade raspberry sauce, apple-cinnamon pancakes, or eggs Benedict. During the summer you'll enjoy this in the patio garden. The center of Stowe is only a stroll away along the recreation path. Here you can browse through the numerous antique and craft shops.

Innkeeper(s): Carolyn & Bill Cook. $99-209. 8 rooms with PB, 2 with FP, 2 suites. Breakfast included in rates. Types of meals: Full gourmet bkfst and veg bkfst. Beds: KQD. Reading lamp, ceiling fan, clock radio and some with hot tubs in room. Air conditioning. TV, VCR, fax, copier, spa, swimming, bicycles, parlor games, telephone and fireplace on premises. Antiquing, art galleries, beach, bicycling, canoeing/kayaking, cross-country skiing, downhill skiing, fishing, golf, hiking, live theater, museums, parks, shopping, tennis, water sports and wineries nearby.

Location: Mountains, with babbling brook on property.

Certificate may be used: April 1-June 30, Sunday-Thursday; Sept. 1-Sept. 25, Sunday-Thursday; Nov. 1-Dec. 23, Sunday-Thursday.

Vergennes   E2

Emerson Guest House

82 Main St
Vergennes, VT 05491-1155
(802)877-3293 Fax:(802)877-3293
Internet: www.emersonhouse.com
E-mail: emersons@sover.net

Circa 1850. This historic 1850s Victorian home is situated on three-and-a-half acres near downtown Vergennes in the heart of Lake Champlain Valley. Choose from six spacious, airy guest rooms filled with antiques and personal collections. Start the day with a fresh breakfast of frittatas and homemade muffins, or French toast with apple praline topping. Then relax in the large backyard and flower gardens or walk to nearby antique shops and restaurants. The historic city of Vergennes is a welcome getaway, with activities such as swimming, boating or fishing in Lake Champlain and biking or hiking along mountain trails. At the end of the day relax on one of our porches or sit in the backyard and watch the sun set.

Innkeeper(s): Susan & Bill Walsh. $65-140. 6 rooms, 3 with PB, 1 suite and 1 conference room. Breakfast included in rates. Types of meals: Full gourmet bkfst, early coffee/tea and snacks/refreshments. Beds: KQDT. Reading lamp, ceiling fan and clock radio in room. TV, fax, copier, bicycles, library, parlor games, telephone, fireplace, croquet and trails on premises. Limited handicap access. Antiquing, art galleries, bicycling, canoeing/kayaking, cross-country skiing, downhill skiing, fishing, golf, hiking, horseback riding, museums, parks, shopping, sporting events, tennis, water sports, wineries and Lake Champlain nearby.

Location: Country.

Certificate may be used: Jan. 1-Dec. 31, Sunday-Thursday, no weekends.

Strong House Inn

94 W Main St
Vergennes, VT 05491-9531
(802)877-3337 Fax:(802)877-2599
Internet: www.stronghouseinn.com
E-mail: innkeeper@stronghouseinn.com

Circa 1834. This Federal-style home boasts views of the Green Mountains and the Adirondack range. Several rooms offer working fireplaces and all are richly appointed. Country breakfasts and afternoon refreshments are served. Nearby Lake Champlain offers boating and fishing. Golf, hiking, skiing and some of the finest cycling in Vermont are all part of the area's myriad of outdoor activities. Innkeeper Mary Bargiel is an avid gardener and decorates the grounds with flowers and herb gardens. The innkeepers offer a selection of special weekends including Valentine's Day, quilting, gardening, murder mystery and psychic weekends.

Innkeeper(s): Hugh & Mary Bargiel. $95-305. 14 rooms with PB, 4 with FP, 1 suite and 1 conference room. Breakfast and snacks/refreshments included in rates. Types of meals: Country bkfst and early coffee/tea. Beds: KQDT. Modem hook-up, data port, cable TV, VCR, reading lamp, stereo, refrigerator, clock radio, telephone, coffeemaker, desk, hot tub/spa and voice mail in room. Central air. Fax, copier, spa, library, parlor games, fireplace and gift shop on premises. Handicap access. Antiquing, art galleries, bicycling, canoeing/kayaking, cross-country skiing, downhill skiing, fishing, golf, hiking, horseback riding, museums, parks, shopping and tennis nearby.

Location: Country.

Publicity: *New York Times, Vermont Magazine, Addison County Independent and RETN.*

"Blissful stay...Glorious breakfast!"

Certificate may be used: Nov. 1-May 15, Sunday-Thursday, subject to availability.

Waitsfield   E3

Lareau Farm Country Inn

PO Box 563, Rt 100
Waitsfield, VT 05673-0563
(802)496-4949 (800)833-0766
Internet: www.lareaufarminn.com
E-mail: lareau@lareaufarminn.com

Circa 1794. This Greek Revival house was built by Simeon Stoddard, the town's first physician. Old-fashioned roses, lilacs, delphiniums, iris and peonies fill the gardens. The inn sits in a wide meadow next to the crystal-clear Mad River. A canoe trip or a refreshing swim are possibilities here.

Innkeeper(s): Susan Easley. $80-135. 13 rooms, 11 with PB, 1 suite and 1 conference room. Breakfast included in rates. Types of meals: Full gourmet bkfst and early coffee/tea. Beds: QD. Reading lamp and desk in room. Swimming, library and fireplace on premises. Antiquing, cross-country skiing, downhill skiing, fishing, live theater and shopping nearby.

Location: Country.

Publicity: *Pittsburgh Press, Philadelphia Inquirer and Los Angeles Times.*

"Hospitality is a gift. Thank you for sharing your gift so freely with us."

Certificate may be used: Dec. 15-April 1 and May 1-June 29, weekdays, holiday weeks excluded.

Mad River Inn

Tremblay Rd, PO Box 75
Waitsfield, VT 05673
(802)496-7900 (800)832-8278 Fax:(802)496-5390
Internet: www.madriverinn.com
E-mail: madriverinn@madriver.com

Circa 1860. Surrounded by the Green Mountains, this Queen Anne Victorian sits on seven scenic acres along the Mad River. The charming inn boasts attractive woodwork throughout, highlighted by ash, bird's-eye maple and cherry. Guest rooms feature European feather beds and include the Hayden Breeze Room, with a King brass bed, large windows and sea relics, and the Abner Doubleday Room, with a Queen ash bed and mementos of baseball's glory days. The inn sports a billiard table, gazebo, organic gardens and a Jacuzzi overlooking the mountains. Guests can walk to a recreation path along the river.

Innkeeper(s): Luc & Karen Maranda. $95-135. 9 rooms with PB. Breakfast and afternoon tea included in rates. Types of meals: Full gourmet bkfst. Beds: KQ. Reading lamp, ceiling fan, turn-down service and desk in room. VCR, fax, spa, parlor games, telephone and fireplace on premises. Antiquing, cross-country skiing, downhill skiing, fishing, live theater, shopping, sporting events and water sports nearby.

Location: Mountains.

Publicity: *Innsider, Victorian Homes, Let's Live, Skiing, AAA Home & Away, Tea Time at the Inn, Travel & Leisure and Ski Magazine.*

"Your hospitality was appreciated, beautiful house and accommodations, great food & friendly people, just to name a few things. We plan to return and we recommend the Mad River Inn to friends & family."

Certificate may be used: Sunday-Thursday, except Dec. 21-Jan. 3, Sept. 21-Oct. 15, based on availability.

Waitsfield Inn

Rt 100, PO Box 969
Waitsfield, VT 05673-0969
(802)496-3979 (800)758-3801 Fax:(802)496-3970
Internet: www.waitsfieldinn.com
E-mail: lodging@waitsfieldinn.com

Circa 1825. This Federal-style inn once served as a parsonage and was home to several state senators of the Richardson family. The 1839 barn offers a Great Room with fireplace and wood-plank floors, or in winter you may enjoy sipping spiced Vermont apple cider and munching on fresh cookies in the sitting room. Guest quarters are furnished with period antiques, quilts or comforters and some rooms have exposed beams or hand stenciling. A full breakfast is served in the dining room, with a choice of 14 delicious items as prepared by the inns chef. As the inn is in the village of Waitsfield, the entire town's sites are nearby including a beautiful covered bridge. Visit Glen Moss Waterfall, fly fish, canoe, try a glider, golf or watch a polo match. Snowshoeing, skiing and visits to the New England Culinary Institute and Ben & Jerry's Ice Cream Factory are popular activities.

Innkeeper(s): Mike & Ronda Kelley. $105-150. 14 rooms with PB. Breakfast included in rates. Types of meals: Full bkfst. Beds: QDT. Fax, copier, library, telephone, fireplace and modem on premises. Antiquing, cross-country skiing, downhill skiing, fishing, golf, live theater, shopping and canoeing nearby.

Location: Village.

Certificate may be used: Sunday-Thursday, January-March and July 1-Sept. 12. Anytime April-June and November-December, all holiday weeks and foliage season excluded.

Wallingford H3

I. B. Munson House

37 S Main St, PO Box 427
Wallingford, VT 05773-0427
(802)446-2860 (888)519-3771 Fax:(802)446-3336
Internet: www.ibmunsoninn.com
E-mail: stay@ibmunsoninn.com

Circa 1856. An Italianate Victorian bed & breakfast, the inn was meticulously restored as the innkeepers preserved many original elements, such as the wood floors, ornately carved mantels and

woodwork. Period antiques and Waverly wallcoverings are featured in the guest rooms, three of which include a fireplace. All seven guest rooms have private baths. Wallingford is a designated historic village, so there are many interesting old homes and buildings to see. Ski areas, shops and restaurants are within a couple of blocks.

Innkeeper(s): Charles & Lisa McClafferty. $130-165. 7 rooms with PB, 3 with FP, 2 suites. Breakfast included in rates. Types of meals: Full gourmet bkfst, veg bkfst and afternoon tea. Beds: Q. Reading lamp, ceiling fan, turn-down service and fireplace in room. Air conditioning. TV, VCR, library, parlor games, telephone and gift shop on premises. Antiquing, art galleries, canoeing/kayaking, cross-country skiing, downhill skiing, fishing, golf, hiking, horse-back riding, live theater, museums, parks and shopping nearby.

Location: Historic village.

Publicity: *The Rotarian, Spring 3100 magazine, Best Recipes B&B Cookbook and Historic Inns B&B Coffee Table book.*

"It was a pleasure to stay at your beautiful historic Bed and Breakfast. Wonderful hospitality! Delicious breakfast - a very special treat!! We will be back."

Certificate may be used: Any night April 1-June 1, excluding Memorial Day weekend, any night Nov. 1-Dec. 1, Sunday-Thursday all year, excluding foliage, subject to availability.

Waterbury D3

The Inn at Blush Hill

784 Blush Hill Rd
Waterbury, VT 05676
(802)244-7529 (800)736-7522 Fax:(802)244-7314
Internet: www.blushhill.com
E-mail: inn@blushhill.com

Circa 1790. This shingled Cape-style house was once a stage-coach stop en route to Stowe and is the oldest inn in Waterbury. A 12-foot-long pine farmhand's table is set near the double fireplace and the kitchen bay window, revealing views of the Worcester Mountains. A

favorite summertime breakfast, served gardenside, is pancakes with fresh blueberries, topped with ice cream and maple syrup.

Innkeeper(s): Pam Gosselin. $89-160. 5 rooms with PB, 1 with FP. Breakfast, afternoon tea and snacks/refreshments included in rates. Types of meals: Full gourmet bkfst and early coffee/tea. Beds: QT. TV, reading lamp, refrigerator, ceiling fan, clock radio, turn-down service and hot tub/spa in room. Air conditioning. Fax, library, parlor games, telephone and fireplace on premises. Antiquing, cross-country skiing, downhill skiing, fishing, golf, live theater, parks, shopping, water sports and Ben & Jerry's ice cream factory nearby.

Location: Mountains.

Publicity: *Vermont, Charlotte Observer, Yankee, New York Times, Ski, New York Post and WCAX Television.*

"Our room was wonderful — especially the fireplace. Everything was so cozy and warm."

Certificate may be used: Anytime, November-April, subject to availability.

Thatcher Brook Inn

PO Box 490, Rt 100 N
Waterbury, VT 05676-0490
(802)244-5911 (800)292-5911 Fax:(802)244-1294
Internet: www.thatcherbrook.com
E-mail: info@thatcherbrook.com

Circa 1899. Listed in the Vermont Register of Historic Buildings, this restored Victorian mansion features a rambling porch with twin gazebos and a covered walkway leading to the historic Wheeler House. Guest rooms are decorated in classic country style. Four rooms have fireplaces, and six have whirlpool tubs.

Innkeeper(s): Lisa & John Fischer. $80-195. 22 rooms with PB, 4 with FP, 1 suite and 1 conference room. Breakfast included in rates. Types of meals: Full bkfst and gourmet dinner. Restaurant on premises. Beds: KQD. Reading lamp, ceiling fan, clock radio, telephone, most have A/C and 6 have whirlpools in room. Fax, copier, parlor games, fireplace and Internet access on premises. Handicap access. Antiquing, bicycling, cross-country skiing, downhill skiing, fishing, hiking, horseback riding, live theater, parks, shopping and water sports nearby.

Location: City. Village.

"I'd have to put on a black tie in Long Island to find food as good as this, and best of all it's in a relaxed country atmosphere."

Certificate may be used: November through August, Sunday through Thursday.

West Dover   K3

Austin Hill Inn

Rt 100, Box 859
West Dover, VT 05356
(802)464-5281 (800)332-7352 Fax:(802)464-1229
Internet: www.austinhillinn.com
E-mail: info@austinhillinn.com

Circa 1950. This family-owned and operated inn is situated between Mt. Snow and Haystack Mountains just outside the historic village of West Dover. Guest rooms feature country decor and furnishings. Romantic amenities include in-room fireplaces and votive candles at turndown. Guests are treated to a hearty New England breakfast, as well as afternoon wine and cheese or home-baked treats. In cool weather, guests enjoy the warm glow of the inn's fireplaces in the common rooms. The Austin Hill Inn is notable for its attention to detail and superior hospitality.

Innkeeper(s): John & Deborah Bailey. $115-195. 11 rooms with PB, 6 with FP, 1 suite and 1 conference room. Breakfast, snacks/refreshments and wine included in rates. Types of meals: Full gourmet bkfst, early coffee/tea and gourmet dinner. Beds: KQDT. TV, VCR, reading lamp, snack bar, clock radio and fireplace in room. Fax, copier, swimming, parlor games, telephone and gift shop on premises. Antiquing, art galleries, bicycling, canoeing/kayaking, cross-country skiing, downhill skiing, fishing, golf, hiking, horseback riding, live theater, parks, shopping, water sports, wineries and chamber music nearby.

Location: Mountains.

Publicity: *Country Inns, Getaways and Greenwich Magazine.*

Certificate may be used: May 1-Sept. 15, Sunday-Thursday.

Snow Goose Inn at Mount Snow

PO Box 366,   259 Rte. 100
West Dover, VT 05356
(802)464-3984 (888)604-7964 Fax:(802)464-5322
Internet: www.snowgooseinn.com
E-mail: gooseinn@aol.com

Circa 1959. Three acres of Vermont countryside create a secluded setting for the Snow Goose Inn. Renovations in 1998 include the addition of Southern pine floors and private decks. Hand-hewn beams from an old country barn were fashioned into a new grand entry and a duplex honeymoon suite was created. (The new suite offers two decks with mountain and valley views, a Jacuzzi tub, fireplace and sitting area.) Most of the other antique-filled rooms also include a fireplace, VCR, stereo and double Jacuzzi tub. Hypo-allergenic feather mattresses and comforters are additional features. Hearty breakfasts include cereals, fresh fruit, juices, breads and entrees such as wild mushrooms and herb scrambled eggs, French toast stuffed with bananas or fresh bagels imported from New York City. Evening wine and cheese is offered on one of the porches with views to

the pond and flower gardens or by fireside in winter.

Innkeeper(s): Philip & Suzanne Waller. $85-395. 13 rooms with PB, 9 with FP, 8 with HT, 2 suites. Breakfast, snacks/refreshments, hors d'oeuvres and wine included in rates. Types of meals: Full gourmet bkfst, veg bkfst and early coffee/tea. Beds: KQDT. Modem hook-up, data port, cable TV, VCR, reading lamp, stereo, refrigerator, ceiling fan, clock radio, turn-down service, desk, fireplace, real wood fireplace and two-person Jacuzzi tubs in room. Air conditioning. Fax, copier, parlor games, 3 acres of informal gardens and telephone on premises. Handicap access. Antiquing, art galleries, bicycling, canoeing/kayaking, cross-country skiing, downhill skiing, fishing, golf, hiking, horseback riding, live theater, museums, parks, shopping, tennis, water sports and wineries nearby.

Location: Country, mountains.

Certificate may be used: Anytime, Sunday-Thursday, subject to availability.

Weston   J3

The Darling Family Inn

815 Rt 100
Weston, VT 05161-5404
(802)824-3223
Internet: www.thedarlingfamilyinn.com
E-mail: info@thedarlingfamilyinn.com

Circa 1830. This two-story inn also features two cottages. Located in the Green Mountains, just minutes from Bromley, Okemo, Magic and Stratton ski areas, the inn provides a taste of life from the early Colonial days. Guest rooms feature handmade quilts crafted locally. The cottages include kitchenettes, and pets are welcome in the cottages if prior arrangements are made.

Innkeeper(s): Chapin & Joan Darling. $85-145. 5 rooms with PB and 2 cottages. Breakfast included in rates. Types of meals: Full bkfst. Reading lamp and turn-down service in room. VCR, swimming, telephone and fireplace on premises. Antiquing, cross-country skiing, downhill skiing, live theater and shopping nearby.

Location: Country, mountains.

Certificate may be used: Sunday through Thursday, excluding Sundays of holiday weekends; January through June; Sept. 1-15; Oct. 15-Dec. 23.

Williston   D3

Catamount B&B

592 Governor Chittenden Rd
Williston, VT 05495
(802)878-2180 (888)680-1011 Fax:(802)879-6066
Internet: www.catamountoutdoor.com
E-mail: lucy@catamountoutdoor.com

Circa 1796. This huge Federal Colonial Revival inn on 500 acres has been in the McCullough family since 1873. In its early years, the elegant homestead sponsored many grand balls, and today the home exudes a sense of rich family history. The inn is the oldest standing building in Williston, and it has been a Williston landmark for more than 200 years. It is located on the family farm where the family owns and operates a recreation center that includes many outdoor activities. The grounds have one of the finest mountain bike facilities available. It has a professionally designed trail network that includes flat, rolling and steep trails that range from single-track to wide. And it has an acre of groomed ice for ice skating and a tree-free sledding hill. Guests who stay in the inn's three guest bedrooms (including one suite) enjoy a hearty continental breakfast each morning with courses such as homemade muffins, seasonal fruits, cereals, coffee and tea and sometimes waffles.

Innkeeper(s): Lucy & Jim McCullough. $75-105. 3 rooms, 1 suite and 1 conference room. Breakfast included in rates. Types of meals: Cont plus, veg bkfst and early coffee/tea. Beds: D. TV, VCR, fax, copier, bicycles, library, parlor games, telephone, fireplace, cross-country skiing, snowshoes, ice skating and 20 miles of trails on premises. Amusement parks, antiquing, art galleries, beach, bicycling, canoeing/kayaking, cross-country skiing, downhill skiing, fishing, golf, hiking, horseback riding, live theater, museums, parks, shopping, sporting events, tennis, water sports, wineries and Burlington- the cultural hub of Vermont nearby.

Location: Country. 500 acres.

Certificate may be used: June 1-Labor Day, Sunday-Thursday; also Columbus Day-May 1, all days.

Wilmington   K3

The Red Shutter Inn

PO Box 636
Wilmington, VT 05363-0636
(802)464-3768 (800)845-7548 Fax:(802)464-5123
Internet: www.redshutterinn.com
E-mail: innkeeper@redshutterinn.com

Circa 1894. This colonial inn sits on a five-acre hillside amid maples, pin oaks and evergreens. Tucked behind the inn is the renovated carriage house; among its charms is a cozy fireplace suite. In the summer, guests can enjoy gourmet dining by candlelight on an awning-covered porch. The Red Shutter Inn, with its fireplaces in the sitting room and dining room, antique furnishings and view of a rushing river, provide a congenial atmosphere. Antique shops, galleries and craft shops are within walking distance.

Innkeeper(s): Lucylee and Gerard Gingras. $130-280. 9 rooms with PB, 3 with FP, 2 suites. Breakfast included in rates. Types of meals: Full bkfst and gourmet dinner. Restaurant on premises. Beds: QD. Cable TV, reading lamp, ceiling fan, whirlpool tub and some with air conditioning in room. TV, library, telephone and fireplace on premises. Antiquing, cross-country skiing, downhill skiing, fishing, parks, shopping and water sports nearby.

Location: Mountains.

Publicity: *USA Weekend.*

"You've made The Red Shutter Inn a cozy and relaxing hideaway."

Certificate may be used: March-June anytime, July-October, Sunday-Thursday, November-Dec. 18, anytime, Dec. 19-February, Sunday-Thursday. Not available holiday weekends, subject to availability.

Trail's End, A Country Inn

5 Trail's End Ln
Wilmington, VT 05363-7925
(802)464-2727 (800)859-2585
E-mail: trailsnd@together.net

Circa 1956. The innkeepers transformed this rustic inn from its 1950s decor into a beautiful romantic bed & breakfast. The game room, where cookies and hot cider are served each day, features elegant wing-back chairs and a pool table, while the living room offers four overstuffed couches in front of a 22-foot Fieldstone fireplace. Each bedroom is decorated in a different color scheme and utilizes brass, white wicker and family heirlooms for a chic country atmosphere.

Innkeeper(s): Kevin Stephens. $110-200. 15 rooms with PB, 6 with FP, 2 suites and 1 conference room. Breakfast and afternoon tea included in rates. Types of meals: Full bkfst and early coffee/tea. Beds: QDT. Cable TV, reading lamp, stereo, refrigerator, ceiling fan, desk, hot tub/spa, clock and microwave in room. Copier, swimming, tennis, library, parlor games, telephone, fireplace and guest refrigerator on premises. Antiquing, cross-country skiing, downhill skiing, fishing, live theater, parks, shopping, water sports and Marlboro Music Festival nearby.

Location: Mountains.

Publicity: *Yankee Magazine, Boston Globe, Inn Times, Snow Country, Sun Country, Changing Times, PM Magazine and Mt. Snow's 40th Anniversary.*

"Thank you again for an absolutely wonderful weekend."

Certificate may be used: March 15-June 15, Sunday-Friday.

Woodstock   H4

Applebutter Inn

Happy Valley Rd
Woodstock, VT 05091
(802)457-4158 (800)486-1734 Fax:(802)457-4158
Internet: www.applebutterinn.com
E-mail: aplbtrn@adelphia.net

Circa 1850. Gracious hospitality and comfort are equally enjoyed at this elegant 1854 country home. Authentically restored, this Federal gabled inn listed in the National Register boasts original wide pine floors, Oriental rugs and rare antiques. Relax by the fire in the Yellow Room or browse through the extensive book collection. Play the Mason & Hamlin grand piano in the Music Room. Several of the spacious and romantic guest bedrooms feature fireplaces. The Cameo Room also has a separate entrance. Sleep well on an 18th century pencil-post bed in the King David Room with a private porch. Sit in the morning sun of the breakfast room and savor a gourmet meal highlighted by Barbara's own applebutter. Play croquet on the expansive lawn, or sit on the porch with afternoon tea and fresh-baked cookies. Located in the tranquil hamlet of Taftsville, seasonal activities and fine dining are close by.

Innkeeper(s): Barbara & Michael. $95-195. 6 rooms with PB and 1 conference room. Breakfast, afternoon tea and snacks/refreshments included in rates. Types of meals: Full gourmet bkfst, veg bkfst and early coffee/tea. Beds: KQD. Cable TV, VCR and clock radio in room. Air conditioning. Fax, copier, library, parlor games, telephone and fireplace on premises. Limited handicap access.

Location: Country, mountains.

Publicity: *Los Angeles Times, Yankee and Food & Wine.*

Certificate may be used: November-April, Sunday-Thursday excluding holiday weeks, subject to availability.

Ardmore Inn

23 Pleasant St, PO Box 466
Woodstock, VT 05091
(802)457-3887 (800)497-9652 Fax:(802)457-9006
Internet: www.ardmorein.com
E-mail: ardmoreinn@aol.com

Circa 1867. This Greek Revival-style inn offers a gentle welcome with its pretty shutters and graceful entrance. Located on an acre in a village setting, it is furnished elegantly. For instance, the Tully Room has four eyebrow windows shedding sunlight on its four-poster queen bed, and there's a sitting area and marble bath. Enjoy breakfasts of Vermont flat bread served with truffle eggs, apple-smoked sausage and asparagus spears.

$135-175. 5 rooms, 1 with FP, 5 suites. Breakfast and snacks/refreshments included in rates. Types of meals: Country bkfst and afternoon tea. Beds: KQD. Reading lamp, refrigerator, clock radio and desk in room. Air conditioning. Fax, copier, bicycles, telephone and fireplace on premises. Antiquing, cross-country skiing, downhill skiing, fishing, golf, live theater, parks, shopping, tennis, mountain biking and fly fishing nearby.

Location: Mountains. Village.

Certificate may be used: Certain holidays excluded. Sunday to Thursday, except Sept. 15-Oct. 31.

Bailey's Mills B&B

1347 Bailey's Mills Rd
Woodstock, VT 05062-0117
(802)484-7809 (800)639-3437 Fax:(802)484-0014
Internet: www.baileysmills.com
E-mail: info@baileysmills.com

Circa 1820. This Federal-style inn features grand porches, 11 fireplaces, a "good-morning" staircase and a ballroom on the third floor. Four generations of Baileys lived in the home, as well as housing mill workers. There also was once a country store on the premises. Guests can learn much about the home and history of the people who lived here through the innkeepers. Two of the guest rooms include a fireplace, and the suite has a private solarium.  There's plenty to do here, from exploring the surrounding 48 acres to relaxing with a book on the porch swing or in a hammock. If you forgot your favorite novel, borrow a book from the inn's 2,200-volume library.

Innkeeper(s): Barbara Thaeder & Don Whitaker. $100-160. 3 rooms with PB, 2 with FP, 1 suite. Breakfast included in rates. Types of meals: Cont plus and early coffee/tea. Beds: KQ. Reading lamp, clock radio and two with fireplace in room. Swimming, library, parlor games, telephone, fireplace, pond, stream and walking trails on premises. Antiquing, cross-country skiing, downhill skiing, fishing, live theater, parks and shopping nearby.

Location: Country.

Publicity: *Vermont Magazine.*

"If words could encapsulate what a wonderful weekend would be, it would have to be 'Bailey's Mills B&B.' Your home is beautiful. It is elegant yet homey."

Certificate may be used: November-May, Sunday-Thursday or call anytime for last-minute openings.

Charleston House

21 Pleasant St
Woodstock, VT 05091-1131
(802)457-3843
Internet: charlestonhouse.com
E-mail: charleston@adelphia.net

Circa 1835. This authentically restored brick Greek Revival town house, in the National Register, welcomes guests with shuttered many-paned windows and window boxes filled with pink blooms. Guest rooms are appointed with period antiques and reproductions, an art collection and Oriental rugs. Some of the rooms boast four-poster beds, and some feature fireplaces and Jacuzzis. A hearty full breakfast starts off the day in the candlelit dining room, and the innkeepers serve afternoon refreshments, as well. Area offerings include winter sleigh rides, snow skiing, auctions, fly fishing, golfing and summer stock theater, to name a few.

Innkeeper(s): Dieter & Willa Nohl. $115-220. 9 rooms with PB. Breakfast included in rates. Types of meals: Full bkfst. Beds: QT. TV in room. Jacuzzis and fireplaces on premises. Antiquing, cross-country skiing, downhill skiing, fishing and golf nearby.

Publicity: *Harbor News, Boston Business Journal, Weekend Getaway, Inn Spots and Special Places.*

Certificate may be used: Nov. 1 to May 31, except holidays.

Village Inn of Woodstock

41 Pleasant St
Woodstock, VT 05091-1146
(802)457-1255 (800)722-4571 Fax:(802)457-3109
Internet: www.villageinnofwoodstock.com
E-mail: stay@villageinnofwoodstock.com

Circa 1899. In a historic village location, this Queen Anne Victorian inn and intimate tavern create the perfect setting for a romantic interlude, weekend getaway or family reunion. Period antique furnishings are accented by original wood floors, oak molding and wainscoting, heavy beveled glass and ornate tin ceilings. Some guest bedrooms feature marble washstands, clawfoot tubs, Oriental rugs, brass and four-poster cherry beds. One boasts a stained-glass window and fireplace. Savor a three-course breakfast in the dining room showcasing antiques, art work and folk art. Relax in the garden, resplendent with pond and fountain.

Innkeeper(s): Evelyn & David Brey. $100-240. 7 rooms with PB, 1 with FP. Breakfast included in rates. Types of meals: Full bkfst, early coffee/tea, lunch, picnic lunch and dinner. Beds: KQD. Cable TV, reading lamp, clock radio, fireplace and wireless Internet access in room. Air conditioning. VCR, parlor games and telephone on premises. Antiquing, art galleries, bicycling, canoeing/kayaking, cross-country skiing, downhill skiing, fishing, golf, hiking, horseback riding, live theater, museums, parks, shopping and tennis nearby.

Location: Mountains. Historic Village.

Certificate may be used: Dec. 1-20, Sunday-Thursday. March 1-31, Sunday-Thursday.

Woodstocker B&B

61 River St Route 4
Woodstock, VT 05091-1227
(802)457-3896 (866)662-1439 Fax:(802)457-3897
Internet: www.woodstockervt.com
E-mail: woodstocker@valley.net

Circa 1830. This early 19th-century, Cape-style inn is located at the base of Mt. Tom at the edge of the village of Woodstock. Hand-hewn wooden beams create a rustic effect. The seven guest rooms and two suites are individually appointed. Buffet-style, full breakfasts get the day off to a great start. Guests can take a short walk across a covered bridge to reach shops and restaurants. Hikers will enjoy trails that wind up and around Mt. Tom. After a busy winter day, come back and enjoy a soak in the five-person whirlpool.

Innkeeper(s): Tom & Nancy Blackford. $85-205. 9 rooms with PB, 2 suites. Breakfast included in rates. Types of meals: Full bkfst and early coffee/tea. Beds: QD. Cable TV, reading lamp and ceiling fan in room. Air conditioning. VCR, fax, copier and telephone on premises. Antiquing, cross-country skiing, downhill skiing, fishing, live theater, shopping, sporting events and water sports nearby.

Location: Mountains. Village.

"You have truly opened your home and heart to create a comfortable and memorable stay."

Certificate may be used: Sunday through Thursday, except July 1-Oct. 20 and Dec. 20-Jan. 1.

Virginia

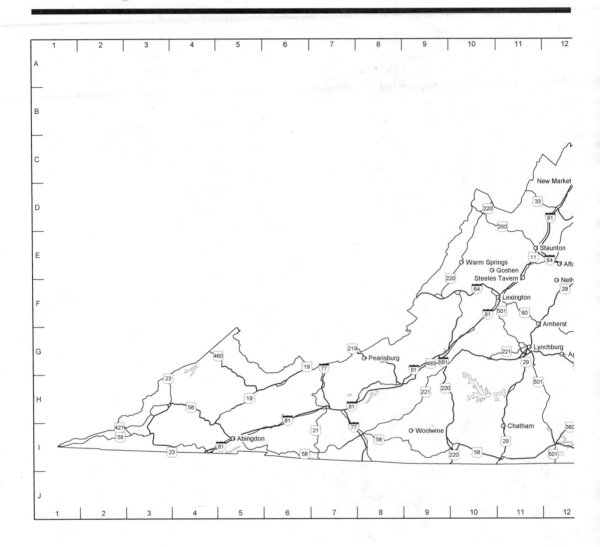

Visit www.iLoveInns.com for photos and more details about each inn.

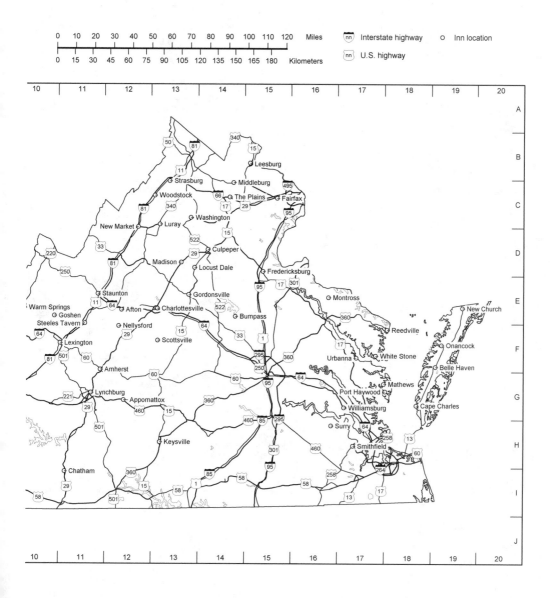

													Miles
0	10	20	30	40	50	60	70	80	90	100	110	120	

													Kilometers
0	15	30	45	60	75	90	105	120	135	150	165	180	

Interstate highway   Inn location

U.S. highway

Abingdon   I5

The Inn on Town Creek

445 E Valley St
Abingdon, VA 24212-1745
(276)628-4560 Fax:(276)628-9611
Internet: www.innontowncreek.com
E-mail: info@innontowncreek.com

Encounter peace and tranquility at this elegant inn that sits on four
wooded acres shaded by dogwood, pine and huge rhododendrons.
The enchanting creek that flows through the scenic grounds is a
tributary of the Holston River. Expect to find gracious southern
hospitality and spacious well-appointed rooms furnished with
antiques and period pieces at this splendid inn. Stay in a large
guest bedroom with Victorian charm. The Brookside Room is a
two-bedroom suite that includes a private entrance, full kitchen,
dining and sitting area overlooking the waterway. An outside covered porch, small kitchen and living room are added features of the
Garden Room. The full daily breakfast is sure to please, and proprietor Linda is delighted to share recipes. Situated in a quiet, tree-
lined neighborhood, it is just a short walk to historic downtown.
Innkeeper(s): Linda Neal. Call for rates. Call inn for details.
Certificate may be used: November through April (Sunday through Thursday)
except during Nascar race weekend in March.

Afton   E12

Afton Mountain Bed & Breakfast

10273 Rockfish Valley Hwy
Afton, VA 22920-2771
(540)456-6844 (800)769-6844 Fax:(540)456-7255
Internet: www.aftonmountain.com
E-mail: stay@aftonmountain.com

Circa 1848. Surrounded by 140-year-old silver maples adorning
10 acres in the foothills of the Blue Ridge Mountains, this
Victorian farmhouse features original heart pine floors and staircase, a stained-glass entryway and a variety of antiques. Air-conditioned guest bedrooms boast luxurious beds for the ultimate in
comfort and include unique furnishings. A sumptuous breakfast
begins with fresh fruit, homemade baked goods and an entree
specialty. Stroll in the formal rose garden or swim in the pool.
Relax on one of the spacious porches with just-baked cookies
and a beverage. Tour scenic Skyline Drive, sample wines at local
award-winning vineyards, golf or ski. Ask about special packages.
Gift certificates are available for the perfect anniversary, birthday,
or romantic getaway. Charlottesville and Monticello are nearby.
Innkeeper(s): Orquida and Dan Ingraham. $70-140. 5 rooms with PB. Breakfast,
afternoon tea and snacks/refreshments included in rates. Types of meals: Full
gourmet bkfst and early coffee/tea. Beds: KQDT. Reading lamp, CD player, ceiling
fan, clock radio, turn-down service and desk in room. Air conditioning. TV, VCR,
fax, copier, swimming, library, parlor games and telephone on premises.
Antiquing, cross-country skiing, downhill skiing, fishing, golf, hiking, horseback
riding, parks, shopping, sporting events, tennis, water sports and wineries nearby.
Location: Mountains.
Certificate may be used: Jan. 1-Sept. 15, Nov. 15-Dec. 31, Sunday-
Thursday, no holidays.

Amherst   F11

Blackberry Ridge Inn

1770 Earley Farm Road
Amherst, VA 24521
(434)946-2723 (877)724-7041 Fax:(434)946-1289
Internet: www.blackberryridge.com
E-mail: info@blackberryridge.com

Circa 1990. Blending in well with the wooded surroundings, this
peaceful cedar inn sits on 100 acres. It boasts a 50-mile panoram-

ic view of five counties from the Blue Ridge Mountains to the
Appalachian Mountains. Inside, the great room is an inviting place
to watch TV or read a book by the fire. Restful guest bedrooms are
named after the women of the family and offer comfortable furnishings. A hot and hearty breakfast is served in the dining
room/parlor, specializing in blackberry French toast. Enjoy the
fresh air, morning mist and quiet walks along whispering streams.
A complimentary dessert is served after sunset each evening.
Family reunions and small group gatherings are welcome.
Innkeeper(s): John & Susan Sarver. $89-109. 5 rooms with PB and 2 confer-
ence rooms. Breakfast and snacks/refreshments included in rates. Types of
meals: Full bkfst, veg bkfst and lunch. Beds: QD. Reading lamp, stereo, ceiling fan and clock radio in room. Central air. TV, VCR, fax, copier, spa, tele-
phone, fireplace and laundry facility on premises. Handicap access.
Antiquing, canoeing/kayaking and downhill skiing nearby.
Location: Country.
Certificate may be used: Anytime, Sunday-Thursday.

Dulwich Manor B&B Inn

107 Farwood Ct
Flat Roch, NC 28731
(434)946-7207 (800)571-9011
Internet: www.thedulwichmanor.com
E-mail: DMRez@centralva.net

Circa 1912. This red Flemish brick and white columned
English Manor sits on five secluded acres at the end of a country lane and in the midst of 97 acres of woodland and meadow.
The Blue Ridge Parkway is minutes away. The entry features a
large center hall and a wide oak staircase. Walls are 14 inches
thick. The 18 rooms include a 50-
foot-long ballroom on the third
floor. The inn is decorated with a
creative mix of antiques, traditional furniture and collectibles.
Innkeeper(s): Mark & Gail Moore. $95-
120. 5 rooms with PB, 2 with FP.
Breakfast included in rates. Types of
meals: Full bkfst and early coffee/tea.
Beds: KQ. Reading lamp, clock radio and two with whirlpool tub in room. Air
conditioning. Parlor games, telephone and fireplace on premises. Antiquing,
downhill skiing, fishing, hiking, parks, shopping, sporting events, water
sports, wineries, historic sites, Monticello and Appomattox Court House and
Natural Bridge nearby.
Location: Mountains. Countryside.
Publicity: *Country Inn and Scene.*
Certificate may be used: Sunday-Thursday, except May and October, holidays and holiday eves. Anytime, December-February, except holidays and
holiday eves.

Appomattox   G12

The Babcock House

Rt 6 Box 1421
Appomattox, VA 24522
(434)352-7532 (800)689-6208 Fax:(434)352-9743

Circa 1884. This columned Greek Revival house occupies
more than an acre in the center of the town's 19th-Century
Homes Walking Tour. Dr. Havilah Babcock, English professor
and noted hunting and fishing author, occupied the home with
his family. Once operated as a boarding house, the home continues its tradition of hospitality and comfort, but now boasts
cable television, private baths, ceiling fans and air conditioning.
Guests still enjoy gathering at the end of the day on the front
porch to share their adventures, which many times includes
visiting Appomattox Courthouse National Historic Park where
General Robert E. Lee surrendered to General Grant. The
innkeepers offer regional dining in their restaurant with a daily

change of menu to reflect seasonal changes in ingredients.
Innkeeper(s): Jerry & Sheila Palamar. $95-120. 6 rooms, 5 with PB, 1 with FP, 1 suite. Breakfast and snacks/refreshments included in rates. Beds: QT. Cable TV, reading lamp, ceiling fan, clock radio, telephone & coffeemaker in room. Central air. VCR, parlor games, fireplace, laundry facility, full service restaurant and catering open for breakfast, lunch & dinner by reservation on premises. Handicap access. Antiquing, bicycling, canoeing/kayaking, fishing & wineries nearby.
Location: Mountains. Small town.
Certificate may be used: Nov. 1-March 31, Sunday-Thursday.

Belle Haven   F19

Bay View Waterfront B&B

35350 Copes Dr
Belle Haven, VA 23306-1952
(757)442-6963 (800)442-6966
Internet: www.bayviewwaterfrontbedandbreakfast.com
E-mail: browning@esva.net

Circa 1800. This rambling inn stretches more than 100 feet across and has five roof levels. There are heart-pine floors, high ceilings and several fireplaces. The hillside location affords bay breezes and wide views of the Chesapeake, Occohannock

Creek and the inn's surrounding 140 acres. The innkeepers are descendants of several generations who have owned and operated Bay View. If you come by water to the inn's deep water dock, look behind Channel Marker 16. Guests can arrange to enjoy a boat tour along the Chesapeake Bay or Atlantic Ocean led by the innkeepers' daughter, U.S. Coast Guard-approved Capt. Mary.
Innkeeper(s): Wayne & Mary Will Browning. $115-175. 3 rooms, 2 with PB, 1 with FP, 1 two-bedroom suite. Breakfast included in rates. Types of meals: Full bkfst. Beds: KQDT. TV, reading lamp, refrigerator, clock radio, telephone and fireplace in room. Air conditioning. VCR, swimming, bicycles, library, parlor games and laundry facility on premises. Antiquing, art galleries, beach, canoeing/kayaking, fishing, golf, live theater, museums, parks, shopping, tennis and water sports nearby.
Location: Country, waterfront.
Publicity: *Rural Living, City and Chesapeake Bay Magazine (Feb. 2003).*

"We loved staying in your home, and especially in the room with a beautiful view of the bay. You have a lovely home and a beautiful location. Thank you so much for your hospitality."
Certificate may be used: Sunday-Thursday, Sept. 15-May 15, excluding holidays and special events.

Bumpass   E14

Rockland Farm Retreat

3609 Lewiston Rd
Bumpass, VA 23024-9659
(540)895-5098
Internet: www.rocklandretreat.com
E-mail: roymxn@aol.com

Circa 1820. The 75 acres of Rockland Farm include pasture land, livestock, vineyard, crops and a farm pond for fishing. The grounds here are said to have spawned Alex Haley's "Roots." Guests can study documents and explore local cemeteries describing life under slavery in the area surrounding this historic home and 18th-century farmlands.
Innkeeper(s): Roy E. Mixon. $79-89. 4 rooms, 3 with PB, 1 suite and 2 conference rooms. Breakfast included in rates. Types of meals: Full bkfst, lunch and dinner. Beds: DT. Reading lamp, clock radio and desk in room. Air conditioning. VCR, parlor games, telephone and fireplace on premises. Amusement parks, antiquing, fishing, parks, shopping and water sports nearby.
Location: Country.
Publicity: *Washington Post and Free Lance-Star.*
Certificate may be used: Non-holiday weekends.

Cape Charles   G18

Cape Charles House

645 Tazewell Ave
Cape Charles, VA 23310-3313
(757)331-4920 Fax:(757)331-4960
Internet: capecharleshouse.com
E-mail: stay@capecharleshouse.com

Circa 1912. A local attorney built this 1912 Colonial Revival home on the site of the town's first schoolhouse. The Cape Charles House is the recipient of the Governor's Award for Virginia Bed and Breakfast Hospitality. Oriental rugs cover lovingly restored hardwood floors. The owners have skillfully combined antiques, heirlooms, artwork, fabrics and collections. Spacious guest bedrooms are named after historically significant townspeople. The premier Julia Wilkins Room features a whirlpool tub/shower and balcony.

Gourmet breakfasts served in the formal dining room may include favorites like fresh mango-stuffed croissants in an egg custard with grated nutmeg and orange liqueur. Enjoy late afternoon wine and cheese as well as tea and sweets. Visit the historic Victorian village and swim the quiet bay beach. Bikes, beach towels, chairs and umbrellas are available.
Innkeeper(s): Bruce & Carol Evans. $100-160. 5 rooms with PB. Breakfast, afternoon tea and snacks/refreshments included in rates. Types of meals: Full gourmet bkfst and early coffee/tea. Beds: KQ. Reading lamp, ceiling fan, clock radio, desk and Jacuzzi (two rooms) in room. Air conditioning. VCR, fax, copier, bicycles, parlor games, telephone and fireplace on premises. Antiquing, fishing, golf, parks, shopping, tennis and water sports nearby.
Location: Small town.
Publicity: *Southern Inns.*

"We'll rave, recommend, and we'll return. The culinary magic of your enchanting breakfasts are beyond comparison, unless you consider the charming effects of your warm and generous spirits."
Certificate may be used: November through March, Sunday-Thursday.

Charlottesville   E13

The Foxfield Inn

2280 Garth Rd
Charlottesville, VA 22901
(434)923-8892 (866)369-3536 Fax:(434)923-0963
Internet: www.foxfield-inn.com
E-mail: stay@foxfield-inn.com

Circa 1951. Experience luxury and peacefulness in this single-story, completely restored colonial home situated on three acres just seven miles from Charlottesville. Guest rooms are tastefully decorated with various luxuries, from four-poster cherry canopy beds to an in-room Jacuzzi, to fireplaces and bay windows. Centrally located near Virginia's historic areas, wineries and Jefferson's Monticello, there are plenty of activities to satisfy every taste for travel. Take a day trip to Washington, D.C., only two hours away, or perhaps a 10-minute drive into Charlottesville to enjoy the amenities of the city. Within walking distance are hiking and biking trails, golf and fishing, as well. Get each day started with gourmet coffee from the coffee bar and a full country breakfast featuring eggs Benedict, scones and fresh fruit.
Innkeeper(s): Mary Pat & John Hulburt. $135-210. 5 rooms with PB, 4 with FP. Breakfast and snacks/refreshments included in rates. Types of meals: Country bkfst and early coffee/tea. Beds: Q. Reading lamp, stereo, ceiling fan, clock radio, turn-down service, fireplace, canopy bed and Bose CD/radio in

room. Central air. TV, VCR, spa, parlor games, telephone and heated outside spa on premises. Limited handicap access. Antiquing, bicycling, canoeing/kayaking, downhill skiing, fishing, golf, hiking, horseback riding, live theater, parks, shopping, sporting events, tennis, wineries and Jefferson's Monticello nearby.
Location: Country.
Certificate may be used: December to March, Monday-Thursday, excluding holidays. July-August, Monday-Thursday, excluding holidays.

The Inn at Monticello
Rt 20 S, 1188 Scottsville Rd
Charlottesville, VA 22902
(434)979-3593 (877)-RELAX-VA
Internet: www.innatmonticello.com
E-mail: stay@innatmonticello.com

Circa 1850. Thomas Jefferson built his own home, Monticello, just two miles from this gracious country home. The innkeepers have preserved the historic ambiance of the area. Rooms boast such pieces as four-poster beds covered with fluffy, down comforters. Some of the guest quarters have private porches or fireplaces. Breakfast at the inn is a memorable gourmet-appointed affair. Aside from the usual homemade rolls, coffee cakes and muffins, guests enjoy such entrees as pancakes or French toast with seasonal fruit, egg dishes and a variety of quiche. The front porch is lined with chairs for those who wish to relax, and the grounds feature several gardens to enjoy.
Innkeeper(s): Norman & Rebecca Lindway. $100-190. 5 rooms with PB, 2 with FP. Breakfast and afternoon tea included in rates. Types of meals: Full gourmet bkfst and early coffee/tea. Beds: KQT. Reading lamp and desk in room. Air conditioning. Fax, parlor games, fireplace and afternoon tea with Virginia wine on premises. Antiquing, downhill skiing, live theater, parks, shopping, sporting events, Blue Ridge Parkway Sky Line Drive and wineries nearby.
Location: Historic, 1 mile to city.
Publicity: *Washington Post, Country Inns, Atlantic Country Magazine, Gourmet and Bon Appetit.*

"What a magnificent room at an extraordinary place. I can't wait to tell all my friends."
Certificate may be used: Sunday-Thursday, January-February, no holidays, $150-$170 rooms only.

Chatham   I11

Sims-Mitchell House B&B
PO Box 429
Chatham, VA 24531-0429
(434)432-0595 (800)967-2867
Internet: www.victorianvilla.com
E-mail: answers@victorianvilla.com

Circa 1870. This Italianate house has 11 fireplaces, original horsehair-based plaster, furnishings from several generations of Mitchells and original art by Southern artists. (Art created by your host also is displayed.) There is a two-bedroom suite and a separate two-bedroom cottage at the side yard offering pastoral views. Hargrave Military Academy and Chatham Hall are within a five-block walk. Patricia, a food historian, has more than 50 books in print and husband Henry is her editor.
Innkeeper(s): Patricia & Henry Mitchell. $75. 2 suites. Breakfast included in rates. Types of meals: Cont plus. Refrigerator, clock radio, telephone and desk in room. Air conditioning. Antiquing nearby.
Location: Rural edge of small town.
Certificate may be used: Monday through Wednesday nights.

Church View   F17

Dragon Run Inn
35 Wares Bridge Rd
Church View, VA 23032
(804)758-5719
Internet: www.dragon-run-inn.com
E-mail: runninn@oasisonline.com

Circa 1913. Built with cypress from Dragon Run Swamp in 1913, this country farm house offers the ambiance of yesterday and the amenities of today. Relax on the large front porch, or play a game on the picnic table under a big shady tree. Planned arrivals with reservations are greeted with fresh flowers, fruit basket, homemade treats and beverages. Keeping in character with the surroundings, guest bedrooms are named after farm animals. Each room boasts antique furnishings, a cheery decor and a romantic Jacuzzi tub. Enjoy a hearty country breakfast before exploring the scenic area. Tour Lighthouse Island, with one of the oldest lighthouses on Chesapeake Bay.
Innkeeper(s): Ivan & Sue Hertgler. $80. 3 rooms with PB. Beds: QD. Reading lamp, CD player, clock radio, desk and Jacuzzi in room. Air conditioning. TV, VCR, library, parlor games and telephone on premises.
Location: Country.
Certificate may be used: Anytime, Sunday-Thursday.

Culpeper   D14

Fountain Hall B&B
609 S East St
Culpeper, VA 22701-3222
(540)825-8200 (800)298-4748 Fax:(540)825-7716
Internet: www.fountainhall.com
E-mail: visit@fountainhall.com

Circa 1859. The well-appointed, oversized guest bedrooms and suites offer comforts galore. Some feature a private porch, whirlpool tub, plush robes and sweeping views of neighboring farms. Enjoy a leisurely breakfast of just-baked flaky croissants with butter and jam, fresh fruits, yogurt, hot and cold cereals and beverages. The surrounding area is steeped in rich American history, and the meticulously landscaped grounds feature seasonal gardens and a lawn groomed for croquet and bocce ball.
Innkeeper(s): Steve & Kathi Walker. $95-150. 6 rooms with PB, 2 suites. Breakfast and snacks/refreshments included in rates. Types of meals: Cont plus and early coffee/tea. Beds: QDT. Modem hook-up, data port, cable TV, VCR, reading lamp, CD player, refrigerator, ceiling fan, clock radio, telephone and desk in room. Air conditioning. Fax, parlor games and fireplace on premises. Handicap access. Antiquing, art galleries, bicycling, canoeing/kayaking, fishing, golf, hiking, horseback riding, museums, parks, shopping and wineries nearby.
Location: Small town.
Publicity: *Culpeper Star Exponent, New York Times, Washington Post, Richmond Channel 8 and Local TV.*

"A great inn you run. We still look back on our stay at Fountain Hall as a standout."
Certificate may be used: Nov. 15-March 31, Sunday to Thursday.

Fairfax   C15

Bailiwick Inn
4023 Chain Bridge Rd.
Fairfax, VA 22030
(703)691-2266 Fax:(703)934-2112
Internet: www.bailiwickinn.com
E-mail: theinn@bailiwickinn.com

Circa 1802. Located across from the county courthouse where George Washington's will is filed, this distinguished three-story Federal brick house recently has been renovated. The first Civil

War casualty occurred on what is now the inn's lawn. The elegant, early Virginia decor is reminiscent of the state's fine plantation mansions. Ask to stay in the Thomas Jefferson Room, a replica of Mr. Jefferson's bed-

room at Monticello. Six-course "Wine Master Dinners" at the inn are featured once a month and include the opportunity for a special package rate for rooms. Every Tuesday and Sunday afternoon teas are featured.

$165-225. 14 rooms, 13 with PB, 1 suite. Breakfast and afternoon tea included in rates. Types of meals: Full gourmet bkfst, gourmet lunch and gourmet dinner. Restaurant on premises. Beds: KQT. Modem hook-up, data port, cable TV, reading lamp, CD player, refrigerator, snack bar, clock radio, telephone, coffeemaker, turn-down service, desk, hot tub/spa, fireplace, Frette towels, sheets, bathrobes and hair dryers in room. Central air. VCR, fax, copier, library, fireplace, 26-seat AAA-rated four diamond restaurant serving breakfast, lunch, tea and cocktails and dinner on premises. Limited handicap access. Amusement parks, antiquing, art galleries, bicycling, canoeing/kayaking, golf, hiking, horseback riding, live theater, museums, parks, shopping, sporting events, tennis, wineries, Mount Vernon, Woodlawn Plantation, Montpelier and many other plantations and historic sites nearby.
Location: City. Historic district in Old Town Fairfax, Va.
Publicity: *Washington Post, Washingtonian Magazine, North American Inns, Fairfax Connection, Inn Times, Mid-Atlantic Country, Victoria, Country Inns, Colonial Homes, The Food Network, Romancing America TV Program and Great Country Inns TV Program.*

"A visit to your establishment clearly transcends any lodging experience that I can recall."
Certificate may be used: All year, except April, May, October.

Fredericksburg   D15

La Vista Plantation

4420 Guinea Station Rd
Fredericksburg, VA 22408-8850
(540)898-8444 (800)529-2823
Internet: www.lavistaplantation.com
E-mail: info@lavistaplantation.com

Circa 1838. La Vista has a long and unusual past, rich in Civil War history. Both Confederate and Union armies camped here, and this is where the Ninth Cavalry was sworn in. It is no wonder then that the house is listed in the National Register of Historic Places. The house, a Classical Revival structure with high ceilings and wide pine floors, sits on 10 acres of pasture and woods. The grounds include a pond stocked with bass. Guest quarters include a spacious room

with a king-size, four-poster bed, fireplace and Empire furniture or the two-bedroom plantation kitchensuite that can accommodate up to six guests and includes a fireplace. Breakfasts feature homemade egg dishes from hens raised on the property.
Innkeeper(s): Michele & Edward Schiesser. $125-150. 3 rooms with PB. Breakfast included in rates. Types of meals: Full bkfst and early coffee/tea. Beds: KQDT. Reading lamp, refrigerator, clock radio, telephone, satellite TV and VCR in room. Air conditioning. Copier, parlor games, fresh brown eggs from resident hens, modem, video and book library, children's library and working fireplaces on premises. Amusement parks, antiquing, fishing, live theater, parks, shopping, sporting events, water sports, pond and rowboat and bird-watching nearby.
Location: Country.
Publicity: *Mid-Atlantic Country, Free Lance Star and Richmond Times Dispatch.*

"Coming here was an excellent choice. La Vista is charming, quiet and restful, all qualities we were seeking. Breakfast was delicious."
Certificate may be used: January and February, Monday-Thursday.

Gordonsville   E13

Sleepy Hollow Farm B&B

16280 Blue Ridge Tpke
Gordonsville, VA 22942-8214
(540)832-5555 (800)215-4804 Fax:(540)832-2515
Internet: www.sleepyhollowfarmbnb.com
E-mail: shfbnb@ns.gemlink.com

Circa 1785. Many generations have added to this brick farmhouse creating somewhat of an optical illusion, as the historic home appears much smaller from a distance. The pink and white room often was visited by a friendly ghost, believed to be a Red Cross nurse during the Civil War, according to local stories. She hasn't been seen since the house was blessed in 1959. Accommodations also are available in Chestnut Cottage, which offers two suites with downstairs sitting areas and bedrooms and baths upstairs. One suite has a fireplace. The other suite includes a deck, full kitchen, whirlpool room and Franklin wood stove. The grounds include abundant wildlife, flower gardens, an herb garden, a gazebo and pond for swimming and fishing.
Innkeeper(s): Beverley Allison & Dorsey Comer. $65-150. 6 rooms with PB, 2 with FP, 3 suites. Breakfast included in rates. Types of meals: Full bkfst, early coffee/tea and snacks/refreshments. Beds: QDT. Cable TV, VCR, reading lamp, refrigerator, clock radio, telephone and desk in room. Air conditioning. Fax, swimming, library, two rooms with whirlpools. In the main house cake and cookies available on sideboard on premises. Antiquing, art galleries, downhill skiing, fishing, golf, hiking, live theater, museums, parks, shopping, sporting events, tennis, wineries, steeplechase race and historic homes nearby.
Location: Country.
Publicity: *Orange County Review, City Magazine, Town & County, Washington Post, New York Times and Country Inn Magazine.*

"This house is truly blessed."
Certificate may be used: Anytime, Sunday-Thursday.

Goshen   E10

The Hummingbird Inn

PO Box 147, 30 Wood Lane
Goshen, VA 24439-0147
(540)997-9065 (800)397-3214
Internet: www.hummingbirdinn.com
E-mail: stay@hummingbirdinn.com

Circa 1853. This early Victorian villa is located in the Shenandoah Valley against the backdrop of the Allegheny Mountains. Both the first and second floors offer wraparound verandas. Furnished with antiques, the inn features a library and sitting room with fireplaces. The rustic den and one guest room comprise the oldest portions of the inn, built around 1780. Dinners are available by advance reservation (Friday and Saturday). An old barn and babbling creek are on the grounds. Lexington, the Virginia Horse Center, Natural Bridge, the Blue Ridge Parkway and antiquing are all nearby.
Innkeeper(s): Pam Miller & Dick Matthews. $120-165. 5 rooms with PB, 4 with FP. Breakfast and snacks/refreshments included in rates. Types of meals: Country bkfst, veg bkfst, early coffee/tea, picnic lunch and dinner. Beds: KQ. Reading lamp, ceiling fan and fireplace in room. Air conditioning. TV, VCR, fax, library, parlor games, telephone, gift shop and trout stream on premises. Limited handicap access. Antiquing, canoeing/kayaking, cross-country skiing,

downhill skiing, fishing, hiking, horseback riding, live theater, museums, parks, shopping, wineries, herb farm, working grist mill and mineral baths nearby.
Location: Mountains.
Publicity: *Blue Ridge Country and Inn Spots and Special Places.*

"We enjoyed our stay so much that we returned two weeks later on our way back for a delicious home-cooked dinner, comfortable attractive atmosphere, and familiar faces to welcome us after a long journey."
Certificate may be used: Dec. 1-May 1, Sunday-Thursday, excluding holidays.

Keysville   H13

The Cottage on New Directions Farm

3422 Briery Rd
Keysville, VA 23947
(434)736-2119
Internet: www.vafarmvacation.com
E-mail: paddyk@hovac.com

Circa 1930. Surrounded by woods and pasture fields, this bungalow-style cottage sits in a private corner of the farm. The covered porch with rockers overlooks an acre pond stocked with channel catfish, crappie, small- and large-mouth bass. Rods and tackle are available. A peaceful tranquility is imparted here, offering a taste of farm life. The two-bedroom, two-bath cottage features a living room and fully equipped kitchen. A gas grill and small washer/dryer are on site. Explore nearby Civil War sites as well as a variety of activities and attractions.
Innkeeper(s): Paddy & Joseph Kernisky. $200-400. 3 rooms, 2 with PB and 1 cottage. Beds: QD. Modem hook-up, TV, VCR, reading lamp, refrigerator, ceiling fan, clock radio, telephone and coffeemaker in room. Bicycles, parlor games, laundry facility, gift shop, stocked fish pond, gas grill, rockers and covered porch on premises. Limited handicap access. Antiquing, canoeing/kayaking, fishing, golf, hiking, live theater, museums, parks, water sports and wineries nearby.
Location: Country. Blue Ridge Mountain.
Certificate may be used: Anytime, subject to availability.

Leesburg   B15

The Norris House Inn & Stone House Tea Room

108 Loudoun St SW
Leesburg, VA 20175-2909
(703)777-1806 (800)644-1806 Fax:(703)771-8051
Internet: www.norrishouse.com
E-mail: inn.keeper@norrishouse.com

Circa 1857. The Norris brothers, Northern Virginia's foremost architects and builders, purchased this building in 1857 and began extensive renovations several years later. They used the

finest wood and brick available, remodeling the exterior to an Eastlake style. Beautifully restored, the inn features built-in bookcases in the library and a cherry fireplace mantel.
Innkeeper(s): Carol Kincaid & Roger Healey. $120-165. 6 rooms, 3 with FP. Breakfast included in rates. Types of meals: Full bkfst, early coffee/tea and afternoon tea. Beds: QT. Reading lamp, clock radio, desk and fireplace in room. Air conditioning. TV, fax, library, parlor games, telephone, wireless Internet and satellite TV on premises. Antiquing, bicycling, fishing, hiking, parks, shopping, water sports and free bike trail planner nearby.
Location: Historic district.
Publicity: *New York Times, Better Homes & Gardens, Washingtonian and Country Home.*

"Thank you for your gracious hospitality. We enjoyed everything about your lovely home, especially the extra little touches that really make the difference."
Certificate may be used: Sunday through Thursday only.

Lexington   F11

Inn at Union Run

Union Run Rd
Lexington, VA 24450
(540)463-9715 (800)528-6466 Fax:(540)463-3526
Internet: www.unionrun.com
E-mail: unionrun@cfw.com

Circa 1883. This inn was named for the spring-fed creek that meanders in front of this restored farmhouse. Union troops, specifically the 2nd and 4th Michigan Calvary, camped on the grounds during the Civil War. The home is surrounded by 10 acres with a fishing pond and brook. The innkeepers have traveled extensively throughout Europe and have brought the influence into their inn. The furnishings, many of which were fashioned out of oak, are a mix of American and Victorian styles.
Innkeeper(s): Roger & Jeanette Serens. $95-120. 8 rooms with PB, 4 with FP and 1 conference room. Breakfast and afternoon tea included in rates. Types of meals: Full bkfst, early coffee/tea, lunch, picnic lunch, snacks/refreshments, dinner and room service. Restaurant on premises. Beds: Q. Reading lamp, refrigerator, ceiling fan, snack bar, clock radio, telephone, turn-down service, desk and Jacuzzis (6 rooms) in room. Air conditioning. Parlor games and fireplace on premises. Handicap access. Antiquing, cross-country skiing, fishing, live theater, museums, parks, shopping, water sports and Civil War sites nearby.
Location: Mountains. Creek-front mountainside property.
Publicity: *News Gazette, Blue Ridge Country and Insider Guide of Virginia.*
Certificate may be used: January to December, excluding October, excludes holidays, Sundays to Thursdays.

Locust Dale   D13

The Inn at Meander Plantation

2333 North James Madison Hwy.
Locust Dale, VA 22948-9701
(540)672-4912 (800)385-4936 Fax:(540)672-0405
Internet: www.meander.net
E-mail: inn@meander.net

Circa 1766. This historic country estate was built by Henry Fry, close friend of Thomas Jefferson who often stopped here on his way to Monticello. The mansion is serenely decorated with elegant antiques and period reproductions, includ-

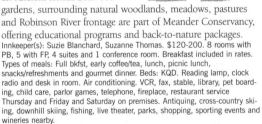

ing four-poster beds. Healthy gourmet breakfasts are prepared by Chef Suzie. Enjoy views of the Blue Ridge Mountains from the rockers on the back porches. Ancient formal boxwood gardens, surrounding natural woodlands, meadows, pastures and Robinson River frontage are part of Meander Conservancy, offering educational programs and back-to-nature packages.
Innkeeper(s): Suzie Blanchard, Suzanne Thomas. $120-200. 8 rooms with PB, 5 with FP, 4 suites and 1 conference room. Breakfast included in rates. Types of meals: Full bkfst, early coffee/tea, lunch, picnic lunch, snacks/refreshments and gourmet dinner. Beds: KQD. Reading lamp, clock radio and desk in room. Air conditioning. VCR, fax, stable, library, pet boarding, child care, parlor games, telephone, fireplace, restaurant service Thursday and Friday and Saturday on premises. Antiquing, cross-country skiing, downhill skiing, fishing, live theater, parks, shopping, sporting events and wineries nearby.
Location: Country.

"Staying at the Inn at Meander Plantation feels like being immersed in another century while having the luxuries and amenities available today."
Certificate may be used: Year-round, Sunday through Thursday, excluding holidays.

Luray   C13

The Ruffner House

440 Ruffner House Rd
Luray, VA 22835-9704
(540)743-7855 (800)969-7855
Internet: www.ruffnerhouse.com
E-mail: info@ruffnerhouse.com

Circa 1739. This 23-acre estate offers scenic pastures with
grazing horses in the heart of the Shenandoah Valley. Peter
Ruffner, the first settler of Page Valley and Luray, built the inn, a
stately manor. Ruffner family members discovered a cavern
opposite the entrance to the Luray Caverns, which were later
discovered. In 1840 the house was sold and no Ruffners occupied it until this year when an 8th-generation Ruffner purchased it. The inn offers handsome antiques, two parlors and
two enticing porches. Guest rooms feature a selection of
amenities including some with fireplaces, Victorian tubs, ceiling
fans and pastoral views. Afternoon tea is offered. A gourmet
breakfast is served in the manor's elegant dining room and will
provide sustenance for a full day of recreation. Visit wineries,
battlefields, the Shenandoah National Park and Luray Caverns
or enjoy horseback riding, canoeing, cycling, golfing or browsing the antique and boutique shops.
Innkeeper(s): Sonia Croucher. $98-150. 6 rooms with PB, 3 with FP.
Breakfast included in rates. Types of meals: Full gourmet bkfst, early
coffee/tea, picnic lunch, snacks/refreshments and gourmet dinner. Beds: QD.
TV, reading lamp, ceiling fan and Victorian soaking tubs (two rooms) in room.
Air conditioning. VCR, parlor games, telephone, fireplace and porches with
rocking chairs and swings on premises. Antiquing, canoeing/kayaking, cross-
country skiing, downhill skiing, fishing, golf, hiking, horseback riding, parks,
shopping, sporting events and wineries nearby.
Location: Country, mountains. 23-acre estate.
Publicity: *Page News & Courier and Washingtonian Magazine.*

*"This is the loveliest inn we have ever stayed in. We were made to feel
very welcome and at ease."*
Certificate may be used: Jan. 15-Sept. 15, Monday-Thursday. Nov. 1-Dec.
15, Monday-Thursday.

Spring Farm B&B

13 Wallace Ave
Luray, VA 22835-9067
(540)843-0606 (866)780-7827 Fax:(540)743-7851
Internet: www.allstarlodging.com
E-mail: allstarlodging@hotmail.com

Circa 1795. Spring Farm is on 10 acres two miles from Luray
Caverns. Hite's Springs run through the land. The Greek
Revival home has double front and back verandas. Rooms feature a mix of antique and new furnishings, and there is a fireplace in the living room. Ask the innkeepers for advice on
shopping, dining and activities in
the Shenandoah and they'll be
happy to help you plan a getaway you'll long remember.
Innkeeper(s): Carlos Ruiz. $75-289. 2
cottages with PB, 9 with FP and 40
cabins. Breakfast, afternoon tea and
snacks/refreshments included in rates.

Types of meals: Full gourmet bkfst, veg bkfst, early coffee/tea, hors d'oeuvres,
wine and gourmet dinner. Restaurant on premises. Beds: KQDT. Cable TV,
VCR, reading lamp, stereo, refrigerator, ceiling fan, clock radio, telephone,
coffeemaker, hot tub/spa and fireplace in room. Central air. Fax, spa, swimming, stable, bicycles, pet boarding, parlor games, laundry facility and free
canoe and tubes on premises. Limited handicap access. Antiquing, art galleries, bicycling, canoeing/kayaking, downhill skiing, fishing, golf, hiking,
horseback riding, museums, parks, shopping, sporting events, tennis, water
sports and wineries nearby.

Location: Mountains. Riverfront properties.
Publicity: *Christmas Tour-Page Courier.*

"Our first, but definitely not our last, visit."
Certificate may be used: Sunday-Thursday, November-March.

The Woodruff Collection of
Victorian Inns

330 Mechanic St
Luray, VA 22835-1808
(540)743-1494 Fax:(540)743-1722
Internet: www.woodruffinns.com
E-mail: woodruffinns@woodruffinns.com

Circa 1882. Prepare to be pampered. The Woodruffs entered the
B&B business after years of experience in hotel management and
restaurant businesses. They have not missed a detail, ensuring a
perfect, relaxing visit. The Rooftop Skylight Fireside Jacuzzi Suite
is often the room of choice because of
its interesting shape and architecture, located where the attic
was before restoration. The
suite boasts skylights, Jacuzzi
tub for two and antique stained
glass. Tasteful antiques and fresh bou-
quets of flowers framed by candlelight add a special ambiance.
Besides the extra attention and comfortable accommodations,
the Woodruffs include coffee and afternoon dessert tea, in-room
coffee or tea and a full fireside breakfast in the rates. Candlelight
sets the mood for the gourmet dinner, and none of the spectacular meals are to be missed. A romantic finish to each evening is a
private dip in one of the garden hot tubs.
Innkeeper(s): Lucas & Deborah Woodruff. $119-289. 5 rooms with PB, 9
with FP, 4 suites and 1 conference room. Breakfast included in rates. Types
of meals: Full bkfst, afternoon tea and gourmet dinner. Beds: KQ. Reading
lamp, clock radio, coffeemaker, desk and coffeemaker in room. Air conditioning. Fax, spa, parlor games, telephone, fireplace, two outdoor gardens,
Jacuzzi tubs for two and afternoon dessert, tea & coffee on premises.
Antiquing, downhill skiing, fishing, parks, shopping, water sports, caverns,
Shenandoah River and Skyline Drive nearby.
Location: Mountains.
Publicity: *Potomac Living, Cascapades Magazine, Blue Ridge Country
Magazine, Cooperative Living, Virginia Wine Gazette, Food and Wine
Magazine, Gourmet Magazine, Washington Times and recipient of Virginia's
gold three cluster wine award.*
Certificate may be used: Jan 5 to March 15, Monday-Thursday, lodging only.

Lynchburg   G11

Federal Crest Inn

1101 Federal St
Lynchburg, VA 24504-3018
(434)845-6155 (800)818-6155 Fax:(434)845-1445
Internet: www.federalcrest.com
E-mail: inn@federalcrest.com

Circa 1909. The guest rooms at Federal Crest are named for the
many varieties of trees and flowers native to Virginia. This handsome red brick home, a fine example of Georgian Revival architecture, features a commanding front entrance flanked by columns
that hold up the second-story veranda. A grand staircase, carved
woodwork, polished floors topped with fine rugs and more
columns create an aura of elegance. Each guest room offers something special and romantic, from a mountain view to a Jacuzzi
tub. Breakfasts are served on fine china, and the first course is
always a freshly baked muffin with a secret message inside.
Innkeeper(s): Ann & Phil Ripley. $135-200. 5 rooms, 4 with PB, 3 with FP, 2
suites and 1 conference room. Breakfast, afternoon tea and snacks/refresh-

ments included in rates. Types of meals: Full bkfst and early coffee/tea. Beds: Q. Cable TV, VCR, reading lamp, clock radio, turn-down service, desk and telephone in room. Air conditioning. Fax, copier, parlor games, telephone, fireplace, gift shop, conference theater with 60-inch TV (Ballroom) with stage, '50s cafe with antique jukebox and video library on premises. Antiquing, fishing, golf, live theater, parks, shopping, sporting events and tennis nearby.
Location: City, mountains. Central Virginia.
Publicity: *Washington Post, News & Advance, Scene and Local ABC.*

"What a wonderful place to celebrate our birthdays and enjoy our last romantic getaway before the birth of our first child."
Certificate may be used: Jan. 2-July 30, Sunday-Thursday.

Peacock Manor Bed & Breakfast, Inc.

1115 Federal St
Lynchburg, VA 24504
(434)528-0626 Fax:(434)528-6007
Internet: www.peacockmanorbb.com
E-mail: peacockmanor@hotmail.com

Circa 1890. Sitting high on a bluff in Federal Hill Historic District, at the foot of Virginia's Blue Ridge Mountains, this intimate European-style bed & breakfast is a Queen Anne Victorian with spectacular views of downtown and across the James River. Trudi and Dennis extend generous Southern hospitality with a New Orleans flair that reflects their upbringing. Swing or rock on the large front porch. Original hardwood floors, Tiffany reproduction stained-glass windows, eight slate fireplaces, Bradbury and Bradbury hand-blocked wallpaper, 11 crystal chandeliers, a heart of pine curved staircase, tall ceilings, and double parlors highlight the impressive interior. Jewel-colored guest bedrooms are a restful retreat and a creative breakfast is prepared from scratch. Sit near a fountain or gazebo on the well-landscaped grounds.
Innkeeper(s): Trudi & Dennis Malik. $110-125. 4 rooms with PB. Breakfast and snacks/refreshments included in rates. Types of meals: Full gourmet bkfst, veg bkfst, early coffee/tea and afternoon tea. Beds: KQDT. Cable TV, VCR, reading lamp, stereo, refrigerator, ceiling fan, snack bar, coffeemaker, turn-down service and fireplace in room. Central air. Fax, copier, bicycles, pet boarding, parlor games and telephone on premises. Antiquing, art galleries, bicycling, canoeing/kayaking, fishing, golf, hiking, live theater, museums, parks, shopping and wineries nearby.
Location: City, mountains. At the foot of the Blue Ridge Mountains, near the Blue Ridge Parkway.
Publicity: *New York Times, Arrington's Bed & Breakfast Journal, News and Advance* and voted past two years "Best Antiques" by Arrington's B&B Journal.
Certificate may be used: Anytime, November-March, subject to availability.

Madison   D13

Dulaney Hollow at Old Rag Mountain B&B Inn

SR 6 Box 215-Scenic VA Byway Rt 231
Madison, VA 22727-9818
(540)923-4470 Fax:(540)923-4841
E-mail: oldragmtninn@nexet.net

Circa 1903. Period furnishings decorate this Victorian manor house on 15 acres of the Blue Ridge Mountains. There is also a cabin, cottage and hayloft suite available amid the shaded lawns and old farm buildings. Enjoy a delicious country breakfast. Take a bicycle jaunt or hike the hills around the Shenandoah River and National Park. Monticello, Charlottesville and Montpelier are within an hour's drive.
Innkeeper(s): Susan & Louis Cable. $85-135. 6 rooms with PB, 1 suite and 2 cottages. Breakfast included in rates. Types of meals: Full gourmet bkfst, early coffee/tea, gourmet lunch, picnic lunch, afternoon tea and gourmet dinner. Beds: QDT. Ceiling fan and desk in room. Air conditioning. VCR, fax, copier, swimming, pet boarding, telephone and Internet access on premises. Antiquing, cross-country skiing, downhill skiing, fishing, golf, live theater, parks, shopping, sporting events, tennis, water sports, wineries, Civil War sites, historic sites and

battlefields, Shenandoah National Park and wildlife preserve nearby.
Location: Mountains, Shenandoah National Park.
Publicity: *Madison Eagle and Charlottesville Daily Progress.*
Certificate may be used: Jan. 1 through Dec. 31 (only on weekday nights, Monday through Thursday; not weekends, not any holidays).

Mathews   G17

Ravenswood Inn

PO Box 1430
Mathews, VA 23109-1430
(804)725-7272
Internet: www.ravenswood-inn.com
E-mail: innkeeper@ravenswood-inn.com

Circa 1913. This intimate waterfront home is located on five acres along the banks of the East River, where passing boats still harvest crabs and oysters. A long screened porch captures river breezes. Most rooms feature a river view and are decorated in Victorian, country, nautical or wicker. Williamsburg, Jamestown and Yorktown are within an hour.
Innkeeper(s): Mrs. Ricky Durham. $70-120. 5 rooms with PB. Breakfast included in rates. Types of meals: Full gourmet bkfst and early coffee/tea. Beds: KQ. Reading lamp and ceiling fan in room. Air conditioning. VCR, spa, telephone and fireplace on premises. Amusement parks, antiquing, live theater, shopping, sporting events and water sports nearby.
Location: Waterfront.
Publicity: *Virginian Pilot and Daily Press.*

"While Ravenswood is one of the most beautiful places we've ever been, it is your love, caring and friendship that has made it such a special place for us."
Certificate may be used: April-November, Sunday-Thursday.

Middleburg   C14

Red Fox Inn

PO Box 385
Middleburg, VA 20117
(540)687-6301 (800)223-1728 Fax:(540)687-6053
Internet: www.redfox.com
E-mail: reservations@redfox.com

Circa 1728. Originally Chinn's Ordinary, the inn was a popular stopping place for travelers between Winchester and Alexandria. During the Civil War, Colonel John Mosby and General Jeb Stuart met here. Guest rooms are furnished in 18th-century decor and most feature four-poster canopy beds.
Innkeeper(s): F. Turner Reuter, Jr. $150-325. 20 rooms with PB and 4 conference rooms. Breakfast included in rates. Types of meals: Cont, lunch and dinner. Restaurant on premises. Beds: KQ. Cable TV and telephone in room. Air conditioning. TV, fax and copier on premises. Handicap access. Antiquing nearby.
Location: Historic town.
Publicity: *Washingtonian, Southern Living, Washington Bride and Virginia Wine Publications.*
Certificate may be used: Sunday-Thursday, all year.

Montross   E16

The Inn at Montross

PO Box 908
Montross, VA 22520
(804)493-0573 Fax:(804)493-9118
E-mail: chefcin@aol.com

Circa 1684. Montross was rebuilt in 1800 on the site of a 17th-century tavern. Operating as an "ordinary" since 1683, parts of the structure have been in continuous use for more than 300 years. It was visited by Burgesses and Justices of the Court (Washington, Lee and Jefferson). The guest rooms feature canopy beds and colonial furnishings. Smoking is allowed here.

Innkeeper(s): Scott Massidda & Cindy Brigman. $65-100. 5 rooms with PB and 1 conference room. Breakfast included in rates. Types of meals: Full gourmet bkfst, gourmet lunch, afternoon tea and gourmet dinner. Restaurant on premises. Beds: Q. Reading lamp and hot tub/spa in room. Air conditioning. TV, VCR, fax, tennis, library, pet boarding, parlor games, fireplace and in-house certified therapeutic massage on premises. Amusement parks, antiquing, fishing, golf, parks, shopping, tennis and water sports nearby.
Location: Historic County/town.
Publicity: *Virginian-Pilot, Travel, Richmond Times-Dispatch, Washington Post and New York Times.*

"Hospitality is Inn!"
Certificate may be used: Feb. 8-Jan. 3, Sunday-Thursday.

Nellysford   F12

The Mark Addy

56 Rodes Farm Dr
Nellysford, VA 22958-9526
(434)361-1101 (800)278-2154
Internet: www.mark-addy.com
E-mail: info@mark-addy.com

Circa 1837. It's not hard to understand why Dr. John Everett, the son of Thomas Jefferson's physician, chose this picturesque, Blue Mountain setting for his home. Everett expanded the simple, four-room farmhouse already present into a gracious manor. The well-appointed guest rooms feature double whirlpool baths, double showers or a clawfoot tub. Beds are covered with vintage linens, feather pillows and cozy, down comforters. There are plenty of relaxing possibilities, including five porches and a hammock set among the trees.
Innkeeper(s): John Storck Maddox. $100-195. 10 rooms with PB, 1 suite. Types of meals: Full gourmet bkfst, early coffee/tea, gourmet lunch, picnic lunch and gourmet dinner. Beds: KQDT. Reading lamp, ceiling fan and Jacuzzi in room. Air conditioning. VCR, library, parlor games and telephone on premises. Handicap access. Antiquing, downhill skiing, fishing, live theater, parks, shopping, sporting events, horseback riding and hiking nearby.
Location: Mountains.
Publicity: *Local paper.*
Certificate may be used: January, March, July-August, November, December, Sunday-Thursday.

New Church   E19

The Garden and The Sea Inn

PO Box 275
New Church, VA 23415-0275
(757)824-0672 (800)824-0672
Internet: www.gardenandseainn.com
E-mail: innkeeper@gardenandseainn.com

Circa 1802. Gingerbread trim, a pair of brightly colored gables and two, adjacent verandas adorn the exterior of this Victorian. A warm, rich Victorian decor permeates the antique-filled guest rooms, an ideal setting for romance. Most rooms include whirlpool tubs. The inn's dining room serves gourmet dinners by reservation. Pets are very welcome.
Innkeeper(s): Tom & Sara Baker. $75-205. 8 rooms with PB and 1 conference room. Breakfast included in rates. Types of meals: Full bkfst, snacks/refreshments and gourmet dinner. Restaurant on premises. Beds: KQ. TV, reading lamp, ceiling fan, clock radio and some with fireplace in room. Air conditioning. VCR, fax, copier, library, parlor games, telephone and outdoor heated pool on premises. Handicap access. Antiquing, beach, fishing, parks, shopping and water sports nearby.
Location: Country.
Publicity: *Washington Post, Modern Bride and Southern Living.*
Certificate may be used: Sunday through Thursday in April, May, June, October and November.

New Market   C12

Cross Roads Inn B&B

9222 John Sevier Rd
New Market, VA 22844-9649
(540)740-4157 (888)740-4157
Internet: www.crossroadsinnva.com
E-mail: lsmith18@juno.com

Circa 1925. This Victorian is full of Southern hospitality. Bountiful breakfasts and homemade treats are served as an afternoon refreshment. The home is decorated with English floral wallpapers, antiques and old family furnishings. Four-poster and canopy beds are topped with fluffy, down comforters. The historic downtown area is within walking distance.
Innkeeper(s): Sharon & Larry Smith. $95-135. 6 rooms with PB. Breakfast included in rates. Types of meals: Full bkfst, early coffee/tea, afternoon tea and snacks/refreshments. Beds: KQDT. Reading lamp, clock radio and several with Jacuzzi or fireplace in room. Air conditioning. VCR, fax, parlor games, telephone and fireplace on premises. Handicap access. Antiquing, downhill skiing, fishing, live theater, parks, shopping, sporting events, water sports and musical summer festivals nearby.
Location: Mountains. Small town.
Certificate may be used: November to September, Sunday-Thursday.

Onancock   F19

Colonial Manor Inn

84 Market St
Onancock, VA 23417-4224
(757)787-3521 Fax:(757)787-2564
Internet: www.colonialmanorinn.com
E-mail: hosts@colonialmanorinn.com

Circa 1882. Adorning the historic waterfront community, this recently renovated Colonial home built in 1882, has since become the oldest operating inn on the state's Eastern Shore. An eclectic blend of antiques and collectibles accents the casually elegant décor of this smoke-free inn. Relax on a comfortable sofa in the living room. Enjoy the inviting enclosed porch with year-round heating and cooling as well as candles that enhance the evening ambiance. Stay in a suite that features a private outside entrance and sitting area. A brick walkway leads to the gazebo with a nearby fountain and two acres of park-like grounds to explore. Breakfast is always a delicious repast served family-style at the huge dining table. Bask on the sun deck or sit on a front lawn chair.
Innkeeper(s): Mr. & Mrs. Tom & Shawn McCulloch. $85-165. 9 rooms with PB. Beds: KQDT.
Certificate may be used: January/February, Sunday-Thursday.

Pearisburg   G8

Inn at River Bend

125 River Ridge Dr.
Pearisburg, VA 24134
(540)921-5211 Fax:(540)921-2720
Internet: www.innatriverbend.com
E-mail: stay@innatriverbend.com

Circa 2003. Expansive views of the New River and the surrounding valley are incredibly breathtaking while staying at this contemporary bed and breakfast. Enjoy refreshments in front of the stone fireplace in a great room with a wall of French doors and windows. Two levels of huge wraparound decks offer an abundance of space to appreciate the scenic beauty and assortment of birds. Watch a movie or gather as a group in the

TV/meeting room. Luxury guest bedrooms are delightful retreats that have access to decks or terraces and feature pressed linens, specialty personal products, stocked refrigerators, and other generous amenities. Several rooms boast whirlpool tubs. After a three-course breakfast, sample some of the area's many outdoor activities. The Appalachian Trail is only two miles away.

Innkeeper(s): Linda & Lynn Hayes. $120-185. 7 rooms with PB and 1 conference room. Breakfast and snacks/refreshments included in rates. Types of meals: Full gourmet bkfst, veg bkfst, early coffee/tea, gourmet lunch, picnic lunch and gourmet dinner. Beds: KQT. Modem hook-up, data port, cable TV, reading lamp, ceiling fan, clock radio, turn-down service and desk in room. Central air. VCR, fax, library, parlor games, telephone, fireplace and gift shop on premises. Handicap access. Antiquing, bicycling, canoeing/kayaking, cross-country skiing, downhill skiing, fishing, golf, hiking, live theater, museums, parks, shopping, sporting events, tennis and wineries nearby.
Location: Country, mountains. Overlooking the New River.
Certificate may be used: Sunday-Thursday, subject to availability.

Port Haywood   G18

Tabb's Creek Inn

PO Box 219 Rt 14 Mathews Co
Port Haywood, VA 23138-0219
(804)725-5136
Internet: www.innvirginia.com
E-mail: tabbscreeklanding@hotmail.com

Circa 1820. Surrounded by 30 acres of woods and located on the banks of Tabb's Creek, this post-Colonial farm features a detached guest cottage. There are maple, elm, magnolia trees and 150 rose bushes on the property. The suites and guest rooms feature fireplaces and antiques. Boats for rowing and canoeing, docks, a swimming pool, and private waterview porches make this an especially attractive getaway for those seeking a dose of seclusion.

Innkeeper(s): Erin Rogers. $125. 7 rooms, 5 with PB, 1 with FP, 2 suites. Breakfast included in rates. Types of meals: Full bkfst and early coffee/tea. Beds: KQD. VCR, reading lamp, stereo, ceiling fan, clock radio, turn-down service and desk in room. Air conditioning. TV, fax, copier, swimming, bicycles, library, telephone and fireplace on premises. Antiquing, fishing and fine restaurants nearby.
Location: Country, waterfront.

"A spot of tea with a bit of heaven. Truly exceptional hosts. The best B&Bs I've happened across!"
Certificate may be used: November to March, Sunday-Thursday.

Reedville   F18

Fleeton Fields B & B

2783 Fleeton Road
Reedville, VA 22539
(804)453-5014 (800)497-8215 Fax:(804)453-5014
Internet: www.fleetonfields.com
E-mail: info@fleetonfields.com

Circa 1945. For a romantic getaway on the Chesapeake Bay, this brick Colonial-style bed and breakfast sits in a park-like setting on 15 tranquil acres at the edge of Fleeton's historic hamlet. Victorian and period furnishings reside amiably with modern amenities. Well-appointed guest suites are spacious and inviting with fresh flowers, soft bathrobes, mini-refrigerators and scenic views. The Garden Suite also features a private entrance, sitting room and fireplace. A multi-course gourmet breakfast is served on fine china, silver and crystal. Explore the

area on a bicycle or on a two-car cable ferry over Little Wicomico River. Launch the inn's canoe or kayak on the pond. Visit the Reedville Fisherman's Museum. The enjoyable activities are endless.

Innkeeper(s): Marguerite Slaughter. $125-165. 3 rooms, 1 with FP, 3 suites. Breakfast included in rates. Types of meals: Full bkfst and early coffee/tea. Beds: Q. Cable TV, VCR, refrigerator, telephone and clocks in room. Central air. TV, fax, copier, bicycles, library and fireplace on premises. Antiquing, art galleries, beach, bicycling, canoeing/kayaking, fishing, golf, hiking, museums, shopping, wineries and Tangier and Smith Island Cruise nearby.
Location: Country, waterfront.
Certificate may be used: November-March, Sunday-Thursday.

Scottsville   F13

High Meadows Vineyard Inn

55 High Meadows Lane
Scottsville, VA 24590-9706
(434)286-2218 (800)232-1832
Internet: www.highmeadows.com
E-mail: peterhmi@aol.com

Circa 1832. Minutes from Charlottesville on the Constitution Highway (Route 20), High Meadows stands on 25 acres of gardens, forests, ponds, a creek and a vineyard. Listed in the National Register, it is actually two historic homes joined by a breezeway as well as three private cottages. The inn is furnished in Federal and Victorian styles. Guests are treated to gracious Virginia hospitality in an elegant and peaceful setting with wine tasting and a romantic candlelight dinner every evening. There are two private hot tubs on the grounds.

Innkeeper(s): Peter Sushka, Mary Jae Abbitt. Rose Farber & Jon Storey. $99-390. 12 rooms with PB, 12 with FP. Restaurant on premises. Beds: KQDT. Reading lamp, refrigerator, clock radio, desk and hot tub/spa in room. Air conditioning. Award-winning restaurant on premises. Antiquing, bicycling, cross-country skiing, downhill skiing, fishing, hiking, shopping, sporting events, water sports and theater nearby.
Location: Mountains. Rural countryside.
Publicity: *Daily Progress, Washington Post, Richmond Times Dispatch, Mid-Atlantic, Washingtonian, Gourmet Magazine and Arrington's Bed & Breakfast Journal.*
Certificate may be used: All year, Sunday-Thursday, non-holidays; Sunday-Friday, Dec. 1-March 1, non-holidays.

Smithfield   H17

Four Square Plantation

13357 Foursquare Rd
Smithfield, VA 23430-8643
(757)365-0749 Fax:(757)365-0749
Internet: www.innvirginia.com
E-mail: foursquareplantation@att.net

Circa 1807. Located in the historic James River area, the original land grant, "Four Square" was established in 1664 and consisted of 640 acres. Now in the National Register and a Virginia Historic Landmark, the Federal style home is called Plantation Plain by Virginia preservationists. The inn is furnished with family period pieces and antiques. The Vaughan Room offers a fireplace, Empire furnishings and access by private staircase. Breakfast is served in the dining room. The inn's four acres provide a setting for weddings and special events. Tour Williamsburg, Jamestown, the James River Plantations and Yorktown nearby.

Innkeeper(s): Roger & Donna. $75-85. 3 rooms with PB, 3 with FP. Breakfast included in rates. Types of meals: Full gourmet bkfst and early coffee/tea. Beds: KQT. Cable TV, reading lamp, ceiling fan, telephone and turn-

down service in room. Air conditioning. VCR, fax, copier and parlor games on premises. Antiquing, golf and shopping nearby.
Location: Country. Three miles from Smithfield.
Publicity: *Daily Press and Virginia Pilot.*
Certificate may be used: Sunday-Thursday, Jan. 1-March 31, July 10-Sept. 1, Nov. 1-Dec. 23, no holidays.

Isle of Wight Inn

1607 S Church St
Smithfield, VA 23430-1831
(757)357-3176 (800)357-3245

Circa 1980. This Colonial inn is located in a historic seaside town, boasting more than 60 homes that date back to the mid-18th century. St. Luke's Church, the oldest in the United States, dating back to 1632, is located near the inn.  Antiques and reproductions fill the rooms, and the suites offer the added amenities of fireplaces and whirlpool tubs. The inn also houses a gift boutique and one of the area's finest antique shops, featuring old clocks and period furniture.
Innkeeper(s): Jackie Madrigel & Bob Hart. $59-119. 9 rooms with PB, 3 with FP, 2 suites and 1 conference room. Breakfast included in rates. Types of meals: Full bkfst and early coffee/tea. Beds: QDT. Cable TV, reading lamp, clock radio, telephone, desk, fireplace (three rooms) and Jacuzzis in room. Air conditioning. VCR, library and parlor games on premises. Handicap access. Amusement parks, antiquing, fishing, live theater, parks, shopping, water sports, Air & Space Museum and Norticus nearby.
Location: Historic small town.
Certificate may be used: Sunday through Thursday, all year, based on availability, excluding holidays.

Staunton   E11

Thornrose House at Gypsy Hill

531 Thornrose Ave
Staunton, VA 24401-3161
(540)885-7026 (800)861-4338
Internet: www.thornrosehouse.com
E-mail: thornros@intelos.net

Circa 1912. A columned veranda wraps around two sides of this gracious red brick Georgian-style house. Two sets of Greek pergolas grace the lawns and there are gardens of azalea, rhododendron and hydrangea. The inn is furnished with a mix of antique oak and walnut period pieces and overstuffed English country chairs. Bircher muesli, and hot-off-the-griddle whole grain banana pecan pancakes are popular breakfast items, served  in the dining room (fireside on cool days). Across the street is a 300-acre park with lighted tennis courts, an 18-hole golf course and swimming pool.
Innkeeper(s): Otis & Suzy Huston. $75-95. 5 rooms with PB. Breakfast and afternoon tea included in rates. Types of meals: Full bkfst. Beds: KQDT. Reading lamp, ceiling fan, clock radio and turn-down service in room. Air conditioning. Telephone and fireplace on premises. Antiquing, fishing, live theater, shopping and sporting events nearby.
Location: City.

"We enjoyed ourselves beyond measure, the accommodations, the food, your helpfulness, but most of all your gracious spirits."
Certificate may be used: Dec. 1-March 31, Sunday through Thursday, no holidays.

Twelfth Night Inn Bed & Breakfast

402 East Beverley St.
Staunton, VA 24401
(540)885-1733 (866)594-5454 Fax:(540)885-4213
Internet: www.12th-night-inn.com
E-mail: visitus@12th-night-inn.com

Circa 1904. Innkeepers/owners John and Juliette impart a Shakespearean flair to the gracious hospitality found at this mansion that was built in the Prairie style. Listen to the birds of this quiet, residential neighborhood while relaxing on the wraparound veranda. Swing in the bench of the landscaped back garden that opens onto a soccer field. A kettle and a stocked refrigerator with drinks are in the upstairs hall for guest use. Stay in a suite with a fireplace or spacious guest bedroom. A breakfast full of delicious homemade treats is enjoyed in the dining room.
Innkeeper(s): Juliette & John Swenson. $85-125. 3 rooms, 1 with PB, 2 suites. Breakfast included in rates. Types of meals: Full gourmet bkfst. Beds: Q. Cable TV, reading lamp, ceiling fan, clock radio, telephone, desk and one suite has fireplace in room. Air conditioning. Parlor games, fireplace and refrigerator on premises. Antiquing, art galleries, fishing, golf, hiking, horseback riding, live theater, museums, parks, shopping, tennis and wineries nearby.
Location: City.
Certificate may be used: Anytime, Sunday-Thursday.

Steeles Tavern   *E11*

Sugar Tree Inn

Highway 56, PO Box 10
Steeles Tavern, VA 24476
(540)377-2197 (800)377-2197
Internet: www.sugartreeinn.com
E-mail: innkeeper@sugartreeinn.com

Circa 1983. A haven of natural beauty sitting on 28 wooded acres high in the Blue Ridge Mountains, this elegantly rustic log inn imparts peace and solitude. Relax on a porch rocker, perfect for bird watching. Stargaze from the hot tub on the mountainside deck. Choose a book or game from the upstairs library. Spacious accommodations include guest bedrooms in the main lodge and log house as well as two suites in the Grey House. Stone fireplaces, whirlpool tubs, separate sitting rooms, outside decks and other pleasing amenities are welcome indulgences. Look out on the wildflowers and chipmunks during a hearty breakfast in the glass-walled dining room. Make reservations for a candlelight dinner with quiet music and Virginia wine, served Wednesday through Saturday at the inn's restaurant. Walk the nature trail by a rushing creek or explore the Appalachian Trail.
Innkeeper(s): Jeff & Becky Chanter. $150-185. 12 rooms, 9 with PB, 12 with FP, 2 suites and 1 cottage. Breakfast and snacks/refreshments included in rates. Types of meals: Country bkfst, early coffee/tea and gourmet dinner. Restaurant on premises. Beds: KQDT. VCR, reading lamp, CD player, ceiling fan, clock radio, coffeemaker, hot tub/spa and fireplace in room. Air conditioning. TV, spa, telephone and gift shop on premises. Limited handicap access. Antiquing, art galleries, bicycling, canoeing/kayaking, cross-country skiing, downhill skiing, fishing, golf, hiking, horseback riding, live theater, museums, parks and shopping nearby.
Location: Mountains.
Publicity: *Washingtonian Magazine "Top 10 Country Inns."*
Certificate may be used: Sunday-Thursday Except Sept. 15-Nov. 15.

Strasburg   C13

Hotel Strasburg

213 S Holliday St
Strasburg, VA 22657-2213
(540)465-9191 (800)488-327 Fax:(540)465-4788
Internet: www.hotelstrasburg.com
E-mail: thehotel@shentel.net

Circa 1902. Experience the romance of the Victorian era at
this three-story hotel, situated on two acres, just one block
from Main Street. Built in 1902 as a hospital, the building was
converted into a hotel in 1915 after a doctor ran off with a
nurse. Since then, it has been the social hub of Strasburg and
offers luxurious accommodations and an exquisite dining area.
Each room of the Victorian Clapboard inn holds the finest array
of antique furnishings, all of which are for sale. Period pieces
are continually brought into the inn from the innkeepers' travels. During their stay, guests enjoy hiking, canoeing, fishing and
visiting nearby Civil War battlefields or taking an hour-long
drive to Washington, D.C. Enjoy the elegance of Victorian
gourmet dining in the hotel's dining room throughout the day.
Innkeeper(s): Gary & Carol Rutherford. $79-175. 29 rooms with PB and 1 con-
ference room. Types of meals: Full bkfst, early coffee/tea, lunch, snacks/refresh-
ments and gourmet dinner. Restaurant on premises. Beds: KQDT. Data port,
cable TV, reading lamp, telephone and some with hot tubs in room. Air conditioning. Fax and copier on premises. Limited handicap access. Antiquing, beach,
bicycling, canoeing/kayaking, downhill skiing, fishing, golf, hiking, horseback riding, live theater, museums, parks, shopping, tennis and wineries nearby.
Location: Small town.
Publicity: *Blue Ridge Country, Washington Post, Washingtonian, Country
Victorian and BBC.*
Certificate may be used: Dec. 1 through March 31, Sunday-Thursday, no
holidays.

Surry   H16

Seward House B&B

PO BOX 352   193 Colonial Trail East
Surry, VA 23883-0352
(757)294-3810

Circa 1901. A long white porch, festooned with gingerbread
and flowers, invites you to an old-fashioned visit at "Grandma's
house." Family pieces and collections from three generations
include toys, needlework and china. Ask for the Seward House
omelet, a house specialty. Afterwards, enjoy the Chippokes
Plantation State Park or cross the James River by ferry and visit
Colonial Williamsburg.
Innkeeper(s): Jackie Bayer & Cindy Erskine. $65-80. 4 rooms, 2 with PB, 1
suite. Breakfast included in rates. Types of meals: Full bkfst, early coffee/tea,
picnic lunch and gourmet dinner. Beds: QDT. Reading lamp and ceiling fan in
room. Air conditioning. VCR, bicycles, telephone and fireplace on premises.
Amusement parks, antiquing, parks and shopping nearby.
Location: Small town - agricultural.
Certificate may be used: Any day during promotion, except holidays.

The Plains   C14

Grey Horse Inn

PO Box 139
The Plains, VA 20198
(540)253-7000 (877)253-7020 Fax:(540)253-7031
Internet: www.greyhorseinn.com
E-mail: innkeeper@greyhorseinn.com

Circa 1880. Built as a Victorian tourist hotel on four acres in
the heart of hunting country, this exclusive yet intimate inn is
well-suited for both the leisure and business traveler. Furnished

with antebellum-era family heirlooms, a refined ambiance is
reflected. Enjoy afternoon tea on one of the relaxing porches
with unspoiled views of the Blue Ridge Mountains beyond the
garden and farmland. Each of the spacious guest bedrooms features a canopy bed, fine linens and personal amenities. Start
the day with a country breakfast before exploring the quaint village setting, nearby wineries or historic Civil War sites.
Innkeeper(s): John & Ellen Hearty. $105-195. 6 rooms. Breakfast included in
rates. Types of meals: Full gourmet bkfst and early coffee/tea. Beds: KQ. Modem
hook-up, data port, cable TV, VCR, reading lamp, refrigerator, clock radio, telephone, turn-down service, desk and hot tub/spa in room. Central air. Fax, copier,
library, pet boarding, parlor games, fireplace and laundry facility on premises.
Handicap access. Antiquing, art galleries, bicycling, canoeing/kayaking, fishing,
golf, hiking, horseback riding, museums, parks, shopping and wineries nearby.
Location: Village.
Certificate may be used: Jan. 2-March 31 except holidays (Valentine's Day)
or July 1-31 except holidays (Independence Day).

Urbanna   F17

Hewick Plantation

VSH 602/615, Box 82
Urbanna, VA 23175
(804)758-4214 Fax:(804)758-4080
Internet: www.hewick.com
E-mail: hewick@gvtech.net

Circa 1678. Built for the Robinson Family with flemish bond
bricks made on the original tobacco plantation, this two-story,
Federal-style Colonial home is listed in the National and State
registers. Situated on 66 acres along the
tidewater, the 11th generation of
Robinson descendants currently
reside at the estate. Spacious
guest bedrooms with high ceilings are furnished with period
antiques, offer generous ameni-
ties and feature gas stoves on the original fireplace hearths. Tall,
stately windows overlook landscaped grounds that include a
gazebo amongst the mature willow oak, pecan, walnut, mulberry and magnolia trees. Glimpses of native wildlife and domestic
farm animals are common. A deluxe continental breakfast may
include quiche, sausage, fresh fruit, yogurt, warm breads or
pastries and beverages. Ask about the resident ghost, and be
sure to visit the region's many historic sites.
Innkeeper(s): Helen Battleson. $119-179. 2 rooms with PB, 2 with FP.
Breakfast included in rates. Types of meals: Cont plus. Beds: KQD. Cable TV,
clock radio and telephone in room. Air conditioning. Fax, parlor games and
fireplace on premises. Antiquing, fishing, parks, shopping and sailing nearby.
Publicity: *Richmond Times, Dispatch, Washington Post, Daily Press,
Pleasant Living, Channel 8 - Richmond, WRIC-TV and TV-Tokyo.*
Certificate may be used: Nov. 15-April 15, Monday through Wednesday.

Warm Springs   E10

Three Hills Inn

PO Box 9
Warm Springs, VA 24484-0009
(540)839-5381 (888)234-4557 Fax:(540)839-5199
Internet: www.3hills.com
E-mail: inn@3hills.com

Circa 1913. Mary Johnston, who wrote the book "To Have and
to Hold," built this inn, which rests on 38 mountainous acres.
In 1917, Mary and her sisters opened the home to guests,
earning a reputation for the home's view of the Allegheny
Mountains and Warm Springs Gap. The innkeepers now offer
lodging in the antique-filled main house or adjacent cottages.

Some rooms include private decks, while others have fireplaces or clawfoot tubs. Each of the cottages includes a kitchen; one has a working fireplace, while another offers a wood-burning stove.

Innkeeper(s): Charlene Fike. $69-189. 10 rooms with PB, 3 with FP, 7 suites and 2 cottages. Breakfast included in rates. Types of meals: Full bkfst. Restaurant on premises. Beds: KQDT. Cable TV, reading lamp, clock radio and desk in room. VCR, fax, copier, child care, parlor games, telephone, fireplace, boardroom that seats 12, conference center that seats 80 and hiking on premises. Antiquing, cross-country skiing, downhill skiing, fishing, hiking, live theater, parks, shopping and thermal "spa" warm spring pools nearby. Location: Mountains.
Publicity: *Listed on "Women of Virginia Historic Trail."*
Certificate may be used: Anytime, except weekends July-October and major (legal) holidays.

Washington   C13

Caledonia Farm - 1812 B&B

47 Dearing Rd (Flint Hill)
Washington, VA 22627
(540)675-3693 (800)262-1812
Internet: www.bnb1812.com

Circa 1812. This gracious Federal-style stone house in the National Register is beautifully situated on 52 acres adjacent to Shenandoah National Park. It was built by a Revolutionary War officer, and his musket is displayed over a mantel. The house, a Virginia Historic Landmark, has been restored with the original Colonial color scheme retained. All rooms have working fireplaces and provide views of Skyline Drive and the Blue Ridge Mountains. The innkeeper is a retired broadcaster.

Innkeeper(s): Phil Irwin. $140. 2 rooms, 2 with FP, 2 suites and 1 conference room. Breakfast and snacks/refreshments included in rates. Types of meals: Full gourmet bkfst and early coffee/tea. Beds: D. VCR, reading lamp, refrigerator, snack bar, clock radio, telephone, turn-down service, desk, hot tub/spa and Skyline Drive view in room. Air conditioning. TV, fax, copier, spa, bicycles, library, parlor games, fireplace, hay ride and lawn games on premises. Antiquing, cross-country skiing, downhill skiing, fishing, live theater, parks, shopping, water sports, wineries, caves, stables and battlefields nearby.
Location: Country, mountains.
Publicity: *Country, Country Almanac, Country Living, Blue Ridge Country, Discovery, Washington Post, Baltimore Sun and Pen TV/Cable 15/PBS X3.*
"We've stayed at many, many B&Bs. This is by far the best!"
Certificate may be used: Anytime, subject to availability, except 3-day holiday weekends and all of October.

Fairlea Farm Bed & Breakfast

636 Mt Salem Ave, PO Box 124
Washington, VA 22747-0124
(540)675-3679 Fax:(540)675-1064
Internet: www.fairleafarm.com
E-mail: longyear@shentel.net

Circa 1960. View acres of rolling hills, farmland and the Blue Ridge Mountains from this fieldstone manor house. Rooms are decorated with crocheted canopies and four-poster beds. Potted plants and floral bedcovers add a homey feel. The stone terrace is set up for relaxing with chairs lined along the edge. As a young surveyor, George Washington laid out the boundaries of the historic village of Little Washington, which is just a 15-minute walk from Fairlea Farm, a working sheep and cattle farm.
Innkeeper(s): Susan & Walt Longyear. $115-185. 3 rooms with PB, 1 suite. Breakfast and afternoon tea included in rates. Types of meals: Full gourmet

bkfst and early coffee/tea. Beds: QT. Reading lamp, refrigerator, turn-down service and desk in room. Air conditioning. VCR, fax, copier, parlor games, telephone and fireplace on premises. Antiquing, fishing, horseback riding, live theater, vineyards, Shenandoah National Park and Civil War battlefields nearby.
Location: Country, mountains. Village/working farm.
Certificate may be used: All year, suite only. Sunday through Thursday, except holidays and not including the month of October.

The Foster-Harris House

PO Box 333
Washington, VA 22747-0333
(540)675-3757 (800)666-0153
Internet: www.fosterharris.com
E-mail: fosterharrisbb@aol.com

Circa 1900. In a historic village surveyed by George Washington in the foothills of the Blue Ridge Mountains, this rural bed and breakfast has extended hospitality since 1900. Just minutes from Shenandoah National Park, be immersed in the natural beauty with gorgeous views. Greeted with refreshments and peaceful surroundings, anticipate a wonderful visit. Relax on the side deck or amid the perennial gardens overlooking the neighboring meadow. Lavish guest bedrooms are pampering retreats. Stay in the spacious Mountain View Suite with a whirlpool tub for two, wood-burning stove and sitting room. After breakfast take a scenic hike or tour one of the many wineries nearby. Faith Mountain Company Store is a unique country store in the renovated 1905 Sperryville School House.
Innkeeper(s): Patrick Corbett. $125-275. 5 rooms with PB, 1 suite. Breakfast and afternoon tea included in rates. Types of meals: Full bkfst. Beds: QD. Reading lamp, ceiling fan, clock radio, turn-down service, hair dryers and French brandy in room. Air conditioning. TV, VCR, fax, library, parlor games, telephone, fireplace and iron/board on premises. Handicap access. Antiquing, cross-country skiing, fishing, live theater and shopping nearby.
Location: Mountains. Rural town.
Publicity: *Richmond Times-Dispatch, Southern Living and Washingtonian.*
Certificate may be used: Jan. 1 to Dec. 31, Sunday-Thursday, except October & September.

Gay Street Inn

PO Box 237, Gay St
Washington, VA 22747
(540)675-3288
Internet: www.gaystreetinn.com
E-mail: gaystinn@shentel.net

Circa 1855. After a day of Skyline Drive, Shenandoah National Park and the caverns of Luray and Front Royal, come home to this stucco, gabled farmhouse. If you've booked the fireplace room, a canopy bed will await you. Furnishings include period Shaker pieces. The innkeepers will be happy to steer you to the most interesting vineyards, organic "pick-your-own" fruit and vegetable farms and Made-In-Virginia food and craft shops. Breakfast and afternoon tea are served in the garden conservatory. Five-star dining is within walking distance at The Inn at Little Washington. The innkeepers can arrange for child care.

Innkeeper(s): Robin & Donna Kevis. $110-135. 4 rooms with PB, 1 with FP, 1 suite. Breakfast and afternoon tea included in rates. Types of meals: Full gourmet bkfst and early coffee/tea. Beds: Q. Reading lamp, clock radio and suite has TV in room. Air conditioning. Fireplace on premises. Limited handicap access. Antiquing, fishing, golf, horseback riding, live theater, parks, shopping, water sports and vineyards nearby.
Location: Mountains. Rural town.
Publicity: *Blue Ridge Country and Food Art.*
"Thank you for a wonderful visit. Your hospitality was superb."
Certificate may be used: Sunday through Thursday, excluding holidays and three-day weekends.

White Stone   F17

Flowering Fields B&B

232 Flowering Field
White Stone, VA 22578-9751
(804)435-6238 Fax:(804)435-6238
E-mail: susan@rivnet.net

Circa 1790. Guests will find plenty to do at this Victorian bed & breakfast. The game room is stocked with a pool table, games, darts, cable TV and a fireplace. The grounds are shared by the innkeepers friendly dogs, cat and several horses. The parlor is a bit more formal, and the music room includes a baby grand piano. Complimentary beverages are available around the clock. The morning begins with a huge breakfast. Innkeeper Lloyd Niziol's famous crab cakes, fresh fruit, omelets, French toast and fried apples are among the possibilities. The innkeepers will plan the meal around guests' dietary restrictions. Guest rooms include items such as a four-poster rice bed, antiques, Queen Anne chairs and Oriental rugs. The innkeepers welcome families with children.
Innkeeper(s): Lloyd Niziol & Susan Moenssens. $75-120. 5 rooms, 2 with PB, 1 suite and 1 conference room. Breakfast, afternoon tea and snacks/refreshments included in rates. Types of meals: Full gourmet bkfst and early coffee/tea. Beds: KQDT. Reading lamp, ceiling fan, clock radio, some cable, some desks and sitting area in room. Air conditioning. VCR, fax, copier, bicycles, library, parlor games, telephone, fireplace, advance notification for handicap access and first-floor room with private bath on premises. Antiquing, fishing, golf, parks, shopping, water sports and Williamsburg nearby.
Certificate may be used: Jan. 1-Dec. 31, Sunday-Thursday, excluding holiday weekends (Thanksgiving, Fourth of July, Memorial, Labor Day, Christmas).

Williamsburg   G17

A Williamsburg White House

718 Jamestown Rd
Williamsburg, VA 23185
(757)229-8580 (866)229-8580
Internet: www.awilliamsburgwhitehouse.com
E-mail: info@awilliamsburgwhitehouse.com

Circa 1904. Just four blocks from historic downtown, this spacious century-old Colonial estate graces a picturesque neighborhood. Decorated around an elegant and traditional presidential theme, the common rooms include the JFK library, where a fireside game of chess can be played while sipping sherry in a leather chair, and the Diplomatic Reception Room where afternoon wine and delicious treats are served. Guest bedrooms are considered Presidential Suites with four-poster and canopy feather beds, robes, sitting areas and motif-matching memorabilia. Enjoy a sumptuous full breakfast in the Reagan Dining Room.
Innkeeper(s): Debbie & John Keane. $115-199. 4 rooms with PB, 3 suites. Breakfast, snacks/refreshments and wine included in rates. Types of meals: Full gourmet bkfst and early coffee/tea. Beds: KQ. Cable TV, clock radio, telephone and turn-down service in room. Central air. Fax, library, parlor games and fireplace on premises. Amusement parks, antiquing, art galleries, bicycling, canoeing/kayaking, fishing, golf, hiking, horseback riding, live theater, museums, parks, shopping, sporting events and wineries nearby.
Location: Country.
Certificate may be used: Jan. 3-Feb. 28, Sunday-Thursday, excluding holidays, subject to availability.

An American Inn - Williamsburg Manor B&B

600 Richmond Rd
Williamsburg, VA 23185
(757)220-8011 (800)422-8011 Fax:(757)220-0245
Internet: www.williamsburg-manor.com
E-mail: Williamsburg@occasions.hrcoxmail.com

Circa 1927. Built during the reconstruction of Colonial Williamsburg, this Georgian brick Colonial is just three blocks

from the historic village. A grand staircase, culinary library, Waverly fabrics, Oriental rugs and antiques are featured. Breakfasts begin with fresh fruits and home-baked breads, followed by a special daily entree. Gourmet regional Virginia dinners also are available.
Innkeeper(s): Laura & Craig Reeves. $79-169. 6 rooms, 4 with PB, 1 suite. Breakfast included in rates. Types of meals: Full gourmet bkfst, veg bkfst, early coffee/tea, gourmet lunch, picnic lunch, afternoon tea, snacks/refreshments and gourmet dinner. Beds: QT. Modem hook-up, cable TV, reading lamp, CD player, ceiling fan, clock radio, telephone and voice mail in room. Central air. VCR, spa, child care, parlor games, fireplace, freshly baked cookies and lemonade on premises. Limited handicap access. Amusement parks, antiquing, art galleries, beach, bicycling, canoeing/kayaking, fishing, golf, hiking, horseback riding, live theater, museums, parks, shopping, sporting events, tennis, water sports and wineries nearby.
Location: City. Colonial Williamsburg.
Publicity: *Virginia Gazette, Williamsburg Magazine, Gourmet Magazine, San Francisco Reader and Daily Press.*

"Lovely accommodations - scrumptious breakfast."
Certificate may be used: Anytime, Sunday-Thursday, not valid April, October, December.

Cedars

616 Jamestown Rd
Williamsburg, VA 23185-3945
(757)229-3591 (800)296-3591 Fax:(757)229-0756
Internet: www.cedarsofwilliamsburg.com
E-mail: btubbs@cedarsbandb.com

Circa 1933. This three-story brick Georgian home is a short walk from Colonial Williamsburg and is located across from William and Mary College. Rooms are decorated with traditional antiques, Colonial reproductions, fireplaces and four-poster or canopy beds. The bountiful breakfasts include a hearty entree, fresh fruits, breads, muffins and cereals.
Innkeeper(s): Grace & Bob Tubbs. $115-300. 10 rooms, 8 with PB, 2 with FP, 2 two-bedroom suites and 1 cottage. Breakfast and snacks/refreshments included in rates. Types of meals: Full gourmet bkfst and early coffee/tea. Beds: KQT. Reading lamp, CD player, refrigerator, ceiling fan, snack bar, clock radio and fireplace in room. Central air. Copier, bicycles, library, parlor games and telephone on premises. Limited handicap access. Amusement parks, antiquing, beach, bicycling, canoeing/kayaking, fishing, golf, hiking, live theater, museums, parks, shopping, sporting events, wineries and historic sites nearby.
Location: City. Colonial Williamsburg.
Publicity: *Williamsburg's lauded Business Appreciation Award.*
Certificate may be used: Jan. 2 through March 13, excluding holiday weekends.

Colonial Gardens

1109 Jamestown Rd
Williamsburg, VA 23185
(757)220-8087 (800)886-9715 Fax:(757)253-1495
Internet: www.colonial-gardens.com
E-mail: innkeeper@widowmaker.com

Circa 1965. If it's summer or spring when you arrive at Colonial Gardens, ask to take your breakfast out to the gardens and breathe in the color and artistry of the innkeeper's picture perfect gardens, or join other guests in the formal dining room. You might want to keep your camera by your side to record the gardens and landscaping of the inn's three acres of towering trees, rhododendrons, impatiens, clematis and the variety of flowering shrubs. The home is appointed with 1800s English and American antiques and there are usually vases of fresh flowers. The Azalea Suite boasts a plantation rice-carved canopy bed, overstuffed chair and a sitting area, while the Library Room features an Empire bed, bookshelves with leather bound books, and an Oriental carpet. The innkeeper's original art is displayed throughout.

Breakfast may include smoked Virginia bacon or sausage and sautéed apples and pecans served with croissant French toast.
Innkeeper(s): Scottie & Wil Phillips. $135-175. 4 rooms with PB, 2 with FP, 2 suites. Breakfast and snacks/refreshments included in rates. Types of meals: Full bkfst, veg bkfst and early coffee/tea. Beds: KQT. Modem hook-up, data port, cable TV, VCR, reading lamp, ceiling fan, clock radio, telephone, turn-down service and 2 suites with fireplace on premises. Central air. Fax, library, parlor games and VCR library on premises. Amusement parks, antiquing, art galleries, golf, live theater, museums, shopping, wineries and plantations nearby.
Location: Small town.
Publicity: *Mid Atlantic Country Magazine, Unique Inns & Bed & Breakfasts of Virginia and Travel & Leisure.*
Certificate may be used: Monday-Thursday, exclusive of all holidays, October and December.

Legacy Of Williamsburg Bed & Breakfast

930 Jamestown Rd
Williamsburg, VA 23185-3917
(757)220-0524 (800)962-4722
Internet: www.legacyofwilliamsburgbb.com
E-mail: legacy@tni.net

Circa 1976. Designed to reflect the ambiance of an 18th century tavern inn, the hardwood pine floors, crown molding, brick fireplaces and candlelight are just the first steps in crossing the threshold of time. Play a game of chance in the Tavern Room. Cards, darts or billiards are popular. Read a book by the fire in the library. Three spacious suites feature comfy terry robes, welcome snacks, personal products, fireplaces and soft comforters on queen beds. Some rooms boast feather beds. A hearty, hot breakfast is served by the host, authentically dressed in period attire in the fireside Keeping Room with music from that era playing in the background. Convenient off-street parking is provided and complimentary beverages are always available. Feel more immersed in history by visiting Colonial Williamsburg just five blocks away. Arrive at William and Mary within five minutes.
Innkeeper(s): Joan & Art Ricker. $135-185. 4 rooms with PB, 3 with FP, 3 suites. Breakfast and afternoon tea included in rates. Types of meals: Full gourmet bkfst, veg bkfst and early coffee/tea. Beds: Q. Modem hook-up, data port, cable TV, reading lamp, refrigerator, telephone, fireplace and clock in room. Central air. VCR, library and parlor games on premises. Amusement parks, antiquing, art galleries, beach, bicycling, fishing, golf, horseback riding, live theater, museums, parks, shopping, tennis, water sports and wineries nearby.
Location: City.
Publicity: *Pam Lanier Inn of the year 1997.*
Certificate may be used: Sunday-Thursday, January-March, Sunday-Thursday, July-September.

Woodstock   C13

Candlewick Inn

127 N Church St
Woodstock, VA 22664
(540)459-8008
Internet: www.candlewickinnllc.com
E-mail: candlewickinnllc@hotmail.com

Circa 1831. Built before the Civil War and listed in the National Register, this fully restored country home is located in a quaint town in the Shenandoah Mountains. Enjoy five o'clock tea or lemonade on the veranda. Romantic guest bedrooms and a suite with a Jacuzzi offer a relaxing getaway for couples with pampering amenities. A bountiful breakfast can be savored in the sun room, formal dining room or on a private deck. Enjoy quiet moments on a porch swing, or stroll through the colorful gardens. Local historic sites are in abundance.
Innkeeper(s): Sharon & Dennis Pike. $85-150. 5 rooms with PB, 1 suite. Breakfast and afternoon tea included in rates. Types of meals: Full gourmet bkfst. Beds: KQ. Cable TV, reading lamp and ceiling fan in room. Air conditioning. Library and parlor games on premises. Antiquing, bicycling, canoeing/kayaking, downhill skiing, fishing, golf, horseback riding, museums,

parks, shopping, sporting events, tennis and wineries nearby.
Location: Mountains. Quaint town in Shenandoah mountains.
Certificate may be used: Sunday-Thursday in August and Sunday-Thursday the week before Easter, subject to availability.

Woolwine   19

The Mountain Rose B&B Inn

1787 Charity Hwy
Woolwine, VA 24185-9733
(276)930-1057 Fax:(276)930-2165
Internet: www.mountainrose-inn.com
E-mail: info@mountainrose-inn.com

Circa 1901. This historic Victorian inn, once the home of the Mountain Rose Distillery, sits on 100 acres of forested hills with plenty of hiking trails. A trout-stocked stream goes through the property and a swimming pool provides recreation.
Each room has an antique mantled fireplace, which have been converted to gas logs. Guests can relax by the pool or in rocking chairs on one of the six porches. The innkeepers look forward to providing guests with casually elegant hospitality in the Blue Ridge
Mountains. The Blue Ridge Parkway, Chateau Morrisette Winery, Mabry Mill, The Reynolds Homestead, Laurel Hill J. EB Stuart Birthplace, Patrick County Courthouse and the Patrick County Historical Museum are located nearby. A three-course breakfast is offered every morning.
Innkeeper(s): Melodie Pogue & Reeves Simms. $115-135. 5 rooms with PB, 5 with FP. Breakfast and snacks/refreshments included in rates. Types of meals: Full gourmet bkfst and early coffee/tea. Beds: KQT. Reading lamp, desk, fireplace, satellite TV and porch access in room. Air conditioning. VCR, fax, copier, swimming, parlor games, telephone, trout-stocked creek and hiking trails on premises. Antiquing, fishing, golf, hiking, parks, shopping, tennis, water sports, wineries and Nascar racing nearby.
Location: Mountains.
Publicity: *Enterprise, Bill Mountain Bugle, New York Times, The Parkway Edition and "Best Romantic Getaway" City Magazine.*
Certificate may be used: Year-round, Sunday-Thursday. Weekends, anytime, December to March, subject to availability.

Old Spring Farm Bed & Breakfast, Ltd.

PO Box 3
Woolwine, VA 24185
(276)930-3404
Internet: www.oldspringfarm.com

Circa 1883. Experience the perfect year-round mountain getaway just 50 miles south of Roanoke in Blue Ridge Wine Country. The farmhouse, Country Retreat House and Studio feature Country French décor accented with period pieces and collectibles. Stay in a themed guest bedroom. The Honeymoon Suite offers romantic accommodations with a Jacuzzi and a gas-log stove. Savor a hearty gourmet breakfast of homemade breads, jams and delectable specialties with farm-raised eggs, meat, fruit and vegetables. Take a farm tour after the morning meal. Picnic at Fairy Stone State Park or hike the Rocky Knob Trails. Visit local wineries and enjoy the peaceful countryside.
Innkeeper(s): Suzanne V. Pabst. $105-150. 6 rooms, 4 with PB and 1 conference room. Types of meals: Full gourmet bkfst, early coffee/tea, picnic lunch, snacks/refreshments and gourmet dinner. Beds: KQDT. TV, reading lamp, ceiling fan and clock radio in room. Central air. VCR, telephone, laundry facility and decks on premises. Limited handicap access. Antiquing, art galleries, canoeing/kayaking, fishing, golf, hiking, horseback riding, museums, shopping, sporting events, wineries, swimming and Winston Cup stock car race nearby.
Location: Mountains.
Certificate may be used: Anytime, subject to availability.

Washington

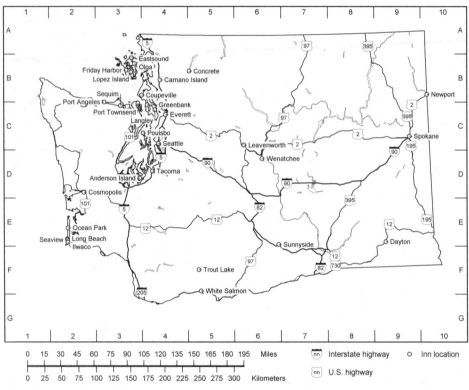

	1	2	3	4	5	6	7	8	9	10	

Map locations:
- Eastsound
- Olga
- Friday Harbor
- Lopez Island
- Concrete
- Camano Island
- Sequim
- Coupeville
- Port Angeles
- Greenbank
- Port Townsend
- Everett
- Langley
- Poulsbo
- Seattle
- Leavenworth
- Wenatchee
- Spokane
- Newport
- Anderson Island
- Tacoma
- Cosmopolis
- Ocean Park
- Long Beach
- Seaview
- Ilwaco
- Sunnyside
- Dayton
- Trout Lake
- White Salmon

| 0 | 15 | 30 | 45 | 60 | 75 | 90 | 105 | 120 | 135 | 150 | 165 | 180 | 195 | Miles |
| 0 | 25 | 50 | 75 | 100 | 125 | 150 | 175 | 200 | 225 | 250 | 275 | 300 | | Kilometers |

Interstate highway · U.S. highway · Inn location

Anderson Island   D3

The Inn at Burg's Landing
8808 Villa Beach Rd
Anderson Island, WA 98303-9785
(253)884-9185 Fax:(425)488-8682
E-mail: innatburgslanding@mailexcite.com

Circa 1987. A short ferry trip from Steilacoom and Tacoma, this log homestead boasts beautiful views of Mt. Rainier, Puget Sound and the Cascade Mountains. The master bedroom features a skylight and a private whirlpool bath. After a full breakfast, guests can spend the day at the inn's private beach. Golf, hiking and freshwater lakes are nearby, and the area has many seasonal activities, including Fourth of July fireworks, the Anderson Island fair and parade in September.

Innkeeper(s): Ken & Annie Burg. $80-130. 4 rooms, 2 with PB. Breakfast included in rates. Types of meals: Full bkfst. Beds: Q. VCR in room. Spa, parlor games and telephone on premises. Amusement parks, downhill skiing, fishing, golf, parks, shopping and tennis nearby.
Location: Waterfront. Puget Sound.
Publicity: *Sunset, Tacoma News Tribune, Portland Oregonian and Seattle Times.*
Certificate may be used: Sunday-Thursday, excluding holidays.

Camano Island   B4

The Inn at Barnum Point
464 S Barnum Rd
Camano Island, WA 98282-8578
(360)387-2256 (800)910-2256 Fax:(360)387-2256
Internet: www.innatbarnumpoint.com
E-mail: barnum@camano.net

Circa 1991. This Cape Cod-style house is located on the bay. Guests enjoy listening to the water lap at the shoreline, watching deer in the orchard and sneaking a kiss under the apple tree. (The orchard was planted by the innkeeper's family in 1904.) The newest accommodation is the 900-square-foot Shorebird Room with deck, fireplace and soaking tub overlooking Port Susan Bay and the Cascade Mountains.

Innkeeper(s): Carolin Barnum Dilorenzo. $110-199. 3 rooms with PB, 3 with FP. Breakfast included in rates. Types of meals: Full gourmet bkfst and early coffee/tea. Beds: Q. TV, VCR, reading lamp, refrigerator, clock radio and telephone in room. Fax, copier, parlor games and fireplace on premises. Antiquing, golf, live theater, parks, shopping and water sports nearby.

Location: Waterfront.

Certificate may be used: Oct. 15-March 15, Sunday through Thursday, no holidays.

Concrete   B5

Cascade Mountain Inn

40418 Pioneer Ln
Concrete, WA 98237
(360)826-4333 (888)652-8127
Internet: cascade-mtn-inn.com
E-mail: casmi2@verizon.net

Circa 1984. Two carved wooden eagles mark the entrance to the Cascade Mountain Inn. Surrounded by scenic farmland, the inn's location in the foothills of the North Cascades, offers splendid mountain views. Five acres of grounds include green lawns, an orchard of cherry, pear, apple and filbert trees and a three-acre pasture for the innkeepers' photogenic black and white Clydesdales. Guest rooms feature some antiques and most have either a view of Sauk Mountain or the foothills of the North Cascades. Creme brulee French toast, or crab and Swiss cheese quiche are house specialties, as well as fresh raspberry muffins. In January and February, bald eagles soar above the inn on their way to the nearby Skagit River where a 1,500-acre eagle preserve attracts up to 300 eagles. The tulip fields of La Conner are close by as well as a multitude of outdoor activities.

Innkeeper(s): Sally & John Brummett. $120. 5 rooms with PB, 1 suite. Types of meals: Full bkfst. Beds: QDT. One-bedroom suite with kitchenette in room.

Publicity: *Country Inns and Sunset.*

"Such a warm wonderful spot, and such nice hospitality."

Certificate may be used: Nov. 1-Jan. 31, Sunday-Thursday.

Cosmopolis   D2

Cooney Mansion Bed & Breakfast

PO Box 54
Cosmopolis, WA 98537-0054
(360)533-0602 (800)977-7823
Internet: www.cooneymansion.com
E-mail: cooney@cooneymansion.com

Circa 1908. This former lumber magnate's home, in a wooded setting, boasts 37 rooms. In the National Register, it was built with a ballroom in the daylight basement, nine bedrooms and eight bathrooms. There are soaking tubs in five of the rooms. The

inn features original mission furnishings, and the Cooney suite has a fireplace, TV and VCR and original "rainfall" shower. Guests can enjoy the National Award Winning Lumber Baron's Breakfast.

Innkeeper(s): Judi & Jim Lohr. $65-185. 8 rooms, 5 with PB, 1 with FP, 1 suite and 1 conference room. Breakfast and afternoon tea included in rates. Types of meals: Country bkfst, veg bkfst and early coffee/tea. Beds: KQDT. Reading lamp, clock radio, one with fireplace, VCR, refrigerator, coffeemaker and most with TV in room. TV, VCR, fax, spa, sauna, tennis, library, parlor games, telephone, fireplace and golf on premises. Antiquing, art galleries, beach, canoeing/kayaking,

fishing, golf, hiking, horseback riding, live theater, museums, parks, shopping, tennis, water sports, whale watching and rain forest nearby.

Location: Country.

Publicity: *Sunset Magazine, Travel & Leisure, Country Inns, Northwest Travel, Seattle Times and Spokane Review.*

"A good B&B should offer the comforts of home, serenity, relaxation and good company. You gave us all we expected and more. Thanks for a romantic weekend."

Certificate may be used: Oct. 15-May 15, Sunday-Thursday.

Coupeville   B4

Captain Whidbey Inn

2072 W Captain Whidbey Inn Rd
Coupeville, WA 98239
(360)678-4097 (800)366-4097 Fax:(360)678-4110
Internet: www.captainwhidbey.com
E-mail: captain@whidbey.net

Circa 1907. Overlooking Whidbey Island's Penn Cove, this log inn has comfortable rooms featuring down comforters, feather beds and views of lagoons and gardens. The Cove Restaurant has a magnificent view and guests can enjoy their meals by the fireplace. Chef/owner James Roberts utilizes local products such as salmon and Penn Cove mussels. The proprietor is also a sailing captain, and guests can book an afternoon on his 52-foot ketch, Cutty Sark. The proprietor's family has run the inn for more than 30 years.

Innkeeper(s): Mendy Mclean-Stone. $95-300. 32 rooms, 20 with PB, 7 with FP and 1 conference room. Types of meals: Full bkfst, lunch, picnic lunch, snacks/refreshments and gourmet dinner. Restaurant on premises. Beds: KQD. Reading lamp, refrigerator, telephone and desk in room. Fax, copier, fireplace, sailing and fishing on premises. Antiquing, shopping and museums nearby.

Location: Ocean community.

Publicity: *Gourmet Magazine and USA-Weekend.*

"I visit and stay here once a year and love it."

Certificate may be used: October-May, Sunday-Thursday, excluding special events/holidays.

Inn at Penn Cove

PO Box 85
Coupeville, WA 98239-0085
(360)678-8000 (800)688-2683
Internet: www.whidbey.net/penncove
E-mail: penncove@whidbey.net

Circa 1887. Two restored historic houses, one a fanciful white and peach Italianate confection in the National Register, comprise the inn. Each house contains only three guest rooms affording a variety of small parlors for guests to enjoy. The most romantic accommodation is Desiree's Room with a fireplace, a whirlpool tub for two and mesmerizing views of Puget Sound and Mt. Baker.

Innkeeper(s): Gladys & Mitchell Howard. $60-125. 6 rooms, 4 with PB, 3 with FP. Breakfast and afternoon tea included in rates. Types of meals: Full gourmet bkfst and veg bkfst. Beds: KQ. Cable TV, reading lamp, ceiling fan, clock radio and hot tub/spa in room. TV, VCR, library, parlor games, telephone, fireplace, pump organ and music box on premises. Antiquing, beach, bicycling, fishing, golf, horseback riding, live theater, museums, parks, shopping and wineries nearby.

Location: Waterside village.

Publicity: *Whidbey News-Times, Country Inns and Glamour.*

"Our hosts were warm and friendly, but also gave us plenty of space and privacy - a good combination."

Certificate may be used: Oct. 15-March 15, Sunday-Friday; March 15-June 15, Sunday-Thursday.

The Victorian B&B

PO Box 761, 602 N Main
Coupeville, WA 98239-0761
(360)678-5305

Circa 1889. This graceful Italianate Victorian sits in the heart of one of the nation's few historic reserves. It was built for German immigrant Jacob Jenne, who became the proprietor of the Central Hotel on Front Street. Noted for having the first running water on the island, the house's old wooden water tower stands in the back garden. An old-fashioned storefront, once the local dentist's office, sits demurely behind a picket fence, now a private hideaway for guests.

Innkeeper(s): Alfred Sasso. $65-100. 3 rooms with PB, 1 suite. Breakfast included in rates. Types of meals: Full bkfst. Beds: Q. TV and telephone in room. VCR on premises. Antiquing, fishing, live theater and shopping nearby.
Location: City.
Publicity: *Seattle Times and Country Inns.*

"If kindness and generosity are the precursors to success (and I certainly hope they are!), your success is assured."

Certificate may be used: Anytime, Sunday through Thursday.

Dayton   E9

The Purple House

415 E Clay St
Dayton, WA 99328-1348
(509)382-3159 (800)486-2574

Circa 1882. History buffs will adore this aptly named bed & breakfast, colored in deep purple tones with white, gingerbread trim. The home, listed in the National Register, is the perfect place to enjoy Dayton, which boasts two historic districts and a

multitude of preserved Victorian homes. Innkeeper Christine Williscroft has filled the home with antiques and artwork. A highly praised cook, Christine prepares the European-style full breakfasts, as well as mouthwatering afternoon refreshments. Guests can relax in the richly appointed parlor or library, and the grounds also include a swimming pool.

Innkeeper(s): D. Christine Williscroft. $85-125. 4 rooms, 2 with PB, 1 with FP, 1 suite. Breakfast and afternoon tea included in rates. Types of meals: Full gourmet bkfst, early coffee/tea, picnic lunch and dinner. Beds: QD. Reading lamp, refrigerator, ceiling fan, clock radio, telephone and desk in room. Air conditioning. VCR, swimming, library, pet boarding, parlor games and fireplace on premises. Handicap access. Antiquing, cross-country skiing, downhill skiing, fishing, live theater, parks, shopping, sporting events and water sports nearby.
Location: City.
Publicity: *Sunset.*

"You have accomplished so very much with your bed & breakfast to make it a very special place to stay."

Certificate may be used: Sunday-Thursday.

Weinhard Hotel

235 E Main St
Dayton, WA 99328-1352
(509)382-4032 Fax:(509)382-2640
Internet: www.weinhard.com

Circa 1890. This luxurious Victorian bed & breakfast, tucked at the base of the scenic Blue Mountains, originally served up spirits as the Weinhard Saloon and Lodge Hall. Guests are transported back to the genteel Victorian era during their stay. After a restful sleep among period pieces, ornate carpeting and ceilings fans, guests might imagine the days when horses and buggies road through town. While the innkeepers have worked to preserve the history of the hotel, they didn't forget such modern luxuries as Jacuzzi tubs in the private baths. The hotel boasts a beautiful Victorian roof garden, a perfect place to relax with a cup of tea or gourmet coffee. For a unique weekend, try the hotel's special Romantic Getaway package. Guests are presented with sparkling wine or champagne and a dozen roses. The package also includes a five-course meal.

Innkeeper(s): Virginia Butler. $70-125. 15 rooms with PB. Breakfast included in rates. Types of meals: Lunch, afternoon tea and gourmet dinner. Restaurant on premises. Beds: Q.
Publicity: *Seattle Times, Daily Journal of Commerce, Sunset Magazine, Lewiston Morning Tribune, San Francisco Examiner and Spokesman Review.*

"It's spectacular! Thank you so much for all your kindness and caring hospitality."

Certificate may be used: Sunday-Thursday, year-round, except May 26-29, July 14-17, Sept. 1-5, excluding special events and holidays.

Eastsound   B3

Turtleback Farm Inn

1981 Crow Valley Rd
Eastsound, WA 98245
(360)376-4914 (800)376-4914
Internet: www.turtlebackinn.com
E-mail: info@turtlebackinn.com

Circa 1895. Guests will delight in the beautiful views afforded from this farmhouse and the newly constructed Orchard House, which overlooks 80 acres of forest and farmland, duck ponds and Mt. Constitution to the east. Rooms feature antique furnishings and many boast views of the farm, orchard or sheep pasture. Beds are covered with wool comforters made from sheep raised on the property. Bon Appetit highlighted some of the breakfast recipes

served at Turtleback; a breakfast here is a memorable affair. Tables set with bone china, silver and fresh linens make way for a delightful mix of fruits, juice, award-winning granola, homemade breads and specialty entrees. Evening guests can settle down with a game or a book in the fire-lit parlor as they enjoy sherry, tea or hot chocolate.

Innkeeper(s): William & Susan C. Fletcher. $90-225. 11 rooms with PB, 4 with FP. Breakfast included in rates. Types of meals: Full bkfst, early coffee/tea and picnic lunch. Beds: KQD. Reading lamp and clock radio in room. Library, parlor games, telephone, fireplace and refrigerator with self-serve beverage bar in dining room on premises. Handicap access. Fishing, live theater, parks, shopping and water sports nearby.
Location: Country.

Publicity: *Los Angeles Times, USA Today, Travel & Leisure, Contra Costa Sun, Seattle Times, Northwest Living, Sunset, Food & Wine, Gourmet, Northwest Travel, New York Times and Alaska Air.*

"A peaceful haven for soothing the soul."

Certificate may be used: November-April, Sunday through Thursday, subject to availability. Holidays and special event dates are excluded.

Everett   C4

Gaylord House

3301 Grand Ave
Everett, WA 98201
(425)339-9153 (888)507-7177 Fax:(425)303-9713
Internet: www.gaylordhouse.com
E-mail: gaylord_house@msn.com

Circa 1908. A shaded front porch surrounded by lush green-ery is an inviting way to enjoy the serenity of this two-story Craftsman home, recently added to the city's historic overlay register. Find a secluded spot amid the 4,000-square-foot house, or listen to Gaylord play the clarinet in the parlor. Guest bedrooms offer different decor that match a variety of tastes, from nautical to floral, Mediterranean or old-fashioned English royalty. Select a teacup from the collection gathered by three generations, then enjoy a gourmet breakfast that may include cheese blintzes, baked apple, pork-apple sausage and fresh raspberries. This historic region is known as the gateway to all the wonders of the Pacific Northwest, between the Cascade Mountains and Puget Sound.

Innkeeper(s): Gaylord, ShirleyAnne, Theresa Schaudies. $68-135. 4 rooms with PB, 1 with FP. Breakfast included in rates. Types of meals: Full gourmet bkfst, veg bkfst, early coffee/tea, gourmet lunch, afternoon tea and gourmet dinner. Beds: Q. Modem hook-up, cable TV, VCR, reading lamp, clock radio, telephone, desk, hot tub/spa and Jacuzzi in room. Central air. Fax, copier, library, parlor games and fireplace on premises. Antiquing, art galleries, cross-country skiing, downhill skiing, fishing, golf, hiking, live theater, parks, tennis and wineries nearby.

Location: City.

Certificate may be used: Anytime, subject to availability.

Friday Harbor   B3

Friday's Historical Inn

PO Box 2023, 35 First St
Friday Harbor, WA 98250
(360)378-5848 (800)352-2632 Fax:(360)378-2881
Internet: www.friday-harbor.com
E-mail: stay@friday-harbor.com

Circa 1891. A visit to San Juan Island should include a stay at this restored turn-of-the-century inn that was originally the San Juan Island Hotel. Gracious service and knowledgeable advice are abundantly shared to ensure a wonderful experi-ence. Choose a romantic guest bedroom or suite featuring a two-person Jacuzzi tub, luxuriously appointed bed and fire-place. A homemade continental breakfast is served daily. Bicycles are available for exploring the island. Lime Kiln Whale Watch Park is perfect for spotting orcas, or ask about taking a charter. Kayaking is just one more of the area's many outdoor adventures.

Innkeeper(s): Laura & Adam Saccio. $55-265. 15 rooms. Breakfast and afternoon tea included in rates. Types of meals: Cont plus and snacks/refresh-ments. Beds: KQDT. Data port, cable TV, VCR, reading lamp, refrigerator, ceiling fan, snack bar, clock radio, coffeemaker, desk, hot tub/spa and fire-place in room. Fax, spa, bicycles, parlor games and fireplace on premises. Handicap access. Antiquing, art galleries, beach, bicycling, canoeing/kayak-ing, fishing, golf, hiking, horseback riding, live theater, museums, parks, shopping, tennis and wineries nearby.

Location: Ocean community.

Certificate may be used: October-March, Sunday-Thursday, subject to availability.

Pear Point Inn

2858 Pear Point Road
Friday Harbor, WA 98250
(360)378-6655 Fax:(360)378-6605
Internet: www.pearpointinn.com
E-mail: pearpointinn@interisland.net

Circa 1995. A new addition to San Juan Island, this contempo-rary inn features modern furnishings that are elegant yet inviting. Surrounded by nature and two public beaches, this bed & break-fast sits on more than seven acres that overlook Griffin Bay to the Olympic Mountains. The great room offers spectacular ocean views, a fireplace sitting area and breakfast dining. The spacious Sun Room boasts a bronze, four-poster bed and a walk-in closet. The Suite is a private one-bedroom guest house with living room, fully equipped kitchen, eating area and balcony. Relax on the glass-front deck with a fountain, or soak in the hot tub.

Innkeeper(s): John Darroudi & Lisa Brown. $135-225. 2 rooms, 1 with PB, 1 suite. Types of meals: Full gourmet bkfst, early coffee/tea, picnic lunch, afternoon tea and snacks/refreshments. Beds: QT. Modem hook-up, cable TV, VCR, reading lamp, stereo, refrigerator, clock radio, telephone, coffeemaker, bathrobes, hair dryers, toiletries and fresh fruit in room. Central air. Fax, copi-er, spa and fireplace on premises. Antiquing, art galleries, beach, bicycling, canoeing/kayaking, fishing, golf, hiking, live theater, museums, parks, shop-ping, water sports and wineries nearby.

Certificate may be used: November through April, except holidays, subject to availability. November to April 30, Monday-Sunday.

San Juan Inn B&B

50 Spring St, Box 776
Friday Harbor, WA 98250-0776
(360)378-2070 (800)742-8210 Fax:(360)378-2027
Internet: www.san-juan.net/sjinn
E-mail: sanjuaninn@rockisland.com

Circa 1873. In the National Register, this old European-style hotel is filled with stained glass, old photographs and flowers picked from the inn's garden. A Victorian settee is situated under a cherry tree within sniffing distance of the lilacs and roses. It's a half-block to the ferry landing.

Innkeeper(s): Steve Judson. $65-225. 10 rooms, 4 with PB, 2 suites. Breakfast included in rates. Types of meals: Cont plus. Beds: KQDT. Cable TV, VCR, reading lamp, refrigerator, ceiling fan, clock radio and hot tub/spa in room. Fax, spa and fireplace on premises. Fishing, live theater, parks, shop-ping and water sports nearby.

Location: City, ocean community.

Certificate may be used: Oct. 15-April 30, Sunday-Thursday.

States Inn

2687 West Valley Rd
Friday Harbor, WA 98250-8164
(360)378-6240 (866)602-2737 Fax:(360)378-6241
Internet: www.statesinn.com
E-mail: info@statesinn.com

Circa 1910. This sprawling ranch home has ten guest rooms, each named and themed for a particular state. The Arizona and New Mexico rooms, often booked by families or couples travel-ing together, can be combined to create a private suite with two bedrooms, a bathroom and a sitting area. The oldest part of the house was built as a country school and later used as a dance hall, before it was relocated to its current 60-acre spread. Baked French toast, accompanied by fresh fruit topped with yogurt sauce and homemade muffins are typical breakfast fare.

Innkeeper(s): Cole & Amy Hull. $68-195. 10 rooms, 8 with PB, 1 with FP, 1 suite. Breakfast and afternoon tea included in rates. Types of meals: Full gourmet bkfst, veg bkfst, early coffee/tea and snacks/refreshments. Beds: KQDT. Reading lamp and clock radio in room. Fax, stable, library, parlor games, telephone, fireplace and working ranch on premises. Handicap access. Antiquing, art galleries, beach, bicycling, canoeing/kayaking, fishing, golf, hiking, horseback riding, live theater, museums, parks, shopping, tennis, water sports, wineries, sea kayaking, whale watching and bird watching nearby.

Location: Country, ocean community. Pastoral valley with stream running through property.

Publicity: *Glamour, Conde Naste, USA Today and CITI TV Vancouver.*

Certificate may be used: Oct. 1 to April 15, entire week.

Tucker House Bed & Breakfast

260 B Street
Friday Harbor, WA 98250
(360)378-2783 (800)965-0123 Fax:(360)378-6437
Internet: www.tuckerhouse.com
E-mail: reservations@rockisland.com

Circa 1898. Only one block from the ferry landing, the white picket fence bordering Tucker House is a welcome sight for guests. The spindled entrance leads to the parlor. The home includes three guest rooms that share a bath. The rooms are decorated with antiques. The innkeepers also offer self-contained cottages that include private baths, kitchenettes, queen beds, TVs and VCRs. All guests enjoy use of the outdoor hot tub. The inn's breakfasts are served in the solarium.

Innkeeper(s): Alan Paschal . $125-300. 10 rooms with PB, 4 with FP, 2 suites, 2 cottages and 1 conference room. Breakfast and snacks/refreshments included in rates. Types of meals: Full gourmet bkfst, veg bkfst, early coffee/tea, gourmet lunch, picnic lunch and room service. Beds: KQDT. Cable TV, VCR, reading lamp, refrigerator, ceiling fan, clock radio, coffeemaker, hot tub/spa, fireplace, private balcony, private entrance, microwave, convection oven and range in room. Spa, parlor games, telephone, fireplace, videos, sun room and sun deck on premises. Limited handicap access. Antiquing, art galleries, beach, bicycling, canoeing/kayaking, fishing, golf, hiking, horseback riding, live theater, museums, parks, shopping, water sports, wineries and dining nearby.

Location: City.

Publicity: *Travel Holiday magazine.*

"A lovely place, the perfect getaway. We'll be back."

Certificate may be used: Oct. 16-April 15.

Greenbank   C4

Guest House Log Cottages

24371-SR 525, Whidbey Island
Greenbank, WA 98253
(360)678-3115
Internet: www.guesthouselogcottages.com
E-mail: guesthse@whidbey.net

Circa 1925. These storybook cottages and log home are nestled within a peaceful forest on 25 acres. The log cabin features stained-glass and criss-cross paned windows that give it the feel of a gingerbread house. Four of the cottages are log construction. Ask for the Lodge and enjoy a private setting with a pond just beyond the deck. Inside are two Jacuzzi tubs, a stone fireplace, king bed, antiques and a luxurious atmosphere.

Innkeeper(s): Don & Mary Jane Creger. $165-325. 6 cottages. Breakfast included in rates. Types of meals: Full bkfst. Beds: KQ. TV, VCR, reading lamp, stereo, refrigerator, ceiling fan, clock radio, telephone, desk, hot tub/spa, kitchen and Jacuzzi in room. Air conditioning. Fax, copier, spa and swimming pool on premises. Antiquing, fishing, golf, parks, shopping and tennis nearby.

Location: Mountains, ocean community. Island - wooded.

Publicity: *Los Angeles Times, Woman's Day, Sunset, Country Inns and Bride's.*

"The wonderful thing is to be by yourselves and rediscover what's important."

Certificate may be used: Midweek Monday, Tuesday, Wednesday, Thursday, either Farm Guest or Carriage House cottages, Nov. 1-March 15.

Ilwaco   E2

Bell Tower Inn

PO Box 922
Ilwaco, WA 98624-0922
(360)642-8686 (888)244-2523 Fax:(360)642-8642
Internet: www.belltowerinn.com
E-mail: innkeeper@belltowerinn.com

Circa 1879. A weathered, shingled New England-style building, the Inn at Ilwaco was originally the Community Presbyterian Church. The former sanctuary is now used for weddings, seminars, concerts and reunions. Some rooms have views of a stream that meanders by and the Columbia River seaport is two blocks away. Excursions include salmon fishing charters, clam digging, horseback riding, and visiting the cranberry bogs.

Innkeeper(s): Mike & Jean Christensen. $79-189. 9 rooms with PB, 2 with FP, 3 suites and 2 conference rooms. Breakfast included in rates. Types of meals: Full gourmet bkfst and early coffee/tea. Beds: KQ. Cable TV and refrigerator in room. VCR, fax, copier, bicycles, library, telephone and fireplace on premises. Amusement parks, antiquing, fishing, golf, live theater, parks, shopping, tennis, water sports and beach nearby.

Location: City, ocean community. Lighthouses, forts.

Certificate may be used: Nov. 1-April 30.

Langley   C4

Saratoga Inn

PO Box 3073
Monterey, CA 93942-3073
(360)221-5801 (800)698-2910 Fax:(360)221-5804
Internet: www.saratogainnwhidbey.com
E-mail: saratogainn@foursisters.com

Circa 1994. This romantic, island inn is located away from the hustle and bustle of Seattle. To reach the inn, guests hop aboard a ferry and take a 20-minute journey from the city to quiet Whidbey Island. The inn offers 15 elegantly appointed guest rooms, each with a fireplace. Each room also boasts a water view. Guests enjoy a full breakfast and afternoon with a variety of goodies. Guests can spend the day exploring the island, or hop aboard the ferry to visit the sites of Seattle. There is a $20 fee for an additional guest in room, except for children less than 5 years old. Saratoga Inn is a Four Sisters Inn.

Innkeeper(s): Cheryl Lambour. $110-275. 15 rooms with PB, 15 with FP. Breakfast and afternoon tea included in rates. Types of meals: Full gourmet bkfst and early coffee/tea. Beds: KQ. Telephone and turn-down service in room. Fax and bicycles on premises. Handicap access.

Certificate may be used: October-June 15, Sunday-Thursday, excluding holidays and special event periods, based on availability.

Leavenworth   C6

Autumn Pond Bed & Breakfast

10388 Titus Rd
Leavenworth, WA 98826-9509
(509)548-4482 (800)222-9661
Internet: www.autumnpond.com
E-mail: info@autumnpond.com

Circa 1992. This modern ranch-style inn is set at the base of the Cascade Mountains and offers stunning views, which one can enjoy from the outdoor hot tub. The interior is welcoming, with bright, country prints on the beds and country furnishings. Exposed beams add a rustic touch to the dining area and living room. Guests can feed the ducks at the pond or fish for trout. After a homemade breakfast, head into Leavenworth and explore the shops and sites of this historic Bavarian town.

Innkeeper(s): John & Jennifer Lorenz. $99-109. 6 rooms with PB. Breakfast included in rates. Types of meals: Full bkfst and early coffee/tea. Beds: Q. Reading lamp and clock radio in room. Air conditioning. Telephone, fireplace and pond on premises. Antiquing, cross-country skiing, downhill skiing, fishing, golf, live theater, parks, shopping, water sports, whitewater rafting, cross country skiing, hiking and mountain biking nearby.

Location: Mountains.

Certificate may be used: March 1 to May 31, Sunday-Thursday only.

Haus Rohrbach Pension

12882 Ranger Rd
Leavenworth, WA 98826-9503
(509)548-7024 (800)548-4477 Fax:(509)548-6455
Internet: www.hausrohrbach.com
E-mail: info@hausrohrbach.com

Circa 1975. Situated on 13 1/2 acres overlooking the village, Haus Rohrbach offers both valley and mountain views and is at the entrance to Tumwater Mountain cycling and hiking trails. Leavenworth is two minutes away. Private fireplaces and whirlpools for two are features of each of three suites. Sourdough pancakes and cinnamon rolls are specialties of the house. Guests often take breakfast out to the deck to enjoy pastoral views that include grazing sheep and a pleasant pond. In the evening, return from white-water rafting, tobogganing, skiing or sleigh rides to soak in the hot tub.

Innkeeper(s): Carol & Mike Wentink. $85-175. 10 rooms, 8 with PB, 3 with FP, 3 suites and 2 conference rooms. Breakfast included in rates. Types of meals: Full bkfst, early coffee/tea, lunch, picnic lunch, snacks/refreshments and dinner. Beds: KQD. Reading lamp, stereo, refrigerator, desk and hot tub/spa in room. Air conditioning. Telephone, fireplace, outdoor pool & hot tub, private gardens, suites with fireplace and double soaking whirlpool tub and beautiful views on premises. Handicap access. Antiquing, cross-country skiing, downhill skiing, fishing, horseback riding, shopping and five miles of hiking and biking paths on Tumwater Mountain nearby.

Location: Mountains. Theme town.

Certificate may be used: Jan. 7 to May 7, Sept. 10 to Oct. 31, Sunday through Thursday. Holiday and festival times are excluded.

Long Beach   E2

A Rendezvous Place Bed and Breakfast

547 Gavilan Canyon Rd
Ruidoso, NM 88345
(360)642-8877 (866)642-8877 Fax:(360)642-8877
Internet: www.rendezvousplace.com
E-mail: info@rendezvousplace.com

Circa 1970. You are asked to honor a Scandinavian custom of removing your shoes upon entering this B&B. White wool carpeting and blond-wood pieces decorate the living room. A recreation room offers a hot tub and Finnish sauna. The Icelandic Room has an antique armoire and hand-painted cabinets, while the Swedish Suite features a two-person soaking tub tucked into a private nook. Breakfast items such as creamed rice, shrimp au gratin and Danish pastries are served smorgasbord-style with the hosts in costume.

Innkeeper(s): David Haines. $88-175. 5 rooms, 4 with PB, 1 two-bedroom suite. Breakfast, afternoon tea and snacks/refreshments included in rates. Types of meals: Full gourmet bkfst and early coffee/tea. Beds: Q. Cable TV, VCR and desk in room. Fax, copier, spa, sauna, bicycles, library, parlor games, telephone and fireplace on premises. Limited handicap access.

Antiquing, art galleries, beach, bicycling, canoeing/kayaking, fishing, golf, hiking, horseback riding, museums, parks and shopping nearby.

Location: Ocean community. Coastal small town.

Certificate may be used: Sunday-Thursday, holidays and festivals excluded.

Boreas Bed & Breakfast Inn

PO Box 1344
Long Beach, WA 98631
(360)642-8069 (888)642-8069 Fax:(360)642-5353
Internet: www.boreasinn.com
E-mail: boreas@boreasinn.com

Circa 1920. This oceanfront inn started as a beach house and was remodeled eclectically with decks and two fireplaces. There are two living rooms that offer views of the dunes. All of the five guest rooms feature ocean, garden or mountain views. Guests can enjoy private time in the hot tub in the enclosed gazebo, take the private path that winds through the dunes to the surf or walk to the boardwalk, restaurants and shopping. There is also a three-bedroom cottage available. Breakfast and spa is not available at the cottage.

Innkeeper(s): Susie Goldsmith & Bill Verner. $135-155. 5 suites, 1 cottage and 1 guest house. Breakfast and snacks/refreshments included in rates. Types of meals: Full gourmet bkfst. Beds: KQT. Reading lamp, CD player, clock radio, desk, hot tub/spa and one with jetted tub in room. VCR, fax, spa, library, parlor games, telephone, fireplace, hypo-allergenic feather beds, pillows, comforters and blankets on premises. Antiquing, art galleries, beach, bicycling, canoeing/kayaking, fishing, golf, hiking, horseback riding, museums, parks, shopping, tennis, water sports, Lewis and Clark discovery trail, Lewis and Clark Interpretive Center and historical sites, birding, lighthouses, art galleries, deep sea fishing and kite flying nearby.

Location: Ocean community, waterfront. Ocean front.

Publicity: Arrington's 2003 & 2004 Most Romantic Hideaway Top 15 in the nation, Business of the Year 2002, Customer Service Award honored by the Better Business Bureau and Enterprise Rent-A-Car for Oregon and SW Washington, Best Places to Kiss in the NW - three Kiss Rating, NW Best Places and Sunset.

Certificate may be used: October-March, Sunday-Thursday, holidays excluded, subject to availability.

Lopez Island   B3

MacKaye Harbor Inn

949 MacKaye Harbor Rd
Lopez Island, WA 98261-8145
(360)468-2253 (888)314-6140 Fax:(360)468-2393
Internet: www.mackayeharborinn.com
E-mail: mackaye@rockisland.com

Circa 1927. Launching a kayak from the inn's sandy beach is a favorite activity here, as well as watching otters, seals and eagles from the waterfront parlor or expansive wraparound porch. Four of the guest rooms boast views of the bay, and there are three acres to explore, including a quarter mile of beach. The home was the first house on the island to have electric lights, as well as its first inn. In the evenings, guests are treated to chocolate truffles and an aperitif to enhance the sunset views. Complimentary mountain bikes are offered for cycling around the island.

Innkeeper(s): Robin & Mike. $89-185. 5 rooms, 3 with PB, 1 with FP, 1 suite and 1 conference room. Breakfast included in rates. Types of meals: Cont plus, early coffee/tea, picnic lunch and afternoon tea. Beds: KQDT. Reading lamp, clock radio, turn-down service and desk in room. Fax, copier, telephone, fireplace and BBQs on premises. Antiquing, bicycling, canoeing/kayaking, fishing, golf, parks and tennis nearby.

Location: Ocean community, waterfront. Sandy beach.

Publicity: Los Angeles Times, Sunset, Northwest and Coastal Living.

Certificate may be used: Oct. 20-March 30, Sunday-Friday, excluding holidays.

Newport   B10

Inn at the Lake

581 S. Shore Diamond Lake Rd
Newport, WA 99156
(509)447-5772 (877)447-5772 Fax:(509)447-0999
Internet: www.innatthelake.net
E-mail: info@innatthelake.com

Circa 1993. A vacation paradise, this Southwestern-style home
offers resort amenities. A family room boasts a gas-log fireplace,
VCR, books and games. The large entertainment deck overlooks
tiered gardens and ponds. Luxurious waterfront suites boast
spacious privacy, fireplaces, double Jacuzzis and lake views. Stay
in the romantic Peach Penthouse Suite with a roof-top deck and
two-person swing. Breakfast is found in each room's refrigerator,
ready to enjoy when desired. Fish for rainbow trout from the
dock, or rent a canoe. Play volleyball on the grass beach before a
refreshing swim. Winter sports also are in abundance.

Innkeeper(s): Robert & Margaret Smith. $95-159. 5 rooms, 1 with FP, 5
suites. Breakfast and snacks/refreshments included in rates. Types of meals:
Cont plus, veg bkfst, afternoon tea and room service. Beds: KQ. Cable TV,
VCR, reading lamp, refrigerator, ceiling fan, clock radio, telephone, coffeemaker, desk, hot tub/spa and fireplace in room. Air conditioning. Fax, copier, swimming, parlor games and fireplace on premises. Beach, bicycling,
cross-country skiing, downhill skiing, fishing, golf, hiking, horseback riding,
live theater, parks, shopping and water sports nearby.

Location: Country, mountains, waterfront.

Certificate may be used: Sunday-Thursday, Nov. 1-April 30, except holidays.

Ocean Park   E2

Whalebone House

2101 Bay Ave
Ocean Park, WA 98640
(360)665-5371 (888)298-3330
Internet: www.whalebonehouse.com
E-mail: stay@whalebonehouse.com

Circa 1889. Proudly listed in the state's Historic Register, this
restored Victorian farmhouse is an example of the area's early
homes that blended the architectural styles of the Pacific
Northwest and coastal Maine. Past the white picket fence and
country gardens, the interior is furnished with a refreshing
assortment of antiques, beach whimsies, primitives and family
heirlooms. Guest bedrooms offer privacy and modern conveniences. Enjoy specialty dishes like Whalebone Hash (smoked
salmon), a vegetable frittata and creme brulee French toast for
sweet and savory breakfast treats. Relax on an enclosed sun
porch or side deck.

Innkeeper(s): Deidre & RD Williams. $120. 4 rooms with PB. Breakfast,
afternoon tea and snacks/refreshments included in rates. Types of meals: Full
gourmet bkfst, veg bkfst, early coffee/tea and picnic lunch. Beds: Q. Reading
lamp and clock radio in room. Fax, library, parlor games, telephone, fireplace,
gift shop and printer on premises. Limited handicap access. Antiquing, art
galleries, beach, bicycling, canoeing/kayaking, golf, hiking, horseback riding,
museums, parks, shopping, Lewis & Clark historic sites, trails, landmarks and
clamming nearby.

Location: Country, ocean community.

Publicity: *Pacific Press, Sunset, Chinook Observer and Best Places to Kiss.*

Certificate may be used: Anytime, subject to availability.

Olga   B3

Buck Bay Farm

716 Pt Lawrence Rd
Olga, WA 98279
(360)376-2908 (888)422-2825
Internet: www.buckbayfarm.com
E-mail: Buckbayfarm@centurytel.net

Circa 1920. This farmhouse is secluded on five acres and is decorated in country style. Down pillows and comforters are a few
homey touches. Homemade breakfasts include items like freshly
baked muffins, scones and biscuits still steaming from the oven.

Innkeeper(s): Sheri Marzolf. $99-135. 5 rooms, 4 with PB, 1 suite.
Breakfast included in rates. Types of meals: Full bkfst and early coffee/tea.
Beds: Q. Reading lamp and clock radio in room. Spa, parlor games and telephone on premises. Handicap access. Antiquing, canoeing/kayaking, fishing,
hiking, live theater, parks, shopping and whale watching nearby.

Location: Country.

Publicity: *Island's Sounder.*

Certificate may be used: Oct. 15-April 15, except holiday weekends.

Port Angeles   C3

Five SeaSuns Bed & Breakfast

1006 S Lincoln St
Port Angeles, WA 98362-7826
(360)452-8248 (800)708-0777 Fax:(360)417-0465
Internet: www.seasuns.com
E-mail: info@seasuns.com

Circa 1926. Take a respite from the rush of today at this
restored, historic home that reflects the 1920s era of sophistication with a sense of romance and refinement. Guest bedrooms
depict the seasons of the year and are furnished with period
antiques. Pleasing amenities include whirlpool or soaking tubs,
balconies and water or mountain
views. Artfully presented
gourmet breakfasts are served by
candlelight with fine china and
silver. Relax on the porch or
wander the picturesque gardens
that highlight the estate-like
grounds. Explore nearby Olympic National Park and the Ediz
Hook Coast Guard Station. The Underground History Walk is
ten blocks. Visit the Makah Indian Museum 75 miles away.

Innkeeper(s): Jan & Bob Harbick. $75-145. 5 rooms with PB, 1 suite and 1
cottage. Breakfast, afternoon tea and snacks/refreshments included in rates.
Types of meals: Full bkfst, veg bkfst, early coffee/tea and picnic lunch. Beds:
QD. Reading lamp and turn-down service in room. TV, VCR, fax, parlor
games, telephone and fireplace on premises. Antiquing, art galleries, beach,
bicycling, canoeing/kayaking, cross-country skiing, fishing, hiking, live theater,
museums, parks, shopping and wineries nearby.

Location: City, ocean community.

Publicity: *Arrington B&B Journal "Best Breakfast" award for 2003 and "Best
Garden" for 2004.*

Certificate may be used: Anytime, November-April, subject to availability
except holiday weekends.

Port Townsend   C3

Ann Starrett Mansion

744 Clay St
Port Townsend, WA 98368-5808
(888)385-3205
Internet: www.starrettmansion.com
E-mail: edel@starrettmansion.com

Circa 1889. George Starrett came from Maine to Port Townsend and became the major residential builder. By 1889, he had constructed one house a week, totaling more than 350 houses. The Smithsonian believes the Ann Starrett's elaborate free-hung spiral staircase is the only one of its type in the United States. A frescoed dome atop the octagonal tower depicts four seasons and four virtues. On the first day of each season, the sun causes a ruby red light to point toward the appropriate painting. The mansion won a "Great American Home Award" from the National Trust for Historic Preservation.

Innkeeper(s): Edel Sokol. $110-185. 11 rooms with PB, 2 with FP, 2 suites, 2 cottages and 2 conference rooms. Breakfast included in rates. Types of meals: Cont. Beds: KQDT. Cable TV, reading lamp, refrigerator, clock radio, telephone and desk in room. Fax and fireplace on premises. Antiquing, cross-country skiing, fishing, live theater, parks, shopping and whale watching nearby.
Location: Seaport Village.
Publicity: *Peninsula, New York Times, Vancouver Sun, San Francisco Examiner, London Times, Colonial Homes, Elle, Leader, Japanese Travel, National Geographic Traveler, Victorian, Historic American Trails, Sunset Magazine, PBS and Day Boy Night Girl.*

"Staying here was like a dream come true."

Certificate may be used: Nov. 1-March 30, Sunday through Thursday, must mention certificate at time of reservation.

Blue Gull Inn B&B

1310 Clay Street
Port Townsend, WA 98368
(360)379-3241 (888)700-0205 Fax:(360)379-5498
Internet: www.bluegullinn.com
E-mail: bluegull@olypen.com

Circa 1868. Proudly gracing the heart of the historic district between uptown and downtown, this Gothic Revival home boasts a Country Victorian decor. Absorb the peaceful ambiance from a rocker on the pillared front porch. Stylish guest bedrooms offer a variety of comfortable amenities. Two rooms can be made adjoining. Private bathrooms boast an oversize shower, clawfoot or whirlpool tub. Breakfast is a culinary treat of gourmet specialties and down-home favorites served in the dining room with an inspiring garden view.

Innkeeper(s): John & Renee Eissinger. $95-185. 6 rooms with PB, 1 suite. Breakfast and snacks/refreshments included in rates. Types of meals: Full bkfst, early coffee/tea and afternoon tea. Beds: QT. Two rooms with whirlpool tubs, spacious bathrooms and one room with private sun porch in room. Charming guest parlor and large dining room on premises. Antiquing, art galleries, beach, bicycling, canoeing/kayaking, golf, hiking, live theater, museums, parks, shopping, water sports, wineries, downtown and waterfront nearby.
Location: Historic Victorian seaport.
Certificate may be used: Oct. 1-April 1.

The English Inn

PO Box 866
Port Townsend, WA 98368
(360)385-5302 (800)254-5302
Internet: www.English-Inn.com
E-mail: stay@english-inn.com

Circa 1885. There is much to enjoy at this distinctive Italianate-style Victorian inn. The parlor's large bay window seat overlooks the impressive Olympic Mountains. Sit by the fire and choose

from a diverse selection of music to listen to. Take the grand staircase to the spacious corner guest bedrooms named after British historical eras. Indulge in a long soak in a clawfoot tub. An assortment of treats is available in the long hallway where a tea/coffee bar is set up on a huge, antique English sideboard near a cozy loveseat. A delectable breakfast is too good to miss in the formal dining room. Gaze at the arbors, pond and colorful flowers while relaxing in the garden gazebo.

Innkeeper(s): Martin & Jennifer MacGillonie. $110-120. 4 rooms with PB. Breakfast included in rates. Types of meals: Full gourmet bkfst, veg bkfst, early coffee/tea, afternoon tea and snacks/refreshments. Beds: Q. Reading lamp and desk in room. Parlor games and fireplace on premises. Antiquing, art galleries, beach, bicycling, canoeing/kayaking, fishing, golf, hiking, live theater, museums, parks, shopping, water sports and wineries nearby.
Location: Victorian seaport.
Certificate may be used: Jan. 1-June 30 and Nov. 1-Dec. 31, Sunday-Thursday.

Holly Hill House B&B

611 Polk St
Port Townsend, WA 98368-6531
(360)385-5619 (800)435-1454 Fax:(360)385-3041
Internet: www.hollyhillhouse.com/rooms.html
E-mail: info@hollyhillhouse.com

Circa 1872. There are 17 holly trees surround this aptly named bed & breakfast, built by Robert C. Hill, the co-founder of the First National Bank of Port Townsend. The cozy, romantic rooms are decorated with florals and lace. Billie's Room affords a view of Admiralty Inlet and Mt. Baker, while Lizette's Room offers Victorian decor and a view of the garden. The Skyview Room includes a wonderful skylight. The spacious Colonel's Room features a picture window with water and mountain views, and the Morning Glory Room is a cozy retreat with lace-trimmed quilts. Expansive breakfasts are served in the dining room, and coffee and tea are always available. The inn's gardens are surrounded by a picket fence and nearly 90 rose bushes.

Innkeeper(s): Nina & Greg Dortch. $94-165. 5 rooms with PB, 1 suite. Breakfast and afternoon tea included in rates. Types of meals: Full bkfst, veg bkfst, early coffee/tea and picnic lunch. Beds: KQ. Reading lamp and clock radio in room. TV, VCR, library, parlor games, fireplace and DVD on premises. Limited handicap access. Antiquing, art galleries, beach, bicycling, canoeing/kayaking, fishing, golf, museums, parks, shopping, water sports and wineries nearby.
Location: City, mountains, ocean community.
Publicity: *Washington State Visitors' Guide, PT Guide, Port Townsend Chamber of Commerce Guide, The Official Guide to American Historic Inns, Bed & Breakfast USA, Bed & Breakfast Homes Best of the West Coast, National Trust Guide, Romantic Getaway Guide and Stash Tea Guide of B&B Inns.*
Certificate may be used: Anytime, Nov. 1-March 15, subject to availability.

Manresa Castle

PO Box 564, 7th & Sheridan
Port Townsend, WA 98368-0564
(360)385-5750 (800)732-1281 Fax:(360)385-5883
Internet: www.manresacastle.com

Circa 1892. When businessman Charles Eisenbeis built the largest private residence in Port Townsend, locals dubbed it "Eisenbeis Castle," because it resembled the castles in Eisenbeis' native Prussia. The home is truly a royal delight to behold, both inside and out. Luxurious European antiques and hand-painted wall coverings decorate the dining room and many of the castle's stately guest rooms. The turret suites are unique and many of the rooms have mountain and water views, but beware of the third floor. Rumors of ghosts in the upper floor have frightened some, but others seek out the "haunted" rooms for a spooky stay. Port Townsend offers a variety of galleries, gift shops and antiquing.

Innkeeper(s): Ron Myhre. $70-175. 40 rooms with PB, 2 suites and 1 conference room. Breakfast included in rates. Types of meals: Gourmet dinner. Restaurant on premises. Beds: KQD. Cable TV, reading lamp, clock radio and telephone in room. Fax, copier and library on premises. Limited handicap access. Antiquing, art galleries, beach, bicycling, canoeing/kayaking, fishing, golf, hiking, live theater, museums, parks, shopping, tennis, water sports and wineries nearby. Location: Mountains.

Publicity: *Island Independent, Leader News, Province Showcase, Sunset Magazine, Oregonian, Northwest Palate Magazine, History Channel and Sightings.*

Certificate may be used: Sunday through Friday, October through May.

Palace Hotel

1004 Water St
Port Townsend, WA 98368-6706
(360)385-0773 (800)962-0741 Fax:(360)385-0780
Internet: www.palacehotelpt.com
E-mail: palacehotel@pc.com

Circa 1889. This old brick hotel has been restored and refurbished in a Victorian style. The Miss Rose Room has a Jacuzzi tub and is on the third floor. Some rooms have kitchenettes. Miss Kitty's Room, with its antique bed and wood-burning stove has great views of Puget Sound and downtown.

Innkeeper(s): Gary Schweitzer. $60-199. 17 rooms. Breakfast included in rates. Types of meals: Cont. Beds: KQDT. TV in room.

Certificate may be used: October to May, except Friday and Saturday nights, excludes holidays and special events. Subject to availability.

Poulsbo   C4

Foxbridge B&B

30680 Hwy 3 NE
Poulsbo, WA 98370
(360)598-5599
Internet: www.sfox.com/foxbridge
E-mail: info@foxbridge.com

Circa 1993. The innkeepers at this Georgian-style home have taken the words bed & breakfast to heart. Each of the comfortable rooms has an individual theme. The Country Garden room is a floral delight with a canopy bed. The Old World room includes a sleigh bed and down comforter. The Foxhunt room is done up in masculine hues with a four-poster bed. Antiques are placed throughout the home. As for the breakfast, each morning brings a new menu. Heart-shaped waffles topped with blueberries and cream might be the fare one morning, while another day could bring eggs Benedict or a smoked-salmon quiche. All are served with cereals and a special starter, perhaps baked nectarines with cream Ambrose.

Innkeeper(s): Hilary Renfer & Gray Odell. $90. 3 rooms with PB. Breakfast and afternoon tea included in rates. Types of meals: Full gourmet bkfst and early coffee/tea. Beds: Q. Reading lamp, turn-down service and desk in room. Fax, library, parlor games, telephone and fireplace on premises. Antiquing, cross-country skiing, fishing, live theater, parks, shopping, water sports and museums nearby. Location: Country.

Certificate may be used: Nov. 1 to May 1.

Seattle   C4

Inn at Harbor Steps

PO Box 3073
Monterey, CA 93942-3073
(206)748-0973 (888)728-8910 Fax:(206)748-0533
Internet: www.innatharborsteps.com
E-mail: inn@harborsteps.com

Circa 1997. This inn is located in the heart of downtown Seattle, within walking distance of antique shops, restaurants, Pike Place Market, boutiques and the Seattle Art Museum. The romantic guest rooms include king-size beds, sitting areas and fireplaces. In-room amenities include refrigerators, data ports and voice mail. The inn has a media room, business center and fitness room. Guest can borrow bicycles. In addition to all these modern amenities, guests are pampered with a gourmet breakfast and afternoon tea. There is a $20 fee for an additional guest in room, except for children less than 5 years old. The inn, one of the Four Sisters Inns, is located at the base of a luxury residential high-rise.

Innkeeper(s): Gregory Crick. $165-230. 28 rooms with PB, 20 with FP and 3 conference rooms. Breakfast, afternoon tea and snacks/refreshments included in rates. Types of meals: Full bkfst. Beds: KQ. Modem hook-up, data port, cable TV, VCR, reading lamp, CD player, refrigerator, ceiling fan, snack bar, clock radio, telephone, coffeemaker, turn-down service, desk, hot tub/spa, voice mail, European balcony and sitting area in room. Central air. TV, fax, spa, swimming, sauna, bicycles, library, parlor games, fireplace, gym, lap pool, sauna, state of the art media room and private parking on premises. Handicap access. Amusement parks, antiquing, art galleries, bicycling, canoeing/kayaking, fishing, golf, hiking, live theater, museums, parks, shopping and sporting events nearby. Location: City.

Certificate may be used: November-April, excluding holidays and special events, based on availability.

Seaview   E2

Shelburne Inn

4415 Pacific Way, PO Box 250
Seaview, WA 98644
(360)642-2442 Fax:(360)642-8904
Internet: www.theshelburneinn.com
E-mail: innkeeper@theshelburneinn.com

Circa 1896. The Shelburne is known as the oldest continuously operating hotel in the state of Washington, and it is listed in the National Register. The front desk at the hotel is a former church altar. Art nouveau stained-glass windows rescued from a church torn down in Morecambe, England, now shed light and color on the dining room. The guest rooms are appointed in antiques. Just a 10-minute walk from the ocean, the inn is situated on the Long Beach Peninsula, a 28-mile stretch of seacoast that includes bird sanctuaries and lighthouses. The inn offers a full gourmet breakfast.

Innkeeper(s): David Campiche & Laurie Anderson. $119-199. 15 rooms with PB, 2 suites and 1 conference room. Breakfast included in rates. Types of meals: Full gourmet bkfst, lunch, gourmet dinner and room service. Restaurant on premises. Beds: QD. Fax and copier on premises. Handicap access. Antiquing and fishing nearby.

Publicity: *Better Homes & Gardens, Bon Appetit, Conde Nast Traveler, Esquire, Gourmet, Food & Wine and Travel & Leisure.*

"Fabulous food. Homey but elegant atmosphere. Hospitable service, like being a guest in an elegant home."

Certificate may be used: Midweek, October through May, excluding holidays.

Sequim   C3

Greywolf Inn

395 Keeler Rd
Sequim, WA 98382-9024
(360)683-5889 (800)914-WOLF Fax:(360)683-1487
Internet: www.greywolfinn.com
E-mail: info@greywolfinn.com

Circa 1973. Built in a farmhouse style, this house is located on five acres. If you prefer a canopy bed, request the Pamela Room and enjoy Bavarian decor. Salmon and egg dishes are presented at breakfast. Decks surround the house, affording views of an occasional eagle, ducks in the pond and Mount Baker. A nature trail provides a pleasant

walk through the fields, tall fir trees and over a small stream. Birdwatching and beachcombing are popular on the Dungeness Spit.

Innkeeper(s): Peggy & Bill Melang.
$80-140. 5 rooms with PB, 1 suite. Breakfast included in rates. Types of meals: Full bkfst, early coffee/tea and picnic lunch. Beds: KQT. TV, reading lamp, ceiling fan, clock radio, coffeemaker, desk and fireplace in room. VCR, fax, library, parlor games, telephone, fireplace and hot tub on premises. Antiquing, art galleries, beach, bicycling, canoeing/kayaking, cross-country skiing, downhill skiing, fishing, golf, hiking, horseback riding, live theater, museums, parks, shopping, tennis, water sports, wineries and casino nearby.
Location: Country.
Certificate may be used: Anytime from Oct. 15-May 15, excluding holiday weekends. Offer limited to three rooms.

Spokane   C9

Fotheringham House

2128 W 2nd Ave
Spokane, WA 99204-0916
(509)838-1891 Fax:(509)838-1807
Internet: www.ior.com/fotheringham
E-mail: innkeeper@fotheringham.net

Circa 1891. A vintage Victorian in the National Register, this inn was built by the first mayor of Spokane, David Fotheringham. There are tin ceilings, a carved staircase, gabled porches and polished woodwork. Victorian furnishings and stained-glass pieces are featured. Across the street is Coeur d'Alene Park and the Patsy Clark Mansion. Walk two blocks to the Elk Public House.

Innkeeper(s): Irene & Paul Jensen. $95-115. 4 rooms. Breakfast included in rates. Types of meals: Full bkfst and early coffee/tea. Reading lamp, clock radio, chocolates and amenities in room. Telephone and fireplace on premises. Antiquing, live theater, museums, shopping and sporting events nearby.
Location: City.
Certificate may be used: Consecutive nights Sunday through Thursday, November-March.

Marianna Stoltz House

427 E Indiana Ave
Spokane, WA 99207-2324
(509)483-4316 (800)978-6587 Fax:(509)483-6773
Internet: www.aimcomm.com/stoltzhouse
E-mail: info@mariannastoltzhouse.com

Circa 1908. Located on a tree-lined street, two miles from downtown Spokane, is this American Four Square Victorian.

It is in the local historic register and features a wraparound porch, high ceilings and leaded-glass windows. Furnishings include Oriental rugs and period pieces. Peach Melba Parfait and Stoltz House Strada are breakfast specialties.

Innkeeper(s): Phyllis & Jim Maguire. $89-99. 4 rooms, 2 with PB, 1 suite. Breakfast included in rates. Types of meals: Full bkfst and early coffee/tea. Beds: KQT. Cable TV, reading lamp, refrigerator, clock radio, telephone and desk in room. Air conditioning. Fax, copier, parlor games, fireplace and piano on premises. Amusement parks, cross-country skiing, downhill skiing, fishing, live theater, parks, shopping and sporting events nearby.
Location: City.
Certificate may be used: Sunday through Thursday, Nov. 15-March 15, holidays excluded.

Waverly Place B&B

709 W Waverly Place
Spokane, WA 99205
(509)328-1856 (866)328-1856 Fax:(509)326-7059
Internet: www.waverlyplace.com
E-mail: waverly@waverlyplace.com

Circa 1900. The first home built in what is now the Corbin Park Historical District, this storybook Victorian offers quiet relaxation and a central location. An inviting parlor boasts beaded pillars and window seats. Choose from spacious park-view rooms or the romantic third-floor turret suite. Wake to hot coffee just outside the door before savoring a full gourmet breakfast in the dining room. Swedish pancakes with huckleberry sauce, sausage, fresh fruit and yogurt are some of the favorite items served. Sit on the veranda with afternoon tea, or swim in the refreshing pool. The sites and shops of downtown are five minutes away.

Innkeeper(s): Marge & Tammy Arndt. $95-125. 3 rooms with PB, 1 suite. Breakfast and afternoon tea included in rates. Types of meals: Full gourmet bkfst, veg bkfst and early coffee/tea. Beds: Q. Reading lamp, clock radio and desk in room. Central air. Fax, swimming, telephone and fireplace on premises. Antiquing, art galleries, bicycling, cross-country skiing, downhill skiing, golf, hiking, live theater, museums, parks, shopping, sporting events, tennis, water sports and wineries nearby.
Location: City.
Certificate may be used: October-April, Sunday-Thursday, subject to availability.

Sunnyside   E6

Sunnyside Inn B&B

800 E Edison Ave
Sunnyside, WA 98944-2206
(509)839-5557 (800)221-4195
Internet: www.sunnysideinn.com
E-mail: sunnyside@sunnysideinn.com

Circa 1919. This wine country inn offers spacious rooms, decorated in a comfortable, country style. Most of the rooms include baths with double Jacuzzi tubs. The one bedroom without a Jacuzzi, includes the home's original early 20th-century fixtures. Two rooms offer fireplaces. A full breakfast is served, as well as evening snacks.

Innkeeper(s): Karen & Don Vlieger. $89-119. 13 rooms with PB, 2 with FP. Breakfast and snacks/refreshments included in rates. Types of meals: Full bkfst. Beds: KQ. Cable TV, reading lamp, refrigerator, ceiling fan, clock radio and telephone in room. Air conditioning. Fireplace on premises. Antiquing, cross-country skiing, fishing, golf, live theater, parks and shopping nearby.
Location: City.
Certificate may be used: Nov. 1-June 30, Sunday-Thursday nights.

Tacoma   D4

Chinaberry Hill - An 1889 Grand Victorian Inn

302 Tacoma Ave N
Tacoma, WA 98403-2737
(253)272-1282 Fax:(253)272-1335
Internet: www.chinaberryhill.com
E-mail: chinaberry@wa.net

Circa 1889. In the 19th century, this Queen Anne was known as far away as China for its wondrous gardens, one of the earliest examples of landscape gardening in the Pacific Northwest. The home, a wedding present from a husband to his bride, is listed in the National Register. The innkeepers have selected a unique assortment of antiques and collectibles to decorate the manor. The house offers two Jacuzzi suites and a guest room, all eclectically decorated with items such as a four-poster rice bed or a canopy bed. There are two lodging options in the Catchpenny Cottage, a restored carriage house steps away from the manor. Guests can stay either in the romantic carriage suite or the Hay Loft, which includes a bedroom, sitting room, clawfoot tub and a unique hay chute. In the mornings, as the innkeepers say, guests enjoy "hearty breakfasts and serious coffee." Not a bad start to a day exploring Antique Row or Pt. Defiance, a 698-acre protected rain forest park with an aquarium, gardens, beaches and a zoo. Seattle is 30 minutes away.
Innkeeper(s): Cecil & Yarrow Wayman. $110-195. 5 rooms with PB, 1 with FP, 4 suites, 1 cottage and 1 guest house. Breakfast and snacks/refreshments included in rates. Types of meals: Full gourmet bkfst, veg bkfst and early coffee/tea. Beds: Q. Modem hook-up, data port, cable TV, reading lamp, clock radio, telephone, turn-down service, desk, hot tub/spa and fireplace in room. Fax, copier, library and parlor games on premises. Antiquing, art galleries, beach, bicycling, canoeing/kayaking, fishing, golf, hiking, live theater, museums, parks, shopping, wineries, whale-watching, boat tours, dinner train Mount Rainier, Mount Saint Helens, Olympic National Forest and ferries nearby.
Location: City. Six blocks to downtown.
Publicity: News Tribune, Habitat, Olympian, Oregonian, Seattle Magazine, Tacoma Weekly, Sunset Magazine, NW best Places, Best Places to Kiss NW, Recommended Country Inns - Pacific Northwest, Seattle P-I, Seattle Magazine, Tacoma News Tribune, Tacoma Reporter, Tacoma Voice, Romantic Days & Nites in Seattle, Unofficial Guide to Bed & Breakfast - Pacific Northwest and Tacoma Grand Home Tour.

"... the highlight of our trip so far - wonderful ...the company, the food, the accommodations, all the best."
Certificate may be used: November, January-March, Monday-Wednesday. Seven days prior to reservation. Excludes holidays and special events.

Trout Lake   F5

The Farm Bed & Breakfast

490 Sunnyside Rd
Trout Lake, WA 98650-9715
(509)395-2488 Fax:(509)395-2127
Internet: www.thefarmbnb.com
E-mail: farmbnb@gorge.net

Circa 1890. Extraordinary views of Mt. Adams and Mt. Hood instill a quiet serenity at this 1890 wooden farmhouse on six acres. Relax on a deck shaded by aspen and weeping willow trees or sit inside by the fire. Two comfortably furnished guest bedrooms feature antique quilts and furniture, fresh flowers and terry robes. Wake up hungry to fully enjoy the generous country breakfast served in the dining room on family heirloom silver, vintage pewter and crystal. Favorites include Dean's homemade huckleberry pancakes, French toast, 400 Mile

Oatmeal and Dutch Babies served with fresh bacon and sausage from Otto's. The gorgeous grounds with barn and arbor are perfect for dream weddings. Trout Lake Festival of the Arts is hosted here each summer, with juried local artists, live music and regional food and drink. Windsurf at Columbia River Gorge Scenic Area or kayak the White Salmon River.
Innkeeper(s): Rosie & Dean Hostetter. $70-88. 2 rooms. Breakfast, afternoon tea and snacks/refreshments included in rates. Types of meals: Full bkfst, early coffee/tea and lunch. Beds: QDT. Desk and clocks in room. VCR, bicycles, telephone and perennial flower gardens on premises. Antiquing, canoeing/kayaking, cross-country skiing, downhill skiing, fishing, shopping, water sports, wineries, Festival of the Arts in July, white water rafting, mountain climbing at Mt. Adams, Mt. St. Helens and Mt. Rainier nearby.
Location: Country.
Certificate may be used: Oct. 15-May 31.

Wenatchee   D6

Apple Country Bed & Breakfast

524 Okanogan Ave
Wenatchee, WA 98801
(509)664-0400 Fax:(509)664-6448
Internet: www.applecountryinn.com
E-mail: innkeepers@applecountryinn.com

Circa 1920. One of the first houses built in the Okanogan Heights area, this Craftsman home with an inviting front porch has been recently renovated. Stay in a spacious guest bedroom in the main house or in the carriage house that offers a one-bedroom apartment. More than just a morning meal, breakfast is highlighted with delicious entrees and fresh-baked breads. Gourmet candlelight dinners are available for an extra charge. After a day of local skiing, soak in the large hot tub.
Innkeeper(s): Jerry & Sandi Anderson. $65-95. 6 rooms, 4 with PB and 1 cottage. Breakfast included in rates. Types of meals: Full gourmet bkfst, veg bkfst, early coffee/tea, picnic lunch and gourmet dinner. Beds: QD. Modem hook-up, cable TV, reading lamp, stereo, clock radio, telephone and hot tub/spa in room. Air conditioning. Spa, bicycles and large porch on premises. Antiquing, bicycling, canoeing/kayaking, cross-country skiing, downhill skiing, fishing, golf, hiking, museums, parks, shopping, water sports and wineries nearby.
Location: City, mountains.
Publicity: Arlington's and Food 911 - Tyler's Ultimate.
Certificate may be used: Anytime, Sunday-Thursday.

White Salmon   F5

Llama Ranch B&B

1980 Hwy 141
White Salmon, WA 98672-8032
(509)395-2786 Fax:(509)395-2557
E-mail: lama1@gorge.net

Circa 1988. Llamas abound at this unique, picturesque ranch, which affords views of Mt. Adams. Innkeeper Jerry Stone offers nature walks through the woods accompanied by some of their friendly llamas. Jerry also offers the unusual amenity of llama boarding. The White Salmon area, located in between the Mt. Adams Wilderness Area and Columbia Gorge, is full of interesting activities, including white-water rafting, horseback riding and berry picking.
Innkeeper(s): Jerry Stone. $59-99. 7 rooms, 2 with PB. Breakfast included in rates. Types of meals: Country bkfst and early coffee/tea. Beds: Q. TV, VCR, copier, spa, stable, library, parlor games, telephone, fireplace, laundry facility, gift shop, creek, ponds and llamas on premises. Antiquing, art galleries, beach, bicycling, canoeing/kayaking, cross-country skiing, downhill skiing, fishing, golf, hiking, horseback riding, live theater, museums, parks, shopping, tennis, water sports and white water rafting nearby.
Location: Country, mountains.
Certificate may be used: Oct. 1-April 30.

Washington, D.C.

Aaron Shipman House

PO Box 12011
Washington, DC 20005-0911
(202)328-3510 (877)893-3233 Fax:(413)582-9669
Internet: www.aaronshipmanhouse.com
E-mail: reservations@bedandbreakfastdc.com

Circa 1887. This three-story Victorian townhouse was built by Aaron Shipman, who owned one of the first construction companies in the city. The turn-of-the-century revitalization of Washington began in Logan Circle, considered to be the city's first truly residential area. During the house's restoration, flower gardens, terraces and fountains were added. Victorian antiques, original wood paneling, stained glass, chandeliers, as well as practical amenities such as air conditioning and laundry facilities, make this a comfortable stay. There is a furnished apartment available, as well.

Innkeeper(s): Charles & Jackie Reed. $75-175. 6 rooms, 5 with PB, 2 with FP, 1 with HT. Breakfast included in rates. Types of meals: Full bkfst. Beds: QDT. Modem hook-up, data port, TV, clock radio, telephone, desk, fireplace (wood burning or decorative) and some with hot tubs in room. Central air. Library, child care, fireplace and laundry facility on premises. Antiquing, art galleries, bicycling, golf, horseback riding, live theater, museums, shopping, tennis, national monuments, Smithsonian, Washington Convention Center and White House nearby.
Location: City.

"This home was the highlight of our stay in Washington! This was a superb home and location. The Reeds treated us better than family."
Certificate may be used: Sunday-Thursday, Jan. 1-March 15, not valid holiday weekends or special events.

Adams Inn

1744 Lanier Pl NW
Washington, DC 20009-2118
(202)745-3600 (800)578-6807 Fax:(202)319-7958
Internet: www.adamsinn.com
E-mail: adamsinn@adamsinn.com

Circa 1908. These restored town houses have fireplaces, a library and parlor, all furnished home-style, as are the guest rooms. Former residents of this neighborhood include Tallulah Bankhead, Woodrow Wilson and Al Jolson. The Adams-Morgan area is home to diplomats, radio and television personalities and government workers. A notable firehouse across the street holds the record for the fastest response of a horse-drawn fire apparatus. Located in the restaurant area, over 100 restaurants and shops are within walking distance.

Innkeeper(s): Anne Owens. $70-115. 25 rooms, 15 with PB. Breakfast included in rates. Types of meals: Cont plus and early coffee/tea. Beds: QDT. Reading lamp and clock radio in room. Air conditioning.

Parlor games, telephone and fireplace on premises. Antiquing, parks and walking distance to Metro and buses nearby.
Location: City.
Publicity: *Travel Host.*

"We enjoyed your friendly hospitality and the home-like atmosphere. Your suggestions on restaurants and help in planning our visit were appreciated."
Certificate may be used: Dec. 1-March 1, Sunday-Thursday.

The Embassy Inn

1627 16th St Nw
Washington, DC 20009-3063
(202)234-7800 (800)423-9111 Fax:(202)234-3309
Internet: www.embassyinndc.com
E-mail: susandcinns@aol.com

Circa 1910. This restored inn is furnished in a Federalist style. The comfortable lobby offers books and evening sherry. Conveniently located, the inn is seven blocks from the Adams Morgan area of ethnic restaurants. The Embassy's philosophy of innkeeping includes providing personal attention and cheerful hospitality. Concierge services are available. The inn does not have an elevator or parking on site.

Innkeeper(s): Susan Stiles. $79-150. 38 rooms with PB. Breakfast included in rates. Types of meals: Cont plus and snacks/refreshments. Beds: DT. Cable TV, reading lamp, clock radio, telephone and free HBO in room. Air conditioning. Fax, copier and Washington Post daily on premises. Antiquing, live theater, museums, parks and White House nearby.
Location: City.
Publicity: *Los Angeles Times, Inn Times, Business Review and N.Y. Times.*

"When I return to D.C., I'll be back at the Embassy."
Certificate may be used: Anytime, subject to availability.

The Windsor Inn

1842 16th St Nw
Washington, DC 20009-3316
(202)667-0300 (800)423-9111 Fax:(202)667-4503
Internet: www.windsorinndc.com
E-mail: susandcinns.@aol.com

Circa 1910. Recently renovated and situated in a neighborhood of renovated townhouses, the Windsor Inn is the sister property to the Embassy Inn. It is larger and offers suites as well as a small meeting room. The refurbished lobby is in an Art Deco style and a private club atmosphere prevails. It is six blocks to the Metro station at Dupont Circle. There are no elevators or parking on site.

Innkeeper(s): Susan Stiles. $89-199. 45 rooms with PB, 2 suites and 1 conference room. Breakfast included in rates. Types of meals: Cont plus and snacks/refreshments. Beds: QDT. TV, reading lamp, clock radio, telephone and some with refrigerators in room. Air conditioning. Fax, copier and daily Washington Post on premises. Antiquing, live theater and parks nearby.
Location: City.
Publicity: *Los Angeles Times, Inn Times, Sunday Telegram, WCUA Press Release and New York Times.*

"Being here was like being home. Excellent service, would recommend."
Certificate may be used: Anytime, subject to availability.

West Virginia

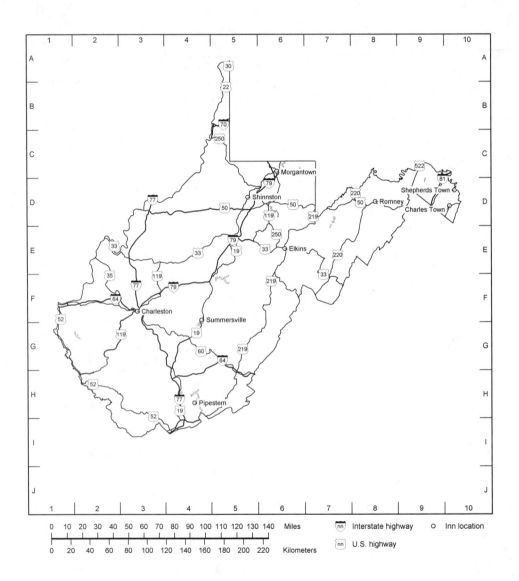

		Miles
0 10 20 30 40 50 60 70 80 90 100 110 120 130 140		

		Kilometers
0 20 40 60 80 100 120 140 160 180 200 220		

nn Interstate highway   o Inn location

nn U.S. highway

Charles Town   D10

Gilbert House B&B of Middleway

PO Box 1104
Charles Town, WV 25414
(304)725-0637
Internet: www.gilberthouse.com
E-mail: gilberthousebb@yahoo.com

Circa 1760. A magnificent graystone of early Georgian design,
the Gilbert House is located in one of the state's oldest European
settlements. Elegant appointments include fine Oriental rugs,
tasteful art and antique furnishings. During restoration, graffiti
found on the upstairs bedroom walls
included an 1832 drawing of the
future President James Polk and a
child's growth chart from the
1800s. The inn is located in the
Colonial era mill village of
Middleway, which contains one of
the country's best collections of log
houses. The village is a mill site on the original settlers' trail into
Shenandoah Valley ("Philadelphia Waggon Road" on Peter
Jefferson's 1755 map of Virginia). Middleway was also the site of
"wizard clip" hauntings during the last decade of the 1700s. The
region was home to members of "Virginia Blues," commanded
by Daniel Morgan during the Revolutionary War.
Innkeeper(s): Bernie Heiler. $110-150. 3 rooms with PB, 2 with FP, 1 suite.
Breakfast included in rates. Types of meals: Full gourmet bkfst. Beds: QT.
Clock radio in room. Air conditioning. TV, VCR, library, parlor games, telephone and fireplace on premises. Antiquing, live theater, parks, shopping,
sports car racing and slots nearby.
Location: 18th-century village.

*"We have stayed at inns for 15 years, and yours is at the top of the
list as best ever!"*

Certificate may be used: At base rate, anytime, Nov. 30-Aug. 15, subject
to availability.

The Washington House Inn

216 S George St
Charles Town, WV 25414-1632
(304)725-7923 (800)297-6957 Fax:(304)728-5150
Internet: www.washingtonhouseinnwv.com
E-mail: emailus@washingtonhouseinnwv.com

Circa 1899. This three-story brick Victorian was built by the
descendants of President Washington's brothers, John Augustine
and Samuel. Carved oak mantels, spacious guest rooms, antique
furnishings and refreshments served on the wraparound veranda
or gazebo make the inn memorable. For business travelers, data
ports are available. Harpers Ferry National Historic Park,
Antietam, and the Shenandoah and Potomac rivers are all within
a 15-minute drive. Thoroughbred racing, slot machines and car
racing are some of the popular area attractions.
Innkeeper(s): Mel & Nina Vogel. $99-175. 7 rooms with PB, 1 suite and 1
conference room. Breakfast and snacks/refreshments included in rates. Types
of meals: Full bkfst and early coffee/tea. Beds: QT. Cable TV, reading lamp,
ceiling fan, clock radio, telephone and desk in room. Air conditioning. VCR,
fax, copier, parlor games, Internet and antiques and collectibles for sale on
premises. Antiquing, fishing, golf, live theater, parks, shopping, water sports,
history, museums, horse racing, car racing and slots nearby.
Location: City.
Publicity: *Washington Post - Feb 03, Good Housekeeping - April 03,
Travel Holiday - May 03, Recreation News - May 03, Woman's Day and
The Today Show.*
Certificate may be used: Sunday-Thursday, Nov. 1-Aug. 31.

Charleston   F3

Benedict Haid Farm

8 Hale St
Charleston, WV 25301-2806
(304)346-1054

Circa 1869. Although no breakfast is served, we couldn't help
including this farm on 350-mountain-top acres because it specializes in raising exotic animals that include llamas, guanacos
and black mountain sheep, as well as donkeys and cows. There
are two rustic cabins for those looking for an economical stay.
Most will prefer the main German-built, hand-hewn log lodge,
which features antique furnishings and a large screened-in deck
with fireplace and hot tub. There is a stocked pond. Bring your
own breakfast.
Innkeeper(s): Bill Pepper. $150-200. 3 rooms and 1 cottage. Beds: D. TV,
reading lamp, clock radio and desk in room. Air conditioning. VCR, bicycles,
parlor games, telephone and fireplace on premises. Cross-country skiing, fishing, horseshoes, croquet and volleyball nearby.
Location: Country, mountains.
Publicity: *Television Travel Show.*

"Like stepping back in time."

Certificate may be used: Anytime, based on availability.

Brass Pineapple B&B

1611 Virginia St E
Charleston, WV 25311-2113
(304)344-0748 (800)CAL-LWVA Fax:(304)344-0748
Internet: www.wvweb.com/brasspineapplebandb
E-mail: pineapp104@aol.com

Circa 1910. Original oak paneling, leaded and stained glass are
among the architectural highlights at this smoke-free inn that
graces the historic district near the Capitol Complex. Guest
bedrooms feature thoughtful amenities including terry robes
and hair dryers as well as technology
for business needs. A full breakfast
consisting of tea, juices, fruit,
muffins, waffles, quiche, basil
tomatoes and cottage fries, is
served in the dining room.
Dietary requirements can be
met upon request.

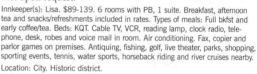

Innkeeper(s): Lisa. $89-139. 6 rooms with PB, 1 suite. Breakfast, afternoon
tea and snacks/refreshments included in rates. Types of meals: Full bkfst and
early coffee/tea. Beds: KQT. Cable TV, VCR, reading lamp, clock radio, telephone, desk, robes and voice mail in room. Air conditioning. Fax, copier and
parlor games on premises. Antiquing, fishing, golf, live theater, parks, shopping,
sporting events, tennis, water sports, horseback riding and river cruises nearby.
Location: City. Historic district.
Publicity: *Mid-Atlantic Country, Country Inns, Gourmet, Charlestonian,
Charleston Daily Mail, Gourmet, Southern Living, Recommended Country
Inns and News 8.*

*"Charming, convenient location, lovely antiques, appealing decor.
Extremely clean; excellent service from Lisa and the staff."*

Certificate may be used: Anytime, except major holidays and vacation periods, subject to availability.

Elkins   E6

Tunnel Mountain B&B

Rt 1, Box 59-1
Elkins, WV 26241-9711
(304)636-1684 (888)211-9123

Circa 1939. Nestled on five acres of wooded land, this three-story Fieldstone home offers privacy in a peaceful setting. Rooms are tastefully decorated with antiques, collectibles and

crafts. Each bedroom boasts a view of the surrounding mountains. The chestnut and knotty pine woodwork accentuate the decor. The fireplace in the large common room is a great place for warming up after a day of touring or skiing. The area is home to a number of interesting events, including a Dulcimer festival and the state's largest festival, the Mountain State Forest Festival.

Innkeeper(s): Anne & Paul Beardslee. $80-90. 3 rooms with PB. Breakfast included in rates. Types of meals: Country bkfst. Beds: QD. Cable TV, reading lamp and clock radio in room. Air conditioning. Parlor games, telephone, fireplace and one great room on premises. Antiquing, art galleries, beach, bicycling, canoeing/kayaking, cross-country skiing, downhill skiing, fishing, golf, hiking, horseback riding, live theater, museums, parks, shopping, sporting events, tennis, water sports, rock climbing and mountain biking nearby.

Location: Mountains.

Publicity: *Blue Ridge Country, Washington Post and WBOY.*

Certificate may be used: November to May, Sunday-Thursday.

Landgraff   H3

Elkhorn Inn & Theatre

PO Box 100
Eckman, WV 24829
(304)862-2031 (800)708-2040 Fax:(304)862-2031
Internet: www.elkhorninnwv.com
E-mail: elisse@elkhorninnwv.com

Circa 1900. Named for the trout-filled Elkhorn Creek that runs behind the inn, this historic Italianate brick building with archways and a balcony on the Coal Heritage Trail has been lovingly restored by Dan and Elisse. Period antiques and 1930s furnishings complement an international art collection. Paintings, prints, ceramics, stained glass, sculpture and textiles are for sale. Stay in a guest bedroom or suite with handmade vintage quilts, clawfoot tubs and bubble baths. A family suite with two adjoining rooms is available. Alto Grande Coffee, offered exclusively at the inn, accompanies a continental breakfast. Located near Pinnacle Rock State Park and Panther State Forest, there are ATV and bike trails on Burke Mountain. McDowell County is also a popular hunting and fishing area.

Innkeeper(s): Elisse & Dan Clark. $55-100. 8 rooms, 2 with PB, 1 two-bedroom suite. Breakfast included in rates. Types of meals: Cont, early coffee/tea, lunch, snacks/refreshments and dinner. Beds: DT. Reading lamp, ceiling fan, clock radio, desk, down quilts and pillows, individual fans and heaters in room. TV, VCR, library, telephone, fireplace, laundry facility, gift shop, balcony and fireplace lounge on premises. Antiquing, canoeing/kayaking, fishing, golf, hiking, live theater, parks, shopping, Pinnacle Rock State Park, Panther State Forest, Blackwolf golf course, Hatfield-McCoy ATV trails, McDowell County trails, stocked trout streams, hunting, summer theatre in Bramwell, outdoor music at Highwall Park, railfan, historic sites, Tamarack, Glade Springs Spa, Winterplace Ski Resort and Beckley Coal Mine Museum nearby.

Location: Country, mountains, waterfront. On Elkhorn Creek, near Pinnacle Rock State Park.

Publicity: *NY Daily News, Charleston Gazette, Charleston Daily Mail, Bluefield Daily Telegraph, Welch News, West Virginia Wild & Wonderful Magazine, Trains Magazine, Blue Ridge Country, The Artists Magazine, ATV Illustrated Magazine, All-Terrain-Vehicle Magazine, Appalachian Journal, WVVA News Channel 6 (NBC), Speed Channel, www.atv.com, www.retreatsonline.com, www.hawk.com, www.trailsheaven.com (Hatfield & McCoy ATV trails) and www.byways.org (Coal Heritage Trail).*

Certificate may be used: Year-round, Sunday-Thursday, subject to availability.

Morgantown   C6

Almost Heaven B&B

391 Scott Ave
Morgantown, WV 26505-8804
(304)296-4007 Fax:(304)296-4007
Internet: www.almostheavenbedandbreakfast.com

Circa 1990. A burgundy-colored door and steps add a hint of color to this white Federal-style house, which is set on two landscaped acres. Inside, guests will find Victorian decor and soft, feather beds. Innkeeper Cookie Coombs prepares a veritable feast for breakfast, with items such as biscuits and gravy, fried potatoes, apple dumplings, fresh fruit and pastries. The inn offers close access to West Virginia University.

Innkeeper(s): Cookie Coombs. $65-150. 5 rooms with PB, 1 suite. Breakfast included in rates. Types of meals: Full bkfst. Beds: KQ. Cable TV, VCR, reading lamp, ceiling fan, clock radio, telephone and desk in room. Air conditioning. Fax, library, parlor games and fireplace on premises. Antiquing, cross-country skiing, fishing, golf, live theater, parks, shopping, sporting events, tennis and water sports nearby.

Location: City, mountains. Woods.

Publicity: *Dominion Post.*

Certificate may be used: Jan. 1-March 15, Sunday-Friday.

Pipestem   H4

Walnut Grove Inn

Hc 78 Box 260
Pipestem, WV 25979-9702
(304)466-6119 (800)701-1237

Circa 1850. Located on 38 acres, this red shingled country farmhouse has a century-old log barn and ancient cemetery with graves of Confederate soldiers and others prior to the Civil War. The farmhouse is decorated eclectically, and the front porch is furnished with rocking chairs and a swing. Swimming, basketball, badminton and horseshoes are available. A gourmet breakfast of biscuits and gravy, fresh eggs and homemade preserves is served in the dining room or screen room.

Innkeeper(s): Mason & Connie Wiley. $80. 5 rooms with PB. Breakfast, afternoon tea and snacks/refreshments included in rates. Types of meals: Full gourmet bkfst and early coffee/tea. Beds: KQDT. Reading lamp and desk in room. Air conditioning. Swimming, parlor games, telephone and fireplace on premises. Antiquing, cross-country skiing, downhill skiing, fishing, live theater, parks, shopping, water sports, whitewater rafting, golf and hiking trails nearby.

Location: Mountains.

Certificate may be used: Weekdays Monday through Thursday, all year; weekdays and weekends, Nov. 1-May 1.

Romney   D8

Hampshire House 1884

165 N Grafton St
Romney, WV 26757-1616
(304)822-7171
Internet: www.hampshirehouse1884.net
E-mail: hhouse@raven-villages.net

Circa 1884. Located near the south branch of the Potomac
River, the garden here has old boxwoods and walnut trees. The
inn features ornate brickwork; tall, narrow windows; and fireplaces with handsome period mantels. A sitting room with a
well-stocked library, a cozy patio
and a music room with an
antique pump organ are favorite
places. On-site massage available. One guest room has been
renovated to allow full wheelchair accessibility.

Innkeeper(s): Jane & Scott Simmons. $85-100. 6 rooms with PB, 3 with FP
and 1 conference room. Breakfast included in rates. Types of meals: Full
bkfst, early coffee/tea and snacks/refreshments. Beds: QDT. Cable TV, VCR,
reading lamp, clock radio and telephone in room. Air conditioning. TV, bicycles, parlor games, fireplace and therapeutic massage on premises. Handicap
access. Antiquing, canoeing/kayaking, fishing, hiking, museums, shopping,
water sports, massage and Civil War museum nearby.

Location: Mountains. South branch Potomac River.

Publicity: *Hampshire Review, Mid-Atlantic Country and Weekend Journal.*

"Your personal attention made us feel at home immediately."

Certificate may be used: November-May 1; weekdays only May 2-Sept. 30
(not honored in October).

Shepherdstown   D10

Thomas Shepherd Inn

PO Box 3634
Shepherdstown, WV 25443
(304)876-3715 (888)889-8952 Fax:(304)876-3313
Internet: www.thomasshepherdinn.com
E-mail: info@thomasshepherdinn.com

Circa 1868. Built as a Lutheran parsonage using Federal architecture, this inn has been renovated to offer gracious hospitality in a traditional style. Spacious common rooms like the large
living room with a fireplace or the book-filled library offer several seating areas with comfortable antique furnishings. The
porch invites quiet relaxation. Appealing guest bedrooms provide a retreat from distractions of phone or television. Savor a
hearty breakfast served family style that may include favorites
like apple cranberry crisp, tomato mushroom and cheese
omelet, local bacon, and poppyseed muffins with homemade
asian pear marmalade.

Innkeeper(s): Jim Ford & Jeanne Muir. $100-150. 6 rooms with PB. Breakfast
included in rates. Types of meals: Full gourmet bkfst, veg bkfst and early cof-
fee/tea. Beds: QD. Reading lamp and clock radio in room. Central air. TV,
VCR, fax, copier, library, parlor games and telephone on premises. Antiquing,
bicycling, canoeing/kayaking, fishing, golf, hiking, horseback riding, live theater, museums, parks, shopping, water sports and wineries nearby.

Location: Small town.

Certificate may be used: November-June, Sunday-Thursday, subject to
availability.

Shinnston   D5

Gillum House Bed & Breakfast

35 Walnut St
Shinnston, WV 26431
(304)592-0177 (888)592-0177 Fax:(304)592-1882
Internet: www.gillumhouse.com
E-mail: relax@gillumhouse.com

Circa 1912. The architectural style of a 1912 house is reflected
in this comfortable inn. Original works of art, painted by the
one of the innkeepers, grace the walls. The second-floor library
offers books to savor and finish reading at home. Antique-filled
guest bedrooms pamper with fresh flowers, candles, Egyptian
cotton or flannel linens, down comforters and fluffy robes.
Breakfast is a healthy, low-fat culinary delight, accented with
locally made maple syrup. The nearby West Fork River Trail
entertains hikers, bicyclists and equestrians.

Innkeeper(s): Kathleen A. Panek. $60-70. 3 rooms and 1 conference room.
Breakfast included in rates. Types of meals: Full bkfst, veg bkfst, early cof-
fee/tea and picnic lunch. Beds: QD. Cable TV, VCR, reading lamp, clock radio
and decorative fireplace in room. Air conditioning. Fax, copier, parlor games,
library, parlor games, telephone, laundry facility, gift shop, overnight stabling
2.5 miles away and escort service provided from I-79 exit on premises.
Antiquing, bicycling, fishing, golf, hiking, museums, parks, shopping, sporting
events, wineries, 9 covered bridges, 7 state parks, Chapel of Perpetual
Adoration, 2 drive-in theaters, several hand-blown glass factories with tours,
historic sites, Mother's Day shrine, rail-trails and birding nearby.

Location: City. 6 miles west of I-79, small city (pop. 2,300).

Publicity: *Pittsburgh Post-Gazette, Clarksburg Exponent-Telegram,
Shinnston News, Akron Beacon Journal, Blue Ridge Outdoors, State
Journal, C-FAX, WBOY, "Inn to Inn Hiking Guide to the Virginias," Off the
Beaten Path- West Virginia, Fourth Edition (vignette), Good Morning West
Virginia and Vol. II.*

Certificate may be used: Anytime, subject to availability, except holidays and
WVU home football weekends.

Summersville   F4

Historic Brock House B&B Inn

1400 Webster Rd
Summersville, WV 26651-1524
(304)872-4887
E-mail: brockhouse@citynet.net

Circa 1890. This Queen Anne farmhouse is the second venture into the bed & breakfast business for innkeepers Margie
and Jim Martin. The exterior looks friendly and inviting, perhaps because of its long history of welcoming guests. The
National Register inn originally served as a hotel and later as a
boarding house. Margie has a degree in design, and her skills
are evident in the cheerful, country rooms. Each of the guest
rooms has a different color scheme and decor. One is decked in
deep blue, another is appointed with flowery bedspreads and
pastel curtains.

Innkeeper(s): Carol Taylor. $70-90. 6 rooms, 4 with PB, 1 suite and 1 con-
ference room. Breakfast, afternoon tea and snacks/refreshments included in
rates. Types of meals: Full gourmet bkfst and early coffee/tea. Beds: QT.
Reading lamp, clock radio and turn-down service in room. Air conditioning.
VCR, fax, library, parlor games, telephone and fireplace on premises.
Antiquing, fishing, live theater, parks, shopping, water sports, white water,
boating and biking nearby.

Location: Mountains.

Certificate may be used: Feb. 1 to Nov. 22, Sunday through Friday.

Wisconsin

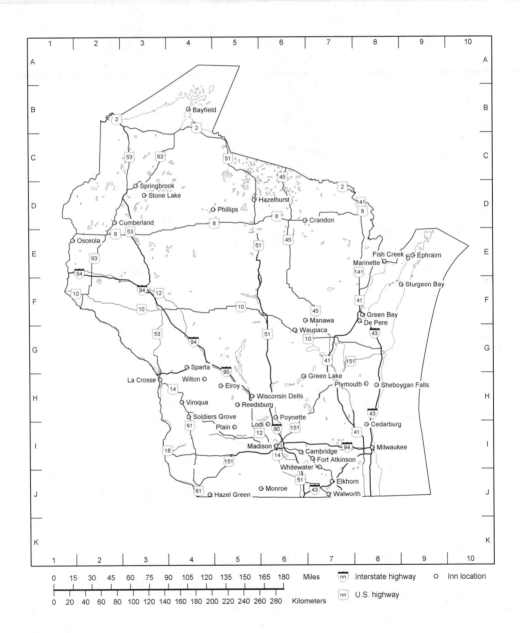

	Miles											
0	15	30	45	60	75	90	105	120	135	150	165	180

	Kilometers														
0	20	40	60	80	100	120	140	160	180	200	220	240	260	280

Interstate highway   O Inn location

U.S. highway

Bayfield   B4

Old Rittenhouse Inn

301 Rittenhouse Ave
Bayfield, WI 54814-0584
(715)779-5111 (800)779-2129
Internet: www.rittenhouseinn.com
E-mail: gourmet@rittenhouseinn.com

Circa 1892. Two historic Queen Anne mansions, a guest house and a private cottage comprise this elegant Victorian inn and gourmet restaurant just a few blocks from downtown. Under massive gables, a wraparound veranda is filled with white wicker furniture, geraniums and petunias. The inn boasts 22 working fireplaces amidst antique furnishings. Well-appointed guest bedrooms and luxury suites offer a variety of romantic amenities that may include whirlpools as well as views of Madeline Island and Lake Superior. The two-story Fountain Cottage is just uphill. For breakfast indulge in baked muffins served with Rittenhouse Jams, Jellies and a cup of coffee accompanied by dishes such as Wild Bayfield Blueberry Crisp or Moonglow Pears Poached in White Zinfandel.

Innkeeper(s): Larry E. Cicero. $99-299. 24 rooms with PB, 19 with FP, 4 suites. Breakfast included in rates. Types of meals: Cont plus, gourmet lunch, gourmet dinner and room service. Restaurant on premises. Beds: KQD. 14 luxury rooms/suites with whirlpool in room. Telephone and fireplace on premises. Handicap access. Shopping nearby.

Location: City.

Publicity: *Wisconsin Trails, Midwest Living, National Geographic Traveler, Country Inns, Minnesota Monthly, Bon Appetit, Gourmet and Better Homes and Gardens.*

"The whole decor, the room, the staff and the food were superb! Your personalities and talents give a great warmth to the inn."

Certificate may be used: Nov. 1 to May 25, Wednesday and Thursday.

Thimbleberry Inn B&B

15021 Pagent Rd, PO Box 1007
Bayfield, WI 54814-1007
(715)779-5757 (800)881-5903 Fax:(715)779-5690
Internet: www.thimbleberryinn.com
E-mail: locey@thimbleberryinn.com

Circa 1992. The waters of Lake Superior sparkle beside the 400-foot shoreline adjacent to this natural wood home. The peaceful forest setting adds to the romance of the rooms, which include fireplaces. Innkeeper Sharon Locey writes a food column and currently is writing her first cookbook. Her culinary expertise makes breakfast a gourmet treat. While enjoying your morning meal, watch for wildlife and bald eagles as they soar over the Loceys' 40 acres. The deck features a cedar hot tub perfect for relaxing after skiing, hiking or just spending the day by the lake's side.

Innkeeper(s): Craig & Sharon Locey. $89-159. 3 rooms with PB, 3 with FP, 1 suite. Breakfast included in rates. Types of meals: Full bkfst and early coffee/tea. Beds: KQ. Reading lamp and clock radio in room. Antiquing, cross-country skiing, downhill skiing, fishing, shopping and sailboat nearby.

Location: Waterfront. On Lake Superior.

Certificate may be used: Jan. 2-May 15, Nov. 1-Dec. 15, Sunday-Thursday.

Cambridge   I6

Covington Manor

W9694 Hwy 12
Cambridge, WI 53523
(608)423-1333 (800)798-7647 Fax:(608)423-9557
Internet: www.covingtonmanorbandb.com
E-mail: donrsimon@msn.com

Circa 1899. Surrounded by gentle hills and lush forests in a small midwestern town, this quaint yet luxurious bed and breakfast offers an idyllic stay. The foyer in the middle of the house leads to a plush parlor, a popular place to read or play chess. Upstairs guest bedrooms and a suite are furnished with family heirlooms and overlook the well-tended gardens or the historic neighborhood. Free long distance phone calls and high-speed Internet access are provided. Gourmet breakfasts are served in the elegant dining room. Lake Ripley is only 5 blocks away to swim or boat. The Fireside Theater is just 15 minutes away. Go for a bike ride on country roads or local trails. Madison and the university are only 20 minutes to the west.

Innkeeper(s): Don & Carol Simon. $95-125. 4 rooms, 3 with PB, 1 two-bedroom suite and 1 conference room. Breakfast and wine included in rates. Types of meals: Full gourmet bkfst, veg bkfst and early coffee/tea. Beds: KQ. Modem hook-up, data port, cable TV, VCR, reading lamp, clock radio, telephone and desk in room. Central air. TV, fax, copier, bicycles, parlor games and fireplace on premises. Antiquing, art galleries, beach, bicycling, canoeing/kayaking, cross-country skiing, fishing, golf, hiking, horseback riding, live theater, parks, shopping, sporting events, tennis and Glacial Drumlin bike trail nearby.

Location: Country. Small village.

Publicity: *We were featured in the Wisconsin State Journal, (November 2003).*

Certificate may be used: Anytime, November-March, Sunday and Monday to Thursday, subject to availability.

Cedarburg   I8

The Washington House Inn

W 62 N 573 Washington Ave
Cedarburg, WI 53012-1941
(262)375-3550 (800)554-4717 Fax:(262)375-9422
Internet: www.washingtonhouseinn.com
E-mail: whinn@execpc.com

Circa 1886. This three-story cream city brick building is in the National Register. Rooms are appointed in a country Victorian style and feature antiques, whirlpool baths, vases of flowers and fireplaces. The original guest registry, more than 100 years old, is displayed proudly in the lobby, and a marble trimmed fireplace is often lit for the afternoon wine and cheese hour. Breakfast is continental and is available in the gathering room, often including recipes from a historic Cedarburg cookbook for items such as homemade muffins, cakes and breads.

Innkeeper(s): Wendy Porterfield. $95-235. 34 rooms with PB, 3 suites and 1 conference room. Breakfast included in rates. Types of meals: Cont plus and snacks/refreshments. Beds: KQD. Cable TV, VCR, reading lamp, ceiling fan, clock radio and telephone in room. Air conditioning. TV, fax, copier and sauna on premises. Antiquing, cross-country skiing, fishing, live theater, parks, shopping and sporting events nearby.

Location: City. Historic district.

Publicity: *Country Home and Chicago Sun-Times.*

Certificate may be used: Sunday-Thursday on $135-$235 rooms, no holidays.

Crandon   **D6**

Courthouse Square B&B

210 E Polk St
Crandon, WI 54520-1436
(715)478-2549 (888)235-1665 Fax:(715)478-2549
Internet: www.courthousesquarebb.com
E-mail: chousebb@charter.net

Circa 1905. Situated on the shores of Surprise Lake, this Victorian Shingle also manages to provide the conveniences of town with its location. The inn features antique and country furnishings, and each of its guest rooms offers a lake or park view. The area provides excellent antiquing and shopping opportunities, in addition to cross-country and downhill skiing. Visitors also enjoy borrowing a bike to explore the town, relaxing on the inn's porch or venturing across the street to a city park.

Innkeeper(s): Les & Bess Aho. $62-70. 3 rooms, 1 with PB. Breakfast included in rates. Types of meals: Full gourmet bkfst, early coffee/tea, afternoon tea and snacks/refreshments. Beds: QDT. Reading lamp, ceiling fan, clock radio, desk, fresh flowers and sweets in room. VCR, parlor games, telephone and fireplace on premises. Antiquing, cross-country skiing, downhill skiing, fishing, parks, shopping and water sports nearby.

Location: Waterfront. Small town.

Certificate may be used: Sunday to Thursday, year-round, except holidays & special events.

Cumberland   **D2**

The Rectory

1575 Second Ave
Cumberland, WI 54829
(715)822-3151
E-mail: therectory@chibardun.net

Circa 1904. This city's unique island setting makes it an ideal stopping point for those exploring the state's lake-rich Northwest. The German Gothic inn, once home to the parish priest, features charming guest rooms, all filled with antiques, heirlooms and items of interest. The Mae Jenet Room, with its striking corner turret, features a doll collection and other unique toys. Breakfasts, served in the roomy parlor, often feature the inn's famous Breakfast Pie. A gaming casino is nearby, and 50 lakes are found within a 10-mile radius of Cumberland.

Innkeeper(s): Ethel Anderson. $75-85. 4 rooms, 2 with PB. Reading lamp, ceiling fan, desk and two with whirlpool tub in room. VCR, telephone, fireplace, piano and garage on premises. Antiquing, cross-country skiing, live theater and shopping nearby.

Location: City. Island.

Certificate may be used: Sunday-Thursday, excluding holidays and special events.

De Pere   **F8**

James St. Inn

201 James St
De Pere, WI 54115-2562
(920)337-0111 (800)897-8483 Fax:(920)337-6135
Internet: www.jamesstreetinn.com
E-mail: jamesst@netnet.net

Circa 1995. An old flour mill on the Fox River is the foundation for this wonderful inn. The comfortable great room is a relaxing place to enjoy a glass of wine with the region's legendary cheese. Spacious waterfront suites feature excellent views and lavish amenities for leisure or business needs; plus,

six penthouse suites were added recently. A generous continental-plus breakfast is served daily.

Innkeeper(s): Kevin Flatley & Joan Hentges. $69-219. 36 rooms with PB, 4 with FP, 32 suites and 1 conference room. Breakfast and snacks/refreshments included in rates. Types of meals: Cont plus and early coffee/tea. Beds: Q. Cable TV, VCR, reading lamp, refrigerator, clock radio, telephone, desk, hot tub/spa, decks over the river and data port on phones in room. Air conditioning. Fax, copier, parlor games and fireplace on premises. Handicap access. Amusement parks, antiquing, cross-country skiing, fishing, live theater, parks, shopping, sporting events and water sports nearby.

Location: Waterfront. Riverfront, historic downtown.

Publicity: *Midwest Living, Newmonth, Green Bay Press-Gazette* and WLUK-*Gastank Getaway.*

Certificate may be used: Jan. 1-April 30 and Nov. 1-Dec. 31, Sunday-Friday.

Elkhorn   **J7**

Ye Olde Manor House

N7622 US Hwy 12
Elkhorn, WI 53121-2758
(262)742-2450 Fax:(262)742-2425
Internet: www.yeoldmanorhouse.com
E-mail: markson@elknet.net

Circa 1905. Located on three tree-shaded acres, this country manor house offers travelers all the simple comforts of home. The guest rooms, living room and dining room are decorated with a variety of antiques and comfortable furniture that inspires a family atmosphere. One room offers a porch and views of Lauderdale Lakes. The B&B offers a full gourmet breakfast each morning.

Innkeeper(s): Stuart & Carolyn Markson. $60-120. 4 rooms, 2 with PB, 1 suite and 1 conference room. Breakfast included in rates. Types of meals: Full gourmet bkfst and early coffee/tea. Beds: QDT. Cable TV, reading lamp and clock radio in room. VCR, fax, copier, parlor games, telephone and fireplace on premises. Antiquing, cross-country skiing, downhill skiing, fishing, golf, live theater, parks, shopping and water sports nearby.

Location: Country.

Certificate may be used: Nov. 1 to March 31, anytime subject to availability; April 1 to Oct. 31, Sunday-Thursday, subject to availability.

Elroy   **H5**

East View B&B

33620 County P Rd
Elroy, WI 53929
(608)463-7564
Internet: www.outspokinadventures.com/eastview
E-mail: eastview@elroynet.com

Circa 1994. This comfortable ranch house offers splendid views of the countryside, with its rolling hills covered with woods. Autumn is a particularly scenic time for a visit, when the trees explode in color. The three guest rooms are simply furnished in a homey, country style with quilts topping the beds. Each room offers a pleasing view. Breakfast comes in several courses, with fresh fruit, homemade breads, a daily entree and finally a dessert. The area provides opportunities for hiking, biking, canoeing or browsing at local craft stores.

Innkeeper(s): Dom & Bev Puechner. $75. 3 rooms with PB. Breakfast included in rates. Types of meals: Full bkfst and early coffee/tea. Beds: QD. Reading lamp, ceiling fan, clock radio, telephone and turn-down service in room. Air conditioning. Walking trails on premises. Amusement parks, antiquing, cross-country skiing, golf and shopping nearby.

Location: Country.

Publicity: *Country Inns and Midwest Living Magazine.*

"What a wonderful treat it was to stay at East View. The view was magnificent and the breakfasts superb."

Certificate may be used: Anytime, subject to availability.

Ephraim   E9

Hillside Hotel B&B

9980 Hwy 42, PO Box 17
Ephraim, WI 54211-0017
(920)854-2417 (800)423-7023 Fax:(920)854-4240
Internet: www.hillsidehotel.com
E-mail: dmcneil@itol.com

Circa 1854. In the National Register, this Victorian country house is the last remaining "grand hotel" of the turn-of-the-century hotels in the area. On the waterfront, Hillside provides views of Eagle Harbor and Green Bay from most of the rooms and the 100-foot veranda. There is a private beach and moorings for small craft. Guest rooms feature antiques, feather beds and four-poster beds. Afternoon tea is offered with scones, petit fours and tea breads, while eggs Benedict is often found on the breakfast menu along with specialty items found locally.

Innkeeper(s): David & Karen McNeil. $79-94. 12 rooms, 2 with FP, 2 cottages and 1 conference room. Breakfast and afternoon tea included in rates. Types of meals: Full gourmet bkfst. Beds: QD. Reading lamp, ceiling fan, turn-down service, (fireplace, clock, AC and refrigerator in cottages) in room. VCR, fax, copier, swimming, parlor games, telephone, fireplace, private beach and small boat moorings available on premises. Amusement parks, antiquing, cross-country skiing, fishing, golf, live theater, parks, shopping, sporting events, tennis, water sports, world-class galleries and musical events nearby.

Location: Waterfront.

Publicity: *Milwaukee Journal, Chicago Tribune and Wisconsin Restaurant Magazine.*

"You have a very nice inn and the breakfasts were great. You all made us feel at home (without the chores) and it was like we'd known you for a long time."

Certificate may be used: Nov. 1 to May 1, Sunday-Friday.

Fish Creek   E9

Thorp House Inn & Cottages

4135 Bluff Ln, PO Box 490
Fish Creek, WI 54212
(920)868-2444
Internet: www.thorphouseinn.com
E-mail: innkeeper@thorphouseinn.com

Circa 1902. Every season surrounds this bed & breakfast inn and its cottages with a natural beauty. Listed in the National Register, an extensive restoration has preserved details like authentic lighting and documentary wallcoverings. Fine antique furnishings and accessories accented with European lace enhance the gracious

ambiance. Relax in the library or by the fire in the double parlor. Warm hospitality is enjoyed on the summer sitting porch with refreshments from the stocked pantry. Choose a well-appointed guest bedroom or stay in one of the

quaint country cottages. A beach house is also available.

Innkeeper(s): Christine & Sverre Falck-Pedersen. $95-195. 5 rooms with PB and 6 cottages. Types of meals: Cont plus and early coffee/tea. Beds: KQDT. Reading lamp, refrigerator, three with whirlpool and two with fireplace in room. Central air. Parlor games, telephone and fireplace on premises. Antiquing, cross-country skiing, fishing, live theater, parks, shopping, water sports, summer art school and music festival nearby.

Location: Small village.

Publicity: *Green Bay Press-Gazette, Milwaukee Journal/Sentinel, McCall's, Minnesota Monthly and Madison PM.*

"Amazing attention to detail from restoration to the furnishings. A very first-class experience."

Certificate may be used: Sunday through Thursday nights, Nov. 6 through May, holidays excluded.

Fort Atkinson   I7

Lamp Post Inn

408 S Main St
Fort Atkinson, WI 53538-2231
(920)563-6561
Internet: www.thelamppostinn.com
E-mail: info@wbba.org

Circa 1878. Prepare to enjoy an authentic Victorian experience at this charming, restored home. Innkeepers Debra and Mike Rusch get into the spirit of things by donning Victorian attire. Each of the guest rooms includes a working Victrola, which guests are encouraged to use and enjoy. Debra and Mike pamper guests with fresh flowers and chocolates. Rooms are furnished completely with antiques. Breakfasts include specialties such as jelly-filled muffins, scones, Swedish puff pancakes and strawberry sorbet.

Innkeeper(s): Debra & Mike Rusch. $70-110. 3 rooms, 2 with PB. Breakfast included in rates. Types of meals: Full gourmet bkfst, early coffee/tea, picnic lunch, afternoon tea and snacks/refreshments. Beds: D. VCR, reading lamp, telephone and Jacuzzi in room. Air conditioning. Parlor games and fireplace on premises.

Location: Small town.

Certificate may be used: Sunday through Thursday, excluding holidays.

Green Bay   F8

The Astor House B&B

637 S Monroe Ave
Green Bay, WI 54301-3614
(920)432-3585 (888)303-6370
Internet: www.astorhouse.com
E-mail: astor@execpc.com

Circa 1888. Located in the Astor Historic District, the Astor House is completely surrounded by Victorian homes. Guests have their choice of five rooms, each uniquely decorated for a range of ambiance, from the Vienna Balconies to the Marseilles Garden to the Hong Kong Retreat. The parlor, veranda and many suites feature a grand view of City Centre's lighted church towers. This home is also the first and only B&B in Green Bay and received the Mayor's Award for Remodeling and Restoration.

Business travelers should take notice of the private phone lines in each room, as well as the ability to hook up a modem.

Innkeeper(s): Greg & Barbara Robinson. $120-159. 5 rooms with PB, 4 with FP, 3 suites. Breakfast included in rates. Types of meals: Cont plus. Beds: KQDT. Cable TV, VCR, reading lamp, stereo, refrigerator, clock radio, telephone, gas fireplaces and double whirlpool tub (4 of 5 rooms) in room. Air conditioning. Amusement parks, antiquing, cross-country skiing, fishing, live theater, parks, shopping, sporting events and water sports nearby.

Location: City.

Publicity: *Chicago Sun-Times and Corporate Reports.*

Certificate may be used: Anytime, Sunday-Thursday, subject to availability.

Green Lake   H6

McConnell Inn

497 S Lawson Dr
Green Lake, WI 54941-8700
(920)294-6430 (888)238-8625
Internet: www.mcconnellinn.com
E-mail: info@mcconnellinn.com

Circa 1901. This stately home features many of its original features, including leaded windows, woodwork, leather wainscoting and parquet floors. Each of the guest rooms includes beds covered with handmade quilts and clawfoot tubs. The grand, master suite comprises the entire third floor and boasts 14-foot vaulted beam ceilings, Victorian walnut furnishings, a Jacuzzi and six-foot oak buffet now converted into a unique bathroom vanity. Innkeeper Mary Jo Johnson, a pastry chef, creates the wonderful pastries that accompany an expansive breakfast with fresh fruit, granola and delectable entrees.

Innkeeper(s): Mary Jo Johnson and Scott Johnson. $60-175. 5 rooms with PB, 2 with FP, 1 suite. Breakfast included in rates. Types of meals: Full gourmet bkfst and early coffee/tea. Beds: KQ. TV, VCR, reading lamp, refrigerator, ceiling fan, clock radio and hot tub/spa in room. Central air. Library, parlor games and telephone on premises. Antiquing, art galleries, beach, bicycling, canoeing/kayaking, cross-country skiing, fishing, golf, hiking, horseback riding, live theater, museums, parks, shopping, sporting events, tennis and water sports nearby.

Certificate may be used: November-April.

Hazel Green   J4

Wisconsin House Stagecoach Inn

2105 Main, PO Box 71
Hazel Green, WI 53811-0071
(887)854-2233
Internet: www.wisconsinhouse.com
E-mail: wishouse@mhtc.net

Circa 1846. Located in southwest Wisconsin's historic lead mining region, this one-time stagecoach stop will delight antique-lovers. The spacious two-story inn once hosted Ulysses S. Grant, whose home is just across the border in Illinois. One of the inn's guest rooms bears his name and features a walnut four-poster bed. Don't miss the chance to join the Dischs on a Saturday evening for their gourmet dinner, served by reservation only.

Innkeeper(s): Ken & Pat Disch. $75-125. 8 rooms, 6 with PB, 2 suites. Breakfast included in rates. Types of meals: Full gourmet bkfst, early coffee/tea and gourmet dinner. Beds: KQDT. Air conditioning. Copier, library, parlor games and telephone on premises. Antiquing, bicycling, cross-country skiing, downhill skiing, fishing, live theater and parks nearby.

Location: City.

Publicity: *Travel & Leisure, Milwaukee Magazine, Chicago Magazine, Milwaukee Journal and Wisconsin Trails.*

Certificate may be used: May through October anytime, rooms with shared baths only. Other months all rooms available.

Hazelhurst   D5

Hazelhurst Inn

6941 Hwy 51
Hazelhurst, WI 54531
(715)356-6571
E-mail: hzhrstbb@newnorth.net

Circa 1969. Situated in the scenic Northwoods, this country inn graces 18 wooded acres that are adjacent to the Bearskin State Trail. Outdoor enthusiasts appreciate the hiking, swimming, fishing, golfing, hunting, snowmobiling, cross-country skiing, horseback riding, boating and the many other activities the area offers. Enjoy a hearty breakfast each morning after a peaceful night's rest in a comfortable guest bedroom. Families are welcome here. Soak up the view from the sitting room or just relax by the fire.

Innkeeper(s): Sharon Goetsch. $60-70. 4 rooms, 1 with PB. Breakfast included in rates. Types of meals: Country bkfst. Beds: Q. Reading lamp, ceiling fan and clock radio in room. VCR, pet boarding, telephone and fireplace on premises. Antiquing, beach, bicycling, canoeing/kayaking, cross-country skiing, fishing, golf, hiking, horseback riding, live theater, museums, shopping, tennis and water sports nearby.

Location: Northwoods.

Certificate may be used: Anytime, subject to availability.

La Crosse   H3

Chateau La Crosse

410 Cass St
La Crosse, WI 54601-4508
(608)796-1090 (800)442-7969 Fax:(608)796-0700
Internet: www.visitor-guide.com/chateaulacrosse
E-mail: chateaulax@aol.com

Circa 1854. Enter a personal fairy tale when you visit this inviting yet stately stone castle. A destination unto itself, it is the oldest stone house in the state that has been continuously occupied since it was built. In the National Register, the finely crafted interior offers elegant fireplaces, gleaming woodwork and elaborately detailed wood floors, renovated at a cost of more than $1 million. Relax in the elegant common rooms, which include a main parlor, drawing room, dining room, library and music room. If it's a special occasion, request the Master Bedroom to enjoy its masterful hand-painted mural ceiling and faux-painted marble walls complete with gold leaf trim. There's a marble wood-burning fireplace, as well. The bath boasts marble floors and a tub of faux marble with a hand-painted mural of cherubs. The gardens offer a fountain, pond and variety of flowering trees such as a Japanese lilac tree. Red hibiscus, lilac, potted palms, elephant ears, hydrangeas and an arbor with roses completes the garden. A full champagne breakfast includes dishes such as quiche, cinnamon toast, French cashew waffles and usually a breakfast dessert such as cheesecake or peach pie. A gourmet restaurant on the premises offers six private dining rooms.

Innkeeper(s): JoAn Lambert Smith. $125-225. 7 rooms with PB and 1 conference room. Breakfast included in rates. Types of meals: Full gourmet bkfst, veg bkfst, early coffee/tea, gourmet lunch, picnic lunch, afternoon tea, snacks/refreshments, gourmet dinner and room service. Beds: KQ. Modem hook-up, data port, cable TV, reading lamp, stereo, ceiling fan, clock radio, telephone, coffeemaker, desk and hot tub/spa in room. Air conditioning. VCR, fax, copier, spa, library, parlor games, fireplace, laundry facility and full champagne breakfast on premises. Handicap access. Antiquing, art galleries, beach, bicycling, canoeing/kayaking, cross-country skiing, downhill skiing, fishing, golf, hiking, live theater, museums, parks, shopping, sporting events and tennis nearby.

Location: City.

Publicity: *LaCrosse Tribune and Home & Garden.*

Certificate may be used: Jan. 2-April 30, (except Feb. 14), Sunday-Thursday, discount is taken off full rate, breakfast not included.

Lodi   I6

Prairie Garden B&B

W13172 Hwy 188
Lodi, WI 53555
(608)592-5187 (800)380-8427 Fax:(608)592-5853
Internet: www.prairiegarden.com
E-mail: prairiegarden@prairiegarden.com

This 19th-century farmhouse offers four guest rooms, each decorated in a pleasant Victorian style. Innkeeper Todd Olson includes family pictures and his aunt's artwork within the decor. In the mornings, he or partner Dennis Stocks, deliver a delicious homemade breakfast to their guests' rooms. The B&B is closed to many attractions, including skiing, a nude beach, a casino, winery and Lake Wisconsin.

Innkeeper(s): Todd Olson & Dennis Stocks. $55-115. 5 rooms, 1 with PB. Breakfast and afternoon tea included in rates. Types of meals: Full bkfst. Beds: D. Cable TV, reading lamp, ceiling fan, clock radio, turn-down service and hot tub/spa in room. Air conditioning. VCR, fax, spa, stable, bicycles, parlor games, telephone and fireplace on premises. Handicap access. Amusement parks, antiquing, cross-country skiing, downhill skiing, fishing, golf, live theater, parks, shopping, sporting events, tennis and water sports nearby.

Location: Country.

Publicity: *In Step Newsmagazine.*

Certificate may be used: Nov. 1 through April 30, Sunday through Thursday.

Victorian Treasure Inn

115 Prairie St
Lodi, WI 53555-1240
(608)592-5199 (800)859-5199 Fax:(608)592-7147
Internet: www.victoriantreasure.com
E-mail: innkeeper@victoriantreasure.com

Circa 1897. Victorian Treasure features seven individually decorated guest rooms spread among two 19th-century Queen Anne Victorians. The interiors boast stained- and leaded-glass windows, pocket doors, rich restored woods and expansive porches. Five suites include a whirlpool tub, fireplace, wet bar, TV/VCR and stereo. Guests are greeted with a wine and cheese reception. Full, gourmet breakfasts may include specialties such as eggs Florentine, herb vegetable quiche, or stuffed French toast topped with a seasonal fruit sauce. Guests enjoy hiking along the National Scenic Ice Age Trail which passes beside the inn.

Innkeeper(s): Renee & Eric Degelau. $119-249. 7 rooms with PB, 4 with FP, 4 two-bedroom and 2 three-bedroom suites and 1 conference room. Breakfast, afternoon tea, snacks/refreshments and wine included in rates. Types of meals: Full gourmet bkfst, veg bkfst, early coffee/tea and room service. Beds: Q. Modem hook-up, data port, cable TV, VCR, reading lamp, stereo, refrigerator, ceiling fan, snack bar, clock radio, telephone, coffeemaker, turn-down service, desk, hot tub/spa, fireplace and six with whirlpools in room. Central air. Fax, copier, library, parlor games, gift shop and gift shop on premises. Antiquing, art galleries, beach, bicycling, canoeing/kayaking, cross-country skiing, downhill skiing, fishing, golf, hiking, horseback riding, live theater, museums, parks, shopping, sporting events, tennis, water sports, eagle watching, Taliesin, House on the Rock, Frank Lloyd Wright, Ice Age Trail and Wollersheim winery nearby.

Location: Small Victorian town.

Publicity: *Recommended Romantic Inns, Wisconsin State Journal, Chicago*

Sun-Times, Milwaukee Magazine, Wisconsin Trails, Victorian Homes and Country Inn Cooking with Gail Greco.

"An elegant, romantic getaway that everyone wants to return to again and again."

Certificate may be used: Sunday-Thursday, November-March, excluding holidays, subject to availability.

Madison   I6

Arbor House, An Environmental Inn

3402 Monroe St
Madison, WI 53711-1702
(608)238-2981
Internet: www.arbor-house.com

Circa 1853. Nature-lovers not only will enjoy the inn's close access to a 1,280-acre nature preserve, they will appreciate the innkeepers' ecological theme. Organic sheets and towels are offered for guests as well as environmentally safe bath products. Arbor House is one of Madison's oldest existing homes and features plenty of historic features, such as romantic reading chairs and antiques, mixed with modern amenities and unique touches. Five guest rooms include a whirlpool tub and three have fireplaces. The Annex guest rooms include private balconies. The innkeepers offer many amenities for business travelers, including value-added corporate rates. The award-winning inn has been recognized as a model of urban ecology. Lake Wingra is within walking distance as are biking and nature trails, bird watching and a host of other outdoor activities. Guests enjoy complimentary canoeing and use of mountain bikes.

Innkeeper(s): John & Cathie Imes. $125-230. 8 rooms with PB, 3 with FP, 1 suite and 1 conference room. Breakfast included in rates. Types of meals: Full bkfst. Beds: KQ. Cable TV, VCR, reading lamp, stereo, ceiling fan, clock radio, telephone and desk in room. Air conditioning. Fax, copier, sauna and fireplace on premises. Handicap access. Antiquing, cross-country skiing, fishing, parks, shopping, sporting events and water sports nearby.

Location: City.

Publicity: *Money Magazine, Coop America, E, New York Times, Natural Home and Offspring.*

"What a delightful treat in the middle of Madison. Absolutely, unquestionably, the best time I've spent in a hotel or otherwise. B&Bs are the only way to go! Thank you!"

Certificate may be used: November-April, Sunday-Thursday, excluding holidays (John Nolen and Cozy Rose guest rooms only).

Manawa   F6

Lindsay House

539 Depot St # 304
Manawa, WI 54949-9562
(920)596-3643
Internet: www.lindsayhouse.com
E-mail: lhbandb@netnet.net

Circa 1892. Built for a prominent local businessman in 1892, this Queen Anne Victorian has been extensively restored. The original woodwork, leaded glass windows and open staircase are accented by antiques and an authentic 19th-century decor. Central heating and air conditioning are modern comforts to appreciate. Relax in one of the elegant parlors. Overlook the front lawn while staying in The Gracious Oak Room or the peaceful backyard gardens from the Secret Garden Room. Enjoy the sunny view of Lindsay Park from The Rose Room. Savor a gourmet breakfast served in the formal dining room. The Little Wolf River and surrounding area offer many outdoor activities.

Innkeeper(s): Judith & Patrick Burkhart. $60-75. 4 rooms with PB. Breakfast and snacks/refreshments included in rates. Types of meals: Full gourmet bkfst and early coffee/tea. Beds: QD. Reading lamp, clock radio and telephone in room. Air conditioning. VCR, child care and parlor games on premises. Antiquing, cross-country skiing, fishing, golf, parks, tennis and eAA (Oshkosh) nearby.

Location: Small town.

Certificate may be used: Dec. 1 to March 30, Sunday-Saturday.

Marinette   E8

Lauerman Guest House

1975 Riverside Ave
Marinette, WI 54143-1218
(715)732-7800 Fax:(715)732-7800
Internet: explorewisconsin.com/lauermanguesthouseinn
E-mail: lauermanguesthouseinn@juno.com

Circa 1910. Regarded as one of the Midwest's most beautiful examples of Colonial Revival architecture, this lavish mansion is an elegant inn that combines modern amenities and impeccable service with traditional surroundings. It was recently restored to reflect its original grace as well as modern conveniences. Gorgeous guest bedrooms with ten-foot ceilings boast a rich decor with period furnishings and family heirlooms. The honeymoon suite features a huge balcony overlooking the Menominee River. A full breakfast is included daily. A buffet lunch is available Tuesday through Friday at a very reasonable rate. Courtesy transportation is provided from the Twin Country Airport.

$85-125. 6 rooms with PB and 1 conference room. Breakfast included in rates. Types of meals: Full bkfst. Restaurant on premises. Beds: QDT. Cable TV, reading lamp, clock radio, desk, hot tub/spa and fireplace in room. Air conditioning. Telephone and fireplace on premises. Limited handicap access. Antiquing, beach, bicycling, canoeing/kayaking, fishing, golf, hiking, live theater, museums, parks, shopping, tennis and water sports nearby.

Location: City. On Manominee River.

Publicity: *Eagle Herald.*

Certificate may be used: Sunday-Thursday nights, Nov. 1-April 30, subject to availability.

Milwaukee   I8

The Brumder Mansion

3046 W Wisconsin Ave
Milwaukee, WI 53208
(414)342-9767 (866)793-3676 Fax:(414)342-4772
Internet: www.brumdermansion.com
E-mail: brumder@execpc.com

Circa 1910. Built in the English Arts & Crafts style, this majestic brick home with Victorian and Gothic elements is furnished with elegant antiques. Common rooms feature huge oak fireplaces and exquisite woodwork, like the foyer's massive Gothic oak stairway. The lavish parlor's comfortable chairs invite relaxation, and the library has a large selection of games, magazines and books. A friendly atmosphere is enhanced with complimentary wine or beverages and homemade snacks or chocolates. Spacious guest bedrooms offer romantic settings with decorative painting and fine linens. Three suites include a double whirlpool, exquisite marble showers, CD player and TV/VCR. Enjoy the many flowers and view of the boulevard from the front porch.

Innkeeper(s): Carol & Bob Hirschi. $79-215. 5 rooms with PB, 3 with FP, 3 suites and 1 conference room. Breakfast and snacks/refreshments included in rates. Types of meals: Cont plus, veg bkfst and early coffee/tea. Beds: KQT.

Cable TV, VCR, reading lamp, CD player, ceiling fan, clock radio, hot tub/spa, fireplace and 3 with whirlpools in room. Central air. Fax, copier, spa, library, parlor games, telephone and fireplace on premises. Antiquing, art galleries, beach, live theater, museums, parks, shopping, sporting events, water sports and wineries nearby.

Location: City.

Publicity: *Milwaukee Magazine and HBO.*

Certificate may be used: Sunday-Thursday, Jan. 2-May 15, except Valentine's Day.

Monroe   J5

Victorian Garden B&B

1720 16th St
Monroe, WI 53566-2643
(608)328-1720 (888)814-7909
Internet: apu.com/vicgard

Circa 1890. The original charm of this blue and white three-story Victorian home still remains today. Antiques and collectibles are found throughout the house, along with a vintage doll and teddy bear collection. Wraparound porches and flower gardens are great for relaxing.
Accommodations include the White Lace and Roses Suite featuring a clawfoot tub and shower for two. The Rosebud Room overlooks the hand-carved Italian fountain, and the Ivy Room is a quiet corner setting. A full breakfast is served in the formal dining room. Local attractions include the Monroe Depot and historic square. Come stay and visit with us, the pleasure is all ours.

Innkeeper(s): Judy & Ron Marsh. $89-109. 3 rooms with PB. Breakfast included in rates. Types of meals: Full bkfst. Beds: QD. Air conditioning. Antiquing, bicycling, cross-country skiing, fishing, golf, hiking, parks and sporting events nearby.

Location: City.

Certificate may be used: Dec. 1-March 31, excluding Dec. 24-Jan. 2, subject to availability, no holidays.

Osceola   E1

St. Croix River Inn

305 River St, PO Box 356
Osceola, WI 54020-0356
(715)294-4248 (800)645-8820
Internet: www.stcroixriverinn.com
E-mail: innkeeper@stcroixriverinn.com

Circa 1908. Timeless elegance is imparted at this meticulously restored stone house that blends old world charm with new world luxuries. Indulge in dramatic vistas from this gorgeous setting on the bluffs of the river. A comfortable ambiance embraces this inn where complimentary coffee is always found in the sitting room. There is also a wine and beverage bar. Select a book or game from the enter-
tainment closet. Videos and CDs are also available for use in the private suites that all feature a fireplace and a hydromassage tub. A sumptuous breakfast served to each room is highlighted with spectacular views of the water.

Innkeeper(s): Vicki LaBelle. $100-200. 6 suites. Breakfast and snacks/refreshments included in rates. Types of meals: Full gourmet bkfst and early coffee/tea. Beds: Q. Cable TV, VCR, reading lamp, stereo, refrigerator, snack bar, clock radio, telephone, coffeemaker, hot tub/spa, fireplace, ultimate bathing experience with premier Acryline tubs and wine in room. Central air. Deck on premises. Handicap access. Antiquing, beach, bicycling, canoeing/kayaking, cross-country skiing, downhill skiing, golf, hiking, live theater, parks, shopping, water sports, snowmobile trails, scenic train ride, dinner cruises, dog sledding, spa services, casino and fine dining nearby.

Location: Country, waterfront.

Publicity: *Chicago Sun-Times, Skyway News and St. Paul Pioneer Press.*

Certificate may be used: Nov. 30 to April 30, Sunday-Thursday.

Phillips   D5

East Highland School House B&B

West 4342, Hwy D
Phillips, WI 54555
(715)339-3492

Circa 1905. Guests are invited to ring the bell at this restored one-room schoolhouse. An addition to the building in 1920 features rooms with rustic exposed beams, brick walls and original light fixtures. Innkeepers Jeanne and Russ Kirchmeyer filled the home with family antiques and turn-of-the-century pieces. Lacy curtains, doilies and hand-hooked rugs lend to the romantic, country atmosphere. Two museums featuring a 1900s kit area, school area and old logging and farming tools have been added to the inn; one in the basement and one in the barn across the street. The kitchen, which once served as a stage for the school, is now where Jeanne prepares the expansive morning meals.

Innkeeper(s): Russ & Jeanne Kirchmeyer. $55-70. 4 rooms. Breakfast included in rates. Types of meals: Full bkfst.

Certificate may be used: Year-round, weekends if available.

Plain   I5

Bettinger House Bed & Breakfast

PO Box 243
Plain, WI 53577
(608)546-2951 Fax:(608)546-2951
Internet: www.bettingerbnb.com
E-mail: bhbb@charter.net

Circa 1904. This two-story brick inn once was home to the town's midwife, (and the innkeeper's grandmother) who delivered more than 300 babies here. The current innkeepers are just as eager to bring new guests into their home. The Elizabeth Room, named for the midwife, boasts a round king-size bed and private bath. Lavish country breakfasts often include potatoes dug from the innkeeper's off-site farm, sour cream cucumbers, breakfast pie with eggs and sausage, rhubarb coffeecake and sorbet. Area attractions are plentiful, including the House on the Rock, St. Anne's Shrine and the Wisconsin River. Be sure to visit the nearby Cedar Grove Cheese Factory.

Innkeeper(s): Jim & Marie Neider. $60-80. 5 rooms, 3 with PB. Breakfast and snacks/refreshments included in rates. Types of meals: Country bkfst. Beds: KQT. Reading lamp and ceiling fan in room. Central air. TV, VCR, library and parlor games on premises. Antiquing, art galleries, beach, bicycling, canoeing/kayaking, cross-country skiing, downhill skiing, fishing, golf, hiking, horseback riding, live theater, parks, shopping, tennis and wineries nearby.

Location: Country. Village.

Certificate may be used: Sunday through Thursday, year-round.

Plymouth   H8

Yankee Hill Inn B&B

405 Collins St
Plymouth, WI 53073-2361
(920)892-2222
Internet: www.yankeehillinn.com
E-mail: yankee@excel.net

Circa 1870. Two outstanding examples of 19th-century architecture comprise this inn, one a striking Italianate Gothic listed in the National Register, and the other a Queen Anne Victorian with many custom touches. Between the two impressive structures, visitors will choose from 12 spacious guest rooms, featuring antique furnishings and handmade quilts. Visitors can walk to downtown, where they will find an antique mall, shopping and fine dining.

Innkeeper(s): Peg Stahlman. $80-111. 12 rooms with PB. Breakfast included in rates. Types of meals: Full bkfst and early coffee/tea. Beds: QD. Reading lamp and clock radio in room. VCR, telephone and fireplace on premises. Antiquing, cross-country skiing, fishing, shopping, bicycling and hiking nearby.

Location: Small city.

Publicity: *Wisconsin Country Life, Milwaukee Journal, Plymouth Review and Wisconsin Trails.*

"You have mastered the art of comfort. All the perfect little touches make this a dream come true. I only regret that we cannot stay forever."

Certificate may be used: Nov. 1-April 30, anytime except holidays or holiday weekends. May 1-Oct. 31, Monday through Thursday only.

Poynette   H6

Jamieson House

407 N Franklin St
Poynette, WI 53955-9490
(608)635-4100 Fax:(608)635-2292
Internet: www.Jamiesonhouse.com
E-mail: jamhouse@execpc.com

Circa 1879. Victorian elegance and proximity to recreational activities and sightseeing attractions help bring enthusiastic guests to this inn, which consists of three different structures. A main house, guest house and schoolhouse are furnished with antiques gathered from the entire Midwest. Four of the rooms have whirlpool tubs, and the inn's breakfast fare is noteworthy. Water sports are just a few miles away on Lake Wisconsin, and Baraboo's Circus World Museum, Madison and the Wisconsin Dells are within easy driving distance.

Innkeeper(s): Heidemarie Hutchison. $85-165. 12 rooms with PB, 1 with FP, 3 suites and 1 conference room. Breakfast included in rates. Types of meals: Full gourmet bkfst, veg bkfst and early coffee/tea. Restaurant on premises. Beds: KQT. Cable TV, VCR, reading lamp, CD player, refrigerator, clock radio, telephone, coffeemaker, desk and hot tub/spa in room. Central air. Fax, copier, spa, bicycles, library, parlor games and fireplace on premises. Amusement parks, antiquing, art galleries, beach, bicycling, canoeing/kayaking, cross-country skiing, downhill skiing, fishing, golf, hiking, horseback riding, live theater, museums, parks, shopping, sporting events, water sports and wineries nearby.

Location: Small Village.

Publicity: *Capital Times, North West News, Poynette Press and Midwest Living.*

Certificate may be used: Sunday-Thursday, anytime, excluding holidays.

Reedsburg   H5

Parkview B&B

211 N Park St
Reedsburg, WI 53959-1652
(608)524-4333 Fax:(608)524-1172
Internet: www.parkviewbb.com
E-mail: info@parkviewbb.com

Circa 1895. Tantalizingly close to Baraboo and Spring Green, this central Wisconsin inn overlooks a city park in the historic district. The gracious innkeepers delight in tending to their guests' desires and offer wake-up coffee and a morning paper. The home's first owners were in the hardware business, so there are many original, unique fixtures, in addition to hardwood floors, intricate woodwork, leaded and etched windows and a suitors' window. The downtown business district is just a block away.

Innkeeper(s): Tom & Donna Hofmann. $75-90. 4 rooms, 2 with PB, 1 with FP. Breakfast and snacks/refreshments included in rates. Types of meals: Full gourmet bkfst, veg bkfst and early coffee/tea. Beds: QT. Reading lamp, CD player, refrigerator, ceiling fan, clock radio and 1 with fireplace in room. Central air. TV, fax and parlor games on premises. Antiquing, art galleries, bicycling, canoeing/kayaking, cross-country skiing, downhill skiing, fishing, golf, hiking, horseback riding, live theater, parks, shopping, wineries and state parks nearby.

Location: City. Population of 8,500 people.

Publicity: *Reedsburg Report and Reedsburg Times-Press.*

"Your hospitality was great! You all made us feel right at home."

Certificate may be used: Sunday-Thursday, May 1-Oct. 31, holidays not included anytime remainder of year.

Sheboygan Falls   H8

The Rochester Inn

504 Water St
Sheboygan Falls, WI 53085-1455
(920)467-3123 Fax:(920)467-9729
Internet: www.rochesterinn.com
E-mail: info@rochesterinn.com

Circa 1848. This Greek Revival inn is furnished with Queen Anne Victorian antiques, wet bars and four-poster beds. The most romantic offerings are the 600-square-foot suites. They include living rooms with camel back couches and wing back chairs on the first floor and bedrooms with double whirlpool tubs on the second floor. Sheboygan Falls is one mile from the village of Kohler.

Innkeeper(s): Sean & Jacquelyn O'Dwanny. $109-170. 6 rooms, 5 with HT, 6 total suites, including 5 two-bedroom suites. Breakfast and snacks/refreshments included in rates. Types of meals: Full gourmet bkfst, early coffee/tea and afternoon tea. Beds: Q. Data port, cable TV, VCR, reading lamp, refrigerator, clock radio, telephone, coffeemaker, desk, hot tub/spa and whirlpool in room. Central air. Laundry facility on premises. Antiquing, art galleries, beach, bicycling, canoeing/kayaking, cross-country skiing, fishing, golf, hiking, horseback riding, parks, shopping, tennis, water sports, black Wolf Run, Whistling Straits and Kohler nearby.

Location: Small town.

Certificate may be used: Sunday-Thursday, Nov. 1-May 1, some restrictions apply.

Soldiers Grove   H4

Old Oak Inn & Acorn Pub

500 Church Street
Soldiers Grove, WI 54655-9777
(608)624-5217
Internet: www.oldoakinn.com
E-mail: oldoak@mwt.net

Circa 1900. Guests will find lodging and dining at this spacious Queen Anne Victorian turreted inn, a mile from town. Beautiful etched and stained glass and woodcarving dominate the interior, while the guest rooms boast antique-style furnishings and imported woodwork. The area is well-known for its antiquing, cross-country skiing and fishing, and many visitors just enjoy soaking up the abundant local scenery. The inn's facilities make it a natural location for meetings and receptions, and it also is popular with those celebrating anniversaries.

Innkeeper(s): Karen Kovars. $48-62. 7 rooms. Types of meals: Full gourmet bkfst, early coffee/tea, gourmet lunch, picnic lunch, afternoon tea, snacks/refreshments and gourmet dinner. Restaurant on premises. Beds: KDT. Cable TV in room. Air conditioning. VCR, telephone and fireplace on premises. Antiquing, cross-country skiing, downhill skiing, fishing, parks, shopping and water sports nearby.

Location: Small town.

Certificate may be used: Nov. 1-March 1, anytime; March 1-Oct. 31, Sunday through Thursday, with reservations.

Sparta   G4

The Franklin Victorian Bed & Breakfast

220 E Franklin St
Sparta, WI 54656-1804
(608)366-1427 (888)594-3822 Fax:(608)366-1226
Internet: www.franklinvictorianbb.com
E-mail: innkeeper@franklinvictorianbb.com

Circa 1900. Escape to this Victorian treasure located in the Hidden Valleys of Southwestern Wisconsin. This area is considered to be the Bicycling Capital of America and the famous Elroy-Sparta state biking trail is nearby. Relax with a book and a homemade treat from the bottomless cookie jar. In the early evening, enjoy a wine and cheese reception. Guest bedrooms are elegant and spacious retreats. After a scrumptious full breakfast, adventures await. Explore Amish country, go hiking, experience Warren Cranfest, cranberry harvesting and an abundance of water and snow sports. This all-season inn offers year-round activities. Ask about Murder Mystery Weekends. Bike storage and shuttles are provided.

Innkeeper(s): Jennifer & Steve Dunn. $80-120. 4 rooms with PB, 1 with FP, 1 suite and 1 conference room. Breakfast included in rates. Types of meals: Full bkfst, early coffee/tea and snacks/refreshments. Beds: KQ. Reading lamp, CD player, ceiling fan, clock radio, coffeemaker, turn-down service, hot tub/spa and fireplace in room. Air conditioning. TV, VCR, parlor games and telephone on premises. Antiquing, art galleries, beach, bicycling, canoeing/kayaking, cross-country skiing, downhill skiing, fishing, golf, hiking, horseback riding, museums, parks, shopping, sporting events, tennis and water sports nearby.

Location: City.

Publicity: *La Crosse Tribune.*

Certificate may be used: Anytime, November-March, subject to availability.

Justin Trails Resort

7452 Kathryn Ave
Sparta, WI 54656-9729
(608)269-4522 (800)488-4521 Fax:(608)269-3280
Internet: www.justintrails.com
E-mail: info@justintrails.com

Circa 1920. Do as little or as much as desired during a visit to this B&B resort in a peaceful valley surrounded by forested hills that invites daydreaming while lounging in an Amish bentwood rocker on private decks, or makes dreams come true of hiking, cross-country skiing, snowshoeing, bird watching, disc golfing and so much more. Cabins and 1920s farmhouse suites feature two-person whirlpool tubs and fireplaces. Kathryn's Room is the first-floor corner garden view room offering easy access to a common area with a coffeemaker, microwave and refrigerator. Enjoy Donna's hearty farm breakfasts that can be delivered to the cabins. The Justin Trails Eatery is open by advance reservation for lunch or dinner made with local produce.

Innkeeper(s): Don & Donna Justin. $100-350. 6 rooms with PB, 5 with FP, 2 suites, 1 cottage, 1 guest house, 2 cabins and 1 conference room. Breakfast included in rates. Types of meals: Full bkfst and veg bkfst. Beds: KQT. Cable TV, VCR, reading lamp, stereo, refrigerator, ceiling fan, clock radio, coffeemaker, fireplace and microwave in room. Central air. Fax, copier, spa, library, pet boarding, telephone, gift shop, snowshoe trails, cross-country skiing, disc golf, massage, and dogsledding on premises. Limited handicap access. Antiquing, bicycling, canoeing/kayaking, cross-country skiing, downhill skiing, fishing, golf, hiking, horseback riding, museums, parks, shopping and Amish country nearby.

Location: Country.

Publicity: *Milwaukee Journal/Sentinel, Wisconsin Trails, Travel America, Family Fun, Family Life and Midwest Living and Chicago Tribune.*

Certificate may be used: Nov. 1-June 30, Monday-Thursday, except holidays.

Springbrook   D3

The Stout Trout B&B

W4244 County F
Springbrook, WI 54875-9801
(715)466-2790

Circa 1900. Located on 40 acres of rolling, wooded countryside, The Stout Trout overlooks a lily-ringed bay on Gull Lake. The lake can be viewed from the living room, dining areas and second-floor guest rooms. The inn features wood-plank floors, folk art, classic prints and country-style furniture. Homemade jams and maple syrup are served.

Innkeeper(s): Kathleen Fredricks. $80-85. 4 rooms with PB. Breakfast included in rates. Types of meals: Full bkfst. Beds: QD. Reading lamp in room. TV and telephone on premises. Antiquing, cross-country skiing, fishing, shopping and sporting events nearby.

Location: Waterfront.

Publicity: *Chicago Tribune, Wisconsin West Magazine and Wisconsin State Journal.*

"Thank you again for the comfortable setting, great food and gracious hospitality!"

Certificate may be used: Nov. 1-May 30, Sunday through Thursday.

Stone Lake   D3

Lake House

5793 Division (on The Lake)
Stone Lake, WI 54876
(715)865-6803
E-mail: tweldon@win.bright.net

Circa 1917. This bed & breakfast is the oldest building in town and began its life as a hotel in Stone Lake's downtown area. Several years later, it was moved to its present lakeside location. Innkeepers Maxine Mashek and Terri Weldon renovated the homes interior, decorating it with antiques. There are plenty of places to relax, including common  areas with fireplaces, a porch or on the deck overlooking the water. In addition to the B&B, there is an art gallery on the premises, featuring works of local artists.

Innkeeper(s): Maxine Mashek & Terri Weldon. $55-75. 4 rooms, 2 with PB, 1 with FP. Breakfast and afternoon tea included in rates. Types of meals: Full gourmet bkfst and early coffee/tea. Beds: QD. VCR, reading lamp, stereo, refrigerator, ceiling fan, clock radio and desk in room. Air conditioning. Fax, swimming, bicycles, library, parlor games, telephone and fireplace on premises. Handicap access. Amusement parks, antiquing, cross-country skiing, downhill skiing, fishing, golf, live theater, parks, shopping and water sports nearby.

Location: Waterfront.

Publicity: *Four Seasons.*

Certificate may be used: March 1 through June 15, Sunday through Thursday.

Sturgeon Bay   F9

Inn at Cedar Crossing

336 Louisiana St
Sturgeon Bay, WI 54235-2422
(920)743-4200 Fax:(920)743-4422
Internet: www.innatcedarcrossing.com
E-mail: innkeeper@innatcedarcrossing.com

Circa 1884. This historic hotel, in the National Register, is a downtown two-story brick building that once housed street-level shops with second-floor apartments for the tailors, shopkeepers and pharmacists who worked below. The upstairs, now guest rooms, is decorated with rich fabrics and wallpapers and fine antiques. The Anniversary Room has a mahogany bed, fireplace and double whirlpool tub. The Victorian-era dining room and pub, both with fireplaces, are on the lower level. The waterfront is three blocks away.

Innkeeper(s): Steve and Kelly Helmann. $75-190. 9 rooms with PB, 6 with FP. Breakfast and snacks/refreshments included in rates. Types of meals: Full gourmet bkfst, early coffee/tea, lunch, picnic lunch, gourmet dinner and room service. Restaurant on premises. Beds: KQ. Cable TV, VCR, reading lamp, clock radio, telephone, double whirlpool tubs and some fireplaces in room. Air conditioning. TV, fax, copier, library, parlor games and fireplace on premises. Antiquing, cross-country skiing, downhill skiing, fishing, live theater, parks, shopping, water sports, art galleries and great biking nearby.

Publicity: *New Month, New York Times, Chicago Sun-Times, Country Inns, Bon Appetit, Gourmet, Green Bay Press Gazette, Midwest Living, Milwaukee Journal, Wisconsin Trails, Conde Nast Traveler and Select Registry.*

"The second-year stay at the inn was even better than the first. I couldn't have found a more romantic place."

Certificate may be used: November through April, Sunday through Thursday (excludes holiday stays).

The Reynolds House B&B

111 So 7th Ave
Sturgeon Bay, WI 54235
(920)746-9771 (877)269-7401 Fax:(920)746-9441
Internet: www.reynoldshousebandb.com
E-mail: jsekula@reynoldshousebandb.com

Circa 1900. A three-story, red-roofed Queen Anne Victorian house, the Reynolds House is painted in two shades of teal and yellow with white trim on its balustrades and brackets. Leaded-glass windows and a stone veranda that wraps around the front of the house are features. Rooms are cheerfully decorated and offer antique beds, attractive bed coverings and wallpapers. Tucked under the gable, the Winesap Suite includes a whirlpool, sitting room and fireplace. The innkeeper's kitchen garden furnishes fresh herbs to accent breakfast dishes, as well as flowers for the table.

Innkeeper(s): Heather Hull. $65-165. 4 rooms with PB, 3 with FP, 1 suite. Breakfast and snacks/refreshments included in rates. Types of meals: Full gourmet bkfst and early coffee/tea. Beds: Q. Cable TV, ceiling fan, clock radio and some with whirlpool in room. Central air. TV, VCR, fax, copier, library, parlor games, telephone and fireplace on premises. Antiquing, art galleries, beach, bicycling, cross-country skiing, fishing, golf, hiking, horseback riding, live theater, museums, parks, shopping, tennis and wineries nearby.

Location: City.

Publicity: *Door County Magazine, Midwest Living Magazine (Voted Best in the Midwest June 2001 & 2003) and Arrington Inn Traveler's (Best Breakfast 2004).*

"Sometimes the last minute things in life are the best!"

Certificate may be used: Nov. 1 through April 30, Monday-Thursday.

Scofield House B&B

PO Box 761
Sturgeon Bay, WI 54235-1849
(920)743-7727 (888)463-0204 Fax:(920)743-7727
Internet: www.scofieldhouse.com
E-mail: scofldhs@charterinternet.net

Circa 1902. Mayor Herbert Scofield, prominent locally in the lumber and hardware business, built this late-Victorian house with a sturdy square tower and inlaid floors that feature intricate borders patterned in cherry, birch, maple, walnut, and red and white oak. Oak moldings throughout the house boast raised designs of bows, ribbons, swags and flowers. Equally lavish decor is featured in the guest rooms with fluffy flowered comforters and cabbage rose wallpapers highlighting romantic antique bedsteads. Baked apple-cinnamon French toast is a house specialty. Modern amenities include many suites with fireplaces and double whirlpools. "Room at the Top" is a sky-lit 900-square-foot suite occupying the whole third floor and furnished with Victorian antiques.

Innkeeper(s): Mike & Carolyn Pietrek. $84-220. 6 rooms with PB, 5 with FP. Breakfast and afternoon tea included in rates. Types of meals: Full gourmet bkfst. Beds: Q. Cable TV, VCR, reading lamp, stereo, refrigerator, ceiling fan, clock radio and double whirlpools in room. Air conditioning. TV, fax, copier, parlor games, telephone, fireplace and free movie library on premises. Antiquing, cross-country skiing, downhill skiing, fishing, live theater, parks, shopping, sporting events and water sports nearby.

Location: Surrounded by 250 miles of shoreline.

Publicity: *Innsider, Glamour, Country, Wisconsin Trails, Green Bay Press Gazette, Chicago Tribune, Milwaukee Sentinel-Journal, Midwest Living, Victorian Decorating & Lifestyle, Country Inns and National Geographic Traveler.*

"You've introduced us to the fabulous world of B&Bs. I loved the porch swing and would have been content on it for the entire weekend."

Certificate may be used: Monday-Thursday, Nov. 15-April 30.

White Lace Inn

16 N 5th Ave
Sturgeon Bay, WI 54235-1795
(920)743-1105 (877)948-5223
Internet: www.WhiteLaceInn.com
E-mail: romance@whitelaceinn.com

Circa 1903. The romantic White Lace Inn is composed of four beautifully restored Victorian houses connected by meandering garden paths. Inviting rooms and suites offer fine antiques and ornate Victorian or canopy beds. The inn's suites include oversized whirlpool baths, fireplaces, white linens, down comforters and many other amenities. Often the site for romantic anniversary celebrations, a favorite suite has a two-sided fireplace, magnificent walnut Eastlake bed, English country fabrics and a whirlpool. Lemonade or hot chocolate and cookies are offered upon arrival. In the morning, the delectable offerings include items such as cherry apple crisp and creamy rice pudding. Year-round activities invite frequent visits — the Festival of Blossoms, the Lighthouse Walk, Cherry Festival and the Classic Wooden Boat event, for instance. Take museums and gallery strolls, and enjoy the area's great restaurants.

Innkeeper(s): Dennis & Bonnie Statz. $70-235. 18 rooms with PB, 15 with FP, 5 suites. Breakfast included in rates. Types of meals: Full bkfst. Beds: KQ. 12 with whirlpool tubs and 9 with fireplace and whirlpool in room. Handicap access. Antiquing, cross-country skiing, fishing, live theater and water sports nearby.

Publicity: *Milwaukee Sentinel, Brides, National Geographic Traveler, Wisconsin Trails, Milwaukee, Country Home and Midwest Living.*

""Each guest room is an overwhelming visual feast, a dazzling fusion of colors, textures and beautiful objects. It is one of these rare gems that established a tradition the day it opened." — Wisconsin Trails

Certificate may be used: Sunday through Thursday, Nov. 1-April 30 with some restrictions, at "high season" rate.

Viroqua H4

Viroqua Heritage Inn B&B's

217 & 220 E Jefferson St
Viroqua, WI 54665
(608)637-3306 (888)443-7466
Internet: www.herinn.com
E-mail: rhodsent@mwt.net

Circa 1890. Considered to be "much, much more than a great night's sleep," this inn offers distinctive lodging in two adjacent 1890s landmark homes in the scenic Hidden Valley Region. These restored Victorian-era architectural jewels showcase gorgeous woodwork, ornate fireplaces and mantles, leaded beveled windows, hardwood floors, spectacular staircases, crystal chandeliers and gasoliers. The baby grand piano in the parlor music room once belonged to silent movie star Coleen Moore. Antique furnishings include a Russian guest bedroom. The Eckhart House boasts a renovated two-room suite with pocket doors and enclosed porch. Breakfast is served by innkeeper Nancy at each guest's desired and chosen time in the Boyle House formal dining room, curved front porch or balcony overlooking the garden.

Innkeeper(s): Nancy Rhodes. $60-120. 8 rooms, 6 with PB, 2 with FP, 1 with WP. Breakfast included in rates. Types of meals: Full bkfst and early coffee/tea. Beds: KQD. TV, reading lamp, clock radio, telephone, coffee pots and one with whirlpool bath in room. Air conditioning. VCR, bicycles, library, child care, parlor games, fireplace, refrigerator, exercise club, whirlpool tub, organic cooking and healing and nurturing spa on premises. Antiquing, cross-country skiing, downhill skiing, fishing, live theater, parks, shopping, water sports, Amish shopping and community built city park nearby.

Location: Wisconsin "Main Street" Town.

Publicity: *Smithsonian Magazine, Readers' Digest and Milwaukee Magazine.*

"Wonderful house, great hosts."

Certificate may be used: Anytime, November-April, subject to availability.

Walworth   J7

Arscott House B&B

PO Box 875, 241 S Main
Walworth, WI 53184-0875
(262)275-3233

Circa 1903. Built by a master carpenter at the turn of the century, this turreted Queen Anne Victorian has been lovingly restored to its original stylings. A new addition is the inn's Arizona Apartment, with Southwestern decor, a spacious sitting room, kitchen and a private, outside entrance. A roomy front porch and two outside decks are favorite relaxing spots, and a full breakfast is available to guests. The inn is just minutes from Lake Geneva's many attractions.

Innkeeper(s): Valerie C. Dudek. $55-200. 2 rooms. Breakfast included in rates. Types of meals: Full bkfst and early coffee/tea. Beds: QDT. Cable TV, VCR, reading lamp, ceiling fan, clock radio, turn-down service, front porch and two decks in room. Air conditioning. Telephone, video library and bike rental on premises. Antiquing, cross-country skiing, downhill skiing, fishing, live theater, parks, shopping, water sports and skydiving nearby.

"Enjoyed your gracious hospitality. Loved the breakfast. Loved your house. We'll be back again. Thank you for making our first anniversary such an enjoyable one."

Certificate may be used: Nov. 1 to April 30, Sunday-Friday.

Waupaca   G6

Crystal River Inn B&B

E1369 Rural Rd
Waupaca, WI 54981-8246
(715)258-5333 (800)236-5789 Fax:(715)258-5310
Internet: www.crystalriver-inn.com
E-mail: crystalriverinn@charter.net

Circa 1853. The stately beauty of this historic Greek Revival farmhouse is rivaled only by its riverside setting. Each room features a view of the water, garden, woods or all three. A Victorian gazebo, down comforters and delicious breakfasts, with pecan sticky buns, a special favorite, add to guests' enjoyment. A recent addition to the inn's offerings include a newly restored historic cottage. With luxurious decor it includes two bedrooms, a living room with fireplace and private porches. It may be reserved singly or together. Exploring the village of Rural, which is in the National Register, will delight those interested in bygone days. Recreational activities abound, with the Chain O'Lakes and a state park nearby.

Innkeeper(s): Lois Sorenson. $68-138. 7 rooms, 5 with PB, 4 with FP, 2 cottages and 1 conference room. Breakfast and snacks/refreshments included in rates. Types of meals: Full bkfst and early coffee/tea. Beds: KQ. TV, reading

lamp, ceiling fan, clock radio, telephone, desk, hot tub/spa and fireplace in room. Central air. VCR, fax and copier on premises. Limited handicap access. Antiquing, art galleries, beach, canoeing/kayaking, cross-country skiing, downhill skiing, golf, hiking, parks, shopping, sporting events, tennis and water sports nearby.

Location: Waterfront. 23 Lakes.

Publicity: *Resorter, Stevens Point Journal, Wisconsin Trails Magazine, Fox Cities Magazine and Appleton Post Crescent.*

"It was like being king for a day."

Certificate may be used: Anytime, subject to availability.

Walkers Barn B&B

E1268 Cleghorn Rd
Waupaca, WI 54981
(715)258-5235 (800)870-0737 Fax:(715)258-5235
Internet: www.walkersbarn.com
E-mail: hospitality@walkersbarn.com

Circa 1985. Three acres surround this country house with a log facade. The inn boasts interiors of barn-board walls and Amish furnishings and quilts. For instance, there are some hand-crafted bedsteads including a four-poster. A large stone fireplace in the living room and woodland views from the dining room enhance the country setting. Dutch pancakes with apple topping and maple butter is a favorite breakfast item. Nearby are antique shops, art galleries, streams for canoeing and back roads for cycling.

Innkeeper(s): Bob & Linda Yerkes. $75-120. 4 rooms with PB, 3 with FP. Breakfast included in rates. Types of meals: Full bkfst and early coffee/tea. Beds: QT. Reading lamp, ceiling fan, clock radio and turn-down service in room. Air conditioning. VCR, telephone and fireplace on premises. Antiquing, cross-country skiing, fishing, golf, parks, shopping and water sports nearby.

Location: Rural.

Certificate may be used: Sept. 1 to June 15, Sunday-Thursday and Nov. 1 to May 1, subject to availability.

Windmill Manor B&B

N2919 Hwy Qq
Waupaca, WI 54981
(920)698-2650 Fax:(715)256-1770
Internet: www.windmill-manor.com
E-mail: windmillmanor@aol.com

Circa 1891. Casual elegance is found at this restored farmhouse with its namesake windmill sitting atop a water tower constructed by the original owner. Eight acres of tranquil beauty and peaceful surroundings enhance a relaxing stay. The sound-insulated guest bedrooms and suite feature fireplaces, Jacuzzi tubs and private balconies with fantastic views. A former caterer, innkeeper Jan creates scrumptious culinary delights for breakfast. An assortment of activity packages are offered, ask about the popular Mystery Weekend.

Innkeeper(s): Jan, Amy & Brian Koch. $85-135. 5 rooms with PB. Types of meals: Full bkfst. Air conditioning. Antiquing, cross-country skiing, fishing, golf, shopping, biking, hiking and boating nearby.

Certificate may be used: Oct. 1-May 1, Sunday-Friday.

Whitewater   I7

Victoria-On-Main B&B

622 W Main St
Whitewater, WI 53190-1855
(262)473-8400
E-mail: viconmain@sbcglobal.net

Circa 1895. This graceful Queen Anne Victorian, shaded by a
tall birch tree, is in the heart of Whitewater National Historic
District, adjacent to the University of Wisconsin. It was built
for Edward Engebretson, mayor of Whitewater. Yellow tulip and
sunny daffodils fill the spring flower beds, while fuchsias and
geraniums bloom in summertime behind a
picket fence. The inn's gables, flower-filled
veranda and three-story turret feature a
handsome green tin roof. Each guest
room is named for a Wisconsin hardwood. The Red Oak Room, Cherry
Room and Bird's Eye Maple Room all
offer handsome antiques in their cor-
responding wood, Laura Ashley
prints, antique sheets, pristine heirloom-laced pillowcases and
down comforters. A hearty breakfast is sometimes served on
the wraparound veranda, and there are kitchen facilities available for light meal preparation. Whitewater Lake and Kettle
Moraine State Forest are five minutes away.

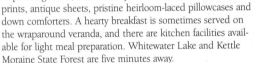

Innkeeper(s): Nancy Wendt. $85-95. 3 rooms, 1 with PB, 1 with FP.
Breakfast included in rates. Types of meals: Full bkfst and early coffee/tea.
Beds: D. Reading lamp and ceiling fan in room. Air conditioning. Telephone
on premises. Antiquing, cross-country skiing, fishing, live theater, parks,
shopping and water sports nearby.

Location: City.

"We loved it. Wonderful hospitality."

Certificate may be used: June through September and January, Sunday
through Thursday.

Wilton   H4

Rice's Whispering Pines B&B

Rt 2 Box 225
Wilton, WI 54670-9606
(608)435-6531

Circa 1896. Guests will find this pleasant place for a getaway.
There are 60 acres surrounding the main farmhouse, ensuring
tranquility during one's stay. Tucked behind the century-old
farmhouse are a bright red barn and grain elevators, adding to
the rural setting. Although not a working farm, the property
has chickens and horses. The comfortable home has been in
the Rice family for three generations. There are three guest
rooms, decorated in a homey country style. One room has a
wilderness scene on the wall behind the white iron and brass
bed. In another room, a swash of fabric, decorated with cream-
colored tassels, is draped at the headboard of the bed, which
rests on a backdrop of a tree. The third room offers two twin
beds, a queen-size bed and a day bed, all dressed in coordinating fabrics. The homestay is close to Amish communities and
the Elroy-Sparta Bicycle Trail.

Innkeeper(s): Bill & Marilyn Rice. $60-70. 3 rooms. Breakfast included in
rates. Types of meals: Full bkfst and early coffee/tea. Beds: QT. Reading lamp
in room. Air conditioning. Telephone on premises. Antiquing, cross-country
skiing, downhill skiing, fishing, parks and shopping nearby.

Location: Country. Hills and valleys.

Publicity: *Summer Fun.*

"We loved the peace and quiet of Whispering Pines."

Certificate may be used: Nov. 1 to March 30, Sunday-Monday, seven days
a week.

Wisconsin Dells   H5

Bowman's Oak Hill Bed and Breakfast

4169 State Hwy 13
Wisconsin Dells, WI 53965
(608)253-5638 (888)253-5631
Internet: bowmansoakhillbedandbreakfast.com
E-mail: bowmansoakhillbb@aol.com

Circa 1969. Thirteen acres of country peacefulness surround
this estate with lawns, gardens, fields and a cottage ranch home
built in the 1960s. This smoke-free, adult retreat is "where
comfort comes with your key." Relaxation is easy on the front
porch wicker furniture or three-season sun porch. Sit in wing-
backed chairs and watch a movie from the video library in the
living room. Afternoon and evening snacks and refreshments
are offered. Air-conditioned guest bedrooms boast family heirloom furniture, sitting areas and cozy robes. Fresh fruit
smoothies are a house specialty for breakfast that includes a
hot egg dish and warm baked goods or pancakes. An outdoor
covered swing and sitting areas provide romantic settings. Walk
in the woods, play croquet or a game of horseshoes.

Innkeeper(s): David and Nancy Bowman. $75-105. 3 rooms, 2 with PB.
Breakfast and snacks/refreshments included in rates. Types of meals: Full
gourmet bkfst, veg bkfst and early coffee/tea. Beds: QD. Reading lamp, ceiling fan, clock radio, turn-down service, desk, antiques, two comfortable
chairs and quilts in room. Air conditioning. TV, VCR, library, parlor games and
telephone on premises. Amusement parks, antiquing, art galleries, bicycling,
canoeing/kayaking, cross-country skiing, downhill skiing, fishing, golf, hiking,
horseback riding, live theater, museums, parks, shopping, water sports and
wineries nearby.

Location: Country. One mile from the center of the River District downtown.

Publicity: *Ad-lit publications.*

Certificate may be used: November-May excluding Memorial Day Weekend,
Sunday-Thursday, subject to availability.

Historic Bennett House

825 Oak St
Wisconsin Dells, WI 53965-1418
(608)254-2500
Internet: www.historicbennetthouse.com
E-mail: richobermeyer@ad-lit.com

Circa 1863. This handsomely restored Greek Revival-style
home, framed by a white picket fence, once housed the Henry
Bennetts. Mr. Bennett's work, displayed in the Smithsonian, is
noted for being the first stop-action photography. His family
recently donated the Bennett photographic studio, located in
town, to the state. It will open as a museum, the ninth historical site in Wisconsin. The National Register home is decorated
in European and Victorian styles and its flower-filled grounds
offer sun and shade gardens.

Innkeeper(s): Gail & Rich Obermeyer. $70-95. 3 rooms, 1 with PB, 1 suite.
Breakfast included in rates. Types of meals: Full gourmet bkfst and early cof-
fee/tea. Beds: QD. Cable TV, VCR, reading lamp, ceiling fan, clock radio,
designer bedding, antiques and armoires in room. Air conditioning. TV,
library, parlor games, telephone, fireplace, gardens, fountain, benches and
picnic table on premises. Amusement parks, antiquing, cross-country skiing,
downhill skiing, live theater, parks, shopping, water sports, river tours, museums, crane and eagles, casino, greyhound racing and Indian mounds nearby.

Location: City.

Publicity: *Milwaukee Journal, Wisconsin State Journal, Midwest Living, Country Life and Travel & Leisure.*

"We felt we were visiting relatives for the weekend and the visit was too short."

Certificate may be used: October through May, Sunday through Thursday.

Terrace Hill B&B

922 River Rd
Wisconsin Dells, WI 53965-1423
(608)254-4724 (800)482-4724
Internet: www.terracehillbb.com
E-mail: info@terracehillbb.com

Circa 1900. A park borders one edge of this B&B, and the Wisconsin River is just across the street, ensuring pleasant surroundings. Decorated in a cheerful mix of Victorian and country, the guest bedrooms offer comfortable furnishings and delightful views. The Park View boasts a canopy bed and a clawfoot tub; other rooms feature whirlpools. A barbecue grill and picnic table are available to use. The inn is just a block and a half from downtown. Private parking is in the rear.

Innkeeper(s): Len, Cookie, Lenard & Lynn Novak. $105-225. 4 rooms with PB. Breakfast and afternoon tea included in rates. Types of meals: Full bkfst and early coffee/tea. Beds: Q. Cable TV, VCR, reading lamp, clock radio, one with clawfoot tub and four with whirlpools in room. Air conditioning. Parlor games, telephone, fireplace and eclectic library on premises. Amusement parks, antiquing, cross-country skiing, downhill skiing, fishing, live theater, parks, shopping and water sports nearby.

Location: City.

Certificate may be used: Sunday through Thursday.

The White Rose Bed & Breakfast

910 River Road
Wisconsin Dells, WI 53965
(608)254-4724 (800)482-4724 Fax:(608)254-4585
Internet: www.thewhiterose.com
E-mail: info@thewhiterose.com

Circa 1903. Just two blocks from the Wisconsin River, this historic Victorian mansion is ornately decorated and boasts original woodwork, stairways and architectural details. Well-appointed guest bedrooms with gorgeous colors and fabrics feature soft lighting and whirlpool baths. A working fireplace is enjoyed in the parlour room. Honeymooners often request the Blue Room or the Master Suite. World-famous omelettes, home-fried potatoes, croissants, fresh fruit, asparagus and Belgium waffles with strawberries and cream are some of the items served for breakfast in the dining room. Walk the lavish gardens, popular for weddings, and swim in the pool. The

nearby Dells, created by the Northern Glacier, reflects ice-age history and provides great hiking and biking trails. Devil's Lake State Park is just 10 miles away.

Innkeeper(s): Marty and Shionagh Stuehler. $80-225. 21 rooms with PB, 5 with FP, 15 with WP and 1 conference room. Breakfast included in rates. Types of meals: Full gourmet bkfst, veg bkfst, early coffee/tea, gourmet lunch, picnic lunch and gourmet dinner. Restaurant on premises. Beds: KQT. Cable TV, VCR, reading lamp, ceiling fan, fireplace and some have whirlpool Jacuzzi in room. Central air. Fax, copier, swimming, parlor games, telephone, fireplace and The Secret Garden Cafe on premises. Limited handicap access. Amusement parks, antiquing, beach, bicycling, canoeing/kayaking, cross-country skiing, downhill skiing, fishing, golf, hiking, horseback riding, parks, shopping, tennis, water sports and wineries nearby.

Location: City.

Publicity: *Isthmus Newspaper, Wisconsin State Journal, Milwaukee State Journal, Janesville Gazette and WNNO radio.*

Certificate may be used: Anytime, November-April, subject to availability.

Wisconsin Dells Thunder Valley B&B Inn

W15344 Waubeek Rd
Wisconsin Dells, WI 53965-9005
(608)254-4145
Internet: www.thundervalleyinn.com
E-mail: neldell@midplains.net

Circa 1870. The Wisconsin Dells area is full of both Scandinavian and Native American heritage, and the innkeepers of this country inn have tried to honor the traditions. The inn even features a Scandinavian gift shop. Chief Yellow Thunder, for whom this inn is named, often camped out on the grounds and surrounding area. The inn's restaurant is highly acclaimed. Everything is homemade, including the wheat the innkeepers grind for the morning pancakes and rolls. There is a good selection of Wisconsin beer and wine, as well. Guests can stay in the Farmhouse, Swedish Guest Hus, or Wee Hus, all of which offer microwaves and refrigerators.

Innkeeper(s): Anita, Kari & Sigrid Nelson. $65-135. 10 rooms with PB. Breakfast included in rates. Types of meals: Full bkfst. Beds: KQD. Air conditioning. Handicap access. International Crane Foundation, Circus Museum, House on Rock, casino, farm animals and dairy nearby.

Location: Country. Farmhouse is only one mile from downtown Wisconsin Dells in the country.

Publicity: *Wisconsin Trails Magazine, Country Inns, Midwest Living Magazine, Chicago Sun-Times, Milwaukee Journal-Sentinel and National Geographic Travel Magazine.*

"Thunder Valley is a favorite of Firstar Club members — delicious food served in a charming atmosphere with warm Scandinavian hospitality."

Certificate may be used: Sunday through Thursday, November through May, except holidays and upon availability. Does not apply to $65 rooms.

Wyoming

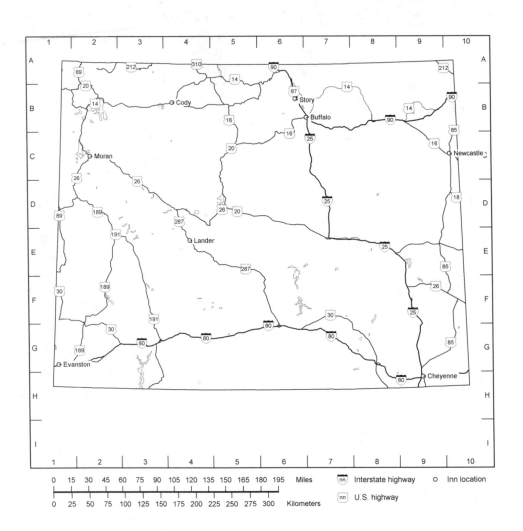

Miles: 0 15 30 45 60 75 90 105 120 135 150 165 180 195

Kilometers: 0 25 50 75 100 125 150 175 200 225 250 275 300

Interstate highway   O Inn location

U.S. highway

Buffalo   B7

Clear Creek Bed & Breakfast

330 S. Main
Buffalo, WY 82834
(307)684-2317 (888)865-6789
Internet: www.clearcreekbb.com
E-mail: slegner@clearcreekbb.com

Circa 1883. Taste Old West history at this modernized
Victorian-era bed & breakfast that is one of the area's oldest
homes. Partake in lively discussions by the parlor's stone and
fossil fireplace, or choose a more cozy sitting area for quiet
reflection. Comfortable leather couches are inviting in the television room. Delightful guest bedrooms and suites reflect the
country locale. The two-room Sagewood Suite is furnished in
white wicker, an iron bed and a clawfoot tub. The Highland
Retreat boasts rustic pine accents and views of the Big Horn
Mountain Range from a private deck. A complete breakfast full
of great home cooking starts the day right.

Innkeeper(s): Susan & Dennis Legner. $55-85. 4 rooms. Breakfast and
snacks/refreshments included in rates. Types of meals: Full bkfst and early
coffee/tea. Reading lamp and clock radio in room. Air conditioning. VCR, parlor games, telephone and fireplace on premises. Antiquing, art galleries, bicycling, canoeing/kayaking, cross-country skiing, downhill skiing, fishing, golf,
hiking, horseback riding, live theater, museums, parks, shopping, tennis and
water sports nearby.

Location: Mountains.

Certificate may be used: January-April, subject to availability.

Cheyenne   H9

A. Drummonds Ranch B&B

399 Happy Jack Rd, Hwy 210
Cheyenne, WY 82007
(307)634-6042 Fax:(307)634-6042
Internet: www.cruising-america.com/drummond.html
E-mail: adrummond@juno.com

Circa 1990. With 120 acres of Wyoming wilderness and a nearby
National Forest and State Park, this Old English-style farmhouse
offers a quiet retreat. Private, outdoor Jacuzzis provide views of the
surrounding area and evening skies filled with stars. Some rooms
include private entrances,
window seats, a fireplace
or a steam sauna. One
unit is completely self-
contained and includes a
small kitchen.

Homemade snacks, beverages and fresh fruit always are available
for guests. Boarding is available for those traveling with horses and
pets. A. Drummonds Ranch is located halfway between Cheyenne
and Laramie. The University of Wyoming is nearby.

Innkeeper(s): Taydie Drummond. $74-175. 4 rooms, 2 with PB, 1 with FP, 1
suite. Breakfast, afternoon tea and snacks/refreshments included in rates.
Types of meals: Full gourmet bkfst, early coffee/tea, lunch, picnic lunch and
gourmet dinner. Beds: QDT. TV, reading lamp, refrigerator, snack bar, clock
radio, telephone, turn-down service and desk in room. VCR, fax, copier,
sauna, bicycles, library, pet boarding, child care, parlor games, fireplace and
private hot tubs on premises. Cross-country skiing, fishing, live theater, parks,
sporting events and water sports nearby.

Location: Mountains.

Publicity: *Country Inns, Country Extra, Inn Times, Adventures West, Colorado
Expressions, Sunset Magazine, Redbook and Wyoming Homes & Living.*

Certificate may be used: October-December, January-April, Monday nights
through Thursday nights.

Adventurers' Country B&B Raven Cry Ranch

3803 I-80 South Service Rd
Cheyenne, WY 82009-8785
(307)632-4087 Fax:(307)632-4087
E-mail: fwhite1@juno.com

Circa 1985. Situated behind an adobe fence, this Southwestern-
style inn rests on a knoll overlooking 102 acres of prairie.
Guests enjoy the tree-lined adobe courtyard, flower gardens and
a front veranda filled with rocking chairs and swings. The inn
offers murder-mystery weekends and a Western Adventure package. Weekly rodeos, a
scenic rail excursion,
and crystal and granite
lakes are nearby.

Innkeeper(s): Fern White.
$70-135. 5 rooms, 4 with
PB, 1 with FP, 1 suite. Breakfast included in rates. Types of meals: Full bkfst,
early coffee/tea, lunch, picnic lunch, afternoon tea, snacks/refreshments,
gourmet dinner and room service. Beds: KQ. Reading lamp, clock radio, telephone and turn-down service in room. VCR, fireplace and horseback activities
on premises. Antiquing, cross-country skiing, downhill skiing, live theater,
parks, shopping and sporting events nearby.

Location: Country. Ranch.

*"The service was superbly personalized with great attention to detail
and a great down-home cowboy atmosphere."*

Certificate may be used: October through April, suite only.

Porch Swing Bed & Breakfast

502 East 24th Street
Cheyenne, WY 82001
(307)778-7182 Fax:(307)778-7182
Internet: www.cruising-america.com/porch.html
E-mail: porchswing@juno.com

At this Victorian inn, breakfast is served on the back porch in
summer and by the dining room fire in cold weather. Guests
can enjoy items like yeast waffles with maple syrup and fresh
strawberries, orange pecan French toast and German pancakes
with Swiss honey butter. All these recipes and more are found in
the innkeepers' cookbook available for sale. The property's summer gardens are colorful and fra-
grant with a variety of perennials,
aromatic and culinary herbs, wildflowers and annuals. The innkeepers would be happy to send you
home with a cutting or seeds of
something that's taken your fancy.

Innkeeper(s): Carole Eppler. $39-66. 3
rooms. Breakfast included in rates. Types of meals: Full bkfst, early coffee/tea &
snacks/refreshments. Reading lamp and clock radio in room. VCR & telephone on
premises. Antiquing, downhill skiing, shopping & sporting events nearby.

Location: City. 25 minutes from mountains.

Certificate may be used: November-March, Sunday-Thursday.

Cody   B4

AKA-Grandma's House - The Lockhart B&B Inn

109 W Yellowstone Ave
Cody, WY 82414-8723
(307)587-6074 (800)377-7255 Fax:(307)587-8644
Internet: www.codyvacationproperties.com
E-mail: info@codyvacationproperties.com

Circa 1890. Once the home of author and journalist Caroline
Lockhart, this Victorian inn has beautiful mountain views from

its veranda. The deck affords a view of the Shoshone River. Rooms are decorated with antiques, old-fashioned beds and a clawfoot tub. Breakfast is served on fine china at your private table in the dining room. Making reservations for dining, river rafting, golfing, rodeo events and more, is offered.

Innkeeper(s): Betty Schmit. $95-145. 7 rooms with PB. Breakfast included in rates. Types of meals: Full bkfst and picnic lunch. Beds: QD. Cable TV, reading lamp, ceiling fan, clock radio, telephone and desk in room. Air conditioning. Fireplace and piano on premises. Antiquing, cross-country skiing, downhill skiing, fishing, live theater, shopping, sporting events and water sports nearby.

Location: City. Overlooking river.

Publicity: *Glamour, AAA Today, National Geographic Traveler, Windsurf, New York Times, Houston Post, Los Angeles Times* and *Home & Garden TV.*

"Just like going to grandma's house, like coming home to family — home away from home."

Certificate may be used: May 1-June 15, Aug. 15-Nov. 15, excluding holidays, discount applied to full rack rates.

Mayor's Inn Bed & Breakfast

1413 Rumsey Ave
Cody, WY 82414
(307)587-0887 (888)217-3001 Fax:(307)587-0890
Internet: www.mayorsinn.com
E-mail: mayorsinn@vcn.com

Circa 1909. Considered the town's first mansion, this stylish two-story, turn-of-the-century home was built for Cody's first elected mayor. A romantic Victorian ambiance is achieved with warm hospitality, antiques, soft lighting, chandeliers and splendid wall and ceiling papers. The parlor inspires nostalgia. The guest bedrooms feature either a brass bed and clawfoot tub, a lodge pole pine bed, jetted tub and western art, or an open, sunny room with double shower. The suite boasts a fresh water hot tub and CD player. Offering private seating, breakfast is served in both of the dining rooms. The Carriage House is a cottage with a fully equipped kitchen.

Innkeeper(s): Bill & DaLeLee Delph. $95-205. 5 rooms, 4 with PB, 1 with HT and 1 cottage. Breakfast included in rates. Types of meals: Full gourmet bkfst and early coffee/tea. Restaurant on premises. Beds: KQD. Cable TV, reading lamp, CD player, clock radio and hot tub/spa in room. Central air. Fax, telephone and wine & spirits in The Back Porch on premises. Antiquing, art galleries, bicycling, canoeing/kayaking, cross-country skiing, downhill skiing, fishing, golf, hiking, horseback riding, museums, parks, shopping and water sports nearby.

Location: Small town.

Publicity: *Cody Enterprise* and *The Telegraph Travel.*

Certificate may be used: Anytime, November-April, subject to availability.

Parson's Pillow B&B

1202 14th St
Cody, WY 82414-3720
(307)587-2382 (800)377-2348 Fax:(307)527-8908
Internet: www.cruising-america.com/parsonspillow
E-mail: ppbb@trib.com

Circa 1991. This historic building originally served as the Methodist-Episcopal Church, Cody's first church. The inn offers a TV and VCR; guest rooms feature antiques and quilts. Clawfoot and oak-framed prairie tubs add to the nostalgia. The Buffalo Bill Historical Center is nearby.

Innkeeper(s): Dorothy & Paul Olson. $75-95. 5 rooms with PB. Breakfast included in rates. Types of meals: Full bkfst and early coffee/tea. Beds: Q. Ceiling fan and clock radio in room. VCR, library, telephone and computer port on premises. Antiquing, cross-country skiing, downhill skiing, fishing, golf, parks, shopping, tennis, water sports and white water rafting nearby.

Location: City.

Certificate may be used: September through May, any day of the week. Subject to availability. One certificate per stay.

Evanston G1

Pine Gables Inn B&B

1049 Center St
Evanston, WY 82930-3432
(307)789-2069
E-mail: pinegabl@allwest.net

Circa 1883. This Eastlake Victorian was built by A.V. Quinn, who ran the company store in town for the Union Pacific railroad. The rooms of this National Register home are filled with antiques, and the carved handmade beds are a highlight. The guest rooms are cheerful with romantic touches. One room features a beautiful antique bed decorated with a hint of ivy and bathroom with a pedestal sink and hand-stenciled walls. The inn's parlor is particularly inviting. Rich, rose-colored walls and white molding are enhanced by stenciling and an ornate ceiling. French doors lead out to the porch. In the mornings, guests feast on items such as waffles, omelettes, quiche, fresh fruit and homemade muffins.

Innkeeper(s): Nephi & Ruby Jensen. $80-155. 6 rooms with PB, 4 with FP. Breakfast included in rates. Types of meals: Full bkfst and early coffee/tea. Beds: KQD. Cable TV, reading lamp, ceiling fan, clock radio, telephone, clawfoot tubs and one with Jacuzzi in room. Parlor games and fireplace on premises. Antiquing, cross-country skiing, fishing, golf, live theater, parks, shopping and tennis nearby.

Certificate may be used: Oct. 1-April 30.

Jackson Hole E6

Sassy Moose Inn

3895 Miles Rd
Jackson Hole, WY 83014
(307)733-1277 (800)356-1277 Fax:(307)739-0793
Internet: www.sassymoose.com
E-mail: craigerwy@aol.com

Circa 1992. All of the rooms at this log-house-style inn have spectacular Teton views. The Mountain Room has a rock fireplace, queen bed and mountain cabin decor. The River Room's decor is dominated by the colors of the Snake River and accented with antiques. The inn is five minutes from Teton Village and the Jackson Hole Ski Resort. Teton Pines Golf Course and Nordic Trails are just across the road. After a day of activities, enjoy sharing your experiences over tea, wine or relaxing in the large hot tub.

Innkeeper(s): Polly Kelley. $139-215. 5 rooms with PB, 5 with FP, 1 suite. Breakfast included in rates. Types of meals: Full bkfst, early coffee/tea and afternoon tea. Beds: KQ. TV, VCR, reading lamp, clock radio and desk in room. Air conditioning. Fax, copier, spa, library, child care, parlor games, telephone, fireplace and limited laundry on premises. Cross-country skiing, downhill skiing, fishing, live theater, parks, shopping and water sports nearby.

Location: Mountains. Snake River.

Certificate may be used: Anytime except January-February and June-September.

Lander   E4

Baldwin Creek B&B

2343 Baldwin Creek Rd
Lander, WY 82520-0866
(307)332-7608

Circa 1991. View roaming wildlife and the breathtaking Wind River Mountains from more than 1,000 square feet of deck attached to this lodge-style log home. Guest rooms include a Jacuzzi tub in a private bath. The inn is open year-round and winter guests can enjoy the Continental Divide Snowmobile Trail and the inn's 10,000 acres. In the summer, mountain bikes are available.

Innkeeper(s): Gary Eaton. $80-90. 6 rooms with PB, 1 suite and 2 conference rooms. Breakfast and snacks/refreshments included in rates. Types of meals: Full gourmet bkfst, early coffee/tea, gourmet lunch, picnic lunch, afternoon tea, gourmet dinner and room service. Beds: QDT. Reading lamp, refrigerator, snack bar, clock radio, turn-down service and desk in room. VCR, fax, spa, pet boarding, parlor games, telephone, fireplace and satellite dish on premises. Antiquing, cross-country skiing, downhill skiing, fishing, parks, shopping and water sports nearby.

Location: Mountains.

Publicity: *Los Angeles Times.*

Certificate may be used: Oct. 1-March 30.

Moran   C2

Diamond D Ranch-Outfitters

Buffalo Valley Rd, Box 211
Moran, WY 83013
(307)543-2479
E-mail: info@diamond-d.com

Located on the scenic Buffalo Valley Road, this log house inn serves many purposes, including being an old hunting lodge, guest ranch, pack trip outfitter, cross-country skiing lodge, and snowmobile and base lodge for touring Yellowstone and Grand Teton national parks. There's a relaxed atmosphere with a flexible schedule. The main lodge has two units each with private baths, and the cabins have two units also with private baths. The staff teaches Western horsemanship and has horses for each guest's ability.

Innkeeper(s): Rod Doty. $99. 16 rooms, 2 suites. Breakfast included in rates. Types of meals: Full bkfst, lunch and dinner. Cable TV, refrigerator, desk and hot tub/spa in room. Telephone and fireplace on premises. Cross-country skiing nearby.

Location: Guest ranch.

Certificate may be used: Nov. 1 to Dec. 15, Jan. 5 to May 15. Sunday through Thursday.

Newcastle   C10

EVA-Great Spirit Ranch B&B

1262 Beaver Creek Rd
Newcastle, WY 82701
(307)746-2537
Internet: www.wyomingbnb-ranchrec.com/evagreatspirit

Circa 1984. Amidst spectacular scenery of mountains and woods, guests will find this modern log home. Although the home is new, it rests on what was an old stagecoach route. A century-old barn is located on the property, as well as ruins of a 19th-century bunkhouse. The interior features hardwood floors and high ceilings, and the guest rooms are comfortably furnished in a modern style. There are two rooms with private baths and two adjoining rooms with a shared bath. Irene offers spring and fall hunting packages, where guests can search for deer, elk and wild turkey on the 525-acre property and adjacent Bureau of Land Management and state lands. The vast acreage borders Black Hills National Forest in South Dakota.

Innkeeper(s): Irene Spillane. $55-75. 4 rooms, 2 with PB. Breakfast included in rates. Types of meals: Full bkfst. Beds: KQT. Reading lamp, clock radio and fans in room. VCR, library, parlor games, telephone, fireplace, cross-country skiing, games and fireplace on premises. Handicap access. Antiquing, downhill skiing, fishing, golf, parks, snowmobile trails and sightseeing nearby.

Location: Mountains.

Publicity: *News Letter Journal.*

"We enjoyed a very homely introduction to the wild west!"

Certificate may be used: Sept. 15 to May 15, Sunday-Saturday. Bed & breakfast stay only. Hunting packages and Romantic Getaways excluded.

Story   B6

Piney Creek Inn B&B

11 Skylark Ln, PO Box 456
Story, WY 82842
(307)683-2911
Internet: www.pineycreekinn.com
E-mail: pineyinn@fiberpipe.net

Circa 1956. There's an abundance of wildlife on the property of this secluded log-house-style inn nestled in the Big Horn Mountains. For the Old West buff, historic sites that are only minutes away include Fort Phil Kearny, Bozeman Trail, Little Big Horn Battlefield, numerous Indian battle sites and museums and galleries. Ranch experiences and trail ride packages are favorites. At the end of the day, relax on the deck or in the common area, where visitors will find a television, books, magazines and games. Guests also can relax by the campfire for conversation and viewing the stars. Historical tours, ranch adventures and trail-ride packages are available.

Innkeeper(s): Vicky Hoff. $85-150. 4 rooms, 3 with PB and 2 cabins. Breakfast and snacks/refreshments included in rates. Types of meals: Full bkfst, early coffee/tea, lunch, picnic lunch and dinner. Beds: KQDT. Reading lamp, ceiling fan, clock radio and desk in room. VCR, spa, library, parlor games, telephone, hot tub, campfire and refrigerator on premises. Handicap access. Antiquing, fishing, golf, live theater, shopping, trail rides and historical tours nearby.

Location: Mountains.

Publicity: *Country.*

Certificate may be used: Nov. 1-April 30, excluding holidays, two-night minimum.

U.S. Territories

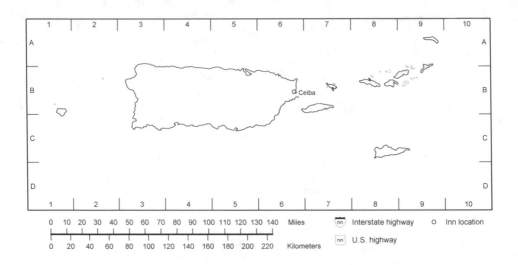

```
Miles          0  10  20  30  40  50  60  70  80  90  100 110 120 130 140
Kilometers     0    20    40    60    80   100  120  140  160  180  200  220
```

(inn) Interstate highway   ○ Inn location
(nn) U.S. highway

Puerto Rico

Ceiba   **B6**

Ceiba Country Inn
PO Box 1067
Ceiba, PR 00735-1067
(787)885-0471 (888)560-2816 Fax:(787)885-0471
Internet: www.geocities.com/countryinn00735
E-mail: prinn@juno.com

Circa 1950. A large Spanish patio is available at this tropical
country inn perched on rolling, green hills. Situated 500 feet
above the valley floor, the inn affords a view of the ocean with
the isle of Culebra on
the horizon. A continen-
tal buffet is served in the
warm and sunny break-
fast room. The inn is
four miles from Puerto
Del Rey, the largest mari-
na in the Caribbean, and 10 miles from Luquillo Beach, which is
a mile of white sand, dotted with coconut palms.

Innkeeper(s): Sue Newbauer & Dick Bray. $75. 9 rooms with PB. Breakfast
included in rates. Types of meals: Cont plus. Beds: QD. Data port, reading
lamp, ceiling fan, clock radio, telephone and small refrigerator in room. Air
conditioning. TV, fax, copier, library and parlor games on premises. Handicap
access. Beach, canoeing/kayaking, fishing, golf, hiking, horseback riding,
shopping, water sports and snorkeling nearby.

Location: Mountains.

Certificate may be used: May-November.

Canada

British Columbia

Courtenay

Belle Vue Bed & Breakfast
5782 Coral Road
Courtenay, BC V9J 1W9
(250)898-8702 (866)898-8702 Fax:(250)898-8703
Internet: www.labellevue.com
E-mail: belvues@yahoo.com

Circa 1994. A pleasurable fusion of East and West blend amiably at this beachfront California Colonial-style home overlooking the Strait of Georgia to the coastal mountains beyond. Become acquainted with American, Chinese, Middle Eastern and European art. Relax on French and Chinese furniture accented by Turkish lamps that highlight Persian carpets. Guest bedrooms boast balcony access and stocked refrigerators. Elderdowns grace the beds, though hypoallergenic alternatives are available. International flavors enhance a delicious breakfast served on English china with Russian silver, Belgian crystal and Thai brass.
Innkeeper(s): Walter & Haideh Jordan. $80-105. 3 rooms with PB. Breakfast included in rates. Types of meals: Full gourmet bkfst, veg bkfst, early coffee/tea and snacks/refreshments. Beds: Q. Cable TV, VCR, reading lamp, refrigerator, telephone, hot tub/spa and whirlpool bath and shower in room. Fax, copier, spa, swimming, library, parlor games, fireplace, boat and kayak and canoe rentals (within walking distance) on premises. Antiquing, art galleries, beach, bicycling, canoeing/kayaking, cross-country skiing, downhill skiing, fishing, golf, hiking, horseback riding, live theater, museums, parks, shopping, tennis, water sports, caving, fossil hunting and bird watching nearby.
Location: Country, waterfront. On the Strait of Georgia, minutes north of Courtenay and Comox.
Certificate may be used: Oct. 15 to April 30, subject to availability.

Galiano Island

Casa De Edrie Holloway
PO BOX 190, 107 Cain Rd, Sturdies
Galiano Island, BC V0N 1-P0
(250)539-2581 Fax:(250)539-5822
E-mail: exceedee@hotmail.com

Circa 1967. Just 300 yards from the Galiano Island ferry stop, this seaside homestay offers comfortable accommodations within walking distance of the bay and beach. Guests can relax in front of a fire with one of the home's many books or strum the ivories on the innkeepers' 1840 grand piano. Rooms include feather beds, and the hosts provide turndown service, as well as indulging guests with plenty of chocolates and a homemade breakfast.

Innkeeper(s): Edrie Gordon Holloway. $75-90. 2 rooms, 1 with PB. Breakfast included in rates. Types of meals: Full gourmet bkfst and early coffee/tea. Beds: DT. Reading lamp and turn-down service in room. Fax, bicycles, library, parlor games, telephone and fireplace on premises. Fishing, parks, shopping, kayaking, cycling and hiking nearby.
Certificate may be used: All year, Sunday to Friday.

Nanoose Bay

Lookout at Schooner Cove
3381 Dolphin Dr
Nanoose Bay, BC V9P 9H7
(250)468-9796 Fax:(250)468-9796
Internet: www.bbcanada.com/490.html
E-mail: thelookout@webtv.net

Circa 1972. Massive rocks, tall trees and a winding path lead to this West Coast contemporary house overlooking Georgia Strait and the mountains. Schooner Cove and its marina are within 500 yards. Located on Vancouver Island, halfway between Victoria and Tofino, the inn offers a wraparound deck the favorite spot for enjoying lingering sunsets, Alaskan cruise ships, eagles, otters and sea lions. Reserve early to get one of the two rooms with private bath.
Innkeeper(s): Marj & Herb Wilkie. $50-80. 2 rooms, 1 with PB, 1 suite. Breakfast included in rates. Types of meals: Full bkfst. Beds: Q. Cable TV, VCR, reading lamp, refrigerator, ceiling fan, clock radio, telephone and desk in room. Fax, copier, library and parlor games on premises. Amusement parks, antiquing, cross-country skiing, downhill skiing, fishing, golf, live theater, parks, shopping, sporting events, tennis and water sports nearby.
Location: Ocean community.

"I must say, we had the most relaxing time with you. Moreover, you served the best breakfast."
Certificate may be used: Oct. 1-April 30, subject to availability, holidays excluded.

Penticton

Riordan House
689 Winnipeg St
Penticton, BC V2A 5N1
(250)493-5997 Fax:(250)493-5997
E-mail: jeortiz@img.net

Circa 1920. Beneath lush vines of English ivy and Virginia creeper, the shingles of this three-story Arts-and-Crafts-style home are a warm pink. Munioned windows, gables and a bay window combine with lush plantings of wisteria and tamarax trees to create an inviting welcome. An antique shop is on the property and of course the home is filled with antiques. In addition to the dining room where breakfasts of freshly baked breads and fruit dishes are served, there are parlors and sitting

Canada

areas for guests' enjoyment as well as the beautiful gardens.
Innkeeper(s): John & Donna Ortiz. $60-95. 4 rooms, 1 with FP. Breakfast included in rates. Types of meals: Full gourmet bkfst and picnic lunch. Beds: QD. Cable TV, VCR, reading lamp and clock radio in room. Air conditioning. Fax, bicycles, library and telephone on premises. Amusement parks, antiquing, cross-country skiing, downhill skiing, fishing, golf, parks, shopping, sporting events, tennis and water sports nearby.
Location: City.
Certificate may be used: Oct. 1-March 1, two-night minimum.

Salt Spring Island

Anne's Oceanfront Hideaway B&B

168 Simson Rd
Salt Spring Island, BC V8K 1E2
(250)537-0851 (888)474-2663 Fax:(250)537-0861
Internet: www.annesoceanfront.com
E-mail: annes@saltspring.com

Circa 1995. The exquisite views of the blue Pacific from the wraparound veranda, living room and guest rooms are a rewarding feature of this 7,000-square-foot Country Victorian inn. However, even without the magnificent setting, you could luxuri-

ate in the amenities, which include a library, fine linens, hydro massage tub, canopy bed or fireplace. A four-course breakfast is served in the dining room. (Ask about the egg blossom and lamb patty entree.)
The quiet setting of oak and arbutus trees, and the ocean path that leads to the sandstone beach are additional pleasures. The inn is also wheelchair accessible, and there's an elevator.
Innkeeper(s): Rick & Ruth-Anne Broad. $185-260. 4 rooms with PB, 4 with FP. Breakfast and snacks/refreshments included in rates. Types of meals: Full bkfst and early coffee/tea. Beds: KQT. Reading lamp, stereo, refrigerator, clock radio, telephone, turn-down service, desk, hot tub/spa, fireplace, robes, slippers and blow dryers in room. Central air. TV, VCR, fax, copier, spa, bicycles, library, parlor games and laundry facility on premises. Handicap access. Art galleries, beach, bicycling, canoeing/kayaking, fishing, golf, hiking, horseback riding, live theater, parks, shopping, tennis, water sports, wineries, Artisan Studio Tours, Salt Spring Saturday Market, Artcraft and Island Gourmet Safari nearby.
Location: Ocean community, waterfront.
Publicity: Fodors, Frommers, NW Best Places, Best Places to Kiss and Westworld.

"We leave relaxed, refreshed and anxious to return. You've thought of every detail and we've so enjoyed the results."
Certificate may be used: Oct. 1 to May 1, Sunday to Friday, (excluding holidays and long weekends), subject to availability.

Sooke

Ocean Wilderness Inn & Spa Retreat

109 W Coast Rd, RR 2
Sooke, BC V0S 1N0
(250)646-2116 (800)323-2116 Fax:(250)646-2317
Internet: www.oceanwildernessinn.com
E-mail: info@oceanwildernessinn.com

Circa 1940. The hot tub spa of this log house inn is in a Japanese gazebo overlooking the ocean. Reserve your time for a private soak, terry bathrobes are supplied. Experience massage and mud treatments, ocean treatments and herbal wraps while meditation enhances your creative expression. The inn will

arrange fishing charters, nature walks, wilderness treks and beach-combing. Coffee is delivered to your room each morning on a silver service. Guests are invited to enjoy breakfast in their room or in the dining lounge. Rooms include antiques, sitting areas and canopy beds. Two of the rooms have hot tubs for two with spectacular ocean and Olympic Mountain views. Rates are in Canadian funds.
Innkeeper(s): Marion J. Rolston. $99-180. 9 rooms with PB. Breakfast included in rates. Types of meals: Full bkfst and early coffee/tea. Beds: KQT. Reading lamp and refrigerator in room. Fax and telephone on premises. Handicap access. Antiquing, fishing, live theater, parks, shopping, whale watching and Galloping Goose biking trail nearby.
Location: Waterfront.
Publicity: Puget Sound Business Journal, Getaways from Vancouver, Travel Holiday Magazine and Seattle Times.

"Thank you for the most wonderful hospitality and accommodations of our entire vacation."
Certificate may be used: Oct. 1 to June 30.

Valemount

Rainbow Retreat B&B

PO Box 138
Valemount, BC V0E 2Z0
(250)566-9747
Internet: www.spiralmountain.com

This authentically fashioned log cabin home rests beside an old fur-trader's route nestled in the Canadian Rockies and surrounded by woods. Guests are sure to see plenty of birds and wildlife, including the occasional deer that march across the grounds. The innkeepers have kept the rustic touch, but added Victorian flair such as stained glass and a grand piano. Hearty breakfasts start off the day and gourmet dinners are made-to-order. The secluded retreat is just a few minutes from Mount Robson Provincial Park, and it's just a short walk to Fraser River, especially popular during the annual salmon spawning run.
Innkeeper(s): Keith Burchnall. $50-70. 2 rooms. Breakfast included in rates. Types of meals: Full bkfst.
Certificate may be used: Anytime, except July and August.

Vernon

Richmond House 1894

4008 Pleasant Valley Rd
Vernon, BC V1T 4M2
(250)549-1767 (866)267-4419
Internet: www.richmondhousebandb.com
E-mail: richmondhouse@home.com

Because of its central location, this Victorian inn is an ideal spot for outdoor enthusiasts to base their daily activities. The ski area of Silverstar Mountain is a 30-minute drive and two major lakes (Okanagan and Kalamalka) are 10 minutes from the inn. Internationally renowned Predator Ridge golf course is 20 minutes away. A fireplace in the living room brings warmth in the winter months, and an outdoor deck and hot tub are enjoyed year-round. The innkeeper can direct you to adventure travel packages and local wineries. Breakfasts include a variety of quiche or stuffed French toast with peach sauce.

Innkeeper(s): Keith Brookes & Colleen Couves. $75. 3 rooms. Breakfast included in rates. Types of meals: Full bkfst. Reading lamp, ceiling fan and clock radio in room. Library, telephone, fireplace and lounge on premises. Antiquing, cross-country skiing, downhill skiing, golf and shopping nearby.

Location: Mountains.

Certificate may be used: Oct. 1-Dec. 22 and Jan. 3-April 30.

Victoria

Claddagh House B&B

1761 Lee Ave
Victoria, BC V8R 4W7
(250)370-2816 (877)377-2816 Fax:(250)592-0228
Internet: www.claddaghhouse.com
E-mail: info@claddaghhouse.com

Circa 1913. In a tranquil neighborhood, hospitality abounds at this romantic Victorian inn, fully modernized. Garden views are found in the sunny guest bedrooms. Ask for the spacious top-floor Tara Suite, an ideal indulgence for two or a perfect family setting. Fresh flowers, Belgian chocolates, a double Jacuzzi and down duvets are lavish rejuvenating touches. Select a satisfying breakfast from a substantial menu, to be made when desired. Relax on the front porch, stroll by the pond and fountain, or experience the diversity of Victoria.

Innkeeper(s): Elaine & Ken Brown. $149-249. 3 rooms, 2 with PB, 1 suite. Breakfast, afternoon tea and snacks/refreshments included in rates. Types of meals: Full gourmet bkfst, early coffee/tea and picnic lunch. Beds: KQDT. Ceiling fan and desk in room. VCR, fax, copier, bicycles, library, parlor games, telephone and fireplace on premises. Antiquing, bicycling, fishing, golf, hiking, live theater, parks, shopping, water sports, whale watching, castle tours, gardens and boating nearby.

Location: Residential.

Certificate may be used: Oct. 1 to May 1, Sunday-Thursday, excluding holidays.

Scholefield House B&B

731 Vancouver St
Victoria, BC V8V 3V4
(250)385-2025 (800)661-1623 Fax:(250)383-3036
Internet: scholefieldhouse.com
E-mail: mail@scholefieldhouse.com

Circa 1892. Located on a quiet street downtown and three blocks from the Empress Hotel, this authentically restored Victorian B&B is shaded by tall trees that line the wide boulevards. A picket fence and gabled front entrance provide an inviting welcome to guests. Rooms are furnished with antiques and period decor, and each has a private bath. The five-course champagne breakfast is served fireside in the Parlor and edible flowers decorate the abundant servings of eggs Florentine, French toast with Brie, smoked salmon and other entrees. Two favorite spots are the private library where guests may enjoy a glass of sherry or tea and coffee and outside, an English herb and rose garden. The innkeeper is an author, who enjoys the historic register home's connection to the original owner, who founded the library in the Legislature Building. Stroll to the Inner Harbour, restaurants, antique shops, and theater in Victoria's flower-filled environment sometimes called "more English than England."

Innkeeper(s): Tana Dineen. $110-185. 3 rooms with PB, 1 with FP, 2 with WP, 1 suite. Breakfast included in rates. Types of meals: Full gourmet bkfst.

Beds: KQ. TV, reading lamp, ceiling fan, clock radio, turn-down service, 2 with Jacuzzi for two and 1 with fireplace in room. VCR, fax, library, parlor games, telephone and Internet access on premises. Antiquing, canoeing/kayaking, fishing, golf, live theater, museums, shopping, whale watching, salmon fishing, gardens and English high tea nearby.

Location: City.

Certificate may be used: Nov. 1-April 30.

Whistler

Belle Neige Bed & Breakfast

8597 Drifter Way
Whistler, BC V0N 1B8
(604)938-9225 Fax:(604)938-9384
E-mail: fun@look.ca

Circa 1993. Peacefully sitting amongst Whistler and Blackcomb Mountains, this new West Coast-style home offers year-round pleasure. The inn's extraordinary panoramic scenery is a breathtaking experience. The guest bedrooms and suites feature the extra comforts of cozy housecoats and goose-down duvets. Italian prosciuto frittata, apple cinnamon pancakes and Quebec-style French toast with pure Canadian maple syrup are some of the items served for breakfast. After a day at the ski resorts, soak in a hot tub Jacuzzi on the treetop-level deck.

Innkeeper(s): Myrna & Todd. $99-189. 1 room, 2 suites. Types of meals: Full gourmet bkfst. Beds: KQT. Reading lamp, refrigerator, clock radio and coffeemaker in room. Spa, bicycles and telephone on premises. Amusement parks, art galleries, beach, bicycling, canoeing/kayaking, cross-country skiing, downhill skiing, fishing, hiking, horseback riding, parks, shopping, sporting events, tennis and water sports nearby.

Location: Mountains.

Publicity: *History Channel and The Origins of Christmas.*

Certificate may be used: April 1-June 30, Oct. 1-Nov. 15, breakfast not included, pending availability.

Golden Dreams B&B

6412 Easy St
Whistler, BC V0N 1B6
(604)932-2667 (800)668-7055 Fax:(604)932-7055
Internet: www.goldendreamswhistler.com
E-mail: ann@goldendreamswhistler.com

Circa 1986. Experience the many secrets of great B&B stays at this established inn. Surrounded by mountain views and the beauty of nature, this West Coast home features a private guest living room with wood fireplace where the innkeepers share their knowledge of the locale. Velour robes, duvets and sherry decanters are provided in the guest bed rooms, which have Victorian, Wild West and Aztec themes. After a wholesome breakfast, valley trail and bus stop are just outside. Whistler village and skiing are only one mile away. Relax in the hot tub and enjoy house wine and snacks. A large BBQ sundeck and guest kitchen are convenient amenities. Town Plaza village condos are also available for families. Discount skiing, sight-seeing passes and airport transport booking services are available.

Innkeeper(s): Ann & Terry Spence. $70-115. 3 rooms, 1 with PB. Breakfast included in rates. Types of meals: Full gourmet bkfst. Beds: QD. Reading lamp, clock radio, bathrobes, slippers and sherry decanter in room. TV, VCR, fax, spa, bicycles, library, telephone, fireplace, BBQ and kitchen on premises. Art galleries, cross-country skiing, downhill skiing, fishing, golf, parks, sporting events, water sports, horseback, rafting and canoeing, trolley tours, bungy jumping and zip trek nearby.

Location: Mountains.

"Great house, great food, terrific people."

Certificate may be used: April 15-June 15 and Sept. 15-Nov. 15, except holidays. Two condos in village December-April only.

New Brunswick

Hillsborough

The Ship's Lantern Inn

17 Pleasant Street
Hillsborough, NB E4H 3A6
(506)734-3221 (866)734-7447 Fax:(506)734-2972
Internet: www.shipslantern.com
E-mail: brendog@nbnet.nb.ca

Circa 1786. Be captivated by the casual elegance of this 18th century Georgian inn with gingerbread trim and large verandas. An included Welcome Package features a variety of treats to choose from. The first floor sitting room is highlighted by an Italian marble fireplace and distinctive antiques. For avid readers or history buffs there are magazines and books to peak interest and provide background of the inn and local area. Generous amenities ensure the feeling of being pleasantly pampered. Several of the guest suites offer whirlpool baths. Select from a breakfast menu in the Lewis or Duffy dining rooms.

Innkeeper(s): Brenda & Cole Belliveau. $115-150. 5 rooms, 1 with PB, 4 suites. Breakfast and snacks/refreshments included in rates. Types of meals: Full gourmet bkfst, early coffee/tea, picnic lunch, gourmet dinner and room service. Restaurant on premises. Beds: KQT. Data port, cable TV, VCR, reading lamp, ceiling fan, snack bar, clock radio, telephone, coffeemaker, turn-down service, desk, whirlpool bathtub, bathrobes and hair dryer in room. Air conditioning. Fax, pet boarding, child care, parlor games, fireplace and laundry facility on premises. Handicap access. Antiquing, art galleries, beach, bicycling, canoeing/kayaking, cross-country skiing, fishing, golf, hiking, horseback riding, museums, parks, shopping, wineries and guided tours nearby.

Location: Scenic country village.

Publicity: *Canadian Country Inns and North American Country Inns.*

Certificate may be used: Anytime, subject to availability.

Rexton

Jardine's Inn

104 Main Street
Rexton, NB E4W 2B3
(506)523-7070 (866)523-7070 Fax:(866)523-7072
Internet: www.jardinesinn.com
E-mail: hudsonj@nb.sympatico.ca

Circa 1850. Nominated as a Provincial Historic Site, this inn was built with deal construction, using three-inch wood that is pegged together upright. Guest bedrooms are named after Jardine ships. Sleep on a sleigh bed with down duvet, and soak in an antique clawfoot tub. Breakfast delights include grapefruit marinated in Grand Marnier, apple blossom tart with maple sauce, citrus French toast and orange juice with a dollop of mango sorbet. Savor afternoon tea and scones in the tea room. A variety of on-site activities are offered. Make reservations for a lobster supper, learn of the area's rich folklore on an Evening Lantern Guided Walking Tour down Water Street and be sure to view the display of artwork and crafts made by local artists.

Innkeeper(s): Jean & Jack Hudson. $89-125. 5 rooms with PB. Breakfast and afternoon tea included in rates. Types of meals: Full bkfst and picnic lunch. Beds: QT. Cable TV, reading lamp, ceiling fan and clock radio in room. TV, VCR, fax, bicycles, parlor games, telephone and gift shop on premises. Antiquing, beach, bicycling, canoeing/kayaking, fishing, golf, hiking, horseback riding, live theater, museums, parks and water sports nearby.

Location: Country.

Certificate may be used: During the month of May and the month of October.

Saint Andrews

Kingsbrae Arms Relais & Chateaux

219 King St
Saint Andrews, NB E5B 1Y1
(506)529-1897 Fax:(506)529-1197
Internet: www.kingsbrae.com
E-mail: kingbrae@nbnet.nb.ca

Circa 1897. With its splendid ocean views and ridgeline location, this shingle-style was built at the turn of the century on a choice piece of land. Today a trip to the manor house is a bit like traveling to a welcoming English country estate. The five guest rooms and three suites have been decorated with the utmost of elegance. Each room has a fireplace, and beds are dressed with fine linens and puffy comforters. Guests might find a room with a canopy bed draped with velvet or perhaps a bath with a clawfoot tub, marble walls and a wood floor. For those who wish to relax, the library is a masculine retreat with a fireplace and dark, exposed wood beams. Guests also can take a swim in the outdoor, heated swimming pool. The innkeepers pamper you with a gourmet morning feast and tea in the afternoon. One also can arrange to enjoy a five-course dinner, as rates are MAP. The inn has a Canada Select five-star rating and holds a four-star rating from Mobile. It has been selected as a Grand Award Winner of Andrew Harper's "Hideaways of the Year."

Innkeeper(s): Harry Chancey & David Oxford. $375-525. 8 rooms with PB, 8 with FP, 3 suites and 1 conference room. Breakfast, afternoon tea, snacks/refreshments and dinner included in rates. Types of meals: Full gourmet bkfst, early coffee/tea, gourmet lunch, picnic lunch and room service. Restaurant on premises. Beds: KQ. Cable TV, VCR, reading lamp, CD player, ceiling fan, clock radio, telephone, coffeemaker, turn-down service, desk, whirlpools and Jacuzzi in room. Air conditioning. Fax, copier, swimming, bicycles, library, parlor games, fireplace, patio and piano on premises. Antiquing, cross-country skiing, fishing, golf, parks, shopping, tennis, water sports and whale watching nearby.

Publicity: *Boston Globe, Atlantic Monthly, Canadian House & Home and CBC TV & Radio.*

Certificate may be used: Nov. 15-April 15, Monday-Thursday.

Nova Scotia

Bridgewater

Fairview Inn Bridgewater

25 Queen Street
Bridgewater, NS B4V 1P1
(902)423-1102 (800)725-8732 Fax:(902)423-8329
Internet: www.nsinns.com
E-mail: info@nsinns.com

Circa 1863. Recently restored, this plantation-style inn is the area's oldest continually operating, and boasts a quiet, relaxed setting for business or leisure. Memorable suites feature historical themes and are enhanced with hardwood floors, antique furnishings, local original artwork and data ports. Stay in a suite with a canopy bed, fireplace and Jacuzzi tub. A satisfying breakfast starts the day. Dine on the covered veranda or fireside in the dining room. Room service is available. Swim in the heated outdoor pool and hot tub.

Innkeeper(s): Mr. Stephen O'Leary. $48-108. 26 rooms with PB, 4 suites.

Breakfast included in rates. Types of meals: Full bkfst, lunch and dinner. Restaurant on premises. Beds: QDT. Modem hook-up, data port, cable TV, VCR, reading lamp, ceiling fan, clock radio, telephone, turn-down service, desk, hot tub/spa, voice mail and fireplace in room. Fax, copier, spa, swimming, fireplace, laundry facility and pool on premises. Antiquing, art galleries, beach, bicycling, canoeing/kayaking, cross-country skiing, fishing, golf, hiking, horseback riding, live theater, museums, parks, shopping, water sports and wineries nearby.

Location: Small town.

Certificate may be used: Anytime, subject to availability.

Gaetz Brook

Elephant's Nest B&B

127 Pleasant Drive
Gaetz Brook, NS B0J 1N0
(902)827-3891 Fax:(902)827-3891
E-mail: elephantsnest@ns.sympatico.ca

Circa 1982. Lakeside tranquility is found at this modern post-and-beam bed & breakfast. Enjoy an acre of delight while sitting on the waterfront in a lush country setting. Contemporary guest bedrooms boast balconies and armchairs to help guests appreciate the view. A full breakfast provides fuel for the assortment of activities offered. Canoeing and kayaking are available, or for the more adventuresome, try sailboarding. Hop on a bike to explore the surrounding scenery. For a nightcap, discuss the day's delights while soaking in the hot tub.

Innkeeper(s): June & John Meehan. $90. 2 rooms with PB. Breakfast and snacks/refreshments included in rates. Types of meals: Full bkfst. Beds: Q. Reading lamp, ceiling fan, clock radio, telephone, desk, balconies and arm chairs in room. TV, VCR, fax, copier, spa, swimming, bicycles, library, parlor games, fireplace, laundry facility, sailboards, canoeing and kayaks on premises. Antiquing, art galleries, beach, canoeing/kayaking, fishing, golf, hiking, museums, parks, shopping and water sports nearby.

Location: Country, waterfront.

Certificate may be used: Nov. 1-April 30, subject to availability.

Halifax

Welcome Inn Halifax

1984 Connaught Ave.
Halifax, NS B3H 4E1
(902)446-6500 (877)288-2999 Fax:(902)835-3805
Internet: www.welcomeinnhalifax.com
E-mail: info@welcomeinnhalifax.com

Circa 1948. Leave stress at home and experience all the comforts and luxuries that are in abundance at this Dutch Colonial-style inn. An appealing ambiance is imparted from the blend of modern and traditional decor. Hardwood and ceramic floors enhance the clean interior. A fireplace highlights the spacious sitting room. Most of the guest bedrooms feature a fireplace, data port, Jacuzzi tub and balcony. A hearty breakfast makes lunch almost unnecessary. Fax and photocopying services are available.

Innkeeper(s): Angela Kidston. $105-155. 3 rooms with PB, 3 with FP. Breakfast included in rates. Types of meals: Full bkfst. Beds: Q. Cable TV, VCR, reading lamp, clock radio, telephone, fireplace and two with a Jacuzzi tub in room. Fax on premises. Art galleries, bicycling, canoeing/kayaking, golf and hiking nearby.

Location: City.

Certificate may be used: Anytime, subject to availability.

West Dover Seaside Cottages

1984 Connaught Ave.
Halifax, NS B3H 4E1
(902)423-1102 (800)725-8732 Fax:(902)423-8329
Internet: www.nsinns.com
E-mail: info@nsinns.com

Peggy's Cove Parkland, a small fishing village is the bordering setting for these seaside accommodations. Stay in modern Hillside Cottages boasting harbor views, one or two bedrooms, full kitchens, balconies, gas grills and picnic tables. Some include fireplaces, as does the Deluxe Boathouse. Built on stilts over the water, the wharf is its deck. Full housekeeping service is provided. Ask about vacation packages and day adventures.
$75-205. 9 cottages. Beds: Q. Cable TV, reading lamp, refrigerator, clock radio and coffeemaker in room. Telephone on premises. Canoeing/kayaking, fishing, golf, hiking and shopping nearby.

Certificate may be used: Anytime, subject to availability.

Liverpool

Lane's Privateer Inn & B&B

27-33 Bristol Ave, PO Box 509
Liverpool, NS B0T 1K0
(902)354-3456 (800)794-3332 Fax:(902)354-7220
Internet: www3.nssympatico.ca/ron.lane
E-mail: ron.lane@ns.sympatico.ca

Circa 1798. For more than 30 years, three generations of the Lane family have run this historic lodge nestled among Nova Scotia's scenic coast and forests. The inn is a participant in "A Taste of Nova Scotia," which features a group of fine eateries that meet strict government standards. Lane's hosts a "Sip and Savour" series throughout the year, featuring wine tastings and gourmet meals. Breakfast at the inn is a treat with specialty menus featuring such items as haddock cakes and eggs Benedict. Nearby Kejimkujik National Park offers plenty of outdoor activities, and beaches are only a few miles away. Liverpool offers many fine shops and restaurants to enjoy.

Innkeeper(s): The Lane Family, Ron, Carol, Susan & Terry. $50-85. 30 rooms, 27 with PB. Breakfast included in rates. Types of meals: Lunch, picnic lunch, afternoon tea, gourmet dinner and room service. Restaurant on premises. Beds: QDT. Antiquing, cross-country skiing, fishing, live theater and water sports nearby.

Publicity: *Encore Travel, Providence and Rhode Island News.*

"Warm and relaxed atmosphere!"

Certificate may be used: Oct. 31-June 1, based on availability.

Lunenburg

Lunenburg Inn

PO Box 1407
Lunenburg, NS B0J 2C0
(902)634-3963 (800)565-3963 Fax:(902)634-9419
Internet: www.lunenburginn.com
E-mail: gail.don@lunenburginn.com

Circa 1893. Recently restored to maintain its classic Victorian beauty, this registered Heritage Property from the late 1800s sits on the edge of the UNESCO World Heritage Site of Old Town. Original woodwork, period colors, decor and antiques blend well with modern conveniences to offer comfort and gracious accommodations. A sun deck and veranda provide relaxing interludes. Guest suites feature whirlpool baths and sitting rooms. Savor a hot breakfast accompanied by seasonal fruit, fresh baked goods and preserves. Year-round activities within a short walk include seasonal festivals, waterfront shops, jogging and cycling trails. Whale watching and harbour tours are available.

Innkeeper(s): Gail and Don Wallace. $80-185. 7 rooms, 5 with PB, 2 suites. Breakfast and afternoon tea included in rates. Types of meals: Full bkfst, veg bkfst and snacks/refreshments. Beds: QT. Reading lamp, ceiling fan, clock radio, desk, suites have air conditioning, whirlpool baths, refrigerator, TV and VCR in room. TV, VCR, fax, copier, library, parlor games, telephone and data port for guest use on premises. Antiquing, art galleries, beach, bicycling, canoeing/kayaking, fishing, golf, hiking, horseback riding, museums, parks, shopping, tennis, water sports, wineries, waterfront, the Fisheries Museum of the Atlantic, scallop draggers, pleasure boats, tall ships, BlueNose II, wooden churches, art galleries, puffins and seals nearby.

Location: Ocean community. Our inn is located on the edge of the National Historic District and UNESCO designated World Heritage Site of Old Town Lunenburg with its classic Victorian and Georgian architecture.

Certificate may be used: April and May, subject to availability, all days.

Peggy's Cove

Peggy's Cove Bed & Breakfast

19 Church Road
Peggy's Cove, NS B3Z 3R7
(902)423-1102 (800)725-8732 Fax:(902)423-8329
Internet: www.NSinns.com
E-mail: info@NSinns.com

Circa 1940. Walk to the world famous Peggy's Cove lighthouse from this yellow farm house with wraparound veranda. Situated in the fishing village, it is on two acres of grounds. Enjoying the sunset views from a private balcony, sipping local wines and soaking in an outdoor hot tub are among the favorite experiences at the inn. A full stick-to-your-ribs breakfast is offered. Once owned by artist Bill de Garthe, the home was originally a fisherman's house. The art studio now features contemporary landscapes and marine art by local Nova Scotian artisans including the resident artist. Carvings and local crafts are also on exhibit.

Innkeeper(s): Paul Matte & Bee Gibson. $95-145. 5 rooms with PB. Breakfast included in rates. Types of meals: Full bkfst. Beds: Q. Cable TV, reading lamp, clock radio and telephone in room. Outdoor hot tub on premises. Antiquing, canoeing/kayaking, fishing, golf, hiking and shopping nearby.

Location: Ocean community.

Certificate may be used: Anytime, subject to availability.

Prospect

Prospect Bed and Breakfast

1758 Prospect Bay Road
Prospect, NS B3H 4E1
(902)423-1102 (800)725-8732 Fax:(902)423-8329
Internet: www.NSinns.com
E-mail: info@NSinns.com

Circa 1854. Surrounded by ocean with magnificent views in all directions, this Victorian home is at the end of a point in the quaint fishing village of Prospect. Originally built as a summer home for the Premiere of Nova Scotia, the large, comfortable rooms feature private baths and are furnished with antiques and original art. Kayak or canoe in the shelter of the bay, or explore one of the nearby, uninhabited islands with gull rookeries and secluded coves. Numerous nature trails on the cliffs

along the coast provide opportunities for hiking and bird or whale watching, accompanied by a stunning view of the sunset. Meals include gourmet breakfasts featuring home-baked goods and complimentary afternoon tea.

Innkeeper(s): Helena Prsala. $95-145. 5 rooms with PB. Breakfast included in rates. Types of meals: Full gourmet bkfst and early coffee/tea. Beds: Q. Cable TV, reading lamp, clock radio and telephone in room. Swimming and beach on premises. Antiquing, art galleries, beach, canoeing/kayaking, golf and hiking nearby.

Location: Waterfront.

Publicity: *National Geographic, Doctors Review, NS Tourism TV, Red Rose and Baby.*

Certificate may be used: Anytime, subject to availability.

Queensland

Surfside Inn

RR2
Hubbards, NS B0J 1T0
(902)857-2417 (800)373-2417 Fax:(902)857-2107
Internet: www.thesurfsideinn.com
E-mail: info@thesurfsideinn.com

Circa 1880. Befitting its name, this Victorian inn overlooks Queensland Beach and all of St. Margaret's Bay. Originally a sea captain's home, restoration has maintained the elegant ambiance of that era while offering present-day amenities. Luxurious guest bedrooms and suites boast whirlpool tubs and lake or ocean views. Breakfast on the deck includes yogurt, secret-recipe granola, maritime brown bread and blueberry preserves. Relax over a delicious dinner by candlelight in the dining room. The bay area offers a variety of land activities and water sports.

Innkeeper(s): Michelle & Bill Batcules. $89-199. 8 rooms with PB. Breakfast included in rates. Types of meals: Cont plus, veg bkfst, snacks/refreshments, gourmet dinner and room service. Restaurant on premises. Beds: QD. Cable TV, VCR, reading lamp, ceiling fan, clock radio and hot tub/spa in room. Fax, copier, spa, swimming, telephone, fireplace and laundry facility on premises. Limited handicap access. Amusement parks, antiquing, art galleries, beach, bicycling, canoeing/kayaking, cross-country skiing, fishing, golf, hiking, horseback riding, live theater, museums, parks, shopping, sporting events, tennis, water sports and wineries nearby.

Location: Waterfront.

Certificate may be used: Oct. 1-May 15, Sunday-Thursday.

Ontario

Aylmer

Ye Olde Apple Yard B&B

49450 College Line, RR 4
Aylmer, ON N5H 2R3
(519)765-2708
E-mail: yeoldeapplyard@gent.net

This Italianate farmhouse is set on acres of secluded countryside. Guests can stroll through the apple orchard or simply relax with a picnic under the trees. Romantic dinners for two can be arranged. Guests can also enjoy the company of the resident farm animals, or simply sit and relax by the fireplace. The area offers many interesting shops and Amish farms.

Innkeeper(s): Tino Smiaris. $65. 2 rooms. Breakfast included in rates. Types of meals: Full bkfst.

Certificate may be used: Monday to Thursday, Nov. 1-April 30.

Chatham

Jordan House

RR #6
Chatham, ON N7M 5J6
(519)436-0839
Internet: www.jordan-house.com
E-mail: reservations@jordan-house.com

Circa 1900. Since 1838 the Jordan family has owned this fifty-acre estate, and hosts John and Barbara act the part of the historic original owners of this Victorian Queen Anne house, in period 1900s attire. Luxury and comfort combine in this large home boasting tastefully decorated rooms furnished with antiques, accented with fresh flowers and featuring an Edwardian decor. Air-conditioned guest bedrooms are named after local and British counties, as well as reflecting the direction they face. Some of the pleasurable amenities include feather bed mattress tops, down duvets and blackout blinds behind draperies. Savor a morning meal full of classic favorites.

Innkeeper(s): John & Barbara Jordan. $85-95. 4 rooms with PB. Breakfast included in rates. Types of meals: Full gourmet bkfst, veg bkfst, early coffee/tea, picnic lunch, afternoon tea, dinner and room service. Beds: KQDT. Modem hook-up, data port, TV, reading lamp, ceiling fan, clock radio, telephone, turn-down service and desk in room. Air conditioning. VCR, library, pet boarding, parlor games and fireplace on premises. Antiquing, art galleries, beach, bicycling, fishing, golf and horseback riding nearby.

Location: Country.

Certificate may be used: Anytime, subject to availability.

Collingwood

Pretty River Valley Country Inn

RR 1
Nottawa, ON L0M IPO
(705)445-7598 Fax:(705)445-7598
Internet: www.prettyriverinn.com
E-mail: inn@cois.on.ca

Circa 1980. Each of the guest rooms at this log inn includes a fireplace, and suites have the added amenity of a double whirlpool tub. The secluded, 120-acre estate offers views of the Pretty River Valley as well as the Blue Mountains. The innkeepers provide an ample breakfast, highlighted by items such as eggs Benedict. A collection of menus from local restaurants is kept on hand. Each season brings outdoor fun. Downhill and cross-country skiing, water sports on the bay and golfing are nearby, and there are plenty of antique shops to explore.

Innkeeper(s): Steve & Diane Szelestowski. $110-145. 8 rooms with PB, 8 with FP, 2 suites and 1 conference room. Breakfast included in rates. Types of meals: Full bkfst. Beds: QT. Refrigerator, clock radio and two with whirlpool in room. Air conditioning. Fax, spa, pet boarding, telephone and fireplace on premises. Antiquing, bicycling, cross-country skiing, downhill skiing, fishing, golf, hiking, parks, shopping, tennis, water sports and kennel across street nearby.

Location: Country, mountains. In valley surrounded by hills.

Publicity: *Toronto Sun and Century Homes.*

Certificate may be used: All year, Sunday to Thursday.

Emsdale

Fernglen Inn

Box 83
Emsdale, ON P0A 1-J0
(705)636-5489 Fax:(705)636-0293
Internet: www.ferngleninn.on.ca
E-mail: fernglen@surenet.net

Circa 1905. Cradled by 120 acres of rolling hills in the Almaguin Highlands, this four-season bed & breakfast was originally a farmhouse. Guest bedrooms in the Main House and Coach House exude an old-country ambiance and are furnished with Canadian antiques, boast private baths, coffee service and snacks. In the morning, indulge in an ample breakfast that is sure to satisfy. Lunch and dinner are available upon request. Besides the inn's private trails for hiking, biking, cross-country skiing, snowmobiling, and snowshoeing, explore the Seguin Trail System and nearby Algonquin and Arrowhead Provincial Parks.

$95. 5 rooms with PB. Breakfast included in rates. Types of meals: Country bkfst, veg bkfst, lunch, picnic lunch and gourmet dinner. Beds: D. Reading lamp, ceiling fan, clock radio, coffeemaker and hot tub/spa in room. Fax, spa, bicycles, parlor games and telephone on premises. Limited handicap access. Antiquing, art galleries, beach, bicycling, canoeing/kayaking, cross-country skiing, fishing, golf, hiking, horseback riding, parks and shopping nearby.

Location: Country. On Trans Canada Hiking Trail.

Certificate may be used: Anytime, subject to availability.

Gananoque

Manse Lane B&B

465 Stone St S
Gananoque, ON K7G 2A7
(613)382-8642 (888)565-6379
Internet: www.bbcanada.com/942.html

Circa 1860. Four comfortable guest rooms, two with a private bath, are available at this bed & breakfast. Breakfasts include items such as cereal, fruit, yogurt, cheeses, breads, bacon and eggs. Guests are within walking distance of local attractions.

Innkeeper(s): Jocelyn & George Bounds. $55-160. 4 rooms, 2 with PB. Breakfast included in rates. Types of meals: Full bkfst, early coffee/tea, afternoon tea and room service. Beds: QT. Reading lamp and desk in room. Air conditioning. Swimming, parlor games, telephone and fireplace on premises. Antiquing, cross-country skiing, fishing, golf, live theater, parks, tennis, water sports, boat cruises and festivals nearby.

"Thoroughly enjoyed the stay. It was great to see you again."
Certificate may be used: Nov. 1 through April 15, seven days a week.

Kingston

Hotel Belvedere

141 King St E
Kingston, ON K7L 2Z9
(613)548-1565 (800)559-0584 Fax:(613)546-4692
Internet: www.hotelbelvedere.com
E-mail: reserve@hotelbelvedere.com

Circa 1880. Hotel Belvedere began its life as a private mansion, built in the Georgian style of architecture. Eventually, it was transformed into a hotel and then into a boarding house.

Thankfully, it has been restored and refurbished back to its original state. The interior boasts the fine woodwork, carved mantels and marble floors one expects in a grand mansion. Elegant guest rooms are decorated in period style with antiques, and beds are dressed with fine white linens. In warm weather, the innkeepers serve a continental breakfast on the private terrace. Guests can enjoy the morning fare in their room or in front of a warm fire in the living room. Secluded three hours from Toronto along the shores of Lake Ontario, Kingston is a charming site for a getaway. Historic homes, museums and dinner cruises are among the offerings in town. The town once served as the capital of Canada.

Innkeeper(s): Donna Mallory & Ian Walsh. $110-250. 20 rooms with PB, 2 suites and 1 conference room. Breakfast included in rates. Types of meals: Cont plus and early coffee/tea. Beds: KQDT. Modem hook-up, data port, TV, reading lamp, telephone, desk and hot tub/spa in room. Air conditioning. Fax, copier, library, fireplace and laundry facility on premises. Limited handicap access. Antiquing, art galleries, beach, bicycling, canoeing/kayaking, cross-country skiing, fishing, golf, hiking, live theater, museums, parks, shopping, sporting events, tennis and water sports nearby.

Location: City.

Publicity: *New York Times, Globe & Mail, National Geographic Traveler, Toronto Star, A Taste of Life and Canadian Travel Show.*

Certificate may be used: Nov. 1 through March 31 on Friday, Saturday, Sunday.

Kitchener

Mornington Crescent Bed & Breakfast

11 Sunbridge Crescent
Kitchener, ON N2K 1T6
(519)763-6557 (877)763-6557
Internet: www.morningtoncres.ca
E-mail: bandb@morningtoncres.ca

Circa 1970. Just minutes from the city, yet this modern bunga-low style bed & breakfast sits peacefully secluded in historic and scenic Menn County. Stay here at any time of the year while traveling for business or leisure. Deluxe guest bedrooms and a suite feature pampering amenities as well as high speed and wireless Internet access. Relax in a double whirlpool tub by candlelight before sleeping in a handcrafted Mennonite bed by a fireplace. A well-stocked library offers videos and reading materials to borrow. After a complete breakfast, made as requested, take one of the walking trails from the back yard. Swim in the heated pool or soak in the hot tub.

Innkeeper(s): Carolyn Steele. $75-120. 4 rooms, 2 with PB, 1 with FP and 1 conference room. Breakfast included in rates. Types of meals: Full bkfst, veg bkfst, early coffee/tea and afternoon tea. Beds: KQT. Cable TV, VCR, read-ing lamp, refrigerator, clock radio, coffeemaker, desk, fireplace and suites have microwave in room. Central air. Fax, copier, spa, swimming, bicycles, library, pet boarding, parlor games, telephone, fireplace, high-speed wireless Internet and heated in-ground pool on premises. Antiquing, bicycling, canoe-ing/kayaking, cross-country skiing, fishing, golf, hiking, horseback riding, live theater, parks and shopping nearby.

Location: City.

Certificate may be used: Anytime, November-April, subject to availability.

New Hamburg

The Waterlot

17 Huron St
New Hamburg, ON N3A 1K1
(519)662-2020 Fax:(519)662-2114
Internet: www.waterlot.com
E-mail: waterlot@waterlot.com

Circa 1844. Located beside a mill pond, this Victorian home boasts an imaginative architecture with gothic gables frosted with gingerbread trim and an unusual cupola. It houses the inn's most important asset, a French-country restaurant, Le Bistro, which seats 125 people. Overlooking the Nith River as it flows through the backyard, the restaurant has been well-known for three decades. Guest rooms are simple and housed beneath each of the inn's twin gables.

Innkeeper(s): Gord & Leslie Elkeer. $80-120. 3 rooms, 1 suite. Breakfast included in rates. Types of meals: Cont plus, lunch, picnic lunch and gourmet dinner. Restaurant on premises. Beds: KQD. Clock radio in room. Fax, copier, parlor games, telephone and fireplace on premises. Amusement parks, antiquing, cross-country skiing, downhill skiing, fishing, golf, live theater, parks, shopping and tennis nearby.

Location: Waterfront.

Certificate may be used: April 1-Feb. 28, (closed March).

Niagara Falls

Bampfield Hall

4761 Zimmerman Ave.
Niagara Falls, ON L2E 3M8
(905)353-8522 (877)353-8522
E-mail: niagbnb@mergetal.com

Circa 1872. Designed with Neo-Gothic architecture, this his-toric home boasts etched glass, a turret, gracefully curved stair-case and patterned wood floors. Family heirlooms and collec-tions are found throughout. Relaxing conversations are popular in the living room, which reflects a 1930s Hollywood decor. Guest bedrooms and a suite are comfortably furnished. The pri-vate Jesters Suite is a top-floor room at the back of the house and boasts a Jacuzzi tub. Enjoy a satisfying breakfast in the large dining room.

Innkeeper(s): David Tetrault. $50-115. 3 rooms with PB. Breakfast included in rates. Types of meals: Full gourmet bkfst and veg bkfst. Beds: KQ. Amusement parks, antiquing, art galleries, beach, bicycling, fishing, golf, hik-ing, horseback riding, live theater, museums, parks, shopping, tennis and wineries nearby.

Location: City.

Certificate may be used: Nov. 1-April 30, Sunday-Thursday, except Christmas, New Year's and Valentine's Day.

Niagara Inn

4300 Simcoe Street
Niagara Falls, ON L2E 1T6
(905)353-8522 (877)353-8522
Internet: www.niagaraniagara.com
E-mail: niagbnb@mergetel.com

Circa 1887. Victorian in design and decor with eclectic accents, this bed & breakfast exudes a feeling of nostalgia. Original detailed woodwork and stained glass reflect the quality craftsmanship of the era. Comfortable guest bedrooms feature antique furnishings. Savor a leisurely breakfast that includes delicious entrees and homemade baked goods. Explore the scenic locale on available bicycles.

Innkeeper(s): David Tetrault. $50-105. 3 rooms with PB. Breakfast included in rates. Types of meals: Full gourmet bkfst and veg bkfst. Beds: Q. Cable TV, reading lamp, refrigerator, ceiling fan and clock radio in room. Air conditioning. TV, bicycles, library and telephone on premises. Limited handicap access. Amusement parks, antiquing, art galleries, beach, bicycling, fishing, golf, hiking, horseback riding, live theater, museums, parks, shopping, tennis, water sports and wineries nearby.

Location: City.

Certificate may be used: Nov. 1-April 30, Sunday-Thursday, excluding Christmas, New Year's and Valentine's Day.

Ottawa

Gasthaus Switzerland Inn

89 Daly Ave
Ottawa, ON K1N 6E6
(613)237-0335 (888)663-0000 Fax:(613)594-3327
Internet: www.gasthausswitzerlandinn.com
E-mail: switzinn@gasthausswitzerlandinn.com

Circa 1872. Constructed from limestone, this Vernacular Classical Revival home served as a military rehabilitation facility during World War I. The inn has welcomed guests since 1985, and proud innkeepers Josef and Sabina provide splendid hospitality with a distinctively European flair. The well-appointed guest bedrooms and romantic suites are comfortably elegant. Some feature fireplaces, double Jacuzzis, CD stereos, four-poster canopy beds and sparkling wine. A traditional Swiss, full breakfast is served buffet style or delivered to the room. Parliament Hill is within an easy walk, as are interesting shops, museums and restaurants.

Innkeeper(s): Sabina & Josef Sauter. $98-248. 22 rooms, 20 with PB, 6 with FP, 2 suites. Breakfast included in rates. Types of meals: Full bkfst. Beds: KQDT. Modem hook-up, data port, cable TV, reading lamp, stereo, clock radio, telephone, desk and some with fireplace in room. Central air. TV, fax, copier, bicycles, fireplace, laundry facility and limited free parking on premises. Antiquing, beach, bicycling, cross-country skiing, downhill skiing, fishing, golf, hiking, horseback riding, live theater, museums, parks, shopping, tennis and cycling nearby.

Location: City. Downtown Ottawa.

Publicity: *The Washington Post, Arrington's Inn Traveler and Travel Travel CFCFTV.*

Certificate may be used: Nov. 15-Jan. 30, Anytime. March 1-April 15, Sunday-Thursday, Honeymoon suite excluded.

Inn on Somerset

282 Somerset St W
Ottawa, ON K2P 0J6
(613)236-9309 (800)658-3564 Fax:(613)237-6842
Internet: www.innonsomerset.com
E-mail: info@innonsomerset.com

Circa 1895. Enjoy a delightful stay at this grand Victorian home built in 1895. Relax in front of the fireplace in the living room or take a leisurely stroll beside the Rideau Canal. Well-appointed guest bedrooms are furnished with period antiques and feature Internet access. Two rooms boast a fireplace and one has a sun porch. A hearty breakfast is served in the gracious dining room from 7:30 to 9 a.m. Work out in the exercise room, use the sauna or be entertained by the home theatre. A washer and dryer are available. The inn is located in the heart of Ottawa, an easy walk to Parliament Hill, shopping and fine restaurants.

Innkeeper(s): George & Richard. $95-130. 11 rooms, 5 with PB, 1 with FP. Breakfast included in rates. Types of meals: Full bkfst. Beds: QDT. Reading lamp, clock radio, telephone and desk in room. Air conditioning. VCR, fax, copier, fireplace and sauna on premises. Antiquing, cross-country skiing,

downhill skiing, live theater, parks, shopping, sporting events and tourist attractions nearby.

Location: City.

Publicity: *Ottawa Citizen.*

Certificate may be used: November through January.

Peterborough

King Bethune Guest House & Spa

270 King St
Peterborough, ON K9J 2S2
(705)743-4101 (800)574-3664
Internet: www.bbcanada.com/165
E-mail: marlis@sympatico.ca

Circa 1893. This brick Victorian is downtown on a quiet tree-shaded street. Restored hardwood floors, original trim throughout, tall ceilings and handsome windows grace the interiors.

Guest rooms are large with ensuite baths and offer antiques, as well as desks, data ports, TVs and VCRs. The Spa Suite has a king bed and private entrance as well as a private hot tub, sauna, steam bath and massage therapy room. There's a restful walled garden with fireplace and patio, a favorite spot for breakfast.

Innkeeper(s): Marlis Lindsay. $104-220. 2 rooms with PB, 1 with HT, 1 suite. Breakfast included in rates. Types of meals: Full bkfst and room service. Beds: KQ. Cable TV, VCR, reading lamp, ceiling fan, clock radio, telephone, turn-down service and desk in room. Sauna, parlor games, fireplace, steambath, massage therapy room and private outdoor garden hot tub on premises. Amusement parks, antiquing, bicycling, cross-country skiing, downhill skiing, fishing, golf, live theater, parks, shopping, sporting events, tennis and water sports nearby.

Location: City.

Publicity: *Canadian Country and Examiner.*

"We still have not found better accommodations anywhere."

Certificate may be used: Jan. 30-Nov. 30, Sunday-Monday.

Toronto

A Rosedale Bed & Breakfast

572 Sherbourne St.
Toronto, ON M4X 1L3
(416)927-0543 (800)360-1382 Fax:(416)966-0962
Internet: www.rosedalebandb.ca
E-mail: mail@rosedalebandb.ca

Circa 1887. Embracing Victorian design in both architecture and decor, this historic inn was recently remodeled. Relax on comfortable European and Asian furnishings by the tiled fireplace in the living room. Guest bedrooms offer a variety of choices. The fireplaced French Room overlooks the garden and fish pond. The spacious Green Suite includes a sleigh bed and eating area with wet bar and refrigerator. The more modern studio boasts teak furniture from India. Enjoy a generous continental breakfast before exploring the many city attractions.

Innkeeper(s): Aries & Michael. $75-140. 7 rooms, 4 with PB. Types of meals: Cont plus and early coffee/tea. Beds: QD. Cable TV, VCR, reading lamp, refrigerator, ceiling fan, clock radio, coffeemaker and desk in room. Central air. Fax, telephone and laundry facility on premises. Art galleries, bicycling, live theater, museums, parks and shopping nearby.

Location: City.

Certificate may be used: November through March, Sunday-Thursday.

Westport

Stepping Stone Inn

328 Centreville Rd, RR 2
Westport, ON K0G 1X0
(613)273-3806 Fax:(613)273-3331
Internet: www.steppingstoneinn.com
E-mail: stepping@rideau.net

Circa 1840. Multi-colored limestone warms in the afternoon
sun on this historic house located on more than 150 acres.
Flower beds surround the wraparound veranda decorated in
white gingerbread and fretwork. Rooms are furnished with
antiques, and there is a solarium and dining room that overlook flower gardens, a pic-
turesque swimming pond and
waterfall. Guest rooms
include luxury suites with
Jacuzzis, fireplaces and
private entrances. Plan
ahead and the inn's chef

will create a custom menu for you. Stepping Stone is popular
for garden weddings and corporate meetings. The grounds offer
a beaver pond, pastures and nature trails. The Rideau Canal
System and many lakes are nearby.

Innkeeper(s): Madeleine Saunders. $75-150. 10 rooms with PB, 3 with FP,
3 suites, 1 cabin and 1 conference room. Breakfast included in rates. Types
of meals: Full gourmet bkfst, early coffee/tea, picnic lunch, afternoon tea and
gourmet dinner. Restaurant on premises. Beds: QT. Reading lamp and 5 with
Jacuzzis in room. Air conditioning. Fax, swimming, telephone and fireplace
on premises. Handicap access. Antiquing, cross-country skiing, fishing, golf,
hiking, live theater, parks, shopping, tennis, water sports and skating nearby.

Certificate may be used: Feb. 1 to Dec. 15, Sunday to Thursday, subject
to availability.

Windsor

Ye Olde Walkerville B & B

1104 Monmouth Rd
Windsor, ON N8Y 3L8
(519)254-1507 Fax:(519)252-5542
Internet: www.wescanada.com
E-mail: walkervillebb@wescanada.com

Circa 1903. Exuding an upscale romantic ambiance and informal friendliness, this Victorian manor provides an adult-oriented
tranquility and relaxation. Excellent service resulting in complete
satisfaction is the accomplished desire of this award-winning bed
& breakfast. Stay in Samantha's Suite or one of the impressive
guest bedrooms, each named after the hosts' grandchildren.
Enjoy cable TV and free local phone calls in a smoke-free environment. Choose a chef-prepared breakfast from a varied menu
selection that is sure to please. Quantities are made-to-order.

Innkeeper(s): Wayne Strong. $189-289. 5 rooms with PB, 1 with FP, 1 suite.
Breakfast included in rates. Types of meals: Full gourmet bkfst, early coffee/tea and picnic lunch. Beds: KQ. Cable TV, VCR, reading lamp,
clock radio, telephone, desk, hot tub/spa and fireplace in room. Central air.
Fax, copier, spa, parlor games and fireplace on premises. Art galleries, bicycling, golf, horseback riding, live theater, museums, parks, shopping, sporting
events and wineries nearby.

Location: City.

Publicity: Windsor Star and CBC.

Certificate may be used: September-November, January-May, Sunday-
Thursday, excludes all holidays.

Prince Edward Island

Cardigan

Cardigan River Inn

57 Owens Wharf Rd.
Cardigan, PE C0A 1G0
(902)583-2331 (800)425-9577 Fax:(902)583-2331
Internet: www.cardiganriverinn.com
E-mail: cardiganriverinn@hotmail.com

Known locally as the Road's End Mansion, this renovated five-
star waterfront estate graces a 26-acre knoll with a generous
amount of salt-river frontage. Listen to music in the living room
by firelight, gaze at the library's waterview and enjoy afternoon
tea in the sunroom. Splendid guest bedrooms feature period
antiques, whirlpool baths with showers, fireplaces, thoughtful
personal amenities and use of an extensive video library. Each
morning choose from a multi-selection menu for breakfast in
the dining room. Manicured grounds boast the area's oldest
and largest linden trees. A gazebo is perfect for watching boats
sail by. Call the inn for additional travel packages.

$145-240. 4 rooms with PB, 3 with FP, 4 with WP, 2 suites. Whirlpool tub
in room.

Certificate may be used: Sept. 9-Oct. 31, Sunday-Friday.

Roseneath B&B

RR #6
Cardigan, PE C0A 1G0
(902)838-4590 (800)823-8933 Fax:(902)838-4590
Internet: www.resebb.ca
E-mail: sleep@rosebb.ca

Circa 1868. Located on 90 acres, this Victorian farm house has
scroll-decorated gables and a wraparound porch. It has been in
the present family since 1920, and the innkeeper's father once
ran the old saw mill. The inn has antiques and quilts, and artwork collected during many years of living overseas. Guests are
welcome to play the pump organ or gramophone or borrow
binoculars for bird watching (bald eagles, blue jays and
herons). Nearby attractions include seal-watching cruises, the
Wood Islands Ferry, Orwell Historic Village and Charlottetown.
Rates are quoted in Canadian dollars.

Innkeeper(s): Edgar & Brenda Dewar. $95-160. 4 rooms with PB. Breakfast
and afternoon tea included in rates. Types of meals: Full bkfst and early cof-
fee/tea. Beds: QDT. Reading lamp, desk and washbasin in room. VCR, fax,
copier, bicycles, library, parlor games and telephone on premises. Cross-country skiing, fishing, golf, live theater, parks, shopping and water sports nearby.

Location: Country.

Certificate may be used: Oct. 30 to May 1, subject to availability. Rates are
in Canadian dollars.

Inns of Interest

African-American History

Wingscorton Farm Inn . . . . . East Sandwich, Mass.
Munro House B&B Day Spa . . . . . Jonesville, Mich.
The Signal House . . . . Ripley, Ohio
The Inn at Weathersfield . . . . Perkinsville, Vt.
Golden Stage Inn . . . . Proctorsville, Vt.
Rockland Farm Retreat . . . . Bumpass, Va.
Sleepy Hollow Farm B&B . . . . Gordonsville, Va.

Animals

Canaan Land Farm B&B . . . . Harrodsburg, Ky.
The Wren's Nest Bed & Breakfast
. . . . West Bloomfield, Mich.
The Shaw House B&B . . . . Georgetown, S.C.
Southwind . . . . Wimberley, Texas
The Garden, Bed & Breakfast Inn
. . . . Spring City, Utah
Llama Ranch B&B . . . . White Salmon, Wash.

Barns

Old Church House Inn . . . . Mossville, Ill.
1794 Watchtide... by the Sea . . . . Searsport, Maine
Brannon-Bunker Inn . . . . Walpole, Maine
Candlelite Inn . . . . Bradford, N.H.
The Inn At Cedar Falls . . . . Logan, Ohio
Cornerstone B&B Inn . . . . Landenberg, Pa.
Jackson Fork Inn LLC . . . . Huntsville, Utah
Waitsfield Inn . . . . Waitsfield, Vt.

Bordellos

Cheyenne Canon Inn . . . . . Colorado Springs, Colo.

Castles

Ravenwood Castle . . . . New Plymouth, Ohio
Manresa Castle . . . . Port Townsend, Wash.

Churches & Parsonages

The Victorian Rose B&B . . . . Ventura, Calif.
Fourteen Lincoln Street, a Chef-Owned
Bed & Breakfast . . . . Niantic, Conn.
Old Church House Inn . . . . Mossville, Ill.
Christopher's B&B . . . . Bellevue, Ky.
Parsonage Inn . . . . Saint Michaels, Md.
The Parsonage Inn . . . . East Orleans, Mass.
The Parsonage on The Green B&B . . . . . Lee, Mass.
The Abbey Bed & Breakfast. . . . . . . Cape May, N.J.
Parson's Pillow B&B . . . . Cody, Wyo.

Civil War

Myrtledene B&B. . . . . Lebanon, Ky.
The General Rufus Putnam House
. . . . Rutland, Mass.
Munro House B&B Day Spa . . . . . Jonesville, Mich.
Anchuca . . . . Vicksburg, Miss.
James Gettys Hotel . . . . Gettysburg, Pa.
The Beechmont B&B Inn . . . . Hanover, Pa.
Chesnut Cottage B&B . . . . Columbia, S.C.
The Inn at Weathersfield . . . . Perkinsville, Vt.
La Vista Plantation . . . . Fredericksburg, Va.

Cookbooks Written by Innkeepers

"Heartstone Inn Breakfast Cookbook"
The Heartstone Inn & Cottages
. . . . Eureka Springs, Ark.
"The Old Yacht Club Inn Cookbook"
The Old Yacht Club Inn. . . . . . Santa Barbara, Calif.
"A Taste of Blue Spruce Inn"
Blue Spruce Inn . . . . Soquel, Calif.
"By Request, The White Oak Cookbook"
The White Oak Inn . . . . Danville, Ohio
Whispering Pines Bed and Breakfast
. . . . Dellroy, Ohio
"Favorite Recipes of Whitestone Country Inn"
Whitestone Country Inn . . . . Kingston, Tenn.
"Recipes from the Kitchen of"
Hill Farm Inn. . . . . Arlington, Vt.
"Trail's End Cookbook"
Trail's End, A Country Inn
. . . . Wilmington, Vt.
"The Inn Tastes of MacKaye Harbor"
MacKaye Harbor Inn . . . . Lopez Island, Wash.
"With Lots of Love"
A. Drummonds Ranch B&B . . . . . Cheyenne, Wyo.

Farms and Orchards

Fool's Cove Ranch B&B . . . . Kingston, Ark.
Apple Blossom Inn B&B. . . . . Ahwahnee, Calif.
Howard Creek Ranch . . . . Westport, Calif.
Black Forest B&B. . . . . . . Colorado Springs, Colo.
Homespun Farm Bed and Breakfast
. . . . Jewett City, Conn.
Canaan Land Farm B&B. . . . . . . Harrodsburg, Ky.
1851 Historic Maple Hill Manor B&B
. . . . Springfield, Ky.
Maple Hill Farm B&B Inn. . . . . . Hallowell, Maine
Wingscorton Farm Inn . . . . . East Sandwich, Mass.
Gilbert's Tree Farm B&B . . . . Rehoboth, Mass.
Horse & Carriage B&B . . . . Jonesville, Mich.
Caverly Farm & Orchard B&B . . . . Bland, Mo.
Grandpa's Farm B&B . . . . Lampe, Mo.
Brass Heart Inn . . . . Chocorua, N.H.
Inn at Ellis River . . . . Jackson, N.H.
Olde Orchard Inn. . . . . . . Moultonborough, N.H.
Apple Valley Inn . . . . Glenwood, N.J.
Berry Hill Gardens B&B. . . . . Bainbridge, N.Y.
Agape Farm B&B and Paintball . . . . . Corinth, N.Y.
The Mast Farm Inn . . . . Valle Crucis, N.C.
Volden Farm. . . . . Luverne, N.D.
Barley Sheaf Farm . . . . Holicong, Pa.
Cedar Hill Farm . . . . Mount Joy, Pa.
Field & Pine B&B. . . . . Shippensburg, Pa.
B&B at Skoglund Farm. . . . . Canova, S.D.
Hill Farm Inn. . . . . Arlington, Vt.
Liberty Hill Farm. . . . . Rochester, Vt.
Rockland Farm Retreat . . . . Bumpass, Va.
Old Spring Farm Bed & Breakfast, Ltd.
. . . . Woolwine, Va.
Turtleback Farm Inn . . . . Eastsound, Wash.

Glacier Viewing

Justin Trails Resort . . . . Sparta, Wis.
Pearson's Pond Luxury Inn & Adventure Spa
. . . . Juneau, Alaska

Gold Mines & Gold Panning

Pearson's Pond Luxury Inn & Adventure Spa
. . . . Juneau, Alaska

Hot Springs

Vichy Hot Springs Resort & Inn
. . . . Ukiah, Calif.
Wiesbaden Hot Springs Spa & Lodgings
. . . . Ouray, Colo.

Inns Built Prior to 1800

1678 Hewick Plantation . . . . Urbanna, Va.
1684 The Inn at Montross . . . . Montross, Va.
1690 Brookside Manor . . . . Wakefield, R.I.
1691 The Great Valley House of Valley Forge
. . . . Valley Forge, Pa.
1696 Old Yarmouth Inn . . . . Yarmouth Port, Mass.
1699 Ashley Manor Inn . . . . Barnstable, Mass.
1700 Elias Child House B&B
. . . . Woodstock, Conn.
1700 Evermay-On-The-Delaware . . . . Erwinna, Pa.
1704 Cornerstone B&B Inn . . . . . Landenberg, Pa.
1709 The Woodbox Inn . . . . . . Nantucket, Mass.
1711 La Hacienda Grande . . . . . Bernalillo, N.M.
1712 Blue Gateways . . . . Wellfleet, Mass.
1714 Pennsbury Inn . . . . Chadds Ford, Pa.
1720 Roseledge Farm B&B . . . . . . Preston, Conn.
1725 1725 Historic Witmer's Tavern Inn & Museum
. . . . Lancaster, Pa.
1727 Apple Blossom B&B. . . . . York, Maine
1728 Red Fox Inn. . . . . Middleburg, Va.
1731 Bird-In-Hand . . . . Coventry, Conn.
1739 The Ruffner House . . . . Luray, Va.
1740 Homespun Farm Bed and Breakfast
. . . . Jewett City, Conn.
1740 Inn at Lower Farm
. . . . North Stonington, Conn.
1740 Red Brook Inn. . . . . Old Mystic, Conn.
1740 High Meadows B&B . . . . Eliot, Maine
1740 Lamb and Lion Inn . . . . Barnstable, Mass.
1740 Barley Sheaf Farm . . . . Holicong, Pa.
1743 The Inn at Mitchell House
. . . . Chestertown, Md.
1745 Olde Rhinebeck Inn . . . . . Rhinebeck, N.Y.
1746 Deacon Timothy Pratt Bed & Breakfast
Inn C.1746 . . . . Old Saybrook, Conn.
1750 Peace With-Inn Bed & Breakfast
. . . . Fryeburg, Maine
1750 The General Rufus Putnam House
. . . . Rutland, Mass.
1750 Carlisle House . . . . Carlisle, Pa.
1750 The Melville House . . . . . . Newport, R.I.
1752 The Olde Stage Coach B&B
. . . . Jennerstown, Pa.
1758 Hammett House Inn . . . . . . Newport, R.I.

1760 Glasgow B&B Inn . . . . Cambridge, Md.
1760 Gilbert House B&B of Middleway
. . . . Charles Town, W.Va.
1763 Wingscorton Farm Inn East Sandwich, Mass.
1764 Colonel Spencer Inn . . . . . . Campton, N.H.
1766 Seven South Street Inn . . . . Rockport, Mass.
1766 1766 Osceola Mill House . . . Gordonville, Pa.
1766 The Inn at Meander Plantation
. . . . Locust Dale, Va.
1767 Birchwood Inn . . . . Lenox, Mass.
1767 Highland Lake Inn B&B
. . . . East Andover, N.H.
1769 The Inn at Millrace Pond . . . . Hope, N.J.
1770 The Parsonage Inn . . . . . East Orleans, Mass.
1770 Ira Allen House . . . . Arlington, Vt.
1771 The Inn on Cove Hill. . . . . . Rockport, Mass.
1772 The Bagley House . . . . Durham, Maine
1772 Jailhouse Inn . . . . Newport, R.I.
1775 Colonel Roger Brown House
. . . . Concord, Mass.
1775 Kanaga House B&B Inn
. . . . New Kingstown, Pa.
1777 Doneckers, The Inns . . . . Ephrata, Pa.
1778 The Inn at Chester . . . . Chester, Conn.
1780 Hotel Saint Pierre . . . . . . New Orleans, La.
1780 Stone Manor . . . . Middletown, Md.
1780 Christine's Bed-Breakfast & Tearoom
. . . . Housatonic, Mass.
1780 Birch Hill Bed & Breakfast . . . Sheffield, Mass.
1780 The Dowds' Country Inn . . . . . . Lyme, N.H.
1782 Abel Darling B&B . . . . Litchfield, Conn.
1783 The Towers B&B. . . . . Milford, Del.
1785 1785 Inn & Restaurant
. . . . North Conway, N.H.
1785 Sleepy Hollow Farm B&B. . . Gordonsville, Va.
1786 Windsor House . . . . . . Newburyport, Mass.
1786 Kenniston Hill Inn . . . . Boothbay, Maine
1786 The Ship's Lantern Inn . . . Hillsborough, N.B.
1786 The Wayside Inn & Meeting Center
. . . . Greenfield Center, N.Y.
1787 Brass Heart Inn . . . . Chocorua, N.H.
1788 Strasburg Village Inn . . . . Strasburg, Pa.
1788 Golden Stage Inn . . . . Proctorsville, Vt.
1789 Longwood . . . . Woodbury, Conn.
1789 Stevens Farm B&B. . . . . Barre, Mass.
1789 Sugar Hill Inn . . . . Sugar Hill, N.H.
1790 Silvermine Tavern . . . . Norwalk, Conn.
1790 Fairhaven Inn . . . . Bath, Maine
1790 Candleberry Inn . . . . Brewster, Mass.
1790 Ivy Lodge . . . . Nantucket, Mass.
1790 Southern Hotel. . . . . . Sainte Genevieve, Mo.
1790 Olde Orchard Inn. . . Moultonborough, N.H.
1790 Hacienda Antigua Inn . . . Albuquerque, N.M.
1790 The Inn at Bingham School
. . . . Chapel Hill, N.C.
1790 1812 on The Perquimans B&B Inn
. . . . Hertford, N.C.
1790 Hillsborough House Inn
. . . . Hillsborough, N.C.
1790 Brownstone Colonial Inn . . . . Reinholds, Pa.
1790 Field & Pine B&B . . . . Shippensburg, Pa.
1790 The Cuthbert House Inn B&B
. . . . Beaufort, S.C.
1790 Hill Farm Inn . . . . Arlington, Vt.
1790 Silver Maple Lodge & Cottages. . . Fairlee, Vt.
1790 The Putney Inn . . . . Putney, Vt.
1790 The Inn at Blush Hill . . . . Waterbury, Vt.
1790 Flowering Fields B&B. . . . . White Stone, Va.

1791 St. Francis Inn . . . . Saint Augustine, Fla.
1791 Sedgwick Inn . . . . Berlin, N.Y.
1792 The Inn at Weathersfield. . . . Perkinsville, Vt.
1793 Cove House . . . . Kennebunkport, Maine
1793 Mill Creek Homestead B&B
. . . . Bird-in-Hand, Pa.
1794 1794 Watchtide... by the Sea
. . . . Searsport, Maine
1794 The Wagener Estate B&B
. . . . Penn Yan, N.Y.
1794 The Whitehall Inn. . . . . New Hope, Pa.
1794 Lareau Farm Country Inn . . . . Waitsfield, Vt.
1795 Canaan Land Farm B&B. . . . Harrodsburg, Ky.
1795 Shiretown Inn on the Island of
Martha's Vineyard . . . . . . Edgartown, Mass.
1795 Spring Farm B&B . . . . Luray, Va.
1796 Catamount B&B . . . . Williston, Vt.
1797 Applebrook B&B. . . . . Jefferson, N.H.
1797 Fitch Hill Inn. . . . . Hyde Park, Vt.
1798 Lane's Privateer Inn & B&B . . Liverpool, N.S.
1799 The Kennebunk Inn . . . . Kennebunk, Maine
1799 Dr. Jonathan Pitney House . . . Absecon, N.J.

Jailhouses

Jailhouse Inn . . . . Newport, R.I.

Literary Figures Asscociated With Inns

Louisa May Alcott
Hawthorne Inn. . . . . Concord, Mass.
Henry Beston
Over Look Inn . . . . Eastham, Mass.
Ralph Waldo Emerson
The Island House . . . . . . Southwest Harbor, Maine
Hawthorne Inn. . . . . Concord, Mass.
Emerson Inn By The Sea . . . . Rockport, Mass.
D.H. Lawrence
Vichy Hot Springs Resort & Inn . . . . . Ukiah, Calif.
Jack London
Vichy Hot Springs Resort & Inn . . . . . Ukiah, Calif.
Nathaniel Hawthorne
The Island House . . . . . . Southwest Harbor, Maine
Hawthorne Inn. . . . . Concord, Mass.
Emerson Inn By The Sea . . . . Rockport, Mass.
Mark Twain (Samuel Clemens)
Vichy Hot Springs Resort & Inn . . . . . Ukiah, Calif.
Edith Wharton
The Gables Inn . . . . Lenox, Mass.

Llama Ranches

1851 Historic Maple Hill Manor B&B
. . . . Springfield, Ky.
Llama Ranch B&B. . . . . White Salmon, Wash.

Log Cabins/Houses

Ocean Wilderness Inn & Spa Retreat . . . Sooke, B.C.
Knickerbocker Mansion Country Inn
. . . . Big Bear Lake, Calif.
Wild Horse Inn Bed and Breakfast. . . . Fraser, Colo.
Canaan Land Farm B&B. . . . . Harrodsburg, Ky.
Trout House Village Resort . . . . Hague, N.Y.
Log Country Inn - B&B of Ithaca . . . . . Ithaca, N.Y.
Heartland Country Resort. . . . Fredericktown, Ohio
The Inn At Cedar Falls . . . . Logan, Ohio
Roddy Tree Ranch . . . . Hunt, Texas
The Inn at Burg's Landing . . . Anderson Island, Wash.
Guest House Log Cottages . . . . . Greenbank, Wash.
A. Drummonds Ranch B&B . . . . . Cheyenne, Wyo.

Movie Locations

Consenting Adults
Rice Hope Plantation Inn Bed & Breakfast
. . . . Moncks Corner, S.C.
Isaac's Storm
C.W. Worth House B&B. . . . . . . Wilmington, N.C.
Maverick
The Mason Place B&B . . . . Loudon, Tenn.
Outbreak
Collingwood Inn Bed & Breakfast . . . Ferndale, Calif.

Old Mills

Silvermine Tavern. . . . . Norwalk, Conn.
Asa Ransom House. . . . . Clarence, N.Y.

Oldest Continuously Operated Inns

1859 Historic National Hotel, A Country Inn
. . . . Jamestown, Calif.
Vichy Hot Springs Resort & Inn . . . . . Ukiah, Calif.
1857 Florida House Inn. . . . . . Amelia Island, Fla.
Emerson Inn By The Sea . . . . Rockport, Mass.
Candlelite Inn . . . . Bradford, N.H.
The Bellevue House . . . . Block Island, R.I.
Smith House Inn . . . . Crosbyton, Texas
Casa Bella Inn. . . . . Pittsfield, Vt.

Plantations

Melhana The Grand Plantation . . . Thomasville, Ga.
Merry Sherwood Plantation. . . . . Berlin, Md.
Rice Hope Plantation Inn Bed & Breakfast
. . . . Moncks Corner, S.C.
La Vista Plantation . . . . Fredericksburg, Va.
The Inn at Meander Plantation . . . Locust Dale, Va.
Four Square Plantation . . . . Smithfield, Va.

Ranches

Howard Creek Ranch . . . . Westport, Calif.
Hasse House and Ranch. . . . . Mason, Texas
A. Drummonds Ranch B&B . . . . . Cheyenne, Wyo.

Revolutionary War

Ashley Manor Inn . . . . Barnstable, Mass.
Colonel Roger Brown House. . . . . . Concord, Mass.
Village Green Inn . . . . Falmouth, Mass.
The Melville House . . . . Newport, R.I.
Gilbert House B&B of Middleway
. . . . Charles Town, W.Va.

Schoolhouses

The Roosevelt Inn . . . . Coeur d' Alene, Idaho
The Bagley House. . . . . Durham, Maine
Old Sea Pines Inn. . . . . Brewster, Mass.
The Inn at Bingham School . . . . . Chapel Hill, N.C.
States Inn. . . . . Friday Harbor, Wash.
East Highland School House B&B . . . Phillips, Wis.

Space Shuttle Launches

The Higgins House . . . . Sanford, Fla.

Stagecoach Stops

Fensalden Inn . . . . Albion, Calif.
Maple Hill Farm B&B Inn. . . . . . . Hallowell, Maine
The Mendon Country Inn . . . . . . Mendon, Mich.
Hacienda Antigua Inn. . . . . . . Albuquerque, N.M.
Hacienda Vargas. . . . . Algodones, N.M.

The Inn at Bingham School . . . . . Chapel Hill, N.C.
Penguin Crossing B&B . . . . Circleville, Ohio
The Olde Stage Coach B&B . . . . . Jennerstown, Pa.
Churchill House Inn . . . . Brandon, Vt.
Casa Bella Inn . . . . Pittsfield, Vt.
Golden Stage Inn . . . . Proctorsville, Vt.
The Inn at Blush Hill . . . . Waterbury, Vt.
Wisconsin House Stagecoach Inn
. . . . Hazel Green, Wis.

Still in the Family

Brae Loch Inn. . . . . Cazenovia, N.Y.
Northern Plantation B&B . . . . Urbana, Ohio
Cedar Hill Farm . . . . Mount Joy, Pa.
Hasse House and Ranch. . . . . Mason, Texas
Catamount B&B . . . . Williston, Vt.
Bay View Waterfront B&B . . . . Belle Haven, Va.
Hewick Plantation . . . . Urbanna, Va.

Taverns

Fensalden Inn . . . . Albion, Calif.
Bird-In-Hand. . . . . Coventry, Conn.
Silvermine Tavern. . . . . Norwalk, Conn.
Red Brook Inn . . . . Old Mystic, Conn.
Chapman Inn . . . . Bethel, Maine
Birchwood Inn . . . . Lenox, Mass.
Bed and Breakfast at Giddings Garden
. . . . Syracuse, N.Y.
Rider's 1812 Inn. . . . . Painesville, Ohio
Doneckers, The Inns . . . . Ephrata, Pa.
James Gettys Hotel . . . . Gettysburg, Pa.
1725 Historic Witmer's Tavern Inn & Museum
. . . . Lancaster, Pa.

Train Stations & Renovated Rail Cars

Inn at Depot Hill . . . . Capitola, Calif.
Featherbed Railroad Company B&B . . . Nice, Calif.

Tunnels, Caves, Secret Passageways

Merry Sherwood Plantation. . . . . Berlin, Md.
Ashley Manor Inn . . . . Barnstable, Mass.
Wingscorton Farm Inn . . . . . East Sandwich, Mass.
Munro Bed & Breakfast Day Spa . . . . . Jonesville, Mich.
Colonel Spencer Inn . . . . Campton, N.H.
1725 Historic Witmer's Tavern Inn & Museum
. . . . Lancaster, Pa.
The Great Valley House of Valley Forge
. . . . Valley Forge, Pa.

Underground Railroad

Monier Manor . . . . Naples, N.Y.
Pheasant Field B&B . . . . Carlisle, Pa.
Rosebelle's Victorian Inn. . . . . Brandon, Vt.
Golden Stage Inn . . . . Proctorsville, Vt.

Unusual Sleeping Places

In a caboose
Featherbed Railroad Company B&B
. . . . Nice, Calif.
In a bank
The Landmark Inn at The Historic Bank of Oberlin
. . . . Oberlin, Kan.
In a trading post
Hacienda Vargas . . . . Algodones, N.M.

On or next to an archaeological dig site
The White Oak Inn . . . . Danville, Ohio
Hewick Plantation . . . . Urbanna, Va.

Waterfalls

The Inn At Cedar Falls . . . . Logan, Ohio

Who Slept/Visited Here

John Adams
1725 Historic Witmer's Tavern Inn & Museum
. . . . Lancaster, Pa.

Louis Armstrong
Hotel Saint Pierre. . . . . New Orleans, La.
John James Audubon
Weston House . . . . Eastport, Maine
Barrymore family
Evermay-On-The-Delaware . . . . Erwinna, Pa.
Big Nose Kay
Plaza Hotel . . . . Las Vegas, N.M.
Billy the Kid
Plaza Hotel . . . . Las Vegas, N.M.
Buffalo Bill Cody
The Inn at Jim Thorpe . . . . Jim Thorpe, Pa.
The Carnegies
1857 Florida House Inn. . . . . . . Amelia Island, Fla.
Grover Cleveland
The Cordova . . . . Ocean Grove, N.J.
Calvin Coolidge
Lehmann House B&B . . . . Saint Louis, Mo.
Echo Lake Inn . . . . Ludlow, Vt.
Jefferson Davis
Anchuca . . . . Vicksburg, Miss.
Thomas Edison
The Inn at Jim Thorpe . . . . Jim Thorpe, Pa.
Echo Lake Inn . . . . Ludlow, Vt.
Dwight D. Eisenhower
Swann Hotel . . . . Jasper, Texas
Errol Flynn
The Mission Inn . . . . Cape May, N.J.
Henry Ford
Echo Lake Inn . . . . Ludlow, Vt.
Clark Gable
Gold Mountain Manor Historic B&B
. . . . Big Bear, Calif.
Cary Grant
The Mulburn Inn . . . . Bethlehem, N.H.
Ulysses S. Grant
Vichy Hot Springs Resort & Inn . . . . . Ukiah, Calif.
1857 Florida House Inn. . . . . . . Amelia Island, Fla.
Aldrich Guest House . . . . Galena, Ill.
Alex Haley
McKay House . . . . Jefferson, Texas
Mrs. Warren Harding
1794 Watchtide... by the Sea . . . . Searsport, Maine
Lillian Hellman
Barley Sheaf Farm . . . . Holicong, Pa.
Mrs. Herbert Hoover
1794 Watchtide... by the Sea . . . . Searsport, Maine
Barbara Hutton
The Mulburn Inn . . . . Bethlehem, N.H.
Andrew Jackson
Cornstalk Hotel. . . . . New Orleans, La.
Thomas Jefferson
1725 Historic Witmer's Tavern Inn & Museum
. . . . Lancaster, Pa.
The Inn at Meander Plantation
. . . . Locust Dale, Va.

Lady Bird Johnson
McKay House . . . . Jefferson, Texas
Abraham Lincoln
Aldrich Guest House . . . . Galena, Ill.
Patchwork Inn . . . . Oregon, Ill.
Carole Lombard
Gold Mountain Manor Historic B&B
. . . . Big Bear, Calif.
Jack London
Vichy Hot Springs Resort & Inn . . . . . Ukiah, Calif.
Marx Brothers
Barley Sheaf Farm . . . . Holicong, Pa.
President William McKinley
Cheshire Cat Inn & Spa. . . . . . Santa Barbara, Calif.
Colonel Taylor Inn B&B and Gift Shop
. . . . Cambridge, Ohio
Captain Cornelius J. Mey
Captain Mey's B&B Inn . . . . Cape May, N.J.
Gram Parsons
Joshua Tree Inn. . . . . Joshua Tree, Calif.
General George Patton
Swann Hotel . . . . Jasper, Texas
S.J. Perlman
Barley Sheaf Farm . . . . Holicong, Pa.
Tyrone Power
The Mission Inn . . . . Cape May, N.J.
Robert Preston
The Mission Inn . . . . Cape May, N.J.
John D. Rockefeller
1857 Florida House Inn. . . . . . . Amelia Island, Fla.
The Inn at Jim Thorpe . . . . Jim Thorpe, Pa.
Eleanor Roosevelt
1794 Watchtide... by the Sea . . . . Searsport, Maine
Theodore Roosevelt
Vichy Hot Springs Resort & Inn . . . . . Ukiah, Calif.
Lehmann House B&B . . . . Saint Louis, Mo.
Lillian Russell
Bayview Hotel . . . . Aptos, Calif.
Martin Sheen
Justin Trails Resort . . . . Sparta, Wis.
General W.T. Sherman
The Cuthbert House Inn B&B. . . . . . Beaufort, S.C.
Robert Louis Stevenson
Vichy Hot Springs Resort & Inn . . . . . Ukiah, Calif.
Harriet Beecher Stowe
Cornstalk Hotel. . . . . New Orleans, La.
William H. Taft
Lehmann House B&B . . . . Saint Louis, Mo.
Mark Twain (Samuel Clemens)
Vichy Hot Springs Resort & Inn . . . . . Ukiah, Calif.
Martin Van Buren
Old Hoosier House. . . . . Knightstown, Ind.
1725 Historic Witmer's Tavern Inn & Museum
. . . . Lancaster, Pa.
George Washington
1725 Historic Witmer's Tavern Inn & Museum
. . . . Lancaster, Pa.
Tennessee Williams
Hotel Saint Pierre. . . . . New Orleans, La.
Woodrow Wilson
The Cordova . . . . Ocean Grove, N.J.
Woolworth Family
The Mulburn Inn . . . . Bethlehem, N.H.

INN EVALUATION FORM

Please copy and complete for each stay and mail to the address shown. Since 1981 we have provided this evaluation form to millions of travelers. This information helps us follow the changes in the inns listed in this guide.

Name of Inn: _____

City and State: _____

Date of Stay: _____

Your Name: _____

Address: _____

City/State/Zip: _____

Phone: (__ __ __) __ __ __ – __ __ __ __

E-mail: _____

Please use the following rating scale for the next items.
1: Outstanding.   2: Good.   3: Average.   4: Fair.   5: Poor.

Location	1	2	3	4	5
Cleanliness	1	2	3	4	5
Food Service	1	2	3	4	5
Privacy	1	2	3	4	5
Beds	1	2	3	4	5
Bathrooms	1	2	3	4	5
Parking	1	2	3	4	5
Handling of reservations	1	2	3	4	5
Attitude of staff	1	2	3	4	5
Overall rating	1	2	3	4	5

Comments on Above: _____

_____

_____

_____

_____

MAIL THE COMPLETED FORM TO:
American Historic Inns, Inc.
PO Box 669
Dana Point, CA 92629-0669
(949) 497-2232
www.iLoveInns.com

AMERICAN HISTORIC INNS
INCORPORATED

iLoveInns.com

PO Box 669
Dana Point
California
92629-0669
(949) 497-2232
Fax (949) 497-9228
www.iLoveInns.com

Order Form

Date: __ __ / __ __ / __ __   Shipped: __ __ / __ __ / __ __

Name: _____

Street: _____

City/State/Zip: _____

Phone: (__ __ __) __ __ __ – __ __ __ __   E-mail: _____

QTY.	Prod. No.	Description	Amount	Total
_____	AHI16	Bed & Breakfasts and Country Inns	$21.95	_____
_____	AHIH9	The Official Guide to American Historic Inns	$16.95	_____
_____	AHIE3	Bed & Breakfast Encyclopedia	$18.95	_____
_____	AHIC2	Bed & Breakfast and Country Inn Travel Club (reg. $59.95)	$49.95	_____

Subtotal _____

California buyers add 7.75% sales tax _____

Shipping and Handling on Encyclopedia Book Orders
STANDARD (10-20 days): $3.50 for first book. Add $1 for each additional copy.
PRIORITY (3-5 days): $8. Add $5 each add'l copy.   2ND-DAY AIR: $11.00. Add $3.50 each add'l copy.

Shipping and Handling on Other Book and Travel Club Orders
STANDARD (10-20 days): $3 for first book. Add 75¢ for each additional copy.
PRIORITY (3-5 days): $5.75. Add $3.50 each add'l copy.   2ND-DAY AIR: $11.00. Add $3.50 each add'l copy. _____

TOTAL _____

❏ Check/Money Order   ❏ Discover   ❏ Mastercard   ❏ Visa   ❏ American Express

Account Number __ __ __ __ __ __ __ __ __ __ __ __ __ __ __ __   Exp. Date __ __ / __ __

Name on card _____

Signature _____

Publications From American Historic Inns

Bed & Breakfast and Country Inns, 16th Edition

By Deborah Edwards Sakach

Imagine the thrill of receiving this unique book with its FREE night certificate as a gift. Now you can let someone else experience the magic of America's country inns with this unmatched offer. *Bed & Breakfasts and Country Inns* is the most talked about guide among inngoers.

This fabulous guide features more than 1,550 inns from across the United States and Canada. Best of all, no other bookstore guide offers a FREE night certificate.* This certificate can be used at any one of the inns featured in the guide.

American Historic Inns, Inc. has been publishing books about bed & breakfasts since 1981. Its books and the FREE night offer have been recommended by many travel writers and editors, and featured in: *The New York Times, Washington Post, Los Angeles Times, Boston Globe, Chicago Sun Times, USA Today, Orange County Register, Baltimore Sun, McCalls, Good Housekeeping, Cosmopolitan, Consumer Reports* and more.

*With purchase of one night at the regular rate required. Subject to limitations.

464 pages, paperback, 500 illustrations   **Price $21.95**

The Official Guide to American Historic Inns

Completely Revised and Updated, Ninth Edition

By Deborah Sakach

A Book of the Month Club and History Book Club Selection

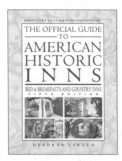

Open the door to America's past with this fascinating guide to historic inns that reflect our colorful heritage. From Dutch Colonials to Queen Anne Victorians, these bed & breakfasts and country inns offer experiences of a lifetime. This special edition guide includes more than 2,400 certified American Historic Inns that provide the utmost in hospitality, beauty, authentic restoration and preservation. Inns have been carefully selected so as to provide readers with the opportunity to visit genuine masterpieces.

With inns dating back to as early as 1600, this guide is filled with treasures waiting to be discovered. Full descriptions, illustrations, guest comments and recommendations all are included to let you know what's in store for you before choosing one of America's Historic Inns.

704 pages, paperback, 1,000 illustrations   **Price $16.95**

The Bed & Breakfast Encyclopedia
Completely Revised and Updated, Third Edition
By Deborah Edwards Sakach & Tiffany Crosswy

This massive guide is the most comprehensive guide on the market today. Packed with detailed listings to more than 2,600 bed & breakfasts and country inns, the Encyclopedia also includes an index to an additional 14,000 inns, detailed state maps and more than 1,200 illustrations. Recipes, helpful phone numbers, information about reservation services and informative articles about bed & breakfast hot spots, the best bed & breakfasts, inns of interest, how to start your own B&B and much, much more.

If you're planning a getaway, this all-inclusive guide is a must!

1,056 pages, paperback, 1,200 illustrations   **Price $18.95**

Bed & Breakfast and Country Inn Travel Club
Membership From American Historic Inns, Inc.

SAVE! SAVE! SAVE! We offer an exclusive discount club that lets you enjoy the excitement of bed & breakfast and country inn travel again and again. As a member of this special club, you'll receive benefits that include savings of 25% to 50% off every night's stay!

Your membership card will entitle you to tremendous savings at some of the finest inns in America. Members receive a guide with more than 1,000 participating bed & breakfasts and country inns to choose from. Plan affordable getaways to inns nearby or visit an area of the country you've always wanted to experience.

The best part of being an American Historic Inns Travel Club Member is that the card can be used as many times as you like.

In addition to your card, you will get a FREE night's stay certificate—truly a club membership that's hard to pass up!

All travel club members receive:
- Travel club card entitling holder to 25% to 50% off lodging.
- FREE night's stay certificate.
- Guide to more than 1,000 participating inns across America.

Membership is good for one year. Free night's stay with purchase of one night at the regular rate. Travel Club card is transferable. Discount and certificate cannot be combined.

Introductory price with full benefits (Reg. $59.95)   **$49.95**

www.iLoveInns.com

"The only online bed & breakfast guide you will ever need.™"

Named "Best B&B Site" by Yahoo! Internet Magazine

- More than 17,000 bed & breakfasts and country inns.
- Color photos and line illustrations.
- Use our easy Innfinder Search to quickly access inns near your destination.
- Online room availability and booking.
- Or use our Advanced Search to look for inns that meet your specific needs.
- Search for inns in our Free Night program.
- Send reservation requests via e-mail.
- See our specially selected Featured Inns.
- Learn about bed & breakfast hot spots across the country.
- Find out where the top inns are, including our famous picks for the Top 10 Most Romantic Inns.